P9-AFF-679

WITHDRAWN

DAVID O. McKAY LIBRARY
BYU-IDAHO

THE SADTLER HANDBOOK

OF

PROTON NMR SPECTRA

INDEX

THE
SADTLER
HANDBOOK

OF

PROTON
NMR
SPECTRA

INDEX

Editor:
William W. Simons
Spectroscopist
Sadtler Research Laboratories, Inc.

SADTLER

Published by
Sadtler Research Laboratories, Inc.
Subsidiary of Block Engineering, Inc.
3316 Spring Garden Street
Philadelphia, Pennsylvania 19104

ISBN 0-8456-0035-4

Library of Congress Catalog Card Number: 78-54281

Co-published for exclusive distribution in Europe by
Heyden & Son Ltd.
Spectrum House, Hillview Gardens
London N.W. 4, England 2JQ

ISBN 0-8550-1442-3

Copyright © 1978, by Sadtler Research Laboratories, Inc. All rights reserved. No part of this book may be reproduced or reformatted in any form, by photostat, microfilm, retrieval system, or any other means, without written permission from Sadtler Research Laboratories, Inc.

Printed in the United States of America

TABLE OF CONTENTS

Page

INTRODUCTION

This second volume of the Sadtler Handbook of NMR Spectra contains the indices for the spectra appearing in the first volume. In addition to the book order index (functional group order) and the alphabetical index, which are identical to those provided with the Sadtler Handbook of Infrared Spectra, this volume contains the Sadtler Chemical Shift Index. Both the Infrared Spec-Finder and the NMR Chemical Shift Indices, are useful means of locating a matching reference spectrum. The Spec-Finder approach has been found more useful with infrared spectra, while the Chemical Shift Indices has proven itself to be a more appropriate method of locating the data required from NMR spectra.

The Chemical Shift index is presented in two forms. One is ordered by chemical shift and the other is presented in a proton type and environment sequence. The chemical shift order set provides the user with all of the proton types and environments which result in a specific chemical shift.

The proton type sequence makes available all of the chemical shifts observed for a specific proton type and environment. Together, these two indices provide the user with a potent tool for obtaining the proton shift information from the 3000 spectra printed in the NMR spectra volume.

In preparing the chemical shift tables which introduce each group of spectra in the text, the complete Chemical Shift Index containing information from 24,000 spectra was used. The methods used to describe and locate the proton types and environments is relatively simple to learn and the few minutes spend studying the system will be amply rewarded through the fund of chemical shift data made available to the teacher, student or chemist who requires it.

NOTE

The spectrum numbers listed in these indices apply only to the spectra in the Sadtler Handbooks of Reference Spectra (Infrared, Proton NMR, Ultraviolet) and do not correspond in any way to the spectrum numbers in the Sadtler Standard Spectra volumes.

1

SPECTRUM NO.   NAME

NORMAL ALKANES

1	PENTANE
2	HEXANE
3	HEPTANE
4	OCTANE
5	NONANE
6	DECANE
7	UNDECANE
8	DODECANE
9	TRIDECANE
10	TETRADECANE
11	PENTADECANE
12	OCTADECANE
13	EICOSANE
14	DOCOSANE
15	TRICOSANE
16	HEXATRIACONTANE

BRANCHED ALKANES

17	2-METHYLBUTANE
18	2,3-DIMETHYLBUTANE
19	2-METHYLPENTANE
20	3-METHYLPENTANE
21	2,2-DIMETHYLPENTANE
22	2,4-DIMETHYLPENTANE
23	3,3-DIMETHYLPENTANE
24	3-ETHYL-2-METHYLPENTANE
25	2,2,3-TRIMETHYLPENTANE
26	2,3,3-TRIMETHYLPENTANE
27	2,2,4-TRIMETHYLPENTANE
28	2,3,4-TRIMETHYLPENTANE
29	2-METHYLHEXANE
30	3-METHYLHEXANE
31	2,5-DIMETHYLHEXANE
32	2-METHYLHEPTANE
33	3,3-DIMETHYLHEPTANE
34	2-METHYLOCTANE
35	4-METHYLOCTANE
36	3-METHYLNONANE
37	2,6,10,14-TETRAMETHYLPENTADECANE

CYCLIC ALKANES

38	ISOPROPYLCYCLOPROPANE
39	cis-1,2-DIMETHYLCYCLOPROPANE
40	1,1,2-TRIMETHYLCYCLOPROPANE
41	DICYCLOPROPYLMETHANE
42	CYCLOPENTANE

SPECTRUM NO.	NAME
88	3-METHYL-1,5-HEPTADIENE
89	5-METHYL-1,3,6-HEPTATRIENE
90	2-METHYL-2-BUTENE
91	2,4,4-TRIMETHYL-2-PENTENE
92	cis-3-METHYL-2-HEXENE
93	2-METHYL-2-HEXENE
94	2,5-DIMETHYL-2-HEXENE
95	2,5-DIMETHYL-2,4-HEXADIENE
96	2,3-DIMETHYL-2-BUTENE

CYCLIC ALKENES

97	CYCLOPENTENE
98	1,2-DIMETHYLCYCLOPENTENE
99	CYCLOHEXENE
100	4-tert-PENTYLCYCLOHEXENE
101	1-VINYL-4-CYCLOHEXENE
102	1-METHYLCYCLOHEXENE
103	1-ETHYLCYCLOHEXENE
104	1,2-DIMETHYLCYCLOHEXENE
105	BI-1-CYCLOHEXEN-1-YL
106	CYCLOOCTENE
107	cis-1,3-DIMETHYL-2-METHYLENECYCLOHEXANE
108	3,3-DIMETHYL-2-METHYLENENORBORNANE
109	2(10)-PINENE
110	(±)-2-PINENE
111	(+)-p-MENTHA-1,8-DIENE
112	1,3-CYCLOHEXADIENE
113	1,4-CYCLOHEXADIENE
114	1,5-CYCLOOCTADIENE
115	3a,4,7,7a-TETRAHYDRO-4,7-METHANOINDENE

ALKYNES

116	3,3-DIMETHYL-1-BUTYNE
117	1-PENTYNE
118	1-HEXYNE
119	1-NONYNE
120	1-DECYNE
121	1-UNDECYNE
122	1-OCTADECYNE
123	1,7-OCTADIYNE
124	1,8-NONADIYNE
125	2-BUTYNE
126	4,4-DIMETHYL-2-PENTYNE
127	4-DECYNE
128	3-UNDECYNE
129	6-DODECYNE
130	2,9-DIMETHYL-5-DECYNE
131	3,9-DODECADIYNE

SPECTRUM NO.   NAME

MONOCYCLIC AROMATICS

SPECTRUM NO.	NAME
358	1,3-DIBROMOBUTANE
359	1,4-DIBROMOBUTANE
360	1,5-DIBROMOPENTANE
361	2,5-DIBROMOHEXANE
362	1,6-DIBROMOHEXANE
363	BROMOCYCLOPENTANE
364	(3-BROMOPROPYL) CYCLOHEXANE
365	BROMOCYCLOHEXANE
366	1-BROMO-3-METHYLCYCLOHEXANE
367	1,4-DIBROMOCYCLOHEXANE
368	3-BROMOPROPENE
369	1,4-DIBROMO-2-BUTENE
370	1,2-DIBROMOETHYLENE
371	*a*-BROMOTOLUENE
372	*a*-BROMO-o-XYLENE
373	*a*-BROMO-p-XYLENE
374	BROMODIPHENYLMETHANE
375	(2-BROMOETHYL) BENZENE
376	*a,a*-DIBROMOTOLUENE
377	*a,a*-DIBROMO-m-XYLENE
378	(1,2-DIBROMOETHYL) BENZENE
379	1,5-DIBROMO-3-PHENYLPENTANE
380	β-BROMOSTYRENE
381	BROMOBENZENE
382	o-BROMOTOLUENE
383	m-BROMOTOLUENE
384	p-BROMOTOLUENE
385	3-BROMO-p-CYMENE
386	1-BROMO-2,4,5-TRIMETHYLBENZENE
387	2-BROMOMESITYLENE
388	p-BROMO-*a,a,a*-TRIFLUOROTOLUENE
389	1-BROMO-2-FLUOROBENZENE
390	1-BROMO-3-FLUOROBENZENE
391	1-BROMO-4-FLUOROBENZENE
392	1-BROMO-2-CHLOROBENZENE
393	1-BROMO-3-CHLOROBENZENE
394	1-BROMO-4-CHLOROBENZENE
395	*a*,m-DIBROMOTOLUENE
396	o-DIBROMOBENZENE
397	m-DIBROMOBENZENE
398	p-DIBROMOBENZENE
399	4-BROMOBIPHENYL
400	1-BROMONAPHTHALENE
401	2-BROMONAPHTHALENE
402	1,4-DIBROMONAPHTHALENE

SPECTRUM NO.   NAME

IODINATED HYDROCARBONS

403	IODOMETHANE
404	IODOETHANE
405	1-IODOPROPANE
406	2-IODOPROPANE
407	1-IODOBUTANE
408	2-IODOBUTANE
409	1-IODO-2-METHYLPROPANE
410	1-IODO-3-METHYLBUTANE
411	1-IODOHEXANE
412	1-IODONONANE
413	1-IODODODECANE
414	1-IODOHEXADECANE
415	DIIODOMETHANE
416	1,2-DIIODOETHANE
417	1,3-DIIODOPROPANE
418	1,4-DIIODOBUTANE
419	1,5-DIIODOPENTANE
420	1,6-DIIODOHEXANE
421	IODOCYCLOPENTANE
422	IODOCYCLOHEXANE
423	3-IODOPROPENE
424	(2-IODOETHYL) BENZENE
425	*a*-IODOTOLUENE
426	IODOBENZENE
427	o-IODOTOLUENE
428	m-IODOTOLUENE
429	p-IODOTOLUENE
430	2-IODO-p-XYLENE
431	m-IODO-*a,a,a*-TRIFLUOROTOLUENE
432	1-FLUORO-4-IODOBENZENE
433	1-CHLORO-2-IODOBENZENE
434	1-BROMO-2-IODOBENZENE
435	1-BROMO-4-IODOBENZENE
436	m-DIIODOBENZENE
437	p-DIIODOBENZENE
438	1-IODONAPHTHALENE

PRIMARY AMINES

439	PROPYLAMINE
440	ISOPROPYLAMINE
441	BUTYLAMINE
442	ISOBUTYLAMINE
443	sec-BUTYLAMINE
444	PENTYLAMINE
445	2-METHYLBUTYLAMINE
446	ISOPENTYLAMINE

SPECTRUM NO.   NAME

SPECTRUM NO.   NAME

QUINOLINES

718	QUINOLINE
719	QUINALDINE
720	LEPIDINE
721	6-METHYLQUINOLINE
722	7-METHYLQUINOLINE
723	8-METHYLQUINOLINE
724	2-CHLOROQUINOLINE
725	6-BROMOQUINOLINE
726	2-IODOQUINOLINE
727	3-AMINOQUINOLINE
728	ISOQUINOLINE
729	1-CHLOROISOQUINOLINE
730	1-CHLORO-3-METHYLISOQUINOLINE
731	4-BROMOISOQUINOLINE

MISCELLANEOUS NITROGEN HETEROAROMATICS

732	4-PHENYLPYRIMIDINE
733	4,6-DICHLOROPYRIMIDINE
734	2-AMINOPYRIMIDINE
735	TETRAMETHYLPYRAZINE
736	2,4,6-TRIPHENYL-s-TRIAZINE
737	2,4,6-TRIS[DI(2-ETHYLHEXYL)AMINO]-S-TRIAZINE
738	BENZIMIDAZOLE
739	2-PROPYLBENZIMIDAZOLE
740	5-METHYLBENZIMIDAZOLE
741	1H-BENZOTRIAZOLE
742	4-CHLOROQUINAZOLINE
743	PURINE
744	9-ETHYLCARBAZOLE
745	9-PHENYLCARBAZOLE
746	ACRIDINE
747	9-AMINOACRIDINE
748	PHENANTHRIDINE
749	BENZO[f]QUINOLINE
750	1,10-PHENANTHROLINE, MONOHYDRATE
751	2,9-DIMETHYL-1,10-PHENANTHROLINE
752	NAPHTHO(1,8-de)TRIAZINE

HYDRAZINES

753	METHYLHYDRAZINE
754	1,1-DIMETHYLHYDRAZINE
755	1-AMINO-4-METHYLPIPERAZINE
756	PHENYLHYDRAZINE
757	(2,5-DICHLOROPHENYL)HYDRAZINE
758	(2,4,6-TRICHLOROPHENYL)HYDRAZINE
759	1,1-DIPHENYLHYDRAZINE
760	HYDRAZOBENZENE

SPECTRUM NO.	NAME
761	1,2-DIMETHYL-1,2-DI-p-TOLYLHYDRAZINE
762	1,2-BIS(4-BIPHENYLYL)-1,2-DIMETHYLHYDRAZINE
763	1,2-DIMESITYL-1,2-DIMETHYLHYDRAZINE
764	2-HYDRAZINOQUINOLINE

AMINE SALTS

765	METHYLAMINE, HYDROCHLORIDE
766	ETHYLAMINE, HYDROCHLORIDE
767	PROPYLAMINE, HYDROCHLORIDE
768	BUTYLAMINE, HYDROCHLORIDE
769	tert-BUTYLAMINE, COMPOUND WITH BORANE
770	OCTYLAMINE, HYDROCHLORIDE
771	2,2,2-TRIFLUOROETHYLAMINE, HYDROCHLORIDE
772	CYCLOBUTYLAMINE, HYDROCHLORIDE
773	2-NORBORNANAMINE, HYDROCHLORIDE
774	ETHYLENEDIAMINE, DIHYDROCHLORIDE
775	ETHYLENEDIAMINE, DIHYDROBROMIDE
776	ETHYLENEDIAMINE, SULFATE
777	1,4-BUTANEDIAMINE, DIHYDROCHLORIDE
778	1,5-PENTANEDIAMINE, DIHYDROCHLORIDE
779	1,6-HEXANEDIAMINE, DIHYDROCHLORIDE
780	2,2'-DITHIOBISETHYLAMINE, DIHYDROCHLORIDE
781	ALLYLAMINE, HYDROCHLORIDE
782	BENZYLAMINE, HYDROCHLORIDE
783	m-BROMOBENZYLAMINE, HYDROCHLORIDE
784	a-METHYLBENZYLAMINE, HYDROCHLORIDE
785	1-METHYL-3-PHENYLPROPYLAMINE, HYDROCHLORIDE
786	p-CHLORO-a,a-DIMETHYLPHENETHYLAMINE, HYDROCHLORIDE
787	ANILINE, HYDROCHLORIDE
788	ANILINE, SULFATE
789	o-TOLUIDINE, HYDROCHLORIDE
790	m-TOLUIDINE, HYDROCHLORIDE
791	p-ANISIDINE, HYDROCHLORIDE
792	2,5-XYLIDINE, HYDROCHLORIDE
793	o-PHENYLENEDIAMINE, DIHYDROCHLORIDE
794	m-PHENYLENEDIAMINE, DIHYDROCHLORIDE
795	p-PHENYLENEDIAMINE, DIHYDROCHLORIDE
796	2-CHLORO-p-PHENYLENEDIAMINE, DIHYDROCHLORIDE
797	DIETHYLAMINE, HYDROCHLORIDE
798	DIISOPROPYLAMINE, HYDROBROMIDE
799	DIBUTYLAMINE, HYDROCHLORIDE
800	DIBUTYLAMINE, HEXAFLUOROSILICATE (2:1)
801	PIPERIDINE, HYDROCHLORIDE
802	PIPERAZINE, MONOHYDROCHLORIDE
803	PIPERAZINE, PHOSPHATE (3:2)
804	DL-N,a-DIMETHYLPHENETHYLAMINE, HYDROCHLORIDE
805	DIBENZYLAMINE, HYDROCHLORIDE
806	N-ETHYLANILINE, HYDROCHLORIDE

SPECTRUM NO.　NAME

807	DIPHENYLAMINE, HYDROCHLORIDE
808	TRIMETHYLAMINE, HYDROCHLORIDE
809	TRIETHYLAMINE, HYDROCHLORIDE
810	TRIOCTYLAMINE, HYDROCHLORIDE
811	2-CHLORO-N,N-DIMETHYLETHYLAMINE, HYDROCHLORIDE
812	2-CHLOROTRIETHYLAMINE, HYDROCHLORIDE
813	N,N-DIMETHYL-1-ADAMANTANAMINE, HYDROCHLORIDE
814	4-(DIMETHYLAMINO)PIPERIDINE, DIHYDROCHLORIDE
815	1-(2-CHLOROETHYL)PIPERIDINE, HYDROCHLORIDE
816	N,N-DIMETHYL-m-PHENYLENEDIAMINE, DIHYDROCHLORIDE
817	N,N-DIETHYL-p-PHENYLENEDIAMINE MONOHYDROCHLORIDE
818	N,N-DIMETHYL-p-PHENYLENEDIAMINE, DIHYDROCHLORIDE
819	N,N,N',N'-TETRAMETHYL-p-PHENYLENEDIAMINE, DIHYDROCHLORIDE
820	HISTAMINE, MONOHYDROCHLORIDE
821	4-BROMOPYRIDINE, MONOHYDROBROMIDE
822	METHYLHYDRAZINE, SULFATE (1:1)
823	(3-CHLORO-p-TOLYL)HYDRAZINE, MONOHYDROCHLORIDE
824	(p-METHOXYPHENYL)HYDRAZINE, MONOHYDROCHLORIDE
825	(2-NAPHTHYL)HYDRAZINE, MONOHYDROCHLORIDE
826	3-HYDRAZINOQUINOLINE, DIHYDROCHLORIDE
827	TETRAETHYLAMMONIUM IODIDE
828	TETRABUTYLAMMONIUM TETRAFLUOROBORATE(1-)
829	DODECYLTRIMETHYLAMMONIUM CHLORIDE, MONOHYDRATE
830	DODECYLTRIMETHYLAMMONIUM BROMIDE
831	HEXADECYLTRIMETHYLAMMONIUM BROMIDE
832	TETRABUTYLAMMONIUM BROMIDE
833	OCTADECYLTRIMETHYLAMMONIUM BROMIDE
834	(2-PROPYNYL)TRIETHYLAMMONIUM BROMIDE
835	1-ADAMANTYLTRIMETHYLAMMONIUM IODIDE
836	BENZYLTRIMETHYLAMMONIUM CHLORIDE
837	BENZYLTRIMETHYLAMMONIUM IODIDE
838	BENZYLTRIMETHYLAMMONIUM HEXAFLUOROANTIMONATE(1-)
839	BENZYLDIMETHYLHEXADECYLAMMONIUM CHLORIDE, HYDRATE
840	PHENYLTRIMETHYLAMMONIUM CHLORIDE
841	PHENYLTRIETHYLAMMONIUM IODIDE
842	1-METHYLPYRIDINIUM IODIDE
843	1-HEXADECYLPYRIDINIUM IODIDE
844	3-AMINO-1-METHYLPYRIDINIUM BROMIDE
845	1,1'-ETHYLENEBIS[PYRIDINIUM BROMIDE]
846	o-METHYLHYDROXYLAMINE, HYDROCHLORIDE
847	PYRIDINE, 1-OXIDE, HYDROCHLORIDE

OXIMES

848	ISOBUTYRALDEHYDE, OXIME
849	HEPTANAL, OXIME
850	GLYOXIME
851	CINNAMALDEHYDE, OXIME

SPECTRUM NO.	NAME
893	3,7-DIMETHYL-6-OCTENOHYDROXAMIC ACID
894	SORBOHYDROXAMIC ACID
895	ISONICOTINOHYDROXAMIC ACID

AZO COMPOUNDS

896	AZOBENZENE
897	m,m'-AZOTOLUENE
898	3,3'-DICHLOROAZOBENZENE
899	p-PHENYLAZOANILINE (C.I. SOLVENT YELLOW 1)
900	N,N-DIMETHYL-p-PHENYLAZOANILINE
901	N,N-DIMETHYL-p[(p-AMINOPHENYL)AZO] ANILINE
902	AZOXYBENZENE
903	trans-4,4'-DICHLOROAZOXYBENZENE

TRIAZENES

904	3-METHYL-1-p-TOLYLTRIAZENE
905	1,3-DIPHENYLTRIAZENE
906	3,3-DIMETHYL-1-PHENYLTRIAZENE

ISOCYANATES

907	ISOCYANIC ACID, METHYL ESTER
908	ISOCYANIC ACID, PROPYL ESTER
909	ISOCYANIC ACID, HEXYL ESTER
910	ISOCYANIC ACID, DODECYL ESTER
911	ISOCYANIC ACID, BICYCLO[2.2.2]OCT-1,4-YLENE ESTER
912	ISOCYANIC ACID, PHENYL ESTER
913	ISOCYANIC ACID, o-TOLYL ESTER
914	ISOCYANIC ACID,a,a,a-TRIFLUORO-o-TOLYL ESTER
915	ISOCYANIC ACID,a,a,a-TRIFLUORO-m-TOLYL ESTER
916	ISOCYANIC ACID, o-FLUOROPHENYL ESTER
917	ISOCYANIC ACID, m-FLUOROPHENYL ESTER
918	ISOCYANIC ACID, METHYLENEDI-p-PHENYLENE ESTER
919	ISOCYANIC ACID, 2,5-XYLYL ESTER
920	ISOCYANIC ACID, 2,5-DICHLOROPHENYL ESTER
921	ISOCYANIC ACID, 4-METHYL-m-PHENYLENE ESTER
922	ISOCYANIC ACID, 1-NAPHTHYL ESTER

CARBODIIMIDES

923	DIISOPROPYLCARBODIIMIDE
924	DICYCLOHEXYLCARBODIIMIDE
925	tert-BUTYL(TRIPHENYLMETHYL)CARBODIIMIDE
926	DITRITYLCARBODIIMIDE
927	DL-o-TOLYLCARBODIIMIDE
928	DI-p-TOLYLCARBODIIMIDE
929	BIS(2,6-DIETHYLPHENYL)CARBODIIMIDE

ISOTHIOCYANATES

930	ISOTHIOCYANIC ACID, METHYL ESTER
931	ISOTHIOCYANIC ACID, BUTYL ESTER
932	ISOTHIOCYANIC ACID, tert-BUTYL ESTER

SPECTRUM NO.   NAME

NITROSO COMPOUNDS

1021	2-METHYL-2-NITROSOPROPANE
1022	4-NITROSODIPHENYLAMINE
1023	N,N-DIMETHYL-p-NITROSOANILINE
1024	N,N-DIETHYL-4-NITROSOANILINE

N-NITROSO COMPOUNDS

1025	N-NITROSODIMETHYLAMINE
1026	N-NITROSODIETHYLAMINE
1027	N-NITROSODIPROPYLAMINE
1028	N-NITROSODICYCLOHEXYLAMINE
1029	1-NITROSOPYRROLIDINE
1030	1-NITROSOPIPERIDINE
1031	N-METHYL-N-NITROSOANILINE
1032	N-NITROSODIPHENYLAMINE

NITRITES

1033	PROPYL NITRITE
1034	sec-BUTYL NITRITE
1035	ISOBUTYL NITRITE
1036	tert-BUTYL NITRITE
1037	ISOPENTYL NITRITE
1038	OCTYL NITRITE

NITRO COMPOUNDS

1039	NITROMETHANE
1040	NITROETHANE
1041	1-NITROPROPANE
1042	2-NITROPROPANE
1043	2-METHYL-2-NITROPROPANE
1044	1-CHLORO-1-NITROETHANE
1045	NITROCYCLOHEXANE
1046	o-NITROTOLUENE
1047	m-NITROTOLUENE
1048	p-NITROTOLUENE
1049	1-ETHYL-2-NITROBENZENE
1050	1-ETHYL-4-NITROBENZENE
1051	2-NITROBIPHENYL
1052	3-NITROBIPHENYL
1053	4-NITROBIPHENYL
1054	1-FLUORO-2-NITROBENZENE
1055	1-FLUORO-4-NITROBENZENE
1056	1-CHLORO-2-NITROBENZENE
1057	1-CHLORO-3-NITROBENZENE
1058	1-CHLORO-4-NITROBENZENE
1059	1-BROMO-2-NITROBENZENE
1060	1-IODO-3-NITROBENZENE
1061	1-IODO-4-NITROBENZENE

SPECTRUM NO.   NAME

1062	N-ETHYL-o-NITROANILINE
1063	2-PENTANONE, (p-NITROPHENYL)HYDRAZONE
1064	BENZ ALDEHYDE, (p-NITROPHENYL)HYDRAZONE
1065	4-NITROAZOBENZENE
1066	o-DINITROBENZENE
1067	m-DINITROBENZENE
1068	4-NITRO-m-XYLENE
1069	1,2-DICHLORO-4-NITROBENZENE
1070	3-NITRO-p-TOLUIDINE
1071	4-NITRO-m-TOLUIDINE
1072	2,4-DINITRO-1-FLUOROBENZENE
1073	1-BROMO-2,4-DINITROBENZENE
1074	N,N-DIMETHYL-3,4-DINITROANILINE
1075	ACETONE, (2,4-DINITROPHENYL)HYDRAZONE
1076	1,3,5-TRINITROBENZENE
1077	4-NITRO-2,6-XYLIDINE

N-NITRO COMPOUNDS

1078	N-NITRODIISOBUTYLAMINE
1079	1,4-DINITROPIPERAZINE

NITRATES

1080	PROPYL NITRATE
1081	ISOPROPYL NITRATE
1082	NITRIC ACID, PENTYL ESTER

SILICON CONTAINING COMPOUNDS

1083	HEXYLSILANE
1084	DIPHENYLSILANE
1085	TETRAETHYLSILANE
1086	ALLYLTRIMETHYLSILANE
1087	DIALLYLDIMETHYLSILANE
1088	DIBENZYLDIPHENYLSILANE
1089	PHENYLTRIMETHYLSILANE
1090	DIDODECYLDIPHENYLSILANE
1091	ETHYLTRIPHENYLSILANE
1092	METHYLTRICHLOROSILANE
1093	1,1,1,3,3,3-HEXAMETHYLDISILAZANE
1094	HEXAMETHYLDISILANE

PHOSPHORUS CONTAINING COMPOUNDS

1095	TRIBUTYLPHOSPHINE
1096	DIPHENYLETHYLPHOSPHINE
1097	TRIMETHYLENEBIS[DIPHENYLPHOSPHINE]
1098	TRI-o-TOLYLPHOSPHINE
1099	TRI-p-TOLYLPHOSPHINE
1100	TRIS(p-CHLOROPHENYL)PHOSPHINE
1101	TETRAETHYLPHOSPHONIUM IODIDE

SPECTRUM NO.   NAME

SPECTRUM NO.	NAME
1102	METHYLTRIPHENYLPHOSPHONIUM BROMIDE
1103	DIMETHYLDODECYLPHOSPHINE OXIDE
1104	DIMETHYLHEXADECYLPHOSPHINE OXIDE
1105	TRI-o-TOLYLPHOSPHINE OXIDE
1106	TRI-m-TOLYLPHOSPHINE OXIDE

SULFIDES

1107	ETHYL METHYL SULFIDE
1108	ETHYL SULFIDE
1109	PROPYL SULFIDE
1110	BUTYL SULFIDE
1111	ISOBUTYL SULFIDE
1112	ISOPENTYL SULFIDE
1113	BIS(2-ETHYLHEXYL) SULFIDE
1114	HEXYL SULFIDE
1115	HEPTYL SULFIDE
1116	DODECYL METHYL SULFIDE
1117	DODECYL ETHYL SULFIDE
1118	DODECYL SULFIDE
1119	ETHYL OCTADECYL SULFIDE
1120	BIS(CHLOROMETHYL) SULFIDE
1121	3-(METHYLTHIO)PROPYLAMINE
1122	3,3'-THIODIPROPIPNITRILE
1123	1,2-BIS(ETHYLTHIO)ETHANE
1124	1,2-BIS(PROPYLTHIO)ETHANE
1125	1,4-BIS(ETHYLTHIO)BUTANE
1126	1,4-BIS(PROPYLTHIO)BUTANE
1127	1,6-BIS(METHYLTHIO)HEXANE
1128	TRITHIOORTHOFORMIC ACID, TRIETHYL ESTER
1129	TRIMETHYLENE SULFIDE
1130	TETRAHYDROTHIOPHENE
1131	TETRAHYDRO-2H-THIOPYRAN
1132	m-DITHIANE
1133	p-DITHIANE
1134	2-METHYL-2-THIAZOLINE
1135	2-(BENZYLAMINO)-2-THIAZOLINE
1136	THIOPHENE
1137	3-METHYLTHIOPHENE
1138	2-CHLOROTHIOPHENE
1139	2,5-DICHLOROTHIOPHENE
1140	2-BROMOTHIOPHENE
1141	3-BROMOTHIOPHENE
1142	2,5-DIBROMOTHIOPHENE
1143	2-IODOTHIOPHENE
1144	2-THIOPHENECARBONITRILE
1145	2-THIOPHENECARBOXALDEHYDE, anti-OXIME

SPECTRUM NO.	NAME
1146	3-NITROTHIOPHENE
1147	2,2'-METHYLENEDITHIOPHENE
1148	3-METHYLISOTHIAZOLE
1149	4-METHYLISOTHIAZOLE
1150	4-PHENYLISOTHIAZOLE
1151	4,5-DIPHENYL-2-METHYLTHIAZOLE
1152	2-BROMOTHIAZOLE
1153	2-AMINOTHIAZOLE
1154	2-AMINO-4-METHYLTHIAZOLE
1155	2-AMINO-5-ETHYL-1,3,4-THIADIAZOLE
1156	2-(ETHYLAMINO)-1,3,4-THIADIAZOLE
1157	2,5-DIPHENYL-p-DITHIIN
1158	BENZYL METHYL SULFIDE
1159	BENZYL ETHYL SULFIDE
1160	p-BROMOPHENYL METHYL SULFIDE
1161	o-(METHYLTHIO)ANILINE
1162	BENZYL p-TOLYL SULFIDE
1163	PHENETHYL PHENYL SULFIDE
1164	PHENYL 3-PHENYLPROPYL SULFIDE
1165	BENZYL p-CHLOROPHENYL SULFIDE
1166	2,2-DIPHENYLVINYL PHENYL SULFIDE
1167	BIS(PHENYLTHIO)METHANE
1168	TETRATHIOORTHOCARBONIC ACID, TETRAPHENYL ESTER
1169	PHENYL SULFIDE
1170	DI-p-TOLYL SULFIDE
1171	BIS(p-CHLOROPHENYL)SULFIDE
1172	4-(PHENYLTHIO)PYRIDINE
1173	BENZYL 2-NAPHTHYL SULFIDE
1174	2-(PHENYLTHIO)QUINOLINE
1175	2-METHYLBENZOTHIAZOLE
1176	2-PHENYLBENZOTHIAZOLE
1177	5-CHLORO-2-METHYLBENZOTHIAZOLE
1178	2,1,3-BENZOTHIADIAZOLE
1179	3-DIBENZOTHIOPHENAMINE
1180	3,7-DINITRODIBENZOTHIOPHENE
1181	PHENOTHIAZINE
1182	3-CHLOROPHENOTHIAZINE

DISULFIDES

1183	BUTYL DISULFIDE
1184	sec-BUTYL DISULFIDE
1185	ISOBUTYL DISULFIDE
1186	tert-BUTYL DISULFIDE
1187	PENTYL DISULFIDE
1188	ISOPENTYL DISULFIDE
1189	DODECYL DISULFIDE
1190	ALLYL DISULFIDE

SPECTRUM NO.   NAME

1235	p-BROMOBENZENETHIOL
1236	o-AMINOBENZENETHIOL
1237	m-AMINOBENZENETHIOL
1238	p-AMINOBENZENETHIOL
1239	3,4-DITHIOLTOLUENE
1240	p-CHLORO-1,3-BENZENEDITHIOL
1241	1-NAPHTHALENETHIOL
1242	2-NAPHTHALENETHIOL

SULFOXIDES

1243	METHYL SULFOXIDE
1244	BUTYLMETHYL SULFOXIDE
1245	BUTYL SULFOXIDE
1246	ISOBUTYL SULFOXIDE
1247	BENZYL SULFOXIDE
1248	PHENYL PROPYL SULFOXIDE
1249	p-IODOPHENYL METHYL SULFOXIDE
1250	p-CHLOROPHENYL 3-PENTYNYL SULFOXIDE
1251	PHENYL SULFOXIDE

SULFONES

1252	METHYL SULFONE
1253	PROPYL SULFONE
1254	BUTYL SULFONE
1255	PENTYL SULFONE
1256	ETHYL VINYL SULFONE
1257	trans-CINNAMYL METHYL SULFONE
1258	STYRYL SULFONE
1259	2,5-DIHYDRO-2,4-DIMETHYLTHIOPHENE, 1,1-DIOXIDE
1260	3,4-DICHLOROTHIOPHENE, 1,1-DIOXIDE
1261	ALLYL PHENYL SULFONE
1262	ALLYL p-TOLYL SULFONE
1263	ALLYL p-CHLOROPHENYL SULFONE
1264	BIS(p-TOLYLSULFONYL)METHANE
1265	PHENYL 2-PROPYNYL SULFONE
1266	3,4-DICHLOROPHENYL 2-PROPYNYL SULFONE
1267	BENZYL p-TOLYL SULFONE
1268	PHENYL p-TOLYL SULFONE
1269	p-TOLYL SULFONE
1270	p-FLUOROPHENYL PHENYL SULFONE
1271	BIS(p-FLUOROPHENYL)SULFONE
1272	PHENYL a,a,a-TRIFLUORO-m-TOLYL SULFONE
1273	2,5-DICHLOROPHENYL PHENYL SULFONE
1274	BIS(p-CHLOROPHENYL) SULFONE
1275	BIS(p-BROMOPHENYL) SULFONE
1276	p-NITROPHENYL PHENYL SULFONE
1277	BENZO[b]THIOPHENE, 1,1-DIOXIDE
1278	2-DIBENZOTHIOPHENAMINE, 5,5-DIOXIDE

SPECTRUM NO.   NAME

SULFONYL HALIDES

SULFONIC ACIDS, SALTS AND ESTERS

SPECTRUM NO.   NAME

SULFURIC ACID ESTERS AND SALTS

1323	SULFUROUS ACID, DIMETHYL ESTER
1324	ETHYL SULFITE
1325	PENTYL SULFITE
1326	SULFURIC ACID, MONOETHYL ESTER, MONOPOTASSIUM SALT
1327	SULFURIC ACID, MONOPENTYL ESTER, SODIUM SALT
1328	SULFURIC ACID, MONOTETRADECYL ESTER, SODIUM SALT
1329	SULFURIC ACID, DIPROPYL ESTER
1330	SULFURIC ACID, BIS(2-CHLOROETHYL) ESTER

THIOAMIDES

1331	THIOACETAMIDE
1332	2-PHENYLTHIOACETAMIDE
1333	THIOBENZAMIDE
1334	6-METHYLTHIOPICOLINAMIDE
1335	THIOBENZANILIDE
1336	N,N-DIMETHYLTHIOFORMAMIDE
1337	N,N-DIMETHYLTHIOACETAMIDE

THIOUREAS

1338	1-METHYL-2-THIOUREA
1339	1-ETHYL-2-THIOUREA
1340	1-PHENYL-2-THIOUREA
1341	2-THIO-1-o-TOLYLUREA
1342	1-(1-NAPHTHYL)-2-THIOUREA
1343	1,1-DIPHENYL-2-THIOUREA
1344	1,3-DIETHYL-2-THIOUREA
1345	1,3-DIISOPROPYL-2-THIOUREA
1346	1,3-DIISOBUTYL-2-THIOUREA
1347	1,3-DIDECYL-2-THIOUREA
1348	1-ETHYL-3-PHENYL-2-THIOUREA
1349	1-ISOPROPYL-3-PHENYL-2-THIOUREA
1350	1-ALLYL-3-PHENYL-2-THIOUREA
1351	THIOCARBANILIDE
1352	1-(o-CHLOROPHENYL)-3-PHENYL-2-THIOUREA
1353	1,1-DIMETHYL-4-(2-NORBORNYL)-3-THIOSEMICARBAZIDE
1354	3-(o-CHLOROPHENYL)-1-DIMETHYL-2-THIOUREA
1355	THIO-1-PIPERIDINECARBOXY-m-TOLUIDIDE
1356	1,1,3,3-TETRAETHYL-2-THIOUREA
1357	NAPHTH[2,3-d]IMIDAZOLINE-2-THIONE
1358	1,5-BIS-HEPTYLIDENE-3-THIOCARBOHYDRAZIDE

SULFONAMIDES

1359	METHANESULFONAMIDE
1360	trans-2-PHENYLETHENESULFONAMIDE
1361	BENZENESULFONAMIDE
1362	o-TOLUENESULFONAMIDE

SPECTRUM NO.	NAME
1363	p-TOLUENESULFONAMIDE
1364	2-MESITYLENESULFONAMIDE
1365	SULFANILAMIDE
1366	N^4-BENZYLIDENESULFANILAMIDE
1367	2-NAPHTHALENESULFONAMIDE
1368	ETHANESULFONO-p-TOLUIDIDE
1369	N-(2-HYDROXYETHYL)-N-(3-HYDROXYPROPYL)-p-TOLUENESULFONAMIDE
1370	p-TOLUENESULFONANILIDE
1371	BENZENESULFONO-o-TOLUIDIDE
1372	p-TOLUENESULFONO-2',6'-XYLIDIDE
1373	N,N-DIMETHYLMETHANESULFONAMIDE
1374	N,N,N',N'-TETRAMETHYL-1,4-PIPERAZINEDISULFONAMIDE
1375	N,N-DIMETHYL-p-TOLUENESULFONAMIDE
1376	1,3-BIS(PHENYLSULFONYL)IMIDAZOLIDINE

SULFAMIDES

1377	N,N'-DICYCLOHEXYLSULFAMIDE
1378	4,4'-DIBROMOSULFANILIDE

ETHERS

1379	ETHYL ETHER
1380	BUTYL METHYL ETHER
1381	PROPYL ETHER
1382	BUTYL ETHYL ETHER
1383	ETHYL ISOBUTYL ETHER
1384	BUTYL ETHER
1385	ISOPENTYL ETHER
1386	HEXYL ETHER
1387	BIS(2-ETHYLHEXYL) ETHER
1388	OCTYL ETHER
1389	DECYL ETHER
1390	ETHYL OCTADECYL ETHER
1391	HEXADECYL ETHER
1392	OCTADECYL ETHER
1393	(2-CHLORO-1,1,2-TRIFLUOROETHYL) ETHYL ETHER
1394	ISOPROPYL PROPYL ETHER
1395	ISOPROPYL ETHER
1396	tert-BUTYL METHYL ETHER
1397	tert-BUTYL ETHYL ETHER
1398	tert-BUTYL ISOPROPYL ETHER
1399	BIS(CHLOROMETHYL) ETHER
1400	3-ISOPROPOXYPROPIONITRILE
1401	2-ETHOXYETHANETHIOL
1402	2,2'-OXYDIETHANETHIOL
1403	ALLYL ETHYL ETHER
1404	BUTYL VINYL ETHER
1405	ISOBUTYL VINYL ETHER

SPECTRUM NO.   NAME

SPECTRUM NO.	NAME
1544	m-NITROPHENYL PHENYL ETHER
1545	o-DIMETHOXYBENZENE
1546	m-DIMETHOXYBENZENE
1547	p-DIMETHOXYBENZENE
1548	1-METHOXY-4-PHENOXYBENZENE
1549	4,4'-OXYDIANISOLE
1550	m-DIPHENOXYBENZENE
1551	2,3-DIMETHYLANISOLE
1552	2,4-DIMETHYLANISOLE
1553	2,6-DICHLOROANISOLE
1554	4-CHLORO-o-ANISIDINE
1555	2,4-DINITROANISOLE
1556	2,6-DINITROANISOLE
1557	2,4-DINITROPHENETOLE
1558	2,5-DIMETHOXYTOLUENE
1559	1,2-DIMETHOXY-4-PROPENYLBENZENE
1560	4-ALLYL-1,2-DIMETHOXYBENZENE
1561	3,4-DIETHOXYANILINE
1562	2,5-DIBUTOXYANILINE
1563	VERATRONITRILE
1564	1,3-DIMETHOXY-4-NITROBENZENE
1565	1,2,3-TRIMETHOXYBENZENE
1566	2,4,6-TRICHLOROANISOLE
1567	2,4,6-TRIBROMOANISOLE
1568	2,4,6-TRINITROANISOLE
1569	1-METHOXYNAPHTHALENE
1570	1-ETHOXYNAPHTHALENE
1571	2-ETHOXYNAPHTHALENE
1572	2-(BENZYLOXY)NAPHTHALENE

FURANS

SPECTRUM NO.	NAME
1573	FURAN
1574	2-METHYLFURAN
1575	2,5-DIMETHYLFURAN
1576	2-FURONITRILE
1577	2-FURANMETHANETHIOL
1578	2-(2-NITROVINYL)FURAN
1579	3-METHYLISOXAZOLE
1580	2-(m-CHLOROPHENYL)-5-PHENYLOXAZOLE
1581	2-(HEXADECYLOXY)PYRIDINE
1582	METHOXYPYRAZINE
1583	3-METHOXYPHENOTHIAZINE
1584	BENZOFURAN
1585	2,5,6-TRIMETHYLBENZOXAZOLE
1586	PHENOXATHIIN
1587	PHENOXATHIIN, 10,10-DIOXIDE

SPECTRUM NO.   NAME

1588	1,3-BENZODIOXOLE
1589	ISOCHROMAN
1590	1,4-BENZODIOXAN
1591	DIBENZO-p-DIOXIN
1592	HYPOCHLOROUS ACID, tert-BUTYL ESTER

SILICON ETHERS

1593	ETHOXYTRIMETHYLSILANE
1594	DIMETHOXYDIPHENYLSILANE
1595	METHYLTRIETHOXYSILANE
1596	ETHYLTRIETHOXYSILANE
1597	3-(TRIETHOXYSILYL)PROPYLAMINE
1598	SILICIC ACID, TETRAMETHYL ESTER
1599	SILICIC ACID, TETRABUTYL ESTER
1600	PENTYL SILICATE
1601	SILICIC ACID, TETRAKIS(2-ETHYLBUTYL)ESTER
1602	SILICIC ACID, TETRAKIS(2-ETHYLHEXYL)ESTER
1603	HEXAMETHYLDISILOXANE
1604	1,3-BIS(CHLOROMETHYL)-1,1,3,3-TETRAMETHYLDISILOXANE
1605	OCTAMETHYLCYCLOTETRASILOXANE

PHOSPHORUS ETHERS

1606	2-ETHYL-1-HEXANOL, PHOSPHITE
1607	2-CHLOROETHANOL, PHOSPHITE (3:1)
1608	PHOSPHOROUS ACID, TRIPHENYL ESTER

PEROXIDES

1609	tert-BUTYL PEROXIDE
1610	1,4-EPIDIOXY-p-MENTH-2-ENE

PRIMARY ALCOHOLS

1611	METHANOL
1612	ETHYL ALCOHOL
1613	PROPYL ALCOHOL
1614	BUTYL ALCOHOL
1615	ISOBUTYL ALCOHOL
1616	PENTYL ALCOHOL
1617	(—)-2-METHYL-1-BUTANOL
1618	3-METHYL-1-BUTANOL
1619	HEXYL ALCOHOL
1620	3-METHYL-1-PENTANOL
1621	4-METHYL-1-PENTANOL
1622	2-ETHYL-1-BUTANOL
1623	HEPTYL ALCOHOL
1624	2,2-DIMETHYL-1-PENTANOL
1625	5-METHYL-1-HEXANOL
1626	1-OCTANOL
1627	2-ETHYL-4-METHYL-1-PENTANOL

SPECTRUM NO.	NAME
1674	2-[2-(ETHOXY)ETHOXY]ETHANOL
1675	2-[2-(BUTOXY)ETHOXY]ETHANOL
1676	2,2'-(2—BUTYNYLENEDIOXY)DIETHANOL
1677	2,3-EPOXY-1-PROPANOL
1678	2-THIOPHENETHANOL
1679	2,2-DIMETHYL-1,3-DIOXOLANE-4-METHANOL
1680	CYCLOHEXANEMETHANOL
1681	4-METHYLCYCLOHEXANEMETHANOL
1682	CYCLOHEXANEETHANOL
1683	3-PIPERIDINEMETHANOL
1684	1-ADAMANTANEMETHANOL
1685	ALLYL ALCOHOL
1686	2-BUTEN-1-OL
1687	3-BUTEN-1-OL
1688	cis-3-HEXEN-1-OL
1689	cis-9-OCTADECEN-1-OL
1690	PHYTOL
1691	2-(ALLYLOXY)ETHANOL
1692	3,4-DIHYDRO-2,5-DIMETHYL-2H-PYRAN-2-METHANOL
1693	2-PROPYN-1-OL
1694	2-BUTYN-1-OL
1695	3-BUTYN-1-OL
1696	2-PENTYN-1-OL
1697	2-NONYN-1-OL
1698	3-NONYN-1-OL
1699	3-DECYN-1-OL
1700	BENZYL ALCOHOL
1701	PHENETHYL ALCOHOL
1702	3-PHENYL-1-PROPANOL
1703	2-(BENZYLMETHYLAMINO)ETHANOL
1704	2-(DIBENZYLAMINO)ETHANOL
1705	2-(BENZYLOXY)ETHANOL
1706	2-(N-ETHYLANILINO)ETHANOL
1707	2-[(p-CHLOROBENZYLIDENE)AMINO]ETHANOL
1708	2-(p-TOLYLTHIO)ETHANOL
1709	(p-TOLYLSULFONYL)METHANOL
1710	2-PHENOXYETHANOL
1711	CINNAMYL ALCOHOL
1712	3-PHENYL-2-BUTEN-1-OL
1713	p-METHYLBENZYL ALCOHOL
1714	p-CYMEN-7-OL
1715	o-FLUOROBENZYL ALCOHOL
1716	p-FLUOROBENZYL ALCOHOL
1717	o-CHLOROBENZYL ALCOHOL
1718	p-AMINOPHENETHYL ALCOHOL
1719	o-NITROBENZYL ALCOHOL

SPECTRUM NO.	NAME
1720	m-NITROBENZYL ALCOHOL
1721	p-NITROBENZYL ALCOHOL
1722	o-METHOXYBENZYL ALCOHOL
1723	p-METHOXYBENZYL ALCOHOL
1724	3-(p-NITROPHENYL)-2-PROPEN-1-OL
1725	1-NAPHTHALENEETHANOL
1726	2-(2-NAPHTHYLOXY)ETHANOL
1727	FLUORENE-9-METHANOL
1728	2-PYRIDINEMETHANOL
1729	4-PYRIDINEMETHANOL
1730	2-BENZIMIDAZOLEMETHANOL
1731	3-QUINOLINEMTHANOL
1732	5-PHENYL-2-PYRIMIDINEETHANOL
1733	FURFURYL ALCOHOL
1734	PIPERONYL ALCOHOL

SECONDARY ALCOHOLS

1735	ISOPROPYL ALCOHOL
1736	2-BUTANOL
1737	3-PENTANOL
1738	2-HEXANOL
1739	2-HEPTANOL
1740	4-HEPTANOL
1741	2,4-DIMETHYL-3-PENTANOL
1742	(+)-2-OCTANOL
1743	4-ETHYL-3-HEXANOL
1744	2,2-DIMETHYL-3-HEXANOL
1745	6-ETHYL-3-OCTANOL
1746	5-ETHYL-2-NONANOL
1747	6-ETHYL-3-DECANOL
1748	2-TRIDECANOL
1749	3,9-DIETHYL-6-TRIDECANOL
1750	1,3-DICHLORO-2-PROPANOL
1751	1,3-DIBROMO-2-PROPANOL
1752	1,3-DIAMINO-2-PROPANOL
1753	3-AMINO-2-BUTANOL
1754	2-(DIMETHYLAMINO)-1-METHYLETHANOL
1755	1-(DIBUTYLAMINO)-2-PROPANOL
1756	a-METHYL-1-PYRROLIDINEETHANOL
1757	4-(TETRADECYLAMINO)-2-BUTANOL, HYDROCHLORIDE
1758	LACTONITRILE
1759	4-METHOXY-4-METHYL-2-PENTANOL
1760	1-[2-(2-METHOXY-1-METHYLETHOXY)-1-METHYLETHOXY]-2-PROPANOL
1761	a-METHYLCYCLOPROPANEMETHANOL
1762	1-CYCLOHEXYLETHANOL
1763	CYCLOBUTANOL
1764	CYCLOPENTANOL

SPECTRUM NO.	NAME
1810	1-ETHYLCYCLOHEXANOL
1811	1-METHYLCYCLOHEPTANOL
1812	2-METHYL-3-BUTEN-2-OL
1813	2-METHYL-3-BUTYNE-2-OL
1814	3-METHYL-1-PENTYN-3-OL
1815	2,4,7,9-TETRAMETHYL-5-DECYNE-4,7-DIOL
1816	1-ETHYLNYLCYCLOHEXANOL
1817	a,a-DIMETHYLBENZYL ALCOHOL
1818	a,a-DIETHYLBENZYL ALCOHOL
1819	2-PHENYL-3-BUTYN-2-OL
1820	a-OCTYLBENZHYDROL
1821	1-p-TOLYLCYCLOHEXANOL
1822	TRIPHENYLMETHANOL

DIOLS

1823	ETHYLENE GLYCOL
1824	1,3-PROPANEDIOL
1825	1,5-PENTANEDIOL
1826	1,6-HEXANEDIOL
1827	1,16-HEXADECANEDIOL
1828	1,2-PROPANEDIOL
1829	1,2-BUTANEDIOL
1830	2,4-PENTANEDIOL
1831	2-METHYL-2,4-PENTANEDIOL
1832	3-METHYL-1,5-PENTANEDIOL
1833	2,5-HEXANEDIOL
1834	2,3-DIMETHYL-2,3-BUTANEDIOL, HYDRATE
1835	2,2-DIETHYL-1,3-PROPANEDIOL
1836	2-ETHYL-1,3-HEXANEDIOL
1837	2,4,4-TRIMETHYL-1,2-PENTANEDIOL
1838	2,4,4-TRIMETHYL-2,3-PENTANEDIOL
1839	2-BUTYL-2-ETHYL-1,3-PROPANEDIOL
1840	3-CHLORO-1,2-PROPANEDIOL
1841	2,2-BIS(BROMOMETHYL)-1,3-PROPANEDIOL
1842	2,2'-IMINODIETHANOL
1843	2,2'-(ETHYLENEDIIMINO)DIETHANOL
1844	3-AMINO-1,2-PROPANEDIOL
1845	DIETHYLENE GLYCOL
1846	TRIETHYLENE GLYCOL
1847	TETRAETHYLENE GLYCOL
1848	GLYCEROL
1849	1,4,7-HEPTANETRIOL
1850	2,2',2''-NITRILOTRIETHANOL
1851	1,1',1''-NITRILOTRI-2-PROPANOL
1852	2,2',2''-NITRILOTRIETHANOL, HYDROCHLORIDE
1853	PENTAERYTHRITOL

SPECTRUM NO. NAME

1854	2,2',2'',2'''-(ETHYLENEDINITRILO)TETRAETHANOL
1855	cis-CYCLOHEXANE-1,2-DIOL
1856	1,4-CYCLOHEXANEDIOL
1857	cis-1,5-CYCLOOCTANEDIOL
1858	2-BUTYNE-1,4-DIOL
1859	2,7-DIMETHYL-3,5-OCTADIYNE-2,7-DIOL
1860	p-XYLENE-*a,a'*-DIOL

CARBOHYDRATES

1861	ERYTHRITOL
1862	XYLITOL
1863	GALACTITOL
1864	D-GLUCITOL
1865	D-(—)-MANNITOL
1866	D-RIBOSE
1867	1-ARABINOPYRANOSE
1868	D-(+)-XYLOSE
1869	L-(+)-RHAMNOSE, HYDRATE
1870	D-(—)-FRUCTOSE
1871	D-(+)-GLUCOSE
1872	D-(+)-MANNOSE
1873	D-(+)-GALACTOSE
1874	SUCROSE

PHENOLS

1875	PHENOL
1876	o-CRESOL
1877	m-CRESOL
1878	p-CRESOL
1879	o-ETHYLPHENOL
1880	m-ETHYLPHENOL
1881	p-ISOPROPYLPHENOL
1882	o-tert-BUTYLPHENOL
1883	p-tert-BUTYLPHENOL
1884	p-PENTYLPHENOL
1885	p-tert-PENTYLPHENOL
1886	p-(1,1,3,3-TETRAMETHYLBUTYL)PHENOL
1887	p-CYCLOHEXYLPHENOL
1888	4,4'-METHYLENEDIPHENOL
1889	p-PHENYLPHENOL
1890	o-FLUOROPHENOL
1891	p-FLUOROPHENOL
1892	o-CHLOROPHENOL
1893	p-CHLOROPHENOL
1894	o-BROMOPHENOL
1895	p-BROMOPHENOL
1896	o-IODOPHENOL

SPECTRUM NO.   NAME

ALDEHYDES

SPECTRUM NO.   NAME

2170	p-(DIMETHYLAMINO)BENZALDEHYDE
2171	m-NITROBENZALDEHYDE
2172	p-NITROBENZALDEHYDE
2173	p-PROPOXYBENZALDEHYDE
2174	p-(PENTYLOXY)BENZALDEHYDE
2175	p-(ALLYLOXY)BENZALDEHYDE
2176	2,5-DIMETHYLBENZALDEHYDE
2177	3,4-DICHLOROBENZALDEHYDE
2178	6-HYDROXY-m-ANISALDEHYDE
2179	5-INDANCARBOXALDEHYDE
2180	FLUORENE-2-CARBOXALDEHYDE
2181	3-PYRENECARBOXALDEHYDE
2182	PYRROLE-2-CARBOXALDEHYDE
2183	3-QUINOLINECARBOXALDEHYDE
2184	5-METHYL-2-THIOPHENECARBOXALDEHYDE
2185	5-NITROFURFURAL
2186	PIPERONAL

ACID HALIDES

2187	PROPIONYL CHLORIDE
2188	BUTYRYL CHLORIDE
2189	3,3-DIMETHYLBUTYRYL CHLORIDE
2190	2,2-DIMETHYLVALERYL CHLORIDE
2191	2-PROPYLVALERYL CHLORIDE
2192	DECANOYL CHLORIDE
2193	LAUROYL CHLORIDE
2194	STEAROYL CHLORIDE
2195	4-CHLOROBUTYRYL CHLORIDE
2196	3-BROMOPROPIONYL CHLORIDE
2197	6-BROMOHEXANOYL CHLORIDE
2198	SUCCINYL CHLORIDE
2199	ADIPOYL CHLORIDE
2200	PIMELOYL CHLORIDE
2201	AZELAOYL CHLORIDE
2202	SEBACOYL CHLORIDE
2203	CYCLOPENTANEPROPIONYL CHLORIDE
2204	CYCLOPENTANECARBONYL CHLORIDE
2205	CYCLOHEXANECARBONYL CHLORIDE
2206	10-UNDECENOYL CHLORIDE
2207	OLEOYL CHLORIDE
2208	SORBOYL CHLORIDE
2209	FUMAROYL CHLORIDE
2210	1-CYCLOHEXENE-1-CARBONYL CHLORIDE
2211	3-CYCLOHEXENE-1-CARBONYL CHLORIDE
2212	HYDROCINNAMOYL CHLORIDE
2213	CHLOROPHENYLACETYL CHLORIDE
2214	BROMODIPHENYLACETYL BROMIDE

SPECTRUM NO.   NAME

2215	PHENOXYACETYL CHLORIDE
2216	2-PHENOXYPROPIONYL CHLORIDE
2217	(p-CHLOROPHENYL)ACETYL CHLORIDE
2218	4-(p-BROMOPHENYL)BUTYRYL CHLORIDE
2219	BENZOYL FLUORIDE
2220	BENZOYL CHLORIDE
2221	BENZOYL BROMIDE
2222	o-TOLUOYL CHLORIDE
2223	p-TOLUOYL CHLORIDE
2224	p-tert-BUTYLBENZOYL CHLORIDE
2225	a,a,a-TRIFLUORO-o-TOLUOYL CHLORIDE
2226	a,a,a-TRIFLUORO-p-TOLUOYL CHLORIDE
2227	o-FLUOROBENZOYL CHLORIDE
2228	m-FLUOROBENZOYL CHLORIDE
2229	o-CHLOROBENZOYL CHLORIDE
2230	m-CHLOROBENZOYL CHLORIDE
2231	p-CHLOROBENZOYL CHLORIDE
2232	o-BROMOBENZOYL CHLORIDE
2233	m-BROMOBENZOYL CHLORIDE
2234	m-BROMOBENZOYL BROMIDE
2235	o-NITROBENZOYL CHLORIDE
2236	m-NITROBENZOYL CHLORIDE
2237	PHTHALOYL CHLORIDE
2238	2,3-DIMETHYLBENZOYL CHLORIDE
2239	3,4-DIMETHYLBENZOYL CHLORIDE
2240	3,5-DIMETHYLBENZOYL CHLORIDE
2241	3-NITRO-p-TOLUOYL CHLORIDE
2242	2-CHLORO-4-NITROBENZOYL CHLORIDE
2243	2-CHLORO-5-NITROBENZOYL CHLORIDE
2244	3,5-DIMETHOXYBENZOYL CHLORIDE
2245	1-NAPHTHOYL CHLORIDE
2246	2-FUROYL CHLORIDE

ANHYDRIDES

2247	ACETIC ANHYDRIDE
2248	PROPIONIC ANHYDRIDE
2249	BUTYRIC ANHYDRIDE
2250	VALERIC ANHYDRIDE
2251	PIVALIC ANHYDRIDE
2252	HEXANOIC ANHYDRIDE
2253	2-ETHYLBUTYRIC ANHYDRIDE
2254	HEPTANOIC ANHYDRIDE
2255	SUCCINIC ANHYDRIDE
2256	METHYLSUCCINIC ANHYDRIDE
2257	(2-DODECEN-1-YL)SUCCINIC ANHYDRIDE
2258	METHYLENESUCCINIC ANHYDRIDE
2259	3-METHYLGLUTARIC ANHYDRIDE

SPECTRUM NO.	NAME
2260	2,2-DIMETHYLGLUTARIC ANHYDRIDE
2261	1,2-CYCLOHEXANEDICARBOXYLIC ANHYDRIDE
2262	DL-CAMPHORIC ANHYDRIDE
2263	MALEIC ANHYDRIDE
2264	CITRACONIC ANHYDRIDE
2265	DIMETHYLMALEIC ANHYDRIDE
2266	BROMOMALEIC ANHYDRIDE
2267	1-CYCLOHEXENE-1,2-DICARBOXYLIC ANHYDRIDE
2268	4-CYCLOHEXENE-1,2-DICARBOXYLIC ACID, ANHYDRIDE
2269	CINNAMIC ANHYDRIDE
2270	BENZOIC ANHYDRIDE
2271	4-METHYLPHTHALIC ANHYDRIDE
2272	5-FLUOROPHTHALIC ANHYDRIDE
2273	1,2,4,5-BENZENETETRACARBOXYLIC 1,2:4,5-DIANHYDRIDE
2274	NAPHTHALIC ANHYDRIDE

AMIDES

SPECTRUM NO.	NAME
2275	ACETAMIDE
2276	PROPIONAMIDE
2277	HEXANAMIDE
2278	HEPTANAMIDE
2279	OCTANAMIDE
2280	MYRISTAMIDE
2281	2-CHLOROACETAMIDE
2282	2,2-DICHLOROACETAMIDE
2283	LACTAMIDE
2284	2-METHOXYACETAMIDE
2285	a-ETHYL-1-CYCLOHEXENE-1-ACETAMIDE
2286	2-PHENYLBUTYRAMIDE
2287	1-NAPHTHALENEACETAMIDE
2288	BENZAMIDE
2289	m-TOLUAMIDE
2290	p-TOLUAMIDE
2291	o-BROMOBENZAMIDE
2292	p-NITROBENZAMIDE
2293	SALICYLAMIDE
2294	2-FURAMIDE
2295	N-ETHYLFORMAMIDE
2296	N-METHYLPROPIONAMIDE
2297	N-BUTYLACETAMIDE
2298	N-METHYLDODECANAMIDE
2299	N-PROPYLDODECANAMIDE
2300	N,N'-METHYLENEBISFORMAMIDE
2301	N,N'-ETHYLENEBISACETAMIDE
2302	N,N'-DI-tert-PENTYLGLUTARAMIDE
2303	2-PIPERIDONE
2304	N-tert-BUTYLACRYLAMIDE

SPECTRUM NO.	NAME
2351	N,N-DIBUTYLPROPIONAMIDE
2352	N,N-DIMETHYLBUTYRAMIDE
2353	N,N-DIETHYLBUTYRAMIDE
2354	N,N-DIPROPYLDECANAMIDE
2355	N,N-DIMETHYLDODECANAMIDE
2356	N,N-DIETHYLLAURAMIDE
2357	N,N-DIMETHYLLACTAMIDE
2358	N,N-DIETHYLACETOACETAMIDE
2359	N,N-DIMETHYL-1-ADAMANTANECARBOXAMIDE
2360	4-ACETYLMORPHOLINE
2361	N-ETHYLFORMANILIDE
2362	N-ETHYL-p-FORMOTOLUIDIDE
2363	N-METHYLACETANILIDE
2364	N-ETHYLACETANILIDE
2365	N-PROPYLACETANILIDE
2366	N-BUTYLACETANILIDE
2367	DIPHENYLFORMAMIDE
2368	N,N-DIPHENYLACETAMIDE
2369	1-BENZOYLPIPERIDINE
2370	N,N,N',N'-TETRAETHYLPHTHALAMIDE
2371	3,4-DIHYDRO-1(2H)-QUINOLINECARBOXALDEHYDE
2372	1-ACETYL-1,2,3,4-TETRAHYDROQUINOLINE
2373	9-ACETYLCARBAZOLE
2374	1-PHENYL-2-PYRROLIDINONE

IMIDES

2375	SUCCINIMIDE
2376	2-METHYLSUCCINIMIDE
2377	GLUTARIMIDE
2378	3-AZASPIRO[5.5]UNDECANE-2,4-DIONE
2379	MALEIMIDE
2380	PHTHALIMIDE
2381	4-NITROPHTHALIMIDE
2382	N-PENTYLSUCCINIMIDE
2383	1-ACETYLHEXAHYDRO-2H-AZEPIN-2-ONE
2384	N-ETHYLMALEIMIDE
2385	N-PHENETHYLMALEIMIDE
2386	N-BENZYLMALEIMIDE
2387	N-(o-CHLOROPHENYL)MALEIMIDE
2388	N-(p-BROMOPHENYL)MALEIMIDE
2389	N-(p-IODOPHENYL)MALEIMIDE
2390	N,N'-m-PHENYLENEDIMALEIMIDE
2391	N-METHYLPHTHALIMIDE
2392	N-(2-CHLOROETHYL)PHTHALIMIDE
2393	N-(BROMOMETHYL)PHTHALIMIDE
2394	N-(2,3-EPOXYPROPYL)PHTHALIMIDE
2395	N-VINYLPHTHALIMIDE

SPECTRUM NO.   NAME

2440	N,N'-DIMETHYLCARBANILIDE
2441	1-PHENYL-2-BENZIMIDAZOLINONE
2442	5,5-DIMETHYLTETRAHYDRO-2(1H)-PYRIMIDINONE

HYDANTOINS, URACILS, BARBITURATES

2443	HYDANTOIN
2444	5-METHYLHYDANTOIN
2445	3-BENZYL-5,5-DIMETHYLHYDANTOIN
2446	5-PHENYLHYDANTOIN
2447	5-METHYL-5-PHENYLHYDANTOIN
2448	3-METHYL-5-PHENYLHYDANTOIN
2449	3-ETHYL-5-PHENYLHYDANTOIN
2450	1,3-DIPHENYLHYDANTOIN
2451	ALLANTOIN
2452	1,3-DIMETHYLURACIL
2453	THYMINE (5-METHYLURACIL)
2454	6-METHYLURACIL
2455	5,6-DIMETHYLURACIL
2456	5-BROMOURACIL
2457	5-IODOURACIL
2458	5-NITROURACIL
2459	5-(1-METHYLBUTYL)BARBITURIC ACID
2460	5,5-DIETHYLBARBITURIC ACID
2461	5,5-DIALLYLBARBITURIC ACID
2462	5,5-DIBENZYLBARBITURIC ACID
2463	5-BENZYLIDENEBARBITURIC ACID
2464	5-ALLYL-5-PHENYLBARBITURIC ACID
2465	1,3,5-TRIS(2-HYDROXYETHYL)-s-TRIAZINE-2,4,6(1H,3H,5H)-TRIONE
2466	1,3-DIPHENYL-5-ETHYL-s-TRIAZINE-2,4,6(1H,3H,5H)-TRIONE
2467	1,4-DIPHENYLSEMICARBAZIDE
2468	4,4-DIPHENYLSEMICARBAZIDE
2469	3-METHYL-2-BUTANONE, SEMICARBAZONE
2470	2-HEPTANONE, SEMICARBAZONE

CARBOXYLIC ACIDS

2471	FORMIC ACID
2472	ACETIC ACID
2473	PROPIONIC ACID
2474	IOSBUTYRIC ACID
2475	DL-2-METHYLBUTYRIC ACID
2476	PIVALIC ACID
2477	2-ETHYLHEXANOIC ACID
2478	2-ETHYL-4-METHYLVALERIC ACID
2479	2-PROPYLVALERIC ACID
2480	LAURIC ACID
2481	2-PENTYLHEPTANOIC ACID
2482	PALMITIC·ACID
2483	CHLOROACETIC ACID

SPECTRUM NO.	NAME
2484	2-CHLOROBUTYRIC ACID
2485	BROMOACETIC ACID
2486	2-BROMOVALERIC ACID
2487	2-BROMOHEPTANOIC ACID
2488	IODOACETIC ACID
2489	2-MERCAPTOPROPIONIC ACID
2490	3-MERCAPTOPROPIONIC ACID
2491	METHOXYACETIC ACID
2492	GLYCOLIC ACID
2493	LACTIC ACID
2494	LEVULINIC ACID
2495	9,12-DIOXOOCTADECANOIC ACID
2496	MALONIC ACID
2497	SUCCINIC ACID
2498	GLUTARIC ACID
2499	ADIPIC ACID
2500	3,3-DIMETHYLGLUTARIC ACID
2501	SUBERIC ACID
2502	DECANEDIOIC ACID
2503	HEXADECANEDIOIC ACID
2504	2,2,3,3,4,4-HEXAFLUOROGLUTARIC ACID
2505	3-CHLOROGLUTARIC ACID
2506	TARTRONIC ACID
2507	L-MALIC ACID
2508	L-(+)-TARTARIC ACID
2509	DL-TARTARIC ACID
2510	1,2,3-PROPANETRICARBOXYLIC ACID
2511	CITRIC ACID
2512	2-THIOPHENEACETIC ACID
2513	CYCLOBUTANECARBOXYLIC ACID
2514	CYCLOHEXANECARBOXYLIC ACID
2515	1,4-CYCLOHEXANEDICARBOXYLIC ACID
2516	3-BUTENOIC ACID
2517	CROTONIC ACID
2518	4-PENTENOIC ACID
2519	3-METHYLCROTONIC ACID
2520	trans-2-HEXENOIC ACID
2521	3-HEPTENOIC ACID
2522	4-METHYL-2-HEPTENOIC ACID
2523	2-ETHYL-2-HEXENOIC ACID
2524	2-DECENOIC ACID
2525	trans-4-DECENOIC ACID
2526	trans-4-UNDECENOIC ACID
2527	trans-4-TRIDECENOIC ACID
2528	OLEIC ACID

SPECTRUM NO.	NAME
2575	o-IODOBENZOIC ACID
2576	m-IODOBENZOIC ACID
2577	p-IODOBENZOIC ACID
2578	p-AMINOBENZOIC ACID
2579	N-PHENYLANTHRANILIC ACID
2580	m-CYANOBENZOIC ACID
2581	o-NITROBENZOIC ACID
2582	p-NITROBENZOIC ACID
2583	m-ANISIC ACID
2584	p-ANISIC ACID
2585	o-ETHOXYBENZOIC ACID
2586	p-PROPOXYBENZOIC ACID
2587	SALICYLIC ACID
2588	p-HYDROXYBENZOIC ACID
2589	4,4'-OXYDIBENZOIC ACID
2590	PHTHALIC ACID
2591	ISOPHTHALIC ACID
2592	TEREPHTHALIC ACID
2593	2,6-DIMETHYLBENZOIC ACID
2594	2,4-DINITROBENZOIC ACID
2595	6-AMINO-m-ANISIC ACID
2596	2,4-CRESOTIC ACID
2597	3-NITROSALICYLIC ACID
2598	VANILLIC ACID
2599	β-RESORCYLIC ACID
2600	PROTOCATECHUIC ACID
2601	4-NITROPHTHALIC ACID
2602	5-NITROISOPHTHALIC ACID
2603	1,3,5-BENZENETRICARBOXYLIC ACID
2604	3-FUROIC ACID
2605	2-FURANACRYLIC ACID
2606	NICOTINIC ACID, HYDROCHLORIDE
2607	3-INDOLEACETIC ACID
2608	PIPERONYLIC ACID
2609	THIOACETIC ACID
2610	THIOBENZOIC ACID

AMINO ACIDS

2611	GLYCINE
2612	SARCOSINE
2613	N-(2-CYANOETHYL)GLYCINE
2614	L-ALANINE
2615	dl-2-AMINOBUTYRIC ACID
2616	2-METHYLALANINE
2617	β-ALANINE
2618	DL-NORVALINE

SALTS OF CARBOXYLIC ACIDS

SPECTRUM NO.　　NAME

2664	SUCCINIC ACID, DISODIUM SALT
2665	NITRILOTRIACETIC ACID, DISODIUM SALT, HYDRATE
2666	NITRILOTRIACETIC ACID, TRISODIUM SALT, HYDRATE
2667	POTASSIUM CITRATE, HYDRATE
2668	(ETHYLENEDINITRILO)TETRAACETIC ACID, DIPOTASSIUM SALT, DIHYDRATE
2669	ACRYLIC ACID, CALCIUM SALT
2670	10-UNDECENOIC ACID, POTASSIUM SALT
2671	SORBIC ACID, POTASSIUM SALT
2672	MALEIC ACID, SODIUM SALT
2673	PHENYLACETIC ACID, SODIUM SALT
2674	1-NAPHTHALENEACETIC ACID, SODIUM SALT
2675	BENZOIC ACID, SODIUM SALT
2676	m-AMINOBENZOIC ACID, SODIUM SALT
2677	p-AMINOBRNZOIC ACID, SODIUM SALT
2678	SODIUM SALICYLATE
2679	p-HYDROXYBENZOIC ACID, MONOSODIUM SALT
2680	PHTHALIC ACID, MONOPOTASSIUM SALT
2681	2-FUROIC ACID, POTASSIUM SALT
2682	SUCCINIC ACID, DIAMMONIUM SALT
2683	BENZOIC ACID, AMMONIUM SALT
2684	SALICYLIC ACID, AMMONIUM SALT
2685	DECYLAMINE, ACETATE (1:1) (SALT)
2686	DODECYLAMINE, ACETATE
2687	HYDROXYLAMINE, ACETATE (SALT)
2688	N,N-DIMETHYL-p-PHENYLENEDIAMINE, OXALATE (2:1)
2689	PIPERAZINE, ADIPATE (1:1)
2690	ETHYLENEDIAMINE, MONO-(+)-TARTRATE

ESTERS

2691	2-ETHYL-1-BUTANOL, FORMAT
2692	FORMIC ACID, HEPTYL ESTER
2693	FORMIC ACID, OCTYL ESTER
2694	ACETIC ACID, METHYL ESTER
2695	ACETIC ACID, 2-ETHYLBUTYL ESTER
2696	ACETIC ACID, 2-ETHYLHEXYL ESTER
2697	ACETIC ACID, DODECYL ESTER
2698	PROPIONIC ACID, sec-BUTYL ESTER
2699	ISOVALERIC ACID, METHYL ESTER
2700	BUTYRIC ACID, ISOPROPYL ESTER
2701	VALERIC ACID, ETHYL ESTER
2702	ISOBUTYRIC ACID, BUTYL ESTER
2703	PIVALIC ACID, ETHYL ESTER
2704	OCTANOIC ACID, METHYL ESTER
2705	VALERIC ACID, PENTYL ESTER
2706	ISOVALERIC ACID, PENTYL ESTER
2707	DECANOIC ACID, METHYL ESTER

SPECTRUM NO.	NAME
2753	ETHYLENE GLYCOL, DIPROPIONATE
2754	1,2-PROPANEDIOL, DIACETATE
2755	1,5-PENTANEDIOL, DIACETATE
2756	TRIETHYLENE GLYCOL, DIACETATE
2757	TRIETHYLENE GLYCOL, BIS(2-ETHYLHEXANOATE)
2758	1,3-DIPALMITIN
2759	1,3-DISTEARIN
2760	TRIOCTANOIN
2761	TRISTEARIN
2762	CITRIC ACID, TRIS(2-ETHYLHEXYL)ESTER, ACETATE
2763	PENTAERYTRITOL, TETRALAURATE
2764	D-SUCROSE, OCTAACETATE
2765	CARBONIC ACID, DIBUTYL ESTER
2766	OXALIC ACID, DIBUTYL ESTER
2767	MALONIC ACID, DIBUTYL ESTER
2768	MALONIC ACID, DI-tert-BUTYL ESTER
2769	MALONIC ACID, DIDODECYL ESTER
2770	PENTYLMALONIC ACID, DIETHYL ESTER
2771	DIETHYLMALONIC ACID, DIMETHYL ESTER
2772	DIBROMOMALONIC ACID, DIETHYL ESTER
2773	SUCCINIC ACID, DIISOPROPYL ESTER
2774	SUCCINIC ACID, DIPENTYL ESTER
2775	GLUTARIC ACID, DIBUTYL ESTER
2776	3,3-DIMETHYLGLUTARIC ACID, DIMETHYL ESTER
2777	ADIPIC ACID, DIETHYL ESTER
2778	ADIPIC ACID, DIISOBUTYL ESTER
2779	AZELAIC ACID, DIMETHYL ESTER
2780	AZELAIC ACID, DIETHYL ESTER
2781	SEBACIC ACID, DIMETHYL ESTER
2782	SEBACIC ACID, BIS(2-ETHYLHEXYL) ESTER
2783	SEBACIC ACID, DIDODECYL ESTER
2784	SEBACIC ACID, BIS(2-BUTOXYETHYL) ESTER
2785	DODECANEDIOIC ACID, DIMETHYL ESTER
2786	1,2-CYCLOPROPANEDICARBOXYLIC ACID, DIETHYL ESTER
2787	1,3-CYCLOHEXANEDICARBOXYLIC ACID, DIMETHYL ESTER
2788	1,2-CYCLOHEXANEDICARBOXYLIC ACID, BIS(2-ETHYLHEXYL) ESTER
2789	IMINODIACETIC ACID, DIETHYL ESTER
2790	MALIC ACID, DIMETHYL ESTER
2791	3-HYDROXYGLUTARIC ACID, DIMETHYL ESTER
2792	TARTARIC ACID, DIBUTYL ESTER
2793	3,3',3''-NITRILOTRIPROPIONIC ACID
2794	NITRILOTRIACETIC ACID, TRIETHYL ESTER
2795	1,1,2,2-ETHANETETRACARBOXYLIC ACID, TETRAETHYL ESTER
2796	1,1,4,4-BUTANETETRACARBOXYLIC ACID, TETRAMETHYL ESTER
2797	PROPIONIC ACID, VINYL ESTER

SPECTRUM NO.   NAME

2798	4-PENTEN-1-OL, ACETATE
2799	2-HEXENOIC ACID, METHYL ESTER
2800	trans-2-HEXEN-1-OL, ACETATE
2801	NONANOIC ACID, ALLYL ESTER
2802	STEARIC ACID, VINYL ESTER
2803	CHLOROACETIC ACID, VINYL ESTER
2804	CHLOROACETIC ACID, ALLYL ESTER
2805	OXALIC ACID, DIALLYL ESTER
2806	SUCCINIC ACID, DIALLYL ESTER
2808	ACRYLIC ACID, ISOBUTYL ESTER
2808	ACRYLIC ACID, 2-ETHYLHEXYL ESTER
2809	ACRYLIC ACID, DODECYL ESTER
2810	METHACRYLIC ACID, ETHYL ESTER
2811	METHACRYLIC ACID, ISOPROPYL ESTER
2812	METHACRYLIC ACID, ISOBUTYL ESTER
2813	METHACRYLIC ACID, DECYL ESTER
2814	CROTONIC ACID, ETHYL ESTER
2815	2-DECENOIC ACID, METHYL ESTER
2816	LINOLENIC ACID, METHYL ESTER
2817	OLEIC ACID, ETHYL ESTER
2818	ELAIDIC ACID, ETHYL ESTER
2819	ELAIDIC ACID, BUTYL ESTER
2820	2-CHLOROACRYLIC ACID, ETHYL ESTER
2821	4-OXO-2-PENTENOIC ACID, METHYL ESTER
2822	RICINOLEIC ACID, METHYL ESTER, ACETATE
2823	TRIOLEIN
2824	5-NORBORNENE-2-CARBOXYLIC ACID, ETHYL ESTER
2826	FUMARIC ACID, DIMETHYL ESTER
2826	FUMARIC ACID, DIISOPROPYL ESTER
2827	FUMARIC ACID, DIHEXYL ESTER
2828	MALEIC ACID, DIISOPROPYL ESTER
2829	MALEIC ACID, DIALLYL ESTER
2830	ETHENETETRACARBOXYLIC ACID, TETRAETHYL ESTER
2831	FORMIC ACID, PHENETHYL ESTER
2832	ACETIC ACID, BENZYL ESTER
2833	ACETIC ACID, PHENETHYL ESTER
2834	a-METHYLBENZYL ALCOHOL, ACETATE
2835	PROPIONIC ACID, PHENETHYL ESTER
2836	ISOBUTYRIC ACID, PHENETHYL ESTER
2837	ISOVALERIC ACID, BENZYL ESTER
2838	ISOVALERIC ACID, PHENETHYL ESTER
2839	p-METHOXYBENZYL ALCOHOL, ACETATE
2840	ACETIC ACID, PHENACYL ESTER
2841	ACETIC ACID, CINNAMYL ESTER
2842	BUTYRIC ACID, CINNAMYL ESTER
2843	ISOVALERIC ACID, CINNAMYL ESTER

SPECTRUM NO.	NAME
2844	BROMOACETIC ACID, BENZYL ESTER
2845	ACRYLIC ACID, BENZYL ESTER
2846	METHACRYLIC ACID, BENZYL ESTER
2847	PHENYLACETIC ACID, BUTYL ESTER
2848	PHENYLACETIC ACID, OCTYL ESTER
2849	4-PHENYLBUTYRIC ACID, METHYL ESTER
2850	3-PHENYLHYDRACRYLIC ACID, ETHYL ESTER
2851	HIPPURIC ACID, METHYL ESTER
2852	METHYLPHENYLMALONIC ACID, DIETHYL ESTER
2853	3,3'-(BENZYLIMINO)DIPROPIONIC ACID, DIETHYL ESTER
2854	o-TOLYLACETIC ACID, ETHYL ESTER
2855	FLUORENE-9-CARBOXYLIC ACID, METHYL ESTER
2856	β-METHYLCINNAMIC ACID, ETHYL ESTER
2857	CINNAMIC ACID, CYCLOHEXYL ESTER
2858	a-CYANOCINNAMIC ACID, ETHYL ESTER
2859	(TRIPHENYLPHOSPHORANYLIDENE)ACETIC ACID, METHYL ESTER
2860	PHENYLACETIC ACID, PHENETHYL ESTER
2861	CINNAMIC ACID, BENZYL ESTER
2862	CINNAMIC ACID, PHENETHYL ESTER
2863	BENZOIC ACID, PROPYL ESTER
2864	BENZOIC ACID, ISOBUTYL ESTER
2865	BENZOIC ACID, 2-(DIMETHYLAMINO)ETHYL ESTER
2866	BENZOIC ACID, PHENETHYL ESTER
2867	DIETHYLENE GLYCOL, DIBENZOATE
2868	8-QUINOLINOL, BENZOATE
2869	o-TOLUIC ACID, METHYL ESTER
2870	p-tert-BUTYLBENZOIC ACID, ETHYL ESTER
2871	m-FLUOROBENZOIC ACID, ETHYL ESTER
2872	o-CHLOROBENZOIC ACID, METHYL ESTER
2873	m-CHLOROBENZOIC ACID, METHYL ESTER
2874	p-CHLOROBENZOIC ACID, METHYL ESTER
2875	p-BROMOBENZOIC ACID, ETHYL ESTER
2876	m-IODOBENZOIC ACID, METHYL ESTER
2877	ANTHRANILIC ACID, HEXYL ESTER
2878	ANTHRANILIC ACID, CYCLOHEXYL ESTER
2879	ANTHRANILIC ACID, PENTYL ESTER
2880	m-AMINOBENZOIC ACID, METHYL ESTER
2881	p-AMINOBENZOIC ACID, METHYL ESTER
2882	p-AMINOBENZOIC ACID, ISOPROPYL ESTER
2883	p-NITROSOBENZOIC ACID, ETHYL ESTER
2884	p-ISOCYANATOBENZOIC ACID, ETHYL ESTER
2885	m-NITROBENZOIC ACID, ETHYL ESTER
2886	p-NITROBENZOIC ACID, METHYL ESTER
2887	o-ANISIC ACID, METHYL ESTER
2888	p-ANISIC ACID, METHYL ESTER

SPECTRUM NO.	NAME
2889	SALICYLIC ACID, ISOPROPYL ESTER
2890	SALICYLIC ACID, BUTYL ESTER
2891	SALICYLIC ACID, PHENETHYL ESTER
2892	m-HYDROXYBENZOIC ACID, METHYL ESTER
2893	p-HYDROXYBENZOIC ACID, ISOPROPYL ESTER
2894	p-HYDROXYBENZOIC ACID, BUTYL ESTER
2895	p-HYDROXYBENZOIC ACID, DODECYL ESTER
2896	PHTHALIC ACID, MONOBUTYL ESTER
2897	PHTHALIC ACID, DIPENTYL ESTER
2898	PHTHALIC ACID, BIS(2-ETHYLHEXYL) ESTER
2899	PHTHALIC ACID, DIALLYL ESTER
2900	TETRACHLOROPHTHALIC ACID, DIPROPYL ESTER
2901	ISOPHTHALIC ACID, DIMETHYL ESTER
2902	ISOPHTHALIC ACID, DIBUTYL ESTER
2903	ISOPHTHALIC ACID, BIS(2-ETHYLHEXYL) ESTER
2904	ISOPHTHALIC ACID, DIALLYL ESTER
2905	5-AMINOISOPHTHALIC ACID, DIMETHYL ESTER
2906	5-NITROISOPHTHALIC ACID, DIMETHYL ESTER
2907	TEREPHTHALIC ACID, DIETHYL ESTER
2908	TEREPHTHALIC ACID, DIBUTYL ESTER
2909	TEREPHTHALIC ACID, DIOCTYL ESTER
2910	2-AMINOTEREPHTHALIC ACID, DIMETHYL ESTER
2911	3,5-DINITROBENZOIC ACID, ETHYL ESTER
2912	3,5-DINITROBENZOIC ACID, CYCLOHEXYL ESTER
2913	3,5-DINITROBENZOIC ACID, BENZYL ESTER
2914	a-RESORCYLIC ACID, METHYL ESTER
2915	3,5-DIMETHOXY-4-HYDROXYBENZOIC ACID, METHYL ESTER
2916	GALLIC ACID, METHYL ESTER
2917	GALLIC ACID, BUTYL ESTER
2918	GALLIC ACID, ISOBUTYL ESTER
2919	GALLIC ACID, DODECYL ESTER
2920	1,2,4,5-BENZENETETRACARBOXYLIC ACID, TETRAMETHYL ESTER
2921	PROPIONIC ACID, PHENYL ESTER
2922	PIVALIC ACID, PHENYL ESTER
2923	TRIFLUOROACETIC ACID, PHENYL ESTER
2924	ACETIC ACID, p-TOLYL ESTER
2925	OCTANOIC ACID, p-TOLYL ESTER
2926	ACETIC ACID, p-NITROPHENYL ESTER
2927	PIVALIC ACID, p-NITROPHENYL ESTER
2928	RESORCINOL, DIACETATE
2929	PHLOROGLUCINOL, TRIACETATE
2930	2-NAPHTHOL, ACETATE
2931	FURFURYL ALCOHOL, ACETATE
2932	PHENYLACETIC ACID, m-TOLYL ESTER
2933	PHENYLACETIC ACID, p-TOLYL ESTER
2934	2-FURANACRYLIC ACID, ETHYL ESTER

SPECTRUM NO.   NAME

2935	2-FUROIC ACID, PROPYL ESTER
2936	2-FUROIC ACID, PENTYL ESTER
2937	5-NITRO-2-FUROIC ACID, ETHYL ESTER
2938	2-PYRIDINEACETIC ACID, METHYL ESTER
2939	NICOTINIC ACID, NONYL ESTER
2940	CARBONIC ACID, DI-p-TOLYL ESTER
2941	CARBONIC ACID, BIS(p-CHLOROPHENYL) ESTER
2942	BENZOIC ACID, BENZYL ESTER
2943	BENZOIC ACID, p-TOLYL ESTER
2944	ETHYLENE GLYCOL, DIBENZOATE
2945	PYROCATECHOL, DIBENZOATE

CYCLIC ESTERS (LACTONES)

2946	4-HYDROXY-2-METHYLBUTYRIC ACID, γ-LACTONE
2947	4-HYDROXYOCTANOIC ACID, γ-LACTONE
2948	3-BROMODIHYDRO-2(3H)-FURANONE
2949	2,4-DIHYDROXY-3,3-DIMETHYLBUTYRIC ACID, γ-LACTONE
2950	3-ACETYL-4,5-DIHYDRO-2(3H)-FURANONE
2951	DIHYDRO-4-PHENYL-2(3H)-FURANONE
2952	2-OXEPANONE
2953	OXACYCLOPENTADECAN-2-ONE
2954	5-METHYL-2(3H)-FURANONE
2955	(o-HYDROXYPHENYL)ACETIC ACID, γ-LACTONE
2956	6-NITROPHTHALIDE
2957	3-CHLOROCOUMARIN
2958	4-HYDROXYCOUMARIN, ACETATE

CHLOROFORMATES

2959	CHLOROFORMIC ACID, BUTYL ESTER
2960	CHLOROFORMIC ACID, 2-ETHYLHEXYL ESTER
2961	CHLOROFORMIC ACID, DODECYL ESTER
2962	CHLOROFORMIC ACID, 2-CHLOROETHYL ESTER
2963	CHLOROFORMIC ACID, 2,2,2-TRICHLOROETHYL ESTER
2964	2,2-DIMETHYL-1,3-PROPANEDIOL, BIS(CHLOROFORMATE)
2965	CHLOROFORMIC ACID, ALLYL ESTER
2966	CHLOROFORMIC ACID, 9-OCTADECENYL ESTER
2967	CHLOROFORMIC ACID, p-NITROBENZYL ESTER
2968	CHLOROFORMIC ACID, PHENYL ESTER
2969	CHLOROFORMIC ACID, p-NITROPHENYL ESTER

ESTERS OF THIO-ACIDS

2970	THIOACETIC ACID S-ETHYL ESTER
2971	THIOBENZOIC ACID, S-BENZYL ESTER
2972	THIOCARBONIC ACID, o-ETHYL S-(2-HYDROXYETHYL) ESTER

CARBAMATES

| 2973 | CARBAMIC ACID, ISOPROPYL ESTER |

SPECTRUM NO.   NAME

2974	CARBAMIC ACID, BUTYL ESTER
2975	CARBAMIC ACID, tert-BUTYL ESTER
2976	CARBAMIC ACID, DODECYL ESTER
2977	CARBAMIC ACID, ALLYL ESTER
2978	CARBAMIC ACID, PHENYL ESTER
2979	CARBAMIC ACID, p-TOLYL ESTER
2980	METHYLCARBAMIC ACID, ETHYL ESTER
2981	PROPYLCARBAMIC ACID, ETHYL ESTER
2982	BUTYLCARBAMIC ACID, METHYL ESTER
2983	METHYLENEDICARBAMIC ACID, DIETHYL ESTER
2984	DIBUTYL CARBAMIC ACID, ETHYL ESTER
2985	1,4-PIPERAZINEDICARBOXYLIC ACID, DIETHYL ESTER
2986	PHENETHYLCARBAMIC ACID, ETHYL ESTER
2987	CARBANILIC ACID, PROPYL ESTER
2988	CARBANILIC ACID, CYCLOHEXYL ESTER
2989	CARBANILIC ACID, DIPHENYLMETHYL ESTER
2990	BUTYLPHENYLCARBAMIC ACID, ETHYL ESTER
2991	DIMETHYLCARBAMIC ACID, PHENYL ESTER
2992	2-OXAZOLIDINONE
2993	s-TRIAZINE-1,3,5(2H,4H,6H)-TRICARBOXYLIC ACID, TRIMETHYL ESTER
2994	3-PHENYL-2-OXAZOLIDINONE
2995	BENZOYL PEROXIDE

ESTERS OF PHOSPHORUS ACIDS

2996	VINYLPHOSPHONIC ACID, BIS(2-CHLOROETHYL) ESTER
2997	PHOSPHORIC ACID, DIETHYL ESTER
2998	N,N-DIETHYLPHOSPHORAMIDIC ACID, DIBUTYL ESTER
2999	PHOSPHORIC ACID, TRIPROPYL ESTER
3000	PHOSPHORIC ACID, TRIBENZYL ESTER

NAME	SPECTRUM NO.
ADIPOYL CHLORIDE	2199
ALANINE, DL-, ETHYL ESTER, HYDROCHLORIDE	2736
ALANINE, DL-, METHYL ESTER, HYDROCHLORIDE	2735
ALANINE, 3-MERCAPTO-, L-(+)-,	2624
ALANINE, 2-METHYL-,	2616
β-ALANINE	2617
L-ALANINE	2614
ALLANTOIN	2451
ALLENE, TETRAPHENYL-,	165
ALLYL ALCOHOL	1685
ALLYLAMINE	474
ALLYLAMINE, HYDROCHLORIDE	781
ALLYLAMINE, N-CYCLOHEXYL-,	570
ALLYLAMINE, N,N-DIMETHYL-,	642
ALLYLAMINE, 2-METHYL-,	475
ALLYLAMINE, N-PHENYL-,	587
ALLYL CHLORIDE	272
AMBER ACID	2497
AMMONIUM BENZENESULFONATE, PHENYLTRIMETHYL-,	1313
AMMONIUM BROMIDE, DODECYLTRIMETHYL-,	830
AMMONIUM BROMIDE, HEXADECYLTRIMETHYL-,	831
AMMONIUM BROMIDE, OCTADECYLTRIMETHYL-,	833
AMMONIUM BROMIDE, (2-PROPYNYL)TRIETHYL-,	834
AMMONIUM BROMIDE, TETRABUTYL-,	832
AMMONIUM CHLORIDE, BENZYLDIMETHYLHEXADECYL-, HYDRATE	839
AMMONIUM CHLORIDE, BENZYLTRIMETHYL-,	836
AMMONIUM CHLORIDE, DODECYLTRIMETHYL-, MONOHYDRATE	829
AMMONIUM CHLORIDE, (2-HYDROXY-ETHYL)TRIMETHYL-,	1657
AMMONIUM CHLORIDE, PHENYLTRIMETHYL-,	840
AMMONIUM HEXAFLUOROANTIMONATE(1-), BENZYLTRIMETHYL,-	838
AMMONIUM IODIDE, 1-ADAMANTYLTRIMETHYL-,	835
AMMONIUM IODIDE, BENZYLTRIMETHYL-,	837
AMMONIUM IODIDE, PHENYLTRIETHYL-,	841
AMMONIUM IODIDE, TETRAETHYL-,	827
AMMONIUM SALICYLATE	2684
AMMONIUM SUCCINATE	2682
AMMONIUM TETRAFLUOROBORATE(1-), TETRABUTYL-,	828
AMYL DISULFIDE	1187
AMYL NITRITE	1037
AMYL SULFONE	1255
ANDROST-5-EN-17-ONE, 3β-HYDROXY-,	2129
ANETHOL	1506
ANILINE	487
ANILINE, HYDROCHLORIDE	787
ANILINE, PICRATE	1940

NAME	SPECTRUM NO.
BENZENE, 1,4-DIBENZOYL-,	2107
BENZENE, m-DIBROMO-,	397
BENZENE, o-DIBROMO-,	396
BENZENE, p-DIBROMO-,	398
BENZENE, (1,2-DIBROMOETHYL)-,	378
BENZENE, m-DICHLORO-,	306
BENZENE, o-DICHLORO-,	305
BENZENE, p-DICHLORO-,	307
BENZENE, 1,2-DICHLORO-4-FLUORO-,	310
BENZENE, 1,2-DICHLORO-4-NITRO-,	1069
BENZENE, p-DICYCLOHEXYL-,	183
BENZENE, m-DIETHYL-,	179
BENZENE, o-DIFLUORO-,	230
BENZENE, 1,3-DIFLUORO-,	231
BENZENE, 1,4-DIFLUORO-,	232
BENZENE, m-DIHYDROXY-,	1911
BENZENE, o-DIHYDROXY-,	1910
BENZENE, p-DIHYDROXY-,	1912
BENZENE, m-DIIODO-,	436
BENZENE, p-DIIODO-,	437
BENZENE, o-DIMETHOXY-,	1545
BENZENE, 1,3-DIMETHOXY-,	1546
BENZENE, 1,4-DIMETHOXY-,	1547
BENZENE, 1,3-DIMETHOXY-4-NITRO-,	1564
BENZENE, 1,2-DIMETHOXY-4-PROPENYL-,	1559
BENZENE, m-DINITRO-,	1067
BENZENE, o-DINITRO-,	1066
BENZENE, 2,4-DINITRO-1-FLUORO-,	1072
BENZENE, 1,3-DINITRO-4-METHOXY-,	1555
BENZENE, m-DIPHENOXY-,	1550
BENZENE, m-DIPHENYL-,	180
BENZENE, o-DIPHENYL-,	176
BENZENE, p-DIPHENYL-,	186
BENZENE, (EPOXYETHYL)-,	1447
BENZENE, ETHOXY-,	1489
BENZENE, 1-ETHOXY-4-NITRO-,	1533
BENZENE, ETHYL-,	134
BENZENE, 1-ETHYL-3-METHYL-,	178
BENZENE, 1-ETHYL-2-NITRO-,	1049
BENZENE, 1-ETHYL-4-NITRO-,	1050
BENZENE, ETHYNYL-,	166
BENZENE, FLUORO-,	223
BENZENE, 1-FLUORO-4-IODO-,	432
BENZENE, 1-FLUORO-2-NITRO-,	1054
BENZENE, 1-FLUORO-4-NITRO-,	1055
BENZENE, IODO-,	426

NAME	SPECTRUM NO.
BENZOFURANONE, 2(3H)-,	2955
BENZOIC ACID	2566
BENZOIC ACID, AMMONIUM SALT	2683
BENZOIC ACID, BENZYL ESTER	2942
BENZOIC ACID, CYCLOHEXYLIDENE-, HYDRAZIDE	2411
BENZOIC ACID, 2-(DIMETHYLAMINO)-, ETHYL ESTER	2865
BENZOIC ACID, ISOBUTYL ESTER	2864
BENZOIC ACID, PHENETHYL ESTER	2866
BENZOIC ACID, PROPYL ESTER	2863
BENZOIC ACID, 8-QUINOLINYL ESTER	2868
BENZOIC ACID, SODIUM SALT	2675
BENZOIC ACID, p-TOLYL ESTER	2943
BENZOIC ACID, m-AMINO-, METHYL ESTER	2880
BENZOIC ACID, m-AMINO-, SODIUM SALT	2676
BENZOIC ACID, p-AMINO-,	2578
BENZOIC ACID, p-AMINO-, ISOPROPYL ESTER	2882
BENZOIC ACID, p-AMINO-, METHYL ESTER	2881
BENZOIC ACID, p-AMINO-, SODIUM SALT	2677
BENZOIC ACID, m-BROMO-,	2573
BENZOIC ACID, o-BROMO-,	2572
BENZOIC ACID, p-BROMO-,	2574
BENZOIC ACID, p-BROMO-, ETHYL ESTER	2875
BENZOIC ACID, p-BROMO-, HYDRAZIDE	2406
BENZOIC ACID, p-tert-BUTYL-, ETHYL ESTER	2870
BENZOIC ACID, m-CHLORO-, METHYL ESTER	2873
BENZOIC ACID, o-CHLORO-, METHYL ESTER	2872
BENZOIC ACID, p-CHLORO-,	2571
BENZOIC ACID, p-CHLORO-, 2,2-DIMETHYLHYDRAZIDE	2410
BENZOIC ACID, p-CHLORO-, METHYL ESTER	2874
BENZOIC ACID, m-CYANO-,	2580
BENZOIC ACID, 3,5-DIHYDROXY-, METHYL ESTER	2914
BENZOIC ACID, 3,5-DIMETHOXY-4-HYDROXY-, METHYL ESTER	2915
BENZOIC ACID, 2,6-DIMETHYL-,	2593
BENZOIC ACID, 2,4-DINITRO-,	2594
BENZOIC ACID, 3,5-DINITRO-, BENZYL ESTER	2913
BENZOIC ACID, 3,5-DINITRO-, CYCLOHEXYL ESTER	2912
BENZOIC ACID, 3,5-DINITRO-, ETHYL ESTER	2911
BENZOIC ACID, o-ETHOXY-,	2585
BENZOIC ACID, m-FLUORO-, ETHYL ESTER	2871
BENZOIC ACID, o-FLUORO-,	2569
BENZOIC ACID, p-FLUORO-,	2570
BENZOIC ACID, m-HYDROXY-, METHYL ESTER	2892
BENZOIC ACID, p-HYDROXY-,	2588
BENZOIC ACID, p-HYDROXY-, BUTYL ESTER	2894
BENZOIC ACID, p-HYDROXY-, DODECYL ESTER	2895

NAME	SPECTRUM NO.
BENZOPHENONE, 2-METHYL-,	2099
BENZOPHENONE, 4-METHYL-,	2100
BENZOPYRAN, 1H-2-, 3,4-DIHYDRO-,	1589
BENZOPYRAN-2-ONE, 2H-1-, 4-HYDROXY-, ACETATE	2958
BENZO (c) QUINOLINE	748
BENZO(f)QUINOLINE	749
p-BENZOQUINONE, 2,5-DI-tert-PENTYL-,	2031
p-BENZOQUINONE, PHENYL-,	2033
p-BENZOQUINONE, TETRAMETHYL-,	2032
BENZOTHIADIAZOLE, 2,1,3-,	1178
BENZOTHIAZOLE, 5-CHLORO-2-METHYL-,	1177
BENZOTHIAZOLE, 2-METHYL-,	1175
BENZOTHIAZOLE, 2-PHENYL-,	1176
BENZO(β)THIOPHENE, 1,1-DIOXIDE	1277
1-BENZOTHIOPHENE, 1,1-DIOXIDE	1277
o-BENZOTOLUIDIDE	2344
p-BENZOTOLUIDIDE	2345
1H-BENZOTRIAZOLE	741
BENZOTRICHLORIDE	289
BENZOTRIFLUORIDE	222
BENZOXAZOLE, 2,5,6-TRIMETHYL-,	1585
BENZOYL BROMIDE	2221
BENZOYL BROMIDE, m-BROMO-,	2234
BENZOYL CHLORIDE	2220
BENZOYL CHLORIDE, m-BROMO-,	2233
BENZOYL CHLORIDE, o-BROMO-,	2232
BENZOYL CHLORIDE, p-tert-BUTYL-,	2224
BENZOYL CHLORIDE, m-CHLORO-,	2230
BENZOYL CHLORIDE, o-CHLORO-,	2229
BENZOYL CHLORIDE, p-CHLORO-,	2231
BENZOYL CHLORIDE, 2-CHLORO-4-NITRO-,	2242
BENZOYL CHLORIDE, 2-CHLORO-5-NITRO-,	2243
BENZOYL CHLORIDE, 3,5-DIMETHOXY-,	2244
BENZOYL CHLORIDE, 2,3-DIMETHYL-,	2238
BENZOYL CHLORIDE, 3,4-DIMETHYL-,	2239
BENZOYL CHLORIDE, 3,5-DIMETHYL-,	2240
BENZOYL CHLORIDE, m-FLUORO-,	2228
BENZOYL CHLORIDE, o-FLUORO-,	2227
BENZOYL CHLORIDE, m-NITRO-,	2236
BENZOYL CHLORIDE, o-NITRO-,	2235
BENZOYL FLUORIDE	2219
BENZOYL PEROXIDE	2995
BENZYL ALCOHOL	1700
BENZYL ALCOHOL, o-CHLORO-,	1717
BENZYL ALCOHOL, a-CYCLOPROPYL-,	1789

NAME	SPECTRUM NO.
BUTANE, 1-BROMO-,	322
BUTANE, 2-BROMO-,	323
BUTANE, 1-BROMO-3-METHYL-,	328
BUTANE, 1-CHLORO-,	236
BUTANE, 2-CHLORO-,	237
BUTANE, 2-CHLORO-2-METHYL-,	241
BUTANE, 1-CHLORO-4-(m-TOLYLOXY)-,	1502
BUTANE, 1,2-DIBROMO-,	357
BUTANE, 1,3-DIBROMO-,	358
BUTANE, 1,4-DIBROMO-,	359
BUTANE, 1,2-DICHLORO-,	262
BUTANE, 1,4-DICHLORO-,	263
BUTANE, 1,1-DICHLORO-3,3-DIMETHYL-,	265
BUTANE, 1,4-DIIODO-,	418
BUTANE, 2,3-DIMETHYL-,	18
BUTANE, 1,2-EPOXY-,	1439
BUTANE, 1-IODO-,	407
BUTANE, 2-IODO-,	408
BUTANE, 1-IODO-3-METHYL-,	410
BUTANE, 2-METHYL-,	17
BUTANE, meso-1,2,3,4-TETRAPHENYL-,	152
1,4-BUTANEDIAMINE	461
1,4-BUTANEDIAMINE, DIHYDROCHLORIDE	777
1,4-BUTANEDIAMINE, N^4, N^4-DIETHYL-1-METHYL-,	626
BUTANEDIOIC ACID	2497
1,2-BUTANEDIOL	1829
2,3-BUTANEDIOL, 2,3-DIMETHYL-, HYDRATE	1834
1,3-BUTANEDIONE, 1-(2-FURYL)-,	2141
1,3-BUTANEDIONE, 1-PHENYL-,	2147
2,3-BUTANEDIONE, DIOXIME	864
1,4-BUTANEDITHIOL	1220
1-BUTANESULFONIC ACID, 4-HYDROXY-, δ-SULTONE	1319
1-BUTANESULFONYL CHLORIDE	1281
BUTANETETRACARBOXYLIC ACID, 1,1,4,4-, TETRAMETHYL ESTER	2796
BUTANETETROL, 1,2,3,4-, ERYTHRO-,	1861
1-BUTANETHIOL, 3-METHYL-,	1205
2-BUTANETHIOL	1203
1-BUTANOL	1614
1-BUTANOL, 2-AMINO-,	1644
1-BUTANOL, 3-AMINO-3-METHYL-,	1645
1-BUTANOL, 1-(DIPHENYLPHOSPHINYL)-,	1659
1-BUTANOL, 2-ETHYL-,	1622
1-BUTANOL, 2-ETHYL-, FORMATE	2691
1-BUTANOL, 2-METHYL-, (-)	1617
1-BUTANOL, 3-METHYL-,	1618

NAME	SPECTRUM NO.
ETHYLAMINE, 2-CHLORO-N,N-DIETHYL-, HYDROCHLORIDE	812
ETHYLAMINE, 2-CHLORO-N,N-DIMETHYL-, HYDROCHLORIDE	811
ETHYLAMINE, 2,2-DIETHOXY-,	1428
ETHYLAMINE, 2,2-DIMETHOXY-,	1427
ETHYLAMINE, N,N-DIMETHYL-,	613
ETHYLAMINE, N,N-DIMETHYL-2-(VINYLOXY)-,	1406
ETHYLAMINE, 2,2'-DITHIOBIS-,	780
ETHYLAMINE, 2,2,2-TRIFLUORO-, HYDROCHLORIDE	771
ETHYLAMINE HYDROCHLORIDE	766
2-ETHYLBUTYL SILICATE	1601
ETHYLENE, 1,2-DIBROMO-,	370
ETHYLENE, trans-1,2-DICHLORO-,	281
ETHYLENE, 1,1-DICHLORO-,	279
ETHYLENE, 1,2-DIPHENYL-, cis-,	158
ETHYLENE, 1,2-DIPHENYL-, trans-,	159
ETHYLENE, TRICHLORO-,	282
ETHYLENE, TRIPHENYL-,	163
ETHYLENEDIAMINE	457
ETHYLENEDIAMINE, DIHYDROBROMIDE	775
ETHYLENEDIAMINE, DIHYDROCHLORIDE	774
ETHYLENEDIAMINE, MONOTARTRATE, (+)	2690
ETHYLENEDIAMINE, SULFATE	776
ETHYLENEDIAMINE, N-BENZYL-,	580
ETHYLENEDIAMINE, N,N'-BIS(1-METHYLHEPTYL)-,	557
ETHYLENEDIAMINE, N,N'-DICINNAMYLIDENE-,	867
ETHYLENEDIAMINE, N,N-DIETHYL-N',-N'-DIMETHYL-,	632
ETHYLENEDIAMINE, N,N'-DIETHYL-N,N'-DIMETHYL-,	633
ETHYLENEDIAMINE, N,N'-DIISOPROPYL-,	556
ETHYLENEDIAMINE, 2,2-DIMETHYL-,	460
ETHYLENEDIAMINE, N-ETHYL-,	463
ETHYLENEDIAMINE, N,N'-DIBENZYLIDENE-,	868
ETHYLENEDIAMINE, N,N'-DIETHYL-,	555
ETHYLENE DIBROMIDE	348
ETHYLENE GLYCOL	1823
ETHYLENE GLYCOL, DIACETATE	2752
ETHYLENE GLYCOL, DIBENZOATE	2944
ETHYLENE GLYCOL, DIPROPIONATE	2753
ETHYLENETETRACARBOXYLIC ACID, 1,1,2,2-, TETRAETHYL ESTER	2830
ETHYL ETHER	1379
2-ETHYLHEXYL SILICATE	1602
ETHYL IODIDE	404
ETHYL MERCAPTAN	1200
ETHYL POTASSIUM SULFATE	1326
ETHYL SULFIDE	1108
ETHYL SULFITE	1324

NAME	SPECTRUM NO.
FORMIC ACID, STYRYL-,	2550
p-FORMOTOLUIDIDE, N-ETHYL-,	2362
FRUCTOSE, D-(-)-,	1870
FUMARIC ACID	2533
FUMARIC ACID, DIHEXYL ESTER	2827
FUMARIC ACID, DIISOPROPYL ESTER	2826
FUMARIC ACID, DIMETHYL ESTER	2825
FUMARIC ACID, METHYL-,	2534
FUMAROYL CHLORIDE	2209
2-FURALDEHYDE, 5-NITRO-,	2185
2-FURAMIDE	2294
FURAN	1573
FURAN, 2,5-DIMETHYL-,	1575
FURAN, 2-(METHOXYMETHYL)TETRAHYDRO-,	1457
FURAN, 2-METHYL-,	1574
FURAN, 2-METHYLTETRAHYDRO-,	1456
FURAN, 2-(2-NITROVINYL)-,	1578
FURAN, TETRAHYDRO-,	1455
2-FURANACRYLIC ACID	2605
2-FURANACRYLIC ACID, ETHYL ESTER	2934
2,5-FURANDIONE	2263
2,5-FURANDIONE, DIHYDRO-,	2255
2-FURANMETHANETHIOL	1577
2-FURANMETHANOL	1733
FURANONE, 2(3H)-, DIHYDRO-4-PHENYL-,	2951
FURFURAN	1573
FURFURYL ALCOHOL	1733
FURFURYL ALCOHOL, ACETATE	2931
FURIL	2133
2-FUROIC ACID, PENTYL ESTER	2936
2-FUROIC ACID, POTASSIUM SALT	2681
2-FUROIC ACID, PROPYL ESTER	2935
2-FUROIC ACID, 5-NITRO-, ETHYL ESTER	2937
3-FUROIC ACID	2604
FUROIN	2023
2-FURONITRILE	1576
2-FUROYL CHLORIDE	2246
GALACTITOL	1863
D-GALACTOSE	1873
GALLIC ACID, BUTYL ESTER	2917
GALLIC ACID, DODECYL ESTER	2919
GALLIC ACID, ISOBUTYL ESTER	2918
GALLIC ACID, METHYL ESTER	2916

NAME	SPECTRUM NO.
HYDRAZINE, METHYL-,	753
HYDRAZINE, METHYL-, SULFATE	822
HYDRAZINE, (2-NAPHTHYL)-, MONOHYDROCHLORIDE	825
HYDRAZINE, PHENYL-,	756
HYDRAZINE, (2,4,6-TRICHLOROPHENYL)-,	758
HYDRAZOBENZENE	760
HYDRINDENE	195
HYDROCINNAMALDEHYDE	2159
HYDROCINNAMIC ACID	2540
HYDROCINNAMIC ACID, *a*-BENZYL-,	2544
HYDROCINNAMONITRILE	973
HYDROCINNAMONITRILE, *β,β*-DIMETHYL-,	974
HYDROCINNAMONITRILE, p-HYDROXY-,	1902
HYDROCINNAMOYL CHLORIDE	2212
HYDROQUINOL	1912
HYDROQUINONE	1912
HYDROQUINONE, 2,6-DICHLORO-,	1943
HYDROQUINONE, PHENYL-,	1931
HYDROXYLAMINE, ACETATE	2687
HYDROXYLAMINE, N-HEXANOYL-,	891
HYDROXYLAMINE, N-ISONICOTINOYL-,	895
HYDROXYLAMINE, o-METHYL-, HYDROCHLORIDE	846
HYDROXYLAMINE, N-SORBOYL-,	894
IMIDAZOLE, 4(OR 5)-(2-AMINOETHYL)-, HYDROCHLORIDE	820
IMIDAZOLIDINE, 1,3-BIS(PHENYLSULFONYL)-,	1376
2,4-IMIDAZOLIDINEDIONE	2443
2,4-IMIDAZOLIDINEDIONE, 3-METHYL-5-PHENYL-,	2448
2-IMIDAZOLIDINETHIONE, 1-(2-HYDROXYETHYL)-,	1664
2-IMIDAZOLIDINONE	2431
2-IMIDAZOLIDINONE, 1-ALLYL-,	2434
2-IMIDAZOLIDINONE, 1-BUTYL-,	2433
2-IMIDAZOLINE, 1,2-DIPHENYL-,	674
INDAN	195
INDAN, 5-ACETYL-,	2108
INDAN, 1,2-EPOXY-,	1453
5-INDANCARBOXALDEHYDE	2179
1,3-INDANDIONE, 5-CHLORO-,	2149
1,3-INDANDIONE, 2,2-DIHYDROXY-, MONOHYDRATE	2150
4-INDANOL	1948
2-INDANONE, OXIME	863
INDANTRIONE, 1,2,3-, MONOHYDRATE	2150
INDENE	199
INDENE, 2,3-DIHYDRO-,	195
INDENE OXIDE	1453
INDOLE	605

NAME	SPECTRUM NO.
ISOTHIOCYANIC ACID, p-FLUOROPHENYL ESTER	941
ISOTHIOCYANIC ACID, HEPTYL ESTER	933
ISOTHIOCYANIC ACID, METHYL ESTER	930
ISOTHIOCYANIC ACID, OCTADECYL ESTER	934
ISOTHIOCYANIC ACID, PHENYL ESTER	938
ISOVALERIC ACID, BENZYL ESTER	2837
ISOVALERIC ACID, CINNAMYL ESTER	2843
ISOVALERIC ACID, CYCLOHEXYL ESTER	2715
ISOVALERIC ACID, METHYL ESTER	2699
ISOVALERIC ACID, PENTYL ESTER	2706
ISOVALERIC ACID, PHENETHYL ESTER	2838
ISOVALERONITRILE	947
ISOXAZOLE, 3-METHYL-,	1579
ITACONIC ANHYDRIDE	2258
KETONE, 1-CYCLOHEXENYL METHYL,	2022
KETONE, CYCLOHEXYL PHENYL,	2084
KETONE, CYCLOPENTYL PHENYL,	2083
KETONE, DICYCLOPROPYL,	1996
KETONE, HEXYL PHENYL,	2049
KETONE, 5-INDANYL METHYL,	2108
KETONE, METHYL ETHYL,	1968
KETONE, METHYL HEXYL,	1974
KETONE, METHYL 2-NORBORNYL,	1998
KETONE, METHYL 6-METHYL-2-PYRIDYL	2111
KETONE, METHYL PHENYL,	2045
KETONE, METHYL 4-PHENYL-4-PIPERIDYL, HYDROCHLORIDE	144
KETONE, METHYL 2-PYRIDYL,	2110
KETONE, METHYL 2-PYRIDYL, PHENYL HYDRAZONE	878
KETONE, PHENYL 3-PYRIDYL,	2112
LACTAMIDE	2283
LACTAMIDE, N,N-DIMETHYL-,	2357
LACTIC ACID	2493
LACTIC ACID, METHYL ESTER	2740
LACTIC ACID, SODIUM SALT, DL-,	2659
LACTONITRILE	1758
LACTONITRILE, 2-METHYL-,	1806
LAURAMIDE, N,N-DIETHYL-,	2356
LAURIC ACID	2480
LAURIC ACID, DODECYL ESTER	2711
LAURIC ACID, SODIUM SALT	2652
LAUROYL CHLORIDE	2193
LEPIDINE	720
L-LEUCINE, N-ACETYL-,	2621
LEVULINIC ACID	2494
LEVULINIC ACID, ISOPENTYL ESTER	2747
LEVULINIC ACID, METHYL ESTER	2746

NAME	SPECTRUM NO.
MENADIONE	2119
p-MENTHA-1,8-DIENE	111
p-MENTHAN-3-OL	1772
p-MENTH-2-ENE, 1,4-EPIDIOXY-,	1610
p-MENTH-1-EN-8-OL	1808
MENTHOL	1772
MESACONIC ACID	2534
MESIDINE	502
MESITOL, a2,a6-BIS(5-tert-BUTYL-6-HYDROXY-m-TOLYL)-,	1936
MESITYLENE	189
MESITYLENE, 2-BROMO-,	387
2-MESITYLENESULFONAMIDE	1364
MESITYL OXIDE	2020
METALDEHYDE	1432
METHACRYLIC ACID, BENZYL ESTER	2846
METHACRYLIC ACID, DECYL ESTER	2813
METHACRYLIC ACID, ETHYL ESTER	2810
METHACRYLIC ACID, ISOBUTYL ESTER	2812
METHACRYLIC ACID, ISOPROPYL ESTER	2811
METHACRYLONITRILE	967
METHALLYLAMINE	475
METHANE, BIS(p-AMINOPHENYL)-,	530
METHANE, BIS(2-CHLOROETHOXY)-,	1411
METHANE, BIS(PHENYLTHIO)-,	1167
METHANE, BIS(p-TOLYLSULFONYL)-,	1264
METHANE, BROMODICHLORO-,	342
METHANE, BROMODIPHENYL-,	374
METHANE, CYCLOPROPYL PHENYL-	144
METHANE, DIBROMO-,	346
METHANE, DICHLORO-,	249
METHANE, DICHLORODIPHENYL-,	288
METHANE, DICYCLOPROPYL-,	41
METHANE, DIETHOXY-,	1410
METHANE, DIIODO-,	415
METHANE, DIMETHOXYDIPHENYL-,	1486
METHANE, DIPHENYL-,	148
METHANE, IODO-,	403
METHANE, NITRO-,	1039
METHANE, TETRAKIS(HYDROXYMETHYL)-,	1853
METHANE, TETRAKIS(PHENYLTHIO)-,	1168
METHANE, TRICHLORO-,	250
METHANE, TRIPHENYL-,	150
METHANEDIAMINE, N,N,N',N'-TETRABUTYL-,	631
METHANEDICARBOXYLIC ACID	2496
METHANESULFONAMIDE	1359
METHANESULFONAMIDE, N,N-DIMETHYL-,	1373

NAME	SPECTRUM NO.
NAPHTHALENE, 1-CHLORO-,	317
NAPHTHALENE, 2-CHLORO-,	318
NAPHTHALENE, 1-(CHLOROMETHYL)-,	316
NAPHTHALENE, DECAHYDRO-, trans-,	52
NAPHTHALENE, 1,4-DIBROMO-,	402
NAPHTHALENE, 2,3-DIMETHYL-,	203
NAPHTHALENE, 2,6-DIMETHYL-,	204
NAPHTHALENE, 2-ETHOXY-,	1570
NAPHTHALENE, 2-ETHOXY-,	1571
NAPHTHALENE, 1-ETHYL-,	201
NAPHTHALENE, 1-ETHYL-1,2,3,4-TETRAHYDRO-,	197
NAPHTHALENE, 1-FLUORO-,	233
NAPHTHALENE, 2-FLUORO-,	234
NAPHTHALENE, 1-IODO-,	438
NAPHTHALENE, 1-METHOXY-,	1569
NAPHTHALENE, 2-METHYL-,	202
NAPHTHALENE, 1,2,3,4-TETRAHYDRO-,	196
NAPHTHALENE, 2,3,6-TRIMETHYL-,	205
1-NAPHTHALENEACETIC ACID, SODIUM SALT	2674
2-NAPHTHALENEACETONITRILE	998
1-NAPHTHALENECARBONITRILE	999
2-NAPHTHALENECARBONITRILE	1000
2,7-NAPHTHALENEDIAMINE	540
1,3-NAPHTHALENEDIOL	1956
1,5-NAPHTHALENEDIOL	1957
2,7-NAPHTHALENEDIOL	1958
2,7-NAPHTHALENEDISULFONIC ACID, DISODIUM SALT	1311
1-NAPHTHALENEETHANOL	1725
1-NAPHTHALENEPROPIONITRILE, 2-HYDROXY-,	1954
2-NAPHTHALENESULFONAMIDE	1367
1-NAPHTHALENESULFONIC ACID, 2-AMINO-,	1293
1-NAPHTHALENESULFONIC ACID, DIHYDRATE	1292
2-NAPHTHALENESULFONIC ACID, SODIUM SALT	1309
1-NAPHTHALENESULFONYL CHLORIDE	1286
1-NAPHTHALENETHIOL	1241
2-NAPHTHALENETHIOL	1242
NAPHTHALENONE, 1(2H)-, 3,4-DIHYDRO-,	2114
NAPHTHALENONE, 1(2H)-, 3,4-DIHYDRO-7-ETHYL-,	2115
NAPHTHALENONE, 3,4-DIHYDRO-7-METHOXY-2(1H)-,	2116
NAPHTH(2,3-D)IMIDAZOLINE-2-THIONE	1357
NAPHTHIONIC ACID, SODIUM SALT, HEMIHYDRATE	1310
NAPHTHOIC ANHYDRIDE	2274
1-NAPHTHOL	1950
1-NAPHTHOL, 6-AMINO-,	1953
1-NAPHTHOL, 2-METHYL-,	1952

NAME	SPECTRUM NO.
PROPADIENE, TETRAPHENYL-,	165
PROPANE, 2,2-BIS(ALLYLOXY)-,	1434
PROPANE, 2,2-BIS(p-(ALLYLOXY)-PHENYL)-,	1539
PROPANE, 1-BROMO-,	320
PROPANE, 2-BROMO-,	321
PROPANE, 1-BROMO-3-CHLORO-2-METHYL-,	344
PROPANE, 1-BROMO-2,2-DIMETHYL-,	329
PROPANE, 1-BROMO-2,3-EPOXY-,	1444
PROPANE, 1-BROMO-2-METHYL-,	324
PROPANE, 2-BROMO-2-METHYL-,	325
PROPANE, 1-CHLORO-,	235
PROPANE, 3-CHLORO-1,2-DIBROMO-,	355
PROPANE, 1-CHLORO-2,3-EPOXY-,	1443
PROPANE, 2-CHLORO-1,3-EPOXY-,	1454
PROPANE, 1-CHLORO-2-METHYL-,	238
PROPANE, 2-CHLORO-2-METHYL-,	239
PROPANE, 1-CYCLOHEXYL-2-METHYL-,	48
PROPANE, 1,2-DIBROMO-,	353
PROPANE, 1,3-DIBROMO-,	354
PROPANE, 1,2-DICHLORO-,	257
PROPANE, 2,2-DICHLORO-,	258
PROPANE, 1,3-DIIODO-,	417
PROPANE, 2,2-DIMETHOXY-,	1433
PROPANE, 1,2-EPOXY-,	1438
PROPANE, 1,2-EPOXY-3-ISOPROPOXY-,	1445
PROPANE, 1,2-EPOXY-3-(m-TOLYLOXY)-,	1540
PROPANE, 1-IODO-,	405
PROPANE, 2-IODO-,	406
PROPANE, 1-IODO-2-METHYL-,	409
PROPANE, 2-METHYL-2-NITRO-,	1043
PROPANE, 2-METHYL-2-NITROSO-,	1021
PROPANE, 2-NITRO-,	1042
PROPANE, 1-NITRO-,	1041
PROPANE, 1,1,2,3,3-PENTACHLORO-,	261
PROPANE, 1,1,1,2-TETRACHLORO-,	260
PROPANE, 1,1,3,3-TETRAMETHOXY-,	1429
PROPANE, 1,2,3-TRIBROMO-,	356
PROPANE, 1,2,3-TRICHLORO-,	259
1,2-PROPANEDIAMINE	459
1,2-PROPANEDIAMINE, N^2,N^2-DIMETHYL-,	625
1,2-PROPANEDIAMINE, 2-METHYL-,	460
1,3-PROPANEDIAMINE	458
1,3-PROPANEDIAMINE, N,N-DIBUTYL-,	465
1,3-PROPANEDIAMINE, N,N-DIETHYL-N'-(1-METHYLDODECYL)-,	629
1,3-PROPANEDIAMINE, N-METHYL-,	464

NAME	SPECTRUM NO.
PROPIONIC ACID, 2-(p-CHLOROPHENOXY)-2-METHYL-,	2562
PROPIONIC ACID, 3-CYANO-, METHYL ESTER	2737
PROPIONIC ACID, 2,3-DICHLORO-, METHYL ESTER	2726
PROPIONIC ACID, 2,3-DICHLORO-2-METHYL-, SODIUM SALT	2655
PROPIONIC ACID, 2,2-DIMETHYL-,	2476
PROPIONIC ACID, 2-FLUORO-, ETHYL ESTER	2720
PROPIONIC ACID, 2-HYDROXY-,	2493
PROPIONIC ACID, 3-HYDROXY-, SODIUM SALT	2660
PROPIONIC ACID, 3-HYDROXY-3-PHENYL-, ETHYL ESTER	2850
PROPIONIC ACID, 2-MERCAPTO-,	2489
PROPIONIC ACID, 3-MERCAPTO-,	2490
PROPIONIC ACID, 3-MERCAPTO-, METHYL ESTER	2738
PROPIONIC ACID, 2-METHYL-,	2474
PROPIONIC ACID, 2-METHYL-, OCTYL ESTER	2708
PROPIONIC ACID, 3,3',3''-NITRILOTRI-, TRIMETHYL ESTER	2793
PROPIONIC ACID, 3-PHENYL-,	2540
PROPIONIC ANHYDRIDE	2248
PROPIONITRILE, 3-BROMO-,	956
PROPIONITRILE, 3-CHLORO-,	954
PROPIONITRILE, 2,2-DIMETHYL-,	948
PROPIONITRILE, 3-HYDROXY-,	1658
PROPIONITRILE, 2-HYDROXY-2-METHYL-,	1806
PROPIONITRILE, 3,3'-IMINODI-,	960
PROPIONITRILE, 3-ISOPROPOXY-,	1400
PROPIONITRILE, 3-PHENYL-,	973
PROPIONITRILE, 3,3'-(PHENYLIMINO)-DI-,	976
PROPIONITRILE, 2,2'-THIODI-,	1122
PROPIONYL CHLORIDE	2187
PROPIONYL CHLORIDE, 3-BROMO-,	2196
PROPIONYL CHLORIDE, 2-PHENOXY-,	2216
PROPIOPHENONE	2046
PROPIOPHENONE, 3-CHLORO-,	2052
PROPIOPHENONE, 2-PHENOXY-,	2090
PROPIOPHENONE, 3-PHENYL-,	2088
PROPIOPHENONE, 2,2,2',4'-TETRAMETHYL-,	2061
PROPYL ALCOHOL	1613
PROPYLAMINE	439
PROPYLAMINE, HYDROCHLORIDE	767
PROPYLAMINE, 1,1-DIMETHYL-,	447
PROPYLAMINE, 3,3'-IMINODI-,	466
PROPYLAMINE, 3,3'-(METHYLIMINO)-DI-,	627
PROPYLAMINE, 1-METHYL-3-PHENYL-, HYDROCHLORIDE	785
PROPYLAMINE, 3-(METHYLTHIO)-,	1121
PROPYLAMINE, 3-PHENYL-,	481
PROPYLAMINE, 3-(TRIETHOXYSILYL)-,	1597

NAME	SPECTRUM NO.
PYROMELLITIC DIANHYDRIDE	2273
PYROMELLITIMIDE	2401
PYRROLE	575
PYRROLE, 2-((DIMETHYLAMINO)-METHYL)-,	677
PYRROLE, 2,5-DIMETHYL-1-PHENYL-,	676
PYRROLE, 1-METHYL-,	675
1H-PYRROLE	575
PYRROLE-2-CARBOXALDEHYDE	2182
PYRROLIDINE	560
PYRROLIDINE, 1-METHYL-,	636
PYRROLIDINE, 1-METHYL-2-(3-PYRIDYL)-,	711
PYRROLIDINE, 1-NITROSO-,	1029
2-PYRROLIDINECARBOXYLIC ACID	2636
2,5-PYRROLIDINEDIONE	2375
1-PYRROLIDINEETHANOL, a-METHYL-,	1756
2-PYRROLIDINONE, 1-PHENYL-,	2374
3-PYRROLINE-2,5-DIONE	2379
QUINALDINE	719
QUINALDINE, 1,2,3,4-TETRAHYDRO-,	602
QUINAZOLINE, 4-CHLORO-,	742
QUININE	1794
QUINOL	1912
QUINOLINE	718
QUINOLINE, 1-ACETYL-1,2,3,4-TETRAHYDRO-,	2372
QUINOLINE, 3-AMINO-,	727
QUINOLINE, 6-BROMO-,	725
QUINOLINE, 2-CHLORO-,	724
QUINOLINE, DECAHYDRO-,	569
QUINOLINE, 2-HYDRAZINO-,	764
QUINOLINE, 3-HYDRAZINO-, DIHYDROCHLORIDE	826
QUINOLINE, 2-IODO-,	726
QUINOLINE, 2-METHYL-,	719
QUINOLINE, 4-METHYL-,	720
QUINOLINE, 6-METHYL-,	721
QUINOLINE, 7-METHYL-,	722
QUINOLINE, 8-METHYL-,	723
QUINOLINE, 2-(PHENYLTHIO)-,	1174
QUINOLINE, 1,2,3,4-TETRAHYDRO-,	601
QUINOLINECARBOXALDEHYDE, 1(2H)-, 3,4-DIHYDRO-,	2371
3-QUINOLINECARBOXALDEHYDE	2183
3-QUINOLINEMETHANOL	1731
2-QUINOLINOL	1961
8-QUINOLINOL	1962
8-QUINOLINOL, BENZOATE	2868
QUINOLONE, 2(1H)-,	1961

CHEMICAL SHIFT INDEX

The chemical shift of a proton is primarily determined by the kind of proton which causes it; e.g. methyl, methylene, vinyl, etc. The shift position is further modified by the shielding or deshielding influence of nearby atoms or groups. This Chemical Shift Index has been devised to correlate chemical shift with structure and to provide a facile method for locating a structure-shift combination.

In any given NMR spectrum there will be a series of signals or peaks (chemical shift in ppm referred to tetramethylsilane) designated by the lower case letters a, b, c, etc. These letters are assigned to the constituent environmentally different proton groups, in alphabetical sequence, from high to low field.

Thus, for the compound shown in Figure 1, the spectrum

a   b   d   c

CH_3-CH_2-CH_2-OH

Figure 1

will consist of four resonance bands. These protons have been arranged into <u>Basic Proton</u> groups and further classified into <u>Environmental</u> groups. The Chemical Shift Index is listed in two different orders:

<u>Set One</u> -- Arranged by increasing magnitude of chemical shift (0 - 18 ppm) - (Figure 2).

<u>Set Two</u> -- In an alphanumeric order based on Basic Proton and Environmental Group codes. (Figure 3).

(Figures 2 and 3 on following page.)

The Set One index is arranged according to increasing chemical shift (third column from left), with the associated data not ordered in any definite pattern. Unequivocal chemical shift assignments are often difficult to specify. For example, p-Chlorotoluene, has the assignments:

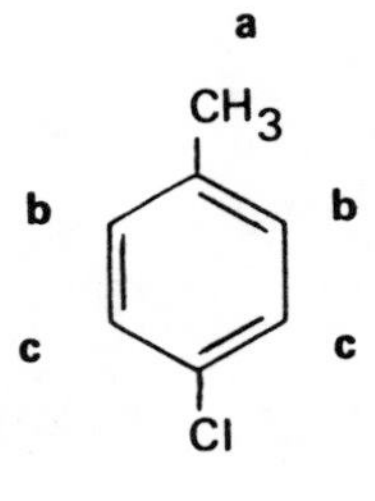

b (protons ortho to methyl group), c (protons ortho to chlorine atom). The corresponding chemical shifts are 6.98 and 7.12. However, the values could be reversed, or b given the value 7.12 and c, 6.98. For such "either-or" assignments, the proton will be coded twice, once for each shift value.

The Set Two index is arranged by Proton and Environmental group sequence as will be detailed later.

Chemical Shift Sequence -- Arranged by increasing magnitude of chemical shift (0 - 18 ppm) -- (Figure 2)

CHEMICAL SHIFT INDEX

ORDERED BY CHEMICAL SHIFT

BOOK NO.	ASSIGN-MENT	CHEM SHIFT - ppm -	PROTON GROUP	ENVIRONMENTAL GROUPS	S	SOLVENT
2324M	C	2.56	CH2	A(C-CH-CH-C(NH-C(=0)))/CH3		CDCL3
2313M	A	2.56	CH2	C(=0)-NH/CH2-CL		CDCL3
1400M	B	2.56	CH2	C:N/CH2-O		CDCL3
574M	C	2.56	CH2	NH-CH2/CH3		CCL4
547M	E	2.56	CH2	NH-C/CH2-CH2		CDCL3
1244M	D	2.56 APP.	CH2	SO-CH2/CH2-CH2		CCL4
1244M	D	2.56 APP.	CH2	SO-CH2/CH3		CCL4
1123M	B	2.56	CH2	S-CH2.2/CH3		CCL4
2075M	A	2.56	CH3	C(=0)-A		CDCL3
1585M	B	2.56	CH3	R5NOA<C=N/O>		CDCL3
773M	C	2.56	CH*R	R6R6BI(CH(NH2)-CH2/CH2-CH*/CH2-CH2)	S	D20
1440M	D	2.56	HCHR	R30<O-CH(CH2.5-CH3)>		CCL4
1442M	D	2.56	HCHR	R30(O-CH(CH2-CH2))		CCL4
688M	C	2.57	CH2	AN(C-CH-CH-N)/CH2-CH2		CCL4
2218M	C	2.57	CH2	A<C-CH-CH-C(BR)>/CH2-CH2		CDCL3
1933M	C	2.57	CH2	A<C-CH-C(C(CH3/CH3/CH3))-C(OH)/CH-C(CH2-A)>		CDCL3
1879M	B	2.57	CH2	A<C-C(OH)>/CH3		CCL4
143M	C	2.57	CH2	A/CH2-CH2		CCL4
2218M	B	2.57	CH2	C(=0)-CL/CH2-CH2		CDCL3
445M	E	2.57	CH2	NH2/CH(CH2/CH3)		CDCL3
579M	C	2.57	CH2	NH-CH2/CH2-CH2		CCL4
1652M	D	2.57	CH2	N(CH2.3/CH2.3)/CH2-OH		CDCL3
1121M	C	2.57	CH2	S-CH3/CH2.2-NH2		D20
1046M	A	2.57	CH3	A(C-C(NO2))		CCL4
1687M	B	2.57	OH	CH2-CH2		CDCL3
179M	B	2.58	CH2	A<C-CH-C(CH2-CH3)>/CH3		CCL4
137M	C	2.58	CH2	A/CH2-CH2		CCL4
141M	C	2.58	CH2	A/CH2-CH2		CCL4
135M	C	2.58	CH2	A/CH2-CH3		CDCL3
542M	C	2.58	CH2	NH-CH2.2/CH2-CH3		CDCL3
958M	D	2.58	CH2	N(CH/CH)/CH2.2-C:N		CCL4

Proton Type Sequence -- In an alphanumeric order based on Basic Proton and Environmental Group identities (Figure 3)

CHEMICAL SHIFT INDEX

ORDERED BY PROTON TYPE

BOOK NO.	ASSIGN-MENT	CHEM SHIFT - ppm -	PROTON GROUP	ENVIRONMENTAL GROUPS	S	SOLVENT
276M	B	5.93	Q2	CH2-CL/CH2-CL		CCL4
2549M	B	6.14	Q2	CH2-C(=0)-OH/A		CDCL3
2521M	E	11.47	Q2	CH2-C(=0)-OH/CH2-CH2		CCL4
274M	E	5.30- 6.15	Q2	CH2-C/CH2-CL		CDCL3
574M	E	5.55	Q2	CH2-NH/CH2-NH		CCL4
572M	D	4.87	Q2	CH2-NH/CH3		CDCL3
1724M	C	6.61 APP.	Q2	CH2-OH/A<C-CH-CH-C(NO2)>		POLYSOL-D
1686M	D	5.57 APP.	Q2	CH2-OH/CH3		CCL4
1711M	C	6.31	Q2	CH2-OH/H/A		CDCL3
2841M	C	6.16	Q2	CH2-0-C(=0)/A		CCL4
2843M	E	6.18	Q2	CH2-0-C(=0)/H/A		CCL4
2842M	E	6.19	Q2	CH2-0-C(=0)/H/A		CCL4
2800M	F	5.61 APP.	Q2	CH2-0-C(=0)/H/CH2.2-CH3		CCL4
2257M	E	5.41 APP.	Q2	CH2-R50/CH2.8-CH3		CDCL3
1257M	C	6.27	Q2	CH2-S02/H/A		CDCL3
1019M	B	6.10 APP.	Q2	CH2-S/H/A		CDCL3
1506M	C	5.91	Q2	CH3/A(C-CH-CH-C(0-CH3))		CCL4
154M	C	5.47 APP.	Q2	CH3/CH2-A		CCL4
88M	F	5.35 APP.	Q2	CH3/CH2-CH		CCL4
83M	E	1.95 APP.	Q2	CH3/CH2-CH2		CCL4
75M	D	5.34 APP.	Q2	CH3/CH2-CH3		CCL4
475M	D	4.70	Q2	CH3/CH2-NH2/H		CCL4
1686M	D	5.57 APP.	Q2	CH3/CH2-OH		CCL4
76M	D	4.90 5.41	Q2	CH3/CH(CH3/CH3)		CCL4
1559M	D	5.91	Q2	CH3/H/A<C-CH-C(0-CH3)-C(O-CH3)>		CDCL3
77M	D	5.31	Q2	CH3/H/CH(CH3/CH3)		CCL4
2018M	D	6.70	Q2	CH3/H/C(=0)-CH3		CCL4
2517M	C	7.04	Q2	CH3/H/C(=0)-OH		CDCL3
2814M	E	6.90	Q2	CH3/H/C(=0)-0-CH2		CCL4
1406M	E	4.68	Q2	CH3/H/0-CH2		CCL4
894M	C	6.06 APP.	Q2	CH3/H/Q2(H/C(=0)-NH/H)		POLYSOL-D

152

Thus, the user of the various indexes can locate spectra which exhibit chemical shift characteristics of a certain proton grouping or he can extract a particular chemical shift from an experimental spectrum and determine the type or kind of proton which could generate such a shift, together with their derivative total spectra.

NMR CODING RULES

As can be expected with any humanly devised coding system, it is almost impossible to anticipate every permutation and combination which could be encountered in the architecture of organic molecules. Thus, after a few minimal ground rules are established and the task of coding proceeds, one is faced with many situations for which the simple rules do not offer an adequate solution. In coding the many thousand compounds we feel that a good many of these questionable situations have been encountered and solved, and the following rules encompass the solutions to the problems.

Fundamentally, each code consists of a series of chemical like notations indicating the Basic Proton and Environmental groups, which can be further modified by certain punctuation symbols. This method of coding allows the use of computer techniques to arrange, print or search the voluminous data. The coding system does not, however, require the use of computers and can be done anywhere, with no mechanical aid other than a pencil.

Basic Proton Group

A basic proton group incorporates the proton under investigation ("coded" proton) in conjunction with the atom or group of atoms to which it is attached. This group is printed in the fourth column from the left of the page in the index.

Environment Group

This is the group to which the basic proton is directly attached and which provides the electronic environment contributing to the chemical shift of the basic proton or protons. This group is located in the fifth column from the left of the page in the index.

S Column

This column is used to signify the presence of a salt in the molecular structure and is important in determining the chemical shift effect of certain groups such as the amines.

Five items of punctuation have been used to indicate certain features, as follows:

1. Slash - / - A slash indicates cessation of coding in one direction along a chain or around a ring, even though the ring or chain continues further. Coding is then initiated in another direction (maintaining alphabetic and numeric priority), beginning from the same branched Basic Proton or Environmental Group which initiated the code. The last code entry does not require that a slash follow it.

    Example:

    a   b
    CH_3-CH_2-NO_2

Assignment	Proton Group	Environment Groups
A	CH3	CH2-NO2
B	CH2	NO2/CH3

2. Parentheses - ( ) - Parentheses indicate branching from a chain: a group shown in parentheses is branched from the group coded directly before the first parenthesis.

    Example:

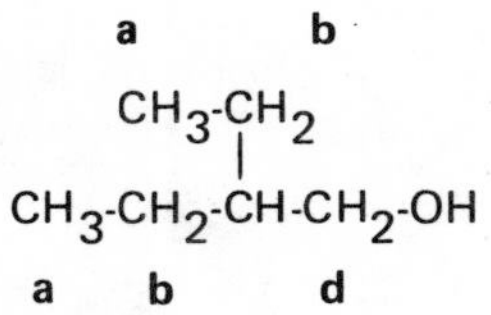

    a   b
    CH_3-CH_2
     |
    CH_3-CH_2-CH-CH_2-OH
    a   b   d

Assignment	Proton Group	Environmental Groups
A	CH3	CH2-CH
B	CH2	CH(CH2/CH2)/CH3
C	OH	CH2-CH
D	CH2	OH/CH(CH2/CH2)

3. Brackets - ⟨ ⟩ - Brackets are used to show ring substitution. A group appearing in brackets is attached to a ring, the type of ring is shown by the code in front of the brackets.

    Example:

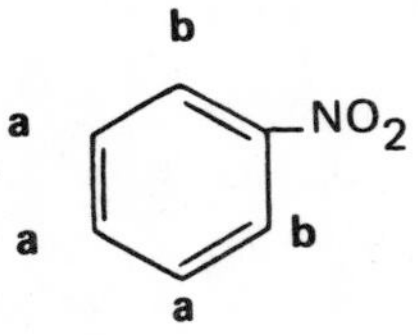

Assignment	Proton Group	Environmental Groups
A	CHA	A⟨CH-C(NO2)⟩
A	CHA	A⟨CH-CH-C(NO2)⟩
B	CHA	A⟨C(NO2)⟩

4. Asterisk - * - If an asterisk follows a Basic Proton or is contained in an Environmental Group, it signifies that the group or atom is part of a ring fusion.

    Example:

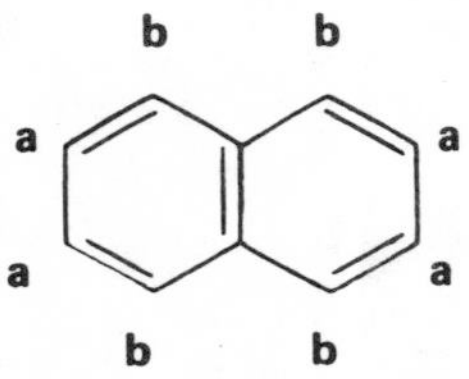

Assignment	Proton Group	Environmental Groups
A	CHA	A⟨CH-C*/CH-CH-C*⟩
B	CHA	A⟨C*⟩

5. Plus and Minus Signs (+, -)   A + or - indicates the type of charge carried by the preceding group (or atom). Quaternary ammonium groups appear as N (+).

Other Symbols Used In Coding

The Chemical Shift Index is generated by computer with the consequent limitations on type style, therefore all characters are upper case and there is no subscripting; for example, the element tin is printed as SN, silicon as SI, etc. and all subscripts are upper case.

BI   --   Whenever BI follows a ring group it indicates the presence of a bicyclic ring, for example,

R6R6BI - Decahydronaphthalene

SPI --   This notation preceded by a ring group indicates the presence of a spiro type ring molecule, for example,

R5R6SPI

R   --   Refers to a cyclic, non-aromatic structure.

RN   --   N refers to the number of sites in a ring.
          examples: R5 is a five membered ring
                      R6 is a six membered ring

A   --   Refers to an aromatic, six-membered ring structure.

S   --   This entry appears in the column titled S whenever there is an acidic and a basic group in the molecule under examination; it signifies the presence of a salt.

CODING PROCEDURE

The simplest method of demonstrating the coding technique is to indicate the coding procedure used for a few representative compounds, then to include more specific rules with examples.

The structure for nitroethane contains two type of protons, designated a and b.

$$\overset{a}{}\quad\overset{b}{}$$

$$CH_3\text{-}CH_2\text{-}NO_2$$

To code proton **a** take CH_3 as the basic proton group and proceed to code as the environmental group, the attached chain through two groups. In coding **b** take the CH_2 as the basic proton group and code two groups (if present) in each direction along the attached chains. The choice of direction in coding attached chains is alphabetic according to element symbol, for example, a chlorine atom (Cl) takes precedence over a flurorine atom (F). All non-carbon atoms take preference over carbon atoms.

The coding sequence for alkyl groups is as follows (in descending order):

$$-C\text{-}, \quad -CH, \quad -CH_2, \quad -CH_3, \quad -C{=}C, \quad -C{\equiv}C\text{-}$$

Example:

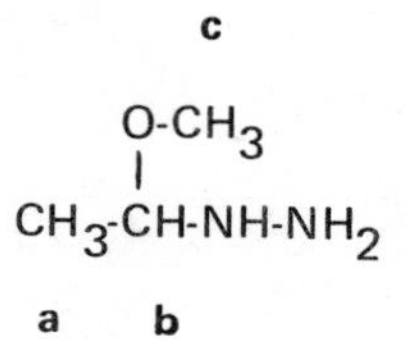

c

O-CH$_3$
|
CH$_3$-CH-NH-NH$_2$

a   b

Assignment	Proton Group	Environmental Groups
A	CH3	CH(NH/O)
B	CH	NH-NH2/O-CH3/CH3
C	CH3	O-CH

Basic coding in cyclic and heterocyclic compounds is the same as for alkyl groups, two groups in each direction from the basic proton group are included, any substituents existing on these two groups are coded similarly but enclosed by parentheses. Cyclic rings and the number of atoms contained in them are designated Rn where n = the number of ring atoms, heterocyclic rings are designated RnZ where Z = the hetero atom.

Example:

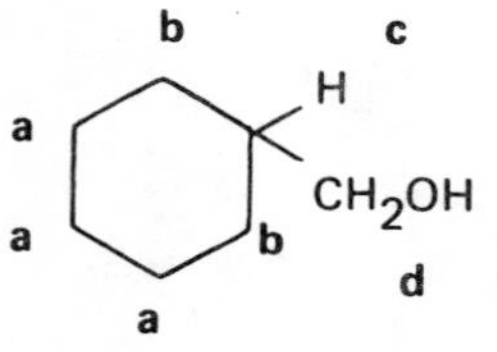

Assignment	Proton Group	Environmental Groups
A	CH2R	R6⟨CH2CH(CH2-OH)/CH2CH2⟩
A	CH2R	R6⟨CH2-CH2/CH2-CH2⟩
B	CH2R	R6⟨CH(CH2-OH)-CH2/CH2-CH2⟩
C	CHR	R6⟨(CH2-OH)/CH2-CH2/CH2-CH2⟩
D	CH2	OH/R6⟨CH-CH2/CH2⟩

Olefinic compounds are represented as follows:

-C=C-	represented as Q
-CH=C-	represented as Q1
-CH=CH- and CH2=C-	represented as Q2
CH2=CH-	represented as Q3
-C=N-	represented as QN

The group or groups attached to the carbon atom of the basic proton is coded first, followed by the groups attached to the remaining carbon atom (geminal, trans, cis- order).

Examples:

Assignment	Proton Group	Environmental Groups
A	CH3	C(=O)-O-Q
B		UNSPECIFIED

Assignment	Proton Group	Environmental Groups
A		UNSPECIFIED
B	Q1	A⟨C-C(CL)⟩/A/C(=O)-OH
C	OH	C(=O)-Q1

Assignment	Proton Group	Environmental Groups
A	CH3	CH2-Q2
B	CH2	Q2(H/C(=O)-OH/H)/CH3
C	Q2	C(=O)-OH/H/CH2-CH3
D	Q2	CH2-CH3/H/C(=O)-OH
E	OH	C(=O)-Q2

Assignment	Proton Group	Environmental Groups
A	CH3	CH2-Q2
B	CH2	Q2(H/H/C(=O)-OH)/CH3
C	Q2	C(=O)-OH/CH2-CH3/H
D	Q2	CH2-CH3/C(=O)-OH/H
E	OH	C(=O)-Q2

Assignment	Proton Group	Environmental Groups
A	CH2	Q3/CH2-CL
B	CH2	CL/CH2-Q3
C	Q3	H/CH2-CH2/H
D	Q3	H/H/CH2-CH2
E	Q3	CH2-CH2/H/H

Assignment	Proton Group	Environmental Groups	S
A	QN	NH2	S
B	QNH	NH2	S
C	NH2	QNH	S

The symbol for any six-membered aromatic ring is A, in aromatic-heterocyclic rings the hetero atom is added after A, e.g., pyridine, AN. In coding aromatic rings substituents re designated as far as the para position before change of direction and coding of remaining substituents as far as the para position. All substituents on the ring are coded up to two groups away from the ring atom.

Examples:

Assignment	Proton Group	Environmental Groups
A	CH3	A⟨C-CH-C(OH)-C(NO2)⟩
B	CHA	A⟨C(OH)-C(NO2)/C(CH3)⟩
C	CHA	A⟨C(CH3)-CH-C(OH)/CH-C(NO2)⟩
D	CHA	A⟨C(NO2)-C(OH)/CH-C(CH3)⟩

The symbol for any six-membered ring is A. For aromatic-heterocyclic rings, the hetero atom is placed after the A, e.g. pyridine, AN. In coding aromatic rings, substituents are identified as far as the para position before changing direction and coding the remaining substituents up to the para position in the opposite direction. All groups are coded up to two groups away from the ring atom.

Assignment	Proton Group	Environmental Groups
A	CH3	ANA⟨C-C*-CH-C(OH)/CH-CH-N⟩
B	CHA	AAN⟨C(OH)-CH-C*/CH-C*-N⟩
C	CHA	AAN⟨C*-C(CH3)/C(OH)⟩
D	CHA	AAN⟨C*-N/CH-C(OH)⟩
E	CHA	ANA⟨C(CH3)-C*/CH-N-C*⟩
F	CHA	ANA⟨N-C*/CH-C(CH3)-C*⟩

Assignment	Proton Group	Environmental Groups
A	CHA	AAA⟨CH-C*-C(NO2)/OH-CH-C*⟩
A	CHA	AAA⟨CH-C*/CH-CH-C*⟩
B	CHA	AAA⟨C*-C(C*-C(NO2)-C*⟩
B	CHA	AAA⟨C*-CH-C*⟩
C	CHA	AAA⟨C*/C*⟩

In some cases individual proton assignments cannot be defined due to the complexity of the chemical shift pattern, therefore a further coding procedure has been incorporated. If there is indication that an assignment could possibly be coded in more than two ways the assignment is not extensively cross-coded, instead it is designated as UNSPECIFIED. One exception has been made in the case of mono-substituted aromatic rings; unspecifiable ring protons are coded once as UNSPECIFIED and one cross-coding referring to the proton ortho to the mono-substitution location.

Examples:

Assignment	Proton Group	Environmental Groups
A	NH	A/A
B		UNSPECIFIED

Assignment	Proton Group	Environmental Groups
A	CH2	CL/A
B	CHA	A⟨C(CH2-CL)⟩
B		UNSPECIFIED

Compounds containing long aliphatic chains also contain assignments which refer to a variable number of protons, in such cases the assignment referring to the chain of similar proton groups is coded as follows:

Examples:

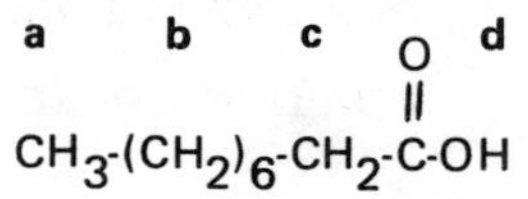

a   b   c   d

O
‖
CH_3-$(CH_2)_6$-CH_2-C-OH

Assignment	Proton Group	Environmental Groups
A	CH3	CH2-CH2
B	**CH2.X**	**CH2.6**
C	CH2	C(=O)-OH/CH2-CH2
D	OH	C(=O)-CH2

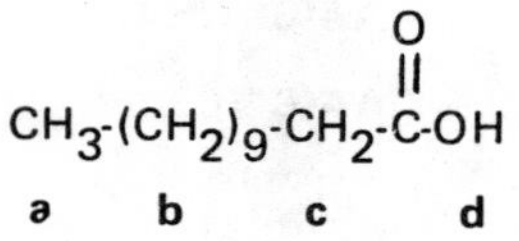

O
‖
CH_3-$(CH_2)_9$-CH_2-C-OH
a   b   c   d

Assignment	Proton Group	Environmental Groups
A	CH3	CH2.10-C(=O)-OH
B	**CH2.9**	**CH2-C(=O)-OH/CH3**
C	CH2	C(=O)-OH/CH2.9-CH3
D	OH	C(=O)-CH2

In compounds containing a carbonyl group, the next atom beyond the carbonyl group should always be coded.

Example:

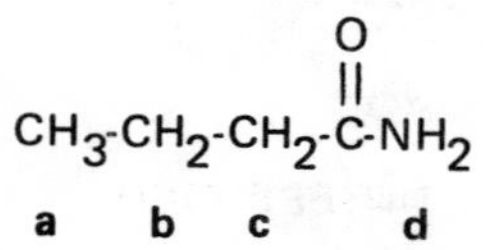

O
‖
CH_3-CH_2-CH_2-C-NH_2
a   b   c   d

Assignment	Proton Group	Environmental Groups
A	**CH3**	**CH2.2-C(=O)-NH2**
B	**CH2**	**CH2-C(=O)-NH2/CH3**
C	**CH2**	**C(=O)-NH2/CH2-CH3**
D	**NH2**	**C(=O)-CH2.2-CH3**

BOOK NO.	ASSIGN-MENT	CHEM SHIFT - ppm -	PROTON GROUP	ENVIRONMENTAL GROUPS	S	SOLVENT
1087M	A	0.01	CH3	SI(CH2/CH2/CH3)		CL2C=CCL2
38M	A	0.02	HCHR	R3<CH(CH(CH3/CH3))-HCH>		CCL4
1086M	A	0.03	CH3	SI(CH2/CH3/CH3)		CCL4
41M	A	0.03	HCHR	R3<CH(CH2-R3)-HCH>		CCL4
1093M	A	0.04	CH3	SI(NH/CH3/CH3)		CCL4
1603M	A	0.04	CH3	SI(O/CH3/CH3)		CCL4
1094M	A	0.04	CH3	SI(SI/CH3/CH3)		CCL4
40M	A	0.05	HCHR	R3<C(CH3/CH3)-CH(CH3)>		CCL4
144M	A	0.08- 0.74	CH2R	R3<CH(CH2-A)-CH2>		CDCL3
1605M	A	0.08	CH3	R80000SISISISI<SI(CH3)-O/O>		CCL4
1593M	A	0.08	CH3	SI(O/CH3/CH3)		CCL4
1789M	A	0.09- 0.64	CH2R	R3<CH(CH(OH/A))-CH2>		CCL4
1761M	A	0.10- 0.80	CH2R	R3<CH(CH(OH/CH3))-CH2>		CDCL3
39M	A	0.11	HCHR	R3<CH(CH3)-CH(CH3)>		CCL4
1595M	A	0.13	CH3	SI(O/O/O)		CDCL3
1604M	A	0.23	CH3	SI(O/CH2/CH3)		CDCL3
1680M	A	0.25- 2.82		UNSPECIFIED		CCL4
1089M	A	0.29	CH3	SI(A/CH3/CH3)		CDCL3
38M	B	0.31	CHR	R3<(CH(CH3/CH3))/HCH-HCH>		CCL4
38M	B	0.31	HCHR	R3<CH(CH(CH3/CH3))-HCH>		CCL4
225M	A	0.32	CH3	A(C-CH-C(F))		CCL4
40M	B	0.33- 0.97	CHR	R3<(CH3)/C(CH3/CH3)-HCH>		CCL4
40M	B	0.33- 0.97	HCHR	R3<C(CH3/CH3)-CH(CH3)>		CCL4
41M	B	0.41	HCHR	R3<CH(CH2-R3)-HCH>		CCL4
1682M	A	0.50- 2.00		UNSPECIFIED		CCL4
1773M	A	0.50- 2.20		UNSPECIFIED		CDCL3
1771M	B	0.50- 2.10		UNSPECIFIED		CDCL3
364M	A	0.50- 2.15		UNSPECIFIED		CCL4
1596M	A	0.53	CH2	SI(O/O/O)/CH3		CCL4
2735M	A	0.57	CH3	CH(NH2/C(=O)-O)	S	D2O
28M	A	0.58- 1.07	CH3	CH(CH/CH3)		CCL4
28M	A	0.58- 1.07	CH3	CH(CH/CH)		CCL4
1085M	A	0.59	CH2	SI(CH2/CH2/CH2)		CCL4
1996M	A	0.60- 1.10	CH2R	R3(CH(C(=O)-R3)-CH2)		CCL4
20M	A	0.62- 1.00	CH3	CH2-CH		CCL4
20M	A	0.62- 1.00	CH3	CH(CH2/CH2)		CCL4
1597M	A	0.64	CH2	SI(O/O/O)/CH2.2-NH2		CDCL3
1668M	B	0.65- 1.90	CH2	CH2-CH2/CH3		CCL4
1668M	B	0.65- 1.90	CH2	CH2-O/CH2-CH3		CCL4
2770M	C	0.65- 1.55	CH2.X	CH2.3		CCL4
553M	A	0.66	NH	CH2-CH2/CH2-CH2		CCL4
543M	A	0.67	NH	CH(CH3/CH3)/CH(CH3/CH3)		CCL4
1885M	A	0.68	CH3	CH2-C		CCL4
2545M	A	0.70- 1.40	CH2	CH2-C/CH3		CDCL3
1450M	A	0.70- 1.70	CH2R	R7R30<CH2-CH2/CH2-CH2>		CCL4
1450M	A	0.70- 1.70	CH2R	R7R30<CH2-CH*/CH2-CH2>		CCL4
2545M	A	0.70- 1.40	CH3	CH2.2-C		CDCL3
1472M	A	0.70	CH3	R600<C(CH3)-HCH/HCH>		CCL4
1771M	A	0.70- 1.15	CH3	R6<CH-CH2/CH2>		CDCL3
1771M	A	0.70- 1.15	CH3	R6<CH-CH(OH)/CH2>		CDCL3
2421M	A	0.70- 2.10		UNSPECIFIED		POLYSOL-D
1778M	A	0.70- 2.10		UNSPECIFIED		POLYSOL-D
586M	A	0.70- 2.20		UNSPECIFIED		CDCL3
1767M	B	0.70- 1.80		UNSPECIFIED		CDCL3
1681M	B	0.70- 2.00		UNSPECIFIED		CCL4
48M	B	0.70- 2.00		UNSPECIFIED		CCL4
1770M	B	0.70- 2.10		UNSPECIFIED		CDCL3
1377M	A	0.70- 2.20		UNSPECIFIED		POLYSOL-D
564M	B	0.71- 1.89	CH2R	R6N(CH2-CH(CH3)/CH2-CH2)		CCL4
564M	B	0.71- 1.89	CH2R	R6N(CH2-CH(CH3)/CH2-CH(CH3))		CCL4
2031M	A	0.71	CH3	CH2-C		CDCL3
49M	A	0.71- 2.00		UNSPECIFIED		CCL4
109M	A	0.72	CH3	R4R6BI(C(CH3)-CH*/CH*)		CCL4
2130M	A	0.72	CH3	R5R6R6R6(C*-CH(CH/CH2)/CH2)		CDCL3
1886M	A	0.73	CH3	C(CH2/CH3/CH3)		CDCL3
547M	A	0.74	NH	C(CH3/CH3)/CH2-CH2		CDCL3
41M	C	0.75 APP.	CHR	R3<(CH2-R3)/HCH-HCH>		CCL4
39M	B	0.75	HCHR	R3<CH(CH3)-CH(CH3)>		CCL4
1818M	A	0.77	CH3	CH2-C		CDCL3
100M	A	0.79	CH3	CH2-C		CCL4
26M	A	0.79 APP.	CH3	CH2-C		CCL4
26M	A	0.79 APP.	CH3	C(CH/CH2/CH3)		CCL4
100M	A	0.79	CH3	C(R6/CH2/CH3)		CCL4
546M	A	0.79	NH	CH2-CH/CH2-CH		CCL4
2771M	A	0.80	CH3	CH2-C		CCL4
138M	A	0.80	CH3	CH2-CH		CCL4
1780M	A	0.80	CH3	R5R6R6R6(C*-CH*(CH(CH2/CH3)))		CDCL3
1780M	D	0.80- 2.40	CH3	R6R6R6R5(C*-CH*/CH2)		CDCL3
1772M	A	0.80	CH3	R6(CH-CH2/CH2)		CDCL3
569M	A	0.80- 1.90		UNSPECIFIED		CDCL3
52M	A	0.80- 1.90		UNSPECIFIED		CCL4

BOOK NO.	ASSIGN-MENT	CHEM SHIFT - ppm -	PROTON GROUP	ENVIRONMENTAL GROUPS	S	SOLVENT
469M	A	0.80- 2.00		UNSPECIFIED		CDCL3
470M	A	0.80- 2.02		UNSPECIFIED		CCL4
145M	A	0.80- 2.10		UNSPECIFIED		CCL4
1217M	A	0.80- 2.10		UNSPECIFIED		CDCL3
1353M	A	0.80- 2.10		UNSPECIFIED		POLYSOL-D
1451M	A	0.80- 2.30		UNSPECIFIED		CDCL3
198M	A	0.80- 2.60		UNSPECIFIED		CCL4
1775M	A	0.80- 2.90		UNSPECIFIED		CCL4
1803M	B	0.80- 1.50		UNSPECIFIED		CCL4
773M	A	0.80- 2.20		UNSPECIFIED	S	D20
559M	B	0.80- 2.10		UNSPECIFIED		CDCL3
107M	B	0.80- 2.30		UNSPECIFIED		CCL4
471M	C	0.80- 2.20		UNSPECIFIED		CDCL3
2130M	E	0.80- 2.10		UNSPECIFIED		CDCL3
2419M	A	0.81	CH3	CH2-C		DMSO-D6
1788M	A	0.81	CH3	CH2-CH		CCL4
33M	A	0.81 APP.		UNSPECIFIED		CCL4
108M	A	0.82	CH2R	R5R5BI(CH*(Q2/CH2))		CDCL3
23M	A	0.82	CH3	CH2-C(CH3/CH3)		CDCL3
26M	B	0.82	CH3	CH(C/CH3)		CCL4
883M	A	0.82- 1.98		UNSPECIFIED		CDCL3
558M	A	0.82- 2.07		UNSPECIFIED		CDCL3
1835M	A	0.83	CH3	CH2-C		CDCL3
1839M	A	0.83	CH3	CH2-C		C3D60
2302M	A	0.83	CH3	CH2-C		CDCL3
2286M	A	0.83	CH3	HCH-CH		CCL4
2207M	A	0.83	CH3	R5R5BI(C(CH3)-C*(HCH-SO3H)/CH*)		D20
2121M	A	0.83- 2.17		UNSPECIFIED		CDCL3
1766M	A	0.83- 2.43		UNSPECIFIED		CCL4
1927M	A	0.84	CH3	CH2-CH2		CDCL3
35M	A	0.84	CH3	CH(CH2/CH2)		CDCL3
23M	B	0.84	CH3	C(CH3/CH2/CH2)		CDCL3
110M	A	0.84	CH3	R4R6BI(C(CH3)-CH*/CH*)		CCL4
2353M	A	0.85- 1.35	CH3	CH2.2-C(=O)-N		D20
1744M	A	0.85	CH3	CH2-CH2		CCL4
1747M	A	0.85	CH3	CH2-CH2		CCL4
2277M	A	0.85	CH3	CH2-CH2		DMSO-D6
2353M	A	0.85- 1.35	CH3	CH2-N		D20
19M	A	0.85	CH3	CH(CH2/CH3)		CCL4
1624M	A	0.85	CH3	C(CH2/CH2/CH3)		CDCL3
448M	A	0.85	CH3	C(CH/CH3/CH3)		CCL4
1744M	A	0.85	CH3	C(CH/CH3/CH3)		CCL4
1683M	A	0.85- 2.00		UNSPECIFIED		CDCL3
2203M	A	0.85- 2.11		UNSPECIFIED		CCL4
1761M	B	0.86	CHR	R3<(CH(OH/CH3))/CH2-CH2>		CDCL3
56M	A	0.86	CH3	CH2-CH		CDCL3
17M	A	0.86	CH3	CH2-CH		CCL4
552M	A	0.86	CH3	CH2-CH2		CDCL3
2652M	A	0.86	CH3	CH2-CH2		D20
37M	A	0.86	CH3	CH(CH2/CH2)		CCL4
37M	A	0.86	CH3	CH(CH2/CH3)		CCL4
22M	A	0.86	CH3	CH(CH2/CH3)		CCL4
24M	A	0.86	CH3	CH(CH/CH3)		CCL4
574M	A	0.86	NH	CH2-Q2/CH2-CH3		CCL4
2543M	A	0.87	CH3	CH2.2-C		DMSO-D6
1659M	A	0.87	CH3	CH2.2-CH		POLYSOL-D
1620M	A	0.87	CH3	CH2-CH		CCL4
449M	A	0.87	CH3	CH2-CH2		CDCL3
13M	A	0.87	CH3	CH2-CH2		CDCL3
1113M	A	0.87	CH3	CH2-CH2		CCL4
47M	A	0.87	CH3	CH2-R6		CCL4
17M	B	0.87	CH3	CH(CH2/CH3)		CCL4
1670M	A	0.88	CH3	CH2.11-O		CDCL3
554M	A	0.88	CH3	CH2.12-NH		CDCL3
1119M	A	0.88	CH3	CH2.17-S		CDCL3
1027M	A	0.88	CH3	CH2.2-N		CCL4
689M	A	0.88	CH3	CH2.3-CH		CCL4
1749M	A	0.88 APP.	CH3	CH2.3-CH		CCL4
160M	A	0.88	CH3	CH2.3-Q1		CCL4
1204M	A	0.88	CH3	CH2.5		CDCL3
1820M	A	0.88	CH3	CH2.7-C		CCL4
2285M	A	0.88	CH3	CH2-CH		CDCL3
494M	A	0.88	CH3	CH2-CH		CCL4
1622M	A	0.88	CH3	CH2-CH		CDCL3
55M	A	0.88	CH3	CH2-CH		CCL4
1746M	A	0.88 APP.	CH3	CH2-CH		CCL4
1749M	A	0.88 APP.	CH3	CH2-CH		CCL4
5M	A	0.88	CH3	CH2-CH2		CDCL3
7M	A	0.88	CH3	CH2-CH2		CCL4
15M	A	0.88	CH3	CH2-CH2		CCL4
2712M	A	0.88	CH3	CH2-CH2		CDCL3

: REPRESENTS TRIPLE BOND, ¬ REPRESENTS AN ARROW AND < AND > REPRESENT BRACKETS.   PAGE   162

BOOK NO.	ASSIGN-MENT	CHEM SHIFT - ppm -	PROTON GROUP	ENVIRONMENTAL GROUPS	S	SOLVENT
2579M	A	0.88	CH3	CH2-CH2		CDCL3
2355M	A	0.88	CH3	CH2-CH2		CCL4
688M	A	0.88	CH3	CH2-CH2		CCL4
1322M	A	0.88	CH3	CH2-CH2		CCL4
1387M	A	0.88	CH3	CH2-CH2		CCL4
2470M	A	0.88	CH3	CH2-CH2		CDCL3
615M	A	0.88	CH3	CH2-CH2		CCL4
2817M	A	0.88	CH3	CH2-CH2		CCL4
2818M	A	0.88	CH3	CH2-CH2		CCL4
467M	A	0.88	CH3	CH2-CH2		CCL4
412M	A	0.88	CH3	CH2-CH2		CCL4
1633M	A	0.88	CH3	CH2-CH2		CDCL3
1689M	A	0.88	CH3	CH2-CH2		CCL4
1632M	A	0.88	CH3	CH2-CH2		CDCL3
1626M	A	0.88	CH3	CH2-CH2		CCL4
1980M	A	0.88	CH3	CH2-CH2		CCL4
143M	A	0.88	CH3	CH2-CH2		CCL4
244M	A	0.88	CH3	CH2-CH2		CCL4
2976M	A	0.88	CH3	CH2-CH2		CDCL3
120M	A	0.88	CH3	CH2-CH2		CCL4
11M	A	0.88	CH3	CH2-CH2		CCL4
86M	A	0.88	CH3	CH2-CH2		CDCL3
60M	A	0.88	CH3	CH2-CH2		CCL4
62M	A	0.88	CH3	CH2-CH2		CCL4
64M	A	0.88	CH3	CH2-CH2		CCL4
1746M	A	0.88 APP.	CH3	CH2-CH2		CCL4
843M	A	0.88	CH3	CH2-CH2	S	DMSO-D6
1651M	A	0.88- 1.28	CH3	CH2-N		CCL4
1459M	A	0.88	CH3	CH2-R500		CCL4
29M	A	0.88	CH3	CH(CH2.3/CH3)		CDCL3
31M	A	0.88	CH3	CH(CH2/CH3)		CCL4
1799M	A	0.88	CH3	CH(CH2/CH3)		CCL4
546M	B	0.88	CH3	CH(CH2/CH3)		CCL4
1780M	B	0.88	CH3	CH(CH2/CH3)		CDCL3
18M	A	0.88	CH3	CH(CH/CH3)		CCL4
1651M	A	0.88- 1.28	CH3	CH(N/CH2)		CCL4
25M	A	0.88 APP.		UNSPECIFIED		CCL4
2763M	A	0.89	CH3	CH2.10-C(=0)-0		CDCL3
1989M	A	0.89	CH3	CH2.11-C(=0)		CDCL3
413M	A	0.89	CH3	CH2.11-I		CCL4
829M	A	0.89	CH3	CH2.11-N(+)	S	CDCL3
830M	A	0.89	CH3	CH2.11-N(+)	S	CDCL3
2783M	A	0.89	CH3	CH2.11-0-C(=0)		CDCL3
2769M	A	0.89	CH3	CH2.11-0-C(=0)		CDCL3
1660M	A	0.89	CH3	CH2.11-S		CDCL3
1189M	A	0.89	CH3	CH2.11-S		CDCL3
1090M	A	0.89	CH3	CH2.11-SI		CCL4
2050M	A	0.89	CH3	CH2.12-C(=0)-A		CDCL3
1328M	A	0.89	CH3	CH2.13-0-S03-NA		POLYSOL-D
1928M	A	0.89	CH3	CH2.15-A		POLYSOL-D
339M	A	0.89	CH3	CH2.15-BR		CCL4
247M	A	0.89	CH3	CH2.15-CL		CCL4
414M	A	0.89	CH3	CH2.15-I		CCL4
833M	A	0.89	CH3	CH2.17-N(+)	S	CDCL3
1390M	A	0.89	CH3	CH2.17-0		CDCL3
624M	A	0.89	CH3	CH2.21-N		CDCL3
1635M	A	0.89	CH3	CH2.23-OH		POLYSOL-D
2354M	A	0.89 APP.	CH3	CH2.2-N		CDCL3
16M	A	0.89	CH3	CH2.34-CH3		POLYSOL-D
2651M	A	0.89	CH3	CH2.3-CH		POLYSOL-D
2650M	A	0.89 APP.	CH3	CH2.3-CH		D20
1884M	A	0.89	CH3	CH2.4-A		CCL4
849M	A	0.89	CH3	CH2.5-QN		CDCL3
161M	A	0.89	CH3	CH2.6-Q1		CCL4
2815M	A	0.89	CH3	CH2.6-Q2		CCL4
1295M	A	0.89	CH3	CH2.6-S03-NA		D20
810M	A	0.89	CH3	CH2.7-N		CDCL3
2848M	A	0.89	CH3	CH2.7-0-C(=0)		CCL4
2527M	A	0.89	CH3	CH2.7-Q2		CCL4
2257M	A	0.89	CH3	CH2.8-Q2		CDCL3
622M	A	0.89	CH3	CH2.9-N		CDCL3
1216M	A	0.89	CH3	CH2.9-NH		CDCL3
1347M	A	0.89	CH3	CH2.9-NH		POLYSOL-D
1389M	A	0.89	CH3	CH2.9-0		CCL4
162M	A	0.89	CH3	CH2.9-Q1		CDCL3
447M	A	0.89	CH3	CH2-C		CDCL3
1803M	A	0.89	CH3	CH2-C		CCL4
1802M	A	0.89 APP.	CH3	CH2-C		CCL4
2021M	A	0.89	CH3	CH2-CH		CCL4
2650M	A	0.89 APP.	CH3	CH2-CH		D20
2895M	A	0.89	CH3	CH2-CH2		CCL4

BOOK NO.	ASSIGN-MENT	CHEM SHIFT - ppm -	PROTON GROUP	ENVIRONMENTAL GROUPS	S	SOLVENT
2919M	A	0.89	CH3	CH2-CH2		C3D60
2939M	A	0.89	CH3	CH2-CH2		CDCL3
2990M	A	0.89	CH3	CH2-CH2		CCL4
2961M	A	0.89	CH3	CH2-CH2		CCL4
2966M	A	0.89	CH3	CH2-CH2		CCL4
8M	A	0.89	CH3	CH2-CH2		CCL4
9M	A	0.89	CH3	CH2-CH2		CCL4
83M	A	0.89	CH3	CH2-CH2		CCL4
57M	A	0.89	CH3	CH2-CH2		CCL4
1M	A	0.89	CH3	CH2-CH2		CCL4
10M	A	0.89	CH3	CH2-CH2		CCL4
92M	A	0.89	CH3	CH2-CH2		CCL4
2M	A	0.89	CH3	CH2-CH2		CCL4
14M	A	0.89	CH3	CH2-CH2		CDCL3
2710M	A	0.89	CH3	CH2-CH2		CCL4
2719M	A	0.89	CH3	CH2-CH2		CDCL3
2697M	A	0.89	CH3	CH2-CH2		CCL4
2356M	A	0.89	CH3	CH2-CH2		CCL4
2365M	A	0.89	CH3	CH2-CH2		CDCL3
2366M	A	0.89	CH3	CH2-CH2		CCL4
2278M	A	0.89	CH3	CH2-CH2		CDCL3
953M	A	0.89	CH3	CH2-CH2		CDCL3
1011M	A	0.89	CH3	CH2-CH2		CCL4
2193M	A	0.89	CH3	CH2-CH2		CDCL3
2049M	A	0.89	CH3	CH2-CH2		CCL4
1317M	A	0.89	CH3	CH2-CH2		CDCL3
1392M	A	0.89	CH3	CH2-CH2		CDCL3
2495M	A	0.89	CH3	CH2-CH2		CDCL3
2480M	A	0.89	CH3	CH2-CH2		CCL4
2524M	A	0.89	CH3	CH2-CH2		CCL4
2528M	A	0.89	CH3	CH2-CH2		CCL4
579M	A	0.89	CH3	CH2-CH2		CCL4
2759M	A	0.89	CH3	CH2-CH2		CDCL3
2822M	A	0.89	CH3	CH2-CH2		CCL4
2758M	A	0.89	CH3	CH2-CH2		CDCL3
2802M	A	0.89	CH3	CH2-CH2		CDCL3
1757M	A	0.89	CH3	CH2-CH2		CDCL3
1634M	A	0.89	CH3	CH2-CH2		CDCL3
1739M	A	0.89	CH3	CH2-CH2		CCL4
1628M	A	0.89	CH3	CH2-CH2		CCL4
1748M	A	0.89	CH3	CH2-CH2		CCL4
1987M	A	0.89	CH3	CH2-CH2		CDCL3
338M	A	0.89	CH3	CH2-CH2		CCL4
341M	A	0.89	CH3	CH2-CH2		CDCL3
119M	A	0.89	CH3	CH2-CH2		CCL4
1623M	A	0.89	CH3	CH2-CH2		CCL4
1103M	A	0.89	CH3	CH2-CH2		CDCL3
1213M	A	0.89	CH3	CH2-CH2		CCL4
1104M	A	0.89	CH3	CH2-CH2		CDCL3
1118M	A	0.89	CH3	CH2-CH2		CCL4
2459M	A	0.89	CH3	CH2-CH2		DMSO-D6
770M	A	0.89	CH3	CH2-CH2	S	D20
1312M	A	0.89	CH3	CH2-CH2	S	CDCL3
19M	B	0.89	CH3	CH2-CH2		CCL4
35M	B	0.89	CH3	CH2-CH2		CDCL3
553M	B	0.89	CH3	CH2-CH2		CCL4
1624M	B	0.89	CH3	CH2-CH2		CDCL3
2761M	A	0.89	CH3	CH2-C(=0)-0		CDCL3
1810M	A	0.89	CH3	CH2-R6		C3F60
453M	A	0.89	CH3	CH(CH2.2/CH3)		CDCL3
1690M	A	0.89 APP.	CH3	CH(CH2.3/CH3)		CCL4
58M	A	0.89	CH3	CH(CH2/CH2)		CCL4
1629M	A	0.89	CH3	CH(CH2/CH2)		CDCL3
48M	A	0.89	CH3	CH(CH2/CH3)		CCL4
32M	A	0.89	CH3	CH(CH2/CH3)		CCL4
34M	A	0.89	CH3	CH(CH2/CH3)		CCL4
1383M	A	0.89	CH3	CH(CH2/CH3)		CCL4
619M	A	0.89	CH3	CH(CH2/CH3)		CDCL3
1615M	A	0.89	CH3	CH(CH2/CH3)		CCL4
2130M	B	0.89	CH3	CH(CH2/CH3)		CDCL3
21M	A	0.89	CH3	C(CH2.2/CH3/CH3)		CDCL3
1629M	A	0.89	CH3	C(CH2/CH3/CH3)		CDCL3
1779M	A	0.89	CH3	R5R5BI<C(CH3)-C*(CH3)/CH*>		CDCL3
2007M	A	0.89	CH3	R5R5BI<C(CH3)-C*(HCH-S03-NA)/CH*>		D20
1779M	A	0.89	CH3	R5R5BI<C*-C(CH3/CH3)/CH(OH)/CH2>		CDCL3
1768M	A	0.89	CH3	R6<CH-CH2/CH2>		CDCL3
1207M	A	0.89	SH	CH2-CH		CCL4
30M	A	0.89 APP.		UNSPECIFIED		CCL4
924M	A	0.89- 2.13		UNSPECIFIED		CDCL3
17M	C	0.90- 1.60	CH	CH2-CH3/CH3/CH3		CCL4
38M	C	0.90 APP.	CH	R3<CH-HCH/HCH>/CH3/CH3		CCL4

BOOK NO.	ASSIGN-MENT	CHEM SHIFT - ppm -	PROTON GROUP	ENVIRONMENTAL GROUPS	S	SOLVENT
39M	C	0.90 APP.	CHR	R3<(CH3)/CH(CH3)-HCH>		CCL4
563M	B	0.90- 1.80	CHR	R6N<(CH3)/CH2-HCH/CH2-HCH>		CCL4
17M	C	0.90- 1.60	CH2	CH(CH3/CH3)/CH3		CCL4
47M	B	0.90- 1.90	CH2	R6/CH3		CCL4
1083M	A	0.90 APP.	CH2	SIH3/CH2.4-CH3		CDCL3
1090M	B	0.90- 1.60	CH2.X	CH2.11		CCL4
563M	B	0.90- 1.80	CH2R	R6N<CH(CH3)-CH2/HCH-NH>		CCL4
1630M	A	0.90	CH3	CH2.CH2		CCL4
2254M	A	0.90	CH3	CH2.S-C(=0)-0		CCL4
629M	A	0.90	CH3	CH2.10-CH		CDCL3
2711M	A	0.90	CH3	CH2.10-CH3		CDCL3
621M	A	0.90	CH3	CH2.11-N		CDCL3
2686M	A	0.90	CH3	CH2.11-NH2		CDCL3
910M	A	0.90	CH3	CH2.11-N=C=0		CCL4
2711M	A	0.90	CH3	CH2.11-0-C(=0)		CDCL3
1116M	A	0.90	CH3	CH2.11-S		CCL4
1117M	A	0.90	CH3	CH2.11-S		CCL4
1012M	A	0.90	CH3	CH2.11-S		CCL4
2482M	A	0.90	CH3	CH2.14-C(=0)-OH		CDCL3
122M	A	0.90	CH3	CH2.15-C:		CCL4
340M	A	0.90	CH3	CH2.16-BR		CDCL3
2194M	A	0.90	CH3	CH2.16-C(=0)-CL		CCL4
934M	A	0.90	CH3	CH2.17-N=		CDCL3
21M	B	0.90	CH3	CH2.2-C		CDCL3
542M	A	0.90 APP.	CH3	CH2.2-NH		CDCL3
1490M	A	0.90	CH3	CH2.2-0		CDCL3
2782M	A	0.90	CH3	CH2.3-CH		CDCL3
29M	B	0.90	CH3	CH2.3-CH		CDCL3
2819M	A	0.90	CH3	CH2.3-0-C(=0)		CDCL3
2481M	A	0.90	CH3	CH2.4-CH		CCL4
618M	A	0.90	CH3	CH2.4-N		CCL4
548M	A	0.90	CH3	CH2.4-NH		CDCL3
2879M	A	0.90	CH3	CH2.4-0-C(=0)		DMSO-D6
2382M	A	0.90	CH3	CH2.4-R5N		CDCL3
1800M	A	0.90	CH3	CH2.5-C		CDCL3
1210M	A	0.90	CH3	CH2.5-CH		CDCL3
1982M	A	0.90	CH3	CH2.5-C(=0)-CH		CCL4
2709M	A	0.90	CH3	CH2.5-C(=0)-0		CCL4
1699M	A	0.90	CH3	CH2.5-C:		CCL4
909M	A	0.90	CH3	CH2.5-N=C=0		CDCL3
2526M	A	0.90	CH3	CH2.5-Q2		CCL4
1472M	B	0.90	CH3	CH2.5-R600		CCL4
1206M	A	0.90	CH3	CH2.5-SH		CCL4
1083M	A	0.90 APP.	CH3	CH2.5-SIH3		CDCL3
168M	A	0.90	CH3	CH2.6-C:		CCL4
951M	A	0.90	CH3	CH2.6-C:N		CCL4
1115M	A	0.90	CH3	CH2.6-S		CCL4
2733M	A	0.90	CH3	CH2.7-CH		CCL4
2801M	A	0.90	CH3	CH2.7-C(=0)-0		CCL4
620M	A	0.90	CH3	CH2.7-N		CCL4
623M	A	0.90	CH3	CH2.7-N		CDCL3
2819M	A	0.90	CH3	CH2.7-Q2		CDCL3
1441M	A	0.90	CH3	CH2.7-R30		CCL4
121M	A	0.90	CH3	CH2.8-C:		CCL4
952M	A	0.90	CH3	CH2.8-C:N		CCL4
1211M	A	0.90	CH3	CH2.8-SH		CDCL3
1988M	A	0.90	CH3	CH2.9-C(=0)-CH2		CCL4
2685M	A	0.90	CH3	CH2.9-NH2		CDCL3
1801M	A	0.90	CH3	CH2-C		CCL4
1796M	A	0.90	CH3	CH2-C		CCL4
2782M	A	0.90	CH3	CH2-CH		CDCL3
454M	A	0.90	CH3	CH2-CH		CDCL3
1627M	A	0.90	CH3	CH2-CH		CCL4
1736M	A	0.90	CH3	CH2-CH		CCL4
1737M	A	0.90	CH3	CH2-CH		CCL4
1743M	A	0.90	CH3	CH2-CH		CCL4
2691M	A	0.90	CH3	CH2-CH		CDCL3
2696M	A	0.90	CH3	CH2-CH		CCL4
2695M	A	0.90	CH3	CH2-CH		CCL4
2698M	A	0.90	CH3	CH2-CH		CDCL3
737M	A	0.90	CH3	CH2-CH		CCL4
545M	A	0.90	CH3	CH2-CH		CCL4
1113M	B	0.90	CH3	CH2-CH		CCL4
1387M	B	0.90	CH3	CH2-CH		CCL4
332M	A	0.90	CH3	CH2-CH2		CCL4
141M	A	0.90	CH3	CH2-CH2		CCL4
334M	A	0.90	CH3	CH2-CH2		CCL4
335M	A	0.90	CH3	CH2-CH2		CCL4
336M	A	0.90	CH3	CH2-CH2		CCL4
142M	A	0.90	CH3	CH2-CH2		CDCL3
242M	A	0.90	CH3	CH2-CH2		CCL4

: REPRESENTS TRIPLE BOND, ¬ REPRESENTS AN ARROW AND < AND > REPRESENT BRACKETS.   PAGE 165

BOOK NO.	ASSIGN-MENT	CHEM SHIFT - ppm -	PROTON GROUP	ENVIRONMENTAL GROUPS	S	SOLVENT
243M	A	0.90	CH3	CH2-CH2		CCL4
248M	A	0.90	CH3	CH2-CH2		CCL4
220M	A	0.90	CH3	CH2-CH2		CCL4
1619M	A	0.90	CH3	CH2-CH2		CCL4
1581M	A	0.90	CH3	CH2-CH2		CDCL3
1501M	A	0.90	CH3	CH2-CH2		CCL4
1600M	A	0.90	CH3	CH2-CH2		CCL4
1208M	A	0.90	CH3	CH2-CH2		CDCL3
1209M	A	0.90	CH3	CH2-CH2		CCL4
1212M	A	0.90	CH3	CH2-CH2		CDCL3
2809M	A	0.90	CH3	CH2-CH2		CCL4
2813M	A	0.90	CH3	CH2-CH2		CCL4
2770M	A	0.90	CH3	CH2-CH2		CCL4
2823M	A	0.90	CH3	CH2-CH2		CCL4
2760M	A	0.90	CH3	CH2-CH2		CCL4
411M	A	0.90	CH3	CH2-CH2		CCL4
451M	A	0.90	CH3	CH2-CH2		CDCL3
444M	A	0.90	CH3	CH2-CH2		CDCL3
454M	A	0.90	CH3	CH2-CH2		CDCL3
465M	A	0.90	CH3	CH2-CH2		CCL4
1985M	A	0.90	CH3	CH2-CH2		CCL4
1986M	A	0.90	CH3	CH2-CH2		CDCL3
1804M	A	0.90	CH3	CH2-CH2		CDCL3
1783M	A	0.90	CH3	CH2-CH2		CCL4
1675M	A	0.90	CH3	CH2-CH2		CDCL3
1742M	A	0.90	CH3	CH2-CH2		CCL4
1631M	A	0.90	CH3	CH2-CH2		CCL4
2925M	A	0.90	CH3	CH2-CH2		CCL4
2909M	A	0.90	CH3	CH2-CH2		CDCL3
2981M	A	0.90	CH3	CH2-CH2		CCL4
4M	A	0.90	CH3	4M		CCL4
82M	A	0.90	CH3	CH2-CH2		CCL4
93M	A	0.90	CH3	CH2-CH2		CCL4
59M	A	0.90	CH3	CH2-CH2		CCL4
63M	A	0.90	CH3	CH2-CH2		CCL4
65M	A	0.90	CH3	CH2-CH2		CCL4
12M	A	0.90	CH3	CH2-CH2		CDCL3
6M	A	0.90	CH3	CH2-CH2		CCL4
44M	A	0.90	CH3	CH2-CH2		CCL4
2721M	A	0.90	CH3	CH2-CH2		CDCL3
2692M	A	0.90	CH3	CH2-CH2		CCL4
2693M	A	0.90	CH3	CH2-CH2		CCL4
2696M	A	0.90	CH3	CH2-CH2		CCL4
2707M	A	0.90	CH3	CH2-CH2		CCL4
2297M	A	0.90	CH3	CH2-CH2		D2O
2298M	A	0.90	CH3	CH2-CH2		CDCL3
2279M	A	0.90	CH3	CH2-CH2		CDCL3
933M	A	0.90	CH3	CH2-CH2		CCL4
1010M	A	0.90	CH3	CH2-CH2		CCL4
857M	A	0.90	CH3	CH2-CH2		CDCL3
737M	A	0.90	CH3	CH2-CH2		CCL4
2153M	A	0.90	CH3	CH2-CH2		CCL4
1384M	A	0.90	CH3	CH2-CH2		CCL4
1386M	A	0.90	CH3	CH2-CH2		CCL4
1358M	A	0.90	CH3	CH2-CH2		CDCL3
1391M	A	0.90	CH3	CH2-CH2		CDCL3
2532M	A	0.90	CH3	CH2-CH2		CCL4
2521M	A	0.90	CH3	CH2-CH2		CCL4
2487M	A	0.90	CH3	CH2-CH2		CCL4
2529M	A	0.90	CH3	CH2-CH2		CDCL3
650M	A	0.90	CH3	CH2-CH2		CCL4
578M	A	0.90	CH3	CH2-CH2		CCL4
617M	A	0.90	CH3	CH2-CH2		CCL4
550M	A	0.90	CH3	CH2-CH2		CDCL3
551M	A	0.90	CH3	CH2-CH2		CDCL3
1972M	A	0.90	CH3	CH2-CH2		CCL4
2413M	A	0.90	CH3	CH2-CH2		DMSO-D6
2299M	A	0.90 APP.	CH3	CH2-CH2		CDCL3
831M	A	0.90	CH3	CH2-CH2	S	CDCL3
839M	A	0.90	CH3	CH2-CH2	S	CDCL3
767M	A	0.90	CH3	CH2-CH2	S	DMSO-D6
2816M	A	0.90	CH3	CH2-Q2		CCL4
1476M	A	0.90	CH3	CH2-R600R600SPI		CCL4
130M	A	0.90	CH3	CH(CH2.2/CH3)		CCL4
1385M	A	0.90	CH3	CH(CH2.2/CH3)		CCL4
1625M	A	0.90	CH3	CH(CH2.4/CH3)		CDCL3
549M	A	0.90	CH3	CH(CH2/CH3)		CCL4
2837M	A	0.90	CH3	CH(CH2/CH3)		CCL4
2838M	A	0.90	CH3	CH(CH2/CH3)		CCL4
442M	A	0.90	CH3	CH(CH2/CH3)		CDCL3
1976M	A	0.90	CH3	CH(CH2/CH3)		CCL4

BOOK NO.	ASSIGN-MENT	CHEM SHIFT - ppm -	PROTON GROUP	ENVIRONMENTAL GROUPS	S	SOLVENT
1979M	A	0.90	CH3	CH(CH2/CH3)		CCL4
139M	A	0.90	CH3	CH(CH2/CH3)		CDCL3
94M	A	0.90	CH3	CH(CH2/CH3)		CCL4
2418M	A	0.90	CH3	CH(CH2/CH3)		POLYSOL-D
1802M	B	0.90	CH3	CH(CH2/CH3)		CCL4
1617M	A	0.90	CH3	CH(HCH/CH2)		CCL4
38M	C	0.90 APP.	CH3	CH(R3/CH3)		CCL4
27M	A	0.90	CH3	C(CH2/CH3/CH3)		CCL4
2129M	A	0.90	CH3	R5R6R6R6(C*-C(=O)/CH2)		CDCL3
46M	A	0.90	CH3	R6(CH-CH2/CH2)		CCL4
36M	A	0.90 APP.		UNSPECIFIED		CCL4
183M	A	0.90- 2.10		UNSPECIFIED		CDCL3
570M	A	0.90- 2.20		UNSPECIFIED		CCL4
2878M	A	0.90- 2.20		UNSPECIFIED		CDCL3
1774M	A	0.90- 2.20		UNSPECIFIED		CDCL3
1006M	A	0.90- 2.27		UNSPECIFIED		CDCL3
270M	A	0.90- 2.50		UNSPECIFIED		CCL4
1997M	A	0.90- 2.60		UNSPECIFIED		CCL4
2155M	A	0.90- 2.60		UNSPECIFIED		CDCL3
47M	B	0.90- 1.90		UNSPECIFIED		CCL4
1448M	A	0.91- 1.60	CH2R	R6R30BI<CH2-CH*/CH2-CH2>		CCL4
1984M	A	0.91	CH3	CH2.2-C(=O)-CH2.8		CCL4
1394M	A	0.91	CH3	CH2.2-O		CCL4
2800M	A	0.91	CH3	CH2.2-Q2		CCL4
452M	A	0.91	CH3	CH2.3-C		CDCL3
1969M	A	0.91	CH3	CH2.3-C(=O)-CH3		CCL4
1652M	A	0.91	CH3	CH2.3-N		CDCL3
1380M	A	0.91	CH3	CH2.3-O		CDCL3
1413M	A	0.91	CH3	CH2.3-O		CCL4
2847M	A	0.91	CH3	CH2.3-O-C(=O)		CCL4
2252M	A	0.91	CH3	CH2.4-C(=O)-O		CDCL3
129M	A	0.91	CH3	CH2.4-C:		CCL4
127M	A	0.91	CH3	CH2.4-C:C		CCL4
1294M	A	0.91	CH3	CH2.4-SO3-NA		D20
1440M	A	0.91	CH3	CH2.5-R30		CCL4
1114M	A	0.91	CH3	CH2.5-S		CCL4
128M	A	0.91	CH3	CH2.6-C:		CCL4
1745M	A	0.91	CH3	CH2-CH		CDCL3
2137M	A	0.91	CH3	CH2-CH		CDCL3
24M	B	0.91	CH3	CH2-CH		CCL4
1747M	B	0.91	CH3	CH2-CH		CCL4
245M	A	0.91	CH3	CH2-CH2		CCL4
246M	A	0.91	CH3	CH2-CH2		CCL4
2479M	A	0.91	CH3	CH2-CH2		CCL4
2757M	A	0.91	CH3	CH2-CH2		CDCL3
2877M	A	0.91	CH3	CH2-CH2		CCL4
439M	A	0.91	CH3	CH2-CH2		CCL4
439M	A	0.91	CH3	CH2-CH2		CCL4
441M	A	0.91	CH3	CH2-CH2		CDCL3
1974M	A	0.91	CH3	CH2-CH2		CCL4
1978M	A	0.91	CH3	CH2-CH2		CDCL3
1983M	A	0.91	CH3	CH2-CH2		CCL4
333M	A	0.91	CH3	CH2-CH2		CCL4
337M	A	0.91	CH3	CH2-CH2		CCL4
1614M	A	0.91	CH3	CH2-CH2		CCL4
1616M	A	0.91	CH3	CH2-CH2		CCL4
1110M	A	0.91	CH3	CH2-CH2		CCL4
85M	A	0.91	CH3	CH2-CH2		CCL4
61M	A	0.91	CH3	CH2-CH2		CCL4
72M	A	0.91	CH3	CH2-CH2		CCL4
1738M	A	0.91	CH3	CH2-CH2		CCL4
2903M	A	0.91	CH3	CH2-CH2		CCL4
2898M	A	0.91	CH3	CH2-CH2		CCL4
1038M	A	0.91	CH3	CH2-CH2		TFA
892M	A	0.91	CH3	CH2-CH2		CDCL3
891M	A	0.91	CH3	CH2-CH2		D20
800M	A	0.91	CH3	CH2-CH2		CDCL3
854M	A	0.91	CH3	CH2-CH2		CCL4
687M	A	0.91	CH3	CH2-CH2		CCL4
2192M	A	0.91	CH3	CH2-CH2		CDCL3
2154M	A	0.91	CH3	CH2-CH2		CCL4
1417M	A	0.91	CH3	CH2-CH2		CCL4
1388M	A	0.91	CH3	CH2-CH2		CCL4
1404M	A	0.91	CH3	CH2-CH2		CCL4
84M	A	0.91 APP.	CH3	CH2-CH2		CCL4
32M	B	0.91	CH3	CH2-CH2		CCL4
34M	B	0.91	CH3	CH2-CH2		CCL4
1085M	B	0.91	CH3	CH2-SI		CDCL3
585M	A	0.91	CH3	CH(CH2.2/CH3)		CCL4
1621M	A	0.91	CH3	CH(CH2.3/CH3/CH3)		CCL4
450M	A	0.91	CH3	CH(CH2/CH3)		CCL4

BOOK NO.	ASSIGN-MENT	CHEM SHIFT - ppm -	PROTON GROUP	ENVIRONMENTAL GROUPS	S	SOLVENT
446M	A	0.91	CH3	CH(CH2/CH3)		CDCL3
1971M	A	0.91	CH3	CH(CH2/CH3)		CCL4
1618M	A	0.91	CH3	CH(CH2/CH3)		CCL4
1205M	A	0.91	CH3	CH(CH2/CH3)		CCL4
856M	A	0.91	CH3	CH(CH2/CH3)		CDCL3
2621M	A	0.91	CH3	CH(CH2/CH3)		POLYSOL-D
1627M	B	0.91	CH3	CH(CH2/CH3)		CCL4
1780M	C	0.91	CH3	CH(R5R6R6R6/CH2)		CDCL3
2130M	C	0.91	CH3	CH(R5R6R6R6/CH2)		CDCL3
1772M	B	0.91	CH3	CH(R6/CH3)		CDCL3
2132M	A	0.91	CH3	R5R5BI<C(CH3)-C*(CH3)/CH*>		POLYSOL-D
563M	A	0.91	CH3	R6N<CH-CH2/CH2>		CCL4
366M	A	0.91	CH3	R6(CH-CH2/CH2)		CCL4
577M	A	0.91	NH	CH2-A/CH2-CH3		CCL4
1887M	A	0.91- 2.18		UNSPECIFIED		CDCL3
1028M	A	0.91- 2.20		UNSPECIFIED		CDCL3
2280M	A	0.92	CH3	CH2.12-C(=0)-NH2		TFA
1970M	A	0.92	CH3	CH2.2-C(=0)-CH2		CDCL3
1798M	A	0.92	CH3	CH2.3-C		CCL4
455M	A	0.92	CH3	CH2.3-CH		CDCL3
2732M	A	0.92	CH3	CH2.3-CH		CDCL3
2705M	A	0.92	CH3	CH2.3-C(=0)-0		CCL4
2041M	A	0.92	CH3	CH2.3-C(=0)-Q2		CDCL3
1653M	A	0.92	CH3	CH2.3-N		CDCL3
1975M	A	0.92	CH3	CH2.4-C(=0)-CH2		CDCL3
1698M	A	0.92	CH3	CH2.4-C:		CCL4
2897M	A	0.92	CH3	CH2.4-0-C(=0)		CCL4
2705M	A	0.92	CH3	CH2.4-0-C(=0)		CCL4
1327M	A	0.92	CH3	CH2.4-0-SO3-NA		D2O
219M	A	0.92	CH3	CH2.5		CCL4
1697M	A	0.92	CH3	CH2.5-C:		CCL4
950M	A	0.92	CH3	CH2.5-C:N		CCL4
1669M	A	0.92	CH3	CH2.5-0		CCL4
598M	A	0.92	CH3	CH2-CH		CDCL3
443M	A	0.92	CH3	CH2-CH		CDCL3
1606M	A	0.92	CH3	CH2-CH		CCL4
1601M	A	0.92	CH3	CH2-CH		CCL4
1602M	A	0.92 APP.	CH3	CH2-CH		CCL4
1617M	B	0.92	CH3	CH2-CH		CCL4
58M	B	0.92	CH3	CH2-CH		CCL4
137M	A	0.92	CH3	CH2-CH2		CCL4
326M	A	0.92	CH3	CH2-CH2		CCL4
1421M	A	0.92	CH3	CH2-CH2		CCL4
1325M	A	0.92	CH3	CH2-CH2		CCL4
2477M	A	0.92	CH3	CH2-CH2		CCL4
544M	A	0.92	CH3	CH2-CH2		D2O
584M	A	0.92	CH3	CH2-CH2		CCL4
2827M	A	0.92	CH3	CH2-CH2		CCL4
1606M	A	0.92	CH3	CH2-CH2		CCL4
70M	A	0.92	CH3	CH2-CH2		CCL4
71M	A	0.92	CH3	CH2-CH2		CCL4
2947M	A	0.92	CH3	CH2-CH2		CCL4
2984M	A	0.92	CH3	CH2-CH2		CCL4
2717M	A	0.92	CH3	CH2-CH2		CCL4
2704M	A	0.92	CH3	CH2-CH2		CCL4
2316M	A	0.92	CH3	CH2-CH2		CDCL3
959M	A	0.92	CH3	CH2-CH2		CCL4
959M	A	0.92	CH3	CH2-CH2		CCL4
2161M	A	0.92	CH3	CH2-CH2		CCL4
1602M	A	0.92 APP.	CH3	CH2-CH2		CCL4
1207M	B	0.92	CH3	CH2-CH2		CCL4
79M	A	0.92	CH3	CH2-Q2		CCL4
445M	A	0.92	CH3	CH(CH2/CH2)		CDCL3
1832M	A	0.92	CH3	CH(CH2/CH2)		CDCL3
2478M	A	0.92	CH3	CH(CH2/CH3)		CCL4
1112M	A	0.92	CH3	CH(CH2/CH3)		CDCL3
855M	A	0.92	CH3	CH(CH2/CH3)		CDCL3
2140M	A	0.92 APP.	CH3	CH(CH2/CH3)		CCL4
27M	B	0.92	CH3	CH(CH2/CH3)		CCL4
1741M	A	0.92	CH3	CH(CH/CH3)		CDCL3
2620M	A	0.92	CH3	CH(CH/CH3)		DMSO-D6
1681M	A	0.92	CH3	R6<CH-CH2/CH2>		CCL4
471M	A	0.92 APP.	CH3	R6<CH-CH2/CH2>		CDCL3
135M	A	0.93	CH3	CH2.2-A		CDCL3
2522M	A	0.93	CH3	CH2.2-CH		CCL4
1740M	A	0.93	CH3	CH2.2-CH		CDCL3
1981M	A	0.93 APP.	CH3	CH2.2-C(=0)-CH2.5		CCL4
1381M	A	0.93	CH3	CH2.2-0		CDCL3
1667M	A	0.93	CH3	CH2.2-0		CDCL3
693M	A	0.93	CH3	CH2.3-AN		CDCL3
456M	A	0.93	CH3	CH2.3-C		CDCL3

BOOK NO.	ASSIGN-MENT	CHEM SHIFT - ppm -	PROTON GROUP	ENVIRONMENTAL GROUPS	S	SOLVENT
2762M	A	0.93 APP.	CH3	CH2.3-CH		CCL4
2071M	A	0.93	CH3	CH2.3-C(=O)-A		CDCL3
1215M	A	0.93	CH3	CH2.3-NH		CDCL3
799M	A	0.93	CH3	CH2.3-NH	S	D2O
1382M	A	0.93	CH3	CH2.3-O		CCL4
2765M	A	0.93	CH3	CH2.3-O-C(=O)-O		CDCL3
2936M	A	0.93	CH3	CH2.4-O-C(=O)		CCL4
1981M	A	0.93 APP.	CH3	CH2.5-C(=O)-CH2.2		CCL4
2475M	A	0.93	CH3	CH2-CH		CDCL3
2744M	A	0.93	CH3	CH2-CH		CCL4
2960M	A	0.93	CH3	CH2-CH		CCL4
2174M	A	0.93	CH3	CH2-CH2		CCL4
2774M	A	0.93	CH3	CH2-CH2		CCL4
1442M	A	0.93	CH3	CH2-CH2		CCL4
240M	A	0.93	CH3	CH2-CH2		CCL4
330M	A	0.93	CH3	CH2-CH2		CCL4
118M	A	0.93	CH3	CH2-CH2		CCL4
1755M	A	0.93	CH3	CH2-CH2		CCL4
1668M	A	0.93	CH3	CH2-CH2		CCL4
2960M	A	0.93	CH3	CH2-CH2		CCL4
2714M	A	0.93	CH3	CH2-CH2		CCL4
949M	A	0.93	CH3	CH2-CH2		CDCL3
2706M	A	0.93 APP.	CH3	CH2-CH2		CDCL3
547M	B	0.93	CH3	CH2-CH2		CDCL3
1839M	B	0.93	CH3	CH2-CH2		C3D6O
2034M	A	0.93	CH3	CH2-C(=O)		CCL4
2747M	A	0.93	CH3	CH(CH2.2/CH3)		CCL4
1801M	B	0.93	CH3	CH(CH2.2/CH3)		CCL4
893M	A	0.93	CH3	CH(CH2/CH2)		CDCL3
2706M	A	0.93 APP.	CH3	CH(CH2/CH3)		CDCL3
1753M	A	0.93- 1.25	CH3	CH(NH2/CH)		CDCL3
1753M	A	0.93- 1.25	CH3	CH(OH/CH)		CDCL3
2008M	A	0.93	CH3	R5R5RI<C(CH3)-C*(CH3)/CH*>		CDCL3
1769M	A	0.93	CH3	R6<CH-CH2/CH2>		CDCL3
477M	A	0.93 APP.	NH2	CH2-CH2		CCL4
53M	A	0.93- 2.17		UNSPECIFIED		CDCL3
1797M	A	0.94	CH3	CH2.2-C		CCL4
331M	A	0.94	CH3	CH2.2-CH		CCL4
2987M	A	0.94	CH3	CH2.2-O-C(=O)		CDCL3
2799M	A	0.94	CH3	CH2.2-Q2		CCL4
2788M	A	0.94	CH3	CH2.3-CH		CCL4
1599M	A	0.94	CH3	CH2.3-O		CCL4
1095M	A	0.94	CH3	CH2.3-P		CDCL3
2788M	A	0.94	CH3	CH2-CH		CCL4
445M	B	0.94	CH3	CH2-CH		CDCL3
1743M	B	0.94	CH3	CH2-CH		CCL4
1745M	B	0.94	CH3	CH2-CH		CDCL3
1613M	A	0.94	CH3	CH2-CH2		CCL4
2066M	A	0.94	CH3	CH2-CH2		CDCL3
2438M	A	0.94	CH3	CH2-CH2		CCL4
2784M	A	0.94	CH3	CH2-CH2		CCL4
2982M	A	0.94	CH3	CH2-CH2		CCL4
2708M	A	0.94	CH3	CH2-CH2		CCL4
2741M	A	0.94	CH3	CH(CH2/CH3)		CCL4
328M	A	0.94	CH3	CH(CH2/CH3)		CCL4
2001M	A	0.94	CH3	R6<CH-C(=O)/CH2>		CCL4
689M	B	0.95- 1.50	CH2	CH2.2-CH/CH3		CCL4
689M	B	0.95- 1.50	CH2	CH2-CH/CH2-CH3		CCL4
1688M	A	0.95	CH2	Q2(H/H/CH2-CH2)/CH3		CCL4
2151M	A	0.95	CH3	CHI.2-C(=O)-H		CCL4
2190M	A	0.95	CH3	CH2.2-C		CCL4
2745M	A	0.95	CH3	CH2.2-CH		CDCL3
2191M	A	0.95	CH3	CH2.2-CH		CCL4
1836M	A	0.95	CH3	CH2.2-CH		CDCL3
327M	A	0.95	CH3	CH2.2-CH		CCL4
1784M	A	0.95	CH3	CH2.2-CH		CDCL3
2842M	A	0.95	CH3	CH2.2-C(=O)-O		CCL4
2700M	A	0.95	CH3	CH2.2-C(=O)-O		CCL4
1787M	A	0.95	CH3	CH2.2-C:		CCL4
1063M	A	0.95	CH3	CH2.2-QN		POLYSOL-D
2351M	A	0.95	CH3	CH2.3-N		CDCL3
1562M	A	0.95	CH3	CH2.3-O		CDCL3
1965M	A	0.95	CH3	CH2.3-O		CDCL3
2743M	A	0.95	CH3	CH2.3-O-C(=O)		CCL4
2775M	A	0.95	CH3	CH2.3-O-C(=O)		CCL4
2896M	A	0.95	CH3	CH2.3-O-C(=O)		CDCL3
2433M	A	0.95	CH3	CH2.3-R5NN		CCL4
1082M	A	0.95	CH3	CH2.4-O-NO2		CDCL3
1187M	A	0.95	CH3	CH2.4-S		CCL4
1836M	A	0.95	CH3	CH2-CH		CDCL3
1644M	A	0.95	CH3	CH2-CH		CDCL3

BOOK NO.	ASSIGN-MENT	CHEM SHIFT - ppm -	PROTON GROUP	ENVIRONMENTAL GROUPS	S	SOLVENT
2808M	A	0.95 APP.	CH3	CH2-CH		CCL4
2767M	A	0.95	CH3	CH2-CH2		CCL4
651M	A	0.95	CH3	CH2-CH2		CCL4
2047M	A	0.95	CH3	CH2-CH2		CCL4
1414M	A	0.95	CH3	CH2-CH2		CCL4
1424M	A	0.95	CH3	CH2-CH2		CCL4
236M	A	0.95	CH3	CH2-CH2		CCL4
2998M	A	0.95	CH3	CH2-CH2		CCL4
2618M	A	0.95	CH3	CH2-CH2		D20
2250M	A	0.95	CH3	CH2-CH2		CDCL3
2808M	A	0.95 APP.	CH3	CH2-CH2		CCL4
664M	A	0.95	CH3	CH2-N		CCL4
78M	A	0.95	CH3	CH2-Q2		CDCL3
75M	A	0.95	CH3	CH2-Q2		CCL4
197M	A	0.95	CH3	CH2-R6A		CCL4
1620M	B	0.95	CH3	CH(CH2.2/CH2)		CCL4
1188M	A	0.95	CH3	CH(CH2.2/CH3)		CCL4
2715M	A	0.95	CH3	CH(CH2/CH3)		CCL4
1346M	A	0.95	CH3	CH(CH2/CH3)		CDCL3
80M	A	0.95	CH3	CH(Q2/CH3)		CCL4
2004M	A	0.95	CH3	C(R6/CH3/CH3)		CDCL3
565M	A	0.95	NHR	R13N<CH2-CH2/CH2-CH2>		CDCL3
2139M	A	0.95		UNSPECIFIED		CCL4
1629M	B	0.95- 1.70		UNSPECIFIED		CDCL3
2352M	A	0.96	CH3	CH2.2-C(=O)-N		D20
2060M	A	0.96	CH3	CH2.3-C(=O)-A		CDCL3
2766M	A	0.96	CH3	CH2.3-O-C(=O)		CDCL3
103M	A	0.96	CH3	CH2-A		CCL4
1034M	A	0.96	CH3	CH2-CH		CCL4
1245M	A	0.96	CH3	CH2-CH2		CDCL3
874M	A	0.96	CH3	CH2-CH2		CCL4
2429M	A	0.96	CH3	CH2-CH2		CDCL3
2523M	A	0.96	CH3	CH2-CH2		CCL4
1126M	A	0.96	CH3	CH2-CH2		CCL4
1534M	A	0.96	CH3	CH2-CH2		CCL4
2917M	A	0.96	CH3	CH2-CH2		C3D60
2709M	B	0.96	CH3	CH(CH2.2/CH3)		CCL4
410M	A	0.96	CH3	CH(CH2/CH3)		CCL4
2807M	A	0.96	CH3	CH(CH2/CH3)		CCL4
2778M	A	0.96	CH3	CH(CH2/CH3)		CCL4
2699M	A	0.96	CH3	CH(CH2/CH3)		CCL4
448M	B	0.96	CH3	CH(NH2/C)		CCL4
77M	A	0.96	CH3	CH(Q2/CH3)		CCL4
1610M	A	0.96	CH3	CH(R600R6BI/CH3)		CCL4
1765M	A	0.96	CH3	R5<CH-CH(OH)/CH2>		CDCL3
1027M	B	0.97	CH3	CH2.2-N		CCL4
1033M	A	0.97	CH3	CH2.2-O-N=O		CCL4
1254M	A	0.97	CH3	CH2.3-SO2		CDCL3
1315M	A	0.97	CH3	CH2.3-SO3		CDCL3
1829M	A	0.97	CH3	CH2-CH		CDCL3
2253M	A	0.97	CH3	CH2-CH		CCL4
2477M	B	0.97	CH3	CH2-CH		CCL4
946M	A	0.97	CH3	CH2-CH2		CCL4
946M	A	0.97	CH3	CH2-CH2		CCL4
2894M	A	0.97	CH3	CH2-CH2		CCL4
2349M	A	0.97	CH3	CH2-CH2		CCL4
616M	A	0.97	CH3	CH2-N		CCL4
661M	A	0.97	CH3	CH2-N		CDCL3
661M	A	0.97	CH3	CH2-N		CDCL3
632M	A	0.97	CH3	CH2-N		CCL4
1037M	A	0.97	CH3	CH(CH2.2/CH3)		CDCL3
1405M	A	0.97	CH3	CH(CH2/CH3)		CCL4
2843M	A	0.97	CH3	CH(CH2/CH3)		CCL4
616M	A	0.97	CH3	CH(N/CH3)		CCL4
76M	A	0.97	CH3	CH(Q2/CH3)		CCL4
88M	A	0.97	CH3	CH(Q3/CH2)		CCL4
55M	B	0.97	CH3	CH(Q3/CH2)		CCL4
1449M	A	0.97	CH3	R3OR6R4BI<C*(O/CH*)>		CCL4
43M	A	0.97	CH3	R5<CH-CH2/CH2>		CCL4
144M	B	0.98 APP.	CHR	R3<(CH2-A)/CH2-CH2>		CDCL3
1789M	B	0.98	CHR	R3<(CH(OH/A))/CH2-CH2>		CCL4
2486M	A	0.98	CH3	CH2.2-CH		CDCL3
2070M	A	0.98	CH3	CH2.2-C(=O)-A		CDCL3
2077M	A	0.98	CH3	CH2.2-C(=O)-A		CCL4
127M	B	0.98	CH3	CH2.2-C:C		CCL4
2156M	A	0.98	CH3	CH2.2-Q2		CDCL3
2520M	A	0.98	CH3	CH2.2-Q2		CCL4
1109M	A	0.98	CH3	CH2.2-S		CCL4
768M	A	0.98	CH3	CH2.3-NH2	S	CDCL3
1223M	A	0.98	CH3	CH2-C		CDCL3
1203M	A	0.98	CH3	CH2-CH		CCL4

BOOK NO.	ASSIGN-MENT	CHEM SHIFT - ppm -	PROTON GROUP	ENVIRONMENTAL GROUPS	S	SOLVENT
1787M	B	0.98	CH3	CH2-CH		CCL4
908M	A	0.98	CH3	CH2-CH2		CDCL3
2157M	A	0.98	CH3	CH2-CH2		CCL4
1255M	A	0.98	CH3	CH2-CH2		CCL4
2890M	A	0.98	CH3	CH2-CH2		CCL4
2701M	A	0.98	CH3	CH2-CH2		CCL4
614M	A	0.98	CH3	CH2-N		CCL4
1439M	A	0.98	CH3	CH2-R30		CCL4
1596M	B	0.98	CH3	CH2-SI		CCL4
1078M	A	0.98	CH3	CH(CH2/CH3)		CDCL3
1035M	A	0.98	CH3	CH(CH2/CH3)		CCL4
2812M	A	0.98	CH3	CH(CH2/CH3)		CCL4
1738M	B	0.98	CH3	CH(OH/CH2)		CCL4
81M	A	0.98	CH3	CH(Q2/CH3)		CCL4
925M	A	0.98	CH3	C(N=C=N/CH3/CH3)		CDCL3
101M	A	0.98- 2.51		UNSPECIFIED		CCL4
2188M	A	0.99	CH3	CH2.2-C(=0)-CL		CDCL3
1201M	A	0.99	CH3	CH2.2-SH		CDCL3
407M	A	0.99	CH3	CH2.3-I		CCL4
931M	A	0.99	CH3	CH2.3-N=C=S		CCL4
2005M	A	0.99 APP.	CH3	CH2.5-R6		CDCL3
1184M	A	0.99	CH3	CH2-CH		CCL4
408M	A	0.99	CH3	CH2-CH		CDCL3
2615M	A	0.99	CH3	CH2-CH		D20
2478M	B	0.99	CH3	CH2-CH		CCL4
1207M	C	0.99	CH3	CH2-CH		CCL4
1124M	A	0.99	CH3	CH2-CH2		CCL4
1244M	A	0.99	CH3	CH2-CH2		CCL4
1183M	A	0.99	CH3	CH2-CH2		CDCL3
1009M	A	0.99	CH3	CH2-CH2		CCL4
2792M	A	0.99	CH3	CH2-CH2		CCL4
557M	A	0.99	CH3	CH2-CH2		CDCL3
322M	A	0.99	CH3	CH2-CH2		CCL4
3M	A	0.99	CH3	CH2-CH2		CCL4
2999M	A	0.99	CH3	CH2-CH2		CDCL3
1968M	A	0.99	CH3	CH2-C(=0)		CCL4
672M	A	0.99	CH3	CH2-N		CCL4
1111M	A	0.99	CH3	CH(CH2/CH3)		CCL4
2619M	A	0.99	CH3	CH(CH/CH3)		D20
568M	A	0.99	CH3	R6NN(CH-NH/HCH)		CDCL3
2005M	A	0.99 APP.	CH3	R6(CH-CH2/CH2)		CDCL3
479M	A	0.99	NH2	CH2-CH		CDCL3
482M	A	0.99	NH2	CH2-CH2		CCL4
1037M	B	1.00- 2.20	CH	CH2.2-NO2/CH3/CH3		CDCL3
20M	B	1.00- 1.50	CH	CH2-CH3/CH2-CH3/CH3		CCL4
58M	C	1.00- 1.80	CH	CH2-Q3/CH2-CH3/CH3		CCL4
26M	C	1.00- 1.82	CH	C(CH2/CH3/CH3)/CH3/CH3		CCL4
100M	C	1.00- 1.60	CHR	R6<(C(CH2/CH3/CH3))/CH2-CH=/CH2-CH2>		CCL4
2060M	B	1.00- 2.05	CH2	CH2.2-C(=0)-A/CH3		CDCL3
2041M	B	1.00- 2.00	CH2	CH2.2-C(=0)-Q2/CH3		CDCL3
799M	B	1.00- 2.00	CH2	CH2.2-NH/CH3	S	D20
2765M	B	1.00- 2.00	CH2	CH2.2-0-C(=0)-0/CH3		CDCL3
2743M	B	1.00- 1.85	CH2	CH2.2-0-C(=0)/CH3		CCL4
1327M	B	1.00- 1.60	CH2	CH2.2-0-S03-NA/CH2-CH3		D20
1599M	B	1.00- 1.70	CH2	CH2.2-0/CH3		CCL4
1327M	B	1.00- 1.60	CH2	CH2.3-0-S03-NA/CH3		D20
2066M	B	1.00- 2.00	CH2	CH2-CH2/CH3		CDCL3
2060M	B	1.00- 2.05	CH2	CH2-C(=0)-A/CH2-CH3		CDCL3
2041M	B	1.00- 2.00	CH2	CH2-C(=0)-Q2/CH2-CH3		CDCL3
2066M	B	1.00- 2.00	CH2	CH2-C(=0)/CH2-CH3		CDCL3
1624M	C	1.00- 1.40	CH2	CH2-C/CH3		CDCL3
799M	B	1.00- 2.00	CH2	CH2-NH/CH2-CH3	S	D20
1027M	C	1.00- 2.05	CH2	CH2-N/CH3		CCL4
2765M	B	1.00- 2.00	CH2	CH2-0-C(=0)-0/CH2-CH3		CDCL3
2743M	B	1.00- 1.85	CH2	CH2-0-C(=0)/CH2-CH3		CCL4
1599M	B	1.00- 1.70	CH2	CH2-0/CH2-CH3		CCL4
20M	B	1.00- 1.50	CH2	CH(CH2/CH3)/CH3		CCL4
58M	C	1.00- 1.80	CH2	CH(CH2/CH3)/CH3		CCL4
1037M	B	1.00- 2.20	CH2	CH(CH3/CH3)/CH2-NO2		CDCL3
2651M	B	1.00- 1.75	CH2	CH(C(=0)-0/CH2.3)/CH3		POLYSOL-D
545M	C	1.00- 1.70	CH2	CH(NH/CH3)/CH3		CCL4
1624M	C	1.00- 1.40	CH2	C(CH2/CH3/CH3)/CH2-CH3		CDCL3
26M	C	1.00- 1.82	CH2	C(CH/CH3/CH3)/CH3		CCL4
2049M	B	1.00- 1.60	CH2.X	CH2.3		CCL4
2525M	B	1.00- 1.70	CH2.X	CH2.3		CCL4
2277M	B	1.00- 1.80	CH2.X	CH2.3		DMSO-D6
548M	B	1.00- 1.90	CH2.X	CH2.3		CDCL3
952M	B	1.00- 1.90	CH2.X	CH2.7		CCL4
1975M	C	1.00- 1.90	CH2.3	CH2-C(=0)-CH2/CH3		CDCL3
2651M	B	1.00- 1.75	CH2.3	CH(C(=0)-0/CH2)/CH3		POLYSOL-D
1095M	B	1.00- 1.90	CH2.3	P(CH2.3/CH2.3)/CH3		CDCL3

BOOK NO.	ASSIGN-MENT	CHEM SHIFT - ppm -	PROTON GROUP	ENVIRONMENTAL GROUPS	S	SOLVENT
1981M	B	1.00- 1.50	CH2.4	CH2-C(=O)-CH2.2/CH3		CCL4
1982M	C	1.00- 1.90	CH2.4	CH2-C(=O)-CH/CH3		CCL4
1669M	B	1.00- 1.80	CH2.4	CH2-O/CH3		CCL4
1083M	B	1.00- 1.70	CH2.4	CH2-SIH3/CH3		CDCL3
161M	B	1.00- 1.70	CH2.5	CH2-Q1/CH3		CCL4
1820M	B	1.00- 1.60	CH2.6	CH2-C/CH3		CCL4
468M	A	1.00- 2.10	CH2R	R5<CH2-CH(NH2)/CH2-CH2>		CDCL3
468M	A	1.00- 2.10	CH2R	R5<CH(NH2)-CH2/CH2-CH2>		CDCL3
1692M	C	1.00- 1.90	CH2R	R60(C(CH2-OH/CH3)-O/CH2-C(CH3)=)		CDCL3
1692M	C	1.00- 1.90	CH2R	R60(C(CH3)=CH/CH2-C(CH2-OH/CH3))		CDCL3
422M	A	1.00- 2.00	CH2R	R6<CH2-CH2/CH2-CH2>		CDCL3
422M	A	1.00- 2.00	CH2R	R6<CH2-CH(I)/CH2-CH2>		CDCL3
1855M	A	1.00- 2.09	CH2R	R6<CH2-CH(OH)/CH2-CH2>		CDCL3
100M	C	1.00- 1.60	CH2R	R6<CH(C(CH2/CH3))-CH2/CH2-CH=>		CCL4
1855M	A	1.00- 2.09	CH2R	R6<CH(OH)-CH(OH)/CH2-CH2>		CDCL3
105M	A	1.00- 1.90	CH2R	R6(CH2-CH=/CH2-CH2)		CCL4
105M	A	1.00- 1.90	CH2R	R6(CH2-C(R6)=/CH2-CH2)		CCL4
1856M	A	1.00- 2.20	CH2R	R6(CH(OH)-CH2/CH2-CH(OH))		D20
1857M	A	1.00- 2.20	CH2R	R8<CH2-CH(OH)/CH2-CH(OH)>		D20
1857M	A	1.00- 2.20	CH2R	R8<CH(OH)-CH2/CH2-CH2>		D20
2863M	A	1.00	CH3	CH2.2-O-C(=O)		CCL4
739M	A	1.00	CH3	CH2.2-R5NNA		POLYSOL-D
828M	A	1.00	CH3	CH2.3-N(+)		CDCL3
323M	A	1.00	CH3	CH2-CH		CDCL3
2903M	B	1.00	CH3	CH2-CH		CCL4
405M	A	1.00	CH3	CH2-CH2		CCL4
1329M	A	1.00	CH3	CH2-CH2		CCL4
2908M	A	1.00	CH3	CH2-CH2		CCL4
2902M	A	1.00	CH3	CH2-CH2		CCL4
1980M	B	1.00	CH3	CH2-C(=O)		CCL4
1650M	A	1.00	CH3	CH2-N		CCL4
626M	A	1.00	CH3	CH2-N		CDCL3
633M	A	1.00	CH3	CH2-N		CCL4
635M	A	1.00	CH3	CH2-N		CCL4
629M	B	1.00	CH3	CH2-N		CDCL3
2138M	A	1.00	CH3	CH2-Q1		CCL4
69M	A	1.00	CH3	CH2-Q2		CCL4
1770M	A	1.00 APP.	CH3	CH2-R6		CDCL3
2864M	A	1.00	CH3	CH(CH2/CH3)		CDCL3
2918M	A	1.00	CH3	CH(CH2/CH3)		C3D60
1977M	A	1.00	CH3	CH(C(=O)-C/CH3)		CCL4
545M	B	1.00 APP.	CH3	CH(NH/CH2)		CCL4
543M	B	1.00	CH3	CH(NH/CH3)		CCL4
625M	A	1.00	CH3	CH(N/CH2)		D20
958M	A	1.00	CH3	CH(N/CH3)		CCL4
1648M	A	1.00	CH3	CH(N/HCH)		D20
67M	A	1.00	CH3	CH(Q3/CH2)		CCL4
2459M	B	1.00	CH3	CH(R6NN/CH2)		DMSO-D6
274M	A	1.00	CH3	C(CH2/CH2/CH3)		CDCL3
2305M	A	1.00	CH3	C(CH2/CH3-CH3)		CDCL3
274M	A	1.00	CH3	C(CH2/CH3/CH3)		CDCL3
460M	A	1.00	CH3	C(NH2/CH2/CH3)		CCL4
547M	C	1.00	CH3	C(NH/CH3/CH3)		CDCL3
82M	B	1.00	CH3	C(Q2/CH3/CH3)		CCL4
54M	A	1.00	CH3	C(Q3/CH3/CH3)		CCL4
562M	A	1.00	CH3	R6N(CH-NH/CH2)		CCL4
564M	A	1.00	CH3	R6N(CH-N/CH2)		CCL4
548M	B	1.00- 1.90	NH	CH2.4-CH3/CH2.4-CH3		CDCL3
578M	B	1.00	NH	CH2-A/CH2-CH2		CCL4
1998M	A	1.00- 2.00		UNSPECIFIED		CDCL3
1794M	A	1.00- 2.00		UNSPECIFIED		POLYSOL-D
2084M	A	1.00- 2.20		UNSPECIFIED		CDCL3
1816M	A	1.00- 2.20		UNSPECIFIED		CDCL3
2988M	A	1.00- 2.20		UNSPECIFIED		CDCL3
2205M	A	1.00- 2.45		UNSPECIFIED		CCL4
1045M	A	1.00- 2.50		UNSPECIFIED		CCL4
1781M	A	1.00- 2.60		UNSPECIFIED		CDCL3
2536M	A	1.00- 2.80		UNSPECIFIED		CDCL3
30M	B	1.00- 1.60		UNSPECIFIED		CCL4
1690M	B	1.00- 1.60		UNSPECIFIED		CCL4
2650M	B	1.00- 1.75		UNSPECIFIED		D20
2762M	B	1.00- 1.75		UNSPECIFIED		CCL4
46M	B	1.00- 1.80		UNSPECIFIED		CCL4
1836M	B	1.00- 1.80		UNSPECIFIED		CDCL3
1621M	B	1.00- 1.90		UNSPECIFIED		CCL4
562M	B	1.00- 1.90		UNSPECIFIED		CCL4
635M	B	1.00- 2.00		UNSPECIFIED		CCL4
2001M	B	1.00- 2.10		UNSPECIFIED		CCL4
472M	B	1.00- 2.20		UNSPECIFIED		CDCL3
1768M	B	1.00- 2.20		UNSPECIFIED		CDCL3
1779M	B	1.00- 2.60		UNSPECIFIED		CDCL3

BOOK NO.	ASSIGN-MENT	CHEM SHIFT - ppm -	PROTON GROUP	ENVIRONMENTAL GROUPS	S	SOLVENT
455M	C	1.00- 1.60		UNSPECIFIED		CDCL3
1839M	C	1.00- 1.60		UNSPECIFIED		C3D6O
1743M	C	1.00- 1.70		UNSPECIFIED		CCL4
29M	C	1.00- 1.80		UNSPECIFIED		CDCL3
453M	C	1.00- 1.90		UNSPECIFIED		CDCL3
1620M	C	1.00- 1.90		UNSPECIFIED		CCL4
24M	C	1.00- 2.00		UNSPECIFIED		CCL4
1210M	C	1.00- 2.00		UNSPECIFIED		CDCL3
2935M	A	1.01	CH3	CH2.2-O-C(=O)		CCL4
1814M	A	1.01	CH3	CH2-C		CCL4
241M	A	1.01	CH3	CH2-C		CCL4
237M	A	1.01	CH3	CH2-CH		CCL4
1080M	A	1.01	CH3	CH2-CH2		CCL4
117M	A	1.01	CH3	CH2-CH2		CCL4
2249M	A	1.01	CH3	CH2-CH2		CCL4
1041M	A	1.01	CH3	CH2-CH2		CCL4
2959M	A	1.01	CH3	CH2-CH2		CCL4
2900M	A	1.01	CH3	CH2-CH2		CDCL3
832M	A	1.01	CH3	CH2-CH2	S	CDCL3
1988M	B	1.01	CH3	CH2-C(=O)-CH2.9		CCL4
2157M	B	1.01	CH3	CH2-Q1		CCL4
71M	B	1.01	CH3	CH2-Q2		CCL4
2460M	A	1.01	CH3	CH2-R6NN		TFA
409M	A	1.01	CH3	CH(CH2/CH3)		CCL4
1185M	A	1.01	CH3	CH(CH2/CH3)		CCL4
1815M	A	1.01	CH3	CH(CH2/CH3)		CDCL3
2035M	A	1.01	CH3	CH(C(=O)-CH2/CH3)		CCL4
440M	A	1.01	CH3	CH(NH2/CH3)		D2O
559M	A	1.01	CH3	CH(NH/CH3)		CDCL3
2006M	A	1.01	CH3	R5R5BI(C(CH3)-CH*/C(=O)-C*(CH3))		CCL4
2262M	A	1.01	CH3	R5R6OBI<C(CH3)-C*(CH3)/CH*>		CDCL3
641M	A	1.01	CH3	R6NN<CH-N(A)/CH2>		CDCL3
481M	A	1.01	NH2	CH2-CH2		CDCL3
2502M	A	1.02- 1.88	CH2.X	CH2.6		DMSO-D6
2586M	A	1.02	CH3	CH2.2-O		POLYSOL-D
1281M	A	1.02	CH3	CH2.3-SO2		CCL4
1248M	A	1.02	CH3	CH2-CH2		CCL4
320M	A	1.02	CH3	CH2-CH2		CCL4
645M	A	1.02	CH3	CH2-N		CDCL3
646M	A	1.02	CH3	CH2-N		CDCL3
1464M	A	1.02	CH3	CH2-R6NO		CCL4
2731M	A	1.02	CH3	CH(CH/CH3)		CDCL3
1755M	B	1.02	CH3	CH(OH/HCH)		CCL4
1837M	A	1.02	CH3	C(CH2/CH3/CH3)		CDCL3
1973M	A	1.02	CH3	C(CH2/CH3/CH3)		CCL4
329M	A	1.02	CH3	C(CH2/CH3/CH3)		CCL4
1838M	A	1.02	CH3	C(CH/CH3/CH3)		CDCL3
2949M	A	1.02	CH3	R5O<C(CH3)-CH(OH)/CH2>		CDCL3
2949M	B	1.02	CH3	R5O<C(CH3)-CH(OH)/CH2>		CDCL3
2002M	A	1.02	CH3	R6(CH-CH2/CH2)		CCL4
2003M	A	1.02	CH3	R6(CH-CH2/CH2)		CCL4
1976M	B	1.02- 1.90		UNSPECIFIED		CCL4
21M	C	1.03- 1.45	CH2	CH2-C/CH3		CDCL3
21M	C	1.03- 1.45	CH2	C(CH3/CH3/CH3)/CH2-CH3		CDCL3
2131M	A	1.03	CH3	CH2-C(=O)		CCL4
1970M	B	1.03	CH3	CH2-C(=O)-CH2.2		CDCL3
2137M	B	1.03	CH3	CH2-Q		CDCL3
2523M	B	1.03	CH3	CH2-Q1		CCL4
238M	A	1.03	CH3	CH(CH2/CH3)		CCL4
557M	B	1.03	CH3	CH(NH/CH2)		CDCL3
556M	A	1.03	CH3	CH(NH/CH3)		D2O
1759M	A	1.03	CH3	CH(OH/HCH)		CCL4
2207M	B	1.03	CH3	R5R5BI(C(CH3)-C*(HCH-SO3H)/CH*)		D2O
1767M	A	1.03	CH3	R6<CH-CH(OH)/CH2>		CDCL3
107M	A	1.03	CH3	R6<CH-C(=CH2)/CH2>		CCL4
2173M	A	1.04	CH3	CH2.2-O		CCL4
1339M	A	1.04	CH3	CH2-NH		DMSO-D6
574M	B	1.04	CH3	CH2-NH		CCL4
1398M	A	1.04	CH3	CH(O/CH3)		CCL4
1627M	C	1.04- 1.83		UNSPECIFIED		CCL4
1617M	C	1.05- 1.81	CH	HCH-OH/CH2-CH3/CH3		CCL4
1617M	C	1.05- 1.81	CH2	CH(HCH/CH3)/CH3		CCL4
83M	B	1.05- 1.50	CH2.X	CH2.3		CCL4
262M	A	1.05	CH3	CH2-CH		CCL4
235M	A	1.05	CH3	CH2-CH2		CCL4
1096M	A	1.05	CH3	CH2-P		CDCL3
2619M	B	1.05	CH3	CH(CH/CH3)		D2O
1982M	B	1.05	CH3	CH(C(=O)-CH2.5/CH3)		CCL4
626M	B	1.05	CH3	CH(NH2/CH2.3)		CDCL3
449M	B	1.05	CH3	CH(NH2/CH2)		CDCL3
443M	B	1.05	CH3	CH(NH2/CH2)		CDCL3

BOOK NO.	ASSIGN-MENT	CHEM SHIFT - ppm -	PROTON GROUP	ENVIRONMENTAL GROUPS	S	SOLVENT
1395M	A	1.05	CH3	CH(O/CH3)		CCL4
2008M	B	1.05	CH3	R5R5RI<C(CH3)-C*(CH3)/CH*>		CDCL3
1463M	A	1.05- 1.30	CH3	R6NO<CH-O/CH2>		CDCL3
2129M	B	1.05	CH3	R6R6R6R5(C*-CH*/CH2)		CDCL3
19M	C	1.05- 1.90		UNSPECIFIED		CCL4
1675M	B	1.06- 1.78	CH2	CH2-CH2/CH3		CDCL3
1675M	B	1.06- 1.78	CH2	CH2-O/CH2-CH3		CDCL3
2470M	B	1.06- 1.68	CH2.X	CH2.3		CDCL3
2822M	B	1.06- 1.78	CH2.X	CH2.5		CCL4
242M	B	1.06- 2.03	CH2.X	CH2.5		CCL4
2657M	A	1.06	CH3	CH2-N		D20
2998M	B	1.06	CH3	CH2-N		CCL4
453M	B	1.06	CH3	CH(NH2/CH2.2)		CDCL3
465M	B	1.06- 1.50		UNSPECIFIED		CCL4
549M	B	1.07- 1.81	CH	CH2-CH2/CH3/CH3		CCL4
549M	B	1.07- 1.81	CH2	CH2-NH/CH(CH3/CH3)		CCL4
977M	A	1.07	CH3	CH2-C		CDCL3
331M	B	1.07	CH3	CH2-CH		CCL4
944M	A	1.07	CH3	CH2-CH2		CCL4
1975M	B	1.07	CH3	CH2-C(=0)-CH2.4		CDCL3
705M	A	1.07	CH3	CH2-N		CDCL3
662M	A	1.07	CH3	CH2-N		CCL4
463M	A	1.07	CH3	CH2-NH		D20
577M	B	1.07	CH3	CH2-NH		CCL4
459M	A	1.07	CH3	CH(NH2/CH2)		CDCL3
1762M	A	1.07	CH3	CH(OH/R6)		CCL4
2776M	A	1.07	CH3	C(CH2-C(=0)-0/CH2-C(=0)-0/CH3		CCL4
265M	A	1.07	CH3	C(CH2/CH3/CH3)		CCL4
2027M	A	1.07	CH3	R6<CH-CH2/CH2>		CCL4
31M	B	1.08- 1.83	CH	CH2-CH2/CH3/CH3		CCL4
1322M	B	1.08- 2.70	CH2	CH2-CH2/CH3		CCL4
1322M	B	1.08- 2.70	CH2	CH2-SO3/CH2-CH3		CCL4
31M	B	1.08- 1.83	CH2	CH(CH3/CH3)/CH2-CH		CCL4
141M	B	1.08- 1.91	CH2.X	CH2.3		CCL4
332M	B	1.08- 1.60	CH2.X	CH2.4		CCL4
2692M	B	1.08- 1.91	CH2.X	CH2.5		CCL4
2484M	A	1.08	CH3	CH2-CH		CDCL3
357M	A	1.08	CH3	CH2-CH		CDCL3
2364M	A	1.08	CH3	CH2-N		CCL4
670M	A	1.08	CH3	CH2-N		CDCL3
663M	A	1.08	CH3	CH2-N		CDCL3
947M	A	1.08	CH3	CH(CH2/CH3)		CCL4
1246M	A	1.08	CH3	CH(CH2/CH3)		CCL4
324M	A	1.08	CH3	CH(CH2/CH3)		CCL4
450M	B	1.08	CH3	CH(NH2/CH2)		CCL4
1647M	A	1.08	CH3	CH(NH/CH3)		CCL4
848M	A	1.08	CH3	CH(QN/CH3)		CCL4
2522M	B	1.08	CH3	CH(Q2/CH2.2)		CCL4
631M	A	1.08	CH3	C(CH2/CH2/CH3)		D20
2964M	A	1.08	CH3	C(CH2/CH3/CH3)		CCL4
2857M	A	1.08- 2.18		UNSPECIFIED		CCL4
1772M	C	1.08- 2.48		UNSPECIFIED		CDCL3
445M	C	1.09- 1.68	CH	CH2-NH2/CH2-CH3/CH3		CDCL3
445M	C	1.09- 1.68	CH2	CH(CH2/CH3)/CH3		CDCL3
22M	B	1.09	CH2	CH(CH3/CH3)/CH(CH3/CH3)		CCL4
444M	B	1.09- 1.66	CH2.X	CH2.3		CDCL3
1616M	B	1.09- 1.80	CH2.X	CH2.3		CCL4
172M	A	1.09	CH3	CH2-A		CCL4
2702M	A	1.09	CH3	CH2-CH2		CCL4
1253M	A	1.09	CH3	CH2-CH2		CCL4
2649M	A	1.09	CH3	CH2-C(=0)-0		D20
2835M	A	1.09	CH3	CH2-C(=0)-0		CCL4
613M	A	1.09	CH3	CH2-N		CDCL3
1706M	A	1.09	CH3	CH2-N		CDCL3
2370M	A	1.09	CH3	CH2-N		CDCL3
853M	A	1.09	CH3	CH2-QN		CDCL3
2417M	A	1.09	CH3	CH(NH/CH3)		POLYSOL-D
1760M	A	1.09	CH3	CH(OH/CH2)		CCL4
1760M	A	1.09	CH3	CH(O/CH2)		CCL4
2469M	A	1.09	CH3	CH(QN/CH3)		CDCL3
91M	A	1.09	CH3	C(Q1/CH3/CH3)		CCL4
2132M	B	1.09	CH3	R5R5RI<C(CH3)-C*(CH3)/CH*>		POLYSOL-D
2132M	B	1.09	CH3	R5R5RI<C*(C(CH3/CH3))-C(=0)/CH2>		POLYSOL-D
2006M	B	1.09	CH3	R5R5RI(C*(C(=0)/CH2/CH2))		CCL4
2144M	A	1.09	CH3	R6(C(CH3)-CH2/CH2)		CDCL3
366M	B	1.09- 2.44		UNSPECIFIED		CCL4
1387M	C	1.09- 1.62		UNSPECIFIED		CCL4
619M	B	1.10- 1.88	CH	CH2-CH2/CH3/CH3		CDCL3
1618M	B	1.10- 1.90	CH	CH2-CH2/CH3/CH3		CCL4
2695M	B	1.10- 1.70	CH	CH2-0-C(=0)/CH2-CH3/CH2-CH3		CCL4
2691M	B	1.10- 1.80	CH	CH2-0-C(=0)/CH2-CH3/CH2-CH3		CDCL3

BOOK NO.	ASSIGN-MENT	CHEM SHIFT - ppm -	PROTON GROUP	ENVIRONMENTAL GROUPS	S	SOLVENT
25M	B	1.10- 1.90	CH	C(CH3/CH3/CH3)/CH2-CH3/CH3		CCL4
56M	B	1.10- 2.10	CH	O3/CH2-CH3/CH2-CH3		CDCL3
693M	B	1.10- 1.90	CH2	CH2.2-AN/CH3		CDCL3
1884M	B	1.10- 1.50	CH2	CH2.2-A/CH2-CH3		CCL4
2732M	C	1.10- 1.70	CH2	CH2.2-CH/CH3		CDCL3
2071M	B	1.10- 2.00	CH2	CH2.2-C(=0)-A/CH3		CDCL3
2252M	B	1.10- 1.55	CH2	CH2.2-C(=0)-0/CH2-CH3		CDCL3
768M	B	1.10- 2.20	CH2	CH2.2-NH2/CH3		CDCL3
1215M	B	1.10- 1.80	CH2	CH2.2-NH/CH3	S	CDCL3
828M	B	1.10- 2.00	CH2	CH2.2-N(+)/CH3		CDCL3
1653M	B	1.10- 1.60	CH2	CH2.2-N/CH3		CDCL3
1652M	B	1.10- 1.80	CH2	CH2.2-N/CH3		CDCL3
2351M	C	1.10- 1.90	CH2	CH2.2-N/CH3		CDCL3
2775M	B	1.10- 1.80	CH2	CH2.2-0-C(=0)/CH3		CCL4
2847M	B	1.10- 1.90	CH2	CH2.2-0-C(=0)/CH3		CCL4
2896M	B	1.10- 2.00	CH2	CH2.2-0-C(=0)/CH3		CDCL3
2766M	B	1.10- 2.05	CH2	CH2.2-0-C(=0)/CH3		CDCL3
1082M	B	1.10- 1.60	CH2	CH2.2-0-NO2/CH2-CH3		CDCL3
1413M	B	1.10- 1.70	CH2	CH2.2-0/CH3		CCL4
1380M	B	1.10- 1.75	CH2	CH2.2-0/CH3		CDCL3
1965M	B	1.10- 2.00	CH2	CH2.2-0/CH3		CDCL3
160M	B	1.10- 1.80	CH2	CH2.2-Q1/CH3		CCL4
2433M	B	1.10- 1.65	CH2	CH2.2-R5NN/CH3		CCL4
1315M	B	1.10- 2.10	CH2	CH2.2-S03/CH3		CDCL3
1187M	B	1.10- 1.60	CH2	CH2.2-S/CH2-CH3		CCL4
1884M	B	1.10- 1.50	CH2	CH2.3-A/CH3		CCL4
2252M	B	1.10- 1.55	CH2	CH2.3-C(=0)-0/CH3		CDCL3
1082M	B	1.10- 1.60	CH2	CH2.3-0-NO2/CH3		CDCL3
1187M	B	1.10- 1.60	CH2	CH2.3-S/CH3		CCL4
693M	B	1.10- 1.90	CH2	CH2-AN/CH2-CH3		CDCL3
137M	B	1.10- 1.80	CH2	CH2-A/CH2-CH3		CCL4
1501M	B	1.10- 1.92	CH2	CH2-A/CH3		CCL4
2174M	B	1.10- 1.60	CH2	CH2-CH2/CH2-CH3		CCL4
2174M	B	1.10- 1.60	CH2	CH2-CH2/CH3		CCL4
2429M	B	1.10- 1.70	CH2	CH2-CH2/CH3		CDCL3
1384M	B	1.10- 1.70	CH2	CH2-CH2/CH3		CCL4
1614M	B	1.10- 1.70	CH2	CH2-CH2/CH3		CCL4
2297M	B	1.10- 1.70	CH2	CH2-CH2/CH3		D20
1414M	B	1.10- 1.72	CH2	CH2-CH2/CH3		CCL4
1404M	B	1.10- 1.80	CH2	CH2-CH2/CH3		CCL4
137M	B	1.10- 1.80	CH2	CH2-CH2/CH3		CCL4
651M	B	1.10- 1.85	CH2	CH2-CH2/CH3		CDCL3
1978M	B	1.10- 1.90	CH2	CH2-CH2/CH3		CCL4
236M	B	1.10- 2.00	CH2	CH2-CH2/CH3		CCL4
2990M	C	1.10- 1.70	CH2	CH2-CH2/CH3		CCL4
71M	C	1.10- 1.70	CH2	CH2-CH2/CH3		CDCL3
2732M	C	1.10- 1.70	CH2	CH2-CH/CH2-CH3		CDCL3
1784M	B	1.10- 1.65	CH2	CH2-CH/CH3		CCL4
2479M	B	1.10- 2.00	CH2	CH2-CH/CH3		POLYSOL-D
1659M	B	1.10- 2.00	CH2	CH2-CH/CH3		CCL4
2191M	B	1.10- 2.10	CH2	CH2-CH/CH3		CCL4
327M	B	1.10- 2.10	CH2	CH2-CH/CH3		CCL4
2522M	C	1.10- 1.70	CH2	CH2-CH/CH3		CCL4
236M	B	1.10- 2.00	CH2	CH2-CL/CH2-CH3		CDCL3
2071M	B	1.10- 2.00	CH2	CH2-C(=0)-A/CH2-CH3		CDCL3
1978M	B	1.10- 1.90	CH2	CH2-C(=0)/CH2-CH3		CCL4
1787M	C	1.10- 1.90	CH2	CH2-C:/CH3		CCL4
2190M	C	1.10- 2.00	CH2	CH2-C/CH3	S	CDCL3
768M	B	1.10- 2.20	CH2	CH2-NH2/CH2-CH3		D20
2297M	B	1.10- 1.70	CH2	CH2-NH/CH2-CH3		CDCL3
2429M	B	1.10- 1.70	CH2	CH2-NH/CH2-CH3		CDCL3
1215M	B	1.10- 1.80	CH2	CH2-NH/CH2-CH3		CDCL3
828M	B	1.10- 2.00	CH2	CH2-N(+)/CH2-CH3		CDCL3
626M	C	1.10- 1.70	CH2	CH2-N/CH2-CH		CDCL3
1653M	B	1.10- 1.60	CH2	CH2-N/CH2-CH3		CDCL3
1652M	B	1.10- 1.80	CH2	CH2-N/CH2-CH3		CCL4
651M	B	1.10- 1.85	CH2	CH2-N/CH2-CH3		CCL4
2990M	C	1.10- 1.70	CH2	CH2-N/CH2-CH3		CDCL3
2351M	C	1.10- 1.90	CH2	CH2-N/CH2-CH3		POLYSOL-D
1849M	A	1.10- 2.00	CH2	CH2-OH/CH2-CH		CCL4
1614M	B	1.10- 1.70	CH2	CH2-OH/CH2-CH3		CCL4
2775M	B	1.10- 1.80	CH2	CH2-0-C(=0)/CH2-CH3		CCL4
2847M	B	1.10- 1.90	CH2	CH2-0-C(=0)/CH2-CH3		CDCL3
2896M	B	1.10- 2.00	CH2	CH2-0-C(=0)/CH2-CH3		CDCL3
2766M	B	1.10- 2.05	CH2	CH2-0-C(=0)/CH2-CH3		CCL4
1413M	B	1.10- 1.70	CH2	CH2-0/CH2-CH3		CCL4
1384M	B	1.10- 1.70	CH2	CH2-0/CH2-CH3		CCL4
1414M	B	1.10- 1.72	CH2	CH2-0/CH2-CH3		CDCL3
1380M	B	1.10- 1.75	CH2	CH2-0/CH2-CH3		CCL4
1404M	B	1.10- 1.80	CH2	CH2-0/CH2-CH3		CDCL3
1965M	B	1.10- 2.00	CH2	CH2-0/CH2-CH3		

BOOK NO.	ASSIGN-MENT	CHEM SHIFT - ppm -	PROTON GROUP	ENVIRONMENTAL GROUPS	S	SOLVENT
160M	B	1.10- 1.80	CH2	CH2-Q1/CH2-CH3		CCL4
71M	C	1.10- 1.70	CH2	CH2-Q2/CH2-CH3		CCL4
2399M	A	1.10- 2.00	CH2	CH2-R5NA/CH2-CH2		CDCL3
2433M	B	1.10- 1.65	CH2	CH2-R5NN/CH2-CH3		CCL4
1315M	B	1.10- 2.10	CH2	CH2-SO3/CH2-CH3		CDCL3
327M	B	1.10- 2.10	CH2	CH(BR/CH3)/CH2-CH3		CCL4
2695M	B	1.10- 1.70	CH2	CH(CH2/CH2)/CH3		CCL4
2691M	B	1.10- 1.80	CH2	CH(CH2/CH2)/CH3		CDCL3
619M	B	1.10- 1.88	CH2	CH(CH3/CH3)/CH2-N		CDCL3
1618M	B	1.10- 1.90	CH2	CH(CH3/CH3)/CH2-OH		CCL4
2191M	B	1.10- 2.10	CH2	CH(C(=O)-CL/CH2.2)/CH2-CH3		CCL4
2479M	B	1.10- 2.20	CH2	CH(C(=O)-OH/CH2)/CH2-CH3		CCL4
2757M	B	1.10- 1.91	CH2	CH(C(=O)-O/CH2)/CH3		CDCL3
25M	B	1.10- 1.90	CH2	CH(C/CH3)/CH3		CCL4
626M	C	1.10- 1.70	CH2	CH(NH2/CH3)/CH2.2-N		CDCL3
598M	C	1.10- 1.80	CH2	CH(NH/CH3)/CH3		CDCL3
1849M	A	1.10- 2.00	CH2	CH(OH/CH2.3)/CH2.2-OH		POLYSOL-D
1784M	B	1.10- 1.65	CH2	CH(OH/CH2)/CH2-CH3		CDCL3
1829M	B	1.10- 1.80	CH2	CH(OH/CH2)/CH3		CDCL3
1787M	C	1.10- 1.90	CH2	CH(OH/CH2)/CH3		CCL4
1659M	B	1.10- 2.00	CH2	CH(OH/P=)/CH2-CH3		POLYSOL-D
2522M	C	1.10- 1.70	CH2	CH(Q2/CH3)/CH2-CH3		CCL4
56M	B	1.10- 2.10	CH2	CH(Q3/CH2)/CH3		CDCL3
2190M	C	1.10- 2.00	CH2	C(C(=O)-CL/CH3/CH3)/CH2-CH3		CCL4
1116M	B	1.10- 1.80	CH2.X	CH2.10		CCL4
2769M	B	1.10- 1.90	CH2.X	CH2.10		CDCL3
829M	B	1.10- 2.10	CH2.X	CH2.10	S	CDCL3
830M	B	1.10- 2.20	CH2.X	CH2.10	S	CDCL3
910M	B	1.10- 1.90	CH2.X	CH2.11		CCL4
2280M	B	1.10- 2.10	CH2.X	CH2.11		TFA
953M	B	1.10- 1.50	CH2.X	CH2.12		CDCL3
1804M	C	1.10- 1.60	CH2.X	CH2.12		CDCL3
892M	B	1.10- 1.60	CH2.X	CH2.14		TFA
122M	B	1.10- 1.70	CH2.X	CH2.14		CCL4
934M	B	1.10- 1.90	CH2.X	CH2.16		CDCL3
833M	B	1.10- 2.10	CH2.X	CH2.16	S	CDCL3
142M	B	1.10- 1.50	CH2.X	CH2.3		CDCL3
2254M	B	1.10- 1.60	CH2.X	CH2.3		CCL4
933M	B	1.10- 1.60	CH2.X	CH2.3		CCL4
411M	B	1.10- 1.65	CH2.X	CH2.3		CCL4
59M	B	1.10- 1.70	CH2.X	CH2.3		CCL4
2487M	B	1.10- 1.75	CH2.X	CH2.3		CCL4
330M	B	1.10- 1.80	CH2.X	CH2.3		CCL4
618M	B	1.10- 1.80	CH2.X	CH2.3		CCL4
1983M	B	1.10- 1.80	CH2.X	CH2.3		CCL4
129M	B	1.10- 1.80	CH2.X	CH2.3		CCL4
1698M	B	1.10- 1.85	CH2.X	CH2.3		CCL4
2382M	B	1.10- 1.90	CH2.X	CH2.3		CDCL3
2757M	B	1.10- 1.91	CH2.X	CH2.3		CDCL3
2897M	B	1.10- 2.00	CH2.X	CH2.3		CCL4
2623M	A	1.10- 1.60	CH2.X	CH2.4		D20
1826M	A	1.10- 1.80	CH2.X	CH2.4		CDCL3
2622M	A	1.10- 1.90	CH2.X	CH2.4		D20
2760M	B	1.10- 1.45	CH2.X	CH2.4		CCL4
2749M	B	1.10- 1.55	CH2.X	CH2.4		CDCL3
2526M	B	1.10- 1.65	CH2.X	CH2.4		CCL4
857M	B	1.10- 1.70	CH2.X	CH2.4		CDCL3
1386M	B	1.10- 1.70	CH2.X	CH2.4		CCL4
849M	B	1.10- 1.80	CH2.X	CH2.4		CDCL3
1697M	B	1.10- 1.80	CH2.X	CH2.4		CCL4
1699M	B	1.10- 1.80	CH2.X	CH2.4		CCL4
550M	B	1.10- 1.80	CH2.X	CH2.4		CDCL3
1987M	B	1.10- 1.80	CH2.X	CH2.4		CDCL3
1114M	B	1.10- 1.90	CH2.X	CH2.4		CCL4
2827M	B	1.10- 1.99	CH2.X	CH2.4		CCL4
2481M	B	1.10- 2.00	CH2.X	CH2.4		CCL4
950M	B	1.10- 2.00	CH2.X	CH2.4		CCL4
1206M	C	1.10- 2.00	CH2.X	CH2.4		CCL4
810M	B	1.10- 1.60	CH2.X	CH2.5		CDCL3
333M	B	1.10- 1.60	CH2.X	CH2.5		CCL4
1038M	B	1.10- 1.60	CH2.X	CH2.5		CCL4
219M	B	1.10- 1.65	CH2.X	CH2.5		CCL4
551M	B	1.10- 1.80	CH2.X	CH2.5		CDCL3
2816M	B	1.10- 1.80	CH2.X	CH2.5		CCL4
951M	B	1.10- 1.90	CH2.X	CH2.5		CCL4
1115M	B	1.10- 1.90	CH2.X	CH2.5		CCL4
168M	B	1.10- 2.00	CH2.X	CH2.5		CCL4
128M	C	1.10- 1.75	CH2.X	CH2.5		CCL4
1211M	B	1.10- 1.50	CH2.X	CH2.6		CDCL3
412M	B	1.10- 1.60	CH2.X	CH2.6		CCL4
2192M	B	1.10- 1.60	CH2.X	CH2.6		CCL4

BOOK NO.	ASSIGN-MENT	CHEM SHIFT - ppm -	PROTON GROUP	ENVIRONMENTAL GROUPS	S	SOLVENT
2939M	B	1.10- 1.60	CH2.X	CH2.6		
2527M	B	1.10- 1.65	CH2.X	CH2.6		CDCL3
620M	B	1.10- 1.70	CH2.X	CH2.6		CCL4
623M	B	1.10- 1.80	CH2.X	CH2.6		CCL4
1221M	B	1.10- 1.91	CH2.X	CH2.6		CDCL3
220M	B	1.10- 1.60	CH2.X	CH2.7		CCL4
121M	B	1.10- 1.85	CH2.X	CH2.7		CCL4
2707M	B	1.10- 1.90	CH2.X	CH2.7		CCL4
1389M	B	1.10- 1.70	CH2.X	CH2.8		CCL4
1347M	B	1.10- 1.80	CH2.X	CH2.8		CCL4
1216M	B	1.10- 1.90	CH2.X	CH2.8		POLYSOL-D
2299M	B	1.10- 1.50	CH2.X	CH2.9		CDCL3
2763M	B	1.10- 1.90	CH2.X	CH2.9		CDCL3
2686M	B	1.10- 1.80	CH2.10	CH2-NH2/CH3		CDCL3
1670M	B	1.10- 1.85	CH2.10	CH2-0/CH3		CDCL3
1660M	B	1.10- 2.00	CH2.10	CH2-S/CH3		CDCL3
1117M	C	1.10- 1.80	CH2.10	CH2-S/CH3		CDCL3
554M	B	1.10- 1.80	CH2.11	CH2-NH/CH3		CCL4
1328M	B	1.10- 1.90	CH2.12	CH2-0-S03-NA/CH3		CDCL3
1928M	B	1.10- 1.80	CH2.14	CH2-A/CH3		POLYSOL-D
2748M	A	1.10- 2.10	CH2.3	CH2-C(=0)-CL/CH2-C(=0)-0		POLYSOL-D
2936M	B	1.10- 2.00	CH2.3	CH2-0-C(=0)/CH3		CDCL3
2879M	B	1.10- 2.00	CH2.3	CH2-0-C(=0)/CH3		CCL4
1294M	B	1.10- 2.10	CH2.3	CH2-S03-NA/CH3		DMSO-D6
1295M	B	1.10- 1.60	CH2.4	CH2.2-S03-NA/CH3		D20
2709M	C	1.10- 2.00	CH2.4	CH2-C(=0)-0/CH3		D20
909M	B	1.10- 1.90	CH2.4	CH2-N=C=0/CH3		CCL4
2815M	B	1.10- 1.75	CH2.5	CH2-Q2/CH3		CDCL3
1204M	B	1.10- 1.90	CH2.5	CH2-SA/CH3		CCL4
1800M	C	1.10- 1.60	CH2.5	C(OH/CH3/CH3)/CH3		CDCL3
1440M	B	1.10- 1.80	CH2.5	R30<CH-0/HCH>/CH3		CDCL3
1472M	D	1.10- 1.70	CH2.5	R600<CH-0/0>/CH3		CCL4
1984M	B	1.10- 1.50	CH2.6	CH2.2-C(=0)-CH2.2/CH3		CCL4
2801M	B	1.10- 1.90	CH2.6	CH2-C(=0)-0/CH3		CCL4
2848M	B	1.10- 1.90	CH2.6	CH2-0-C(=0)/CH3		CCL4
1441M	B	1.10- 1.60	CH2.7	R30<CH-0/HCH>/CH3		CCL4
1988M	C	1.10- 1.90	CH2.8	CH2-C(=0)-CH2/CH3		CCL4
162M	B	1.10- 1.70	CH2.8	CH2-Q1/CH3		CCL4
1763M	A	1.10- 2.50	CH2R	R4(CH2-CH(OH)/CH2)		CDCL3
1763M	A	1.10- 2.50	CH2R	R4(CH(OH)-CH2/CH2)		CCL4
712M	A	1.10- 1.80	CH2R	R5N<CH2-CH2/CH2-CH2>		CCL4
712M	A	1.10- 1.80	CH2R	R5N<CH2-N(CH2-AN)/CH2-CH2>		CDCL3
2537M	A	1.10- 1.60	CH2R	R5R5BI(CH*(CH(C(=0)-OH)/CH=)		CDCL3
1776M	A	1.10- 1.80	CH2R	R6<CH2-CH(OH)/CH2-CH2>		CCL4
1776M	A	1.10- 1.80	CH2R	R6<CH2-C(A/A)/CH2-CH2>		CDCL3
367M	A	1.10- 2.60	CH2R	R6(CH(BR)-CH2/CH2-CH(BR))		CDCL3
649M	A	1.10	CH3	CH2-N		CDCL3
593M	A	1.10	CH3	CH2-NH		CCL4
1091M	A	1.10	CH3	CH2-SI		CDCL3
1851M	A	1.10	CH3	CH(OH/CH2)		CDCL3
1748M	B	1.10	CH3	CH(OH/CH2)		CDCL3
848M	B	1.10	CH3	CH(QN/CH3)		CCL4
89M	A	1.10	CH3	CH(Q2/Q3)		CCL4
2500M	A	1.10	CH3	C(CH2/CH2/CH3)		CCL4
2189M	A	1.10	CH3	C(CH2/CH3/CH3)		POLYSOL-D
447M	B	1.10	CH3	C(NH2/CH2/CH3)		CCL4
1802M	C	1.10	CH3	C(OH/CH2/CH2)		CDCL3
2007M	B	1.10	CH3	R5R5BI<C(CH3)-C*(HCH-S03-NA)/CH*>		CCL4
2262M	B	1.10	CH3	R5R60BI<C(CH3)-C*(CH3)/CH*>		D20
475M	A	1.10	NH2	CH2-Q2		CDCL3
1810M	B	1.10 APP.	OH	R6(C(CH2-CH3)-CH2/CH2-CH2)		CCL4
1211M	B	1.10- 1.50	SH	CH2.8-CH3		C3F60
964M	A	1.10- 2.10		UNSPECIFIED		CDCL3
365M	A	1.10- 2.40		UNSPECIFIED		CCL4
2514M	A	1.10- 2.60		UNSPECIFIED		CCL4
2787M	A	1.10- 2.80		UNSPECIFIED		CCL4
2696M	B	1.10- 1.60		UNSPECIFIED		CCL4
1602M	B	1.10- 1.60		UNSPECIFIED		CCL4
84M	B	1.10- 1.70		UNSPECIFIED		CCL4
1749M	B	1.10- 1.70		UNSPECIFIED		CCL4
2819M	B	1.10- 1.80		UNSPECIFIED		CCL4
1625M	B	1.10- 1.80		UNSPECIFIED		CDCL3
1985M	B	1.10- 1.85		UNSPECIFIED		CDCL3
2808M	B	1.10- 1.87		UNSPECIFIED		CCL4
2783M	B	1.10- 1.90		UNSPECIFIED		CCL4
2898M	B	1.10- 1.90		UNSPECIFIED		CDCL3
1986M	B	1.10- 1.90		UNSPECIFIED		CCL4
2705M	B	1.10- 1.90		UNSPECIFIED		CDCL3
2706M	B	1.10- 1.90		UNSPECIFIED		CCL4
1769M	B	1.10- 2.00		UNSPECIFIED		CDCL3
2782M	B	1.10- 2.00		UNSPECIFIED		CDCL3

: REPRESENTS TRIPLE BOND, ¬ REPRESENTS AN ARROW AND < AND > REPRESENT BRACKETS.   PAGE   177

BOOK NO.	ASSIGN-MENT	CHEM SHIFT - ppm -	PROTON GROUP	ENVIRONMENTAL GROUPS	S	SOLVENT
2495M	B	1.10- 2.00		UNSPECIFIED		CDCL3
2711M	B	1.10- 2.00		UNSPECIFIED		CDCL3
2140M	B	1.10- 2.10		UNSPECIFIED		CCL4
1765M	B	1.10- 2.20		UNSPECIFIED		CDCL3
2788M	B	1.10- 2.30		UNSPECIFIED		CCL4
2002M	B	1.10- 2.40		UNSPECIFIED		CCL4
2715M	B	1.10- 2.50		UNSPECIFIED		CCL4
1745M	C	1.10- 1.80		UNSPECIFIED		CDCL3
127M	C	1.10- 1.80		UNSPECIFIED		CCL4
2459M	C	1.10- 1.80		UNSPECIFIED		DMSO-D6
629M	C	1.10- 1.90		UNSPECIFIED		CDCL3
2478M	C	1.10- 2.00		UNSPECIFIED		CCL4
2129M	C	1.10- 2.10		UNSPECIFIED		CDCL3
2005M	C	1.10- 2.60		UNSPECIFIED		CDCL3
1801M	D	1.10- 1.70		UNSPECIFIED		CCL4
2250M	B	1.11- 1.97	CH2	CH2-CH2/CH3		CDCL3
1245M	B	1.11- 2.08	CH2	CH2-CH2/CH3		CDCL3
2250M	B	1.11- 1.97	CH2	CH2-C(=0)-0/CH2-CH3		CDCL3
615M	B	1.11- 1.75	CH2	CH2-N/CH3		CCL4
1245M	B	1.11- 2.08	CH2	CH2-S(=0)/CH2-CH3		CDCL3
2628M	A	1.11- 2.00	CH2.X	CH2.3		D20
2877M	B	1.11- 1.96	CH2.X	CH2.4		CCL4
2138M	B	1.11	CH3	CH2-C(=0)-CH2		CCL4
2138M	B	1.11	CH3	CH2-C(=0)-Q1		CCL4
131M	A	1.11	CH3	CH2-C:		CCL4
128M	B	1.11	CH3	CH2-C:		CCL4
2350M	A	1.11	CH3	CH2-N		D20
2361M	A	1.11	CH3	CH2-N		CDCL3
1026M	A	1.11	CH3	CH2-N		CCL4
2356M	B	1.11	CH3	CH2-N		CDCL3
555M	A	1.11	CH3	CH2-NH		CCL4
1397M	A	1.11	CH3	CH2-0		CCL4
2990M	B	1.11	CH3	CH2-0-C(=0)		CDCL3
2731M	B	1.11	CH3	CH(CH/CH3)		CDCL3
1754M	A	1.11	CH3	CH(OH/CH2)		CCL4
1736M	B	1.11	CH3	CH(OH/CH2)		CCL4
1739M	B	1.11	CH3	CH(OH/CH2)		CCL4
1977M	B	1.11	CH3	C(C(=0)-CH/CH3/CH3)		CDCL3
452M	B	1.11	CH3	C(NH2/CH2.3/CH3)		CCL4
2008M	C	1.11	CH3	R5R5BI<C*-C(=0)/C(CH3/CH3)/CH2>		CCL4
2029M	A	1.11	CH3	R6<C(CH3)-CH2/CH2>		CCL4
1205M	B	1.11	SH	CH2-CH2		CCL4
1209M	B	1.11	SH	CH2-CH2		CDCL3
893M	D	1.11- 2.33		UNSPECIFIED		CCL4
2982M	B	1.12- 1.64	CH2	CH2-CH2/CH3		CCL4
2982M	B	1.12- 1.64	CH2	CH2-NH/CH2-CH3		CCL4
27M	C	1.12	CH2	C(CH3/CH3/CH3)/CH(CH3/CH3)		CDCL3
1255M	B	1.12- 2.15	CH2.X	CH2.3		CDCL3
1974M	B	1.12- 1.72	CH2.X	CH2.4		CCL4
2276M	A	1.12	CH3	CH2-C(=0)		CDCL3
2358M	A	1.12	CH3	CH2-N		CCL4
2347M	A	1.12	CH3	CH2-NH		CDCL3
583M	A	1.12	CH3	CH2-R5NN		CDCL3
2449M	A	1.12	CH3	CH(C(=0)-CH3/CH2)		POLYSOL-D
1994M	A	1.12	CH3	CH(C(=0)-NH/CH3)		CCL4
2317M	A	1.12	CH3	CH(C(=0)-0/CH3)		CCL4
2836M	A	1.12	CH3	CH(C(=0)/CH3)		CDCL3
2152M	A	1.12	CH3	CH(NH/CH2)		CCL4
598M	B	1.12	CH3	CH(OH/CH2)		CCL4
1742M	B	1.12 APP.	CH3	CH(OH/CH2)		CCL4
1746M	B	1.12	CH3	CH(OH/HCH)		CCL4
1831M	A	1.12	CH3	CH(0/CH3)		CCL4
1445M	A	1.12	CH3	CH(0/CH3)		CCL4
1394M	B	1.12	CH3	C(CH2/CH2/CH3)		D20
631M	B	1.12	CH3	C(OH/CH2.2/CH2)		CCL4
1801M	C	1.12	CH3	C(OH/CH2/CH3)		CCL4
1799M	B	1.12	CH3	C(OH/R6/CH3)		CCL4
1808M	A	1.12	CH3	C(0-CH/CH3/CH3)		CCL4
1398M	B	1.12	CH3	C(0/CH3/CH3)		CCL4
1396M	A	1.12	CH3	R60<CH-CH2/CH2>		CDCL3
2259M	A	1.12	CH3	UNSPECIFIED		CCL4
959M	B	1.12- 2.08		UNSPECIFIED		CCL4
959M	B	1.12- 2.08		UNSPECIFIED		CCL4
1525M	A	1.13	CH3	CH2-N		CCL4
1379M	A	1.13	CH3	CH2-0		CCL4
1480M	A	1.13	CH3	CH2-0		CDCL3
1593M	B	1.13	CH3	CH2-0		CCL4
2702M	B	1.13	CH3	CH(C(=0)-0/CH3)		CCL4
1756M	A	1.13	CH3	CH(OH/CH2)		CDCL3
1828M	A	1.13	CH3	CH(OH/HCH)		CDCL3
1397M	B	1.13	CH3	C(0/CH3/CH3)		CCL4

BOOK NO.	ASSIGN-MENT	CHEM SHIFT - ppm -	PROTON GROUP	ENVIRONMENTAL GROUPS	S	SOLVENT
1456M	A	1.13	CH3	R5O<CH-O/CH2-CH2>		CCL4
567M	A	1.13	CH3	R6NN<CH-NH/CH2>		CDCL3
2442M	A	1.13	CH3	R6NN<C(CH3)-CH2/CH2>		TFA
1802M	D	1.13- 1.78		UNSPECIFIED		CCL4
2792M	B	1.14- 1.95	CH2	CH2-CH2/CH3		CCL4
2792M	B	1.14- 1.95	CH2	CH2-O-C(=O)/CH2-CH3		CCL4
2473M	A	1.14	CH3	CH2-C(=O)-O		CDCL3
2362M	A	1.14	CH3	CH2-N		CDCL3
817M	A	1.14	CH3	CH2-N	S	D2O
1423M	A	1.14	CH3	HCH-O		CCL4
40M	C	1.14	CH3	R3<CH-C(CH3/CH3)/HCH>		CCL4
40M	C	1.14	CH3	R3<C(CH3)-CH(CH3)/HCH>		CCL4
460M	B	1.14	NH2	CH2-C		CCL4
460M	B	1.14	NH2	C(CH2/CH3/CH3)		CCL4
2714M	B	1.14- 2.00		UNSPECIFIED		CCL4
2947M	B	1.14- 2.07		UNSPECIFIED		CCL4
1562M	B	1.15- 2.08	CH2	CH2.2-O/CH3		CDCL3
1254M	B	1.15- 2.15	CH2	CH2.2-SO2/CH3		CDCL3
1562M	B	1.15- 2.08	CH2	CH2-O/CH2-CH3		CDCL3
1254M	B	1.15- 2.15	CH2	CH2-SO2/CH2-CH3		CDCL3
891M	B	1.15- 1.94	CH2.X	CH2.3		CDCL3
1325M	B	1.15- 2.00	CH2.X	CH2.3		CCL4
1209M	C	1.15- 1.85	CH2.X	CH2.6		CCL4
2753M	A	1.15	CH3	CH2-C(=O)-O		CDCL3
1696M	A	1.15	CH3	CH2-C:		CCL4
2295M	A	1.15	CH3	CH2-NH		D2O
1383M	B	1.15	CH3	CH2-O		CCL4
2986M	A	1.15	CH3	CH2-O-C(=O)		CCL4
1833M	A	1.15	CH3	CH(OH)-HCH		CCL4
1796M	B	1.15	CH3	C(OH/CH2/CH3)		CCL4
39M	D	1.15	CH3	R3<CH-CH(CH3)/HCH>		CCL4
2784M	B	1.15- 1.91		UNSPECIFIED		CCL4
326M	B	1.16- 1.70	CH2	CH2-CH2/CH2-CH3		CCL4
326M	B	1.16- 1.70	CH2	CH2-CH2/CH3		CCL4
1009M	B	1.16- 2.13	CH2	CH2-CH2/CH3		CCL4
2618M	B	1.16- 2.10	CH2	CH2-CH/CH3		D2O
1009M	B	1.16- 2.13	CH2	CH2-S/CH2-CH3		CCL4
2477M	C	1.16- 1.90	CH2	CH(C(=O)-O/CH2)/CH3		CCL4
2618M	B	1.16- 2.10	CH2	CH(NH2/C(=O)-O/CH2-CH3		D2O
2477M	C	1.16- 1.90	CH2.X	CH2.3		CCL4
1880M	A	1.16	CH3	CH2-A		CDCL3
2351M	B	1.16	CH3	CH2-C(=O)-N		CDCL3
2797M	A	1.16	CH3	CH2-C(=O)-O		CCL4
2698M	B	1.16	CH3	CH2-C(=O)-O		CDCL3
1410M	A	1.16	CH3	CH2-O		CDCL3
1481M	A	1.16	CH3	CH2-O		CDCL3
1382M	B	1.16	CH3	CH2-O		CCL4
1425M	A	1.16	CH3	HCH-O		CCL4
602M	A	1.16	CH3	R6NA<CH-NH/HCH>		CDCL3
1692M	A	1.16	CH3	R6O(C(CH2-OH)-O/CH2-CH2)		CDCL3
1811M	A	1.16	CH3	R7<C(OH)-CH2/CH2>		CCL4
1804M	B	1.16	OH	C(CH2/CH2/CH2)		CDCL3
1222M	A	1.16	SH	CH2-CH2		CCL4
441M	B	1.17- 1.57	CH2	CH2-CH2/CH3		CDCL3
544M	B	1.17- 1.63	CH2	CH2-CH2/CH3		D2O
2917M	B	1.17- 1.89	CH2	CH2-CH2/CH3		C3D6O
547M	D	1.17- 1.65	CH2	CH2-CH2/CH3		CDCL3
441M	B	1.17- 1.57	CH2	CH2-NH2/CH2-CH3		CDCL3
544M	B	1.17- 1.63	CH2	CH2-NH/CH2-CH3		D2O
547M	D	1.17- 1.65	CH2	CH2-NH/CH2-CH3		CDCL3
2917M	B	1.17- 1.89	CH2	CH2-O-C(=O)/CH2-CH3		C3D6O
1280M	A	1.17	CH3	CH2.2-SO2		CCL4
1879M	A	1.17	CH3	CH2-A		CCL4
2296M	A	1.17	CH3	CH2-C(=O)-NH		CDCL3
2248M	A	1.17	CH3	CH2-C(=O)-O		CCL4
653M	A	1.17	CH3	CH2-N		CDCL3
2104M	A	1.17	CH3	CH2-N		CDCL3
1412M	A	1.17	CH3	CH2-O		CCL4
1612M	A	1.17	CH3	CH2-OH		CCL4
344M	A	1.17	CH3	CH(CH2/CH2)		CDCL3
2475M	B	1.17	CH3	CH(C(=O)-O/CH2)		CDCL3
2703M	A	1.17	CH3	C(C(=O)-O/CH3/CH3)		CCL4
2419M	B	1.17	CH3	C(NH/CH2/CH3)		DMSO-D6
1798M	B	1.17	CH3	C(OH/CH2.3/CH3)		CCL4
1472M	C	1.17	CH3	R600<C(CH3)-HCH/HCH>		CCL4
1092M	A	1.17	CH3	SI(CL/CL/CL)		CCL4
1092M	A	1.17	CH3	SI(CL/CL/CL)		CCL4
443M	C	1.17	NH2	CH(CH2/CH3)		CDCL3
1200M	A	1.17	SH	CH2-CH3		CCL4
1460M	A	1.17- 1.70		UNSPECIFIED		CCL4
2285M	B	1.17- 2.30		UNSPECIFIED		CDCL3

BOOK NO.	ASSIGN-MENT	CHEM SHIFT - ppm -	PROTON GROUP	ENVIRONMENTAL GROUPS	S	SOLVENT
2903M	C	1.17- 1.99		UNSPECIFIED		CCL4
2003M	B	1.18- 2.28	CHR	R6((CH3)/CH2-CH2/CH2-CH2)		CCL4
240M	B	1.18- 2.01	CH2	CH2-CH2/CH2/CH3		CCL4
118M	B	1.18- 1.65	CH2	CH2-CH2/CH3		CCL4
2908M	B	1.18- 1.93	CH2	CH2-CH2/CH3		CCL4
240M	B	1.18- 2.01	CH2	CH2-CH2/CH3		CCL4
118M	B	1.18- 1.65	CH2	CH2-C:CH/CH2-CH3		CCL4
2908M	B	1.18- 1.93	CH2	CH2-O-C(=O)/CH2-CH3		CCL4
1738M	C	1.18- 1.71	CH2.X	CH2.3		CCL4
1442M	B	1.18- 1.55	CH2.X	CH2.9		CCL4
2003M	B	1.18- 2.28	CH2R	R6(CH(CH3)-CH2/CH2-C(=O))		CCL4
491M	A	1.18	CH3	CH2-A		CDCL3
2324M	A	1.18	CH3	CH2-A		CDCL3
2046M	A	1.18	CH3	CH2-C(=O)		CDCL3
1666M	A	1.18	CH3	CH2-O		CCL4
2384M	A	1.18	CH3	CH2-R5N		CDCL3
2048M	A	1.18	CH3	CH(C(=O)/CH3)		CCL4
1349M	A	1.18	CH3	CH(NH/CH3)		POLYSOL-D
1400M	A	1.18	CH3	CH(O/CH3)		CDCL3
126M	A	1.18	CH3	C(C:C/CH3/CH3)		CCL4
1797M	B	1.18	CH3	C(OH/CH2.2/CH3)		CCL4
1831M	B	1.18	CH3	C(OH/HCH/CH3)		CCL4
1759M	B	1.18	CH3	C(O/HCH/CH3)		CCL4
2949M	A	1.18	CH3	R50<C(CH3)-CH(OH)/CH2>		CDCL3
2949M	B	1.18	CH3	R50<C(CH3)-CH(OH)/CH2>		CDCL3
466M	A	1.18	NH	CH2-CH2/CH2-CH2		CDCL3
485M	A	1.18	NH2	CH2-A		CCL4
466M	A	1.18	NH2	CH2-CH2		CDCL3
1220M	A	1.18	SH	CH2-CH2		CCL4
1221M	A	1.18	SH	CH2-CH2		CCL4
2959M	B	1.19- 2.05	CH2	CH2-CH2/CH3		CCL4
1534M	B	1.19- 2.08	CH2	CH2-CH2/CH3		CCL4
832M	B	1.19- 2.10	CH2	CH2-CH2/CH3	S	CDCL3
832M	B	1.19- 2.10	CH2	CH2-N(+)/CH2-CH3	S	CDCL3
2959M	B	1.19- 2.05	CH2	CH2-O-C(=O)/CH2-CH3		CCL4
1534M	B	1.19- 2.08	CH2	CH2-O/CH2-CH3		CCL4
41M	D	1.19	CH2	R3<CH-CH2/CH2>/R3<CH-CH2/CH2>		CCL4
134M	A	1.19	CH3	CH2-A		CCL4
500M	A	1.19	CH3	CH2-A		CDCL3
503M	A	1.19	CH3	CH2-A		CCL4
2315M	A	1.19	CH3	CH2-C(=O)		CDCL3
2358M	B	1.19 APP.	CH3	CH2-N		CDCL3
1348M	A	1.19	CH3	CH2-NH		CDCL3
1426M	A	1.19	CH3	CH2-O		CCL4
1436M	A	1.19	CH3	CH2-O		CCL4
1493M	A	1.19	CH3	CH2-O		CCL4
1390M	B	1.19	CH3	CH2-O		CDCL3
1596M	C	1.19	CH3	CH2-O		CCL4
2850M	A	1.19	CH3	CH2-O-C(=O)		CCL4
1159M	A	1.19	CH3	CH2-S		CCL4
1830M	A	1.19	CH3	CH(OH/CH2)		CCL4
1485M	A	1.19	CH3	CH(O/O)		CCL4
1609M	A	1.19	CH3	C(O/CH3/CH3)		CCL4
457M	A	1.19	NH2	CH2-CH2		CCL4
456M	B	1.19	NH2	C(CH2.3/CH2.3/CH2.3)		CDCL3
1206M	B	1.19	SH	CH2.5-CH3		CCL4
1385M	B	1.20- 2.00	CH	CH2.2-O/CH3/CH3		CCL4
585M	B	1.20- 2.10	CH	CH2.2/CH3/CH3		CDCL3
1112M	B	1.20- 2.00	CH	CH2-CH2/CH3/CH3		CDCL3
2004M	B	1.20- 1.85	CHR	R6<(C(CH3/CH3/CH3))/HCH-CH2/HCH-CH2>		CDCL3
931M	B	1.20- 2.10	CH2	CH2.2-N=C=S/CH3		CCL4
1382M	C	1.20- 1.80	CH2	CH2.2-O		CCL4
70M	B	1.20- 1.60	CH2	CH2-CH2/CH3		CCL4
1417M	B	1.20- 1.70	CH2	CH2-CH2/CH3		CCL4
2902M	B	1.20- 2.08	CH2	CH2-CH2/CH3		CCL4
1183M	B	1.20- 2.14	CH2	CH2-CH2/CH3		CDCL3
2984M	C	1.20- 1.75	CH2	CH2-CH2/CH3		CCL4
1740M	B	1.20- 1.70	CH2	CH2-CH/CH3		CDCL3
2543M	B	1.20- 1.40	CH2	CH2-C/CH3		DMSO-D6
585M	B	1.20- 2.10	CH2	CH2-NH/CH(CH3/CH3)		CDCL3
931M	B	1.20- 2.10	CH2	CH2-N=C=S/CH2-CH3		CCL4
2984M	C	1.20- 1.75	CH2	CH2-N/CH2-CH3		CCL4
2902M	B	1.20- 2.08	CH2	CH2-O-C(=O)/CH2-CH3		CCL4
1417M	B	1.20- 1.70	CH2	CH2-O/CH2-CH3		CCL4
1382M	C	1.20- 1.80	CH2	CH2-O/CH2-CH3		CCL4
70M	B	1.20- 1.60	CH2	CH2-Q2/CH2-CH3		CCL4
1183M	B	1.20- 2.14	CH2	CH2-S/CH2-CH3		CDCL3
1112M	B	1.20- 2.00	CH2	CH2-S/CH(CH3/CH3)		CDCL3
23M	C	1.20	CH2	CH3/C(CH3/CH3/CH2)		CDCL3
1385M	B	1.20- 2.00	CH2	CH(CH3/CH3)/CH2-O		CCL4
450M	C	1.20	CH2	CH(NH2/CH3)/CH(CH3/CH3)		CCL4

BOOK NO.	ASSIGN-MENT	CHEM SHIFT - ppm -	PROTON GROUP	ENVIRONMENTAL GROUPS	S	SOLVENT
1740M	B	1.20- 1.70	CH2	CH(OH/CH2.2)/CH2-CH3		
1223M	B	1.20- 1.60	CH2	C(SH/CH2.3/CH3)/CH3		CDCL3
2755M	A	1.20- 1.90	CH2.X	CH2.3		CDCL3
2200M	A	1.20- 2.05	CH2.X	CH2.3		CCL4
419M	A	1.20- 2.20	CH2.X	CH2.3		CCL4
2197M	A	1.20- 2.20	CH2.X	CH2.3		CDCL3
957M	A	1.20- 2.10	CH2.X	CH2.4		CCL4
1456M	B	1.20- 2.20	CH2R	R50<CH2-0/CH2-CH(CH3)>		CCL4
1456M	B	1.20- 2.20	CH2R	R50<CH(CH3)-0/CH2-CH2>		CCL4
638M	A	1.20- 1.80	CH2R	R6N(CH2-CH2/CH2-CH2)		CCL4
638M	A	1.20- 1.80	CH2R	R6N(CH2-N(CH2-R6N)/CH2-CH2)		CCL4
2261M	A	1.20- 2.30	CH2R	R6R50(CH2-CH*/CH2-CH2)		CDCL3
2261M	A	1.20- 2.30	CH2R	R6R50(CH*-C(=0)/CH2-CH2)		CDCL3
1497M	A	1.20	CH3	CH2-A		CCL4
179M	A	1.20	CH3	CH2-A		CCL4
538M	A	1.20	CH3	CH2-A		CCL4
2921M	A	1.20	CH3	CH2-C(=0)-0		CDCL3
1356M	A	1.20	CH3	CH2-N		CCL4
2370M	B	1.20	CH3	CH2-N		CDCL3
2347M	B	1.20	CH3	CH2-N		CDCL3
1416M	A	1.20	CH3	CH2-0		CDCL3
1431M	A	1.20	CH3	CH2-0		CDCL3
1401M	A	1.20	CH3	CH2-0		CDCL3
1403M	A	1.20	CH3	CH2-0		CDCL3
1674M	A	1.20	CH3	CH2-0		CDCL3
1865M	A	1.20	CH3	CH2-0-C(=0)		CCL4
2853M	A	1.20	CH3	CH2-0-C(=0)		CDCL3
2824M	A	1.20	CH3	CH2-0-C(=0)		CDCL3
2751M	A	1.20	CH3	CH2-0-C(=0)		CCL4
2824M	B	1.20	CH3	CH2-0-C(=0)		DMSO-D6
2981M	B	1.20	CH3	CH2-0-C(=0)		CCL4
2551M	A	1.20	CH3	CH2-Q1		CCL4
138M	B	1.20	CH3	CH(A/CH2)		CDCL3
494M	B	1.20	CH3	CH(A/CH2)		CCL4
1881M	A	1.20	CH3	CH(A/CH3)		CCL4
2474M	A	1.20	CH3	CH(C(=0)-0/CH3)		CDCL3
2708M	B	1.20	CH3	CH(C(=0)-0/CH3)		CCL4
1782M	A	1.20	CH3	CH(OH/Q2)		CCL4
1422M	A	1.20	CH3	CH(0/0)		CCL4
1795M	A	1.20	CH3	C(OH/CH3/CH3)		CCL4
1459M	B	1.20	CH3	R500<C(CH2-CH3)-0/0>		CCL4
756M	A	1.20	CH3	R60<C(CH3)-C(C(=0)-0-CH2)=/CH=>		CCL4
2130M	D	1.20	CH3	R6R6R6R5(C*-CH*/CH2)		CCL4
602M	B	1.20- 2.15	HCHR	R6NA<CH(CH3)-NH/HCH-C*>		CDCL3
2004M	B	1.20- 1.85	HCHR	R6<CH(C(CH3/CH3/CH3))-HCH/CH2-C(=0)>		CDCL3
459M	B	1.20	NH2	CH2-CH		CDCL3
451M	B	1.20	NH2	CH2-CH2		CDCL3
459M	B	1.20	NH2	CH(CH2/CH3)		CDCL3
1213M	B	1.20	SH	CH2-CH2		CDCL3
2953M	A	1.20- 2.00		UNSPECIFIED		CCL4
858M	A	1.20- 2.10		UNSPECIFIED		CDCL3
1777M	A	1.20- 2.30		UNSPECIFIED		CDCL3
2912M	A	1.20- 2.30		UNSPECIFIED		CDCL3
33M	B	1.20 APP.		UNSPECIFIED		CDCL3
1797M	C	1.20- 1.60		UNSPECIFIED		CCL4
2006M	C	1.20- 2.20		UNSPECIFIED		CCL4
2207M	C	1.20- 2.65		UNSPECIFIED		CCL4
1222M	B	1.21- 1.98	CH2.X	CH2.7		CDCL3
1312M	B	1.21 APP.	CH2.X	CH2.9		CCL4
492M	A	1.21	CH3	CH2-A	S	CDCL3
1933M	A	1.21	CH3	CH2-A		CDCL3
178M	A	1.21	CH3	CH2-A		CDCL3
685M	A	1.21	CH3	CH2-AN		CCL4
2350M	B	1.21	CH3	CH2-C(=0)-N		D20
2852M	A	1.21	CH3	CH2-0-C(=0)		CCL4
2854M	A	1.21	CH3	CH2-0-C(=0)		CCL4
2818M	B	1.21	CH3	CH2-0-C(=0)		CCL4
2984M	B	1.21	CH3	CH2-0-C(=0)		CCL4
744M	A	1.21	CH3	CH2-R5NAA		CDCL3
1117M	B	1.21	CH3	CH2-S		CCL4
686M	A	1.21	CH3	CH(AN/CH3)		CDCL3
479M	B	1.21	CH3	CH(A/CH2)		CDCL3
486M	A	1.21	CH3	CH(A/CH3)		CCL4
1714M	A	1.21	CH3	CH(A/CH3)		CCL4
182M	A	1.21	CH3	CH(A/CH3)		CCL4
385M	A	1.21	CH3	CH(A/CH3)		CDCL3
1792M	A	1.21	CH3	CH(OH/CH2)		CCL4
2698M	C	1.21	CH3	CH(0-C(=0)/CH2)		CDCL3
2727M	A	1.21	CH3	CH(0-C(=0)/CH3)		CCL4
1423M	B	1.21	CH3	CH(0/0)		CCL4
2061M	A	1.21	CH3	C(C(=0)-A/CH3/CH3)		CCL4

BOOK NO.	ASSIGN- MENT	CHEM SHIFT - ppm -	PROTON GROUP	ENVIRONMENTAL GROUPS	S	SOLVENT
2476M	A	1.21	CH3	C(C(=0)-OH/CH3/CH3)		CDCL3
116M	A	1.21	CH3	C(C:/CH3/CH3)		CCL4
1021M	A	1.21	CH3	C(N=0/CH3/CH3)		CDCL3
1800M	B	1.21	CH3	C(OH/CH2.5/CH3)		CDCL3
1759M	C	1.21	CH3	C(O/HCH/CH3)		CCL4
2031M	B	1.21	CH3	C(R6/CH2/CH3)		CDCL3
2946M	A	1.21	CH3	R50<CH-C(=0)/CH2>		CCL4
2260M	A	1.21	CH3	R60(C(CH3)-C(=0)/CH2)		CDCL3
1809M	A	1.21	CH3	R6<C(OH)-CH2/CH2>		CDCL3
445M	D	1.21	NH2	CH2-CH		CDCL3
474M	A	1.21	NH2	CH2-Q3		CDCL3
473M	A	1.21	NH2	CH2-R6R6R6TRI		CDCL3
1126M	B	1.21- 1.91		UNSPECIFIED		CCL4
1091M	B	1.22	CH2	SI(A/A/A)/CH3		CDCL3
295M	A	1.22	CH3	CH2-A		CCL4
375M	A	1.22	CH3	CH2-A		CCL4
2059M	A	1.22	CH3	CH2-A		CCL4
2115M	A	1.22	CH3	CH2-AR6		CDCL3
2187M	A	1.22	CH3	CH2-C(=0)-CL		CDCL3
2428M	A	1.22	CH3	CH2-NH		CDCL3
1344M	A	1.22	CH3	CH2-NH		CCL4
1595M	B	1.22	CH3	CH2-O		CDCL3
1597M	B	1.22	CH3	CH2-O		CDCL3
2786M	A	1.22	CH3	CH2-O-C(=0)		CCL4
2817M	B	1.22	CH3	CH2-O-C(=0)		CCL4
592M	A	1.22	CH3	CH(A/CH3)		CDCL3
493M	A	1.22	CH3	CH(A/CH3)		CDCL3
136M	A	1.22	CH3	CH(A/CH3)		CCL4
1917M	A	1.22	CH3	CH(A/CH3)		CDCL3
923M	A	1.22	CH3	CH(N=C=/CH3)		CDCL3
2357M	A	1.22	CH3	CH(OH/C(=0))		CCL4
2773M	A	1.22	CH3	CH(O-C(=0)/CH3)		CCL4
2973M	A	1.22	CH3	CH(O-C(=0)/CH3)		CDCL3
2700M	B	1.22	CH3	CH(O-C(=0)/CH3)		CCL4
1424M	B	1.22	CH3	CH(O/O)		CCL4
216M	A	1.22	CH3	CH/CH3/AAA		CDCL3
1645M	A	1.22	CH3	C(NH2/CH2/CH3)		CDCL3
447M	C	1.22	NH2	C(CH2/CH3/CH3)		CDCL3
37M	B	1.22 APP.		UNSPECIFIED		CCL4
552M	B	1.23 APP.	CH2.X	CH2.16		CDCL3
190M	A	1.23	CH3	CH2-A		CCL4
1024M	A	1.23	CH3	CH2-N		CDCL3
1428M	A	1.23	CH3	CH2-O		CDCL3
1408M	A	1.23	CH3	CH2-O		CCL4
2856M	A	1.23	CH3	CH2-O-C(=0)		CCL4
2777M	A	1.23	CH3	CH2-O-C(=0)		CCL4
2983M	A	1.23	CH3	CH2-O-C(=0)		CDCL3
2703M	B	1.23	CH3	CH2-O-C(=0)		CCL4
2970M	A	1.23	CH3	CH2-S		CCL4
1107M	A	1.23	CH3	CH2-S		CCL4
1108M	A	1.23	CH3	CH2-S		CCL4
1321M	A	1.23	CH3	CH(SO3/CH3)		CCL4
1885M	B	1.23	CH3	C(A/CH2/CH3)		CCL4
1831M	C	1.23	CH3	C(OH/HCH/CH3)		CCL4
1812M	A	1.23	CH3	C(OH/Q3/CH3)		CCL4
1433M	A	1.23	CH3	C(O/OCH3)		CCL4
555M	B	1.23	NH	CH2.2-NH/CH2-CH3		CDCL3
1428M	A	1.23	NH2	CH2-CH		CDCL3
15M	B	1.24	CH2.X	CH2.21		CCL4
2780M	A	1.24	CH3	CH2-O-C(=0)		CDCL3
2814M	A	1.24	CH3	CH2-O-C(=0)		CCL4
2824M	A	1.24	CH3	CH2-O-C(=0)		CCL4
2980M	A	1.24	CH3	CH2-O-C(=0)		CDCL3
2824M	B	1.24	CH3	CH2-O-C(=0)		CCL4
1119M	B	1.24	CH3	CH2-S		CDCL3
1345M	A	1.24	CH3	CH(NH/CH3)		CDCL3
1438M	A	1.24	CH3	R30(CH-O/HCH)		CCL4
1199M	A	1.24	SH	CH3		CDCL3
1203M	B	1.24	SH	CH(CH2/CH3)		CCL4
1808M	B	1.24- 2.29		UNSPECIFIED		CCL4
2747M	B	1.25- 1.95	CH	CH2.2-O-C(=0)/CH3/CH3		CCL4
2M	B	1.25	CH2	CH2-CH2/CH2-CH3		CCL4
2M	B	1.25	CH2	CH2-CH2/CH3		CCL4
1M	B	1.25 APP.	CH2	CH2-CH2/CH3		CCL4
1M	B	1.25 APP.	CH2	CH2-CH3/CH2-CH3		CCL4
2747M	B	1.25- 1.95	CH2	CH(CH3/CH3)/CH2-O-C(=0)		CCL4
1748M	C	1.25	CH2	CH(OH/CH3)/CH2-CH2		CCL4
10M	B	1.25	CH2.X	CH2.12		CCL4
338M	B	1.25 APP.	CH2.X	CH2.12		CCL4
1633M	B	1.25 APP.	CH2.X	CH2.16		CDCL3
1390M	C	1.25 APP.	CH2.X	CH2.16		CDCL3

BOOK NO.	ASSIGN-MENT	CHEM SHIFT - ppm -	PROTON GROUP	ENVIRONMENTAL GROUPS	S	SOLVENT
13M	B	1.25	CH2.X	CH2.18		CDCL3
7M	B	1.25	CH2.X	CH2.9		CCL4
1748M	C	1.25	CH2.X	CH2.9		CCL4
1156M	A	1.25	CH3	CH2-NH		POLYSOL-D
2724M	A	1.25	CH3	CH2-0-C(=0)		CCL4
2770M	B	1.25	CH3	CH2-0-C(=0)		CCL4
1125M	A	1.25	CH3	CH2-S		CDCL3
1193M	A	1.25	CH3	CH2-S		CCL4
501M	A	1.25	CH3	CH(A/CH3)		CDCL3
2725M	A	1.25	CH3	CH(0-C(=0)/CH3)		CCL4
2754M	A	1.25	CH3	CH(0-C(=0)/HCH)		CCL4
2251M	A	1.25	CH3	C(C(=0)-0/CH3/CH3)		CCL4
109M	B	1.25	CH3	R4R6BI(C(CH3)-CH*/CH*)		CCL4
1466M	A	1.25 APP.	NH2	CH2-CH2		CCL4
1747M	C	1.25		UNSPECIFIED		CCL4
449M	C	1.25		UNSPECIFIED		CDCL3
1746M	C	1.25 APP.		UNSPECIFIED		CCL4
35M	C	1.25 APP.		UNSPECIFIED		CDCL3
94M	D	1.26- 2.08	CH	CH2-Q1/CH3/CH3		CCL4
1104M	B	1.26	CH2	CH2-CH2/CH3		CDCL3
2702M	C	1.26- 1.84	CH2	CH2-CH2/CH3		CCL4
2702M	C	1.26- 1.84	CH2	CH2-0-C(=0)/CH2-CH3		CCL4
100M	B	1.26	CH2	C(R6/CH3/CH3)/CH3		CCL4
94M	D	1.26- 2.08	CH2	Q1(CH3/CH3)/CH(CH3/CH3)		CCL4
2895M	B	1.26	CH2.X	CH2.10		CCL4
9M	B	1.26	CH2.X	CH2.11		CCL4
1757M	B	1.26 APP.	CH2.X	CH2.12		CDCL3
11M	B	1.26	CH2.X	CH2.13		CCL4
1104M	B	1.26	CH2.X	CH2.13		CDCL3
2719M	B	1.26	CH2.X	CH2.15		CDCL3
2759M	B	1.26	CH2.X	CH2.15		CDCL3
1634M	B	1.26	CH2.X	CH2.18		CDCL3
624M	B	1.26 APP.	CH2.X	CH2.20		CDCL3
929M	A	1.26	CH3	CH2-A		CDCL3
1049M	A	1.26	CH3	CH2-A		CCL4
827M	A	1.26	CH3	CH2-N(&)	S	D20
827M	A	1.26	CH3	CH2-N(T)	S	D20
2985M	A	1.26	CH3	CH2-0-C(=0)		CDCL3
2750M	A	1.26	CH3	CH2-0-C(=0)	S	D20
1256M	A	1.26	CH3	CH2-S02		CCL4
1757M	B	1.26 APP.	CH3	CH(OH/CH2)		CDCL3
1834M	A	1.26	CH3	C(OH/C/CH3)		CDCL3
2262M	C	1.26	CH3	R5R60BI<C*-C(=0)/C(CH3/CH3)/CH2>		CDCL3
32M	C	1.26		UNSPECIFIED		CCL4
553M	C	1.27	CH2	CH2.8		CCL4
1103M	B	1.27	CH2	CH2-CH2/CH3		CDCL3
8M	B	1.27	CH2.X	CH2.10		CCL4
64M	B	1.27 APP.	CH2.X	CH2.12		CCL4
2710M	B	1.27	CH2.X	CH2.14		CCL4
1392M	B	1.27	CH2.X	CH2.16		CDCL3
1119M	C	1.27 APP.	CH2.X	CH2.16		CDCL3
2712M	B	1.27	CH2.X	CH2.19		CDCL3
1103M	B	1.27	CH2.X	CH2.9		CDCL3
86M	B	1.27	CH2.X	UNSPECIFIED		CDCL3
2482M	B	1.27 APP.	CH2.12	CH2-CH2-C(=0)-OH/CH3		CDCL3
2685M	B	1.27 APP.	CH2.8	CH2-NH2/CH3		CDCL3
1050M	A	1.27	CH3	CH2-A		CCL4
2795M	A	1.27	CH3	CH2-0-C(=0)		CDCL3
2749M	A	1.27	CH3	CH2-0-C(=0)		CDCL3
2811M	A	1.27	CH3	CH(0-C(=0)/CH3)		CCL4
2828M	A	1.27	CH3	CH(0-C(=0)/CH3)		CCL4
1837M	B	1.27	CH3	C(OH/CH2/CH2)		CDCL3
110M	B	1.27	CH3	R4R6BI(C(CH3)-CH*/CH*)		CCL4
1869M	A	1.27	CH3	R60<CH-0/CH(OH)>		D20
115M	A	1.27	HCH	R5R5BIR5<CH*(CH*/CH=)/CH*(CH*/CH)>		CCL4
115M	B	1.27	HCH	R5R5BIR5<CH*(CH*/CH=)/CH*(CH*/CH)>		CCL4
737M	B	1.27 APP.		UNSPECIFIED		CCL4
467M	B	1.27 APP.		UNSPECIFIED		CCL4
274M	B	1.28	CH2	C(CH2/CH3/CH3)/C(CH3/CH3/CH3)		CDCL3
2976M	B	1.28 APP.	CH2.X	CH2.10		CDCL3
2697M	B	1.28	CH2.X	CH2.10		CCL4
1118M	B	1.28	CH2.X	CH2.11		CCL4
1632M	B	1.28	CH2.X	CH2.12		CDCL3
247M	B	1.28 APP.	CH2.X	CH2.13		CCL4
843M	B	1.28	CH2.X	CH2.13	S	DMSO-D6
65M	B	1.28	CH2.X	CH2.14		CCL4
2761M	B	1.28 APP.	CH2.X	CH2.14		CDCL3
2194M	B	1.28 APP.	CH2.X	CH2.14		CCL4
248M	B	1.28	CH2.X	CH2.15		CCL4
12M	B	1.28	CH2.X	CH2.16		CDCL3
1980M	C	1.28	CH2.X	CH2.5		CCL4

BOOK NO.	ASSIGN-MENT	CHEM SHIFT - ppm -	PROTON GROUP	ENVIRONMENTAL GROUPS	S	SOLVENT
2785M	A	1.28 APP.	CH2.X	CH2.6		CDCL3
4M	B	1.28	CH2.X	CH2.6		CCL4
143M	B	1.28	CH2.X	CH2.6		CCL4
5M	B	1.28	CH2.X	CH2.7		CDCL3
62M	B	1.28	CH2.X	CH2.8		CCL4
6M	B	1.28	CH2.X	CH2.8		CCL4
244M	B	1.28	CH2.X	CH2.8		CCL4
1317M	B	1.28 APP.	CH2.X	CH2.8		CDCL3
2355M	B	1.28	CH2.X	CH2.9		CCL4
2961M	B	1.28	CH2.X	CH2.9		CCL4
413M	B	1.28 APP.	CH2.9	CH2.2-I/CH3		CCL4
995M	A	1.28	CH3	CH2-N		CDCL3
1123M	A	1.28	CH3	CH2-S		CCL4
1244M	B	1.28	CH3	CH2-SO		CCL4
1184M	B	1.28	CH3	CH(S/CH2)		CCL4
1231M	A	1.28	CH3	C(A/CH3/CH3)		CCL4
1883M	A	1.28	CH3	C(A/CH3/CH3)		CDCL3
2818M	C	1.28 APP.		UNSPECIFIED		CCL4
93M	B	1.29	CH2	CH2-Q1/CH3		CCL4
1835M	B	1.29	CH2	C(CH2/CH2/CH2)/CH3		CDCL3
2503M	A	1.29	CH2.X	CH2.10		POLYSOL-D
2919M	B	1.29	CH2.X	CH2.10		C3D60
2050M	B	1.29 APP.	CH2.X	CH2.10		CDCL3
621M	B	1.29 APP.	CH2.X	CH2.10		CDCL3
337M	B	1.29 APP.	CH2.X	CH2.11		CCL4
2758M	B	1.29	CH2.X	CH2.12		CDCL3
246M	B	1.29 APP.	CH2.X	CH2.12		CCL4
414M	B	1.29 APP.	CH2.X	CH2.13		CCL4
339M	B	1.29 APP.	CH2.X	CH2.13		CCL4
831M	B	1.29 APP.	CH2.X	CH2.13	S	CDCL3
839M	B	1.29 APP.	CH2.X	CH2.13	S	CDCL3
1391M	B	1.29	CH2.X	CH2.14		CDCL3
340M	B	1.29 APP.	CH2.X	CH2.14		CDCL3
1213M	C	1.29	CH2.X	CH2.14		CCL4
2802M	B	1.29	CH2.X	CH2.15		CDCL3
341M	B	1.29 APP.	CH2.X	CH2.16		CDCL3
14M	B	1.29	CH2.X	CH2.20		CDCL3
1927M	B	1.29 APP.	CH2.X	CH2.4		CDCL3
3M	B	1.29	CH2.X	CH2.5		CCL4
1208M	B	1.29	CH2.X	CH2.5		CDCL3
1689M	B	1.29	CH2.X	CH2.6		CCL4
1626M	B	1.29 APP.	CH2.X	CH2.6		CCL4
2298M	B	1.29	CH2.X	CH2.8		CDCL3
2480M	B	1.29	CH2.X	CH2.8		CCL4
622M	B	1.29 APP.	CH2.X	CH2.8		CDCL3
335M	B	1.29 APP.	CH2.X	CH2.8		CCL4
2652M	B	1.29	CH2.X	CH2.9		D20
336M	B	1.29	CH2.X	CH2.9		CCL4
1189M	B	1.29 APP.	CH2.X	CH2.9		CDCL3
1989M	B	1.29 APP.	CH2.X	CH2.9		CDCL3
1012M	B	1.29 APP.	CH2.X	CH2.9		CCL4
2356M	C	1.29	CH2.X	CH2.9		CCL4
2579M	B	1.29	CH2.X	CH2-8		CDCL3
1635M	B	1.29 APP.	CH2.22	CH2-OH/CH3		POLYSOL-D
16M	B	1.29	CH2.34	CH3/CH3		POLYSOL-D
2010M	A	1.29	CH2R	R13(CH2-CH2/CH2-CH2)		CCL4
631M	C	1.29	CH3	CH2-N		D20
1522M	A	1.29	CH3	CH2-O		CDCL3
2810M	A	1.29	CH3	CH2-O-C(=O)		CCL4
2789M	A	1.29	CH3	CH2-O-C(=O)		CCL4
2794M	A	1.29	CH3	CH2-O-C(=O)		CDCL3
2730M	A	1.29	CH3	CH2-O-C(=O)		CCL4
2734M	A	1.29	CH3	CH2-O-C(=O)		CCL4
2934M	A	1.29	CH3	CH2-O-C(=O)		CDCL3
2733M	B	1.29	CH3	CH2-O-C(=O)		CCL4
2744M	B	1.29	CH3	CH2-O-C(=O)		CCL4
2701M	B	1.29	CH3	CH2-O-C(=O)		CCL4
2745M	B	1.29	CH3	CH2-O-C(=O)		CDCL3
2466M	A	1.29	CH3	CH2-R6NNN		CDCL3
1128M	A	1.29	CH3	CH2-S		CCL4
478M	A	1.29	CH3	CH(NH2/A)		CCL4
2348M	A	1.29	CH3	CH(N/CH3)		CCL4
1735M	A	1.29	CH3	CH(OH/CH3)		CCL4
2626M	A	1.29	CH3	CH(OH/CH)		D20
1761M	C	1.29	CH3	CH(OH/R3)		CDCL3
2826M	A	1.29	CH3	CH(O-C(=O)/CH3)		CCL4
2325M	A	1.29	CH3	C(A/CH3/CH3)		CDCL3
2190M	B	1.29	CH3	C(C(=O)-CL/CH2.2/CH3)		CCL4
2302M	B	1.29	CH3	C(NH/CH2/CH3)		CDCL3
1610M	B	1.29	CH3	R600R6BI<C*-O/CH=/CH2>		CCL4
455M	B	1.29	NH2	CH(CH2.3/CH2.3)		CDCL3

BOOK NO.	ASSIGN-MENT	CHEM SHIFT - ppm -	PROTON GROUP	ENVIRONMENTAL GROUPS	S	SOLVENT
454M	B	1.29		UNSPECIFIED		
36M	B	1.29 APP.		UNSPECIFIED		CDCL3
2817M	C	1.29		UNSPECIFIED		CCL4
1799M	C	1.29		UNSPECIFIED		CCL4
34M	C	1.29 APP.		UNSPECIFIED		CCL4
452M	C	1.29 APP.		UNSPECIFIED		CCL4
1188M	B	1.30- 2.05	CH	CH2.2-S/CH3/CH3		CDCL3
120M	B	1.30	CH2	CH2-CH2/CH3		CCL4
617M	B	1.30	CH2	CH2-CH2/CH3		CCL4
1424M	C	1.30- 1.69	CH2	CH2-CH2/CH3		CCL4
2998M	C	1.30- 1.91	CH2	CH2-CH2/CH3		CCL4
2745M	C	1.30- 2.10	CH2	CH2-CH/CH3		CCL4
617M	B	1.30	CH2	CH2-N/CH2-CH3		CDCL3
2998M	C	1.30- 1.91	CH2	CH2-0/CH2CH3		CCL4
1424M	C	1.30- 1.69	CH2	CH2-0/CH2-CH3		CCL4
1622M	B	1.30	CH2	CH(CH2/CH2)/CH3		CCL4
1188M	B	1.30- 2.05	CH2	CH(CH3/CH3)/CH2-S		CDCL3
2745M	C	1.30- 2.10	CH2	CH(C(=0)-0/C(=0)-CH3)/CH2-CH3		CCL4
462M	A	1.30 APP.	CH2.X	CH2.10		CDCL3
1212M	B	1.30	CH2.X	CH2.10		CDCL3
2809M	B	1.30	CH2.X	CH2.10		CDCL3
63M	B	1.30 APP.	CH2.X	CH2.10		CCL4
1581M	B	1.30	CH2.X	CH2.13		CCL4
778M	A	1.30- 2.30	CH2.X	CH2.3		CDCL3
85M	B	1.30	CH2.X	CH2.4	S	TFA
44M	B	1.30	CH2.X	CH2.4		CCL4
334M	B	1.30	CH2.X	CH2.4		CCL4
1739M	C	1.30 APP.	CH2.X	CH2.4		CCL4
120M	B	1.30	CH2.X	CH2.5		CCL4
2005M	B	1.30	CH2.X	CH2.5		CCL4
61M	B	1.30	CH2.X	CH2.6		CDCL3
2966M	B	1.30	CH2.X	CH2.6		CCL4
2154M	B	1.30	CH2.X	CH2.7		CCL4
1628M	B	1.30	CH2.X	CH2.7		CDCL3
2257M	B	1.30	CH2.X	CH2.7		CCL4
243M	B	1.30	CH2.X	CH2.7		CDCL3
1011M	B	1.30	CH2.X	CH2.7		CCL4
2354M	B	1.30 APP.	CH2.X	CH2.7		CCL4
2813M	B	1.30	CH2.X	CH2.8		CDCL3
2193M	B	1.30	CH2.X	CH2.8		CCL4
1630M	B	1.30	CH2.X	CH2.8		CDCL3
1631M	B	1.30	CH2.X	CH2.9		CCL4
245M	B	1.30 APP.	CH2.X	CH2.9		CCL4
2733M	C	1.30 APP.	CH2.6	CH2-CH/CH3		CCL4
1030M	A	1.30- 2.00	CH2R	R6N(CH2-CH2/CH2-CH2)		CCL4
815M	A	1.30- 2.20	CH2R	R6N(CH2-CH2/CH2-CH2)		CDCL3
815M	A	1.30- 2.20	CH2R	R6N(CH2-N(CH2-CH2)/CH2-CH2)	S	D20
1030M	A	1.30- 2.20	CH2R	R6N(CH2-N(=0)/CH2-CH2)	S	D20
1131M	A	1.30- 2.10	CH2R	R6S<CH2-CH2/CH2-CH2>		CDCL3
1131M	A	1.30- 2.10	CH2R	R6S<CH2-S/CH2-CH2>		CCL4
146M	A	1.30- 2.00	CH2R	R6<CH2-CH=/CH2-CH2>		CCL4
184M	A	1.30- 2.00	CH2R	R6<CH2-CH=/CH2-CH2>		CCL4
184M	A	1.30- 2.00	CH2R	R6<CH2-C(A<C-CH-CH-C(CH3)>)=/CH2-CH2>		CCL4
146M	A	1.30- 2.00	CH2R	R6<CH2-C(A)=/CH2-CH2>		CCL4
2515M	A	1.30- 2.30	CH2R	R6<CH(C(=0)-OH)-CH2/CH2-CH(C(=0)-OH)>		TFA
834M	A	1.30	CH3	CH2-N		POLYSOL-D
766M	A	1.30	CH3	CH2-NH2		D20
841M	A	1.30	CH3	CH2-N(+)	S	CDCL3
1499M	A	1.30	CH3	CH2-0		CCL4
2211M	A	1.30	CH3	CH2-0		DMSO-D6
2830M	A	1.30	CH3	CH2-0-C(=0)		CDCL3
2720M	A	1.30	CH3	CH2-0-C(=0)		CCL4
2736M	A	1.30	CH3	CH2-0-C(=0)		D20
2741M	B	1.30	CH3	CH2-0-C(=0)	S	CCL4
2732M	B	1.30	CH3	CH2-0-C(=0)		CDCL3
756M	B	1.30	CH3	CH2-0-C(=0)		CCL4
2731M	C	1.30	CH3	CH2-0-C(=0)		CDCL3
945M	A	1.30	CH3	CH(C:N/CH3)		CCL4
2659M	A	1.30	CH3	CH(OH/C(=0)-0)		D20
1210M	B	1.30	CH3	CH(SH/CH2.5)		CDCL3
1203M	C	1.30	CH3	CH(SH/CH2)		CCL4
769M	A	1.30	CH3	C(NH2/CH3/CH3)		CDCL3
1838M	B	1.30	CH3	C(OH/CH/CH3)		CDCL3
1186M	A	1.30	CH3	C(S/CH3/CH3)		CCL4
1449M	B	1.30	CH3	R4R6BIR30<C(CH3)-CH*/CH*>		CCL4
1966M	A	1.30	CH3	R5NN<C(CH3)-NH/C(=0)>		CDCL3
1475M	A	1.30	CH3	R600R600SPI<CH-0/0>		CDCL3
2713M	A	1.30- 2.05		UNSPECIFIED		CCL4
1821M	A	1.30- 2.10		UNSPECIFIED		CDCL3
269M	A	1.30- 2.50		UNSPECIFIED		CDCL3
2528M	B	1.30		UNSPECIFIED		CCL4

: REPRESENTS TRIPLE BOND, ¬ REPRESENTS AN ARROW AND < AND > REPRESENT BRACKETS.   PAGE   185

BOOK NO.	ASSIGN-MENT	CHEM SHIFT - ppm -	PROTON GROUP	ENVIRONMENTAL GROUPS	S	SOLVENT
2823M	B	1.30 APP.		UNSPECIFIED		CCL4
456M	C	1.30 APP.		UNSPECIFIED		CDCL3
1610M	C	1.30- 2.15		UNSPECIFIED		CCL4
2007M	C	1.30- 2.70		UNSPECIFIED		D20
82M	C	1.31	CH2	CH2-Q2/CH3		CCL4
443M	D	1.31	CH2	CH(NH2/CH3)/CH3		CDCL3
55M	C	1.31	CH2	CH(Q3/CH3)/CH3		CCL4
72M	B	1.31 APP.	CH2.X	CH2.3		CCL4
2279M	B	1.31 APP.	CH2.X	CH2.4		CDCL3
2524M	B	1.31	CH2.X	CH2.5		CCL4
1742M	C	1.31	CH2.X	CH2.5		CDCL3
2554M	A	1.31 APP.	CH2.X	CH2.6		D20
2670M	A	1.31	CH2.X	CH2.6	S	CCL4
2693M	B	1.31	CH2.X	CH2.6		CCL4
1388M	B	1.31	CH2.X	CH2.6		DMSO-D6
1827M	A	1.31 APP.	CH2.14	CH2-OH/CH2-OH		CCL4
2786M	B	1.31	CH2R	R3<CH(C(=0)-0-CH2)-CH(C(=0)-0-CH2)>		CDCL3
1561M	A	1.31	CH3	CH2-0		CDCL3
2729M	A	1.31	CH3	CH2-0-C(=0)		CCL4
2972M	A	1.31	CH3	CH2-0-C(=0)		D20
1326M	A	1.31	CH3	CH2-0-S03-K		CCL4
1200M	B	1.31	CH3	CH2-SH		CCL4
1202M	A	1.31	CH3	CH(SH/CH3)		CCL4
1437M	A	1.31	CH3	C(0/0/0)		CDCL3
1223M	C	1.31	CH3	C(SH/CH2.3/CH2)		CDCL3
2376M	A	1.31	CH3	R5N<CH-C(=0)/HCH>		CCL4
1679M	A	1.31	CH3	R500<C(CH3)-0/0>		POLYSOL-D
2444M	A	1.31	CH3	R6NN<CH-NH/C(=0)>		CDCL3
2278M	B	1.31	CH3.X	CH2.3		CDCL3
483M	A	1.31	NH2	CH2-A		CDCL3
471M	B	1.31	NH2	R6<CH-CH2/CH2>		CDCL3
1201M	B	1.31	SH	CH2.2-CH3		CDCL3
557M	C	1.31		UNSPECIFIED		CCL4
1113M	C	1.31 APP.		UNSPECIFIED		CCL4
109M	C	1.31- 2.60		UNSPECIFIED		CDCL3
446M	B	1.32	CH2	CH(CH3/CH3)/CH2-NH2		CCL4
360M	A	1.32- 2.20	CH2.X	CH2.3		CCL4
2781M	A	1.32 APP.	CH2.X	CH2.4		CCL4
60M	B	1.32 APP.	CH2.X	CH2.4		CCL4
2532M	B	1.32	CH2.X	CH2.5		CCL4
119M	B	1.32	CH2.X	CH2.5		CCL4
600M	A	1.32	CH3	CH2-NH		CDCL3
2882M	A	1.32	CH3	CH(0-C(=0)/CH3)		CDCL3
696M	A	1.32	CH3	C(AN/CH3/CH3)		CDCL3
1886M	B	1.32	CH3	C(A/CH2/CH3)		CCL4
140M	A	1.32	CH3	C(A/CH3/CH3)		CCL4
1434M	A	1.32	CH3	C(0/0/CH3)		CDCL3
2142M	A	1.32	CH3	R4<C(CH3)-C(=0)/C(=0)>		CCL4
581M	A	1.32	NH	CH2-A/CH2-A		CCL4
1744M	B	1.32	OH	CH(C/CH2)		CDCL3
2529M	B	1.32		UNSPECIFIED		CCL4
1606M	B	1.32		UNSPECIFIED		CCL4
2960M	B	1.32 APP.		UNSPECIFIED		CCL4
1207M	D	1.32		UNSPECIFIED		CCL4
688M	B	1.33 APP.	CH2	CH2-CH2/CH3		CCL4
92M	B	1.33	CH2	CH2-Q1/CH3		CCL4
688M	B	1.33 APP.	CH2.X	CH2.2		CCL4
2704M	B	1.33	CH2.X	CH2.4		CCL4
1010M	B	1.33	CH2.X	CH2.5		CCL4
2997M	A	1.33	CH3	CH2-0		CCL4
2820M	A	1.33	CH3	CH2-0-C(=0)		CCL4
1101M	A	1.33	CH3	CH2-P(+)	S	CDCL3
1368M	A	1.33	CH3	CH2-S02		CDCL3
798M	A	1.33	CH3	CH(NH/CH3)	S	D20
1592M	A	1.33	CH3	C(0/CH3/CH3)		CDCL3
1809M	B	1.33	OH	R6<C(OH)-CH2/CH2>		CDCL3
2011M	A	1.33 APP.		UNSPECIFIED		CDCL3
1601M	B	1.34	CH	CH2-0/CH2-CH3/CH2-CH3		CCL4
1601M	B	1.34	CH2	CH(CH2/CH2)/CH3		CCL4
2153M	B	1.34	CH2.X	CH2.3		CCL4
1358M	B	1.34	CH2.X	CH2.4		CDCL3
770M	B	1.34	CH2.X	CH2.5	S	D20
1489M	A	1.34	CH3	CH2-0		CCL4
2875M	A	1.34	CH3	CH2-0-C(=0)		CCL4
1324M	A	1.34	CH3	CH2-S03		CCL4
1483M	A	1.34	CH3	CH(0/A)		CCL4
1483M	B	1.34	CH3	CH(0/A)		CCL4
2870M	A	1.34	CH3	C(A/CH3/CH3)		CCL4
2922M	A	1.34	CH3	C(C(=0)-0-A/CH3/CH3)		CDCL3
573M	A	1.34	NH	CH2-Q1/CH2-Q1		CDCL3
569M	B	1.34	NHR	R6NR6(CH*-CH2/CH2-CH2)		CDCL3

BOOK NO.	ASSIGN-MENT	CHEM SHIFT - ppm -	PROTON GROUP	ENVIRONMENTAL GROUPS	S	SOLVENT
1810M	C	1.34		UNSPECIFIED		
1969M	B	1.35 APP.	CH2	CH2.2-C(=O)-CH3/CH3		C3F60
2501M	A	1.35	CH2	CH2-CH2/CH2-CH2		CCL4
2721M	B	1.35 APP.	CH2	CH2-CH2/CH2-CH3		DMSO-D6
57M	B	1.35	CH2	CH2-CH2/CH3		CDCL3
2721M	B	1.35 APP.	CH2	CH2-CH2/CH3		CCL4
57M	B	1.35	CH2	CH2-O3/CH2-CH3		CDCL3
447M	D	1.35	CH2	C(NH2/CH3/CH3)/CH3		CCL4
264M	A	1.35- 2.12	CH2.X	CH2.3		CDCL3
1619M	B	1.35 APP.	CH2.X	CH2.4		CCL4
2909M	B	1.35	CH2.X	CH2.5		CCL4
451M	C	1.35	CH2.X	CH2.5		CDCL3
1513M	A	1.35	CH3	CH2-O		CDCL3
1518M	A	1.35	CH3	CH2-O		CCL4
1393M	A	1.35	CH3	CH2-O		CDCL3
130M	B	1.36	CH2	CH2-C:/CH(CH3/CH3)		CCL4
1644M	B	1.36 APP.	CH2	CH(NH2/HCH)/CH3		CCL4
2925M	B	1.36	CH2.X	CH2.4		CDCL3
1498M	A	1.36	CH3	CH2-O		CCL4
1500M	A	1.36	CH3	CH2-O		CCL4
1561M	B	1.36	CH3	CH2-O		CCL4
2858M	A	1.36	CH3	CH2-O-C(=O)		CDCL3
2307M	A	1.36	CH3	CH(NH/A)		CDCL3
2740M	A	1.36	CH3	CH(OH/C(=O)-O)		CCL4
2893M	A	1.36	CH3	CH(O-C(=O)/CH3)		CCL4
1483M	A	1.36	CH3	CH(O/A)		CDCL3
1483M	B	1.36	CH3	CH(O/A)		CCL4
694M	A	1.36	CH3	C(AN/CH3/CH3)		CCL4
472M	A	1.36	NH2	R7<CH-CH2/CH2>		CCL4
687M	B	1.37 APP.	CH2	CH2-CH2/CH2-CH3		CDCL3
687M	B	1.37 APP.	CH2	CH2-CH2/CH3		CCL4
1744M	C	1.37 APP.	CH2	CH2-CH/CH3		CCL4
1744M	C	1.37 APP.	CH2	CH(OH/C)/CH2-CH3		CCL4
2202M	A	1.37	CH2.X	CH2.4		CCL4
1798M	C	1.37 APP.	CH2.3	C(OH/CH3/CH3)/CH3		CCL4
201M	A	1.37	CH3	CH2-AA		CCL4
1570M	A	1.37	CH3	CH2-O		CCL4
2772M	A	1.37	CH3	CH2-O-C(=O)		CDCL3
2870M	B	1.37	CH3	CH2-O-C(=O)		CCL4
1432M	A	1.37	CH3	CH(O-CH/O-CH)		CCL4
1081M	A	1.37	CH3	CH(O-NO2/CH3)		CDCL3
1993M	A	1.37	CH3	C(OH/C(=O)/CH3)		CCL4
1679M	B	1.37	CH3	P500<C(CH3)-O/O>		CDCL3
448M	C	1.37	NH2	CH(C/CH3)		CCL4
450M	D	1.38- 2.14	CH	CH2-CH/CH3/CH3		CCL4
28M	B	1.38- 1.98	CH	CH(CH3/CH3)/CH(CH3/CH3)/CH3		CCL4
28M	B	1.38- 1.98	CH	CH(CH/CH3)/CH3/CH3		CCL4
2366M	B	1.38	CH2	CH2-CH2/CH3		CCL4
334M	B	1.38	CH2	CH2-CH2/CH3		CCL4
1755M	C	1.38 APP.	CH2	CH2-CH2/CH3		CDCL3
1755M	C	1.38 APP.	CH2	CH2-N/CH2-CH3		CCL4
1736M	C	1.38	CH2	CH(OH/CH3)/CH3		CCL4
1600M	B	1.38	CH2.X	CH2.3		CCL4
1783M	B	1.38 APP.	CH2.X	CH2.3		CCL4
2780M	B	1.38 APP.	CH2.X	CH2.3		CDCL3
266M	A	1.38- 2.30	CH2R	R5<CH2-CH(CL)/CH2-CH2>		CCL4
2083M	A	1.38- 2.15	CH2R	R5<CH2-CH(C(=O)-A)/CH2-CH2>		CCL4
266M	A	1.38- 2.30	CH2R	R5<CH(CL)-CH2/CH2-CH2>		CCL4
2083M	A	1.38- 2.15	CH2R	R5<CH(C(=O)-A)-CH2/CH2-CH2>		CCL4
812M	A	1.38	CH3	CH2-N	S	D20
1062M	A	1.38	CH3	CH2-NH		CCL4
1525M	B	1.38	CH3	CH2-O		CCL4
2884M	A	1.38	CH3	CH2-O-C(=O)		CDCL3
804M	A	1.38	CH3	CH(NH/CH2)	S	CDCL3
2283M	A	1.38	CH3	CH(OH/C(=O))		D20
1936M	A	1.38	CH3	C(A/CH3/CH3)		CDCL3
2927M	A	1.38	CH3	C(C(=O)-O/CH3/CH3)		CDCL3
2445M	A	1.38	CH3	R5NN<C(CH3)-NH/C(=O)>		CDCL3
2438M	B	1.39	CH2	CH2-CH2/CH3		CCL4
2438M	B	1.39	CH2	CH2-N/CH2-CH3		CCL4
1737M	B	1.39	CH2	CH(OH/CH2)/CH3		CCL4
2206M	A	1.39	CH2.X	CH2.5		CCL4
1623M	B	1.39 APP.	CH2.X	CH2.5		CCL4
2708M	C	1.39	CH2.X	CH2.5		CCL4
565M	B	1.39 APP.	CH2R	R13N<CH2-CH2/CH2-CH2>		CDCL3
565M	B	1.39 APP.	CH2R	R13N<CH2-NH/CH2-CH2>		CDCL3
806M	A	1.39	CH3	CH2-NH	S	D20
2871M	A	1.39	CH3	CH2-O-C(=O)		CCL4
1316M	A	1.39	CH3	CH2-SO3		CCL4
2889M	A	1.39	CH3	CH(O-C(=O)/CH3)		CDCL3
1034M	B	1.39	CH3	CH(O-N=O/CH2)		CCL4

BOOK NO.	ASSIGN-MENT	CHEM SHIFT - ppm -	PROTON GROUP	ENVIRONMENTAL GROUPS	S	SOLVENT
2224M	A	1.39	CH3	C(A/CH3/CH3)		CDCL3
948M	A	1.39	CH3	C(C:N/CH3/CH3)		CCL4
1859M	A	1.39	CH3	C(OH/C:/CH3)		DMSO-D6
2120M	A	1.39	CH3	C(R6A/CH3/CH3)		CDCL3
1259M	A	1.39	CH3	R5S<CH-SO2/CH=>		CDCL3
1759M	D	1.39- 2.11	HCH	C(O/CH3/CH3)/CH(OH/CH3)		CCL4
572M	A	1.39	NH	CH2-Q2/CH2-Q2		CDCL3
626M	D	1.39 APP.	NH2	CH(CH2.3/CH3)		CDCL3
1741M	C	1.40- 2.10	CH	CH(OH/CH)/CH3/CH3		CDCL3
407M	B	1.40 APP.	CH2	CH2.2-I/CH3		CCL4
2161M	B	1.40	CH2	CH2-CH2/CH3		CCL4
2161M	B	1.40	CH2	CH2-Q1/CH2-CH3		CCL4
357M	B	1.40- 2.50	CH2	CH(BR/HCH)/CH3		CDCL3
2010M	B	1.40- 1.95	CH2R	R13(CH2-C(=O)/CH2-CH2)		CCL4
2824M	C	1.40- 2.30	CH2R	R5R5BI<CH*(CH=/CH2)/CH(C(=O)-O-CH2)-CH*>		CCL4
2824M	C	1.40- 2.30	CH2R	R5R5RI<CH*(CH=/CH2)/CH*(CH=/CH(C(=O)-O-CH2))>		CCL4
2132M	C	1.40- 2.40	CH2R	R5R5RI<CH*(C(=O)/C(CH3/CH3))/CH2-C*(CH3)>		POLYSOL-D
2008M	D	1.40- 2.30	CH2R	R5R5RI<C(=O)-C*(CH3)/CH*(C(=O)/C)>		CDCL3
2132M	C	1.40- 2.40	CH2R	R5R5RI<C*(CH3)-C(=O)/C(CH3/CH3))/CH2-CH*>		POLYSOL-D
2008M	D	1.40- 2.30	CH2R	R5R5RI<C*((CH3)/C(=O)/C)/C(=O)-CH*>		CDCL3
363M	A	1.40- 2.32	CH2R	R5<CH2-CH(BR)/CH2-CH2>		CCL4
363M	A	1.40- 2.32	CH2R	R5<CH(BR)-CH2/CH2-CH2>		CCL4
2204M	A	1.40- 2.25	CH2R	R5(CH2-CH(C(=O)-CL)/CH2-CH2)		CCL4
2204M	A	1.40- 2.25	CH2R	R5(CH(C(=O)-CL)-CH2/CH2-CH2)		CCL4
104M	A	1.40- 1.69	CH2R	R6<CH2-C(=O)=/CH2-CH2>		CCL4
965M	A	1.40- 2.35	CH2R	R6<CH(C:N)-CH2/CH2-CH(C:N)>		CDCL3
2535M	A	1.40- 1.90	CH2R	R6(CH2-CH=/CH2-CH2)		CCL4
2535M	A	1.40- 1.90	CH2R	R6(CH2-C(C(=O)-OH)=/CH2-CH2)		CCL4
1517M	A	1.40	CH3	CH2-O		CCL4
2563M	A	1.40	CH3	CH2-O		CDCL3
2907M	A	1.40	CH3	CH2-O-C(=O)		CDCL3
2937M	A	1.40	CH3	CH2-O-C(=O)		CDCL3
1882M	A	1.40	CH3	C(A/CH3/CH3)		CCL4
1933M	B	1.40	CH3	C(A/CH3/CH3)		CDCL3
786M	A	1.40	CH3	C(NH2/CH2/CH3)	S	D20
2304M	A	1.40	CH3	C(NH/CH3/CH3)		CDCL3
1223M	D	1.40	CH3	C(SH/CH2.3/CH3)		CDCL3
1202M	B	1.40	SH	CH(CH3/CH3)		CCL4
2779M	A	1.40 APP.		UNSPECIFIED		CCL4
2952M	A	1.40- 2.00		UNSPECIFIED		CCL4
2158M	A	1.40- 2.72		UNSPECIFIED		CCL4
197M	B	1.40- 2.10		UNSPECIFIED		CCL4
1597M	C	1.40- 1.90		UNSPECIFIED		CDCL3
44M	C	1.40- 2.00		UNSPECIFIED		CCL4
2349M	B	1.41	CH2	CH2-CH2/CH3		CCL4
579M	B	1.41 APP.	CH2	CH2-CH2/CH3		CCL4
579M	B	1.41 APP.	CH2	CH2-NH/CH2-CH3		CCL4
2349M	B	1.41	CH2	CH2-N/CH2-CH3		CCL4
2521M	B	1.41	CH2	CH2-Q2/CH3		CCL4
2800M	B	1.41	CH2	CH2-Q2/CH3		CCL4
1026M	B	1.41	CH3	CH2-N		CDCL3
2723M	A	1.41	CH3	CH2-O-C(=O)		CDCL3
1793M	A	1.41	CH3	CH(OH/A)		CCL4
1219M	A	1.41	CH3	CH(SH/CH2)		CDCL3
1814M	B	1.41	CH3	C(OH/C:C/CH2)		CCL4
1104M	C	1.41	CH3	P(=O/CH2/CH3)		CDCL3
2256M	A	1.41	CH3	R5O<CH-C(=O)/CH2>		CDCL3
1831M	D	1.41	HCH	C(OH/CH3/CH3)/CH(OH/CH3)		CCL4
1204M	C	1.41	SH	CH2.6-CH3		CDCL3
1127M	A	1.42	CH2	CH2-CH2/CH2-CH2		CCL4
2644M	A	1.42- 2.28	CH2	CH2-NH2/CH2-CH	S	D20
1127M	A	1.42	CH2	CH2-S/CH2-CH2		CCL4
2644M	A	1.42- 2.28	CH2	CH(NH2/C(=O)-OH)/CH2-CH2	S	D20
637M	A	1.42 APP.	CH2R	R6N<CH2-CH2/CH2-CH2>		CCL4
637M	A	1.42 APP.	CH2R	R6N<CH2-N(CH3)/CH2-CH2>		CCL4
45M	A	1.42	CH2R	R6<CH2-CH2/CH2-CH2>		CCL4
1512M	A	1.42	CH3	CH2-O		CCL4
1533M	A	1.42	CH3	CH2-O		CDCL3
2076M	A	1.42	CH3	CH2-O		CDCL3
2885M	A	1.42	CH3	CH2-O-C(=O)		CCL4
1216M	C	1.42	NH	CH2.2-SH/CH2.9-CH3		CDCL3
322M	B	1.43 APP.	CH2	CH2-CH2/CH3		CCL4
2493M	A	1.43	CH3	CH(OH/C(=O)-OH)		D20
568M	B	1.43	NHR	R6NN(CH(CH3)-HCH/HCH-CH(CH3))		CDCL3
856M	B	1.44	CH	CH2-CH2/CH3/CH3		CDCL3
856M	B	1.44	CH2	CH(CH3/CH3)/CH2-QN		CDCL3
2774M	B	1.44	CH2.X	CH2.3		CCL4
1155M	A	1.44	CH3	CH2-R5NNS		TFA
2768M	A	1.44	CH3	C(O-C(=O)/CH3/CH3)		CCL4
1103M	C	1.44	CH3	P(=O/CH2/CH3)		CDCL3
2717M	B	1.45	CH2	CH2-CH2/CH3		CCL4

BOOK NO.	ASSIGN-MENT	CHEM SHIFT - ppm -	PROTON GROUP	ENVIRONMENTAL GROUPS	S	SOLVENT
2981M	C	1.45	CH2	CH2-NH/CH3		CCL4
2717M	B	1.45	CH2	CH2-0/CH2-CH3		CCL4
560M	A	1.45	CH2R	R5N<CH2-NH/CH2-CH2>		C6H6
1452M	A	1.45- 2.02	CH2R	R8R30R30(CH*-0/CH2-CH*)		CCL4
809M	A	1.45	CH3	CH2-N		CDCL3
797M	A	1.45	CH3	CH2-NH	S	CDCL3
1571M	A	1.45	CH3	CH2-0	S	CDCL3
2883M	A	1.45	CH3	CH2-0-C(=0)		CDCL3
1287M	A	1.45	CH3	CH2-S03-H		CDCL3
2310M	A	1.45	CH3	CH(NH/A)		CDCL3
2975M	A	1.45	CH3	C(0-C(=0)/CH3/CH3)		CDCL3
932M	A	1.45	CH3	QN(CH3/CH3/=C=S)		CCL4
1799M	D	1.46	CH	CH2-CH2/CH3/CH3		CCL4
18M	B	1.46	CH	CH(CH3/CH3)/CH3/CH3		CCL4
1796M	C	1.46	CH2	C(OH/CH3/CH3)/CH3		CCL4
2625M	A	1.46	CH3	C(NH2/C(=0)-OH/HCH)		D20
1212M	C	1.46	SH	CH2-CH2		CDCL3
711M	A	1.46- 2.55		UNSPECIFIED		CCL4
1110M	B	1.47	CH2	CH2-CH2/CH3		CCL4
461M	A	1.47	CH2	CH2-NH2/CH2-CH2		D20
578M	C	1.47	CH2	CH2-NH/CH3		CCL4
1110M	B	1.47	CH2	CH2-S/CH2-CH3		CCL4
2541M	A	1.47	CH3	CH(C(=0)-OH/A)		CCL4
974M	A	1.47	CH3	C(A/CH2/CH3)		CCL4
2305M	B	1.47	CH3	C(NH/CH2/CH3)		CDCL3
1467M	A	1.47	CH3	C(R6N0/C:N/CH3)		CDCL3
478M	B	1.47	NH2	CH(A/CH3)		CCL4
468M	B	1.47	NH2	R5<CH-CH2/CH2>		CDCL3
1421M	B	1.48	CH2	CH2-CH2/CH3		CCL4
439M	B	1.48	CH2	CH2-NH2		CCL4
439M	B	1.48	CH2	CH2-NH2/CH3		CCL4
1421M	B	1.48	CH2	CH2-0/CH2-CH3		CCL4
1837M	C	1.48	CH2	C(OH/CH2/CH3)/C(CH3/CH3/CH3)		CDCL3
98M	B	1.48- 1.97	CH2R	R5<CH2-C(CH3)=/CH2-C(CH3)>		CCL4
473M	B	1.48	CH2R	R6R6R6TRI<CH*(CH2/CH2)/CH*(CH2/CH2)>		CDCL3
2614M	A	1.48	CH3	CH(NH2/C(=0)-0)		D20
1934M	A	1.48	CH3	C(A/CH3/CH3)		CDCL3
90M	A	1.48	CH3	Q1(CH3/CH3)		CCL4
1833M	B	1.48	HCH	CH(OH/CH3)/HCH-CH		CCL4
1833M	C	1.48	HCH	CH(OH/CH3)/HCH-CH		CCL4
482M	B	1.49 APP.	CH2	CH2-A/CH2-CH2		CCL4
2486M	B	1.49	CH2	CH2-CH/CH3		CDCL3
482M	B	1.49 APP.	CH2	CH2-NH2/CH2-CH2		CCL4
542M	B	1.49	CH2	CH2-NH/CH3		CDCL3
1613M	B	1.49	CH2	CH2-OH/CH3		CCL4
1830M	B	1.49	CH2	CH(OH/CH3)/CH(OH/CH3)		CCL4
2741M	C	1.49 APP.	CH2	CH(OH/C(=0)-0)/CH(CH3/CH3)		CCL4
1803M	C	1.49	CH2	C(OH/CH/CH2)/CH3		CCL4
1825M	A	1.49 APP.	CH2.X	CH2.3		D20
949M	B	1.49	CH2.X	CH2.3		CDCL3
801M	A	1.49- 2.18	CH2R	R6NH<CH2-CH2/CH2-CH2>	S	CDCL3
801M	A	1.49- 2.18	CH2R	R6NH<CH2-NH/CH2-CH2>	S	CDCL3
2585M	A	1.49	CH3	CH2-0		CCL4
2911M	A	1.49	CH3	CH2-0-C(=0)		CDCL3
237M	B	1.49	CH3	CH(CL/CH2)		CCL4
1815M	B	1.49	CH3	C(OH/C:C/CH2)		CDCL3
552M	C	1.49	NH	CH2-CH2/CH3		CDCL3
567M	B	1.49	NHR	R6NN<CH(CH3)-CH2/CH2-CH(CH3)>		CDCL3
446M	C	1.49	NH2	CH2-CH2		CDCL3
469M	B	1.49	NH2	CH2-R6		CDCL3
1776M	B	1.49	OH	R6<CH-C(A/A)/CH2>		CDCL3
2778M	B	1.50- 2.10	CH	CH2-0-C(=0)/CH3/CH3		CCL4
779M	A	1.50 APP.	CH2	CH2.2-NH2/CH2.3-NH2	S	D20
1281M	B	1.50	CH2	CH2.2-S02/CH3		CCL4
420M	A	1.50	CH2	CH2-CH2/CH2-CH2		CCL4
2767M	B	1.50	CH2	CH2-CH2/CH3		CCL4
2778M	B	1.50- 2.10	CH2	CH2-C(=0)-0/CH2-C(=0)-0		CCL4
2767M	B	1.50	CH2	CH2-0-C(=0)/CH2-CH3		CCL4
1394M	C	1.50	CH2	CH2-0/CH3		CCL4
2523M	C	1.50	CH2	CH2-Q1/CH3		CCL4
2799M	B	1.50	CH2	CH2-Q2/CH3		CCL4
2021M	B	1.50	CH2	CH(Q2/CH2)/CH3		CCL4
1203M	D	1.50	CH2	CH(SH/CH3)/CH3		CCL4
1439M	B	1.50	CH2	R30<CH-0/HCH>/CH3		CCL4
772M	A	1.50- 2.60	CH2R	R4(CH2-CH(NH2)/CH2)	S	D20
772M	A	1.50- 2.60	CH2R	R4(CH(NH2)-CH2/CH2)	S	D20
2537M	B	1.50-22.40	CH2R	R5R5RI(CH(C(=0)-OH)-CH*/CH*(CH=/CH2))		CCL4
42M	A	1.50	CH2R	R5<CH2-CH2/CH2-CH2>		CCL4
2720M	B	1.50	CH3	CH(F/C(=0)-0)		CCL4
2616M	A	1.50	CH3	C(NH2/C(=0)-0/CH3)		D20
115M	A	1.50	HCH	R5R5RIR5<CH*(CH*/CH=)/CH*(CH*/CH)>		CCL4

BOOK NO.	ASSIGN-MENT	CHEM SHIFT - ppm -	PROTON GROUP	ENVIRONMENTAL GROUPS	S	SOLVENT
115M	B	1.50	HCH	R5R5BIR5<CH*(CH*/CH=)/CH*(CH*/CH)>		CCL4
1505M	A	1.50	NH2	CH2-A		CDCL3
1224M	A	1.50	SH	CH2-A		CCL4
115M	C	1.50- 3.40		UNSPECIFIED		CCL4
1969M	C	1.51 APP.	CH2	CH2-C(=O)-CH3/CH2-CH3		CCL4
2299M	C	1.51	CH2	CH2-NH/CH3		CDCL3
874M	B	1.51	CH2	CH2-QN/CH3		CCL4
1684M	A	1.51 APP.	CH2R	R6R6R6TRI<CH*(CH2/CH2)/CH*(CH2/CH2)>		POLYSOL-D
1008M	A	1.51	CH3	CH2-S		CDCL3
241M	B	1.51	CH3	C(CL/CH2/CH3)		CCL4
1817M	A	1.51	CH3	C(OH/A/CH3)		CDCL3
486M	B	1.51	NH2	CH2-A		CCL4
444M	C	1.51	NH2	CH2-CH2		CDCL3
470M	B	1.51	NH2	R6<CH-CH2/CH2>		CCL4
2378M	A	1.51 APP.		UNSPECIFIED		CDCL3
1809M	C	1.51 APP.		UNSPECIFIED		CDCL3
1449M	C	1.51- 2.11		UNSPECIFIED		CCL4
2843M	B	1.52	CH	CH2-C(=O)-O/CH3/CH3		CCL4
1884M	C	1.52	CH2	CH2-A/CH2.2-CH3		CCL4
362M	A	1.52 APP.	CH2	CH2-CH2/CH2-CH2		CCL4
2499M	A	1.52	CH2	CH2-C(=O)-O/CH2-CH2		DMSO-D6
131M	B	1.52	CH2	CH2-C:/CH2.2-C:		CCL4
1087M	B	1.52	CH2	SI(CH2/CH3/CH3)/Q3(H/H/H)		CL2C=CCL2
124M	A	1.52 APP.	CH2.X	CH2.3		CDCL3
51M	A	1.52	CH2R	R8(CH2-CH2/CH2-CH2)		CCL4
106M	A	1.52	CH2R	R8(CH2-CH=CH/CH2-CH2)		CCL4
785M	A	1.52	CH3	CH(NH2/CH2)	S	TFA
2834M	A	1.52	CH3	CH(O-C(=O)/A)		CDCL3
2489M	A	1.52	CH3	CH(SH/C(=O)-OH)		CCL4
476M	A	1.52	NH2	CH2-A		CDCL3
1832M	B	1.53	CH	CH2-CH2/CH2-CH2/CH3		CDCL3
800M	B	1.53	CH2	CH2-CH2/CH3		D20
800M	B	1.53	CH2	CH2-NH/CH2-CH3		D20
494M	C	1.53	CH2	CH(A/CH3)/CH3		CCL4
1832M	B	1.53	CH2	CH(CH2/CH3)/CH2-OH		CDCL3
50M	A	1.53	CH2R	R7<CH2-CH2/CH2-CH2>		CDCL3
1813M	A	1.53	CH3	C(OH/C:CH/CH3)		CDCL3
1408M	B	1.53	CH3	Q2(H/H/O-CH2)		CCL4
1408M	B	1.53	CH3	Q3(H/O-CH2/H)		CCL4
1779M	C	1.53	OH	R5R5BI<CH-C*(CH3)/CH2>		CDCL3
561M	A	1.53 APP.		UNSPECIFIED		CDCL3
2701M	C	1.54 APP.	CH2	CH2-CH2/CH3		CCL4
1981M	C	1.54	CH2	CH2-C(=O)-CH2.5/CH3		CCL4
2701M	C	1.54 APP.	CH2	CH2-C(=O)-O/CH2-CH3		CCL4
1989M	C	1.54	CH2	CH2-C(=O)/CH2.9-CH3		CDCL3
1466M	B	1.54	CH2	CH2-NH2/CH2-R6NO		CCL4
584M	B	1.54	CH2	CH2-NH/CH3		CCL4
2520M	B	1.54	CH2	CH2-Q2/CH3		CCL4
2156M	B	1.54	CH2	CH2-Q2/CH3		CDCL3
886M	A	1.54	CH2R	R6N<CH2-CH2/CH2-CH2>		CCL4
886M	A	1.54	CH2R	R6N<CH2-N(QN(A))/CH2-CH2>		CCL4
1557M	A	1.54	CH3	CH2-O		CDCL3
1807M	A	1.54	CH3	C(OH/SO3-NA/CH3)		D20
1811M	B	1.54		UNSPECIFIED		CCL4
2781M	B	1.55 APP.	CH2	CH2-C(=O)-O/CH2-CH2		CCL4
117M	B	1.55	CH2	CH2-C:CH/CH3		CCL4
953M	C	1.55	CH2	CH2-C:N/CH2-CH2		CDCL3
458M	A	1.55	CH2	CH2-NH2/CH2-NH2		D20
2698M	D	1.55	CH2	CH(O-C(=O)/CH3)/CH3		CDCL3
1459M	C	1.55	CH2	R500<C(CH3)/O/O>/CH3		CCL4
1476M	B	1.55	CH2	R600R600SPI<CH-O/O>/CH3		CCL4
1040M	A	1.55	CH3	CH2-NO2		CDCL3
92M	C	1.55	CH3	Q1(H/CH3/CH2-CH2)		CCL4
1833M	B	1.55	HCH	CH(OH/CH3)/HCH-CH		CCL4
1833M	C	1.55	HCH	CH(OH/CH3)/HCH-CH		CCL4
1831M	E	1.55	HCH	C(OH/CH3/CH3)/CH(OH/CH3)		CCL4
563M	C	1.55	NHR	R6N<HCH-CH2/HCH-CH2>		CCL4
1984M	C	1.56	CH2	CH2-C(=O)-CH2.2/CH2.6-CH3		CCL4
1984M	C	1.56	CH2	CH2-C(=O)-CH2.8/CH3		CCL4
2365M	B	1.56	CH2	CH2-N/CH3		CDCL3
854M	B	1.56	CH2	CH2-QN/CH3		CDCL3
2475M	C	1.56 APP.	CH2	CH(C(=O)-O/CH3)/CH3		CDCL3
1645M	B	1.56	CH2	C(NH2/CH3/CH3)/CH2-OH		CDCL3
1086M	B	1.56	CH2	SI(CH3/CH3/CH3)/Q3		CCL4
2639M	A	1.56	CH3	CH(NH2/C(=O)-NH)		D20
1692M	B	1.56	CH3	R6O(C=CH/CH2)		CDCL3
104M	B	1.56	CH3	R6<C=C(CH3)/CH2>		CCL4
571M	A	1.56	NH	CH2-Q3		CDCL3
1622M	C	1.56	OH	CH2-CH		CDCL3
1788M	B	1.57	CH2	CH(OH/A)/CH3		CCL4
1223M	E	1.57	CH2.3	C(SH/CH2/CH3)/C(SH/CH3/CH3)		CDCL3

BOOK NO.	ASSIGN-MENT	CHEM SHIFT - ppm -	PROTON GROUP	ENVIRONMENTAL GROUPS	S	SOLVENT
103M	B	1.57	CH2R	R6<CH2-CH=/CH2-CH2>		CCL4
103M	B	1.57	CH2R	R6<CH2-C(CH2-CH2)=/CH2-CH2>		CCL4
1991M	A	1.57	CH3	CH(CL/C(=O)-CH3)		CCL4
1042M	A	1.57	CH3	CH(NO2/CH3)		CDCL3
1908M	A	1.57	CH3	C(A/A/CH3)		POLYSOL-D
1036M	A	1.57	CH3	C(O-NO/CH3/CH3)		CDCL3
83M	C	1.57	CH3	Q2(CH2-CH2)		CCL4
98M	A	1.57	CH3	R5<C=C(CH3)/CH2>		CCL4
2354M	C	1.58	CH2	CH2.N/CH3		CDCL3
2503M	B	1.58	CH2	CH2-C(=O)-OH/CH2.12-C(=O)-OH		POLYSOL-D
1972M	B	1.58	CH2	CH2-C(=O)/CH3		CCL4
2413M	B	1.58	CH2	CH2-C(=O)/CH3		DMSO-D6
464M	A	1.58	CH2	CH2-NH/CH2-NH2		D2O
650M	B	1.58	CH2	CH2-N/CH3		CCL4
2157M	C	1.58	CH2	CH2-Q1/CH3		CCL4
1815M	C	1.58	CH2	C(OH/C:C/CH3)/CH(CH3/CH3)		CDCL3
1104M	D	1.58 APP.	CH2	P(=O/CH3/CH3)/CH2-CH2		CDCL3
1021M	B	1.58	CH3	C(+)(N/CH3/CH3)		CDCL3
90M	B	1.58 APP.	CH3	Q1(CH3/CH3)		CCL4
1218M	A	1.58	NH	CH2-CH2/CH2-CH2		CDCL3
1225M	A	1.58	SH	CH2-A		CCL4
2490M	A	1.58	SH	CH2-CH2		CCL4
1218M	A	1.58	SH	CH2-CH2		CDCL3
442M	B	1.59	CH	CH2-NH2/CH3/CH3		CDCL3
142M	C	1.59	CH2	CH2-A/CH2-CH2		CDCL3
946M	B	1.59	CH2	CH2-CH2/CH3		CCL4
946M	B	1.59	CH2	CH2-CH2/CH3		CCL4
1970M	C	1.59	CH2	CH2-C(=O)-CH2/CH3		CDCL3
2352M	B	1.59	CH2	CH2-C(=O)-N/CH3		D2O
2785M	B	1.59	CH2	CH2-C(=O)-O/CH2-CH2		CDCL3
2760M	C	1.59	CH2	CH2-C(=O)-O/CH2-CH2		CCL4
946M	B	1.59	CH2	CH2-C:N/CH2-CH3		CCL4
946M	B	1.59	CH2	CH2-C:N/CH2-CH3		CCL4
1667M	B	1.59	CH2	CH2-O/CH3		CDCL3
1063M	B	1.59	CH2	CH2-ON/CH3		POLYSOL-D
1109M	B	1.59	CH2	CH2-S/CH3		CCL4
138M	C	1.59 APP.	CH2	CH(A/CH3)/CH3		CCL4
2621M	B	1.59 APP.	CH2	CH(NH/C(=O)-OH)/CH(CH3/CH3)		POLYSOL-D
1758M	A	1.59	CH3	CH(OH/C:N)		CDCL3
2562M	A	1.59	CH3	C(O/C(=O)-OH/CH3)		CDCL3
92M	D	1.59	CH3	Q1(CH2-CH2/CH3/H)		CCL4
893M	B	1.59	CH3	Q1(CH3/CH2-CH2)		CDCL3
893M	C	1.59	CH3	Q1(CH3/CH2-CH2)		CDCL3
76M	B	1.59	CH3	Q2(CH(CH3/CH3))		CCL4
554M	C	1.59	NH	CH2.12-CH3/CH2.12-CH3		CDCL3
551M	C	1.59	NH	CH2-CH2/CH2-CH2		CDCL3
462M	B	1.59	NH2	CH2.1I-NH2		CDCL3
22M	C	1.60	CH	CH2-CH/CH3/CH3		CCL4
546M	C	1.60	CH	CH2-NH/CH3/CH3		CCL4
331M	C	1.60 APP.	CH2	CH2-CH		CCL4
2894M	B	1.60	CH2	CH2-CH2/CH3		CCL4
2689M	A	1.60	CH2	CH2-C(=O)-OH/CH2-CH2		D2O
2579M	C	1.60	CH2	CH2-C(=O)-OH/CH2-CH2		CDCL3
2480M	C	1.60	CH2	CH2-C(=O)-O/CH2-CH2		CCL4
2279M	C	1.60	CH2	CH2-C(=O)/CH2-CH2		CDCL3
2278M	C	1.60 APP.	CH2	CH2-C(=O)/CH2-CH2		CDCL3
627M	A	1.60	CH2	CH2-N/CH2-NH2		CDCL3
1649M	A	1.60	CH2	CH2-N/CH2-OH		CCL4
2894M	B	1.60	CH2	CH2-O-C(=O)/CH2-CH3		CCL4
1381M	B	1.60	CH2	CH2-O/CH3		CDCL3
1211M	C	1.60	CH2	CH2-SH/CH2.6-CH3		CDCL3
1124M	B	1.60	CH2	CH2-S/CH3		CCL4
2253M	B	1.60	CH2	CH(C(=O)-O/CH2)/CH3		CCL4
1184M	C	1.60	CH2	CH(S/CH3)/CH3		CCL4
1885M	C	1.60	CH2	C(A/CH3/CH3)/CH3		CCL4
1103M	D	1.60 APP.	CH2	P(=O/CH3/CH3)/CH2-CH2		CDCL3
2513M	A	1.60- 2.70	CH2R	R4<CH2-CH(C(=O)-OH)/CH2>		CDCL3
2513M	A	1.60- 2.70	CH2R	R4<CH(C(=O)-OH)-CH2/CH2>		CDCL3
1457M	A	1.60- 2.12	CH2R	R50<CH2-O/CH2-CH(CH2-O)>		CCL4
1457M	A	1.60- 2.12	CH2R	R50<CH(CH2-O)-O/CH2-CH2>		CCL4
43M	B	1.60 APP.	CH2R	R5<CH2-CH(CH3)/CH2-CH2>		CCL4
43M	B	1.60 APP.	CH2R	R5<CH2-CH(CH3)/CH2-CH2>		CCL4
2439M	A	1.60 APP.	CH2R	R6N<CH2-CH2/CH2-CH2>		CDCL3
2439M	A	1.60 APP.	CH2R	R6N<CH2-N(C(=O)-R6N)/CH2-CH2>		CDCL3
814M	A	1.60- 2.70	CH2R	R6N<CH(N(CH3/CH3))-CH2/CH2-NH>	S	D2O
1319M	A	1.60- 2.50	CH2R	R6OS<CH2-O/CH2-CH2>		CDCL3
1319M	A	1.60- 2.50	CH2R	R6OS<CH2-SO2/CH2-CH2>		CDCL3
2022M	A	1.60	CH2R	R6<CH2-CH=/CH2-CH2>		CCL4
2022M	A	1.60	CH2R	R6<CH2-C(C(=O)-CH3)=/CH2-CH2>		CCL4
2411M	A	1.60 APP.	CH2R	R6(CH2-CH2/CH2-CH2)		CDCL3
2411M	A	1.60 APP.	CH2R	R6(CH2-C(=N-NH)/CH2-CH2)		CDCL3

BOOK NO.	ASSIGN-MENT	CHEM SHIFT - ppm -	PROTON GROUP	ENVIRONMENTAL GROUPS	S	SOLVENT
257M	A	1.60	CH3	CH(CL/CH2)		CCL4
2736M	B	1.60	CH3	CH(NH2/C(=0)-0)	S	D20
1935M	A	1.60	CH3	C(A/A/CH3)		CDCL3
93M	C	1.60	CH3	Q1(CH3/CH2-CH2/H)		CCL4
94M	B	1.60	CH3	Q1(CH3/CH2-CH)		CCL4
94M	C	1.60	CH3	Q1(CH3/CH2-CH)		CCL4
93M	D	1.60	CH3	Q1(CH3/H/CH2-CH2)		CCL4
75M	B	1.60	CH3	Q2(CH2-CH3)		CCL4
441M	C	1.60	NH2	CH2-CH2		CDCL3
1402M	A	1.60	SH	CH2-CH2		CCL4
1401M	B	1.60	SH	CH2-CH2		CDCL3
102M	A	1.60 APP.		UNSPECIFIED		CCL4
147M	A	1.60- 2.33		UNSPECIFIED		CDCL3
111M	C	1.60- 2.40		UNSPECIFIED		CCL4
2151M	B	1.61	CH2	CH2-C(=0)-H/CH3		CCL4
2404M	A	1.61	CH2	CH2-C(=0)-NH/CH2.2-C(=0)-NH		D20
2761M	C	1.61	CH2	CH2-C(=0)-0/CH2.14-CH3		CDCL3
2779M	B	1.61	CH2	CH2-C(=0)-0/CH2-CH2		CCL4
2777M	B	1.61	CH2	CH2-C(=0)-0/CH2-CH2		CCL4
2704M	C	1.61	CH2	CH2-C(=0)-0/CH2-CH2		CCL4
908M	B	1.61	CH2	CH2-N=C=0/CH3		CDCL3
2419M	C	1.61	CH2	C(NH/CH3/CH3)/CH3		DMSO-D6
1814M	C	1.61	CH2	C(OH/C:C/CH3)/CH3		CCL4
465M	C	1.61	CH2	N(CH2/CH2)/CH2-CH2		CCL4
1764M	A	1.61 APP.	CH2R	R5(CH2-CH(OH)/CH2-CH2)		CCL4
1764M	A	1.61 APP.	CH2R	R5(CH(OH)-CH2/CH2-CH2)		CCL4
239M	A	1.61	CH3	C(CL/CH3/CH3)		CCL4
588M	A	1.61	CH3	C(NH/C:CH/CH3)		CDCL3
1043M	A	1.61	CH3	C(NO2/CH3/CH3)		CCL4
1806M	A	1.61	CH3	C(OH/C:N/CH3)		CDCL3
1808M	C	1.61	CH3	R6(C=CH/CH2)		CCL4
1215M	C	1.61	NH	CH2.2-SH/CH2.3-CH3		CDCL3
1215M	C	1.61	SH	CH2.2-NH		CDCL3
2890M	B	1.62 APP.	CH2	CH2-CH2/CH3		CCL4
2501M	B	1.62	CH2	CH2-C(=0)-0/CH2-CH2		DMSO-D6
2780M	C	1.62	CH2	CH2-C(=0)-0/CH2-CH2		CDCL3
2758M	C	1.62	CH2	CH2-C(=0)-0/CH2-CH2		CDCL3
2298M	C	1.62 APP.	CH2	CH2-C(=0)/CH2-CH2		CDCL3
2629M	A	1.62	CH2	CH2-NH/CH2-CH		D20
2890M	B	1.62 APP.	CH2	CH2-0-C(=0)/CH2-CH3		CCL4
2629M	A	1.62	CH2	CH(NH2/C(=0)-0)/CH2-CH2		D20
2369M	A	1.62	CH2R	R6N<CH2-CH2/CH2>		CCL4
2369M	A	1.62	CH2R	R6N<CH2-N(C(=0)-A)/CH2-CH2>		CCL4
99M	A	1.62 APP.	CH2R	R6<CH2-CH=/CH2-CH2>		CCL4
77M	B	1.62	CH3	Q2(H/CH(CH3/CH3)/H)		CCL4
96M	A	1.62	CH3	Q(CH3/CH3/CH3)		CDCL3
1634M	C	1.62	OH	CH2-CH2		CDCL3
2139M	B	1.62 APP.		UNSPECIFIED		CCL4
135M	B	1.63	CH2	CH2-A/CH3		CDCL3
1244M	C	1.63 APP.	CH2	CH2-CH2/CH3		CCL4
2353M	B	1.63	CH2	CH2-C(=0)-N/CH3		D20
2749M	C	1.63	CH2	CH2-C(=0)-OH/CH2.6-C(=0)-0		CDCL3
2252M	C	1.63	CH2	CH2-C(=0)-0/CH2.2-CH3		CDCL3
2254M	C	1.63	CH2	CH2-C(=0)-0/CH2.3-CH3		CCL4
2749M	C	1.63	CH2	CH2-C(=0)-0/CH2.6-C(=0)-OH		CDCL3
466M	B	1.63	CH2	CH2-NH/CH2-NH2		CDCL3
1244M	C	1.63 APP.	CH2	CH2-SO/CH2-CH3		CCL4
1355M	A	1.63	CH2R	R6N<CH2-CH2/CH2-CH2>		CDCL3
1355M	A	1.63	CH2R	R6N<CH2-N/CH2-CH2>		CDCL3
1539M	A	1.63	CH3	C(A/A/CH3)		CDCL3
88M	B	1.63	CH3	Q2(CH2-CH)		CCL4
111M	A	1.63	CH3	Q2(R6(CH-CH2/CH2))		CCL4
2316M	B	1.64	CH2	CH2-C(=0)/CH3		CDCL3
2623M	B	1.64	CH2	CH2-NH2/CH2-CH2		D20
767M	B	1.64	CH2	CH2-NH2/CH3	S	DMSO-D6
2011M	B	1.64	CH2R	R15<CH2-C(=0)/CH2-CH2>		CDCL3
2090M	A	1.64	CH3	CH(0/C(=0)-A)		CDCL3
1632M	C	1.64	OH	CH2-CH2		CDCL3
1741M	B	1.64	OH	CH(CH/CH)		CDCL3
2727M	B	1.65 APP.	CH2.X	CH2.3		CCL4
1478M	A	1.65	CH2R	R700<CH2-0/CH2-CH2>		CCL4
91M	B	1.65- 1.71	CH3	Q1(CH3/C)		CCL4
643M	A	1.65	CH3	Q1(CH3/N)		CDCL3
110M	C	1.65	CH3	R4R6BI(C=CH/CH*)		CCL4
267M	A	1.65 APP.		UNSPECIFIED		CCL4
2143M	C	1.65- 2.70		UNSPECIFIED		CCL4
1248M	B	1.66	CH2	CH2-SO/CH3		CCL4
319M	A	1.66	CH3	CH2-BR		CCL4
1615M	B	1.67	CH	CH2-OH/CH3/CH3		CCL4
2842M	B	1.67	CH2	CH2-C(=0)-0/CH3		CCL4
944M	B	1.67	CH2	CH2-C:N/CH3		CCL4

BOOK NO.	ASSIGN-MENT	CHEM SHIFT - ppm -	PROTON GROUP	ENVIRONMENTAL GROUPS	S	SOLVENT
634M	A	1.67	CH2	CH2-N/CH2-N		CDCL3
2708M	D	1.67	CH2	CH2-O-C(=O)/CH2-CH2		CCL4
1201M	C	1.67	CH2	CH2-SH/CH3		CDCL3
1690M	C	1.67 APP.	CH3	Q1(CH2.3-CH/CH2-OH)		CCL4
1748M	D	1.67	OH	CH(CH2/CH3)		CCL4
130M	C	1.68	CH	CH2.2-C:/CH3/CH3		CCL4
27M	D	1.68	CH	CH2-C/CH3/CH3		CCL4
2946M	B	1.68- 2.82	CHR	R50<(CH3)/C(=O)-O/CH2-CH2>		CCL4
123M	A	1.68	CH2	CH2-C:/CH2-CH2		CDCL3
1643M	A	1.68	CH2	CH2-OH/CH2-NH2		D20
2987M	B	1.68	CH2	CH2-O-C(=O)/CH3		CDCL3
1187M	C	1.68 APP.	CH2	CH2-S/CH2.2-CH3		CCL4
1189M	C	1.68	CH2	CH2-S/CH2.9-CH3		CDCL3
689M	C	1.68 APP.	CH2	CH(AN/CH2.3)/CH2.2-CH3		CCL4
2946M	B	1.68- 2.82	CH2R	R50<CH(CH3)-C(=O)/CH2-O>		CCL4
971M	A	1.68 APP.	CH2R	R6(CH2-CH=/CH2-CH2)		CCL4
971M	A	1.68 APP.	CH2R	R6(CH2-C(C:N)=/CH2-CH2)		CCL4
893M	B	1.68	CH3	Q1(CH3/CH2-CH2)		CDCL3
893M	C	1.68	CH3	Q1(CH3/CH2-CH2)		CDCL3
573M	B	1.68	CH3	Q1(CH3/CH2-NH)		CDCL3
154M	A	1.68	CH3	Q2(CH2-A)		CCL4
2447M	A	1.68	CH3	R5NN(C(A)-NH/C(=O))		DMSO-D6
549M	C	1.68	NH	CH2-CH2/CH2-CH2		CCL4
2738M	A	1.68	SH	CH2.2-C(=O)-O		CDCL3
1219M	B	1.68	SH	CH2-CH		CDCL3
2418M	B	1.69	CH	CH2-NH/CH3/CH3		POLYSOL-D
963M	A	1.69	CH2	CH2-CH2/CH2-CH2		CDCL3
2249M	B	1.69	CH2	CH2-C(=O)-O/CH3		CCL4
2049M	C	1.69	CH2	CH2-C(=O)/CH2-CH2		CCL4
963M	A	1.69	CH2	CH2-C:N/CH2-CH2		CDCL3
958M	B	1.69	CH2	CH2-N/CH2-C:N		CCL4
1653M	C	1.69	CH2	CH2-N/CH2-OH		CDCL3
1327M	C	1.69	CH2	CH2-O-SO3-NA/CH2.2-CH3		D20
1220M	B	1.69	CH2	CH2-SH/CH2-CH2		CCL4
1125M	B	1.69	CH2	CH2-S/CH2-CH2		CDCL3
935M	A	1.69	CH2R	R6R6R6TRI<CH*(CH2/CH2)/CH*(CH2/CH2)>		CDCL3
835M	A	1.69	CH2R	R6R6R6TRI(CH*(CH2/CH2)/CH*(CH2/CH2))	S	D20
175M	A	1.69 APP.	CH2R	R6<CH2-CH=/CH2-CH2>		CCL4
175M	A	1.69 APP.	CH2R	R6<CH2-C(A<C-C(CH3)>)=/CH2-CH2>		CCL4
2210M	A	1.69 APP.	CH2R	R6(CH2-CH=/CH2-CH2)		CCL4
2210M	A	1.69 APP.	CH2R	R6(CH2-C(C(=O)-CL)/CH2-CH2)		CCL4
334M	C	1.69	CH3	CH(BR/CH2)		CCL4
627M	B	1.69	CH3	N(CH2/CH2)		CDCL3
93M	C	1.69	CH3	Q1(CH3/CH2-CH2/H)		CCL4
93M	D	1.69	CH3	Q1(CH3/H/CH2-CH2)		CCL4
69M	B	1.69	CH3	Q2(CH2-CH3/H/H)		CCL4
1686M	A	1.69	CH3	Q2(CH2-OH)		CCL4
1427M	A	1.69	NH2	CH2-CH		CCL4
446M	D	1.70	CH	CH2-CH2/CH3/CH3		CDCL3
1078M	B	1.70- 2.64	CH	CH2-N/CH3/CH3		CDCL3
248M	C	1.70 APP.	CH2	CH2-CL/CH2-CH2		CCL4
2482M	C	1.70	CH2	CH2-C(=O)-OH/CH2.12-CH3		CDCL3
2554M	B	1.70 APP.	CH2	CH2-C(=O)-OH/CH2-CH2		CDCL3
2925M	C	1.70	CH2	CH2-C(=O)-O/CH2-CH2		CCL4
2700M	C	1.70	CH2	CH2-C(=O)-O/CH3		CCL4
2193M	C	1.70	CH2	CH2-C(=O)/CH2-CH2		CDCL3
779M	B	1.70	CH2	CH2-NH2/CH2.4-NH2	S	D20
770M	C	1.70	CH2	CH2-NH2/CH2-CH2	S	D20
2554M	B	1.70 APP.	CH2	CH2-O/CH2-CH2		CDCL3
2999M	B	1.70	CH2	CH2-O/CH3		CDCL3
1097M	A	1.70	CH2	CH2-P/CH2-P		CDCL3
1886M	C	1.70	CH2	C(A/CH3/CH3)/C(CH3/CH3/CH3)		CDCL3
2302M	C	1.70	CH2	C(NH/CH3/CH3)/CH3		CDCL3
79M	B	1.70- 2.24	CH2	Q2(H/CH2-CH3/H)/CH3		CCL4
1460M	B	1.70- 2.40	CH2R	R50<CH2-O/CH2-CH(CH2-O)>		CCL4
1460M	B	1.70- 2.40	CH2R	R50<CH(CH2-O)-O/CH2-CH2>		CCL4
813M	A	1.70	CH2R	R6R6R6TRI(CH*(CH2/CH2)/CH*(CH2/CH2))	S	D20
2026M	A	1.70- 2.50	CH2R	R6<CH2-C(=O)/CH2-C(CL)=>		CCL4
2026M	A	1.70- 2.50	CH2R	R6<C(=O)-CH=/CH2-CH2>		CCL4
323M	B	1.70	CH3	CH(BR/CH2)		CDCL3
321M	A	1.70	CH3	CH(BR/CH3)		CCL4
125M	A	1.70	CH3	C:C-CH3		CCL4
94M	B	1.70	CH3	Q1(CH3/CH2-CH)		CCL4
94M	C	1.70	CH3	Q1(CH3/CH2-CH)		CCL4
70M	C	1.70	CH3	Q2(CH2-CH2)		CCL4
72M	C	1.70	CH3	Q2(CH2-CH2)		CCL4
1782M	B	1.70	CH3	Q2(CH(OH/CH3)/H/H)		CCL4
1223M	F	1.70	SH	C(CH2.3/CH2/CH3)		CDCL3
1223M	F	1.70	SH	C(CH2.3/CH3/CH3)		CDCL3
2027M	C	1.70- 2.60		UNSPECIFIED		CCL4
2202M	B	1.71	CH2	CH2-C(=O)-CL/CH2.6-C(=O)-CL		CCL4

BOOK NO.	ASSIGN-MENT	CHEM SHIFT - ppm -	PROTON GROUP	ENVIRONMENTAL GROUPS	S	SOLVENT
2712M	C	1.71 APP.	CH2	CH2-C(=0)-O/CH2-CH2		CDCL3
2961M	C	1.71 APP.	CH2	CH2-O-C(=0)/CH2-CH2		CCL4
1490M	B	1.71	CH2	CH2-O/CH3		CDCL3
2586M	B	1.71	CH2	CH2-O/CH3		POLYSOL-D
1295M	C	1.71	CH2	CH2-SO3-NA/CH2.4-CH3		D2O
268M	A	1.71	CH2R	R6R6R6TRI<CH*(CH2/CH2)/CH*(CH2/CH2)>		CDCL3
473M	C	1.71	CH2R	R6R6R6TRI<C*(CH2/NH2)-CH2/CH*(CH2/CH2)>		CDCL3
2009M	A	1.71 APP.	CH2R	R7<CH2-CH2/CH2-CH2>		CDCL3
2009M	A	1.71 APP.	CH2R	R7<CH2-C(=0)/CH2-CH2>		CDCL3
327M	C	1.71	CH3	CH(BR/CH2.2)		CCL4
1992M	A	1.71	CH3	CH(BR/C(=0))		CCL4
2216M	A	1.71	CH3	CH(O/C(=0)-CL)		CCL4
126M	B	1.71	CH3	C:C-C		CCL4
91M	C	1.71- 1.65	CH3	Q1(CH3/C)		CCL4
95M	A	1.71	CH3	Q1(Q1/CH3)		CCL4
111M	B	1.71	CH3	R6(C=CH/CH2)		CCL4
119M	C	1.72	CH	:C-CH2		CCL4
687M	C	1.72 APP.	CH2	CH2-AN/CH2-CH2		CCL4
2050M	C	1.72	CH2	CH2-C(=0)-A/CH2.10-CH3		CDCL3
2070M	B	1.72	CH2	CH2-C(=0)-A/CH3		CDCL3
2077M	B	1.72	CH2	CH2-C(=0)-A/CH3		CCL4
2194M	C	1.72	CH2	CH2-C(=0)-CL/CH2.14-CH3		CCL4
2192M	C	1.72	CH2	CH2-C(=0)/CH2-CH2		CCL4
2047M	B	1.72	CH2	CH2-C(=0)/CH3		CCL4
1121M	A	1.72	CH2	CH2-NH2/CH2-S		D2O
2935M	B	1.72	CH2	CH2-O-C(=0)/CH3		CCL4
1033M	B	1.72	CH2	CH2-O-N=O/CH3		CCL4
237M	C	1.72	CH2	CH(CL/CH3)/CH3		CCL4
1684M	B	1.72 APP.	CH2R	R6R6R6TRI<C*((CH2-OH)/CH2/CH2)/CH*(CH2/CH2)>		POLYSOL-D
2359M	A	1.72	CH2R	R6R6R6TRI(CH*(CH2/CH2)/CH*(CH2/CH2))		CDCL3
2364M	B	1.72	CH3	C(=0)-N		CCL4
2366M	C	1.72	CH3	C(=0)-N		CCL4
573M	C	1.72	CH3	Q1(CH3/CH2-NH)		CDCL3
68M	A	1.72	CH3	Q2(CH3/H/H)		CDCL3
1504M	A	1.72	NH2	CH2-A		CDCL3
2025M	A	1.72- 2.58		UNSPECIFIED		CCL4
410M	B	1.73 APP.	CH	CH2-CH2/CH3/CH3		CCL4
409M	B	1.73	CH	CH2-I/CH3/CH3		CCL4
118M	C	1.73	CH	:C-CH2		CCL4
2863M	B	1.73	CH2	CH2-O-C(=0)/CH3		CCL4
410M	B	1.73 APP.	CH2	CH(CH3/CH3)/CH2-I		CCL4
1034M	C	1.73	CH2	CH(O-N=O/CH3)/CH3		CCL4
241M	C	1.73	CH2	C(CL/CH3/CH3)/CH3		CCL4
2818M	D	1.73- 2.30	CH2	C(=0)-O-CH2/CH2-CH2		CCL4
2818M	D	1.73- 2.30	CH2	Q2(CH2-CH2)/CH2-CH2		CCL4
280M	A	1.73	CH3	Q1(CL/CL)		CDCL3
475M	B	1.73	CH3	Q2(CH2-NH2/H/H)		CCL4
87M	A	1.73	CH3	Q2(Q2(CH3))		CCL4
120M	C	1.74	CH	C-CH2		CCL4
247M	C	1.74	CH2	CH2-CL/CH2.13-CL		CCL4
244M	C	1.74	CH2	CH2-CL/CH2-CH2		CCL4
933M	C	1.74	CH2	CH2-N=C=S/CH2-CH2		CCL4
1038M	C	1.74	CH2	CH2-ONO/CH2-CH2		CCL4
2798M	A	1.74	CH2	CH2-O-C(=0)/CH2-Q3		CCL4
1082M	C	1.74	CH2	CH2-O-NO2/CH2.2-CH3		CDCL3
2636M	A	1.74- 2.60	CH2R	R5N<CH2-NH/CH2-CH(C(=0)-OH)>		D2O
2636M	A	1.74- 2.60	CH2R	R5N<CH(C(=0)-OH)-NH/CH2-CH2>		D2O
2013M	A	1.74	CH3	R6N<C((CH3)-NH/CH2>	S	CDCL3
1629M	C	1.74	OH	CH2-CH2		CDCL3
122M	C	1.75	CH	:C-CH2.15		CCL4
2188M	B	1.75	CH2	CH2-C(=0)-CL/CH3		CDCL3
2721M	C	1.75	CH2	CH2-O-C(=0)/CH2-CH2		CDCL3
1080M	B	1.75	CH2	CH2-O-NO2/CH3		CCL4
1329M	B	1.75	CH2	CH2-O/CH3		CCL4
408M	B	1.75	CH2	CH(I/CH3)/CH3		CDCL3
2655M	A	1.75	CH3	C(CL/C(=0)-O/CH2)	S	D2O
1819M	A	1.75	CH3	C(OH/A/C:C)		CDCL3
1250M	A	1.75	CH3	C:C-CH2.2		CDCL3
2453M	A	1.75	CH3	R6NN<C=CH/C(=0)>		DMSO-D6
756M	C	1.75	CH3	R6O<C-O/=CH>		CCL4
2286M	B	1.75 APP.	HCH	CH(C(=0)/A)/CH3		CCL4
2286M	C	1.75 APP.	HCH	CH(C(=0)/A)/CH3		CCL4
328M	B	1.76	CH	CH2-CH2/CH3/CH3		CCL4
243M	C	1.76	CH2	CH2-CL/CH2-CH2		CCL4
892M	C	1.76	CH2	CH2-C(=0)/CH2-CH2		TFA
2173M	B	1.76	CH2	CH2-O/CH3		CCL4
328M	B	1.76	CH2	CH(CH3/CH3)/CH2-CH2		CCL4
1756M	B	1.76	CH2R	R5N<CH2-N(CH2-CH)/CH2-CH2>		CDCL3
361M	A	1.76	CH3	CH(BR/CH2)		CDCL3
2730M	B	1.76	CH3	CH(BR/CH2)		CCL4
1762M	B	1.76		UNSPECIFIED		CCL4

: REPRESENTS TRIPLE BOND. ¬ REPRESENTS AN ARROW AND < AND > REPRESENT BRACKETS.   PAGE 194

BOOK NO.	ASSIGN-MENT	CHEM SHIFT - ppm -	PROTON GROUP	ENVIRONMENTAL GROUPS	S	SOLVENT
235M	B	1.77	CH2	CH2-CL/CH2		CCL4
240M	C	1.77	CH2	CH2-CL/CH2-CH2		CCL4
245M	C	1.77	CH2	CH2-CL/CH2-CH2		CCL4
2199M	A	1.77	CH2	CH2-C(=0)/CH2-CH2		CDCL3
2770M	D	1.77	CH2	CH(C(=0)-0/C(=0)-0)/CH2-CH2		CCL4
2031M	C	1.77	CH2	C(R6/CH3/CH3)/CH3		CDCL3
2303M	A	1.77	CH2R	R6N<CH2-C(=0)/CH2-CH2>		CCL4
325M	A	1.77	CH3	C(BR/CH3/CH3)		CCL4
2852M	B	1.77	CH3	C(C(=0)-0/C(=0)-0/A)		CCL4
1805M	A	1.77	CH3	C(OH/CBR3/CH3)		CDCL3
2383M	A	1.77		UNSPECIFIED		CDCL3
1205M	C	1.78- 1.92	CH	CH2-CH2/CH3/CH3		CCL4
2206M	B	1.78	CH2	CH2-C(=0)/CH2-CH2		CCL4
777M	A	1.78	CH2	CH2-NH2/CH2-CH2	S	D2O
1824M	A	1.78	CH2	CH2-OH/CH2-OH		D2O
1205M	C	1.78- 1.92	CH2	CH(CH3/CH3)/CH2-SH		CCL4
60M	C	1.78- 2.47	CH2	Q3(H/H/H)/CH2-CH2		CCL4
636M	A	1.78	CH2R	R5N<CH2-N(CH3)/CH2-CH2>		CDCL3
421M	A	1.78	CH2R	R5<CH2-CH(I)/CH2-CH2>		CCL4
358M	A	1.78	CH3	CH(BR/CH2)		CCL4
95M	B	1.78	CH3	Q1(Q1/CH3)		CCL4
1506M	A	1.78	CH3	Q2(A(C-CH-CH-C(0-CH3))/CH3		CCL4
572M	B	1.78	CH3	Q2(CH2-NH)		CDCL3
640M	A	1.78	NHR	R6NN(CH2-CH2-N)		CDCL3
1462M	A	1.78	NHR	R6NO(CH2-CH2/CH2-CH2)		CCL4
1798M	D	1.78	OH	C(CH2.3/CH3/CH3)		CCL4
737M	C	1.79	CH	CH2-N/CH2-CH2/CH2-CH3		CCL4
1111M	B	1.79	CH	CH2-S/CH3/CH3		CCL4
117M	C	1.79	CH	:C-CH2		CCL4
121M	C	1.79	CH	:C-CH2.8		CCL4
2939M	C	1.79	CH2	CH2-0-C(=0)/CH2-CH2		CDCL3
2542M	A	1.79	CH2	CH(C(=0)-OH/A)/CH2-CH		DMSO
196M	A	1.79	CH2R	R6A(CH2-C*/CH2-CH2)		CDCL3
2000M	A	1.79	CH2R	R6(CH2-CH2/CH2-CH2)		CCL4
2000M	A	1.79	CH2R	R6(CH2-C(=0)/CH2-CH2)		CCL4
550M	C	1.79	NH	CH2-CH2/CH2-CH2		CDCL3
1818M	B	1.79	OH	C(A/CH2/CH2)		CDCL3
1662M	A	1.79	SH	CH2-CH		CDCL3
2532M	C	1.79- 2.47		UNSPECIFIED		CCL4
2741M	D	1.80 APP.	CH	CH2-CH/CH3/CH3		CCL4
1383M	C	1.80	CH	CH2-0/CH3/CH3		CCL4
88M	C	1.80- 2.40	CH	Q3/CH2-Q2/CH3		CCL4
341M	C	1.80	CH2	CH2-BR/CH2-CH2		CDCL3
2498M	A	1.80	CH2	CH2-C(=0)-0/CH2-C(=0)-0		DMSO-D6
407M	C	1.80 APP.	CH2	CH2-I/CH2-CH3		CCL4
481M	B	1.80	CH2	CH2-NH2/CH2-A		CDCL3
2909M	C	1.80	CH2	CH2-0-C(=0)/CH2-CH2		CDCL3
2900M	B	1.80	CH2	CH2-0-C(=0)/CH3		CDCL3
1581M	C	1.80	CH2	CH2-0/CH2-CH2		CDCL3
2174M	C	1.80	CH2	CH2-0/CH2-CH2		CCL4
331M	D	1.80 APP.	CH2	CH(BR/CH2.2)/CH3		CCL4
331M	D	1.80 APP.	CH2	CH(BR/CH2)/CH2-CH3		CCL4
1429M	A	1.80	CH2	CH(0/0)/CH(0/0)		CCL4
1688M	B	1.80- 2.45	CH2	OH/CH2-Q2		CCL4
71M	D	1.80- 2.25	CH2	Q2(CH2-CH3/CH2)/CH2-CH2		CCL4
88M	C	1.80- 2.40	CH2	Q2(CH3)/CH(Q3/CH3)		CCL4
2262M	D	1.80- 2.60	CH2R	R5R60BI<CH*(C/C(=0))/CH2-C*(CH3)>		CDCL3
2262M	D	1.80- 2.60	CH2R	R5R60BI<C*(C(=0)/C/CH3)/CH2-CH*>		CDCL3
1688M	B	1.80- 2.45	CH3	CH2-Q2		CCL4
960M	A	1.80	NH	CH2-CH2/CH2-CH2		CDCL3
484M	A	1.80	NH2	CH2-A		CDCL3
439M	C	1.80- 2.40	NH2	CH2-CH2		CCL4
439M	C	1.80- 2.40	NH2	CH2-CH2		CCL4
2816M	C	1.80- 2.40		UNSPECIFIED		CCL4
110M	D	1.80- 2.60		UNSPECIFIED		CCL4
139M	B	1.81	CH	CH2-A/CH3/CH3		CDCL3
43M	C	1.81 APP.	CHR	R5<(CH3)/CH2-CH2/CH2-CH2>		CCL4
412M	C	1.81	CH2	CH2-I/CH2-CH2		CCL4
831M	C	1.81	CH2	CH2-N(+)/CH2-CH2	S	CDCL3
1369M	A	1.81	CH2	CH2-N/CH2-OH		CDCL3
1253M	B	1.81	CH2	CH2-SO2/CH3		CCL4
1012M	C	1.81	CH2	CH2-S/CH2.9-CH3		CCL4
334M	D	1.81 APP.	CH2	CH(BR/CH3)/CH2-CH2		CCL4
1455M	A	1.81	CH2R	R50(CH2-0/CH2-CH2)		CDCL3
2469M	B	1.81	CH3	QN(CH(CH3/CH3)/NH-C(=0))		CDCL3
1712M	A	1.81	CH3	Q1(A/H/CH2-OH)		CDCL3
894M	A	1.81	CH3	Q2(H/Q2/H)		POLYSOL-D
1227M	A	1.81	SH	CH2-A		CDCL3
1246M	B	1.82- 2.80	CH	CH2-S(=0)/CH3/CH3		CCL4
1312M	C	1.82	CH2	CH2-AN/CH2-CH2	S	CDCL3
322M	C	1.82	CH2	CH2-BR/CH2-CH3		CCL4

BOOK NO.	ASSIGN-MENT	CHEM SHIFT - ppm -	PROTON GROUP	ENVIRONMENTAL GROUPS	S	SOLVENT
414M	C	1.82	CH2	CH2-I/CH2.13-CH3		CCL4
411M	C	1.82	CH2	CH2-I/CH2-CH2		CCL4
1702M	A	1.82	CH2	CH2-OH/CH2-A		CCL4
1011M	C	1.82	CH2	CH2-S/CH2-CH2		CCL4
323M	C	1.82	CH2	CH(BR/CH3)/CH3		CDCL3
2744M	C	1.82	CH2	CH(C(=O)-O/C(=O)-CH3)/CH3		CCL4
2305M	C	1.82	CH2	C(NH/CH3/CH3)/C(CH3/CH3/CH3)		CDCL3
1818M	C	1.82	CH2	C(OH/A/CH2)/CH3		CDCL3
1246M	B	1.82- 2.80	CH2	S(=O)-CH2/CH(CH3/CH3)		CCL4
1448M	B	1.82 APP.	CH2R	R6R30BI<CH*-O/CH2-CH2>		CCL4
2267M	A	1.82	CH2R	R6R5O<CH2-C*=/CH2-CH2>		CDCL3
2365M	C	1.82	CH3	C(=O)-N		CDCL3
2470M	C	1.82	CH3	QN(CH2-CH2/NH-C(=O))		CDCL3
2671M	A	1.82	CH3	Q2(H/H/Q2)		D2O
73M	A	1.82	CH3	Q2(Q3/H/H)		CCL4
442M	C	1.82	NH2	CH2-CH		CDCL3
413M	C	1.83	CH2	CH2-I/CH2.9-CH3		CCL4
839M	C	1.83	CH2	CH2-N(+)/CH2-CH2	S	CDCL3
1010M	C	1.83	CH2	CH2-S/CH2-CH2 _		CCL4
601M	A	1.83	CH2R	R6NA<CH2-NH/CH2-C*>		CDCL3
611M	A	1.83	CH2R	R6R5NA<CH2-C*=/CH2-CH2>		CDCL3
1694M	A	1.83	CH3	C:C		CCL4
1217M	B	1.83	NH	R6/CH2.2-SH		CDCL3
1217M	B	1.83	SH	CH2.2-NH		CDCL3
338M	C	1.84	CH2	CH2-BR/CH2-CH2		CCL4
810M	C	1.84	CH2	CH2-N/CH2.5-CH3		CDCL3
104M	C	1.84	CH2R	R6<C(CH3)=C(CH3)/CH2-CH2>		CCL4
404M	A	1.84	CH3	CH2-I		CCL4
353M	A	1.84	CH3	CH(BR)-HCH		CCL4
332M	C	1.85	CH2	CH2-BR/CH2-CH2		CCL4
326M	C	1.85	CH2	CH2-BR/CH2-CH2		CCL4
2775M	C	1.85	CH2	CH2-C(=O)-O/CH2-C(=O)-O		CCL4
405M	B	1.85	CH2	CH2-I/CH3		CCL4
2137M	C	1.85	CH2	CH(C(=O)-CH3/C(=O)-CH3)/CH3		CDCL3
2771M	B	1.85	CH2	C(C(=O)-O/C(=O)-O/CH2)/CH3		CCL4
2277M	C	1.85- 2.25	CH2	C(=O)-HNH/CH2-CH2		DMSO-D6
97M	A	1.85	CH2R	R5<CH2-CH=/CH2-CH=>		CCL4
2004M	C	1.85- 2.60	CH2R	R6<C(=O)-CH2/HCH-CH(C(CH3/CH3/CH3))>		CDCL3
2028M	A	1.85	CH3	R6<C=C(CL)/C(=O)>		CCL4
2004M	C	1.85- 2.60	HCHR	R6<CH(C(CH3/CH3/CH3))-HCH/CH2-C(=O)>		CDCL3
1662M	B	1.85	SH	CH(CH2/CH2)		CDCL3
339M	C	1.86	CH2	CH2-BR/CH2.13-CH3		CCL4
335M	C	1.86	CH2	CH2-BR/CH2-CH2		CCL4
219M	C	1.86	CH2	CH2-F/CH2.3-CH3		CCL4
2363M	A	1.86	CH3	C(=O)-N		CDCL3
1559M	A	1.86	CH3	Q2(H/A<C-CH-C(O-CH3)-C(O-CH3)>/H)		CDCL3
1767M	C	1.86	HCHR	R6<CH(OH)-CH(CH3)/CH2-CH2>		CDCL3
1219M	C	1.86	SH	CH(CH2/CH3)		CDCL3
333M	C	1.87	CH2	CH2-BR/CH2-CH2		CCL4
336M	C	1.87	CH2	CH2-BR/CH2-CH2		CCL4
337M	C	1.87	CH2	CH2-BR/CH2-CH2		CCL4
2218M	A	1.87	CH2	CH2-C(=O)/CH2-A		CDCL3
865M	A	1.87 APP.	CH2R	R6(CH2-C(=N-OH)/CH2-CH2)		CDCL3
784M	A	1.87	CH3	CH(NH2/A)	S	TFA
74M	A	1.87	CH3	Q2(Q2(CH3/H/H)/H/H)		CCL4
1820M	C	1.87	OH	C(A/A/CH2.7)		CCL4
340M	C	1.88	CH2	CH2-BR/CH2.14-CH3		CDCL3
330M	C	1.88	CH2	CH2-BR/CH2-CH2		CCL4
220M	C	1.88	CH2	CH2-F/CH2-CH2		CCL4
420M	B	1.88	CH2	CH2-I/CH2-CH2		CCL4
262M	B	1.88	CH2	CH(CL/CH2)/CH3		CCL4
2615M	B	1.88	CH2	CH(NH2/C(=O)-O)/CH3		D2O
102M	B	1.88	CH2R	R6<CH=C(CH3)/CH2-CH2>		CCL4
102M	B	1.88	CH2R	R6<C(CH3)=CH/CH2-CH2>		CCL4
260M	A	1.88	CH3	CH(CL/C)		CCL4
2146M	A	1.88	CH3	C(=O)-Q1		CCL4
854M	C	1.88	CH3	QN(CH2-CH2/OH)		CDCL3
857M	C	1.88	CH3	QN(CH2-CH2/OH)		CDCL3
1259M	B	1.88	CH3	R5S<C=CH/CH2>		CDCL3
2812M	B	1.89	CH	CH2-O-C(=O)/CH3/CH3		CCL4
116M	B	1.89	CH	:C-C		CCL4
362M	B	1.89 APP.	CH2	CH2-BR/CH2-CH2		CCL4
320M	B	1.89	CH2	CH2-BR/CH3		CCL4
1502M	A	1.89	CH2	CH2-CL/CH2.2-O		CCL4
1502M	A	1.89	CH2	CH2-O/CH2.2-CL		CCL4
2543M	C	1.89	CH2	C(A/CH2/CH2)/CH2-CH3		DMSO-D6
2042M	A	1.89	CH3	C(=O)-Q1		CDCL3
853M	B	1.89	CH3	QN(CH2-CH3/OH)		CDCL3
855M	B	1.89	CH3	QN(CH2-CH/OH)		CDCL3
2018M	A	1.89	CH3	Q2(H/C(=O)-CH3/H)		CCL4
2814M	B	1.89	CH3	Q2(H/C(=O)-O-CH2/H)		CCL4

BOOK NO.	ASSIGN-MENT	CHEM SHIFT - ppm -	PROTON GROUP	ENVIRONMENTAL GROUPS	S	SOLVENT
2517M	A	1.89	CH3	Q2(H/C(=O)-O/H)		CDCL3
2530M	A	1.89	CH3	Q2(Q2-C(=O)-OH)		CDCL3
1800M	D	1.89	OH	C(CH2.5/CH3/CH3)		CDCL3
1774M	B	1.89	OH	R6<CH-CH(A)/HCH>		CDCL3
103M	C	1.89		UNSPECIFIED		CCL4
1971M	C	1.90- 2.37	CH	CH2-C(=O)/CH3/CH3		CCL4
1405M	B	1.90	CH	CH2-O/CH3/CH3		CCL4
67M	B	1.90- 2.50	CH	Q3/CH2-Q3/CH3		CCL4
1774M	C	1.90- 2.70	CHR	R6<(A)/CH(OH)-HCH/CH2-CH2>		CDCL3
2849M	A	1.90	CH2	CH2-C(=O)-O/CH2-A		CCL4
739M	B	1.90	CH2	CH2-R5NNA/CH3		POLYSOL-D
1971M	C	1.90- 2.37	CH2	C(=O)-CH3/CH(CH3/CH3)		CCL4
1787M	D	1.90- 2.40	CH2	C:C/CH2-CH3		CCL4
1787M	D	1.90- 2.40	CH2	C:C/CH(OH/CH2)		CCL4
67M	B	1.90- 2.50	CH2	Q3/CH(Q3/CH3)		CCL4
1756M	C	1.90- 2.90	CH2	R5N<N-CH2-CH2>/CH(OH/CH3)		CDCL3
1756M	C	1.90- 2.90	CH2R	R5N<N(CH2-CH)-CH2/CH2-CH2>		CDCL3
1130M	A	1.90	CH2R	R5S<CH2-S/CH2-CH2>		CCL4
911M	A	1.90	CH2R	R6R6BI<C*(N=C=O/CH2/CH2)/CH2-C*(N=C(O)>		CDCL3
100M	D	1.90 APP.	CH2R	P6<CH(C(CH2/CH3/CH3))-CH2/CH=CH>		CCL4
100M	D	1.90 APP.	CH2R	R6<CH=CH/CH2-CH(C(CH2/CH3/CH3))>		CCL4
1776M	C	1.90 APP.	CH2R	R6<C(A/A)-CH(OH)/CH2-CH2>		CDCL3
105M	B	1.90- 2.50	CH2R	R6(CH=C(R6)/CH2-CH2)		CCL4
105M	B	1.90- 2.50	CH2R	R6(C(R6)=CH/CH2-CH2)		CCL4
2525M	A	1.90	CH3	CH2.4-Q2		CCL4
408M	C	1.90	CH3	CH(I/CH2)		CDCL3
2309M	A	1.90	CH3	C(=O)-NH		CDCL3
2301M	A	1.90	CH3	C(=O)-NH		POLYSOL-D
2310M	B	1.90	CH3	C(=O)-NH		CDCL3
2685M	C	1.90	CH3	C(=O)-OH		CDCL3
2833M	A	1.90	CH3	C(=O)-O-CH2		CCL4
856M	C	1.90	CH3	QN(CH2-CH2/OH)		CDCL3
888M	A	1.90	CH3	QN(NH-A/A)		CDCL3
2020M	A	1.90	CH3	Q1(CH3/C(=O)-CH3)		CDCL3
2743M	C	1.90	CH3	Q1(OH/C(=O)-O-CH2.3)		CCL4
2811M	B	1.90	CH3	Q2(C(=O)-O-CH/H/H)		CCL4
1158M	A	1.90	CH3	S-CH2		CCL4
1774M	C	1.90- 2.70	HCHR	R6<CH(OH)-CH(A)/CH2-CH2>		CDCL3
641M	B	1.90	NHR	R6NN<CH2-CH(CH3)/CH2-CH2>		CDCL3
1577M	A	1.90	SH	CH2-R50		CDCL3
238M	B	1.91	CH	CH2-CL/CH3/CH3		CCL4
1656M	A	1.91	CH2	CH2-NH2/CH2-OH	S	D20
406M	A	1.91	CH3	CH(I/CH3)		CCL4
2621M	C	1.91	CH3	C(=O)-NH		POLYSOL-D
2686M	C	1.91	CH3	C(=O)-OH		CDCL3
2810M	B	1.91	CH3	Q2(C(=O)-O-CH2/H/H)		CCL4
1757M	C	1.91		UNSPECIFIED		CDCL3
1346M	B	1.92	CH	CH2-N/CH3/CH3		CDCL3
1185M	B	1.92	CH	CH2-S/CH3/CH3		CCL4
263M	A	1.92	CH2	CH2-CL/CH2-CH2		CCL4
2302M	D	1.92- 2.61	CH2	CH2-C(=O)/CH2-C(=O)		CDCL3
1164M	A	1.92	CH2	CH2-S/CH2-A		CCL4
2302M	D	1.92- 2.61	CH2	C(=O)-NH/CH2-CH2		CDCL3
1948M	A	1.92	CH2R	R5A(CH2-C*/CH2-C*)		CDCL3
2371M	A	1.92	CH2R	R6NA<CH2-N(C(=O)-H)/CH2-C*>		CDCL3
2260M	B	1.92	CH2R	R6O(C(CH3/CH3)-C(=O)/CH2-C(=O))		CDCL3
2620M	B	1.92	CH3	C(=O)-NH		DMSO-D6
2358M	C	1.92	CH3	Q1(OH/C(=O)-N		CDCL3
2812M	C	1.92	CH3	Q2(C(=O)-O-CH2/H/H)		CCL4
2813M	C	1.92	CH3	Q2(C(=O)-O-CH2/H/H)		CCL4
2208M	A	1.92	CH3	Q2(Q2(C(=O)-CL))		CCL4
2950M	A	1.92- 3.02	HCHR	R50<CH(C(=O)-CH3)-C(=O)/CH2-O>		CCL4
324M	B	1.93	CH	CH2-BR/CH3/CH3		CCL4
124M	B	1.93	CH	:C-CH2		CDCL3
2733M	D	1.93	CH2	CH(BR/C(=O)-O)/CH2.6-CH3		CCL4
1450M	B	1.93 APP.	CH2R	R7R3O<CH*-O/CH2-CH2>		CCL4
2403M	A	1.93	CH3	C(=O)-NH		CDCL3
2839M	A	1.93	CH3	C(=O)-O-CH2		CCL4
2319M	A	1.93	CH3	C(=O)-Q1		DMSO-D6
1684M	C	1.93	CH*R	R6R6R6TRI<CH2-C*(CH2-OH)/CH2-CH*/CH2-CH*>		POLYSOL-D
1815M	D	1.93	OH	C(C:C/CH2/CH3)		CDCL3
418M	A	1.94	CH2	CH2-I/CH2-CH2		CCL4
2627M	A	1.94 APP.	CH2	CH(NH/C(=O)-OH)/CH2-S		POLYSOL-D
813M	B	1.94	CH2R	R6R6R6TRI(C*(N(CH3/CH3)/CH2/CH2)/CH*(CH2/CH2))	S	D20
813M	B	1.94	CH2R	R6R6R6TRI(C*(N(CH3/CH3))-CH2/CH*(CH2/CH2))	S	D20
2729M	B	1.94	CH3	C(BR/C(=O)-O/CH3)		CDCL3
2696M	C	1.94	CH3	C(=O)-O-CH2		CCL4
2143M	A	1.94	CH3	C(=R5/OH)		CCL4
943M	A	1.94	CH3	C:N		CCL4
2627M	A	1.94 APP.	CH3	S-CH2.2		POLYSOL-D
576M	A	1.94	NHR	R6N<CH2-CH=/CH2-CH2>		CDCL3

BOOK NO.	ASSIGN-MENT	CHEM SHIFT - ppm -	PROTON GROUP	ENVIRONMENTAL GROUPS	S	SOLVENT
2846M	A	1.94	Q2	C(=0)-0-CH2/H/H		CDCL3
1815M	E	1.95 APP.	CH	CH2-C/CH3/CH3		CDCL3
2372M	A	1.95	CHR	R6NA<CH2-N(C(=0)-CH3)/CH2-C*>		CDCL3
93M	E	1.95	CH2	Q1(H/CH3/CH3)/CH2-CH3		CCL4
85M	C	1.95	CH2	Q2(CH2)/CH2-CH2		CCL4
83M	D	1.95 APP.	CH2	Q2(CH3)/CH2-CH2		CCL4
2819M	C	1.95 APP.	CH2	Q2(H/CH2.7-CH3/H)/CH2.6-C(=0)-0		CDCL3
2819M	C	1.95 APP.	CH2	Q2(H/CH2.7-C(=0)-0/H)/CH2.7-CH3		CDCL3
2822M	C	1.95	CH3	C(=0)-0-CH		CCL4
2697M	C	1.95	CH3	C(=0)-0-CH2		CCL4
2713M	B	1.95	CH3	C(=0)-0-R8		CCL4
1063M	C	1.95 APP.	CH3	QN(CH2.2-CH3/NH-A)		POLYSOL-D
2519M	A	1.95	CH3	Q1(CH3/H/C(=0)-OH)		CCL4
83M	E	1.95 APP.	Q2	CH2-CH2/CH3		CCL4
83M	E	1.95 APP.	Q2	CH3/CH2-CH2		CCL4
2822M	D	1.95- 2.42		UNSPECIFIED		CCL4
1979M	B	1.96- 2.34	CH	CH2-C(=0)/CH3/CH3		CCL4
1695M	A	1.96	CH	:C-CH-CH2		CCL4
2796M	A	1.96	CH2	CH(C(=0)-0-CH3/C(=0)-0-CH3)/CH2-CH		CDCL3
1979M	B	1.96- 2.34	CH2	C(=0)-CH2/CH(CH3/CH3)		CCL4
2817M	D	1.96	CH2	C(=0)-0-CH2/CH2-CH2		CCL4
1690M	D	1.96	CH2	Q1(CH3/CH2-0H)/CH2.2-CH		CCL4
86M	C	1.96	CH2	Q2(CH2-CH2)/CH2-CH2		CDCL3
82M	D	1.96	CH2	Q2(H/C(CH3/CH3/CH3)/H)/CH2-CH3		CCL4
2832M	A	1.96	CH3	C(=0)-0-CH2		CCL4
2798M	B	1.96	CH3	C(=0)-0-CH2		CCL4
2695M	C	1.96	CH3	C(=0)-0-CH2		CCL4
2699M	B	1.97	CH	CH2-C(=0)-0/CH3/CH3		CCL4
947M	B	1.97	CH	CH2-C:N/CH3/CH3		CCL4
2807M	B	1.97	CH	CH2-0-C(=0)/CH3/CH3		CCL4
2651M	C	1.97	CH	C(=0)-0-CA/CH2.3-CH3/CH2-CH3		POLYSOL-D
1637M	A	1.97	CH2	CH2-CL/CH2-0H		CCL4
1480M	B	1.97	CH2	CH(0/A)/CH2-C:N		CDCL3
92M	E	1.97	CH2	Q1(CH3/H/CH3)/CH2-CH3		CCL4
2527M	C	1.97	CH2	Q2(H/CH2.2-C(=0)-OH/H)/CH2.6-CH3		CCL4
84M	C	1.97 APP.	CH2	Q2(H/CH2-CH2/H)/CH2-CH2		CCL4
84M	C	1.97 APP.	CH2	Q2(H/CH2-CH2/H)/CH2-CH3		CCL4
2966M	C	1.97	CH2	Q2(H/CH2-CH2)/CH2-CH2		CCL4
1689M	C	1.97	CH2	Q2(H/CH2-CH2)/CH2-CH2		CCL4
99M	B	1.97	CH2R	R6<CH=CH/CH2-CH2>		CCL4
2348M	B	1.97	CH3	C(=0)-N		CCL4
2755M	B	1.97	CH3	C(=0)-0-CH2		CCL4
2800M	C	1.97	CH3	C(=0)-0-CH2		CCL4
2027M	B	1.97	CH3	R6<C=CH/CH2>		CCL4
473M	D	1.97	CH*R	R6R6R6TRI<CH2-C*(CH2-NH2)/CH2-CH*/CH2-CH*>		CDCL3
1627M	D	1.97	OH	CH2-CH		CCL4
1035M	B	1.98	CH	CH2-0-N=/OCH3/CH3		CCL4
855M	C	1.98- 2.40	CH	CH2-QN/CH3/CH3		CDCL3
123M	B	1.98	CH	:C-CH2		CDCL3
843M	C	1.98	CH2	CH2-AN/CH2-CH2	S	DMSO-D6
361M	B	1.98	CH2	CH(BR/CH3)/CH2-CH		CDCL3
855M	C	1.98- 2.40	CH2	QN(CH3/OH)/CH(CH3/CH3)		CDCL3
75M	C	1.98	CH2	Q2(CH3)/CH3		CCL4
2529M	C	1.98	CH2	Q2(H/CH2-CH2/H)/CH2-CH2		CDCL3
58M	D	1.98	CH2	Q3/CH(CH2/CH3)		CCL4
2145M	A	1.98	CH2R	R6(CH2-C(=0)/CH2-C(OH)=)		CCL4
2349M	C	1.98	CH3	C(=0)-N		CCL4
2275M	A	1.98	CH3	C(=0)-NH2		D20
2717M	C	1.98	CH3	C(=0)-0-CH2		CCL4
2360M	A	1.98	CH3	C(=0)-R6NO		CCL4
2146M	B	1.98	CH3	Q1(OH/C(=0)-CH2)		CCL4
967M	A	1.98	CH3	Q2(C:N/H/H)		CCL4
1096M	B	1.99	CH2	P(A/A)/CH3		CDCL3
2257M	C	1.99	CH2	Q2(CH2-R50)/CH2.7-CH3		CDCL3
72M	D	1.99	CH2	Q2(CH3)/CH2-CH2		CCL4
2525M	C	1.99	CH2	Q2(H/CH2.2-C(=0)-OH/H)/CH2.3-CH3		CCL4
2338M	A	1.99	CH3	A(C-CH-C(CH3)-C(NH-C(=0)))		CDCL3
2297M	C	1.99	CH3	C(=0)-NH		D20
2687M	A	1.99	CH3	C(=0)-0H	S	D20
2762M	C	1.99	CH3	C(=0)-0-C		CCL4
2841M	A	1.99	CH3	C(=0)-0-CH2		CCL4
167M	A	1.99	CH3	C:C		CDCL3
2160M	A	1.99	CH3	Q1(C(=0)-H/A)		CCL4
2954M	A	1.99	CH3	R50<C-0/=CH>		CCL4
2021M	C	2.00 APP.	CH	Q2(H/C(=0)-CH3/H)/CH2-CH3/CH2-CH3		CCL4
1996M	B	2.00	CHR	R3((C(=0)-R3)-CH2/CH2)		CCL4
2560M	A	2.00	CH2	CH2-C(=0)-0H/CH2-A	S	D20
1041M	B	2.00	CH2	CH2-NO2/CH3		CCL4
849M	C	2.00- 2.60	CH2	QN(H/OH)/CH2.4-CH3		CDCL3
70M	D	2.00	CH2	Q2(CH3)/CH2-CH2		CCL4
2526M	C	2.00	CH2	Q2(H/CH2.2-C(=0)-0H/H)/CH2.4-CH3		CCL4

: REPRESENTS TRIPLE BOND, ¬ REPRESENTS AN ARROW AND < AND > REPRESENT BRACKETS.

BOOK NO.	ASSIGN-MENT	CHEM SHIFT - ppm -	PROTON GROUP	ENVIRONMENTAL GROUPS	S	SOLVENT
2528M	C	2.00	CH2	Q2(H/H/CH2-CH2)/CH2-CH2		CCL4
65M	C	2.00	CH2	Q3(H/H/H)/CH2-CH2		CCL4
63M	C	2.00	CH2	Q3/CH2-CH2		CCL4
1473M	A	2.00- 2.70	CH2	R6NO<N-CH2/CH2>/R600<CH-O/CH2>		CDCL3
2637M	A	2.00- 2.80	CH2R	R5N(CH(OH)-CH2/CH(C(=O)-OH)-NH)		D20
2129M	D	2.00- 2.50	CH2R	R5R6R6R6(C(=O)-C*(CH3)/CH2-CH*)		CDCL3
1473M	A	2.00- 2.70	CH2R	R6NO<N(CH2-R600)-CH2/CH2-O>		CDCL3
2268M	A	2.00- 2.90	CH2R	R6R50<CH*-C(=O)/CH=CH>		CDCL3
2129M	D	2.00- 2.50	CH2R	R6R6R6R5(CH*-CH*/CH=C*)		CDCL3
184M	B	2.00- 2.50	CH2R	R6<CH=C(A<C-CH-CH-C(CH3)>)/CH2-CH2>		CCL4
146M	B	2.00- 2.50	CH2R	R6<CH=C(A)/CH2-CH2>		CCL4
184M	B	2.00- 2.50	CH2R	R6<C(A<C-CH-CH-C(CH3)>)=CH/CH2-CH2>		CCL4
146M	B	2.00- 2.50	CH2R	R6<C(A)=CH/CH2-CH2>		CCL4
2535M	B	2.00- 2.50	CH2R	R6(C(C(=0)-OH)=CH/CH2-CH2)		CCL4
497M	A	2.00	CH3	A<C-C(NH2)-CH-C(CH3)>		CCL4
595M	A	2.00	CH3	A<C-C(NH-CH2)>		CDCL3
495M	B	2.00	CH3	A(C-C(CH3)-C(NH2))		CCL4
495M	A	2.00	CH3	A(C-C(NH2)/C(CH3))		CCL4
2036M	A	2.00	CH3	C(=0)-CH2		CCL4
2931M	A	2.00	CH3	C(=0)-0-CH2		CCL4
2694M	A	2.00	CH3	C(=0)-0-CH3		CCL4
756M	D	2.00	CH3	R60<C-0/=C(C(=0)-0-CH2)>		CCL4
1127M	B	2.00	CH3	S-CH2		CCL4
1801M	E	2.00	OH	C(CH2.2/CH2/CH3)		CCL4
2764M	A	2.00- 2.20		UNSPECIFIED		CDCL3
1794M	B	2.00- 3.70		UNSPECIFIED		POLYSOL-D
1998M	C	2.00- 3.10		UNSPECIFIED		CDCL3
2786M	C	2.01	CHR	R3<(C(=0)-0-CH2)/CH(C(=0)-0-CH2)-CH2>		CCL4
1281M	C	2.01	CH2	CH2-S02/CH2-CH3		CCL4
1016M	A	2.01	CH2	CH2-S/CH2-CH2		CDCL3
2487M	C	2.01	CH2	CH(BR/C(=0)-OH)/CH2-CH2		CCL4
69M	C	2.01	CH2	Q2(CH3/H/H)/CH3		CCL4
2800M	D	2.01 APP.	CH2	Q2(H/CH2-0-C(=0)/H)/CH2-CH3		CCL4
2823M	C	2.01 APP.	CH2	Q2(H/H/CH2-CH2)/CH2-CH2		CCL4
2028M	B	2.01 APP.	CH2R	R6<CH2-C(=0)/CH2-C(CL)=>		CCL4
1971M	B	2.01	CH3	C(=0)-CH2		CCL4
2752M	A	2.01	CH3	C(=0)-0-CH2.2		CCL4
864M	A	2.01	CH3	QN(QN(OH/CH3)/OH)		POLYSOL-D
2032M	A	2.01	CH3	R6<C=C(CH3)/C(=0)>		CDCL3
1116M	C	2.01	CH3	S-CH2.11		CCL4
192M	A	2.01- 2.28		UNSPECIFIED		CCL4
2620M	C	2.02	CH	CH(NH/C(=0)-0)/CH3/CH3		DMSO-D6
2521M	C	2.02	CH2	Q2(CH2-C(=0)-OH)/CH2-CH3		CCL4
195M	A	2.02	CH2R	R5A<CH2-C*/CH2-C*>		CDCL3
1999M	A	2.02 APP.	CH2R	R5<CH2-C(=0)/CH2-CH2>		CCL4
1999M	A	2.02 APP.	CH2R	R5<C(=0)-CH2/CH2-CH2>		CCL4
935M	B	2.02	CH2R	R6R6R6TRI<C*(QN(=S)/CH2/CH2)/CH*(CH2/CH2)>		CDCL3
2359M	B	2.02	CH2R	R6R6R6TRI(C*(C(=0)-N/CH2/CH2)/CH*(CH2/CH2))		CDCL3
1132M	A	2.02	CH2R	R6SS<CH2-S/CH2-S>		POLYSOL-D
2144M	B	2.02	CH2R	R6(C(OH)=CH/C(CH3/CH3)-CH2)		CDCL3
2144M	B	2.02	CH2R	R6(C(=0)-CH=/C(CH3/CH3)-CH2)		CDCL3
496M	A	2.02	CH3	A(C-C(NH2)/CH-C(CH3))		CCL4
1372M	A	2.02	CH3	A(C-C(NH-S02)-C(CH3))		CDCL3
1044M	A	2.02	CH3	CH(CL/NO2)		CCL4
2337M	A	2.02	CH3	C(=0)-NH		DMSO-D6
2211M	B	2.02	CH3	C(=0)-NH		DMSO-D6
676M	A	2.02	CH3	R5N<C=CH/N(A)>		CDCL3
935M	B	2.02	CH*	R6R6R6TRI<CH2-C*(QN(=S))/CH2-CH*/CH2-CH*>		CDCL3
2359M	B	2.02	CH*R	R6R6R6TRI(CH2-C*(C(=0)-N)/CH2-CH*/CH2-CH*)		CDCL3
1749M	C	2.02	OH	CH(CH2.2/CH2.2)		CCL4
78M	B	2.03	CH2	Q2(H/H/CH2-CH3)		CDCL3
59M	C	2.03	CH2	Q3/CH2-CH2		CCL4
2108M	A	2.03	CH2R	R5A(CH2-C*/CH2-C*)		CDCL3
421M	B	2.03	CH2R	R5<CH(I)-CH2/CH2-CH2>		CCL4
536M	A	2.03	CH3	A<C-C(NH2)-CH-C(NH2)>		CDCL3
2336M	A	2.03	CH3	C(=0)-NH		POLYSOL-D
2834M	B	2.03	CH3	C(=0)-0-CH		CDCL3
566M	A	2.03	NHR	R6NN<CH2-CH2/CH2-CH2>		CDCL3
2259M	B	2.04- 3.15	CHR	R60<(CH3)/CH2-C(=0)-0/CH2-C(=0)>		CDCL3
359M	A	2.04	CH2	CH2-RR/CH2-CH2		CCL4
2732M	D	2.04	CH2	CH(BR/C(=0)-0)/CH2.2-CH3		CDCL3
2484M	B	2.04	CH2	CH(CL/C(=0)-OH)/CH3		CDCL3
57M	C	2.04	CH2	Q3(H/H/H)/CH2-CH2		CCL4
62M	C	2.04	CH2	Q3/CH2-CH2		CCL4
2259M	B	2.04- 3.15	CH2R	R60<C(=0)-0-C(=0)/CH(CH3)-CH2>		CDCL3
528M	A	2.04	CH3	A<C-C(NH2)/CH-C(I)>		POLYSOL-D
488M	A	2.04	CH3	A(C-C(NH2))		CCL4
1107M	B	2.04	CH3	S-CH2		CCL4
2012M	A	2.04		UNSPECIFIED		CDCL3
2918M	B	2.05	CH	CH2-0-C(=0)/CH3/CH3		C3D60
274M	C	2.05	CH2	Q2(CH2-CL)/C(CH2/CH3/CH3)		CDCL3

BOOK NO.	ASSIGN-MENT	CHEM SHIFT - ppm -	PROTON GROUP	ENVIRONMENTAL GROUPS	S	SOLVENT
61M	C	2.05	CH2	Q3/CH2-CH2		CCL4
2321M	B	2.05	CH3	A(C-C(NH-C(=O)))		CDCL3
1997M	B	2.05	CH3	C(=O)-CH2		CCL4
1968M	B	2.05	CH3	C(=O)-CH2		CCL4
2321M	A	2.05	CH3	C(=O)-NH		CDCL3
2323M	A	2.05	CH3	C(=O)-NH		DMSO-D6
2455M	A	2.05	CH3	R6NN<C=C(CH3)/C(=O)>		TFA
1633M	C	2.05	OH	CH2-CH2		CDCL3
1743M	D	2.05	OH	CH(CH/CH2)		CCL4
55M	D	2.06	CH	Q3/CH2-CH3/CH3		CCL4
2486M	C	2.06	CH2	CH(BR/C(=O)-OH)/CH2-CH3		CDCL3
2798M	C	2.06	CH2	Q3(H/H/H)/CH2-CH2		CCL4
1973M	B	2.06	CH3	C(=O)-CH2		CCL4
1974M	C	2.06	CH3	C(=O)-CH2		CCL4
1976M	C	2.06	CH3	C(=O)-CH2		CCL4
2368M	A	2.06	CH3	C(=O)-N		CDCL3
2322M	A	2.06	CH3	C(=O)-NH		CDCL3
2472M	A	2.06	CH3	C(=O)-OH		CCL4
2947M	C	2.07- 2.66	CH2R	R50<C(=O)-O/CH2-CH(CH2-CH2)>		CCL4
2114M	A	2.07	CH2R	R6A<CH2-C*/CH2-C(=O)>		CCL4
835M	B	2.07	CH2R	R6R6R6TRI(C*(N(+)(CH3/CH3/CH3))-CH2/CH*(CH2/CH2))	S	D20
835M	B	2.07	CH2R	R6R6R6TRI(C*(N(+)(CH3/CH3/CH3)/CH2/CH2)/CH*(CH2/CH2))	S	D20
2339M	A	2.07	CH3	A<C-CH-C(NH-C(=O))-C(CH3)>		CDCL3
502M	A	2.07	CH3	A<C-C(NH2)-C(CH3)/CH-C(CH3)>		CCL4
251M	A	2.07	CH3	CH(CL/CL)		CCL4
1969M	D	2.07	CH3	C(=O)-CH2.3		CCL4
2324M	B	2.07	CH3	C(=O)-NH		CDCL3
2754M	B	2.07 APP.	CH3	C(=O)-O-CH		CCL4
2754M	B	2.07 APP.	CH3	C(=O)-O-HCH		CCL4
1199M	B	2.07	CH3	SH		CDCL3
2286M	B	2.07 APP.	HCH	CH(C(=O)/A)/CH3		CCL4
2286M	C	2.07 APP.	HCH	CH(C(=O)/A)/CH3		CCL4
2789M	B	2.07	NH	CH2-C(=O)-O/CH2-C(=O)-O		CCL4
1660M	C	2.07	OH	CH2.2-S		CDCL3
2650M	C	2.07	OH	C(=O)-NA/CH2.3-CH3/CH2-CH3		D20
2838M	C	2.08	CH	CH2-C(=O)-O/CH3/CH3		CCL4
2864M	B	2.08	CH	CH2-O-C(=O)/CH3/CH3		CDCL3
2838M	B	2.08	CH2	C(=O)-O-CH2/CH(CH3/CH3)		CCL4
161M	C	2.08	CH2	Q1(A/A)/CH2.5-CH3		CCL4
64M	C	2.08	CH2	Q3/CH2-CH2		CCL4
1029M	A	2.08	CH2R	R5N<CH2-N(NO)/CH2-CH2>		D20
576M	B	2.08 APP.	CH2R	R6N<CH=CH/CH2-NH>		CDCL3
1461M	A	2.08	CH2R	R6O(CH=CH/CH2-O)		CCL4
422M	B	2.08 APP.	CH2R	R6<CH(I)-CH2/CH2-CH2>		CDCL3
2058M	A	2.08	CH3	A<C-C(CH3)-C(C(=O)-CH3)-C(CH3)/CH-C(CH3)>		CDCL3
500M	B	2.08	CH3	A<C-C(NH2)-C(CH2-CH3)>		CDCL3
515M	A	2.08	CH3	A(C-C(NH2)/CH-C(CL))		CCL4
2627M	B	2.08	CH3	C(=O)-NH		POLYSOL-D
2756M	A	2.08	CH3	C(=O)-O-CH2		CDCL3
2141M	A	2.08	CH3	Q1(OH/C(=O)-R50)		CCL4
2030M	A	2.08	CH3	R6<C=CH/C(=O)>		CDCL3
568M	C	2.08- 3.09	HCHR	R6NN(NH-HCH/CH(CH3)-NH)		CDCL3
603M	A	2.08	NHR	R6NA(CH2-C*/CH2-CH2)		CCL4
955M	A	2.09	CH2	CH2-CL/CH2-C:N		CCL4
1280M	B	2.09	CH2	CH2-SO2/CH3		CCL4
2670M	B	2.09	CH2	C(=O)-O-K/CH2-CH2	S	D20
2715M	C	2.09 APP.	CH2	C(=O)-O-R6/CH(CH3/CH3)		CCL4
119M	D	2.09 APP.	CH2	C:CH/CH2-CH2		CCL4
129M	C	2.09	CH2	C:C/CH2.3-CH3		CCL4
160M	C	2.09	CH2	Q1(A/A)/CH2.2-CH3		CCL4
2670M	B	2.09	CH2	Q3(H/H/H)/CH2-CH2	S	D20
2640M	A	2.09	CH3	A<C-C(CH3)-CH-C(CH3)/CH-C(NH2)>		CCL4
2338M	C	2.09	CH3	A(C-C(NH-C(=O))/CH-C(CH3))		CDCL3
2019M	A	2.09	CH3	C(=O)-CH2		CCL4
2039M	A	2.09	CH3	C(=O)-CH2		CCL4
2335M	A	2.09	CH3	C(=O)-NH		DMSO-D6
2338M	B	2.09	CH3	C(=O)-NH		CDCL3
1075M	A	2.09	CH3	QN(CH3/NH-A)		CDCL3
1075M	B	2.09	CH3	QN(CH3/NH-A)		CDCL3
2265M	A	2.09	CH3	R50(C=C(CH3)/C(=O))		CDCL3
569M	C	2.09	CH*R	R6NR6(CH2-CH2/CH2-CH2)		CDCL3
1208M	C	2.09	SH	CH2-CH2		CDCL3
2837M	B	2.10	CH	CH2-C(=O)-O/CH3/CH3		CCL4
1640M	A	2.10	CH2	CH2-BR/CH2-OH		CDCL3
2837M	B	2.10	CH2	C(=O)-O-CH2/CH(CH3/CH3)		CCL4
120M	D	2.10	CH2	C:CH/CH2-CH2		CCL4
127M	D	2.10	CH2	C:C-CH2.2/CH2.3-CH3		CCL4
127M	D	2.10	CH2	C:C-CH2.4/CH2-CH3		CCL4
128M	D	2.10 APP.	CH2	C:C/CH2.5-CH3		CCL4
130M	D	2.10	CH2	C:C/CH2-CH		CCL4
128M	D	2.10 APP.	CH2	C:C/CH3		CCL4

BOOK NO.	ASSIGN-MENT	CHEM SHIFT - ppm -	PROTON GROUP	ENVIRONMENTAL GROUPS	S	SOLVENT
465M	D	2.10- 2.55	CH2	N(CH2/CH2)/CH2-CH2		CCL4
162M	C	2.10	CH2	Q1(A/A)/CH2.8-CH3		CDCL3
2206M	C	2.10	CH2	Q3/CH2-CH2		CCL4
2374M	A	2.10	CH2R	R5N(CH2-N(A)/CH2-C(=O))		CDCL3
2115M	B	2.10	CH2R	R6A<CH2-C*/CH2-C(=O)>		CDCL3
1683M	B	2.10- 2.70	CH2R	R6N(NH-CH2/CH(CH2-OH)-CH2)		CDCL3
2130M	F	2.10- 2.55	CH2R	R6R6R6R5(C(=O)-CH=/CH2-C*(CH3))		CDCL3
858M	B	2.10- 2.65	CH2R	R8(C(=NOH)-CH2/CH2-CH2)		CDCL3
537M	A	2.10	CH3	A(C-C(NH2)-C(CH3)/CH-C(NH2))		CDCL3
589M	A	2.10	CH3	A(C-C(NH-CH3))		CDCL3
2747M	C	2.10	CH3	C(=O)-CH2.2		CCL4
2330M	A	2.10	CH3	C(=O)-NH		DMSO-D6
2331M	A	2.10	CH3	C(=O)-NH		DMSO-D6
2325M	B	2.10	CH3	C(=O)-NH		CDCL3
157M	A	2.10	CH3	Q2(A/H/H)		CCL4
637M	B	2.10	CH3	R6N<N-CH2/CH2>		CCL4
1121M	B	2.10	CH3	S-CH2.3		D20
465M	D	2.10- 2.55	NH2	CH2-CH2		CCL4
1670M	C	2.10	OH	CH2.2-O		CDCL3
1791M	A	2.10	OH	CH(A/CH2)		CDCL3
1834M	B	2.10	OH	C(C/CH3/CH3)		CDCL3
970M	A	2.10 APP.	UNSPECIFIED			CCL4
2038M	A	2.11	CH2	A(C-CH-CH-C(OH))/CH2-C(=O)		CDCL3
379M	A	2.11	CH2	CH(CH2/A)/CH2-BR		CCL4
2038M	A	2.11	CH2	C(=O)-CH3/CH2-A		CDCL3
2413M	C	2.11	CH2	C(=O)-NH/CH2-CH3		DMSO-D6
122M	D	2.11	CH2	C:CH/CH2.14-CH3		CCL4
118M	D	2.11	CH2	C:CH/CH2-CH2		CCL4
131M	C	2.11 APP.	CH2	C:C/CH2.3-C:		CCL4
131M	C	2.11 APP.	CH2	C:C/CH3		CCL4
66M	A	2.11	CH2	Q3(H/H/H)/CH2-Q3		CCL4
1371M	A	2.11	CH3	A<C-C(NH-SO2)>		DMSO-D6
511M	A	2.11	CH3	A(C-C(F)/CH-C(NH2))		CCL4
2746M	A	2.11	CH3	C(=O)-CH2		CCL4
1967M	A	2.11	CH3	C(=O)-CH3		CDCL3
2327M	A	2.11	CH3	C(=O)-NH		CDCL3
2327M	A	2.11	CH3	C(=O)-NH		CDCL3
2332M	A	2.11	CH3	C(=O)-NH		CDCL3
2340M	A	2.11	CH3	C(=O)-NH		CDCL3
2334M	A	2.11	CH3	C(=O)-NH		DMSO-D6
2718M	A	2.11	CH3	C(=O)-O-CH2		CDCL3
1998M	B	2.11 APP.	CH3	C(=O)-R5R5BI		CDCL3
2843M	C	2.12 APP.	CH2	C(=O)-O-CH2/CH(CH3/CH3)		CCL4
2699M	C	2.12	CH2	C(=O)-O-CH3/CH(CH3/CH3)		CCL4
117M	D	2.12	CH2	C:CH/CH2-CH3		CCL4
1699M	C	2.12	CH2	C:C/CH2.4-CH3		CCL4
874M	C	2.12	CH2	QN(NH-A)/CH2-CH3		CCL4
2179M	A	2.12	CH2R	R5A<CH2-C*/CH2-C*>		CCL4
2377M	A	2.12	CH2R	R6N<CH2-C(=O)/CH2-C(=O)>		TFA
106M	B	2.12	CH2R	R8(CH=CH-CH2/CH2.5)		CCL4
1966M	B	2.12	CH3	A<C-C(NH-CH2)/CH-C(CH3)>		CDCL3
1918M	A	2.12	CH3	A<C-C(OH)-C(CH2-Q3)>		CCL4
1914M	A	2.12	CH3	A(C-C(CH3)-CH-C(OH))		CCL4
1914M	A	2.12	CH3	A(C-C(CH3)/CH-C(OH))		CCL4
2744M	D	2.12	CH3	C(=O)-CH		CCL4
1995M	A	2.12	CH3	C(=O)-CH2		CCL4
2924M	A	2.12	CH3	C(=O)-O-A		CCL4
2018M	B	2.12	CH3	C(=O)-Q2		CCL4
633M	B	2.12	CH3	N(CH2/CH2)		CCL4
632M	B	2.12	CH3	N(CH2/CH3)		CCL4
1134M	A	2.12	CH3	R5NS<C=N/S>		CCL4
1214M	A	2.12	SH	CH(HCH/HCH)		CCL4
1651M	B	2.12- 2.89	UNSPECIFIED			CCL4
2652M	C	2.13	CH2	C(=O)-O-NO/CH2CH2		CCL4
2029M	B	2.13	CH2R	R6<C(=O)-CH=/C(CH3/CH3)-CH2>		CCL4
2061M	B	2.13	CH3	A<C-CH-C(CH3)-C(C(=O)-C)>		CCL4
2339M	B	2.13	CH3	A<C-C(NH-C(=O))-CH-C(CH3)>		CDCL3
1551M	A	2.13	CH3	A<C-C(O-CH3)/C(CH3)>		CDCL3
191M	A	2.13	CH3	A(C-C(CH3)-C(CH3)/C(CH3))		CCL4
1989M	D	2.13	CH3	C(=O)-CH2.11		CDCL3
2339M	C	2.13	CH3	C(=O)-NH		CDCL3
2840M	A	2.13	CH3	C(=O)-O-CH2		CDCL3
2147M	A	2.13	CH3	Q1(OH/C(=O)-A)		CDCL3
2195M	A	2.14	CH2	CH2-CL/CH2-C(=O)		CCL4
2623M	C	2.14	CH2	C(=O)-OH/CH2-CH2		D20
673M	A	2.14 APP.	CH2R	R6N<CH=CH/CH2-N(CH3)>		CCL4
112M	A	2.14	CH2R	R6<CH=CH/CH2-CH=>		CDCL3
596M	A	2.14	CH3	A<C-CH-CH-C(NH-CH2)>		CCL4
1913M	A	2.14	CH3	A<C-C(OH)/C(CH3)>		CDCL3
2716M	A	2.14	CH3	C(=O)-O-CH2		CDCL3
2021M	D	2.14	CH3	C(=O)-Q2		CCL4

BOOK NO.	ASSIGN-MENT	CHEM SHIFT - ppm -	PROTON GROUP	ENVIRONMENTAL GROUPS	S	SOLVENT
644M	A	2.14	CH3	N(CH2/CH3)		CCL4
610M	A	2.14	CH3	N(CH2/CH3)		DMSO-D6
1812M	B	2.14	OH	C(Q3/CH3/CH3)		CCL4
1820M	D	2.15	CH2	C(OH/A/A)/CH2.6-CH3		CCL4
2622M	B	2.15	CH2	C(=O)-OH/CH2-CH2		D2O
121M	D	2.15	CH2	C:CH/CH2.7-CH3		CCL4
1698M	C	2.15	CH2	C:C/CH2.3-CH3		CCL4
175M	B	2.15 APP.	CH2R	R6<CH=C(A<C-C(CH3)>)/CH2-CH2>		CCL4
175M	B	2.15 APP.	CH2R	R6<C(A<C-C(CH3)>)=CH/CH2-CH2>		CCL4
2119M	A	2.15	CH3	AA<C-C(=O)-C*/CH-C(=O)-C*>		CDCL3
499M	A	2.15	CH3	A<C-CH-C(NH2)/CH-C(CH3)>		CCL4
2640M	B	2.15	CH3	A<C-C(CH3)-CH-C(NH2)/CH-C(CH3)>		CCL4
2640M	B	2.15	CH3	A<C-C(NH2)-CH-C(CH3)/CH-C(CH3)>		CCL4
2974M	A	2.15	CH3	A<C-C(NH-C(=O))/CH-C(BR)>		CDCL3
2321M	B	2.15	CH3	A(C-C(NH-C(=O)))		CDCL3
2321M	A	2.15	CH3	C(=O)-NH		CDCL3
2020M	B	2.15 APP.	CH3	C(=O)-Q1		CDCL3
2022M	B	2.15	CH3	C(=O)-R6		CCL4
2020M	B	2.15 APP.	CH3	Q1(CH3/C(=O)-CH3)		CDCL3
1154M	A	2.15	CH3	R5NS<C=CH/N=>	S	D2O
711M	B	2.15	CH3	R5N(N-CH2/CH2)		CCL4
1837M	D	2.15	OH	C(CH2/CH2/CH3)		CDCL3
2815M	C	2.16	CH2	Q2(H/C(=O)-O-CH3/H)/CH2.5-CH3		CCL4
2799M	C	2.16	CH2	Q2(H/C(=O)-O-CH3/H)/CH2-CH3		CCL4
268M	B	2.16 APP.	CH2R	R6R6R6TRI<C*((CL)/CH2/CH2)/CH*(CH2/CH2)>		CDCL3
502M	B	2.16	CH3	A<C-CH-C(CH3)-C(NH2)/CH-C(CH3)>		CCL4
496M	B	2.16	CH3	A<C-CH-C(CH3)-C(NH2)>		CCL4
386M	A	2.16	CH3	A(C-C(CH3)-CH-C(BR)/CH-C(CH3))		CDCL3
386M	A	2.16	CH3	A(C-C(CH3)-CH-C(CH3)/CH-C(BR))		CDCL3
2329M	A	2.16	CH3	C(=O)-NH		CDCL3
268M	B	2.16 APP.	CH*R	R6R6R6TRI<CH2-C*(CL)/CH2-CH*/CH2-CH*>		CDCL3
2140M	C	2.16 APP.		UNSPECIFIED		CCL4
1754M	B	2.17	CH2	N(CH3/CH3)/CH(OH/CH3)		CDCL3
497M	B	2.17	CH3	A<C-CH-C(NH2)-C(CH3)>		CCL4
1926M	A	2.17	CH3	A<C-CH-C(OH)-C(OH)>		CDCL3
1876M	A	2.17	CH3	A<C-C(OH)>		CCL4
521M	A	2.17	CH3	A(C-CH-C(BR)-C(NH2))		CDCL3
1239M	A	2.17	CH3	A(C-CH-C(SH)-C(SH))		CDCL3
193M	A	2.17	CH3	A(C-C(CH3)-CH-C(CH3)/CH-C(CH3))		CDCL3
2494M	A	2.17	CH3	C(=O)-CH2		CDCL3
2326M	A	2.17	CH3	C(=O)-NH		CDCL3
2328M	A	2.17	CH3	C(=O)-NH		CDCL3
2706M	C	2.18	CH2	C(=O)-O-CH2/CH(CH3/CH3)		CDCL3
2700M	D	2.18	CH2	C(=O)-O-CH/CH2-CH3		CCL4
695M	A	2.18	CH3	AN<C-CH-C(CH3)-N/CH-C(CH3)>		CCL4
490M	A	2.18	CH3	A<C-CH-CH-C(NH2)>		CCL4
503M	B	2.18	CH3	A<C-CH-C(CH2-CH3)-C(NH2)/CH-C(CH2-CH3)>		CCL4
430M	A	2.18	CH3	A<C-CH-C(I)-C(CH3)>		CCL4
1498M	B	2.18	CH3	A<C-C(O-CH2)>		CCL4
1558M	A	2.18	CH3	A<C-C(O-CH3)/CH-C(O-CH3)>		CCL4
1877M	A	2.18	CH3	A(C-CH-C(OH))		CCL4
1915M	A	2.18	CH3	A(C-CH-C(OH)/CH-C(CH3))		CCL4
1916M	A	2.18	CH3	A(C-C(OH)-C(CH3))		CCL4
1494M	A	2.18	CH3	A(C-C(O-CH3))		CCL4
2928M	A	2.18	CH3	C(=O)-O-A		CCL4
1075M	A	2.18	CH3	QN(CH3/NH-A)		CDCL3
1075M	B	2.18	CH3	QN(CH3/NH-A)		CDCL3
1755M	D	2.18	HCH	N(CH2/CH2)/CH(OH/CH3)		CCL4
1740M	C	2.18	OH	CH(CH2.2/CH2.2)		CDCL3
77M	C	2.19	CH	Q2(H/CH3/H)/CH3/CH3		CCL4
785M	B	2.19	CH2	CH(NH2/CH3)/CH2-A	S	TFA
2356M	D	2.19	CH2	C(=O)-N/CH2-CH2		CCL4
2022M	C	2.19	CH2R	R6<CH=C(C(=O)-CH3)/CH2-CH2>		CCL4
2022M	C	2.19	CH2R	R6<C(C(=O)-CH3)=CH/CH2-CH2>		CCL4
187M	A	2.19	CH3	A<C(CH3)/C(CH3)>		CDCL3
660M	A	2.19	CH3	A<C-CH-CH-C(N(CH3/CH3))>		CCL4
1552M	A	2.19	CH3	A<C-CH-C(CH3)-C(O-CH3)>		CDCL3
498M	A	2.19	CH3	A<C-C(CH3)-CH-C(NH2)>		CDCL3
498M	A	2.19	CH3	A<C-C(CH3)/CH-C(NH2)>		CDCL3
2058M	B	2.19	CH3	A<C-C(C(=O)-CH3)-C(CH3)-C(CH3)/C(CH3)>		CDCL3
1227M	B	2.19	CH3	A(C-C(CH3)-CH-C(CH2-SH)/CH-C(CH2-SH))		CDCL3
191M	B	2.19	CH3	A(C-C(CH3)-CH-C(CH3)-C(CH3))		CCL4
532M	A	2.19	CH3	A(C-C(NH2)/CH-C(A(C-CH-C(CH3)-C(NH2))))		CDCL3
480M	A	2.19	CH3	C(NH2/A/CH3)		CCL4
2742M	A	2.19	CH3	C(=O)-CH2		CDCL3
2743M	D	2.19	CH3	C(=O)-CH2		CCL4
2930M	A	2.19	CH3	C(=O)-O-AA		CDCL3
628M	A	2.19	CH3	N(CH2/CH3)		D2O
625M	B	2.19	CH3	N(CH/CH3)		D2O
2519M	B	2.19	CH3	Q1(CH3/H/C(=O)-OH)		CCL4
278M	A	2.19	CH3	Q1(CL/CH2-CL)		CCL4

BOOK NO.	ASSIGN-MENT	CHEM SHIFT - ppm -	PROTON GROUP	ENVIRONMENTAL GROUPS	S	SOLVENT
2264M	A	2.19	CH3	R50(C=CH/C(=0))		
450M	E	2.19 APP.	NH2	CH(CH2/CH3)		CCL4
1802M	E	2.19	OH	C(CH2/CH2/CH3)		CCL4
188M	A	2.19 APP.		UNSPECIFIED		CCL4
2731M	D	2.20	CH	CH(BR/C(=0)-0)/CH3/CH3		CCL4
81M	B	2.20 APP.	CH	Q2(H/CH(CH3/CH3)/H)/CH3/CH3		CDCL3
471M	D	2.20- 3.10	CHR	R6<(NH2)/CH2-CH2/CH2-CH2>		CCL4
2632M	A	2.20	CH2	CH(NH2/C(=0)-OH)/CH2-C(=0)		CDCL3
891M	C	2.20	CH2	C(=0)-NH/CH2-CH2		D20
2298M	D	2.20	CH2	C(=0)-NH/CH2-CH2		CDCL3
2355M	C	2.20	CH2	C(=0)-N/CH2-CH2		CDCL3
2501M	C	2.20	CH2	C(=0)-OH/CH2-CH2		CCL4
2518M	A	2.20- 2.70	CH2	C(=0)-OH/CH2-Q3		DMSO-D6
2709M	D	2.20	CH2	C(=0)-0-CH2.2/CH2.4-CH3		CDCL3
2714M	C	2.20	CH2	C(=0)-0-R6/CH2-CH3		CCL4
124M	C	2.20	CH2	C:CH/CH2-CH2		CCL4
1697M	C	2.20	CH2	C:C/CH2.4-CH3		CDCL3
459M	C	2.20- 2.65	CH2	NH2/CH(NH2/CH3)		CCL4
2470M	D	2.20	CH2	ON(CH3/NH-C(=0))/CH2-CH2		CDCL3
2524M	C	2.20	CH2	Q2(C(=0)-OH)/CH2-CH2		CDCL3
2817M	E	2.20	CH2	Q2(H/H/CH2-CH2)/CH2-CH2		CCL4
2518M	A	2.20- 2.70	CH2	Q3/CH2-C(=0)-OH		CCL4
2948M	A	2.20- 3.27	CH2R	R50(CH(BR)-C(=0)/CH2-0)		CDCL3
755M	B	2.20- 3.30	CH2R	R6NN<N(CH3)-CH2/CH2-N(NH2)>		CCL4
755M	B	2.20- 3.00	CH2R	R6NN<N(NH2)-CH2/CH2-N(CH3)>		CDCL3
1463M	B	2.20- 3.20	CH2R	R6NO<NH-CH2/CH(CH3)-0>		CDCL3
2303M	B	2.20	CH2R	R6N<CH2-NH/CH2-CH2>		CDCL3
2303M	B	2.20	CH2R	R6N<C(=0)-NH/CH2-CH2>		CCL4
691M	A	2.20	CH3	AN(C-CH-N-C(CH3))		CCL4
1878M	A	2.20	CH3	A<C-CH-CH-C(OH)>		CDCL3
1923M	A	2.20	CH3	A<C-C(OH)/CH-C(S-CH3)>		CDCL3
593M	B	2.20	CH3	A(C-CH-CH-C(NH-CH2))		CDCL3
1230M	A	2.20	CH3	A(C-CH-CH-C(SH))		CDCL3
489M	A	2.20	CH3	A(C-CH-C(NH2))		CDCL3
2322M	B	2.20	CH3	A(C-CH-C(NH-C(=0)))		CCL4
174M	A	2.20	CH3	A(C-C(CH3))		CDCL3
258M	A	2.20	CH3	C(CL/CL/CH3)		CCL4
2141M	B	2.20	CH3	C(=0)-CH2		CCL4
2341M	A	2.20	CH3	C(=0)-NH		CCL4
2247M	A	2.20	CH3	C(=0)-0-C(=0)		CDCL3
2017M	A	2.20	CH3	C(=0)-Q3		CCL4
403M	A	2.20	CH3	I		CCL4
1649M	B	2.20	CH3	N(CH2/CH3)		CDCL3
634M	B	2.20	CH3	N(CH2/CH3)		CCL4
1648M	B	2.20	CH3	N(CH/CH3)		CDCL3
627M	C	2.20	NH2	CH2-CH2		D20
2137M	D	2.20 APP.		UNSPECIFIED		CDCL3
344M	B	2.21	CH	CH2-BR/CH2-CL/CH3		CDCL3
2139M	C	2.21	CH2	C(=0)-CH2/CH2-CH3		CCL4
2278M	D	2.21	CH2	C(=0)-NH2/CH2-CH2		CDCL3
2279M	D	2.21	CH2	C(=0)-NH2/CH2-CH2		CDCL3
2299M	D	2.21	CH2	C(=0)-NH/CH2-CH2		CDCL3
2499M	B	2.21	CH2	C(=0)-OH/CH2-CH2		DMSO-D6
2849M	B	2.21	CH2	C(=0)-0-CH3/CH2.2-A		CCL4
2707M	C	2.21	CH2	C(=0)-0-CH3/CH2-CH2		CCL4
2139M	C	2.21	CH2	C(=0)-Q1/CH2-CH3		CCL4
947M	C	2.21	CH2	C:N/CH(CH3/CH3)		CCL4
624M	C	2.21 APP.	CH2	N(CH3/CH3)/CH2.20-CH3		CDCL3
1097M	B	2.21	CH2	P(A/A)/CH2-CH2		CDCL3
857M	D	2.21	CH2	QN(CH3/OH)/CH2-CH2		CDCL3
2520M	C	2.21	CH2	Q2(H/C(=0)-OH/H)/CH2-CH3		CCL4
1784M	C	2.21	CH2	Q3/CH(OH/CH2.2)		CDCL3
2003M	C	2.21 APP.	CH2R	R6(C(=0)-CH2/CH2-CH(CH3))		CCL4
1952M	A	2.21	CH3	AA(C-C(OH)-C*/CH-CH-C*)		CDCL3
2423M	A	2.21	CH3	A<C-CH-CH-C(NH-C(=0))>		DMSO-D6
1162M	A	2.21	CH3	A<C-CH-CH-C(S-CH2)>		POLYSOL-D
1966M	C	2.21	CH3	A<C-CH-C(CH3)-C(NH-CH2)>		CDCL3
2932M	A	2.21	CH3	A<C-CH-C(0-C(=0)-CH2)>		CCL4
1925M	A	2.21	CH3	A<C-C(OH)-C(OH)>		CDCL3
2397M	A	2.21	CH3	A<C-C(R5NA<N-C(=0)/C(=0)>)>		CDCL3
591M	A	2.21	CH3	A(C-CH-CH-C(NH-CH3))		CDCL3
663M	B	2.21	CH3	A(C-CH-CH-C(N(CH2/CH2)))		CDCL3
1099M	A	2.21	CH3	A(C-CH-CH-C(P(A/A)))		CDCL3
1936M	B	2.21	CH3	A(C-CH-C(CH2-A)-C(OH)/CH-C(CH2-A))		CDCL3
387M	A	2.21	CH3	A(C-CH-C(CH3)-C(BR)/CH-C(CH3))		CCL4
763M	A	2.21	CH3	A(C-CH-C(CH3)-C(N(N/CH3))/CH-C(CH3))		CDCL3
1936M	B	2.21	CH3	A(C-CH-C(C(CH3/CH3/CH3))-C(OH)/CH-C(CH2-A))		CDCL3
1917M	B	2.21	CH3	A(C-CH-C(OH)-C(CH(CH3/CH3)))		CDCL3
495M	B	2.21	CH3	A(C-C(CH3)-C(NH2))		CCL4
1077M	A	2.21	CH3	A(C-C(NHT)-C(CH3)/CH-C(NO2))		CDCL3
495M	A	2.21	CH3	A(C-C(NH2)/C(CH3))		CCL4

BOOK NO.	ASSIGN-MENT	CHEM SHIFT - ppm -	PROTON GROUP	ENVIRONMENTAL GROUPS	S	SOLVENT
1994M	B	2.21	CH3	C(=0)-CH		CDCL3
2745M	D	2.21	CH3	C(=0)-CH		CDCL3
2319M	B	2.21	CH3	C(=0)-CH2		DMSO-D6
2974M	B	2.21	CH3	C(=0)-NH		CDCL3
2143M	B	2.21	CH3	C(=0)-R5		CCL4
2372M	B	2.21	CH3	C(=0)-R6NA		CDCL3
624M	C	2.21 APP.	CH3	N(CH2.21/CH3)		CDCL3
1406M	A	2.21	CH3	N(CH2.2/CH3)		CCL4
623M	C	2.21	CH3	N(CH2.7/CH2.7)		CDCL3
622M	C	2.21	CH3	N(CH2.9-CH3/CH3)		CDCL3
642M	A	2.21	CH3	N(CH2/CH3)		CDCL3
609M	A	2.21	CH3	R5NA<C=C(CH3)/C*>		CDCL3
673M	B	2.21	CH3	R6N<N-CH2/CH2>		CCL4
2619M	C	2.22	CH	CH(NH2/C(=0)-OH)/CH3/CH3		D20
2001M	C	2.22 APP.	CHR	R6<(CH3)/C(=0)-CH2/CH2-CH2>		CCL4
2502M	B	2.22	CH2	C(=0)-OH/CH2-CH2		DMSO-D6
2705M	C	2.22	CH2	C(=0)-O-CH2.4		CCL4
2835M	B	2.22	CH2	C(=0)-O-CH2/CH3		CCL4
123M	C	2.22	CH2	C:CH/CH2-CH2 ¬		CDCL3
853M	C	2.22	CH2	QN(CH3/OH)/CH3		CDCL3
2460M	B	2.22	CH2	R6NN<C(CH2-CH3)-C(=0)/C(=0)>/CH3		TFA
98M	C	2.22	CH2R	R5<C(CH3)=C(CH3)/CH2-CH2>		CCL4
2001M	C	2.22 APP.	CH2R	R6<C(=0)-CH(CH3)/CH2-CH2>		CCL4
971M	B	2.22 APP.	CH2R	R6(CH=C(C:N)/CH2-CH2)		CCL4
971M	B	2.22 APP.	CH2R	R6(C(C:N)=CH/CH2-CH2)		CCL4
1708M	A	2.22	CH3	A<C-CH-CH-C(S-CH2.2)>		CCL4
1932M	A	2.22	CH3	A<C-CH-C(OH)-C(CH2-Q3)/CH-C(CH3)>		CDCL3
1932M	A	2.22	CH3	A<C-C(CH2-Q3)-C(OH)/CH-C(CH3)>		CDCL3
664M	B	2.22	CH3	A<C-C(N(CH2/CH2))-CH-C(CH3)>		CCL4
2323M	B	2.22	CH3	A(C-CH-CH-C(NH-C(=0)))		DMSO-D6
224M	A	2.22	CH3	A(C-C(F))		CCL4
2338M	C	2.22	CH3	A(C-C(NH-C(=0))/CH-C(CH3))		CDCL3
2338M	B	2.22	CH3	C(=0)-NH		CDCL3
2929M	A	2.22	CH3	C(=0)-O-A		CDCL3
1703M	A	2.22	CH3	N(CH2/CH2)		CDCL3
677M	A	2.22	CH3	N(CH2/CH3)		CDCL3
630M	A	2.22	CH3	N(CH2/CH3)		CDCL3
1574M	A	2.22	CH3	R50<C-O/=CH>		CCL4
1137M	A	2.22	CH3	R5S<C=CH/CH=>		CCL4
813M	C	2.22	CH*R	R6R6R6TRI(CH2-C*(N(CH3/CH3))/CH2-CH*/CH2-CH*)	S	D20
1753M	B	2.22	NH2	CH(CH/CH3)		CDCL3
1753M	B	2.22	OH	CH(CH/CH3)		CDCL3
2489M	B	2.22	SH	CH(C(=0)-OH/CH3)		CCL4
194M	A	2.22		UNSPECIFIED		CDCL3
2276M	B	2.23	CH2	C(=0)-NH2/CH3		CDCL3
2710M	C	2.23	CH2	C(=0)-O-CH3/CH2-CH2		CCL4
2781M	C	2.23	CH2	C(=0)-O-CH3/CH2-CH2		CCL4
2727M	C	2.23	CH2	C(=0)-O-CH/CH2-CH2		CCL4
1696M	B	2.23	CH2	C:C/CH3		CCL4
622M	D	2.23	CH2	N(CH3/CH3)/CH2.8-CH3		CDCL3
637M	C	2.23 APP.	CH2R	R6N<N(CH3)-CH2/CH2-CH2>		CCL4
189M	A	2.23	CH3	A<C-CH-C(CH3)/CH-C(CH3)>		CCL4
662M	B	2.23	CH3	A<C-CH-C(N(CH2/CH2))>		CCL4
226M	A	2.23	CH3	A(C-CH-CH-C(F))		CCL4
1993M	B	2.23	CH3	C(=0)-C		CDCL3
609M	B	2.23	CH3	R5NA<C=C(CH3)/NH>		CDCL3
1575M	A	2.23	CH3	R50<C=CH/O>		CDCL3
1438M	B	2.23	HCHR	R30(O-CH(CH3))		CCL4
1772M	D	2.23	OH	R6(CH-CH(CH(CH3/CH3))/CH2)		CDCL3
2296M	B	2.24	CH2	C(=0)-NH/CH3		CDCL3
2801M	C	2.24	CH2	C(=0)-O-CH2/CH2.6-CH3		CCL4
2842M	C	2.24	CH2	C(=0)-O-CH2/CH2-CH3		CCL4
692M	A	2.24	CH3	AN<C-CH-N/CH-C(CH3)>		CCL4
885M	A	2.24	CH3	A<C-CH-CH-C(QN(N(CH3/CH3))>		CCL4
590M	A	2.24	CH3	A<C-CH-C(NH-CH3)>		CDCL3
1913M	B	2.24	CH3	A<C-C(CH3)-C(OH)>		CDCL3
1341M	A	2.24	CH3	A<C-C(NH-C(=S))>		DMSO-D6
1552M	B	2.24	CH3	A<C-C(O-CH3)/CH-C(CH3)>		CDCL3
175M	C	2.24	CH3	A<C-C(R6<C=CH/CH2>)>		CCL4
1195M	A	2.24	CH3	A<C-C(S-S)>		CCL4
1301M	A	2.24	CH3	A(C-CH-C(CH3)-C(SO3NA))	S	D20
428M	A	2.24	CH3	A(C-CH-C(I))		CCL4
1499M	B	2.24	CH3	A(C-CH-C(O-CH2))		CCL4
2147M	B	2.24	CH3	C(=0)-CH2		CDCL3
708M	A	2.24	CH3	N(CH2/CH3)		CDCL3
2704M	D	2.25	CH2	C(=0)-O-CH3/CH2-CH2		CCL4
854M	D	2.25	CH2	QN(CH3/OH)/CH2-CH3		CDCL3
2000M	B	2.25	CH2R	R6(C(=0)-CH2/CH2-CH2)		CCL4
384M	A	2.25	CH3	A(C-CH-CH-C(BR))		CCL4
761M	A	2.25	CH3	A(C-CH-CH-C(N(N/CH3)))		CDCL3
659M	A	2.25	CH3	A(C-CH-C(N(CH3/CH3)))		CCL4

BOOK NO.	ASSIGN-MENT	CHEM SHIFT - ppm -	PROTON GROUP	ENVIRONMENTAL GROUPS	S	SOLVENT
823M	A	2.25	CH3	A(C-C(CL)-CH-C(NH-NH2))	S	DMSO-D6
860M	A	2.25	CH3	QN(A/OH)		CDCL3
2138M	C	2.26	CH2	C(=O)-CH2/CH3		CCL4
2498M	B	2.26	CH2	C(=O)-OH/CH2-CH2		DMSO-D6
2138M	C	2.26	CH2	C(=O)-Q1/CH3		CCL4
2339M	B	2.26	CH3	A<C-C(NH-C(=O))-CH-C(CH3)>		CDCL3
429M	A	2.26	CH3	A(C-CH-CH-C(I))		CDCL3
1500M	B	2.26	CH3	A(C-CH-CH-C(O-CH2))		CCL4
385M	B	2.26	CH3	A(C-CH-C(BR)-C(CH(CH3/CH3)))		CDCL3
665M	A	2.26	CH3	A(C-C(N(CH3/CH3))-C(CH3))		CDCL3
2358M	D	2.26	CH3	C(=O)-CH2		CDCL3
2131M	B	2.26	CH3	C(=O)-C(=O)		CCL4
2339M	C	2.26	CH3	C(=O)-NH		CDCL3
639M	A	2.26	CH3	R6NN<N-CH2/CH2>		CDCL3
2218M	C	2.27	CH2	A<C-CH-CH-C(BR)>/CH2-CH2		CDCL3
2218M	B	2.27	CH2	C(=O)-CL/CH2-CH2		CDCL3
2503M	C	2.27	CH2	C(=O)-OH/CH2.13		POLYSOL-D
2689M	B	2.27	CH2	C(=O)-OH/CH2-CH2		D20
2777M	C	2.27	CH2	C(=O)-O-CH2/CH2-CH2		CCL4
2784M	C	2.27	CH2	C(=O)-O-CH2/CH2-CH2		CCL4
944M	C	2.27	CH2	C:N/CH2-CH3		CCL4
1063M	D	2.27	CH2	QN(CH3/NH-A)/CH2-CH3		POLYSOL-D
2523M	D	2.27	CH2	Q1(C(=O)-OH/CH2-CH2)/CH3		CCL4
2523M	D	2.27	CH2	Q1(C(=O)-OH/CH2-CH3)/CH2-CH3		CCL4
683M	A	2.27	CH3	AN(C-CH-N)		CCL4
2979M	A	2.27	CH3	A<C-CH-CH-C(O-C(=O)-NH2)>		DMSO-D6
1551M	B	2.27	CH3	A<C-C(CH3)-C(O-CH3)>		CDCL3
181M	A	2.27	CH3	A(C-CH-CH-C(CH3))		CCL4
2333M	A	2.27	CH3	C(=O)-NH		CDCL3
613M	B	2.27	CH3	N(CH2/CH3)		CDCL3
1579M	A	2.27	CH3	R5NO(C=N/CH=)		CCL4
2257M	D	2.27- 3.40		UNSPECIFIED		CDCL3
358M	B	2.28	CH2	CH(BR/CH3)/CH2-BR		CCL4
265M	B	2.28	CH2	C(CH3/CH3/CH3)/CH(CL/CL)		CCL4
1973M	C	2.28	CH2	C(=O)-CH3/C(CH3/CH3/CH3)		CCL4
2404M	B	2.28	CH2	C(=O)-NH/CH2.3-C(=O)-NH		D20
2783M	C	2.28	CH2	C(=O)-O-CH2.11/CH2.7-C(=O)-O		CDCL3
2711M	C	2.28	CH2	C(=O)-O-CH2.11/CH2.9-CH3		CDCL3
2823M	D	2.28	CH2	C(=O)-O-CH2/CH2-CH2		CCL4
2779M	C	2.28	CH2	C(=O)-O-CH3/CH2-CH2		CCL4
2823M	D	2.28	CH2	C(=O)-O-CH2/CH2-CH2		CCL4
856M	D	2.28 APP.	CH2	QN(CH3/OH)/CH2-CH2		CDCL3
1713M	A	2.28	CH3	A<C-CH-CH-C(CH2-OH)>		CCL4
182M	B	2.28	CH3	A<C-CH-CH-C(CH(CH3/CH3))>		CCL4
664M	C	2.28	CH3	A<C-CH-C(N(CH2/CH2)-C(CH3)>		CCL4
1495M	A	2.28	CH3	A<C-CH-C(O-CH3)>		CCL4
658M	A	2.28	CH3	A<C-C(N(CH3/CH3))>		CCL4
285M	A	2.28	CH3	A(C-CH-CH-C(CH2-CL))		CCL4
2924M	B	2.28	CH3	A(C-CH-CH-C(O-C(=O)-CH3))		CCL4
177M	A	2.28	CH3	A(C-CH-C(CH3))		CCL4
1496M	A	2.28	CH3	A(C/CH-CH-C(O-CH3))		CDCL3
273M	A	2.28	CH3	C(=O)-NH		DMSO-D6
2970M	B	2.28	CH3	C(=O)-S		CCL4
1755M	E	2.28	HCH	N(CH2/CH2)/CH(OH/CH3)		CCL4
1442M	C	2.28	HCHR	R30(O-CH(CH2-CH2))		CCL4
1790M	A	2.28	OH	CH(A/A)		CCL4
2477M	D	2.29	CH	C(=O)-OH/CH2-CH2/CH2-CH3		CCL4
2757M	C	2.29	CH	C(=O)-O-CH2/CH2-CH2/CH2-CH3		CDCL3
2253M	C	2.29	CH	C(=O)-O-C(=O)-CH/CH2-CH3/CH2-CH3		CCL4
625M	C	2.29- 2.95	CH	N(CH3/CH3)/CH2-NH2/CH3		D20
1217M	C	2.29	CHR	R6((NH-CH2.2)/CH2-CH2/CH2-CH2)		CDCL3
2778M	C	2.29	CH2	CH2-C(=O)-O/CH2-C(=O)-O		CCL4
417M	A	2.29	CH2	CH2-I/CH2-I		CCL4
1970M	D	2.29	CH2	C(=O)-CH2.2/CH3		CDCL3
2316M	C	2.29	CH2	C(=O)-NH/CH2-CH3		CDCL3
2354M	D	2.29	CH2	C(=O)-N/CH2.7-CH3		CDCL3
2775M	D	2.29	CH2	C(=O)-O-CH2.3/CH2.2-C(=O)-O		CCL4
2819M	D	2.29	CH2	C(=O)-O-CH2.3/CH2.6-Q2		CDCL3
2782M	C	2.29	CH2	C(=O)-O-CH2/CH2.7-C(=O)-O		CDCL3
2780M	D	2.29	CH2	C(=O)-O-CH2/CH2-CH2		CDCL3
2760M	D	2.29	CH2	C(=O)-O-CH/CH2-CH2		CCL4
2760M	D	2.29	CH2	C(=O)-O-HCH/CH2-CH2		CCL4
950M	C	2.29	CH2	C:N/CH2.4-CH3		CCL4
952M	C	2.29	CH2	C:N/CH2.7-CH3		CCL4
625M	C	2.29- 2.95	CH2	NH2/CH(N/CH3)		D20
620M	C	2.29	CH2	N(CH2.7/CH2.7)/CH2.6-CH3		CCL4
634M	C	2.29 APP.	CH2	N(CH3/CH3)/CH2-CH2		CDCL3
2137M	E	2.29	CH2	Q(C(=O)-CH3/OH/CH3)/CH3		CDCL3
97M	B	2.29	CH2R	R5<CH=CH/CH2-CH2>		CCL4
133M	A	2.29	CH3	A		CCL4
216M	B	2.29	CH3	AAA<C-C*-CH/CH-CH-CH-C*-C*>		CDCL3

BOOK NO.	ASSIGN-MENT	CHEM SHIFT - ppm -	PROTON GROUP	ENVIRONMENTAL GROUPS	S	SOLVENT
684M	A	2.29	CH3	AN(C-CH-CH-N)		CCL4
690M	A	2.29	CH3	AN(C-CH-C(CH3)-N)		CDCL3
373M	A	2.29	CH3	A<C-CH-CH-C(CH2-BR)>		CCL4
2933M	A	2.29	CH3	A<C-CH-CH-C(O-C(=O)-CH2)>		CDCL3
377M	A	2.29	CH3	A<C-CH-C(CH(BR/BR))>		CCL4
790M	A	2.29	CH3	A<C-CH-C(NH2)>	S	POLYSOL-D
187M	B	2.29	CH3	A<C-C(CH3)-C(CH3)>		CDCL3
304M	A	2.29	CH3	A<C-C(CL)-CH-C(F)>		CCL4
294M	A	2.29	CH3	A(C-CH-CH-C(CL))		CCL4
1370M	A	2.29	CH3	A(C-CH-CH-C(SO2-NH))		CDCL3
919M	A	2.29	CH3	A(C-CH-C(QN(=O))-C(CH3))		CCL4
2099M	A	2.29	CH3	A(C-C(C(=O)-A))		CCL4
661M	B	2.29	CH3	A(C-C(N(CH2/CH2)))		CDCL3
661M	B	2.29	CH3	A(C-C(N(CH2/CH2)))		CDCL3
913M	A	2.29	CH3	A(C-C(N=C=O))		CCL4
921M	A	2.29	CH3	A(C-C(N=C=O)-CH-C(N=C=O))		CCL4
919M	A	2.29	CH3	A(C-C(QN(=O))-CH-C(CH3))		CCL4
1991M	B	2.29	CH3	C(=O)-CH		CCL4
464M	B	2.29	CH3	NH-CH2		D20
1754M	C	2.29	CH3	N(CH2/CH3)		CDCL3
607M	A	2.29	CH3	R5NA<C=CH/C*>		CDCL3
755M	A	2.29	CH3	R6NN<N-CH2/CH2>		CDCL3
1161M	A	2.29	CH3	S-A		CCL4
773M	B	2.29	CH*R	R6R6BI(CH2-CH*/CH2-CH(NH2)/CH2-CH2)	S	D20
835M	C	2.29	CH*R	R6R6R6TRI(CH2-C*(N(+)(CH3/CH3/CH3))/CH2-CH*/CH2-CH*)	S	D20
1440M	C	2.29	HCHR	R30<O-CH(CH2.5-CH3)>		CCL4
1441M	C	2.29	HCHR	R30<O-CH(CH2.7-CH3)>		CCL4
1838M	C	2.29	OH	C(CH/CH3/CH3)		CDCL3
1814M	D	2.30	CH	:C-C		CCL4
2256M	B	2.30- 3.55	CHR	R50<(CH3)/C(=O)-O/CH2-C(=O)>		CDCL3
567M	C	2.30- 3.10	CHR	R6NN<(CH3)/NH-CH2/CH2-NH>		CDCL3
562M	D	2.30- 3.20	CHR	R6N((CH3)/NH-CH2/CH2-CH2)		CCL4
2643M	A	2.30	CH2	CH(NH2/C(=O)-OH)/CH2-NH2	S	D20
1981M	D	2.30 APP.	CH2	C(=O)-CH2.2/CH2.4-CH3		CCL4
1984M	D	2.30	CH2	C(=O)-CH2.2/CH2.7-CH3		CCL4
1981M	D	2.30 APP.	CH2	C(=O)-CH2.5/CH2-CH3		CCL4
1984M	D	2.30	CH2	C(=O)-CH2.8/CH2-CH3		CCL4
2528M	D	2.30	CH2	C(=O)-OH/CH2-CH2		CCL4
2649M	B	2.30	CH2	C(=O)-O-CD/CH3		D20
2763M	C	2.30	CH2	C(=O)-O-CH2/CH2.9-CH3		CDCL3
2701M	D	2.30	CH2	C(=O)-O-CH2/CH2-CH2		CCL4
2785M	C	2.30	CH2	C(=O)-O-CH3/CH2-CH2		CDCL3
2712M	D	2.30	CH2	C(=O)-O-CH3/CH2-CH2		CDCL3
2761M	D	2.30	CH2	C(=O)-O-CH/CH2.15-CH3		CDCL3
2698M	E	2.30	CH2	C(=O)-O-CH/CH3		CDCL3
2761M	D	2.30	CH2	C(=O)-O-HCH/CH2.15-CH3		CDCL3
958M	C	2.30	CH2	C:N/CH2.2-N		CCL4
946M	C	2.30	CH2	C:N/CH2-CH2		CCL4
946M	C	2.30	CH2	C:N/CH2-CH2		CCL4
617M	C	2.30	CH2	N(CH2/CH2)/CH2-CH2		CCL4
1358M	C	2.30	CH2	QN(NH-C(=S))/CH2-CH2		CDCL3
1785M	A	2.30	CH2	Q3/CH(OH/Q3)		CDCL3
2256M	B	2.30- 3.55	CH2R	R50<C(=O)-O/CH(CH3)-C(=O)>		CDCL3
567M	C	2.30- 3.10	CH2R	R6NN<NH-CH(CH3)/CH2-NH>		CDCL3
562M	D	2.30- 3.20	CH2R	R6N(NH-CH(CH3)/CH2-CH2)		CCL4
2117M	A	2.30	CH3	AR60<C-CH-C*-C(=O)/CH-CH-C*>		CDCL3
904M	A	2.30	CH3	A<C-CH-CH-C(N=N-NH)>		CDCL3
870M	A	2.30	CH3	A<C-CH-CH-C(QN(O2))>		CDCL3
184M	C	2.30	CH3	A<C-CH-CH-C(R6<C=CH/CH2>)>		CCL4
1196M	A	2.30	CH3	A<C-CH-CH-C(S-S)>		CDCL3
293M	A	2.30	CH3	A<C-CH-C(CL)>		CCL4
1468M	A	2.30	CH3	A<C-CH-C(R6NO<N-CH2/CH2>)>		CDCL3
1229M	A	2.30	CH3	A<C-CH-C(SH)>		CDCL3
2854M	B	2.30	CH3	A<C-C(CH2-C(=O)-O)>		CCL4
483M	B	2.30	CH3	A<C-C(CH2-NH2)>		CDCL3
2061M	C	2.30	CH3	A<C-C(C(=O)-C)/CH-C(CH3)>		CCL4
430M	B	2.30	CH3	A<C-C(I)-CH-C(CH3)>		CCL4
185M	A	2.30	CH3	A(C-CH-CH-C(CH2.2-A))		CDCL3
485M	B	2.30	CH3	A(C-CH-CH-C(CH2-NH2))		CCL4
2345M	A	2.30	CH3	A(C-CH-CH-C(NH-C(=O)))		CDCL3
1368M	B	2.30	CH3	A(C-CH-CH-C(NH-SO2))		CDCL3
928M	A	2.30	CH3	A(C-CH-CH-C(QN(=N-A)))		CDCL3
1268M	A	2.30	CH3	A(C-CH-CH-C(SO2-A))		CDCL3
1170M	A	2.30	CH3	A(C-CH-CH-C(S-A))		CDCL3
383M	A	2.30	CH3	A(C-CH-C(BR))		CCL4
1291M	A	2.30	CH3	A(C-C(NH2)-CH-C(SO3-H))		DMSO-D6
763M	B	2.30	CH3	A(C-C(N(N/CH3))-C(CH3)/CH-C(CH3))		CDCL3
606M	A	2.30	CH3	R5NA<C-NH/=CH>		CDCL3
1690M	E	2.30	OH	CH2-Q1		CCL4
1813M	B	2.30	OH	C(C:CH/CH3/CH3)		CDCL3
628M	B	2.30- 2.81		UNSPECIFIED		D20

BOOK NO.	ASSIGN-MENT	CHEM SHIFT - ppm -	PROTON GROUP	ENVIRONMENTAL GROUPS	S	SOLVENT
2481M	C	2.31	CH	C(=O)-OH/CH2.4-CH3/CH2.4-CH3		CCL4
2545M	B	2.31	CH2	C(C(=O)-OH/A/A)/CH2-CH3		CDCL3
1983M	C	2.31	CH2	C(=O)-CH2/CH2-CH2		CCL4
1985M	C	2.31	CH2	C(=O)-CH2/CH2-CH2		CCL4
1972M	C	2.31	CH2	C(=O)-CH2/CH2-CH3		CCL4
2351M	D	2.31	CH2	C(=O)-N/CH3		CDCL3
2554M	C	2.31	CH2	C(=O)-OH/CH2-CH2		CDCL3
2500M	B	2.31	CH2	C(=O)-OH/C(CH2/CH3/CH3)		POLYSOL-D
951M	C	2.31	CH2	C:N/CH2.5-CH3		CCL4
953M	D	2.31	CH2	C:N/CH2-CH2		CDCL3
473M	E	2.31	CH2	NH2/R6R6TRI<C*(CH2/CH2/CH2)>		CDCL3
546M	D	2.31	CH2	NH-CH2/CH(CH3/CH3)		CCL4
623M	D	2.31	CH2	N(CH2.7/CH3)/CH2.6-CH3		CDCL3
615M	C	2.31	CH2	N(CH2/CH2)/CH2-CH3		CCL4
2953M	B	2.31	CH2R	R150<C(=O)-O/CH2-CH2>		CDCL3
205M	A	2.31	CH3	AA<C-C(CH3)-CH-C*/CH-C*>		CDCL3
203M	A	2.31	CH3	AA<C-C(CH3)-CH-C*/CH-C*>		CDCL3
696M	B	2.31	CH3	AN<C-CH-C(C(CH3/CH3/CH3))-N/CH-C(C(CH3/CH3/CH3))>		CDCL3
2940M	A	2.31	CH3	A<C-CH-C(O-C(=O)-O)>		CCL4
178M	B	2.31	CH3	A<C-CH-C(CH2-CH3)>		CDCL3
299M	A	2.31	CH3	A<C-CH-C(CL)-C(CH3)>		CCL4
2596M	A	2.31	CH3	A<C-CH-C(OH)-C(C(=O)-OH)>		POLYSOL-D
1502M	B	2.31	CH3	A<C-CH-C(O-CH2.4)>		CCL4
1540M	A	2.31	CH3	A<C-CH-C(O-CH2)>		CCL4
2239M	A	2.31 APP.	CH3	A<C-C(CH3)-CH-C(C(=O)-CL)>		CCL4
2239M	A	2.31 APP.	CH3	A<C-C(CH3)/CH-C(C(=O)-CL)>		CCL4
299M	A	2.31	CH3	A<C-C(CL)-CH-C(CH3)>		CCL4
2557M	A	2.31	CH3	A(C-CH-CH-C(CH2-C(=O)-O))		CDCL3
1269M	A	2.31	CH3	A(C-CH-CH-C(SO2-A))		CDCL3
1312M	D	2.31	CH3	A(C-CH-CH-C(SO3))	S	CDCL3
1364M	A	2.31	CH3	A(C-CH-C(CH3)-C(SO2-NH2)/CH-C(CH3))		TFA
386M	B	2.31	CH3	A(C-C(BR)-CH-C(CH3)/CH-C(CH3))		CDCL3
2344M	A	2.31	CH3	A(C-C(NH-C(=O)))		CDCL3
1992M	B	2.31	CH3	C(=O)-CH		CCL4
2865M	A	2.31	CH3	N(CH2.2/CH3)		CDCL3
1353M	B	2.31 APP.	CH*R	R5R5BI<CH2-CH*/CH2-CH(NH-C(=S))/CH2-CH2>		POLYSOL-D
1353M	B	2.31 APP.	CH*R	R5R5BI<CH(NH-C(=S))-CH2/CH2-CH*/CH2-CH2>		POLYSOL-D
1439M	C	2.31	HCHR	R30<O-CH(CH2-CH3)>		CCL4
562M	C	2.31	NHR	R6N(CH(CH3)-CH2/CH2-CH2)		CCL4
1704M	A	2.31	OH	CH2.2-N		CDCL3
2749M	D	2.32 APP.	CH2	C(=O)-OH/CH2.7-C(=O)-O		CDCL3
2579M	D	2.32	CH2	C(=O)-OH/CH2-CH2		CDCL3
2749M	D	2.32 APP.	CH2	C(=O)-O-CH2/CH2.7-C(=O)-OH		CDCL3
1699M	D	2.32	CH2	C:C/CH2-OH		CCL4
2157M	D	2.32	CH2	Q1(C(=O)-H/CH2-CH3)/CH2-CH3		CCL4
1159M	B	2.32	CH2	S-CH2/CH3		CCL4
1111M	C	2.32	CH2	S-CH2/CH(CH3/CH3)		CCL4
2028M	C	2.32	CH2R	R6<C(=O)-C(CH3)=/CH2-CH2>		CCL4
2210M	B	2.32 APP.	CH2R	R6(CH=C(C(=O)-CL)/CH2-CH2)		CCL4
2210M	B	2.32 APP.	CH2R	R6(C(=O)-CL)=CH/CH2-CH2)		CCL4
1585M	A	2.32	CH3	AR5NO<C-C(CH3)-CH-C*/CH-C*-N=>		CDCL3
1585M	A	2.32	CH3	AR5NO<C-C(CH3)-CH-C*/CH-C*-O>		CDCL3
2925M	D	2.32	CH3	A<C-CH-CH-C(O-C(=O)-CH2)>		CCL4
1355M	B	2.32	CH3	A<C-CH-C(NH-C(=S))>		CDCL3
792M	A	2.32	CH3	A<C-C(NH2)-CH-C(CH3)>	S	D2O
1228M	A	2.32	CH3	A<C-C(SH)>		CDCL3
387M	B	2.32	CH3	A(C(BR)-C(CH3)/CH-C(CH3))		CCL4
2056M	A	2.32	CH3	A(C-CH-CH-C(C(=O)-CH3))		CCL4
544M	C	2.32	CH3	NH-CH2		D2O
1149M	A	2.32	CH3	R5NS<C=CH/CH=>		CCL4
467M	C	2.32- 2.88		UNSPECIFIED		CCL4
2479M	C	2.33	CH	C(=O)-OH/CH2-CH2/CH2-CH2		CCL4
2459M	D	2.33	CHR	R6NN((CH(CH2/CH3))/C(=O)-NH/C(=O)-NH)		DMSO-D6
2748M	B	2.33	CH2	C(=O)-CH3/CH2.4-C(=O)-CL		CDCL3
2480M	D	2.33	CH2	C(=O)-OH/CH2-CH2		CCL4
2527M	D	2.33	CH2	C(=O)-OH/CH2-Q2		CCL4
2719M	C	2.33	CH2	C(=O)-O-CH2/CH2-CH2		CDCL3
957M	B	2.33	CH2	C:N/CH2-CH2		CCL4
949M	C	2.33	CH2	C:N/CH2-CH2		CDCL3
613M	C	2.33	CH2	N(CH3/CH3)/CH3		CDCL3
2527M	D	2.33	CH2	Q2(H/CH2.7-CH3/H)/CH2-C(=O)-OH		CCL4
2156M	C	2.33	CH2	Q2(H/C(=O)-H/H)/CH2-CH3		CDCL3
114M	A	2.33	CH2R	R8<CH=CH/CH2-CH=>		CCL4
484M	B	2.33	CH3	A<C-CH-C(CH2-NH2)>		CDCL3
2057M	A	2.33	CH3	A<C-CH-C(C(=O)-CH3)-C(CH3)>		CCL4
2238M	A	2.33	CH3	A<C-C(CH3)-C(C(=O)-CL)>		CCL4
2564M	A	2.33	CH3	A(C-CH-CH-C(Q2(H/C(=O)-OH/H)))		DMSO-D6
975M	A	2.33	CH3	N(CH/CH3)		CDCL3
588M	B	2.33	CH:	:C-C(NH/CH3/CH3)		CDCL3
1628M	C	2.33	OH	CH2-CH2		CCL4
1711M	A	2.33	OH	CH2-Q2		CDCL3

BOOK NO.	ASSIGN-MENT	CHEM SHIFT - ppm -	PROTON GROUP	ENVIRONMENTAL GROUPS	S	SOLVENT
979M	A	2.34 APP.	CH2	C(A/C:N/CH2.2)/CH2-C:N		DMSO-D6
1988M	D	2.34 APP.	CH2	C(=O)-CH2.9/CH3		CCL4
1988M	D	2.34 APP.	CH2	C(=O)-CH2/CH2.8-CH3		CCL4
1980M	D	2.34	CH2	C(=O)-CH2/CH2-CH2		CCL4
2034M	B	2.34	CH2	C(=O)-CH2/CH3		CCL4
1976M	D	2.34	CH2	C(=O)-CH3/CH2-CH2		CCL4
2154M	C	2.34	CH2	C(=O)-H/CH2-CH2		CDCL3
2529M	D	2.34	CH2	C(=O)-OH/CH2-CH2		CDCL3
1464M	B	2.34 APP.	CH2	R6NO(N-CH2/CH2)/CH3		CCL4
1464M	B	2.34 APP.	CH2R	R6NO(N(CH2-CH3)-CH2/CH2-O)		CCL4
2943M	A	2.34	CH3	A<C-CH-CH-C(O-C(=O)-A)>		CCL4
1821M	B	2.34	CH3	A<C-CH-CH-C(R6<C(OH)-CH2/CH2>)>		CDCL3
286M	A	2.34	CH3	A<C-C(CH2-CL)-CH-C(CH2-CL)/CH-C(CH3)>		CDCL3
308M	A	2.34	CH3	A<C-C(CL)-CH-C(CL)>		CCL4
927M	A	2.34	CH3	A<C-C(N=C=N)>		CCL4
2289M	A	2.34	CH3	A(C-CH-C(C(=O)-NH2))		CDCL3
1430M	A	2.34	CH3	N(CH2/CH2)		CCL4
636M	B	2.34	CH3	R5N<N-CH2/CH2>		CDCL3
1817M	B	2.34	OH	C(A/CH3/CH3) _		CDCL3
2153M	C	2.35	CH2	CH2-C(=O)/CH2-CH2		CCL4
1982M	D	2.35	CH2	C(=O)-CH/CH2.4-CH3		CCL4
2315M	B	2.35	CH2	C(=O)-NH/CH3		CDCL3
2759M	C	2.35 APP.	CH2	C(=O)-O-CH2/CH2-CH2		CDCL3
2776M	B	2.35	CH2	C(=O)-O-CH3/C(CH2/CH3/CH3)		CCL4
633M	C	2.35 APP.	CH2	N(CH2/CH3)/CH2-N		CCL4
633M	C	2.35 APP.	CH3	N(CH2/CH3)/CH3		CCL4
1466M	C	2.35	CH2	R6NO(N-CH2/CH2)/CH2-CH2		CCL4
1466M	C	2.35	CH2R	R6NO(N-CH2/CH2-O)		CCL4
872M	A	2.35	CH3	A<C-CH-CH-C(QN(A))>		CDCL3
1106M	A	2.35	CH3	A<C-CH-C(P(=O/A/A))>		CDCL3
2240M	A	2.35	CH3	A(C-CH-C(C(=O)-CL)/CH-C(CH3))		CCL4
2926M	A	2.35	CH3	C(=O)-O-A		CDCL3
754M	A	2.35	CH3	N(NH2/CH3)		CCL4
2759M	C	2.35 APP.	OH	CH(CH2/CH2)		CDCL3
2475M	D	2.36	CH	C(=O)-OH/CH2-CH3/CH3		CDCL3
2522M	D	2.36	CH	Q2(H/C(=O)-OH/H)/CH2.2-CH3/CH3		CCL4
354M	A	2.36	CH2	CH2-BR/CH2-BR		CCL4
1980M	E	2.36	CH2	C(=O)-CH2/CH3		CCL4
1974M	D	2.36	CH2	C(=O)-CH3/CH2-CH2		CCL4
2151M	C	2.36	CH2	C(=O)-H/CH2-CH3		CCL4
2758M	D	2.36	CH2	C(=O)-O-CH2/CH2-CH2		CDCL3
2797M	B	2.36	CH2	C(=O)-O-Q3/CH3		CCL4
973M	A	2.36	CH2	C:N/CH2-A		CDCL3
2010M	C	2.36	CH2R	R13(C(=O)-CH2/CH2-CH2)		CCL4
721M	A	2.36	CH3	AAN(C-CH-C*/CH-CH-C*)		CDCL3
2362M	B	2.36	CH3	A<C-CH-CH-C(N(C(=O)-H/CH2))>		CDCL3
2101M	A	2.36	CH3	A(C-CH-C(C(=O)-A))		CDCL3
2093M	A	2.36	CH3	A(C-CH-CH-C(C(=O)-Q2))		CDCL3
382M	A	2.36	CH3	A(C-C(BR))		CCL4
372M	A	2.36	CH3	A(C-C(CH2-BR))		CCL4
427M	A	2.36	CH3	A(C-C(I))		CDCL3
1192M	A	2.36	CH3	S-S		CCL4
1821M	C	2.36	OH	R6<C(A<C-CH-CH-C(CH3)>)-CH2/CH2>		CDCL3
1970M	E	2.37	CH2	C(=O)-CH2/CH2-CH3		CDCL3
1969M	E	2.37	CH2	C(=O)-CH3/CH2.2-CH3		CCL4
2482M	D	2.37	CH2	C(=O)-OH/CH2.13-CH3		CDCL3
2525M	D	2.37 APP.	CH2	C(=O)-OH/CH2-Q2		CCL4
2526M	D	2.37 APP.	CH2	C(=O)-OH/CH2-Q2		CCL4
2473M	B	2.37	CH2	C(=O)-OH/CH3		CDCL3
2753M	B	2.37	CH2	C(=O)-O-CH2/CH3		CDCL3
2252M	D	2.37	CH2	C(=O)-O-C(=O)-CH2.4/CH2.3-CH3		CDCL3
168M	C	2.37	CH2	C:C/CH2.5-CH3		CCL4
2525M	D	2.37 APP.	CH2	Q2(H/CH2.4-CH3/H)/CH2-C(=O)-OH		CCL4
2526M	D	2.37 APP.	CH2	Q2(H/CH2.5-CH3/H)/CH2-C(=O)-OH		CCL4
1687M	A	2.37	CH2	Q3/CH2-OH		CDCL3
1113M	D	2.37	CH2	S-CH2/CH(CH2/CH2)		CCL4
673M	C	2.37 APP.	CH2R	R6N<N(CH3)-CH2/CH2-CH=>		CCL4
1776M	D	2.37 APP.	CH2R	R6<CH(OH)-C(A/A)/CH2-CH2>		CDCL3
695M	B	2.37	CH3	AN<C-N-C(CH3)/CH-C(CH3)>		CCL4
1302M	A	2.37	CH3	A(C-CH-CH-C(SO3-BA))	S	D2O
292M	A	2.37	CH3	A(C-C(CL))		CDCL3
2821M	A	2.37	CH3	C(=O)-Q2		CDCL3
2609M	A	2.37	CH3	C(=O)-5H		CCL4
2152M	B	2.38	CH	C(=O)-H/CH3/CH3		CCL4
2478M	D	2.38	CH	C(=O)-OH/CH2-CH-CH2-CH3		CCL4
1975M	D	2.38	CH2	C(=O)-CH2/CH2.3-CH3		CDCL3
1997M	C	2.38 APP.	CH2	C(=O)-CH3/R5		CCL4
2353M	C	2.38	CH2	C(=O)-N/CH2-CH3		D2O
2853M	B	2.38	CH2	C(=O)-O-CH2/CH2-N		CDCL3
2664M	A	2.38	CH2	C(=O)-O-NA/CH2-C(=O)-O		D2O
2802M	C	2.38	CH2	C(=O)-O-Q3/CH2-CH2		CDCL3

BOOK NO.	ASSIGN-MENT	CHEM SHIFT - ppm -	PROTON GROUP	ENVIRONMENTAL GROUPS	S	SOLVENT
1695M	B	2.38	CH2	C:CH/CH2-OH		CCL4
1698M	D	2.38	CH2	C:C/CH2-OH		CCL4
621M	C	2.38	CH2	N(CH2.11/CH2.11)/CH2.10-CH3		CDCL3
619M	C	2.38 APP.	CH2	N(CH2/CH2)/CH2-CH		CDCL3
959M	C	2.38	CH2	N(CH2/CH2)/CH2-CH2		CCL4
959M	C	2.38	CH2	N(CH2/CH2)/CH2-CH2		CCL4
2411M	B	2.38 APP.	CH2R	R6(C(=N-NH)-CH2/CH2-CH2)		CDCL3
2128M	A	2.38	CH3	AR6A<C-C(CH3)-CH-C*/CH-C*-C(=0)>		CDCL3
172M	B	2.38	CH3	A(C-CH-CH-C(A(C-C(CH2-CH3))))		CCL4
2105M	A	2.38	CH3	A(C-CH-CH-C(C(=0)-A))		CDCL3
881M	A	2.38	CH3	A(C-CH-CH-C(QN(QN)))		CDCL3
1372M	B	2.38	CH3	A(C-CH-CH-C(SO2-NH))		CDCL3
2455M	B	2.38	CH3	R6NN<C-NH/=C(CH3)>		TFA
1923M	B	2.38	CH3	S-A		CDCL3
2376M	B	2.38	HCHR	R5N<C(=0)-NH/CH(CH3)-C(=0)>		CDCL3
2719M	D	2.38 APP.	OH	CH2-CH		CDCL3
2719M	D	2.38 APP.	OH	CH(CH2/CH2)		CDCL3
635M	C	2.39 APP.	CHR	R6<(N(CH2/CH2))/CH2-CH2/CH2-CH2>		CCL4
139M	C	2.39	CH2	A/CH(CH3/CH3)		CDCL3
1987M	C	2.39	CH2	C(=0)-CH2/CH2-CH2		CDCL3
1480M	C	2.39 APP.	CH2	C:N/CH2-CH		CDCL3
155M	A	2.39	CH2	Q3/CH2-A		CDCL3
638M	B	2.39 APP.	CH2R	R6N(N(CH2-R6N)-CH2/CH2-CH2)		CCL4
2145M	D	2.39	CH2R	R6(C(OH)=C(C(=0)-CH3)/CH2-CH2)		CCL4
2145M	B	2.39	CH2R	R6(C(=0)-C(C(=0)-CH3)=/CH2-CH2)		CCL4
1267M	A	2.39	CH3	A<C-CH-CH-C(SO2-CH2)>		POLYSOL-D
1290M	A	2.39	CH3	A<C-CH-C(SO2-OH)-C(NH2)>		DMSO-D6
2238M	B	2.39	CH3	A<C-C(C(=0)-CL)/C(CH3)>		CCL4
2100M	A	2.39	CH3	A(C-CH-CH-C(C(=0)-A))		CDCL3
2062M	A	2.39	CH3	A(C-CH-CH-C(C(=0)-CH2))		CDCL3
985M	A	2.39	CH3	A(C-CH-C(C:N))		CCL4
1098M	A	2.39	CH3	A(C-C(P(A/A)))		CDCL3
2950M	B	2.39	CH3	C(=0)-R50		CCL4
558M	B	2.39	CH3	NH-R6		CDCL3
643M	B	2.39	CH3	N(Q1/CH3)		CDCL3
878M	A	2.39	CH3	QN(AN(C-N)/NH-A)		DMSO-D6
2454M	A	2.39	CH3	R6NN<C-NH/=CH>		TFA
2412M	A	2.39	HCHR	R5NN<C(=0)-NH/CH(A)-NH>		DMSO-D6
2412M	B	2.39	HCHR	R5NN<C(=0)-NH/CH(A)-NH>		DMSO-D6
560M	B	2.39	NHR	R5N<CH2-CH2/CH2-CH2>		C6H6
1770M	C	2.39	OH	R6<CH-CH(CH2-CH3)/CH2>		CDCL3
145M	B	2.40 APP.	CHR	R6((A)/CH2-CH2/CH2-CH2)		CCL4
503M	C	2.40	CH2	A<C-C(NH2)-C(CH2-CH3)/CH-C(CH3)>/CH3		CCL4
491M	B	2.40	CH2	A(C-C(NH2))/CH3		CDCL3
1978M	C	2.40	CH2	C(=0)-CH2/CH2-CH2		CDCL3
1986M	C	2.40	CH2	C(=0)-CH2/CH2-CH2		CDCL3
2495M	C	2.40 APP.	CH2	C(=0)-CH2/CH2-CH2		CDCL3
2019M	B	2.40 APP.	CH2	C(=0)-CH3/CH2-Q3		CCL4
1968M	C	2.40	CH2	C(=0)-CH3/CH3		CCL4
2495M	C	2.40 APP.	CH2	C(=0)-OH/CH2-CH2		CDCL3
2738M	B	2.40- 3.00	CH2	C(=0)-O-CH3/CH2-SH		CDCL3
2254M	D	2.40	CH2	C(=0)-O-C(=0)-CH2.5/CH2.4-CH3		CCL4
2249M	C	2.40	CH2	C(=0)-O-C(=0)/CH2-CH3		CCL4
963M	B	2.40	CH2	C:N/CH2-CH2		CDCL3
627M	D	2.40	CH2	NH2/CH2-CH2		CDCL3
460M	C	2.40	CH2	NH2/C(NH2/CH3/CH3)		CCL4
550M	D	2.40	CH2	NH-CH2/CH2-CH2		CDCL3
551M	D	2.40	CH2	NH-CH2/CH2-CH2		CDCL3
618M	C	2.40	CH2	N(CH2.4/CH2.4)/CH2.3-CH3		CCL4
853M	D	2.40	CH2	QN(CH3/OH)/CH3		CDCL3
2139M	D	2.40	CH2	Q1(OH/C(=0)-CH2.2)/CH2-CH3		CCL4
2019M	B	2.40 APP.	CH2	Q3(H/H/H)/CH2-C(=0)		CCL4
2738M	B	2.40- 3.00	CH2	SH/CH2-C(=0)-O		CDCL3
569M	D	2.40- 3.27	CH2R	R6NR6(NH-CH*/CH2-CH2)		CDCL3
722M	A	2.40	CH3	AAN<C-CH-C*-N/CH-CH-C*>		CCL4
205M	B	2.40	CH3	AA<C-CH-C*/CH-CH-C*>		CDCL3
2060M	C	2.40	CH3	A<C-CH-CH-C(C(=0)-CH2.3)>		CDCL3
1262M	A	2.40	CH3	A<C-CH-CH-C(SO2-CH2)>		CDCL3
1068M	A	2.40	CH3	A<C-CH-C(CH3)-C(NO2)>		CDCL3
897M	A	2.40	CH3	A<C-CH-C(N=N-A)>		CDCL3
1369M	B	2.40	CH3	A(C-CH-CH-C(SO2-N))		CDCL3
1321M	B	2.40	CH3	A(C-CH-CH-C(SO3-CH))		CCL4
2058M	C	2.40	CH3	C(=0)-A		CDCL3
2044M	A	2.40	CH3	C(=0)-C:		CDCL3
1331M	A	2.40	CH3	C(=S)-NH2		DMSO-D6
1331M	A	2.40	CH3	C(=S)-NH2		DMSO-D6
552M	D	2.40	CH3	NH-CH2		CDCL3
1431M	B	2.40	CH3	N(CH2/CH2)		CDCL3
569M	D	2.40- 3.27	CH*R	R6NR6(NH-CH2/CH2-CH2)		CDCL3
602M	C	2.40- 2.90	HCHR	R6NA<C*/HCH-CH(CH3)>		CDCL3
1795M	B	2.40	OH	C(CH3/C(3/CH3)		CCL4

BOOK NO.	ASSIGN-MENT	CHEM SHIFT - ppm -	PROTON GROUP	ENVIRONMENTAL GROUPS	S	SOLVENT
1218M	B	2.40- 3.16		UNSPECIFIED		CDCL3
632M	C	2.40 APP.		UNSPECIFIED		CCL4
2115M	C	2.40- 3.10		UNSPECIFIED		CDCL3
1215M	D	2.40- 3.00		UNSPECIFIED		CDCL3
1216M	D	2.40- 3.10		UNSPECIFIED		CDCL3
1813M	C	2.41	CH	C-C		CDCL3
977M	B	2.41	CH2	C(A/A/C:N)/CH3		CDCL3
2352M	C	2.41	CH2	C(=0)-N/CH2-CH3		D20
2350M	C	2.41	CH2	C(=0)-N/CH3		D20
2660M	A	2.41	CH2	C(=0)-0-NA/CH2-OH		D20
1649M	C	2.41	CH2	N(CH3/CH3)/CH2-CH2		CCL4
1117M	D	2.41	CH2	S-CH2/CH2.10-CH3		CCL4
1118M	C	2.41	CH2	S-CH2/CH2-CH2		CCL4
1116M	D	2.41	CH2	S-CH3/CH2.10-CH3		CCL4
2015M	A	2.41	CH2R	R6N<C(=0)-CH2/CH2-N(CH2-A)>		CDCL3
209M	A	2.41	CH3	AR5A<C-CH-C*/CH-CH-C*>		CDCL3
1284M	A	2.41	CH3	A<C-CH-C(SO2-CL)-C(CH3)>		CCL4
1070M	A	2.41	CH3	A<C-C(NO2)-CH-C(NH2)>		CDCL3
986M	A	2.41	CH3	A(C-CH-CH-C(C:N))		CCL4
309M	A	2.41	CH3	A(C-C(CL)/C(CL))		CCL4
2593M	A	2.41	CH3	A(C-C(C(=0)-OH)-C(CH3))		CDCL3
2534M	A	2.41	CH3	Q1(C(=0)-OH/H/C(=0)-OH)		TFA
283M	A	2.42	CH	:C-CH2		CCL4
570M	B	2.42 APP.	CHR	R6<(NH-CH2)/CH2-CH2/CH2-CH2>		CCL4
500M	C	2.42	CH2	A<C-C(NH2)-C(CH3)>/CH3		CDCL3
1653M	D	2.42	CH2	N(CH2.3/CH2.3)/CH2.2-CH3		CDCL3
614M	B	2.42 APP.	CH2	N(CH2/CH2)/CH3		CCL4
1755M	F	2.42 APP.	CH2	N(CH2/HCH)/CH2-CH2		CCL4
1110M	C	2.42	CH2	S-CH2/CH2-CH2		CCL4
1127M	C	2.42	CH2	S-CH3/CH2-CH2		CCL4
639M	B	2.42	CH2R	R6NN<N(CH3)-CH2/CH2-N(CH(A/A))>		CDCL3
639M	B	2.42	CH2R	R6NN<N(CH(A/A))-CH2/CH2-N(CH3)>		CDCL3
2260M	C	2.42	CH2R	R60(C(=0)-0/CH2-C(CH3/CH3))		CDCL3
204M	A	2.42	CH3	AA<C-CH-C*>		CCL4
1709M	A	2.42	CH3	A<C-CH-CH-C(SO2-CH2)>		CDCL3
2165M	A	2.42	CH3	A<C-CH-C(C(=0)-H)>		CCL4
1322M	C	2.42	CH3	A(C-CH-CH-C(SO3-CH2))		CCL4
2059M	B	2.42	CH3	C(=0)-A		CCL4
2056M	B	2.42	CH3	C(=0)-A		CCL4
2037M	A	2.42	CH3	C(=0)-CH		CDCL3
1746M	D	2.42	OH	CH(CH2/CH3)		CCL4
538M	B	2.43	CH2	A<C-C(NH2)-C(CH2-CH3)-C(NH2)>/CH3		CDCL3
2014M	A	2.43	CH2	A/CH2-R6N		CDCL3
1975M	E	2.43	CH2	C(=0)-CH2.4/CH3		CDCL3
1989M	E	2.43	CH2	C(=0)-CH3/CH2.1n		CDCL3
2497M	A	2.43	CH2	C(=0)-OH/CH2-C(=0)-0		DMSO-D6
2793M	A	2.43	CH2	C(=0)-0-CH3/CH2-N		CDCL3
2248M	B	2.43	CH2	C(=0)-0-C(=0)/CH3		CCL4
1117M	E	2.43	CH2	S-CH2.11/CH3		CCL4
1114M	C	2.43	CH2	S-CH2.5/CH2.4-CH3		CCL4
1126M	C	2.43	CH2	S-CH2/CH2-CH2		CCL4
1126M	C	2.43	CH2	S-CH2/CH2-CH3		CCL4
1107M	C	2.43	CH2	S-CH3/CH3		CCL4
2011M	C	2.43	CH2R	R15<C(=0)-CH2/CH2-CH2>		CDCL3
712M	B	2.43	CH2R	R5N<N(CH2-AN)-CH2/CH2-CH2>		CDCL3
735M	A	2.43	CH3	ANN(C-N-C(CH3)-C(CH3)/C(CH3)-N)		CDCL3
792M	B	2.43	CH3	A<C-CH-C(NH2)-C(CH3)>	S	D20
1375M	A	2.43	CH3	A(C-CH-CH-C(SO2-N))		CDCL3
2045M	A	2.43	CH3	C(=0)-A		CCL4
2958M	A	2.43	CH3	C(=0)-0-R60A		CDCL3
1784M	D	2.43	OH	CH(CH2/CH2.2)		CDCL3
2702M	D	2.44 APP.	CH	C(=0)-0-CH2/CH3/CH3		CCL4
848M	C	2.44	CH	QN(OH)/CH3/CH3		CCL4
1109M	C	2.44	CH2	S-CH2.2/CH2-CH3		CCL4
215M	A	2.44	CH3	AAA<C-CH-C*/CH-CH-C*>		CDCL3
2223M	A	2.44	CH3	A<C-CH-CH-C(C(=0)-CL)>		CCL4
1264M	A	2.44	CH3	A<C-CH-CH-C(SO2-CH2)>		POLYSOL-D
2057M	B	2.44 APP.	CH3	A<C-C(C(=0)-CH3)-CH-C(CH3)>		CCL4
2057M	B	2.44 APP.	CH3	C(=0)-A		CCL4
2667M	A	2.44	HCH	C(=0)-0-K/C(OH/C(=0)-0-K/HCH	S	D20
2667M	B	2.44	HCH	C(=0)-0-K/C(OH/C(=0)-0-K/HCH	S	D20
1701M	A	2.44	OH	CH2-CH2		CDCL3
2836M	B	2.45	CH	C(=0)-0-CH2.2/CH3/CH3		CCL4
1753M	C	2.45- 3.90	CH	NH2/CH(OH/CH3)/CH3		CDCL3
1753M	C	2.45- 3.90	CH	OH/CH(NH2/CH3)/CH3		CDCL3
183M	B	2.45	CHR	R6((A(C-CH-CH-C(R6)))/CH2-CH2/CH2-CH2)		CDCL3
1927M	C	2.45	CH2	A<C-C(OH)-CH-C(OH)>/CH2-CH2		CDCL3
2747M	D	2.45	CH2	C(=0)-CH3/CH2-C(=0)-0		CCL4
2925M	E	2.45	CH2	C(=0)-0-A/CH2-CH2		CCL4
1213M	D	2.45	CH2	SH/CH2-CH2		CCL4
1115M	C	2.45	CH2	S-CH2.6/CH2.5-CH3		CCL4

BOOK NO.	ASSIGN-MENT	CHEM SHIFT - ppm -	PROTON GROUP	ENVIRONMENTAL GROUPS	S	SOLVENT
1465M	A	2.45	CH2R	R6NO<N(CH2-Q3)-CH2/CH2-O>		CDCL3
2267M	B	2.45	CH2R	P6R50<C*-C(=O)/CH2-CH2>		CDCL3
2126M	A	2.45	CH3	AR6A<C-CH-C*-C(=O)/CH-CH-C*>		CCL4
1048M	A	2.45	CH3	A(C-CH-CH-C(NO2))		CDCL3
1047M	A	2.45	CH3	A(C-CH-C(NO2))		CCL4
1160M	A	2.45	CH3	S-A		CDCL3
691M	B	2.46	CH3	AN(C-N-CH-C(CH3))		CDCL3
1363M	A	2.46	CH3	A(C-CH-CH-C(SO2-NH2))		TFA
2072M	A	2.46	CH3	C(=O)-A		CCL4
1445M	B	2.46	HCHR	R30<O-CH(CH2-O)>		CCL4
1765M	C	2.47 APP.	CHR	R5<(CH3)/CH(OH)-CH2/CH2-CH2>		CDCL3
1887M	B	2.47	CHR	R6<(A<C-CH-CH-C(OH)>)/CH2-CH2/CH2-CH2>		CDCL3
2632M	B	2.47	CH2	C(=O)-NH2/CH2-CH		D20
2921M	B	2.47	CH2	C(=O)-O-A/CH3		CCL4
2138M	D	2.47	CH2	Q1(OH/C(=O)-CH2)/CH3		CCL4
1204M	D	2.47	CH2	SH/CH2.5		CDCL3
1108M	B	2.47	CH2	S-CH2/CH3		CCL4
682M	A	2.47	CH3	AN(C-N)		CCL4
740M	A	2.47	CH3	AR5NN(C-CH-C*-N=/CH-CH-C*)		CDCL3
2567M	A	2.47	CH3	A<C-CH-CH-C(C(=O)-OH)		TFA
1816M	B	2.48	CH	C-R6		CDCL3
2469M	C	2.48	CH	QN(NH-C(=O)/CH3)/CH3/CH3		CDCL3
1884M	D	2.48	CH2	A<C-CH-CH-C(OH)>/CH2.3-CH3		CCL4
2250M	C	2.48	CH2	C(=O)-O-C(=O)/CH2-CH2		CDCL3
959M	D	2.48	CH2	C:N/CH2-CH2		CCL4
959M	D	2.48	CH2	C:N/CH2-CH2		CCL4
974M	B	2.48	CH2	C:N/C(A/CH3/CH3)		CCL4
1652M	C	2.48	CH2	N(CH2.2/CH2.3)/CH2.2-CH3		CDCL3
1851M	B	2.48	CH2	N(CH2/CH2)/CH(OH/CH3)		CDCL3
635M	D	2.48	CH2	N(CH2/R6)/CH3		CCL4
616M	B	2.48	CH2	N(CH/CH)/CH3		CCL4
2161M	C	2.48	CH2	Q1(C(=O)-H/H/A)/CH2-CH2		CCL4
636M	C	2.48	CH2R	R5N<N(CH3)-CH2/CH2-CH2>		CDCL3
608M	A	2.48	CH3	AR5N<C-C*-CH=CH>		CDCL3
2078M	A	2.48	CH3	A<C-C(C(=O)-CH3)/CH-C(OH)>		DMSO-D6
2078M	A	2.48	CH3	C(=O)-A		DMSO-D6
2108M	B	2.48	CH3	C(=O)-AR5		CDCL3
859M	A	2.48	CH3	QN(A/OH)		CCL4
2708M	E	2.49	CH	C(=O)-O-CH2/CH3/CH3		CCL4
1266M	A	2.49	CH	:C-CH2		CDCL3
559M	C	2.49	CHR	R6((NH-CH)/CH2-CH2/CH2-CH2)		CDCL3
2633M	A	2.49	CH2	CH(NH3(+)/C(=O)-OH)/CH2-C(=O)-O		TFA
2791M	A	2.49	CH2	C(=O)-O-CH3/CH(OH/CH2)		CCL4
2773M	B	2.49	CH2	C(=O)-O-CH/CH2-C(=O)-O		CCL4
979M	B	2.49 APP.	CH2	C:N/CH2-C		DMSO-D6
442M	D	2.49	CH2	NH2/CH(CH3/CH3)		CDCL3
646M	B	2.49	CH2	N(CH2/CH2)/CH3		CDCL3
1206M	D	2.49	CH2	SH/CH2.4-CH3		CCL4
1205M	D	2.49	CH2	SH/CH2-CH		CCL4
1222M	C	2.49	CH2	SH/CH2-CH2		CCL4
1209M	D	2.49	CH2	SH/CH2-CH2		CCL4
1207M	E	2.49	CH2	SH/CH(CH2/CH2)		CCL4
1119M	D	2.49	CH2	S-CH2/CH2.16-CH3		CDCL3
1124M	C	2.49	CH2	S-CH2/CH2-CH3		CCL4
2024M	A	2.49	CH2R	R5<C(=O)-CH=/CH2-C(CL)=>		CCL4
2116M	A	2.49	CH2R	R6A<C(=O)-CH2/CH2-C*>		CDCL3
2029M	C	2.49	CH2R	R6<C(CL)=CH/C(CH3/CH3)-CH2>		CCL4
2009M	B	2.49	CH2R	R7<C(=O)-CH2/CH2-CH2>		CDCL3
202M	A	2.49	CH3	AA<C-CH-C*/CH-CH-C*>		CDCL3
1283M	A	2.49	CH3	A<C-CH-CH-C(SO2-CL)>		CDCL3
2055M	A	2.49	CH3	A<C-C(C(=O)-CH3)>		CCL4
2290M	A	2.49	CH3	A(C-CH-CH-(C(=O)-NH2))		TFA
789M	A	2.49	CH3	A(C-C(NH2))	S	D20
2055M	B	2.49	CH3	C(=O)-A		CCL4
2109M	A	2.49	CH3	C(=O)-AR600		CDCL3
2383M	B	2.49	CH3	C(=O)-R7N		CDCL3
563M	D	2.49	HCHR	R6N<NH-HCH/CH2-CH(CH3)>		CCL4
1726M	A	2.49	OH	CH2-CH2		CDCL3
1665M	A	2.49	OH	CH2-CH2		CDCL3
152M	A	2.50- 3.30	CH	A/CH(A/CH2)/CH2-A		CDCL3
1982M	E	2.50	CH	C(=O)-CH2.5/CH3/CH3		CCL4
1501M	C	2.50	CH2	A<C-CH-CH-C(O-CH3)>/CH2-CH3		CCL4
1928M	C	2.50	CH2	A<C-C(OH)-CH-C(OH)>/CH2.14-CH3		POLYSOL-D
152M	A	2.50- 3.30	CH2	A/CH(A/CH)		CDCL3
2746M	B	2.50	CH2	C(=O)-CH3/CH2-C(=O)-O		CCL4
2682M	A	2.50	CH2	C(=O)-O-NH4/CH2-C(=O)-O	S	D20
1902M	A	2.50	CH2	C:N/CH2-A		CDCL3
1217M	D	2.50- 3.10	CH2	NH-R6/CH2-SH		CDCL3
626M	E	2.50 APP.	CH2	N(CH2.3/CH2)/CH3		CDCL3
1650M	B	2.50	CH2	N(CH2/CH2)/CH2-OH		CCL4
1221M	C	2.50	CH2	SH/CH2-CH2		CCL4

BOOK NO.	ASSIGN-MENT	CHEM SHIFT - ppm -	PROTON GROUP	ENVIRONMENTAL GROUPS	S	SOLVENT
1217M	D	2.50- 3.10	CH2	SH/CH2-NH		CDCL3
198M	B	2.50- 3.00	CH2R	R5AR6(C*/CH2-CH*)		CCL4
198M	B	2.50- 3.00	CH2R	R6AR5(C*/CH2-CH2)		CCL4 .
2378M	B	2.50	CH2R	R6NR6SPI<C*(CH2/CH2)-CH2/C(=0)-NH>		CDCL3
730M	A	2.50	CH3	ANA(C-N-C(CL)-C*/CH-C*)		CDCL3
690M	B	2.50	CH3	AN(C-N/CH-C(CH3))		CDCL3
2068M	A	2.50	CH3	C(=0)-A		CCL4
2065M	A	2.50	CH3	C(=0)-A		CCL4
2069M	A	2.50	CH3	C(=0)-A		CDCL3
1148M	A	2.50	CH3	R5NS<C=N/CH=>		CCL4
1752M	A	2.50	HCH	NH2/CH(OH/HCH)		D20
2758M	E	2.50 APP.	OH	CH(CH2/CH2)		CDCL3
1646M	A	2.50- 2.90		UNSPECIFIED		CDCL3
629M	D	2.50 APP.		UNSPECIFIED		CDCL3
494M	D	2.51	CH	A<C-C(NH2)>/CH2-CH3/CH3		CCL4
892M	D	2.51	CH2	C(=0)-NH/CH2-CH2		TFA
2774M	C	2.51	CH2	C(=0)-0-CH2/CH2-C(=0)-0		CCL4
955M	B	2.51	CH2	C:N/CH2-CH2		CCL4
553M	D	2.51	CH2	NH-CH2/CH2-CH2		CCL4
708M	B	2.51	CH2	N(CH3/CH3)/CH2-NH		CDCL3
1406M	B	2.51	CH2	N(CH3/CH3/CH2-0		CCL4
1220M	C	2.51 APP.	CH2	SH/CH2-CH2		CCL4
2538M	A	2.51 APP.	CH2R	R6<CH(C(=0)-OH)-CH(C(=0)-OH)/CH=CH>		C3D6O
1071M	A	2.51	CH3	A<C-C(NO2)/CH-C(NH2)S		POLYSOL-D
2222M	A	2.51	CH3	A(C-C(C(=0)-CL))		CCL4
984M	A	2.51	CH3	A((C-C(C:N))		CCL4
2076M	B	2.51	CH3	C(=0)-A		CDCL3
2145M	C	2.51	CH3	C(=0)-R6		CCL4
1353M	C	2.51	CH3	N(NH/CH3)		POLYSOL-D
2856M	B	2.51	CH3	Q1(A/C(=0)-0-CH2)		CCL4
138M	D	2.52 APP.	CH	A/CH2-CH3/CH3		CCL4
492M	B	2.52	CH2	A<C-CH-C(NH2)>/CH3		CDCL3
469M	C	2.52	CH2	NH2/R6		CDCL3
549M	D	2.52	CH2	NH-CH2/CH2-CH		CCL4
544M	D	2.52	CH2	NH-CH2/CH2-CH2		D20
645M	B	2.52	CH2	N(CH2/CH2)/CH3		CDCL3
1650M	C	2.52	CH2	N(CH2/CH2)/CH3		CCL4
1430M	B	2.52	CH2	N(CH2/CH3)/CH(0/0)		CCL4
1101M	B	2.52	CH2	P(+)(CH2/CH2/CH2)/CH3	S	CDCL3
1201M	D	2.52	CH2	SH/CH2-CH3		CDCL3
1200M	C	2.52	CH2	SH/CH3		CCL4
1660M	D	2.52	CH2	S-CH2.2/CH2.10-CH3		CDCL3
1125M	C	2.52	CH2	S-CH2/CH2-CH2		CDCL3
2114M	B	2.52	CH2R	R6A<C(=0)-C*/CH2-CH2>		CCL4
1105M	A	2.52	CH3	A<C-C(P(=0/A/A))>		CDCL3
2074M	A	2.52	CH3	C(=0)-A		POLYSOL-D
1243M	A	2.52	CH3	S(=0)-CH3		CCL4
2074M	A	2.52	CH3	S-A		POLYSOL-D
1497M	B	2.53	CH2	A<C-CH-CH-C(0-CH3)>/CH3		CCL4
134M	B	2.53	CH2	A/CH3		CCL4
144M	C	2.53	CH2	A/R3		CDCL3
2617M	A	2.53	CH2	C(=0)-OH/CH2-NH2		D20
578M	D	2.53	CH2	NH-CH2/CH2-CH3		CCL4
464M	C	2.53	CH2	NH-CH3/CH2-CH2		D20
1211M	D	2.53	CH2	SH/CH2.7-CH3		CDCL3
1208M	D	2.53	CH2	SH/CH2-CH2		CDCL3
1112M	C	2.53	CH2	S-CH2/CH2-CH		CDCL3
1334M	A	2.53	CH3	AN<C-N-C(C(=S)-NH2)>		POLYSOL-D
2063M	A	2.53	CH3	C(=0)-A		CCL4
2317M	B	2.54	CH	C(=0)-NH/CH3/CH3		POLYSOL-D
1693M	A	2.54	CH	C-CH2		CDCL3
482M	C	2.54	CH2	NH2/CH2-CH2		CCL4
552M	E	2.54	CH2	NH-CH3/CH2-CH2		CDCL3
1119M	E	2.54	CH2	S-CH2.17/CH3		CDCL3
2627M	C	2.54	CH2	S-CH3/CH2-CH		POLYSOL-D
2184M	A	2.54	CH3	R5S(C-S/CH-CH)		CDCL3
2012M	B	2.54	CH*R	R6R6R6TRI<C(=0)-CH*/CH2-CH*/CH2-CH*>		CDCL3
1441M	D	2.54	HCHR	R30<0-CH(CH2.7-CH3)>		CCL4
1767M	D	2.54	OH	R6<CH-CH(CH3)/HCH>		CDCL3
2474M	B	2.55	CH	C(=0)-OH/CH3/CH3		CCL4
190M	B	2.55	CH2	A<C-CH-C(CH2-CH3)/CH-C(CH2-CH3)>/CH3		CCL4
1880M	B	2.55	CH2	A<C-CH-C(OH)>/CH3		CDCL3
2560M	B	2.55	CH2	C(=0)-OH/CH2.2-A	S	D20
1250M	B	2.55	CH2	C:C-CH3/CH2-S0		CDCL3
960M	B	2.55	CH2	C:N/CH2-NH		CDCL3
1212M	D	2.55	CH2	SH/CH2-CH2		CDCL3
1185M	C	2.55	CH2	S-S/CH(CH3/CH3)		CCL4
2374M	B	2.55	CH2R	R5N(C(=0)-N(A)/CH2-CH2)		CDCL3
1470M	A	2.55	CH2R	R60S<S-CH2/CH2-0>		CCL4
2064M	A	2.55	CH3	C(=0)-A		CCL4
1439M	D	2.55	HCHR	R30<0-CH(CH2-CH3)>		CCL4

BOOK NO.	ASSIGN-MENT	CHEM SHIFT - ppm -	PROTON GROUP	ENVIRONMENTAL GROUPS	S	SOLVENT
2324M	C	2.56	CH2	A(C-CH-CH-C(NH-C(=O)))/CH3		CDCL3
2313M	A	2.56	CH2	C(=O)-NH/CH2-CL		CDCL3
1400M	B	2.56	CH2	C:N/CH2-O		CDCL3
574M	C	2.56	CH2	NH-CH2/CH3		CCL4
547M	E	2.56	CH2	NH-C/CH2-CH2		CDCL3
1244M	D	2.56 APP.	CH2	SO-CH2/CH2-CH2		CCL4
1244M	D	2.56 APP.	CH2	SO-CH2/CH3		CCL4
1123M	B	2.56	CH2	S-CH2.2/CH3		CCL4
2075M	A	2.56	CH3	C(=O)-A		CDCL3
1585M	B	2.56	CH3	R5NOA<C=N/O>		CDCL3
773M	C	2.56	CH*R	R6R6BI(CH(NH2)-CH2/CH2-CH*/CH2-CH2)	S	D2O
1440M	D	2.56	HCHR	R30<O-CH(CH2.5-CH3)>		CCL4
1442M	D	2.56	HCHR	R30(O-CH(CH2-CH2))		CCL4
688M	C	2.57	CH2	AN(C-CH-CH-N)/CH2-CH2		CCL4
2218M	C	2.57	CH2	A<C-CH-CH-C(BR)>/CH2-CH2		CDCL3
1933M	C	2.57	CH2	A<C-CH-C(C(CH3/CH3/CH3))-C(OH)/CH-C(CH2-A)>		CDCL3
1879M	B	2.57	CH2	A<C-C(OH)>/CH3		CCL4
143M	C	2.57	CH2	A/CH2-CH2		CCL4
2218M	B	2.57	CH2	C(=O)-CL/CH2-CH2		CDCL3
445M	E	2.57	CH2	NH2/CH(CH2/CH3)		CDCL3
579M	C	2.57	CH2	NH-CH2/CH2-CH2		CCL4
1652M	D	2.57	CH2	N(CH2.3/CH2.3)/CH2-OH		CDCL3
1121M	C	2.57	CH2	S-CH3/CH2.2-NH2		D2O
1046M	A	2.57	CH3	A(C-C(NO2))		CCL4
1687M	B	2.57	OH	CH2-CH2		CDCL3
179M	B	2.58	CH2	A<C-CH-C(CH2-CH3)>/CH3		CCL4
137M	C	2.58	CH2	A/CH2-CH2		CCL4
141M	C	2.58	CH2	A/CH2-CH2		CCL4
135M	C	2.58	CH2	A/CH2-CH3		CDCL3
542M	C	2.58	CH2	NH-CH2.2/CH2-CH3		CDCL3
958M	D	2.58	CH2	N(CH/CH)/CH2.2-C:N		CCL4
2551M	B	2.58	CH2	Q1(A/C(=O)-OH)/CH3		CDCL3
2394M	A	2.58- 2.95	CH2R	R30(O-CH(HCH-R5NA))		CDCL3
1131M	B	2.58	CH2R	R6S<S-CH2/CH2-CH2>		CCL4
1068M	B	2.58	CH3	A<C-C(NO2)/CH-C(CH3)>		CDCL3
1444M	A	2.58	HCHR	R30<O-CH(CH2-BR)>		CCL4
1443M	A	2.58	HCHR	R30(O-CH(HCH-CL))		CCL4
1443M	B	2.58	HCHR	R30(O-CH(HCH-CL))		CCL4
2951M	A	2.58	HCHR	R50<C(=O)-O/CH(A)-HCH>		CDCL3
2951M	B	2.58	HCHR	R50<C(=O)-O/CH(A)-HCH>		CDCL3
557M	D	2.58	NH	CH(CH2/CH3)/CH2-CH2		CDCL3
1838M	D	2.58	OH	CH(C/C)		CDCL3
448M	D	2.59	CH	NH2/C(CH3/CH3/CH3)/CH3		CCL4
76M	C	2.59	CH	Q2(CH3)/CH3/CH3		CCL4
685M	B	2.59	CH2	AN<C-CH-CH-N>/CH3		CCL4
172M	C	2.59	CH2	A(C-C(A(C-CH-CH-C(CH3))))/CH3		CCL4
142M	D	2.59	CH2	A/CH2-CH2		CDCL3
2494M	B	2.59 APP.	CH2	C(=O)-CH3/CH2-C(=O)-O		CDCL3
2850M	B	2.59	CH2	C(=O)-O-CH2/CH(OH/A)		CCL4
554M	D	2.59	CH2	NH-CH2.12/CH2.11-CH3		CDCL3
705M	B	2.59	CH2	N(CH2/CH2)/CH3		CDCL3
1703M	B	2.59	CH2	N(CH2/CH3)/CH2-OH		CDCL3
1088M	A	2.59	CH2	SI(A/A/CH2)/A		CDCL3
2952M	B	2.59	CH2R	R60<C(=O)-O/CH2-CH2>		CCL4
2869M	A	2.59	CH3	A(C-C(C(=O)-O-CH3))		CDCL3
2067M	A	2.59	CH3	C(=O)-A		CCL4
2080M	A	2.59	CH3	C(=O)-A		DMSO-D6
1438M	C	2.59	HCHR	R30(O-CH(CH3))		CCL4
1624M	D	2.59	OH	CH2-C		CDCL3
1705M	A	2.59	OH	CH2-CH2		CCL4
2544M	A	2.60- 3.30	CH	C(=O)-OH/CH2-A/CH2-A		CDCL3
804M	C	2.60- 3.12	CH	NH-CH3/CH2-A/CH3	S	CDCL3
80M	B	2.60	CH	Q2(H/H/CH(CH3/CH3))/CH3/CH3		CCL4
2376M	C	2.60- 3.30	CHR	R5N<(CH3)/C(=O)-NH/HCH-C(=O)>>		CDCL3
564M	C	2.60	CHR	R6N((CH3)/N-CH(CH3)/CH2-CH2)		CCL4
693M	C	2.60	CH2	AN(C-CH-N/CH-C(CH2.3-CH3))		CDCL3
178M	C	2.60	CH2	A<C-CH-C(CH3)>/CH3		CDCL3
2544M	A	2.60- 3.30	CH2	A/CHNC(=O)-OH/CH2)/A		CDCL3
482M	D	2.60	CH2	A/CH2-CH2		CCL4
1865M	B	2.60	CH2	CH(C(=O)-O/C(=O))/CH(C(=O)-O/C(=O))		CDCL3
1995M	B	2.60	CH2	C(=O)-CH3/CH2-C(=O)		CCL4
2806M	A	2.60	CH2	C(=O)-O-CH2/CH2-C(=O)-O		CCL4
461M	B	2.60	CH2	NH2/CH2-CH2		D2O
580M	A	2.60 APP.	CH2	NH2/CH2-NH		D2O
457M	B	2.60	CH2	NH2/CH2-NH2		CCL4
548M	C	2.60	CH2	NH-CH2.4/CH2.3-CH3		CDCL3
580M	A	2.60 APP.	CH2	NH-CH2/CH2-NH2		D2O
463M	B	2.60	CH2	NH-CH2/CH3		D2O
577M	C	2.60	CH2	NH-CH2/CH3		CCL4
2461M	A	2.60	CH2	Q3/R6NN<C(CH2-Q3)-C(=O)/C(=O)>		DMSO-D6
641M	C	2.60- 3.26	CH2R	R6NN<NH-CH2/CH(CH3)-N(A)>		CDCL3

BOOK NO.	ASSIGN-MENT	CHEM SHIFT - ppm -	PROTON GROUP	ENVIRONMENTAL GROUPS	S	SOLVENT
611M	B	2.60	CH2R	R6R5NA<C*-C*/CH2-CH2>		CDCL3
611M	B	2.60	CH2R	R6R5NA<C*-NH/CH2-CH2>		CDCL3
2111M	A	2.60	CH3	AN(C-N-C(C(=O)-CH3))		CDCL3
2113M	A	2.60	CH3	C(=O)-AA		CCL4
2132M	D	2.60	CH*R	R5R5BI<C(=O)-C(=O)/C(CH3/CH3)-C*(CH3)/CH2-CH2>		POLYSOL-D
1446M	A	2.60	HCHR	R30<O-CH(Q3)>		CDCL3
2376M	C	2.60- 3.30	HCHR	R5N<C(=O)-NH/CH(CH3)-C(=O)>		CDCL3
1837M	E	2.60	OH	CH2-C		CDCL3
1768M	C	2.60	OH	R6<CH-CH2/CH2>		CDCL3
2035M	B	2.61	CH	C(=O)-CH2/CH3/CH3		CCL4
529M	A	2.61	CH2	A<C-CH-CH-C(NH2)>/CH2-NH2		CDCL3
2849M	C	2.61	CH2	A/CH2.2-C(=O)-O		CCL4
2041M	C	2.61	CH2	C(=O)-Q2/CH2.2-CH3		CDCL3
1658M	A	2.61	CH2	C:N/CH2-OH		CDCL3
441M	D	2.61	CH2	NH2/CH2-CH2		CDCL3
464M	D	2.61	CH2	NH2/CH2-CH2		D20
454M	C	2.61	CH2	NH2/CH(CH2/CH2)		CDCL3
1124M	D	2.61	CH2	S-CH2/CH2-S		CCL4
1318M	A	2.61	CH2R	R5OS<CH2-O/CH2-SO2>		CDCL3
603M	B	2.61	CH2R	R6NA(C*/CH2-NH)		CCL4
1467M	B	2.61	CH2R	R6NO<N(C(C:N/CH3/CH3))-CH2/CH2-O>		CDCL3
2145M	D	2.61	CH2R	R6(C(OH)=C(C(=O)-CH3)/CH2-CH2)		CCL4
2145M	B	2.61	CH2R	R6(C(=O)-C(C(=O)-CH3)=/CH2-CH2)		CCL4
753M	A	2.61	CH3	NH-NH2		CCL4
1007M	A	2.61	CH3	S-C:N		CCL4
2008M	E	2.61	CH*R	R5R5BI<C(=O)-CH2/C(CH3/CH3)-C*/CH2-C(=O)>		CDCL3
1447M	A	2.61	HCHR	R30(O-CH(A))		CCL4
1184M	D	2.62	CH	S-S/CH2-CH3/CH3		CCL4
1702M	B	2.62	CH2	A/CH2-CH2		CCL4
2747M	E	2.62	CH2	C(=O)-O-CH2.2/CH2-C(=O)-CH3		CCL4
2737M	A	2.62	CH2	C(=O)-O-CH3/CH2-C:N		CCL4
2737M	A	2.62	CH2	C:N/CH2-C(=O)-O		CCL4
458M	B	2.62	CH2	NH2/CH2-CH2		D20
556M	B	2.62	CH2	NH-CH/CH2-NH		D20
1854M	A	2.62 APP.	CH2	N(CH2/CH2)/CH2-N		CDCL3
1854M	A	2.62 APP.	CH2	N(CH2/CH2)/CH2-OH		CDCL3
2079M	A	2.62	CH3	C(=O)-A		CDCL3
2110M	A	2.62	CH3	C(=O)-AN		CCL4
1337M	A	2.62	CH3	C(=S)-N		CDCL3
765M	A	2.62	CH3	NH2	S	D20
591M	B	2.62	CH3	NH-A		CDCL3
658M	B	2.62	CH3	N(A/CH3)		CCL4
1752M	B	2.62	HCH	NH2/CH(OH/HCH)		D20
1805M	B	2.62	OH	C(CBR3/CH3/CH3)		CDCL3
545M	D	2.63	CH	NH-CH/CH2-CH3/CH3		CCL4
1819M	B	2.63	CH	:C-C		CDCL3
1445M	C	2.63	CHR	R30<(CH2-O)/O-HCH>		CCL4
1718M	A	2.63	CH2	A<C-CH-CH-C(NH2)>/CH2-OH		POLYSOL-D
2280M	C	2.63	CH2	C(=O)-NH2/CH2.11-CH3		TFA
1844M	A	2.63	CH2	NH2/CH(OH/CH2)		D20
1653M	E	2.63	CH2	N(CH2.3/CH2.3)/CH2.2-OH		CDCL3
1704M	B	2.63	CH2	N(CH2/CH2)/CH2-OH		CDCL3
2271M	A	2.63	CH3	AR50<C-CH-C*-C(=O)/CH-CH-C*>		CDCL3
2082M	A	2.63	CH3	C(=O)-A		CDCL3
1523M	A	2.63	CH3	NH-A		POLYSOL-D
1781M	B	2.63 APP.	HCHR	R6S(S-HCH/CH2-CH2)		CDCL3
1781M	B	2.63 APP.	HCHR	R6S(S-HCH/CH(OH)-CH2)		CDCL3
598M	D	2.63	NH	A<C-CH-CH-C(NH-CH)>/CH(CH2/CH3)>		CDCL3
1672M	A	2.63	NH2	CH2.2-0		CDCL3
1672M	A	2.63	OH	CH2.2-0		CDCL3
964M	B	2.64	CHR	R6<((C:N)/CH2-CH2/CH2-CH2>		CCL4
470M	C	2.64	CHR	R6<(NH2)/CH2-CH2/C-CH2>		CCL4
481M	C	2.64	CH2	A/CH2-CH2		CDCL3
2036M	B	2.64	CH2	C(=O)-CH3/CH2-A		CCL4
1954M	A	2.64	CH2	C:N/CH2-AA		POLYSOL-D
1431M	C	2.64	CH2	N(CH2/CH3)/CH(O/O)		CDCL3
1187M	D	2.64	CH2	S-S/CH2.3-CH3		CCL4
565M	C	2.64	CH2R	R13N<NH-CH2/CH2-CH2>		CDCL3
719M	A	2.64	CH3	ANA<C-N-C*/CH-CH-C*>		CCL4
1364M	B	2.64	CH3	A(C-C(SO2-NH2)-C(CH3)/CH-C(CH3))		TFA
2081M	A	2.64	CH3	C(=O)-A		CDCL3
1648M	C	2.65	CH	N(CH3/CH3)/HCH-OH/CH3		D20
2059M	C	2.65	CH2	A(C-CH-CH-C(C(=O)-CH3))/CH3		CCL4
439M	D	2.65	CH2	NH2/CH2-CH2		CCL4
439M	D	2.65	CH2	NH2/CH2-CH3		CCL4
463M	C	2.65 APP.	CH2	NH2/CH2-NH		D20
555M	C	2.65	CH2	NH-CH2.2/CH3		CDCL3
463M	C	2.65 APP.	CH2	NH-CH2/CH2-NH2		D20
1540M	B	2.65	CH2R	R30<O-CH(CH2-O)>		CCL4
113M	A	2.65	CH2R	R6<CH=CH/CH=CH>		CDCL3
2164M	A	2.65	CH3	A<C-C(C(=O)-H)>		CCL4

BOOK NO.	ASSIGN-MENT	CHEM SHIFT - ppm -	PROTON GROUP	ENVIRONMENTAL GROUPS	S	SOLVENT
1362M	A	2.65	CH3	A<C-C(SO2-NH2)>		DMSO-D6
1301M	B	2.65	CH3	A(C-C(SO3NA)/CH-C(CH3))		D2O
2746M	C	2.66	CH2	C(=O)-O-CH3/CH2-C(=O)	S	CCL4
1647M	B	2.66	CH2	NH-CH/CH2-OH		CCL4
1193M	B	2.66	CH2	S-S/CH3		CCL4
2127M	A	2.66	CH3	AR6A(C-C*-C(=O)-C*/CH-CH-C(CH3))		CDCL3
2312M	A	2.66	CH3	NH-C(=O)		CDCL3
2410M	A	2.66	CH3	N(NH/CH3)		CDCL3
689M	D	2.67	CH	AN<C-N>/CH2.3-CH3/CH2.3-CH3		CCL4
155M	B	2.67	CH2	A/CH2-Q3		CDCL3
2495M	D	2.67	CH2	C(=O)-CH2/CH2-C(=O)		CDCL3
2540M	A	2.67	CH2	C(=O)-OH/CH2-A		CCL4
1248M	C	2.67	CH2	SO-A/CH2-CH3		CDCL3
2016M	A	2.67	CH2R	R6S(C(=O)-CH2/CH2-S)		CDCL3
720M	A	2.67	CH3	ANA(C-C*/CH-CH-N)		CCL4
582M	A	2.67	CH3	NH-A		CCL4
1788M	C	2.67	OH	CH(A/CH2)		CDCL3
2285M	C	2.68	CH	C(=O)-NH2/R6<C=CH/CH2>/CH2-CH3		CDCL3
477M	B	2.68 APP.	CH2	A/CH2-NH2		CCL4
462M	C	2.68	CH2	NH2/CH2.11-NH2		CDCL3
1121M	D	2.68	CH2	NH2/CH2.2-S		D2O
1597M	D	2.68	CH2	NH2/CH2.2-SI		CDCL3
465M	E	2.68	CH2	NH2/CH2-CH2		CCL4
1661M	A	2.68	CH2	SH/CH2-OH		D2O
1245M	C	2.68	CH2	S(=O)-CH2/CH2-CH2		CDCL3
2073M	A	2.68	CH3	C(=O)-A		CDCL3
945M	B	2.69	CH	C:N/CH3/CH3		CCL4
1439M	E	2.69	CHR	R30<(CH2-CH3)/O-HCH>		CCL4
2515M	B	2.69	CHR	R6<(C(=O)-OH)/CH2-CH2/CH2-CH2>		TFA
1164M	C	2.69	CH2	A/CH2-CH2		CCL4
2159M	A	2.69	CH2	C(=O)-H/CH2-A		CDCL3
976M	A	2.69	CH2	C:N/CH2-N		DMSO-D6
444M	D	2.69	CH2	NH2/CH2-CH2		CDCL3
1427M	B	2.69	CH2	NH2/CH(O/O)		CCL4
2657M	B	2.69	CH2	N(CH2/CH2)/CH3		D2O
1401M	C	2.69	CH2	SH/CH2-O		CDCL3
1164M	B	2.69	CH2	S-A/CH2-CH2		CCL4
1128M	B	2.69	CH2	S-CH/CH3		CCL4
1188M	C	2.69	CH2	S-S/CH2-CH		CCL4
560M	C	2.69	CH2R	R5N<NH-CH2/CH2-CH2>		C6H6
601M	B	2.69	CH2R	R6NA<C*/CH2-CH2>		CDCL3
1589M	A	2.69	CH2R	R60A<C*/CH2-O>		CCL4
2111M	B	2.69	CH3	C(=O)-AN		CDCL3
590M	B	2.69	CH3	NH-A		CDCL3
1375M	B	2.69	CH3	N(SO2/CH3)		CDCL3
1777M	B	2.69	OH	R7<CH-CH2/CH2>		CDCL3
2824M	D	2.69- 3.28		UNSPECIFIED		CCL4
455M	D	2.70	CH	NH2/CH2.3/CH2.3		CDCL3
1440M	E	2.70	CHR	R30<(CH2.5-CH3)/O-HCH>		CCL4
197M	C	2.70	CHR	R6A((CH2-CH3)/C*/CH2-CH2)		CCL4
2788M	C	2.70	CHR	R6<(C(=O)-O-CH2)/CH(C(=O)-O-CH2)-CH2/CH2-CH2>		CCL4
147M	B	2.70	CH2	A/CH2-CH2		CDCL3
2494M	C	2.70	CH2	C(=O)-OH/CH2-C(=O)		CDCL3
2725M	B	2.70	CH2	C(=O)-O-CH/CH2-CL		CCL4
1643M	B	2.70	CH2	NH2/CH2-CH2		D2O
466M	C	2.70	CH2	NH2/CH2-CH2		CDCL3
451M	D	2.70	CH2	NH2/CH2-CH2		CDCL3
481M	D	2.70	CH2	NH2/CH2-CH2		CDCL3
1466M	D	2.70	CH2	NH2/CH2-CH2		CCL4
466M	C	2.70	CH2	NH-CH2/CH2-CH2		CDCL3
557M	E	2.70	CH2	NH-CH/CH2-NH		CDCL3
1850M	A	2.70	CH2	N(CH2/CH2)/CH2-OH		D2O
2865M	B	2.70	CH2	N(CH3/CH3)/CH2-O-C(=O)		CDCL3
1402M	B	2.70	CH2	SH/CH2-O		CCL4
1189M	D	2.70	CH2	S-S/CH2.10-CH3		CDCL3
2382M	C	2.70	CH2R	R5N<C(=O)-N(CH2.4-CH3)/CH2-C(=O)>		CDCL3
197M	C	2.70	CH2R	R6A(C*/CH2-CH2)		CCL4
815M	B	2.70- 3.80	CH2R	R6N(N(CH2-CH2)-CH2/CH2-CH2)	S	D2O
2026M	B	2.70	CH2R	R6<C(CL)=CH/CH2-CH2>		CCL4
2383M	C	2.70	CH2R	R7N(C(=O)-N(C(=O)-CH3)/CH2-CH2)		CDCL3
1284M	B	2.70	CH3	A<C-C(SO2-CL)-CH-C(CH3)>		CCL4
2241M	A	2.70	CH3	A(C-C(NO2)-CH-C(C(=O)-CL))		CCL4
2373M	A	2.70	CH3	C(=O)-R5NAA		CDCL3
253M	A	2.70	CH3	C-CL3		CCL4
592M	B	2.70	CH3	NH-A		CDCL3
2416M	A	2.70	CH3	NH-C(=O)-NH2		D2O
1151M	A	2.70	CH3	R5NS<C=N/S>		CDCL3
1249M	A	2.70	CH3	SO-A		CDCL3
2667M	A	2.70	HCH	C(=O)-O-K/C(OH/C(=O)-O-K/HCH	S	D2O
2667M	B	2.70	HCH	C(=O)-O-K/C(OH/C(=O)-O-K/HCH	S	D2O
1822M	A	2.70 APP.	OH	C(A/A/A)		CDCL3

BOOK NO.	ASSIGN-MENT	CHEM SHIFT - ppm -	PROTON GROUP	ENVIRONMENTAL GROUPS	S	SOLVENT
1814M	E	2.70	OH	C(C:C/CH2/CH3)		CCL4
479M	C	2.71 APP.	CH	A/CH2-NH2/CH3		CDCL3
1994M	C	2.71	CH	C(=O)-CH3/CH2-OH/CH3		CDCL3
1441M	E	2.71	CHR	R30<(CH2.7-CH3)/O-HCH>		CCL4
2205M	B	2.71	CHR	R6<(C(=O)-CL/CH2-CH2/CH2-CH2>		CCL4
965M	B	2.71	CHR	R6<(C:N)/CH2-CH2/CH2-CH2>		CDCL3
970M	B	2.71 APP.	CHR	R6((C:N)/CH2-CH=/CH2-CH2)		CCL4
1485M	B	2.71	CH2	A/CH2-O		CCL4
2131M	C	2.71	CH2	C(=O)-C(=O)/CH3		CCL4
2724M	B	2.71	CH2	C(=O)-O-CH2/CH2-CL		CCL4
446M	E	2.71	CH2	NH2/CH2-CH		CDCL3
479M	C	2.71 APP.	CH2	NH2/CH(A/CH3)		CDCL3
627M	E	2.71	CH2	N(CH2/CH3)/CH2-CH2		CDCL3
2816M	D	2.71	CH2	Q2(H/H/CH2-Q2)/Q2(H/H/CH2-CH3)		CCL4
638M	C	2.71	CH2	R6N(N-CH2/CH2)/R6N(N-CH2/CH2)		CCL4
1219M	D	2.71	CH2	SH/CH(SH/CH3)		CDCL3
1660M	E	2.71	CH2	S-CH2.11/CH2-OH		CDCL3
1123M	C	2.71	CH2	S-CH2/CH2-S		CCL4
2015M	B	2.71	CH2R	R6N<N(CH2-A)-CH2/CH2-C(=O)>		CDCL3
2028M	D	2.71	CH2R	R6<C(CL)=C(CH3)/CH2-CH2>		CCL4
1177M	A	2.71	CH3	R5NSA<C=N/S>		CDCL3
1453M	A	2.71	HCHR	P5R30A<C*/CH*(O/CH*)>		CCL4
1645M	C	2.71	NH2	C(CH2.2/CH3/CH3)		CDCL3
2038M	B	2.71	OH	A(C-CH-CH-C(CH2-CH2))		CDCL3
1635M	C	2.71	OH	CH2.23-CH3		POLYSOL-D
1645M	C	2.71	OH	CH2.2-C		CDCL3
1745M	D	2.71	OH	CH(CH2/CH2)		CDCL3
2191M	C	2.72	CH	C(=O)-CL/CH2.2-CH3/CH2.2-CH3		CCL4
1644M	C	2.72	CH	NH2/HCH-OH/CH2-CH3		CDCL3
2372M	C	2.72	CHR	R6NA<C*/CH2-CH2>		CDCL3
1843M	A	2.72	CH2	NH-CH2/CH2-NH		D20
555M	D	2.72	CH2	NH-CH2/CH2-NH		CDCL3
1843M	A	2.72	CH2	NH-CH2/CH2-OH		D20
630M	B	2.72	CH2	N(CH3/CH3)/N(CH3/CH3)		CDCL3
1462M	B	2.72	CH2R	R6NO(NH-CH2/CH2-O)		CCL4
2741M	E	2.72	OH	CH(C(=O)-O/CH2)		CCL4
1819M	C	2.72	OH	C(A/C:C/CH3)		CDCL3
687M	D	2.73	CH2	AN<C-N>/CH2-CH2		CCL4
295M	B	2.73	CH2	A<C-C(CL)>/CH3		CCL4
973M	B	2.73	CH2	A/CH2-C:N		CDCL3
2986M	B	2.73	CH2	A/CH2-NH		CCL4
1484M	A	2.73	CH2	A/CH2-O		CDCL3
1642M	A	2.73	CH2	NH2/CH2-OH		CDCL3
2986M	C	2.73	CH2	NH-C(=O)/CH2-A		CCL4
2853M	C	2.73	CH2	N(CH2/CH2)/CH2-C(=O)-O		CDCL3
1442M	E	2.74	CHR	R30((CH2-CH2)/O-HCH)		CCL4
1050M	B	2.74	CH2	A<C-CH-CH-C(NO2)>/CH3		CCL4
375M	B	2.74	CH2	A<C-C(BR)>/CH3		CCL4
2490M	B	2.74 APP.	CH2	CH2-C(=O)-O/SH		CCL4
2490M	B	2.74 APP.	CH2	C(=O)-OH/CH2-SH		CCL4
1842M	A	2.74	CH2	NH-CH2/CH2-OH		D20
1902M	B	2.75	CH2	A<C-CH-CH-C(OH)>/CH2-C:N		CDCL3
379M	B	2.75- 3.40	CH2	BR/CH2-CH		CCL4
1604M	B	2.75	CH2	CL/SI(O/CH3/CH3)		CDCL3
1122M	A	2.75	CH2	C:N/CH2-S		CDCL3
767M	C	2.75	CH2	NH2/CH2-CH3	S	DMSO-D6
1122M	B	2.75	CH2	S-CH2.2/CH2-C:N		CDCL3
196M	B	2.75	CH2R	R6A(C*/CH2-CH2)		CDCL3
2117M	B	2.75	CH2R	R60A<C(=O)-C*/CH2-O>		CDCL3
2437M	A	2.75	CH3	N(C(=O)/CH3)		3.40
1669M	C	2.75	OH	CH2.2-O		CCL4
2537M	C	2.75- 3.30		UNSPECIFIED		CCL4
592M	C	2.76	CH	A<C-CH-CH-C(NH-CH3)>/CH3/CH3		CDCL3
1428M	B	2.76	CH2	NH2/CH(O/O)		CDCL3
1701M	B	2.77	CH2	A/CH2-OH		CDCL3
1130M	B	2.77	CH2R	R5S<S-CH2/CH2-CH2>		CCL4
2118M	A	2.77	CH2R	R60A(C(=O)-C*/CH2-O)		CDCL3
2038M	C	2.77	CH3	C(=O)-CH2		CDCL3
2612M	A	2.77	CH3	NH-CH2		D20
1175M	A	2.77	CH3	R5NSA(C=N/S)		CDCL3
1761M	D	2.77	OH	CH(R3/CH3)		CDCL3
556M	C	2.78	CH	NH-CH2/CH3/CH3		D20
2510M	A	2.78	CH2	C(=O)-OH/CH(C(=O)-O/CH2)		D20
962M	A	2.78	CH2	C:N/CH2-C:N		CDCL3
1948M	B	2.78 APP.	CH2R	R5A(C*-C(OH)/CH2-CH2)		CDCL3
1948M	B	2.78 APP.	CH2R	R5A(C*/CH2-CH2)		CDCL3
804M	B	2.78	CH3	NH-CH	S	CDCL3
2436M	A	2.78	CH3	NH-C(=O)		CDCL3
2980M	B	2.78	CH3	NH-C(=O)-O		CDCL3
813M	D	2.78	CH3	N(R6R6R6TRI/CH3)	S	D20
1373M	A	2.78	CH3	SO2-N	S	CDCL3

BOOK NO.	ASSIGN-MENT	CHEM SHIFT - ppm -	PROTON GROUP	ENVIRONMENTAL GROUPS	S	SOLVENT
1451M	B	2.78 APP.	CH*R	R8R30<0-CH*/CH2-CH2>		
1783M	C	2.78	OH	CH(Q3/CH2)		CDCL3
2309M	B	2.79	CH2	A/CH2-NH		CCL4
2860M	A	2.79	CH2	A/CH2-0-C(=0)		CDCL3
2077M	C	2.79	CH2	C(=0)-A/CH2-CH3		CCL4
2189M	B	2.79	CH2	C(=0)-CL/C(CH3/CH3/CH3)		CCL4
2686M	D	2.79	CH2	NH2/CH2.10-CH3		CDCL3
2793M	B	2.79	CH2	N(CH2.2/CH2.2)/CH2-C(=0)-0		CDCL3
2375M	A	2.79	CH2R	R5N<C(=0)-NH/CH2-C(=0)>		D20
2377M	B	2.79	CH2R	R6N<C(=0)-NH/CH2-CH2>		TFA
673M	D	2.79	CH2R	R6N<N(CH3)-CH2/CH=CH>		CCL4
599M	A	2.79	CH3	NH-AA		CDCL3
1288M	A	2.79	CH3	NH-CH2		D20
665M	B	2.79	CH3	N(A/CH3)		CDCL3
659M	B	2.79	CH3	N(A/CH3)		CCL4
660M	B	2.79	CH3	N(A/CH3)		CCL4
1677M	A	2.79	HCHR	R30<0-CH(HCH-OH)>		D20
1443M	A	2.79	HCHR	R30(0-CH(HCH-CL))		CCL4
1443M	B	2.79	HCHR	R30(0-CH(HCH-CL))		CCL4
2412M	A	2.79	HCHR	R5NN<C(=0)-NH/CH(A)-NH>		DMSO-D6
2412M	B	2.79	HCHR	R5NN<C(=0)-NH/CH(A)-NH>		DMSO-D6
2014M	B	2.79 APP.		UNSPECIFIED		CDCL3
216M	C	2.80	CH	AAA/CH3/CH3		CCL4
182M	C	2.80	CH	A<C-CH-CH-C(CH3)>/CH3/CH3		CDCL3
493M	B	2.80	CH	A<C-CH-CH-C(NH2)>/CH3/CH3		CCL4
1438M	D	2.80	CHR	R30((CH3)/0-HCH)		CDCL3
883M	B	2.80 APP.	CHR	R6<(QN(N(CH3/CH3)))/CH2-CH2/CH2-CH2>		CDCL3
929M	B	2.80	CH2	A<C-C(N=C=N)-C(CH2-CH3)>/CH3		CDCL3
1164M	C	2.80	CH2	A/CH2-CH2		CCL4
954M	A	2.80	CH2	C:N/CH2-CL		CCL4
2685M	D	2.80	CH2	NH2/CH2.8-CH3		CDCL3
1164M	B	2.80	CH2	S-A/CH2-CH2		CCL4
2013M	B	2.80	CH2R	R6N<C(=0)-CH2/C(CH3/CH3)-NH>	S	CDCL3
561M	B	2.80	CH2R	R6N(NH-CH2/CH2-CH2)		CDCL3
1683M	C	2.80- 3.30	CH2R	R6N(NH-CH2/CH2-CH2)		CDCL3
723M	A	2.80	CH3	AAN<C-C*-N>		CCL4
1963M	A	2.80	CH3	ANA<C-C*/CH-C(OH)-N>		TFA
2298M	E	2.80	CH3	NH-C(=0)		CDCL3
2296M	C	2.80	CH3	NH-C(=0)-CH2		CDCL3
1338M	A	2.80	CH3	NH-C(=S)		DMSO-D6
669M	A	2.80	CH3	N(A/CH3)		CDCL3
883M	B	2.80 APP.	CH3	N(QN/CH3)		CDCL3
2007M	D	2.80	HCH	S03-NA/R5R5BI<C*-C(=0)/C(CH3/CH3)/CH2>		D20
2951M	A	2.80	HCHR	R50<C(=0)-0/CH(A)-HCH>		CDCL3
2951M	B	2.80	HCHR	R50<C(=0)-0/CH(A)-HCH>		CDCL3
1881M	B	2.81	CH	A<C-CH-CH-C(OH)>/CH3/CH3		CDCL3
453M	D	2.81	CH	NH2/CH2.2-CH/CH3		CDCL3
443M	E	2.81	CH	NH2/CH2-CH3/CH3		CDCL3
1203M	E	2.81	CH	SH/CH2-CH3/CH3		CCL4
2036M	C	2.81	CH2	A/CH2-C(=0)		CCL4
2070M	C	2.81	CH2	C(=0)-A/CH2-CH3		CDCL3
1295M	D	2.81	CH2	S03-NA/CH2.5-CH3		D20
2371M	B	2.81	CH2R	R6NA<C*/CH2-CH2>		CDCL3
774M	A	2.81	CH3	NH-NH	S	D20
671M	A	2.81	CH3	N(AA/CH3)		CCL4
1900M	A	2.81	CH3	N(A/CH3)		CDCL3
2207M	D	2.81	HCH	S03H/R5R5BI(C*(C(=0)/C/CH2))		D20
1738M	D	2.81	OH	CH(CH2/CH3)		CCL4
1760M	C	2.81- 4.09		UNSPECIFIED		CCL4
2308M	A	2.82	CH2	A/CH(NH/CH2)		DMSO-D6
2071M	C	2.82	CH2	C(=0)-A/CH2.2-CH3		CDCL3
2047M	C	2.82	CH2	C(=0)-A/CH2-CH3		CCL4
2730M	C	2.82 APP.	CH2	C(=0)-0-CH2/CH(BR/CH3)		CCL4
477M	C	2.82 APP.	CH2	NH2/CH2-A		CCL4
1642M	B	2.82	NH2	CH2-CH2		CDCL3
1642M	B	2.82	OH	CH2-CH2		CDCL3
1793M	B	2.82	OH	CH(A/CH3)		CCL4
686M	B	2.83	CH	AN<C-CH-CH-N>/CH3/CH3		CDCL3
136M	B	2.83	CH	A/CH3/CH3		CCL4
785M	C	2.83	CH2	A/CH2-CH	S	TFA
2311M	A	2.83	CH2	A/CH2-NH		CDCL3
1672M	B	2.83	CH2	NH2/CH2-0		CDCL3
1662M	C	2.83	CH2	SH/CH(SH/CH2)		CDCL3
2970M	C	2.83	CH2	S-C(=0)-CH3/CH3		CCL4
566M	B	2.83	CH2R	R6NN<NH-CH2/CH2-NH>		CDCL3
1132M	B	2.83	CH2R	R6SS<S-CH2/CH2-CH2>		POLYSOL-D
1374M	A	2.83	CH3	N(S02/CH3)		CDCL3
2631M	A	2.83	HCH	C(=0)-NH2/CH(NH2/C(=0)-OH)		D20
2505M	A	2.83	HCH	C(=0)-OH/CH(CL/HCH)		D20
1734M	A	2.83	OH	CH2-AR500		CDCL3
459M	D	2.84	CH	NH2/CH2-NH2/CH3		CDCL3

BOOK NO.	ASSIGN- MENT	CHEM SHIFT - ppm -	PROTON GROUP	ENVIRONMENTAL GROUPS	S	SOLVENT
2790M	A	2.84	CH2	C(=O)-O-CH3/CH(OH/C(=O)-O)		CDCL3
1255M	C	2.84	CH2	SO2-CH2/CH2-CH2		CCL4
1452M	B	2.84 APP.	CH*R	R30R*R30(O-CH*/CH2-CH2)		CCL4
2262M	E	2.84	CH*R	R5R60BI<C(=O)-O/C(CH3/CH3)-C*/CH2-CH2>		CDCL3
2630M	A	2.84 APP.	HCH	C(=O)-NH2/CH(NH2/C(=O)-OH)>		D2O
1444M	B	2.84	HCHR	R30<O-CH(CH2-RR)>		CCL4
486M	C	2.85	CH	A<C-CH-CH-C(CH2-NH2)>/CH3/CH3		CCL4
1714M	B	2.85	CH	A<C-CH-CH-C(CH2-OH)>/CH3/CH3		CCL4
1647M	C	2.85	CH	NH-CH2.2/CH3/CH3		CCL4
2838M	D	2.85	CH2	A/CH2-O-C(=O)		CCL4
2194M	D	2.85	CH2	C(=O)-CL/CH2.15-CH3		CCL4
2024M	B	2.85	CH2R	R5<C(CL)=CH/CH2-C(=O)>		CCL4
1133M	A	2.85	CH2R	R6SS(S-CH2/CH2-S)		CCL4
589M	B	2.85	CH3	NH-A		CDCL3
648M	A	2.85	CH3	N(A/CH3)		CCL4
666M	A	2.85	CH3	N(A/CH3)		CDCL3
1524M	A	2.85	CH3	N(A/CH3)		CDCL3
1373M	B	2.85	CH3	N(SO2/CH3)	S	CDCL3
1625M	C	2.85	OH	CH2.4-CH		CDCL3
185M	B	2.86	CH2	A(C-CH-CH-C(CH3))/CH2-A		CDCL3
2049M	D	2.86	CH2	C(=O)-A/CH2-CH2		CCL4
2193M	D	2.86	CH2	C(=O)-CL/CH2-CH2		CDCL3
529M	B	2.86	CH2	NH2/CH2-A		CDCL3
211M	A	2.86	CH2R	R6AA<C*/CH2-C*>		CDCL3
668M	A	2.86	CH3	N(A/CH3)		CDCL3
1787M	E	2.86	OH	CH(CH2/CH2)		CCL4
1769M	C	2.86	OH	R6<CH-CH2/CH2>		CDCL3
1210M	D	2.87	CH	SH/CH2.5-CH3/CH3		CDCL3
2560M	C	2.87	CH2	A<C-C(NH2)>/CH2.2-C(=O)-OH	S	D2O
2385M	A	2.87	CH2	A/CH2-R5N		POLYSOL-D
2192M	D	2.87	CH2	C(=O)-CL/CH2-CH2		CCL4
885M	B	2.87	CH3	N(QN/CH3)		CCL4
1257M	A	2.87	CH3	SO2-CH2		CDCL3
1689M	D	2.87	OH	CH2-CH2		CCL4
626M	F	2.88	CH	NH2/CH2.3-N/CH3		CDCL3
543M	C	2.88	CH	NH-CH/CH3/CH3		CCL4
89M	B	2.88	CH	Q2(Q3)/Q3/CH3		CCL4
1049M	B	2.88	CH2	A(C-C(NO2))/CH3		CCL4
2835M	C	2.88	CH2	A/CH2-O-C(=O)		CCL4
2202M	C	2.88	CH2	C(=O)-CL/CH2.7-C(=O)-CL		CCL4
2188M	C	2.88	CH2	C(=O)-CL/CH2-CH3		CDCL3
2203M	B	2.88	CH2	C(=O)-CL/CH2-R5		CCL4
1122M	A	2.88	CH2	C:N/CH2-S		CDCL3
1122M	B	2.88	CH2	S-CH2.2/CH2-C:N		CDCL3
1003M	A	2.88	CH3	N(C:N/CH3)		CCL4
501M	B	2.89	CH	A<C-C(NH2)-C(CH(CH3/CH3))>/CH3/CH3		CDCL3
149M	A	2.89	CH2	A/CH2-A		CDCL3
2212M	A	2.89	CH2	A/CH2-C(=O)-CL		CCL4
2159M	B	2.89	CH2	A/CH2-C(=O)-H		CDCL3
2836M	C	2.89	CH2	A/CH2-O-C(=O)		CCL4
2200M	B	2.89	CH2	C(=O)-CL/CH2-CH2		CCL4
2633M	B	2.89	CH2	C(=O)-O-CH2/CH2-CH		TFA
1294M	C	2.89	CH2	SO3-NA/CH2.3-CH3		D2O
1708M	B	2.89	CH2	S-A/CH2-OH		CCL4
2108M	C	2.89	CH2R	R5A(C*/CH2-CH2)		CDCL3
865M	B	2.89 APP.	CH2R	R6(C(=N-OH)-C(=N-OH)/CH2-CH2)		CDCL3
751M	A	2.89	CH3	ANAAN<C-N-C*-C*/CH-CH-C*>		POLYSOL-D
1901M	A	2.89	CH3	N(A/CH3)		POLYSOL-D
761M	B	2.89	CH3	N(N/A)		CDCL3
763M	C	2.89	CH3	N(N/A)		CDCL3
1449M	D	2.89	CH*	R30R6R4BI<O-C*(CH3)/CH2-CH*>		CCL4
1703M	C	2.89	OH	CH2-CH2		CDCL3
1796M	D	2.89	OH	C(CH2/CH3/CH3)		CCL4
2121M	B	2.90	CHR	R6<(R6A<CH=CH/C(=O)>)/CH2-CH2/CH2-CH2>		CDCL3
2831M	A	2.90	CH2	A/CH2-O-C(=O)		CCL4
1163M	A	2.90	CH2	A/CH2-S		CDCL3
2060M	D	2.90	CH2	C(=O)-A/CH2.2-CH3		CDCL3
2066M	C	2.90	CH2	C(=O)-A/CH2-CH2		CDCL3
2628M	B	2.90	CH2	NH2/CH2-CH2		D2O
739M	C	2.90	CH2	R5NNA<C=N/NH>/CH2-CH3		POLYSOL-D
195M	B	2.90	CH2R	R5A(C*/CH2-CH2)		CDCL3
2114M	C	2.90	CH2R	R6A<C*/CH2-CH2>		CCL4
652M	A	2.90	CH3	N(A/CH2)		CCL4
884M	A	2.90	CH3	N(QN/CH3)		CCL4
2511M	A	2.90	HCH	C(=O)-OH/C(OH/C(=O)-O/HCH)		D2O
1446M	B	2.90	HCHR	R30<O-CH(Q3)>		CDCL3
2791M	B	2.90	OH	CH(CH2/CH2)		CCL4
1735M	B	2.90	OH	CH(CH3/CH3)		CCL4
2507M	A	2.91	CH2	C(=O)-OH/CH(OH/C(=O)-OH)		D2O
2418M	C	2.91	CH2	NH-C(=O)-NH2/CH(CH3/CH3)		POLYSOL-D
2998M	D	2.91	CH2	N(P/CH2)/CH3		CCL4

BOOK NO.	ASSIGN-MENT	CHEM SHIFT - ppm -		PROTON GROUP	ENVIRONMENTAL GROUPS	S	SOLVENT
2998M	E	2.91		CH2	N(P/CH2)/CH3		CCL4
1678M	A	2.91		CH2	R5S<C=CH/S>/CH2-OH		CCL4
1253M	C	2.91		CH2	SO2-CH2/CH2-CH3		CCL4
2179M	B	2.91		CH2R	R5A<C*/CH2-CH2>		CCL4
603M	C	2.91		CH2R	R6NA(NH-CH2/CH2-C*)		CCL4
822M	A	2.91		CH3	NH-NH2		D20
2426M	A	2.91		CH3	N(C(=0)/CH3)	S	CDCL3
2355M	D	2.91	APP.	CH3	N(C(=0)/CH3)		CCL4
1450M	C	2.91		CH*R	R7R30<0-CH*/CH2-CH2>		CCL4
1677M	B	2.91		HCHR	R30<0-CH(HCH-OH)>		D20
1706M	B	2.91		OH	CH2-CH2		CDCL3
472M	C	2.92		CHR	R7<(NH2)/CH2-CH2/CH2-CH2>		CDCL3
2197M	B	2.92		CH2	C(=0)-CL/CH2.4-RR		CCL4
2206M	D	2.92		CH2	C(=0)-CL/CH2-CH2		CCL4
811M	A	2.92		CH3	N(CH2/CH3)	S	D20
2129M	E	2.92		OH	R6R6R6R5(CH-CH2/CH2)		CDCL3
713M	A	2.93		CH2	AN<C-CH-N>/CH2-AN		CDCL3
2540M	B	2.93		CH2	A/CH2-C(=0)-OH		CDCL3
2050M	D	2.93		CH2	C(=0)-A/CH2.11-CH3		CDCL3
2187M	B	2.93		CH2	C(=0)-CL/CH3		CDCL3
1654M	A	2.93		CH2	NH-NH2/CH2-OH		D20
664M	D	2.93		CH2	N(A/CH2)/CH3		CCL4
642M	B	2.93		CH2	N(CH3/CH3)/Q3		CDCL3
1010M	D	2.93		CH2	S-C:N/CH2-CH2		CCL4
1011M	D	2.93		CH2	S-C:N/CH2-CH2		CCL4
2862M	A	2.94		CH2	A/CH2-0-C(=0)		CCL4
2046M	B	2.94		CH2	C(=0)-A/CH3		CDCL3
2748M	C	2.94		CH2	C(=0)-CL/CH2.4-C(=0)-0		CDCL3
2199M	B	2.94		CH2	C(=0)-CL/CH2-CH2		CDCL3
1250M	C	2.94		CH2	SO-A/CH2-C:C		CDCL3
1012M	D	2.94		CH2	S-C:N/CH2.10-CH3		CCL4
808M	A	2.94		CH3	N(CH3/CH3)	S	D20
2352M	D	2.94		CH3	N(C(=0)-CH2.2/CH3)		D20
1448M	C	2.94		CH*	R6R30BI<0-CH*/CH2-CH2>		CCL4
1713M	B	2.94		OH	CH2-A		CCL4
1254M	C	2.95		CH2	SO2-CH2.3/CH2.2-CH3		CDCL3
1025M	A	2.95		CH3	N(NO/CH3)		CCL4
2630M	B	2.95	APP.	HCH	C(=0)-NH2/CH(NH2/C(=0)-OH)>		D20
2866M	A	2.96		CH2	A/CH2-0-C(=0)		CCL4
1297M	A	2.96	APP.	CH2	C:N/CH2-SO3		D20
960M	C	2.96		CH2	NH-CH2/CH2-C:N		CDCL3
1183M	C	2.96		CH2	S-S/CH2-CH2		CDCL3
1447M	B	2.96		HCHR	R30(0-CH(A))		CCL4
563M	E	2.96		HCHR	R6N<NH-HCH/CH2-CH(CH3)>		CCL4
173M	A	2.97		CH2	A<C-CH-CH-C(A)>/CH2-A		CDCL3
173M	A	2.97		CH2	A/CH2-A		CDCL3
1791M	B	2.97		CH2	CH(OH/A)/A		CDCL3
956M	A	2.97		CH2	C:N/CH2-BR		CCL4
584M	C	2.97		CH2	NH-A/CH2-CH3		CCL4
1256M	B	2.97		CH2	SO2-Q3/CH3		CCL4
1009M	C	2.97		CH2	S-C:N/CH2-CH2		CCL4
2116M	B	2.97		CH2R	R6A<C*/CH2-C(=0)>		CDCL3
576M	C	2.97		CH2R	R6N<NH-CH2/CH2-CH=>		CDCL3
2342M	A	2.97		CH3	NH-C(=0)		CDCL3
710M	A	2.97		CH3	N(AN/CH3)		CDCL3
2642M	A	2.97		CH3	N(CH2/CH3)	S	D20
2435M	A	2.97		CH3	N(C(=0)/CH3)		CDCL3
814M	B	2.97		CH3	N(R6N/CH3)	S	D20
1317M	C	2.97		CH3	SO3-CH2		CDCL3
2631M	B	2.97		HCH	C(=0)-NH2/CH(NH2/C(=0)-OH)		D20
1747M	D	2.97		OH	CH(CH2/CH2)		CCL4
450M	F	2.98		CH	NH2/CH2-CH/CH3		CCL4
559M	D	2.98		CH	NH-R6/CH3/CH3		CDCL3
2622M	C	2.98		CH2	NH2/CH2-CH2		D20
2623M	D	2.98		CH2	NH2/CH2-CH2		D20
661M	C	2.98		CH2	N(A/CH2)/CH3		CDCL3
661M	C	2.98		CH2	N(A/CH2)/CH3		CDCL3
631M	D	2.98		CH2	N(CH2/CH2)/C(CH2/CH3/CH3)		D20
2972M	B	2.98		CH2	S-C(=0)-0/CH2-OH		CCL4
2016M	B	2.98		CH2R	R6S(S-CH2/CH2-C(=0))		CDCL3
900M	A	2.98		CH3	N(A/CH3)		CDCL3
901M	A	2.98		CH3	N(A/CH3)		DMSO-D6
1445M	D	2.98		HCHR	R30<0-CH(CH2-0)>		CCL4
2543M	D	2.99		CH2	C(=0)-OH/C(A/CH2/CH2.2)		DMSO-D6
1155M	B	2.99		CH2	R5NNS<C=N/S>/CH3		TFA
1020M	A	2.99		CH2R	R5NA<C*/CH2-NH>		CDCL3
2357M	B	2.99		CH3	N(C(=0)/CH3)		CCL4
835M	D	2.99		CH3	N(+)(R6R6R6TRI/CH3/CH3)	S	D20
958M	E	3.00		CH	N(CH/CH2.3)/CH3/CH3		CCL4
1662M	D	3.00	APP.	CH	SH/CH2-OH/CH2-SH		CDCL3
1219M	E	3.00		CH	SH/CH2-SH/CH3		CDCL3

BOOK NO.	ASSIGN-MENT	CHEM SHIFT - ppm -	PROTON GROUP	ENVIRONMENTAL GROUPS	S	SOLVENT
1377M	B	3.00	CHR	R6<(NH-SO2)/CH2-CH2/CH2-CH2>		POLYSOL-D
778M	B	3.00- 3.70	CH2	NH2/CH2-CH2	S	TFA
1465M	B	3.00	CH2	R6NO<N-CH2/CH2>/Q3		CDCL3
1008M	B	3.00	CH2	S-C:N/CH3		CDCL3
1129M	A	3.00	CH2R	R4S<CH2-S/CH2>		CDCL3
2255M	A	3.00	CH2R	R5O<C(=0)-O/CH2-C(=0)>		CDCL3
2448M	A	3.00	CH3	R5NN<N-C(=0)/C(=0)>		CDCL3
1315M	C	3.00	CH3	SO3-CH2.3		CDCL3
754M	B	3.00	NH2	N(CH3/CH3)		CCL4
1871M	A	3.00- 4.10		UNSPECIFIED		D20
1741M	D	3.01	CH	OH/CH(CH3/CH3)/CH(CH3/CH3)		CDCL3
2613M	A	3.01	CH2	C:N/CH2-NH		D20
593M	C	3.01	CH2	NH-A/CH3		CDCL3
810M	D	3.01	CH2	N(CH2.7/CH2.7)/CH2.6-CH3		CDCL3
1016M	B	3.01	CH2	S-C:N/CH2-CH2		CDCL3
641M	D	3.01 APP.	CH2R	R6NN<NH-CH2/CH2-N(A)>		CDCL3
641M	D	3.01 APP.	CH2R	R6NN<N(A)-CH(CH3)/CH2-NH>		CDCL3
2170M	A	3.01	CH3	N(A/CH3)		CDCL3
907M	A	3.01	CH3	N=C=0		CDCL3
616M	C	3.02	CH	N(CH/CH2)/CH3/CH3		CCL4
786M	B	3.02	CH2	A(C-CH-CH-C(CL))/C(NH2/CH3/CH3)	S	D20
2212M	B	3.02	CH2	C(=0)-CL/CH2-A		CCL4
2438M	C	3.02	CH2	N(C(=0)/CH2)/CH2-CH2		CCL4
762M	A	3.02	CH3	N(N/A)		CDCL3
1644M	D	3.02	NH2	CH(HCH/CH2)		CDCL3
1644M	D	3.02	OH	HCH-CH		CDCL3
201M	B	3.03	CH2	AA<C-C*>/CH3		CCL4
1503M	A	3.03	CH2	A<C-CH-CH-C(O-CH3)>/CH2-BR		CCL4
2521M	D	3.03	CH2	C(=0)-OH/Q2(CH2-CH2)		CCL4
770M	D	3.03	CH2	NH2/CH2-CH2	S	D20
583M	B	3.03	CH2	NH-A/CH3		CCL4
800M	C	3.03	CH2	NH-CH2/CH2-CH2		D20
797M	B	3.03	CH2	NH-CH2/CH3	S	CDCL3
1359M	A	3.03	CH3	SO2-NH2		POLYSOL-D
440M	B	3.04	CH	NH2/CH3/CH3		D20
1771M	C	3.04	CHR	R6<(OH)/CH(CH3)-CH2/CH2-CH2>		CDCL3
585M	C	3.04	CH2	NH-A/CH2-CH		CDCL3
2420M	A	3.04	CH2	NH-C(=0)/CH2-NH		DMSO-D6
2359M	C	3.04	CH3	N(C(=0)/CH3)		CDCL3
779M	C	3.05	CH2	NH2/CH2.5-NH2	S	D20
1468M	B	3.05	CH2R	R6NO<N(A<C-CH-C(CH3)>)-CH2/CH2-0>		CDCL3
839M	D	3.05	H	OH	S	CDCL3
1762M	C	3.05	OH	CH(R6/CH3)		CCL4
1226M	A	3.05	SH	C(A/A/A)		CDCL3
2768M	B	3.06	CH2	C(=0)-O-C/C(=0)-O-C		CCL4
1757M	D	3.06	CH2	NH-CH2/CH2-CH		CDCL3
1757M	D	3.06	CH2	NH-CH2/CH2-CH2		CDCL3
2991M	A	3.06	CH3	N(C(=0)-O/CH3)		CDCL3
1977M	C	3.07	CH	C(=0)-C/CH3/CH3		CCL4
1202M	C	3.07	CH	SH/CH3/CH3		CCL4
2891M	A	3.07	CH2	A/CH2-O-C(=0)		CDCL3
777M	B	3.07	CH2	NH2/CH2-CH2	S	D20
780M	B	3.07	CH2	NH2/CH2-S		D20
799M	C	3.07	CH2	NH/CH2.2-CH3	S	D20
1684M	D	3.07	CH2	OH/R6R6R6TRI<C*(CH2/CH2/CH2)>		POLYSOL-D
1163M	B	3.07	CH2	S-A/CH2-A		CDCL3
780M	A	3.07	CH2	S-S/CH2-NH2		D20
1320M	A	3.07	CH3	SO3-A		CDCL3
1675M	C	3.07	OH	CH2-CH2		CDCL3
166M	A	3.08	CH	:C-A		CDCL3
2088M	A	3.08	CH2	A/CH2-C(=0)		CDCL3
424M	A	3.08	CH2	A/CH2-I		CDCL3
2088M	B	3.08	CH2	C(=0)-A/CH2-A		CDCL3
766M	B	3.08	CH2	NH2/CH3	S	D20
2981M	D	3.08	CH2	NH-C(=0)-O/CH2-CH3		CCL4
2954M	B	3.08	CH2R	R5O<C(=0)-O/CH=C(CH3)>		CCL4
640M	B	3.08	CH2R	R6NN(NH/CH2-N)		CDCL3
640M	B	3.08	CH2R	R6NN(N(A)/CH2-NH)		CDCL3
2505M	B	3.08	HCH	C(=0)-OH/CH(CL/HCH)		D20
2511M	B	3.08	HCH	C(=0)-OH/C(OH/C(=0)-O/HCH)		D20
1816M	C	3.08	OH	R6(C(C:CH)-CH2/CH2)		CDCL3
2538M	B	3.09	CHR	R6<(C(=0)-OH)/CH(C(=0)-O)-CH2/CH2-CH=>		C3D60
1725M	A	3.09	CH2	AA-C-C*/CH2-OH		CCL4
2195M	B	3.09	CH2	C(=0)-CL/CH2-CH2		CCL4
768M	C	3.09	CH2	NH2/CH2.2-CH3	S	CDCL3
2982M	C	3.09	CH2	NH-C(=0)-O/CH2-CH2		CCL4
2666M	A	3.09	CH2	N(CH2/CH2)/C(=0)-O-NA		D20
1383M	D	3.09	CH2	O-CH2/CH(CH3/CH3)		CCL4
2464M	A	3.09	CH2	Q3/R6NN<C(A)-C(=0)/C(=0)>		DMSO-D6
1316M	B	3.09	CH2	SO3-CH3/CH3		CCL4
1476M	C	3.09- 3.82	CH2R	R6OOR6OOSPI<C*(HCH/CH2)-HCH/O-CH(CH2-CH3)>		CCL4

BOOK NO.	ASSIGN-MENT	CHEM SHIFT - ppm -	PROTON GROUP	ENVIRONMENTAL GROUPS	S	SOLVENT
1487M	A	3.09	CH3	O-C		CCL4
1453M	B	3.09	HCHR	R5R30A<C*/CH*(O/CH*)>		CCL4
1476M	C	3.09- 3.82	HCHR	R600R600SPI<C*(HCH/CH2)-CH2/O-CH(CH2-CH3)>		CCL4
1723M	A	3.09	OH	CH2-A		CCL4
1782M	C	3.09	OH	CH(Q2/CH3)		CCL4
1829M	C	3.10- 3.80	CH	OH/CH2-OH/CH2-CH3		CDCL3
1265M	A	3.10	CH	:C-CH2		POLYSOL-D
814M	C	3.10- 3.95	CHR	R6N<(N(CH3/CH3))/CH2-CH2/CH2-CH2>	S	D20
409M	C	3.10	CH2	I/CH(CH3/CH3)		CCL4
2644M	B	3.10	CH2	NH2/CH2-CH2	S	D20
2358M	E	3.10- 3.60	CH2	N(C(=O)-CH2/CH2>		CDCL3
2358M	E	3.10- 3.60	CH2	N(C(=O)-Q1/CH2>		CDCL3
2998M	D	3.10	CH2	N(P/CH2)/CH3		CCL4
2998M	E	3.10	CH2	N(P/CH2)/CH3		CCL4
1829M	C	3.10- 3.80	CH2	OH/CH(OH/CH2)		CDCL3
968M	A	3.10	CH2	Q3/C:N		CCL4
2433M	C	3.10	CH2	R5NN<N-C(=O)/CH2>/CH2.2-CH3		CCL4
2624M	A	3.10	CH2	SH/CH(NH2/C(=O)-OH)		D20
1368M	C	3.10	CH2	SO2-NH/CH3		CDCL3
814M	C	3.10- 3.95	CH2R	R6N<NH-CH2/CH2-CH(N(CH3/CH3))>	S	D20
838M	A	3.10	CH3	N(+)(CH2/CH3/CH3)		POLYSOL-D
1433M	B	3.10	CH3	O-C		CCL4
1700M	A	3.10	OH	CH2-A		CCL4
1761M	E	3.11	CH	OH/R3/CH3		CDCL3
2663M	A	3.11	CH2	C(=O)-O-NA/C(=O)-O-NA	S	D20
1023M	A	3.11	CH3	N(A/CH3)		CDCL3
1074M	A	3.11	CH3	N(A/CH3)		DMSO-D6
2352M	E	3.11	CH3	N(C(=O)-CH2.2/CH3)		D20
1486M	A	3.11	CH3	O-C		CDCL3
1396M	B	3.11	CH3	O-C		CCL4
1252M	A	3.11	CH3	SO2-CH3		D20
1722M	A	3.11	OH	CH2-A		CDCL3
1994M	D	3.11	OH	CH2-CH		CDCL3
1742M	D	3.11	OH	CH(CH2/CH3)		CCL4
1771M	D	3.11	OH	R6<CH-CH(CH3)/CH2>		CDCL3
1767M	E	3.12	CHR	R6<(OH)/CH(CH3)-CH2/HCH-CH2>		CDCL3
2516M	A	3.12	CH2	C(=O)-OH/Q3		CDCL3
412M	D	3.12	CH2	I/CH2-CH2		CCL4
475M	C	3.12	CH2	NH2/Q2(CH3/H/H)		CCL4
574M	D	3.12	CH2	NH-CH2/Q2(CH2-NH)		CCL4
672M	B	3.12	CH2	N(AA/CH2)/CH3		CCL4
1481M	B	3.12	CH2	O-C/CH3		CDCL3
1663M	A	3.12	CH2	SO3-K/CH2-OH		D20
199M	A	3.12	CH2R	R5A(C*/CH=CH)		CCL4
711M	C	3.12	CH2R	R5N(N(CH3)-CH2/CH(AN(C-CH-N))-CH2)		CCL4
1674M	B	3.12	OH	CH2.2-O		CCL4
1719M	A	3.12	OH	CH2-A		CDCL3
1744M	D	3.13	CH	OH/C(CH3/CH3/CH3)/CH2-CH2		CCL4
404M	B	3.13	CH2	I/CH3		CCL4
572M	C	3.13	CH2	NH-CH2/Q2(CH3)		CDCL3
2770M	E	3.14	CH	C(=O)-O-CH2/C(=O)-O-CH2/CH2-CH2		CCL4
413M	D	3.14	CH2	I/CH2.10-CH3		CCL4
414M	D	3.14	CH2	I/CH2.14-CH3		CCL4
411M	D	3.14	CH2	I/CH2-CH2		CCL4
1288M	B	3.14- 3.58	CH2	NH-CH3/CH2-SO3H		D20
1288M	B	3.14- 3.58	CH2	SO3H/CH2-NH		D20
601M	C	3.14	CH2R	R6NA<NH-C*/CH2-CH2>		CDCL3
802M	A	3.14	CH2R	R6NN(NH-CH2/CH2-NH)	S	D20
2414M	A	3.14	CH3	N(N/C(=O)-A)		CDCL3
1917M	C	3.15	CH	A(C-C(OH)-CH-C(CH3))/CH3/CH3		CDCL3
1838M	E	3.15	CH	OH/C(OH/CH3/CH3)/C(CH3/CH3/CH3)		CDCL3
1445M	E	3.15- 3.90	CH	O-CH2/CH3/CH3		CCL4
1540M	C	3.15	CHR	R30<(CH2-O)/O-CH2>		CCL4
329M	B	3.15	CH2	BR/C(CH3/CH3/CH3)		CCL4
405M	C	3.15	CH2	I/CH2-CH3		CCL4
2429M	C	3.15	CH2	NH-C(=O)/CH2-CH2		CDCL3
1410M	B	3.15	CH2	O-CH2/CH3		CDCL3
1445M	E	3.15- 3.90	CH2	O-CH/R30<CH-O/HCH>		CCL4
1297M	B	3.15 APP.	CH2	SO3-NA/CH2-C:N		D20
1785M	B	3.15	OH	CH(Q3/CH2)		CDCL3
1460M	C	3.15- 4.10		UNSPECIFIED		CCL4
2440M	A	3.16	CH3	N(C(=O)-N/A)		CDCL3
496M	C	3.16	NH2	A(C-C(CH3)-CH-C(CH3))		CCL4
1231M	B	3.16	SH	A(C-CH-CH-C(C(CH3/CH3/CH3)))		CCL4
1868M	A	3.16- 4.19		UNSPECIFIED		D20
1443M	C	3.17	CHR	R30((HCH-CL)-O-HCH)		CCL4
924M	B	3.17	CHR	R6((N=C=N)/CH2-CH2/CH2-CH2)		CDCL3
410M	C	3.17	CH2	I/CH2-CH		CCL4
418M	B	3.17	CH2	I/CH2-CH2		CCL4
1656M	B	3.17	CH2	NH2/CH2.2-OH	S	D20
650M	C	3.17	CH2	N(A/CH2)/CH2-CH3		CCL4

BOOK NO.	ASSIGN-MENT	CHEM SHIFT - ppm -	PROTON GROUP	ENVIRONMENTAL GROUPS	S	SOLVENT
670M	B	3.17	CH2	N(A/CH2)/CH3		CDCL3
631M	E	3.17	CH2	N(CH2/CH2)/CH3		D20
2354M	E	3.17	CH2	N(C(=0)-CH2.8/CH2.2)/CH2-CH3		CDCL3
1319M	B	3.17	CH2R	R60S<S02-0/CH2-CH2>		CDCL3
537M	B	3.17	NH2	A(C-CH-C(CH3)-C(NH2)/CH-C(CH3))		CDCL3
537M	B	3.17	NH2	A(C-C(CH3)-CH-C(NH2)/C(CH3))		CDCL3
2762M	D	3.18	CH2	C(=0)-0-CH2/C(0-C(=0)/C(=0)-0/CH2)		CCL4
2617M	B	3.18	CH2	NH2/CH2-C(=0)-0		D20
1655M	A	3.18	CH2	NH2/CH2-OH	S	D20
1759M	E	3.18	CH3	0-C		CCL4
848M	D	3.19	CH	QN(OH)/CH3/CH3		CCL4
2513M	B	3.19	CHR	R4<(C(=0)-0H)/CH2-CH2/CH2>		CDCL3
2204M	B	3.19	CHR	R5((C(=0)-CL)/CH2-CH2/CH2-CH2)		CCL4
1770M	D	3.19	CHR	R6<(0H)/CH(CH(CH3)-CH2/CH2-CH2>		CDCL3
407M	D	3.19	CH2	I/CH2.2-CH3		CCL4
424M	B	3.19	CH2	I/CH2-A		CDCL3
573M	D	3.19	CH2	NH-CH2/Q1(CH3/CH3)		CDCL3
2297M	D	3.19	CH2	NH-C(=0)/CH2-CH2		D20
2657M	C	3.19	CH2	N(CH2/CH2)/C(=0)-0-NA		D20
2984M	D	3.19	CH2	N(C(=0)-0/CH2)/CH2-CH2		CCL4
1387M	D	3.19	CH2	0-CH2/CH(CH2/CH2)		CCL4
2442M	B	3.19	CH2R	R6NN<NH-C(=0)/C(CH3/CH3)-CH2>		TFA
2439M	B	3.19	CH2R	R6N<N(C(=0)-R6N)-CH2/CH2/CH2-CH2>		CDCL3
1475M	B	3.19- 3.69	CH2R	R600R600SPI<0-CH(CH3)/C*(HCH/CH2)-HCH>		CDCL3
1437M	B	3.19	CH3	0-C		CCL4
1475M	B	3.19- 3.69	HCHR	R600R600SPI<0-CH(CH3)/C*(HCH/CH2)-CH2>		CDCL3
1647M	D	3.19	NH	CH(CH3/CH3)/CH2.2-OH		CCL4
502M	C	3.19	NH2	A<C-C(CH3)-CH-C(CH3)/C(CH3)>		CCL4
1647M	D	3.19	OH	CH2.2-NH		CCL4
1754M	D	3.19	OH	CH(CH2/CH3)		CDCL3
2744M	E	3.20	CH	C(=0)-0-CH2/C(=0)-CH3/CH2-CH3		CCL4
1775M	B	3.20- 4.00	CHR	R6<(0H)/CH(A)-CH2/CH2-CH2>		CCL4
2088M	A	3.20	CH2	A/CH2-C(=0)		CDCL3
2088M	B	3.20	CH2	C(=0)-A/CH2-A		CDCL3
419M	B	3.20	CH2	I/CH2.4-I		CDCL3
420M	C	3.20	CH2	I/CH2-CH2		CCL4
600M	B	3.20	CH2	NH-AA/CH3		CCL4
2299M	E	3.20	CH2	NH-C(=0)/CH2-CH3		CDCL3
570M	C	3.20	CH2	NH-R6/Q3		CCL4
828M	C	3.20	CH2	N(+)(CH2.3/CH2.3/CH2.3)/CH2.2-CH3		CDCL3
1428M	C	3.20- 3.90	CH2	0-CH/CH3		CDCL3
801M	B	3.20	CH2R	R6NH<NH-CH2/CH2-CH2>	S	CDCL3
593M	D	3.20	NH	A(C-CH-CH-C(CH3))/CH2-CH3		CDCL3
449M	D	3.20	NH2	CH(CH2/CH3)		CDCL3
1755M	G	3.20	OH	CH(HCH/CH3)		CCL4
1855M	B	3.20	OH	R6<CH-CH(OH)/CH2>		CDCL3
1872M	A	3.20- 4.00		UNSPECIFIED		D20
1869M	B	3.20- 4.10		UNSPECIFIED		D20
1669M	D	3.20- 3.80		UNSPECIFIED		CCL4
2286M	D	3.21	CH	C(=0)-HNH/A/HCH-CH3		CCL4
586M	B	3.21	CHR	R6((NH-A)/CH2-CH2/CH2-CH2)		CDCL3
1924M	A	3.21	CH2	A(C-CH-C(0-CH3)-C(OH))/Q3		CCL4
809M	B	3.21	CH2	N(CH2/CH2)/CH3	S	CDCL3
2354M	F	3.21	CH2	N(C(=0)-CH2.8/CH2.2)/CH2-CH3		CDCL3
2645M	A	3.21	CH2	SH/CH(NH2/C(=0)-OH)	S	D20
904M	B	3.21	CH3	NH-N=N-A		CDCL3
1422M	B	3.21	CH3	0-CH		CCL4
503M	D	3.21	NH2	A<C-C(CH2-CH3)-CH-C(CH3)/C(CH2-CH3)>		CCL4
497M	C	3.21	NH2	A<C-C(CH3)/CH-C(CH3)>		CCL4
755M	C	3.21	NH2	R6NN<N-CH2/CH2)		CDCL3
2510M	B	3.22	CH	C(=0)-0H/CH2-C(=0)-0/CH2-C(=0)-0		D20
2629M	B	3.22	CH	NH2/C(=0)-0H/CH2-CH2		D20
1214M	B	3.22	CH	SH/HCH-CL/HCH-CL		CCL4
1732M	A	3.22	CH2	ANN<C-N-CH-C(A)/N>/CH2-OH		CDCL3
1444M	C	3.22	CH2	BR/R30<CH-0/HCH>		CCL4
2767M	C	3.22	CH2	C(=0)-0-CH2/C(=0)-0-CH2		CCL4
571M	B	3.22	CH2	NH-CH2/Q3		CDCL3
2629M	B	3.22	CH2	NH-QNH(NH2)/CH2-CH2		D20
651M	C	3.22	CH2	N(A/CH2)/CH2-CH2		CCL4
662M	C	3.22	CH2	N(A/CH2)/CH3		CCL4
2349M	D	3.22	CH2	N(C(=0)/CH2)/CH2-CH2		CCL4
1435M	A	3.22	CH3	0-CH		CCL4
2261M	B	3.22	CH*R	R6R50(C(=0)-0/CH2-CH2)		CDCL3
1789M	C	3.22	OH	CH(A/R3)		CCL4
663M	C	3.23	CH2	N(A/CH2)/CH3		CDCL3
1129M	B	3.23	CH2R	R4S<S-CH2/CH2>		CDCL3
1318M	B	3.23	CH2R	R50S<S02-0/CH2-CH2>		CDCL3
2303M	C	3.23	CH2R	R6N<NH-C(=0)/CH2-CH2>		CCL4
2363M	B	3.23	CH3	N(C(=0)/A)		CDCL3
906M	A	3.23	CH3	N(N=/CH3)		CCL4
1657M	A	3.23	CH3	N(+)(CH2/CH3/CH3)	S	CDCL3

BOOK NO.	ASSIGN-MENT	CHEM SHIFT - ppm -	PROTON GROUP	ENVIRONMENTAL GROUPS	S	SOLVENT
1429M	B	3.23	CH3	O-CH		CCL4
1409M	A	3.23	CH3	O-CH2		CCL4
2391M	A	3.23	CH3	R5NA<N-C(=O)/C(=O)>		TFA
583M	C	3.23	NH	A/CH2-CH3		CCL4
538M	C	3.23	NH2	A<C-C(CH2-CH3)-CH-C(NH2)/CH-C(CH2-CH3)>		CDCL3
488M	B	3.23	NH2	A(C-C(CH3))		CCL4
324M	C	3.24	CH2	BR/CH(CH3/CH3)		CCL4
2301M	B	3.24	CH2	NH-C(=O)-CH3/CH2-NH		POLYSOL-D
827M	B	3.24	CH2	N(&)(CH2/CH2/CH2)/CH3	S	D2O
1369M	C	3.24	CH2	N(SO2/CH2)/CH2-OH		CDCL3
827M	B	3.24	CH2	N(T)(CH2/CH2/CH2)/CH3	S	D2O
909M	C	3.24	CH2	N=C=O/CH2.4-CH3		CDCL3
1631M	C	3.24	OH	CH2-CH2		CCL4
2740M	B	3.24	OH	CH(C(=O)-O/CH3)		CCL4
978M	A	3.25	CH	CH(C:N/A)/A/CH2-A		CDCL3
2394M	B	3.25	CHR	R30((HCH-R5NA)/O-CH2)		CDCL3
2084M	B	3.25	CHR	R6((C(=O)-A)/CH2-CH2/CH2-CH2)		CDCL3
1560M	A	3.25	CH2	A<C-CH-C(O-CH3)-C(O-CH3)>/Q3		CCL4
978M	A	3.25	CH2	CH(A/CH)/A		CDCL3
2549M	A	3.25	CH2	C(=O)-OH/Q2(A)		CDCL3
803M	A	3.25	CH2R	R6NN(NH-CH2/CH2-NH)	S	D2O
490M	B	3.25	NH2	A<C-CH-CH-C(CH3)>		CCL4
1668M	C	3.25	OH	CH2-CH2		CCL4
1918M	B	3.26	CH2	Q3/A<C-C(OH)-C(CH3)>		CCL4
1287M	B	3.26	CH2	SO3-H/CH3		CDCL3
1484M	B	3.26	CH3	O-CH2		CDCL3
1228M	B	3.26	SH	A<C-C(CH3)>		CDCL3
598M	E	3.27	CH	NH-A/CH2-CH3/CH3		CDCL3
1677M	C	3.27	CHR	R30<(HCH-OH)/O-HCH>		D2O
154M	B	3.27	CH2	A/Q2(CH3)		CCL4
649M	B	3.27	CH2	N(A/CH2)/CH3		CCL4
2356M	E	3.27	CH2	N(C(=O)/CH2)/CH3		CCL4
1615M	C	3.27	CH2	OH/CH(CH3/CH3)		CCL4
1624M	E	3.27	CH2	OH/C(CH2/CH3/CH3)		CDCL3
1298M	A	3.27	CH2	SO3-NA/CH2-SO3-NA		D2O
1376M	A	3.27	CH2R	R5NN<N(SO2-A)-CH2/CH2-N(SO2-A)>		POLYSOL-D
1134M	B	3.27	CH2R	R5NS<N=C(CH3)/CH2-S		CCL4
1336M	A	3.27	CH3	N(C(=S)-H/CH3)		CDCL3
1102M	A	3.27	CH3	P(+)(A/A/A)	S	CDCL3
2207M	E	3.27	HCH	SO3H/R5R5BI(C*(C(=O)/C/CH2))		D2O
2007M	E	3.27	HCH	SO3-NA/R5R5BI<C*-C(=O)/C(CH3/CH3)/CH2>		D2O
2640M	C	3.27	NH2	A<C-C(CH3)-CH-C(CH3)/CH-C(CH3)>		CCL4
1673M	A	3.27	OH	CH2-CH2		CDCL3
1751M	A	3.27	OH	CH(CH2/CH2)		CCL4
1426M	B	3.28	CH2	BR/CH(O/O)		CCL4
257M	B	3.28- 3.78	CH2	CL/CH(CL/CH3)		CCL4
2198M	A	3.28	CH2	C(=O)-CL/CH2-C(=O)-CL		CDCL3
2405M	A	3.28	CH2	C(=O)-NH-NH2/A(C-CH-CH-C(NH2))		POLYSOL-D
1339M	B	3.28	CH2	NH-C(=S)/CH3		DMSO-D6
2370M	C	3.28	CH2	N(C(=O)-A/CH2)/CH3		CDCL3
1644M	E	3.28	HCH	OH/CH(NH2/CH2)		CDCL3
1472M	E	3.28	HCHR	R600<O-CH(CH2.5-CH3)/C(CH3/CH3)>		CCL4
533M	A	3.28	NH2	A(C-C(NH2))		CDCL3
1708M	C	3.28	OH	CH2.2-S		CCL4
1641M	A	3.28	OH	CH2-C		CDCL3
417M	B	3.29	CH2	I/CH2-CH2		CCL4
2295M	B	3.29	CH2	NH-C(=O)/CH3		D2O
1525M	C	3.29	CH2	N(A/CH2)/CH3		CCL4
2351M	E	3.29	CH2	N(C(=O)-CH2/CH2.3)/CH2.2-CH3		CDCL3
910M	C	3.29	CH2	N=C=O/CH2.10-CH3		CCL4
908M	C	3.29	CH2	N=C=O/CH2-CH3		CDCL3
1384M	C	3.29	CH2	O-CH2/CH2-CH2		CCL4
1386M	C	3.29	CH2	O-CH2/CH2-CH2		CCL4
2784M	D	3.29- 3.68	CH2	O-CH2/CH2-CH2		CCL4
2784M	D	3.29- 3.68	CH2	O-CH2/CH2-O-C(=O)		CCL4
1190M	A	3.29	CH2	S-S/Q3		CCL4
1135M	A	3.29	CH2R	R5NS(S-C(NH-CH2)=/CH2-N=)		CDCL3
1354M	A	3.29	CH3	N(C(=S)/CH3)		POLYSOL-D
839M	E	3.29	CH3	N(+)(CH2/CH2/CH3)	S	CDCL3
1546M	A	3.29	CH3	O-A		CCL4
1419M	A	3.29	CH3	O-CH2		CCL4
1479M	A	3.29	CH3	O-CH2		CDCL3
591M	C	3.29	NH	A(C-CH-CH-C(CH3))/CH3		CDCL3
499M	B	3.29	NH2	A<C-CH-C(CH3)/CH-C(CH3)>		CCL4
669M	B	3.29	NH2	A(C-CH-CH-C(N(CH3/CH3)))		CDCL3
2628M	C	3.30	CH	NH2/C(=O)-OH/CH2-CH2		D2O
1844M	B	3.30- 3.90	CH	OH/CH2-NH2/CH2-OH		D2O
1446M	C	3.30	CHR	R30<(Q3)/O-HCH>		CDCL3
1456M	C	3.30- 4.00	CHR	R50<(CH3)/O-CH2/CH2-CH2>		CCL4
602M	D	3.30	CHR	R6NA<(CH3)/NH-C*/HCH-HCH>		CDCL3
1463M	C	3.30- 4.00	CHR	R6NO<(CH3)/O-CH(CH3)/CH2-NH>		CDCL3

BOOK NO.	ASSIGN-MENT	CHEM SHIFT - ppm -	PROTON GROUP	ENVIRONMENTAL GROUPS	S	SOLVENT
1856M	B	3.30- 3.90	CHR	R6((OH)/CH2-CH2/CH2-CH2)		D2O
1873M	A	3.30- 4.30	CHR	UNSPECIFIED		D2O
2462M	A	3.30	CH2	A/R6NN(C(CH2-A)-C(=O)/C(=O))		DMSO-D6
364M	B	3.30	CH2	BR/CH2.2-R6		CCL4
2743M	E	3.30	CH2	C(=O)-O-CH2.3/C(=O)-CH3		CCL4
474M	B	3.30	CH2	NH2/Q3		CDCL3
1062M	B	3.30	CH2	NH-A/CH3		CCL4
1346M	C	3.30	CH2	NH-C(=S)/CH(CH3/CH3)		CDCL3
1706M	D	3.30	CH2	N(A/CH2)/CH2-OH		CDCL3
1706M	C	3.30	CH2	N(A/CH2)/CH3		CDCL3
1844M	B	3.30- 3.90	CH2	OH/CH(OH/CH2)		D2O
207M	A	3.30	CH2R	R5AA(C*/CH2-C*)		CDCL3
1456M	C	3.30- 4.00	CH2R	R5O<O-CH(CH3)/CH2-CH2>		CCL4
2689M	C	3.30	CH2R	R6NN(NH-CH2/CH2-NH)		D2O
576M	D	3.30	CH2R	R6N<CH=CH/NH-CH2>		CDCL3
1336M	B	3.30	CH3	N(C(=S)-H/CH3)		CDCL3
837M	A	3.30	CH3	N(+)/CH2/CH3/CH3)		POLYSOL-D
930M	A	3.30	CH3	N=C=S		CDCL3
1427M	C	3.30	CH3	O-CH		CCL4
1430M	C	3.30	CH3	O-CH		CCL4
1420M	A	3.30	CH3	O-CH2		CCL4
1760M	B	3.30	CH3	O-CH2		CCL4
1492M	A	3.30	CH3	O-CH2.2		CCL4
1380M	C	3.30	CH3	O-CH2.3		CDCL3
2452M	A	3.30	CH3	R6NN(N-C(=O)/C(=O))		CDCL3
491M	C	3.30	NH2	A(C-C(CH2-CH3))		CDCL3
1699M	E	3.30 APP.	OH	CH2.2-C:		CCL4
1717M	A	3.30	OH	CH2-A		CDCL3
1737M	C	3.30	OH	CH(CH2/CH2)		CCL4
1993M	C	3.30	OH	C(C(=O)/CH3/CH3)		CDCL3
1230M	B	3.30	SH	A(C-CH-CH-C(CH3))		CDCL3
1691M	A	3.30- 3.75		UNSPECIFIED		CCL4
1867M	A	3.30- 4.20		UNSPECIFIED		D2O
1473M	B	3.30- 4.00		UNSPECIFIED		CDCL3
1414M	C	3.30- 3.80		UNSPECIFIED		CCL4
1668M	D	3.30- 3.74		UNSPECIFIED		CCL4
1670M	D	3.30- 3.80		UNSPECIFIED		CDCL3
1667M	D	3.30- 3.85		UNSPECIFIED		CDCL3
1369M	D	3.30- 4.20		UNSPECIFIED		CDCL3
385M	C	3.31	CH	A(C-C(BR)-CH-C(CH3))/CH3/CH3		CDCL3
262M	C	3.31- 4.16	CH	CL/CH2-CL/CH2-CH3		CCL4
468M	C	3.31	CHR	R5<(NH2)/CH2-CH2/CH2-CH2>		CDCL3
338M	D	3.31	CH2	BR/CH2-CH2		CCL4
262M	C	3.31- 4.16	CH2	CL/CH(CL/CH2)		CCL4
2643M	B	3.31	CH2	NH2/CH2-CH	S	D2O
2347M	C	3.31	CH2	N(C(=O)-H/CH2)/CH3		CDCL3
1388M	C	3.31	CH2	O-CH2/CH2-CH2		CCL4
1457M	B	3.31	CH2	O-CH3/R5O<CH-O/CH2>		CCL4
1394M	D	3.31	CH2	O-CH/CH2-CH3		CCL4
1480M	D	3.31	CH2	O-CH/CH3		CDCL3
1374M	B	3.31	CH2R	R6NN<N(SO2-N)-CH2/CH2-N(SO2-N)>		CDCL3
886M	B	3.31	CH2R	R6N<N(QN(A))-CH2/CH2-CH2>		CCL4
1337M	B	3.31	CH3	N(C(=S)/CH3)		CDCL3
1415M	A	3.31	CH3	O-CH2		CCL4
1457M	B	3.31	CH3	O-CH2		CCL4
584M	D	3.31	NH	A/CH2-CH2		CCL4
1698M	E	3.31	OH	CH2.2-C:		CCL4
1240M	A	3.31	SH	A<C-CH-C(SH)-C(CL)>		CCL4
1240M	B	3.31	SH	A<C-C(CL)/CH-C(SH)>		CCL4
2986M	B	3.32	CH2	A/CH2-NH		CCL4
335M	D	3.32	CH2	BR/CH2-CH2		CCL4
238M	C	3.32	CH2	CL/CH(CH3/CH3)		CCL4
2146M	C	3.32	CH2	C(=O)-CH2/C(=O)-CH3		CCL4
2986M	C	3.32	CH2	NH-C(=O)/CH2-A		CCL4
812M	B	3.32	CH2	N(CH2.2/CH3)/CH3	S	D2O
1680M	B	3.32	CH2	OH/R6<CH-CH2/CH2>		CCL4
1681M	C	3.32	CH2	OH/R6<CH-CH2/CH2>		CCL4
1385M	C	3.32	CH2	O-CH2.2/CH2-CH		CCL4
1431M	D	3.32- 3.90	CH2	O-CH/CH3		CDCL3
1397M	C	3.32	CH2	O-C/CH3		CCL4
820M	A	3.32	CH2	R5NN(C=CH/N)/CH2-NH2	S	D2O
2552M	A	3.32	CH3	O-CH		CDCL3
487M	A	3.32	NH2	A		CCL4
489M	B	3.32	NH2	A(C-CH-C(CH3))		CCL4
511M	B	3.32	NH2	A(C-CH-C(CH3)-C(F))		CCL4
1733M	A	3.32	OH	CH2-R5O		CDCL3
328M	C	3.33	CH2	BR/CH2-CH		CCL4
332M	D	3.33	CH2	BR/CH2-CH2		CCL4
326M	D	3.33	CH2	BR/CH2-CH2		CCL4
644M	B	3.33	CH2	N(CH3/CH3)/A		CCL4
153M	A	3.33	CH2	Q3/A		CCL4

BOOK NO.	ASSIGN-MENT	CHEM SHIFT - ppm -	PROTON GROUP	ENVIRONMENTAL GROUPS	S	SOLVENT
1469M	A	3.33	CH2R	R6NO(O-CH2/CH2-NH)		
510M	A	3.33	NH2	A<C-CH-CH-C(F)>	S	D20
1662M	E	3.33	OH	CH2-CH		CCL4
336M	D	3.34	CH2	BR/CH2-CH2		CDCL3
337M	D	3.34	CH2	BR/CH2-CH2		CCL4
319M	B	3.34	CH2	BR/CH3		CCL4
2769M	C	3.34	CH2	C(=O)-O/CH2.11/C(=O)-O-CH2.11		CDCL3
1611M	A	3.34	CH3	OH		CCL4
582M	B	3.34	NH	A/CH3		CCL4
494M	E	3.34	NH2	A<C-C(CH(CH2/CH3))>		CCL4
2143M	D	3.35	CHR	R5<(C(=O)-CH3)-C(=O)/CH2>		CCL4
151M	A	3.35	CH2	A/CH(A/A)		CDCL3
339M	D	3.35	CH2	BR/CH2.14-CH3		CCL4
333M	D	3.35	CH2	BR/CH2-CH2		CCL4
1382M	D	3.35	CH2	O-CH2/CH2.2-CH3		CCL4
585M	D	3.35	NH	A/CH2.2-CH		CDCL3
495M	C	3.35	NH2	A(C-C(CH3)-C(CH3))		CCL4
480M	B	3.35	NH2	C(A/CH3/CH3)		CCL4
1241M	A	3.35	SH	AA(C-C*)		CDCL3
1874M	A	3.35- 4.33		UNSPECIFIED		D20
1737M	D	3.36	CH	OH/CH2-CH3/CH2-CH3		CCL4
2421M	B	3.36	CHR	R6<(NH-C(=O)-NH2)/CH2-CH2/CH2-CH2>		POLYSOL-D
1932M	B	3.36	CH2	A<C-C(OH)-CH-C(CH3)/C(CH3)>/Q3		CDCL3
320M	C	3.36	CH2	BR/CH2-CH3		CCL4
708M	C	3.36	CH2	NH-AN/CH2-N		CDCL3
995M	B	3.36	CH2	N(A/CH2)/CH3		CDCL3
2353M	D	3.36	CH2	N(C(=O)-CH2.2/CH2)/CH3		D20
2350M	D	3.36	CH2	N(C(=O)-CH2-CH2)/CH3		D20
819M	A	3.36	CH3	N(A/CH3)	S	D20
1423M	C	3.36	HCH	O-CH/CH3		CCL4
592M	D	3.36	NH	A<C-CH-CH-C(CH(CH3/CH3))>/CH3		CDCL3
753M	B	3.36	NH	NH2/CH3		CCL4
753M	B	3.36	NH2	NH-CH3		CCL4
1954M	B	3.37	CH2	AA<C-C*/C(OH)>/CH2-C:N		POLYSOL-D
362M	C	3.37	CH2	BR/CH2-CH2		CCL4
2496M	A	3.37	CH2	C(=O)-OH/C(=O)-OH		POLYSOL-D
2742M	B	3.37	CH2	C(=O)-O-CH3/C(=O)-CH3		CDCL3
2347M	D	3.37	CH2	N(C(=O)-H/CH2)/CH3		CDCL3
1683M	D	3.37	CH2	OH/R6N(CH-CH2/CH2)		CDCL3
1381M	C	3.37	CH2	O-CH2.2/CH2-CH3		CDCL3
1380M	D	3.37	CH2	O-CH3/CH2.2-CH3		CDCL3
1828M	B	3.37	HCH	OH/CH(OH/CH3)		CDCL3
1536M	A	3.37	SH	A<C-CH-CH-C(O-CH3)>		CDCL3
1772M	E	3.38	CHR	R6)(OH)/CH(CH(CH3/CH3))-CH2/CH2-CH(CH3))		CDCL3
360M	B	3.38	CH2	BR/CH2-CH2		CCL4
330M	D	3.38	CH2	BR/CH2-CH2		CCL4
2789M	C	3.38	CH2	NH-CH2/C(=O)-O-CH2		CCL4
2104M	B	3.38	CH2	N(A/CH2)/CH3		CDCL3
1392M	C	3.38	CH2	O-CH2/CH2-CH2		CDCL3
2717M	D	3.38	CH2	O-CH2/CH2-CH2		CCL4
1379M	B	3.38	CH2	O-CH2/CH3		CCL4
1383M	E	3.38	CH2	O-CH2/CH3		CCL4
1405M	C	3.38	CH2	O-Q3/CH(CH3/CH3)		CCL4
1015M	A	3.38	CH2	S-C:N/CH2-S		POLYSOL-D
2433M	D	3.38	CH2R	R5NN<NH-C(=O)/CH2-N(CH2.3-CH3)>		CCL4
2433M	D	3.38	CH2R	R5NN<N(CH2.3-CH3)-C(=O)/CH2-NH>		CCL4
2739M	A	3.38	CH3	O-CH2		CCL4
1665M	B	3.38	CH3	O-CH2		CDCL3
586M	C	3.38	NH	A/R6		CDCL3
500M	D	3.38	NH2	A<C-C(CH2-CH3)/C(CH3)>		CDCL3
1712M	B	3.38	OH	CH2-Q1		CDCL3
1233M	A	3.38	SH	A<C-CH-C(CL)-C(CL)>		CCL4
341M	D	3.39	CH2	BR/CH2-CH2		CDCL3
322M	D	3.39	CH2	BR/CH2-CH2		CCL4
2052M	A	3.39	CH2	C(=O)-A/CH2-CL		CDCL3
780M	B	3.39	CH2	NH2/CH2-S		D20
1347M	C	3.39	CH2	NH-C(=S)/CH2.8-CH3		POLYSOL-D
1156M	B	3.39	CH2	NH-R5NNS/CH3		POLYSOL-D
1413M	C	3.39	CH2	O-CH2.2/CH2.2-CH3		CCL4
1382M	E	3.39	CH2	O-CH2.3/CH3		CCL4
780M	A	3.39	CH2	S-S/CH2-NH2		D20
2434M	A	3.39	CH2R	R5NN<NH-C(=O)/CH2-N(CH2-Q3)>		POLYSOL-D
2434M	A	3.39	CH2R	R5NN<N(CH2-Q3)-C(=O)/CH2-NH>		POLYSOL-D
2636M	B	3.39	CH2R	R5N<NH-CH(C(=O)-OH)/CH2-CH2>		D20
1031M	A	3.39	CH3	N(N=O/A)		CDCL3
590M	C	3.39	NH	A<C-CH-C(CH3)>/CH3		CDCL3
589M	C	3.39	NH	A(C-C(CH3))/CH3		CDCL3
536M	B	3.39	NH2	A<C-CH-C(NH2)-C(CH3)>		CDCL3
536M	B	3.39	NH2	A<C-C(CH3)/CH-C(NH2)>		CDCL3
1739M	D	3.39	OH	CH(CH2/CH3)		CCL4
1229M	B	3.39	SH	A<C-CH-C(CH3)>		CDCL3

BOOK NO.	ASSIGN- MENT	CHEM SHIFT - ppm -	PROTON GROUP	ENVIRONMENTAL GROUPS	S	SOLVENT
2796M	B	3.40	CH	C(=O)-O-CH3/C(=O)-O-CH3/CH2.2-CH		CDCL3
1444M	D	3.40 APP.	CHR	R3O<(CH2-BR)/O-HCH>		CCL4
2197M	C	3.40	CH2	BR/CH2.4-C(=O)-CL		CCL4
957M	C	3.40	CH2	BR/CH2-CH2		CCL4
240M	D	3.40	CH2	CL/CH2-CH2		CCL4
775M	A	3.40	CH2	NH2/CH2-NH2		D20
2350M	E	3.40	CH2	N(C(=O)-CH2/CH2)/CH3		D20
834M	B	3.40	CH2	N(+)(CH2/CH2/CH2)/CH3		POLYSOL-D
1827M	B	3.40	CH2	OH/CH2.15-OH		DMSO-D6
1672M	D	3.40- 3.80	CH2	OH/CH2-O		CDCL3
1672M	D	3.40- 3.80	CH2	O-CH2.2/CH2-OH		CDCL3
1390M	D	3.40	CH2	O-CH2/CH2.16-CH3		CDCL3
1417M	C	3.40	CH2	O-CH2/CH2-CH2		CCL4
1391M	C	3.40	CH2	O-CH2/CH2-CH2		CDCL3
1424M	D	3.40	CH2	O-CH/CH2-CH2		CCL4
836M	A	3.40	CH3	N(+)(CH2/CH3/CH3)	S	CDCL3
2491M	A	3.40	CH3	O-CH2		D20
1673M	B	3.40	CH3	O-CH2		CDCL3
1617M	D	3.40	HCH	OH/CH(CH2/CH3)		CCL4
1617M	E	3.40	HCH	OH/CH(CH2/CH3)		CCL4
1623M	C	3.40	OH	CH2-CH2		CCL4
1750M	C	3.40- 4.40	OH	CH(CH2/CH2)		CDCL3
1756M	D	3.40	OH	CH(CH2/CH3)		CDCL3
1759M	F	3.40	OH	CH(HCH/CH3)		CCL4
1862M	A	3.40- 3.80		UNSPECIFIED		D20
1707M	A	3.40- 4.00		UNSPECIFIED		CDCL3
1676M	A	3.40- 4.10		UNSPECIFIED		CDCL3
1836M	C	3.40- 4.20		UNSPECIFIED		CDCL3
1747M	E	3.41	CH	OH/CH2-CH2/CH2-CH3		CCL4
340M	D	3.41	CH2	BR/CH2.15-CH3		CDCL3
1503M	B	3.41	CH2	BR/CH2-A		CCL4
359M	B	3.41	CH2	BR/CH2-CH2		CCL4
2139M	E	3.41	CH2	C(=O)-CH2.2/C(=O)-CH2.2		CCL4
2690M	A	3.41	CH2	NH2/CH2-NH2		D20
2353M	E	3.41	CH2	N(C(=O)-CH2.2/CH2)/CH3		D20
1421M	C	3.41	CH2	O-CH2/CH2-CH2		CCL4
1296M	A	3.41	CH2	SO3-NA/CH2-BR	S	D20
829M	C	3.41	CH3	N(+)(CH2.11/CH3/CH3)	S	CDCL3
866M	A	3.41	CH3	QN(A)		CDCL3
2452M	B	3.41	CH3	R6NN(N-C(=O)/CH=)		CDCL3
588M	C	3.41	NH	A/C(C:CH/CH3/CH3)		CDCL3
1725M	B	3.41	OH	CH2.2-AA		CCL4
1792M	B	3.41	OH	CH(CH2/CH3)		CCL4
1738M	E	3.42	CH	OH/CH2-CH3		CCL4
1743M	E	3.42	CH	OH/CH(CH2/CH2)/CH2-CH3		CCL4
776M	A	3.42	CH2	NH2/CH2-NH2	S	D20
832M	C	3.42 APP.	CH2	N(+)(CH2/CH2/CH2)/CH2-CH2	S	CDCL3
1412M	B	3.42	CH2	O-CH2.2/CH3		CCL4
1425M	B	3.42	HCH	O-CH/CH3		CCL4
1658M	B	3.42	OH	CH2-CH2		CDCL3
1235M	A	3.42	SH	A<C-CH-CH-C(BR)>		CDCL3
1762M	D	3.43	CH	OH/R6/CH3		CCL4
1773M	B	3.43	CHR	R6<(OH)/CH(R6)-CH2/CH2-CH2>		CDCL3
2146M	D	3.43	CH2	A/C(=O)-CH2		CCL4
2146M	D	3.43	CH2	A/C(=O)-O1		CCL4
243M	D	3.43	CH2	CL/CH2-CH2		CCL4
2613M	B	3.43	CH2	NH-CH2/CH2-C:N		D20
737M	D	3.43	CH2	N(ANNN/CH2)/CH(CH2/CH2)		CCL4
653M	B	3.43	CH2	N(A/CH2)/CH3		CDCL3
677M	B	3.43	CH2	N(CH3/CH3)/R5N<C=CH/NH>		CDCL3
1627M	E	3.43	CH2	OH/CH(CH2/CH2)		CCL4
1667M	C	3.43	CH2	O-CH2.2/CH2-CH3		CDCL3
816M	A	3.43	CH3	N(A/CH3)		D20
2284M	A	3.43	CH3	O-CH2	S	CDCL3
493M	C	3.43	NH2	A<C-CH-CH-C(CH(CH3/CH3))>		CDCL3
498M	B	3.43	NH2	A<C-CH-C(CH3)-C(CH3)>		CDCL3
1561M	C	3.43	NH2	A(C-CH-C(O-CH2)-C(O-CH2))		CDCL3
1535M	A	3.43	SH	A(C-CH-C(O-CH3))		CDCL3
242M	C	3.44	CH2	CL/CH2-CH2		CCL4
244M	D	3.44	CH2	CL/CH2-CH2		CCL4
2860M	B	3.44	CH2	C(=O)-O-CH2/A		CCL4
1675M	D	3.44	CH2	O-CH2/CH2-CH2		CDCL3
2985M	B	3.44	CH2R	R6NN<N(C(=O)-O-CH2)-CH2/CH2-N(C(=O)-O-CH2)>		CDCL3
818M	A	3.44	CH3	N(A/CH3)	S	D20
1639M	A	3.45	CH2	BR/CH2-OH		CCL4
235M	C	3.45	CH2	CL/CH2-CH3		CCL4
1650M	D	3.45	CH2	OH/CH2-N		CCL4
2360M	B	3.45	CH2R	R6NO<N(C(=O)-CH3)-CH2/CH2-O>		CCL4
2360M	C	3.45	CH2R	R6NO<O-CH2/CH2-N(C(=O)-CH3)>		CCL4
532M	B	3.45	NH2	A(C-C(CH3)-CH-C(A(C-CH-C(CH3)-C(NH2))))		CDCL3
1242M	A	3.45	SH	AA(C-CH-C*/CH-CH-C*)		CDCL3

BOOK NO.	ASSIGN-MENT	CHEM SHIFT - ppm -	PROTON GROUP	ENVIRONMENTAL GROUPS	S	SOLVENT
1749M	D	3.46	CH	OH/CH2.2-CH/CH2.CH		CCL4
246M	C	3.46	CH2	CL/CH2-CH2		CCL4
245M	D	3.46	CH2	CL/CH2-CH2		CCL4
248M	D	3.46	CH2	CL/CH2-CH2		CCL4
1390M	E	3.46	CH2	O-CH2.17/CH3		CDCL3
1419M	B	3.46 APP.	CH2	O-CH2/CH2-O		CCL4
1419M	B	3.46 APP.	CH2	O-CH3/CH2-O		CCL4
1191M	A	3.46	CH2	S-CH2/A		CS2
1648M	D	3.46	HCH	OH/CH(N/CH3)		D2O
1679M	C	3.46	OH	CH2-R500		CCL4
2048M	B	3.47	CH	C(=0)-A/CH3/CH3		CCL4
2745M	E	3.47	CH	C(=0)-O-CH2/C(=0)-CH3/CH2.2-CH3		CDCL3
2138M	E	3.47	CH2	C(=0)-CH2/C(=0)-CH2		CCL4
1839M	D	3.47	CH2	OH/C(CH2/CH2/CH2)		C3D6O
1412M	C	3.47	CH2	O-CH2/CH2-O		CCL4
2449M	B	3.47	CH2	R5NN<N-C(=0)/C(=0)>/CH3		CDCL3
2369M	B	3.47	CH2R	R6N<N(C(=0)-A)-CH2/CH2-CH2>		CCL4
492M	C	3.47	NH2	A<C-CH-C(CH2-CH3)>		CDCL3
1832M	C	3.47	OH	CH2-CH2		CDCL3
1778M	B	3.48	CHR	R6R6<(OH)/CH2-CH*/CH2-CH2>		POLYSOL-D
247M	D	3.48	CH2	CL/CH2.1J-CH3		CCL4
2039M	B	3.48	CH2	C(=0)-CH3/AR500(C-CH-C*-O/CH-CH-C*)		CCL4
2312M	B	3.48	CH2	C(=0)-NH/A		CDCL3
2848M	C	3.48	CH2	C(=0)-O-CH2.7/A		CCL4
2309M	C	3.48	CH2	NH-C(=0)-CH3/CH2-A		CDCL3
1024M	B	3.48	CH2	N(A/CH2)/CH3		CDCL3
1027M	D	3.48	CH2	N(N=0/CH2.2)/CH2-CH3		CCL4
1635M	D	3.48	CH2	OH/CH2.22-CH3		POLYSOL-D
1413M	D	3.48	CH2	O-CH2.3/CH2-O		CCL4
1420M	B	3.48 APP.	CH2	O-CH2/CH2-O		CCL4
1420M	B	3.48 APP.	CH2	O-CH3/CH2-O		CCL4
1337M	C	3.48	CH3	N(C(=S)/CH3)		CDCL3
830M	C	3.48	CH3	N(+)(CH2.11/CH3/CH3)	S	CDCL3
2268M	B	3.48 APP.	CH*R	R6R50<C(=0)-O/CH2-CH=>		CDCL3
353M	B	3.48	HCH	BR/CH(BR/CH3)		CDCL3
353M	C	3.48	HCH	BR/CH(BR/CH3)		CCL4
1443M	D	3.48	HCH	CL/R30		CCL4
1443M	E	3.48	HCH	CL/R30		CCL4
596M	B	3.48	NH	A<C-CH-CH-C(CH3)>/CH2-A		CCL4
2412M	B	3.48	NHR	R5NN<NH-C(=0)/CH(A)-HCH>		DMSO-D6
602M	E	3.48	NHR	R6NA<C*/CH-(CH3)-HCH>		CDCL3
1846M	A	3.48	OH	CH2-CH2		CDCL3
1680M	C	3.48	OH	CH2-R6		CCL4
1745M	E	3.49	CH	OH/CH2-CH2/CH2-CH3		CDCL3
2129M	F	3.49	CHR	R6R6R6R5((OH)/CH2-C*=/CH2-CH2)		CDCL3
2129M	F	3.49	CHR	R6R6R6R5(=C*-CH2/CH2-CH*)		CDCL3
1766M	B	3.49	CHR	R6((OH)/CH2-CH2/CH2-CH2)		CCL4
236M	C	3.49	CH2	CL/CH2-CH2		CCL4
820M	B	3.49	CH2	NH2/CH2-R5NN	S	D2O
2370M	D	3.49	CH2	N(C(=0)-A/CH2)/CH3		CDCL3
1626M	C	3.49	CH2	OH/CH2-CH2		CCL4
1689M	E	3.49	CH2	OH/CH2-CH2		CCL4
1692M	D	3.49 APP.	CH2	OH/R60(C(CH3)-O/CH2)		CDCL3
1415M	B	3.49	CH2	O-CH2/CH2-O		CCL4
1403M	B	3.49	CH2	O-CH2/CH3		CDCL3
1415M	B	3.49	CH2	O-CH3/CH2-O		CCL4
1485M	C	3.49 APP.	CH2	O-CH/CH2-A		CCL4
2382M	D	3.49	CH2	R5N<N-C(=0)/C(=0)>/CH2.3-CH3		CDCL3
831M	D	3.49	CH3	N(+)(CH2/CH3/CH3)	S	CDCL3
1677M	D	3.49	HCH	OH/R30<CH-O/HCH>		D2O
515M	B	3.49	NH2	A(C-C(CH3)-CH-C(CL))		CCL4
1682M	B	3.49	OH	CH2.2-R6		CCL4
1692M	D	3.49 APP.	OH	CH2-R60		CDCL3
1684M	E	3.49	OH	CH2-R6R6R6TRI		POLYSOL-D
1806M	B	3.49	OH	C(C:N/CH3/CH3)		CDCL3
1864M	A	3.49- 4.05		UNSPECIFIED		D2O
1780M	E	3.49		UNSPECIFIED		CDCL3
2626M	B	3.50	CH	NH2/C(=0)-OH/CH(OH/CH3)		D2O
2718M	B	3.50- 4.00	CH	OH/CH2-O-C(=0)/CH2-OH		CDCL3
2489M	C	3.50	CH	SH/C(=0)-OH/CH3		CCL4
1457M	C	3.50- 4.08	CHR	R50<(CH2-0)/0-CH2/CH2-CH2>		CCL4
2854M	C	3.50	CH2	C(=0)-O-CH2/A<C-C(CH3)>		CCL4
2428M	B	3.50	CH2	NH-C(=0)/CH3		CDCL3
1852M	A	3.50	CH2	N(CH2/CH2)/CH2-OH	S	D2O
839M	F	3.50 APP.	CH2	N(+)(CH2/CH3/CH3)/CH2-CH2	S	CDCL3
1621M	C	3.50	CH2	OH/CH2.2-CH		CCL4
1616M	C	3.50	CH2	OH/CH2-CH2		CCL4
1619M	C	3.50	CH2	OH/CH2-CH2		CCL4
1630M	C	3.50	CH2	OH/CH2-CH2		CCL4
1623M	D	3.50	CH2	OH/CH2-CH2		CCL4
1613M	C	3.50	CH2	OH/CH2-CH3		CCL4

BOOK NO.	ASSIGN-MENT	CHEM SHIFT - ppm -	PROTON GROUP	ENVIRONMENTAL GROUPS	S	SOLVENT
2718M	B	3.50- 4.00	CH2	OH/CH(OH/CH2)		CDCL3
1835M	C	3.50	CH2	OH/C(CH2/CH2/CH2)		CDCL3
1674M	C	3.50	CH2	O-CH2.2/CH2-OH		CCL4
1674M	C	3.50	CH2	O-CH2.2/CH3		CCL4
1419M	C	3.50	CH2	O-CH2/CH2-O		CCL4
1417M	D	3.50	CH2	O-CH2/CH2-O		CCL4
2717M	E	3.50	CH2	O-CH2/CH2-O		CCL4
1416M	B	3.50 APP.	CH2	O-CH2/CH3		CDCL3
2431M	A	3.50	CH2R	R5NN<NH-C(=O)/CH2-NH>		CDCL3
1457M	C	3.50- 4.08	CH2R	R5O<O-CH(CH2-O)/CH2-CH2>		CDCL3
833M	C	3.50	CH3	N(+)(CH2.17/CH3/CH3)	S	CDCL3
2726M	A	3.50- 4.15	HCH	CL/CH(CL/C(=O)-O)		CCL4
1828M	C	3.50	HCH	OH/CH(OH/CH3)		CDCL3
1425M	C	3.50	HCH	O-CH/CH3		CCL4
1237M	A	3.50	NH2	A<C-CH-C(SH)>		CDCL3
508M	A	3.50	NH2	A<C-C(F)>		CCL4
2468M	A	3.50	NH2	NH-C(=O)		CDCL3
1630M	C	3.50	OH	CH2-CH2		CCL4
2850M	C	3.50	OH	CH(A/CH2)		CCL4
1237M	A	3.50	SH	A<C-CH-C(NH2)>		CDCL3
1671M	A	3.50- 3.90		UNSPECIFIED		CDCL3
1710M	A	3.50- 4.00		UNSPECIFIED		CCL4
1870M	A	3.50- 4.20		UNSPECIFIED		D2O
1866M	A	3.50- 4.30		UNSPECIFIED		D2O
1781M	C	3.50- 4.05		UNSPECIFIED		CDCL3
798M	B	3.51	CH	NH-CH/CH3/CH3	S	D2O
1394M	E	3.51	CH	O-CH2.2/CH3/CH3		CCL4
1768M	D	3.51	CHR	R6<(OH)/CH2-CH2/CH2-CH2>		CDCL3
804M	D	3.51	CH2	A/CH(NH/CH3)	S	CDCL3
1640M	B	3.51	CH2	BR/CH2.2-OH		CDCL3
354M	B	3.51	CH2	BR/CH2-CH2		CCL4
2196M	A	3.51 APP.	CH2	BR/CH2-C(=O)		CCL4
264M	B	3.51	CH2	CL/CH2-CH2		CCL4
2727M	D	3.51	CH2	CL/CH2-CH2		CCL4
2196M	A	3.51 APP.	CH2	C(=O)-CL/CH2-BR		CCL4
2320M	A	3.51	CH2	C(=O)-NH/C(=O)-NH		DMSO-D6
2358M	F	3.51	CH2	C(=O)-N/C(=O)-CH3		CDCL3
2847M	C	3.51	CH2	C(=O)-O-CH2.3/A		CCL4
806M	B	3.51	CH2	NH-A/CH3	S	D2O
1344M	B	3.51	CH2	NH-C(=S)/CH3		CCL4
647M	A	3.51	CH2	N(CH2/CH2)/A		CCL4
934M	C	3.51	CH2	N=C=S/CH2.16-CH3		CDCL3
933M	D	3.51	CH2	N=C=S/CH2-CH2		CCL4
1702M	C	3.51	CH2	OH/CH2-CH2		CCL4
1631M	D	3.51	CH2	OH/CH2-CH2		CCL4
1665M	C	3.51	CH2	OH/CH2-O		CDCL3
1665M	D	3.51	CH2	O-CH3/CH2-OH		CDCL3
2658M	A	3.51	CH2	SH/C(=O)-O-NA	S	D2O
2116M	C	3.51	CH2R	R6A<C*/C(=O)-CH2>		CDCL3
1472M	F	3.51	HCHR	R600<O-CH(CH2.5-CH3)/C(CH3/CH3)>		CCL4
1666M	B	3.51 APP.		UNSPECIFIED		CCL4
2542M	B	3.52	CH	C(=O)-OH/A/CH2-CH2		DMSO
1395M	B	3.52	CH	O-CH/CH3/CH3		CCL4
1774M	D	3.52	CHR	R6<(OH)/CH(A)-CH2/HCH-CH2>		CDCL3
358M	C	3.52	CH2	BR/CH2-CH		CCL4
1491M	A	3.52	CH2	BR/CH2-O		CDCL3
1502M	C	3.52	CH2	CL/CH2.3-O		CCL4
263M	B	3.52	CH2	CL/CH2-CH2		CCL4
2311M	B	3.52	CH2	NH-C(=O)/CH2-A		CDCL3
610M	B	3.52	CH2	N(CH3/CH3)/R5NA(C=CH/C*)		DMSO-D6
1356M	B	3.52	CH2	N(C(=S)/CH2)/CH3		CDCL3
829M	D	3.52	CH2	N(+)(CH3/CH3/CH3)/CH2.10-CH3	S	CDCL3
1618M	C	3.52	CH2	OH/CH2-CH		CCL4
1614M	C	3.52	CH2	OH/CH2-CH2		CCL4
1672M	C	3.52	CH2	O-CH2.2/CH2-NH2		CDCL3
1420M	C	3.52	CH2	O-CH2/CH2-O		CCL4
1401M	D	3.52	CH2	O-CH2/CH3		CDCL3
1436M	B	3.52	CH2	O-CH/CH3		CCL4
1688M	C	3.52	CH2	O2(H/H/CH2-CH3)/CH2-OH		CCL4
1029M	B	3.52	CH2R	R5N<N(NO)-CH2/CH2-CH2>		D2O
1462M	C	3.52	CH2R	R6NO(O-CH2/CH2-NH)		CCL4
2688M	A	3.52	CH3	N(A/CH3)		TFA
667M	A	3.52	CH3	N(A/CH3)		TFA
1083M	C	3.52	H	SIH2-CH2.5		CDCL3
1617M	D	3.52	HCH	OH/CH(CH2/CH3)		CCL4
1617M	E	3.52	HCH	OH/CH(CH2/CH3)		CCL4
1423M	D	3.52	HCH	O-CH/CH3		CCL4
1238M	A	3.52	NH2	A<C-CH-CH-C(SH)>		CDCL3
1650M	E	3.52	OH	CH2-CH2		CCL4
1238M	A	3.52	SH	A<C-CH-CH-C(NH2)>		CDCL3
1239M	B	3.52	SH	A(C-C(SH)-CH-C(CH3))		CDCL3

BOOK NO.	ASSIGN-MENT	CHEM SHIFT - ppm -	PROTON GROUP	ENVIRONMENTAL GROUPS	S	SOLVENT
923M	B	3.53	CH	N=C=/CH3/CH3		CDCL3
1752M	C	3.53	CH	OH/HCH-NH2/HCH-NH2		D20
956M	B	3.53	CH2	BR/CH2-C:N		CCL4
2034M	C	3.53	CH2	C(=0)-CH2/A		CCL4
1679M	D	3.53	CH2	OH/R500<CH-O/CH2>		CCL4
1484M	C	3.53	CH2	O-CH3/CH2-A		CDCL3
815M	C	3.53	CH2	R6N(N-CH2/CH2)/CH2-CL	S	D20
2360M	B	3.53	CH2R	R6NO<N(C(=0)-CH3)-CH2/CH2-0>		CCL4
2360M	C	3.53	CH2R	R6NO<O-CH2/CH2-N(C(=0)-CH3)>		CCL4
1507M	A	3.53	CH3	O-A		CCL4
520M	A	3.53	NH2	A(C-CH-CH-C(BR))		CDCL3
1704M	C	3.54	CH2	OH/CH2-N		CDCL3
1652M	E	3.54	CH2	OH/CH2-N		CDCL3
1642M	C	3.54	CH2	OH/CH2-NH2		CDCL3
1622M	D	3.54	CH2	OH/CH(CH2/CH2)		CDCL3
2637M	B	3.54 APP.	CH2R	R5N(NH-CH(C(=0)-OH)/CH(OH)-CH2)		D20
526M	A	3.54	NH2	A(C-CH-C(I))		CDCL3
2619M	D	3.55	CH	NH2/C(=0)-OH/CH(CH3/CH3)		D20
344M	C	3.55	CH2	BR/CH(CH2/CH3)		CDCL3
2195M	C	3.55	CH2	CL/CH2-CH2		CCL4
344M	C	3.55	CH2	CL/CH(CH2/CH3)		CDCL3
2314M	A	3.55	CH2	C(=0)-NH/A		CDCL3
2673M	A	3.55	CH2	C(=0)-O-NA/A	S	D20
1703M	D	3.55	CH2	N(CH2/CH3)/A		CDCL3
931M	C	3.55	CH2	N=C=S/CH2.2-CH3		CCL4
1628M	D	3.55	CH2	OH/CH2-CH2		CCL4
1847M	A	3.55	CH2	OH/CH2-0		CCL4
1421M	D	3.55 APP.	CH2	O-CH2/CH2-0		CCL4
1402M	C	3.55	CH2	O-CH2/CH2-SH		CCL4
2384M	B	3.55	CH2	R5N<N-C(=0)/C(=0)>/CH3		CDCL3
2137M	F	3.56	CH	C(=0)-CH3/C(=0)-CH3/CH2-CH3		CDCL3
343M	A	3.56	CH2	BR/CH2-CL		CCL4
1841M	A	3.56	CH2	BR/C(CH2/CH2/CH2)		POLYSOL-D
2319M	C	3.56	CH2	C(=0)-NH/C(=0)-CH3		DMSO-D6
645M	C	3.56	CH2	N(CH2/CH2)/A		CDCL3
646M	C	3.56	CH2	N(CH2/CH2)/A		CDCL3
2853M	D	3.56	CH2	N(CH2/CH2)/A		CDCL3
811M	B	3.56	CH2	N(CH3/CH3)/CH2-CL	S	D20
1657M	B	3.56	CH2	N(+)(CH3/CH3/CH3)/CH2-OH	S	CDCL3
1849M	B	3.56	CH2	OH/CH2.2-CH		POLYSOL-D
1620M	D	3.56	CH2	OH/CH2-CH		CCL4
1826M	B	3.56	CH2	OH/CH2-CH2		CDCL3
1682M	C	3.56	CH2	OH/CH2-R6		CCL4
1674M	C	3.56	CH2	O-CH2.2/CH2-0		CCL4
1674M	D	3.56	CH2	O-CH2/CH2-0		CCL4
1020M	B	3.56	CH2R	R5NA<NH-C*/CH2-C*>		CDCL3
1443M	D	3.56	HCH	CL/R30		CCL4
1443M	E	3.56	HCH	CL/R30		CCL4
1787M	F	3.57	CH	OH/CH2-C:/CH2-CH3		CCL4
530M	A	3.57	CH2	A(C-CH-CH-C(NH2))/A(C-CH-CH-C(NH2))		DMSO-D6
2557M	B	3.57	CH2	C(=0)-OH/A(C-CH-CH-C(CH3))		CDCL3
812M	C	3.57	CH2	N(CH2/CH2)/CH2-CL	S	D20
1708M	D	3.57	CH2	OH/CH2-S		CCL4
1225M	B	3.57	CH2	SH/A<C-CH-CH-C(CL)>		CCL4
1464M	C	3.57	CH2R	R6NO(O-CH2/CH2-N(CH2-CH3))		CCL4
829M	E	3.57	H	OH	S	CDCL3
2532M	D	3.58	CH	OH/CH2-Q2/CH2-CH2		CCL4
2559M	A	3.58	CH2	C(=0)-OH/A(C-CH-C(F))		CDCL3
2611M	A	3.58	CH2	NH2/C(=0)-OH		D20
1078M	C	3.58	CH2	N(NO2/CH2)/CH(CH3/CH3)		CDCL3
833M	D	3.58	CH2	N(+)(CH3/CH3/CH3)/CH2.16-CH3	S	CDCL3
1647M	E	3.58	CH2	OH/CH2-NH		CCL4
1612M	B	3.58	CH2	OH/CH3		CCL4
2717M	F	3.58	CH2	O-CH2/CH2-0-C(=0)		CCL4
1426M	C	3.58 APP.	CH2	O-CH/CH3		CCL4
1158M	B	3.58	CH2	S-CH3/A		CCL4
1019M	A	3.58	CH2	S-C:N/Q2(H/A/H)		CDCL3
1466M	E	3.58	CH2R	R6NO(O-CH2/CH2-N)		CCL4
501M	C	3.58	NH2	A<C-C(CH(CH3/CH3))/C(CH(CH3/CH3))>		CDCL3
519M	A	3.58	NH2	A(C-CH-C(BR))		CDCL3
513M	A	3.58	NH2	A(C-CH-C(CL))		CDCL3
1764M	B	3.58	OH	R5(CH-CH2/CH2)		CCL4
1863M	A	3.59- 3.81	CH	OH/CH(OH/CH)/CH2-OH		CDCL3
1755M	H	3.59	CH	OH/HCH-N/CH3		CCL4
1751M	B	3.59	CH2	BR/CH(OH/CH2)		CDCL3
2563M	B	3.59	CH2	C(=0)-OH/A<C-CH-CH-C(O-CH2)>		CDCL3
1649M	D	3.59	CH2	OH/CH2-CH2		CCL4
1633M	D	3.59	CH2	OH/CH2-CH2		CDCL3
1863M	A	3.59- 3.81	CH2	OH/CH(OH/CH)		CDCL3
1411M	A	3.59	CH2	O-CH2/CH2-CL		CCL4
1401M	E	3.59	CH2	O-CH2/CH2-SH		CDCL3

BOOK NO.	ASSIGN-MENT	CHEM SHIFT - ppm -	PROTON GROUP	ENVIRONMENTAL GROUPS				S	SOLVENT
1492M	B	3.59	CH2	O-CH3/CH2-O					CCL4
1593M	C	3.59	CH2	O-SI/CH3					CCL4
2955M	A	3.59	CH2R	R5OA<C*/C(=O)-O>					CDCL3
2776M	C	3.59	CH3	O-C(=O)-CH2					CCL4
2707M	D	3.59	CH3	O-C(=O)-CH2					CCL4
2816M	E	3.59	CH3	O-C(=O)-CH2.7-Q?					CCL4
1323M	A	3.59	CH3	O-S(=O/O)					CCL4
587M	A	3.59	NH	A/CH2-Q3					CDCL3
527M	A	3.59	NH2	A(C-CH-CH-C(I))					CDCL3
1848M	A	3.60	CH	OH/CH2-OH/CH2-OH					D20
1727M	A	3.60- 4.20	CHR	R5AA<(CH2-OH)/C*/C*>					POLYSOL-D
1679M	E	3.60- 4.30	CHR	R500<(CH2-OH)/O-C(CH3/CH3)/CH2-O>					CCL4
773M	D	3.60	CHR	R6R6BI((NH2)/CH*(CH2/CH2)/CH2-CH*)				S	D20
1006M	B	3.60	CHR	R6<(N:C)/CH2-CH2/CH2-CH2>					CDCL3
2146M	E	3.60	CH2	A/Q1(OH/C(=O)-CH3)					CCL4
955M	C	3.60	CH2	CL/CH2-CH2					CCL4
781M	A	3.60	CH2	NH2/Q3				S	POLYSOL-D
587M	B	3.60	CH2	NH-A/Q3					CDCL3
1026M	C	3.60	CH2	N(NO/CH2)/CH3					CDCL3
1004M	A	3.60	CH2	N-C:N/Q3					CCL4
1625M	D	3.60	CH2	OH/CH2.3-CH					CDCL3
1825M	B	3.60	CH2	OH/CH2-CH2					D20
1698M	F	3.60	CH2	OH/CH2-C:					CCL4
1699M	F	3.60	CH2	OH/CH2-C:					CCL4
1646M	B	3.60	CH2	OH/CH2-NH					CDCL3
1705M	C	3.60	CH2	OH/CH2-O					CCL4
2465M	A	3.60	CH2	OH/CH2-R6N3					DMSO-D6
1651M	C	3.60	CH2	OH/CH(N/CH3)					CCL4
1727M	A	3.60- 4.20	CH2	OH/R5AA<CH-C*/C*>					POLYSOL-D
1389M	C	3.60	CH2	O-CH2.9/CH2.8-CH3					CCL4
1847M	B	3.60	CH2	O-CH2/CH2-O					CCL4
1847M	B	3.60	CH2	O-CH2/CH2-OH					CCL4
1705M	B	3.60	CH2	O-CH2/CH2-OH					CCL4
1404M	C	3.60	CH2	O-Q3/CH2-CH2					CCL4
2015M	C	3.60	CH2	R6N<N-CH2/CH2>/A					CDCL3
1679M	E	3.60- 4.30	CH2R	R500<O-C(CH3/CH3)/CH(CH2-OH)-O>					CCL4
2781M	D	3.60	CH3	O-C(=O)-CH2					CCL4
2822M	E	3.60	CH3	O-C(=O)-CH2					CCL4
2849M	D	3.60	CH3	O-C(=O)-CH2.3					CCL4
2982M	D	3.60	CH3	O-C(=O)-NH					CCL4
2787M	B	3.60	CH3	O-C(=O)-R6					CCL4
1598M	A	3.60	CH3	O-SI					CDCL3
357M	C	3.60	HCH	BR/CH(BR/CH2)					CDCL3
509M	A	3.60	NH2	A<C-CH-C(F)>					CDCL3
2662M	B	3.60- 4.10		UNSPECIFIED				S	D20
1675M	E	3.60 APP.		UNSPECIFIED					CDCL3
1740M	D	3.61	CH	OH/CH2.2/CH2.2					CDCL3
1739M	E	3.61	CH	OH/CH2-CH2/CH3					CCL4
2539M	A	3.61	CH2	A/C(=O)-OH					CDCL3
655M	A	3.61 APP.	CH2	CL/CH2-N					POLYSOL-D
2035M	C	3.61	CH2	C(=O)-CH/A					CCL4
655M	A	3.61 APP.	CH2	N(A/CH2.2)/CH2-CL					POLYSOL-D
1704M	D	3.61	CH2	N(CH2/CH2.2)/A					CDCL3
2990M	D	3.61	CH2	N(C(=O)-O/A)/CH2-CH2					CCL4
1632M	D	3.61	CH2	OH/CH2-CH2					CDCL3
1703M	E	3.61	CH2	OH/CH2-N					CDCL3
1506M	B	3.61	CH3	O-A					CCL4
1523M	B	3.61	CH3	O-A					POLYSOL-D
2779M	D	3.61	CH3	O-C(=O)-CH2					CCL4
2746M	D	3.61	CH3	O-C(=O)-CH2					CCL4
2699M	D	3.61	CH3	O-C(=O)-CH2					CCL4
2710M	D	3.61	CH3	O-C(=O)-CH2					CCL4
2704M	E	3.61	CH3	O-C(=O)-CH2					CCL4
1594M	A	3.61	CH3	O-SI					CDCL3
275M	A	3.61	HCH	CL/CH(CL/Q3)					CCL4
275M	B	3.61	HCH	CL/CH(CL/Q3)					CCL4
2972M	C	3.61	OH	CH2-CH2					CCL4
1697M	D	3.61 APP.	OH	CH2-C:					CCL4
2541M	B	3.62	CH	C(=O)-OH/A/CH3					CCL4
785M	D	3.62	CH	NH2/CH2-CH2/CH3				S	TFA
1736M	D	3.62	CH	OH/CH2-CH3/CH3					CCL4
712M	C	3.62	CH2	AN<C-N>/R6N<N-CH2/CH2>					CDCL3
972M	A	3.62	CH2	A/C:N					CCL4
981M	A	3.62	CH2	C:N/A<C-CH-CH-C(CL)>					CCL4
980M	A	3.62	CH2	C:N/A<C-C(F)>					CCL4
2612M	B	3.62	CH2	NH-CH3/C(=O)-OH					D20
1637M	B	3.62	CH2	OH/CH2-CH2					CCL4
1634M	D	3.62	CH2	OH/CH2-CH2					CDCL3
1706M	E	3.62	CH2	OH/CH2-N					CDCL3
1848M	B	3.62	CH2	OH/CH(OH/CH2)					D20
1853M	A	3.62	CH2	OH/C(CH2/CH2/CH2)					D20

BOOK NO.	ASSIGN-MENT	CHEM SHIFT - ppm -	PROTON GROUP	ENVIRONMENTAL GROUPS	S	SOLVENT
1606M	C	3.62	CH2	O-P/CH(CH2/CH2)		CCL4
1159M	C	3.62	CH2	S-CH2/A		CCL4
2992M	A	3.62	CH2R	R5NO<NH-C(=O)/CH2-O>		CDCL3
2258M	A	3.62	CH2R	R5O<C(=O)-O/C(=HCH)-C(=O)>		CDCL3
1558M	B	3.62	CH3	O-A		CCL4
2799M	D	3.62	CH3	O-C(=O)-Q2		CCL4
675M	A	3.62	CH3	R5N<N-CH=/CH=>		CDCL3
1644M	F	3.62	HCH	OH/CH(NH2/CH)		CDCL3
1648M	E	3.62	HCH	OH/CH(N/CH3)		D2O
595M	B	3.62	NH	A<C-C(CH3)>/CH2-A		CDCL3
601M	D	3.62	NHR	R6NA<C*/CH2/CH2>		CDCL3
1522M	B	3.62	NH2	A(C-CH-C(O-CH2))		CDCL3
1784M	E	3.63	CH	OH/CH2-Q3/CH2.2-CH3		CDCL3
1400M	C	3.63	CH	O-CH2/CH3/CH3		CDCL3
1636M	B	3.63	CH2	CL/CH2-OH		CDCL3
2932M	B	3.63	CH2	C(=O)-O-A/A		CCL4
2656M	A	3.63	CH2	I/C(=O)-O-NA	S	D2O
817M	B	3.63	CH2	N(A/CH2)/CH3	S	D2O
1643M	C	3.63	CH2	OH/CH2-CH2		D2O
1636M	A	3.63	CH2	OH/CH2-CL		CDCL3
1854M	B	3.63	CH2	OH/CH2-N		CDCL3
1416M	C	3.63 APP.	CH2	O-CH2/CH2-O		CDCL3
1400M	C	3.63	CH2	O-CH/CH2-C		CDCL3
2149M	A	3.63	CH2R	R5A<C(=O)-C*/C(=O)-C*>		TFA
1471M	A	3.63	CH2R	R600<O-CH2/CH2-O>		CCL4
2712M	E	3.63	CH3	O-C(=O)-CH2		CDCL3
2815M	D	3.63	CH3	O-C(=O)-Q2		CCL4
2787M	C	3.63	CH3	O-C(=O)-R6		CCL4
2625M	B	3.63	HCH	OH/C(NH2/C(=O)-OH/CH3)		D2O
1702M	D	3.63 APP.	OH	CH2-CH2		CCL4
1673M	C	3.63		UNSPECIFIED		CDCL3
2607M	A	3.64	CH2	C(=O)-OH/R5NA<C-C*/=CH>		DMSO
580M	B	3.64	CH2	NH-CH2.2/A		D2O
2668M	A	3.64	CH2	N(CH2/CH2)/CH2-N		D2O
1718M	B	3.64	CH2	OH/CH2-A		POLYSOL-D
1850M	B	3.64	CH2	OH/CH2-N		D2O
2756M	B	3.64	CH2	O-CH2/CH2-O		CDCL3
1224M	B	3.64	CH2	SH/A		CCL4
1259M	C	3.64	CH2R	R5S<SO2-CH(CH3)/C(CH3)=CH>		CDCL3
1501M	D	3.64	CH3	O-A		CCL4
2793M	C	3.64	CH3	O-C(=O)-CH2.2		CDCL3
1652M	F	3.64	OH	CH2.2-N		CDCL3
1746M	E	3.65	CH	OH/CH2-CH2/CH3		CCL4
2083M	B	3.65	CHR	R5<(C(=O)-A)/CH2-CH2/CH2-CH2>		CCL4
2366M	D	3.65	CH2	N(A/C(=O))/CH2-CH2		CCL4
1629M	D	3.65	CH2	OH/CH2-CH		CDCL3
1832M	D	3.65	CH2	OH/CH2-CH		CDCL3
1824M	B	3.65	CH2	OH/CH2-CH2		D2O
1845M	A	3.65	CH2	OH/CH2-O		CDCL3
1687M	C	3.65	CH2	OH/CH2-Q3		CDCL3
1845M	A	3.65	CH2	O-CH2/CH2-OH		CDCL3
1528M	A	3.65	CH3	O-A		CDCL3
2785M	D	3.65	CH3	O-C(=O)-CH2		CDCL3
2694M	B	3.65	CH3	O-C(=O)-CH3		CCL4
2855M	A	3.65	CH3	O-C(=O)-R5AA		CDCL3
522M	A	3.65	NH2	A(C-CH-C(CL)-C(BR))		CDCL3
1296M	B	3.66	CH2	BR/CH2-SO3	S	D2O
1840M	A	3.66 APP.	CH2	CL/CH(OH/CH2)		D2O
1348M	B	3.66	CH2	NH-C(=S)/CH3		CDCL3
1840M	A	3.66 APP.	CH2	OH/CH(OH/CH2)		D2O
2757M	D	3.66	CH2	O-CH2/CH2-O		CDCL3
1601M	C	3.66	CH2	O-SI/CH(CH2/CH2)		CCL4
1748M	E	3.67	CH	OH/CH2-CH2/CH3		CCL4
641M	E	3.67	CHR	R6NN<(CH3)/N(A)-CH2/CH2-NH>		CDCL3
252M	A	3.67	CH2	CL/CH2-CL		CCL4
1607M	A	3.67	CH2	CL/CH2-O		CDCL3
2040M	A	3.67	CH2	C(=O)-CH2/A		CDCL3
2794M	B	3.67	CH2	N(CH2/CH2)/C(=O)-O-CH2		CDCL3
830M	D	3.67	CH2	N(+)(CH3/CH3/CH3)/CH2.10-CH3	S	CDCL3
1695M	C	3.67	CH2	OH/CH2-C:CH		CCL4
1678M	B	3.67	CH2	OH/CH2-R5S		CCL4
1600M	C	3.67	CH2	O-SI/CH2-CH2		CCL4
1602M	C	3.67	CH2	O-SI/CH(CH2/CH2)		CCL4
1478M	B	3.67	CH2R	R700<O-CH2/CH2-CH2>		CCL4
2771M	C	3.67	CH3	O-C(=O)-C		CCL4
2938M	A	3.67	CH3	O-C(=O)-CH2		CDCL3
2742M	C	3.67	CH3	O-C(=O)-CH2		CDCL3
2748M	D	3.67	CH3	O-C(=O)-CH2.5		CDCL3
1695M	C	3.67	OH	CH2-CH2		CCL4
1619M	D	3.67	OH	CH2-CH2		CCL4
1683M	E	3.67	OH	CH2-R6N		CDCL3

BOOK NO.	ASSIGN-MENT	CHEM SHIFT - ppm -	PROTON GROUP	ENVIRONMENTAL GROUPS	S	SOLVENT
1846M	B	3.67		UNSPECIFIED		CDCL3
1742M	E	3.68	CH	OH/CH2-CH2/CH3		CCL4
348M	A	3.68	CH2	BR/CH2-BR		CDCL3
2313M	B	3.68	CH2	CL/CH2-C(=O)		CDCL3
578M	E	3.68	CH2	NH-CH2/A		CCL4
2613M	C	3.68	CH2	NH-CH2/C(=O)-OH		D20
1823M	A	3.68	CH2	OH/CH2-OH		D20
1841M	B	3.68	CH2	OH/C(CH2/CH2/CH2)		POLYSOL-D
2756M	C	3.68	CH2	O-CH2/CH2-O-C(=O)		CDCL3
1493M	B	3.68	CH2	O-CH/CH3		CCL4
1280M	C	3.68	CH2	SO2-CL/CH2-CH3		CCL4
1299M	A	3.68	CH2	SO3-NA/Q3		D20
1510M	A	3.68	CH3	O-A		CCL4
1495M	B	3.68	CH3	O-A		CCL4
2839M	B	3.68	CH3	O-A		CCL4
1236M	A	3.68	NH2	A<C-C(SH)>		CDCL3
1236M	A	3.68	SH	A<C-C(NH2)>		CDCL3
2348M	C	3.69	CH	N(C(=O)/CH)/CH3/CH3		CCL4
1447M	C	3.69	CHR	R30((A)/O-HCH).		CCL4
2951M	C	3.69	CHR	R50<(A)/HCH-O/HCH-C(=O)>		CDCL3
1750M	A	3.69	CH2	CL/CH(OH/CH2)		CDCL3
2558M	A	3.69	CH2	C(=O)-OH/A<C-C(F)>		CDCL3
2734M	B	3.69	CH2	I/C(=O)-O-CH2		CCL4
579M	D	3.69	CH2	NH-CH2/A		CCL4
976M	B	3.69	CH2	N(A/CH2.2)/CH2-C:N		DMSO-D6
2365M	D	3.69	CH2	N(C(=O)/A)/CH2-CH3		D20
2364M	C	3.69	CH2	N(C(=O)/A)/CH3		CCL4
831M	E	3.69	CH2	N(+)(CH3/CH3/CH3)/CH2-CH2	S	CDCL3
1725M	C	3.69	CH2	OH/CH2-AA		CCL4
1843M	B	3.69	CH2	OH/CH2-NH		D20
1842M	B	3.69	CH2	OH/CH2-NH		D20
1661M	B	3.69	CH2	OH/CH2-SH		D20
2719M	E	3.69	CH2	OH/CH(OH/CH2)		CDCL3
2399M	B	3.69	CH2	R5NA(N-C(=O)/C(=O))/CH2-CH2		CDCL3
2385M	B	3.69	CH2	R5N<N-C(=O)/C(=O)>/CH2-A		POLYSOL-D
1281M	D	3.69	CH2	SO2-CL/CH2.2-CH3		CCL4
1461M	B	3.69	CH2R	R60(O-CH2/CH2-CH=)		CCL4
840M	A	3.69	CH3	N(&)(A/CH3/CH3)	S	D20
1515M	A	3.69	CH3	O-A		CDCL3
1722M	B	3.69	CH3	O-A		CDCL3
1723M	B	3.69	CH3	O-A		CCL4
1558M	C	3.69	CH3	O-A		CCL4
1497M	C	3.69	CH3	O-A		CCL4
2739M	B	3.69	CH3	O-C(=O)-CH2		CCL4
2791M	C	3.69	CH3	O-C(=O)-CH2		CCL4
708M	D	3.69	NH	AN<C-N>/CH2-CH2		CDCL3
1239M	C	3.69	SH	A(C-C(SH)-CH-C(CH3))		CDCL3
2615M	C	3.70	CH	NH2/C(=O)-OH/CH2-CH3		D20
2614M	B	3.70	CH	NH2/C(=O)-OH/CH3		D20
1398M	A	3.70	CH	O-C/CH3/CH3		CCL4
1888M	A	3.70	CH2	A<C-CH-CH-C(OH)>/A<C-CH-CH-C(OH)>		DMSO-D6
343M	B	3.70	CH2	CL/CH2-BR		CCL4
954M	B	3.70	CH2	CL/CH2-C:N		CCL4
416M	A	3.70	CH2	I/CH2-I		CDCL3
581M	B	3.70	CH2	NH-CH2/A		CCL4
577M	D	3.70	CH2	NH-CH2/A		CCL4
1705M	C	3.70	CH2	OH/CH2-O		CCL4
1705M	B	3.70	CH2	O-CH2/CH2-OH		CCL4
2757M	E	3.70	CH2	O-CH2/CH2-O-C(=O)		CDCL3
1406M	C	3.70	CH2	O-Q3/CH2-N		CCL4
1577M	B	3.70	CH2	SH/R50(C=CH/O)		CDCL3
1465M	C	3.70	CH2R	R6NO<O-CH2/CH2-N(CH2-Q3)>		CDCL3
1467M	C	3.70	CH2R	R6NO<O-CH2/CH2-N(C(C:N/CH3/CH3))>		CDCL3
1313M	A	3.70	CH3	N(+)(A/CH3/CH3)		POLYSOL-D
1520M	A	3.70	CH3	O-A		CCL4
1511M	A	3.70	CH3	O-A		CCL4
1488M	A	3.70	CH3	O-A		CCL4
2178M	A	3.70	CH3	O-A		CCL4
2595M	A	3.70	CH3	O-A		POLYSOL-D
1924M	B	3.70	CH3	O-A		CCL4
2337M	B	3.70	CH3	O-A		DMSO-D6
1583M	A	3.70	CH3	O-AR6NSA		DMSO-D6
506M	A	3.70	NH2	A<C-CH-C(CF3)>		CDCL3
2792M	C	3.70	OH	CH(C(=O)-O/CH)		CCL4
2661M	B	3.70- 4.20		UNSPECIFIED	S	D20
2140M	D	3.71	CH	C(=O)-CH3/C(=O)-CH3/CH2-CH		CCL4
2618M	C	3.71	CH	NH2/C(=O)-OH/CH2-CH2		D20
2950M	C	3.71	CHR	R50<(C(=O)-CH3)/C(=O)-O/HCH-CH2>		CCL4
1765M	D	3.71	CHR	R5<(OH)/CH(CH3)-CH2/CH2-CH2>		CDCL3
2724M	C	3.71	CH2	CL/CH2-C(=O)-O		CCL4
2996M	A	3.71	CH2	CL/CH2-O		CCL4

BOOK NO.	ASSIGN-MENT	CHEM SHIFT - ppm -	PROTON GROUP	ENVIRONMENTAL GROUPS	S	SOLVENT
2488M	A	3.71	CH2	I/C(=O)-OH		CDCL3
486M	D	3.71	CH2	NH2/A<C-CH-CH-C(CH(CH3/CH3))>		CCL4
1701M	C	3.71	CH2	OH/CH2-A		CDCL3
1665M	C	3.71	CH2	OH/CH2-O		CDCL3
1660M	F	3.71	CH2	OH/CH2-S		CDCL3
1994M	E	3.71	CH2	OH/CH(C(=O)-CH3/CH3)		CDCL3
1665M	D	3.71	CH2	O-CH3/CH2-OH		CDCL3
1408M	C	3.71	CH2	O-Q2/CH3		CCL4
1599M	C	3.71	CH2	O-SI/CH2.2-CH3		CCL4
1455M	B	3.71	CH2R	R5O(O-CH2/CH2-CH2)		CDCL3
1025M	B	3.71	CH3	N(NO/CH3)		CCL4
1519M	A	3.71	CH3	O-A		CDCL3
1547M	A	3.71	CH3	O-A		CDCL3
1548M	A	3.71	CH3	O-A		CDCL3
1516M	A	3.71	CH3	O-A		CCL4
2425M	A	3.71	CH3	O-A		POLYSOL-D
1560M	B	3.71	CH3	O-A		CCL4
1535M	B	3.71	CH3	O-A		CDCL3
1503M	C	3.71	CH3	O-A		CCL4
2790M	B	3.71	CH3	O-C(=O)-CH2		CDCL3
2738M	C	3.71	CH3	O-C(=O)-CH2.2		CDCL3
1214M	C	3.71	HCH	CL/CH(SH/HCH)		CCL4
1839M	E	3.71	OH	CH2-C		C3D6O
1613M	D	3.71	OH	CH2-CH2		CCL4
2417M	B	3.72	CH	NH-C(=O)-NH2/CH3/CH3		POLYSOL-D
1637M	C	3.72	CH2	CL/CH2-CH2		CCL4
2962M	A	3.72	CH2	CL/CH2-O-C(=O)		CDCL3
485M	C	3.72	CH2	NH2/A(C-CH-CH-C(CH3))		CCL4
1640M	C	3.72	CH2	OH/CH2.2-BR		CDCL3
2972M	D	3.72	CH2	OH/CH2-S		CCL4
1792M	C	3.72	CH2	O-A/CH(OH/CH3)		CCL4
2180M	A	3.72	CH2R	R5AA(C*-CH-C(C(=O)-H)/C*)		CDCL3
1545M	A	3.72	CH3	O-A		CCL4
1554M	A	3.72	CH3	O-A		CDCL3
1569M	A	3.72	CH3	O-AA		CCL4
2737M	B	3.72	CH3	O-C(=O)-CH2.2		CCL4
1562M	C	3.72	NH2	A<C-C(O-CH2.3)/CH-C(O-CH2.3)>		CDCL3
2725M	C	3.73	CH2	CL/CH2-C(=O)-O		CCL4
1656M	C	3.73	CH2	OH/CH2.2-NH2	S	D20
1355M	C	3.73	CH2R	R6N<N(C(=S)-NH)-CH2/CH2-CH2>		CDCL3
1494M	B	3.73	CH3	O-A		CCL4
2851M	A	3.73	CH3	O-C(=O)-CH2		CDCL3
1861M	A	3.74 APP.	CH	OH/CH(OH/CH2)/CH2-OH		D20
2665M	A	3.74	CH2	N(CH2/CH2)/C(=O)-O-NA		D20
2662M	A	3.74	CH2	OH(CH(OH/CH))	S	D20
1654M	B	3.74	CH2	OH/CH2-NH		D20
1861M	A	3.74 APP.	CH2	OH/CH(OH/CH)		D20
1521M	A	3.74	CH3	O-A		CDCL3
1505M	B	3.74	CH3	O-A		CDCL3
2740M	C	3.74	CH3	O-C(=O)-CH		CCL4
1649M	E	3.74	OH	CH2-CH2		CCL4
2661M	A	3.75 APP.	CH	OH/CH(OH/CH)/CH2-OH	S	D20
1833M	D	3.75	CH	OH/HCH-HCH/CH3		CCL4
1028M	B	3.75	CHR	R6<(N(NO/R6))/CH2-CH2/CH2-CH2>		CDCL3
1028M	C	3.75	CHR	R6<(N(NO/R6))/CH2-CH2/CH2-CH2>		CDCL3
1855M	C	3.75	CHR	R6<(OH)/CH(OH)-CH2/CH2-CH2>		CDCL3
1227M	C	3.75	CH2	A(C-C(CH2-SH)-CH-C(CH3)/CH-C(CH3))/SH		CDCL3
705M	C	3.75	CH2	N(CH2/CH2)/AN<C-N>		CDCL3
2661M	A	3.75 APP.	CH2	OH/CH(OH/CH)	S	D20
2796M	C	3.75	CH3	C-C(=O)-CH		CDCL3
1549M	A	3.75	CH3	O-A		POLYSOL-D
1524M	B	3.75	CH3	O-A		CDCL3
1771M	E	3.75	OH	R6<CH-CH(CH3)/CH2>		CDCL3
1596M	D	3.76	CH2	O-SI/CH3		CCL4
208M	A	3.76	CH2R	AR5A(C*/C*)		CDCL3
1474M	A	3.76	CH2R	R6OOR6OOSPI<O-CH2/C*(CH2/CH2/CH2)		CDCL3
1508M	A	3.76	CH3	O-A		CDCL3
1536M	B	3.76	CH3	O-A		CDCL3
1851M	C	3.77 APP.	CH	OH/CH2-N/CH3		CDCL3
1857M	B	3.77	CHR	R8<(OH)/CH2-CH2/CH2-CH2>		D20
2728M	A	3.77	CH2	BR/C(=O)-O-CH3		CCL4
1662M	F	3.77	CH2	OH/CH(SH/CH2)		CDCL3
2434M	B	3.77	CH2	R5NN<N-C(=O)/CH2>/Q3		POLYSOL-D
1496M	B	3.77	CH3	O-A		CDCL3
2728M	A	3.77	CH3	O-C(=O)-CH2		CCL4
2859M	A	3.77	CH3	O-C(=O)-CH=		TFA
2993M	A	3.77	CH3	O-C(=O)-R6NNN		CDCL3
507M	A	3.77	NH2	A<C-CH-CH-C(CF3)>		CDCL3
666M	B	3.78	CH2	A<C-CH-CH-C(N(CH3/CH3))>/A<C-CH-CH-C(N(CH3/CH3))>		CDCL3
1653M	F	3.78	CH2	OH/CH2.2-N		CDCL3
1949M	A	3.78	CH2R	R5AA<C*/C*>		POLYSOL-D

BOOK NO.	ASSIGN- MENT	CHEM SHIFT - ppm -	PROTON GROUP	ENVIRONMENTAL GROUPS	S	SOLVENT
2374M	C	3.78	CH2R	R5N(N(A)-C(=O)/CH2-CH2)		CDCL3
1030M	B	3.78	CH2R	R6N(N(N=O)-CH2/CH2-CH2)		CDCL3
1906M	A	3.78	CH3	O-A		CDCL3
2116M	D	3.78	CH3	O-AR6		CDCL3
275M	A	3.78	HCH	CL/CH(CL/Q3)		CCL4
275M	B	3.78	HCH	CL/CH(CL/Q3)		CCL4
594M	A	3.78	NH	A/CH2-A		CDCL3
1554M	B	3.78	NH2	A(C-C(O-CH3)-CH-C(CL))		CDCL3
1678M	C	3.78	OH	CH2.2-R5S		CCL4
2632M	C	3.79	CH	NH2/C(=O)-OH/CH2-CH2		D2O
1754M	E	3.79	CH	OH/CH2-N/CH3		CDCL3
1756M	E	3.79	CH	OH/CH2-R5N/CH3		CDCL3
2372M	D	3.79	CHR	R6NA<N(C(=O)-CH3)-C*/CH2-CH2>		CDCL3
1411M	B	3.79	CH2	CL/CH2-O		CCL4
1636M	B	3.79	CH2	CL/CH2-OH		CDCL3
2512M	A	3.79	CH2	C(=O)-OH/R5S<C=CH/S>		CDCL3
2933M	B	3.79	CH2	C(=O)-O-A/A		CDCL3
1505M	C	3.79	CH2	NH2/A<C-CH-C(O-CH3)>		CDCL3
483M	C	3.79	CH2	NH2/A<C-C(CH3)2		CDCL3
2751M	B	3.79	CH2	NH-C(=O)/C(=O)-O-CH2		DMSO-D6
1636M	A	3.79	CH2	OH/CH2-CL		CDCL3
2660M	B	3.79	CH2	OH/CH2-C(=O)-O		D2O
1418M	A	3.79 APP.	CH2	O-CH2/CH2-O		CDCL3
2867M	A	3.79	CH2	O-CH2/CH2-O-C(=O)		CCL4
1418M	A	3.79 APP.	CH2	O-Q3/CH2-O		CDCL3
1458M	A	3.79	CH2R	R500<O-CH2/CH2-O>		CCL4
1468M	C	3.79	CH2R	R6NO<O-CH2/CH2-N(A<C-CH-C(CH3)>)>		CDCL3
1589M	B	3.79	CH2R	R60A<O-CH2/CH2-C*>		CCL4
1537M	A	3.79	CH3	O-A		CDCL3
1551M	C	3.79	CH3	O-A		CDCL3
1552M	C	3.79	CH3	O-A		CDCL3
2790M	C	3.79	CH3	O-C(=O)-CH		CDCL3
769M	B	3.79	H	BH2		CDCL3
769M	B	3.79	NH2	C(CH3/CH3/CH3)		CDCL3
1620M	E	3.79	OH	CH2.2-CH		CCL4
1240M	A	3.79	SH	A<C-CH-C(SH)-C(CL)>		CCL4
1240M	B	3.79	SH	A<C-C(CL)/CH-C(SH)>		CCL4
1828M	D	3.80	CH	OH/HCH-OH/CH3		CDCL3
1259M	D	3.80	CHR	R5S<(CH3)/SO2-CH2/CH=C(CH3)>		CDCL3
1777M	C	3.80	CHR	R7<(OH)/CH2-CH2/CH2-CH2>		CDCL3
1929M	A	3.80	CH2	A(C-C(OH)-CH-C(OH))/A		DMSO-D6
1330M	A	3.80	CH2	CL/CH2-O		CDCL3
2392M	A	3.80	CH2	CL/CH2-R5NA		CDCL3
423M	A	3.80	CH2	I/Q3		CCL4
484M	C	3.80	CH2	NH2/A<C-CH-C(CH3)>		CDCL3
2362M	C	3.80	CH2	N(C(=O)-H/A)/CH3		CDCL3
2778M	D	3.80	CH2	O-C(=O)-CH2.3/CH(CH3/CH3)		CCL4
1597M	E	3.80	CH2	O/SI/CH3		CDCL3
867M	A	3.80	CH2	QN(Q2(A))/CH2-QN		CDCL3
2392M	B	3.80	CH2	R5NA<N-C(=O)/C(=O)>/CH2-CL		CDCL3
1261M	A	3.80	CH2	SO2-A/Q3		CDCL3
2371M	C	3.80	CH2R	R6NA<N(C(=O)-H)-C*/CH2-CH2>		CDCL3
603M	D	3.80	CH2R	R6NA(NH-CH2/C*)		CCL4
1132M	C	3.80	CH2R	R6SS<S-CH2/S-CH2>		POLYSOL-D
2398M	A	3.80	CH3	O-A		CDCL3
2244M	A	3.80	CH3	O-A		CCL4
2887M	A	3.80	CH3	O-A		CCL4
2077M	D	3.80	CH3	O-A		CCL4
2887M	A	3.80	CH3	O-C(=O)-A		CCL4
2880M	A	3.80	CH3	O-C(=O)-A		CDCL3
2916M	A	3.80	CH3	O-C(=O)-A		POLYSOL-D
2825M	A	3.80	CH3	O-C(=O)-Q2		CDCL3
1314M	A	3.80	CH3	O-SO3-K		D2O
353M	B	3.80	HCH	BR/CH(BR/CH3)		CCL4
353M	C	3.80	HCH	BR/CH(BR/CH3)		CCL4
356M	A	3.80	HCH	BR/CH(BR/HCH)		CCL4
356M	B	3.80	HCH	BR/CH(BR/HCH)		CCL4
1070M	B	3.80	NH2	A<C-CH-C(NO2)-C(CH3)>		CDCL3
1936M	C	3.81	CH2	A(C-C(OH)-C(C(CH3/CH3/CH3))/CH-C(CH3))/A(C-C(OH)-C(CH2-A)/CH-C(CH3))		CDCL3
2634M	A	3.81	CH2	NH-A/C(=O)-OH		DMSO-D6
2639M	B	3.81	CH2	NH-C(=O)-CH/C(=O)-OH		D2O
2361M	B	3.81	CH2	N(C(=O)-H/A)/CH3		CDCL3
1645M	D	3.81	CH2	OH/CH2-C		CDCL3
1499M	C	3.81	CH2	O-A/CH3		CCL4
1595M	C	3.81	CH2	O-SI/CH3		CDCL3
1263M	A	3.81	CH2	SO2-A/Q3		CDCL3
1262M	B	3.81	CH2	SO2-A/Q3		CDCL3
1470M	B	3.81	CH2R	R6OS<O-CH2/CH2-S>		CCL4
1567M	A	3.81	CH3	O-A		CCL4
2869M	B	3.81	CH3	O-C(=O)-A		CDCL3

BOOK NO.	ASSIGN-MENT	CHEM SHIFT - ppm -	PROTON GROUP	ENVIRONMENTAL GROUPS	S	SOLVENT
357M	D	3.81	HCH	BR/CH(BR/CH2)		CDCL3
2394M	C	3.81	HCH	R5NA(N-C(=0)/C(=0))/R3O(CH-0/CH2)		CDCL3
539M	A	3.81	NH2	AA(C-C*)		CDCL3
512M	A	3.81	NH2	A(C-C(CL))		CCL4
1778M	C	3.81	OH	R6R6<CH-CH2/CH2>		POLYSOL-D
2644M	C	3.82	CH	NH2/C(=0)-OH/CH2-CH2	S	D20
148M	A	3.82	CH2	A/A		CCL4
355M	A	3.82	CH2	BR/CH(BR/CH2)		CCL4
1562M	D	3.82	CH2	0-A/CH2.?-CH3		CDCL3
1522M	C	3.82	CH2	0-A/CH3		CDCL3
1328M	C	3.82	CH2	0-SO3-NA/CH2.12-CH3		POLYSOL-D
209M	B	3.82	CH2R	R5AA<C*-CH-C(CH3)/C*>		CDCL3
1459M	D	3.82	CH2R	R500<0-C/CH2-0>		CCL4
1529M	A	3.82	CH3	0-A		CDCL3
2584M	A	3.82	CH3	0-A		DMSO-D6
2888M	B	3.82	CH3	0-A		CDCL3
2888M	A	3.82	CH3	0-C(=0)-A		CDCL3
2881M	A	3.82	CH3	0-C(=0)-A		CDCL3
2821M	B	3.82	CH3	0-C(=0)-Q2		CDCL3
521M	B	3.82	NH2	A(C-C(BR)-CH-C(CH3))		CDCL3
2844M	A	3.83	CH2	BR/C(=0)-CH2		CDCL3
2465M	B	3.83	CH2	R6N3<N-C(=0)/C(=0)-N>/CH2-OH		DMSO-D6
863M	A	3.83 APP.	CH2R	R5A(C*/C(=NOH)-CH2)		CDCL3
2135M	A	3.83	CH3	0-A		CDCL3
1563M	A	3.83	CH3	0-A		CDCL3
2357M	C	3.83	OH	CH(C(=0)/CH3)		CCL4
2938M	B	3.84	CH2	C(=0)-0-CH3/AN(C-N)		CDCL3
2638M	A	3.84	CH2	NH2/C(=0)-NH		D20
2638M	B	3.84	CH2	NH-C(=0)/C(=0)-OH		D20
1553M	A	3.84	CH3	0-A		CCL4
1514M	A	3.84	CH3	0-A		CDCL3
791M	A	3.84	CH3	0-A	S	D20
1527M	A	3.84	CH3	0-A	S	POLYSOL-D
1559M	B	3.84	CH3	0-A		CDCL3
2910M	A	3.84	CH3	0-C(=0)-A		POLYSOL-D
2735M	B	3.84	CH3	0-C(=0)-CH	S	D20
899M	A	3.84	NH2	A(C-CH-CH-C(N=N-A))		CDCL3
1404M	D	3.84	Q3	H/0-CH2/H		CCL4
1232M	A	3.84	SH	A<C-C(CL)/CH-C(CL)>		CCL4
772M	B	3.85	CHR	R4((NH2)/CH2-CH?/CH2)	S	D20
476M	B	3.85	CH2	NH2/A		CDCL3
656M	A	3.85	CH2	N(A/CH2)/Q3		CCL4
1639M	B	3.85	CH2	OH/CH2-BR		CCL4
1658M	C	3.85	CH2	OH/CH2-C:N		CDCL3
1655M	B	3.85	CH2	OH/CH2-NH2	S	D20
1490M	C	3.85	CH2	0-A/CH2-CH3		CDCL3
1247M	A	3.85	CH2	S(=0)-CH2/A		CDCL3
2583M	A	3.85	CH3	0-A		DMSO-D6
824M	A	3.85	CH3	0-A	S	D20
2872M	A	3.85	CH3	0-C(=0)-A		CCL4
2726M	B	3.85	CH3	0-C(=0)-CH		CCL4
1316M	C	3.85	CH3	SO3-CH2		CCL4
1234M	A	3.85	SH	A(C-C(CL)-CH-C(CL)/CH-C(CL))		CDCL3
2141M	C	3.86	CH2	C(=0)-R50/C(=0)-CH3		CCL4
2998M	F	3.86	CH2	0-P/CH2-CH2		CCL4
1257M	B	3.86	CH2	Q2(H/A/H)/SO2-CH3		CDCL3
1565M	A	3.86	CH3	0-A		CDCL3
1531M	A	3.86	CH3	0-A		CDCL3
2914M	A	3.86	CH3	0-C(=0)-A		DMSO-D6
1405M	D	3.86	Q3	H/0-CH2/H		CCL4
1770M	E	3.87	CHR	R6<(OH)/CH(CH2-CH3)-CH2/CH2-CH2>		CDCL3
918M	A	3.87	CH2	A<C-CH-CH-C(N=C=0)>/A<C-CH-CH-C(N=C=0)>		POLYSOL-D
2052M	B	3.87	CH2	CL/CH2-C(=0)		CDCL3
2823M	E	3.87- 4.42	CH2	0-C(=0)-CH2/CH(0-C(=0)/CH2)		CCL4
1509M	A	3.87	CH3	0-A		CDCL3
2888M	B	3.87	CH3	0-A		CDCL3
1563M	B	3.87	CH3	0-A		CDCL3
1559M	C	3.87	CH3	0-A		CDCL3
2888M	A	3.87	CH3	0-C(=0)-A		CDCL3
1453M	C	3.87	CH*R	R3OR5A<0-CH*/HCH-C*>		CCL4
757M	A	3.87 APP.	NH	NH2/A<C-C(CL)/CH-C(CL)>		CDCL3
757M	A	3.87 APP.	NH2	NH-A		CDCL3
237M	D	3.88	CH	CL/CH2-CH3/CH3		CCL4
1789M	D	3.88	CH	OH/A/R3<CH-CH2/CH2>		CCL4
1840M	B	3.88	CH	OH/CH2-CL/CH2-OH		D20
368M	A	3.88	CH2	BR/Q3		CCL4
259M	A	3.88	CH2	CL/CH(CL/CH2)		CCL4
415M	A	3.88	CH2	I/I		CCL4
1504M	B	3.88 APP.	CH2	NH2/A<C-C(0-CH3)>		CDCL3
1502M	D	3.88	CH2	0-A/CH2.3-CL		CCL4
1566M	A	3.88	CH3	0-A		CDCL3

BOOK NO.	ASSIGN-MENT	CHEM SHIFT - ppm -	PROTON GROUP	ENVIRONMENTAL GROUPS	S	SOLVENT
2075M	B	3.88	CH3	O-A		CDCL3
1504M	B	3.88 APP.	CH3	O-A		CDCL3
2873M	A	3.88	CH3	O-C(=O)-A		CCL4
834M	C	3.88	CH:	:C-CH2		POLYSOL-D
2880M	B	3.88	NH2	A<C-CH-C(C(=O)-O-CH3)>		CDCL3
1769M	D	3.89	CHR	R6<(OH)/CH2-CH2/CH2-CH2>		CDCL3
771M	A	3.89	CH2	NH2/CF3	S	D20
1562M	E	3.89	CH2	O-A/CH2.2-CH3		CDCL3
2284M	B	3.89	CH2	O-CH3/C(=O)-NH2		CDCL3
2812M	D	3.89	CH2	O-C(=O)-Q2/CH(CH3/CH3)		CCL4
2807M	C	3.89	CH2	O-C(=O)-Q3/CH(CH3/CH3)		CCL4
1434M	B	3.89	CH2	O-C/Q3		CCL4
1564M	A	3.89	CH3	O-A		CDCL3
1530M	A	3.89	CH3	O-A		CCL4
1532M	A	3.89	CH3	O-A		CCL4
2096M	A	3.89	CH3	O-A		POLYSOL-D
2876M	A	3.89	CH3	O-C(=O)-A		CDCL3
2874M	A	3.89	CH3	O-C(=O)-A		CDCL3
2915M	A	3.89	CH3	O-C(=O)-A		CDCL3
2905M	A	3.89	CH3	O-C(=O)-A		POLYSOL-D
846M	A	3.89	CH3	O-NH2	S	D20
378M	A	3.89 APP.	HCH	BR/CH(BR/A)		CDCL3
1406M	D	3.89	Q3	H/O-CH2.2/H		CCL4
1933M	D	3.90	CH2	A<C-C(OH)-C(C(CH3/CH3/CH3))/CH-C(CH2-CH3)>/ A<C-C(OH)-C(C(CH3/CH3/CH3))/CH-C(CH2-CH3)>		CDCL3
2638M	A	3.90	CH2	NH2/C(=O)-NH		D20
2638M	B	3.90	CH2	NH-C(=O)/C(=O)-OH		D20
2668M	B	3.90	CH2	N(CH2/CH2.2)/C(=O)-O-K		D20
1518M	B	3.90	CH2	O-A/CH3		CDCL3
1513M	B	3.90	CH2	O-A/CH3		CCL4
1407M	A	3.90	CH2	O-CH2/Q3		CCL4
2739M	C	3.90	CH2	O-CH3/C(=O)-O-CH3		CCL4
2696M	D	3.90	CH2	O-C(=O)-CH3/CH(CH2/CH2)		CCL4
2994M	A	3.90	CH2R	R5NO<N(A)-C(=O)/CH2-O>		CDCL3
1794M	C	3.90	CH3	O-AAN		POLYSOL-D
356M	A	3.90	HCH	BR/CH(BR/HCH)		CCL4
356M	B	3.90	HCH	BR/CH(BR/HCH)		CCL4
1626M	D	3.90	OH	CH2-CH2		CCL4
1617M	F	3.90	OH	HCH-CH		CCL4
331M	E	3.91	CH	BR/CH2.2-CH3/CH2-CH3		CCL4
2643M	C	3.91	CH	NH2/C(=O)-OH/CH2.2-NH2	S	D20
811M	C	3.91	CH2	CL/CH2-N	S	D20
2306M	A	3.91	CH2	NH-C(=O)/Q3		CDCL3
2586M	C	3.91	CH2	O-A/CH2-CH3		POLYSOL-D
1489M	B	3.91	CH2	O-A/CH3		CCL4
1500M	C	3.91	CH2	O-A/CH3		CCL4
2211M	C	3.91	CH2	O-A/CH3		DMSO-D6
2383M	D	3.91	CH2R	R7N(N(C(=O)-CH3)-C(=O)/CH2-CH2)		CDCL3
2892M	A	3.91	CH3	O-C(=O)-A		CDCL3
2625M	C	3.91	HCH	OH/C(NH2/C(=O)-OH/CH3)		D20
1414M	D	3.91	Q3	H/O-CH2/H		CCL4
2485M	A	3.92	CH2	BR/C(=O)-OH		CDCL3
1332M	A	3.92	CH2	C(=S)-NH2/A		POLYSOL-D
2646M	A	3.92	CH2	NH2/C(=O)-NH	S	D20
1686M	B	3.92	CH2	OH/Q2(CH3)		CCL4
2554M	D	3.92	CH2	O-A/CH2-CH2		CDCL3
1498M	C	3.92	CH2	O-A/CH3		CCL4
2695M	D	3.92	CH2	O-C(=O)-CH3/CH(CH2/CH2)		CCL4
1538M	A	3.92	CH3	O-A		CDCL3
2598M	A	3.92	CH3	O-A		DMSO-D6
2915M	B	3.92	CH3	O-A		CDCL3
1564M	B	3.92	CH3	O-A		CDCL3
1214M	D	3.92	HCH	CL/CH(SH/HCH)		CCL4
1677M	E	3.92	HCH	OH/R30<CH-O/HCH>		D20
1827M	C	3.92	OH	CH2.16-OH		DMSO-D6
2719M	F	3.93 APP.	CH	OH/CH2-O-C(=O)/CH2-OH		CDCL3
1783M	D	3.93	CH	OH/Q3/CH2-CH2		CCL4
2655M	B	3.93	CH2	CL/C(CL/C(=O)-O/CH3)	S	D20
1663M	B	3.93	CH2	OH/CH2-SO3-K		D20
1837M	F	3.93	CH2	OH/C(OH/CH2/CH3)		CDCL3
2173M	C	3.93	CH2	O-A/CH2-CH3		CCL4
505M	A	3.93	NH2	A<C-CH-CH-C(A)>		C3H60
1841M	C	3.93	OH	CH2-C		POLYSOL-D
1525M	D	3.94	CH2	O-A/CH3		CCL4
2788M	D	3.94	CH2	O-C(=O)-R6/CH(CH2.3/CH2)		CCL4
1325M	C	3.94	CH2	O-S(=O)-O/CH2-CH2		CCL4
1664M	A	3.94	CH2	R5NN<N-C(=S)/CH2>/CH2-OH		TFA
1322M	D	3.94	CH2	SO3-A/CH2-CH2		CCL4
2901M	A	3.94	CH3	O-C(=O)-A		CDCL3
2394M	D	3.94	HCH	R5NA(N-C(=O)/C(=O))/R30(CH-O/CH2)		CDCL3
1664M	A	3.94	NH	R5NN<C(=S)-N(CH2-CH2)/CH2-CH2>		TFA

BOOK NO.	ASSIGN-MENT	CHEM SHIFT - ppm -	PROTON GROUP	ENVIRONMENTAL GROUPS	S	SOLVENT
1830M	C	3.95	CH	OH/CH2-CH/CH3		CCL4
267M	B	3.95	CHR	R6((CL)/CH2-CH2/CH2-CH2)		CCL4
1570M	B	3.95	CH2	O-AA/CH3		CCL4
1540M	D	3.95	CH2	O-A/R3O<CH-O/CH2>		CDCL3
600M	C	3.95	NH	AA<C-C*>/CH2-CH3		CCL4
518M	A	3.95	NH2	A(C-C(BR))		CCL4
1863M	B	3.96 APP.	CH	OH/CH(OH/CH)/CH(OH/CH2)		CDCL3
355M	B	3.96	CH2	CL/CH(BR/CH2)		CDCL3
2561M	A	3.96	CH2	C(=O)-OH/A<C-CH-CH-C(NO2)>		CCL4
868M	A	3.96	CH2	QN(A)/CH2-QN		TFA
2920M	A	3.96	CH3	O-C(=O)-A		CDCL3
1732M	B	3.96	OH	CH2.2-ANN		CDCL3
254M	A	3.97	CH2	CL/CH(CL/CL)		CDCL3
1852M	B	3.97	CH2	OH/CH2-N		CDCL3
1638M	A	3.97	CH2	OH/CH(CL/CL)	S	D20
1561M	D	3.97	CH2	O-A/CH3		CCL4
1691M	B	3.97	CH2	O-CH2.2/Q3		CDCL3
1403M	C	3.97	CH2	O-CH2/Q3		CCL4
2949M	C	3.97	CH2R	R5O<O-C(=O)/C(CH3/CH3)-CH(OH)>		CDCL3
1526M	A	3.97	CH3	O-A		CDCL3
1582M	A	3.97	CH3	O-ANN	S	POLYSOL-D
2886M	A	3.97	CH3	O-C(=O)-A		CDCL3
759M	A	3.97	NH2	N(A/A)		CDCL3
1759M	G	3.98	CH	OH/HCH-C/CH3		CCL4
815M	D	3.98	CH2	CL/CH2-R6N		CCL4
2641M	A	3.98	CH2	NH2/C(=O)-NH	S	D20
2642M	B	3.98	CH2	N(CH3/CH3)/C(=O)-OH		D20
1726M	B	3.98	CH2	OH/CH2-O	S	D20
2762M	E	3.98 APP.	CH2	O-C(=O)-CH2/CH(CH2.3/CH2)		CDCL3
2697M	D	3.98	CH2	O-C(=O)-CH3/CH2-CH2		CCL4
1469M	B	3.98	CH2R	R6NO(NH-CH2/CH2-O)		CCL4
1615M	D	3.98	OH	CH2-CH	S	D20
334M	E	3.99	CH	BR/CH2-CH2/CH3		CCL4
1694M	B	3.99	CH	CH2-C:C		CCL4
1735M	C	3.99	CH	OH/CH3/CH3		CCL4
369M	A	3.99	CH2	BR/Q2(CH2-BR)		CCL4
812M	D	3.99	CH2	CL/CH2-N		CDCL3
272M	A	3.99	CH2	CL/Q3	S	D20
2641M	B	3.99	CH2	OH/CH(NH/C(=O)-OH)		CCL4
2174M	D	3.99	CH2	O-A/CH2-CH2		D20
1517M	B	3.99	CH2	O-A/CH3		CCL4
2848M	D	3.99	CH2	O-C(=O)-CH2/CH2.6-CH3		CCL4
2999M	C	3.99	CH2	O-P/CH2-CH3		CCL4
727M	A	3.99	NH2	ANA(C-CH-N-C*/CH-C*)		CDCL3
523M	A	3.99	NH2	A<C-C(BR)-CH-C(BR)>		CDCL3
516M	A	3.99	NH2	A<C-C(CL)-CH-C(CL)>		CDCL3
1736M	E	3.99	OH	CH(CH2/CH3)		CDCL3
2630M	C	4.00	CH	NH2/C(=O)-OH/HCH-C(=O)-NH2		CCL4
1779M	D	4.00	CHR	R5R5BI<(OH)/C*((CH3)/C*/CH2)/CH2-CH*>		D20
1492M	C	4.00	CH2	O-A/CH2-O		CDCL3
2775M	E	4.00	CH2	O-C(=O)-CH2.3/CH2.2-CH3		CCL4
2798M	D	4.00	CH2	O-C(=O)-CH3/CH2-CH2		CCL4
2702M	E	4.00	CH2	O-C(=O)-CH/CH2-CH2		CCL4
2986M	D	4.00	CH2	O-C(=O)-NH/CH3		CCL4
674M	A	4.00	CH2R	R5NN<N(A)-C(A)=/CH2-N=>		CCL4
674M	A	4.00	CH2R	R5NN<N=C(A)/CH2-N(A)>		CDCL3
1135M	B	4.00	CH2R	R5NS(N=C(NH-CH2)/CH2-S)		CDCL3
2722M	A	4.00	CH3	O-C(=O)-C-CL3		CDCL3
2754M	C	4.00	HCH	O-C(=O)-CH3/CH(O-C(=O)/CH3)		CCL4
535M	A	4.00	NH2	A<C-CH-CH-C(NH2)>		CCL4
1418M	B	4.00	Q3	H/O-CH2/H		DMSO-D6
478M	C	4.01	CH	NH2/A/CH3		CDCL3
1282M	A	4.01	CH2	CL/CH2-SO2		CCL4
2705M	D	4.01	CH2	O-C(=O)-CH2.3/CH2.3-CH3		CCL4
2774M	D	4.01	CH2	O-C(=O)-CH2/CH2-CH2		CCL4
2824M	E	4.01	CH2	O-C(=O)-R5R5BI/CH3		CCL4
2824M	F	4.01	CH2	O-C(=O)-R5R5BI/CH3		CCL4
1282M	A	4.01	CH2	SO2-CL/CH2-CL		CCL4
1461M	C	4.01	CH2R	R6O(O-CH2/CH=CH)		CCL4
1453M	D	4.01	CH*R	R3OR5A<O-CH*/C*>		CCL4
1693M	B	4.01	OH	CH2-C		CDCL3
1696M	C	4.01	OH	CH2-C:		CCL4
1404M	E	4.01	Q3	H/H/O-CH2		CCL4
2631M	C	4.02	CH	NH2/C(=O)-OH/HCH-C(=O)-NH2		D20
998M	A	4.02	CH2	AA(C-CH-C*/CH-CH-C*)/C:N		POLYSOL-D
349M	A	4.02	CH2	BR/C(BR/F2)		CCL4
2400M	A	4.02	CH2	N(CH2/CH2)/A		CDCL3
1690M	F	4.02	CH2	OH/Q1(CH2.3-CH/CH3)		CDCL3
1512M	B	4.02	CH2	O-A/CH3		CCL4
2563M	C	4.02	CH2	O-A/CH3		CCL4
2782M	D	4.02	CH2	O-C(=O)-CH2.8/CH(CH2/CH2.3)		CDCL3

BOOK NO.	ASSIGN-MENT	CHEM SHIFT - ppm -	PROTON GROUP	ENVIRONMENTAL GROUPS	S	SOLVENT
2755M	C	4.02	CH2	O-C(=O)-CH3/CH2-CH2		CCL4
2466M	B	4.02	CH2	R6NNN(N-C(=O)/C(=O))/CH3		CDCL3
2946M	C	4.02- 4.42	CH2R	R5O<O-C(=O)/CH2-CH(CH3)>		CCL4
2906M	A	4.02	CH3	O-C(=O)-A		CDCL3
525M	A	4.02	NH2	A<C-C(I)>		CDCL3
1786M	A	4.02	OH	Q1(H/CH2-CL/CL)		CCL4
1786M	A	4.02	OH	Q1(H/CL/CH2-CL)		CCL4
257M	C	4.03	CH	CL/CH2-CL/CH3		CCL4
2624M	B	4.03	CH	NH2/C(=O)-OH/CH2-SH		D2O
1751M	C	4.03	CH	OH/CH2-BR/CH2-BR		CDCL3
2444M	B	4.03	CHR	R6NN<(CH3)/NH-C(=O)/C(=O)-NH>		POLYSOL-D
2804M	A	4.03	CH2	CL/C(=O)-O-CH2		CCL4
277M	A	4.03	CH2	CL/Q2(H/CL/H)		CDCL3
277M	B	4.03	CH2	CL/Q2(H/H/CL)		CDCL3
2147M	C	4.03	CH2	C(=O)-A/C(=O)-CH3		CDCL3
2747M	F	4.03	CH2	O-C(=O)-CH2.2/CH2-CH		CCL4
2709M	E	4.03	CH2	O-C(=O)-CH2.5/CH2-CH		CCL4
2847M	D	4.03	CH2	O-C(=O)-CH2/CH2.2-CH3		CCL4
2981M	E	4.03	CH2	O-C(=O)-NH/CH3_		CCL4
2990M	E	4.03	CH2	O-C(=O)-N/CH3		CCL4
2808M	C	4.03	CH2	O-C(=O)-Q3/CH(CH2/CH2)		CCL4
1965M	C	4.03	CH2	O-P=/CH2.2-CH3		CDCL3
599M	B	4.03	NH	AA(C-C*)		CDCL3
2881M	B	4.03	NH2	A(C-CH-CH-C(C(=O)-O-CH3))		CDCL3
1405M	E	4.03	Q3	H/H/O-CH2		CCL4
327M	D	4.04	CH	BR/CH2.2-CH3/CH3		CCL4
2741M	F	4.04	CH	OH/C(=O)-O-CH2/CH2-CH		CCL4
2918M	C	4.04	CH2	O-C(=O)-A/CH(CH3/CH3)		C3D6O
2818M	E	4.04	CH2	O-C(=O)-CH2/CH3		CCL4
2976M	C	4.04	CH2	O-C(=O)-NH2/CH2-CH2		CDCL3
1324M	B	4.04	CH2	SO3-CH2/CH3		CCL4
1556M	A	4.04	CH3	O-A		CDCL3
631M	F	4.04 APP.		UNSPECIFIED		D2O
2731M	E	4.05	CH	BR/C(=O)-O-CH2/CH(CH3/CH3)		CDCL3
1750M	B	4.05	CH	OH/CH2-CL/CH2-CL		CDCL3
1353M	D	4.05	CHR	R5R5BI<(NH-C(=S))/CH*(CH2/CH2)/CH2-CH*>		POLYSOL-D
2483M	A	4.05	CH2	CL/C(=O)-OH		CCL4
276M	A	4.05	CH2	CL/Q2(CH2-CL)		CCL4
1657M	C	4.05	CH2	OH/CH2-N(+)	S	CDCL3
1685M	A	4.05	CH2	OH/Q3		CCL4
1393M	B	4.05	CH2	O-CF2/CH3		CCL4
2711M	D	4.05	CH2	O-C(=O)-CH2.10/CH2.10-CH3		CDCL3
2783M	D	4.05	CH2	O-C(=O)-CH2.8/CH2.10-CH3		CDCL3
2853M	E	4.05	CH2	O-C(=O)-CH2/CH3		CDCL3
1162M	B	4.05	CH2	S-A/A		POLYSOL-D
1718M	C	4.05	NH2	A<C-CH-CH-C(CH2.2-OH)>		POLYSOL-D
2405M	B	4.05	NH2	A(C-CH-CH-C(CH2-C(=O)-NH))		POLYSOL-D
2405M	B	4.05	NH2	NH-C(=O)-CH2		POLYSOL-D
1363M	B	4.05 APP.	NH2	SO2-A		TFA
1718M	C	4.05	OH	CH2.2-A		POLYSOL-D
1714M	C	4.05	OH	CH2-A		CCL4
1681M	D	4.05	OH	CH2-R6		CCL4
1758M	B	4.05	OH	CH(C:N/CH3)		CDCL3
2392M	A	4.06	CH2	CL/CH2-R5NA		CDCL3
283M	B	4.06	CH2	CL/C:CH		CCL4
783M	A	4.06	CH2	NH2/A(C-CH-C(BR))	S	POLYSOL-D
1005M	A	4.06	CH2	N(C:N/CH2)/A		CDCL3
1027M	E	4.06	CH2	N(N=O/CH2.2)/CH2-CH3		CCL4
1534M	C	4.06	CH2	O-A/CH2-CH2		CCL4
2819M	E	4.06	CH2	O-C(=O)-CH2.7/CH2.2-CH3		CDCL3
2777M	D	4.06	CH2	O-C(=O)-CH2/CH3		CCL4
2850M	D	4.06	CH2	O-C(=O)-CH2/CH3		CCL4
2817M	F	4.06	CH2	O-C(=O)-CH2/CH3		CCL4
2997M	B	4.06	CH2	O-P=/CH3		CCL4
1327M	D	4.06	CH2	O-SO3-NA/CH2.3-CH3		D2O
2392M	B	4.06	CH2	R5NA<N-C(=O)/C(=O)>/CH2-CL		CDCL3
1266M	B	4.06	CH2	SO2-A/C:CH		CDCL3
408M	D	4.07	CH	I/CH2-CH3/CH3		CDCL3
274M	D	4.07	CH2	CL/Q2(CH2-C)		CDCL3
596M	C	4.07	CH2	NH-A/A		CCL4
2743M	F	4.07	CH2	O-C(=O)-CH2/CH2.2-CH3		CCL4
2706M	D	4.07	CH2	O-C(=O)-CH2/CH2-CH2		CDCL3
2703M	C	4.07	CH2	O-C(=O)-C/CH3		CCL4
2984M	E	4.07	CH2	O-C(=O)-N/CH3		CCL4
2743M	F	4.07	CH2	O-C(=O)-Q1/CH2.2-CH3		CCL4
1165M	A	4.07	CH2	S-A/A		POLYSOL-D
361M	C	4.08	CH	BR/CH2-CH2/CH3		CDCL3
978M	B	4.08	CH	C:N/CH(A/CH2)/A		CDCL3
1757M	E	4.08	CH	OH/CH2-CH2/CH3		CDCL3
1792M	D	4.08	CH	OH/CH2-O/CH3		CCL4
2548M	A	4.08	CH2	N(A/CH2)/C(=O)-OH		POLYSOL-D

BOOK NO.	ASSIGN-MENT	CHEM SHIFT - ppm -	PROTON GROUP	ENVIRONMENTAL GROUPS	S	SOLVENT
2854M	D	4.08	CH2	O-C(=O)-CH2/CH3		CCL4
2786M	D	4.08	CH2	O-C(=O)-R3/CH3		CCL4
534M	A	4.08	NH2	A(C-CH-C(NH2))		POLYSOL-D
1406M	E	4.08	Q3	H/H/O-CH2.2		CCL4
2733M	E	4.09	CH	BR/C(=O)-O-CH2/CH2.7-CH3		CCL4
2795M	B	4.09	CH	C(=O)-O-CH2/C(=O)-O-CH2/CH(C(=O)-O/C(=O)-O)		CDCL3
2659M	B	4.09	CH	OH/C(=O)-O-NA/CH3		D20
351M	A	4.09	CH2	BR/CH(BR/BR)		CCL4
1712M	C	4.09	CH2	OH/Q1(H/A/CH3)		CDCL3
1726M	C	4.09	CH2	O-AA/CH2-OH		CDCL3
2076M	C	4.09	CH2	O-A/CH3		CDCL3
2824M	E	4.09	CH2	O-C(=O)-R5R5BI/CH3		CCL4
2824M	F	4.09	CH2	O-C(=O)-R5R5BI/CH3		CCL4
378M	B	4.09 APP.	HCH	BR/CH(BR/A)		CDCL3
1835M	D	4.09	OH	CH2-C		CDCL3
1414M	E	4.09	Q3	H/H/O-CH2		CCL4
323M	D	4.10	CH	BR/CH2-CH3/CH3		CDCL3
357M	E	4.10	CH	BR/HCH-BR/CH2-CH3		CDCL3
271M	A	4.10- 4.90	CHR	R6<(CL)/CH(CL)-CH(CL)/CH(CL)-CH(CL)>		POLYSOL-D
2217M	A	4.10	CH2	C(=O)-CL/A(C-CH-CH-C(CL))		CDCL3
2646M	B	4.10	CH2	NH-C(=O)/C(=O)-OH		D20
2491M	B	4.10	CH2	O-CH3/C(EO)-OH	S	D20
2864M	C	4.10	CH2	O-C(=O)-A/CH(CH3/CH3)		CDCL3
2763M	D	4.10	CH2	O-C(=O)-CH2.10/C(CH2/CH2/CH2)		CDCL3
2767M	D	4.10	CH2	O-C(=O)-CH2/CH2-CH2		CCL4
2718M	C	4.10	CH2	O-C(=O)-CH3/CH(OH/CH2>		CDCL3
2692M	C	4.10	CH2	O-C(=O)-H/CH2-CH2		CCL4
2693M	C	4.10	CH2	O-C(=O)-H/CH2-CH2		CCL4
2691M	C	4.10	CH2	O-C(=O)-H/CH(CH2/CH2)		CDCL3
2987M	C	4.10	CH2	O-C(=O)-NH/CH2-CH3		CDCL3
2813M	D	4.10	CH2	O-C(=O)-Q2/CH2-CH2		CCL4
2809M	C	4.10	CH2	O-C(=O)-Q3/CH2-CH2		CCL4
1607M	B	4.10	CH2	O-P/CH2-CL		CDCL3
744M	B	4.10	CH2	R5AA(N-C*/C*)		CDCL3
1079M	A	4.10	CH2R	R6NN<N(NO2)-CH2/CH2-N(NO2)>		DMSO-D6
2760M	E	4.10	HCH	O-C(=O)-CH2/CH(O-C(=O)/HCH)		CCL4
2764M	B	4.10- 4.40		UNSPECIFIED		CDCL3
1785M	C	4.11	CH	OH/Q3/CH2-Q3		CDCL3
1732M	C	4.11	CH2	OH/CH2-ANN		CDCL3
1694M	C	4.11	CH2	OH/C:C-CH3		CCL4
1571M	B	4.11	CH2	O-AA/CH3		CDCL3
1533M	B	4.11	CH2	O-A/CH3		CDCL3
2784M	E	4.11	CH2	O-C(=O)-CH2/CH2-O		CCL4
2751M	C	4.11	CH2	O-C(=O)-CH2/CH3		DMSO-D6
2780M	E	4.11	CH2	O-C(=O)-CH2/CH3		CDCL3
2708M	F	4.11	CH2	O-C(=O)-CH/CH2-CH2		CCL4
2964M	B	4.11	CH2	O-C(=O)-CL/C(CH2/CH3/CH3)		CCL4
2980M	C	4.11	CH2	O-C(=O)-NH/CH3		CDCL3
2765M	C	4.11	CH2	O-C(=O)-O-CH2.3/CH2.2-CH3		CDCL3
2856M	C	4.11	CH2	O-C(=O)-Q1/CH3		CCL4
2814M	C	4.11	CH2	O-C(=O)-Q2/CH3		CCL4
2953M	C	4.11	CH2R	R150<O-C(=O)/CH2-CH2>		CDCL3
1664M	B	4.11 APP.	CH2R	R5NN<NH-C(=S)/CH2-N(CH2-CH2)>		TFA
1664M	B	4.11 APP.	CH2R	R5NN<N(CH2-CH2)-C(=S)/CH2-NH>		TFA
1134M	C	4.11	CH2R	R5NS<S-C(CH3)=/CH2-N=>		CCL4
2803M	A	4.11	CH3	CL/C(=O)-O-Q3		CDCL3
1161M	B	4.11	NH2	A<C-C(S-CH3)>		CCL4
1614M	D	4.11	OH	CH2-CH2		CCL4
1618M	D	4.11	OH	CH2-CH2		CCL4
1686M	C	4.11	OH	CH2-Q2		CCL4
1611M	B	4.11	OH	CH3		CCL4
2639M	C	4.12	CH	NH2/C(=O)-NH/CH3		D20
278M	B	4.12	CH2	CL/Q1(CL/CH3)		CCL4
1026M	D	4.12	CH2	N(NO/CH2)/CH3		CDCL3
2717M	G	4.12	CH2	O-C(=O)-CH3/CH2-O		CCL4
1326M	B	4.12	CH2	O-SO3-K/CH3		D20
1773M	C	4.12	OH	R6<CH-CH(R6)/CH2>		CDCL3
2759M	D	4.13 APP.	CH	OH/CH2-O-C(=O)-CH2-O-C(=O)		CDCL3
365M	B	4.13	CHR	R6((BR)/CH2-CH2/CH2-CH2)		CCL4
1786M	B	4.13	CH2	CL/Q1(CL/H/OH)		CCL4
2749M	E	4.13	CH2	O-C(=O)-CH2.8/CH3		CDCL3
2769M	D	4.13	CH2	O-C(=O)-CH2/CH2.10-CH3		CDCL3
2730M	D	4.13	CH2	O-C(=O)-CH2/CH3		CCL4
2789M	D	4.13	CH2	O-C(=O)-CH2/CH3		CCL4
2759M	D	4.13 APP.	CH2	O-C(=O)-CH2/CH(OH/CH2)		CDCL3
2719M	G	4.13	CH2	O-C(=O)-CH2/CH(OH/CH2)		CDCL3
2770M	F	4.13	CH2	O-C(=O)-CH/CH3		CCL4
756M	E	4.13	CH2	O-C(=O)-R60/CH3		CCL4
2754M	D	4.13	HCH	O-C(=O)-CH3/CH(O-C(=O)/CH3)		CCL4
1621M	D	4.13	OH	CH2.3-CH		CCL4
1782M	D	4.14	CH	OH/Q2(CH3/H/H)/CH3		CCL4

BOOK NO.	ASSIGN-MENT	CHEM SHIFT - ppm -	PROTON GROUP	ENVIRONMENTAL GROUPS	S	SOLVENT
2636M	C	4.14	CHR	R5N<(C(=O)-OH)/NH-CH2/CH2-CH2>		D2O
2054M	A	4.14	CH2	C(=O)-A/C:N		CDCL3
841M	B	4.14	CH2	N(+)(A/CH2/CH2)/CH3		CDCL3
2919M	C	4.14	CH2	O-C(=O)-A/CH2-CH2		C3D6O
2734M	C	4.14	CH2	O-C(=O)-CH2/CH3		CCL4
2724M	D	4.14	CH2	O-C(=O)-CH2/CH3		CCL4
2744M	F	4.14	CH2	O-C(=O)-CH/CH3		CCL4
2983M	B	4.14	CH2	O-C(=O)-NH/CH3		CDCL3
2985M	C	4.14	CH2	O-C(=O)-R6NN/CH3		CDCL3
353M	D	4.15 APP.	CH	BR/HCH-BR/CH3		CCL4
1483M	C	4.15	CH	O-CH/A/CH3		CCL4
1483M	D	4.15	CH	O-CH/A/CH3		CCL4
936M	A	4.15	CH2	N=C=S/Q3		CCL4
2810M	C	4.15	CH2	O-C(=O)-Q2/CH3		CCL4
1329M	C	4.15	CH2	O-SO2-O/CH2-CH3		CCL4
1017M	A	4.15	CH2	S-C:N/A		CDCL3
2761M	E	4.15	HCH	O-C(=O)-CH2.16/CH(O-C(=O)/HCH)		CDCL3
2626M	C	4.16	CH	OH/CH(NH2/C(=O)-O)/CH3		D2O
2662M	C	4.16	CH	OH/C(=O)-O-NA/CH(OH/CH)	S	D2O
1831M	F	4.16	CH	OH/HCH-C/CH3		CCL4
1763M	B	4.16	CHR	R4((OH)/CH2-CH2/CH2)		CCL4
2852M	C	4.16	CH2	O-C(=O)-C/CH3		CCL4
679M	A	4.16	CH3	R5NNNN(N-N=/C(A)=)		CDCL3
2951M	D	4.16	HCHR	R5O<O-C(=O)/CH(A)-HCH>		CDCL3
2951M	E	4.16	HCHR	R5O<O-C(=O)/CH(A)-HCH>		CDCL3
1418M	C	4.16	Q3	H/H/O-CH2		CDCL3
1696M	D	4.17	CH2	OH/C:C		CCL4
2827M	C	4.17	CH2	O-C(=O)-Q2/CH2-CH2		CCL4
2281M	A	4.18	CH2	CL/C(=O)-NH2		D2O
2860M	C	4.18	CH2	O-C(=O)-CH2/CH2-A		CCL4
1173M	A	4.18	CH2	S-AA/A		CDCL3
758M	A	4.18 APP.	NH	NH2/A(C-C(CL)-CH-C(CL)/C(CL))		CDCL3
1020M	C	4.18	NHR	R5NA<C*/CH2-CH2>		CDCL3
758M	A	4.18 APP.	NH2	NH-A		CDCL3
2487M	D	4.19	CH	BR/C(=O)-OH/CH2-CH2		CCL4
259M	B	4.19	CH	CL/CH2-CL/CH2-CL		CCL4
2620M	D	4.19	CH	NH-C(=O)/C(=O)-OH/CH(CH3/CH3)		DMSO-D6
2758M	F	4.19	CH	OH/CH2-O-C(=O)/CH2-O-C(=O)		CDCL3
2740M	D	4.19	CH	OH/C(=O)-O-CH3/CH3		CCL4
2287M	A	4.19	CH2	C(=O)-NH2/AA<C-C*>		TFA
1697M	E	4.19	CH2	OH/C:C		CCL4
1491M	B	4.19	CH2	O-A/CH2-BR		CDCL3
2898M	C	4.19	CH2	O-C(=O)-A/CH(CH2/CH2)		CCL4
2750M	B	4.19	CH2	O-C(=O)-CH2/CH3	S	D2O
2794M	C	4.19	CH2	O-C(=O)-CH2/CH3		CDCL3
2701M	E	4.19	CH2	O-C(=O)-CH2/CH3		CCL4
2758M	F	4.19	CH2	O-C(=O)-CH2/CH(OH/CH2)		CDCL3
2752M	B	4.19	CH2	O-C(=O)-CH3/CH2-O-C(=O)		CCL4
2733M	F	4.19	CH2	O-C(=O)-CH/CH3		CCL4
1030M	C	4.19	CH2R	R6N(N(N=O)-CH2/CH2-CH2)		CDCL3
1568M	A	4.19	CH3	O-A		CDCL3
1555M	A	4.19	CH3	O-A		POLYSOL-D
1638M	B	4.19	OH	CH2-CH		CCL4
358M	D	4.20	CH	BR/CH2-CH2/CH3		CCL4
2732M	E	4.20	CH	BR/C(=O)-O-CH2)/CH2.3-CH3		CDCL3
2735M	C	4.20	CH	NH2/C(=O)-O-CH3/CH3	S	D2O
277M	B	4.20	CH2	CL(Q2(H/H/CL)		CDCL3
277M	A	4.20	CH2	CL/Q2(H/CL/H)		CDCL3
2148M	A	4.20	CH2	C(=O)-A/Q1(OH/C(=O)-A)		POLYSOL-D
2851M	B	4.20	CH2	NH-C(=O)/C(=O)-O-CH3		CDCL3
2838M	E	4.20	CH2	O-C(=O)-CH2/CH2-A		CCL4
2720M	C	4.20	CH2	O-C(=O)-CH/CH3		CCL4
2795M	C	4.20	CH2	O-C(=O)-CH/CH3		CDCL3
2745M	F	4.20	CH2	O-C(=O)-CH/CH3		CDCL3
2741M	G	4.20	CH2	O-C(=O)-CH/CH3		CCL4
2960M	C	4.20	CH2	O-C(=O)-CL/CH(CH2/CH2)		CCL4
2935M	C	4.20	CH2	O-C(=O)-R5O/CH2-CH3		CCL4
2996M	B	4.20 APP.	CH2	O-P/CH2-CL		CCL4
1317M	D	4.20	CH2	SO3-CH3/CH2-CH2		CDCL3
2952M	C	4.20	CH2R	R6O<O-C(=O)/CH2-CH2>		CCL4
1720M	A	4.20	OH	CH2-A		CDCL3
1766M	C	4.20	OH	R6(CH-CH2/CH2)		CCL4
151M	B	4.21	CH	A/A/CH2-A		CDCL3
321M	B	4.21	CH	BR/CH3/CH3		CCL4
2736M	C	4.21	CH	NH2/C(=O)-O-CH2/CH3	S	D2O
1764M	C	4.21	CHR	R5((OH)/CH2-CH2/CH2-CH2)		CCL4
2085M	A	4.21	CH2	C(=O)-A/A		TFA
961M	A	4.21	CH2	C:N/C:N		DMSO-D6
2897M	C	4.21	CH2	O-C(=O)-A/CH2.3-CH3		CCL4
2879M	C	4.21	CH2	O-C(=O)-A/CH2.3-CH3		DMSO-D6
2877M	C	4.21	CH2	O-C(=O)-A/CH2-CH2		CCL4

BOOK NO.	ASSIGN-MENT	CHEM SHIFT - ppm -	PROTON GROUP	ENVIRONMENTAL GROUPS	S	SOLVENT
2756M	D	4.21	CH2	O-C(=O)-CH3/CH2-O		CDCL3
2836M	D	4.21	CH2	O-C(=O)-CH/CH2-A		CCL4
1865M	C	4.21	CH2	O-C(=O)-CH/CH3		CDCL3
2729M	C	4.21	CH2	O-C(=O)-C/CH3		CDCL3
2934M	B	4.21	CH2	O-C(=O)-Q2/CH3		CDCL3
1029M	C	4.21	CH2R	R5N<N(NO)-CH2/CH2-CH2>		D2O
1640M	D	4.21	OH	CH2.3-BR		CDCL3
1688M	D	4.21	OH	CH2-CH2		CCL4
639M	C	4.22	CH	R6NN<N-CH2/CH2>/A/A		CDCL3
2949M	D	4.22	CHR	R5O<(OH)/C(=O)-O/C(CH3/CH3)-CH2>		CDCL3
594M	B	4.22	CH2	NH-A/A		CDCL3
1350M	A	4.22	CH2	NH-C(=S)/Q3		CDCL3
1711M	B	4.22	CH2	OH/Q2(H/A/H)		CDCL3
2863M	C	4.22	CH2	O-C(=O)-A/CH2-CH3		CCL4
2903M	D	4.22	CH2	O-C(=O)-A/CH(CH2/CH2)		CCL4
2835M	D	4.22	CH2	O-C(=O)-CH2/CH2-A		CCL4
2792M	D	4.22	CH2	O-C(=O)-CH/CH2-CH2		CCL4
2731M	F	4.22	CH2	O-C(=O)-CH/CH3		CCL4
2732M	F	4.22	CH2	O-C(=O)-CH/CH3		CDCL3
2936M	C	4.22	CH2	O-C(=O)-R5O/CH2.3-CH3		CCL4
2450M	A	4.22	CH2R	R5NN(N(A)-C(=O)/C(=O)-N(A))		CDCL3
1039M	A	4.22	CH3	NO2		CCL4
2882M	B	4.22	NH2	A<C-CH-CH-C(C(=O)-O-CH)>		CDCL3
1845M	B	4.22	OH	CH2-CH2		CDCL3
1991M	C	4.23	CH	CL/C(=O)-CH3/CH3		CCL4
1427M	D	4.23	CH	O-CH3/O-CH3/CH2-NH2		CCL4
1693M	C	4.23	CH2	OH/C:CH		CDCL3
1676M	B	4.23	CH2	O-CH2/C:C		CDCL3
1315M	D	4.23	CH2	SO3-CH3/CH2.2-CH3		CDCL3
1590M	A	4.23	CH2R	R600A<O-C*/CH2-O>		CDCL3
2760M	F	4.23	HCH	O-C(=O)-CH2/CH(O-C(=O)/HCH)		CCL4
1198M	A	4.24	NH2	A(C-C(S-S))		CDCL3
269M	B	4.25- 4.75	CHR	R6R6R6TRI<(CL)/CH*(CH2/CH2)/CH*(CH2/CH2)>		CDCL3
2674M	A	4.25	CH2	C(=O)-ONA/AA<C-C*>	S	D2O
2422M	A	4.25	CH2	NH-C(=O)-NH2/A		POLYSOL-D
2917M	C	4.25	CH2	O-C(=O)-A/CH2-CH2		C3D6O
2757M	F	4.25	CH2	O-C(=O)-CH/CH2-O		CDCL3
1167M	A	4.25	CH2	S-A/S-A		CDCL3
2971M	A	4.25	CH2	S-C(=O)/A		CDCL3
2961M	D	4.26	CH2	O-C(=O)-CL/CH2-CH2		CCL4
2283M	B	4.27	CH	OH/C(=O)-NH2/CH3		D2O
2318M	A	4.27	CH2	CL/C(=O)-NH		DMSO-D6
2086M	A	4.27	CH2	C(=O)-A/A<C-CH-CH-C(CL)>		POLYSOL-D
782M	A	4.27	CH2	NH2/A	S	D2O
2894M	C	4.27	CH2	O-C(=O)-A/CH2-CH2		CCL4
2966M	D	4.27	CH2	O-C(=O)-CL/CH2-CH2		CCL4
2766M	C	4.27	CH2	O-C(=O)-C(=O)-O/CH2.2-CH3		CDCL3
2972M	E	4.27	CH2	O-C(=O)-S/CH3		CCL4
2109M	B	4.27	CH2R	R600A<O-C*/CH2-O>		CDCL3
1408M	D	4.27	Q2	CH3/O-CH2/H		CCL4
2484M	C	4.28	CH	CL/C(=O)-OH/CH2-CH3		CDCL3
1472M	G	4.28	CHR	R600<(CH2.5-CH3)/O-HCH/O-HCH>		CCL4
2432M	A	4.28	CH2	NH-C(=O)-NH/A		POLYSOL-D
1641M	B	4.28	CH2	OH/C(BR/BR/BR)		CDCL3
2585M	B	4.28	CH2	O-A/CH3		CCL4
2908M	C	4.28	CH2	O-C(=O)-A/CH2-CH2		CCL4
1147M	A	4.28	CH2	R5S(C=CH/S)/R5S(=CH/S)		CDCL3
1833M	E	4.28	OH	CH(HCH/CH3)		CCL4
2486M	D	4.29	CH	BR/C(=O)-OH/CH2.2-CH3		CDCL3
406M	B	4.29	CH	I/CH3/CH3		CCL4
1476M	D	4.29	CHR	R600R600SPI<(CH2-CH3)/O-HCH/O-CH2>		CCL4
1045M	B	4.29	CHR	R6((NO2)/CH2-CH2/CH2-CH2)		CCL4
709M	A	4.29	CH2	NH-AN/A		DMSO-D6
2492M	A	4.29	CH2	OH/C(=O)-OH		D2O
1724M	A	4.29	CH2	OH/Q2(A<C-CH-CH-C(NO2)>)		POLYSOL-D
1858M	A	4.29	CH2	OH/Q3-CH2		D2O
2890M	C	4.29	CH2	O-C(=O)-A/CH2-CH2		CCL4
2870M	C	4.29	CH2	O-C(=O)-A/CH3		CCL4
2820M	B	4.29	CH2	O-C(=O)-Q2/CH3		CCL4
2443M	A	4.29	CH2R	R5NN<NH-C(=O)/C(=O)-NH>		TFA
2950M	D	4.29	CH2R	R5O<O-C(=O)/HCH-CH(C(=O)-CH3)>		CCL4
2761M	F	4.29	HCH	O-C(=O)-CH2.16/CH(O-C(=O)/HCH)		CDCL3
1639M	C	4.29	OH	CH2-CH2		CCL4
356M	C	4.30	CH	BR/HCH-BR/HCH-BR		CCL4
2621M	D	4.30	CH	NH-C(=O)-CH3/C(=O)-OH/CH2-CH		POLYSOL-D
1480M	E	4.30	CH	O-CH2/A/CH2-CH2		CDCL3
1581M	D	4.30	CH2	O-AN/CH2-CH2		CDCL3
2902M	C	4.30	CH2	O-C(=O)-A/CH2-CH2		CDCL3
2895M	C	4.30	CH2	O-C(=O)-A/CH2-CH2		CCL4
2900M	C	4.30	CH2	O-C(=O)-A/CH2-CH3		CDCL3
2753M	C	4.30	CH2	O-C(=O)-CH2/CH2-O-C(=O)		CDCL3

BOOK NO.	ASSIGN-MENT	CHEM SHIFT - ppm -	PROTON GROUP	ENVIRONMENTAL GROUPS	S	SOLVENT
2736M	D	4.30	CH2	O-C(=O)-CH/CH3	S	D2O
2831M	B	4.30	CH2	O-C(=O)-H/CH2-A		CCL4
2830M	B	4.30	CH2	O-C(=O)-Q		CDCL3
2070M	D	4.30	NH2	A<C-CH-CH-C(C(=O)-CH2.2)>		CDCL3
1077M	B	4.30	NH2	A(C-C(CH3)-CH-C(NO2)/C(CH3))		CDCL3
2718M	D	4.30	OH	CH2-CH		CDCL3
1829M	D	4.30	OH	CH2-CH		CDCL3
2718M	D	4.30	OH	CH(CH2/CH2)		CDCL3
1829M	D	4.30	OH	CH(CH2/CH2)		CDCL3
2791M	D	4.31	CH	OH/CH2-C(=O)-O/CH2-C(=O)-O		CCL4
220M	D	4.31	CH2	F/CH2-CH2		CCL4
1041M	C	4.31	CH2	NO2/CH2-CH3		CCL4
2875M	B	4.31	CH2	O-C(=O)-A/CH3		CCL4
2871M	B	4.31	CH2	O-C(=O)-A/CH3		CCL4
2959M	C	4.31	CH2	O-C(=O)-CL/CH2-CH2		CCL4
2124M	A	4.31	CH2R	R6AA(C*/C*)		CDCL3
355M	C	4.32	CH	BR/CH2-BR/CH2-CL		CCL4
2308M	B	4.32	CH	NH-C(=O)-H/CH2-A/CH2-A		DMSO-D6
1345M	B	4.32	CH	NH-C(=S)/CH3/CH3		CDCL3
421M	C	4.32	CHR	R5<(I)/CH2-CH2/CH2-CH2>		CCL4
367M	B	4.32	CHR	R6((BR)/CH2-CH2/CH2-CH2)		CDCL3
373M	B	4.32	CH2	BR/A<C-CH-CH-C(CH3)>		CCL4
2314M	B	4.32	CH2	NH-C(=O)/A		CDCL3
2721M	D	4.32	CH2	O-C(=O)-CF3/CH2-CH2		CDCL3
2862M	B	4.32	CH2	O-C(=O)-Q2/CH2-A		CCL4
395M	A	4.33	CH2	BR/A<C-CH-C(BR)>		CDCL3
371M	A	4.34	CH2	BR/A		CCL4
1786M	C	4.34	CH2	CL/Q1(CL/OH/H)		CCL4
2313M	C	4.34	CH2	NH-C(=O)/A		CDCL3
2884M	B	4.34	CH2	O-C(=O)-A/CH3		CDCL3
2772M	B	4.34	CH2	O-C(=O)-C/CH3		CCL4
2858M	B	4.34	CH2	O-C(=O)-Q1/CH3		CDCL3
844M	A	4.34	CH3	AN<N(+)-CH-C(NH2)>		D2O
266M	B	4.35	CHR	R5<(CL)/CH2-CH2>		CCL4
219M	D	4.35	CH2	F/CH2.4-CH3		CCL4
1714M	D	4.35	CH2	OH/A<C-CH-CH-C(CH(CH3/CH3))>		CCL4
1479M	B	4.35	CH2	O-CH3/A		CDCL3
2939M	D	4.35	CH2	O-C(=O)-AN/CH2-CH2		CDCL3
2909M	D	4.35	CH2	O-C(=O)-A/CH2-CH2		CDCL3
1265M	B	4.35	CH2	SO2-A/C:CH		POLYSOL-D
2726M	C	4.36	CH	CL/C(=O)-O-CH3/HCH-CL		CCL4
1659M	C	4.36	CH	OH/P(=O/A/A)/CH2.2-CH3		POLYSOL-D
422M	C	4.36	CHR	R6<(I)/CH2-CH2/CH2-CH2>		CDCL3
2148M	B	4.36	CH2	C(=O)-A/C(=O)-Q1		POLYSOL-D
2994M	B	4.36	CH2R	R5NO<O-C(=O)/CH2-N(A)>		CDCL3
2357M	D	4.37	CH	OH/C(=O)-N/CH3		CCL4
1429M	C	4.37	CH	O-CH3/O-CH3/CH2-CH		CCL4
805M	A	4.37	CH2	NH-CH2/A	S	TFA
1713M	C	4.37	CH2	OH/A<C-CH-CH-C(CH3)>		CCL4
1557M	B	4.37	CH2	O-A/CH3		CDCL3
2896M	C	4.37	CH2	O-C(=O)-A/CH2.2-CH3		CDCL3
1788M	D	4.38	CH	OH/A/CH2-CH3		CCL4
2690M	B	4.38	CH	OH/C(=O)-OH/CH(OH/C(=O)-OH)		D2O
363M	B	4.38	CHR	R5<(BR)/CH2-CH2/CH2-CH2>		CCL4
756M	F	4.38	CHR	R6O<=C(CH3)-O/C(CH3/CH3)-C(C(=O)-O-CH2)=>		CCL4
425M	A	4.38	CH2	I/A		CDCL3
2071M	D	4.38	NH2	A<C-CH-CH-C(C(=O)-CH2.3)>		CDCL3
2426M	B	4.38	NH2	C(=O)-N		CDCL3
1828M	E	4.38	OH	CH(HCH/CH3)		CDCL3
1828M	E	4.38	OH	HCH-CH		CDCL3
1992M	C	4.39	CH	BR/C(=O)-CH3/CH3		CCL4
372M	B	4.39	CH2	BR/A(C-C(CH3))		CCL4
2062M	B	4.39	CH2	BR/C(=O)-A		CDCL3
834M	D	4.39	CH2	N(+)(CH2/CH2/CH2)/C:CH		POLYSOL-D
2907M	B	4.39	CH2	O-C(=O)-A/CH3		CDCL3
517M	A	4.39	NH2	A<C-C(CL)-CH-C(CL)/C(CL)>		CDCL3
1916M	B	4.39	OH	A(C-C(CH3)/C(CH3))		CCL4
2730M	E	4.40	CH	BR/CH2-C(=O)-O/CH3		CCL4
2493M	B	4.40	CH	OH/C(=O)-OH/CH3		D2O
1428M	D	4.40	CH	O-CH2/O-CH2/CH2-NH2		CDCL3
1430M	D	4.40	CH	O-CH3/O-CH3/CH2-N		CCL4
2947M	D	4.40 APP.	CHR	R5O<(CH2-CH2)/O-C(=O)/CH2-CH2>		CCL4
350M	A	4.40	CH2	BR/C(CL/CL/CL)		CCL4
285M	B	4.40	CH2	CL/A(C-CH-CH-C(CH3))		CCL4
1040M	B	4.40	CH2	NO2/CH3		CDCL3
1723M	C	4.40	CH2	OH/A<C-CH-CH-C(O-CH3)>		CCL4
1716M	A	4.40	CH2	OH/A(C-CH-CH-C(F))		CDCL3
1409M	B	4.40	CH2	O-CH3/O-CH3		CCL4
2885M	B	4.40	CH2	O-C(=O)-A/CH3		CCL4
1080M	C	4.40	CH2	O-NO2/CH2-CH3		CCL4
1014M	A	4.40	CH2	S-C:N/S-C:N		CDCL3

BOOK NO.	ASSIGN-MENT	CHEM SHIFT - ppm -	PROTON GROUP	ENVIRONMENTAL GROUPS	S	SOLVENT
1612M	C	4.40	OH	CH2-CH3		CCL4
652M	B	4.41	CH2	N(A/CH3)/A		CCL4
1700M	B	4.41	CH2	OH/A		CCL4
2866M	B	4.41	CH2	O-C(=O)-A/CH2-A		CCL4
2865M	C	4.41	CH2	O-C(=O)-A/CH2-N		CDCL3
2867M	B	4.41	CH2	O-C(=O)-A/CH2-O		CCL4
2800M	E	4.41	CH2	O-C(=O)-CH3/Q2(H/CH2.2-CH3/H)		CCL4
2723M	B	4.41	CH2	O-C(=O)-C/CH3		CDCL3
531M	A	4.41	NH2	A<C-CH-CH-C(A<C-CH-CH-C(NH2)>)>		DMSO-D6
1616M	D	4.41	OH	CH2-CH2		CCL4
2627M	D	4.42	CH	NH-C(=O)-CH3/C(=O)-OH/CH2.2-S		POLYSOL-D
2792M	E	4.42	CH	OH/C(=O)-O-CH2/CH(OH/C(=O)-O)		CCL4
311M	A	4.42	CH2	CL/A<C-CH-C(CL)-C(CL)>		CCL4
540M	A	4.42	NH2	AA<C-CH-C*/CH-CH-C*>		POLYSOL-D
1724M	B	4.42	OH	CH2-Q2		POLYSOL-D
2948M	B	4.43 APP.	CHR	R50((BR)/C(=O)-O/CH2-CH2)		CCL4
2053M	A	4.43	CH2	BR/C(=O)-A		CDCL3
1734M	B	4.43	CH2	OH/AR500<C-CH-C*-O/CH-CH-C*>		CDCL3
2948M	B	4.43 APP.	CH2R	R50(O-C(=O)/CH2-CH(BR))		CCL4
2949M	E	4.43	OH	R50<CH-C(=O)/C((CH3/CH3)>		CDCL3
261M	A	4.44	CH	CL/CH-CL2/CH-CL2		CCL4
2937M	B	4.44	CH2	O-C(=O)-R50/CH3		CDCL3
1267M	B	4.44	CH2	SO2-A/A		POLYSOL-D
1483M	C	4.45	CH	O-CH/A/CH3		CCL4
1483M	D	4.45	CH	O-CH/A/CH3		CCL4
1454M	A	4.45- 5.00	CHR	R40((CL)/CH2-O/CH2)		CCL4
1135M	C	4.45	CH2	NH-R5NS/A		CDCL3
2883M	B	4.45	CH2	O-C(=O)-A/CH3		CDCL3
1035M	C	4.45	CH2	O-N=O/CH(CH3/CH3)		CCL4
1454M	A	4.45- 5.00	CH2R	R40(O-CH2/CH(CL))		CCL4
1709M	B	4.45	OH	CH2-SO2		CDCL3
1715M	A	4.46	CH2	OH/A(C-C(F))		CCL4
2645M	B	4.47	CH	NH2/C(=O)-OH/CH2-SH	S	D20
2633M	C	4.47	CH	NH3(+)/C(=O)-OH/CH2.2-C(=O)-O		TFA
1482M	A	4.47	CH2	O-CH2/A		CCL4
1082M	D	4.47	CH2	O-NO2/CH2.3-CH3		CDCL3
1523M	C	4.47	NH	A<C-CH-CH-C(O-CH3)>/CH3		POLYSOL-D
2797M	C	4.47	Q3	H/O-C(=O)-CH2/H		CCL4
275M	C	4.48	CH	CL/Q3(H/H/H)/HCH-CL		CCL4
284M	A	4.48	CH2	CL/A		CCL4
653M	C	4.48	CH2	N(A/CH2)/A		CDCL3
838M	B	4.48	CH2	N(+)(CH3/CH3/CH3)/A		POLYSOL-D
1539M	B	4.48	CH2	O-A/Q3		CDCL3
2801M	D	4.48	CH2	O-C(=O)-CH2.7/Q3		CCL4
2977M	A	4.48	CH2	O-C(=O)-NH2/Q3		CCL4
2992M	B	4.48	CH2R	R5NO<O-C(=O)/CH2-NH>		CDCL3
2117M	C	4.48	CH2R	R60A<O-C*/CH2-C(=O)>		CDCL3
2436M	B	4.48	NH	C(=O)-N/CH3		CDCL3
1882M	B	4.48	OH	A<C-C(C(CH3/CH3/CH3))>		CCL4
2811M	C	4.49	CH	O-C(=O)-Q2/CH3/CH3		CCL4
1422M	C	4.50	CH	O-CH3/O-CH3/CH3		CCL4
2637M	C	4.50- 4.90	CHR	R5N(OH/CH2-NH/CH2-CH(C(=O)-OH))		D20
2637M	C	4.50- 4.90	CHR	R5N((C(=O)-OH)/NH-CH2/CH2-CH(OH))		D20
286M	B	4.50	CH2	CL/A<C-C(CH3)-CH-C(CH3)/CH-C(CH2-CL)>		CDCL3
1733M	B	4.50	CH2	OH/R50(C=CH/O)		CDCL3
1318M	C	4.50	CH2R	R50S<O-SO2/CH2-CH2>		CDCL3
1636M	C	4.50	OH	CH2-CH2		CDCL3
1349M	B	4.51	CH	NH-C(=S)/CH3/CH3		POLYSOL-D
1867M	B	4.51	CHR	R60<(OH)/O-CH2/CH2-CH(OH)-CH(OH)>		D20
2983M	C	4.51	CH2	NH-C(=O)-O/NH-C(=O)-O		CDCL3
2430M	A	4.51	CH2	NH-C(=O)/OH		DMSO-D6
1860M	A	4.51	CH2	OH/A<C-CH-CH-C(CH2-OH)>		DMSO-D6
2911M	B	4.51	CH2	O-C(=O)-A/CH3		CDCL3
107M	C	4.51	CH2	R6<=C-CH(CH3)/CH(CH3)>		CCL4
1018M	A	4.51	CH2	S-C:N/A<C-C(CL)/C(CL)>		CDCL3
1867M	B	4.51	CH2R	R60<O-CH(OH)/CH(OH)-CH(OH)>		D20
2409M	A	4.51	NH2	NH-C(=O)		DMSO-D6
1715M	B	4.51	OH	CH2-A		CCL4
1830M	D	4.51- 4.88	OH	CH(CH2/CH3)		CCL4
2802M	D	4.51	Q3	H/O-C(=O)-CH2/H		CDCL3
366M	C	4.52	CHR	R6((BR)/CH2-CH(CH3)/CH2-CH2)		CCL4
2565M	A	4.52	CH2	O-A/C(=O)-OH		POLYSOL-D
1330M	B	4.52	CH2	O-SO3/CH2-CL		CDCL3
1475M	C	4.52	HCHR	R600R600SPI<O-CH(CH3)/C*(HCH/CH2)-CH2>		CDCL3
2406M	A	4.52	NH	NH2/C(=O)-A		DMSO
2406M	A	4.52	NH2	NH-C(=O)		DMSO
1826M	C	4.52	OH	CH2-CH2		CDCL3
2891M	B	4.53	CH2	O-C(=O)-A/CH2-A		CDCL3
2806M	B	4.53	CH2	O-C(=O)-CH2.2/Q3		CCL4
2118M	B	4.53	CH2R	R60A(O-C*/CH2-C(=O))		CDCL3
2859M	B	4.53	CH=	=P(A/A/A)/C(=O)-O-CH3		TFA

BOOK NO.	ASSIGN-MENT	CHEM SHIFT - ppm -		PROTON GROUP	ENVIRONMENTAL GROUPS	S	SOLVENT
1849M	C	4.53		OH	CH2.3-CH		POLYSOL-D
1849M	C	4.53		OH	CH(CH2.3/CH2.3)		POLYSOL-D
2346M	A	4.54		CH2	NH-C(=O)/A		CDCL3
1705M	D	4.54		CH2	O-CH2/A		CCL4
2962M	B	4.54		CH2	O-C(=O)-CL/CH2-CL		CDCL3
842M	A	4.54		CH3	AN<N(+)>		POLYSOL-D
2465M	C	4.54		OH	CH2-CH2		DMSO-D6
260M	B	4.55		CH	CL/CCL3/CH3		CCL4
2790M	D	4.55		CH	OH/C(=O)-O-CH3/CH2-C(=O)-O		CDCL3
1485M	D	4.55		CH	O-CH2/O-CH2/CH3		CCL4
1776M	E	4.55		CHR	R6<(OH)/C(A/A)-CH2/CH2-CH2>		CDCL3
1907M	A	4.55		CH2	OH/A(C-C(OH))		DMSO-D6
1410M	C	4.55		CH2	O-CH2/O-CH2		CDCL3
1319M	C	4.55		CH2R	R6OS<O-SO2/CH2-CH2>		CDCL3
1476M	E	4.55		HCHR	R6OOR6OOSPI<C*(HCH/CH2)-CH2/O-CH(CH2-CH3)>		CCL4
2407M	A	4.55	APP.	NH	NH2/C(=O)-A		DMSO-D6
2407M	A	4.55	APP.	NH2	NH-C(=O)-A		DMSO-D6
1460M	D	4.56		CHR	R6O<(O-CH2)/O-CH2/CH2-CH2>		CCL4
1376M	B	4.56		CH2R	R5NN<N(SO2-A)-CH2/N(SO2-A)-CH2>		POLYSOL-D
528M	B	4.56		NH2	A<C-C(CH3)-CH-C(I)>		POLYSOL-D
1424M	E	4.57		CH	O-CH2/O-CH2/CH3		CCL4
2175M	A	4.57		CH2	O-A/Q3		CCL4
109M	D	4.57	APP.	CH2	R4R6BI(=C-CH*/CH2)		CCL4
1475M	D	4.58		CHR	R6OOR6OOSPI<(CH3)/O-HCH/O-CH2>		CDCL3
2829M	A	4.58		CH2	O-C(=O)-Q2/Q3		CCL4
2951M	D	4.58		HCHR	R5O<O-C(=O)/CH(A)-HCH>		CDCL3
2951M	E	4.58		HCHR	R5O<O-C(=O)/CH(A)-HCH>		CDCL3
504M	A	4.58		NH2	A<C-C(A)>		DMSO-D6
1423M	E	4.59		CH	O-HCH/O-HCH/CH3		CCL4
654M	A	4.59		CH2	N(A/CH2)/A		CDCL3
937M	A	4.59		CH2	N=C=S/A		CDCL3
524M	A	4.59		NH2	A<C-C(BR)-CH-C(BR)/C(BR)>		CDCL3
1758M	C	4.60		CH	OH/C:N/CH3		CDCL3
1426M	D	4.60		CH	O-CH2/O-CH2/CH2-BR		CCL4
1431M	E	4.60		CH	O-CH2/O-CH2/CH2-N		CDCL3
1871M	B	4.60		CHR	R6O<(OH)/O-CH(CH2-OH)/CH(OH)-CH(OH)>		D2O
1873M	B	4.60		CHR	R6(OH/O-CH/CH(OH))		D2O
1181M	A	4.60		CH2	CL/A<C-C(CL)>		CCL4
1722M	C	4.60		CH2	OH/A(C-C(O-CH3))		CDCL3
1589M	C	4.60		CH2R	R6OA<O-CH2/C*>		CCL4
2408M	A	4.60	APP.	NH	NH2/C(=O)-AN		CDCL3
1966M	D	4.60		NHR	R5NN<C(=O)-N(CH2-NH)/C(CH3/CH3)-C(=O)>		CDCL3
2408M	A	4.60	APP.	NH2	NH-C(=O)		CDCL3
1685M	B	4.60		OH	CH2-Q3		CCL4
1312M	E	4.61		CH2	AN(N)/CH2-CH2	S	CDCL3
1709M	C	4.61		CH2	OH/SO2-A		CDCL3
2841M	B	4.61		CH2	O-C(=O)-CH3/Q2(A)		CCL4
1033M	C	4.61		CH2	O-N=O/CH2-CH3		CCL4
1854M	C	4.61		OH	CH2-CH2		CDCL3
1657M	D	4.61		OH	CH2-CH2	S	CDCL3
70M	E	4.61		Q2	CH2-CH2/CH3		CCL4
68M	B	4.61		Q2	Q2(H/CH3/CH3)		CDCL3
2412M	D	4.62		CHR	R5NN<(A)/NH-NH/HCH-C(=O)>		DMSO-D6
1038M	D	4.62		CH2	ONO/CH2-CH2		CCL4
2843M	D	4.62		CH2	O-C(=O)-CH2/Q2(H/A/H)		CCL4
2804M	B	4.62		CH2	O-C(=O)-CH2/Q3		CCL4
1478M	C	4.62		CH2R	R7OO<O-CH2/O-CH2>		CCL4
1135M	D	4.62		NH	R5NS(C=N/S)/CH2-A		CDCL3
862M	A	4.62		NH2	A<C-C(QN(A/OH))>		POLYSOL-D
72M	F	4.62		Q2	CH2-CH2/CH3		CCL4
69M	D	4.62		Q2	H/CH2-CH3/CH3		CCL4
69M	D	4.62		Q2	H/CH3/CH2-CH2		CCL4
2641M	C	4.63		CH	NH-C(=O)-CH2/C(=O)-OH/CH2-OH		D2O
2507M	B	4.63		CH	OH/C(=O)-OH/CH2-C(=O)-OH		D2O
2944M	A	4.63		CH2	O-C(=O)-A/CH2-O-C(=O)		CDCL3
2386M	A	4.63		CH2	R5N(N-C(=O)/C(=O))/A		CDCL3
530M	B	4.63		NH2	A(C-CH-CH-C(CH2-A))		DMSO-D6
2445M	B	4.64		CH2	R5NN<N-C(=O)/C(=O)>/A		CDCL3
1865M	D	4.65		CH	C(=O)-O-CH2/C(=O)-A/CH2-CH		CDCL3
1042M	B	4.65		CH	NO2/CH3/CH3		CDCL3
1717M	B	4.65		CH2	OH/A<C-C(CL)>		CDCL3
1321M	C	4.66		CH	SO3-A/CH3/CH3		CCL4
2051M	A	4.66		CH2	CL/C(=O)-A		CDCL3
2842M	D	4.66		CH2	O-C(=O)-CH2.2/Q2(H/A/H)		CCL4
71M	E	4.66		Q2	CH2-CH3/CH2-CH2		CCL4
2803M	B	4.66		Q3	H/O-C(=O)-CH2/H		CDCL3
2553M	A	4.67		CH2	O-A/C(=O)-OH		C3H6O
1886M	D	4.67		OH	A(C-CH-CH-C(C(CH2/CH3/CH3)))		CDCL3
2508M	A	4.68		CH	OH/C(=O)-OH/CH/CH(OH/C(=O)-OH)		D2O
1868M	B	4.68		CHR	R6O<(OH)/O-CH2/CH(OH)-CH(OH)>		D2O
2714M	D	4.68		CHR	R6<(O-C(=O)-CH2)/CH2-CH2/CH2-CH2>		CCL4

BOOK NO.	ASSIGN-MENT	CHEM SHIFT - ppm -	PROTON GROUP	ENVIRONMENTAL GROUPS	S	SOLVENT
1408M	E	4.68	Q2	CH3/H/O-CH2		CCL4
2505M	C	4.69	CH	CL/HCH-C(=O)-OH/HCH-C(=O)-OH		D2O
2716M	B	4.69	CH2	O-C(=O)-CH3/C:N		CDCL3
1907M	B	4.69	OH	CH2-A		DMSO-D6
111M	D	4.69	Q2	R6(CH-CH2/CH2)/CH3		CCL4
2715M	D	4.70	CHR	R6((O-C(=O)-CH2)/CH2-CH2/CH2-CH2)		CCL4
1037M	C	4.70	CH2	NO2/CH2-CH		CDCL3
1664M	C	4.70	CH2	OH/CH2-R5NN		TFA
1411M	C	4.70	CH2	O-CH2/O-CH2		CCL4
1851M	D	4.70	OH	CH(CH2/CH3)		CDCL3
475M	D	4.70	Q2	CH3/CH2-NH2/H		CCL4
1782M	F	4.70	Q2	H/CH3/CH(OH/CH3)		CCL4
1782M	E	4.70	Q2	H/CH(OH/CH3)/CH3		CCL4
843M	D	4.71	CH2	AN(N(+))/CH2-CH2	S	DMSO-D6
1729M	A	4.71	CH2	OH/AN(C-CH-CH-N)		CDCL3
2805M	A	4.71	CH2	O-C(=O)-C(=O)-O/Q3		CCL4
1953M	A	4.71	NH2	AA<C-CH-C*/CH-CH-C*>		DMSO-D6
1899M	A	4.71	NH2	A(C-CH-C(OH))		DMSO
1953M	A	4.71	OH	AA<C-C*>		DMSO-D6
2899M	A	4.72	CH2	O-C(=O)-A/Q3		CCL4
1831M	G	4.72	OH	C(HCH/CH3/CH3)		CCL4
2653M	A	4.73	CH2	F/C(=O)-O-NA		D2O
67M	C	4.75- 5.20	Q3	CH2-CH		CCL4
67M	C	4.75- 5.20	Q3	CH(CH2/CH3)		CCL4
2764M	C	4.75- 5.80		UNSPECIFIED		CDCL3
784M	B	4.77	CH	NH2/A/CH3	S	TFA
2822M	F	4.77	CH	O-C(=O)-CH3/CH2-Q2/CH2-CH2		CCL4
1917M	D	4.77	OH	A(C-C(CH(CH3/CH3))/CH-C(CH3))		CDCL3
62M	D	4.77- 6.06	Q3	CH2-CH2		CCL4
2797M	D	4.77	Q3	H/H/O-C(=O)-CH2		CCL4
2552M	B	4.78	CH	O-CH3/C(=O)-OH/A		CDCL3
2153M	D	4.78	CH2	C(=O)-H/CH2-CH2		CCL4
1728M	A	4.78	CH2	OH/AN<C-N>		CDCL3
1720M	B	4.78	CH2	OH/A<C-CH-C(NO2)>		CDCL3
2965M	A	4.78	CH2	O-C(=O)-CL/Q3(H/H/H)		CCL4
2396M	A	4.78	CH2	R5NA(N-C(=O)/C(=O))/A		DMSO-D6
54M	B	4.78	Q3	H/H/C(CH3/CH3/CH3)		CCL4
2509M	A	4.79	CH	OH/C(=O)-OH/CH(OH/C(=O)-O)		D2O
1425M	D	4.79	CH	O-HCH/O-HCH/Q3		CCL4
2988M	B	4.79	CHR	R6((O-C(=O)-NH)/CH2-CH2/CH2-CH2)		CDCL3
1721M	A	4.79	CH2	OH/A<C-CH-CH-C(NO2)>		C3H6O
1918M	C	4.79	OH	A<C-C(CH2-Q3)/C(CH3)>		CCL4
1087M	C	4.79 APP.	Q3	H/CH2-SI/H		CL2C=CCL2
1087M	C	4.79 APP.	Q3	H/H/CH2-SI		CL2C=CCL2
1435M	B	4.80	CH	O-CH3/O-CH3/O-CH3		CCL4
1128M	C	4.80	CH	S-CH2/S-CH2/S-CH2		CCL4
2855M	B	4.80	CHR	R5AA<(C(=O)-O-CH3)-C*/C*>		CDCL3
1731M	A	4.80	CH2	OH/ANA(C-CH-N-C*/CH-C*)		CDCL3
2215M	A	4.80	CH2	O-A/C(=O)-CL		CCL4
1458M	B	4.80	CH2R	R500<O-CH2/O-CH2>		CCL4
1474M	B	4.80	CH2R	R600R600SPI<O-CH2/O-CH2>		CDCL3
475M	E	4.80	Q2	H/CH3/CH2-NH2		CCL4
975M	B	4.81	CH	N(CH3/CH3)/A/C:N		CDCL3
1791M	C	4.81	CH	OH/A/CH2-A		CDCL3
1869M	C	4.81	CHR	R6O<(OH)/O-CH(CH3)/CH(OH)-CH(OH)>		D2O
54M	C	4.82	Q3	H/C(CH3/CH3/CH3)/H		CCL4
2802M	E	4.82	Q3	H/H/O-C(=O)-CH2		CDCL3
1028M	B	4.83	CHR	R6<(N(NO/R6))/CH2-CH2/CH2-CH2>		CDCL3
1028M	C	4.83	CHR	R6<(N(NO/R6))/CH2-CH2/CH2-CH2>		CDCL3
2713M	C	4.83	CHR	R8<(O-C(=O)-CH3)/CH2-CH2/CH2-CH2>		CCL4
316M	A	4.83	CH2	CL/AA<C-C*>		CCL4
1120M	A	4.83	CH2	CL/S-CH2		CDCL3
88M	D	4.83	Q3	H/CH(CH2/CH3)/H		CCL4
2609M	B	4.83	SH	C(=O)-CH3		CCL4
1913M	C	4.84	OH	A<C-C(CH3)-C(CH3)>		CDCL3
2698M	F	4.85	CH	O-C(=O)-CH2/CH2-CH3/CH3		CDCL3
1785M	D	4.85- 5.38	Q3	CH2-CH		CDCL3
1785M	D	4.85- 5.38	Q3	CH(OH/CH2)		CDCL3
2216M	B	4.86	CH	O-A/C(=O)-CL/CH3		CCL4
1866M	B	4.86- 5.16	CHR	R50<(OH)/O-CH(CH2-OH)/CH(OH)-CH(OH)>		D2O
1086M	C	4.86 APP.	Q3	CH2-SI		CCL4
57M	D	4.86	Q3	H/CH2-CH2/H		CCL4
64M	D	4.86	Q3	H/CH2-CH2/H		CCL4
2720M	D	4.87	CH	F/C(=O)-O-CH2/CH3		CCL4
2857M	B	4.87	CHR	R6<(O-C(=O)-Q2)/CH2-CH2/CH2-CH2>		CCL4
2963M	A	4.87	CH2	O-C(=O)-CL/C-CL3		CCL4
764M	A	4.87	NH	NH2/ANA<C-N-C*/CH-CH-C*>		POLYSOL-D
764M	A	4.87	NH2	NH-ANA		POLYSOL-D
1831M	H	4.87	OH	CH(HCH/CH3)		CCL4
572M	D	4.87	Q2	CH2-NH/CH3		CDCL3
60M	D	4.87	Q3	H/CH2-CH2/H		CCL4

BOOK NO.	ASSIGN-MENT	CHEM SHIFT - ppm -	PROTON GROUP	ENVIRONMENTAL GROUPS	S	SOLVENT
59M	D	4.87	Q3	H/CH2-CH2/H		CCL4
2904M	A	4.88	CH2	O-C(=O)-A/Q3		CDCL3
1264M	B	4.88	CH2	SO2-A/SO2-A		POLYSOL-D
2975M	B	4.88	NH2	C(=O)-O-C		CDCL3
1716M	B	4.88	OH	CH2-A		CDCL3
2743M	G	4.88	Q1	C(=O)-O-CH2.3/OH/CH3		CCL4
63M	D	4.88	Q3	H/CH2-CH2/H		CCL4
65M	D	4.88	Q3	H/CH2-CH2/H		CCL4
55M	E	4.88	Q3	H/CH(CH2/CH3)/H		CCL4
1812M	C	4.88	Q3	H/C(OH/CH3/CH3)/H		CCL4
2973M	B	4.89	CH	O-C(=O)-NH2/CH3/CH3		CDCL3
1872M	B	4.89	CHR	R6O((OH)/O-CH(CH2-OH)/CH(OH)-CH(OH))		D20
1782M	F	4.89	Q2	H/CH3/CH(OH/CH3)		CCL4
1782M	E	4.89	Q2	H/CH(OH/CH3)/CH3		CCL4
·2461M	B	4.89- 5.91	Q3	CH2-R6NN		DMSO-D6
61M	D	4.89	Q3	H/CH2-CH2/H		CCL4
1794M	D	4.89	Q3	H/R6R6N*BI<CH-CH*/CH2>/H		POLYSOL-D
76M	D	4.90- 5.41	Q2	CH3/CH(CH3/CH3)		CCL4
76M	D	4.90- 5.41	Q2	CH(CH3/CH3)/CH3		CCL4
74M	B	4.90	Q2	H/CH3/Q2(CH3/H/H)		CCL4
57M	E	4.90	Q3	H/H/CH2-CH2		CCL4
64M	E	4.90	Q3	H/H/CH2-CH2		CCL4
65M	E	4.90	Q3	H/H/CH2-CH2		CCL4
56M	C	4.90	Q3	H/H/CH(CH2/CH2)		CDCL3
101M	B	4.90	Q3	H/R6<CH-CH2/CH2>/H		CCL4
2037M	B	4.91	CH	BR/A/CH(BR/C(=O))		CDCL3
1432M	B	4.91	CH	O-CH/O-CH/CH3		CDCL3
2839M	C	4.91	CH2	O-C(=O)-CH3/A<C-CH-CH-C(O-CH3)>		CCL4
1932M	C	4.91 APP.	OH	A<C-C(CH2-Q3)-C(CH3)/CH-C(CH3)>		CDCL3
1883M	B	4.91	OH	A(C-CH-CH-C((C(CH3/CH3/CH3)))		CDCL3
58M	E	4.91 APP.	Q3	CH2-CH		CCL4
66M	B	4.91	Q3	H/CH2-CH2/H		CCL4
2019M	C	4.91	Q3	H/CH2-CH2/H		CCL4
2670M	C	4.91	Q3	H/CH2-CH2/H	S	D20
423M	B	4.91	Q3	H/CH2-I/H		CCL4
1932M	C	4.91 APP.	Q3	H/H/CH2-A		CDCL3
59M	E	4.91	Q3	H/H/CH2-CH2		CCL4
60M	E	4.91	Q3	H/H/CH2-CH2		CCL4
55M	F	4.91	Q3	H/H/CH(CH2/CH3)		CCL4
1794M	E	4.91	Q3	H/H/R6R6N*BI<CH-CH*/CH2>		POLYSOL-D
2700M	E	4.92	CH	O-C(=O)-CH2.2/CH3/CH3		CCL4
2727M	E	4.92	CH	O-C(=O)-CH2/CH3/CH3		CCL4
1013M	A	4.92	CH2	CL/S-C:N		CCL4
2400M	B	4.92	CH2	N(CH2/CH2)/R5NA(N-C(=O)/C(=O))		CDCL3
1084M	A	4.92	H	SI(A/A/H)		CDCL3
2976M	D	4.92	NH2	C(=O)-O-CH2		CDCL3
63M	E	4.92	Q3	H/H/CH2-CH2		CCL4
2449M	C	4.93	CHR	R5NN<(A)/NH-C(=O)/C(=O)-N>		CDCL3
837M	B	4.93	CH2	N(+)(CH3/CH3/CH3)/A		POLYSOL-D
2402M	A	4.93	NH2	R5NA<N-C(=O)/C(=O)>		DMSO
1727M	B	4.93	OH	CH2-R5AA		POLYSOL-D
·73M	B	4.93	Q2	H/CH3/Q3		CCL4
73M	B	4.93	Q2	H/Q3/CH3		CCL4
1783M	E	4.93	Q3	H/CH(OH/CH2)/H		CCL4
346M	A	4.94	CH2	BR/BR		CCL4
2931M	B	4.94	CH2	O-C(=O)-CH3/R5O(C-O/=CH)		CCL4
61M	E	4.94	Q3	H/H/CH2-CH2		CCL4
2803M	C	4.94	Q3	H/H/O-C(=O)-CH2		CDCL3
1730M	A	4.95	CH2	OH/R5NNA(C=N/NH)		DMSO-D6
1887M	C	4.95	OH	A<C-CH-CH-C(R6<CH-CH2/CH2>)>		CDCL3
2798M	E	4.95	Q3	H/CH2-CH2/H		CCL4
88M	E	4.95	Q3	H/H/CH(CH2/CH3)		CCL4
2773M	C	4.96	CH	O-C(=O)-CH2/CH3/CH3		CCL4
2464M	B	4.96- 6.13	Q3	CH2-R6NN		DMSO-D6
66M	C	4.96	Q3	H/H/CH2-CH2		CCL4
2973M	C	4.97	NH2	C(=O)-O-CH		CDCL3
155M	C	4.97	Q3	H/CH2-CH2/H		CDCL3
2019M	D	4.97	Q3	H/H/CH2-CH2		CCL4
2670M	D	4.97	Q3	H/H/CH2-CH2	S	D20
3000M	A	4.98	CH2	O-P=/A		CDCL3
1924M	C	4.98	Q3	CH2-A		CCL4
101M	C	4.98	Q3	H/H/R6<CH-CH2/CH2>		CCL4
2850M	E	4.99	CH	OH/A/CH2-C(=O)-O		CCL4
2878M	B	4.99	CHR	R6<(O-C(=O)-A)/CH2-CH2/CH2-CH2>		CDCL3
839M	G	4.99	CH2	N(+)(CH2/CH3/CH3)/A	S	CDCL3
1719M	B	4.99	CH2	OH/A<C-C(NO2)>		CDCL3
2837M	C	4.99	CH2	O-C(=O)-CH2/A		CCL4
2832M	B	4.99	CH2	O-C(=O)-CH3/A		CCL4
56M	D	4.99	Q3	H/CH(CH2/CH2)/H		CDCL3
153M	B	4.99	Q3	H/H/CH2-A		CCL4
2307M	B	5.00	CH	NH-C(=O)/A/CH3		CCL4

BOOK NO.	ASSIGN-MENT	CHEM SHIFT - ppm -	PROTON GROUP	ENVIRONMENTAL GROUPS	S	SOLVENT
1436M	C	5.00	CH	O-CH2/O-CH2/O-CH2		CCL4
2823M	F	5.00- 5.60	CH	O-C(=0)-CH2/CH2-O-C(=0)/CH2-O-C(=0)		CCL4
2448M	B	5.00	CHR	R5NN<(A)/NH-C(=0)/C(=0)-N(CH3)>		CDCL3
2986M	E	5.00 APP.	NH	C(=0)-O-CH2/CH2-CH2		CCL4
1338M	B	5.00- 8.00	NH	C(=S)-NH2/CH3		DMSO-D6
1338M	B	5.00- 8.00	NH2	C(=S)-NH		DMSO-D6
2823M	F	5.00- 5.60	Q2	CH2-CH2/CH2-CH2/H		CCL4
80M	C	5.00	Q2	CH(CH3/CH3)/CH(CH3/CH3)/H		CCL4
74M	C	5.00	Q2	H/Q2(CH3/H/H)/CH3		CCL4
1425M	E	5.00- 5.50	Q3	CH(O/O)		CCL4
1932M	D	5.00	Q3	H/CH2-A/H		CCL4
570M	D	5.00 APP.	Q3	H/CH2-NH/H		CDCL3
2798M	F	5.00	Q3	H/H/CH2-CH2		CCL4
2506M	A	5.01	CH	OH/C(=0)-OH/C(=0)-OH		D2O
1966M	E	5.01	CH2	NH-A/R5NN<N-C(=0)/C(=0)>		CDCL3
2300M	A	5.01	CH2	NH-C(=0)/NH-C(=0)		CDCL3
157M	B	5.01	Q2	H/A/CH3		TFA
2206M	E	5.01	Q3	H/CH2-CH2/H		CCL4
1434M	C	5.01	Q3	H/CH2-O/H		CCL4
155M	D	5.01	Q3	H/H/CH2-CH2		CCL4
2395M	A	5.01	Q3	H/R5NA<N-C(=0)/C(=0)>/H		CDCL3
2403M	B	5.02	NH	NH2/C(=0)-CH3		CDCL3
2403M	B	5.02	NH2	NH-C(=0)		CDCL3
1728M	B	5.02	OH	CH2-AN		CDCL3
1560M	C	5.02 APP.	Q3	CH2-A		CCL4
1918M	D	5.02 APP.	Q3	CH2-A		CCL4
89M	C	5.02 APP.	Q3	CH(Q2/CH3)		CCL4
153M	C	5.02	Q3	H/CH2-A/H		CCL4
2518M	B	5.02	Q3	H/CH2-CH2/H		CDCL3
73M	C	5.02	Q3	H/Q2/H		CCL4
89M	C	5.02 APP.	Q3	Q2(CH(Q3/CH3))		CCL4
514M	A	5.03	NH2	A(C-CH-CH-C(CL))		DMSO
571M	C	5.03	Q3	H/CH2-NH/H		CDCL3
2546M	A	5.04	CH	A/A/C(=0)-OH		CDCL3
2828M	B	5.04	CH	O-C(=0)-Q2/CH3/CH3		CCL4
2555M	A	5.05	CH	OH/C(=0)-OH/A		DMSO
2725M	D	5.05	CH	O-C(=0)-CH2/CH3/CH3		CCL4
893M	E	5.05	Q1	CH2-CH2/CH3/CH3		CDCL3
1688M	E	5.05- 5.70	Q2	CH2-CH2/CH2-CH3/H		CCL4
1688M	E	5.05- 5.70	Q2	CH2-CH3/CH2-CH2/H		CCL4
1190M	B	5.05	Q3	H/CH2-S/H		CCL4
570M	E	5.05 APP.	Q3	H/H/CH2-NH		CCL4
836M	B	5.06	CH2	N(+)(CH3/CH3/CH3)/A		CDCL3
1784M	F	5.06 APP.	Q3	CH2-CH	S	CDCL3
2826M	B	5.07	CH	O-C(=0)-Q2/CH3/CH3		CCL4
1279M	A	5.07	CH2	SO2-F/A		POLYSOL-D
1685M	C	5.07	Q3	H/CH2-OH/H		CCL4
2206M	F	5.07	Q3	H/H/CH2-CH2		CCL4
1894M	A	5.08	OH	A<C-C(BR)>		CDCL3
474M	C	5.08	Q3	H/CH2-NH2/H		CDCL3
587M	C	5.08	Q3	H/CH2-NH/H		CDCL3
2518M	C	5.08	Q3	H/H/CH2-CH2		CDCL3
2980M	D	5.09	NH	C(=0)-O-CH2/CH3		CDCL3
93M	F	5.09	Q1	CH2-CH2/CH3/CH3		CCL4
368M	B	5.09	Q3	H/CH2-BR/H		CCL4
378M	C	5.10	CH	BR/A/HCH-BR		CDCL3
2310M	C	5.10	CH	NH-C(=0)-CH3/A/CH3		CDCL3
2754M	E	5.10	CH	O-C(=0)-CH3/HCH-O-C(=0)/CH3		CCL4
2954M	C	5.10	CHR	R50<=C(CH3)-O/CH2-C(=0)>		CCL4
1869M	D	5.10	CHR	R60<(OH)/O-CH(CH3)/CH(OH)-CH(OH)>		D2O
1572M	A	5.10	CH2	O-AA/A		CDCL3
706M	A	5.10	NH2	AN(C-N)		CDCL3
1860M	B	5.10	OH	CH2-A		DMSO-D6
94M	E	5.10	Q1	CH2-CH/CH3/CH3		CCL4
2358M	G	5.10	Q1	C(=0)-N/OH/CH3		CDCL3
656M	B	5.10 APP.	Q3	CH2-N		CCL4
1350M	B	5.10	Q3	CH2-NH		CDCL3
1691M	C	5.10	Q3	CH2-O/H/H		CCL4
1687M	D	5.10	Q3	H/CH2-CH2/H		CDCL3
968M	B	5.10- 5.65	Q3	H/CH2-C:N/H		CCL4
968M	B	5.10- 5.65	Q3	H/H/CH2-C:N		CCL4
73M	D	5.10	Q3	H/H/Q2		CCL4
1446M	D	5.10- 5.70	Q3	R30<CH-O/HCH>		CDCL3
1793M	C	5.11	CH	OH/A(C-C(CL)/CH-C(CL))/CH3		CCL4
1990M	A	5.11	CH2	F/C(=0)-CH2		CDCL3
2845M	A	5.11	CH2	O-C(=0)-Q3/A		CCL4
2993M	B	5.11	CH2R	R6NNN<N(C(=0)-O-CH3)-CH2/N(C(=0)-O-CH3)-CH2>		CDCL3
91M	D	5.11	Q1	C(CH3/CH3/CH3)/CH3/CH3		CCL4
156M	A	5.11	Q3	H/A/H		CCL4
2306M	B	5.11	Q3	H/CH2-NH/H		CDCL3
642M	C	5.11	Q3	H/CH2-N/H		CDCL3

BOOK NO.	ASSIGN-MENT	CHEM SHIFT - ppm -	PROTON GROUP	ENVIRONMENTAL GROUPS	S	SOLVENT
1407M	B	5.11	Q3	H/CH2-O/H		CCL4
1812M	D	5.11	Q3	H/H C(OH/CH3/CH3)		CCL4
571M	D	5.11	Q3	H/H/CH2-NH		CDCL3
1190M	C	5.11	Q3	H/H/CH2-S		CCL4
1263M	B	5.11	Q3	H/H/CH2-SO2		CDCL3
1261M	B	5.11	Q3	H/H/CH2-SO2		CDCL3
1477M	A	5.12	CH2R	R6000<0-CH2/0-CH2>		DMSO-D6
90M	C	5.12	Q1	CH3/CH3/CH3		CCL4
2516M	B	5.12	Q3	H/H/CH2-C(=0)-OH		CDCL3
474M	D	5.12	Q3	H/H/CH2-NH2		CDCL3
1262M	C	5.12	Q3	H/H/CH2-SO2		CDCL3
1934M	B	5.13	OH	A<C-C(C(CH3/CH3/CH3))/CH-C(A<C-CH-C(C(CH3/CH3/CH3))-C(OH)/CH-C(C(CH3/CH3/CH3))>/C(C(CH3/CH3/CH3))>		CDCL3
2801M	E	5.13	Q3	H/CH2-0-C(=0)/H		CCL4
587M	D	5.13	Q3	H/H/CH2-NH		CDCL3
2446M	A	5.14	CHR	R5NN<(A)/NH-C(=0)/C(=0)-NH>		DMSO-D6
2977M	B	5.14	Q3	H/CH2-0-C(=0)/H		CCL4
1687M	E	5.14	Q3	H/H/CH2-CH2		CDCL3
1081M	B	5.15	CH	0-NO2/CH3/CH3		CCL4
272M	B	5.15	Q3	H/CH2-CL/H		CCL4
2829M	B	5.15	Q3	H/CH2-0-C(=0)/H		CCL4
1465M	D	5.15	Q3	H/CH2-R6NO/H		CDCL3
1783M	F	5.15	Q3	H/H/CH(OH/CH2)		CCL4
2761M	G	5.16	CH	0-C(=0)-CH2.16/HCH-0-C(=0)/HCH-0-C(=0)		CDCL3
2912M	B	5.16	CHR	R6((0-C(=0)-A)/CH2-CH2/CH2-CH2)		CDCL3
92M	F	5.16	Q1	CH3/CH2-CH2/CH3		CCL4
1403M	D	5.16	Q3	H/CH2-0/H		CDCL3
1691M	D	5.16	Q3	H/CH2-0/H		CCL4
423M	C	5.16	Q3	H/H/CH2-I		CCL4
642M	D	5.16	Q3	H/H/CH2-N		CDCL3
1434M	D	5.16	Q3	H/H/CH2-0		CCL4
110M	E	5.17	CHR	R4R6BI(=C(CH3)-CH*/CH2-CH*)		CCL4
2861M	A	5.17	CH2	0-C(=0)-Q2/A		CCL4
2846M	B	5.17	CH2	0-C(=0)-Q2/A		CDCL3
2806M	C	5.17	Q3	H/CH2-0-C(=0)/H		CCL4
1876M	B	5.18	OH	A<C-C(CH3)>		CCL4
2516M	C	5.18	Q3	H/CH2-C(=0)-OH/H		CDCL3
2306M	C	5.18	Q3	H/H/CH2-NH		CDCL3
2760M	G	5.19	CH	0-C(=0)-CH2/HCH-0-C(=0)/HCH-0-C(=0)		CCL4
1872M	C	5.19	CHR	R60((OH)/0-CH(CH2-OH)/CH(OH)-CH(OH))		D20
1653M	G	5.19	OH	CH2.3-N		CDCL3
2790M	E	5.19	OH	CH(C(=0)-0/CH2)		CDCL3
2434M	C	5.19	Q3	CH2-R5NN		POLYSOL-D
1407M	C	5.19	Q3	H/H/CH2-0		CCL4
1465M	E	5.19	Q3	H/H/CH2-R6NO		CDCL3
1794M	F	5.20- 5.60	CH	ANA<C-C*-CH-C(0-CH3)/CH-CH-N>/R6R6N*BI<CH-N*/CH2>		POLYSOL-D
1871M	C	5.20	CHR	R60<(OH)/0-CH(CH2-OH)/CH(OH)-CH(OH)>		D20
2844M	B	5.20	CH2	0-C(=0)-CH2/A		CDCL3
1952M	B	5.20	OH	AA(C-C*/C(CH3))		CDCL3
1895M	A	5.20	OH	A(C-CH-CH-C(BR))		CDCL3
1794M	F	5.20- 5.60	OH	CH(ANA/R6R6N*BI)		POLYSOL-D
87M	B	5.20- 5.80	Q2	CH3/Q2(CH3)		CCL4
2801M	F	5.20	Q3	H/H/CH2-0-C(=0)		CCL4
2882M	C	5.21	CH	0-C(=0)-A/CH3/CH3		CDCL3
2089M	A	5.21	CH2	0-A/C(=0)-A		CDCL3
2942M	A	5.21	CH2	0-C(=0)-A/A		CCL4
2417M	C	5.21 APP.	NH2	C(=0)-NH		POLYSOL-D
2419M	D	5.21	NH2	C(=0)-NH		DMSO-D6
2319M	D	5.21	Q1	C(=0)-CH3/OH/NH-A		DMSO-D6
2899M	B	5.21	Q3	H/CH2-0-C(=0)/H		CCL4
2804M	C	5.21	Q3	H/CH2-0-C(=0)/H		CCL4
1403M	E	5.21	Q3	H/H/CH2-0		CDCL3
1685M	D	5.21	Q3	H/H/CH2-OH		CCL4
2977M	C	5.21	Q3	H/H/CH2-0-C(=0)		CCL4
2633M	D	5.22	CH2	0-C(=0)-CH2.2/A		TFA
2418M	D	5.22	NH2	C(=0)-NH		POLYSOL-D
2805M	B	5.22	Q3	H/CH2-0-C(=0)/H		CCL4
1539M	C	5.22	Q3	H/CH2-0/H		CDCL3
103M	D	5.23	CHR	R6<=C(CH2-CH3)-CH2/CH2-CH2>		CCL4
2905M	B	5.23	NH2	A<C-CH-C(C(=0)-0-CH3)/CH-C(C(=0)-0-CH3)>		POLYSOL-D
2829M	C	5.23	Q3	H/H/CH2-0-C(=0)		CCL4
2806M	D	5.23	Q3	H/H/CH2-0-C(=0)		CCL4
1867M	C	5.24	CHR	R60<(OH)/0-CH2/CH(OH)-CH(OH)>		D20
221M	A	5.24	CH2	F/A		CCL4
82M	E	5.24	Q2	CH2-CH2/H/C(CH3/CH3/CH3)		CCL4
2981M	F	5.25	NH	C(=0)-0-CH2/CH2-CH2		CCL4
1689M	F	5.25	Q2	CH2-CH2/CH2-CH2/H		CCL4
1004M	B	5.25	Q3	H/CH2-N/H		CCL4
1901M	B	5.26	CH	A<C-CH-CH-C(N(CH3/CH3))>/A<C-CH-CH-C(N(CH3/CH3))>/A<C-CH-CH-C(OH)>		POLYSOL-D
573M	E	5.26	Q1	CH2-NH/CH3/CH3		CDCL3

BOOK NO.	ASSIGN-MENT	CHEM SHIFT - ppm -	PROTON GROUP	ENVIRONMENTAL GROUPS	S	SOLVENT
368M	C	5.26	Q3	H/H/CH2-BR		CCL4
2893M	B	5.27	CH	O-C(=O)-A/CH3/CH3		CDCL3
2430M	B	5.27	OH	CH2-NH		DMSO-D6
81M	C	5.27	Q2	CH(CH3/CH3)/H/CH(CH3/CH3)		CCL4
936M	B	5.27	Q3	H/CH2-N=/H		CCL4
1868M	C	5.28	CHR	R6O<(OH)/O-CH2/CH(OH)-CH(OH)>		D2O
249M	A	5.28	CH2	CL/CL		CCL4
1931M	A	5.28	OH	A<C-CH-C(A)-C(OH)>		CDCL3
1931M	A	5.28	OH	A<C-C(A)-CH-C(OH)>		CDCL3
1920M	A	5.28	OH	A(C-CH-C(CL)/CH-C(CL))		CDCL3
2528M	E	5.28	Q2	CH2-CH2/CH2-CH2/H		CCL4
2817M	G	5.28	Q2	CH2-CH2/CH2-CH2/H		CCL4
2175M	B	5.28	Q3	H/CH2-O/H		CCL4
2889M	B	5.29	CH	O-C(=O)-A/CH3/CH3		CDCL3
994M	A	5.29	NH2	A<C-CH-C(C:N)>		POLYSOL-D
2422M	B	5.29	NH2	C(=O)-NH		POLYSOL-D
2146M	F	5.29	Q1	C(=O)-CH2/OH/CH3		CCL4
2146M	F	5.29	Q1	C(=O)-CH3/OH/CH2-A		CCL4
296M	A	5.29	Q3	H/A<C-C(CL)>/H		CCL4
1263M	C	5.29	Q3	H/CH2-SO2/H		CDCL3
1262M	D	5.29	Q3	H/CH2-SO2/H		CDCL3
272M	C	5.29	Q3	H/H/CH2-CL		CCL4
2816M	F	5.29 APP.		UNSPECIFIED		CCL4
102M	C	5.30 APP.	CHR	R6<=C(CH3)-CH2/CH2-CH2>		CCL4
1873M	C	5.30	CHR	R6(OH/O-CH/CH(OH))		D2O
1808M	D	5.30	CHR	R6(=C(CH3)-CH2/CH2-CH(C(OH/CH3/CH3)))		CCL4
2840M	B	5.30	CH2	O-C(=O)-CH3/C(=O)-A		CDCL3
2982M	E	5.30	NH	C(=O)-O-CH3/CH2-CH2		CCL4
2431M	B	5.30	NHR	R5NN<C(=O)-NH/CH2-CH2>		CDCL3
2818M	F	5.30	Q2	CH2-CH2/CH2-CH2		CCL4
2966M	E	5.30	Q2	CH2-CH2/CH2-CH2/H		CCL4
78M	C	5.30	Q2	CH2-CH3/CH2-CH3/H		CDCL3
274M	E	5.30- 6.15	Q2	CH2-CL/CH2-C		CDCL3
274M	E	5.30- 6.15	Q2	CH2-C/CH2-CL		CDCL3
1261M	C	5.30	Q3	H/CH2-SO2/H		CDCL3
2804M	D	5.30	Q3	H/H/CH2-O-C(=O)		CCL4
89M	D	5.30- 6.60		UNSPECIFIED		CCL4
1780M	F	5.31	CHR	R6R6R6R5((OH)/CH2-C*/CH2-CH2)		CDCL3
1923M	C	5.31	OH	A<C-C(CH3)-CH-C(S-CH3)>		CDCL3
2023M	A	5.31	OH	CH(C(=O)/R5O)		DMSO
643M	C	5.31	Q1	N(CH3/CH3)/CH3/CH3		CDCL3
77M	D	5.31	Q2	CH3/H/CH(CH3/CH3)		CCL4
77M	D	5.31	Q2	CH(CH3/CH3)/H/CH3		CCL4
157M	C	5.31	Q2	H/CH3/A		CCL4
2904M	B	5.31	Q3	H/CH2-O-C(=O)/H		CDCL3
2899M	C	5.31	Q3	H/H/CH2-O-C(=O)		CCL4
1890M	A	5.32	OH	A<C-C(F)>		CCL4
84M	D	5.32 APP.	Q2	CH2-CH2/H/CH2-CH2		CCL4
781M	B	5.32	Q3	H/CH2-NH2/H	S	POLYSOL-D
2037M	C	5.33	CH	BR/C(=O)-CH3/CH(BR/A)		CDCL3
86M	D	5.33	Q2	CH2-CH2/CH2-CH2		CDCL3
1004M	C	5.33	Q3	H/H/CH2-N		CCL4
2805M	C	5.33	Q3	H/H/CH2-O-C(=O)		CCL4
85M	D	5.34	Q2	CH2-CH2/CH2-CH2		CCL4
75M	D	5.34 APP.	Q2	CH2-CH3/CH3		CCL4
75M	D	5.34 APP.	Q2	CH3/CH2-CH3		CCL4
1299M	B	5.34 APP.	Q3	CH2-SO3-NA		D2O
879M	A	5.35	NH2	QN(QN/A)		CDCL3
1690M	G	5.35	Q1	CH2-OH/CH2.3-CH/CH3		CCL4
2822M	G	5.35 APP.	Q2	CH2-CH/CH2-CH2		CCL4
88M	F	5.35 APP.	Q2	CH2-CH/CH3		CCL4
88M	F	5.35 APP.	Q2	CH3/CH2-CH		CCL4
936M	C	5.35	Q3	H/H/CH2-N=		CCL4
2175M	C	5.35	Q3	H/H/CH2-O		CCL4
1539M	D	5.35	Q3	H/H/CH2-O		CDCL3
2610M	A	5.35	SH	C(=O)-A		CDCL3
873M	A	5.37	NH2	QN(AA<C-C*>)		POLYSOL-D
1892M	A	5.37	OH	A<C-C(CL)>		CDCL3
79M	C	5.37	Q2	CH2-CH3/H/CH2-CH3		CCL4
2819M	F	5.38	Q2	CH2.7-CH3/H/CH2.7-C(=O)-O		CDCL3
2819M	F	5.38	Q2	CH2.7-C(=O)-O/H/CH2.7-CH3		CDCL3
2451M	A	5.39	CHR	R5NN<(NH-C(=O)-NH2)/NH-C(=O)/C(=O)-NH>		DMSO-D6
111M	E	5.39	CHR	R6(=C(CH3)-CH2/CH2-CH(Q2(CH3)))		CCL4
2103M	A	5.39	NH2	A<C-CH-C(C(=O)-A)>		DMSO-D6
2421M	C	5.39	NH2	C(=O)-NH		POLYSOL-D
2139M	F	5.39	Q1	C(=O)-CH2.2/OH/CH2.2-CH3		CCL4
2529M	E	5.39	Q2	CH2-CH2/H/CH2-CH2		CDCL3
2813M	E	5.39	Q2	H/O-C(=O)-CH2/CH3		CCL4
2965M	B	5.39	Q3	H/CH2-O-C(=O)/H		CCL4
1034M	D	5.40	CH	O-N=O/CH2-CH3/CH3		CCL4
785M	E	5.40- 7.00	H	CL	S	TFA

: REPRESENTS TRIPLE BOND, ¬ REPRESENTS AN ARROW AND < AND > REPRESENT BRACKETS. PAGE 249

BOOK NO.	ASSIGN-MENT	CHEM SHIFT - ppm -	PROTON GROUP	ENVIRONMENTAL GROUPS	S	SOLVENT
785M	E	5.40- 7.00	NH2	CH(CH2/CH3)	S	TFA
1914M	B	5.40	OH	A(C-CH-C(CH3)-C(CH3))		CCL4
1924M	D	5.40	OH	A(C-C(O-CH3)-CH-C(CH2-Q3))		CCL4
2532M	E	5.40	Q2	CH2-CH2/CH2-CH/H		CCL4
2532M	E	5.40	Q2	CH2-CH/CH2-CH2/H		CCL4
82M	F	5.40	Q2	C(CH3/CH3/CH3)/H/CH2-CH2		CCL4
2304M	B	5.40- 6.50	Q3	C(=O)-NH		CDCL3
966M	A	5.40- 6.10	Q3	C:N/H/H		CCL4
966M	A	5.40- 6.10	Q3	H/C:N/H		CCL4
115M	D	5.41 APP.	CHR	R5R5RIR5<CH*(CH*/HCH(/=CH-CH*>		CCL4
1874M	B	5.41	CHR	R60<(O-R50)/O-CH(CH2-OH)/CH(OH)-CH(OH)>		D20
2144M	C	5.41	CHR	R6(=C(OH)-CH2/C(=O)-CH2)		CDCL3
2967M	A	5.41	CH2	O-C(=O)-CL/A<C-CH-CH-C(NO2)>		CDCL3
1921M	A	5.41	OH	A<C-C(BR)-CH-C(RR)>		CCL4
1898M	A	5.41	OH	A(C-CH-CH-C(I))		CDCL3
2257M	E	5.41 APP.	Q2	CH2.8-CH3/CH2-R50		CDCL3
2257M	E	5.41 APP.	Q2	CH2-R50/CH2.8-CH3		CDCL3
2090M	B	5.42	CH	O-A/C(=O)-A/CH3		CDCL3
597M	A	5.42	NH	A/A		CCL4
2138M	F	5.42	Q1	C(=O)-CH2/OH/CH2-CH3		CCL4
2904M	C	5.42	Q3	H/H/CH2-O-C(=O)		CDCL3
2965M	C	5.42	Q3	H/H/CH2-O-C(=O)		CCL4
845M	A	5.43	CH2	AN(N(+))/CH2-AN	S	D20
2527M	E	5.43	Q2	CH2.2-C(=O)-OH/H/CH2.7-CH3		CCL4
2527M	E	5.43	Q2	CH2.7-CH3/H/CH2.2-C(=O)-OH		CCL4
2811M	D	5.43	Q2	H/C(=O)-O-CH/CH3		CCL4
2913M	A	5.44	CH2	O-C(=O)-A		CDCL3
67M	D	5.45- 6.15	Q3	CH2-CH		CCL4
67M	D	5.45- 6.15	Q3	CH(CH2/CH3)		CCL4
1885M	D	5.46	OH	A(C-CH-CH-C(C(CH2/CH3/CH3)))		CCL4
275M	D	5.46 APP.	Q3	H/CH(CL/HCH)/H		CCL4
1179M	A	5.47	NH2	AR5SA(C-CH-C*-S/CH-CH-C*)		DMSO
1859M	B	5.47	OH	C(C:/CH3/CH3)		DMSO-D6
2526M	E	5.47	Q2	CH2.2-C(=O)-OH/H/CH2.5-CH3		CCL4
2526M	E	5.47	Q2	CH2.5-CH3/H/CH2.2-C(=O)-OH		CCL4
154M	C	5.47 APP.	Q2	CH2-A/CH3		CCL4
154M	C	5.47 APP.	Q2	CH3/CH2-A		CCL4
2812M	E	5.47	Q2	H/C(=O)-O-CH2/CH3		CCL4
100M	E	5.48	CHR	R6<=CH-CH2/CH2-CH2>		CCL4
100M	E	5.48	CHR	R6<=CH-CH2/CH2-CH(C(CH2/CH3/CH3))>		CCL4
114M	B	5.48	CHR	R8<=CH-CH2/CH2-CH2>		CCL4
2956M	A	5.48	CH2R	R50A<O-C(=O)/C*>		CDCL3
2420M	B	5.48	NH2	C(=O)-NH		DMSO-D6
1763M	C	5.48	OH	R4(CH-CH2/CH2)		CCL4
2525M	E	5.48	Q2	CH2.2-C(=O)-OH/H/CH2.4-CH3		CCL4
2525M	E	5.48	Q2	CH2.4-CH3/H/CH2-C(=O)-OH		CCL4
175M	D	5.49	CHR	R6<=C(A<C-C(CH3)>)-CH2/CH2-CH2>		CCL4
1731M	B	5.49	OH	CH2-ANA		CDCL3
2810M	D	5.49	Q2	H/C(=O)-O-CH2/CH3		CCL4
150M	A	5.50	CH	A/A/A		CDCL3
279M	A	5.50	Q2	CL/CL		CCL4
781M	C	5.50	Q3	H/H/CH2-NH2	S	POLYSOL-D
2669M	A	5.50- 6.30		UNSPECIFIED		D20
1399M	A	5.51	CH2	CL/O-CH2		CDCL3
2305M	D	5.51	Q3	H/C(=O)-NH/H		CDCL3
2213M	A	5.52	CH	CL/C(=O)-CL/A		CCL4
1879M	C	5.52	OH	A<C-C(CH2-CH3)>		CCL4
1659M	D	5.52	OH	CH(P=/CH2.2)		POLYSOL-D
2846M	C	5.52	Q2	H/C(=O)-O-CH2/CH3		CDCL3
1350M	C	5.52- 6.20	Q3	CH2-NH		CDCL3
2425M	B	5.53	NH2	C(=O)-NH		POLYSOL-D
2393M	A	5.54	CH2	BR/R5NA<N-C(=O)/C(=O)>		CDCL3
2521M	E	5.54 APP.	Q2	CH2-CH2/CH2-C(=O)-OH		CCL4
106M	C	5.54	Q2	R8(CH2-CH2/CH2-CH2/H)		CCL4
1896M	A	5.55	OH	A(C-C(I))		CDCL3
574M	E	5.55	Q2	CH2-NH/CH2-NH		CCL4
1686M	D	5.57 APP.	Q2	CH2-OH/CH3		CCL4
1686M	D	5.57 APP.	Q2	CH3/CH2-OH		CCL4
673M	E	5.58	CHR	R6N<=CH-CH2/CH2-CH2>		CCL4
673M	E	5.58	CHR	R6N<=CH-CH2/CH2-N(CH3)>		CCL4
99M	C	5.58	CHR	R6<=CH-CH2/CH2-CH2>		CCL4
2412M	E	5.58	NHR	R5NN<NH-CH(A)/C(=O)-HCH>		DMSO-D6
275M	E	5.58 APP.	Q3	H/H/CH(CL/HCH)		CCL4
1790M	B	5.59	CH	OH/A/A^		CCL4
156M	B	5.59	Q3	H/H/A		CCL4
1493M	C	5.60	CH	O-A/O-CH2/O-CH2		CCL4
56M	E	5.60	Q3	CH(CH2/CH2)/H/H		CDCL3
296M	B	5.60	Q3	H/H/A<C-C(CL)>		CCL4
101M	D	5.61	CHR	R6<=CH-CH2/CH2-CH2>		CCL4
101M	D	5.61	CHR	R6<=CH-CH2/CH2-CH(Q3)>		CCL4
604M	A	5.61	NH	AA/A		CCL4

BOOK NO.	ASSIGN-MENT	CHEM SHIFT - ppm -	PROTON GROUP	ENVIRONMENTAL GROUPS	S	SOLVENT
2751M	D	5.61	NH2	C(=0)-NH		DMSO-D6
2800M	F	5.61 APP.	Q2	CH2.2-CH3/H/CH2-0-C(=0)		CCL4
2800M	F	5.61 APP.	Q2	CH2-0-C(=0)/H/CH2.2-CH3		CCL4
2306M	D	5.61 APP.	Q3	H/C(=0)-NH/H		CDCL3
1259M	E	5.63	CHR	R5S<=C(CH3)-CH2/CH(CH3)-S02>		CDCL3
2419M	E	5.63	NH	C(=0)-NH2/C(CH2/CH3/CH3)		DMSO-D6
88M	G	5.63 APP.	Q3	CH(CH2/CH3)/H/H		CCL4
2302M	E	5.64	NH	C(=0)-CH2/C(CH2/CH3/CH3)		CDCL3
1461M	D	5.65	CHR	R60(=CH-CH2/CH2-0)		CCL4
1461M	E	5.65	CHR	R60(=CH-CH2/CH2-0)		CCL4
970M	C	5.65	CHR	R6(=CH-CH2/CH2-CH2)		CCL4
970M	C	5.65	CHR	R6(=CH-CH2/CH2-CH(C:N))		CCL4
2996M	C	5.65- 6.88	Q3	P(=0/0/0)		CCL4
97M	C	5.66	CHR	R5<=CH-CH2/CH2-CH2>		CCL4
2285M	D	5.66	CHR	R6<=C(CH(C(=0)/CH2))-CH2/CH2-CH2>		CDCL3
59M	F	5.66 APP.	Q3	CH2-CH2/H/H		CCL4
64M	F	5.66 APP.	Q3	CH2-CH2/H/H		CCL4
65M	F	5.66 APP.	Q3	CH2-CH2/H/H		CCL4
2536M	B	5.67 APP.	CHR	R8(=CH-CH2/CH2-CH2)		CDCL3
57M	F	5.67 APP.	Q3	CH2-CH2/H/H		CCL4
2798M	G	5.67	Q3	CH2-CH2/H/H		CCL4
1425M	F	5.67	Q3	CH(0/0)		CCL4
2158M	B	5.68	CHR	R6<=CH-CH2/CH2-CH2>		CCL4
2158M	B	5.68	CHR	R6<=CH-CH2/CH2-CH(C(=0)-H)>		CCL4
113M	B	5.68	CHR	R6<=CH-CH2/CH2-CH=>		CDCL3
1919M	A	5.68	OH	A<C-C(CL)-CH-C(CL)>		CDCL3
60M	F	5.68 APP.	Q3	CH2-CH2/H/H		CCL4
351M	B	5.69	CH	BR/BR/CH2-BR		CCL4
2538M	C	5.69	CHR	R6<=CH-CH2/CH2-CH(C(=0)-OH)>		C3060
1365M	A	5.69	NH2	A<C-CH-CH-C(S02-NH2)>		DMSO-D6
2519M	C	5.69	Q1	C(=0)-OH/CH3/CH3		CCL4
1087M	D	5.69 APP.	Q3	CH2-SI/H/H		CL2C=CCL2
2537M	D	5.70- 6.40	CHR	R5R5RI(=CH-CH*/CH*(CH2/CH2))		CCL4
2537M	D	5.70- 6.40	CHR	R5R5RI(=CH-CH*/CH*(CH(C(=0)-OH)/CH2))		CCL4
2130M	G	5.70	CHR	R6R6R6R5(=C*-CH2/C(=0)-CH2)		CDCL3
105M	C	5.70 APP.	CHR	R6(=C(R6)-CH2/CH2-CH2)		CCL4
2451M	B	5.70 APP.	NH	C(=0)-NH2/R5NN<=CH-NH/C(=0)>		DMSO-D6
901M	B	5.70	NH2	A(C-CH-CH-C(N=N-A))		DMSO-D6
2451M	B	5.70 APP.	NH2	C(=0)-NH		DMSO-D6
66M	D	5.70	Q3	CH2-CH2/H/H		CCL4
63M	F	5.70	Q3	CH2-CH2/H/H		CCL4
55M	G	5.70	Q3	CH(CH2/CH3)/H/H		CCL4
2208M	B	5.70- 6.70		UNSPECIFIED		CCL4
2452M	C	5.71	CHR	R6NN(=CH-N(CH3)/C(=0)-N(CH3))		CDCL3
2027M	C	5.71	CHR	R6<=C(CH3)-CH2/C(=0)-CH2>		CCL4
2429M	D	5.71	NH	C(=0)-NH/CH2-CH2		CDCL3
889M	A	5.71	NH	QN(A)/A		DMSO-D6
2878M	C	5.71	NH2	A<C-C(C(=0)-0-R6)>		CDCL3
2977M	D	5.71 APP.	NH2	C(=0)-0-CH2		CCL4
1933M	E	5.71 APP.	OH	A<C-C(C(CH3/CH3/CH3))-CH-C(CH2-CH3)/C(CH2-A)>		CDCL3
1937M	A	5.71	OH	A(C-C(BR)-CH-C(BR)/C(BR))		CCL4
889M	A	5.71	QNH	NH-A/A		DMSO-D6
278M	C	5.71	Q1	CH2-CL/CL/CH3		CCL4
2522M	E	5.71	Q2	C(=0)-OH/H/CH(CH2.2/CH3)		CCL4
2799M	E	5.71	Q2	C(=0)-0-CH3/H/CH2.2-CH3		CCL4
2815M	E	5.71	Q2	C(=0)-0-CH3/H/CH2.6-CH3		CCL4
2809M	D	5.71	Q3	H/C(=0)-0-CH2/H		CCL4
58M	F	5.72	Q3	CH2-CH		CCL4
61M	F	5.72	Q3	CH2-CH2/H/H		CCL4
1190M	D	5.72	Q3	CH2-S/H/H		CCL4
2845M	B	5.72	Q3	H/C(=0)-0-CH2/H		CCL4
2807M	D	5.72	Q3	H/H/C(=0)-0-CH2		CCL4
2877M	D	5.73	NH2	A<C-C(C(=0)-CH2)>		CCL4
1915M	B	5.73	OH	A(C-CH-C(CH3)/CH-C(CH3))		CCL4
2530M	B	5.73	Q2	C(=0)-OH/Q2(CH3)		CDCL3
2808M	D	5.73	Q3	H/C(=0)-0-CH2/H		CCL4
2417M	D	5.74	NH	C(=0)-NH2/CH(CH3/CH3)		POLYSOL-D
2019M	E	5.75	Q3	CH2-CH2/H/H		CCL4
570M	F	5.75 APP.	Q3	CH2-NH/H/H		CCL4
2434M	D	5.75	Q3	CH2-R5NN		POLYSOL-D
1638M	C	5.76	CH	CL/CL/CH2-OH		CCL4
576M	E	5.76 APP.	CHR	R6N<=CH-CH2/CH2-CH2>		CDCL3
576M	E	5.76 APP.	CHR	R6N<=CH-CH2/CH2-NH>		CDCL3
541M	A	5.76	NH2	AAA<C-C*/CH-C*>		DMSO
2524M	D	5.76	Q2	C(=0)-OH/CH2-CH2		CCL4
1263M	D	5.76	Q3	CH2-S02/H/H		CDCL3
265M	C	5.77	CH	CL/CL/CH2-C		CCL4
2824M	G	5.77- 6.22	CHR	R5R5RI<=CH-CH*/CH*(CH2/CH2)>		CCL4
2824M	G	5.77- 6.22	CHR	R5R5RI<=CH-CH*/CH*(CH(C(=0)-0-CH2)/CH2)>		CCL4
2520M	D	5.77	Q2	C(=0)-OH/H/CH2.2-CH3		CCL4
968M	C	5.77	Q3	CH2-C:N/H/H		CCL4

BOOK NO.	ASSIGN-MENT	CHEM SHIFT - ppm -	PROTON GROUP	ENVIRONMENTAL GROUPS	S	SOLVENT
656M	C	5.77	Q3	CH2-N		CCL4
1261M	D	5.77	Q3	CH2-SO2/H/H		CDCL3
1925M	B	5.78	OH	A<C-C(OH)-C(CH3)>		CDCL3
1925M	B	5.78	OH	A<C-C(OH)/C(CH3)>		CDCL3
1785M	E	5.78 APP.	Q3	CH2-CH		CDCL3
2670M	E	5.78	Q3	CH2-CH2/H/H	S	D2O
1785M	E	5.78 APP.	Q3	CH(OH/CH2)		CDCL3
1783M	G	5.78 APP.	Q3	CH(OH/CH2)/H/H		CCL4
254M	B	5.79	CH	CL/CL/CH2-CL		CDCL3
2023M	B	5.79	CH	OH/C(=O)-R5O/R5O(C=CH/O)		DMSO
2423M	B	5.79	NH2	C(=O)-NH		DMSO-D6
2814M	D	5.79	Q2	C(=O)-O-CH2/H/CH3		CCL4
967M	B	5.79 APP.	Q2	H/CH3/C:N		CCL4
967M	B	5.79 APP.	Q2	H/C:N/CH3		CCL4
2977M	E	5.79	Q3	CH2-O-C(=O)/H/H		CCL4
1262M	E	5.79	Q3	CH2-SO2/H/H		CDCL3
1461M	D	5.80	CHR	R6O(=CH-CH2/CH2-O)		CCL4
1461M	E	5.80	CHR	R6O(=CH-CH2/CH2-O)		CCL4
1924M	E	5.80	Q3	CH2-A		CCL4
2518M	D	5.80	Q3	CH2-CH2/H/H		CDCL3
1687M	F	5.80	Q3	CH2-CH2/H/H		CDCL3
587M	E	5.80	Q3•	CH2-NH/H/H		CDCL3
936M	D	5.80 APP.	Q3	CH2-N=/H/H		CCL4
1004M	D	5.80 APP.	Q3	CH2-N/H/H		CCL4
2829M	D	5.80	Q3	CH2-O-C(=O)/H/H		CCL4
1434M	E	5.80	Q3	CH2-O/H/H		CCL4
54M	D	5.80	Q3	C(CH3/CH3/CH3)/H/H		CCL4
1794M	G	5.80	Q3	R6R6N*BI<CH-CH*/CH2>/H/H		POLYSOL-D
277M	C	5.80- 6.50		UNSPECIFIED		CDCL3
1575M	B	5.81	CHR	R5O<=C(CH3)-O/CH=C(CH3)>		CDCL3
1935M	B	5.81	DH	A(C-C(BR)-CH-C(C(A/CH3/CH3))/C(BR))		CDCL3
2305M	E	5.81	NH	C(=O)-Q3/C(CH2/CH3/CH3)		CDCL3
155M	E	5.81	Q3	CH2-CH2/H/H		CDCL3
1691M	E	5.81	Q3	H/H/CH2-O		CCL4
2517M	B	5.82	Q2	C(=O)-OH/H/CH3		CDCL3
1408M	F	5.82	Q2	O-CH2/CH3/H		CCL4
1784M	G	5.82	Q3	CH2-CH		CDCL3
642M	E	5.82	Q3	CH2-N/H/H		CDCL3
2801M	G	5.82	Q3	CH2-O-C(=O)/H/H		CCL4
1407M	D	5.82	Q3	CH2-O/H/H		CCL4
2017M	B	5.82 APP.	Q3	C(=O)-CH3/H/H		CCL4
1574M	B	5.83	CHR	R5O<=C(CH3)-O/CH=CH>		CCL4
112M	B	5.83	CHR	R6<=CH-CH2/CH=CH>		CDCL3
112M	B	5.83	CHR	R6<=CH-CH=/CH2-CH2>		CDCL3
2671M	B	5.83	Q2	C(=O)-OK/Q2(CH3)		D2O
571M	E	5.83	Q3	CH2-NH/H/H		CDCL3
1086M	D	5.83	Q3	CH2-SI		CCL4
534M	B	5.84	CHA	A(C(NH2)/C(NH2))		POLYSOL-D
982M	A	5.84	Q2	C:N/H/A		CCL4
1918M	E	5.84	Q3	CH2-A		CCL4
2206M	G	5.84	Q3	CH2-CH2/H/H		CCL4
1734M	C	5.85	CH2R	R5OOA<O-C*/O-C*>		CDCL3
2039M	C	5.85	CH2R	R5OOA(O-C*/O-C*)		CCL4
1927M	D	5.85	OH	A<C-CH-C(OH)-C(CH2-CH2)>		CDCL3
1927M	D	5.85	OH	A<C-C(CH2-CH2)/CH-C(OH)>		CDCL3
153M	D	5.85 APP.	Q3	CH2-A/H/H		CCL4
2286M	E	5.86	HNH	C(=O)-CH		CCL4
2286M	F	5.86	HNH	C(=O)-CH		CCL4
280M	B	5.86	Q1	CH3/CL/CL		CDCL3
1932M	E	5.86	Q3	CH2-A/H/H		CDCL3
1465M	F	5.86	Q3	CH2-R6NO/H/H		CDCL3
1154M	B	5.87	NH2	R5NS<C=N/S>	S	D2O
1926M	B	5.87	OH	A<C-C(OH)-CH-C(CH3)>		CDCL3
1926M	B	5.87	OH	A<C-C(OH)/CH-C(CH3)>		CDCL3
1560M	D	5.87	Q3	CH2-A		CCL4
2516M	D	5.87	Q3	CH2-C(=O)-OH/H/H		CDCL3
2806M	E	5.87	Q3	CH2-O-C(=O)/H/H		CCL4
1044M	B	5.88	CH	CL/NO2/CH3		CCL4
2025M	B	5.88	CHR	R6<=CH-CH2/C(=O)-CH2>		CCL4
2424M	A	5.88	NH2	C(=O)-NH		DMSO-D6
2306M	E	5.88	Q3	CH2-NH/H/H		CDCL3
1685M	E	5.88	Q3	CH2-OH/H/H		CCL4
101M	E	5.88	Q3	R6<CH-CH2/CH2>/H/H		CCL4
251M	B	5.89	CH	CL/CH/CH3		CCL4
1588M	A	5.89	CH2R	R5OOA<O-C*/O-C*>		CCL4
890M	A	5.89	NH	QN(NH-A/A)/A		CDCL3
2469M	D	5.89	NH2	C(=O)-NH		CDCL3
95M	C	5.89	Q1	Q1(CH3/CH3)/CH3/CH3		CCL4
2804M	E	5.89	Q3	CH2-O-C(=O)/H/H		CCL4
2834M	C	5.90	CH	O-C(=O)-CH3/A/CH3		CDCL3
115M	E	5.90 APP.	CHR	R5R5BIR5<CH*-CH*/=CH-CH2>		CCL4

BOOK NO.	ASSIGN-MENT	CHEM SHIFT - ppm -	PROTON GROUP	ENVIRONMENTAL GROUPS	S	SOLVENT
115M	E	5.90 APP.	CHR	R5R5BIR5<=CH-CH*/CH2-CH*>		CCL4
2468M	B	5.90	NH	NH2/C(=O)-N		CDCL3
272M	D	5.90 APP.	Q3	CH2-CL/H/H		CCL4
2899M	D	5.90	Q3	CH2-O-C(=O)/H/H		CCL4
2965M	D	5.90	Q3	CH2-O-C(=O)/H/H		CCL4
1546M	B	5.90- 7.40		UNSPECIFIED		CCL4
255M	A	5.91	CH	CL/CL/CH(CL/CL)		CDCL3
2654M	A	5.91	CH	F/F/C(=O)-O-NA		D20
534M	C	5.91	CHA	A(C(NH2)-CH-C(NH2))		POLYSOL-D
676M	B	5.91	CHR	R5N<=C(CH3)-N(A)/CH=C(CH3)>		CDCL3
1506M	C	5.91	Q2	CH3/A(C-CH-CH-C(O-CH3))		CCL4
1559M	D	5.91	Q2	CH3/H/A<C-CH-CH-C(O-CH3)-C(O-CH3)>		CDCL3
894M	B	5.91	Q2	C(=O)-NH/H/Q2(H/CH3/H)		POLYSOL-D
368M	D	5.91	Q3	CH2-BR/H/H		CCL4
2421M	D	5.92	NH	C(=O)-NH2/R6		POLYSOL-D
2470M	E	5.92	NH2	C(=O)-NH		CDCL3
2915M	C	5.92	OH	A<C-C(O-CH3)-CH-C(C(=O)-O-CH3)/C(O-CH3)>		CDCL3
2021M	E	5.92	Q2	C(=O)-CH3/H/CH(CH2/CH2)		CCL4
2805M	D	5.92	Q3	CH2-O-C(=O)/H/H		CCL4
1812M	E	5.92	Q3	C(OH/CH3/CH3)/H/H		CCL4
276M	B	5.93	Q2	CH2-CL/CH2-CL		CCL4
87M	C	5.93	Q2	Q2(CH3)/CH3		CCL4
2258M	B	5.94	HCH	=R50<C-C(=O)/CH2-C(=O)>		CDCL3
2258M	C	5.94	HCH	=R50<C-C(=O)/CH2-C(=O)>		CDCL3
2175M	D	5.94	Q3	CH2-O/H/H		CCL4
1403M	F	5.94	Q3	CH2-O/H/H		CDCL3
2314M	C	5.95	NH	C(=O)-CH2/CH2-A		CDCL3
275M	F	5.95 APP.	Q3	CH(CL/HCH)/H/H		CCL4
667M	B	5.97	CH	A<C-CH-CH-C(N(CH3/CH3))>/A<C-CH-CH-C(N(CH3/CH3))>/ A<C-CH-CH-C(N(CH3/CH3))>		TFA
536M	C	5.97	CHA	A<C(NH2)-C(CH3)/C(NH2)>		CDCL3
1154M	C	5.97	CHR	R5NS<=C(CH3)-N=/S-C(NH2)=>	S	D20
1393M	C	5.98	CH	CL/F/CF2-O		CCL4
184M	D	5.98	CHR	R6<=C(A<C-CH-CH-C(CH3)>)-CH2/CH2-CH2>		CCL4
161M	D	5.98	Q1	CH2.6-CH3/A/A		CCL4
423M	D	5.98	Q3	CH2-I/H/H		CCL4
1947M	A	5.99	CHA	A<C(OH)-CH-C(OH)/C(OH)>		C3H60
1899M	B	5.99 APP.	CHA	A(C(NH2)-CH-C(OH))		DMSO
1899M	B	5.99 APP.	CHA	A(C(OH)-CH-C(NH2))		DMSO
1965M	D	5.99 APP.	H	P(=O/O/O)		CDCL3
160M	D	5.99	Q1	CH2.3-CH3/A/A		CCL4
2811M	E	5.99	Q2	H/CH3/C(=O)-O-CH		CCL4
2820M	C	5.99	Q2	H/C(=O)-O-CH2/CL		CCL4
781M	D	6.00	H	CL	S	POLYSOL-D
2418M	E	6.00	NH	C(=O)-NH2/CH2-CH		POLYSOL-D
781M	D	6.00	NH2	CH2-Q3	S	POLYSOL-D
2276M	C	6.00- 7.50	NH2	C(=O)-CH2		CDCL3
2141M	D	6.00	Q1	C(=O)-R50/OH/CH3		CCL4
2018M	C	6.00	Q2	C(=O)-CH3/H/CH3		CCL4
474M	E	6.00	Q3	CH2-NH2/H/H		CDCL3
1299M	C	6.00	Q3	CH2-SO3-NA		D20
1256M	C	6.00- 7.00		UNSPECIFIED		CCL4
1525M	E	6.00- 6.30		UNSPECIFIED		CCL4
261M	B	6.01	CH	CL/CL/CH(CL/CH)		CCL4
2268M	C	6.01 APP.	CHR	R6R50<=CH-CH2/CH2-CH*>		CDCL3
146M	C	6.01	CHR	R6<=C(A)-CH2/CH2-CH2>		CCL4
2186M	A	6.01	CH2R	R500A(O-C*/O-C*)		CDCL3
2420M	C	6.01	NH	C(=O)-NH2/CH2-CH2		DMSO-D6
1947M	B	6.01	OH	A<C-CH-C(OH)/CH-C(OH)>		C3H60
369M	B	6.01	Q2	CH2-BR/CH2-BR		CDCL3
2671M	C	6.01- 6.53	Q2	CH3/Q2(C(=O)-OK)		D20
2530M	C	6.01- 6.51	Q2	C(=O)-OH/Q2(CH3)		CDCL3
2530M	C	6.01- 6.51	Q2	Q2(C(=O)-OH)/CH3		CDCL3
2671M	C	6.01- 6.53	Q2	Q2(C(=O)-OK)/CH3		D20
2904M	D	6.01	Q3	CH2-O-C(=O)/H/H		CDCL3
2454M	B	6.02	CHR	R6NN<=C(CH3)-NH/C(=O)-NH>		TFA
2813M	F	6.02	Q2	H/CH3/O-C(=O)-CH2		CCL4
2395M	B	6.02	Q3	H/H/R5NA<N-C(=O)/C(=O)>		CDCL3
536M	D	6.03	CHA	A<C(NH2)-CH-C(NH2)/CH-C(CH3)>		CDCL3
2304M	C	6.03	NH	C(=O)-Q3/C(CH3/CH3/CH3)		CDCL3
2856M	D	6.03	Q1	C(=O)-O-CH2/A/CH3		CCL4
2808M	E	6.03 APP.	Q3	C(=O)-O-CH2/H/H		CCL4
352M	A	6.04	CH	BR/BR/CH(BR/BR)		CCL4
2812M	F	6.04	Q2	H/CH3/C(=O)-O-CH2		CCL4
511M	C	6.05- 6.37	CHA	A(C(NH2)-CH-C(CH3)/CH-C(F))		CCL4
511M	C	6.05- 6.37	CHA	A(C(NH2)/C(CH3)-C(F))		CCL4
1899M	C	6.06	CHA	A(C(NH2)/C(OH))		DMSO
894M	C	6.06 APP.	Q2	CH3/H/Q2(H/C(=O)-NH/H)		POLYSOL-D
2810M	E	6.06	Q2	H/CH3/C(=O)-O-CH2		CCL4
1539M	E	6.06	Q3	CH2-O/H/H		CDCL3
575M	A	6.07	CHR	R5N(=CH-NH/CH=CH)		CCL4

BOOK NO.	ASSIGN-MENT	CHEM SHIFT - ppm -	PROTON GROUP	ENVIRONMENTAL GROUPS	S	SOLVENT
2026M	C	6.07	CHR	R6<=C(CL)-CH2/C(=O)-CH2>		CCL4
162M	D	6.07	Q1	CH2.9-CH3/A/A		CDCL3
2608M	A	6.08	CH2R	R500A<O-C*/O-C*>		POLYSOL-D
499M	C	6.09	CHA	A<C(NH2)-CH-C(CH3)/C(CH3)>		CCL4
677M	C	6.09 APP.	CHR	R5N<=CH-NH/CH=C(CH2-N)>		CDCL3
677M	C	6.09 APP.	CHR	R5N<=C(CH2-N)-NH/CH=CH>		CDCL3
1692M	E	6.09	CHR	R60(=C(CH3)-CH2/O-C(CH2-OH/CH3))		CDCL3
2029M	D	6.09	CHR	R6<=C(CL)-CH2/C(=O)-CH2>		CCL4
1880M	C	6.09	OH	A<C-CH-C(CH2-CH3)>		CDCL3
2828M	C	6.09	Q2	C(=O)-O-CH/C(=O)-O-CH/H		CCL4
2305M	F	6.09 APP.	Q3	C(=O)-NH/H/H		CDCL3
2807M	E	6.09 APP.	Q3	C(=O)-O-CH2/H/H		CCL4
2305M	G	6.09 APP.	Q3	H/H/C(=O)-NH		CDCL3
256M	A	6.10	CH	CL/CL/C		CCL4
345M	A	6.10	CH	CL/F/C(BR/F2)		CCL4
1345M	C	6.10	NH	C(=S)-NH/CH(CH3/CH3)		CDCL3
2020M	C	6.10	Q1	C(=O)-CH3/CH3/CH3		CDCL3
1019M	B	6.10 APP.	Q2	CH2-S/H/A		CDCL3
2672M	A	6.10	Q2	C(=O)-ONA/C(=O)-ONA/H		D2O
675M	B	6.11	CHR	R5N<=CH-N(CH3)/CH=CH>		CDCL3
2024M	C	6.11	CHR	R5<=C(CL)-CH2/C(=O)-CH2>		CCL4
707M	A	6.11	NH2	AN<C-N-CH-C(CL)>		DMSO-D6
2910M	B	6.11	NH2	A<C-C(C(=O)-O-CH3)/CH-C(C(=O)-O-CH3)>		POLYSOL-D
2279M	E	6.11	NH2	C(=O)-CH2		CDCL3
1875M	A	6.11	OH	A		CDCL3
1071M	B	6.12	NH2	A<C-CH-C(CH3)-C(NO2)>		POLYSOL-D
2147M	D	6.12	Q1	C(=O)-A/OH/CH3		CDCL3
2846M	D	6.12	Q2	H/CH3/C(=O)-O-CH2		CDCL3
1408M	G	6.12	Q2	O-CH2/H/CH3		CCL4
1579M	B	6.13	CHR	R5NO(=CH-O/C(CH3)=N)		CCL4
1574M	C	6.13	CHR	R5O<=CH-O/CH=C(CH3)>		CCL4
2156M	D	6.13	Q2	C(=O)-H/H/CH2.2-CH3		CDCL3
1577M	C	6.14	CHR	R5O(=C(CH2-SH)-O/CH=CH)		CDCL3
2549M	B	6.14	Q2	CH2-C(=O)-OH/A		CDCL3
1948M	C	6.15	OH	AR5(C-C*/CH2-OH)		CDCL3
2829M	E	6.15	Q2	C(=O)-O-CH2/C(=O)-O-CH2		CCL4
509M	B	6.15- 6.60		UNSPECIFIED		CDCL3
489M	C	6.15- 6.55		UNSPECIFIED		CCL4
2432M	B	6.16	NH	C(=O)-NH/CH2-A		POLYSOL-D
2841M	C	6.16	Q2	CH2-O-C(=O)/A		CCL4
1561M	E	6.18 APP.	CHA	A(C(NH2)-CH-C(O-CH2)/CH-C(O-CH2))		CDCL3
1561M	E	6.18 APP.	CHA	A(C(O-CH2)-C(O-CH2)/C(NH2))		CDCL3
606M	B	6.18	CHR	R5NA<C*/=C(CH3)-NH>		CDCL3
595M	C	6.18	CH2	NH-A/A		CDCL3
2843M	E	6.18	Q2	CH2-O-C(=O)/H/A		CCL4
2809M	E	6.18	Q3	C(=O)-O-CH2/H/H		CCL4
2017M	C	6.18 APP.	Q3	H/C(=O)-CH3		CCL4
374M	A	6.19	CH	BR/A/A		CDCL3
1562M	F	6.19	CHA	A<C(O-CH2.3)-CH-C(NH2)/CH-C(O-CH2.3)>		CDCL3
1348M	C	6.19	NH	C(=S)-NH/CH2-CH3		CDCL3
2842M	E	6.19	Q2	CH2-O-C(=O)/H/A		CCL4
2305M	F	6.19 APP.	Q3	C(=O)-NH/H/H		CDCL3
2845M	C	6.19 APP.	Q3	C(=O)-O-CH2/H/H		CCL4
2305M	G	6.19 APP.	Q3	H/HC(=O)-NH		CDCL3
1350M	D	6.20 APP.	NH	C(=S)-NH/CH2-Q3		CDCL3
2285M	E	6.20 APP.	NH2	C(=O)-CH		CDCL3
1522M	D	6.20 APP.		UNSPECIFIED		CDCL3
1929M	B	6.21	CHA	A(C(OH)-CH-C(OH)/CH-C(CH2-A))		DMSO-D6
888M	B	6.21	NH	QN(CH3/A)/A		CDCL3
1506M	D	6.21	Q2	A(C-CH-CH-C(O-CH3))/CH3		CCL4
966M	B	6.22	Q3	H/H/C:N		CCL4
709M	B	6.23	NH	AN<C-CH-N>/CH2-A		DMSO-D6
2298M	F	6.23	NH	C(=O)-CH2/CH3		CDCL3
1786M	D	6.23	Q1	OH/CL/CH2-CL		CCL4
497M	D	6.25	CHA	A<C(NH2)-C(CH3)/C(CH3)>		CCL4
1577M	D	6.25	CHR	R5O(=CH-O/CH=C(CH2-SH))		CDCL3
2278M	E	6.25	NH2	C(=O)-CH2		CDCL3
1562M	G	6.26	CHA	A<C(NH2)-C(O-CH2.3)/C(O-CH2.3)>		CDCL3
894M	D	6.26	Q2	Q2(H/C(=O)-NH/H)/H/CH3		POLYSOL-D
874M	D	6.26- 7.40		UNSPECIFIED		CCL4
1729M	B	6.27	OH	CH2-AN		CDCL3
2556M	A	6.27	OH	C(C(=O)-OH/A/A)		C3H6O
2556M	A	6.27	OH	C(=O)-C		C3H6O
1257M	C	6.27	Q2	CH2-SO2/H/A		CDCL3
2531M	A	6.27	Q2	C(=O)-OH/CL/H		POLYSOL-D
1927M	E	6.28	CHA	A<C(OH)-C(CH2-CH2)/C(OH)>		CDCL3
199M	B	6.28	CHR	R5A(=CH-C*/CH2-C*)		CCL4
1610M	D	6.28	CHR	R600R6BI<=CH-C*(CH(CH3/CH3))/C*((CH3)/O/CH2)>		CCL4
1377M	C	6.28	NH	SO2-NH/R6		POLYSOL-D
2148M	C	6.28	Q1	C(=O)-A/OH/CH2-C(=O)-A		POLYSOL-D
2605M	A	6.28	Q2	C(=O)-OH/H/R5O<C=CH/O>		CDCL3

BOOK NO.	ASSIGN-MENT	CHEM SHIFT - ppm -	PROTON GROUP	ENVIRONMENTAL GROUPS	S	SOLVENT
2934M	C	6.28	Q2	C(=O)-O-CH2/H/R50(C=OH/O)		CDCL3
2017M	D	6.28 APP.	Q3	H/C(=O)-CH3		CCL4
499M	D	6.29	CHA	A<C(CH3)-CH-C(NH2)/C(CH3)>		CCL4
1928M	D	6.29	CHA	A<C(OH)-CH-C(OH)/CH-C(CH2.15-CH3)>		POLYSOL-D
2182M	A	6.29	CHR	R5N<=CH-NH/CH-C(C(=O)-H)>		CDCL3
1733M	C	6.29 APP.	CHR	R50(=CH-O/CH=C(CH2-OH))		CDCL3
2931M	C	6.29	CHR	R50(=CH-O/CH=C(CH2-O-C(=O)))		CCL4
1733M	C	6.29 APP.	CHR	R50(=C(CH2-OH)-O/CH=CH)		CDCL3
2931M	C	6.29	CHR	R50(=C(CH2-O-C(=O))-O/CH=CH)		CCL4
2751M	E	6.29	NH	C(=O)-NH2/CH2-C(=O)-O		DMSO-D6
1278M	A	6.29	NH2	AR5SA(C-CH-C*-C*/CH-CH-C*)		DMSO
2306M	F	6.29 APP.	Q3	C(=O)-NH/H/H		CDCL3
2306M	F	6.29 APP.	Q3	H/H/C(=O)-NH		CDCL3
508M	B	6.29- 7.10		UNSPECIFIED		CCL4
1573M	A	6.30	CHR	R50(=CH-O/CH=CH)		CCL4
2862M	C	6.30	Q2	C(=O)-O-CH2/H/A		CCL4
488M	C	6.30- 7.10		UNSPECIFIED		CCL4
491M	D	6.30- 7.10		UNSPECIFIED		CDCL3
651M	D	6.30- 7.25		UNSPECIFIED		CCL4
2282M	A	6.31	CH	CL/CL/C(=O)-NH2		C3H6O
537M	C	6.31	CHA	A(C(NH2)-CH-C(CH3)/C(CH3)-C(NH2))		CDCL3
1711M	C	6.31	Q2	CH2-OH/H/A		CDCL3
596M	D	6.32	CHA	A<C(NH-CH2)-CH-C(CH3)>		CCL4
1927M	F	6.32	CHA	A<C(OH)-CH-C(OH)/CH-C(CH2-CH2)>		CDCL3
2879M	D	6.32	NH2	A<C-C(C(=O)-O-CH2.4)>		DMSO-D6
1404M	F	6.32	Q3	O-CH2/H/H		CCL4
583M	D	6.32- 7.23		UNSPECIFIED		CCL4
584M	E	6.32- 7.25		UNSPECIFIED		CCL4
490M	C	6.33	CHA	A<C(NH2)/CH-C(CH3)>		CCL4
1915M	C	6.33	CHA	A(C(OH)-CH-C(CH3)/C(CH3))		CCL4
1893M	A	6.33	OH	A(C-CH-CH-C(CL))		CDCL3
601M	E	6.34	CHA	AR6N<C*-NH-CH2>		CDCL3
497M	E	6.34	CHA	A<C(CH3)-CH-C(NH2)/CH-C(CH3)		CCL4
522M	B	6.34	CHA	A(C(NH2)-CH-C(CL)/CH-C(BR))		CDCL3
1902M	C	6.34	OH	A<C-CH-CH-C(CH2.2-C:N)>		CDCL3
2807M	F	6.34	Q3	H/C(=O)-O-CH2/H		CCL4
73M	E	6.34 APP.	Q3	Q2/H/H		CCL4
1583M	B	6.35	CHA	AR6NSA<C(O-CH3)-CH-C*/CH-C*-NH>		DMSO-D6
2422M	C	6.35	NH	C(=O)-NH2/CH2-A		POLYSOL-D
1406M	F	6.35	Q3	O-CH2.2/H/H		CCL4
662M	D	6.35 APP.		UNSPECIFIED		CCL4
706M	B	6.36	CHA	AN(C(NH2)-N)		CDCL3
496M	D	6.36	CHA	A(C(NH2)-C(CH3)/CH-C(CH3))		CCL4
678M	A	6.36	CHR	R5NN<=CH-N(A)/CH=N>		CDCL3
281M	A	6.36	Q2	CL/H/CL		CCL4
1877M	C	6.36- 6.70		UNSPECIFIED		CCL4
650M	D	6.36- 7.20		UNSPECIFIED		CCL4
2877M	E	6.37- 6.71	CHA	A<CH-C(C(=O)-O-CH2)-C(NH2)>		CCL4
2877M	E	6.37- 6.71	CHA	A<C(NH2)-C(C(=O)-O-CH2)>		CCL4
1928M	E	6.37	CHA	A<C(OH)-C(CH2.15-CH3)/C(OH)>		POLYSOL-D
527M	B	6.37	CHA	A(C(NH2)/CH-C(I))		CDCL3
2157M	E	6.37	Q1	CH2-CH2/C(=O)-H/CH2-CH3		CCL4
2808M	F	6.37	Q3	H/H/C(=O)-O-CH2		CCL4
1405M	F	6.37	Q3	O-CH2/H/H		CCL4
1237M	B	6.38	CHA	A<C(NH2)-CH-C(SH)>		CDCL3
605M	A	6.38	CHR	R5NA(C*/CH-NH)		CCL4
1359M	B	6.38	NH2	SO2-CH3		POLYSOL-D
2861M	B	6.38	Q2	C(=O)-O-CH2/H/A		CCL4
1414M	F	6.38	Q3	O-CH2/H/H		CCL4
1583M	C	6.39	CHA	AR6NSA<C*-S-C*/C(O-CH3)>		DMSO-D6
602M	F	6.39	CHA	AR6N<C*-NH-CH(CH3)>		CDCL3
535M	B	6.39	CHA	A<C(NH2)/CH-C(NH2)>		DMSO-D6
590M	D	6.39 APP.	CHA	A<C(NH-CH3)-CH-C(CH3)>		CDCL3
590M	D	6.39 APP.	CHA	A<C(NH-CH3)/CH3>		CDCL3
1929M	C	6.39	CHA	A(C(OH)-C(CH2-A)/C(OH))		DMSO-D6
2599M	A	6.39	CHA	A(C(OH)-C(C(=O)-OH)/C(OH))		DMSO
1881M	C	6.39	OH	A<C-CH-CH-C(CH(CH3/CH3))>		CDCL3
1559M	E	6.39	Q2	A<C-CH-C(O-CH3)>/H/CH3		CDCL3
2845M	D	6.39	Q3	H/H/C(=O)-O-CH2		CCL4
2809M	F	6.39	Q3	H/H/C(=O)-O-CH2		CCL4
1960M	A	6.40	CHA	ANN<CH-N-C(OH)/CH-N>		DMSO-D6
2640M	D	6.40	CHA	A<C(NH2)-C(CH3)/C(CH3)-C(CH3)>		CCL4
582M	C	6.40	CHA	A<C(NH-CH3)>		CCL4
591M	D	6.40	CHA	A(C(NH-CH3)/CH-C(CH3))		CDCL3
608M	B	6.40	CHR	R5NA<=CH-NH/C*-C(CH3)>		CDCL3
2023M	C	6.40 APP.	CHR	R50(=CH-O/CH=C(CH(OH/C(=O))))		DMSO
2023M	C	6.40 APP.	CHR	R50(=C(CH(OH/C(=O)))-O/CH=CH)		DMSO
1610M	E	6.40	CHR	R600R6BI<=CH-C*(CH3)/C*((CH(CH3/CH3))/O/CH2)>		CCL4
2031M	D	6.40	CHR	R6(=C(C(CH2/CH3/CH3))-C(=O)/C(=O)-CH=)		CDCL3
2857M	C	6.40	Q2	C(=O)-O-R6/H/A		CCL4
1931M	B	6.40- 6.85		UNSPECIFIED		CDCL3

BOOK NO.	ASSIGN-MENT	CHEM SHIFT - ppm -	PROTON GROUP	ENVIRONMENTAL GROUPS	S	SOLVENT
512M	B	6.40- 7.30		UNSPECIFIED		CCL4
1502M	E	6.40- 6.80		UNSPECIFIED		CCL4
2087M	A	6.41	CH	BR/C(=O)-A/A		CDCL3,
492M	D	6.41	CHA	A<C(NH2)-CH-C(CH2-CH3)>		CDCL3
519M	B	6.41	CHA	A(C(NH2)-CH-C(BR))		CDCL3
575M	B	6.41	CHR	R5N(NH-CH=/≡CH-CH=)		CCL4
2263M	A	6.41	CHR	R50(=CH-C(=O)/C(=O)-O)		D20
2575M	A	6.41	OH	C(=O)-A		C3D60
2201M	A	6.41	Q2	C(=O)-OH/A		CDCL3
2550M	A	6.41	Q2	C(=O)-OH/H/A		CDCL3
659M	C	6.41 APP.		UNSPECIFIED		CCL4
600M	D	6.42	CHA	AA<C(NH-CH2)-C*/CH-CH-C*>		CCL4
528M	C	6.42	CHA	A<C(NH2)-C(CH3)/CH-C(I)>		POLYSOL-D
510M	B	6.42	CHA	A<C(NH2)/CH-C(F)>		CCL4
648M	B	6.42- 6.72	CHA	A(CH-CH-C(N(CH3/CH3)))		CCL4
648M	B	6.42- 6.72	CHA	A(C(N(CH3/CH3)))		CCL4
2934M	D	6.42	CHR	R50(=CH-O/CH=C(Q2(H/C(=O)-O-CH2/H)))		CDCL3
2983M	D	6.42	NH	C(=O)-O-CH2/CH2-NH		CDCL3
2434M	E	6.42	NHR	R5NN<C(=O)-N(CH2-Q3)/CH2-CH2>		POLYSOL-D
2992M	C	6.42	NHR	R5NO<C(=O)-O/CH2-CH2>		CDCL3
1071M	C	6.43	CHA	A<C(NH2)/C(CH3)-C(NO2)S		POLYSOL-D
1932M	F	6.43	CHA	A<C(OH)-C(CH2-Q3)-C(CH3)/C(CH3)>		CDCL3
487M	B	6.44	CHA	A(C(NH2))		CCL4
2936M	D	6.44	CHR	R50<=CH-O/CH=C(C(=O)-O-CH2.4)>		CCL4
848M	E	6.44	H	QN(OH/CH)		CCL4
1936M	D	6.44	OH	A(C-C(CH2-A)-CH-C(CH3)/C(CH2-A))		CDCL3
1936M	D	6.44	OH	A(C-C(C(CH3/CH3/CH3))-CH-C(CH3)/C(CH2-A))		·CDCL3
849M	E	6.44	QN	CH2.5-CH3/OH		CDCL3
708M	E	6.45	CHA	AN<CH-N-C(NH-CH2)>		CDCL3
708M	E	6.45	CHA	AN<C(NH-CH2)-N>		CDCL3
1237M	C	6.45	CHA	A<C(NH2)/C(SH)>		CDCL3
1523M	D	6.45	CHA	A<C(NH-CH3)/CH-C(O-CH3)>		POLYSOL-D
2548M	B	6.45- 6.85	CHA	A(CH-CH-C(N(CH2/CH2)))		POLYSOL-D
652M	C	6.45- 6.75	CHA	A(CH-CH-C(N(CH2/CH3)))		CCL4
1916M	C	6.45- 6.95	CHA	A(CH-C(CH3)-C(OH)/CH-C(CH3))		CCL4
1915M	D	6.45	CHA	A(C(CH3)-CH-C(OH)/C(CH3))		CCL4
1916M	C	6.45- 6.95	CHA	A(C(CH3)-C(OH)-C(CH3))		CCL4
593M	E	6.45	CHA	A(C(NH-CH2)/CH-C(CH3))		CDCL3
2548M	B	6.45- 6.85	CHA	A(C(N(CH2/CH2)))		POLYSOL-D
652M	C	6.45- 6.75	CHA	A(C(N(CH2/CH3)))		CCL4
2599M	B	6.45	CHA	A(C(OH)-CH-C(OH)/CH-C(C(=O)-OH))		DMSO
2286M	E	6.45	HNH	C(=O)-CH		CCL4
2286M	F	6.45	HNH	C(=O)-CH		CCL4
1878M	B	6.45	OH	A<C-CH-CH-C(CH3)>		CDCL3
1786M	E	6.45	Q1	OH/CH2-CL/CL		CCL4
1876M	C	6.45- 7.12		UNSPECIFIED		CCL4
2039M	D	6.45- 6.76		UNSPECIFIED		CCL4
1540M	E	6.45- 7.25		UNSPECIFIED		CCL4
495M	D	6.46	CHA	A(C(CH3)-C(CH3)-C(NH2))		CCL4
495M	D	6.46	CHA	A(C(NH2)-C(CH3)-C(CH3))		CCL4
1914M	C	6.46 APP.	CHA	A(C(OH)-CH-C(CH3)/CH-C(CH3))		CCL4
1914M	C	6.46 APP.	CHA	A(C(OH)/C(CH3)-C(CH3))		CCL4
2141M	E	6.46	CHR	R50<=CH-O/CH=C(C(=O)-Q1)>		CCL4
1712M	D	6.46	Q1	CH2-OH/CH3/A		CDCL3
525M	B	6.47	CHA	A<CH-C(I)-C(NH2)>		CDCL3
1945M	A	6.47 APP.	CHA	A<C(OH)-C(OH)/CH-C(OH)>		C3H60
538M	D	6.47	CHA	A<C(NH2)-C(CH2-CH3)/C(CH2-CH3)-C(NH2)>		CDCL3
592M	E	6.47	CHA	A<C(NH-CH3)/CH-C(CH(CH3/CH3))>		CDCL3
1945M	A	6.47 APP.	CHA	A<C(OH)-C(OH)>		C3H60
2935M	D	6.47	CHR	R50<=CH-O/CH=C(C(=O)-O-CH2.2)>		CCL4
2435M	B	6.47	NH	C(=O)-N/A		CDCL3
2919M	D	6.47	OH	A<C-C(OH)-CH-C(C(=O)-O-CH2)/C(OH)>		C3D60
2919M	D	6.47	OH	A<C-C(OH)-C(OH)-C(C(=O)-O-CH2)>		C3D60
2021M	F	6.47	Q2	CH(CH2/CH2)/H/C(=O)-CH3		CCL4
706M	C	6.48	CHA	AN(CH-N-C(NH2))		CDCL3
494M	F	6.48	CHA	A<C(NH2)-C(CH(CH2/CH3))>		CCL4
1153M	A	6.48	CHR	R5NS(N=C(NH2)/≡CH-S)		DMSO-D6
2605M	B	6.48	CHR	R50<=CH-O/CH=C(Q2(H/C(=O)-OH/H))>		CDCL3
1418M	D	6.48	Q3	O-CH2/H/H		CDCL3
377M	B	6.49	CH	BR/BR/A<C-CH-C(CH3)>		CCL4
599M	C	6.49	CHA	AA(C(NH-CH3)-C*/CH-CH-C*)		CDCL3
498M	C	6.49	CHA	A<C(NH2)-CH-C(CH3)/CH-C(CH3)>		CDCL3
492M	E	6.49	CHA	A<C(NH2)/C(CH2-CH3)>		CDCL3
660M	C	6.49	CHA	A<C(N(CH3/CH3))/CH-C(CH3)>		CCL4
1911M	A	6.49 APP.	CHA	A<C(OH)-CH-C(OH)>		C3H60
1882M	C	6.49	CHA	A<C(OH)-C(C(CH3/CH3/CH3))>		CCL4
1911M	A	6.49 APP.	CHA	A<C(OH)/C(OH)>		C3H60
1564M	C	6.49	CHA	A<C(O-CH3)-CH-C(O-CH3)/CH-C(NO2)>		CDCL3
526M	B	6.49	CHA	A(C(NH2)-CH-C(I))		CDCL3
530M	C	6.49	CHA	A(C(NH2)/CH-C(CH2-A))		DMSO-D6
1946M	A	6.49	CHA	A(C(OH)-CH-C(OH)/CH-C(OH))		D20

BOOK NO.	ASSIGN-MENT	CHEM SHIFT - ppm -	PROTON GROUP	ENVIRONMENTAL GROUPS	S	SOLVENT
752M	A	6.49	NHR	R6NNNAA(N=N/C*)		DMSO
282M	A	6.49	Q1	CL/CL/CL		CCL4
2564M	B	6.49	Q2	C(=0)-OH/H/A(C-CH-CH-C(CH3))		DMSO-D6
2269M	A	6.49	Q2	C(=0)-O-C(=0)/H/A		CDCL3
710M	B	6.50	CHA	AN<C(N(CH3/CH3))/CH-N>		CDCL3
1020M	D	6.50	CHA	AR5N<C*-NH-CH2/CH-C(S-C:N)>		CDCL3
590M	E	6.50	CHA	A<C(CH3)-CH-C(NH-CH3)>		CDCL3
1071M	D	6.50	CHA	A<C(NH2)-CH-C(CH3)/CH-C(NO2)>		POLYSOL-D
587M	F	6.50	CHA	A<C(NH-CH2)>		CDCL3
654M	B	6.50- 6.80	CHA	A(CH-CH-C(N(CH2/CH2)))		CDCL3
1499M	D	6.50	CHA	A(C(CH3)-CH-C(O-CH2))		CCL4
152M	B	6.50- 7.30	CHA	A(C(CH(CH/CH2)))		CDCL3
515M	C	6.50	CHA	A(C(NH2)-C(CH3)/CH-C(CL))		CCL4
654M	B	6.50- 6.80	CHA	A(C(N(CH2/CH2)))		CDCL3
1499M	D	6.50	CHA	A(C(O-CH2)-CH-C(CH3))		CCL4
2958M	B	6.50	CHR	R60A<=C(O-C(=0)-CH3)-C*/C(=0)-O>		CDCL3
1346M	D	6.50	NH	C(=S)-NH/CH2-CH		CDCL3
2410M	B	6.50- 8.50	NH	N(CH3/CH3)/C(=0)-A		CDCL3
2289M	B	6.50 APP.	NH2	C(=0)-A		CDCL3
1360M	A	6.50 APP.	NH2	SO2-Q2		POLYSOL-D
1468M	D	6.50- 6.85		UNSEPECIFIED		CDCL3
876M	A	6.50- 7.70		UNSPECIFIED		C3H6O
905M	A	6.50- 8.05		UNSPECIFIED		CDCL3
1890M	B	6.50- 7.20		UNSPECIFIED		CCL4
152M	B	6.50- 7.30		UNSPECIFIED		CDCL3
225M	B	6.50- 7.40		UNSPECIFIED		CCL4
1494M	C	6.50- 7.20		UNSPECIFIED		CCL4
1879M	D	6.50- 7.20		UNSPECIFIED		CCL4
1569M	B	6.51	CHA	AA(C(O-CH3)/CH-CH-C*)		CCL4
2879M	E	6.51	CHA	A<CH-C(C(=0)-O-CH2.4)-C(NH2)>		DMSO-D6
2405M	C	6.51	CHA	A(C(NH2)/CH-C(CH2-C(=0)-NH))		POLYSOL-D
585M	E	6.51	CHA	A(C(NH-CH2.2))		CDCL3
2148M	D	6.51	Q1	C(=0)-CH2/OH/A		POLYSOL-D
2820M	D	6.51	Q2	H/CL/C(=0)-O-CH2		CCL4
1877M	B	6.51	OH	A(C-CH-C(CH3))		CCL4
540M	B	6.52	CHA	AA<C*-CH-C(NH2)/C(NH2)>		POLYSOL-D
1238M	B	6.52	CHA	A<C(NH2)/CH-C(SH)>		CDCL3
595M	D	6.52	CHA	A<C(NH-CH2)-C(CH3)>		CDCL3
598M	F	6.52	CHA	A<C(NH-CH)/CH-C(NH-CH)>		CDCL3
586M	D	6.52	CHA	A(C(NH-R6))		CDCL3
1498M	D	6.52- 7.18		UNSPECIFIED		CCL4
1062M	C	6.53	CHA	A<CH-C(NH-CH2)-C(NO2)>		CCL4
1718M	D	6.53	CHA	A<C(NH2)/CH-C(CH2.2-OH)>		POLYSOL-D
498M	D	6.53	CHA	A<C(NH2)/C(CH3)-C(CH3)>		CDCL3
1198M	B	6.53	CHA	A(CH-C(S-S)-C(NH2))		CDCL3
1924M	F	6.53 APP.	CHA	A(C(CH2-Q3)-CH-C(O-CH3)/CH-C(OH))		CCL4
668M	B	6.53	CHA	A(C(N(CH3/CH3))/CH-C(BR))		CDCL3
1917M	E	6.53	CHA	A(C(OH)-C(CH(CH3/CH3))/C(CH3))		CDCL3
1924M	F	6.53 APP.	CHA	A(C(O-CH3)-C(OH)/C(CH2-Q3))		CCL4
1157M	A	6.53	CHR	R6SS<=C(A)-S/S-C(A)=>		CDCL3
2258M	B	6.53	HCH	=R50<C-C(=0)/CH2-C(=0)>		CDCL3
2258M	C	6.53	HCH	=R50<C-C(=0)/CH2-C(=0)>		CDCL3
2428M	C	6.53	NH	C(=0)-NH/CH2-CH3		CDCL3
1891M	A	6.53	OH	A<C-CH-CH-C(F)>		CDCL3
2549M	C	6.53	Q2	A/CH2-C(=0)-OH		CDCL3
602M	G	6.54	CHA	AR6N<CH-C*-HCH/CH-CH-C*>		CDCL3
2878M	D	6.54	CHA	A<C(NH2)-C(C(=0)-O-R6)>		CDCL3
1944M	A	6.54	CHA	A<C(OH)-C(NO2)-C(OH)>		POLYSOL-D
518M	B	6.54	CHA	A(CH-C(BR)-C(NH2))		CDCL3
2042M	B	6.54	Q1	C(=0)-CH3/A/A		CDCL3
875M	A	6.54- 7.66		UNSPECIFIED		DMSO
1161M	C	6.55 APP.	CHA	A<CH-C(S-CH3)-C(NH2)>		CCL4
492M	F	6.55	CHA	A<C(CH2-CH3)-CH-C(NH2)>		CDCL3
1161M	C	6.55 APP.	CHA	A<C(NH2)-C(S-CH3)>		CCL4
1926M	C	6.55	CHA	A<C(OH)-C(OH)/C(CH3)>		CDCL3
649M	C	6.55 APP.	CHA	A(CH-CH-C(N(CH2/CH2)))		CCL4
231M	A	6.55- 7.10	CHA	A(C(F)-CH-C(F))		CDCL3
231M	A	6.55- 7.10	CHA	A(C(F)/C(F))		CDCL3
521M	C	6.55	CHA	A(C(NH2)-C(BR)/CH-C(CH3))		CDCL3
649M	C	6.55 APP.	CHA	A(C(N(CH2/CH2)))		CCL4
2335M	B	6.55	CHA	A(C(OH)-CH-C(NH-C(=0)))		DMSO-D6
1576M	A	6.55	CHR	R50(=CH-O/CH=C(C:N)		CCL4
2578M	A	6.55	NH2	A<C-CH-CH-C(C(=0)-OH)>		C3H6O
2578M	A	6.55	OH	C(=0)-A		C3H6O
2843M	F	6.55	Q2	A/H/CH2-O-C(=0)		CCL4
1182M	A	6.55- 7.20		UNSPECIFIED		DMSO-D6
1510M	B	6.55- 6.95		UNSPECIFIED		CCL4
1535M	C	6.55- 6.95		UNSPECIFIED		CDCL3
1955M	A	6.56	CHA	AA<C(OH)-C(NO)-C*/CH-C*>		CDCL3
1932M	G	6.56	CHA	A<C(CH3)-C(CH2-Q3)-C(OH)/C(CH3)>		CDCL3
507M	B	6.56	CHA	A<C(NH2)/CH-C(CF3)>		CDCL3

BOOK NO.	ASSIGN-MENT	CHEM SHIFT - ppm -	PROTON GROUP	ENVIRONMENTAL GROUPS	S	SOLVENT
2091M	A	6.56	CHR	R50<=CH-O/CH=C(Q2(H/C(=O)-A/H))>		CDCL3
1372M	C	6.56	NH	SO2-A/A(C-CH-CH-C(CH3))		CDCL3
1880M	D	6.56- 6.90		UNSPECIFIED		CDCL3
1961M	A	6.57	CHA	ANA<C(OH)-N-C*/CH-C*>		DMSO
601M	F	6.57	CHA	AR6N<CH-C*-CH2/CH-CH-C*>		CDCL3
582M	D	6.57	CHA	A<CH-CH-C(NH-CH3)>		CCL4
656M	D	6.57	CHA	A<CH-CH-C(N(CH2/CH2))>		CCL4
1237M	D	6.57	CHA	A<C(SH)-CH-C(NH2)>		CDCL3
520M	B	6.57	CHA	A(C(NH2)/CH-C(BR))		CDCL3
675M	C	6.57	CHR	R5N<=CH-CH=/N(CH3)-CH=>		CDCL3
1711M	D	6.57	Q2	A/H/CH2-OH		CDCL3
707M	B	6.58	CHA	AN<C(NH2)-N/CH-C(CL)>		DMSO-D6
523M	B	6.58	CHA	A<C(NH2)-C(BR)/CH-C(BR)>		CDCL3
2070M	E	6.58	CHA	A<C(NH2)/CH-C(C(=O)-CH2.2)>		CDCL3
995M	C	6.58	CHA	A<C(N(CH2/CH2))/CH-C(C:N)>		CDCL3
1913M	D	6.58	CHA	A<C(OH)-C(CH3)-C(CH3)>		CDCL3
1564M	D	6.58	CHA	A<C(O-CH3)-C(NO2)/C(O-CH3)>		CDCL3
1565M	B	6.58	CHA	A<C(O-CH3)-C(O-CH3)>		CDCL3
594M	C	6.58	CHA	A(C(NH-CH2))		CDCL3
2914M	B	6.58	CHA	A(C(OH)-CH-C(C(=O)-O-CH3)/C(OH))		DMSO-D6
1578M	A	6.58	CHR	R50<=CH-O/CH=C(Q2(H/NO2/H))>		CDCL3
971M	C	6.58	CHR	R6(=C(C:N)-CH2/CH2-CH2)		CCL4
2309M	D	6.58	NH	C(=O)-CH3/CH2.2-A		CDCL3
158M	A	6.58	Q2	A/A/H		CDCL3
504M	B	6.58- 7.20		UNSPECIFIED		DMSO-D6
886M	C	6.58- 7.25		UNSPECIFIED		CCL4
539M	B	6.59	CHA	AA(C(NH2)-C*/CH-CH-C*)		CDCL3
695M	C	6.59	CHA	AN<C(CH3)-N-C(CH3)/C(CH3)>		CCL4
1948M	D	6.59	CHA	AR5(C(OH)-C*-CH2/CH-CH-C*)		CDCL3
595M	E	6.59	CHA	A<CH-C(CH3)-C(NH-CH2)>		CDCL3
2878M	E	6.59	CHA	A<CH-C(C(=O)-O-R6)-C(NH2)>		CDCL3
1236M	B	6.59	CHA	A<C(NH2)-C(SH)>		CDCL3
2071M	E	6.59	CHA	A<C(NH2)/CH-C(C(=O)-CH2.3)>		CDCL3
487M	C	6.59 APP.	CHA	A(CH-CH-C(NH2))		CCL4
586M	E	6.59	CHA	A(CH-CH-C(NH-R6))		CDCL3
1896M	B	6.59	CHA	A(CH-C(I)-C(OH))		CDCL3
670M	C	6.59	CHA	A(C(NH2)/CH-C(N(CH2/CH2)))		CDCL3
663M	D	6.59	CHA	A(C(N(CH2/CH2))/CH-C(CH3))		CDCL3
670M	C	6.59	CHA	A(C(N(CH2/CH2))/CH-C(NH2))		CDCL3
1898M	B	6.59	CHA	A(C(OH)/CH-C(I))		CDCL3
1499M	E	6.59	CHA	A(C(O-CH2)/C(CH3))		CCL4
1584M	A	6.59	CHR	R50A<=CH-O/C*>		CCL4
2681M	A	6.59	CHR	R50<=CH-O/CH=C(C(=O)-O-K)>	S	D20
1019M	C	6.59	Q2	A/H/CH2-S		CDCL3
2821M	C	6.59	Q2	C(=O)-O-CH3/H/C(=O)-CH3		CDCL3
156M	C	6.59	Q3	A/H/H		CCL4
1558M	D	6.59 APP.		UNSPECIFIED		CCL4
287M	A	6.60	CH	CL/CL/A		CCL4
540M	C	6.60	CHA	AA<C(NH2)-CH-C*/CH-C*>		POLYSOL-D
1570M	C	6.60	CHA	AA(C(O-CH2)-C*/CH-CH-C*)		CDCL3
2634M	B	6.60	CHA	A<CH-CH-C(NH-CH2)>		DMSO-D6
760M	A	6.60	CHA	A<CH-CH-C(NH-NH)>		DMSO-D6
2063M	B	6.60- 7.10	CHA	A<C(F)-CH-C(F)/CH-C(C(=O)-CH3)>		CCL4
2063M	B	6.60- 7.10	CHA	A<C(F)-C(C(=O)-CH3)/C(F)>		CCL4
516M	B	6.60	CHA	A<C(NH2)-C(CL)/CH-C(CL)>		CDCL3
493M	D	6.60	CHA	A<C(NH2)/CH-C(CH(CH3/CH3))>		CDCL3
2634M	B	6.60	CHA	A<C(NH-CH2)>		DMSO-D6
588M	D	6.60- 7.40	CHA	A<C(NH-C)>		CDCL3
1023M	B	6.60	CHA	A<C(N(CH3/CH3))/CH-C(N=O)>		CDCL3
518M	C	6.60	CHA	A(C(NH2)-C(BR))		CDCL3
1198M	C	6.60	CHA	A(C(NH2)=C(S-S))		CDCL3
514M	B	6.60	CHA	A(C(NH2)/CH-C(CL))		DMSO
899M	B	6.60	CHA	A(C(NH2)/CH-C(N=N-A))		CDCL3
589M	D	6.60	CHA	A(C(NH-CH3)-C(CH3))		CDCL3
2934M	E	6.60	CHR	R50(=C(Q2(H/C(=O)-O-CH2/H))-O/CH=CH)		CDCL3
2264M	B	6.60	CHR	R50(=O(CH3)-C(=O)/C(=O)-O)		CCL4
2918M	D	6.60 APP.	OH	A<C-C(OH)-CH-C(C(=O)-O-CH2)/C(OH)>		C3D60
2918M	D	6.60 APP.	OH	A<C-C(OH)-C(OH)/CH-C(C(=O)-O-CH2)>		C3D60
917M	A	6.60- 7.42		UNSPECIFIED		CDCL3
234M	A	6.60- 7.80		UNSPECIFIED		CDCL3
2334M	B	6.60- 7.08		UNSPECIFIED		DMSO-D6
1892M	B	6.60- 7.38		UNSPECIFIED		CDCL3
604M	B	6.60- 7.55		UNSPECIFIED		CCL4
1495M	C	6.60		UNSPECIFIED		CCL4
1554M	C	6.60		UNSPECIFIED		CDCL3
198M	C	6.60- 7.10		UNSPECIFIED		CCL4
1489M	C	6.60- 7.30		UNSPECIFIED		CCL4
1512M	C	6.60- 7.35		UNSPECIFIED		CCL4
2932M	C	6.60- 7.38		UNSPECIFIED		CCL4
1589M	D	6.60- 7.15		UNSPECIFIED		CCL4
1583M	D	6.60- 7.15		UNSPECIFIED		DMSO-D6

BOOK NO.	ASSIGN-MENT	CHEM SHIFT - ppm -	PROTON GROUP	ENVIRONMENTAL GROUPS	S	SOLVENT
588M	D	6.60- 7.40		UNSPECIFIED		CDCL3
2987M	D	6.60- 7.50		UNSPECIFIED		CDCL3
1560M	E	6.60		UNSPECIFIED		CCL4
494M	G	6.60- 7.11		UNSPECIFIED		CCL4
376M	A	6.61	CH	BR/BR/A		CDCL3
1953M	B	6.61	CHA	AA<C(NH2)-CH-C*/CH-C*-C(OH)>		DMSO-D6
862M	B	6.61	CHA	A<CH-C(QN(A/OH))-C(NH2)>		POLYSOL-D
503M	E	6.61	CHA	A<C((CH2-CH3)-C(NH2)-C(CH2-CH3)/C(CH3)>		CCL4
1926M	D	6.61	CHA	A<C(CH3)-CH-C(OH)/CH-C(OH)>		CDCL3
529M	C	6.61	CHA	A<C(NH2)/CH-C(CH2.2-NH2)>		CDCL3
656M	E	6.61	CHA	A<C(N(CH2/CH2))>		CCL4
585M	F	6.61	CHA	A(CH-CH-C(NH-CH2.2))		CDCL3
2244M	B	6.61	CHA	A(C(O-CH3)-CH-C(C(=O)-CL)/C(O-CH3))		CCL4
2448M	C	6.61	NHR	R5NN<C(=O)-N(CH3)/CH(A)-C(=O)>		CDCL3
1724M	C	6.61 APP.	Q2	A<C-CH-CH-C(NO2)>/CH2-OH		POLYSOL-D
2842M	F	6.61	Q2	A/H/CH2-O-C(=O)		CCL4
380M	A	6.61	Q2	BR/A		CCL4
1724M	C	6.61 APP.	Q2	CH2-OH/A<C-CH-CH-C(NO2)>		POLYSOL-D
1918M	F	6.62	CHA	A<CH-C(CH2-Q3)-C(OH)/CH-C(CH3)>		CCL4
531M	B	6.62	CHA	A<C(NH2)/CH-C(A<C-CH-CH-C(NH2)>)>		DMSO-D6
2882M	D	6.62	CHA	A<C(NH2)/CH-C(C(=O)-O-CH)>		CDCL3
666M	C	6.62	CHA	A<C(N(CH3/CH3))/CH-C(CH2-A)>		CDCL3
1923M	D	6.62	CHA	A<C(OH)-C(CH3)/CH-C(S-CH3)>		CDCL3
669M	C	6.62 APP.	CHA	A(C(N(CH3/CH3)))		CDCL3
2104M	C	6.62	CHA	A(C(N(CH2/CH2))/CH-C(C(=O)-A))		CDCL3
669M	C	6.62 APP.	CHA	A(C(N(CH3/CH3))/CH-C(NH2))		CDCL3
1946M	B	6.62	CHA	A(C(OH)-C(OH)/C(OH))		D20
1277M	A	6.62	CHR	R5SA(=CH-SO2/C*)		CDCL3
2312M	C	6.62	NH	C(=O)-CH2/CH3		CDCL3
2284M	C	6.62 APP.	NH2	C(=O)-CH2		CDCL3
2841M	D	6.62	Q2	A/CH2-O-C(=O)		CCL4
1138M	A	6.62- 7.01		UNSPECIFIED		CDCL3
177M	B	6.62- 7.08		UNSPECIFIED		CCL4
502M	D	6.63	CHA	A<C(CH3)-C(NH2)-C(CH3)/C(CH3)>		CCL4
1901M	C	6.63	CHA	A<C(N(CH3/CH3))/CH-C(CH(A/A))>		POLYSOL-D
885M	C	6.63	CHA	A<C(QN(N(CH3/CH3)))/CH-C(CH3)>		CCL4
594M	D	6.63	CHA	A(CH-CH-C(NH-CH2))		CDCL3
2881M	C	6.63	CHA	A(C(NH2)/CH-C(C(=O)-O-CH3))		CDCL3
655M	B	6.63	CHA	A(C(N(CH2.2/CH2.2)))		POLYSOL-D
2170M	B	6.63	CHA	A(C(N(CH3/CH3))/CH-C(C(=O)-H))		CDCL3
2386M	B	6.63	CHR	R5N(=CH-C(=O)/C(=O)-N(CH2-A))		CDCL3
2030M	B	6.63	CHR	R6<=C(CH3)-C(=O)/C(=O)-CH=>		CDCL3
2116M	E	6.64	CHA	AR6<C*-CH2-C(=O)/C(O-CH3)>		CDCL3
587M	G	6.64	CHA	A<CH-CH-C(NH-CH2)>		CDCL3
1706M	F	6.64	CHA	A<CH-C(N(CH2/CH2))>		CDCL3
500M	E	6.64	CHA	A<CH-C(CH2-CH3)-C(NH2)/CH-C(CH3)>		CDCL3
1236M	C	6.64	CHA	A<CH-C(SH)-C(NH2)>		CDCL3
1365M	B	6.64	CHA	A<C(NH2)/CH-C(SO2-NH2)>		DMSO-D6
2133M	A	6.64	CHR	R5O<=CH-O/CH=C(C(=O)-C(=O))>		CDCL3
2023M	D	6.64	CHR	R5O(=CH-O/CH=C(C(=O)-CH))		DMSO
1139M	A	6.64	CHR	R5S<=C(CL)-S/CH=C(CL)>		CCL4
370M	A	6.64	Q2	BR/BR/H		CCL4
877M	A	6.64- 7.39		UNSPECIFIED		CDCL3
1098M	B	6.64- 7.30		UNSPECIFIED		CDCL3
2596M	B	6.65	CHA	A<C(CH3)-CH-C(OH)/CH-C(C(=O)-OH)>		POLYSOL-D
757M	B	6.65	CHA	A<C(CL)-CH-C(NH-NH2)/CH-C(CL)>		CDCL3
1024M	C	6.65	CHA	A<C(N(CH2/CH2))/CH-C(N=O)>		CDCL3
1562M	H	6.65	CHA	A<C(O-CH2.3)-C(NH2)/CH-C(O-CH2.3)>		CDCL3
589M	E	6.65	CHA	A(CH-C(CH3)-C(NH-CH3))		CDCL3
1519M	B	6.65	CHA	A(CH-C(I)-C(O-CH3))		CDCL3
1500M	D	6.65	CHA	A(C(O-CH2)/CH-C(CH3))		CCL4
1506M	E	6.65	CHA	A(C(O-CH3)/CH-C(Q2(CH3)))		CCL4
1493M	D	6.65- 7.40	CHA	A(C(O-CH))		CCL4
2277M	D	6.65 APP.	HNH	C(=O)-CH2		DMSO-D6
1966M	F	6.65	NH	A<C-C(CH3)-CH-C(CH3)>/CH2-R5NN		CDCL3
224M	B	6.65- 7.27		UNSPECIFIED		CCL4
1875M	B	6.65- 7.32		UNSPECIFIED		CDCL3
1527M	B	6.65- 7.05		UNSPECIFIED	S	POLYSOL-D
1907M	C	6.65- 7.20		UNSPECIFIED		DMSO-D6
1715M	C	6.65- 7.45		UNSPECIFIED		CCL4
1493M	D	6.65- 7.40		UNSPECIFIED		CCL4
496M	E	6.66	CHA	A(C(CH3)-CH-C(CH3)/CH-C(NH2))		CCL4
2533M	A	6.66	Q2	C(=O)-OH/H/C(=O)-OH		DMSO-D6
1088M	B	6.66- 7.09		UNSPECIFIED		CDCL3
2595M	B	6.67	CHA	A<C(NH2)-C(C(=O)-OH)/CH-C(O-CH3)>		POLYSOL-D
2078M	B	6.67	CHA	A<C(OH)/C(CH3)-C(C(=O)-CH3)>		DMSO-D6
533M	B	6.67	CHA	A(CH-C(NH2)-C(NH2))		CDCL3
533M	B	6.67	CHA	A(C(NH2)-C(NH2))		CDCL3
900M	B	6.67	CHA	A(C(N(CH3/CH3))/CH-C(N=N-A))		CDCL3
2294M	A	6.67	CHR	R5O(=CH-O/CH=C(C(=O)-NH2))		DMSO
2121M	C	6.67	CHR	R6A<=C(R6<CH-CH2/CH2>)-C(=O)/C(=O)-C*>		CDCL3

BOOK NO.	ASSIGN-MENT	CHEM SHIFT - ppm -	PROTON GROUP	ENVIRONMENTAL GROUPS	S	SOLVENT
1344M	'C	6.67	NH	C(=S)-NH/CH2-CH3		CCL4
302M	A	6.67- 7.40		UNSPECIFIED		CCL4
1551M	D	6.68	CHA	A<C(CH3)-C(CH3)-C(O-CH3)>		CDCL3
532M	C	6.68	CHA	A(C(NH2)-C(CH3)/CH-C(A(C-CH-C(CH3)-C(NH2))))		CDCL3
1513M	C	6.68	CHA	A(C(O-CH2)/CH-C(CL))		CCL4
1521M	B	6.68	CHA	A(C(O-CH3)/CH-C(I))		CDCL3
199M	C	6.68	CHR	R5A(C*/=CH-CH2)		CCL4
2310M	D	6.68	NH	C(=O)-CH3/CH(A/CH3)		CDCL3
2041M	D	6.68	Q2	C(=O)-CH2.3/H/A		CDCL3
2440M	B	6.68- 7.18		UNSPECIFIED		CDCL3
597M	B	6.68- 7.38		UNSPECIFIED		CDCL3
1925M	C	6.68		UNSPECIFIED		CDCL3
189M	B	6.69	CHA	A<C(CH3)-CH-C(CH3)/C(CH3)>		CCL4
192M	B	6.69	CHA	A<C(CH3)-C(CH3)/C(CH3)>		CCL4
1913M	E	6.69	CHA	A<C(CH3)-C(CH3)-C(OH)>		CDCL3
653M	D	6.69	CHA	A<C(N(CH2/CH2))>		CDCL3
1884M	E	6.69	CHA	A<C(OH)/CH-C(CH2.4-CH3)>		CCL4
1888M	B	6.69	CHA	A<C(OH)/CH-C(CH2-A)>		DMSO-D6
1878M	C	6.69	CHA	A<C(OH)/CH-C(CH3)>		CDCL3
1552M	D	6.69	CHA	A<C(O-CH3)-C(CH3)/CH-C(CH3)>		CDCL3
1523M	E	6.69	CHA	A<C(O-CH3)/CH-C(NH-CH3)>		POLYSOL-D
519M	C	6.69	CHA	A(C(BR)/C(NH2))		CDCL3
522M	C	6.69	CHA	A(C(CL)-C(BR)/C(NH2))		CDCL3
511M	D	6.69	CHA	A(C(F)-C(CH3)/CH-C(NH2))		CCL4
1910M	A	6.69	CHA	A(C(OH)-C(OH))		POLYSOL-D
1895M	B	6.69	CHA	A(C(OH)/CH-C(BR))		CDCL3
1516M	B	6.69	CHA	A(C(O-CH3)/CH-C(BR))		CCL4
608M	C	6.69	CHR	R5NA<=CH-C*/NH-C*>		CDCL3
677M	D	6.69	CHR	R5N<=CH-CH=/NH-C(CH2-N)=>		CDCL3
2091M	B	6.69	CHR	R5O<=C(Q2(H/C(=O)-A/H))-O/CH=CH>		CDCL3
2433M	E	6.69	NHR	R5NN<C(=O)-N(CH2.3-CH3)/CH2-CH2>		CCL4
1897M	A	6.70- 7.00	CHA	A<CH-C(I)/CH-C(OH)>		POLYSOL-D
759M	B	6.70- 7.30	CHA	A<C(N(NH2/A))>		CDCL3
2078M	C	6.70	CHA	A<C(OH)-CH-C(CH3)/CH-C(C(=O)-CH3)>		DMSO-D6
1897M	A	6.70- 7.00	CHA	A<C(OH)-CH-C(I)>		POLYSOL-D
1901M	D	6.70	CHA	A<C(OH)/CH-C(CH(A/A))>		POLYSOL-D
1908M	B	6.70	CHA	A<C(OH)/CH-C(C(A/CH3/CH3))>		POLYSOL-D
2215M	B	6.70- 7.40	CHA	A<C(O-CH2)>		CCL4
2090M	C	6.70- 7.30	CHA	A<C(O-CH)>		CDCL3
884M	B	6.70- 7.30	CHA	A<C(QN-N)>		CCL4
655M	C	6.70	CHA	A(CH-CH-C(N(CH2.2/CH2.2)))		POLYSOL-D
901M	C	6.70	CHA	A(C(NH2)/CH-C(N=N-A))		DMSO-D6
901M	D	6.70	CHA	A(C(N(CH3/CH3))/CH-C(N=N-A))		DMSO-D6
1886M	E	6.70	CHA	A(C(OH)/CH-C(C(CH2/CH3/CH3)))		CDCL3
1550M	A	6.70 APP.	CHA	A(C(O-A)-CH-C(O-A))		CDCL3
1550M	A	6.70 APP.	CHA	A(C(O-A)/C(O-A))		CDCL3
1561M	F	6.70	CHA	A(C(O-CH2)-C(O-CH2)/CH-C(NH2))		CDCL3
1519M	C	6.70	CHA	A(C(O-CH3)-C(I))		CDCL3
2246M	A	6.70	CHR	R5O<=CH-O/CH=C(C(=O)-CL)>		CCL4
2308M	D	6.70- 7.80	NH	C(=O)-H/CH(CH2/CH2)		DMSO-D6
2018M	D	6.70	Q2	CH3/H/C(=O)-CH3		CCL4
389M	A	6.70- 7.60		UNSPECIFIED		CCL4
994M	B	6.70- 7.05		UNSPECIFIED		POLYSOL-D
884M	B	6.70- 7.30		UNSPECIFIED		CCL4
759M	B	6.70- 7.30		UNSPECIFIED		CDCL3
2215M	B	6.70- 7.40		UNSPECIFIED		CCL4
2559M	B	6.70- 7.50		UNSPECIFIED		CDCL3
658M	C	6.70- 7.18		UNSPECIFIED		CCL4
2090M	C	6.70- 7.30		UNSPECIFIED		CDCL3
2103M	C	6.70- 7.30		UNSPECIFIED		DMSO-D6
1355M	D	6.70- 7.40		UNSPECIFIED		CDCL3
603M	E	6.70- 7.20		UNSPECIFIED		CCL4
2116M	F	6.71	CHA	AR6<C(O-CH3)-CH-C*/CH-C*-CH2>		CDCL3
976M	C	6.71	CHA	A<CH-CH-C(N(CH2.2/CH2.2))>		DMSO-D6
1517M	C	6.71	CHA	A<CH-C(BR)-C(O-CH2)>		CCL4
664M	E	6.71	CHA	A<C(CH3-CH-C(N(CH2/CH2))/CH-C(CH3)>		CCL4
525M	C	6.71	CHA	A<C(NH2)-C(I)>		CDCL3
2596M	C	6.71	CHA	A<C(OH)-C(C(=O)-OH)/C(CH3)>		POLYSOL-D
2336M	B	6.71	CHA	A<C(OH)/CH-C(NH-C(=O)-CH3)>		POLYSOL-D
1503M	D	6.71	CHA	A<C(O-CH3)/CH-C(CH2.2-BR)>		CCL4
1501M	E	6.71	CHA	A<C(O-CH3)/CH-C(CH2-CH2)>		CCL4
1497M	D	6.71	CHA	A<C(O-CH3)/CH-C(CH2-CH3)>		CCL4
1917M	F	6.71	CHA	A(C(CH3)-CH-C(OH)/CH-C(CH(CH3/CH3)))		CDCL3
1920M	B	6.71	CHA	A(C(CL)-CH-C(CL)/C(OH))		CDCL3
921M	B	6.71	CHA	A(C(N=C=O)-C(CH3)/C(N=C=O))		CCL4
1924M	G	6.71	CHA	A(C(OH)-C(O-CH3)/CH-C(CH2-Q3))		CCL4
1893M	B	6.71	CHA	A(C(OH)/CH-C(CL))		CDCL3
1710M	B	6.71	CHA	A(C(O-CH2))		CCL4
1518M	C	6.71	CHA	A(C(O-CH2)/CH-C(BR))		CDCL3
2387M	A	6.71	CHR	R5N(=CH-C(=O)/C(=O)-N(A(C-C(CL))))		CDCL3
1142M	A	6.71	CHR	R5S<=C(BR)-S/CH=C(BR)>		CCL4

BOOK NO.	ASSIGN-MENT	CHEM SHIFT - ppm -	PROTON GROUP	ENVIRONMENTAL GROUPS	S	SOLVENT
1678M	D	6.71	CHR	R5S<=C(CH2.2-OH)-S/CH=CH>		CCL4
2430M	C	6.71	NH	C(=O)-NH/CH2-OH		DMSO-D6
849M	D	6.71	QN	CH2.5-CH3/OH		CDCL3
2826M	C	6.71	Q2	C(=O)-O-CH/H/C(=O)-O-CH		CCL4
223M	A	6.71- 7.43		UNSPECIFIED		CCL4
1734M	D	6.71 APP.		UNSPECIFIED		CDCL3
2890M	D	6.72	CHA	A<CH-C(C(=O)-O-CH2)-C(OH)>		CCL4
1706M	G	6.72	CHA	A<C(N(CH2/CH2))>		CDCL3
1926M	E	6.72	CHA	A<C(OH)-C(OH)/CH-C(CH3)>		CDCL3
674M	B	6.72	CHA	A<C(R5NN<N-C(A)=/CH2>)>		CDCL3
1239M	D	6.72	CHA	A(C(CH3)-CH-C(SH)/CH-C(SH))		CDCL3
191M	C	6.72	CHA	A(C(CH3)-C(CH3)-C(CH3)/CH-C(CH3))		CCL4
496M	F	6.72	CHA	A(C(CH3)-C(NH2)/C(CH3))		CCL4
761M	C	6.72	CHA	A(C(N(N/CH3))/CH-C(CH3))		CDCL3
1511M	B	6.72	CHA	A(C(O-CH3)/CH-C(CL))		CCL4
2384M	C	6.72	CHR	R5N<=CH-C(=O)/C(=O)-N(CH2-CH3)>		CDCL3
1143M	A	6.72	CHR	R5S<=CH-S/CH=C(I)>		CDCL3
2892M	B	6.72 APP.	OH	A(C-CH-C(C(=O)-O-CH3))		CDCL3
1257M	D	6.72	Q2	A/H/CH2-SO2		CDCL3
190M	C	6.73	CHA	A<C(CH2-CH3)-CH-C(CH2-CH3)/C(CH2-CH3)>		CCL4
304M	B	6.73	CHA	A<C(F)-CH-C(CL)/CH-C(CH3)>		CCL4
505M	B	6.73	CHA	A<C(NH2)/CH-C(A)>		C3H6O
1723M	D	6.73	CHA	A<C(O-CH3)/CH-C(CH2-OH)>		CCL4
2605M	C	6.73	CHR	R5O<=C(Q2(H/C(=O)-OH))-O/CH=CH>		CDCL3
1939M	A	6.73	OH	A<C-C(NO2)-CH-C(NO2)/C(NO2)>		C3D6O
2828M	D	6.73	Q2	C(=O)-O-CH/H/C(=O)-O-CH		CCL4
1894M	B	6.74	CHA	A<CH-C(BR)-C(OH)>		CDCL3
1882M	D	6.74	CHA	A<CH-C(C(CH3/CH3/CH3))-C(OH)>		CCL4
1505M	D	6.74 APP.	CHA	A<C(CH2-NH2)-CH-C(O-CH3)>		CDCL3
1505M	D	6.74 APP.	CHA	A<C(O-CH3)-CH-C(CH2-NH2)>		CDCL3
1710M	C	6.74	CHA	A(CH-CH-C(O-CH2))		CCL4
534M	D	6.74	CHA	A(CH-C(NH2)/CH-C(NH2))		POLYSOL-D
919M	B	6.74- 6.90	CHA	A(C(CH3)-CH-C(QN(=O))/CH-C(CH3))		CCL4
1885M	E	6.74	CHA	A(C(OH)/CH-C(C(CH2/CH3/CH3)))		CCL4
919M	B	6.74- 6.90	CHA	A(C(QN(=O))-C(CH3)/C(CH3))		CCL4
1953M	D	6.75- 7.10	CHA	AA<C(OH)-C*/CH-CH-C*>		DMSO-D6
1953M	D	6.75- 7.10	CHA	AA<C*-CH-C(NH2)/CH-CH-C(OH)>		DMSO-D6
1948M	E	6.75	CHA	AR5(C*-CH2-CH2/CH-CH-C(OH))		CDCL3
602M	H	6.75- 7.20	CHA	AR6N<CH-C*-NH/CH-CH-C*>		CDCL3
602M	H	6.75- 7.20	CHA	AR6N<C*-HCH-HCH>		CDCL3
889M	B	6.75- 7.10	CHA	A<CH-CH-C(NH-QN)>		DMSO-D6
916M	A	6.75- 7.20	CHA	A<C(F)-C(N=C=O)>		CCL4
510M	C	6.75	CHA	A<C(F)/CH-C(NH2)>		CCL4
940M	A	6.75- 7.55	CHA	A<C(F)/C(N=C=S)>		CCL4
506M	B	6.75	CHA	A<C(NH2)-CH-C(CF3)>		CDCL3
1070M	C	6.75	CHA	A<C(NH2)-CH-C(NO2)/CH-C(CH3)>		CDCL3
1062M	D	6.75	CHA	A<C(NH-CH2)-C(NO2)>		CCL4
889M	B	6.75- 7.10	CHA	A<C(NH-QN)>		DMSO-D6
1887M	D	6.75	CHA	A<C(OH)/CH-C(R6<CH-CH2/CH2>)>		CDCL3
1542M	A	6.75	CHA	A<C(O-A)/CH-C(BR)>		CCL4
2839M	D	6.75	CHA	A<C(O-CH3)/CH-C(CH2-O-C(=O))>		CCL4
519M	D	6.75- 7.06	CHA	A(CH-C(BR)/CH-C(NH2))		CDCL3
2887M	B	6.75- 7.07	CHA	A(CH-C(C(=O)-O-CH3)-C(O-CH3))		CCL4
519M	D	6.75- 7.06	CHA	A(C(BR)-CH-C(NH2))		CDCL3
2038M	D	6.75	CHA	A(C(CH2-CH2)/CH-C(OH))		CDCL3
1883M	C	6.75	CHA	A(C(OH)/CH-C(C(CH3/CH3/CH3)))		CDCL3
1507M	B	6.75	CHA	A(C(O-CH3)-C(A))		CCL4
2887M	B	6.75- 7.07	CHA	A(C(O-CH3)-C(C(=O)-O-CH3))		CCL4
607M	B	6.75	CHR	R5NA<N(H)-C*/=C(CH3)-C*>		CDCL3
1260M	A	6.75	CHR	R5S<SO2-CH=/=C(CL)-C(CL)>		CDCL3
2989M	B	6.75- 7.50		UNSPECIFIED		CDCL3
2119M	B	6.76	CHA	AA<C(=O)-C*/C(CH3)-C(=O)-C*>		CDCL3
1310M	A	6.76	CHA	AA(C(NH2)-C*/CH-C(SO3-NA)-C*)		D2O
1545M	B	6.76	CHA	A<CH-C(O-CH3)-C(O-CH3)>		CCL4
497M	F	6.76	CHA	A<C(CH3)-C(NH2)/CH-C(CH3)>		CCL4
1943M	A	6.76	CHA	A<C(CL)-C(OH)-C(CL)/C(OH)>		POLYSOL-D
2879M	F	6.76	CHA	A<C(NH2)-C(C(=O)-O-CH2.4)>		DMSO-D6
2578M	B	6.76	CHA	A<C(NH2)/CH-C(C(=O)-OH)>		C3H6O
760M	B	6.76	CHA	A<C(NH-NH)>		DMSO-D6
1517M	D	6.76	CHA	A<C(O-CH2)-C(BR)>		CCL4
1551M	E	6.76	CHA	A<C(O-CH3)-C(CH3)-C(CH3)>		CDCL3
1545M	B	6.76	CHA	A<C(O-CH3)-C(O-CH3)>		CCL4
427M	B	6.76	CHA	A(C(CH3)-C(I))		CDCL3
901M	C	6.76	CHA	A(C(NH2)/CH-C(N=N-A))		DMSO-D6
901M	D	6.76	CHA	A(C(N(CH3/CH3))/CH-C(N=N-A))		DMSO-D6
605M	B	6.76	CHR	R5NA(NH-C*/CH-C*)		CCL4
2296M	D	6.76	NH	C(=O)-CH2/CH3		CDCL3
610M	C	6.76- 7.71		UNSPECIFIED		DMSO-D6
2640M	E	6.77	CHA	A<C(CH3)-C(NH2)/C(CH3)-C(CH3)>		CCL4
2880M	C	6.77	CHA	A<C(NH2)-CH-C(C(=O)-O-CH3)>		CDCL3
1902M	D	6.77	CHA	A<C(OH)/CH-C(CH2.2-C:N)>		CDCL3

BOOK NO.	ASSIGN-MENT	CHEM SHIFT - ppm -	PROTON GROUP	ENVIRONMENTAL GROUPS	S	SOLVENT
1515M	B	6.77	CHA	A(C(O-CH3)-CH-C(BR))		CDCL3
2425M	C	6.77	CHA	A(C(O-CH3)/CH-C(NH-C(=O)-NH2))		POLYSOL-D
1137M	B	6.77 APP.	CHR	R5S<=CH-S/C(CH3)=CH>		CCL4
1137M	B	6.77 APP.	CHR	R5S<=C(CH3)-CH=/S-CH=>		CCL4
318M	A	6.78	CHA	AA<C-C*-CH/C(CL)>		CDCL3
1588M	B	6.78	CHA	A<CH-C*-O>		CCL4
432M	A	6.78	CHA	A<C(F)/CH-C(I)>		CDCL3
1881M	D	6.78	CHA	A<C(OH)/CH-C(CH(CH3/CH3))>		CDCL3
1588M	B	6.78	CHA	A<C*-O>		CCL4
1899M	D	6.78	CHA	A(CH-C(NH2)/CH-C(OH))		DMSO
387M	C	6.78	CHA	A(C(CH3)-C(BR)-C(CH3)/C(CH3))		CCL4
2385M	C	6.78	CHR	R5N<=CH-C(=O)/C(=O)-N(CH2.2-A)>		POLYSOL-D
2030M	C	6.78	CHR	R6<=CH-C(=O)/C(=O)-CH=>		CDCL3
2030M	C	6.78	CHR	R6<=CH-C(=O)/C(=O)-C(CH3)=>		CDCL3
2022M	D	6.78	CHR	R6<=C(C(=O)-CH3)-CH2/CH2-CH2>		CCL4
1541M	A	6.78- 7.40		UNSPECIFIED		CDCL3
392M	A	6.78- 7.60		UNSPECIFIED		CCL4
2328M	B	6.78- 7.40		UNSPECIFIED		CDCL3
734M	A	6.79	CHA	ANN<CH-N-C(NH2)/CH-N>		D20
1591M	A	6.79 APP.	CHA	AR600A<CH-C*-O/CH-CH-C*>		CDCL3
1591M	A	6.79 APP.	CHA	AR600A<C*-O-C*>		CDCL3
436M	A	6.79	CHA	A<CH-C(I)/CH-C(I)>		CDCL3
536M	E	6.79	CHA	A<C(CH3)-C(NH2)/CH-C(NH2)>		CDCL3
490M	D	6.79	CHA	A<C(CH3)/CH-C(NH2)>		CCL4
862M	C	6.79	CHA	A<C(NH2)-C(QN(A/OH))>		POLYSOL-D
976M	D	6.79	CHA	A<C(N(CH2.2/CH2.2))>		DMSO-D6
2178M	B	6.79	CHA	A<C(OH)-C(C(=O)-H)/CH-C(O-CH3)>		CCL4
1891M	B	6.79	CHA	A<C(OH)/CH-C(F)>		CDCL3
1492M	D	6.79 APP.	CHA	A<C(O-CH2.2)>		CCL4
1792M	E	6.79	CHA	A<C(O-CH2)>		CCL4
1520M	B	6.79	CHA	A<C(O-CH3)-CH-C(I)>		CCL4
309M	B	6.79- 7.28	CHA	A(CH-C(CL)-C(CH3)/CH-C(CL))		CCL4
526M	C	6.79	CHA	A(CH-C(I)/CH-C(NH2))		CDCL3
763M	D	6.79	CHA	A(C(CH3)-C(N(N/CH3))-C(CH3)/C(CH3))		CDCL3
309M	B	6.79- 7.28	CHA	A(C(CL)-C(CH3)-C(CL))		CCL4
1304M	A	6.79	CHA	A(C(NH2)/CH-C(SO3-NA))		D20
921M	C	6.79	CHA	A(C(N=C=O)-CH-C(N=C=O)/CH-C(CH3))		CCL4
1912M	A	6.79	CHA	A(C(OH)/CH-C(OH))		D20
1722M	D	6.79	CHA	A(C(O-CH3)-C(CH2-OH))		CDCL3
1496M	C	6.79	CHA	A(C(O-CH3)/CH-C(CH3))		CDCL3
1524M	C	6.79	CHA	A(C(O-CH3)/CH-C(N(CH3/CH3)))		CDCL3
1547M	B	6.79	CHA	A(C(O-CH3)/CH-C(O-CH3))		CDCL3
2379M	A	6.79	CHR	R5N(=CH-C(=O)/C(=O)-NH)		POLYSOL-D
1140M	A	6.79	CHR	R5S<=CH-S/CH=C(BR)>		CCL4
2415M	A	6.79	NH2	C(=O)-NH2		POLYSOL-D
1884M	F	6.79	OH	A<C-CH-CH-C(CH2.4-CH3)>		CCL4
2827M	D	6.79 APP.	Q2	C(=O)-O-CH2/H/C(=O)-O-CH2		CCL4
188M	B	6.79 APP.		UNSPECIFIED		CCL4
980M	B	6.79- 7.52		UNSPECIFIED		CCL4
375M	C	6.79- 7.23		UNSPECIFIED		CCL4
347M	A	6.80	CH	BR3		CCL4
671M	B	6.80- 8.30	CHA	AA(C*-C(N(CH3/CH3)))		CCL4
1581M	E	6.80	CHA	AN<CH-N-C(O-CH2)>		CDCL3
1581M	E	6.80	CHA	AN<C(O-CH2)-N>		CDCL3
1278M	B	6.80	CHA	AR5SA(C(NH2)-CH-C*/CH-C*-SO2)		DMSO
1488M	B	6.80	CHA	A<CH-CH-C(O-CH3)>		CCL4
674M	C	6.80- 7.20	CHA	A<CH-CH-C(R5NN<N-C(A)=/CH2>)>		CDCL3
501M	D	6.80	CHA	A<CH-C(CH(CH3/CH3))-C(NH2)/CH-C(CH(CH3/CH3))>		CDCL3
674M	C	6.80- 7.20	CHA	A<CH-C(R5NN<N-C(A)=/CH2>)>		CDCL3
1918M	G	6.80 APP.	CHA	A<C(CH2-Q3)-C(OH)-C(CH3)>		CCL4
1918M	G	6.80 APP.	CHA	A<C(CH3)-C(OH)-C(CH2-Q3)>		CCL4
2677M	A	6.80	CHA	A<C(NH2)/CH-C(C(=O)-ONA)>		D20
664M	F	6.80	CHA	A<C(N(CH2/CH2))-C(CH3)/C(CH3)>		CCL4
926M	A	6.80- 7.30	CHA	A<C(N=C=N)>		CDCL3
1548M	D	6.80- 7.40	CHA	A<C(O-A)>		CDCL3
2089M	B	6.80- 7.40	CHA	A<C(O-CH2)>		CDCL3
2211M	D	6.80	CHA	A<C(O-CH2)/CH-C(NH-C(=O))>		DMSO-D6
1488M	B	6.80	CHA	A<C(O-CH3)>		CCL4
1548M	B	6.80	CHA	A<C(O-CH3)/CH-C(O-A)>		CDCL3
878M	B	6.80	CHA	A(CH-CH-C(NH-QN))		DMSO-D6
1514M	B	6.80	CHA	A(CH-C(BR)-C(O-CH3))		CDCL3
495M	E	6.80	CHA	A(CH-C(NH2)-C(CH3)/CH-C(CH3))		CCL4
2988M	C	6.80- 7.50	CHA	A(C(NH-C(=O)-O))		CDCL3
657M	A	6.80- 7.40	CHA	A(C(N(A/A)))		CDCL3
2299M	F	6.80	NH	C(=O)-CH2/CH2-CH2		CDCL3
2979M	B	6.80	NH2	C(=O)-O-A		DMSO-D6
164M	A	6.80	Q1	Q1(A/A)/A/A		CDCL3
301M	A	6.80- 7.25		UNSPECIFIED		CCL4
657M	A	6.80- 7.40		UNSPECIFIED		CDCL3
1543M	A	6.80- 7.60		UNSPECIFIED		CDCL3
227M	A	6.80- 7.70		UNSPECIFIED		CCL4

BOOK NO.	ASSIGN-MENT	CHEM SHIFT - ppm -	PROTON GROUP	ENVIRONMENTAL GROUPS	S	SOLVENT
210M	A	6.80- 7.80		UNSPECIFIED		CDCL3
233M	A	6.80- 7.81		UNSPECIFIED		CDCL3
1542M	B	6.80- 7.30		UNSPECIFIED		CCL4
2089M	B	6.80- 7.40		UNSPECIFIED		CDCL3
890M	B	6.80- 7.40		UNSPECIFIED		CDCL3
2928M	B	6.80- 7.43		UNSPECIFIED		CCL4
2342M	B	6.80- 7.70		UNSPECIFIED		CDCL3
671M	B	6.80- 8.30		UNSPECIFIED		CCL4
151M	C	6.80- 7.30		UNSPECIFIED		CDCL3
377M	C	6.80- 7.35		UNSPECIFIED		CCL4
2988M	C	6.80- 7.50		UNSPECIFIED		CDCL3
888M	C	6.80- 7.50		UNSPECIFIED		CDCL3
1349M	C	6.80- 7.55		UNSPECIFIED		POLYSOL-D
608M	D	6.80- 7.20		UNSPECIFIED		CDCL3
661M	D	6.80- 7.30		UNSPECIFIED		CDCL3
661M	D	6.80- 7.30		UNSPECIFIED		CDCL3
1548M	D	6.80- 7.40		UNSPECIFIED		CDCL3
1956M	B	6.81	CHA	AA<C*/C(OH)-CH-C(OH)>		C3H6O
1505M	E	6.81	CHA	A<C(CH2-NH2)/C(O-CH3)>		CDCL3
194M	B	6.81	CHA	A<C(CH3)-C(CH3)-C(CH3)/C(CH3)-C(CH3)>		CDCL3
506M	C	6.81	CHA	A<C(NH2)/C(CF3)>		CDCL3
1539M	F	6.81	CHA	A<C(O-CH2)/CH-C(C(A/CH3))>		CDCL3
2077M	E	6.81	CHA	A<C(O-CH3)/CH-C(C(=O)-CH2.2)>		CCL4
1528M	B	6.81	CHA	A<C(O-CH3)/CH-C(QN(A))>		CDCL3
1536M	C	6.81	CHA	A<C(O-CH3)/CH-C(SH)>		CDCL3
530M	D	6.81	CHA	A(C(CH2-A)/CH-C(NH2))		DMSO-D6
226M	B	6.81	CHA	A(C(F)/CH-C(CH3))		CCL4
1678M	E	6.81	CHR	R5S<=CH-S/CH=C(CH2.2-OH)>		CCL4
2634M	C	6.81 APP.	NH	A/CH2-C(=O)-O		DMSO-D6
2634M	C	6.81 APP.	OH	C(=O)-CH2		DMSO-D6
867M	B	6.81 APP.	Q2	A/QN(CH2.2-QN)		CDCL3
867M	B	6.81 APP.	Q2	QN(CH2.2-QN)/A		CDCL3
2558M	B	6.81- 7.45		UNSPECIFIED		CDCL3
1229M	C	6.81- 7.33		UNSPECIFIED		CDCL3
1949M	B	6.82	CHA	AR5A<C(OH)-CH-C*/CH-C*-C*>		POLYSOL-D
2109M	C	6.82	CHA	AR600<C*-O-CH2/CH-C(C(=O)-CH3)>		CDCL3
2117M	D	6.82	CHA	AR60<C*-O-CH2/CH-C(CH3)>		CDCL3
641M	F	6.82	CHA	A<CH-CH-C(R6NN<N-CH(CH3)/CH2>)>		CDCL3
2326M	B	6.82	CHA	A<C(NH-C(=O))-CH-C(F)>		CDCL3
2216M	C	6.82	CHA	A<C(O-CH)>		CCL4
426M	A	6.82- 7.45	CHA	A(CH-CH-C(I))		CCL4
2467M	A	6.82 APP.	CHA	A(CH-CH-C(NH-NH))		DMSO
2978M	A	6.82- 7.40	CHA	A(CH-CH-C(O-C(=O)-NH2))		DMSO
426M	A	6.82- 7.45	CHA	A(CH-C(I))		CCL4
2978M	A	6.82- 7.40	CHA	A(CH-C(O-C(=O)-NH2))		DMSO
2322M	C	6.82	CHA	A(C(CH3)-CH-C(NH-C(=O)))		CDCL3
1914M	D	6.82	CHA	A(C(CH3)-C(CH3)/CH-C(OH))		CCL4
2467M	A	6.82 APP.	CHA	A(C(NH-NH))		DMSO
2924M	C	6.82	CHA	A(C(O-C(=O)-CH3)/CH-C(CH3))		CCL4
1147M	B	6.82 APP.	CHR	R5S(=CH-S/CH=C(CH2-R55))		CDCL3
1147M	B	6.82 APP.	CHR	R5S(=C(CH2-R5S)-S/CH=CH)		CDCL3
1258M	A	6.82	Q2	SO2-Q2/H/A		CDCL3
2607M	B	6.82- 7.70		UNSPECIFIED		DMSO
2186M	B	6.83	CHA	AR500(C*-O-CH2/CH-C(C(=O)-H))		CDCL3
1792M	F	6.83	CHA	A<CH-CH-C(O-CH2)>		CCL4
596M	E	6.83	CHA	A<C(CH3)/CH-C(NH-CH2)>		CCL4
2565M	B	6.83	CHA	A<C(O-CH2)/CH-C(O-CH2)>		POLYSOL-D
1910M	B	6.83	CHA	A(CH-C(OH)-C(OH))		POLYSOL-D
1929M	D	6.83	CHA	A((C(CH2-A)-C(OH)/CH-C(OH))		DMSO-D6
2604M	A	6.83	CHR	R50<=CH-O/C((C(=O)-OH)=CH>		POLYSOL-D
1289M	A	6.83	OH	SO2-A		DMSO
1166M	A	6.83	Q1	S-A/A/A		CDCL3
2799M	F	6.83	Q2	CH2.2-CH3/H/C(=O)-O-CH3		CCL4
2395M	C	6.83	Q3	R5NA<N-C(=O)/C(=O)>/H/H		CDCL3
1530M	B	6.83- 7.85		UNSPECIFIED		CCL4
1590M	B	6.84	CHA	AR600<CH-C*-O/CH-CH-C*>		CDCL3
1590M	B	6.84	CHA	AR600<C*-O-CH2>		CDCL3
2339M	D	6.84	CHA	A<C(CH3)-CH-C(NH-C(=O))/CH-C(CH3)>		CDCL3
2080M	B	6.84	CHA	A<C(OH)-C(C(=O)-CH3)/CH-C(OH)>		DMSO-D6
2894M	D	6.84	CHA	A<C(OH)/CH-C(C(=O)-O-CH2)>		CCL4
2563M	D	6.84	CHA	A<C(O-CH2)/CH-C(CH2-C(=O)-OH)>		CDCL3
1504M	C	6.84	CHA	A<C(O-CH3)/C(CH2-NH2)>		CDCL3
2338M	D	6.84	CHA	A((C(CH3)-CH-C(CH3)/CH-C(NH-C(=O)))		CDCL3
2815M	F	6.84	Q2	CH2.6-CH3/H/C(=O)-O-CH3		CCL4
2531M	B	6.84	Q2	CL/C(=O)-OH/H		POLYSOL-D
2033M	A	6.84		UNSPECIFIED		CDCL3
764M	B	6.85	CHA	ANA<C(NH-NH2)-N-C*/CH-C*>		POLYSOL-D
1928M	F	6.85	CHA	A<C(CH2.15-CH3)-C(OH)/CH-C(OH)>		POLYSOL-D
939M	A	6.85- 7.35	CHA	A<C(F)-C(N=C=S)>		CCL4
2890M	E	6.85	CHA	A<C(OH)-C(C(=O)-O-CH2)>		CCL4
1563M	C	6.85	CHA	A<C(O-CH3)-C(O-CH3)/CH-C(C:N)>		CDCL3

BOOK NO.	ASSIGN-MENT	CHEM SHIFT - ppm -	PROTON GROUP	ENVIRONMENTAL GROUPS	S	SOLVENT
2337M	C	6.85	CHA	A<C(O-CH3)/CH-C(NH-C(=O))>		DMSO-D6
2923M	A	6.85- 7.50	CHA	A<C(O-C(=O)-CF3)>		CDCL3
1722M	E	6.85	CHA	A(CH-C(CH2-OH)-C(O-CH3))		CDCL3
1509M	B	6.85	CHA	A(CH-C(CL)-C(O-CH3))		CDCL3
2891M	C	6.85	CHA	A(CH-C(OH)-C(C(=O)-O-CH2))		CDCL3
521M	D	6.85	CHA	A(C(CH3)-CH-C(BR)/CH-C(NH2))		CDCL3
2125M	A	6.85	CHR	AR7A(C*/CH-C*)		CCL4
2120M	B	6.85	CHR	R6A(=C(C(CH3/CH3/CH3))-C(=O)/C(=O)-C*)		CDCL3
2923M	A	6.85- 7.50		UNSPECIFIED		CDCL3
297M	A	6.85- 7.55		UNSPECIFIED		CCL4
2955M	B	6.85- 7.46		UNSPECIFIED		CDCL3
872M	B	6.85- 7.55		UNSPECIFIED		CDCL3
1453M	E	6.85- 7.50		UNSPECIFIED		CCL4
1559M	F	6.85 APP.		UNSPECIFIED		CDCL3
1927M	G	6.86	CHA	A<C(CH2-CH2)-C(OH)/CH-C(OH)>		CDCL3
2825M	B	6.86	Q2	C(=O)-O-CH3/H/C(=O)-O-CH3		CDCL3
1953M	C	6.87	CHA	AA<C*/C(NH2)>		DMSO-D6
1882M	E	6.87	CHA	A<CH-C(OH)-C(C(CH3/CH3/CH3))>		CCL4
299M	B	6.87	CHA	A<C(CH3)-CH-C(CL)/CH-C(CH3)>		CCL4
2929M	B	6.87	CHA	A<C(O-C(=O)-CH3)-CH-C(O-C(=O)-CH3)/C(O-C(=O)-CH3)>		CDCL3
1240M	C	6.87	CHA	A<C(SH)-CH-C(SH)/CH-C(CL)>		CCL4
1553M	B	6.87	CHA	A(CH-C(CL)-C(O-CH3)/CH-C(CL))		CCL4
193M	B	6.87	CHA	A(C(CH3)-C(CH3)/C(CH3)-C(CH3))		CDCL3
1889M	A	6.87	CHA	A(C(OH)/CH-C(A))		DMSO
2895M	D	6.87	CHA	A(C(OH)/CH-C(C(=O)-O-CH2))		CCL4
1529M	B	6.87	CHA	A(C(O-CH3)-C(QN(OH)))		CDCL3
2184M	B	6.87	CHR	R5S(C(CH3)-S/CH-C(C(=O)-H))		CDCL3
1153M	B	6.87	NH2	R5NS(C=N/S)		DMSO-D6
2156M	E	6.87	Q2	CH2.2-CH3/H/C(=O)-H		CDCL3
1105M	B	6.87- 7.62		UNSPECIFIED		CDCL3
178M	D	6.87- 7.39		UNSPECIFIED		CDCL3
1179M	B	6.88	CHA	AR5SA(C(NH2)-CH-C*/CH-C*-C*)		DMSO
885M	D	6.88	CHA	A<C(CH3)/CH-C(QN(N(CH3/CH3)))>		CCL4
2103M	B	6.88	CHA	A<C(NH2)-CH-C(C(=O)-A)>		DMSO-D6
1909M	A	6.88	CHA	A<C(OH)/CH-C(A<C-CH-CH-C(OH)>)>		DMSO-D6
2925M	F	6.88	CHA	A<C(O-C(=O)-CH2)/CH-C(CH3)>		CCL4
807M	A	6.88	CHA	A(CH-CH-C(NH-A))	S	DMSO
2554M	E	6.88 APP.	CHA	A(CH-CH-C(O-CH2))		CDCL3
433M	A	6.88	CHA	A(CH-C(CL)-C(I))		CCL4
2889M	C	6.88	CHA	A(CH-C(C(=O)-O-CH)-C(OH))		CDCL3
433M	A	6.88	CHA	A(CH-C(I)-C(CL))		CCL4
2562M	B	6.88	CHA	A(C(CL)/CH-C(O-C))		CDCL3
1491M	C	6.88	CHA	A(C(O-CH2.2))		CDCL3
2554M	E	6.88 APP.	CHA	A(C(O-CH2))		CDCL3
1514M	C	6.88	CHA	A(C(O-CH3)-C(BR))		CDCL3
2888M	C	6.88	CHA	A(C(O-CH3)/CH-C(C(=O)-O-CH3))		CDCL3
640M	C	6.88	CHA	A(C(R6NN(N/CH2-CH2-NH)))		CDCL3
1341M	B	6.88	NH2	C(=S)-NH		DMSO-D6
2523M	E	6.88	Q1	CH2-CH2/CH2-CH3/C(=O)-OH		CCL4
906M	B	6.88- 7.50		UNSPECIFIED		CCL4
1966M	G	6.88		UNSPECIFIED		CDCL3
2989M	A	6.89	CH	O-C(=O)-NH/A/A		CDCL3
1957M	A	6.89	CHA	AA<C(OH)-C*/CH-CH-C*>		DMSO-D6
699M	A	6.89	CHA	AN<CH-N-C(F)>		CCL4
601M	G	6.89	CHA	AR6N<C*-CH2-CH2>		CDCL3
2118M	C	6.89	CHA	AR6O(C*-O-CH2/CH-C(CL))		CDCL3
660M	D	6.89	CHA	A<C(CH3)/CH-C(N(CH3/CH3))>		CCL4
2079M	B	6.89	CHA	A<C(OH)-C(C(=O)-CH3)/CH-C(CL)>		CDCL3
2173M	D	6.89	CHA	A<C(O-CH2.2)/CH-C(C(=O)-H)>		CCL4
641M	G	6.89	CHA	A<C(R6NN<N-CH(CH3)/CH2>)>		CDCL3
312M	A	6.89- 7.46	CHA	A(CH-C(CL)-C(CL)/CH-C(CL))		CDCL3
429M	B	6.89	CHA	A(C(CH3)/CH-C(I))		CDCL3
312M	A	6.89- 7.46	CHA	A(C(CL)-C(CL)-C(CL))		CDCL3
2512M	B	6.89 APP.	CHR	R5S<=CH-S/CH=C(CH2-C(=O)-OH)>		CDCL3
2512M	B	6.89 APP.	CHR	R5S<=C(CH2-C(=O)-OH)-S/CH=CH>		CDCL3
1365M	C	6.89	NH2	SO2-A		DMSO-D6
722M	B	6.90- 7.30	CHA	AAN<CH-N-C*/CH-C*>		CCL4
722M	B	6.90- 7.30	CHA	AAN<C(CH3)-CH-C*/CH-C*>		CCL4
696M	C	6.90	CHA	AN<C(C(CH3/CH3/CH3))-N-C(C(CH3/CH3/CH3))/C(CH3)>		CDCL3
2608M	B	6.90	CHA	AR500<C*-O-CH2/CH-C(C(=O)-OH)>		POLYSOL-D
1481M	D	6.90- 7.30	CHA	A<CH-CH-C(C(O/A/A))>		CDCL3
2320M	B	6.90- 7.34	CHA	A<CH-CH-C(NH-C(=O))>		DMSO-D6
434M	A	6.90	CHA	A<CH-C(BR)-C(I)>		CCL4
1481M	D	6.90- 7.30	CHA	A<CH-C(C(O/A/A))>		CDCL3
595M	F	6.90- 7.35	CHA	A<CH-C(NH-CH2)-C(CH3)>		CDCL3
2320M	B	6.90- 7.34	CHA	A<CH-C(NH-C(=O))>		DMSO-D6
1903M	A	6.90	CHA	A<CH-C(OH)-C(NO2)>		CCL4
2212M	C	6.90- 7.40	CHA	A<C(CH2.2-C(=O)-CL)>		CCL4
500M	F	6.90	CHA	A<C(CH2-CH3)-C(NH2)-C(CH3)>		CDCL3
2058M	D	6.90	CHA	A<C(CH3)-C(CH3)-C(C(=O)-CH3)/C(CH3)-C(CH3)>		CDCL3
500M	F	6.90	CHA	A<C(CH3)-C(NH2)-C(CH2-CH3)>		CDCL3

BOOK NO.	ASSIGN-MENT	CHEM SHIFT - ppm -	PROTON GROUP	ENVIRONMENTAL GROUPS	S	SOLVENT
595M	F	6.90- 7.35	CHA	A<C(CH3)-C(NH-CH2)>		CDCL3
2547M	A	6.90- 7.50	CHA	A<C(C(C(=O)-OH/A/A))>		DMSO-D6
391M	A	6.90	CHA	A<C(F)/CH-C(BR)>		CCL4
2676M	A	6.90	CHA	A<C(NH2)-CH-C(C(=O)-O-NA)>		D2O
887M	A	6.90- 7.45	CHA	A<C(NH-QN)>		POLYSOL-D
1919M	B	6.90	CHA	A<C(OH)-C(CL)/CH-C(CL)>		CDCL3
1549M	B	6.90	CHA	A<C(O-A)/CH-C(O-CH3)>		POLYSOL-D
1548M	C	6.90	CHA	A<C(O-A)/CH-C(O-CH3)>		CDCL3
2595M	C	6.90	CHA	A<C(O-CH3)-CH-C(C(=O)-OH)/CH-C(NH2)>		POLYSOL-D
1549M	B	6.90	CHA	A<C(O-CH3)/CH-C(O-A)>>		POLYSOL-D
2921M	C	6.90- 7.50	CHA	A<C(O-C(=O)-CH2)>		CCL4
2933M	C	6.90	CHA	A<C(O-C(=O)-CH2)/CH-C(CH3)>		CDCL3
2922M	B	6.90- 7.60	CHA	A<C(O-C(=O)-C)>		CDCL3
160M	E	6.90- 7.60	CHA	A<C(Q1(A/CH2.3-CH3))>		CCL4
161M	E	6.90- 7.50	CHA	A<C(Q1(A/CH2.6-CH3))>		CCL4
1776M	F	6.90- 7.60	CHA	A<C(R6<C(A)-CH(OH)/CH2>)>		CDCL3
2318M	B	6.90- 7.50	CHA	A(CH-CH-C(NH-C(=O)))		DMSO-D6
2315M	C	6.90- 7.42	CHA	A(CH-CH-C(NH-C(=O)))		CDCL3
2316M	E	6.90- 7.70	CHA	A(CH-CH-C(NH-C(=O)))		CDCL3
2593M	B	6.90- 7.35	CHA	A(CH-C(CH3)-C(C(=O)-OH)/CH-C(CH3))		CDCL3
305M	A	6.90- 7.55	CHA	A(CH-C(CL)-C(CL))		CCL4
230M	A	6.90- 7.40	CHA	A(CH-C(F)-C(F))		CDCL3
428M	B	6.90	CHA	A(CH-C(I)/CH-C(CH3))		CCL4
489M	D	6.90	CHA	A(CH-C(NH2)/CH-C(CH3))		CCL4
2318M	B	6.90- 7.50	CHA	A(CH-C(NH-C(=O)))		DMSO-D6
2315M	C	6.90- 7.42	CHA	A(CH-C(NH-C(=O)))		CDCL3
2316M	E	6.90- 7.70	CHA	A(CH-C(NH-C(=O)))		CDCL3
424M	C	6.90- 7.35	CHA	A(C(CH2-CH2))		CDCL3
2400M	C	6.90- 7.30	CHA	A(C(CH2-N))		CDCL3
2593M	B	6.90- 7.35	CHA	A(C(CH3)-C(C(=O)-OH)-C(CH3))		CDCL3
2338M	E	6.90	CHA	A(C(CH3)-C(NH-C(=O))/C(CH3))		CDCL3
181M	B	6.90	CHA	A(C(CH3)/CH-C(CH3))		CCL4
305M	A	6.90- 7.55	CHA	A(C(CL)-C(CL))		CCL4
230M	A	6.90- 7.40	CHA	A(C(F)-C(F))		CDCL3
1716M	C	6.90	CHA	A(C(F)/CH-C(CH2-OH))		CDCL3
941M	A	6.90	CHA	A(C(F)/CH-C(N=C=S))		CCL4
1340M	A	6.90- 7.60	CHA	A(C(NH-C(=S)))		DMSO
1074M	B	6.90	CHA	A(C(N(CH3/CH3))-CH-C(NO2)/CH-C(NO2))		DMSO-D6
2990M	F	6.90- 7.40	CHA	A(C(N(C(=O)-O/CH2)))		CCL4
762M	B	6.90	CHA	A(C(N(N/CH3))/CH-C(A))		CDCL3
2586M	D	6.90	CHA	A(C(O-CH2.2)/CH-C(C(=O)-OH))		POLYSOL-D
1608M	A	6.90- 7.50	CHA	A(C(O-P))		CDCL3
2374M	D	6.90- 7.80	CHA	A(C(R5N(N-C(=O)/CH2)))		CDCL3
1136M	A	6.90	CHR	R5S(=CH-S/CH=CH)		CCL4
2814M	E	6.90	Q2	CH3/H/C(=O)-O-CH2		CCL4
887M	A	6.90- 7.45		UNSPECIFIED		POLYSOL-D
1608M	A	6.90- 7.50		UNSPECIFIED		CDCL3
2547M	A	6.90- 7.50		UNSPECIFIED		DMSO-D6
1340M	A	6.90- 7.60		UNSPECIFIED		DMSO
228M	A	6.90- 7.65		UNSPECIFIED		CDCL3
1544M	A	6.90- 7.65		UNSPECIFIED		CDCL3
2343M	A	6.90- 7.70		UNSPECIFIED		DMSO
715M	A	6.90- 7.70		UNSPECIFIED		CDCL3
1352M	A	6.90- 7.80		UNSPECIFIED		DMSO
2569M	A	6.90- 7.82		UNSPECIFIED		POLYSOL-D
714M	A	6.90- 7.90		UNSPECIFIED		CDCL3
913M	B	6.90- 7.20		UNSPECIFIED		CCL4
1550M	B	6.90- 7.40		UNSPECIFIED		CDCL3
1515M	C	6.90- 7.20		UNSPECIFIED		CDCL3
609M	C	6.90- 7.25		UNSPECIFIED		CDCL3
2400M	C	6.90- 7.30		UNSPECIFIED		CDCL3
424M	C	6.90- 7.35		UNSPECIFIED		CDCL3
2212M	C	6.90- 7.40		UNSPECIFIED		CCL4
2921M	C	6.90- 7.50		UNSPECIFIED		CCL4
1507M	C	6.90- 7.55		UNSPECIFIED		CCL4
2994M	C	6.90- 7.60		UNSPECIFIED		CDCL3
199M	D	6.90- 7.40		UNSPECIFIED		CCL4
2374M	D	6.90- 7.80		UNSPECIFIED		CDCL3
161M	E	6.90- 7.50		UNSPECIFIED		CCL4
160M	E	6.90- 7.60		UNSPECIFIED		CCL4
2319M	E	6.90- 7.75		UNSPECIFIED		DMSO-D6
2990M	F	6.90- 7.40		UNSPECIFIED		CCL4
1776M	F	6.90- 7.60		UNSPECIFIED		CDCL3
1174M	A	6.91	CHA	ANA<C(S-A)-N-C*/CH-C*>		CDCL3
709M	C	6.91 APP.	CHA	AN<CH-N/CH-C(CH2-A)>		DMSO-D6
709M	C	6.91 APP.	CHA	AN<C(NH-CH2)-CH-N>		DMSO-D6
682M	B	6.91 APP.	CHA	AN(CH-C(CH3)-N)		CCL4
682M	B	6.91 APP.	CHA	AN(C(CH3)-N)		CCL4
1504M	D	6.91	CHA	A<CH-C(CH2-NH2)-C(O-CH3)>		CDCL3
1520M	C	6.91	CHA	A<CH-C(I)/CH-C(O-CH3)>		CCL4
662M	E	6.91	CHA	A<CH-C(N(CH2/CH2))/CH-C(CH3)>		CCL4

BOOK NO.	ASSIGN-MENT	CHEM SHIFT - ppm -	PROTON GROUP	ENVIRONMENTAL GROUPS	S	SOLVENT
1718M	E	6.91	CHA	A<C(CH2.2-OH)/CH-C(NH2)>		POLYSOL-D
1552M	E	6.91 APP.	CHA	A<C(CH3)-CH-C(CH3)/CH-C(O-CH3)>		CDCL3
1552M	E	6.91 APP.	CHA	A<C(CH3)-C(O-CH3)/C(CH3)>		CDCL3
310M	A	6.91	CHA	A<C(F)-CH-C(CL)/CH-C(CL)>		CDCL3
1891M	C	6.91	CHA	A<C(F)/CH-C(OH)>		CDCL3
1921M	B	6.91	CHA	A<C(OH)-C(BR)/CH-C(BR)>		CCL4
2076M	D	6.91	CHA	A<C(O-CH2)/CH-C(C(=O)-CH3)>		CDCL3
1532M	B	6.91	CHA	A<C(O-CH3)/CH-C(NO2)>		CCL4
2178M	C	6.91	CHA	A<C(O-CH3)/C(C(=O)-H)-C(OH)>		CCL4
665M	C	6.91	CHA	A(CH-C(CH3)-C(N(CH3/CH3))/CH-C(CH3))		CDCL3
665M	C	6.91	CHA	A(C(CH3)-C(N(CH3/CH3))-C(CH3))		CDCL3
1230M	C	6.91	CHA	A(C(CH3)/CH-C(SH))		CDCL3
303M	A	6.91	CHA	A(C(F)/CH-C(CL))		CDCL3
823M	B	6.91	CHA	A(C(NH-NH2)-CH-C(CL)/CH-C(CH3))	S	DMSO-D6
1946M	C	6.91	CHA	A(C(OH)-C(OH)/CH-C(OH))		D20
1533M	C	6.91	CHA	A(C(O-CH2)/CH-C(NO2))		CDCL3
1509M	C	6.91	CHA	A(C(O-CH3)-C(CL))		CDCL3
1537M	B	6.91	CHA	A(C(O-CH3)/CH-C(SO2-A))		CDCL3
1141M	A	6.91	CHR	R5S<=CH-S/C(BR)=CH>		CDCL3
2025M	C	6.91	CHR	R6<=CH-C(=O)/CH2-CH2>		CCL4
2162M	A	6.91	Q2	C(=O)-H/H/A<C-CH-CH-C(NO2)>		DMSO-D6
209M	C	6.91- 7.98		UNSPECIFIED		CDCL3
2061M	D	6.91 APP.		UNSPECIFIED		CCL4
1172M	A	6.92	CHA	AN<C(S-A)/CH-N>		CDCL3
601M	H	6.92	CHA	AR6N<CH-CH-NH/CH-CH-C*>		CDCL3
397M	A	6.92	CHA	A<CH-C(BR)/CH-C(BR)>		CCL4
506M	D	6.92	CHA	A<C(CF3)-CH-C(NH2)>		CDCL3
1878M	D	6.92	CHA	A<C(CH3)/CH-C(OH)>		CDCL3
1708M	E	6.92	CHA	A<C(CH3)/CH-C(S-CH2.2)>		CCL4
2175M	E	6.92	CHA	A<C(O-CH2)/CH-C(C(=O)-H)>		CCL4
2135M	B	6.92	CHA	A<C(O-CH3)/CH-C(C(=O)-C(=O))>		CDCL3
2979M	C	6.92	CHA	A<C(O-C(=O)-NH2)/CH-C(CH3)>		DMSO-D6
2553M	B	6.92 APP.	CHA	A(CH-CH-C(O-CH2))		C3H6O
591M	E	6.92	CHA	A(C(CH3)/CH-C(NH-CH3))		CDCL3
1920M	C	6.92	CHA	A(C(CL)-CH-C(OH)/C(CL))		CDCL3
2553M	B	6.92 APP.	CHA	A(C(O-CH2))		C3H6O
2174M	E	6.92	CHA	A(C(O-CH2)/CH-C(C(=O)-H))		CCL4
1578M	B	6.92	CHR	R5O<=C(Q2(H/NO2/H))-O/CH=CH>		CDCL3
1586M	A	6.92		UNSPECIFIED		CDCL3
179M	C	6.92 APP.		UNSPECIFIED		CCL4
1228M	C	6.92- 7.40		UNSPECIFIED		CDCL3
1936M	E	6.92		UNSPECIFIED		CDCL3
1490M	D	6.93 APP.	CHA	A<CH-CH-C(O-CH2.2)>		CDCL3
2216M	D	6.93	CHA	A<CH-CH-C(O-CH)>		CCL4
1884M	G	6.93	CHA	A<C(CH2.4-CH3)/CH-C(OH)>		CCL4
498M	E	6.93	CHA	A<C(CH3)-C(CH3)/CH-C(NH2)>		CDCL3
1490M	D	6.93 APP.	CHA	A<C(O-CH2.2)>		CDCL3
1529M	C	6.93	CHA	A(CH-C(QN(OH))-C(O-CH3))		CDCL3
2893M	C	6.93	CHA	A(C(OH)/CH-C(C(=O)-O-CH))		CDCL3
1508M	B	6.93	CHA	A(C(O-CH3)/CH-C(A))		CDCL3
1339M	C	6.93	NH2	C(=O)-NH		DMSO-D6
2522M	F	6.93	Q2	CH(CH2.2/CH3)/H/C(=O)-OH		CCL4
672M	C	6.93- 8.42		UNSPECIFIED		CCL4
1913M	F	6.94	CHA	A<CH-C(OH)-C(CH3)/CH-C(CH3)>		CDCL3
1877M	D	6.94	CHA	A(CH-C(OH)/CH-C(CH3))		CCL4
2451M	C	6.94	NHR	R5NN<C(=O)-NH/CH(NH-C(=O)-NH2)-C(=O)>		DMSO-D6
687M	E	6.95	CHA	AN<CH-N-C(CH2-CH2)>		CCL4
691M	C	6.95	CHA	AN(C(CH3)-N/CH-C(CH3))		CDCL3
232M	A	6.95	CHA	A<C(F)/CH-C(F)>		CCL4
2335M	C	6.95- 7.20	CHA	A(CH-C(NH-C(=O))/CH-C(OH))		DMSO-D6
2892M	C	6.95- 7.48	CHA	A(CH-C(OH)/CH-C(C(=O)-O-CH3)		CDCL3
384M	B	6.95	CHA	A(C(CH3)/CH-C(BR))		CCL4
1500M	E	6.95	CHA	A(C(CH3)/CH-C(O-CH2))		CCL4
515M	D	6.95 APP.	CHA	A(C(CL)-CH-C(CH3)/CH-C(NH2))		CCL4
515M	D	6.95 APP.	CHA	A(C(CL)/C(CH3)-C(NH2))		CCL4
2914M	C	6.95	CHA	A(C(C(=O)-O-CH3)-CH-C(OH)/C(OH))		DMSO-D6
2335M	C	6.95- 7.20	CHA	A(C(NH-C(=O))-CH-C(OH))		DMSO-D6
2892M	C	6.95- 7.48	CHA	A(C(OH)-CH-C(C(=O)-O-CH3))		CDCL3
2891M	D	6.95	CHA	A(C(OH)-C(C(=O)-O-CH2))		CDCL3
1153M	C	6.95	CHR	R5NS(S-C(NH2)=/=CH-N=)		DMSO-D6
778M	C	6.95 APP.	NH2	CH2-CH2	S	TFA
383M	B	6.95- 7.30		UNSPECIFIED		CCL4
2462M	B	6.95- 7.40		UNSPECIFIED		DMSO-D6
2055M	C	6.95- 7.45		UNSPECIFIED		CCL4
1949M	C	6.95- 7.50		UNSPECIFIED		POLYSOL-D
174M	B	6.95		UNSPECIFIED		CCL4
870M	C	6.95- 7.56		UNSPECIFIED		CDCL3
688M	D	6.96	CHA	AN(C(CH2-CH2)/CH-N)		CCL4
2293M	A	6.96	CHA	A<CH-C(C(=O)-NH2)-C(OH)>		DMSO-D6
1534M	D	6.96	CHA	A<CH-C(O-CH2)-C(NO2)>		CCL4
1491M	D	6.96	CHA	A(CH-CH-C(O-CH2.2))		CDCL3

BOOK NO.	ASSIGN-MENT	CHEM SHIFT - ppm -	PROTON GROUP	ENVIRONMENTAL GROUPS	S	SOLVENT
2405M	D	6.96	CHA	A(C(CH2-C(=O)-NH)/CH-C(NH2))		POLYSOL-D
593M	F	6.96	CHA	A(C(CH3)/CH-C(NH-CH2))		CDCL3
2889M	D	6.96	CHA	A(C(OH)-C(C(=O)-O-CH))		CDCL3
2313M	D	6.96 APP.	NH	C(=O)-CH2/CH2-A		CDCL3
689M	E	6.97 APP.	CHA	AN<CH-N-C(CH(CH2.3/CH2.3))>		CCL4
689M	E	6.97 APP.	CHA	AN<C(CH(CH2.3/CH2.3))-N>		CCL4
690M	C	6.97	CHA	AN(C/CH3)-N/C(CH3))		CDCL3
2684M	A	6.97	CHA	A<CH-C(C(=O)-O-NH4)-C(OH)>		D2O
1237M	E	6.97	CHA	A<CH-C(NH2)/CH-C(SH)>		CDCL3
430M	C	6.97 APP.	CHA	A<C(CH3)-CH-C(I)/CH-C(CH3)>		CCL4
430M	C	6.97 APP.	CHA	A<C(CH3)-C(I)/CH-C(CH3)>		CCL4
390M	A	6.97	CHA	A<C(F)-CH-C(BR)>		CCL4
509M	C	6.97	CHA	A<C(F)-CH-C(NH2)>		CDCL3
2678M	A	6.97 APP.	CHA	A<C(OH)-C(C(=O)-ONA)>		D2O
2398M	B	6.97	CHA	A<C(O-CH3)/CH-C(R5NA<N-C(=O)/C(=O)>)>		CDCL3
526M	D	6.97	CHA	A(C(I)/C(NH2))		CDCL3
2182M	B	6.97	CHR	R5N<=C(C(=O)-H)-NH/CH=CH>		CDCL3
1930M	A	6.97		UNSPECIFIED		POLYSOL-D
541M	B	6.98	CHA	AAA<C*/C(NH2)-C*>		DMSO
684M	B	6.98	CHA	AN(C(CH3)/CH-N)		CCL4
1948M	F	6.98	CHA	AR5(CH-C*-CH2/CH-C(OH)-C*)		CDCL3
1525M	F	6.98	CHA	A<CH-C(N(CH2/CH2))/CH-C(O-CH2)>		CCL4
529M	D	6.98	CHA	A<C(CH2.2-NH2)/CH-C(NH2)>		CDCL3
2218M	D	6.98	CHA	A<C(CH2-CH2)/CH-C(BR)>		CDCL3
1501M	F	6.98	CHA	A<C(CH2-CH2)/CH-C(O-CH3)>		CCL4
139M	D	6.98	CHA	A<C(CH2-CH)>		CDCL3
286M	C	6.98	CHA	A<C(CH3)-C(CH2-CL)/C(CH3)-C(CH2-CL)>		CDCL3
918M	B	6.98	CHA	A<C(N=C=O)/CH-C(CH2-A)>		POLYSOL-D
1894M	C	6.98	CHA	A<C(OH)-C(BR)>		CDCL3
1522M	E	6.98	CHA	A(CH-C(NH2)/CH-C(O-CH3))		CDCL3
386M	C	6.98	CHA	A(C(CH3)-C(BR)/C(CH3)-C(CH3))		CDCL3
294M	B	6.98	CHA	A(C(CH3)/CH-C(CL))		CCL4
294M	C	6.98	CHA	A(C(CL)/CH-C(CH3))		CCL4
1896M	C	6.98	CHA	A(C(OH)-C(I))		CDCL3
2075M	C	6.98	CHA	A(C(O-CH3)/CH-C(C(=O)-CH3))		CDCL3
1148M	B	6.98	CHR	R5NS<=C-S/C(CH3)=N>		CCL4
1140M	C	6.98	CHR	R5S<S-C(BR)=/=CH-CH=>		CCL4
1140M	B	6.98	CHR	R5S<=C(BR)-S/CH=CH>		CCL4
752M	B	6.98- 7.37		UNSPECIFIED		DMSO
139M	D	6.98		UNSPECIFIED		CDCL3
697M	A	6.99	CHA	AN<CH-N-C(A)>		CDCL3
690M	D	6.99	CHA	AN(C(CH3)-CH-C(CH3)/CH-N)		CDCL3
1161M	D	6.99	CHA	A<CH-C(NH2)-C(S-CH3)>		CCL4
664M	G	6.99	CHA	A<C(CH3)-C(N(CH2/CH2))/CH-C(CH3)>		CCL4
373M	C	6.99	CHA	A<C(CH3)/CH-C(CH2-BR)>		CCL4
182M	D	6.99	CHA	A<C(CH3)/CH-C(CH(CH3/CH3))>		CCL4
184M	E	6.99	CHA	A<C(CH3)/CH-C(R6<C=CH/CH2>)>		CCL4
182M	D	6.99	CHA	A<C(CH(CH3/CH3))/CH-C(CH3)>		CCL4
1232M	B	6.99	CHA	A<C(CL)-CH-C(SH)/CH-C(CL)>		CCL4
304M	C	6.99	CHA	A<C(CL)-C(CH3)/C(F)>		CCL4
2327M	B	6.99	CHA	A<C(F)/CH-C(NH-C(=O))>		CDCL3
2600M	A	6.99	CHA	A<C(OH)-C(OH)/CH-C(C(=O)-OH)>		DMSO-D6
487M	D	6.99	CHA	A(CH-C(NH2))		CCL4
659M	D	6.99	CHA	A(CH-C(N(CH3/CH3))/CH-C(CH3))		CCL4
2327M	B	6.99	CHA	A(C(F)/CH-C(NH-C(=O)))		CDCL3
2038M	E	6.99	CHA	A(C(OH)/CH-C(CH2-CH2))		CDCL3
2389M	A	6.99	CHR	R5N(=CH-C(=O)/C(=O)-N(A(C-CH-CH-C(I))))		TFA
163M	A	6.99	Q1	A/A/A		CDCL3
1096M	C	6.99- 7.44		UNSPECIFIED		CDCL3
1569M	C	6.99- 7.50		UNSPECIFIED		CCL4
197M	D	6.99		UNSPECIFIED		CCL4
1163M	D	6.99- 7.51		UNSPECIFIED		CDCL3
1958M	A	7.00	CHA	AA<C(OH)-CH-C*/CH-C*>		C3D6O
438M	A	7.00	CHA	AA(CH-C(I)-C*/CH-C*)		CDCL3
1584M	B	7.00- 7.30	CHA	AR5O<CH-C*-CH=/CH-CH-C*>		CCL4
1584M	B	7.00- 7.30	CHA	AR5O<C*-O-CH=>		CCL4
678M	B	7.00- 7.55	CHA	A<CH-CH-C(R5NN<N-N=/CH=>)>		CDCL3
187M	C	7.00	CHA	A<CH-C(CH3)-C(CH3)/CH-C(CH3)>		CDCL3
2876M	B	7.00	CHA	A<CH-C(I)/CH-C(C(=O)-O-CH3)>		CDCL3
1526M	B	7.00	CHA	A<CH-C(NH2)-C(O-CH3)>	S	POLYSOL-D
2317M	C	7.00	CHA	A<CH-C(NH-C(=O)-CH)>		POLYSOL-D
2678M	B	7.00 APP.	CHA	A<CH-C(OH)-C(C(=O)-ONA)>		D2O
1565M	C	7.00	CHA	A<CH-C(O-CH3)-C(O-CH3)/CH-C(O-CH3)>		CDCL3
678M	B	7.00- 7.55	CHA	A<CH-C(R5NN<N-N=/CH=>)>		CDCL3
1933M	F	7.00	CHA	A<C(CH2-A)-C(OH)-C(C(CH3/CH3/CH3))/C(CH2-CH3)>		CDCL3
1888M	C	7.00	CHA	A<C(CH2-A)/CH-C(OH)>		DMSO-D6
1267M	C	7.00- 7.30	CHA	A<C(CH2-SO2)>		POLYSOL-D
1495M	D	7.00	CHA	A<C(CH3)-CH-C(O-CH3)>		CCL4
187M	C	7.00	CHA	A<C(CH3)-C(CH3)-C(CH3)>		CDCL3
1901M	E	7.00	CHA	A<C(CH(A/A))/CH-C(N(CH3/CH3))>		POLYSOL-D
1901M	E	7.00	CHA	A<C(CH(A/A))/CH-C(OH)>		POLYSOL-D

BOOK NO.	ASSIGN-MENT	CHEM SHIFT - ppm -	PROTON GROUP	ENVIRONMENTAL GROUPS	S	SOLVENT
516M	C	7.00	CHA	A<C(CL)-CH-C(CL)/CH-C(NH2)>		CDCL3
1820M	E	7.00- 7.40	CHA	A<C(C(OH/A/CH2.7))>		CCL4
2414M	B	7.00- 7.60	CHA	A<C(C(=O)-N)>		CDCL3
987M	A	7.00- 7.90	CHA	A<C(C:N)-C(F)>		CDCL3
1348M	D	7.00- 7.70	CHA	A<C(NH-C(=S))>		CDCL3
2361M	C	7.00- 7.60	CHA	A<C(N(C(=O)-H/CH2))>		CDCL3
2598M	B	7.00	CHA	A<C(OH)-C(O-CH3)/CH-C(C(=O)-OH)>		DMSO-D6
1528M	C	7.00- 7.40	CHA	A<C(QN(A<C-CH-CH-C(O-CH3)>))>		CDCL3
162M	E	7.00- 7.50	CHA	A<C(Q1(A/CH2.9-CH3))>		CDCL3
2042M	C	7.00- 7.50	CHA	A<C(Q1(A/C(=O)-CH3))>		CDCL3
146M	D	7.00- 7.45	CHA	A<C(R6<C=CH/CH2>)>		CCL4
1233M	B	7.00	CHA	A<C(SH)-CH-C(CL)/CH-C(CL)>		CCL4
2597M	A	7.00	CHA	A(CH-C(NO2)-C(OH)/CH-C(C(=O)-OH))		POLYSOL-D
1499M	F	7.00	CHA	A(CH-C(O-CH2)/CH-C(CH3))		CCL4
2040M	B	7.00- 7.40	CHA	A(C(CH2-C(=O)-CH2))		CDCL3
1301M	C	7.00- 7.20	CHA	A(C(CH3)-CH-C(CH3)/CH-C(SO3NA))	S	D2O
1301M	C	7.00- 7.20	CHA	A(C(CH3)-C(SO3NA)/C(CH3))	S	D2O
226M	C	7.00	CHA	A(C(CH3)-CH-C(F))		CCL4
1099M	B	7.00- 7.40	CHA	A(C(CH3)/CH-C(P(A/A)))		CDCL3
1099M	B	7.00- 7.40	CHA	A(C(P(A/A))/CH-C(CH3))		CDCL3
746M	A	7.00- 7.80	CHA	UNSPECIFIED		CCL4
1678M	F	7.00	CHR	R5S<=CH-CH=/S-C(CH2.2-OH)>		CCL4
1342M	A	7.00	NH2	C(=S)-NH		POLYSOL-D
1155M	C	7.00- 9.00	NH2	R5NNS<C=N/S>		TFA
1155M	C	7.00- 9.00	OH	C(=O)-CF3		TFA
2671M	D	7.00	Q2	Q2(CH3)/C(=O)-OK)		D2O
1348M	D	7.00- 7.70		UNSEPCIFIED		CDCL3
869M	A	7.00- 7.60		UNSPECIFIED		CDCL3
180M	A	7.00- 7.70		UNSPECIFIED		CDCL3
922M	A	7.00- 7.90		UNSPECIFIED		CDCL3
140M	B	7.00- 7.35		UNSPECIFIED		CCL4
2040M	B	7.00- 7.40		UNSPECIFIED		CDCL3
2467M	B	7.00- 7.45		UNSPECIFIED		DMSO
2329M	B	7.00- 7.50		UNSPECIFIED		CDCL3
2344M	B	7.00- 7.50		UNSPECIFIED		CDCL3
2971M	B	7.00- 7.50		UNSPECIFIED		CDCL3
2414M	B	7.00- 7.60		UNSPECIFIED		CDCL3
1354M	B	7.00- 7.60		UNSPECIFIED		POLYSOL-D
1267M	C	7.00- 7.30		UNSPECIFIED		POLYSOL-D
2869M	C	7.00- 7.40		UNSPECIFIED		CDCL3
1528M	C	7.00- 7.40		UNSPECIFIED		CDCL3
2042M	C	7.00- 7.50		UNSPECIFIED		CDCL3
2361M	C	7.00- 7.60		UNSPECIFIED		CDCL3
744M	C	7.00- 7.60		UNSPECIFIED		CDCL3
539M	C	7.00- 7.85		UNSPECIFIED		CDCL3
764M	C	7.00- 7.85		UNSPECIFIED		POLYSOL-D
1571M	C	7.00- 7.90		UNSPECIFIED		CDCL3
792M	C	7.00- 7.50		UNSPECIFIED	S	D2O
296M	D	7.00- 7.30		UNSPECIFIED		CCL4
156M	D	7.00- 7.40		UNSPECIFIED		CCL4
146M	D	7.00- 7.45		UNSPECIFIED		CCL4
2114M	D	7.00- 7.50		UNSPECIFIED		CCL4
1725M	D	7.00- 8.00		UNSPECIFIED		CCL4
1820M	E	7.00- 7.40		UNSPECIFIED		CCL4
600M	E	7.00- 7.50		UNSPECIFIED		CCL4
162M	E	7.00- 7.50		UNSPECIFIED		CDCL3
1950M	A	7.01	CHA	AA(C(OH)-C*)		C3H6O
683M	B	7.01	CHA	AN(CH-N/CH-C(CH3))		CCL4
683M	C	7.01	CHA	AN(C(CH3)-CH-N)		CCL4
2123M	A	7.01	CHA	AR5A<C(F)-CH-C*/CH-C*-C*>		CDCL3
1922M	A	7.01	CHA	A<CH-C(CL)-C(OH)/CH-C(NO2)>		CDCL3
666M	D	7.01	CHA	A<C(CH2-A)/CH-C(N(CH3/CH3))>		CDCL3
1713M	D	7.01	CHA	A<C(CH2-OH)/CH-C(CH3)>		CCL4
2339M	E	7.01	CHA	A<C(CH3)-C(NH-C(=O))/CH-C(CH3)>		CDCL3
1713M	D	7.01	CHA	A<C(CH3)/CH-C(CH2-OH)>		CCL4
2423M	C	7.01	CHA	A<C(CH3)/CH-C(NH-C(=O))>		DMSO-D6
1162M	C	7.01	CHA	A<C(CH3)/CH-C(S-CH2)>		POLYSOL-D
592M	F	7.01	CHA	A<C(CH(CH3/CH3))/CH-C(NH-CH3)>		CDCL3
2919M	E	7.01	CHA	A<C(OH)-C(OH)-C(OH)/C(C(=O)-O-CH2)>		C3D6O
1372M	D	7.01 APP.	CHA	A(CH-C(CH3)-C(NH-SO2)/CH-C(CH3))		CDCL3
1372M	D	7.01 APP.	CHA	A(C(CH3)-C(NH-SO2)-C(CH3))		CDCL3
663M	E	7.01	CHA	A(C(CH3)/CH-C(N(CH2/CH2)))		CDCL3
2924M	D	7.01	CHA	A(C(CH3)/CH-C(O-C(=O)-CH3))		CCL4
1350M	E	7.01- 7.59	CHA	A(C(NH-C(=S)))		CDCL3
1032M	A	7.01	CHA	A(C(N(N=O/A)))		CDCL3
1176M	A	7.01- 7.55		UNSPECIFIED		CDCL3
1951M	A	7.01- 7.86		UNSPECIFIED		C3H6O
2942M	B	7.01- 7.49		UNSPECIFIED		CCL4
2974M	C	7.01- 7.72		UNSPECIFIED		CDCL3
175M	E	7.01 APP.		UNSPECIFIED		CCL4
1350M	E	7.01- 7.59		UNSPECIFIED		CDCL3

BOOK NO.	ASSIGN-MENT	CHEM SHIFT - ppm -	PROTON GROUP	ENVIRONMENTAL GROUPS	S	SOLVENT
1241M	B	7.02	CHA	AA(CH-C*/CH-C(SH)-C*)		CDCL3
687M	F	7.02	CHA	AN<C(CH2-CH2)-N>		CCL4
685M	C	7.02	CHA	AN<C(CH2-CH3)/CH-N>		CCL4
196M	C	7.02 APP.	CHA	AR6(CH-C*-CH2)		CDCL3
196M	C	7.02 APP.	CHA	AR6(C*-CH2-CH2)		CDCL3
2587M	A	7.02	CHA	A<CH-C(C(=O)-OH)-C(OH)>		TFA
299M	C	7.02	CHA	A<C(CH3)-C(CL)/CH-C(CH3)>		CCL4
2362M	D	7.02	CHA	A<C(N(C(=O)-H/CH2)/CH-C(CH3)>		CDCL3
2293M	B	7.02	CHA	A<C(OH)-C(C(=O)-NH2)>		DMSO-D6
2178M	D	7.02	CHA	A<C(O-CH3)-CH-C(C(=O)-H)/CH-C(OH)>		CCL4
1563M	D	7.02	CHA	A<C(O-CH3)-C(O-CH3)/C(C:N)>		CDCL3
919M	C	7.02	CHA	A(C(CH3)-C(QN(=O))/CH-C(CH3))		CCL4
285M	C	7.02	CHA	A(C(CH3)/CH-C(CH2-CL))		CCL4
514M	C	7.02	CHA	A(C(CL)/CH-C(NH2))		DMSO
380M	B	7.02	Q2	A/BR		CCL4
2441M	A	7.02 APP.		UNSPECIFIED		DMSO-D6
2868M	A	7.02- 7.54		UNSPECIFIED		CDCL3
1195M	B	7.02 APP.		UNSPECIFIED		CDCL3
374M	B	7.02- 7.51		UNSPECIFIED		CDCL3
984M	B	7.02- 7.66		UNSPECIFIED		CCL4
1717M	C	7.02- 7.51		UNSPECIFIED		CDCL3
2341M	B	7.03	CHA	AN<CH-N-C(NH-C(=O)) >		CDCL3
2585M	C	7.03	CHA	A<CH-C(C(=O)-OH)-C(O-CH2)>		CCL4
1503M	C	7.03	CHA	A<C(CH2.2-BR)/CH-C(O-CH3)>		CCL4
1902M	E	7.03	CHA	A<C(CH2.2-C:N)/CH-C(OH)>		CDCL3
1497M	E	7.03	CHA	A<C(CH2-CH3)/CH-C(O-CH3)>		CCL4
1070M	D	7.03	CHA	A<C(CH3)-C(NO2)/CH-C(NH2)>		CDCL3
501M	E	7.03	CHA	A<C(CH(CH3/CH3))-C(NH2)-C(CH(CH3/CH3))>		CDCL3
493M	E	7.03	CHA	A<C(CH(CH3/CH3))/CH-C(NH2)>		CDCL3
1881M	E	7.03	CHA	A<C(CH3/CH3))/CH-C(OH)>		CDCL3
1534M	E	7.03	CHA	A<C(O-CH2)-C(NO2)>		CCL4
2096M	B	7.03	CHA	A<C(O-CH3)/CH-C(C(=O)-Q2)>		POLYSOL-D
1923M	E	7.03	CHA	A<C(S-CH3)-CH-C(CH3)/CH-C(OH)>		CDCL3
393M	A	7.03	CHA	A(CH-C(BR)/CH-C(CL))		CCL4
518M	D	7.03	CHA	A(CH-C(NH2)-C(BR))		CDCL3
652M	D	7.03	CHA	A(CH-C(N(CH2/CH3)))		CCL4
1227M	D	7.03	CHA	A(C(CH2-SH)-C(CH2-SH)/C(CH3)-C(CH3))		CDCL3
2323M	C	7.03	CHA	A(C(CH3)/CH-C(NH-C(=O)))		DMSO-D6
526M	E	7.03	CHA	A(C(I)-CH-C(NH2))		CDCL3
2520M	E	7.03	Q2	CH2.2-CH3/H/C(=O)-OH		CCL4
2821M	D	7.03	Q2	C(=O)-CH3/H/C(=O)-O-CH3		CDCL3
1961M	B	7.03- 7.81		UNSPECIFIED		DMSO
605M	C	7.03 APP.		UNSPECIFIED		CCL4
483M	D	7.03- 7.32		UNSPECIFIED		CDCL3
639M	D	7.03- 7.53		UNSPECIFIED		CDCL3
694M	B	7.04	CHA	AN<C(C(CH3/CH3/CH3))-N-C(C(CH3/CH3/CH3))>		CCL4
929M	C	7.04	CHA	A<C(CH2-CH3)-C(N=C=N)/CH-C(CH2-CH3)>		CDCL3
929M	C	7.04	CHA	A<C(CH2-CH3)-C(N=C=N)-C(CH2-CH3)>		CDCL3
308M	B	7.04 APP.	CHA	A<C(CH3)-C(CL)/CH-C(CL)>		CCL4
304M	D	7.04	CHA	A<C(CH3)-C(CL)/CH-C(F)>		CCL4
308M	B	7.04 APP.	CHA	A<C(CL)-CH-C(CL)/CH-C(CH3)>		CCL4
1908M	C	7.04	CHA	A<C(C(A/CH3/CH3))/CH-C(OH)>		POLYSOL-D
2684M	B	7.04	CHA	A<C(OH)-C(C(=O)-O-NH4)>		D2O
2324M	D	7.04	CHA	A(C(CH2-CH3)/CH-C(NH-C(=O)))		CDCL3
485M	D	7.04	CHA	A(C(CH2-NH2)/CH-C(CH3))		CCL4
133M	B	7.04	CHA	A(C(CH3))		CCL4
1364M	C	7.04	CHA	A(C(CH3)-C(SO2-NH2)-C(CH3)/C(CH3))		TFA
485M	D	7.04	CHA	A(C(CH3)/CH-C(CH2-NH2))		CCL4
1100M	A	7.04- 7.50	CHA	A(C(CL)/CH-C(P(A/A)))		CDCL3
1100M	A	7.04- 7.50	CHA	A(C(P(A/A))/CH-C(CL))		CDCL3
133M	B	7.04	CHA	UNSPECIFIED		CCL4
605M	D	7.04 APP.	NHR	R5NA(C*/CH-CH)		CCL4
2534M	B	7.04	Q1	C(=O)-OH/CH3/C(=O)-OH		TFA
370M	B	7.04	Q2	BR/H/BR		CCL4
2524M	E	7.04	Q2	CH2-CH2/C(=O)-OH		CCL4
2517M	C	7.04	Q2	CH3/H/C(=O)-OH		CDCL3
851M	A	7.04	Q2	QN(OH)/A		DMSO
1962M	A	7.04- 7.41		UNSPECIFIED		CDCL3
606M	C	7.04		UNSPECIFIED		CDCL3
1726M	D	7.04- 7.60		UNSPECIFIED		CDCL3
1954M	C	7.05- 7.45	CHA	AA<CH-C*-C(CH2.2-C:N)/CH-CH-C*>		POLYSOL-D
1954M	C	7.05- 7.45	CHA	AA<CH-C*/CH-CH-C*>		POLYSOL-D
719M	B	7.05	CHA	ANA<C(CH3)-N-C*/CH-C*>		CCL4
492M	G	7.05	CHA	A<CH-C(NH2)/CH-C(CH2-CH3)>		CDCL3
1332M	B	7.05- 7.45	CHA	A<C(CH2-C(=S))>		POLYSOL-D
425M	B	7.05- 7.45	CHA	A<C(CH2-I)>		CDCL3
2940M	B	7.05	CHA	A<C(CH3)/CH-C(O-C(=O)-O)>		CCL4
1196M	B	7.05	CHA	A<C(CH3)/CH-C(S-S)>		CDCL3
2850M	F	7.05- 7.45	CHA	A<C(CH(OH/CH2))>		CCL4
2910M	C	7.05	CHA	A<C(C(=O)-O-CH3)-CH-C(NH2)/CH-C(C(=O)-O-CH3)>		POLYSOL-D
168M	D	7.05- 7.50	CHA	A<C(C:C)>		CCL4

BOOK NO.	ASSIGN-MENT	CHEM SHIFT - ppm -	PROTON GROUP	ENVIRONMENTAL GROUPS	S	SOLVENT
290M	A	7.05	CHA	A<C(F)/CH-C(C-CL3)>		CCL4
2940M	B	7.05	CHA	A<C(O-C(=O)-O)/CH-C(CH3)>		CCL4
2856M	E	7.05- 7.55	CHA	A<C(Q1(CH3/C(=O)-O-CH2))>		CCL4
2842M	G	7.05- 7.45	CHA	A<C(Q2(H/CH2-O-C(=O)/H))>		CCL4
867M	C	7.05- 7.50	CHA	A<C(Q2(QN))>		CDCL3
676M	C	7.05- 7.60	CHA	A<C(R5N<N-C(CH3)=/C(CH3)=>		CDCL3
640M	D	7.05	CHA	A(CH-CH-C(R6NN(N/CH2-CH2-NH)))		CDCL3
649M	D	7.05 APP.	CHA	A(CH-C(N(CH2/CH2)))		CCL4
761M	D	7.05	CHA	A(C(CH3)/CH-C(N(N/CH3)))		CDCL3
1239M	E	7.05	CHA	A(C(SH)-C(SH)/C(CH3))		CDCL3
1167M	B	7.05- 7.55	CHA	A(C(S-CH2))		CDCL3
2681M	B	7.05	CHR	R5O<=C(C(=O)-O-K)-O/CH=CH>	S	D2O
1137M	C	7.05	CHR	R5S<=CH-C(CH3)=/S-CH=>		CCL4
2043M	A	7.05	Q2	C(=O)-Q2/H/A		CDCL3
2122M	A	7.05- 7.70		UNSPECIFIED		CCL4
425M	B	7.05- 7.45		UNSPECIFIED		CDCL3
1332M	B	7.05- 7.45		UNSPECIFIED		POLYSOL-D
1167M	B	7.05- 7.55		UNSPECIFIED		CDCL3
2450M	B	7.05- 7.65		UNSPECIFIED		CDCL3
790M	B	7.05- 7.40		UNSPECIFIED	S	POLYSOL-D
978M	C	7.05		UNSPECIFIED		CDCL3
867M	C	7.05- 7.50		UNSPECIFIED		CDCL3
676M	C	7.05- 7.60		UNSPECIFIED		CDCL3
505M	C	7.05- 7.62		UNSPECIFIED		C3H6O
168M	D	7.05- 7.50		UNSPECIFIED		CCL4
2856M	E	7.05- 7.55		UNSPECIFIED		CCL4
2850M	F	7.05- 7.45		UNSPECIFIED		CCL4
2842M	G	7.05- 7.45		UNSPECIFIED		CCL4
1952M	C	7.06	CHA	AA(C(CH3)-C(OH)-C*/CH-C*)		CDCL3
705M	D	7.06	CHA	AN<CH-N-C(CH2-N)>		CDCL3
712M	D	7.06	CHA	AN<CH-N-C(CH2-R6N)>		CDCL3
713M	B	7.06	CHA	AN<C(CH2.2-AN)/CH-N>		CDCL3
590M	F	7.06	CHA	A<CH-C(NH-CH3)/CH-C(CH3)>		CDCL3
1502M	F	7.06	CHA	A<CH-C(O-CH2.4)/CH-C(CH3)>		CCL4
2080M	C	7.06	CHA	A<C(OH)-CH-C(C(=O)-CH3)/CH-C(OH)>		DMSO-D6
2679M	A	7.06	CHA	A<C(OH)/CH-C(C(=O)-O-NA)>		D2O
1905M	A	7.06	CHA	A<C(OH)/CH-C(NO2)>		C3H6O
2435M	C	7.06	CHA	A(CH-CH-C(NH-C(=O)))		CDCL3
396M	A	7.06	CHA	A(CH-C(BR)-C(BR))		CCL4
928M	B	7.06	CHA	A(C(CH3)/CH-C(QN(=N-A)))		CDCL3
2389M	B	7.06	CHA	A(C(I)/CH-C(R5N(N-C(=O)/C(=O))))		TFA
817M	C	7.06	CHA	A(C(N(CH2/CH2))/CH-C(NH2))	S	D2O
928M	B	7.06	CHA	A(C(QN(=N-A))/CH-C(CH3))		CDCL3
2884M	C	7.06	CHA	A(C(QN(=O))/CH-C(C(=O)-O-CH2))		CDCL3
2141M	F	7.06	CHR	R5O<=C(C(=O)-Q1)-O/CH=CH>		CCL4
2851M	C	7.06	NH	C(=O)-A/CH2-C(=O)-O		CDCL3
1181M	B	7.06- 7.51		UNSPECIFIED		CCL4
878M	C	7.06- 7.46		UNSPECIFIED		DMSO-D6
2372M	E	7.06- 7.40		UNSPECIFIED		CDCL3
760M	C	7.07	CHA	A<CH-C(NH-NH)>		DMSO-D6
656M	F	7.07	CHA	A<CH-C(N(CH2/CH2))>		CCL4
1894M	D	7.07	CHA	A<CH-C(OH)-C(BR)>		CDCL3
1911M	B	7.07	CHA	A<CH-C(OH)/CH-C(OH)>		C3H6O
1551M	F	7.07	CHA	A<CH-C(O-CH3)-C(CH3)/CH-C(CH3)>		CDCL3
918M	C	7.07	CHA	A<C(CH2-A)/CH-C(N=C=O)>		POLYSOL-D
1714M	E	7.07	CHA	A<C(CH2-OH)/CH-C(CH(CH3/CH3))>		CCL4
2057M	C	7.07	CHA	A<C(CH3)-CH-C(C(=O)-CH3)/CH-C(CH3)>		CCL4
2057M	C	7.07	CHA	A<C(CH3)-C(C(=O)-CH3)/CH-C(CH3)>		CCL4
2943M	B	7.07	CHA	A<C(CH3)/CH-C(O-C(=O)-A)>		CCL4
1714M	E	7.07	CHA	A<C(CH(CH3/CH3))/CH-C(CH2-OH)>		CCL4
2588M	A	7.07	CHA	A<C(OH)/CH-C(C(=O)-OH)>		C3H6O
1538M	B	7.07	CHA	A<C(O-CH3)/CH-C(SO2-CL)>		CDCL3
2943M	B	7.07	CHA	A<C(O-C(=O)-A)/CH-C(CH3)>		CCL4
1235M	B	7.07	CHA	A<C(SH)/CH-C(BR)>		CDCL3
148M	B	7.07 APP.	CHA	A(C(CH2-A))		CCL4
134M	C	7.07	CHA	A(C(CH2-CH3))		CCL4
428M	C	7.07	CHA	A(C(CH3)-CH-C(I))		CCL4
1170M	B	7.07	CHA	A(C(CH3)/CH-C(S-A))		CDCL3
1917M	G	7.07	CHA	A(C(CH(CH3/CH3))-C(OH)/CH-C(CH3))		CDCL3
2365M	E	7.07- 7.60	CHA	A(C(N(C(=O)/CH2))		CDCL3
2388M	A	7.07	CHR	R5N<=CH-C(=O)/C(=O)-N(A<C-CH-CH-C(BR)>)>		POLYSOL-D
2936M	E	7.07	CHR	R5O<=C(C(=O)-O-CH2.4)-O/CH=CH>		CCL4
927M	B	7.07		UNSPECIFIED		CCL4
148M	B	7.07 APP.		UNSPECIFIED		CCL4
293M	B	7.07 APP.		UNSPECIFIED		CCL4
134M	C	7.07		UNSPECIFIED		CCL4
2363M	C	7.07- 7.59		UNSPECIFIED		CDCL3
2365M	E	7.08- 7.60		UNSPECIFIED		CDCL3
1175M	B	7.08- 7.53	CHA	AR5NS(CH-C*-N=/CH-CH-C*)		CDCL3
1175M	B	7.08- 7.53	CHA	AR5NS(CH-C*-S/CH-CH-C*)		CDCL3
582M	E	7.08	CHA	A<CH-C(NH-CH3)>		CCL4

BOOK NO.	ASSIGN-MENT	CHEM SHIFT - ppm -	PROTON GROUP	ENVIRONMENTAL GROUPS	S	SOLVENT
2933M	D	7.08	CHA	A<C(CH3)/CH-C(O-C(=O)-CH2)>		CDCL3
870M	B	7.08	CHA	A<C(CH3)/CH-C(QN(Q2))>		CDCL3
870M	B	7.08	CHA	A<C(QN(Q2))/CH-C(CH3)>		CDCL3
163M	B	7.08	CHA	A<C(Q1(A/A))>		CDCL3
1887M	E	7.08	CHA	A<C(R6<CH-CH2/CH2>)/CH-C(OH)>		CDCL3
385M	D	7.08 APP.	CHA	A(CH-C(CH(CH3/CH3))-C(BR)/CH-C(CH3))		CDCL3
2322M	D	7.08	CHA	A(CH-C(NH-C(=O))/CH-C(CH3))		CDCL3
185M	C	7.08	CHA	A(C(CH2.2-A)/CH-C(CH3))		CDCL3
385M	D	7.08 APP.	CHA	A(C(CH3)-CH-C(BR)/CH-C(CH(CH3/CH3)))		CDCL3
589M	F	7.08	CHA	A(C(CH3)-C(NH-CH3))		CDCL3
185M	C	7.08	CHA	A(C(CH3)/CH-C(CH2.2-A))		CDCL3
2345M	B	7.08	CHA	A(C(CH3)/CH-C(NH-C(=O)))		CDCL3
1022M	A	7.08	CHA	A(C(NH-A)/CH-C(N=O))		POLYSOL-D
824M	B	7.08	CHA	A(C(O-CH3)/CH-C(NH-NH2))	S	D20
1506M	F	7.08	CHA	A(C(Q2(CH3))/CH-C(O-CH3))		CCL4
1192M	B	7.08- 7.55	CHA	A(C(S-S))		CCL4
159M	A	7.08	Q2	A/H/A		CDCL3
2209M	A	7.08	Q2	C(=O)-CL/H/C(=O)-CL		CCL4
296M	C	7.08	Q3	A<C-C(CL)>/H/H		CCL4
2945M	A	7.08- 7.63		UNSPECIFIED		CDCL3
2872M	B	7.08- 7.50		UNSPECIFIED		CCL4
163M	B	7.08		UNSPECIFIED		CDCL3
2321M	C	7.08		UNSPECIFIED		CDCL3
1956M	C	7.08- 7.85		UNSPECIFIED		C3H6O
172M	D	7.08- 7.28		UNSPECIFIED		CCL4
1192M	B	7.08- 7.55		UNSPECIFIED		CCL4
2854M	E	7.08		UNSPECIFIED		CCL4
686M	C	7.09	CHA	AN<C(CH(CH3/CH3))/CH-N>		CDCL3
1236M	D	7.09	CHA	A<CH-C(NH2)-C(SH)>		CDCL3
137M	D	7.09	CHA	A<C(CH2-CH2)>		CCL4
920M	A	7.09 APP.	CHA	A<C(CL)-CH-C(N=C=O)/CH-C(CL)>		CDCL3
920M	A	7.09 APP.	CHA	A<C(CL)/C(N=C=O)-C(CL)>		CDCL3
2587M	B	7.09	CHA	A<C(OH)-C(C(=O)-OH)>		TFA
1903M	B	7.09	CHA	A<C(OH)-C(NO2)>		CCL4
1091M	C	7.09- 7.37	CHA	A(CH-CH-C(SI(A/A/CH2)))		CDCL3
1091M	C	7.09- 7.37	CHA	A(CH-C(SI(A/A/CH2)))		CDCL3
2056M	C	7.09	CHA	A(C(CH3)/CH-C(C(=O)-CH3))		CCL4
1496M	D	7.09	CHA	A(C(CH3)/CH-C(O-CH3))		CDCL3
136M	C	7.09	CHA	A(C(CH(CH3/CH3)))		CCL4
2316M	D	7.09	CHA	A(C(NH-C(=O)))		CDCL3
1378M	A	7.09	CHA	A(C(NH-SO2)/CH-C(BR))		POLYSOL-D
791M	B	7.09	CHA	A(C(O-CH3)/CH-C(NH2))	S	D20
1230M	D	7.09	CHA	A(C(SH)/CH-C(CH3))		CDCL3
1147M	C	7.09	CHR	R5S(=CH-CH=/S-C(CH2-R5S)=)		CDCL3
2535M	C	7.09 APP.	CHR	R6(=C(C(=O)-OH)-CH2/CH2-CH2)		CCL4
390M	B	7.09- 7.43		UNSPECIFIED		CCL4
145M	C	7.09		UNSPECIFIED		CCL4
136M	C	7.09		UNSPECIFIED		CCL4
611M	C	7.09		UNSPECIFIED		CDCL3
137M	D	7.09		UNSPECIFIED		CCL4
1958M	B	7.10	CHA	AA<C*-CH-C(OH)/C(OH)>		C3D6O
727M	B	7.10	CHA	ANA(C*/C(NH2)-CH-N)		CDCL3
704M	A	7.10	CHA	AN(CH-N/CH-C(BR))		CCL4
1486M	B	7.10- 7.40	CHA	A<CH-CH-C(C(O/O/A))>		CDCL3
2863M	D	7.10- 7.60	CHA	A<CH-CH-C(C(=O)-O-CH2.2)>		CCL4
1333M	A	7.10- 7.50	CHA	A<CH-CH-C(C(=S)-HNH)>		POLYSOL-D
674M	D	7.10- 7.35	CHA	A<CH-CH-C(R5NN<C=N/N(A)>)>		CDCL3
395M	B	7.10	CHA	A<CH-C(BR)/CH-C(CH2-BR)>		CDCL3
1486M	B	7.10- 7.40	CHA	A<CH-C(C(O/O/A))>		CDCL3
2238M	C	7.10	CHA	A<CH-C(C(=O)-CL)-C(CH3)/CH-C(CH3)>		CCL4
2863M	D	7.10- 7.60	CHA	A<CH-C(C(=O)-O-CH2.2)>		CCL4
1333M	A	7.10- 7.50	CHA	A<CH-C(C(=S)-HNH)>		POLYSOL-D
2069M	B	7.10	CHA	A<CH-C(I)/CH-C(C(=O)-CH3)>		CDCL3
1054M	A	7.10- 7.50	CHA	A<CH-C(NO2)-C(F)>		CCL4
674M	D	7.10- 7.35	CHA	A<CH-C(R5NN<C=N/N(A)>)>		CDCL3
1930M	B	7.10- 7.70	CHA	A<C(A<C-CH-C(OH)-C(OH)>)>		POLYSOL-D
143M	D	7.10	CHA	A<C(CH2-CH2)>		CCL4
709M	D	7.10- 7.50	CHA	A<C(CH2-NH)>		DMSO-D6
646M	D	7.10- 7.50	CHA	A<C(CH2-N)>		CDCL3
1723M	E	7.10	CHA	A<C(CH2-OH)/CH-C(O-CH3)>		CCL4
1068M	C	7.10	CHA	A<C(CH3)-CH-C(CH3)/CH-C(NO2)>		CDCL3
904M	C	7.10	CHA	A<C(CH3)/CH-C(N=N-NH)>		CDCL3
2925M	G	7.10	CHA	A<C(CH3)/CH-C(O-C(=O)-CH2)>		CCL4
170M	A	7.10- 7.70	CHA	A<C(C:C)>		CDCL3
1054M	A	7.10- 7.50	CHA	A<C(F)-C(NO2)>		CCL4
157M	D	7.10- 7.52	CHA	A<C(Q2(CH3/H/H))>		CCL4
1151M	C	7.10- 7.65	CHA	A<C(R5NS<C=C(A)/N=>)>		CDCL3
1151M	B	7.10- 7.65	CHA	A<C(R5NS<C=C(A)/S>)>		CDCL3
1090M	C	7.10- 7.60	CHA	A<C(SI(A/CH2.11/CH2.11))>		CCL4
1923M	F	7.10	CHA	A<C(S-CH3)/C(CH3)-C(OH)>		CDCL3
288M	A	7.10- 7.85	CHA	A<C-C(CL/CL/A)>		CCL4

BOOK NO.	ASSIGN-MENT	CHEM SHIFT - ppm -	PROTON GROUP	ENVIRONMENTAL GROUPS	S	SOLVENT
169M	A	7.10- 7.65	CHA	A<C-C(C:C-A)>		CCL4
2411M	C	7.10- 7.50	CHA	A(CH-CH-C(C(=O)-NH))		CDCL3
2411M	C	7.10- 7.50	CHA	A(CH-C(C(=O)-NH))		CDCL3
1198M	D	7.10	CHA	A(CH-C(NH2)-C(S-S))		CDCL3
807M	B	7.10- 7.40	CHA	A(CH-C(NH-A))	S	DMSO
648M	C	7.10	CHA	A(CH-C(N(CH3/CH3)))		CCL4
1710M	D	7.10	CHA	A(CH-C(O-CH2))		CCL4
1509M	D	7.10- 7.50	CHA	A(CH-C(O-CH3)-C(CL))		CDCL3
1535M	D	7.10	CHA	A(CH-C(O-CH3)/CH-C(SH))		CDCL3
762M	C	7.10- 7.68	CHA	A(C(A(C-CH-CH-C(N(N/CH3)))))		CCL4
1485M	E	7.10 APP.	CHA	A(C(CH2.2-O))		CCL4
1702M	E	7.10	CHA	A(C(CH2-CH2))		CCL4
921M	D	7.10	CHA	A(C(CH3)-C(N=C=O)/CH-C(N=C=O))		CCL4
138M	E	7.10	CHA	A(C(CH(CH2/CH3)))		CDCL3
1509M	D	7.10- 7.50	CHA	A(C(CL)-C(O-CH3))		CDCL3
1893M	C	7.10	CHA	A(C(CL)/CH-C(OH))		CCL4
1513M	D	7.10	CHA	A(C(CL)/CH-C(O-CH2))		CDCL3
2214M	A	7.10- 7.60	CHA	A(C(C(BR/C(=O)-BR/A)))		CDCL3
167M	B	7.10- 7.50	CHA	A(C(C:C)) --		DMSO
807M	B	7.10- 7.40	CHA	A(C(NH-A))	S	DMSO
1306M	B	7.10- 7.65	CHA	A(C(NH-A))	S	CDCL3
1818M	D	7.10- 7.60	CHA	A(C(OH/CH2/CH2))		CDCL3
1097M	C	7.10- 7.60	CHA	A(C(P(A/CH2)))		CDCL3
165M	A	7.10- 7.50	CHA	A(C(Q2/A))		CDCL3
1239M	F	7.10	CHA	A(C(SH)-C(SH)/CH-C(CH3))		CCL4
1136M	B	7.10	CHR	R5S(S-CH=/=CH-CH=)		CCL4
1144M	A	7.10	CHR	R5S(=CH-S/CH=C(C:N))		POLYSOL-D
1347M	D	7.10	NH	C(=S)-NH/CH2.9-CH3		CCL4
2161M	D	7.10	Q1	A/C(=O)-H/CH2-CH2		POLYSOL-D
1360M	B	7.10	Q2	A/H/SO2-NH2		CDCL3
165M	A	7.10- 7.50		UNSPECIFIED		CDCL3
902M	A	7.10- 7.59		UNSPECIFIED		CDCL3
2214M	A	7.10- 7.60		UNSPECIFIED		DMSO
1343M	A	7.10- 7.60		UNSPECIFIED		CCL4
1150M	A	7.10- 7.64		UNSPECIFIED		CDCL3
1335M	A	7.10- 7.70		UNSPECIFIED		CDCL3
745M	A	7.10- 7.70		UNSPECIFIED		CDCL3
170M	A	7.10- 7.70		UNSPECIFIED		CDCL3
914M	A	7.10- 7.80		UNSPECIFIED		CCL4
382M	B	7.10		UNSPECIFIED		CDCL3
2397M	B	7.10- 7.40		UNSPECIFIED		CDCL3
167M	B	7.10- 7.50		UNSPECIFIED		CDCL3
211M	B	7.10- 7.50		UNSPECIFIED		POLYSOL-D
1022M	B	7.10- 7.50		UNSPECIFIED		CDCL3
1166M	B	7.10- 7.55		UNSPECIFIED		POLYSOL-D
873M	B	7.10- 7.55		UNSPECIFIED		CDCL3
697M	B	7.10- 7.65		UNSPECIFIED		CCL4
2222M	B	7.10- 7.65		UNSPECIFIED		CDCL3
1151M	B	7.10- 7.65		UNSPECIFIED		CDCL3
2123M	B	7.10- 7.65		UNSPECIFIED		CDCL3
173M	B	7.10- 7.70		UNSPECIFIED.		POLYSOL-D
1930M	B	7.10- 7.70		UNSPECIFIED		CDCL3
1174M	B	7.10- 7.80		UNSPECIFIED		DMSO
1306M	B	7.10- 7.65		UNSPECIFIED	S	CCL4
372M	C	7.10 APP.		UNSPECIFIED		CCL4
1193M	C	7.10- 7.50		UNSPECIFIED		DMSO-D6
889M	C	7.10- 7.50		UNSPECIFIED		DMSO
1179M	C	7.10- 7.53		UNSPECIFIED		CCL4
201M	C	7.10- 7.55		UNSPECIFIED		CCL4
1090M	C	7.10- 7.60		UNSPECIFIED		CCL4
1049M	C	7.10- 7.60		UNSPECIFIED		CDCL3
1097M	C	7.10- 7.60		UNSPECIFIED		CDCL3
1151M	C	7.10- 7.65		UNSPECIFIED		DMSO
762M	C	7.10- 7.68		UNSPECIFIED		CCL4
541M	C	7.10- 7.80		UNSPECIFIED		CDCL3
143M	D	7.10		UNSPECIFIED		DMSO-D6
646M	D	7.10- 7.50		UNSPECIFIED		CCL4
709M	D	7.10- 7.50		UNSPECIFIED		CDCL3
157M	D	7.10- 7.52		UNSPECIFIED		CDCL3
1570M	D	7.10- 7.55		UNSPECIFIED		CDCL3
1818M	D	7.10- 7.60		UNSPECIFIED		D20
599M	D	7.10- 7.85		UNSPECIFIED		CCL4
2560M	D	7.10- 7.60		UNSPECIFIED	S	CCL4
1702M	E	7.10		UNSPECIFIED		CCL4
138M	E	7.10		UNSPECIFIED		POLYSOL-D
1485M	E	7.10 APP.		UNSPECIFIED		CCL4
862M	E	7.10- 7.60		UNSPECIFIED		TFA
317M	A	7.11	CHA	AA<CH-C(CL)-C*/CH-C*>		CDCL3
1963M	B	7.11	CHA	ANA<C(OH)-N-C*/C(CH3)-C*>		CDCL3
730M	B	7.11	CHA	ANA(C*/C(CH3)-N-C(CL))		
740M	B	7.11	CHA	AR5NN(C(CH3)-CH-C*/CH-C*-NH)		

BOOK NO.	ASSIGN-MENT	CHEM SHIFT - ppm -	PROTON GROUP	ENVIRONMENTAL GROUPS	S	SOLVENT
2116M	G	7.11	CHA	AR6<C*-CH2-CH2/CH-C(O-CH3)>		CDCL3
434M	B	7.11	CHA	A<CH-C(I)-C(BR)>		CCL4
862M	D	7.11	CHA	A<CH-C(NH2)-C(QN(A/OH))>		POLYSOL-D
2880M	D	7.11	CHA	A<CH-C(NH2)/CH-C(C(=O)-O-CH3)>		CDCL3
2634M	D	7.11	CHA	A<CH-C(NH-CH2)>		DMSO-D6
2333M	B	7.11	CHA	A<CH-C(NH-C(=O)¡-C(NO2)>		CDCL3
2849M	E	7.11 APP.	CHA	A<C(CH2.3-C(=O)-O)>		CCL4
311M	B	7.11	CHA	A<C(CH2-CL)-CH-C(CL)/CH-C(CL)>		CCL4
486M	E	7.11 APP.	CHA	A<C(CH2-NH2)/CH-C(CH(CH3/CH3))>		CCL4
154M	D	7.11	CHA	A<C(CH2-Q2)>		CCL4
1821M	D	7.11	CHA	A<C(CH3)/CH-C(R6<C-(OH)-CH2/CH2>)>		CDCL3
486M	E	7.11 APP.	CHA	A<C(CH(CH3/CH3)¡/CH-C(CH2-NH2)>		CCL4
299M	D	7.11	CHA	A<C(CL)-C(CH3)/C(CH3)>		CCL4
1240M	D	7.11	CHA	A<C(CL)-C(SH)/CH-C(SH)>		CCL4
2585M	D	7.11	CHA	A<C(O-CH2)-C(C(=O)-OH)>		CCL4
1160M	B	7.11	CHA	A<C(S-CH3)/CH-C(BR)>		CDCL3
427M	C	7.11 APP.	CHA	A(CH-C(CH3)-C(I))		CDCL3
1510M	C	7.11	CHA	A(CH-C(CL)/CH-C(O-CH3))		CCL4
427M	C	7.11 APP.	CHA	A(CH-C(I)-C(CH3))		CDCL3
654M	C	7.11	CHA	A(CH-C(N(CH2/CH2)))		CDCL3
176M	A	7.11	CHA	A(C(A(C-C(A))))		CDCL3
2833M	D	7.11	CHA	A(C(CH2-CH2))		CCL4
1074M	C	7.11	CHA	A(C(NO2)-C(NO2)/C(N(CH3/CH3)))		DMSO-D6
2969M	A	7.11	CHA	A(C(O-C(=O)-CL)/CH-C(NO2))		DMSO-D6
183M	C	7.11	CHA	A(C(R6)/CH-C(R6))		CDCL3
2935M	E	7.11	CHR	R5O<=C(C(=O)-O-CH2.2)-O/CH=CH>		CCL4
1576M	B	7.11	CHR	R5O(=C(C:N)-O/CH=CH)		CCL4
1141M	B	7.11	CHR	R5S<S-CH=/=C(BR)-CH=>		CDCL3
1366M	A	7.11	NH2	SO2-A		DMSO-D6
1367M	A	7.11	NH2	SO2-AA		POLYSOL-D
880M	A	7.11	QN	Q2(A)/QN(Q2)		CDCL3
880M	A	7.11	Q2	A/QN(QN)		CDCL3
894M	E	7.11	Q2	Q2(H/CH3/H)/H/C(=O)-NH		POLYSOL-D
399M	A	7.11- 7.63		UNSPECIFIED		CDCL3
154M	D	7.11		UNSPECIFIED		CCL4
2833M	D	7.11		UNSPECIFIED		CCL4
2849M	E	7.11 APP.		UNSPECIFIED		CCL4
205M	C	7.12	CHA	AA<C(CH3)-CH-C*/CH-C*>		CDCL3
723M	B	7.12	CHA	ANA<CH-N-C*/CH-C*>		CCL4
739M	D	7.12	CHA	AR5NN<CH-C*-NH/CH-CH-C*>		POLYSOL-D
739M	D	7.12	CHA	AR5NN<CH-C*-N=/CH-CH-C*>		POLYSOL-D
2047M	D	7.12- 7.55	CHA	A<CH-CH-C(C(=O)-CH2)>		CCL4
2047M	D	7.12- 7.55	CHA	A<CH-C(C(=O)-CH2)>		CCL4
525M	D	7.12	CHA	A<CH-C(NH2)-C(I)>		CDCL3
587M	H	7.12	CHA	A<CH-C(NH-CH2)>		CDCL3
1468M	E	7.12	CHA	A<CH-C(R6NO<N-CH2/CH2>)/CH-C(CH3)>		CDCL3
482M	E	7.12	CHA	A<C(CH2-CH2)>		CCL4
204M	B	7.12	CHA	A<C(CH3)-CH-C*/CH-C*>		CCL4
757M	C	7.12 APP.	CHA	A<C(CL)-C(NH-NH2)/CH-C(CL)>		CDCL3
757M	C	7.12 APP.	CHA	A<C(CL)/C(NH-NH2)-C(CL)>		CDCL3
1481M	C	7.12 APP.	CHA	A<C(C(O/A/A))>		CDCL3
1270M	A	7.12	CHA	A<C(F)/CH-C(SO2-A)>		CDCL3
528M	D	7.12	CHA	A<C(I)-CH-C(CH3)/CH-C(NH2)>		POLYSOL-D
1897M	B	7.12	CHA	A<C(I)-CH-C(OH)>		POLYSOL-D
1063M	E	7.12	CHA	A<C(NH-QN)/CH-C(NO2)>		POLYSOL-D
2916M	B	7.12	CHA	A<C(OH)-C(OH)-C(OH)/C(C(=O)-O-CH3)>		POLYSOL-D
1526M	C	7.12	CHA	A<C(O-CH3)-C(NH2)>	S	POLYSOL-D
594M	E	7.12	CHA	A(CH-C(NH-CH2))		CDCL3
586M	F	7.12	CHA	A(CH-C(NH-R6))		CDCL3
2557M	C	7.12	CHA	A(C(CH2-C(=O)-O)/CH-C(CH3))		CDCL3
652M	E	7.12	CHA	A(C(CH2-N))		CCL4
1716M	D	7.12	CHA	A(C(CH2-OH)/CH-C(F))		CDCL3
2557M	C	7.12	CHA	A(C(CH3)/CH-C(CH2-C(=O)-O))		CDCL3
294M	B	7.12	CHA	A(C(CH3)/CH-C(CL))		CCL4
1312M	F	7.12	CHA	A(C(CH3)/CH-C(SO3))	S	CDCL3
313M	A	7.12	CHA	A(C(CL)-CH-C(CL)/CH-C(CL))		CCL4
294M	C	7.12	CHA	A(C(CL)/CH-C(CH3))		CCL4
1370M	B	7.12 APP.	CHA	A(C(NH-SO2))		CDCL3
2244M	C	7.12	CHA	A(C(O-CH3)-CH-C(O-CH3)/C(C(=O)-CL))		CCL4
2182M	C	7.12	CHR	R5N<=CH-CH=/NH-C(C(=O)-H)=>		CDCL3
1140M	C	7.12	CHR	R5S<S-C(BR)=/=CH-CH=>		CCL4
1140M	B	7.12	CHR	R5S<=C(BR)-S/CH=CH>		CCL4
171M	A	7.12- 7.63		UNSPECIFIED		CDCL3
1370M	B	7.12 APP.		UNSPECIFIED		CDCL3
202M	B	7.12- 7.91		UNSPECIFIED		CDCL3
1481M	C	7.12 APP.		UNSPECIFIED		CDCL3
1173M	C	7.12- 7.58		UNSPECIFIED		CDCL3
1164M	D	7.12		UNSPECIFIED		CCL4
484M	D	7.12		UNSPECIFIED		CDCL3
652M	E	7.12		UNSPECIFIED		CCL4
482M	E	7.12		UNSPECIFIED		CCL4

: REPRESENTS TRIPLE BOND, ¬ REPRESENTS AN ARROW AND < AND > REPRESENT BRACKETS.   PAGE   273

BOOK NO.	ASSIGN-MENT	CHEM SHIFT - ppm -	PROTON GROUP	ENVIRONMENTAL GROUPS	S	SOLVENT
2146M	G	7.12 APP.		UNSPECIFIED		CCL4
718M	A	7.13	CHA	ANA<CH-N-C*/CH-C*>		CCL4
711M	D	7.13	CHA	AN(CH-N/CH-C(R5N(CH-CH2/CH2)))		CCL4
381M	A	7.13 APP.	CHA	A<CH-CH-C(BR)>		CCL4
2867M	C	7.13- 7.63	CHA	A<CH-CH-C(C(=O)-O-CH2)>		CCL4
653M	E	7.13	CHA	A<CH-CH-C(N(CH2/CH2))>		CDCL3
381M	A	7.13 APP.	CHA	A<CH-C(BR)>		CCL4
2867M	C	7.13- 7.63	CHA	A<CH-C(C(=O)-O-CH2)>		CCL4
2877M	F	7.13	CHA	A<CH-C(NH2)-C(C(=O)-O-CH2)>		CCL4
653M	E	7.13	CHA	A<CH-C(N(CH2/CH2))>		CDCL3
1517M	E	7.13	CHA	A<CH-C(O-CH2)-C(BR)>		CCL4
141M	D	7.13	CHA	A<C(CH2-CH2)>		CCL4
2239M	B	7.13	CHA	A<C(CH3)-C(CH3)/CH-C(C(=O)-CL)>		CCL4
1068M	D	7.13	CHA	A<C(CH3)-C(NO2)/C(CH3)>		CDCL3
1919M	C	7.13	CHA	A<C(CL)-CH-C(CL)/CH-C(OH)>		CDCL3
394M	A	7.13	CHA	A<C(CL)/CH-C(BR)>		CCL4
1539M	G	7.13	CHA	A<C(C(A/CH3/CH3)/CH-C(O-CH2)>		CDCL3
2871M	C	7.13	CHA	A<C(F)-CH-C(C(=O)-O-CH2)>		CCL4
229M	A	7.13	CHA	A<C(F)/CH-C(CF3)>		CCL4
585M	G	7.13	CHA	A(CH-C(NH-CH2.2))		CDCL3
589M	G	7.13	CHA	A(CH-C(NH-CH3)-C(CH3))		CDCL3
1231M	C	7.13	CHA	A(C(C(CH3/CH3/CH3)/CH-C(SH))		CCL4
1231M	C	7.13	CHA	A(C(SH)/CH-C(C(CH3/CH3/CH3)))		CCL4
2512M	C	7.13	CHR	R5S<=CH-CH=/S-C(CH2-C(=O)-OH)=>		CDCL3
2445M	C	7.13	NHR	R5NN<C(=O)-N(CH2-A)/C(CH3/CH3)-C(=O)>		CDCL3
912M	A	7.13		UNSPECIFIED		CDCL3
1889M	B	7.13- 7.70		UNSPECIFIED		DMSO
141M	D	7.13		UNSPECIFIED		CCL4
2986M	F	7.13		UNSPECIFIED		CCL4
699M	B	7.14	CHA	AN<CH-C(F)-N>		CCL4
681M	A	7.14	CHA	AN(CH-N)		CCL4
2115M	D	7.14	CHA	AR6<C*-CH2-CH2/CH-C(CH2-CH3)>		CDCL3
1880M	E	7.14	CHA	A<CH-C(OH)/CH-C(CH2-CH3)>		CDCL3
147M	C	7.14	CHA	A<C(CH2-CH2)>		CDCL3
153M	E	7.14	CHA	A<C(CH2-O3)>		CCL4
1225M	C	7.14	CHA	A<C(CH2-SH)/CH-C(CL)>		CCL4
2979M	D	7.14	CHA	A<C(CH3)/CH-C(O-C(=O)-NH2)>		DMSO-D6
1225M	C	7.14	CHA	A<C(CL)/CH-C(CH2-SH)>		CCL4
1238M	C	7.14	CHA	A<C(SH)/CH-C(NH2)>		CDCL3
1708M	F	7.14	CHA	A<C(S-CH2.2)/CH-C(CH3)>		CCL4
2548M	C	7.14	CHA	A(CH-C(N(CH2/CH2)))		POLYSOL-D
477M	D	7.14	CHA	A(C(CH2-CH2))		CCL4
823M	C	7.14	CHA	A(C(CL)-C(CH3)/C(NH-NH2))	S	DMSO-D6
1572M	B	7.14- 7.53		UNSPECIFIED		CDCL3
2043M	B	7.14- 7.80		UNSPECIFIED		CDCL3
147M	C	7.14		UNSPECIFIED		CDCL3
477M	D	7.14		UNSPECIFIED		CCL4
153M	E	7.14		UNSPECIFIED		CCL4
1242M	B	7.15	CHA	AA(C(SH)-CH-C*/CH-C*)		CDCL3
721M	B	7.15	CHA	ANA(CH-N-C*/CH-C*)		CDCL3
1728M	C	7.15	CHA	AN<CH-N-C(CH2-OH)>		CDCL3
2938M	C	7.15	CHA	AN(CH-N-C(CH2-C(=O)-O))		CDCL3
701M	A	7.15	CHA	AN(CH-N/CH-C(CL))		CCL4
2373M	B	7.15- 7.55	CHA	AR5NA<CH-C*-C*/CH-CH-C*>		CDCL3
2373M	B	7.15- 7.55	CHA	AR5NA<CH-C*-N(C(=O)-CH3)/CH-CH-C*>		CDCL3
1492M	E	7.15	CHA	A<CH-CH-C(O-CH2.2)>		CCL4
1594M	B	7.15- 7.45	CHA	A<CH-CH-C(SI(O/O/A))>		CDCL3
2065M	B	7.15- 7.63	CHA	A<CH-C(CL)/CH-C(C(=O)-CH3)>		CCL4
1492M	E	7.15	CHA	A<CH-C(O-CH2.2)>		CCL4
1594M	B	7.15- 7.45	CHA	A<CH-C(SI(O/O/A))>		CDCL3
2035M	D	7.15 APP.	CHA	A<C(CH2-C(=O)-CH)>		CCL4
376M	B	7.15- 7.68	CHA	A<C(CH(BR/BR))>		CDCL3
2552M	C	7.15- 7.60	CHA	A<C(CH(O/C(=O)-OH))>		CDCL3
2065M	B	7.15- 7.63	CHA	A<C(CL)-CH-C(C(=O)-CH3)>		CCL4
310M	B	7.15	CHA	A<C(CL)-C(CL)/C(F)>		CDCL3
2049M	E	7.15- 7.55	CHA	A(CH-CH-C(C(=O)-CH2))		CCL4
2045M	B	7.15- 7.50	CHA	A(CH-CH-C(C(=O)-CH3))		CCL4
2084M	C	7.15- 7.60	CHA	A(CH-CH-C(C(=O)-R6))		CDCL3
899M	C	7.15- 7.60	CHA	A(CH-CH-C(N=N-A))		CDCL3
1084M	B	7.15- 7.43	CHA	A(CH-CH-C(SI(A/H/H)))		CDCL3
2049M	E	7.15- 7.55	CHA	A(CH-C(C(=O)-CH2))		CCL4
2045M	B	7.15- 7.50	CHA	A(CH-C(C(=O)-CH3))		CCL4
2084M	C	7.15- 7.60	CHA	A(CH-C(C(=O)-R6))		CDCL3
899M	C	7.15- 7.60	CHA	A(CH-C(N=N-A))		CDCL3
1896M	D	7.15	CHA	A(CH-C(OH)-C(I))		CDCL3
1084M	B	7.15- 7.43	CHA	A(CH-C(SI(A/H/H)))		CDCL3
142M	E	7.15	CHA	A(C(CH2-CH2))		CDCL3
1370M	C	7.15	CHA	A(C(CH3)/CH-C(SO2-NH))		CDCL3
2555M	B	7.15- 7.60	CHA	A(C(CH(OH/C(=O)-OH)))		DMSO
1793M	D	7.15	CHA	A(C(CL)-CH-C(CH(OH/CH3))/CH-C(CL))		CCL4
1793M	D	7.15	CHA	A(C(CL)-C(CH(OH/CH3))/CH-C(CL))		CCL4

BOOK NO.	ASSIGN-MENT	CHEM SHIFT - ppm -	PROTON GROUP	ENVIRONMENTAL GROUPS	S	SOLVENT
1817M	C	7.15- 7.60	CHA	A(C(C(OH/CH3/CH3)))		CDCL3
941M	B	7.15	CHA	A(C(N=C=S)/CH-C(F))		CCL4
159M	B	7.15- 7.65	CHA	A(C(Q2(H/A/H)))		CDCL3
2228M	A	7.15- 7.70	CHA	UNSPECIFIED		CCL4
2093M	B	7.15- 7.75	CHA	UNSPECIFIED		CDCL3
216M	D	7.15- 7.80	CHA	UNSPECIFIED		CDCL3
2390M	A	7.15	CHR	R5N<=CH-C(=0)/C(=0)-N(A<C-CH-C(R5N<N-C(=0)/C(=0)>)>)>		DMSO-D6
1574M	D	7.15	CHR	R50<0-C(CH3)=/=CH-CH>		CCL4
1291M	B	7.15 APP.	H	S03-A		DMSO-D6
2277M	E	7.15 APP.	HNH	C(=0)-CH2		DMSO-D6
1291M	B	7.15 APP.	NH2	A(C-C(CH3)/CH-C(S03-H))		DMSO-D6
915M	A	7.15- 7.55		UNSPECIFIED		CDCL3
298M	A	7.15- 7.60		UNSPECIFIED		CDCL3
2957M	A	7.15- 7.70		UNSPECIFIED		CDCL3
212M	A	7.15- 7.90		UNSPECIFIED		CDCL3
825M	A	7.15- 7.60		UNSPECIFIED	S	DMSO-D6
150M	B	7.15 APP.		UNSPECIFIED		CDCL3
1032M	B	7.15- 7.58		UNSPECIFIED		CDCL3
2064M	B	7.15- 7.60		UNSPECIFIED		CCL4
2555M	B	7.15- 7.60		UNSPECIFIED		DMSO
159M	B	7.15- 7.65		UNSPECIFIED		CDCL3
376M	B	7.15- 7.68		UNSPECIFIED		CDCL3
2866M	C	7.15		UNSPECIFIED		CCL4
295M	C	7.15 APP.		UNSPECIFIED		CCL4
2468M	C	7.15- 7.40		UNSPECIFIED		CDCL3
1817M	C	7.15- 7.60		UNSPECIFIED		CDCL3
2466M	C	7.15- 7.60		UNSPECIFIED		CDCL3
2552M	C	7.15- 7.60		UNSPECIFIED		CDCL3
1242M	C	7.15- 7.75		UNSPECIFIED		CDCL3
2860M	D	7.15		UNSPECIFIED		CCL4
2035M	D	7.15 APP.		UNSPECIFIED		CCL4
142M	E	7.15		UNSPECIFIED		CDCL3
207M	B	7.16	CHA	AAR5(C*-CH2-CH2)		CDCL3
2083M	C	7.16- 7.60	CHA	A<CH-CH-C(C(=0)-R5)>		CCL4
2083M	C	7.16- 7.60	CHA	A<CH-C(C(=0)-R5)>		CCL4
973M	C	7.16	CHA	A<C(CH2-CH2)>		CDCL3
2831M	C	7.16	CHA	A<C(CH2-CH2)>		CCL4
1483M	E	7.16	CHA	A<C(CH(0/CH3))>		CCL4
184M	F	7.16	CHA	A<C(R6<C=CH/CH2>)/CH-C(CH3)>		CCL4
2838M	F	7.16	CHA	A(C(CH2-CH2))		CCL4
1368M	D	7.16 APP.	CHA	A(C(CH3)/CH-C(NH-S02))		CDCL3
1368M	D	7.16 APP.	CHA	A(C(NH-S02)/CH-C(CH3))		CDCL3
1198M	E	7.16	CHA	A(C(S-S)-C(NH2))		CDCL3
1277M	B	7.16	CHR	R5SA(S02-C*/=CH-C*)		CDCL3
1483M	F	7.16		A<C(CH(0/CH3))>		CCL4
2387M	B	7.16- 7.60		UNSPECIFIED		CDCL3
973M	C	7.16		UNSPECIFIED		CDCL3
2831M	C	7.16		UNSPECIFIED		CCL4
1483M	E	7.16		UNSPECIFIED		CCL4
1483M	F	7.16		UNSPECIFIED		CCL4
2838M	F	7.16		UNSPECIFIED		CCL4
1953M	E	7.17	CHA	AA<CH-C*/CH-C(OH)-C*>		DMSO-D6
2930M	B	7.17	CHA	AA<C(0-C(=0)-CH3)-CH-C*/CH-C*>		CDCL3
1885M	F	7.17	CHA	ANC(C(CH2/CH3/CH3))/CH-C(OH))		CCL4
713M	C	7.17	CHA	AN<CH-N/CH-C(CH2.2-AN)>		CDCL3
692M	B	7.17	CHA	AN<C(CH3)-CH-N/C(CH3)>		CCL4
612M	A	7.17	CHA	AR5NA<CH-C*-C*/CH-CH-C*>		C3H60
1177M	B	7.17	CHA	AR5NS<C(CL)-CH-C*/CH-C*-S>		CDCL3
1163M	C	7.17	CHA	A<C(CH2-CH2)>		CDCL3
1191M	B	7.17	CHA	A<C(CH2-S)>		CS2
2227M	A	7.17	CHA	A<C(F)-C(C(=0)-CL)>		CCL4
1240M	E	7.17	CHA	A<C(SH)-C(CL)/C(SH)>		CCL4
2059M	D	7.17	CHA	A(C(CH2-CH3)/CH-C(C(=0)-CH3))		CCL4
1886M	F	7.17	CHA	A(C(C(CH2/CH3/CH3))/CH-C(OH))		CDCL3
988M	A	7.17	CHA	A(C(F)/CH-C(C:N))		CDCL3
2532M	F	7.17	OH	CH(CH2/CH2)		CCL4
2532M	F	7.17	OH	C(=0)-CH2		CCL4
1191M	B	7.17		UNSPECIFIED		CS2
2550M	B	7.17- 7.69		UNSPECIFIED		CDCL3
607M	C	7.17		UNSPECIFIED		CDCL3
1163M	C	7.17		UNSPECIFIED		CDCL3
2034M	D	7.17		UNSPECIFIED		CCL4
747M	A	7.18- 7.83	CHA	AANA(CH-C*-C(NH2)/CH-CH-C*)		DMSO-D6
747M	A	7.18- 7.83	CHA	AANA(CH-C*-N/CH-CH-C*)		DMSO-D6
720M	B	7.18	CHA	ANA(C(CH3)-C*/CH-N-C*)		CDCL3
1020M	E	7.18	CHA	AR5N<C(S-C:N)-CH-C*/CH-C*-NH>		CDCL3
1706M	H	7.18	CHA	A<CH-C(N(CH2/CH2))>		CDCL3
523M	C	7.18	CHA	A<C(BR)-CH-C(BR)/CH-C(NH2)>		CDCL3
435M	A	7.18	CHA	A<C(BR)/CH-C(I)>		CDCL3
2836M	E	7.18 APP.	CHA	A<C(CH2.2-0-C(=0))>		CCL4
373M	D	7.18	CHA	A<C(CH2-BR)/CH-C(CH3)>		CCL4

: REPRESENTS TRIPLE BOND, ￢ REPRESENTS AN ARROW AND < AND > REPRESENT BRACKETS.   PAGE 275

BOOK NO.	ASSIGN-MENT	CHEM SHIFT - ppm -	PROTON GROUP	ENVIRONMENTAL GROUPS	S	SOLVENT
2848M	E	7.18 APP.	CHA	A<C(CH2-C(=0)-0)>		CCL4
577M	E	7.18	CHA	A<C(CH2-NH)>		CCL4
1788M	E	7.18	CHA	A<C(CH(OH/CH2))>		CCL4
517M	B	7.18	CHA	A<C(CL)-C(NH2)-C(CL)/C(CL)>		CDCL3
1712M	E	7.18 APP.	CHA	A<C(Q1(CH3/CH2-OH/H))>		CDCL3
1775M	C	7.18 APP.	CHA	A<C(R6<CH-CH(OH)/CH2>)>		CCL4
1162M	D	7.18	CHA	A<C(S-CH2)/CH-C(CH3)>		POLYSOL-D
640M	E	7.18	CHA	A(CH-C(R6NN(N/CH2-CH2-NH)))		CDCL3
152M	C	7.18 APP.	CHA	A(C(CH2-CH))		CDCL3
285M	D	7.18	CHA	A(C(CH2-CL)/CH-C(CH3))		CCL4
2217M	B	7.18	CHA	A(C(CH2-C(=0)-CL)/CH-C(CL))		CDCL3
1790M	C	7.18	CHA	A(C(CH(OH/A)))		CCL4
1511M	C	7.18	CHA	A(C(CL)/CH-C(O-CH3))		CCL4
1271M	A	7.18	CHA	A(C(F)/CH-C(SO2))		CDCL3
1141M	C	7.18	CHR	R5S<S-CH=/=CH-C(BR)=>		CDCL3
784M	C	7.18 APP.	NH2	CH(A/CH3)	S	TFA
1169M	A	7.18		UNSPECIFIED		CCL4
2112M	A	7.18- 7.69		UNSPECIFIED		CDCL3
728M	A	7.18- 7.89		UNSPECIFIED		CCL4
292M	B	7.18		UNSPECIFIED		CDCL3
317M	B	7.18- 7.77		UNSPECIFIED		CCL4
316M	B	7.18- 8.12		UNSPECIFIED		CCL4
1790M	C	7.18		UNSPECIFIED		CCL4
1775M	C	7.18 APP.		UNSPECIFIED		CCL4
152M	C	7.18 APP.		UNSPECIFIED		CDCL3
2371M	D	7.18		UNSPECIFIED		CDCL3
1788M	E	7.18		UNSPECIFIED		CCL4
577M	E	7.18		UNSPECIFIED		CCL4
1712M	E	7.18 APP.		UNSPECIFIED		CDCL3
2836M	E	7.18 APP.		UNSPECIFIED		CCL4
2848M	E	7.18 APP.		UNSPECIFIED		CCL4
1730M	B	7.19	CHA	AR5NN(CH-C*-NH/CH-CH-C*)		DMSO-D6
1730M	B	7.19	CHA	AR5NN(CH-C*-N=/CH-CH-C*)		DMSO-D6
1278M	C	7.19	CHA	AR5SA(C*-C*/C(NH2))		DMSO
2052M	C	7.19- 7.69	CHA	A<CH-CH-C(C(=0)-CH2)>		CDCL3
2052M	C	7.19- 7.69	CHA	A<CH-C(C(=0)-CH2)>		CDCL3
994M	C	7.19	CHA	A<CH-C(NH2)/CH-C(C:N)>		POLYSOL-D
976M	E	7.19	CHA	A<CH-C(N(CH2.2/CH2.2))>		DMSO-D6
1792M	G	7.19	CHA	A<CH-C(O-CH2)>		CCL4
1488M	C	7.19	CHA	A<CH-C(O-CH3)>		CCL4
2835M	E	7.19	CHA	A<C(CH2-CH2)>		CCL4
2563M	E	7.19	CHA	A<C(CH2-C(=0)-OH)/CH-C(O-CH2)>		CDCL3
1504M	E	7.19	CHA	A<C(CH2-NH2)-C(O-CH3)>		CDCL3
579M	E	7.19	CHA	A<C(CH2-NH)>		CCL4
578M	F	7.19	CHA	A<C(CH2-NH)>		CCL4
596M	F	7.19 APP.	CHA	A<C(CH2-NH)>		CCL4
644M	C	7.19	CHA	A<C(CH2-N)>		CCL4
1700M	C	7.19	CHA	A<C(CH2-OH)>		CCL4
1162M	E	7.19 APP.	CHA	A<C(CH2-S)>		POLYSOL-D
2362M	E	7.19	CHA	A<C(CH3)/CH-C(N(C(=0)-H/CH2))>		CDCL3
1882M	F	7.19	CHA	A<C(C(CH3/CH3/CH3))-C(OH)>		CCL4
1822M	B	7.19	CHA	A<C(C(OH/A/A))>		CDCL3
1520M	D	7.19	CHA	A<C(I)-CH-C(O-CH3)>		CCL4
480M	C	7.19	CHA	A<C(NH2/CH3/CH3)>		CCL4
1064M	A	7.19	CHA	A<C(NH-QN)/CH-C(NO2)>		POLYSOL-D
1070M	E	7.19	CHA	A<C(NO2)-C(CH3)/C(NH2)>		CDCL3
2941M	A	7.19	CHA	A<C(O-C(=0)-0)/CH-C(CL)>		CDCL3
655M	D	7.19	CHA	A(CH-C(N(CH2.2/CH2.2)))		POLYSOL-D
1722M	F	7.19	CHA	A(CH-C(O-CH3)-C(CH2-OH))		CDCL3
521M	E	7.19	CHA	A(C(BR)-C(NH2)/C(CH3))		CDCL3
135M	D	7.19 APP.	CHA	A(C(CH2.2-CH3))		CDCL3
1929M	E	7.19 APP.	CHA	A(C(CH2-A))		DMSO-D6
2862M	D	7.19	CHA	A(C(CH2-CH2)		CCL4
1701M	D	7.19	CHA	A(C(CH2-CH2))		CDCL3
1484M	D	7.19	CHA	A(C(CH2-CH2))		CDCL3
2036M	D	7.19 APP.	CHA	A(C(CH2-CH2))		CCL4
155M	F	7.19	CHA	A(C(CH2-CH2))		CDCL3
1372M	E	7.19	CHA	A(C(CH3)/CH-C(SO2-NH))		CDCL3
379M	C	7.19 APP.	CHA	A(C(CH(CH2/CH2)))		CCL4
303M	B	7.19	CHA	A(C(CL)/CH-C(F))		CDCL3
1904M	A	7.19	CHA	A(C(OH)-CH-C(NO2))		DMSO
380M	C	7.19 APP.	CHA	A(C(Q2(BR)))		CCL4
1143M	B	7.19	CHR	R5S<=C(I)-S/CH=CH>		CDCL3
1353M	E	7.19	NH	C(=S)-NH/R5R5BI<CH-CH*/CH2>		POLYSOL-D
608M	E	7.19 APP.	NHR	R5NA<C*/CH=CH>		CDCL3
2160M	B	7.19	Q1	A/C(=0)-H/CH3		CCL4
1056M	A	7.19- 7.59		UNSPECIFIED		CDCL3
680M	A	7.19- 7.69		UNSPECIFIED		CDCL3
1822M	B	7.19		UNSPECIFIED		CDCL3
149M	B	7.19		UNSPECIFIED		CDCL3
2099M	B	7.19 APP.		UNSPECIFIED		CCL4

BOOK NO.	ASSIGN-MENT	CHEM SHIFT - ppm -	PROTON GROUP	ENVIRONMENTAL GROUPS	S	SOLVENT
1371M	B	7.19 APP.		UNSPECIFIED		DMSO-D6
2180M	B	7.19- 7.51		UNSPECIFIED		CDCL3
644M	C	7.19		UNSPECIFIED		CCL4
2307M	C	7.19		UNSPECIFIED		CCL4
1700M	C	7.19		UNSPECIFIED		CCL4
380M	C	7.19 APP.		UNSPECIFIED		CCL4
379M	C	7.19 APP.		UNSPECIFIED		CCL4
1341M	C	7.19 APP.		UNSPECIFIED		DMSO-D6
1241M	C	7.19- 7.50		UNSPECIFIED		CDCL3
1701M	D	7.19		UNSPECIFIED		CDCL3
2862M	D	7.19		UNSPECIFIED		CCL4
1484M	D	7.19		UNSPECIFIED		CDCL3
2036M	D	7.19 APP.		UNSPECIFIED		CCL4
135M	D	7.19 APP.		UNSPECIFIED		CDCL3
579M	E	7.19		UNSPECIFIED		CCL4
2835M	E	7.19		UNSPECIFIED		CCL4
1929M	E	7.19 APP.		UNSPECIFIED		DMSO-D6
1162M	E	7.19 APP.		UNSPECIFIED		POLYSOL-D
578M	F	7.19		UNSPECIFIED		CCL4
155M	F	7.19		UNSPECIFIED		CDCL3
596M	F	7.19 APP.		UNSPECIFIED		CCL4
342M	A	7.20	CH	BR/CL/CL		CCL4
703M	A	7.20	CHA	AN<CH-N-C(BR)>		CCL4
700M	A	7.20	CHA	AN<CH-N-C(CL)>		CCL4
1585M	D	7.20	CHA	AR5NO<C*-N=C(CH3)/C(CH3)-C(CH3)>		CDCL3
1585M	C	7.20	CHA	AR5NO<C*-O-C(CH3)=/C(CH3)-C(CH3)>		CDCL3
2179M	C	7.20	CHA	AR5<C*-CH2-CH2/CH-C(C(=O)-H)>		CCL4
2050M	E	7.20- 7.60	CHA	A<CH-CH-C(C(=O)-CH2.12)>		CDCL3
2865M	D	7.20- 7.60	CHA	A<CH-CH-C(C(=O)-O-CH2.2)>		CDCL3
2995M	A	7.20- 7.80	CHA	A<CH-CH-C(C(=O)-O-O-C(=O))>		CDCL3
1313M	B	7.20- 7.45	CHA	A<CH-CH-C(N(+)(CH3/CH3/CH3))>		POLYSOL-D
1064M	B	7.20- 7.50	CHA	A<CH-CH-C(QN(NH-A))>		POLYSOL-D
2858M	C	7.20- 7.60	CHA	A<CH-CH-C(Q1(C(=O)-CH2/C:N))>		CDCL3
1157M	B	7.20- 7.48	CHA	A<CH-CH-C(R6SS(C=CH/S>)>		CDCL3
1270M	B	7.20- 7.65	CHA	A<CH-CH-C(SO2-A)>		CDCL3
1261M	E	7.20- 7.75	CHA	A<CH-CH-C(SO2-CH2)>		CDCL3
2050M	E	7.20- 7.60	CHA	A<CH-C(C(=O)-CH2.12)>		CDCL3
2865M	D	7.20- 7.60	CHA	A<CH-C(C(=O)-O-CH2.2)>		CDCL3
2995M	A	7.20- 7.80	CHA	A<CH-C(C(=O)-O-O-C(=O))>		CDCL3
431M	A	7.20	CHA	A<CH-C(I)/CH-C(CF3)>		CCL4
2879M	G	7.20	CHA	A<CH-C(NH2)-C(C(=O)-O-CH2.4)>		DMSO-D6
2878M	F	7.20	CHA	A<CH-C(NH2)-C(C(=O)-O-R6)>		CDCL3
506M	E	7.20	CHA	A<CH-C(NH2)/CH-C(CF3)>		CDCL3
1313M	B	7.20- 7.45	CHA	A<CH-C(N(+)(CH3/CH3/CH3))>		POLYSOL-D
1064M	B	7.20- 7.50	CHA	A<CH-C(QN(NH-A))>		POLYSOL-D
2858M	C	7.20- 7.60	CHA	A<CH-C(Q1(C(=O)-O-CH2/C:N))>		CDCL3
1157M	B	7.20- 7.48	CHA	A<CH-C(R6SS<C=CH/S>)>		CDCL3
1270M	B	7.20- 7.65	CHA	A<CH-C(SO2-A)>		CDCL3
1261M	E	7.20- 7.75	CHA	A<CH-C(SO2-CH2)>		CDCL3
2385M	D	7.20 APP.	CHA	A<C(CH2.2-R5N)>		POLYSOL-D
286M	D	7.20	CHA	A<C(CH2-CL)-C(CH3)/C(CH2-CL)-C(CH3)>		CDCL3
2932M	D	7.20	CHA	A<C(CH2-C(=O)-O)>		CCL4
581M	C	7.20	CHA	A<C(CH2-NH)>		CCL4
2432M	C	7.20 APP.	CHA	A<C(CH2-NH)>		POLYSOL-D
2839M	E	7.20	CHA	A<C(CH2-O-C(=O))/CH-C(O-CH3)>		CCL4
1158M	C	7.20	CHA	A<C(CH2-S)>		CCL4
479M	D	7.20 APP.	CHA	A<C(CH(CH2/CH3))>		CDCL3
975M	C	7.20- 7.60	CHA	A<C(CH(N/C:N))>		CDCL3
1197M	A	7.20	CHA	A<C(CL)/CH-C(S-S)>		CDCL3
1232M	C	7.20	CHA	A<C(C1)-C(SH)/CH-C(CL)>		CCL4
1487M	B	7.20- 7.60	CHA	A<C(C(O/O/O))>		CCL4
1563M	E	7.20	CHA	A<C(C:N)-CH-C(O-CH3)/CH-C(O-CH3)>		CDCL3
528M	E	7.20	CHA	A<C(I)/C(CH3)-C(NH2)>		POLYSOL-D
2917M	D	7.20	CHA	A<C(OH)-C(OH)-C(OH)/C(C(=O)-O-CH2)>		C3D6O
938M	A	7.20 APP.	CHA	A<C(QN(=S))>		CCL4
164M	B	7.20	CHA	A<C(Q1(A/Q1))>		CDCL3
164M	C	7.20	CHA	A<C(Q1(A/Q1))>		CDCL3
2843M	G	7.20 APP.	CHA	A<C(Q2(H/CH2-O-C(=O)/H))>		CCL4
2041M	E	7.20- 7.65	CHA	A<C(Q2(H/C(=O)-CH2.3/H))>		CDCL3
1360M	C	7.20- 7.70	CHA	A<C(Q2(H/SO2-NH2/H))>		POLYSOL-D
158M	B	7.20	CHA	A<C(Q2)>		CDCL3
1774M	E	7.20 APP.	CHA	A<C(R6<CH-CH(OH)/CH2>)>		CDCL3
1172M	B	7.20- 7.65	CHA	A<C(S-AN)>		CDCL3
2099M	C	7.20- 7.50	CHA	A(CH-CH-C(C(=O)-A))		CCL4
2840M	C	7.20- 7.70	CHA	A(CH-CH-C(C(=O)-CH2))		CDCL3
2163M	A	7.20- 7.60	CHA	A(CH-CH-C(C(=O)-H))		CCL4
900M	C	7.20- 7.60	CHA	A(CH-CH-C(N=N-A))		CDCL3
2099M	C	7.20- 7.50	CHA	A(CH-C(C(=O)-A))		CCL4
2840M	C	7.20- 7.70	CHA	A(CH-C(C(=O)-CH2))		CDCL3
2163M	A	7.20- 7.60	CHA	A(CH-C(C(=O)-H))		CCL4
2576M	A	7.20	CHA	A(CH-C(I)/CH-C(C(=O)-OH))		POLYSOL-D

BOOK NO.	ASSIGN-MENT	CHEM SHIFT - ppm -	PROTON GROUP	ENVIRONMENTAL GROUPS	S	SOLVENT
2435M	D	7.20- 7.50	CHA	A(CH-C(NH-C(=0)))		CDCL3
900M	C	7.20- 7.60	CHA	A(CH-C(N=N-A))		CDCL3
1519M	D	7.20	CHA	A(CH-C(O-CH3)-C(I))		CDCL3
1508M	C	7.20- 7.70	CHA	A(C(A(C-CH-CH-C(O-CH3))))		CDCL3
532M	D	7.20	CHA	A(C(A(C-CH-C(CH3)-C(NH2)))-CH-C(CH3)/CH-C(NH2))		CDCL3
393M	B	7.20 APP.	CHA	A(C(BR)-CH-C(CL))		CCL4
2159M	C	7.20 APP.	CHA	A(C(CH2.2-C(=0)-H))		CDCL3
2088M	C	7.20 APP.	CHA	A(C(CH2-CH2))		CDCL3
481M	E	7.20 APP.	CHA	A(C(CH2-CH2))		CDCL3
978M	D	7.20	CHA	A(C(CH2-CH))		CDCL3
2853M	F	7.20	CHA	A(C(CH2-N))		CDCL3
2832M	C	7.20	CHA	A(C(CH2-0-C(=0)))		CCL4
2837M	D	7.20	CHA	A(C(CH2-0-C(=0)))		CCL4
823M	D	7.20	CHA	A(C(CH3)-C(CL)/CH-C(NH-NH2))	S	DMSO-D6
1291M	C	7.20	CHA	A(C(CH3)-C(NH2)/CH-C(SO3-H))		DMSO-D6
2101M	B	7.20	CHA	A(C(CH3)/CH-C(C(=0)-A))		CDCL3
2541M	C	7.20 APP.	CHA	A(C(CH(C(=0)-OH/CH3)))		CCL4
393M	B	7.20 APP.	CHA	A(C(CL)-CH-C(BR))		CCL4
1553M	C	7.20	CHA	A(C(CL)-C(O-CH3)-C(CL))		CCL4
2044M	B	7.20- 7.70	CHA	A(C(C:C))		CDCL3
1055M	A	7.20	CHA	A(C(F)/CH-C(NO2))		CCL4
2435M	D	7.20- 7.50	CHA	A(C(NH-C(=0)))		CDCL3
1031M	B	7.20- 7.60	CHA	A(C(N(N=0/CH3)))		CDCL3
2589M	A	7.20	CHA	A(C(O-A)OCH-C(C(=0)-OH))		DMSO
2583M	B	7.20	CHA	A(C(O-CH3)-CH-C(C(=0)-OH))		DMSO-D6
2201M	B	7.20- 7.60	CHA	A(C(O2(C(=0)-OH)))		CDCL3
1089M	B	7.20- 7.65	CHA	A(C(SI(CH3/CH3/CH3)))		CDCL3
2292M	A	7.20	NH2	C(=0)-A		DMSO
938M	A	7.20 APP.		UNSPECIFIED		CCL4
1052M	A	7.20- 7.65		UNSPECIFIED		CDCL3
2168M	A	7.20- 7.70		UNSPECIFIED		CCL4
1580M	A	7.20- 7.80		UNSPECIFIED		CDCL3
726M	A	7.20- 7.80		UNSPECIFIED		CDCL3
2245M	A	7.20- 7.80		UNSPECIFIED		CCL4
2094M	A	7.20- 8.00		UNSPECIFIED		CDCL3
1292M	A	7.20- 8.30		UNSPECIFIED		TFA
164M	B	7.20		UNSPECIFIED		CDCL3
1165M	B	7.20 APP.		UNSPECIFIED		POLYSOL-D
1031M	B	7.20- 7.60		UNSPECIFIED		CDCL3
438M	B	7.20- 7.60		UNSPECIFIED		CDCL3
1487M	B	7.20- 7.60		UNSPECIFIED		CCL4
2201M	B	7.20- 7.60		UNSPECIFIED		CDCL3
1172M	B	7.20- 7.65		UNSPECIFIED		CDCL3
1089M	B	7.20- 7.65		UNSPECIFIED		CDCL3
2287M	B	7.20- 7.65		UNSPECIFIED		TFA
1342M	B	7.20- 7.65		UNSPECIFIED		POLYSOL-D
2087M	B	7.20- 7.70		UNSPECIFIED		CDCL3
2044M	B	7.20- 7.70		UNSPECIFIED		CDCL3
783M	B	7.20- 7.75		UNSPECIFIED	S	POLYSOL-D
2832M	C	7.20		UNSPECIFIED		CCL4
1158M	C	7.20		UNSPECIFIED		CCL4
164M	C	7.20		UNSPECIFIED		CDCL3
581M	C	7.20		UNSPECIFIED		CCL4
2088M	C	7.20 APP.		UNSPECIFIED		CDCL3
2159M	C	7.20 APP.		UNSPECIFIED		CDCL3
2541M	C	7.20 APP.		UNSPECIFIED		CCL4
2432M	C	7.20 APP.		UNSPECIFIED		POLYSOL-D
730M	C	7.20- 7.50		UNSPECIFIED		CDCL3
975M	C	7.20- 7.60		UNSPECIFIED		CDCL3
723M	C	7.20- 7.60		UNSPECIFIED		CCL4
1508M	C	7.20- 7.70		UNSPECIFIED		CDCL3
1360M	C	7.20- 7.70		UNSPECIFIED		POLYSOL-D
2091M	C	7.20- 7.80		UNSPECIFIED		CDCL3
978M	D	7.20		UNSPECIFIED		CDCL3
2837M	D	7.20		UNSPECIFIED		CCL4
2932M	D	7.20		UNSPECIFIED		CCL4
479M	D	7.20 APP.		UNSPECIFIED		CDCL3
2385M	D	7.20 APP.		UNSPECIFIED		POLYSOL-D
481M	E	7.20 APP.		UNSPECIFIED		CDCL3
1774M	E	7.20 APP.		UNSPECIFIED		CDCL3
2041M	E	7.20- 7.65		UNSPECIFIED		CDCL3
2148M	E	7.20- 7.65		UNSPECIFIED		POLYSOL-D
2853M	F	7.20		UNSPECIFIED		CDCL3
2843M	G	7.20 APP.		UNSPECIFIED		CCL4
250M	A	7.21	CH	CL/CL/CL		CCL4
2108M	D	7.21	CHA	AR5(C*-CH2-CH2/CH-C(C(=0)-CH3))		CDCL3
2127M	B	7.21	CHA	AR6A(C(CH3)-C*-C(=0)/CH-C(CH3)-C*)		CDCL3
2317M	D	7.21	CHA	A<CH-CH-C(NH-C(=0)-CH)S		POLYSOL-D
1505M	F	7.21	CHA	A<CH-C(O-CH3)/CH-C(CH2-NH2)>		CDCL3
641M	H	7.21	CHA	A<CH-C(R6NN<N-CH(CH3)/CH2)>		CDCL3
2309M	E	7.21 APP.	CHA	A<C(CH2.2-NH)>		CDCL3

BOOK NO.	ASSIGN-MENT	CHEM SHIFT - ppm -	PROTON GROUP	ENVIRONMENTAL GROUPS	S	SOLVENT
1791M	D	7.21 APP.	CHA	A<C(CH2-CH)>		CDCL3
2312M	D	7.21	CHA	A<C(CH2-C(=O))>		CDCL3
2086M	B	7.21 APP.	CHA	A<C(CH2-C(=O)-A)/CH-C(CL)>		POLYSOL-D
2847M	E	7.21 APP.	CHA	A<C(CH2-C(=O)-O)>		CCL4
595M	G	7.21 APP.	CHA	A<C(CH2-NH)>		CDCL3
2060M	E	7.21	CHA	A<C(CH3)/CH-C(=O)-CH2.3)>		CDCL3
1483M	E	7.21	CHA	A<C(CH(O/CH3))>		CCL4
1483M	F	7.21	CHA	A<C(CH(O/CH3))>		CCL4
2086M	B	7.21 APP.	CHA	A<C(CL)/CH-C(CH2-C(=O)-A)>		POLYSOL-D
1520M	E	7.21	CHA	A<C(I)/C(O-CH3)>		CCL4
887M	B	7.21 APP.	CHA	A<C(QN(NH-A))>		POLYSOL-D
2134M	A	7.21- 7.65	CHA	A(CH-CH-C(C(=O)-C(=O)))		CCL4
2134M	A	7.21- 7.65	CHA	A(CH-C(C(=O)-C(=O)))		CCL4
520M	C	7.21	CHA	A(C(BR)/CH-C(NH2))		CDCL3
1218M	C	7.21	CHA	A(C(CH2-CH2))		CDCL3
654M	D	7.21 APP.	CHA	A(C(CH2-N))		CDCL3
2564M	C	7.21	CHA	A(C(CH3)/CH-C(Q2(H/C(=O)-OH/H)))		DMSO-D6
2338M	F	7.21	CHA	A(C(NH-C(=O)-C(CH3)/CH-C(CH3))		CDCL3
824M	C	7.21	CHA	A(C(NH-NH2)/CH-C(O-CH3)))	S	D20
1531M	B	7.21	CHA	A(C(O-CH3)-CH-C(NO2))		CDCL3
1447M	D	7.21	CHA	A(C(R30))		CCL4
1170M	C	7.21	CHA	A(C(S-A)/CH-C(CH3))		CDCL3
2266M	A	7.21	CHR	R50<=C(BR)-C(=O)/C(=O)-O>		CDCL3
2453M	B	7.21	CHR	R6NN<NH-C(=O)/=C(CH3)-C(=O)>		DMSO-D6
1362M	B	7.21	NH2	SO2-A		DMSO-D6
2803M	D	7.21	Q3	O-C(=O)-CH2/H/H		CDCL3
942M	A	7.21 APP.		UNSPECIFIED		CCL4
2229M	A	7.21- 7.58		UNSPECIFIED		CCL4
1218M	C	7.21		UNSPECIFIED		CDCL3
1447M	D	7.21		UNSPECIFIED		CCL4
1159M	D	7.21		UNSPECIFIED		CCL4
478M	D	7.21		UNSPECIFIED		CCL4
2312M	D	7.21		UNSPECIFIED		CDCL3
654M	D	7.21 APP.		UNSPECIFIED		CDCL3
1791M	D	7.21 APP.		UNSPECIFIED		CDCL3
2314M	D	7.21 APP.		UNSPECIFIED		CDCL3
1483M	E	7.21		UNSPECIFIED		CCL4
2847M	E	7.21 APP.		UNSPECIFIED		CCL4
2309M	E	7.21 APP.		UNSPECIFIED		CDCL3
1483M	F	7.21		UNSPECIFIED		CCL4
595M	G	7.21 APP.		UNSPECIFIED		CDCL3
1957M	B	7.22	CHA	AA<CH-C*-C(OH)/CH-C(OH)-C*>		DMSO-D6
1954M	D	7.22	CHA	AA<C(OH)-C(CH2.2-C:N)-C*/CH-C*>		POLYSOL-D
725M	A	7.22	CHA	ANA<CH-N-C*/CH-C*>		CCL4
702M	A	7.22	CHA	AN<CH-C(CL)-C(CL)/CH-N>		CDCL3
706M	D	7.22	CHA	AN(CH-C(NH2)-N)		CDCL3
738M	A	7.22	CHA	AR5NN<C*-NH-CH=>		DMSO-D6
738M	A	7.22	CHA	AR5NN<C*-N=CH>		DMSO-D6
2610M	B	7.22- 7.67	CHA	A<CH-CH-C(C(=O)-SH)>		CDCL3
306M	A	7.22	CHA	A<CH-C(CL)/CH-C(CL)>		CCL4
2610M	B	7.22- 7.67	CHA	A<CH-C(C(=O)-SH)>		CDCL3
2326M	C	7.22	CHA	A<CH-C(F)/CH-C(NH-C(=O))>		CDCL3
1490M	E	7.22	CHA	A<CH-C(O-CH2.2)>		CDCL3
2014M	C	7.22 APP.	CHA	A<C(CH2.2-R6N)		CDCL3
395M	C	7.22	CHA	A<C(CH2-RR)-CH-C(BR)>		CDCL3
2311M	C	7.22 APP.	CHA	A<C(CH2-CH2)>		CDCL3
653M	F	7.22	CHA	A<C(CH2-N)>		CDCL3
306M	A	7.22	CHA	A<C(CL)-CH-C(CL)>		CCL4
516M	D	7.22	CHA	A<C(CL)-C(NH2)/C(CL)>		CDCL3
2326M	C	7.22	CHA	A<C(F)/C(NH-C(=O))>		CDCL3
904M	D	7.22	CHA	A<C(N=N-NH)/CH-C(CH3)>		CDCL3
291M	A	7.22 APP.	CHA	A<C-C(CL>		CCL4
2554M	F	7.22	CHA	A(CH-C(O-CH2))		CDCL3
371M	B	7.22	CHA	A(C(CH2-RR))		CCL4
1224M	C	7.22	CHA	A(C(CH2-SH))		CCL4
2100M	B	7.22	CHA	A(C(CH3)/CH-C(C(=O)-A))		CDCL3
881M	B	7.22	CHA	A(C(CH3)/CH-C(QN(QN)))		CDCL3
2367M	A	7.22		UNSPECIFIED		CCL4
2092M	A	7.22- 7.80		UNSPECIFIED		CDCL3
371M	B	7.22		UNSPECIFIED		CCL4
1950M	B	7.22- 7.60		UNSPECIFIED		C3H60
851M	B	7.22- 7.82		UNSPECIFIED		DMSO
974M	C	7.22		UNSPECIFIED		CCL4
1224M	C	7.22		UNSPECIFIED		CCL4
2540M	C	7.22		UNSPECIFIED		CDCL3
2014M	C	7.22 APP.		UNSPECIFIED		CDCL3
2311M	C	7.22 APP.		UNSPECIFIED		CDCL3
727M	C	7.22- 7.65		UNSPECIFIED		CDCL3
2958M	C	7.22- 7.79		UNSPECIFIED		CDCL3
1731M	C	7.22- 7.80		UNSPECIFIED		CDCL3
653M	F	7.22		UNSPECIFIED		CDCL3

BOOK NO.	ASSIGN-MENT	CHEM SHIFT - ppm -	PROTON GROUP	ENVIRONMENTAL GROUPS	S	SOLVENT
2286M	G	7.22		UNSPECIFIED		CCL4
132M	A	7.23	CHA	A		CCL4
749M	A	7.23	CHA	ANAA<CH-N-C</CH-C*-C*>		CDCL3
2346M	B	7.23	CHA	AN<CH-N/CH-C(C(=O)-NH)>		CDCL3
1959M	A	7.23	CHA	AN<CH-N/CH-C(OH)>		DMSO-D6
1959M	A	7.23	CHA	AN<C(OH)-CH-N>		DMSO-D6
2575M	B	7.23	CHA	A<CH-C(I)-C(C(=O)-OH)>		C3D60
1944M	B	7.23	CHA	A<CH-C(OH)-C(NO2)/CH-C(OH)>		POLYSOL-D
1504M	F	7.23 APP.	CHA	A<CH-C(O-CH3)-C(CH2-NH2)>		CDCL3
2556M	B	7.23- 7.72	CHA	A<C(C(OH/C(=O)-OH/A)>		C3H60
2545M	C	7.23	CHA	A<C(C(C(=O)-OH/A/CH2.2)>		CDCL3
1527M	C	7.23	CHA	A<C(NH-NH2)-C(O-CH3)>	S	POLYSOL-D
2918M	E	7.23	CHA	A<C(OH)-C(OH)-C(OH)/C(C(=O)-O-CH2)>		C3D60
2851M	D	7.23- 7.58	CHA	A(CH-CH-C(C(=O)-NH))		CDCL3
1194M	A	7.23	CHA	A(CH-CH-C(S-S))		CDCL3
2851M	D	7.23- 7.58	CHA	A(CH-C(C(=O)-NH))		CDCL3
1194M	A	7.23	CHA	A(CH-C(S-S))		CDCL3
532M	E	7.23	CHA	A(C(A(C-CH-C(CH3)-C(NH2)))/C(CH3)-C(NH2))		CDCL3
2062M	C	7.23	CHA	A(C(CH3)/CH-C(C(=O)-CH2))		CDCL3
986M	B	7.23	CHA	A(C(CH3)/CH-C(C:N))		CCL4
1269M	B	7.23	CHA	A(C(CH3)/CH-C(SN2-A))		CDCL3
307M	A	7.23	CHA	A(C(CL)/CH-C(CL))		CCL4
1883M	D	7.23	CHA	A(C(C(C(CH3/CH3/CH3))/CH-C(OH))		CDCL3
1226M	B	7.23 APP.	CHA	A(C(C(SH/A/A)))		CDCL3
1306M	A	7.23	CHA	A(C(NH-A)-C(SO3NA)/CH-C(NO2))	S	DMSO
848M	F	7.23	H	QN(OH/CH)		CCL4
2802M	F	7.23	Q3	O-C(=O)-CH2/H/H		CDCL3
2968M	A	7.23 APP.		UNSPECIFIED		CCL4
401M	A	7.23- 7.80		UNSPECIFIED		CCL4
2232M	A	7.23- 7.83		UNSPECIFIED		CCL4
1059M	A	7.23- 7.95		UNSPECIFIED		CDCL3
1226M	B	7.23 APP.		UNSPECIFIED		CDCL3
2556M	B	7.23- 7.72		UNSPECIFIED		C3H60
2545M	C	7.23		UNSPECIFIED		CDCL3
2186M	C	7.24	CHA	AR500(C*-O-CH2/C(C(=O)-H))		CDCL3
863M	B	7.24 APP.	CHA	AR5(CH-C*-CH2/CH-CH-C*)		CDCL3
863M	B	7.24 APP.	CHA	AR5(C*-CH2-C(=NOH))		CDCL3
2220M	A	7.24- 7.78	CHA	A<CH-CH-C(C(=O)-CL)>		CCL4
2220M	A	7.24- 7.78	CHA	A<CH-C(C(=O)-CL)>		CCL4
531M	C	7.24	CHA	A<C(A<C-CH-CH-C(NH2)>)/CH-C(NH2)>		DMSO-D6
2544M	B	7.24 APP.	CHA	A<C(CH2-CH)>		CDCL3
981M	B	7.24	CHA	A<C(CH2-C:N)/CH-C(CL)>		CCL4
144M	D	7.24	CHA	A<C(CH2-R3)>		CDCL3
2223M	B	7.24	CHA	A<C(CH3)/CH-C(C(=O)-CL)>		CCL4
1233M	C	7.24	CHA	A<C(CL)-C(CL)/CH-C(SH)>		CCL4
981M	B	7.24	CHA	A<C(CL)/CH-C(CH2-C:N)>		CCL4
2080M	D	7.24	CHA	A<C(OH)/C(C(=O)-CH3)-C(OH)>		DMSO-D6
2074M	B	7.24	CHA	A<C(S-CH3)/CH-C(C(=O)-CH3)>		POLYSOL-D
1514M	D	7.24	CHA	A(CH-C(O-CH3)-C(BR))		CDCL3
1722M	G	7.24	CHA	A(C(CH2-OH)-C(O-CH3))		CDCL3
2562M	C	7.24	CHA	A(C(O-C)/CH-C(CL))		CDCL3
2797M	E	7.24	Q3	O-C(=O)-CH2/H/H		CCL4
2544M	B	7.24 APP.		UNSPECIFIFD		CDCL3
716M	A	7.25	CHA	AN<CH-N-C(AN<C-N>)>		CDCL3
195M	C	7.25 APP.	CHA	AR5<CH-C*-CH2/CH-CH-C*>		CDCL3
195M	C	7.25 APP.	CHA	AR5<C*-CH2-CH2>		CDCL3
2086M	C	7.25- 7.60	CHA	A<CH-CH-C(C(=O)-CH2)>		POLYSOL-D
2090M	D	7.25- 7.55	CHA	A<CH-CH-C(C(=O)-CH)>		CDCL3
1865M	E	7.25- 7.68	CHA	A<CH-CH-C(C(=O)-CH)>		CDCL3
2219M	A	7.25- 7.80	CHA	A<CH-CH-C(C(=O)-F)>		CCL4
1659M	E	7.25- 7.62	CHA	A<CH-CH-C(P(=O/A/CH))>		POLYSOL-D
2086M	C	7.25- 7.60	CHA	A<CH-C(C(=O)-CH2)>		POLYSOL-D
2090M	D	7.25- 7.55	CHA	A<CH-C(C(=O)-CH)>		CDCL3
1865M	E	7.25- 7.68	CHA	A<CH-C(C(=O)-CH)>		CDCL3
2219M	A	7.25- 7.80	CHA	A<CH-C(C(=O)-F)>		CCL4
1659M	E	7.25- 7.62	CHA	A<CH-C(P(=O/A/CH))>		POLYSOL-D
804M	E	7.25	CHA	A<C(CH2-CH)>	S	CDCL3
2422M	D	7.25 APP.	CHA	A<C(CH2-NH)>		POLYSOL-D
1480M	F	7.25	CHA	A<C(CH(O/CH2))>		CDCL3
2436M	C	7.25	CHA	A<C(N(C(=O)/A))>		CDCL3
1557M	C	7.25	CHA	A<C(O-CH2)-C(NO2)/CH-C(NO2)>		CDCL3
2927M	B	7.25	CHA	A<C(O-C(=O)-C)/CH-C(NO2)>		CDCL3
1019M	D	7.25	CHA	A<C(Q2(H/CH2-S/H))>		CDCL3
2951M	F	7.25 APP.	CHA	A<C(R50<CH-HCH/HCH>)>		CDCL3
2553M	C	7.25	CHA	A(CH-C(O-CH2))		C3H60
522M	D	7.25	CHA	A(C(BR)-C(CL)/CH-C(NH2))		CDCL3
668M	C	7.25	CHA	A(C(BR)/CH-C(N(CH3/CH3)))		CDCL3
2313M	E	7.25	CHA	A(C(CH2-NH))		CDCL3
1482M	B	7.25	CHA	A(C(CH2-O))		CCL4
1479M	C	7.25 APP.	CHA	A(C(CH2-O))		CDCL3
2240M	B	7.25	CHA	A(C(CH3)-CH-C(C(=O)-CL)/C(CH3))		CCL4

BOOK NO.	ASSIGN-MENT	CHEM SHIFT - ppm -	PROTON GROUP	ENVIRONMENTAL GROUPS	S	SOLVENT
2322M	E	7.25	CHA	A(C(NH-C(=O))-CH-C(CH3))		CDCL3
2160M	C	7.25- 7.65	CHA	A(C(Q1(C(=O)-H/CH3)))		CCL4
2447M	B	7.25- 7.60	CHA	A(C(R5NN(C(CH3)-NH/C(=O))))		DMSO-D6
1273M	A	7.25- 7.70		UNSPECIFIED		CDCL3
2106M	A	7.25- 8.08		UNSPECIFIED		POLYSOL-D
1482M	B	7.25		UNSPECIFIED		CCL4
2447M	B	7.25- 7.60		UNSPECIFIED		DMSO-D6
880M	B	7.25- 7.70		UNSPECIFIED		CDCL3
2390M	B	7.25- 7.70		UNSPECIFIED		DMSO-D6
1106M	B	7.25- 7.75		UNSPECIFIED		CDCL3
2072M	B	7.25- 7.80		UNSPECIFIED		CCL4
718M	B	7.25- 8.30		UNSPECIFIED		CCL4
2436M	C	7.25		UNSPECIFIED		CDCL3
1479M	C	7.25 APP.		UNSPECIFIED		CDCL3
1362M	C	7.25- 7.50		UNSPECIFIED		DMSO-D6
2160M	C	7.25- 7.65		UNSPECIFIED		CCL4
1277M	C	7.25- 7.77		UNSPECIFIED		CDCL3
1719M	C	7.25- 7.90		UNSPECIFIED		CDCL3
1019M	D	7.25		UNSPECIFIED		CDCL3
2422M	D	7.25 APP.		UNSPECIFIED		POLYSOL-D
2313M	E	7.25		UNSPECIFIED		CDCL3
804M	E	7.25		UNSPECIFIED		CDCL3
1480M	F	7.25		UNSPECIFIED	S	CDCL3
2951M	F	7.25 APP.		UNSPECIFIED		CDCL3
1020M	F	7.26	CHA	AR5N<C*-CH2-CH2/C(S-C:N)>		CDCL3
2346M	C	7.26	CHA	A<C(CH2-NH)>		CDCL3
920M	B	7.26	CHA	A<C(CL)-C(N=C=O)/CH-C(CL)>		CDCL3
1707M	B	7.26	CHA	A<C(CL)/CH-C(QN(CH2,2-OH))>		CDCL3
1268M	B	7.26	CHA	A(C(CH3)/CH-C(Sn2-A))		DMSO
2542M	C	7.26	CHA	A(C(CH(C(=O)-OH/CH2)))		CCL4
2841M	E	7.26	CHA	A(C(Q2(CH2-O-C(=O))))		DMSO
2542M	C	7.26		UNSPECIFIED		CDCL3
2346M	C	7.26		UNSPECIFIED		CCL4
719M	C	7.26- 7.70		UNSPECIFIED		CCL4
2841M	E	7.26		UNSPECIFIED		D20
2676M	B	7.27	CHA	A<CH-C(NH2)/CH-C(C(=O)-O-NA)>		DMSO-D6
2308M	C	7.27	CHA	A<C(CH2-CH)>		DMSO-D6
1860M	C	7.27	CHA	A<C(CH2-OH)/CH-C(CH2-O')>		CCL4
2852M	D	7.27	CHA	A<C(C(C(=O)-O/C(=O)-O/CH3))>		C3H60
2570M	A	7.27	CHA	A<C(F)/CH-C(C(=O)-OH)>		POLYSOL-D
2427M	A	7.27 APP.	CHA	A<C(N(C(=O)-NH2/A))>		CDCL3
231M	B	7.27	CHA	A(CH-C(F)/CH-C(F))		CDCL3
386M	D	7.27	CHA	A(C(BR)-C(CH3)/C(CH3)-C(CH3))		CDCL3
2891M	E	7.27	CHA	A(C(CH2-CH2))		CDCL3
2085M	B	7.27	CHA	A(C(CH2-C(=O)))		CDCL3
2539M	B	7.27	CHA	A(C(CH2-C(=O)-OH))		CCL4
972M	B	7.27	CHA	A(C(CH2-C:N))		CCL4
221M	B	7.27	CHA	A(C(CH2-F))		CDCL3
594M	F	7.27	CHA	A(C(CH2-NH))		CCL4
1322M	E	7.27	CHA	A(C(CH3)/CH-C(Sn3-CH2))		CCL4
1152M	A	7.27	CHR	R5NS<=CH-N=/S-C(BR)=>		CDCL3
1143M	C	7.27	CHR	R5S<=CH-CH=/S-C(I)=>		POLYSOL-D
2427M	A	7.27 APP.		UNSPECIFIED		CCL4
221M	B	7.27		UNSPECIFIED		CCL4
647M	B	7.27		UNSPECIFIED		CDCL3
2539M	B	7.27		UNSPECIFIED		CCL4
972M	B	7.27		UNSPECIFIED		DMSO-D6
2308M	C	7.27		UNSPECIFIED		CCL4
2852M	D	7.27		UNSPECIFIED		CCL4
1789M	E	7.27		UNSPECIFIED		CDCL3
2891M	E	7.27		UNSPECIFIED		CDCL3
594M	F	7.27		UNSPECIFIED		CDCL3
691M	D	7.28	CHA	AN(C(CH3)-CH=N/CH-C(CH3))		CDCL3
2117M	E	7.28	CHA	AR60<C(CH3)-CH-C*/CH-C*-O>		CCL4
2221M	A	7.28- 7.90	CHA	A<CH-CH-C(C(=O)-BR)>		CDCL3
879M	B	7.28 APP.	CHA	A<CH-CH-C(QN(QN/NH2))>		CCL4
2068M	B	7.28	CHA	A<CH-C(BR)/CH-C(C(=O)-CH3)>		CCL4
2221M	A	7.28- 7.90	CHA	A<CH-C(C(=O)-BR)>		CCL4
2871M	D	7.28	CHA	A<CH-C(F)/CH-C(C(=O)-O-CH2)>		CDCL3
879M	B	7.28 APP.	CHA	A<CH-C(QN(QN/NH2))>		CDCL3
3000M	B	7.28	CHA	A<C(CH2-O)>		CDCL3
897M	B	7.28 APP.	CHA	A<C(CH3)-CH-C(N=N-A)>		CCL4
2238M	D	7.28	CHA	A<C(CH3)-C(CH3)-C(C(=O)-CL)>		CDCL3
1919M	D	7.28	CHA	A<C(CL)-C(OH)/C(CL)>		POLYSOL-D
1171M	A	7.28 APP.	CHA	A<C(CL)/CH-C(S-A)>		CCL4
1232M	D	7.28	CHA	A<C(CL)/C(SH)-C(CL)>		DMSO-D6
2543M	E	7.28 APP.	CHA	A<C(C(CH2/CH2.2/CH2.2))>		CDCL3
925M	B	7.28 APP.	CHA	A<C(C(N=C=N/A/A))>		POLYSOL-D
1897M	C	7.28	CHA	A<C(I)/C(OH)>		CDCL3
2991M	B	7.28	CHA	A<C(O-C(=O)-N)>		CDCL3
1088M	C	7.28 APP.	CHA	A<C(SI(A/CH2/CH2))>		CDCL3

BOOK NO.	ASSIGN-MENT	CHEM SHIFT - ppm -	PROTON GROUP	ENVIRONMENTAL GROUPS	S	SOLVENT
1171M	A	7.28 APP.	CHA	A<C(S-A)/CH-C(CL)>		POLYSOL-D
1161M	E	7.28	CHA	A<C(S-CH3)-C(NH2)>		CCL4
852M	A	7.28 APP.	CHA	A(CH-CH-C(CH=NOH))		CDCL3
852M	A	7.28 APP.	CHA	A(CH-C(CH=NOH))		CDCL3
1491M	E	7.28	CHA	A(CH-C(O-CH2.2))		CDCL3
284M	B	7.28	CHA	A(C(CH2-CL))		CCL4
1135M	E	7.28	CHA	A(C(CH2-NH))		CDCL3
1173M	B	7.28	CHA	A(C(CH2-S))		CDCL3
1321M	D	7.28	CHA	A(C(CH3)/CH-C(Sn3-CH))		CCL4
758M	B	7.28	CHA	A(C(CL)-C(NH-NH2)-C(CL)/C(CL))		CDCL3
2325M	C	7.28	CHA	A(C(C(CH3/CH3/CH3))/CH-C(NH-C(=O)))		CDCL3
2325M	D	7.28	CHA	A(C(NH-C(=O))/CH-C(C(CH3/CH3/CH3)))		CDCL3
1711M	E	7.28	CHA	A(C(Q2(H/CH2-OH/H)))		CDCL3
2574M	A	7.28 APP.	OH	C(=O)-A		DMSO-D6
886M	D	7.28	QN	R6N<N-CH2/CH2>/A		CCL4
1173M	B	7.28		UNSPECIFIED		CDCL3
284M	B	7.28		UNSPECIFIED		CCL4
2991M	B	7.28		UNSPECIFIED		CDCL3
3000M	B	7.28		UNSPECIFIED		CDCL3
925M	B	7.28 APP.		UNSPECIFIED		CDCL3
1088M	C	7.28 APP.		UNSPECIFIED		CDCL3
2345M	C	7.28- 7.59		UNSPECIFIED		CDCL3
1135M	E	7.28		UNSPECIFIED		CDCL3
1711M	E	7.28		UNSPECIFIED		CDCL3
2543M	E	7.28 APP.		UNSPECIFIED		DMSO-D6
721M	C	7.29	CHA	AAN(C*/CH-C(CH3))		CDCL3
724M	A	7.29	CHA	ANA<C(CL)-N-C*/CH-C*>		CDCL3
1334M	B	7.29	CHA	AN<C(CH3)-N-C(C(=S)-NH2)>		POLYSOL-D
700M	B	7.29	CHA	AN<C(CL)-N>		CCL4
2938M	D	7.29	CHA	AN(C(CH2-C(=O)-O)-N)		CDCL3
1727M	C	7.29 APP.	CHA	AR5A<CH-C*-CH(CH2-OH)/CH-CH-C*>		POLYSOL-D
1727M	C	7.29 APP.	CHA	AR5A<CH-C*-C*/CH-CH-C*>		POLYSOL-D
866M	B	7.29	CHA	A<CH-CH-C(QN(CH3))>		CDCL3
2216M	E	7.29	CHA	A<CH-C(O-CH)>		CCL4
866M	B	7.29	CHA	A<CH-C(QN(CH3))>		CDCL3
397M	B	7.29	CHA	A<C(BR)-CH-C(BR)>		CCL4
398M	A	7.29	CHA	A<C(BR)/CH-C(BR)>		CDCL3
1542M	C	7.29	CHA	A<C(BR)/CH-C(O-A)>		CCL4
580M	C	7.29 APP.	CHA	A<C(CH2-NH)>		D20
1704M	E	7.29 APP.	CHA	A<C(CH2-N)>		CDCL3
937M	B	7.29 APP.	CHA	A<C(CH2-N=C=S)>		CDCL3
2845M	E	7.29	CHA	A<C(CH2-O-C(=O))>		CCL4
1284M	C	7.29	CHA	A<C(CH3)-C(SO2-CL)/CH-C(CH3)>		CCL4
1267M	D	7.29	CHA	A<C(CH3)/CH-C(Sn2-CH2)>		POLYSOL-D
2310M	E	7.29	CHA	A<C(CH(NH/CH3))>		CDCL3
1233M	D	7.29	CHA	A<C(CL)-C(CL)/C(SH)>		CCL4
1566M	B	7.29	CHA	A<C(CL)-C(O-CH3)-C(CL)/C(CL)>		CDCL3
2423M	D	7.29	CHA	A<C(NH-C(=O))/CH-C(CH3)>		DMSO-D6
2595M	D	7.29	CHA	A<C(O-CH3)/C(C(=O)-OH)-C(NH2)>		POLYSOL-D
163M	C	7.29	CHA	A<C(Q1(A/A))>		CDCL3
1151M	C	7.29	CHA	A<C(R5NS<C=C(A)/N=>)>		CDCL3
1151M	B	7.29	CHA	A<C(R5NS<C=C(A)/S>)>		CDCL3
1168M	A	7.29 APP.	CHA	A(CH-CH-C(S-C))		CDCL3
1168M	A	7.29 APP.	CHA	A(CH-C(S-C))		CDCL3
1935M	C	7.29	CHA	A(C(BR)-C(OH)-C(BR)/C(C(A/CH3/CH3)))		CDCL3
1516M	C	7.29	CHA	A(C(BR)/CH-C(O-CH3))		CCL4
476M	C	7.29	CHA	A(C(CH2-NH2))		CDCL3
2396M	B	7.29	CHA	A(C(CH2-R5NA))		DMSO-D6
2386M	C	7.29 APP.	CHA	A(C(CH2-R5N))		CDCL3
1247M	B	7.29	CHA	A(C(CH2-S(=O)))		CDCL3
860M	B	7.29	CHA	A(C(CL)/CH-C(QN(CH3/OH)))		CDCL3
2322M	F	7.29	CHA	A(C(NH-C(=O))/C(CH3))		CDCL3
2425M	D	7.29	CHA	A(C(NH-C(=O)-NH2)/CH-C(O-CH3))		POLYSOL-D
2294M	B	7.29	CHR	R5O(=C(C(=O)-NH)-O/CH=CH)		DMSO
2452M	D	7.29	CHR	R6NN(=CH-C(=O)/N(CH3)-C(=O))		CDCL3
2346M	D	7.29	NH	C(=O)-AN/CH2-A		CDCL3
2306M	G	7.29	NH	C(=O)-Q3/CH2-Q3		CDCL3
885M	E	7.29	QN	N(CH3/CH3)/A<C-CH-CH-C(CH3)>		CCL4
990M	A	7.29- 7.85		UNSPECIFIED		CDCL3
1151M	B	7.29		UNSPECIFIED		CDCL3
1247M	B	7.29		UNSPECIFIED		CDCL3
2396M	B	7.29		UNSPECIFIED		DMSO-D6
937M	B	7.29 APP.		UNSPECIFIED		CDCL3
2126M	B	7.29- 8.38		UNSPECIFIED		CCL4
476M	C	7.29		UNSPECIFIED		CDCL3
1151M	C	7.29		UNSPECIFIED		CDCL3
163M	C	7.29		UNSPECIFIED		CDCL3
2386M	C	7.29 APP.		UNSPECIFIED		CDCL3
580M	C	7.29 APP.		UNSPECIFIED		D20
2930M	C	7.29- 7.90		UNSPECIFIED		CDCL3
2845M	E	7.29		UNSPECIFIED		CCL4

BOOK NO.	ASSIGN-MENT	CHEM SHIFT - ppm -	PROTON GROUP	ENVIRONMENTAL GROUPS	S	SOLVENT
2310M	E	7.29		UNSPECIFIED		CDCL3
1704M	E	7.29 APP.		UNSPECIFIED		CDCL3
748M	A	7.30- 7.72	CHA	AANA<CH-C*-C*/CH-CH-C*>		CDCL3
748M	A	7.30- 7.72	CHA	AANA<CH-C*/CH-CH-C*>		CDCL3
998M	B	7.30- 7.65	CHA	AA(CH-C*/CH-CH-C*)		POLYSOL-D
998M	B	7.30- 7.65	CHA	AA(C(CH2-C:N)-CH-C*/CH-C*)		POLYSOL-D
1952M	D	7.30	CHA	AA(C*/CH-C(CH3)-C(OH))		CDCL3
2111M	C	7.30	CHA	AN(C(CH3)-N-C(C(=0)-CH3))		CDCL3
1584M	C	7.30- 7.60	CHA	AR50<CH-C*-O/CH-CH-C*>		CCL4
1584M	C	7.30- 7.60	CHA	AR50<C*-CH=CH>		CCL4
2089M	C	7.30- 7.65	CHA	A<CH-CH-C(C(=0)-CH2)>		CDCL3
2095M	A	7.30- 7.70	CHA	A<CH-CH-C(C(=0)-Q2)>		POLYSOL-D
1366M	C	7.30- 7.60	CHA	A<CH-CH-C(QN(A<C-CH-CH-C(SO2-NH2)>))>		DMSO-D6
2096M	C	7.30- 7.55	CHA	A<CH-CH-C(Q2(H/H/C(=0)-A))>		POLYSOL-D
2873M	B	7.30	CHA	A<CH-C(CL)/CH-C(C(=0)-O-CH3)>		CCL4
2089M	C	7.30- 7.65	CHA	A<CH-C(C(=0)-CH2)>		CDCL3
2866M	D	7.30	CHA	A<CH-C(C(=0)-O-CH2)>		CCL4
2095M	A	7.30- 7.70	CHA	A<CH-C(C(=0)-Q2)>		POLYSOL-D
1366M	C	7.30- 7.60	CHA	A<CH-C(QN(A<C-CH-CH-C(SO2-NH2)>))>		DMSO-D6
2096M	C	7.30- 7.55	CHA	A<CH-C(Q2(H/H/C(=0)-A))>		POLYSOL-D
1934M	C	7.30	CHA	A<C(A<C-CH-CH-C(C(CH3/CH3/CH3))-C(OH)/CH-C(C(CH3/CH3/CH3))>-CH-C(C(CH3/CH3/CH3))/C(C(CH3/CH3/CH3))-C(OH)>		CDCL3
1931M	C	7.30	CHA	A<C(A<C-C(OH)/CH-C(OH)>)>		CDCL3
1235M	C	7.30	CHA	A<C(BR)/CH-C(SH)>		CDCL3
1050M	C	7.30	CHA	A<C(CH2-CH3)/CH-C(NO2)>		CCL4
2933M	E	7.30	CHA	A<C(CH2-C(=0)-0)>		CDCL3
1005M	B	7.30	CHA	A<C(CH2-N)>		CDCL3
1703M	F	7.30	CHA	A<C(CH2-N)>		CDCL3
2445M	D	7.30	CHA	A<C(CH2-R5NN)>		CDCL3
2567M	B	7.30	CHA	A<C(CH3)/CH-C(C(=0)-OH)>		TFA
314M	A	7.30	CHA	A<C(CL)-CH-C(CL)/C(CL)>		CDCL3
308M	C	7.30	CHA	A<C(CL)-C(CH3)/C(CL)>		CCL4
2410M	C	7.30	CHA	A<C(CL)/CH-C(C(=0)-NH)>		CDCL3
2103M	D	7.30- 7.90	CHA	A<C(C(=0)-A)>		DMSO-D6
2880M	E	7.30	CHA	A<C(NH2)/C(C(=0)-O-CH3)>		CDCL3
2336M	C	7.30	CHA	A<C(NH-C(=0)-CH3)/CH-C(OH)>		POLYSOL-D
2398M	C	7.30	CHA	A<C(R5NA<N-C(=0)/C(C(=0)>)/CH-C(O-CH3)>		CDCL3
1536M	D	7.30	CHA	A<C(SH)/CH-C(O-CH3)>		CDCL3
1376M	C	7.30- 8.00	CHA	A<C(SO2-R5NN)>		POLYSOL-D
732M	A	7.30- 7.55	CHA	A(CH-CH-C(ANN(C-N-CH-N)))		CDCL3
836M	C	7.30- 7.60	CHA	A(CH-CH-C(CH2-N(+)))	S	CDCL3
2054M	B	7.30- 7.70	CHA	A(CH-CH-C(C(=0)-CH2))		CDCL3
2085M	C	7.30- 7.60	CHA	A(CH-CH-C(C(=0)-CH2))		CDCL3
2088M	D	7.30- 7.55	CHA	A(CH-CH-C(C(=0)-CH2))		CDCL3
2344M	C	7.30- 7.65	CHA	A(CH-CH-C(C(=0)-NH))		CDCL3
1268M	C	7.30- 7.60	CHA	A(CH-CH-C(SO2-A))		CDCL3
732M	A	7.30- 7.55	CHA	A(CH-C(ANN(C-N-CH-N)))		CDCL3
836M	C	7.30- 7.60	CHA	A(CH-C(CH2-N(+)))	S	CDCL3
2054M	B	7.30- 7.70	CHA	A(CH-C(C(=0)-CH2))		CDCL3
2085M	C	7.30- 7.60	CHA	A(CH-C(C(=0)-CH2))		CDCL3
2088M	D	7.30- 7.55	CHA	A(CH-C(C(=0)-CH2))		CDCL3
2289M	C	7.30	CHA	A(CH-C(C(=0)-NH2)/CH-C(CH3))		CDCL3
2344M	C	7.30- 7.65	CHA	A(CH-C(C(=0)-NH))		CDCL3
1268M	C	7.30- 7.60	CHA	A(CH-C(SO2-A))		CDCL3
384M	C	7.30	CHA	A(C(BR)/CH-C(CH3))		CCL4
1895M	C	7.30	CHA	A(C(BR)/CH-C(OH))		CDCL3
839M	H	7.30- 7.80	CHA	A(C(CH2-N(+)))	S	CDCL3
2289M	C	7.30	CHA	A(C(CH3)-CH-C(C(=0)-NH2))		CDCL3
1048M	B	7.30	CHA	A(C(CH3)/CH-C(NO2))		CDCL3
1369M	E	7.30	CHA	A(C(CH3)/CH-C(SO2-N))		CDCL3
2335M	D	7.30	CHA	A(C(NH-C(=0))/C(OH))		DMSO-D6
2549M	D	7.30 APP.	CHA	A(C(Q2(CH2-C(=0)-OH)))		CDCL3
186M	A	7.30- 7.75	CHA	UNSPECIFIED		CDCL3
2931M	D	7.30	CHR	R50(O-C(CH2-O-C(=0))=/=CH-CH=)		CCL4
1577M	E	7.30	CHR	R50(=CH-CH=/O-C(CH2-SH)=)		CDCL3
883M	C	7.30	QN	N(CH3/CH3)/R6<CH-CH2/CH2>		CDCL3
2530M	D	7.30	Q2	CH3/Q2(C(=0)-OH		CDCL3
222M	A	7.30- 7.70		UNSPECIFIED		CCL4
2102M	A	7.30- 7.80		UNSPECIFIED		CDCL3
1251M	A	7.30- 7.80		UNSPECIFIED		CDCL3
1286M	A	7.30- 7.80		UNSPECIFIED		POLYSOL-D
731M	A	7.30- 7.85		UNSPECIFIED		CDCL3
2568M	A	7.30- 8.00		UNSPECIFIED		POLYSOL-D
1005M	B	7.30		UNSPECIFIED		CDCL3
749M	B	7.30- 7.80		UNSPECIFIED		CDCL3
2113M	B	7.30- 8.09		UNSPECIFIED		CCL4
2227M	B	7.30- 8.30		UNSPECIFIED		CCL4
1931M	C	7.30		UNSPECIFIED		CDCL3
2989M	C	7.30 APP.		UNSPECIFIED		CDCL3
1376M	C	7.30- 8.00		UNSPECIFIED		POLYSOL-D
645M	D	7.30		UNSPECIFIED		CDCL3

: REPRESENTS TRIPLE BOND, ¬ REPRESENTS AN ARROW AND < AND > REPRESENT BRACKETS.   PAGE   283

BOOK NO.	ASSIGN-MENT	CHEM SHIFT - ppm -	PROTON GROUP	ENVIRONMENTAL GROUPS	S	SOLVENT
2445M	D	7.30		UNSPECIFIED		CDCL3
2549M	D	7.30 APP.		UNSPECIFIED		CDCL3
1248M	D	7.30- 7.70		UNSPECIFIED		CCL4
2103M	D	7.30- 7.90		UNSPECIFIED		DMSO-D6
2896M	D	7.30- 8.05		UNSPECIFIED		CDCL3
2933M	E	7.30		UNSPECIFIED		CDCL3
1703M	F	7.30		UNSPECIFIED		CDCL3
839M	H	7.30- 7.80		UNSPECIFIED	S	CDCL3
1794M	H	7.31	CHA	AAN<C(O-CH3)-CH-C*/CH-C*-N>		POLYSOL-D
203M	B	7.31	CHA	AA<CH-C*/CH-CH-C*>		CDCL3
882M	A	7.31	CHA	AN<CH-N-C(QN(QN(AN)))>		CDCL3
693M	D	7.31	CHA	AN(C(CH2.3-CH3)-CH-N/C(CH2.3-CH3))		CDCL3
2186M	D	7.31	CHA	AR500(C(C(=O)-H)-CH-C*/CH-C*-O)		CDCL3
2115M	E	7.31	CHA	AR6<C(CH2-CH3)-CH-C*/CH-C*-CH2>		CDCL3
2388M	B	7.31	CHA	A<C(BR)/CH-C(R5N<N-C(=O)/C(=O)>)>		POLYSOL-D
2846M	E	7.31 APP.	CHA	A<C(CH2-O-C(=O))>		CDCL3
2176M	A	7.31	CHA	A<C(CL)-CH-C(CL)/CH-C(C(=O)-H)>		CDCL3
989M	A	7.31	CHA	A<C(F)-C(C:N)-C(F)>		DMSO-D6
2339M	F	7.31	CHA	A<C(NH-C(=O))-C(CH3)/C(CH3)>		CDCL3
2448M	D	7.31	CHA	A<C(R5NN<CH-NH/C(=O)>)>		CDCL3
2675M	A	7.31- 7.64	CHA	A(CH-CH-C(C(=O)-O-NA))		D20
2675M	A	7.31- 7.64	CHA	A(CH-C(C(=O)-O-NA))		D20
1556M	B	7.31	CHA	A(CH-C(NO2)-C(O-CH3)/CH-C(NO2))		CDCL3
1529M	D	7.31	CHA	A(CH-C(O-CH3)-C(QN(OH)))		CDCL3
1518M	D	7.31	CHA	A(C(BR)/CH-C(O-CH2))		CDCL3
786M	C	7.31	CHA	A(C(CH2-C)/CH-C(CL))	S	D20
1907M	D	7.31	CHA	A(C(CH2-OH)-C(OH))		DMSO-D6
378M	D	7.31	CHA	A(C(CH(BR/HCH)))		CDCL3
2862M	E	7.31 APP.	CHA	A(C(Q2(H/C(=O)-O-CH2/H)))		CCL4
2893M	D	7.31	OH	A(C-CH-CH-C(C(=O)-O-CH))		CDCL3
2164M	B	7.31		UNSPECIFIED		CCL4
2861M	C	7.31		UNSPECIFIED		CCL4
2448M	D	7.31		UNSPECIFIED		CDCL3
378M	D	7.31		UNSPECIFIED		CDCL3
2862M	E	7.31 APP.		UNSPECIFIED		CCL4
2846M	E	7.31 APP.		UNSPECIFIED		CDCL3
785M	F	7.31		UNSPECIFIED	S	TFA
1952M	E	7.32 APP.	CHA	AA(CH-C*-C(OH)/CH-CH-C*)		CDCL3
1952M	E	7.32 APP.	CHA	AA(CH-C*/CH-CH-C*)		CDCL3
1729M	C	7.32	CHA	AN(C(CH2-OH)/CH-N)		CDCL3
2855M	C	7.32 APP.	CHA	AR5A<CH-C*-C*/CH-CH-C*>		CDCL3
2855M	C	7.32 APP.	CHA	AR5A<C*-CH(C(=O)-O-CH3)-C*>		CDCL3
1587M	A	7.32	CHA	AR60SA<C*-O-C*>		TFA
2107M	A	7.32- 7.72	CHA	A<CH-CH-C(C(=O)-A)>		CDCL3
2107M	A	7.32- 7.72	CHA	A<CH-C(C(=O)-A)>		CDCL3
2890M	F	7.32	CHA	A<CH-C(OH)-C(C(=O)-O-CH2)>		CCL4
2673M	B	7.32	CHA	A<C(CH2-C(=O)-O)>	S	D20
1709M	D	7.32	CHA	A<C(CH3)/CH-C(SO2-CH2)>		CDCL3
2067M	B	7.32	CHA	A<C(CL)-CH-C(C(=O)-CH3)/CH-C(CL)>		CCL4
310M	C	7.32	CHA	A<C(CL)-C(CL)/CH-C(F)>		CDCL3
2067M	B	7.32	CHA	A<C(CL)-C(C(=O)-CH3)/CH-C(CL)>		CCL4
2370M	E	7.32 APP.	CHA	A<C(C(=O)-N)>		CDCL3
2926M	B	7.32	CHA	A<C(O-C(=O)-CH3)/CH-C(NO2)>		CDCL3
1236M	E	7.32	CHA	A<C(SH)-C(NH2)>		CDCL3
2573M	A	7.32	CHA	A(CH-C(BR)/CH-C(C(=O)-OH))		POLYSOL-D
2370M	E	7.32 APP.	CHA	A(CH-C(C(=O)-N))		CDCL3
1302M	B	7.32	CHA	A(C(CH3)/CH-C(SO3-BA))	S	D20
2546M	B	7.32	CHA	A(C(CH(C(=O)-OH/A)))		CDCL3
2834M	D	7.32	CHA	A(C(CH(O-C(=O)/CH3))		CDCL3
2217M	C	7.32	CHA	A(C(CL)/CH-C(CH2-C(=O)-CL))		CDCL3
2330M	B	7.32	CHA	A(C(CL)/CH-C(NH-C(=O)))		DMSO-D6
2324M	E	7.32	CHA	A(C(NH-C(=O))/CH-C(CH2-CH3))		CDCL3
2937M	C	7.32	CHR	R50(=C(C(=O)-O-CH2)-O/CH=C(NO2))		CDCL3
2937M	C	7.32	CHR	R50(=C(NO2)-O/CH=C(C(=O)-O-CH2))		CDCL3
2834M	D	7.32		UNSPECIED		CDCL3
698M	A	7.32- 7.73		UNSPECIFIED		CDCL3
1053M	A	7.32- 7.89		UNSPECIFIED		C3H60
2546M	B	7.32		UNSPECIFIED		CDCL3
2673M	B	7.32		UNSPECIFIED		CDCL3
2100M	C	7.32- 7.84		UNSPECIFIED	S	D20
999M	A	7.33	CHA	AA(CH-C(C:N)-C*/CH-C*)		CDCL3
1018M	B	7.33 APP.	CHA	A<CH-C(CL)-C(CH2-S)/CH-C(CL)>		CDCL3
2218M	E	7.33	CHA	A<C(BR)/CH-C(CH2-CH2)>		CDCL3
1791M	E	7.33 APP.	CHA	A<C(CH(OH/CH2))>		CDCL3
1018M	B	7.33 APP.	CHA	A<C(CL)-C(CH2-S)-C(CL)>		CDCL3
2369M	C	7.33	CHA	A<C(C(=O)-R6N)>		CCL4
2368M	B	7.33	CHA	A<C(N(C(=O)/A))>		CDCL3
2915M	D	7.33	CHA	A<C(O-CH3)-C(OH)-C(O-CH3)/C(C(=O)-O-CH3)>		CDCL3
2446M	B	7.33	CHA	A<C(R5NN<CH-NH/C(=O)>)>		DMSO-D6
1320M	B	7.33 APP.	CHA	A<C(SO3-CH3)>		CDCL3
2048M	C	7.33	CHA	A(CH-CH-C(C(=O)-CH))		CCL4

BOOK NO.	ASSIGN-MENT	CHEM SHIFT - ppm -	PROTON GROUP	ENVIRONMENTAL GROUPS	S	SOLVENT
2048M	C	7.33	CHA	A(CH-C(C(=O)-CH))		CCL4
1378M	B	7.33	CHA	A(C(BR)/CH-C(NH-SO2))		POLYSOL-D
1705M	E	7.33	CHA	A(C(CH2-O))		CCL4
992M	A	7.33- 7.90		UNSPECIFIED		7.90
2368M	B	7.33		UNSPECIFIED		CDCL3
2446M	B	7.33		UNSPECIFIED		DMSO-D6
1320M	B	7.33 APP.		UNSPECIFIED		CDCL3
1046M	B	7.33 APP.		UNSPECIFIED		CCL4
2369M	C	7.33		UNSPECIFIED		CCL4
2449M	D	7.33		UNSPECIFIED		CDCL3
1705M	E	7.33		UNSPECIFIED		CCL4
1791M	E	7.33 APP.		UNSPECIFIED		CDCL3
540M	D	7.34	CHA	AA<C*/CH-C(NH2)>		POLYSOL-D
2340M	B	7.34	CHA	AA(CH-C*)		CDCL3
1062M	E	7.34	CHA	A<CH-C(NO2)-C(NH-CH2)>		CCL4
2633M	E	7.34	CHA	A<C(CH2-O-C(=O))>		TFA
1262M	F	7.34	CHA	A<C(CH3)/CH-C(SO2-CH2)>		CDCL3
1196M	C	7.34	CHA	A<C(S-S)/CH-C(CH3)>		CDCL3
289M	A	7.34	CHA	A(CH-CH-C(CCL3))		CCL4
289M	A	7.34	CHA	A(CH-C(CCL3))		CCL4
518M	E	7.34	CHA	A(C(BR)-C(NH2))		CDCL3
1375M	C	7.34	CHA	A(C(CH3)/CH-C(SO2-N))		CDCL3
871M	A	7.34		UNSPECIFIED		CDCL3
2633M	E	7.34		UNSPECIFIED		TFA
746M	B	7.35	CHA	AANA<C-C*-N/CH-CH-CH-C*>		CCL4
721M	D	7.35	CHA	AAN(C(CH3)-CH-C*/CH-C*-N)		CDCL3
729M	A	7.35	CHA	ANA(C*/CH-N-C(CL))		CDCL3
705M	E	7.35- 7.75	CHA	AN<CH-C(CH2-N)-N>		CDCL3
705M	E	7.35- 7.75	CHA	AN<C(CH2-N)-N>		CDCL3
1728M	D	7.35	CHA	AN<C(CH2-OH)-N>		CDCL3
683M	B	7.35	CHA	AN(CH-N/CH-C(CH3))		CCL4
683M	C	7.35	CHA	AN(C(CH3)-CH-N)		CCL4
2118M	D	7.35	CHA	AR60(C(CL)-CH-C*/CH-C*-O)		CDCL3
868M	B	7.35	CHA	A<CH-CH-C(QN)>		CDCL3
2286M	A	7.35- 7.85	CHA	A<CH-C(C(=O)-NH2)>		TFA
868M	B	7.35	CHA	A<CH-C(QN)>		CDCL3
507M	C	7.35	CHA	A<C(CF3)/CH-C(NH2)>		CDCL3
2015M	D	7.35 APP.	CHA	A<C(CH2-R6N)>		CDCL3
204M	C	7.35- 7.65	CHA	A<C(CH3)/C*>		CCL4
2941M	B	7.35	CHA	A<C(CL)/CH-C(O-C(=O)-O)>		CDCL3
995M	D	7.35	CHA	A<C(C:N)/CH-C(N(CH2/CH2))>		CDCL3
204M	C	7.35- 7.65	CHA	A<C*-CH-C(CH3)/CH-C(CH3)>		CCL4
385M	E	7.35	CHA	A(C(BR)-C(CH(CH3/CH3))/C(CH3))		CDCL3
2037M	D	7.35 APP.	CHA	A(C(CH(BR/CH)))		CDCL3
313M	B	7.35	CHA	A(C(CL)-C(CL)/CH-C(CL))		CCL4
1234M	B	7.35	CHA	A(C(CL)-C(CL)/C(SH)-C(CL))		CDCL3
2282M	B	7.35 APP.	NH2	C(=O)-CH		C3H6O
884M	C	7.35	QN	N(CH3/CH3)/A		CCL4
2037M	D	7.35 APP.		UNSPECIFIED		CDCL3
2015M	D	7.35 APP.		UNSPECIFIED		CDCL3
708M	F	7.36	CHA	AN<CH-C(NH-CH2)-N>		CDCL3
1819M	D	7.36	CHA	A<CH-CH-C(C(OH/C:C/CH3))>		CDCL3
1819M	D	7.36	CHA	A<CH-C(C(OH/C:C/CH3))>		CDCL3
1921M	C	7.36	CHA	A<C(BR)-CH-C(BR)/CH-C(OH)>		CCL4
395M	D	7.36	CHA	A<C(BR-CH-C(CH2-BR)>		CDCL3
311M	C	7.36	CHA	A<C(CL)-C(CL)/CH-C(CH2-CL)>		CCL4
2870M	D	7.36	CHA	A<C(C(CH3/CH3/CH3))/CH-C(C(=O)-O-CH2)>		CCL4
2680M	F	7.36	CHA	A<C(C(=O)-O-CH3)-CH-C(NH2)>		CDCL3
1821M	E	7.36	CHA	A<C(R6<C(OH)-CH2/CH2>)/CH-C(CH3)>		CDCL3
301M	B	7.36	CHA	A(C(CL)-C(F))		CCL4
1249M	B	7.36	CHA	A(C(I)/CH-C(SO-CH3))		CDCL3
1146M	B	7.36	CHR	R5S<S-CH=/=CH-C(NO2)=>		CCL4
1146M	A	7.36	CHR	R5S<=CH-S/C(NO2)=CH>		CCL4
2301M	C	7.36	NH	C(=O)-CH3/CH2.2-NH		POLYSOL-D
1368M	E	7.36	NH	SO2-CH2/A(C-CH-CH-C(CH3))		CDCL3
982M	B	7.36	Q2	A/H/C:N		CCL4
1000M	A	7.36- 7.97		UNSPECIFIED		CDCL3
1257M	E	7.36 APP.		UNSPECIFIED		CDCL3
2408M	B	7.37	CHA	AN(CH-N-C(C(=O)-NH))		CDCL3
2165M	B	7.37	CHA	A<CH-C(C(=O)-H)/CH-C(CH3)>		CCL4
897M	C	7.37	CHA	A<CH-C(N=N-A)/CH-C(CH3)>		CDCL3
394M	B	7.37	CHA	A<C(BR)/CH-C(CL)>		CCL4
2424M	B	7.37	CHA	A<C(BR)/CH-C(NH-C(=O))>		DMSO-D6
2165M	B	7.37	CHA	A<C(CH3)-CH-C(C(=O)-H)>		CCL4
2424M	B	7.37	CHA	A<C(NH-C(=O))/CH-C(BR)>		DMSO-D6
1366M	B	7.37	CHA	A<C(QN(A))/CH-C(SO2-NH2)>		DMSO-D6
896M	A	7.37	CHA	A(CH-CH-C(N=N))		CDCL3
176M	B	7.37	CHA	A(CH-C(A)-C(A))		CDCL3
896M	A	7.37	CHA	A(CH-C(N=N))		CDCL3
2887M	C	7.37	CHA	A(CH-C(O-CH3)-C(C(=O)-O-CH3))		CCL4
1363M	C	7.37	CHA	A(C(CH3)/CH-C(SO2-NH2))		TFA

BOOK NO.	ASSIGN-MENT	CHEM SHIFT - ppm -	PROTON GROUP	ENVIRONMENTAL GROUPS	S	SOLVENT
527M	C	7.37	CHA	A(C(I)/CH-C(NH2))		CDCL3
1573M	B	7.37	CHR	R50(=CH-CH=/O-CH=)		CCL4
985M	B	7.37		UNSPECIFIED		CCL4
287M	B	7.37 APP.		UNSPECIFIED		CCL4
215M	B	7.38	CHA	AAA<C(CH3)-CH-C*/CH-C*-C*>		CDCL3
207M	C	7.38	CHA	AAR5(CH-C*-CH2/CH-C*)		CDCL3
2939M	E	7.38	CHA	AN(CH-N/CH-C(C(=0)-O-CH2))		CDCL3
1585M	D	7.38	CHA	AR5NO<C*=N-C(CH3)/C(CH3)-C(CH3)>		CDCL3
1585M	C	7.38	CHA	AR5NO<C*-O-C(CH3)=/C(CH3)-C(CH3)>		CDCL3
2608M	C	7.38	CHA	AR500<C*-O-CH2/C(O(=0)-OH)>		POLYSOL-D
2844M	C	7.38 APP.	CHA	A<C(CH2-O-C(=0))>		CDCL3
1017M	B	7.38	CHA	A<C(CH2-S)>		CDCL3
2079M	C	7.38	CHA	A<C(CL)-CH-C(C(=0)-CH3)/CH-C(OH)>		CDCL3
977M	C	7.38 APP.	CHA	A<C(C(A/C:N/CH2))>		CDCL3
1351M	A	7.38	CHA	A<C(NH-C(=S))>		CDCL3
164M	B	7.38	CHA	A<C(Q1(A/Q1))>		CDCL3
164M	C	7.38	CHA	A<C(Q1(A/Q1))>		CDCL3
2161M	E	7.38	CHA	A<C(Q1(H/C(=0)-H/CH2-CH2))>		CCL4
1197M	B	7.38	CHA	A<C(S-S)/CH-C(CL)>		CDCL3
2551M	C	7.38	CHA	A<Q1(C(=0)-OH/CH2-CH3)>		CDCL3
2234M	A	7.38	CHA	A(CH-C(BR)/CH-C(C(=0)-BR))		CCL4
1047M	B	7.38	CHA	A(CH-C(NO2)/CH-C(CH3))		CCL4
200M	A	7.38	CHA	A(CH-C*/CH-CH-C*)		CCL4
1047M	B	7.38	CHA	A(C(CH3)-CH-C(NO2))		CCL4
433M	B	7.38 APP.	CHA	A(C(CL)-C(I))		CCL4
2874M	B	7.38	CHA	A(C(CL)/CH-C(C(=0)-O-CH3))		CDCL3
1733M	D	7.38	CHR	R50(=CH-CH=/O-C(CH2-OH)=)		CDCL3
1340M	B	7.38	NH2	C(=S)-NH		DMSO
2208M	C	7.38	Q2	Q2(CH3)/C(=0)-CL		CCL4
1351M	A	7.38		UNSPECIFIED		CDCL3
1017M	B	7.38		UNSPECIFIED		CDCL3
164M	B	7.38		UNSPECIFIED		CDCL3
789M	B	7.38		UNSPECIFIED	S	D20
164M	C	7.38		UNSPECIFIED		CDCL3
2551M	C	7.38		UNSPECIFIED		CDCL3
977M	C	7.38 APP.		UNSPECIFIED		CDCL3
2844M	C	7.38 APP.		UNSPECIFIED		CDCL3
205M	D	7.38 APP.		UNSPECIFIED		CDCL3
1357M	A	7.39	CHA	AAR5NN(CH-C*/CH-CH-C*)		DMSO-D6
1293M	A	7.39	CHA	AA<C(NH2)-C(SO2-OH)-C*/CH-C*>		DMSO-D6
2110M	B	7.39	CHA	AN<CH-N-C(C(=0)-CH3)>		CCL4
611M	D	7.39	CHA	AR5NR6<C*-C*-CH2>		CDCL3
2233M	A	7.39	CHA	A<CH-C(BR)/CH-C(C(=0)-CL)>		CCL4
1526M	D	7.39	CHA	A<CH-C(O-CH3)-C(NH2)>	S	POLYSOL-D
1289M	B	7.39- 8.00	CHA	A<C(A<C-CH-CH-C(SO2-OH)>)>		DMSO
1160M	C	7.39	CHA	A<C(BR)/CH-C(S-CH3)>		CDCL3
1284M	D	7.39	CHA	A<C(CH3)-CH-C(SO2-CL)/CH-C(CH3)>		CCL4
631M	G	7.39	CHA	A<C(CH(C(=0)-O/CH2))>		D20
311M	D	7.39	CHA	A<C(CL)-C(CL)/C(CH2-CL)>		CCL4
306M	B	7.39	CHA	A<C(CL)/C(CL)>		CCL4
2676M	C	7.39	CHA	A<C(NH2)/C(C(=0)-O-NA)>		D20
2464M	C	7.39	CHA	A<C(R6NN<C(CH2-O3)-C(=0)/C(=0)>)>		DMSO-D6
1276M	A	7.39- 7.69	CHA	A(CH-CH-C(SO2-A))		CDCL3
1276M	A	7.39- 7.69	CHA	A(CH-C(SO--A))		CDCL3
1234M	C	7.39	CHA	A(C(CL)-C(CL)/C(CL)-C(SH))		CDCL3
2066M	D	7.39	CHA	A(C(CL)/CH-C(C(=0)-CH2))		CDCL3
991M	A	7.39	CHA	A(C(CL)/CH-C(C:N))		CDCL3
903M	A	7.39 APP.	CHA	A(C(CL)/CH-C(N(=N-A/=0)))		CDCL3
903M	A	7.39 APP.	CHA	A(C(CL)/CH-C(N=N(=0/A)))		CDCL3
1580M	B	7.39	CHR	R5NO<=C(A)-O/N=C(A<C-CH-C(CL)>)>		CDCL3
2210M	C	7.39	CHR	R6(=C(C(=0)-CL)-CH2/CH2-CH2)		CCL4
611M	D	7.39	NHR	R5NAR6<C*-CH2/C*>		CDCL3
1955M	B	7.39- 7.65		UNSPECIFIED		CDCL3
1289M	B	7.39- 8.00		UNSPECIFIED		DMSO
2464M	C	7.39		UNSPECIFIED		DMSO-D6
631M	G	7.39		UNSPECIFIED		D20
402M	A	7.40	CHA	AA<C(BR)-C*/CH-C(BR)-C*>		CDCL3
712M	E	7.40	CHA	AN<C(CH2-R6N)-N>		CDCL3
682M	C	7.40	CHA	AN(CH-N-C(CH3))		CCL4
1587M	B	7.40	CHA	AR60SA<CH-C*-SO2/CH-CH-C*>		TFA
736M	A	7.40- 7.90	CHA	A<CH-CH-C(ANNN<C-N-C(A)-N/N-C(A)>)>		TFA
841M	C	7.40- 7.85	CHA	A<CH-CH-C(N(+)(CH2/CH2/CH2))>		CDCL3
859M	B	7.40 APP.	CHA	A<CH-CH-C(QN(CH3/OH))>		CCL4
736M	A	7.40- 7.90	CHA	A<CH-C(ANNN<C-N-C(A)-N/N-C(A)>)>		TFA
993M	A	7.40	CHA	A<CH-C(BR)/CH-C(C:N)>		CDCL3
841M	C	7.40- 7.85	CHA	A<CH-C(N(+)(CH2/CH2/CH2))>		CDCL3
859M	B	7.40 APP.	CHA	A<CH-C(QN(CH3/OH))>		CCL4
391M	B	7.40	CHA	A<C(BR)/CH-C(F)>		CCL4
1272M	A	7.40- 8.35	CHA	A<C(CF3)/C(SO2-A)>		CDCL3
837M	C	7.40- 7.90	CHA	A<C(CH2-N(+))>		POLYSOL-D
1290M	B	7.40 APP.	CHA	A<C(CH3)-CH-C(SO2-OH)/CH-C(NH2)>		DMSO-D6

BOOK NO.	ASSIGN-MENT	CHEM SHIFT - ppm -	PROTON GROUP	ENVIRONMENTAL GROUPS	S	SOLVENT
2213M	B	7.40	CHA	A<C(CH(CL/C(=0)¡)>		CCL4
2176M	B	7.40	CHA	A<C(CL)-C(C(=0)-H)/C(CL)>		CDCL3
296M	E	7.40	CHA	A<C(CL)-C(Q3)>		CCL4
1290M	B	7.40 APP.	CHA	A<C(NH2)-C(SO2-OH)/CH-C(CH3)>		DMSO-D6
2327M	C	7.40	CHA	A<C(NH-C(=0))/CH-C(F)>		CDCL3
2412M	F	7.40	CHA	A<C(R5NN<CH-NH/HCH>)>		DMSO-D6
1272M	B	7.40- 8.35	CHA	A<C(SO2-A)>		CDCL3
1065M	A	7.40- 7.65	CHA	A(CH-CH-C(N=N-A¡)		CDCL3
898M	A	7.40 APP.	CHA	A(CH-C(CL)/CH-C(N=N-A))		CDCL3
1065M	A	7.40- 7.65	CHA	A(CH-C(N=N-A))		CDCL3
2913M	B	7.40	CHA	A(C(CH2-0-C(=0)¡)		CDCL3
898M	A	7.40 APP.	CHA	A(C(CL)-CH-C(N=N-A))		CDCL3
2325M	C	7.40	CHA	A(C(C(CH3/CH3/CH3))/CH-C(NH-C(=0)))		CDCL3
437M	A	7.40	CHA	A(C(I)/CH-C(I))		CDCL3
817M	D	7.40	CHA	A(C(NH2)/CH-C(N(CH2/CH2)))	S	D20
2325M	D	7.40	CHA	A(C(NH-C(=0))/CH-C(C(CH3/CH3/CH3)))		CDCL3
2327M	C	7.40	CHA	A(C(NH-C(=0))/CH-C(F))		CDCL3
2311M	D	7.40	NH	C(=0)-CF3/CH2-CH2		CDCL3
1258M	B	7.40 APP.	Q2	A/H/SO2-Q2		CDCL3
2166M	A	7.40 APP.	UNSPECIFIED	UNSPECIFIED		CCL4
2183M	A	7.40- 8.10		UNSPECIFIED		CDCL3
2213M	B	7.40		UNSPECIFIED		CCL4
2913M	B	7.40		UNSPECIFIED		CDCL3
2125M	B	7.40		UNSPECIFIED		CCL4
729M	B	7.40- 7.65		UNSPECIFIED		CDCL3
724M	B	7.40- 7.82		UNSPECIFIED		CDCL3
2407M	B	7.40- 7.90		UNSPECIFIED		DMSO-D6
999M	B	7.40- 8.08		UNSPECIFIED		CDCL3
1963M	C	7.40- 7.90		UNSPECIFIED		TFA
1527M	D	7.40		UNSPECIFIED	S	POLYSOL-D
2412M	F	7.40		UNSPECIFIED		DMSO-D6
213M	A	7.41	CHA	AAA<C-CH-C*/CH-CH-C*>		CDCL3
1310M	B	7.41	CHA	AA(CH-C*-C(SO3-NA)/CH-CH-C*)		D20
609M	D	7.41 APP.	CHA	AR5N<C*-C(CH3)=C(CH3)>		CDCL3
2109M	D	7.41 APP.	CHA	AR600<C(C(=0)-CH3)-CH-C*/CH-C*-0>		CDCL3
2109M	D	7.41 APP.	CHA	AR600<C*-0-CH2/C(C(=0)-CH3)>		CDCL3
2944M	B	7.41	CHA	A<CH-CH-C(C(=0)-0-CH2)>		CDCL3
2944M	B	7.41	CHA	A<CH-C(C(=0)-0-CH2)>		CDCL3
2898M	D	7.41	CHA	A<CH-C(C(=0)-0-CH2)-C(C(=0)-0-CH2)>		CCL4
982M	C	7.41	CHA	A<CNQ2(H/C:N/H))>		CCL4
1732M	D	7.41 APP.	CHA	A<C(ANN<C-CH-N-C(CH2.2-OH)/CH-N>)>		CDCL3
381M	B	7.41 APP.	CHA	A<C(BR)>		CCL4
1283M	B	7.41	CHA	A<C(CH3)/CH-C(SO2-CL)>		CDCL3
2269M	B	7.41	CHA	A<C(Q2(H/C(=0)-0-C(=0)/H))>		CDCL3
2230M	A	7.41	CHA	A(CH-C(CL)/CH-C(C(=0)-CL))		CCL4
1178M	A	7.41	CHR	R6R5NS<=CH-C*/CH=CH>		CDCL3
609M	D	7.41 APP.	NHR	R5NA<C*/C(CH3)=C(CH3)>		CDCL3
2934M	F	7.41	Q2	R5O(C=CH/0)/H/C(=0)-0-CH2		CDCL3
1360M	D	7.41	Q2	SO2-NH2/H/A		POLYSOL-D
2269M	B	7.41		UNSPECIFIED		CDCL3
982M	C	7.41		UNSPECIFIED		CCL4
1732M	D	7.41 APP.		UNSPECIFIED		CDCL3
707M	C	7.42	CHA	AN<C(CL)-CH-N/CH-C(NH2)>		DMSO-D6
606M	D	7.42	CHA	AR5N<C*-CH=C(CH3)>		CDCL3
2902M	D	7.42	CHA	A<CH-C(C(=0)-0-CH2)/CH-C(C(=0)-0-CH2)>		CCL4
1279M	B	7.42 APP.	CHA	A<C(CH2-SO2-F)>		POLYSOL-D
1264M	C	7.42	CHA	A<C(CH3)/CH-C(SO2-CH2)>		POLYSOL-D
300M	A	7.42	CHA	A<C(CL)/CH-C(CF3)>		CCL4
1274M	A	7.42	CHA	A<C(CL)/CH-C(SO2-A)>		CDCL3
2057M	D	7.42	CHA	A<C(C(=0)-CH3)-C(CH3)/C(CH3)>		CCL4
674M	E	7.42	CHA	A<C(R5NN<C=N/N(A)>)>		CDCL3
2572M	A	7.42 APP.	CHA	A(CH-C(BR)-C(C(=0)-OH))		DMSO
2572M	A	7.42 APP.	CHA	A(CH-C(C(=0)-OH)-C(BR))		DMSO
2891M	F	7.42	CHA	A(CH-C(C(=0)-0-CH2)-C(OH))		CDCL3
1531M	C	7.42	CHA	A(CH-C(NO2)/CH-C(0-CH3))		CDCL3
2889M	E	7.42	CHA	A(CH-C(OH)-C(C(=0)-OH))		CDCL3
679M	B	7.42- 7.84	CHA	A(C(R5NNNN(C=N/N(CH3))))		CDCL3
1358M	D	7.42	QN	CH2-CH2/NH-C(=S)		CDCL3
679M	B	7.42- 7.84		UN		CDCL3
1279M	B	7.42 APP.		UNSPECIFIED		POLYSOL-D
402M	B	7.43	CHA	AA<CH-C*-C(BR)/CH-CH-C*>		CDCL3
694M	C	7.43	CHA	AN<CH-C(C(CH3/CH3/CH3))-N/CH-C(C(CH3/CH3/CH3))>		CCL4
713M	D	7.43	CHA	AN<C(CH2.2-AN)/CH-N>		CDCL3
2903M	E	7.43	CHA	A<CH-C(C(=0)-0-CH2)/CH-C(C(=0)-0-CH2)>		CCL4
1909M	B	7.43	CHA	A<C(A<C-CH-CH-C(OH)>)/CH-C(OH)>		DMSO-D6
504M	C	7.43	CHA	A<C(A<C-C(NH2)>)>		DMSO-D6
1894M	E	7.43	CHA	A<C(BR)-C(OH)>		CDCL3
1481M	E	7.43 APP.	CHA	A<C(C(0/A/A))>		CDCL3
2910M	D	7.43	CHA	A<C(NH2)-C(C(=0)-0-CH3)/C(C(=0)-0-CH3)>		POLYSOL-D
2583M	C	7.43	CHA	A(CH-C(0-CH3)/CH-C(C(=0)-OH))		DMSO-D6
1889M	C	7.43	CHA	A(C(A)/CH-C(OH)¡		DMSO

BOOK NO.	ASSIGN-MENT	CHEM SHIFT - ppm -	PROTON GROUP	ENVIRONMENTAL GROUPS	S	SOLVENT
2290M	B	7.43	CHA	A(C(CH3)/CH-C(C(=O)-NH2))		TFA
313M	C	7.43	CHA	A(C(CL)-C(CL)/C(CL))		CCL4
2321M	D	7.43	NH	C(=O)-CH3/A(C-C(CH3))		CDCL3
1941M	A	7.43 APP.		UNSPECIFIED		DMSO
504M	C	7.43		UNSPECIFIED		DMSO-D6
1962M	B	7.44	CHA	ANA(CH-N-C*/CH-C*)		CDCL3
741M	A	7.44	CHA	AR5NNN<CH-C*-NH/CH-CH-C*>		CDCL3
741M	A	7.44	CHA	AR5NNN<CH-C*-N=/CH-CH-C*>		CDCL3
2678M	C	7.44	CHA	A<CH-C(C(=O)-ONA)-C(OH)>		D2O
805M	B	7.44	CHA	A<C(CH2-NH)>	S	TFA
2857M	D	7.44	CHA	A<C(Q2(H/C(=O)-∩-R6/H))>		CCL4
2098M	B	7.44	CHA	A(C(C(=O)-A))		CDCL3
791M	C	7.44	CHA	A(C(NH2)/CH-C(O-CH3))	S	D2O
2444M	C	7.44	NHR	R6NN<C(=O)-NH/CH(CH3)-C(=O)>		POLYSOL-D
805M	B	7.44		UNSPECIFIED	S	TFA
2857M	D	7.44		UNSPECIFIED		CCL4
687M	G	7.45	CHA	AN<CH-C(CH2-CH2)-N>		CCL4
612M	B	7.45 APP.	CHA	AR5NA<C*-NH-C*>		C3H6O
2943M	C	7.45	CHA	A<CH-CH-C(C(=O)-O-A)>		CCL4
2943M	C	7.45	CHA	A<CH-C(C(=O)-O-A)>		CCL4
2331M	C	7.45	CHA	A<C(BR)/CH-C(NH-C(=O))>		DMSO-D6
2676M	D	7.45	CHA	A<C(C(=O)-O-NA)-CH-C(NH2)>		D2O
2331M	B	7.45	CHA	A<C(NH-C(=O))/CH-C(BR)>		DMSO-D6
2323M	D	7.45	CHA	A(C(NH-C(=O))/CH-C(CH3))		DMSO-D6
2327M	D	7.45 APP.	NH	C(=O)-CH3/A<C-CH-CH-C(F)>		CDCL3
2327M	D	7.45 APP.	NH	C(=O)-CH3/A(C-CH-CH-C(F))		CDCL3
206M	A	7.46 APP.	CHA	AA<CH-C*/CH-CH-C*>		CDCL3
2409M	B	7.46	CHA	AN<CH-N/CH-C(C(=O)-NH)>		DMSO-D6
861M	A	7.46	CHA	A<CH-CH-C(QN(A/OH))>		CDCL3
1534M	F	7.46	CHA	A<CH-C(NO2)-C(O-CH2)>		CCL4
2684M	C	7.46	CHA	A<CH-C(OH)-C(C(=O)-O-NH4)>		D2O
861M	A	7.46	CHA	A<CH-C(QN(A/OH))>		CDCL3
375M	D	7.46	CHA	A<C(BR)-C(CH2-CH3)>		CCL4
1517M	F	7.46	CHA	A<C(BR)-C(O-CH2)>		CCL4
2873M	C	7.46	CHA	A<C(CL)-CH-C(C(=O)-O-CH3)>		CCL4
2231M	A	7.46	CHA	A<C(CL)/CH-C(C(=O)-CL)>		CDCL3
2463M	A	7.46	CHA	A(CH-CH-C(CH=R6NN))		DMSO
2463M	A	7.46	CHA	A(CH-C(CH=R6NN))		DMSO
382M	C	7.46	CHA	A(C(BR)-C(CH3))		CCL4
393M	C	7.46	CHA	A(C(BR)/C(CL))		CCL4
786M	D	7.46	CHA	A(C(CL)/CH-C(CH2-C))	S	D2O
1058M	A	7.46	CHA	A(C(CL)/CH-C(NO2))		CDCL3
1145M	A	7.46	CHR	R5S<=CH-S/CH=C(QN(OH))>		TFA
215M	C	7.46- 7.87		UNSPECIFIED		CDCL3
751M	B	7.47	CHA	ANAAN<C(CH3)-N-C*/CH-C*>		POLYSOL-D
689M	F	7.47	CHA	AN<CH-C(CH(CH2.3/CH2.3))-N>		CCL4
395M	E	7.47	CHA	A<C(BR)/C(CH2-BR)>		CDCL3
2033M	B	7.47	CHA	A<C(R6<C=CH/C(=O)>)>		CDCL3
2098M	A	7.47 APP.	CHA	A(CH-CH-C(C(=O)-A))		CDCL3
2046M	C	7.47 APP.	CHA	A(CH-CH-C(C(=O)-CH2))		CDCL3
2098M	A	7.47 APP.	CHA	A(CH-C(C(=O)-A))		CDCL3
2046M	C	7.47 APP.	CHA	A(CH-C(C(=O)-CH2))		CDCL3
986M	C	7.47	CHA	A(C(C:N)/CH-C(CH3))		CCL4
2332M	B	7.47	CHA	A(C(NH-C(=O)-CH3)/CH-C(QN(OH)))		POLYSOL-D
1584M	D	7.47	CHR	R5OA<=CH-C*/O-C*>		CCL4
2033M	B	7.47		UNSPECIFIED		CDCL3
722M	C	7.48	CHA	AAN<C*/CH-C(CH3)>		CCL4
203M	C	7.48	CHA	AA<C*/C(CH3)-C(CH3)>		CDCL3
2897M	D	7.48	CHA	A<CH-C(C(=O)-O-CH2.4)-C(C(=O)-O-CH2.4)>		CCL4
2899M	E	7.48	CHA	A<CH-C(C(=O)-O-CH2)-C(C(=O)-O-CH2)>		CCL4
1720M	C	7.48	CHA	A<CH-C(NO2)/CH-C(CH2-OH)>		CDCL3
2211M	E	7.48	CHA	A<C(NH-C(=O))/CH-C(O-CH2)>		DMSO-D6
2337M	D	7.48	CHA	A<C(NH-C(=O))/CH-C(O-CH3)>		DMSO-D6
2864M	D	7.48	CHA	A(CH-CH-C(C(=O)-O-CH2))		CDCL3
2864M	D	7.48	CHA	A(CH-C(C(=O)-O-CH2))		CDCL3
428M	D	7.48	CHA	A(C(I)-CH-C(CH3))		CCL4
1898M	C	7.48	CHA	A(C(I)/CH-C(OH))		CDCL3
1091M	D	7.48	CHA	A(C(SI(A/A/CH2)))		CDCL3
1194M	B	7.48	CHA	A(C(S-S))		CDCL3
575M	C	7.48	NHR	R5N(CH=CH/CH=CH)		CCL4
1578M	C	7.48	Q2	R5O<C=CH/O>/H/NO2		CDCL3
2181M	A	7.48- 8.07		UNSPECIFIED		CDCL3
703M	B	7.49 APP.	CHA	AN<CH-C(BR)-N>		CCL4
703M	B	7.49 APP.	CHA	AN<C(BR)-N>		CCL4
612M	C	7.49	CHA	AR5NA<CH-C*-NH/CH-CH-C*>		C3H6O
740M	C	7.49	CHA	AR5NN(C*-N=CH/C(CH3))		CDCL3
2051M	B	7.49 APP.	CHA	A<CH-CH-C(C(=O)-CH2)>		CDCL3
2051M	B	7.49 APP.	CHA	A<CH-C(C(=O)-CH2)>		CDCL3
388M	A	7.49	CHA	A<C(CF3)/CH-C(BR)>		CCL4
667M	C	7.49	CHA	A<C(CH(A/A))/CH-C(N(CH3/CH3))>		TFA
2067M	C	7.49	CHA	A<C(CL)/C(C(=O)-CH3)-C(CL)>		CCL4

BOOK NO.	ASSIGN-MENT	CHEM SHIFT - ppm -	PROTON GROUP	ENVIRONMENTAL GROUPS	S	SOLVENT
979M	C	7.49 APP.	CHA	A<C(C(C:N/CH2.2/CH2.2))>		DMSO-D6
1486M	C	7.49	CHA	A<C(C(O/O/A))>		CDCL3
2905M	C	7.49	CHA	A<C(NH2)-CH-C(C(=O)-O-CH3)/C(C(=O)-O-CH3)>		POLYSOL-D
1724M	D	7.49	CHA	A<C(Q2(CH2-OH))/CH-C(NO2)>		POLYSOL-D
1508M	D	7.49	CHA	A(C(A)/CH-C(O-CH3))		CDCL3
396M	B	7.49	CHA	A(C(BR)-C(BR))		CCL4
1514M	E	7.49	CHA	A(C(BR)-C(O-CH3))		CDCL3
2875M	C	7.49	CHA	A(C(BR)/CH-C(C(=O)-O-CH2))		CCL4
1072M	A	7.49	CHA	A(C(F)-C(NO2)/CH-C(NO2))		CDCL3
1940M	A	7.49 APP.	CHA	A(C(NH2))		DMSO
2141M	G	7.49	CHR	R50<=CH-CH=/O-C(C(=O)-Q1)=>		CCL4
2605M	D	7.49	CHR	R50<=CH-CH=/O-C(Q2(H/C(=O)-OH/H))=>		CDCL3
2023M	E	7.49 APP.	CHR	R50(=CH-CH=/O-C(CH(OH/C(=O)))=)		DMSO
2934M	G	7.49	CHR	R50(=CH-CH=/O-C(Q2(H/C(=O)-O-CH2/H))=)		CDCL3
2023M	E	7.49 APP.	CHR	R50(=C(C(=O)-CH)-O/CH=CH)		DMSO
760M	D	7.49	NH	NH-A/A		DMSO-D6
607M	D	7.49	NHR	R5NA<C*/CH=C>		CDCL3
1940M	A	7.49 APP.	NHR	UNSPECIFIED		DMSO
979M	C	7.49 APP.		UNSPECIFIED		DMSO-D6
1794M	I	7.50 APP.	CHA	AAN<C*-C(CH(OH/R6R6N*BI))/C(O-CH3)>		POLYSOL-D
1794M	I	7.50 APP.	CHA	ANA<C(CH(OH/R6R6N*BI))-C*/CH-N-C*>		POLYSOL-D
2400M	D	7.50- 7.90	CHA	AR5N(CH-C*-C(=O)/CH-CH-C*)		CDCL3
605M	E	7.50	CHA	AR5N(C*)		CCL4
2400M	D	7.50- 7.90	CHA	AR5N(C*-C(=O)-N(CH2-N))		CDCL3
1265M	C	7.50- 7.85	CHA	A<CH-CH-C(SO2-CH2)>		POLYSOL-D
1371M	C	7.50- 7.80	CHA	A<CH-CH-C(SO2-NH)>		DMSO-D6
1313M	C	7.50- 7.70	CHA	A<CH-CH-C(SO3(-))>		POLYSOL-D
2293M	C	7.50	CHA	A<CH-C(OH)-C(C(=O)-NH2)>		DMSO-D6
1265M	C	7.50- 7.85	CHA	A<CH-C(SO2-CH2)>		POLYSOL-D
1371M	C	7.50- 7.80	CHA	A<CH-C(SO2-NH)>		DMSO-D6
1313M	C	7.50- 7.70	CHA	A<CH-C(SO3(-))>		POLYSOL-D
524M	B	7.50	CHA	A<C(BR)-C(NH2)-C(BR)/C(BR)>		CDCL3
838M	C	7.50 APP.	CHA	A<C(CH2-N(+))>		POLYSOL-D
1263M	E	7.50	CHA	A<C(CL)/CH-C(SO2-CH2)>		CDCL3
435M	B	7.50	CHA	A<C(I)/CH-C(BR)>		CDCL3
2364M	D	7.50	CHA	A<C(N(C(=O)/CH2))>		CCL4
2859M	C	7.50- 8.10	CHA	A<C(P(=CH/A/A))>		TFA
678M	C	7.50- 7.90	CHA	A<C(R5NN<N-N=/CH=>)>		CDCL3
1365M	D	7.50	CHA	A<C(SO2-NH2)/CH-C(NH2)>		DMSO-D6
1305M	A	7.50- 7.75	CHA	A(CH-CH-C(N=N-A))		DMSO
2901M	B	7.50	CHA	A(CH-C(C(=O)-O-CH3)/CH-C(C(=O)-O-CH3))		CDCL3
1060M	A	7.50	CHA	A(CH-C(I)/CH-C(NO2))		DMSO
1305M	A	7.50- 7.75	CHA	A(CH-C(N=N-A))		DMSO
860M	C	7.50	CHA	A(CQN(CH3/OH))/CH-C(CL))		CDCL3
1793M	E	7.50	CHA	A(C(CH(OH/CH3)-C(CL)/C(CL))		CCL4
2635M	A	7.50 APP.	CHA	A(C(C(C(NH2/C(=O)-OH/A)))		TFA
2583M	D	7.50- 7.80	CHA	A(C(C(C(=O)-OH)-CH-C(O-CH3))		DMSO-D6
2583M	D	7.50- 7.80	CHA	A(C(O-CH3)/C(C(=O)-OH))		DMSO-D6
678M	C	7.50- 7.90	CHR	R5NN<=CH-CH=/N(A)-N=>		CDCL3
1339M	D	7.50	NH	C(=S)-NH2/CH2-CH3		DMSO-D6
823M	E	7.50- 9.50	NH	NH2/A(C-CH-C(CL)-C(CH3))	S	DMSO-D6
823M	E	7.50- 9.50	NH2	NH-A	S	DMSO-D6
2635M	A	7.50 APP.		UNSPECIFIED		TFA
983M	A	7.50 APP.		UNSPECIFIED		CCL4
1001M	A	7.50- 8.00		UNSPECIFIED		CDCL3
826M	A	7.50- 8.15		UNSPECIFIED	S	D20
993M	B	7.50- 7.95		UNSPECIFIED		CDCL3
725M	B	7.50- 8.05		UNSPECIFIED		CCL4
838M	C	7.50 APP.		UNSPECIFIED		POLYSOL-D
2859M	C	7.50- 8.10		UNSPECIFIED		TFA
2364M	D	7.50		UNSPECIFIED		CCL4
1278M	E	7.50- 8.05		UNSPECIFIED		DMSO
1367M	B	7.51 APP.	CHA	AA<CH-C*/CH-CH-C*>		POLYSOL-D
717M	A	7.51	CHA	AN(C(AN(C-CH-CH-N))/CH-N)		CDCL3
739M	E	7.51	CHA	AR5NN<C*-NH-C(CH2.2-CH3)=>		POLYSOL-D
739M	E	7.51	CHA	AR5NN<C*-N=C(CH2.2-CH3)>		POLYSOL-D
1903M	C	7.51	CHA	A<CH-C(NO2)-C(OH)>		CCL4
523M	D	7.51	CHA	A<C(BR)-C(NH2)-C(BR)>		CDCL3
784M	D	7.51	CHA	A<C(CH(NH2/CH3))>	S	TFA
788M	A	7.51	CHA	A<C(NH2)>	S	TFA
787M	A	7.51	CHA	A<C(NH2)>	S	DMSO-D6
2441M	B	7.51	CHA	A<C(R5NA<N-C*/C(=O)>)>		DMSO-D6
2590M	A	7.51	CHA	A(CH-C(C(=O)-OH)-C(C(=O)-OH))		POLYSOL-D
428M	E	7.51	CHA	A(C(I)/C(CH3))		CCL4
2978M	B	7.51	CHA	A(C(O-C(=O)-NH2))		DMSO
1910M	C	7.51	OH	A(C-C(OH))		POLYSOL-D
2041M	F	7.51	Q2	A/H/C(=O)-CH2.3		CDCL3
2605M	E	7.51	Q2	R50<C=CH/O>/H/C(=O)-OH		CDCL3
788M	A	7.51		UNSPECIFIED	S	TFA
787M	A	7.51		UNSPECIFIED	S	DMSO-D6
2441M	B	7.51		UNSPECIFIED		DMSO-D6

BOOK NO.	ASSIGN-MENT	CHEM SHIFT - ppm -	PROTON GROUP	ENVIRONMENTAL GROUPS	S	SOLVENT
784M	D	7.51		UNSPECIFIED	S	TFA
733M	A	7.52	CHA	ANN<C(CL)-N/C(CL)-N>		CDCL3
2179M	D	7.52	CHA	AR5<C(C(=O)-H)-CH-C*/CH-C*-CH2>		CCL4
2683M	A	7.52 APP.	CHA	A<CH-CH-C(C(=O)-O-NH4)>		D2O
2575M	C	7.52	CHA	A<CH-C(C(=O)-OH)-C(I)>		C3D6O
2683M	A	7.52 APP.	CHA	A<CH-C(C(=O)-O-NH4)>		D2O
315M	A	7.52	CHA	A<C(CL)-C(CL)/C(CL)-C(CL)>		CDCL3
2224M	B	7.52	CHA	A<C(C(CH3/CH3/CH3))/CH-C(C(=O)-CL)>		CDCL3
2600M	B	7.52	CHA	A<C(C(=O)-OH)-CH-C(OH)/CH-C(OH)>		DMSO-D6
2326M	D	7.52	CHA	A<C(F)-CH-C(NH-C(=O))>		CDCL3
897M	D	7.52- 7.85	CHA	A<C(N=N-A)-CH-C(CH3)>		CDCL3
897M	D	7.52- 7.85	CHA	A<C(N=N-A)/C(CH3)>		CDCL3
2566M	A	7.52	CHA	A(CH-CH-C(C(=O)-OH))		CCL4
2097M	A	7.52	CHA	A(CH-CH-C(C(=O)-Q2))		CDCL3
2566M	A	7.52	CHA	A(CH-C(C(=O)-OH))		CCL4
2097M	A	7.52	CHA	A(CH-C(C(=O)-Q2))		CDCL3
852M	B	7.52	CHA	A(C(CH=NOH))		CDCL3
1291M	D	7.52	CHA	A(C(SO3-H)-CH-C(NH2)/CH-C(CH3))		DMSO-D6
2246M	B	7.52	CHR	R50<=C(C(=O)-CL)-O/CH=CH>		CCL4
207M	D	7.53	CHA	AAR5(C*/CH-CH-C*)		CDCL3
1309M	A	7.53	CHA	AA<CH-C*/CH-CH-C*>	S	DMSO-D6
205M	E	7.53	CHA	AA<C*-CH-C(CH3)/CH-C(CH3)>		CDCL3
746M	C	7.53	CHA	ANAA<C-C*-CH/C*-CH>		CCL4
1057M	A	7.53	CHA	A<CH-C(CL)/CH-C(NO2)>		CDCL3
2585M	E	7.53	CHA	A<CH-C(O-CH2)-C(C(=O)-OH)>		CCL4
300M	B	7.53	CHA	A<C(CF3)/CH-C(CL)>		CCL4
1250M	D	7.53	CHA	A<C(CL)/CH-C(SO-CH2.2)>		CDCL3
1521M	C	7.53	CHA	A(C(I)/CH-C(O-CH3))		CDCL3
2936M	F	7.53	CHR	R50<=CH-CH=/O-C(C(=O)-O-CH2.4)=>		CCL4
2124M	B	7.53		UNSPECIFIED		CDCL3
2180M	C	7.53- 7.91		UNSPECIFIED		CDCL3
1267M	E	7.54	CHA	A<C(SO2-CH2)/CH-C(CH3)>		POLYSOL-D
2315M	D	7.54	CHA	A(C(NH-C(=O)))		CDCL3
1945M	B	7.54	OH	A<C-C(OH)-C(OH)>		C3H6O
1945M	B	7.54	OH	A<C-C(OH)/C(OH)>		C3H6O
1310M	C	7.55	CHA	AA(CH-C*-C(NH2)/CH-CH-C*)		D2O
1002M	A	7.55	CHA	AN<CH-N/CH-C(C:N)>		CDCL3
681M	B	7.55	CHA	AN(CH-CH-N)		CCL4
1177M	C	7.55	CHA	AR5NS<C*-S-C(CH3)=/CH-C(CL)>		CDCL3
2904M	E	7.55	CHA	A<CH-C(C(=O)-O-CH2/CH-C(C(=O)-O-CH2)>		CDCL3
397M	C	7.55	CHA	A<C(BR)/C(BR)>		CCL4
430M	D	7.55	CHA	A<C(I)-C(CH3)/C(CH3)>		CCL4
806M	C	7.55 APP.	CHA	A<C(NH-CH2)>	S	D2O
1707M	C	7.55	CHA	A<C(QN(CH2.2-OH))/CH-C(CL)>		CDCL3
879M	C	7.55 APP.	CHA	A<C(QN(QN/NH2))>		CDCL3
429M	C	7.55	CHA	A(C(I)/CH-C(CH3))		CDCL3
840M	B	7.55- 8.00		UNSPECIFIED	S	D2O
873M	C	7.55- 8.00		UNSPECIFIED		POLYSOL-D
806M	C	7.55 APP.		UNSPECIFIED	S	D2O
1949M	D	7.56	CHA	AR5A<C*-C*/CH-C(OH)>		POLYSOL-D
2608M	D	7.56	CHA	AR500<C(C(=O)-OH)-CH-C*/CH-C*-O>		POLYSOL-D
1937M	B	7.56	CHA	A(C(BR)-C(OH)-C(BR)/C(BR))		CCL4
2571M	A	7.56	CHA	A(C(CL)/CH-C(C(=O)-OH))		DMSO
1084M	C	7.56	CHA	A(C(SI(A/H/H)))		CDCL3
1152M	B	7.56	CHR	R5NS<=CH-S/N=C(BR)>		CCL4
606M	E	7.56	NHR	R5NA<C*/C(CH3)=CH>		CDCL3
1241M	D	7.57	CHA	AA(C*)		CDCL3
2270M	A	7.57 APP.	CHA	A(CH-CH-C(C(=O)-O-C(=O)))		CDCL3
2081M	B	7.57	CHA	A(CH-C(C(=O)-CH3/CH-C(C(=O)-CH3))		CDCL3
2270M	A	7.57 APP.	CHA	A(CH-C(C(=O)-O-C(=O)))		CDCL3
991M	B	7.57	CHA	A(C(C:N)/CH-C(CL))		CDCL3
969M	A	7.57	NH2	Q1(C:N/C:N)		DMSO-D6
2862M	F	7.57	Q2	A/H/C(=O)-O-CH2		CCL4
1581M	F	7.58	CHA	AN<CH-C(O-CH2)-N>		CDCL3
740M	D	7.58	CHA	AR5NN(C*-NH-CH=/CH-C(CH3))		CDCL3
1300M	A	7.58	CHA	A<CH-CH-C(SO3-NA)>	S	D2O
1300M	A	7.58	CHA	A<CH-C(SO3-NA)>	S	D2O
2177M	A	7.58	CHA	A<C(CL)-C(CL)/CH-C(C(=O)-H)>		CCL4
432M	B	7.58	CHA	A<C(I)/CH-C(F)>		CDCL3
2291M	A	7.58 APP.	CHA	A(C(BR)-C(C(=O)-NH2))		TFA
1896M	E	7.58	CHA	A(C(I)-C(OH))		CDCL3
820M	C	7.58	CHR	R5NN(=C(CH2.2-NH2)-N=/NH-CH=)	S	D2O
2935M	F	7.58	CHR	R50<=CH-CH=/O-C(C(=O)-O-CH2.2)=>		CCL4
1146M	B	7.58	CHR	R5S<S-CH=/=CH-C(NO2)=>		CCL4
1146M	A	7.58	CHR	R5S<=CH-S/C(NO2)=CH>		CCL4
2291M	A	7.58 APP.		UNSPECIFIED		TFA
720M	C	7.58 APP.		UNSPECIFIED		CDCL3
712M	F	7.59	CHA	AN<CH-C(CH2-R6N)-N>		CDCL3
701M	B	7.59	CHA	AN(C(CL)-CH-N)		CCL4
1949M	E	7.59	CHA	AR5A<C*-C*>		POLYSOL-D
607M	E	7.59	CHA	AR5N<C*-C(CH3)=CH>		CDCL3

BOOK NO.	ASSIGN-MENT	CHEM SHIFT - ppm -	PROTON GROUP	ENVIRONMENTAL GROUPS	S	SOLVENT
2179M	E	7.59	CHA	AR5<C*-CH2-CH2/C(C(=O)-H)>		CCL4
2120M	C	7.59- 7.87	CHA	AR6(CH-C*-C(=O)/CH-CH-C*)		CDCL3
2885M	C	7.59	CHA	A<CH-C(NO2)/CH-C(C(=O)-O-CH2)>		CCL4
2587M	C	7.59	CHA	A<CH-C(OH)-C(C(=O)-OH)>		TFA
2591M	A	7.59	CHA	A<CH-C(=O)-OH/CH-C(=O)-OH>		POLYSOL-D
431M	B	7.59	CHA	A<C(CF3)-CH-C(I)>		CCL4
782M	B	7.59	CHA	A<C(CH2-NH2)>	S	D20
2055M	D	7.59	CHA	A<C(C(=O)-CH3)-C(CH3)>		CCL4
796M	A	7.59 APP.	CHA	A<C(NH2)-CH-C(CL)/CH-C(NH2)>	S	D20
796M	A	7.59 APP.	CHA	A<C(NH2)-C(CL)/CH-C(NH2)>	S	D20
2598M	C	7.59	CHA	A<C(O-CH3)-C(OH)/C(C(=O)-OH)>		DMSO-D6
1157M	C	7.59	CHA	A<C(R5SS<C=CH/S>)>		CDCL3
2564M	D	7.59	CHA	A(C(Q2(H/C(=O)-OH/H))/CH-C(CH3))		DMSO-D6
1578M	D	7.59	CHR	R50<=CH-CH=/O-C(Q2(H/NO2/H))=>		CDCL3
2184M	C	7.59	CHR	R5S(C(C(=O)-H)-S/CH-C(CH3))		CDCL3
877M	B	7.59	NH	QN(A(C-C(CL)))/A		CCL4
2225M	A	7.59- 8.12		UNSPECIFIED		D20
782M	B	7.59		UNSPECIFIED	S	DMSO-D6
1357M	B	7.60	CHA	AAR5NN(C*-NH-C(=S)/C*)		CCL4
1569M	D	7.60	CHA	AA(C*/CH-CH-C(O-CH3))		CDCL3
2167M	A	7.60	CHA	A<CH-C(CL)/CH-C(C(=O)-H)>		CCL4
388M	B	7.60	CHA	A<C(BR)/CH-C(CF3)>		TFA
2561M	B	7.60	CHA	A<C(CH2-C(=O)-O)/CH-C(NO2)>		CDCL3
2967M	B	7.60	CHA	A<C(CH2-O-C(=O))/CH-C(NO2)>		CDCL3
2167M	A	7.60	CHA	A<C(CL)-CH-C(C(=O)-H)>		CCL4
2165M	C	7.60	CHA	A<C(C(=O)-H)-CH-C(CH3)>		CCL4
2165M	C	7.60	CHA	A<C(C(=O)-H)/C(CH3)>		CDCL3
436M	B	7.60	CHA	A<C(I)-CH-C(I)>		POLYSOL-D
2317M	E	7.60	CHA	A<C(NH-C(=O)-CH)>		POLYSOL-D
1555M	B	7.60	CHA	A<C(O-CH3)-C(NO2)/CH-C(NO2)>		CDCL3
1250M	E	7.60	CHA	A<C(SO-CH2.2)/CH-C(CL)>		CCL4
1567M	B	7.60	CHA	A(C(BR)-C(O-CH3)-C(BR)/C(BR))		CDCL3
2102M	B	7.60	CHA	A(C(BR)/CH-C(C(=O)-A))		CCL4
2241M	B	7.60	CHA	A(C(CH3)-C(NO2)/CH-C(C(=O)-CL))		CCL4
2230M	B	7.60	CHA	A(C(CL)-CH-C(C(=O)-CL))		CDCL3
898M	B	7.60- 7.90	CHA	A(C(CL)/C(N=N-A))		CDCL3
2102M	B	7.60	CHA	A(C(C(=O)-A)/CH-C(BR))		DMSO
2467M	C	7.60	CHA	A(C(NH-C(=O)))		CDCL3
898M	B	7.60- 7.90	CHA	A(C(N=N-A)-CH-C(CL))		CDCL3
1372M	F	7.60	CHA	A(C(SO2-NH)/CH-C(CH3))		POLYSOL-D
2604M	B	7.60	CHR	R50<=CH-C(C(=O)-OH)=/O-CH=>		CCL4
1576M	C	7.60	CHR	R50(O-C(C:N)=/=CH)		CCL4
1144M	B	7.60 APP.	CHR	R5S(S-C(C:N)=/=CH-CH=)		CCL4
1144M	B	7.60 APP.	CHR	R5S(=C(C:N)-S/CH=CH)		TFA
805M	C	7.60 APP.	NH	CH2-A/CH2-A	S	POLYSOL-D
1908M	D	7.60	OH	A<C-CH-CH-C(C(A/CH3/CH3))>		CCL4
214M	A	7.60		UNSPECIFIED		D20
2674M	B	7.60- 8.50		UNSPECIFIED	S	CDCL3
1258M	C	7.60		UNSPECIFIED		CDCL3
1173M	D	7.60- 7.85		UNSPECIFIED		POLYSOL-D
1954M	E	7.61	CHA	AA<C*/CH-C(OH)-C(CH2.2-C:N)>		CDCL3
2938M	E	7.61	CHA	AN(CH-C(CH2-C(=O)-O)-N)		CDCL3
1175M	C	7.61- 8.04	CHA	AR5NS(C*-N=C(CH3))		CDCL3
1175M	C	7.61- 8.04	CHA	AR5NS(C*-S-C(CH3)=)		CDCL3
2127M	C	7.61	CHA	AR6A(CH-C*-C(=O)/CH-CH-C*)		TFA
1587M	C	7.61	CHA	AR60SA<CH-C*-O/CH-CH-C*>		CDCL3
2333M	C	7.61	CHA	A<CH-C(NO2)-C(NH-C(=O))>		DMSO-D6
2331M	C	7.61	CHA	A<C(BR)/CH-C(NH-C(=O))>		DMSO-D6
2331M	B	7.61	CHA	A<C(NH-C(=O))/CH-C(BR)>		DMSO-D6
2600M	C	7.61	CHA	A<C(OH)-C(OH)/C(C(=O)-OH)>		CDCL3
1594M	C	7.61	CHA	A<C(SI(O/O/A))>		D20
2680M	A	7.61	CHA	A(CH-C(C(=O)-O-K)-C(C(=O)-O-K))		DMSO-D6
2318M	C	7.61	CHA	A(C(NH-C(=O)))		POLYSOL-D
2332M	C	7.61	CHA	A(C(QN(OH))/CH-C(NH-C(=O)-CH3))		DMSO-D6
2564M	E	7.61	Q2	A(C-CH-CH-C(CH3))/H/C(=O)-OH		CDCL3
2340M	C	7.61 APP.		UNSPECIFIED		DMSO
1179M	D	7.61- 8.16		UNSPECIFIED		CDCL3
218M	A	7.62	CHA	AAAA<C-CH-C*/CH-CH-C*>		CDCL3
215M	D	7.62	CHA	AAA<C*-CH-C(CH3)/CH-C*>		CDCL3
215M	D	7.62	CHA	AAA<C*/CH-C*>		DMSO
1964M	B	7.62	CHA	AAN(CH-C*-C(NO2)/CH-CH-C*)		DMSO
1964M	A	7.62	CHA	AAN(CH-C*-C(OH)/CH-CH-C*)		CCL4
201M	D	7.62	CHA	AA<C*>		CDCL3
203M	D	7.62	CHA	AA<C*-CH-C(CH3)>		CDCL3
732M	B	7.62	CHA	ANN(C(A)-N/CH-N)		CCL4
711M	E	7.62	CHA	AN(C(R5N(CH-CH2/CH2))-CH-N)		DMSO
1278M	D	7.62	CHA	AR5SA(C*-SO2-C*/CH-C(NH2))		TFA
1361M	A	7.62 APP.	CHA	A<CH-CH-C(SO2-NH2)>		TFA
1361M	A	7.62 APP.	CHA	A<CH-C(SO2-NH2)>		CCL4
2068M	C	7.62	CHA	A<C(BR)-CH-C(C(=O)-CH3)>		CCL4
1921M	D	7.62	CHA	A<C(BR)-C(OH)/C(BR)>		

BOOK NO.	ASSIGN-MENT	CHEM SHIFT - ppm -	PROTON GROUP	ENVIRONMENTAL GROUPS	S	SOLVENT
1721M	B	7.62	CHA	A<C(CH2-OH)/CH-C(NO2)>		C3H6O
2897M	E	7.62	CHA	A<C(C(=O)-O-CH2.4)-C(C(=O)-O-CH2.4)>		CCL4
866M	C	7.62	CHA	A<C(QN(CH3))>		CDCL3
2406M	B	7.62	CHA	A(C(BR)/CH-C(C(=O)-NH))		DMSO
2292M	B	7.62	CHA	A(C(C(=O)-NH2)/C(NO2))		DMSO
2892M	D	7.62	CHA	A(C(C(=O)-O-CH3)-CH-C(OH))		CDCL3
2892M	D	7.62	CHA	A(C(OH)/C(C(=O)-O-CH3))		CDCL3
1304M	B	7.62	CHA	A(C(SO3-NA)/CH-C(NH2))		D20
2185M	A	7.62 APP.	CHR	R50<=C(C(=O)-H)-O/CH=C(NO2)>		CDCL3
2185M	A	7.62 APP.	CHR	R50<=C(NO2)-O/CH=C(C(=O)-H)>		CDCL3
2339M	G	7.62	NH	C(=O)-CH3/A<C-C(CH3)/CH-C(CH3)>		CDCL3
1102M	B	7.62- 8.08		UNSPECIFIED	S	CDCL3
2119M	C	7.63 APP.	CHA	AA<CH-C*-C(=O)/CH-CH-C*>		CDCL3
1293M	B	7.63	CHA	AA<CH-C*/CH-CH-C*>		DMSO-D6
2871M	E	7.63	CHA	A<C(F)/C(C(=O)-O-CH2)>		CCL4
525M	E	7.63	CHA	A<C(I)-C(NH2)>		CDCL3
1069M	A	7.63	CHA	A(C(CL)-C(CL)/CH-C(NO2))		CCL4
2170M	C	7.63	CHA	A(C(C(=O)-H)/CH-C(N(CH3/CH3)))		CDCL3
2289M	D	7.63	CHA	A(C(C(=O)-NH2)=CH-C(CH3))		CDCL3
2289M	D	7.63	CHA	A(C(C(=O)-NH2)/C(CH3))		CDCL3
901M	E	7.63	CHA	A(C(N=N-A)/CH-C(NH2))		DMSO-D6
901M	F	7.63	CHA	A(C(N=N-A)/CH-C(N(CH3/CH3)))		DMSO-D6
2133M	B	7.63	CHR	R50<=C(C(=O)-C(=O))-O/CH=CH>		CDCL3
969M	B	7.63	Q1	NH2/C:N/C:N		DMSO-D6
2861M	D	7.63	Q2	A/H/C(=O)-O-CH2		CCL4
600M	F	7.64 APP.	CHA	AA<C*>		CCL4
600M	F	7.64 APP.	CHA	AA<C*-C(NH-CH2)>		CCL4
2855M	D	7.64 APP.	CHA	AR5A<CH-C*-CH(C(=O)-O-CH3)/CH-CH-C*>		CDCL3
2855M	D	7.64 APP.	CHA	AR5A<C*-C*>		CDCL3
229M	B	7.64	CHA	A<C(CF3)/CH-C(F)>		CCL4
1720M	D	7.64	CHA	A<C(CH2-OH)-CH-C(NO2)>		CDCL3
2388M	C	7.64	CHA	A<C(R5N<N-C(=O)/C(=O)>)/CH-C(BR)>		POLYSOL-D
2573M	B	7.64	CHA	A(C(BR)-CH-C(C(=O)-OH))		POLYSOL-D
2101M	C	7.64	CHA	A(C(C(=O)-A)/CH-C(CH3))		CDCL3
1529M	E	7.64	CHA	A(C(QN(OH))-C(O-CH3))		CDCL3
2681M	C	7.64	CHR	R50<O-C(C(=O)-O-K)=/=CH-CH>	S	D20
1958M	C	7.65	CHA	AA<C*/CH-C(OH)>		C3D6O
206M	B	7.65- 8.05	CHA	AA<C-C*/CH-CH-CH-C*>		CDCL3
438M	C	7.65	CHA	AA(C*)		CDCL3
434M	C	7.65	CHA	A<C(BR)-C(I)>		CCL4
2898M	E	7.65	CHA	A<C(C(=O)-O-CH2)-C(C(=O)-O-CH2)>		CCL4
434M	D	7.65	CHA	A<C(I)-C(BR)>		CCL4
1526M	E	7.65	CHA	A<C(NH2)-C(O-CH3)>	S	POLYSOL-D
1275M	A	7.65	CHA	A(C(BR)/CH-C(SO2-A))		CDCL3
426M	B	7.65	CHA	A(C(I))		CCL4
816M	B	7.65- 8.00	CHA	A(C(NH2)/CH-C(N(CH3/CH3)))	S	D20
816M	B	7.65- 8.00	CHA	A(C(N(CH3/CH3))/CH-C(NH2))	S	D20
1375M	D	7.65	CHA	A(C(SO2-N)/CH-C(CH3))		CDCL3
1168M	B	7.65	CHA	A(C(S-C))		CDCL3
2307M	D	7.65	NH	C(=O)-H/CH(A/CH3)		CCL4
1370M	D	7.65	NH	SO2-A/A		CDCL3
2271M	B	7.65- 8.10		UNSPECIFIED		CDCL3
1342M	C	7.65- 8.20		UNSPECIFIED		POLYSOL-D
1293M	C	7.66	CHA	AA<CH-C*-C(SO2-OH)/CH-CH-C*>		DMSO-D6
1957M	C	7.66	CHA	AA<C*-C(OH)/CH-CH-C(OH)>		DMSO-D6
738M	B	7.66	CHA	AR5NN<CH-C*N=/CH-CH-C*>		DMSO-D6
738M	B	7.66	CHA	AR5NN<CH-C*-NH/CH-CH-C*>		DMSO-D6
1730M	C	7.66	CHA	AR5NN(C*-NH-C(CH2-OH)=)		DMSO-D6
1730M	C	7.66	CHA	AR5NN(C*-N=C(CH2-OH))		DMSO-D6
1054M	B	7.66	CHA	A<CH-C(F)-C(NO2)>		CCL4
186M	B	7.66	CHA	A<C(A)/CH-C(A)>		CDCL3
793M	A	7.66	CHA	A(CH-C(NH2)-C(NH2))	S	D20
988M	B	7.66	CHA	A(C(C:N)/CH-C(F))		CDCL3
793M	A	7.66	CHA	A(C(NH2)-C(NH2))	S	D20
1955M	C	7.67	CHA	AA<C*/CH-C(OH)-C(NO)>		CDCL3
1176M	B	7.67	CHA	AR5NS(C*-S-C(A)=)		CDCL3
1057M	B	7.67	CHA	A<C(CL)-CH-C(NO2)>		CDCL3
2079M	D	7.67	CHA	A<C(CL)/C(C(=O)-CH3)-C(OH)>		CDCL3
2598M	D	7.67	CHA	A<C(C(=O)-OH)-CH-C(O-CH3)/CH-C(OH)>		DMSO-D6
2899M	F	7.67	CHA	A<C(C(=O)-O-CH2)-C(C(=O)-O-CH2)>		CCL4
868M	C	7.67	CHA	A<C(QN)>		CDCL3
2073M	B	7.67	CHA	A(CH-C(NO2)/CH-C(C(=O)-CH3))		CDCL3
2240M	C	7.67	CHA	A(C(C(=O)-CL)-CH-C(CH3)/C(CH3))		CCL4
2134M	B	7.67- 8.02	CHA	A(C(C(=O)-C(=O)))		CCL4
1291M	E	7.67	CHA	A(C(NH2)-C(CH3)/C(SO3-H))		DMSO-D6
2857M	E	7.67	Q2	A/H/C(=O)-O-R6		CCL4
794M	A	7.67 APP.		UNSPECIFIED	S	D20
700M	C	7.68	CHA	AN<CH-C(CL)-N>		CCL4
2121M	D	7.68 APP.	CHA	AR6<CH-C*-C(=O)/CH-CH-C*>		CDCL3
2169M	A	7.68 APP.	CHA	A<C(BR)/CH-C(C(=O)-H)>		CDCL3
1303M	A	7.68	CHA	A<C(BR)/CH-C(SO3-NA)>	S	D20

BOOK NO.	ASSIGN-MENT	CHEM SHIFT - ppm -	PROTON GROUP	ENVIRONMENTAL GROUPS	S	SOLVENT
2177M	B	7.68	CHA	A<C(CL)-C(CL)/C(C(=O)-H)>		CCL4
1819M	E	7.68	CHA	A<C(C(OH/C:C/CH3))>		CDCL3
2169M	A	7.68 APP.	CHA	A<C(C(=O)-H)/CH-C(BR)>		CDCL3
2334M	C	7.68	CHA	A<C(NH-C(=O))-C(OH)>		DMSO-D6
2330M	C	7.68	CHA	A(C(NH-C(=O))/CH-C(CL))		DMSO-D6
200M	B	7.68	CHA	A(C*)		CCL4
751M	C	7.69	CHA	AANAN<C*/CH-C*>		POLYSOL-D
1952M	F	7.69	CHA	AA(C*)		CDCL3
1728M	E	7.69	CHA	AN<CH-C(CH2-OH)-N>		CDCL3
2111M	D	7.69	CHA	AN(CH-C(C(=O)-CH3)-N/CH-C(CH3))		CDCL3
1727M	D	7.69 APP.	CHA	AR5A<C*-CH(CH2-OH)-C*>		POLYSOL-D
1727M	D	7.69 APP.	CHA	AR5A<C*-C*>		POLYSOL-D
2117M	F	7.69	CHA	AR60<C*-C(=O)-CH2/C(CH3)>		CDCL3
2173M	E	7.69	CHA	A<C(C(=O)-H)/CH-C(O-CH2.2)>		CCL4
2410M	D	7.69	CHA	A<C(C(=O)-NH)/CH-C(CL)>		CDCL3
1064M	C	7.69	CHA	A<C(QN(NH-A))>		POLYSOL-D
2572M	B	7.69 APP.	CHA	A(C(BR)-C(C(=O)-OH))		DMSO
836M	D	7.69	CHA	A(C(CH2-N(+)))	S	CDCL3
2056M	D	7.69	CHA	A(C(C(=O)-CH3)/CH-C(CH3))		CCL4
2572M	B	7.69 APP.	CHA	A(C(C(=O)-OH)-C(BR))		DMSO
2887M	D	7.69	CHA	A(C(C(=O)-O-CH3)-C(O-CH3))		CCL4
1531M	D	7.69	CHA	A(C(NO2)/C(O-CH3))		CDCL3
1369M	F	7.69	CHA	A(C(SO2-N)/CH-C(CH3))		CDCL3
2467M	D	7.69	NH	NH-C(=O)/A		DMSO
1156M	C	7.69	NH	R5NNS<C=N/S>/CH2-CH3		POLYSOL-D
1954M	F	7.70	CHA	AA<C*>		POLYSOL-D
1570M	E	7.70	CHA	AA(C*)		CDCL3
2341M	C	7.70	CHA	AN<CH-C(NH-C(=O))-N>		CDCL3
2399M	C	7.70	CHA	AR5N(CH-C*-C(=O)/CH-CH-C*)		CDCL3
2108M	E	7.70	CHA	AR5(C(C(=O)-CH3)-CH-C*/CH-C*-CH2)		CDCL3
1266M	C	7.70	CHA	A<C(CL)-C(CL)/CH-C(SO2-CH2)>		CDCL3
2329M	C	7.70	CHA	A<C(CL)/C(NH-C(=O))>		CDCL3
2078M	D	7.70	CHA	A<C(C(=O)-CH3)-C(CH3)/CH-C(OH)>		DMSO-D6
2890M	G	7.70	CHA	A<C(C(=O)-O-CH2)-C(OH)>		CCL4
1335M	B	7.70	CHA	A<C(C(=S)-NH)>		CDCL3
1534M	G	7.70	CHA	A<C(NO2)-C(O-CH2)>		CCL4
1023M	C	7.70	CHA	A<C(N=O)/CH-C(N(CH3/CH3))>		CDCL3
2099M	D	7.70	CHA	A(C(C(=O)-A))		CCL4
1321M	E	7.70	CHA	A(C(SO3-CH)/CH-C(CH3))		CCL4
2633M	F	7.70	NH3(+)	CH(C(=O)-OH/CH2.2)		TFA
1928M	G	7.70	OH	A<C-CH-C(OH)-C(CH2.15-CH3)>		POLYSOL-D
1928M	G	7.70	OH	A<C-C(CH2.15-CH3)/CH-C(OH)>		POLYSOL-D
2895M	E	7.70	OH	A(C-CH-CH-C(C(=O)-O-CH2))		CCL4
2235M	A	7.70- 7.99		UNSPECIFIED		CCL4
1285M	A	7.70- 8.05		UNSPECIFIED		CDCL3
742M	A	7.70- 8.30		UNSPECIFIED		TFA
998M	C	7.70- 8.00		UNSPECIFIED		POLYSOL-D
1726M	E	7.70 APP.		UNSPECIFIED		CDCL3
2148M	F	7.70- 8.15		UNSPECIFIED		POLYSOL-D
825M	B	7.71	CHA	AA<C*/CH-C(NH-NH2)>	S	DMSO-D6
1334M	C	7.71	CHA	AN<CH-C(C(=S)-NH2)-N/CH-C(CH3)>		POLYSOL-D
878M	D	7.71	CHA	AN(CH-C(QN(CH3/NH-A))-N)		DMSO-D6
2398M	D	7.71	CHA	AR5N<CH-C*-C(=O)/CH-CH-C*>		CDCL3
211M	C	7.71	CHA	AR6A<C*-C*>		CDCL3
2574M	B	7.71	CHA	A<C(BR)/CH-C(C(=O)-OH)>		DMSO-D6
1922M	B	7.71	CHA	A<C(CL)-C(OH)-C(NO2)>		CDCL3
2239M	C	7.71 APP.	CHA	A<C(C(=O)-CL)-CH-C(CH3)/CH-C(CH3)>		CCL4
2239M	C	7.71 APP.	CHA	A<C(C(=O)-CL)/C(CH3)-C(CH3)>		CCL4
2577M	A	7.71	CHA	A<C(I)/CH-C(C(=O)-OH)>		DMSO-D6
667M	D	7.71	CHA	A<C(N(CH3/CH3))/CH-C(CH(A/A))>		TFA
2174M	F	7.71	CHA	A(C(C(=O)-H)/CH-C(O-CH2))		CCL4
2590M	B	7.71	CHA	A(C(C(=O)-OH)-C(C(=O)-OH))		POLYSOL-D
2599M	C	7.71	CHA	A(C(C(=O)-OH)-C(OH)/CH-C(OH))		DMSO
1519M	E	7.71	CHA	A(C(I)-C(O-CH3))		CDCL3
901M	E	7.71	CHA	A(C(N=N-A)/CH-C(NH2))		DMSO-D6
901M	F	7.71	CHA	A(C(N=N-A)/CH-C(N(CH3/CH3)))		DMSO-D6
1370M	E	7.71	CHA	A(C(SO2-NH)/CH-C(CH3))		CDCL3
1322M	F	7.71	CHA	A(C(SO3-CH2)/CH-C(CH3))		CCL4
427M	D	7.71	CHA	A(C-(I)-C(CH3))		CDCL3
2456M	A	7.71	CHR	R6NN(=C(BR)-C(=O)/NH-C(=O))		DMSO
1572M	C	7.71		UNSPECIFIED		CDCL3
1950M	C	7.72	CHA	AA(C*-C(OH))		C3H6O
750M	B	7.72	CHA	ANAAN<CH-N-C*/CH-C*>		C3H6O
2272M	A	7.72	CHA	AR50(C(F)-CH-C*/CH-C*C(=O))		CDCL3
2164M	C	7.72	CHA	A<C(C(=O)-H)-C(CH3)>		CCL4
2175M	F	7.72	CHA	A<C(C(=O)-H)/CH-C(O-CH2)>		CCL4
2596M	D	7.72	CHA	A<C(C(=O)-OH)-C(OH)/CH-C(CH3)>		POLYSOL-D
881M	C	7.72	CHA	A(C(QN(QN))/CH-C(CH3))		CDCL3
2294M	C	7.72	NH2	C(=O)-R50		DMSO
2917M	E	7.72	OH	A<C-C(OH)-CH-C(C(=O)-O-CH2)/C(OH)>		C3D6O
2917M	E	7.72	OH	A<C-C(OH)-C(OH)/CH-C(C(=O)-O-CH2)>		C3D6O

BOOK NO.	ASSIGN-MENT	CHEM SHIFT - ppm -	PROTON GROUP	ENVIRONMENTAL GROUPS	S	SOLVENT
2555M	C	7.72 APP.	OH	CH(C(=O)-OH/A)		DMSO
2555M	C	7.72 APP.	OH	C(=O)-CH		DMSO
2150M	A	7.72	OH	R5A(C(OH)-C(=O)/C(=O))		DMSO
2043M	C	7.72	Q2	A/H/C(=O)-Q2		CDCL3
895M	A	7.73	CHA	AN(C(C(=O)-NH)/CH-N)		DMSO
2395M	D	7.73	CHA	AR5N<CH-C*-C(=O)>		CDCL3
2226M	A	7.73	CHA	A<C(CF3)/CH-C(C(=O)-CL)>		CDCL3
2070M	F	7.73	CHA	A<C(C(=O)-CH2.2)/CH-C(NH2)>		CDCL3
1528M	D	7.73	CHA	A<C(QN(A))/CH-C(O-CH3)>		CDCL3
2872M	C	7.73	CHA	A(C(C(=O)-O-CH3)-C(CL))		CCL4
876M	B	7.73	QN	A/NH-A		C3H6O
2550M	C	7.73	Q2	A/H/C(=O)-OH		CDCL3
704M	B	7.74	CHA	AN(C(BR)-CH-N)		CCL4
2397M	C	7.74	CHA	AR5N<CH-C*-C(=O)/CH-CH-C*>		CDCL3
2118M	E	7.74	CHA	AR6O(C*-C(=O)-CH2/C(CL))		CDCL3
2580M	A	7.74	CHA	A(CH-C(C(=O)-OH)/CH-C(C:N))		DMSO
882M	B	7.75	CHA	AN<CH-C(QN(QN(AN)))-N>		CDCL3
2581M	A	7.75	CHA	A<CH-C(C(=O)-OH)-C(NO2)>		C3H6O
2581M	A	7.75	CHA	A<CH-C(NO2)-C(C(=O)-OH)>		C3H6O
2071M	F	7.75	CHA	A<C(C(=O)-CH2.3)/CH-C(NH2)>		CDCL3
2879M	H	7.75	CHA	A<C(C(=O)-O-CH2.4)-C(NH2)>		DMSO-D6
2877M	G	7.75	CHA	A<C(C(=O)-O-CH2)-C(NH2)>		CCL4
2320M	C	7.75	CHA	A<C(NH-C(=O))>		DMSO-D6
2104M	D	7.75	CHA	A(C(C(=O)-A)/CH-C(N(CH2/CH2)))		CDCL3
2059M	E	7.75	CHA	A(C(C(=O)-CH3)/CH-C(CH2-CH3))		CCL4
1049M	D	7.75	CHA	A(C(NO2)-C(CH2-CH3))		CCL4
1312M	G	7.75	CHA	A(C(SO3)/CH-C(CH3))	S	CDCL3
1051M	A	7.75		UNSPECIFIED		CDCL3
1310M	D	7.76	CHA	AA(C*-C(NH2))		D20
2408M	C	7.76	CHA	AN(CH-C(C(=O)-NH)-N)		CDCL3
2392M	C	7.76	CHA	AR5N<CH-C*-C(=O)/CH-CH-C*>		CDCL3
2108M	F	7.76	CHA	AR5(C*-CH2-CH2/C(C(=O)-CH3))		CDCL3
2871M	F	7.76	CHA	A<C(C(=O)-O-CH2)-CH-C(F)>		CCL4
872M	C	7.76	CHA	A<C(QN(A))/CH-C(CH3)>		CDCL3
2345M	D	7.76	CHA	A(C(C(=O)-NH))		CDCL3
1531M	E	7.76	CHA	A(C(NO2)-CH-C(O-CH3))		CDCL3
1302M	C	7.76	CHA	A(C(SO3-BA)/CH-C(CH3))	S	D20
716M	B	7.77	CHA	AN<CH-C(AN<C-N>)-N>		CDCL3
699M	C	7.77	CHA	AN<C(F)-N>		CCL4
2910M	E	7.77	CHA	A<C(C(=O)-O-CH3)-C(NH2)/CH-C(C(C=O)-O-CH3)>		POLYSOL-D
1313M	D	7.77	CHA	A<C(N(+)(CH3/CH3/CH3))>		POLYSOL-D
1290M	C	7.77	CHA	A<C(SO2-OH)-C(NH2)/C(CH3)>		DMSO-D6
433M	C	7.77 APP.	CHA	A(C(I)-C(CL))		CCL4
1022M	C	7.77	CHA	A(C(N=O)/CH-C(NH-A))		POLYSOL-D
2096M	D	7.77 APP.		UNSPECIFIED		POLYSOL-D
749M	C	7.78	CHA	AANA<C*/CH-C*-N>		CDCL3
702M	B	7.78	CHA	AN<C(CL)-C(CL)-N>		CDCL3
2956M	B	7.78	CHA	AR5O<C*-CH2-O/CH-C(NO2)>		CDCL3
2128M	B	7.78	CHA	AR6A<CH-C*-C(VO)/CH-CH-C*>		CDCL3
2065M	C	7.78	CHA	A<C(C(=O)-CL)-CH-C(CL)>		CCL4
861M	B	7.78	CHA	A<C(QN(A/OH))>		CDCL3
1262M	G	7.78	CHA	A<C(SO2-CH2)/CH-C(CH3)>		CDCL3
180M	B	7.78	CHA	A(C(A)/C(A))		CDCL3
795M	A	7.78	CHA	A(C(NH2)/CH-C(NH2))	S	D20
2292M	C	7.78	CHA	A(C(NO2)/CH-C(C(=O)-NH2))		DMSO
2133M	C	7.78	CHR	R50<O-C(C(=O)-C(=O))/=CH-CH=>		CDCL3
1578M	E	7.78	Q2	NO2/H/R50<C=CH/O>		CDCL3
1311M	A	7.79	CHA	AA<C*/CH-C(SO3-NA)>		D20
844M	B	7.79 APP.	CHA	AN<CH-C-N(+)(CH3)/CH-C(NH2)>		D20
844M	B	7.79 APP.	CHA	AN<C(NH2)-CH-N(+)(CH3)>		D20
709M	E	7.79	CHA	AN<N/C(NH-CH2)>		DMSO-D6
2399M	D	7.79	CHA	AR5N(C*-C(=O)-N(CH2-CH2))		CDCL3
2272M	B	7.79	CHA	AR5O(C(F)/C*-C(=O)-O)		CDCL3
1052M	B	7.79	CHA	A<C(A)-CH-C(NO2)>		CDCL3
2233M	B	7.79	CHA	A<C(BR)-CH-C(C(=O)-CL)>		CCL4
434M	C	7.79	CHA	A<C(BR)-C(I)>		CCL4
2069M	C	7.79	CHA	A<C(C(=O)-CH3)-CH-C(I)>		CDCL3
2069M	C	7.79	CHA	A<C(I)-CH-C(C(=O)-CH3)>		CDCL3
434M	D	7.79	CHA	A<C(I)-C(BR)>		CCL4
1024M	D	7.79 APP.	CHA	A<C(N=O)/CH-C(N(CH2/CH2))>		CDCL3
1709M	E	7.79	CHA	A<C(SO2-CH2)/CH-C(CH3)>		CDCL3
1303M	B	7.79	CHA	A<C(SO3-NA)/CH-C(BR)>	S	D20
2234M	B	7.79	CHA	A(C(BR)-CH-C(C(=O)-BR))		CCL4
2163M	B	7.79	CHA	A(C(C(=O)-H))		CCL4
818M	C	7.79	CHA	A(C(NH2)/CH-C(N(CH3/CH3)))	S	D20
1056M	B	7.79	CHA	A(C(NO2)-C(CL))		CDCL3
818M	B	7.79	CHA	A(C(N(CH3/CH3))/CH-C(NH2))	S	D20
899M	D	7.79 APP.	CHA	A(C(N=N-A))		CDCL3
899M	D	7.79 APP.	CHA	A(C(N=N-A)/CH-C(NH2))		CDCL3
1537M	C	7.79	CHA	A(C(SO2-A)/CH-C(O-CH3))		CDCL3
2162M	B	7.79	Q2	A<C-CH-CH-C(NO2)>/H/C(=O)-H		DMSO-D6

BOOK NO.	ASSIGN-MENT	CHEM SHIFT - ppm -	PROTON GROUP	ENVIRONMENTAL GROUPS	S	SOLVENT
2095M	B	7.79 APP.		UNSPECIFIED		POLYSOL-D
825M	C	7.80	CHA	AA<C*>	S	DMSO-D6
825M	C	7.80	CHA	AA<C*-CH-C(NH-NH2)>	S	DMSO-D6
604M	C	7.80	CHA	AA(CH-C*-C(NH-A)/CH-CH-C*)		CCL4
604M	C	7.80	CHA	AA(CH-C*/CH-CH-C*)		CCL4
2402M	B	7.80 APP.	CHA	AR5N<CH-C*-C(=O)/CH-CH-C*>		DMSO
2402M	B	7.80 APP.	CHA	AR5N<C*-C(=O)-N(NH2)>		DMSO
2112M	B	7.80	CHA	A<C(C(=O)-AN)>		CDCL3
2077M	F	7.80	CHA	A<C(C(=O)-CH2.2)/CH-C(O-CH3)>		CCL4
2068M	D	7.80	CHA	A<C(C(=O)-CH3)-CH-C(BR)>		CCL4
2167M	B	7.80	CHA	A<C(C(=O)-H)-CH-C(CL)>		CDCL3
2176M	C	7.80	CHA	A<C(C(=O)-H)-C(CL)/CH-C(CL)>		CDCL3
2894M	E	7.80	CHA	A<C(C(=O)-O-CH2)/CH-C(OH)>		CCL4
2905M	D	7.80	CHA	A<C(C(=O)-O-CH3)-CH-C(NH2)/C(C(=O)-O-CH3)>		POLYSOL-D
2237M	A	7.80	CHA	A(CH-C(C(=O)-CL)-CL)/C(C(=O)-CL))		CCL4
2243M	A	7.80	CHA	A(C(CE)-C(C(=O)-CE)/CH-C(NO2))		DMSO
2045M	C	7.80	CHA	A(C(C(=O)-CH3))		CCL4
2851M	E	7.80	CHA	A(C(C(=O)-NH))		CDCL3
2891M	G	7.80	CHA	A(C(C(=O)-O-CH2)-C(OH))		CDCL3
1269M	C	7.80	CHA	A(C(SO2-A)/CH-C(CH3))		CDCL3
2325M	E	7.80	NH	C(=O)-CH3/A(C-CH-CH-C(C(CH3/CH3/CH3)))		CDCL3
1938M	A	7.80 APP.	OH	A(C-C(I)-CH-C(I)/C(I))		DMSO
875M	B	7.80	QN	Q2(A)/NH-A		DMSO
2551M	D	7.80	Q1	A/C(=O)-OH/CH2-CH3		CDCL3
2201M	C	7.80	Q2	A/C(=O)-OH		CDCL3
2269M	C	7.80	Q2	A/H/C(=O)-O-C(=O)		CDCL3
1305M	B	7.80- 8.07		UNSPECIFIED		DMSO
2287M	C	7.80 APP.		UNSPECIFIED		TFA
748M	B	7.81	CHA	AANA<C*-CH-N>		CDCL3
1954M	G	7.81	CHA	AA<C*-C(CH2.2-C:N)-C(OH)>		POLYSOL-D
2110M	C	7.81	CHA	AN<CH-C(C(=O)-CH3)-N>		CCL4
2111M	E	7.81	CHA	AN(C(C(=O)-CH3)-N-C(CH3))		CDCL3
2396M	C	7.81	CHA	ARSN(C*-C(=O)-N(CH2-A))		DMSO-D6
2396M	C	7.81	CHA	AR5N(CH-C*-C(=O)/CH-CH-C*)		DMSO-D6
1289M	C	7.81 APP.	CHA	A<C(A)/CH-C(SO2-OH)>		DMSO
2074M	C	7.81	CHA	A<C(C(=O)-CH3)/CH-C(S-CH3)>		POLYSOL-D
1544M	B	7.81	CHA	A<C(NO2)/C(O-A)>		CDCL3
1264M	D	7.81	CHA	A<C(SO2-CH2)/CH-C(CH3)>		POLYSOL-D
1263M	F	7.81	CHA	A<C(SO2-CH2)/CH-C(CL)>		CDCL3
1284M	E	7.81	CHA	A<C(SO2-CL)-C(CH3)/C(CH3)>		CCL4
1289M	C	7.81 APP.	CHA	A<C(SO2-OH)/CH-C(A)>		DMSO
783M	C	7.81	CHA	A(C(BR)/C(CH2-NH2))	S	POLYSOL-D
2166M	B	7.81 APP.	CHA	A(C(C(=O)-H)-C(CL))		CCL4
2342M	C	7.81	CHA	A(C(C(=O)-NH))		CDCL3
2343M	B	7.81	CHA	A(C(NH-C(=O)))		DMSO
1268M	D	7.81	CHA	A(C(SO2-A)/CH-C(CH3))		CDCL3
726M	B	7.82	CHA	AAN(C*-N-C(I))		CDCL3
722M	D	7.82	CHA	ANA<C*/CH-CH-N>		CCL4
719M	D	7.82	CHA	ANA<C*/CH-C(CH3)-N>		CCL4
721M	E	7.82	CHA	ANA(C*-CH-C(CH3)/CH-CH-N)		CDCL3
2395M	E	7.82	CHA	AR5N<C*-C(=O)-N(Q3)>		CDCL3
2394M	E	7.82 APP.	CHA	AR5N(CH-C*-C(=O)/CH-CH-C*)		CDCL3
2394M	E	7.82 APP.	CHA	AR5N(C*-C(=O)-N(HCH-R30))		C3H6O
1053M	B	7.82	CHA	A<C(A)/CH-C(NO2)>		CCL4
2065M	D	7.82	CHA	A<C(CL)/C(C(=O)-CH3)		CCL4
2168M	B	7.82	CHA	A<C(C(=O)-H)-C(BR)>		D2O
2677M	B	7.82	CHA	A<C(C(=O)-ONA)/CH-C(NH2)>		CDCL3
2876M	C	7.82	CHA	A<C(I)-CH-C(C(=O)-O-CH3)>		CDCL3
1274M	B	7.82	CHA	A<C(SO2-A)/CH-C(CL)>		CDCL3
2147M	F	7.82	CHA	A(C(C(=O)-CH2))		CCL4
2228M	B	7.82	CHA	A(C(C(=O)-CL)-CH-C(F))		CDCL3
2411M	D	7.82	CHA	A(C(C(=O)-NH))		CDCL3
2147M	F	7.82	CHA	A(C(C(=O)-Q1))		CDCL3
900M	D	7.82	CHA	A(C(N=N-A))		CDCL3
900M	D	7.82	CHA	A(C(N=N-A)/CH-C(N(CH3/CH3)))		TFA
2389M	C	7.82	CHA	A(C(R5N(N-C(=O)/C(=O)))/CH-C(I))		CDCL3
1275M	B	7.82	CHA	A(C(SO2-A)/CH-C(BR))		CCL4
2246M	C	7.82	CHR	R50<O-C(C(=O)-CL)=/=CH-CH=>		DMSO
2294M	D	7.82	CHR	R50(=CH-CH=/O-C(C(=O)-NH2))		DMSO
850M	A	7.82	QN	QN(OH)/OH		CDCL3
2373M	C	7.83	CHA	AR5NA<C*-C*>		CDCL3
2373M	D	7.83	CHA	AR5NA<C*-N(C(=O)-CH3)-C*>		CDCL3
2398M	E	7.83	CHA	AR5N<C*-C(=O)-N(A<C-CH-CH-C(O-CH3)>)>		CDCL3
2060M	F	7.83	CHA	A<C(C(=O)-CH2.3)/CH-C(CH3)>		C3H6O
2578M	C	7.83	CHA	A<C(C(=O)-OH)/CH-C(NH2)>		CCL4
289M	B	7.83	CHA	A(C(CCL3))		CDCL3
2062M	D	7.83	CHA	A(C(C(=O)-CH2)/CH-C(CH3))		CCL4
2875M	D	7.83	CHA	A(C(C(=O)-O-CH2)/CH-C(BR))		CDCL3
2881M	D	7.83	CHA	A(C(C(=O)-O-CH3)/CH-C(NH2))		CDCL3
2328M	C	7.83	NH	C(=O)-CH3/A<C-C(CL)>		CCL4
2307M	E	7.84	CH	(=O)/NH-CH		

BOOK NO.	ASSIGN-MENT	CHEM SHIFT - ppm -	PROTON GROUP	ENVIRONMENTAL GROUPS	S	SOLVENT
723M	D	7.84	CHA	ANA<C*/CH-CH-N>		CCL4
2393M	B	7.84	CHA	AR5N<CH-C*-C(=O)/CH-CH-C*>		CDCL3
2391M	B	7.84	CHA	AR5N<CH-C*-C(=O)/CH-CH-C*>		TFA
2391M	B	7.84	CHA	AR5N<C*-C(=O)-N(CH3)>		TFA
2238M	E	7.84	CHA	A<C(C(=O)-CL)-C(CH3)-C(CH3)>		CCL4
1068M	E	7.84	CHA	A<C(NO2)-C(CH3)/CH-C(CH3)>		CDCL3
2889M	F	7.84	CHA	A(C(C(=O)-O-CH)-C(OH)))		CDCL3
819M	B	7.84	CHA	A(C(N(CH3/CH3))/CH-C(N(CH3/CH3)))	S	D2O
1363M	D	7.84	CHA	A(C(SO2-NH2)/CH-C(CH3))		TFA
1062M	F	7.84	NH	A<C-C(NO2)>/CH2-CH3		CCL4
1367M	C	7.85 APP.	CH	AA<C*-CH-C(SO2-NH2)>		POLYSOL-D
1964M	B	7.85	CHA	AAN(CH-C*-C(NO2)/CH-CH-C*)		DMSO
1964M	A	7.85	CHA	AAN(CH-C*-C(OH)/CH-CH-C*)		DMSO
201M	E	7.85	CHA	AA<C*-C(CH2-CH3)>		CCL4
2236M	A	7.85	CHA	A<CH-C(NO2)/CH-C(C(=O)-CL)>		CDCL3
2171M	A	7.85	CHA	A<CH-C(NO2)/CH-C(C(=O)-H)>		CDCL3
796M	B	7.85	CHA	A<C(CL)-C(NH2)/C(NH2)>	S	D2O
2167M	C	7.85	CHA	A<C(CL)/C(C(=O)-H)>		CDCL3
2048M	D	7.85	CHA	A(C(C(=O)-CH))..		CCL4
1177M	D	7.86	CHA	AR5NS<C*-N=C(CH3)/C(CL)>		CDCL3
2380M	A	7.86	CHA	AR5N(CH-C*-C(=O)/CH-CH-C*)		DMSO
2380M	A	7.86	CHA	AR5N(C*-C(=O)-NH)		DMSO
2063M	C	7.86	CHA	A<C(C(=O)-CH3)-C(F)/CH-C(F)>		CCL4
2882M	E	7.86	CHA	A<C(C(=O)-O-CH)/CH-C(NH2)>		CDCL3
1543M	B	7.86	CHA	A<C(NO2)-C(O-A)>		CDCL3
1249M	C	7.86	CHA	A(C(SO-CH3)/CH-C(I))		CDCL3
1293M	D	7.87	CHA	AA<C*>		DMSO-D6
989M	B	7.87	CHA	A<CH-C(F)-C(C:N)/CH-C(F)>		DMSO-D6
2047M	E	7.87	CHA	A<C(C(=O)-CH2)>		CCL4
871M	B	7.87	CHA	A<C(QN(A))>		CDCL3
1371M	D	7.87	CHA	A<C(SO2-NH)>		DMSO-D6
1301M	D	7.87	CHA	A(C(SO3NA)-C(CH3)/CH-C(CH3))	S	D2O
2595M	E	7.87	NH2	A<C-C(C(=O)-OH)-CH-C(O-CH3)>		POLYSOL-D
2595M	E	7.87	OH	C(=O)-A		POLYSOL-D
727M	D	7.88	CHA	AAN(C*-N)		CDCL3
2107M	B	7.88	CHA	A<C(C(=O)-A)>		CDCL3
2052M	D	7.88	CHA	A<C(C(=O)-CH2)>		CDCL3
2870M	E	7.88	CHA	A<C(C(=O)-O-CH2)/CH-C(C(CH3/CH3/CH3))>		CCL4
290M	B	7.88	CHA	A<C(C-CL3)/CH-C(F)>		CCL4
859M	C	7.88	CHA	A<C(QN(CH3/OH))>		CCL4
1266M	D	7.88	CHA	A<C(SO2-CH2)-CH-C(CL)/CH-C(CL)>		CDCL3
2406M	C	7.88	CHA	A(C(C(=O)-NH)/CH-C(BR))		DMSO
2576M	B	7.88	CHA	A(C(I)-CH-C(C(=O)-OH))		POLYSOL-D
1077M	C	7.88	CHA	A(C(NO2)-CH-C(CH3)/C(CH3)-C(NH2))		CDCL3
896M	B	7.88	CHA	A(C(N=N))		CDCL3
2457M	A	7.88	CHR	R6NN<=C(I)-C(=O)/NH-C(=O)>		DMSO
2957M	B	7.88	CHR	R60A(C*/=C(CL)-C(=O))		CDCL3
217M	A	7.89	CHA	AAAA<C-C*-CH/CH-C*-CH>		CCL4
2245M	B	7.89	CHA	AA<C*/CH-CH-C(C(=O)-CL)>		CCL4
2114M	E	7.89	CHA	AR6<C*-C(=O)-CH2>		CCL4
2115M	F	7.89	CHA	AR6<C*-C(=O)-CH2/C(CH2-CH3)>		CDCL3
2177M	C	7.89	CHA	A<C(C(=O)-H)-CH-C(CL)/CH-C(CL)>		CCL4
2873M	D	7.89	CHA	A<C(C(=O)-O-CH3)-CH-C(CL)>		CCL4
2878M	G	7.89	CHA	A<C(C(=O)-O-R6)-C(NH2)>		CDCL3
1333M	B	7.89	CHA	A<C(C(=S)-HNH)>		POLYSOL-D
1071M	E	7.89	CHA	A<C(NO2)-C(CH3)/CH-C(NH2)>		POLYSOL-D
1659M	F	7.89 APP.	CHA	A<C(P(=O/A/CH))>		POLYSOL-D
1261M	F	7.89	CHA	A<C(SO2-CH2)>		CDCL3
1067M	A	7.89	CHA	A(CH-C(NO2)/CH-C(NO2))		CCL4
2840M	D	7.89	CHA	A(C(C(=O)-CH2))		CDCL3
2049M	F	7.89	CHA	A(C(C(=O)-CH2))		CCL4
2066M	E	7.89	CHA	A(C(C(=O)-CH2)/CH-C(CL))		CDCL3
2344M	D	7.89 APP.	CHA	A(C(C(=O)-NH))		CDCL3
1046M	C	7.89	CHA	A(C-C(NO2)-C(CH3))		CCL4
2023M	F	7.89	CHR	R50(=CH-CH=/0-C(C(=O)-CH)=)		DMSO
1178M	B	7.89	CHR	R6R5NS<=CH-CH=/C*=N>		CDCL3
2344M	D	7.89 APP.	NH	C(=O)-A/A(C-C(CH3))		CDCL3
1309M	B	7.89 APP.		UNSPECIFIED	S	DMSO-D6
218M	B	7.90	CHA	AAAA<C-C*-CH/CH-CH-CH-C*-C*>		CDCL3
722M	E	7.90	CHA	AAN<C*-N/C(CH3)>		CCL4
2110M	D	7.90	CHA	AN<C(C(=O)-CH3)-N>		CCL4
2136M	A	7.90	CHA	AR5A<CH-C*-C(=O)/CH-C*>		TFA
996M	A	7.90	CHA	A<C(A<C-CH-CH-C(C:N)>)/CH-C(C:N)>		TFA
2051M	C	7.90	CHA	A<C(C(=O)-CH2)>		CDCL3
2581M	B	7.90	CHA	A<C(C(=O)-OH)-C(NO2)>		C3H6O
2574M	C	7.90	CHA	A<C(C(=O)-OH)/CH-C(BR)>		DMSO-D6
2577M	B	7.90	CHA	A<C(C(=O)-OH)/CH-C(I)>		DMSO-D6
2610M	C	7.90	CHA	A<C(C(=O)-SH)>		CDCL3
996M	A	7.90	CHA	A<C(C:N)/CH-C(A<C-CH-CH-C(C:N)>)>		TFA
431M	C	7.90	CHA	A<C(I)-CH-C(CF3)>		CCL4
2575M	D	7.90	CHA	A<C(I)-C(C(=O)-OH)>		C3D6O

BOOK NO.	ASSIGN-MENT	CHEM SHIFT - ppm -	PROTON GROUP	ENVIRONMENTAL GROUPS	S	SOLVENT
1544M	C	7.90	CHA	A<C(NO2)-CH-C(O-A)>		CDCL3
2581M	B	7.90	CHA	A<C(NO2)-C(C(=0)-OH)>		C3H6O
2162M	C	7.90	CHA	A<C(O2(H/C(=0)-H/H))/CH-C(NO2)>		DMSO-D6
1270M	C	7.90 APP.	CHA	A<C(SO2-A)>		CDCL3
1270M	C	7.90 APP.	CHA	A<C(SO2-A)/CH-CH-C(F)>		CDCL3
1283M	C	7.90	CHA	A<C(SO2-CL)/CH-C(CH3)>		CDCL3
2054M	C	7.90	CHA	A(C(C(=0)-CH2))		CDCL3
2088M	E	7.90	CHA	A(C(C(=0)-CH2))		CDCL3
2895M	F	7.90	CHA	A(C(C(=0)-O-CH2)/CH-C(OH))		CCL4
2869M	D	7.90	CHA	A(C(C(=0)-O-CH3)-C(CH3))		CDCL3
1268M	E	7.90	CHA	A(C(SO2-A))		CDCL3
2831M	D	7.90	H	C(=0)-O-CH2		CCL4
2013M	C	7.90-11.20	NHR	R6N<C(CH3/CH3)-CH2/C(CH3/CH3)-CH2>	S	CDCL3
1941M	B	7.90	NH2	A(C-C(CL))		DMSO
1941M	B	7.90	OH	A(C-C(NO2)-CH-C(NO2)/C(NO2))		DMSO
2482M	E	7.90- 8.90	OH	C(=0)-CH2.14-CH3		CDCL3
877M	C	7.90	QN	A(C-C(CL))/NH-A		CDCL3
750M	C	7.91	CHA	AANAN<C*/CH-C*>		C3H6O
749M	D	7.91	CHA	AANA<C*-N/CH-C*>		CDCL3
1286M	B	7.91 APP.	CHA	AA<C*-C(SO2-CL)>		POLYSOL-D
1286M	B	7.91 APP.	CHA	AA<C*/CH-CH-C(SO2-CL)>		POLYSOL-D
401M	B	7.91	CHA	AA(C(BR)/C*)		CCL4
1961M	C	7.91	CHA	ANA<C*/CH-C(OH)-N>		DMSO
2397M	D	7.91	CHA	AR5N<C*-C(=0)-N(A<C-C(CH3)>)>		CDCL3
2120M	D	7.91- 8.20	CHA	AR6(C*-C(=0)-CH=)		CDCL3
2120M	D	7.91- 8.20	CHA	AR6(C*-C(=0)-C(C(CH3/CH3/CH3))=)		CDCL3
2050M	F	7.91	CHA	A<C(C(=0)-CH2.1?)>		CDCL3
2076M	E	7.91	CHA	A<C(C(=0)-CH3)/CH-C(O-CH2)>		CDCL3
2688M	B	7.91	CHA	A<C(NH2)/CH-C(N(CH3/CH3))>		TFA
2072M	C	7.91	CHA	A<C(NO2)-C(C(=0)-CH3)>		CCL4
2688M	B	7.91	CHA	A<C(N(CH3/CH3))/CH-C(NH2)>		TFA
889M	D	7.91	CHA	A<C(QN(NH-A))>		DMSO-D6
1362M	D	7.91	CHA	A<C(SO2-NH2)-C(CH3)>		DMSO-D6
2237M	B	7.91	CHA	A(C(C(=0)-CL)-G(C(=0)-CL))		CCL4
2084M	D	7.91	CHA	A(C(C(=0)-R6))		CDCL3
2971M	C	7.91	CHA	A(C(C(=0)-S))		CDCL3
2883M	C	7.91	CHA	A(C(NO)/CH-C(C(=0)-O-CH2))		CDCL3
2692M	D	7.91	H	C(=0)-O-CH2		CCL4
2621M	E	7.91	NH	C(=0)-CH3/CH(C(=0)-OH/CH2)		POLYSOL-D
1940M	B	7.91	NH2	A		DMSO
1940M	B	7.91	OH	A(C-C(NO2)-CH-C(NO2)/C(NO2))		DMSO
1367M	D	7.92 APP.	CHA	AA<C(SO2-NH2)-CH-C*/CH-C*>		POLYSOL-D
1367M	D	7.92 APP.	CHA	AA<C*/CH-C(SO2-NH2)>		POLYSOL-D
2873M	E	7.92	CHA	A<C(CL)/C(C(=0)-O-CH3)>		CCL4
2107M	C	7.92	CHA	A<C(C(=0)-A)/CH-C(C(=0)-A))>		CDCL3
2678M	D	7.92	CHA	A<C(C(=0)-ONA)-C(OH)>		D2O
1300M	B	7.92	CHA	A<C(SO3-NA)>	S	D2O
2046M	D	7.92 APP.	CHA	A(C(C(=0)-CH2))		CDCL3
2290M	C	7.92	CHA	A(C(C(=0)-NH2)/CH-C(CH3))		TFA
1065M	B	7.92 APP.	CHA	A(C(N=N-A))		CDCL3
1065M	B	7.92 APP.	CHA	A(C(N=N-A)/CH-C(NO2))		CDCL3
1276M	B	7.92 APP.	CHA	A(C(SO2-A))		CDCL3
2451M	D	7.92	NHR	R5NN<C(=0)-NH/C(=0)-CH(NH-C(=0)-NH2)>		DMSO-D6
1794M	J	7.93	CHA	AAN<C*-N/CH-C(O-CH3)>		POLYSOL-D
1964M	E	7.93	CHA	ANA(N-C(OH)-C*/C(NO2)-C*)		DMSO
706M	E	7.93	CHA	AN(N-C(NH2))		CDCL3
2392M	D	7.93	CHA	AR5N<C*-C(=0)-N(CH2-CH2)>		CDCL3
697M	C	7.93	CHA	A<C(AN<C-N>)>		CDCL3
2620M	E	7.93	NH	C(=0)-CH3/CH(C(=0)-O/CH)		DMSO-D6
2119M	D	7.94 APP.	CHA	AA<C*-C(=0)>		CDCL3
2119M	D	7.94 APP.	CHA	AA<C*-C(=0)-C(CH3)>		CDCL3
707M	D	7.94	CHA	AN<N-C(NH2)/C(CL)>		DMSO-D6
2135M	C	7.94	CHA	A<C(C(=0)-C(=0))/CH-C(O-CH3)>		CDCL3
2219M	B	7.94	CHA	A<C(C(=0)-F)>		CCL4
2866M	E	7.94	CHA	A<C(C(=0)-O-CH3)>		CCL4
2876M	D	7.94	CHA	A<C(C(=0)-O-CH3)-CH-C(I)>		CDCL3
1075M	C	7.94	CHA	A(C(NH-QN)-C(NO2)/CH-C(NO2))		CDCL3
1047M	C	7.94	CHA	A(C(NO2)-CH-C(CH3))		CCL4
1047M	C	7.94	CHA	A(C(NO2)/C(CH3))		CCL4
877M	D	7.94	CHA	A(C(QN(NH-A))-C(CL))		CDCL3
1273M	B	7.94	CHA	A(C(SO2-A))		CDCL3
213M	B	7.95	CHA	AAA<C*/CH-CH-CH-C*>		CDCL3
731M	B	7.95	CHA	AAN(C*-C(BR))		CDCL3
1357M	C	7.95	CHA	AAR5NN(C*-CH-C*)		DMSO-D6
2274M	A	7.95	CHA	AAR6O<CH-C*-C(=0)/CH-C*>		TFA
724M	C	7.95	CHA	ANA<C*/CH-C(CL)-N>		CDCL3
2086M	D	7.95	CHA	A<C(C(=0)-CH2)>		POLYSOL-D
2601M	A	7.95	CHA	A<C(C(=0)-OH)-C(C(=0)-OH)/CH-C(NO2)>		D2O
2083M	D	7.95	CHA	A<C(C(=0)-R5)>		CCL4
1366M	D	7.95	CHA	A<C(QN(A<C-CH-CH-C(SO2-NH2)>))>		DMSO-D6
1580M	C	7.95	CHA	A<C(R5NO<C=N/O>)-CH-C(CL)>		CDCL3

BOOK NO.	ASSIGN-MENT	CHEM SHIFT - ppm -	PROTON GROUP	ENVIRONMENTAL GROUPS	S	SOLVENT
1361M	B	7.95 APP.	CHA	A<C(SO2-NH2)>		TFA
2586M	E	7.95	CHA	A(C(C(=0)-OH)/CH-C(0-CH2.2))		POLYSOL-D
2884M	D	7.95	CHA	A(C(C(=0)-0-CH2)/CH-C(QN(=0)))		CDCL3
2874M	C	7.95	CHA	A(C(C(=0)-0-CH3)/CH-C(CL))		CDCL3
1271M	B	7.95	CHA	A(C(SO2)/CH-C(F))		CDCL3
2308M	E	7.95	H	C(=0)-NH		DMSO-D6
867M	D	7.95	QN	Q2(A)/CH2.2-QN		CDCL3
2097M	B	7.95	Q2	C(=0)-A/H/C(=0)-A		CDCL3
218M	C	7.96	CHA	AAAA<C-C*-CH/CH-C*-C*>		CDCL3
2121M	E	7.96 APP.	CHA	AR6<C*-C(=0)-CH=>		CDCL3
2121M	E	7.96 APP.	CHA	AR6<C*-C(=0)-C(R6<CH-CH2/CH2>)=>		CDCL3
2223M	C	7.96	CHA	A<C(C(=0)-CL)/CH-C(CH3)>		CCL4
2858M	D	7.96	CHA	A<C(Q)(C(=0)-0-CH2/C:N)>		CDCL3
2893M	E	7.96	CHA	A(C(C(=0)-0-CH)/CH-C(OH))		CDCL3
2693M	D	7.96	H	C(=0)-0-CH2		CCL4
2338M	G	7.96	NH	C(=0)-CH3/A(C-C(CH3)-CH-C(CH3))		CDCL3
2684M	D	7.97	CHA	A<C(C(=0)-0-NH4)-C(OH)>		D20
431M	D	7.97	CHA	A<C(I)/C(CF3)>		CCL4
1366M	E	7.97	CHA	A<C(SO2-NH2)/CH-C(QN(A))>		DMSO-D6
2075M	D	7.97	CHA	A(C(C(=0)-CH3)/CH-C(0-CH3))		CDCL3
2573M	C	7.97	CHA	A(C(C(=0)-OH)-CH-C(BR))		POLYSOL-D
1351M	B	7.97 APP.	NH	C=S-NH/A		CDCL3
747M	B	7.98	CHA	AANA(C*-C(NH2)-C*)		DMSO-D6
1174M	C	7.98	CHA	AAN<C*-N-C(S-A)>		CDCL3
1731M	D	7.98	CHA	AAN(C*N)		CDCL3
2089M	D	7.98	CHA	A<C(C(=0)-CH2)>		CDCL3
2908M	D	7.98	CHA	A<C(C(=0)-0-CH2)/CH-C(C(=0)-0-CH2)>		CCL4
1564M	E	7.98	CHA	A<C(NO2)-C(0-CH3)/CH-C(0-CH3)>		CDCL3
1538M	C	7.98	CHA	A<C(SO2-CL)/CH-C(0-CH3)>		CDCL3
2234M	C	7.98	CHA	A(C(C(=0)-BR)-CH-C(BR))		CCL4
2085M	D	7.98	CHA	A(C(C(=0)-CH2))		CDCL3
2230M	C	7.98	CHA	A(C(C(=0)-CL)-CH-C(CL))		CCL4
2343M	C	7.98	CHA	A(C(C(=0)-NH))		DMSO
2942M	C	7.98	CHA	A(C(C(=0)-0-CH2))		CCL4
2675M	B	7.98	CHA	A(C(C(=0)-0-NA))		D20
2093M	C	7.98	CHA	A(C(C(=0)-Q2)/CH-C(CH3))		CDCL3
2686M	E	7.98	NH2	CH2.11-CH3		CDCL3
2686M	E	7.98	OH	C(=0)-CH3		CDCL3
721M	F	7.99	CHA	AAN(C*-N/CH-C(CH3))		CDCL3
1311M	B	7.99	CHA	AA<C(SO3-NA)-CH-C*/CH-C*>		D20
438M	D	7.99	CHA	AA.(C*/CH-CH-C(I))		CDCL3
1962M	C	7.99	CHA	ANA(C*/CH-CH-N)		CDCL3
1312M	H	7.99	CHA	AN(CH-N(CH2-CH2))	S	CDCL3
1176M	C	7.99 APP.	CHA	AR5NS(C*-N=C(A))		CDCL3
2393M	C	7.99	CHA	AR5N<C*-C(=0)-N(CH2-BR)>		CDCL3
2068M	E	7.99	CHA	A<C(BR)/C(C(=0)-CH3)>		CCL4
2683M	B	7.99	CHA	A<C(C(=0)-0-NH4)>		D20
2888M	D	7.99	CHA	A(C(C(=0)-0-CH3)/CH-C(0-CH3))		CDCL3
818M	C	7.99	CHA	A(C(NH2)/CH-C(N(CH3/CH3)))	S	D20
818M	B	7.99	CHA	A(C(N(CH3/CH3))/CH-C(NH2))	S	D20
1176M	C	7.99 APP.	CHA	A(C(R5NSA(C=N/S)))		CDCL3
729M	C	8.00	CHA	AAN(C*-C(CL)-N)		CDCL3
922M	B	8.00	CHA	AA(C*-C(N=C=0))		CDCL3
2868M	B	8.00	CHA	ANA(C*/CH-CH-N)		CDCL3
2128M	C	8.00	CHA	AR6A<C*-C(=0)-C*/C(CH3)-C(CH3)>		CDCL3
2232M	B	8.00	CHA	A<C(C(=0)-CL)-C(BR)>		CCL4
2587M	D	8.00	CHA	A<C(C(=0)-OH)-C(OH)>		TFA
2867M	D	8.00	CHA	A<C(C(=0)-0-CH2)>		CCL4
1903M	D	8.00	CHA	A<C(NO2)-C(OH)>		CCL4
2288M	B	8.00	CHA	A<C-C(C(=0)-NH2)>		TFA
997M	A	8.00	CHA	A(CH-C(C:N)-C(C:N))		TFA
2576M	C	8.00	CHA	A(C(C(=0)-OH)-CH-C(I))		POLYSOL-D
2571M	B	8.00	CHA	A(C(C(=0)-OH)/CH-C(CL))		DMSO
2868M	B	8.00	CHA	A(C(C(=0)-0-AAN))		CDCL3
2680M	B	8.00	CHA	A(C(C(=0)-0-K)-C(C(=0)-0-K))		D20
2092M	B	8.00 APP.	CHA	A(C(C(=0)-Q2))		CDCL3
997M	A	8.00	CHA	A(C(C:N)-C(C:N))		TFA
1556M	C	8.00	CHA	A(C(NO2)-C(0-CH3)-C(NO2))		CDCL3
2894M	F	8.00	OH	A<C-CH-CH-C(C(=0)-0-CH2)>		CCL4
2095M	C	8.00- 8.30		UNSPECIFIED		POLYSOL-D
719M	E	8.01	CHA	AAN<C*-N-C(CH3)>		CCL4
233M	B	8.01	CHA	AA<C*-C(F)>		CDCL3
438M	E	8.01	CHA	AA(C*-C(I))		CDCL3
741M	B	8.01	CHA	AR5NNN<C*-NH-N=>		CDCL3
741M	B	8.01	CHA	AR5NNN<C*-N=N>		CDCL3
2087M	C	8.01	CHA	A<C(C(=0)-CH)>		CDCL3
2229M	B	8.01	CHA	A<C(C(=0)-CL)-C(CL)>		CCL4
2863M	E	8.01	CHA	A<C(C(=0)-0-CH2.2)>		CCL4
2091M	D	8.01	CHA	A<C(C(=0)-Q2)>		CDCL3
1063M	F	8.01	CHA	A<C(NO2)/CH-C(NH-QN)>		POLYSOL-D
1265M	D	8.01	CHA	A<C(SO2-CH2)>		POLYSOL-D

BOOK NO.	ASSIGN-MENT	CHEM SHIFT - ppm -	PROTON GROUP	ENVIRONMENTAL GROUPS	S	SOLVENT
1313M	E	8.01	CHA	A<C(SO3(-))>		POLYSOL-D
2945M	B	8.01	CHA	A(C(C(=0)-0-A))		CDCL3
1061M	A	8.01 APP.	CHA	A(C(I)/CH-C(NO2))		DMSO
1061M	A	8.01 APP.	CHA	A(C(NO2)/CH-C(I))		DMSO
904M	E	8.01	NH	N=N-A/CH3		CDCL3
730M	D	8.02	CHA	AAN(C*-C(CL)-N)		CDCL3
2221M	B	8.02	CHA	A<C(C(=0)-BR)>		CCL4
2231M	B	8.02	CHA	A<C(C(=0)-CL)/CH-C(CL)>		CDCL3
2293M	D	8.02	CHA	A<C(C(=0)-NH2)-C(OH)>		DMSO-D6
2569M	B	8.02	CHA	A<C(C(=0)-OH)-C(F)>		POLYSOL-D
2567M	C	8.02	CHA	A<C(C(=0)-OH)/CH-C(CH3)>		TFA
2407M	C	8.02	CHA	A<C(NO2)-C(C(=0)-NH)>		DMSO-D6
2230M	D	8.02	CHA	A(C(CL)/C(C(=0)-CL))		CCL4
1938M	B	8.02	CHA	A(C(I)-C(OH)-C(I)/C(I))		DMSO
2295M	C	8.02	H	C(=0)-NH		D20
1953M	F	8.03	CHA	AA<C*-C(OH)-CH-C(NH2)>		DMSO-D6
1731M	E	8.03	CHA	ANA(C*/C(CH2-OH)-CH-N)		CDCL3
2127M	D	8.03	CHA	AR6A(C*-C(=0)-C*)		CDCL3
1587M	D	8.03	CHA	AR6OSA<C*-SO2-C*>		TFA
2090M	E	8.03	CHA	A<C(C(=0)-CH)>		CDCL3
2233M	C	8.03	CHA	A<C(C(=0)-CL)-CH-C(BR)>		CCL4
2865M	E	8.03	CHA	A<C(C(=0)-0-CH2.2)>		CDCL3
1054M	C	8.03	CHA	A<C(NO2)-C(F)>		CCL4
1050M	D	8.03	CHA	A<C(NO2)/CH-C(CH2-CH3)>		CCL4
2097M	C	8.03	CHA	A(C(C(=0)-Q2))		CDCL3
1963M	D	8.04	CHA	AAN<C*-N-C(OH)>		TFA
720M	D	8.04	CHA	AAN(C*-N)		CDCL3
1293M	E	8.04	CHA	AA<C*/CH-C(NH2)-C(SO2-OH)>		DMSO-D6
1241M	E	8.04	CHA	AA(C*-C(SH))		CDCL3
744M	D	8.04	CHA	AR5NA(C*-C*)		CDCL3
2381M	A	8.04	CHA	AR5N<C*-C(=0)-NH/CH-C(NO2)>		POLYSOL-D
2220M	B	8.04	CHA	A<C(C(=0)-CL)>		CCL4
2944M	C	8.04	CHA	A<C(C(=0)-0-CH2)>		CDCL3
2920M	B	8.04	CHA	A<C(C(=0)-0-CH3)-C(C(=0)-0-CH3)/C(C(=0)-0-CH3)-C(C(=0)-0-CH3)>		CDCL3
2679M	B	8.04	CHA	A<C(C(=0)-0-NA)/CH-C(OH)>		D20
436M	C	8.04	CHA	A<C(I)/C(I)>		CDCL3
2345M	E	8.04	NH	C(=0)-A/A(C-CH-CH-C(CH3))		CDCL3
875M	C	8.04	NH	QN(Q2(A))/A		DMSO
2332M	D	8.04	QN	A(C-CH-CH-C(NH-C(=0)-CH3)/OH		POLYSOL-D
2082M	B	8.05	CHA	A<C(C(=0)-CH3)/CH-C(C(=0)-CH3)>		CDCL3
2902M	E	8.05 APP.	CHA	A<C(C(=0)-0-CH2)-CH-C(C(=0)-0-CH2)>		CCL4
1720M	E	8.05	CHA	A<C(NO2)-CH-C(CH2-OH)>		CDCL3
1719M	D	8.05	CHA	A<C(NO2)-C(CH2-OH)>		CDCL3
1922M	C	8.05	CHA	A<C(OH)-C(CL)>		CDCL3
1074M	D	8.05	CHA	A(C(NO2)-C(NO2)/CH-C(N(CH3/CH3)))		DMSO-D6
402M	C	8.06	CHA	AA<C*-C(BR)>		CDCL3
1952M	G	8.06	CHA	AA(C*-C(OH)-C(CH3))		CDCL3
1942M	A	8.06	CHA	AN<CH-N>		POLYSOL-D
1865M	F	8.06	CHA	A<C(C(=0)-CH)>		CDCL3
2224M	C	8.06	CHA	A<C(C(=0)-CL)/CH-C(C(CH3/CH3/CH3))>		CDCL3
2575M	E	8.06	CHA	A<C(C(=0)-OH)-C(I)>		C3D60
2995M	B	8.06	CHA	A<C(C(=0)-0-0-C(=0))>		CDCL3
1062M	G	8.06	CHA	A<C(NO2)-C(NH-CH2)>		CCL4
2864M	E	8.06	CHA	A(C(C(=0)-0-CH2))		CDCL3
2627M	E	8.06	NH	C(=0)-CH3/CH(C(=0)-OH/CH2.2)		POLYSOL-D
1064M	D	8.06	QN	A/NH-A		POLYSOL-D
708M	G	8.07	CHA	AN<N-C(NH-CH2)>		CDCL3
2401M	A	8.07	CHA	AR5NR5N<C*-C(=0)-NH/C*-C(=0)-NH>		DMSO
1580M	D	8.07	CHA	A<C(CL)/C(R5N0<C=N/0>)>		CDCL3
2907M	C	8.07	CHA	A<C(C(=0)-0-CH2)/CH-C(C(=0)-0-CH2)>		CDCL3
1724M	E	8.07	CHA	A<C(NO2)/CH-C(Q2(CH2-OH))>		POLYSOL-D
2234M	D	8.07	CHA	A(C(BR)/C(C(=0)-BR))		CCL4
768M	D	8.07	H	CL	S	CDCL3
2691M	D	8.07	H	C(=0)-0-CH2		CDCL3
768M	D	8.07	NH2	CH2.3-CH3	S	CDCL3
2149M	B	8.07 APP.	UNSPECIFIED			TFA
2112M	C	8.08	CHA	AN<C(C(=0)-A)-CH-N>		CDCL3
1066M	A	8.08	CHA	A<CH-C(NO2)-C(NO2)>		DMSO-D6
2585M	F	8.08	CHA	A<C(C(=0)-OH)-C(0-CH2)>		CCL4
1052M	C	8.08	CHA	A<C(NO2)-CH-C(A)>		CDCL3
732M	C	8.08 APP.	CHA	A(C(ANN(C-N-CH-N)))		CDCL3
2463M	B	8.08	CHA	A(C(CH=R6NN))		DMSO
1069M	B	8.08	CHA	A(C(NO2)-CH-C(CL)/CH-C(CL))		CCL4
1306M	C	8.08	CHA	A(C(NO2)-CH-C(SO3NA)/CH-C(NH-A))	S	DMSO
1276M	C	8.08	CHA	A(C(SO2-A)/CH-C(NO2))		CDCL3
2347M	E	8.08	H	C(=0)-N		CDCL3
1310M	E	8.09	CHA	AA(C(SO3-NA)-C*/CH-C(NH2)-C*)		D20
2346M	E	8.09	CHA	AN<C(C(=0)-NH)-CH-N>		CDCL3
1959M	B	8.09	CHA	AN<N-CH-C(OH)>		DMSO-D6
2373M	C	8.09	CHA	AR5NA<C*-C*>		CDCL3

BOOK NO.	ASSIGN-MENT	CHEM SHIFT - ppm -	PROTON GROUP	ENVIRONMENTAL GROUPS	S	SOLVENT
2373M	D	8.09	CHA	AR5NA<C*-N(C(=O)-CH3)-C*>		CDCL3
2172M	A	8.09	CHA	A<C(C(=O))/CH-C(NO2)>		CDCL3
2235M	B	8.09	CHA	A(C(NO2)-C(C(=O)-CL)>		CCL4
1073M	A	8.09	CHA	A(C(BR)-C(NO2)/CH-C(NO2))		CDCL3
2594M	A	8.09	CHA	A(C(C(=O)-OH)-C(NO2)/CH-C(NO2))		DMSO
2597M	B	8.09	CHA	A(C(C(=O)-OH)-C(OH)-C(NO2))		POLYSOL-D
2589M	B	8.09	CHA	A(C(C(=O)-OH)/CH-C(O-A))		DMSO
2597M	B	8.09	CHA	A(C(NO2)-C(OH)-C(C(=O)-OH))		POLYSOL-D
1058M	B	8.09	CHA	A(C(NO2)/CH-C(CL))		CDCL3
903M	B	8.09	CHA	A(C(N=N(=O/A))/CH-C(CL))		CDCL3
2303M	D	8.09	NHR	R6N<C(=O)-CH2/CH2-CH2>		CCL4
1000M	B	8.10	CHA	AA<C*/C(C:N)>		CDCL3
2340M	D	8.10	CHA	AA(C*/C(NH-C(=O)))		CDCL3
1582M	B	8.10	CHA	ANN<N-CH-C(O-CH3)/CH-N>		CDCL3
1582M	B	8.10	CHA	ANN<N/C(O-CH3)-N>		CDCL3
709M	F	8.10	CHA	AN<N-CH-C(NH-CH2)>		DMSO-D6
847M	A	8.10	CHA	AN(CH-N(>O))	S	D20
878M	E	8.10	CHA	AN(C(QN(CH3/NH-A))-N)		DMSO-D6
2136M	B	8.10	CHA	AR5A<C*/CH-CH-C*>		TFA
1266M	E	8.10	CHA	A<C(CL)-C(CL)/C(SO2-CH2)>		CDCL3
1057M	C	8.10 APP.	CHA	A<C(CL)/C(NO2)>		CDCL3
1057M	C	8.10 APP.	CHA	A<C(NO2)-CH-C(CL)>		CDCL3
1064M	E	8.10	CHA	A<C(NO2)/CH-C(NH-QN)>		POLYSOL-D
2580M	B	8.10	CHA	A(C(C:N)-CH-C(C(=O)-OH))		DMSO
1048M	C	8.10	CHA	A(C(NO2)/CH-C(CH3))		CDCL3
1533M	D	8.10	CHA	A(C(NO2)/CH-C(O-CH2))		CDCL3
2300M	B	8.10	NH	C(=O)-H/CH2-NH		TFA
206M	C	8.11	CHA	AA<C-C*/C(AA)-CH-CH-C*>		CDCL3
999M	C	8.11	CHA	AA(C*-C(C:N))		CDCL3
1002M	B	8.11	CHA	AN<C(C:N)-CH-N>		CDCL3
2592M	A	8.11	CHA	A<C(C(=O)-OH)/CH-C(C(=O)-OH)>		DMSO-D6
2570M	B	8.11	CHA	A<C(C(=O)-OH)/CH-C(F)>		C3H6O
2588M	B	8.11	CHA	A<C(C(=O)-OH)/CH-C(OH)>		C3H6O
2909M	E	8.11	CHA	A<C(C(=O)-O-CH2)/CH-C(C(=O)-O-CH2)>		CDCL3
2096M	E	8.11	CHA	A<C(C(=O)-Q2)/CH-C(O-CH3)>		POLYSOL-D
1720M	F	8.11	CHA	A<C(NO2)/C(CH2-OH)>		CDCL3
841M	D	8.11	CHA	A<C(N(+)(CH2/CH2/CH2))>		CDCL3
2106M	B	8.11	CHA	A(C(C(=O)-A)/C(C(=O)-A))		POLYSOL-D
2270M	B	8.11	CHA	A(C(C(=O)-O-C(=O)))		CDCL3
866M	D	8.11	QN	A/CH3		CDCL3
887M	C	8.11	QN	NH-A/A		POLYSOL-D
1569M	E	8.12	CHA	AA(C*-C(O-CH3))		CCL4
692M	C	8.12	CHA	AN<N-CH-C(CH3)/C(CH3)>		CCL4
612M	D	8.12	CHA	AR5NA<C*-C*>		C3H6O
2125M	C	8.12	CHA	AR7A(C*-C(=O)-C*)		CCL4
2943M	D	8.12	CHA	A<C(C(=O)-O-A)>		CCL4
2903M	F	8.12	CHA	A<C(C(=O)-O-CH2)-CH-C(C(=O)-O-CH2)>		CCL4
1532M	C	8.12	CHA	A<C(NO2)/CH-C(O-CH3)>		CCL4
2969M	B	8.12	CHA	A(C(NO2)/CH-C(O-C(=O)-CL))		DMSO-D6
740M	E	8.12	CHR	R5NNA(=N-C*/NH-C*)		CDCL3
1707M	D	8.12	QN	A<C-CH-CH-C(CL)>/CH2.2-OH		CDCL3
751M	D	8.13	CHA	ANAAN<C*/CH-C(CH3)-N>		POLYSOL-D
882M	C	8.13	CHA	AN<C(QN(QN(AN))j-N>		CDCL3
844M	C	8.13 APP.	CHA	AN<N(+)(CH3)-CH-C(NH2)>		D20
844M	C	8.13 APP.	CHA	AN<N(+)(CH3)/C(NH2)>		D20
745M	B	8.13	CHA	AR5NA<C*-C*>		CDCL3
1180M	A	8.13	CHA	AR5SA<C-C*-C*/CH-C(NO2)-CH-C*-S>		DMSO
2081M	C	8.13	CHA	A(C(C(=O)-CH3)-CH-C(C(=O)-CH3))		CDCL3
2566M	B	8.14	CHA	A(C(C(=O)-OH))		CCL4
2685M	E	8.14	NH2	CH2.9-CH3		CDCL3
2685M	E	8.14	OH	C(=O)-CH3		CDCL3
873M	D	8.14	QN	AA<C-C*>/NH2		POLYSOL-D
870M	D	8.14	QN	Q2(A)/A<C-CH-CH-C(CH3)>		CDCL3
2183M	B	8.15	CHA	AAN<C*-N>		CDCL3
317M	C	8.15	CHA	AA<C*-C(CL)>		CCL4
400M	A	8.15	CHA	AA<C-C*-C(BR)>		CCL4
2408M	D	8.15	CHA	AN(C(C(=O)-NH)-N)		CDCL3
2328M	D	8.15	CHA	A<C(NH-C(=O))-C(CL)>		CDCL3
2333M	D	8.15	CHA	A<C(NH-C(=O))-C(NO2)>		CDCL3
1905M	B	8.15	CHA	A<C(NO2)/CH-C(OH)>		C3H6O
2573M	D	8.15	CHA	A(C(BR)/C(C(=O)-OH))		POLYSOL-D
801M	C	8.15	NH	R6NH<CH2-CH2/CH2-CH2>	S	CDCL3
869M	B	8.15	QN	Q2(A)/A		CDCL3
2242M	A	8.15- 8.45		UNSPECIFIED		CDCL3
1286M	C	8.16	CHA	AA<C(SO2-CL)-C*/CH-CH-C*>		POLYSOL-D
729M	D	8.16	CHA	ANA(N-C(CL)-C*/CH-C*)		CDCL3
1911M	C	8.16	OH	A<C-CH-C(OH)>		C3H6O
748M	C	8.17	CHA	AANA<C*-N>		CDCL3
2069M	D	8.17	CHA	A<C(I)/C(C(=O)-CH3)>		CDCL3
1149M	B	8.17	CHR	R5NS<S-N=/=C(CH3)-CH=>		CCL4
1149M	B	8.17	CHR	R5NS<=N-S/C(CH3)=CH>		CCL4

BOOK NO.	ASSIGN-MENT	CHEM SHIFT - ppm -	PROTON GROUP	ENVIRONMENTAL GROUPS	S	SOLVENT
2635M	B	8.17	NH2	C(C(=O)-OH/A/A)		TFA
1956M	D	8.18	CHA	AA<C*-C(OH)>		C3H6O
2409M	C	8.18	CHA	AN<C(C(=O)-NH)-CH-N>		DMSO-D6
699M	D	8.18	CHA	AN<N-C(F)>		CCL4
1581M	G	8.18	CHA	AN<N-C(O-CH3)>		CDCL3
1721M	C	8.18	CHA	A<C(NO2)/CH-C(CH2-OH)>		C3H6O
2241M	C	8.18	CHA	A(C(C(=O)-CL)-CH-C(NO2)/CH-C(CH3))		CCL4
2580M	C	8.18- 8.50	CHA	A(C(C(=O)-OH)-CH-C(C:N))		DMSO
2580M	C	8.18- 8.50	CHA	A(C(C(=O)-OH)/C(C:N))		DMSO
903M	C	8.18	CHA	A(C(N(=N-A/=O))/CH-C(CL))		CDCL3
1145M	B	8.18	CHR	R5S<=C(QN(OH))-S/CH=CH>		TFA
2467M	E	8.18	NH	NH-A/C(=O)-NH		DMSO
843M	E	8.19	CHA	AN(CH-N(+)(CH2-CH2))	S	DMSO-D6
2233M	D	8.19	CHA	A<C(BR)/C(C(=O)-CL)>		CCL4
2222M	C	8.19	CHA	A(C(C(=O)-CL)-C(CH3))		CCL4
2901M	C	8.19	CHA	A(C(C(=O)-O-CH3)-CH-C(C(=O)-O-CH3))		CDCL3
2425M	E	8.19	NH	C(=O)-NH2/A(C-CH-CH-C(O-CH3))		POLYSOL-D
2916M	C	8.19	OH	A<C-C(OH)-CH-C(C(=O)-O-CH3)/C(OH)>		POLYSOL-D
2916M	C	8.19	OH	A<C-C(OH)-CH-C(OH)/CH-C(C(=O)-O-CH3)>		POLYSOL-D
1001M	B	8.20	CHA	AAA<C*/C(C:N)-C*>		CDCL3
2150M	B	8.20	CHA	AR5(CH-C*-C(=O)/CH-CH-C*)		DMSO
2150M	B	8.20	CHA	AR5(C*-C(=O)-C(OH/OH))		DMSO
2226M	B	8.20	CHA	A<C(C(=O)-CL)/CH-C(CF3)>		CDCL3
2591M	B	8.20	CHA	A<C(C(=O)-OH)-CH-C(C(=O)-OH)>		POLYSOL-D
1055M	B	8.20 APP.	CHA	A(C(NO2)/CH-C(F))		CCL4
902M	B	8.20 APP.	CHA	A(C(N(¬O)=N))		CDCL3
902M	B	8.20 APP.	CHA	A(C(N=N(¬O)))		CDCL3
2604M	C	8.20	CHR	R5O<=C(C(=O)-OH)-CH=/O-CH=>		POLYSOL-D
2293M	E	8.20 APP.	NH2	C(=O)-A		DMSO-D6
2078M	E	8.20-10.20	OH	A<C-CH-C(CH3)-C(C(=O)-CH3)>		DMSO-D6
2858M	E	8.20	Q1	A/C(=O)-O-CH2/C:N		CDCL3
852M	C	8.21	CH	=NOH/A		CDCL3
1582M	C	8.21	CHA	ANN<N-C(O-CH3)/CH-N>		CDCL3
1959M	C	8.21	CHA	AN<N/C(OH)>		DMSO-D6
2582M	A	8.21	CHA	A(C(C(=O)-OH)/CH-C(NO2))		DMSO-D6
1060M	B	8.21 APP.	CHA	A(C(I)-CH-C(NO2))		DMSO
1060M	B	8.21 APP.	CHA	A(C(NO2)-CH-C(I))		DMSO
2272M	C	8.22	CHA	AR5O(C*-C(=O)-O/CH-C(F))		CDCL3
2471M	A	8.22	H	C(=O)-OH		D20
273M	B	8.22	NH2	SO2-R5NNS		DMSO-D6
691M	E	8.23	CHA	AN(N-C(CH3)/C(CH3))		CDCL3
2162M	D	8.23	CHA	A<C(NO2)/CH-C(Q2(H/C(=O)-H/H))>		DMSO-D6
1528M	E	8.23	QN	A<C-CH-CH-C(O-CH3)>/A		CDCL3
1146M	C	8.24	CHR	R5S<S-CH=/=C(NO2)-CH=>		CCL4
2340M	E	8.24	NH	C(=O)-CH3/AA(C-CH-C*)		CDCL3
894M	F	8.24	NH	C(=O)-Q2/OH		POLYSOL-D
894M	F	8.24	OH	NH-C(=O)-Q2		POLYSOL-D
1001M	C	8.25 APP.	CHA	AAA<C*-C(C:N)>		CDCL3
710M	C	8.25	CHA	AN<N/CH-C(N(CH3/CH3))>		CDCL3
2904M	F	8.25	CHA	A<C(C(=O)-O-CH2)-CH-C(C(=O)-O-CH2)>		CDCL3
749M	E	8.26	CHA	AAAN<C*-C*>		CDCL3
541M	D	8.26	CHA	AAA<C*-C*>		DMSO
842M	B	8.26	CHA	AN<CH-N(+)(CH3)>		POLYSOL-D
1066M	B	8.26	CHA	A<C(NO2)-C(NO2)>		DMSO-D6
1053M	C	8.26	CHA	A<C(NO2)/CH-C(A)>		C3H6O
2886M	B	8.26	CHA	A(C(C(=O)-O-CH3)/CH-C(NO2))		CDCL3
2886M	B	8.26	CHA	A(C(NO2)/CH-C(C(=O)-O-CH3))		CDCL3
2341M	D	8.27 APP.	CHA	AN<C(NH-C(=O))-N>		CDCL3
703M	C	8.27	CHA	AN<N-C(BR)>		CCL4
2341M	D	8.27 APP.	CHA	AN<N-C(NH-C(=O))>		CDCL3
2967M	C	8.27	CHA	A<C(NO2)/CH-C(CH2-O-C(=O))>		CDCL3
2362M	F	8.27	H	C(=O)-N		CDCL3
2571M	C	8.27	OH	C(=O)-A		DMSO
1309M	C	8.28	CHA	AA<C*/C(SO3-NA)	S	DMSO-D6
2927M	C	8.28	CHA	A<C(NO2)/CH-C(O-C(=O)-C)>		CDCL3
2073M	C	8.28	CHA	A(C(C(=O)-CH3)-CH-C(NO2))		CDCL3
868M	D	8.28	QN	A/CH2-CH2		CDCL3
1964M	D	8.29	CHA	AAN(C*-C(NO2))		DMSO
1964M	C	8.29	CHA	AAN(C*-C(OH)-N)		DMSO
1960M	B	8.29	CHA	ANN<N-C(OH)-N>		DMSO-D6
845M	B	8.29	CHA	AN(CH-N(+)(CH2-CH2))	S	D20
2939M	F	8.29	CHA	AN(C(C(=O)-O-CH2)-CH-N)		CDCL3
2171M	B	8.29	CHA	A<C(C(=O)-H)-CH-C(NO2)>		CDCL3
2171M	C	8.29	CHA	A<C(NO2)-CH-C(C(=O)-H)>		CDCL3
1285M	B	8.29	CHA	A<C(NO2)-C(SO2-CL)>		CDCL3
2926M	C	8.29	CHA	A<C(NO2)/CH-C(O-C(=O)-CH3)>		CDCL3
1307M	A	8.29	CHA	A<C(SO3-NA)-C(NO2)/CH-C(NO2)>		D20
783M	D	8.29	H	CL	S	POLYSOL-D
783M	D	8.29	NH2	CH2-A	S	POLYSOL-D
2463M	C	8.30	CH	R6NN(=C-C(=O)/C(=O))/A		DMSO
702M	C	8.30	CHA	AN<N-C(CL)-C(CL)>		CDCL3

BOOK NO.	ASSIGN-MENT	CHEM SHIFT - ppm -		PROTON GROUP	ENVIRONMENTAL GROUPS	S	SOLVENT
693M	E	8.30		CHA	AN(N-CH-C(CH2.3-CH3)/C(CH2.3-CH3))		CDCL3
2128M	D	8.30		CHA	AR6A<C*-C(=0)-C*>		CDCL3
1052M	D	8.30		CHA	A<C(NO2)/C(A)>		CDCL3
1069M	C	8.30		CHA	A(C(CL)-C(CL)/C(NO2))		CCL4
1075M	D	8.30		CHA	A(C(NO2)-CH-C(NO2)/CH-C(NH-QN))		CDCL3
2582M	B	8.30		CHA	A(C(NO2)/CH-C(C(=0)-OH))		DMSO-D6
1276M	D	8.30		CHA	A(C(NO2)/CH-C(SO2-A))		CDCL3
738M	C	8.30		CHR	R5NNA<NH-C*/=N-C*>		DMSO-D6
2361M	D	8.30		H	C(=0)-N		CDCL3
887M	D	8.30- 9.30		NH	QN(A)/A		POLYSOL-D
1955M	D	8.31		CHA	AA<C*-C(NO)-C(OH)>		CDCL3
1353M	F	8.31		NH	N(CH3/CH3)/C(=S)-NH		POLYSOL-D
2113M	C	8.32		CHA	AA<C*/C(C(=0)-CH3>		CCL4
2136M	C	8.32		CHA	AR5A<C*-C(=0)-C(=0)/CH-CH-C*>		TFA
1273M	C	8.32		CHA	A(C(CL)/C(SO2-A)-C(CL))		CDCL3
2883M	D	8.32		CHA	A(C(C(=0)-O-CH2)/CH-C(NO))		CDCL3
1065M	C	8.32		CHA	A(C(NO2)/CH-C(N=N-A))		CDCL3
767M	C	8.32		NH2	CH2-CH2	S	DMSO-D6
1958M	D	8.32		OH	AA<C-CH-C*/CH-CH-C*>		C3D6O
1570M	F	8.33		CHA	AA<C*-C(O-CH2))		CDCL3
1172M	C	8.33		CHA	AN<N/CH-C(S-A)>		CDCL3
2876M	E	8.33		CHA	A<C(I)/C(C(=0)-O-CH3)>		CDCL3
2561M	C	8.33		CHA	A<C(NO2)/CH-C(CH2-C(=0)-O)>		TFA
2446M	C	8.34		NHR	R5NN<C(=0)-NH/CH(A)-C(=0)>		DMSO-D6
1583M	E	8.34		NHR	R6NSAA<C*/C*>		DMSO-D6
748M	D	8.35 APP.		CHA	AANA<C*-C*>		CDCL3
683M	D	8.35		CHA	AN(N-CH-C(CH3))		CCL4
690M	E	8.35		CHA	AN(N-C(CH3)/CH-C(CH3))		CDCL3
683M	D	8.35		CHA	AN(N/C(CH3))		CCL4
2576M	D	8.35		CHA	A(C(I)/C(C(=0)-OH))		POLYSOL-D
1145M	C	8.35		CHR	R5S<S-C(QN(OH))=/=CH-CH=>		TFA
1951M	B	8.35		OH	AA<C-CH-C*/CH-CH-C*>		C3H6O
688M	E	8.36		CHA	AN(N/CH-C(CH2-CH2))		CCL4
700M	D	8.37		CHA	AN<N-C(CL)>		CCL4
682M	D	8.37		CHA	AN(N-C(CH3))		CCL4
684M	C	8.37		CHA	AN(N/CH-C(CH3))		CCL4
1312M	I	8.38		CHA	AN(CH-CH-N(CH2-CH2))	S	CDCL3
2124M	C	8.38		CHA	AR6A(C*-C(=0)-C*)		CDCL3
2300M	C	8.38		H	C(=0)-NH		TFA
2315M	E	8.38		NH	C(=0)-CH2/A		CDCL3
2405M	E	8.38		NH	NH2/C(=0)-CH2		POLYSOL-D
2245M	C	8.39		CHA	AA<C(C(=0)-CL)-C*/CH-CH-C*>		CCL4
734M	B	8.39		CHA	ANN<N-C(NH2)-N>		D2O
2172M	B	8.39		CHA	A<C(NO2)/CH-C(C(=0))>		CDCL3
1073M	B	8.39		CHA	A(C(NO2)-CH-C(NO2)/CH-C(BR))		CDCL3
1579M	C	8.39		CHR	R5NO(=CH-C(CH3)=/O-N=)		CCL4
2423M	E	8.39		NH	C(=0)-NH2/A<C-CH-C(CH3)>		DMSO-D6
872M	D	8.39		QN	A<C-CH-CH-C(CH3)>/A		CDCL3
216M	E	8.40 APP.		CHA	AAA<C*-CH/CH-CH-C*-C*>		CDCL3
216M	E	8.40 APP.		CHA	AAA<C*-C*CH-CH-C(CH3)-C*-CH>		CDCL3
213M	C	8.40		CHA	AAA<C*/C*>		CDCL3
1311M	C	8.40		CHA	AA<C*-CH-C(SO3-NA)/C(SO3-NA)>		D2O
1334M	D	8.40		CHA	AN<C(C(=S)-NH2)-N-C(CH3)>		POLYSOL-D
871M	C	8.40		QN	A/A		CDCL3
1950M	D	8.41		CHA	AA(C*)		C3H6O
750M	D	8.41		CHA	ANAAN<C*/CH-CH-N>		C3H6O
821M	A	8.41		CHA	AN<C(BR)/CH-N>	S	D2O
685M	D	8.41		CHA	AN<N/CH-C(CH2-CH3)>		CCL4
847M	B	8.41		CHA	AN(CH-CH-N(>O))	S	D2O
701M	C	8.41		CHA	AN(N-CH-C(CL))		CCL4
1729M	D	8.41		CHA	AN(N/CH-C(CH2-OH))		CDCL3
2073M	D	8.41		CHA	A(C(NO2)-CH-C(C(=0)-CH3))		CDCL3
880M	C	8.41		Q2	QN(QN)/A		CDCL3
716M	C	8.42		CHA	AN<C(AN<C-N>)-N>		CDCL3
2243M	B	8.42		CHA	A(C(NO2)-CH-C(C(=0)-CE)/CH-C(CE))		DMSO
2378M	C	8.42		NHR	R6NR6SPI<C(=0)-CH2/C(=0)-CH2>		CDCL3
728M	B	8.43		CHA	ANA(N-CH-C*/CH-C*)		CCL4
687M	H	8.43		CHA	AN<N-C(CH2-CH2)>		CCL4
686M	D	8.43		CHA	AN<N/CH-C(CH(CH3/CH3))>		CDCL3
1557M	D	8.43		CHA	A<C(NO2)-CH-C(NO2)/CH-C(O-CH2)>		CDCL3
1367M	E	8.45		CHA	AA<C*/C(SO2-NH2)>		POLYSOL-D
1308M	A	8.45		CHA	A<C(SO3-NA)-CH-C(SO3-NA)/C(SO3-NA)>		D2O
2316M	F	8.45		NH	C(=0)-CH2/A		CDCL3
1332M	C	8.45 APP.		NH2	C(=S)-CH2		POLYSOL-D
848M	G	8.45		OH	QN(H/CH)		CCL4
2274M	B	8.46		CHA	AAR6O<C*/CH-CH-C*>		TFA
826M	B	8.46		CHA	ANA<C*/C(NH-NH2)-CH-N>	S	D2O
2601M	B	8.46		CHA	A<C(NO2)-CH-C(C(=0)-OH)/CH-C(C(=0)-OH)>		D2O
2648M	A	8.46		H	C(=0)-O-LI		D2O
747M	C	8.48		CHA	AANA(C*-N-C*)		DMSO-D6
727M	E	8.48		CHA	ANA(N-C*/C(NH2)-CH-C*)		CDCL3

BOOK NO.	ASSIGN-MENT	CHEM SHIFT - ppm -	PROTON GROUP	ENVIRONMENTAL GROUPS	S	SOLVENT
704M	C	8.48	CHA	AN(N-CH-C(BR))		CCL4
736M	B	8.48	CHA	A<C(ANNN<C-N-C(A)-N/N-C(A)>)>		TFA
2647M	A	8.48	H	C(=O)-O-CA		D2O
1956M	E	8.48	OH	AA<C-CH-C*/CH-C(OH)-C*>	S	C3H6O
689M	G	8.49	CHA	AN<N-C(CH(CH2.3/CH2.3))>		CCL4
714M	B	8.49	CHA	AN<N-C(Q2(AN<C-CH-N>))>		CDCL3
2381M	B	8.49	CHA	AR5N<C*-C(=O)-NH/C(NO2)>		POLYSOL-D
2236M	B	8.49	CHA	A<C(C(=O)-CL)-CH-C(NO2)>		CDCL3
2236M	C	8.49	CHA	A<C(NO2)-CH-C(C(=O)-CL)>		CDCL3
2081M	D	8.49	CHA	A(C(C(=O)-CH3)/C(C(=O)-CH3))		CDCL3
1060M	C	8.49	CHA	A(C(I)/C(NO2))		DMSO
2241M	D	8.49	CHA	A(C(NO2)-C(CH3)/C(C(=O)-CL))		CCL4
1350M	F	8.49	NH	C(=S)-NH/A		CDCL3
1529M	F	8.49	QN	A(C-C(OH))/OH		CDCL3
713M	E	8.49 APP.		UNSPECIFIED		CDCL3
2367M	B	8.50	CH	(=O)/N(A/A)		CCL4
1964M	D	8.50	CHA	AAN(C*-C(NO2))		DMSO
1964M	C	8.50	CHA	AAN(C*-C(OH)-N)		DMSO
1728M	F	8.50	CHA	AN<N-C(CH2-OH)>		CDCL3
1555M	C	8.50	CHA	A<C(NO2)-CH-C(NO2)/CH-C(O-CH3)>		POLYSOL-D
1156M	D	8.50	CHR	R5NNS<=N-N=/S-C(NH-CH2)=>		POLYSOL-D
2326M	E	8.50	NH	C(=O)-CH3/A<C-CH-C(F)>		CDCL3
1292M	B	8.51	CHA	AA<C*-C(SO3-H)>		TFA
681M	C	8.51	CHA	AN(N)		CCL4
2938M	F	8.51	CHA	AN(N-C(CH2-C(=O)-O))		CDCL3
878M	F	8.51	CHA	AN(N-C(QN(CH3/NH-A)))		DMSO-D6
2171M	B	8.51	CHA	A<C(C(=O)-H)-CH-C(NO2)>		CDCL3
2171M	C	8.51	CHA	A<C(NO2)-CH-C(C(=O)-H)>		CDCL3
1306M	D	8.51	CHA	A(C(NO2)/C(SO3NA)-C(NH-A))	S	DMSO
1942M	B	8.52	CHA	AN<CH-CH-N>		POLYSOL-D
705M	F	8.52	CHA	AN<N-C(CH2-N)>		CDCL3
712M	G	8.52	CHA	AN<N-C(CH2-R6N)>		CDCL3
715M	B	8.52 APP.	CHA	AN<N/CH-C(Q2(AN))>		CDCL3
711M	F	8.52	CHA	AN(N-CH-C(R5N(CH-CH2/CH2)))		CCL4
701M	D	8.52	CHA	AN(N/C(CL))		CCL4
2601M	C	8.52	CHA	A<C(NO2)/C(C(=O)-OH)-C(C(=O)-OH)>		D2O
2095M	D	8.52	CHA	A<C(NO2)/C(Q2(C(=O)-A))>		POLYSOL-D
1148M	C	8.52	CHR	R5NS<S-N=/=CH-C(CH3)=>		CCL4
1150M	B	8.52	CHR	R5NS<S-N=/=C(A)-CH=>		CCL4
1150M	C	8.52	CHR	R5NS<=N-S/C(A)=CH>		CCL4
2447M	C	8.52	NHR	R5NN(C(=O)-NH/C(A/CH3)-C(=O))		DMSO-D6
214M	B	8.53	CHA	AAA(C*-C*)		CCL4
2606M	A	8.53	CHA	AN(CH-N/CH-C(C(=O)-OH))	S	D2O
2408M	E	8.53	CHA	AN(N-C(C(=O)-NH))		CDCL3
2902M	F	8.53	CHA	A<C(C(=O)-O-CH2)/C(C(=O)-O-CH2)>		CCL4
215M	E	8.54 APP.	CHA	AAA<C*-C*>		CDCL3
215M	E	8.54 APP.	CHA	AAA<C*-C*/CH-C(CH3)>		CDCL3
873M	E	8.54	CHA	AA<C*-C(QN(NH2))>		POLYSOL-D
1942M	C	8.54	CHA	A<C(NO2)-C(OH)-C(NO2)/C(NO2)>		POLYSOL-D
749M	F	8.55	CHA	ANAA<C*-C*/CH-CH-C>		CDCL3
2346M	F	8.55	CHA	AN<N-CH-C(C(=O)-NH)>		CDCL3
1145M	D	8.55	QN	R5S<C-S/=CH>/OH		TFA
742M	B	8.56	CHA	AANN(C*-C(CL)-N)		TFA
2903M	G	8.56	CHA	A<C(C(=O)-O-CH2)/C(C(=O)-O-CH2)>		CCL4
781M	E	8.56	Q3	CH2-NH2/H/H	S	POLYSOL-D
541M	E	8.57	CHA	AAA<C*-C(NH2)>		DMSO
1307M	B	8.57	CHA	A<C(NO2)-CH-C(NO2)/CH-C(SO3-NA)>		D2O
2183M	C	8.58	CHA	ANA<C*/C(C(=O)-H)-CH-N>		CDCL3
711M	G	8.58	CHA	AN(N/C(R5N(CH-CH2/CH2)))		CCL4
2469M	E	8.58	NH	QN(CH(CH3/CH3)/CH3)/C(=O)-NH2		CDCL3
714M	C	8.59	CHA	AN<N-CH-C(Q2(AN<C-N>))>		CDCL3
697M	D	8.59	CHA	AN<N-C(A)>		CDCL3
1067M	B	8.59	CHA	A(C(NO2)-CH-C(NO2))		CCL4
2594M	B	8.59	CHA	A(C(NO2)-CH-C(NO2)/CH-C(C(=O)-OH))		DMSO
1366M	F	8.59	QN	A/A<C-CH-CH-C(SO2-NH2)>		DMSO-D6
2381M	C	8.60	CHA	AR5N<C(NO2)-CH-C*/CH-C*-C(=O)>		POLYSOL-D
1072M	B	8.60	CHA	A(C(NO2)-CH-C(NO2)/CH-C(F))		CDCL3
891M	D	8.60	NH	OH/C(=O)-CH2		CDCL3
891M	D	8.60	OH	NH-C(=O)		CDCL3
743M	A	8.60- 9.12		UNSPECIFIED		DMSO-D6
2273M	A	8.61	CHA	AR5OR5O<C*-C(=O)-O/C*-C(=O)-O>		DMSO-D6
2956M	C	8.61	CHA	AR5O<C(NO2)-CH-C*/CH-C*-CH2>		CDCL3
2236M	B	8.61	CHA	A<C(C(=O)-CL)-CH-C(NO2)>		CDCL3
2236M	C	8.61	CHA	A<C(NO2)-CH-C(C(=O)-CL)>		CDCL3
1182M	B	8.61	NHR	R6NSAA<C*/C*>		DMSO-D6
1962M	D	8.61	OH	AAN(C-C*-N)		CDCL3
731M	C	8.62	CHA	ANA(N-CH-C*/C(BR)-C*)		CDCL3
2868M	C	8.62	CHA	ANA(N-C*-C(O-C(=O)-A)/CH-CH-C*)		CDCL3
1307M	C	8.62	CHA	A<C(NO2)-C(SO3-NA)/C(NO2)>		D2O
1150M	B	8.62	CHR	R5NS<S-N=/=C(A)-CH=>		CCL4
1150M	C	8.62	CHR	R5NS<=N-S/C(A)=CH>		CCL4

: REPRESENTS TRIPLE BOND, ￢ REPRESENTS AN ARROW AND < AND > REPRESENT BRACKETS.   PAGE   303

BOOK NO.	ASSIGN-MENT	CHEM SHIFT - ppm -	PROTON GROUP	ENVIRONMENTAL GROUPS	S	SOLVENT
2424M	C	8.62	NH	C(=O)-NH2/A<C-CH-CH-C(BR)>		DMSO-D6
1348M	E	8.62	NH	C(=S)-NH/A		CDCL3
881M	D	8.62	QN	A(C-CH-CH-C(CH3)/QN(A))		CDCL3
1001M	D	8.63 APP.	CHA	AAA<C*-C*>		CDCL3
2245M	D	8.63	CHA	AA<C*-C(C(=O)-CL)>		CCL4
698M	B	8.63	CHA	AN<N/CH-C(A)>		CDCL3
2901M	D	8.63	CHA	A(C(C(=O)-O-CH3)/C(C(=O)-O-CH3))		CDCL3
1180M	B	8.64	CHA	AR5SA<C-C(NO2)-CH-C*-S/CH-C*-C*>		DMSO
2591M	C	8.64	CHA	A(C(C(=O)-OH)-CH-C(C(=O)-OH)>		POLYSOL-D
2978M	C	8.64	NH2	C(=O)-O-A		DMSO
1555M	D	8.65	CHA	A<C(NO2)-C(O-CH3)/C(NO2)>		POLYSOL-D
1794M	K	8.66	CHA	ANA<N-C*/CH-C(CH(OH/R6R6N*BI))-C*>		POLYSOL-D
704M	D	8.66	CHA	AN(N/C(BR))		CCL4
1940M	C	8.66	CHA	A(C(NO2)-C(OH)-C(NO2)/C(NO2))		DMSO
716M	D	8.67	CHA	AN<N-C(AN<C-N>)>		CDCL3
843M	F	8.67	CHA	AN(CH-CH-N(+)(CH2-CH2))	S	DMSO-D6
2171M	D	8.67	CHA	A<C(NO2)/C(C(=O)-H)>		CDCL3
2467M	F	8.67	NH	C(=O)-NH/A		DMSO
882M	D	8.67	QN	AN<C-N>/QN(AN<C-N>)		CDCL3
218M	D	8.68	CHA	AAAA<C-C*-C*/CH-C*-CH>		CDCL3
847M	C	8.68	CHA	AN(N(>O))	S	D20
1557M	E	8.69	CHA	A<C(NO2)-C(O-CH2)/C(NO2)>		CDCL3
1941M	C	8.69	CHA	A(C(NO2)-C(OH)-C(NO2)/C(NO2))		DMSO
893M	F	8.69	NH	OH/C(=O)-CH2		CDCL3
893M	F	8.69	OH	NH-C(=O)		CDCL3
732M	D	8.70	CHA	ANN(N-CH-N/CH-C(A))		CDCL3
2409M	D	8.70	CHA	AN<N-CH-C(C(=O)-NH>		DMSO-D6
882M	E	8.70	CHA	AN<N-C(QN(QN(AN))) >		CDCL3
1073M	C	8.70	CHA	A(C(NO2)-C(BR)/C(NO2))		CDCL3
2594M	C	8.70	CHA	A(C(NO2)-C(C(=O)-OH)/C(NO2))		DMSO
1730M	D	8.70	NHR	R5NNA(C*/C(CH2-OH)=N)		DMSO-D6
1730M	D	8.70	OH	CH2-R5NNA		DMSO-D6
2274M	C	8.71	CHA	AAR60<C*-C(=O)-O/CH-CH-C*>		TFA
1962M	E	8.71	CHA	ANA(N-C*-C(OH)/CH-CH-C*)		CDCL3
2110M	E	8.71	CHA	AN<N-C(C(=O)-CH3)>		CCL4
717M	B	8.71	CHA	AN(N/CH-C(AN(C-CH-CH-N)))		CDCL3
842M	C	8.72	CHA	AN<CH-CH-N(+)(CH3)>		POLYSOL-D
2603M	A	8.72	CHA	A(C(C(=O)-OH)-CH-C(C(=O)-OH)/C(C(=O)-OH))		DMSO
2073M	E	8.72	CHA	A(C(NO2)/C(C(=O)-CH3))		CDCL3
2322M	G	8.72	NH	C(=O)-CH3/A(C-CH-C(CH3))		CDCL3
218M	E	8.73	CHA	AAAA<C-C*-C*/CH-CH-CH-C*-CH>		CDCL3
720M	E	8.73	CHA	ANA(N-C*/CH-C(CH3)-C*)		CDCL3
2333M	E	8.74	CHA	A<C(NO2)-C(NH-C(=O))>		CDCL3
2329M	D	8.74	NH	C(=O)-CH3/A<C-CH-C(CL)>		CDCL3
541M	F	8.75	CHA	AAA<C*-C*>		DMSO
1731M	F	8.75	CHA	ANA(N-C*/C(CH2-OH)-CH-C*)		CDCL3
895M	B	8.76	CHA	AN(N/CH-C(C(=O)-NH))		DMSO
2956M	D	8.76	CHA	AR50<C*-C(=O)-O/C(NO2)>		CDCL3
2470M	F	8.76	NH	QN(CH2-CH2/CH3)/C(=O)-NH2		CDCL3
2336M	D	8.76	OH	A<C-CH-CH-C(NH-C(=O)-CH3)>		POLYSOL-D
821M	B	8.77	CHA	AN<N/CH-C(BR)>	S	D20
2939M	G	8.77	CHA	AN(N-CH-C(C(=O)-O-CH2))		CDCL3
721M	G	8.78	CHA	ANA(N-C*/CH-CH-C*)		CDCL3
2112M	D	8.78	CHA	AN<N-CH-C(C(=O)-A)>		CDCL3
2904M	G	8.78	CHA	A<C(C(=O)-O-CH2)/C(C(=O)-O-CH2)>		CDCL3
1354M	E	8.78	NH	C(=S)-N/A<C-C(CL)>		POLYSOL-D
1899M	E	8.78	OH	A(C-CH-C(NH2))		DMSO
2553M	D	8.78	OH	C(=O)-CH2		C3H6O
723M	E	8.79	CHA	ANA<N-C*-C(CH3)/CH-CH-C*>		CCL4
722M	F	8.79	CHA	ANA<N-C*/CH-CH-C*>		CCL4
1732M	E	8.79	CHA	ANN<N-C(CH2.2-OH)-N/C(A)>		CDCL3
714M	D	8.79	CHA	AN<N/C(Q2(AN<C-N>))>		CDCL3
2602M	A	8.80	CHA	A<C(C(=O)-OH)-CH-C(NO2)/C(C(=O)-OH)>		DMSO
2602M	A	8.80	CHA	A<C(NO2)-CH-C(C(=O)-OH)/C(C(=O)-OH)>		DMSO
2458M	A	8.80	CHR	R6NN(=C(NO2)-C(=O)/NH-C(=O))		DMSO
845M	C	8.81	CHA	AN(CH-CH-N(+)(CH2-CH2))	S	D20
2371M	E	8.81	H	C(=O)-R6NA		CDCL3
725M	C	8.82	CHA	ANA<N-C*/CH-CH-C*>		CCL4
1310M	F	8.83	CHA	AA(C*-C(SO3-NA))		D20
749M	G	8.83	CHA	ANAA<N-C*/CH-CH-C*>		CDCL3
718M	C	8.84	CHA	ANA<N-C*/CH-CH-C*>		CCL4
820M	D	8.84	CHR	R5NN(=N-C(CH2.2-NH2)/NH-CH=)	S	D20
1930M	C	8.86	OH	A<C-C(OH)-CH-C(A)>		POLYSOL-D
1930M	C	8.86	OH	A<C-C(OH)/CH-C(A)>		POLYSOL-D
733M	B	8.89	CHA	ANN<N-C(CL)/N-C(CL)>		CDCL3
1942M	D	8.89	CHA	AN<N>		POLYSOL-D
1002M	C	8.89	CHA	AN<N-CH-C(C:N)>		CDCL3
1180M	C	8.89	CHA	AR5SA<C-C*-S/C(NO2)-CH-CH-C*-C*>		DMSO
2243M	C	8.90	CHA	A(C(NO2)/C(C(=O)-CL)-C(CL))		DMSO
2346M	G	8.92	CHA	AN<N/C(C(=O)-NH)>		CDCL3
1950M	E	8.92	OH	AA(C-C*)		C3H6O

BOOK NO.	ASSIGN-MENT	CHEM SHIFT - ppm -	PROTON GROUP	ENVIRONMENTAL GROUPS	S	SOLVENT
1002M	D	8.93	CHA	AN<N/C(C:N)>		CDCL3
1568M	B	8.93	CHA	A<C(NO2)-C(O-CH3)-C(NO2)/C(NO2)>		CDCL3
1072M	C	8.93	CHA	A(C(NO2)-C(F)/C(NO2))		CDCL3
2236M	D	8.94	CHA	A<C(NO2)/C(C(=O)-CL)>		CDCL3
826M	C	8.95	CHA	ANA<N-C*/C(NH-NH2)-CH-C*>	S	D2O
1943M	B	8.95	OH	A<C-CH-C(CL)-C(OH)/CH-C(CL)>		POLYSOL-D
1341M	D	8.96	NH	C(=S)-NH2/A<C-C(CH3)>		DMSO-D6
2112M	E	8.97	CHA	AN<N/C(C(=O)-A)>		CDCL3
1888M	D	8.97	OH	A<C-CH-CH-C(CH2-A)>		DMSO-D6
2503M	D	8.97	OH	C(=O)-CH2.14		POLYSOL-D
2906M	B	8.98	CHA	A(C(C(=O)-O-CH3)-CH-C(NO2)/C(C(=O)-O-CH3))		CDCL3
2906M	B	8.98	CHA	A(C(NO2)-CH-C(C(=O)-O-CH3)/C(C(=O)-O-CH3))		CDCL3
1956M	F	8.98	OH	AA<C-C*/CH-C(OH)>		C3H6O
1954M	H	8.99 APP.	OH	AA<C-C(CH2.2-C:N)-C*/CH-CH-C*>		POLYSOL-D
1949M	F	8.99	OH	AR5A<C-CH-C*-CH2/CH-CH-C*>		POLYSOL-D
845M	D	9.01	CHA	AN(N(+)(CH2-CH2))	S	D2O
1067M	C	9.01	CHA	A(C(NO2)/C(NO2))		CCL4
731M	D	9.02	CHA	ANA(N-CH-C(BR)/C*)		CDCL3
2409M	E	9.04	CHA	AN<N/C(C(=O)-NH)>		DMSO-D6
1293M	F	9.06	CHA	AA<C*-C(SO2-OH)-C(NH2)>		DMSO-D6
2557M	D	9.07	OH	C(=O)-CH2		CDCL3
1929M	F	9.08	OH	A(C-CH-C(OH)-C(CH2-A))		DMSO-D6
1929M	F	9.08	OH	A(C-C(CH2-A)/CH-C(OH))		DMSO-D6
854M	E	9.08	OH	QN(CH2-CH2/CH3)		CDCL3
855M	D	9.08	OH	QN(CH2-CH/CH3)		CDCL3
2457M	B	9.10	NHR	R6NN<C(=O)-C(I)=/C(=O)-NH>		DMSO
2457M	B	9.10	NHR	R6NN<C(=O)-NH/CH=C(I)>		DMSO
2911M	C	9.11 APP.	CHA	A<C(NO2)-CH-C(NO2)/C(C(=O)-O-CH2)>		CDCL3
2911M	C	9.11 APP.	CHA	A<C(NO2)-CH-C(NO2)/C(C(=O)-O-CH2)>		CDCL3
1075M	E	9.11	CHA	A(C(NO2)-C(NH-QN)/C(NO2))		CDCL3
2572M	C	9.11	OH	C(=O)-A		DMSO
1076M	A	9.12	CHA	A<C(NO2)-CH-C(NO2)/C(NO2)>		DMSO-D6
1939M	B	9.13	CHA	A<C(NO2)-C(OH)-C(NO2)/C(NO2)>		C3D6O
2913M	C	9.13	CHA	A(C(NO2)-CH-C(C(=O)-O-CH2)/C(NO2))		CDCL3
2913M	C	9.13	CHA	A(C(NO2)-CH-C(NO2)/C(C(=O)-O-CH2))		CDCL3
1349M	D	9.13	NH	C(=S)-NH/A		POLYSOL-D
2080M	E	9.14	OH	A<C-CH-C(C(=O)-CH3)-C(OH)>		DMSO-D6
1312M	J	9.16	CHA	AN(N(CH2-CH2))	S	CDCL3
876M	C	9.16	NH	QN(A)/A		C3H6O
2538M	D	9.17	OH	C(=O)-R6		C3D6O
748M	E	9.18	CHA	ANAA<N-C*/C*>		CDCL3
842M	D	9.18	CHA	AN<N(+)(CH3)>		POLYSOL-D
843M	G	9.18	CHA	AN(N(+)(CH2-CH2))	S	DMSO-D6
750M	E	9.19	CHA	ANAAN<N-C*-C*/CH-CH-C*>		C3H6O
2912M	C	9.19 APP.	CHA	A(C(NO2)-CH-C(C(=O)-O-R6)/C(NO2))		CDCL3
2912M	C	9.19 APP.	CHA	A(C(NO2)-CH-C(NO2)/C(C(=O)-O-R6))		CDCL3
1336M	C	9.19	H	C(=S)-N		CDCL3
2604M	D	9.19	OH	C(=O)-R5O		POLYSOL-D
1290M	D	9.20 APP.	NH2	A<C-C(SO2-OH)-CH-C(CH3)>		DMSO-D6
1331M	B	9.20	NH2	C(=S)-CH3		DMSO-D6
1331M	B	9.20	NH2	C(=S)-CH3		DMSO-D6
1909M	C	9.20	OH	A<C-CH-CH-C(A<C-CH-CH-C(OH)>)>		DMSO-D6
1290M	D	9.20 APP.	OH	SO2-A		DMSO-D6
804M	F	9.21	NH	CH(CH2/CH3)/CH3	S	CDCL3
2336M	E	9.21	NH	C(=O)-CH3/A<C-CH-CH-C(OH)>		POLYSOL-D
1335M	C	9.22	NH	C(=S)-A/A		CDCL3
1907M	E	9.22	OH	A(C-C(CH2-OH))		DMSO-D6
2939M	H	9.24	CHA	AN/N/C(C(=O)-O-CH2))		CDCL3
1306M	E	9.24	NH	A(C-C(SO3NA)-CH-C(NO2))/A	S	DMSO
1897M	D	9.24	OH	A<C-CH-C(I)>		POLYSOL-D
2600M	D	9.27 APP.		UNSPECIFIED		DMSO-D6
732M	E	9.28	CHA	ANN(N-C(A)/N)		CDCL3
2606M	B	9.28 APP.	CHA	AN(C(C(=O)-OH)-CH-N)	S	D2O
2606M	B	9.28 APP.	CHA	AN(N-CH-C(C(=O)-OH))	S	D2O
2183M	D	9.31	CHA	ANA<N-C*/C(C(=O)-H)-CH-C*>		CDCL3
1333M	C	9.32	HNH	C(=S)-A		POLYSOL-D
1905M	C	9.32	OH	A<C-CH-CH-C(NO2)>		C3H6O
2157M	F	9.33	H	C(=O)-Q1		CCL4
2494M	D	9.33	OH	C(=O)-CH2		CDCL3
860M	D	9.33	OH	QN(A/CH3)		CDCL3
1529M	G	9.34	OH	QN(A(C-C(O-CH3)))		CDCL3
797M	C	9.35	NH	CH2-CH3/CH2-CH3	S	DMSO-D6
1371M	E	9.36	NH	SO2-A/A<C-C(CH3)>		DMSO-D6
2334M	E	9.37	NH	C(=O)-CH3/A<C-C(OH)>		POLYSOL-D
1943M	C	9.37	OH	A<C-C(CL)-CH-C(OH)/C(CL)>		DMSO-D6
2334M	D	9.37	OH	A<C-C(NH-C(=O))>		CDCL3
857M	E	9.39	OH	QN(CH2-CH2/CH3)		DMSO-D6
2592M	B	9.41	OH	C(=O)-A		DMSO-D6
2335M	E	9.43	NH	C(=O)-CH3/A(C-CH-C(OH))		DMSO-D6
878M	G	9.43	NH	QN(AN(C-N)/CH3)/A		CCL4
2161M	F	9.47	H	C(=O)-Q1		CCL4

BOOK NO.	ASSIGN-MENT	CHEM SHIFT - ppm -	PROTON GROUP	ENVIRONMENTAL GROUPS	S	SOLVENT
2182M	D	9.48	H	C(=O)-R5N		CDCL3
2562M	D	9.48	OH	C(=O)-C		CDCL3
1889M	D	9.49	OH	A(C-CH-CH-C(A))		DMSO
2332M	E	9.50	OH	QN(A(C-CH-CH-C(NH-C(=O)-CH3)))		POLYSOL-D
2376M	D	9.51	NHR	R5N<C(=O)-CH(CH3)/C(=O)-HCH		CDCL3
1063M	G	9.52	NH	QN(CH2.2-CH3/CH3)/A<C-CH-CH-C(NO2)>		POLYSOL-D
2444M	D	9.52	NHR	R6NN<C(=O)-NH/C(=O)-CH(CH3)>		POLYSOL-D
2606M	C	9.53	CHA	AN(N/C(C(=O)-OH))	S	D2O
2156M	F	9.53	H	C(=O)-Q2		CDCL3
1293M	G	9.53	NH2	AA<C-C(SO2-OH)-C*/CH-CH-C*>		DMSO-D6
1293M	G	9.53	OH	SO2-AA		DMSO-D6
742M	C	9.55	CHA	ANNA(N-C(CL)-C*/N-C*)		TFA
2411M	E	9.55	NH	N=R6/C(=O)-A		CDCL3
853M	E	9.55	OH	QN(CH2-CH3/CH3)		CDCL3
853M	E	9.55	OH	QN(CH3/CH2-CH3)		CDCL3
2160M	D	9.57	H	C(=O)-Q1		CCL4
2152M	C	9.58	H	C(=O)-CH		CCL4
2317M	F	9.58	NH	C(=O)-CH/A		POLYSOL-D
1957M	D	9.58	OH	AA<C-C*>		DMSO-D6
2914M	D	9.59	OH	A(C-CH-CH-C(C(=O)-O-CH3)/CH-C(OH))		DMSO-D6
1352M	B	9.60	NH	C(=S)-NH/A(C-C(CL))		DMSO
2413M	D	9.60	NH	NH-C(=O)/C(=O)-CH2		DMSO-D6
1342M	D	9.61	NH	C(=S)-NH2/AA<C-C*>		POLYSOL-D
2594M	D	9.61	OH	C(=O)-A		DMSO
825M	D	9.63		UNSPECIFIED	S	DMSO-D6
2158M	C	9.64	H	C(=O)-R6		CCL4
1333M	D	9.65	HNH	C(=S)-A		POLYSOL-D
2170M	D	9.66	H	C(=O)-A		CDCL3
2155M	B	9.66	H	C(=O)-R6		CDCL3
1340M	C	9.66	NH	C(=S)-NH2/A		DMSO
2151M	D	9.68	H	C(=O)-CH2.2		CCL4
2178M	E	9.70	OH	A<C-C(C(=O)-H)-CH-C(O-CH3)>		CCL4
2159M	D	9.71	H	C(=O)-CH2.2		CDCL3
2211M	F	9.71	NH	C(=O)-CH3/A<C-CH-CH-C(O-CH2)>		DMSO-D6
2337M	E	9.71	NH	C(=O)-CH3/A<C-CH-CH-C(O-CH3)>		DMSO-D6
2186M	E	9.72	H	C(=O)-AR500		CDCL3
2153M	E	9.72	H	C(=O)-CH2		CCL4
2570M	C	9.72	OH	C(=O)-A		C3H6O
2154M	D	9.73	H	C(=O)-CH2		CDCL3
2323M	E	9.74	NH	C(=O)-CH3/A(C-CH-CH-C(CH3))		DMSO-D6
2500M	C	9.74	OH	C(=O)-CH2		POLYSOL-D
2334M	E	9.75	NH	C(=O)-CH3/A<C-C(OH)>		DMSO-D6
2334M	D	9.75	OH	A<C-C(NH-C(=O))>		DMSO-D6
2184M	D	9.76	CH	(=O)/R5S(C-S/CH-CH)		CDCL3
2162M	E	9.76	H	C(=O)-Q2		DMSO-D6
2588M	C	9.76	OH	A<C-CH-CH-C(C(=O)-OH)>		C3H6O
2588M	C	9.76	OH	C(=O)-A		C3H6O
2173M	F	9.78	H	C(=O)-A		CCL4
787M	B	9.78	NH2	A	S	DMSO-D6
1334M	E	9.79 APP.	NH2	C(=S)-AN		POLYSOL-D
1526M	F	9.80	H	CL	S	POLYSOL-D
2174M	G	9.80	H	C(=O)-A		CCL4
1526M	F	9.80	NH2	A<C-C(O-CH3)>	S	POLYSOL-D
849M	F	9.80	OH	QN(CH2.5-CH3)		CDCL3
2175M	G	9.82	H	C(=O)-A		CCL4
2179M	F	9.82	H	C(=O)-AR5		CCL4
856M	E	9.83	OH	QN(CH2-CH2/CH3)		CDCL3
2185M	B	9.87	H	C(=O)-R5O		CDCL3
2165M	D	9.91	H	C(=O)-A		CCL4
852M	D	9.91	OH	N=CH		CDCL3
2180M	D	9.93	H	C(=O)-AR5A		CDCL3
2320M	D	9.93	NH	C(=O)-CH2/A		DMSO-D6
1959M	D	9.93	OH	AN<C-CH-N>		DMSO-D6
2163M	C	9.94	H	C(=O)-A		CCL4
2341M	E	9.94	NH	C(=O)-CH3/AN<C-N>		CDCL3
2177M	D	9.95	H	C(=O)-A		CCL4
2181M	B	9.96	CHR	AAAA(C*-C(C(=O)-H)/CH-C*)		CDCL3
2169M	B	9.97	H	C(=O)-A		CDCL3
2885M	D	10.00 APP.	CHA	A<C(C(=O)-O-CH2)-CH-C(NO2)>		CCL4
2885M	D	10.00 APP.	CHA	A<C(NO2)-CH-C(C(=O)-O-CH2)>		CCL4
2167M	D	10.00	H	C(=O)-A		CDCL3
2144M	D	10.00	OH	R6(C=CH/CH2)		CDCL3
2330M	D	10.03	NH	C(=O)-CH3/A(C-CH-CH-C(CL))		DMSO-D6
2495M	E	10.03	OH	C(=O)-CH2		CDCL3
2331M	D	10.04	NH	C(=O)-CH3/A<C-CH-CH-C(BR)>		DMSO-D6
2530M	E	10.04	OH	C(=O)-Q2		CDCL3
2319M	F	10.05	NH	C(=O)-CH2/A		DMSO-D6
2319M	F	10.05	NH	Q1(OH)-C(=O)/A		DMSO-D6
2516M	E	10.08	OH	C(=O)-CH2		CDCL3
1358M	E	10.10	NH	QN(CH2-CH2)/C(=S)-NH		CDCL3
2455M	C	10.10	NH	R6NN<C(=O)-NH/C(CH3)=(CH3)>		TFA

BOOK NO.	ASSIGN-MENT	CHEM SHIFT - ppm -	PROTON GROUP	ENVIRONMENTAL GROUPS	S	SOLVENT
2455M	C	10.10	NH	R6NN<C(=0)-NH/C(=0)-C(CH3)=>		TFA
1378M	C	10.11	NH	S02-NH/A(C-CH-CH-C(BR))		POLYSOL-D
2172M	C	10.18	H	C(=0)-A		CDCL3
2171M	E	10.19	H	C(=0)-A		CDCL3
2454M	C	10.19	NHR	R6NN<C(=0)-NH/C(CH3)=CH>		TFA
2454M	D	10.19	NHR	R6NN<C(=0)-NH/C(=0)-CH=>		TFA
2599M	D	10.20		UNSPECIFIED		DMSO
2343M	D	10.21	NH	C(=0)-A/A		DMSO
2164M	D	10.22	H	C(=0)-A		CCL4
2183M	E	10.23	H	C(=0)-ANA		CDCL3
807M	C	10.26	NH	A/A		DMSO
2318M	D	10.27	NH	C(=0)-CH2/A	S	DMSO-D6
2333M	F	10.27	NH	C(=0)-CH3/A<C-C(NO2)>		CDCL3
2168M	C	10.30	H	C(=0)-A		CCL4
1960M	C	10.30	OH	ANN<C-N/N>		DMSO-D6
790M	C	10.31	H	CL		POLYSOL-D
790M	C	10.31	NH2	A<C-CH-C(CH3)>	S	POLYSOL-D
1904M	E	10.31	OH	A(C-CH-C(NO2))	S	DMSO
2580M	D	10.32	OH	C(=0)-A		DMSO
2605M	F	10.32	OH	C(=0)-Q2		CDCL3
2176M	D	10.35	H	C(=0)-A		CDCL3
1944M	C	10.35	OH	A<C-C(NO2)-C(OH)>		POLYSOL-D
2181M	C	10.39	H	C(=0)-AAAA		CDCL3
2885M	E	10.40	CHA	A<C(NO2)/C(C(=0)-O-CH2)>		CCL4
1903M	E	10.46	OH	A<C-C(NO2)>		CCL4
2166M	C	10.48	H	C(=0)-A		CCL4
2545M	D	10.48	OH	C(=0)-C		CDCL3
864M	B	10.48	OH	QN(QN(OH/CH3)/CH3)		POLYSOL-D
2473M	C	10.49	OH	C(=0)-CH2		CDCL3
2178M	F	10.50	H	C(=0)-A		CCL4
2544M	C	10.58	OH	C(=0)-CH		CDCL3
2585M	G	10.59	OH	C(=0)-A		CCL4
2485M	B	10.59	OH	C(=0)-CH2		CDCL3
2543M	F	10.59	OH	C(=0)-CH2		DMSO-D6
2379M	B	10.60	NHR	R5N(C(=0)-CH=/C(=0)-CH=)		POLYSOL-D
2546M	C	10.60	OH	C(=0)-CH		CDCL3
2475M	E	10.60	OH	C(=0)-CH		CDCL3
2598M	E	10.63	OH	A<C-C(O-CH3)-CH-C(C(=0)-OH)>		DMSO-D6
2598M	E	10.63	OH	C(=0)-A		DMSO-D6
2456M	B	10.65	NHR	R6NN(C(=0)-C(BR)=/C(=0)-NH)		DMSO
2607M	C	10.66	OH	C(=0)-CH2		DMSO
2581M	C	10.67	OH	C(=0)-A		C3H6O
2554M	G	10.68	OH	C(=0)-CH2		CDCL3
1287M	C	10.70	H	S03-CH2		CDCL3
2563M	F	10.70	OH	C(=0)-CH2		CDCL3
2891M	H	10.72	OH	A(C-C(C(=0)-O-CH2))		CDCL3
2446M	D	10.74	NHR	R5NN<C(=0)-NH/C(=0)-CH(A)>		DMSO-D6
2608M	E	10.80	OH	C(=0)-AR500		POLYSOL-D
2488M	B	10.80	OH	C(=0)-CH2		CDCL3
2518M	E	10.81	OH	C(=0)-CH2		CDCL3
610M	D	10.83	NHR	R5NA(C*/CH=C(CH2-N)-C*)		DMSO-D6
2539M	C	10.88	OH	C(=0)-CH2		CDCL3
2579M	E	10.88	OH	C(=0)-CH2		CDCL3
2596M	E	10.90	OH	A<C-C(C(=0)-OH)/CH-C(CH3)>		POLYSOL-D
2596M	E	10.90	OH	C(=0)-A		POLYSOL-D
2889M	G	10.92	OH	A(C-C(C(=0)-O-CH))		CDCL3
2540M	D	10.92	OH	C(=0)-CH2		CDCL3
2586M	F	10.95	OH	C(=0)-A		POLYSOL-D
2480M	E	10.96	OH	C(=0)-CH2		CCL4
1922M	D	10.97	OH	A<C-C(CL)/C(NO2)>		CDCL3
1075M	F	11.00	NH	QN(CH3/CH3)/A(C-C(NO2-CH-C(NO2))		CDCL3
2558M	C	11.00	OH	C(=0)-CH2		CDCL3
2621M	F	11.01	OH	C(=0)-CH		POLYSOL-D
2502M	C	11.05	OH	C(=0)-CH2		DMSO-D6
2997M	C	11.06	OH	P(=0/0/0)		CCL4
2489M	D	11.09	OH	C(=0)-CH		CCL4
2441M	C	11.10	NHR	R5NA<C*/C(=0)-N(A)>		DMSO-D6
1064M	F	11.14	NH	QN(A)/A<C-CH-CH-C(NO2)>		POLYSOL-D
2182M	E	11.20 APP.	NH	R5N<=C(C(=0)-H-CH/CH=CH>		CDCL3
2573M	E	11.21	OH	C(=0)-A		POLYSOL-D
2201M	D	11.21	OH	C(=0)-Q2		CDCL3
2483M	B	11.22	OH	C(=0)-CH2		CCL4
2549M	E	11.28	OH	C(=0)-CH2		CDCL3
2380M	B	11.29	NHR	R5NA(C(=0)-C*/C(=0)-C*)		DMSO
2499M	C	11.32	OH	C(=0)-CH2		DMSO-D6
2381M	D	11.33	NHR	R5NA<C(=0)-C*/C(=0)-C*>		POLYSOL-D
2461M	C	11.38	NHR	R6NN<C(=0)-NH/C(=0)-C(CH2-Q3/CH2-Q3)>		DMSO-D6
2080M	F	11.40	OH	A<C-C(C(=0)-CH3)-CH-C(OH)>		DMSO-D6
2593M	C	11.40	OH	C(=0)-A		CDCL3
2401M	B	11.42	NHR	R5NAR5N<C(=0)-C*/C(=0)-C*>		DMSO
2521M	E	11.47	Q2	CH2-C(=0)-OH/CH2-CH2		CCL4

BOOK NO.	ASSIGN-MENT	CHEM SHIFT - ppm -	PROTON GROUP	ENVIRONMENTAL GROUPS	S	SOLVENT
2512M	D	11.49	OH	C(=0)-CH2		CDCL3
2481M	D	11.50	OH	C(=0)-CH		CCL4
2541M	D	11.50	OH	C(=0)-CH		CCL4
2496M	B	11.50	OH	C(=0)-CH2		POLYSOL-D
2490M	C	11.50	OH	C(=0)-CH2		CCL4
810M	E	11.51	H	CL		CDCL3
2603M	B	11.53	OH	C(=0)-A		DMSO
2484M	D	11.57	OH	C(=0)-CH		CDCL3
739M	F	11.58	NHR	R5NNA<C*/C(CH2.2-CH3)=N>		POLYSOL-D
2552M	D	11.58	OH	C(=0)-CH		CDCL3
2749M	F	11.60	OH	C(=0)-CH2.8		CDCL3
2464M	D	11.64	NHR	R6NN<C(=0)-NH/C(=0)-C(A/CH2-Q3)>		DMSO-D6
2501M	D	11.67	OH	C(=0)-CH2		DMSO-D6
2548M	D	11.68	OH	C(=0)-CH2		POLYSOL-D
2458M	B	11.69	NHR	R6NN(C(=0)-NH/CH=C(NO2))		DMSO
2458M	B	11.69	NHR	R6NN(C(=0)-NH/C(=0)-C(NO2)=)		DMSO
2591M	D	11.70	CHA	A<C(C(=0)-OH)/C(C(=0)-OH)>		POLYSOL-D
2290M	D	11.70 APP.	NH2	C(=0)-A		TFA
2537M	E	11.70	OH	C(=0)-R5R5BI		CCL4
2536M	C	11.72	OH	C(=0)-R8		CDCL3
2526M	F	11.73	OH	C(=0)-CH2.2		CCL4
2498M	C	11.74	OH	C(=0)-CH2		DMSO-D6
2551M	E	11.76	OH	C(=0)-Q1		CDCL3
1961M	D	11.78	OH	ANA<C-N-C*/CH-CH-C*>		DMSO
2486M	E	11.78	OH	C(=0)-CH		CDCL3
2565M	C	11.79	OH	C(=0)-CH2		POLYSOL-D
2517M	D	11.79	OH	C(=0)-Q2		CDCL3
2627M	F	11.80	OH	C(=0)-CH		POLYSOL-D
2497M	B	11.80	OH	C(=0)-CH2		DMSO-D6
2525M	F	11.80	OH	C(=0)-CH2.2		CCL4
2620M	F	11.85	OH	C(=0)-CH		DMSO-D6
2576M	E	11.86	OH	C(=0)-A		POLYSOL-D
2528M	F	11.86	OH	C(=0)-CH2		CCL4
2559M	C	11.89	OH	C(=0)-CH2		CDCL3
2590M	C	11.90	OH	C(=0)-A		POLYSOL-D
2472M	B	11.90	OH	C(=0)-CH3		CCL4
2550M	D	11.90	OH	C(=0)-Q2		CDCL3
2527M	F	11.91	OH	C(=0)-CH2.2		CCL4
2520M	F	11.91	OH	C(=0)-Q2		CCL4
2743M	H	11.93	OH	Q1(CH3/C(=0)-0-CH2.3)		CCL4
2513M	C	11.99	OH	C(=0)-R4		CDCL3
2105M	G	12.00	OH	A(C-C(C(=0)-A))		CDCL3
2514M	B	12.00	OH	C(=0)-R6		CCL4
2602M	B	12.01	OH	C(=0)-A		DMSO
2476M	B	12.01	OH	C(=0)-C		CDCL3
2478M	E	12.01	OH	C(=0)-CH		CCL4
2079M	E	12.02	OH	A<C-C(C(=0)-CH3)-CH-C(CL)>		CDCL3
2589M	C	12.02	OH	C(=0)-A		DMSO
2477M	E	12.09	OH	C(=0)-CH		CCL4
2487M	E	12.13	OH	C(=0)-CH		CCL4
2522M	G	12.15	OH	C(=0)-Q2		CCL4
2519M	D	12.22	OH	C(=0)-Q1		CCL4
2479M	D	12.23	OH	C(=0)-CH		CCL4
2531M	C	12.27	OH	C(=0)-Q2		POLYSOL-D
2533M	B	12.28	OH	C(=0)-Q2(H/C(=0)-OH/H)		DMSO-D6
2523M	F	12.34	OH	C(=0)-Q1		CCL4
2524M	F	12.35	OH	C(=0)-Q2		CCL4
2535M	D	12.42	OH	C(=0)-R6		CCL4
2896M	E	12.48	OH	C(=0)-A		CDCL3
740M	F	12.49	NHR	R5NNA(C*/CH=N)		CDCL3
2597M	C	12.49	OH	A(C-C(NO2)/C(C(=0)-OH))		POLYSOL-D
2597M	C	12.49	OH	C(=0)-A		POLYSOL-D
2504M	A	12.53	OH	C(=0)-CF2		POLYSOL-D
2569M	C	12.57	OH	C(=0)-A		POLYSOL-D
1357M	D	12.62	NHR	R5NNAA(C*/C(=S)-NH)		DMSO-D6
2568M	B	12.70	OH	C(=0)-A		POLYSOL-D
2583M	E	12.80	OH	C(=0)-A		DMSO-D6
2566M	C	12.82	OH	C(=0)-A		CCL4
2293M	F	13.10	OH	A<C-C(C(=0)-NH2)>		DMSO-D6
2143M	E	13.27	OH	C(=R5/CH3)		CCL4
2143M	E	13.27	OH	R5<C=C(C(=0)-CH3)/CH2>		CCL4
741M	C	14.49	NHR	R5NNNA<N=N-C*/C*>		CDCL3
2146M	H	15.02	OH	Q1(CH3/C(=0)-CH2)		CCL4
2141M	H	15.03	OH	Q1(CH3/C(=0)-R50)		CCL4
2138M	G	15.16	OH	Q1(CH2-CH3/C(=0)-CH2)		CCL4
2139M	G	15.24	OH	Q1(CH2.2-CH3/C(=0)-CH2.2)		CCL4
2137M	G	16.60	OH	Q(CH3/C(=0)-CH3/CH2-CH3)		CDCL3

BOOK NO.	ASSIGN-MENT	CHEM SHIFT - ppm -	PROTON GROUP	ENVIRONMENTAL GROUPS	S	SOLVENT
216M	C	2.80	CH	AAA/CH3/CH3		CDCL3
1367M	C	7.85 APP.	CH	AA<C*-CH-C(SO2-NH2)>		POLYSOL-D
1794M	F	5.20- 5.60	CH	ANA<C-C*-CH-C(O-CH3)/CH-CH-N>/R6R6N*BI<CH-N*/CH2>		POLYSOL-D
686M	B	2.83	CH	AN<C-CH-CH-N>/CH3/CH3		CDCL3
689M	D	2.67	CH	AN<C-N>/CH2.3-CH3/CH2.3-CH3		CCL4
486M	C	2.85	CH	A<C-CH-CH-C(CH2-NH2)>/CH3/CH3		CCL4
1714M	B	2.85	CH	A<C-CH-CH-C(CH2-OH)>/CH3/CH3		CCL4
182M	C	2.80	CH	A<C-CH-CH-C(CH3)>/CH3/CH3		CCL4
493M	B	2.80	CH	A<C-CH-CH-C(NH2)>/CH3/CH3		CDCL3
592M	C	2.76	CH	A<C-CH-CH-C(NH-CH3)>/CH3/CH3		CDCL3
667M	B	5.97	CH	A<C-CH-CH-C(N(CH3/CH3))>/A<C-CH-CH-C(N(CH3/CH3))>/ A<C-CH-CH-C(N(CH3/CH3))>		TFA
1901M	B	5.26	CH	A<C-CH-CH-C(N(CH3/CH3))>/A<C-CH-CH-C(N(CH3/CH3))>/ A<C-CH-CH-C(OH)>		POLYSOL-D
1881M	B	2.81	CH	A<C-CH-CH-C(OH)>/CH3/CH3		CDCL3
494M	D	2.51	CH	A<C-C(NH2)>/CH2-CH3/CH3		CCL4
501M	B	2.89	CH	A<C-C(NH2)-C(CH(CH3/CH3))>/CH3/CH3		CDCL3
385M	C	3.31	CH	A(C-C(BR)-CH-C(CH3))/CH3/CH3		CDCL3
1917M	C	3.15	CH	A(C-C(OH)-CH-C(CH3))/CH3/CH3		CDCL3
150M	A	5.50	CH	A/A/A		CDCL3
151M	B	4.21	CH	A/A/CH2-A		CDCL3
2546M	A	5.04	CH	A/A/C(=O)-OH		CDCL3
138M	D	2.52 APP.	CH	A/CH2-CH3/CH3		CCL4
479M	C	2.71 APP.	CH	A/CH2-NH2/CH3		CDCL3
136M	B	2.83	CH	A/CH3/CH3		CCL4
152M	A	2.50- 3.30	CH	A/CH(A/CH2)/CH2-A		CDCL3
347M	A	6.80	CH	BR3		CCL4
374M	A	6.19	CH	BR/A/A		CDCL3
2037M	B	4.91	CH	BR/A/CH(BR/C(=O))		CDCL3
378M	C	5.10	CH	BR/A/HCH-BR		CDCL3
376M	A	6.61	CH	BR/BR/A		CDCL3
377M	B	6.49	CH	BR/BR/A<C-CH-C(CH3)>		CCL4
351M	B	5.69	CH	BR/BR/CH2-BR		CCL4
352M	A	6.04	CH	BR/BR/CH(BR/BR)		CCL4
331M	E	3.91	CH	BR/CH2.2-CH3/CH2-CH3		CCL4
327M	D	4.04	CH	BR/CH2.2-CH3/CH3		CCL4
355M	C	4.32	CH	BR/CH2-BR/CH2-CL		CCL4
361M	C	4.08	CH	BR/CH2-CH2/CH3		CDCL3
358M	D	4.20	CH	BR/CH2-CH2/CH3		CCL4
334M	E	3.99	CH	BR/CH2-CH2/CH3		CCL4
323M	D	4.10	CH	BR/CH2-CH3/CH3		CDCL3
2730M	E	4.40	CH	BR/CH2-C(=O)-O/CH3		CCL4
321M	B	4.21	CH	BR/CH3/CH3		CCL4
342M	A	7.20	CH	BR/CL/CL		CCL4
2087M	A	6.41	CH	BR/C(=O)-A/A		CDCL3
1992M	C	4.39	CH	BR/C(=O)-CH3/CH3		CCL4
2037M	C	5.33	CH	BR/C(=O)-CH3/CH(BR/A)		CDCL3
2486M	D	4.29	CH	BR/C(=O)-OH/CH2.2-CH3		CDCL3
2487M	D	4.19	CH	BR/C(=O)-OH/CH2-CH2		CCL4
2732M	E	4.20	CH	BR/C(=O)-O-CH2/CH2.3-CH3		CDCL3
2733M	E	4.09	CH	BR/C(=O)-O-CH2/CH2.7-CH3		CCL4
2731M	E	4.05	CH	BR/C(=O)-O-CH2/CH(CH3/CH3)		CDCL3
357M	E	4.10	CH	BR/HCH-BR/CH2-CH3		CDCL3
353M	D	4.15 APP.	CH	BR/HCH-BR/CH3		CCL4
356M	C	4.30	CH	BR/HCH-BR/HCH-BR		CCL4
130M	C	1.68	CH	CH2.2-C:/CH3/CH3		CCL4
1037M	B	1.00- 2.20	CH	CH2.2-NO2/CH3/CH3		CDCL3
2747M	B	1.25- 1.95	CH	CH2.2-O-C(=O)/CH3/CH3		CCL4
1385M	B	1.20- 2.00	CH	CH2.2-O/CH3/CH3		CCL4
1188M	B	1.30- 2.05	CH	CH2.2-S/CH3/CH3		CCL4
585M	B	1.20- 2.10	CH	CH2.?/CH3/CH3		CDCL3
139M	B	1.81	CH	CH2-A/CH3/CH3		CDCL3
344M	B	2.21	CH	CH2-BR/CH2-CL/CH3		CDCL3
324M	B	1.93	CH	CH2-BR/CH3/CH3		CCL4
1832M	B	1.53	CH	CH2-CH2/CH2-CH2/CH3		CDCL3
549M	B	1.07- 1.81	CH	CH2-CH2/CH3/CH3		CCL4
619M	B	1.10- 1.88	CH	CH2-CH2/CH3/CH3		CDCL3
1112M	B	1.20- 2.00	CH	CH2-CH2/CH3/CH3		CDCL3
410M	B	1.73 APP.	CH	CH2-CH2/CH3/CH3		CCL4
328M	B	1.76	CH	CH2-CH2/CH3/CH3		CCL4
1205M	C	1.78- 1.92	CH	CH2-CH2/CH3/CH3		CCL4
1799M	D	1.46	CH	CH2-CH2/CH3/CH3		CCL4
446M	D	1.70	CH	CH2-CH2/CH3/CH3		CDCL3
31M	B	1.08- 1.83	CH	CH2-CH2/CH3/CH3		CCL4
856M	B	1.44	CH	CH2-CH2/CH3/CH3		CDCL3
1618M	B	1.10- 1.90	CH	CH2-CH2/CH3/CH3		CCL4
20M	B	1.00- 1.50	CH	CH2-CH3/CH2-CH3/CH3		CCL4
17M	C	0.90- 1.60	CH	CH2-CH3/CH3/CH3		CCL4
22M	C	1.60	CH	CH2-CH3/CH3/CH3		CCL4
450M	D	1.38- 2.14	CH	CH2-CH/CH3/CH3		CCL4
2741M	D	1.80 APP.	CH	CH2-CH/CH3/CH3		CCL4

BOOK NO.	ASSIGN-MENT	CHEM SHIFT - ppm -	PROTON GROUP	ENVIRONMENTAL GROUPS	S	SOLVENT
238M	B	1.91	CH	CH2-CL/CH3/CH3		CCL4
2699M	B	1.97	CH	CH2-C(=O)-O/CH3/CH3		CCL4
2843M	B	1.52	CH	CH2-C(=O)-O/CH3/CH3		CCL4
2837M	B	2.10	CH	CH2-C(=O)-O/CH3/CH3		CCL4
2838M	C	2.08	CH	CH2-C(=O)-O/CH3/CH3		CCL4
1979M	B	1.96- 2.34	CH	CH2-C(=O)/CH3/CH3		CCL4
1971M	C	1.90- 2.37	CH	CH2-C(=O)/CH3/CH3		CCL4
1694M	B	3.99	CH	CH2-C:C		CCL4
947M	B	1.97	CH	CH2-C:N/CH3/CH3		CCL4
27M	D	1.68	CH	CH2-C/CH3/CH3		CCL4
1815M	E	1.95 APP.	CH	CH2-C/CH3/CH3		CDCL3
409M	B	1.73	CH	CH2-I/CH3/CH3		CCL4
445M	C	1.09- 1.68	CH	CH2-NH2/CH2-CH3/CH3		CDCL3
442M	B	1.59	CH	CH2-NH2/CH3/CH3		CDCL3
546M	C	1.60	CH	CH2-NH/CH3/CH3		CCL4
2418M	B	1.69	CH	CH2-NH/CH3/CH3		POLYSOL-D
737M	C	1.79	CH	CH2-N/CH2-CH2/CH2-CH3		CCL4
1078M	B	1.70- 2.64	CH	CH2-N/CH3/CH3		CDCL3
1346M	B	1.92	CH	CH2-N/CH3/CH3		CDCL3
1615M	B	1.67	CH	CH2-OH/CH3/CH3		CCL4
2695M	B	1.10- 1.70	CH	CH2-O-C(=O)/CH2-CH3/CH2-CH3		CCL4
2691M	B	1.10- 1.80	CH	CH2-O-C(=O)/CH2-CH3/CH2-CH3		CDCL3
2778M	B	1.50- 2.10	CH	CH2-O-C(=O)/CH3/CH3		CCL4
2812M	B	1.89	CH	CH2-O-C(=O)/CH3/CH3		CCL4
2807M	B	1.97	CH	CH2-O-C(=O)/CH3/CH3		CCL4
2864M	B	2.08	CH	CH2-O-C(=O)/CH3/CH3		CDCL3
2918M	B	2.05	CH	CH2-O-C(=O)/CH3/CH3		C3D6O
1035M	B	1.98	CH	CH2-O-N=/OCH3/CH3		CCL4
1601M	B	1.34	CH	CH2-O/CH2-CH3/CH2-CH3		CCL4
1405M	B	1.90	CH	CH2-O/CH3/CH3		CCL4
1383M	C	1.80	CH	CH2-O/CH3/CH3		CCL4
855M	C	1.98- 2.40	CH	CH2-ON/CH3/CH3		CDCL3
94M	D	1.26- 2.08	CH	CH2-Q1/CH3/CH3		CCL4
58M	C	1.00- 1.80	CH	CH2-Q3/CH2-CH3/CH3		CCL4
1246M	B	1.82- 2.80	CH	CH2-S(=O)/CH3/CH3		CCL4
1111M	B	1.79	CH	CH2-S/CH3/CH3		CCL4
1185M	B	1.92	CH	CH2-S/CH3/CH3		CCL4
2731M	D	2.20	CH	CH(BR/C(=O)-O)/CH3/CH3		CDCL3
18M	B	1.46	CH	CH(CH3/CH3)/CH3/CH3		CCL4
28M	B	1.38- 1.98	CH	CH(CH3/CH3)/CH(CH3/CH3)/CH3		CCL4
28M	B	1.38- 1.98	CH	CH(CH/CH)/CH3/CH3		CCL4
978M	A	3.25	CH	CH(C:N/A)/A/CH2-A		CDCL3
2619M	C	2.22	CH	CH(NH2/C(=O)-OH)/CH3/CH3		D2O
2620M	C	2.02	CH	CH(NH/C(=O)-O)/CH3/CH3		DMSO-D6
1741M	C	1.40- 2.10	CH	CH(OH/CH)/CH3/CH3		CDCL3
260M	B	4.55	CH	CL/CCL3/CH3		CCL4
237M	D	3.88	CH	CL/CH2-CH3/CH3		CCL4
262M	C	3.31- 4.16	CH	CL/CH2-CL/CH2-CH3		CCL4
259M	B	4.19	CH	CL/CH2-CL/CH2-CL		CCL4
257M	C	4.03	CH	CL/CH2-CL/CH3		CCL4
261M	A	4.44	CH	CL/CH-CL2/CH-CL2		CCL4
251M	B	5.89	CH	CL/CH/CH3		CCL4
287M	A	6.60	CH	CL/CL/A		CCL4
256M	A	6.10	CH	CL/CL/C		CCL4
265M	C	5.77	CH	CL/CL/CH2-C		CCL4
254M	B	5.79	CH	CL/CL/CH2-CL		CDCL3
1638M	C	5.76	CH	CL/CL/CH2-OH		CCL4
261M	B	6.01	CH	CL/CL/CH(CL/CH)		CCL4
255M	A	5.91	CH	CL/CL/CH(CL/CL)		CDCL3
250M	A	7.21	CH	CL/CL/CL		CCL4
2282M	A	6.31	CH	CL/CL/C(=O)-NH2		C3H6O
1991M	C	4.23	CH	CL/C(=O)-CH3/CH3		CCL4
2213M	A	5.52	CH	CL/C(=O)-CL/A		CCL4
2484M	C	4.28	CH	CL/C(=O)-OH/CH2-CH3		CDCL3
2726M	C	4.36	CH	CL/C(=O)-O-CH3/HCH-CL		CCL4
1393M	C	5.98	CH	CL/F/CF2-O		CCL4
345M	A	6.10	CH	CL/F/C(BR/F2)		CCL4
2505M	C	4.69	CH	CL/HCH-C(=O)-OH/HCH-C(=O)-OH		D2O
1044M	B	5.88	CH	CL/NO2/CH3		CCL4
275M	C	4.48	CH	CL/Q3(H/H/H)/HCH-CL		CCL4
26M	C	1.00- 1.82	CH	C(CH2/CH3/CH3)/CH3/CH3		CCL4
25M	B	1.10- 1.90	CH	C(CH3/CH3/CH3)/CH2-CH3/CH3		CCL4
2048M	B	3.47	CH	C(=O)-A/CH3/CH3		CCL4
1982M	E	2.50	CH	C(=O)-CH2.5/CH3/CH3		CCL4
2035M	B	2.61	CH	C(=O)-CH2/CH3/CH3		CCL4
1994M	C	2.71	CH	C(=O)-CH3/CH2-OH/CH3		CDCL3
2140M	D	3.71	CH	C(=O)-CH3/C(=O)-CH3/CH2-CH		CCL4
2137M	F	3.56	CH	C(=O)-CH3/C(=O)-CH3/CH2-CH3		CDCL3
2191M	C	2.72	CH	C(=O)-CL/CH2.2-CH3/CH2.2-CH3		CCL4
1977M	C	3.07	CH	C(=O)-C/CH3/CH3		CCL4
2286M	D	3.21	CH	C(=O)-HNH/A/HCH-CH3		CCL4

BOOK NO.	ASSIGN-MENT	CHEM SHIFT - ppm -	PROTON GROUP	ENVIRONMENTAL GROUPS	S	SOLVENT
2152M	B	2.38	CH	C(=O)-H/CH3/CH3		CCL4
2285M	C	2.68	CH	C(=O)-NH2/R6<C=CH/CH2>/CH2-CH3		CDCL3
2317M	B	2.54	CH	C(=O)-NH/CH3/CH3		POLYSOL-D
2542M	B	3.52	CH	C(=O)-OH/A/CH2-CH2		DMSO
2541M	B	3.62	CH	C(=O)-OH/A/CH3		CCL4
2481M	C	2.31	CH	C(=O)-OH/CH2.4-CH3/CH2.4-CH3		CCL4
2544M	A	2.60- 3.30	CH	C(=O)-OH/CH2-A/CH2-A		CDCL3
2479M	C	2.33	CH	C(=O)-OH/CH2-CH2/CH2-CH2		CCL4
2477M	D	2.29	CH	C(=O)-OH/CH2-CH2/CH2-CH3		CCL4
2475M	D	2.36	CH	C(=O)-OH/CH2-CH3/CH3		CDCL3
2478M	D	2.38	CH	C(=O)-OH/CH2-CH/CH2-CH3		CCL4
2510M	B	3.22	CH	C(=O)-OH/CH2-C(=O)-O/CH2-C(=O)-O		D20
2474M	B	2.55	CH	C(=O)-OH/CH3/CH3		CCL4
2651M	C	1.97	CH	C(=O)-O-CA/CH2.3-CH3/CH2-CH3		POLYSOL-D
2836M	B	2.45	CH	C(=O)-O-CH2.2/CH3/CH3		CCL4
2757M	C	2.29	CH	C(=O)-O-CH2/CH2-CH2/CH2-CH3		CDCL3
2702M	D	2.44 APP.	CH	C(=O)-O-CH2/CH3/CH3		CCL4
2708M	E	2.49	CH	C(=O)-O-CH2/CH3/CH3		CCL4
1865M	D	4.65	CH	C(=O)-O-CH2/C(=O)-A/CH2-CH		CDCL3
2745M	E	3.47	CH	C(=O)-O-CH2/C(=O)-CH3/CH2.2-CH3		CDCL3
2744M	E	3.20	CH	C(=O)-O-CH2/C(=O)-CH3/CH2-CH3		CCL4
2770M	E	3.14	CH	C(=O)-O-CH2/C(=O)-O-CH2/CH2-CH2		CCL4
2795M	B	4.09	CH	C(=O)-O-CH2/C(=O)-O-CH2/CH(C(=O)-O/C(=O)-O)		CDCL3
2796M	B	3.40	CH	C(=O)-O-CH3/C(=O)-O-CH3/CH2.2-CH		CDCL3
2253M	C	2.29	CH	C(=O)-O-C(=O)-CH/CH2-CH3/CH2-CH3		CCL4
1813M	C	2.41	CH	C-C		CDCL3
1693M	A	2.54	CH	C-CH2		CDCL3
120M	C	1.74	CH	C-CH2		CCL4
1816M	B	2.48	CH	C-R6		CDCL3
945M	B	2.69	CH	C:N/CH3/CH3		CCL4
978M	B	4.08	CH	C:N/CH(A/CH2)/A		CDCL3
2720M	D	4.87	CH	F/C(=O)-O-CH2/CH3		CCL4
2654M	A	5.91	CH	F/F/C(=O)-O-NA		D20
1617M	C	1.05- 1.81	CH	HCH-OH/CH2-CH3/CH3		CCL4
408M	D	4.07	CH	I/CH2-CH3/CH3		CDCL3
406M	B	4.29	CH	I/CH3/CH3		CCL4
784M	B	4.77	CH	NH2/A/CH3	S	TFA
478M	C	4.01	CH	NH2/A/CH3		CCL4
453M	D	2.81	CH	NH2/CH2.2-CH/CH3		CDCL3
626M	F	2.88	CH	NH2/CH2.3-N/CH3		CDCL3
455M	D	2.70	CH	NH2/CH2.3/CH2.3		CDCL3
785M	D	3.62	CH	NH2/CH2-CH2/CH3	S	TFA
443M	E	2.81	CH	NH2/CH2-CH3/CH3		CDCL3
450M	F	2.98	CH	NH2/CH2-CH/CH3		CCL4
459M	D	2.84	CH	NH2/CH2-NH2/CH3		CDCL3
440M	B	3.04	CH	NH2/CH3/CH3		D20
1753M	C	2.45- 3.90	CH	NH2/CH(OH/CH3)/CH3		CDCL3
448M	D	2.59	CH	NH2/C(CH3/CH3/CH3)/CH3		CCL4
2639M	C	4.12	CH	NH2/C(=O)-NH/CH3		D20
2643M	C	3.91	CH	NH2/C(=O)-OH/CH2.2-NH2	S	D20
2629M	B	3.22	CH	NH2/C(=O)-OH/CH2-CH2		D20
2628M	C	3.30	CH	NH2/C(=O)-OH/CH2-CH2		D20
2618M	C	3.71	CH	NH2/C(=O)-OH/CH2-CH2		D20
2632M	C	3.79	CH	NH2/C(=O)-OH/CH2-CH2		D20
2644M	C	3.82	CH	NH2/C(=O)-OH/CH2-CH2	S	D20
2615M	C	3.70	CH	NH2/C(=O)-OH/CH2-CH3		D20
2624M	B	4.03	CH	NH2/C(=O)-OH/CH2-SH		D20
2645M	B	4.47	CH	NH2/C(=O)-OH/CH2-SH	S	D20
2614M	B	3.70	CH	NH2/C(=O)-OH/CH3		D20
2619M	D	3.55	CH	NH2/C(=O)-OH/CH(CH3/CH3)		D20
2626M	B	3.50	CH	NH2/C(=O)-OH/CH(OH/CH3)		D20
2630M	C	4.00	CH	NH2/C(=O)-OH/HCH-C(=O)-NH2		D20
2631M	C	4.02	CH	NH2/C(=O)-OH/HCH-C(=O)-NH2		D20
2736M	C	4.21	CH	NH2/C(=O)-O-CH2/CH3	S	D20
2735M	C	4.20	CH	NH2/C(=O)-O-CH3/CH3	S	D20
1644M	C	2.72	CH	NH2/HCH-OH/CH2-CH3		CDCL3
2633M	C	4.47	CH	NH3(+)/C(=O)-OH/CH2.2-C(=O)-O		TFA
598M	E	3.27	CH	NH-A/CH2-CH3/CH3		CDCL3
1647M	C	2.85	CH	NH-CH2.2/CH3/CH3		CCL4
556M	C	2.78	CH	NH-CH2/CH3/CH3		D20
804M	C	2.60- 3.12	CH	NH-CH3/CH2-A/CH3	S	CDCL3
545M	D	2.63	CH	NH-CH/CH2-CH3/CH3		CCL4
798M	B	3.51	CH	NH-CH/CH3/CH3	S	D20
543M	C	2.88	CH	NH-CH/CH3/CH3		CCL4
2641M	C	4.63	CH	NH-C(=O)-CH2/C(=O)-OH/CH2-OH		D20
2310M	C	5.10	CH	NH-C(=O)-CH3/A/CH3		CDCL3
2627M	D	4.42	CH	NH-C(=O)-CH3/C(=O)-OH/CH2.2-S		POLYSOL-D
2621M	D	4.30	CH	NH-C(=O)-CH3/C(=O)-OH/CH2-CH		POLYSOL-D
2308M	B	4.32	CH	NH-C(=O)-H/CH2-A/CH2-A		DMSO-D6
2417M	B	3.72	CH	NH-C(=O)-NH2/CH3/CH3		POLYSOL-D
2307M	B	5.00	CH	NH-C(=O)/A/CH3		CCL4

BOOK NO.	ASSIGN-MENT	CHEM SHIFT - ppm -	PROTON GROUP	ENVIRONMENTAL GROUPS	S	SOLVENT
2620M	D	4.19	CH	NH-C(=O)/C(=O)-OH/CH(CH3/CH3)		DMSO-D6
1345M	B	4.32	CH	NH-C(=S)/CH3/CH3		CDCL3
1349M	B	4.51	CH	NH-C(=S)/CH3/CH3		POLYSOL-D
559M	D	2.98	CH	NH-R6/CH3/CH3		CDCL3
1042M	B	4.65	CH	NO2/CH3/CH3		CDCL3
975M	B	4.81	CH	N(CH3/CH3)/A/C:N		CDCL3
625M	C	2.29- 2.95	CH	N(CH3/CH3)/CH2-NH2/CH3		D20
1648M	C	2.65	CH	N(CH3/CH3)/HCH-OH/CH3		D20
958M	E	3.00	CH	N(CH/CH2.3)/CH3/CH3		CCL4
616M	C	3.02	CH	N(CH/CH2)/CH3/CH3		CCL4
2348M	C	3.69	CH	N(C(=O)/CH)/CH3/CH3		CCL4
923M	B	3.53	CH	N=C=/CH3/CH3)		CDCL3
1793M	C	5.11	CH	OH/A(C-C(CL)/CH-C(CL))/CH3		CCL4
1790M	B	5.59	CH	OH/A/A		CCL4
1791M	C	4.81	CH	OH/A/CH2-A		CDCL3
1788M	D	4.38	CH	OH/A/CH2-CH3		CCL4
2850M	E	4.99	CH	OH/A/CH2-C(=0)-O		CCL4
1789M	D	3.88	CH	OH/A/R3<CH-CH2/CH2>		CCL4
1749M	D	3.46	CH	OH/CH2.2-CH/CH2.CH		CCL4
1740M	D	3.61	CH	OH/CH2.2/CH2.2		CDCL3
1751M	C	4.03	CH	OH/CH2-BR/CH2-BR		CDCL3
1747M	E	3.41	CH	OH/CH2-CH2/CH2-CH3		CCL4
1745M	E	3.49	CH	OH/CH2-CH2/CH2-CH3		CDCL3
1738M	E	3.42	CH	OH/CH2-CH2/CH3		CCL4
1739M	E	3.61	CH	OH/CH2-CH2/CH3		CCL4
1746M	E	3.65	CH	OH/CH2-CH2/CH3		CCL4
1748M	E	3.67	CH	OH/CH2-CH2/CH3		CCL4
1742M	E	3.68	CH	OH/CH2-CH2/CH3		CCL4
1757M	E	4.08	CH	OH/CH2-CH2/CH3		CDCL3
1737M	D	3.36	CH	OH/CH2-CH3/CH2-CH3		CCL4
1736M	D	3.62	CH	OH/CH2-CH3/CH3		CCL4
1830M	C	3.95	CH	OH/CH2-CH/CH3		CCL4
1750M	B	4.05	CH	OH/CH2-CL/CH2-CL		CDCL3
1840M	B	3.88	CH	OH/CH2-CL/CH2-OH		D20
2791M	D	4.31	CH	OH/CH2-C(=0)-O/CH2-C(=0)-O		CCL4
1787M	F	3.57	CH	OH/CH2-C:/CH2-CH3		CCL4
1844M	B	3.30- 3.90	CH	OH/CH2-NH2/CH2-OH		D20
1851M	C	3.77 APP.	CH	OH/CH2-N/CH3		CDCL3
1754M	E	3.79	CH	OH/CH2-N/CH3		CDCL3
1829M	C	3.10- 3.80	CH	OH/CH2-OH/CH2-CH3		CDCL3
1848M	A	3.60	CH	OH/CH2-OH/CH2-OH		D20
2718M	B	3.50- 4.00	CH	OH/CH2-0-C(=0)/CH2-OH		CDCL3
2719M	F	3.93 APP.	CH	OH/CH2-0-C(=0)/CH2-OH		CDCL3
2759M	D	4.13 APP.	CH	OH/CH2-0-C(=0)/CH2-0-C(=0)		CDCL3
2758M	F	4.19	CH	OH/CH2-0-C(=0)/CH2-0-C(=0)		CDCL3
1792M	D	4.08	CH	OH/CH2-0/CH3		CCL4
2532M	D	3.58	CH	OH/CH2-Q2/CH2-CH2		CCL4
1784M	E	3.63	CH	OH/CH2-Q3/CH2.2-CH3		CDCL3
1756M	E	3.79	CH	OH/CH2-R5N/CH3		CDCL3
1735M	C	3.99	CH	OH/CH3/CH3		CCL4
1743M	E	3.42	CH	OH/CH(CH2/CH2)/CH2-CH3		CCL4
1741M	D	3.01	CH	OH/CH(CH3/CH3)/CH(CH3/CH3)		CDCL3
1753M	C	2.45- 3.90	CH	OH/CH(NH2/CH3)/CH3		CDCL3
2626M	C	4.16	CH	OH/CH(NH2/C(=0)-0)/CH3		D20
1861M	A	3.74 APP.	CH	OH/CH(OH/CH2)/CH2-OH		D20
1863M	A	3.59- 3.81	CH	OH/CH(OH/CH)/CH2-OH		CDCL3
2661M	A	3.75 APP.	CH	OH/CH(OH/CH)/CH2-OH	S	D20
1863M	B	3.96 APP.	CH	OH/CH(OH/CH)/CH(OH/CH2)		CDCL3
1744M	D	3.13	CH	OH/C(CH3/CH3/CH3)/CH2-CH2		CCL4
1838M	E	3.15	CH	OH/C(OH/CH3/CH3)/C(CH3/CH3/CH3)		CDCL3
2283M	B	4.27	CH	OH/C(=0)-NH2/CH3		D20
2357M	D	4.37	CH	OH/C(=0)-N/CH3		CCL4
2555M	A	5.05	CH	OH/C(=0)-OH/A		DMSO
2507M	B	4.63	CH	OH/C(=0)-OH/CH2-C(=0)-OH		D20
2493M	B	4.40	CH	OH/C(=0)-OH/CH3		D20
2508M	A	4.68	CH	OH/C(=0)-OH/CH(OH/C(=0)-OH)		D20
2690M	B	4.38	CH	OH/C(=0)-OH/CH(OH/C(=0)-OH)		D20
2509M	A	4.79	CH	OH/C(=0)-OH/CH(OH/C(=0)-0)		D20
2506M	A	5.01	CH	OH/C(=0)-OH/C(=0)-OH		D20
2741M	F	4.04	CH	OH/C(=0)-0-CH2/CH2-CH		CCL4
2792M	E	4.42	CH	OH/C(=0)-0-CH2/CH(OH/C(=0)-0)		CCL4
2790M	D	4.55	CH	OH/C(=0)-0-CH3/CH2-C(=0)-0		CDCL3
2740M	D	4.19	CH	OH/C(=0)-0-CH3/CH3		CCL4
2659M	B	4.09	CH	OH/C(=0)-0-NA/CH3		D20
2662M	C	4.16	CH	OH/C(=0)-0-NA/CH(OH/CH)	S	D20
2023M	B	5.79	CH	OH/C(=0)-R50/R50(C=CH/0)		DMSO
1758M	C	4.60	CH	OH/C:N/CH3		CDCL3
1831M	F	4.16	CH	OH/HCH-C/CH3		CCL4
1759M	G	3.98	CH	OH/HCH-C/CH3		CCL4
1833M	D	3.75	CH	OH/HCH-HCH/CH3		CCL4
1752M	C	3.53	CH	OH/HCH-NH2/HCH-NH2		D20

BOOK NO.	ASSIGN-MENT	CHEM SHIFT - ppm -	PROTON GROUP	ENVIRONMENTAL GROUPS	S	SOLVENT
1755M	H	3.59	CH	OH/HCH-N/CH3		CCL4
1828M	D	3.80	CH	OH/HCH-OH/CH3		CDCL3
1659M	C	4.36	CH	OH/P(=O/A/A)/CH2.2-CH3		POLYSOL-D
1782M	D	4.14	CH	OH/Q2(CH3/H/H)/CH3		CCL4
1783M	D	3.93	CH	OH/Q3/CH2-CH2		CCL4
1785M	C	4.11	CH	OH/Q3/CH2-Q3		CDCL3
1761M	E	3.11	CH	OH/R3/CH3		CDCL3
1762M	D	3.43	CH	OH/R6/CH3		CCL4
2090M	B	5.42	CH	O-A/C(=O)-A/CH3		CDCL3
2216M	B	4.86	CH	O-A/C(=O)-CL/CH3		CCL4
1493M	C	5.60	CH	O-A/O-CH2/O-CH2		CCL4
1394M	E	3.51	CH	O-CH2.2/CH3/CH3		CCL4
1480M	E	4.30	CH	O-CH2/A/CH2-CH2		CDCL3
1400M	C	3.63	CH	O-CH2/CH3/CH3		CDCL3
1445M	E	3.15- 3.90	CH	O-CH2/CH3/CH3		CCL4
1426M	D	4.60	CH	O-CH2/O-CH2/CH2-BR		CCL4
1431M	E	4.60	CH	O-CH2/O-CH2/CH2-N		CDCL3
1428M	D	4.40	CH	O-CH2/O-CH2/CH2-NH2		CDCL3
1485M	D	4.55	CH	O-CH2/O-CH2/CH3		CCL4
1424M	E	4.57	CH	O-CH2/O-CH2/CH3		CCL4
1436M	C	5.00	CH	O-CH2/O-CH2/O-CH2		CCL4
2552M	B	4.78	CH	O-CH3/C(=O)-OH/A		CDCL3
1429M	C	4.37	CH	O-CH3/O-CH3/CH2-CH		CCL4
1430M	D	4.40	CH	O-CH3/O-CH3/CH2-N		CCL4
1427M	D	4.23	CH	O-CH3/O-CH3/CH2-NH2		CCL4
1422M	C	4.50	CH	O-CH3/O-CH3/CH3		CCL4
1435M	B	4.80	CH	O-CH3/O-CH3/O-CH3		CCL4
1483M	C	4.15	CH	O-CH/A/CH3		CCL4
1483M	C	4.45	CH	O-CH/A/CH3		CCL4
1483M	D	4.15	CH	O-CH/A/CH3		CCL4
1483M	D	4.45	CH	O-CH/A/CH3		CCL4
1395M	B	3.52	CH	O-CH/CH3/CH3		CCL4
1432M	B	4.91	CH	O-CH/O-CH/CH3		CDCL3
2893M	B	5.27	CH	O-C(=O)-A/CH3/CH3		CDCL3
2889M	B	5.29	CH	O-C(=O)-A/CH3/CH3		CDCL3
2882M	C	5.21	CH	O-C(=O)-A/CH3/CH3		CDCL3
2761M	G	5.16	CH	O-C(=O)-CH2.16/HCH-O-C(=O)/HCH-O-C(=O)		CDCL3
2700M	E	4.92	CH	O-C(=O)-CH2.2/CH3/CH3		CCL4
2698M	F	4.85	CH	O-C(=O)-CH2/CH2-CH3/CH3		CDCL3
2823M	F	5.00- 5.60	CH	O-C(=O)-CH2/CH2-O-C(=O)/CH2-O-C(=O)		CCL4
2773M	C	4.96	CH	O-C(=O)-CH2/CH3/CH3		CCL4
2725M	D	5.05	CH	O-C(=O)-CH2/CH3/CH3		CCL4
2727M	E	4.92	CH	O-C(=O)-CH2/CH3/CH3		CCL4
2760M	G	5.19	CH	O-C(=O)-CH2/HCH-O-C(=O)/HCH-O-C(=O)		CCL4
2834M	C	5.90	CH	O-C(=O)-CH3/A/CH3		CDCL3
2822M	F	4.77	CH	O-C(=O)-CH3/CH2-Q2/CH2-CH2		CCL4
2754M	E	5.10	CH	O-C(=O)-CH3/HCH-O-C(=O)/CH3		CCL4
2973M	B	4.89	CH	O-C(=O)-NH2/CH3/CH3		CDCL3
2989M	A	6.89	CH	O-C(=O)-NH/A/A		CDCL3
2828M	B	5.04	CH	O-C(=O)-Q2/CH3/CH3		CCL4
2826M	B	5.07	CH	O-C(=O)-Q2/CH3/CH3		CCL4
2811M	C	4.49	CH	O-C(=O)-Q2/CH3/CH3		CCL4
1398M	C	3.70	CH	O-C/CH3/CH3		CCL4
1423M	E	4.59	CH	O-HCH/O-HCH/CH3		CCL4
1425M	D	4.79	CH	O-HCH/O-HCH/Q3		CCL4
1081M	B	5.15	CH	O-NO2/CH3/CH3		CCL4
1034M	D	5.40	CH	O-N=O/CH2-CH3/CH3		CCL4
2469M	C	2.48	CH	QN(NH-C(=O)/CH3)/CH3/CH3		CDCL3
848M	C	2.44	CH	QN(OH)/CH3/CH3		CCL4
848M	D	3.19	CH	QN(OH)/CH3/CH3		CCL4
76M	C	2.59	CH	Q2(CH3)/CH3/CH3		CCL4
77M	C	2.19	CH	Q2(H/CH3/H)/CH3/CH3		CCL4
81M	B	2.20 APP.	CH	Q2(H/CH(CH3)/H)/CH3/CH3		CCL4
2021M	C	2.00 APP.	CH	Q2(H/C(=O)-CH3/H)/CH2-CH3/CH2-CH3		CCL4
2522M	D	2.36	CH	Q2(H/C(=O)-OH/H)/CH2.2-CH3/CH3		CCL4
80M	B	2.60	CH	Q2(H/H/CH(CH3/CH3))/CH3/CH3		CCL4
89M	B	2.88	CH	Q2(Q3)/Q3/CH3		CCL4
56M	B	1.10- 2.10	CH	Q3/CH2-CH3/CH2-CH3		CDCL3
55M	D	2.06	CH	Q3/CH2-CH3/CH3		CCL4
88M	C	1.80- 2.40	CH	Q3/CH2-Q2/CH3		CCL4
67M	B	1.90- 2.50	CH	Q3/CH2-Q3/CH3		CCL4
38M	C	0.90 APP.	CH	R3<CH-HCH/HCH>/CH3/CH3		CCL4
639M	C	4.22	CH	R6NN<N-CH2/CH2>/A/A		CDCL3
2463M	C	8.30	CH	R6NN(=C-C(=O)/C(=O))/A		DMSO
1210M	D	2.87	CH	SH/CH2.5-CH3/CH3		CDCL3
1203M	E	2.81	CH	SH/CH2-CH3/CH3		CCL4
1662M	D	3.00 APP.	CH	SH/CH2-OH/CH2-SH		CDCL3
1219M	E	3.00	CH	SH/CH2-SH/CH3		CDCL3
1202M	C	3.07	CH	SH/CH3/CH3		CCL4
2489M	C	3.50	CH	SH/C(=O)-OH/CH3		CCL4
1214M	B	3.22	CH	SH/HCH-CL/HCH-CL		CCL4

BOOK NO.	ASSIGN-MENT	CHEM SHIFT - ppm -	PROTON GROUP	ENVIRONMENTAL GROUPS	S	SOLVENT
1321M	C	4.66	CH	SO3-A/CH3/CH3		CCL4
1128M	C	4.80	CH	S-CH2/S-CH2/S-CH2		CCL4
1184M	D	2.62	CH	S-S/CH2-CH3/CH3		CCL4
2307M	E	7.84	CH	(=0)/NH-CH		CCL4
2367M	B	8.50	CH	(=0)/N(A/A)		CCL4
2184M	D	9.76	CH	(=0)/R5S(C-S/CH-CH)		CDCL3
852M	C	8.21	CH	=NOH/A		CDCL3
166M	A	3.08	CH	:C-A		CDCL3
116M	B	1.89	CH	:C-C		CCL4
1819M	B	2.63	CH	:C-C		CDCL3
1814M	D	2.30	CH	:C-C		CCL4
283M	A	2.42	CH	:C-CH2		CCL4
1266M	A	2.49	CH	:C-CH2		CDCL3
1265M	A	3.10	CH	:C-CH2		POLYSOL-D
124M	B	1.93	CH	:C-CH2		CDCL3
123M	B	1.98	CH	:C-CH2		CDCL3
119M	C	1.72	CH	:C-CH2		CCL4
118M	C	1.73	CH	:C-CH2		CCL4
117M	C	1.79	CH	:C-CH2		CCL4
122M	C	1.75	CH	:C-CH2.15		CCL4
121M	C	1.79	CH	:C-CH2.8		CCL4
1695M	A	1.96	CH	:C-CH2-CH2		CCL4
132M	A	7.23	CHA	A		CCL4
218M	A	7.62	CHA	AAAA<C-CH-C*/CH-CH-C*>		CDCL3
218M	B	7.90	CHA	AAAA<C-C*-CH/CH-CH-CH-C*>		CDCL3
217M	A	7.89	CHA	AAAA<C-C*-CH/CH-CH-CH>		CCL4
218M	C	7.96	CHA	AAAA<C-C*-CH/CH-C*-C*>		CDCL3
218M	E	8.73	CHA	AAAA<C-C*-C*/CH-CH-CH-C*-CH>		CDCL3
218M	D	8.68	CHA	AAAA<C-C*-C*/CH-C*-CH>		CDCL3
749M	E	8.26	CHA	AAAN<C*-C*>		CDCL3
215M	B	7.38	CHA	AAA<C(CH3)-CH-C*/CH-C*-C*>		CDCL3
215M	C	7.62	CHA	AAA<C*-CH-C(CH3)/CH-C*>		CDCL3
216M	E	8.40 APP.	CHA	AAA<C*-CH/CH-CH-C*-C*>		CDCL3
1001M	C	8.25 APP.	CHA	AAA<C*-C(C:N)>		CDCL3
541M	E	8.57	CHA	AAA<C*-C(NH2)>		DMSO
216M	E	8.40 APP.	CHA	AAA<C*-C*CH-CH-C(CH3)-C*-CH>		CDCL3
541M	D	8.26	CHA	AAA<C*-C*>		DMSO
1001M	D	8.63 APP.	CHA	AAA<C*-C*>		CDCL3
215M	E	8.54 APP.	CHA	AAA<C*-C*>		CDCL3
541M	F	8.75	CHA	AAA<C*-C*>		DMSO
215M	E	8.54 APP.	CHA	AAA<C*-C*/CH-C(CH3)>		CDCL3
213M	B	7.95	CHA	AAA<C*/CH-CH-CH-C*>		CDCL3
215M	D	7.62	CHA	AAA<C*/CH-C*>		CDCL3
1001M	B	8.20	CHA	AAA<C*/C(C:N)-C*>		CDCL3
541M	B	6.98	CHA	AAA<C*/C(NH2)-C*>		DMSO
213M	C	8.40	CHA	AAA<C*/C*>		CDCL3
213M	A	7.41	CHA	AAA<C-CH-C*/CH-CH-C*>		CDCL3
214M	B	8.53	CHA	AAA(C*-C*)		CCL4
751M	C	7.69	CHA	AANAN<C*/CH-C*>		POLYSOL-D
750M	C	7.91	CHA	AANAN<C*/CH-C*>		C3H6O
748M	A	7.30- 7.72	CHA	AANA<CH-C*-C*/CH-CH-C*>		CDCL3
748M	A	7.30- 7.72	CHA	AANA<CH-C*/CH-CH-C*>		CDCL3
748M	B	7.81	CHA	AANA<C*-CH-N>		CDCL3
748M	D	8.35 APP.	CHA	AANA<C*-C*>		CDCL3
748M	C	8.17	CHA	AANA<C*-N>		CDCL3
749M	D	7.91	CHA	AANA<C*-N/CH-C*>		CDCL3
749M	C	7.78	CHA	AANA<C*/CH-C*-N>		CDCL3
746M	B	7.35	CHA	AANA<C-C*-N/CH-CH-CH-C*>		CCL4
747M	A	7.18- 7.83	CHA	AANA(CH-C*-C(NH2)/CH-CH-C*)		DMSO-D6
747M	A	7.18- 7.83	CHA	AANA(CH-C*-N/CH-CH-C*)		DMSO-D6
747M	B	7.98	CHA	AANA(C*-C(NH2)-C*)		DMSO-D6
747M	C	8.48	CHA	AANA(C*-N-C*)		DMSO-D6
742M	B	8.56	CHA	AANN(C*-C(CL)-N)		TFA
722M	B	6.90- 7.30	CHA	AAN<CH-N-C*/CH-C*>		CCL4
722M	B	6.90- 7.30	CHA	AAN<C(CH3)-CH-C*/CH-C*>		CCL4
1794M	H	7.31	CHA	AAN<C(O-CH3)-CH-C*/CH-C*-N>		POLYSOL-D
1794M	I	7.50 APP.	CHA	AAN<C*-C(CH(OH/R6R6N*BI))/C(O-CH3)>		POLYSOL-D
2183M	B	8.15	CHA	AAN<C*-N>		CDCL3
719M	E	8.01	CHA	AAN<C*-N-C(CH3)>		CCL4
1963M	D	8.04	CHA	AAN<C*-N-C(OH)>		TFA
1174M	C	7.98	CHA	AAN<C*-N-C(S-A)>		CDCL3
1794M	J	7.93	CHA	AAN<C*-N/CH-C(O-CH3)>		POLYSOL-D
722M	E	7.90	CHA	AAN<C*-N/C(CH3)>		CCL4
722M	C	7.48	CHA	AAN<C*/CH-C(CH3)>		CCL4
1964M	B	7.62	CHA	AAN(CH-C*-C(NO2)/CH-CH-C*)		DMSO
1964M	B	7.85	CHA	AAN(CH-C*-C(NO2)/CH-CH-C*)		DMSO
1964M	A	7.62	CHA	AAN(CH-C*-C(OH)/CH-CH-C*)		DMSO
1964M	A	7.85	CHA	AAN(CH-C*-C(OH)/CH-CH-C*)		DMSO
721M	D	7.35	CHA	AAN(C(CH3)-CH-C*/CH-CH-C*-N)		CDCL3
1731M	D	7.98	CHA	AAN(C*N)		CDCL3
731M	B	7.95	CHA	AAN(C*-C(BR))		CDCL3

BOOK NO.	ASSIGN-MENT	CHEM SHIFT - ppm -	PROTON GROUP	ENVIRONMENTAL GROUPS	S	SOLVENT
729M	C	8.00	CHA	AAN(C*-C(CL)-N)		CDCL3
730M	D	8.02	CHA	AAN(C*-C(CL)-N)		CDCL3
1964M	D	8.29	CHA	AAN(C*-C(NO2))		DMSO
1964M	D	8.50	CHA	AAN(C*-C(NO2))		DMSO
1964M	C	8.29	CHA	AAN(C*-C(OH)-N)		DMSO
1964M	C	8.50	CHA	AAN(C*-C(OH)-N)		DMSO
727M	D	7.88	CHA	AAN(C*-N)		CDCL3
720M	D	8.04	CHA	AAN(C*-N)		CDCL3
726M	B	7.82	CHA	AAN(C*-N-C(I))		CDCL3
721M	F	7.99	CHA	AAN(C*-N/CH-C(CH3))		CDCL3
721M	C	7.29	CHA	AAN(C*/CH-C(CH3))		CDCL3
1357M	A	7.39	CHA	AAR5NN(CH-C*/CH-CH-C*)		DMSO-D6
1357M	C	7.95	CHA	AAR5NN(C*-CH-C*)		DMSO-D6
1357M	B	7.60	CHA	AAR5NN(C*-NH-C(=S)/C*)		DMSO-D6
207M	C	7.38	CHA	AAR5(CH-C*-CH2/CH-C*)		CDCL3
207M	B	7.16	CHA	AAR5(C*-CH2-CH2)		CDCL3
207M	D	7.53	CHA	AAR5(C*/CH-CH-C*)		CDCL3
2274M	A	7.95	CHA	AAR60<CH-C*-C(=O)/CH-C*>		TFA
2274M	C	8.71	CHA	AAR60<C*-C(=O)-O/CH-CH-C*>		TFA
2274M	B	8.46	CHA	AAR60<C*/CH-CH-C*>		TFA
317M	A	7.11	CHA	AA<CH-C(CL)-C*/CH-C*>		CCL4
402M	B	7.43	CHA	AA<CH-C*-C(BR)/CH-CH-C*>		CDCL3
1954M	C	7.05- 7.45	CHA	AA<CH-C*-C(CH2.2-C:N)/CH-CH-C*>		POLYSOL-D
1957M	B	7.22	CHA	AA<CH-C*-C(OH)/CH-C(OH)-C*>		DMSO-D6
1293M	C	7.66	CHA	AA<CH-C*-C(SO2-OH)/CH-CH-C*>		DMSO-D6
2119M	C	7.63 APP.	CHA	AA<CH-C*-C(=O)/CH-CH-C*>		CDCL3
206M	A	7.46 APP.	CHA	AA<CH-C*/CH-CH-C*>		CDCL3
1309M	A	7.53	CHA	AA<CH-C*/CH-CH-C*>	S	DMSO-D6
203M	B	7.31	CHA	AA<CH-C*/CH-CH-C*>		CDCL3
1367M	B	7.51 APP.	CHA	AA<CH-C*/CH-CH-C*>		POLYSOL-D
1293M	B	7.63	CHA	AA<CH-C*/CH-CH-C*>		DMSO-D6
1954M	C	7.05- 7.45	CHA	AA<CH-C*/CH-CH-C*>		POLYSOL-D
1953M	E	7.17	CHA	AA<CH-C*/CH-C(OH)-C*>		DMSO-D6
402M	A	7.40	CHA	AA<C(BR)-C*/CH-C(BR)-C*>		CDCL3
205M	C	7.12	CHA	AA<C(CH3)-CH-C*/CH-C*>		CDCL3
2245M	C	8.39	CHA	AA<C(C(=O)-CL)-C*/CH-CH-C*>		CCL4
540M	C	6.60	CHA	AA<C(NH2)-CH-C*/CH-C*>		POLYSOL-D
1953M	B	6.61	CHA	AA<C(NH2)-CH-C*/CH-C*-C(OH)>		DMSO-D6
1293M	A	7.39	CHA	AA<C(NH2)-C(SO2-OH)-C*/CH-C*>		DMSO-D6
600M	D	6.42	CHA	AA<C(NH-CH2)-C*/CH-CH-C*>		CCL4
1958M	A	7.00	CHA	AA<C(OH)-CH-C*/CH-C*>		C3D60
1954M	D	7.22	CHA	AA<C(OH)-C(CH2.2-C:N)-C*/CH-C*>		POLYSOL-D
1955M	A	6.56	CHA	AA<C(OH)-C(NO)-C*/CH-C*>		CDCL3
1957M	A	6.89	CHA	AA<C(OH)-C*/CH-C*>		DMSO-D6
1953M	D	6.75- 7.10	CHA	AA<C(OH)-C*/CH-CH-C*>		DMSO-D6
2930M	B	7.17	CHA	AA<C(O-C(=O)-CH3)-CH-C*/CH-C*>		CDCL3
1286M	C	8.16	CHA	AA<C(SO2-CL)-C*/CH-CH-C*>		POLYSOL-D
1367M	D	7.92 APP.	CHA	AA<C(SO2-NH2)-CH-C*/CH-C*>		POLYSOL-D
1311M	B	7.99	CHA	AA<C(SO3-NA)-CH-C*/CH-C*>		D20
2119M	B	6.76	CHA	AA<C(=O)-C*/C(CH3)-C(=O)-C*>		CDCL3
825M	C	7.80	CHA	AA<C*>	S	DMSO-D6
201M	D	7.62	CHA	AA<C*>		CCL4
1293M	D	7.87	CHA	AA<C*>		DMSO-D6
600M	F	7.64 APP.	CHA	AA<C*>		CCL4
1954M	F	7.70	CHA	AA<C*>		POLYSOL-D
203M	D	7.62	CHA	AA<C*-CH-C(CH3)>		CDCL3
205M	E	7.53	CHA	AA<C*-CH-C(CH3)/CH-C(CH3)>		CDCL3
1953M	D	6.75- 7.10	CHA	AA<C*-CH-C(NH2)/CH-CH-C(OH)>		DMSO-D6
540M	B	6.52	CHA	AA<C*-CH-C(NH2)/C(NH2)>		POLYSOL-D
825M	C	7.80	CHA	AA<C*-CH-C(NH-NH2)>	S	DMSO-D6
1958M	B	7.10	CHA	AA<C*-CH-C(OH)/C(OH)>		C3D60
1311M	C	8.40	CHA	AA<C*-CH-C(SO3-NA)/C(SO3-NA)>		D20
402M	C	8.06	CHA	AA<C*-C(BR)>		CDCL3
1954M	G	7.81	CHA	AA<C*-C(CH2.2-C:N)-C(OH)>		POLYSOL-D
201M	E	7.85	CHA	AA<C*-C(CH2-CH3)>		CCL4
317M	C	8.15	CHA	AA<C*-C(CL)>		CCL4
2245M	D	8.63	CHA	AA<C*-C(C(=O)-CL)>		CCL4
233M	B	8.01	CHA	AA<C*-C(F)>		CDCL3
600M	F	7.64 APP.	CHA	AA<C*-C(NH-CH2)>		CCL4
1955M	D	8.31	CHA	AA<C*-C(NO)-C(OH)>		CDCL3
1956M	D	8.18	CHA	AA<C*-C(OH)>		C3H60
1953M	F	8.03	CHA	AA<C*-C(OH)-CH-C(NH2)>		DMSO-D6
1957M	C	7.66	CHA	AA<C*-C(OH)/CH-CH-C(OH)>		DMSO-D6
873M	E	8.54	CHA	AA<C*-C(ON(NH2))>		POLYSOL-D
1286M	B	7.91 APP.	CHA	AA<C*-C(SO2-CL)>		POLYSOL-D
1293M	F	9.06	CHA	AA<C*-C(SO2-OH)-C(NH2)>		DMSO-D6
1292M	B	8.51	CHA	AA<C*-C(SO3-H)>		TFA
2119M	D	7.94 APP.	CHA	AA<C*-C(=O)>		CDCL3
2119M	D	7.94 APP.	CHA	AA<C*-C(=O)-C(CH3)>		CDCL3
2245M	B	7.89	CHA	AA<C*/CH-CH-C(C(=O)-CL)>		CCL4
1286M	B	7.91 APP.	CHA	AA<C*/CH-CH-C(SO2-CL)>		POLYSOL-D

BOOK NO.	ASSIGN-MENT	CHEM SHIFT - ppm -	PROTON GROUP	ENVIRONMENTAL GROUPS	S	SOLVENT
540M	D	7.34	CHA	AA<C*/CH-C(NH2)>		POLYSOL-D
1293M	E	8.04	CHA	AA<C*/CH-C(NH2)-C(SO2-OH)>		DMSO-D6
825M	B	7.71	CHA	AA<C*/CH-C(NH-NH2)>	S	DMSO-D6
1958M	C	7.65	CHA	AA<C*/CH-C(OH)>		C3D6O
1954M	E	7.61	CHA	AA<C*/CH-C(OH)-C(CH2.2-C:N)>		POLYSOL-D
1955M	C	7.67	CHA	AA<C*/CH-C(OH)-C(NO)>		CDCL3
1367M	D	7.92 APP.	CHA	AA<C*/CH-C(SO2-NH2)>		POLYSOL-D
1311M	A	7.79	CHA	AA<C*/CH-C(SO3-NA)>		D2O
203M	C	7.48	CHA	AA<C*/C(CH3)-C(CH3)>		CDCL3
2113M	C	8.32	CHA	AA<C*/C(C(=O)-CH3>		CCL4
1000M	B	8.10	CHA	AA<C*/C(C:N)>		CDCL3
1953M	C	6.87	CHA	AA<C*/C(NH2)>		DMSO-D6
1956M	B	6.81	CHA	AA<C*/C(OH)-CH-C(OH)>		C3H6O
1367M	E	8.45	CHA	AA<C*/C(SO2-NH2)>		POLYSOL-D
1309M	C	8.28	CHA	AA<C*/C(SO3-NA)	S	DMSO-D6
318M	A	6.78	CHA	AA<C-C*-CH/C(CL)>		CDCL3
400M	A	8.15	CHA	AA<C-C*-C(BR)>		CCL4
206M	B	7.65- 8.05	CHA	AA<C-C*/CH-CH-CH-C*>		CDCL3
206M	C	8.11	CHA	AA<C-C*/C(AA)-CH-CH-C*>		CDCL3
999M	A	7.33	CHA	AA(CH-C(C:N)-C*/CH-C*)		CDCL3
438M	A	7.00	CHA	AA(CH-C(I)-C*/CH-C*)		CDCL3
2340M	B	7.34	CHA	AA(CH-C*)		CDCL3
1310M	C	7.55	CHA	AA(CH-C*-C(NH2)/CH-CH-C*)		D2O
604M	C	7.80	CHA	AA(CH-C*-C(NH-A)/CH-CH-C*)		CCL4
1952M	E	7.32 APP.	CHA	AA(CH-C*-C(OH)/CH-CH-C*)		CDCL3
1310M	B	7.41	CHA	AA(CH-C*-C(SO3-NA)/CH-CH-C*)		D2O
998M	B	7.30- 7.65	CHA	AA(CH-C*/CH-CH-C*)		POLYSOL-D
604M	C	7.80	CHA	AA(CH-C*/CH-CH-C*)		CCL4
1952M	E	7.32 APP.	CHA	AA(CH-C*/CH-CH-C*)		CDCL3
1241M	B	7.02	CHA	AA(CH-C*/CH-C(SH)-C*)		CDCL3
401M	B	7.91	CHA	AA(C(BR)/C*)		CCL4
998M	B	7.30- 7.65	CHA	AA(C(CH2-C:N)-CH-C*/CH-C*)		POLYSOL-D
1952M	C	7.06	CHA	AA(C(CH3)-C(OH)-C*/CH-C*)		CDCL3
539M	B	6.59	CHA	AA(C(NH2)-C*/CH-CH-C*)		CDCL3
1310M	A	6.76	CHA	AA(C(NH2)-C*/CH-C(SO3-NA)-C*)		D2O
599M	C	6.49	CHA	AA(C(NH-CH3)-C*/CH-CH-C*)		CDCL3
1950M	A	7.01	CHA	AA(C(OH)-C*)		C3H6O
1570M	C	6.60	CHA	AA(C(O-CH2)-C*/CH-CH-C*)		CDCL3
1569M	B	6.51	CHA	AA(C(O-CH3)/CH-CH-C*)		CCL4
1242M	B	7.15	CHA	AA(C(SH)-CH-C*/CH-C*)		CDCL3
1310M	E	8.09	CHA	AA(C(SO3-NA)-C*/CH-C(NH2)-C*)		D2O
438M	C	7.65	CHA	AA(C*)		CDCL3
1241M	D	7.57	CHA	AA(C*)		CDCL3
1950M	D	8.41	CHA	AA(C*)		C3H6O
1570M	E	7.70	CHA	AA(C*)		CDCL3
1952M	F	7.69	CHA	AA(C*)		CDCL3
999M	C	8.11	CHA	AA(C*-C(C:N))		CDCL3
438M	E	8.01	CHA	AA(C*-C(I))		CDCL3
1310M	D	7.76	CHA	AA(C*-C(NH2))		D2O
671M	B	6.80- 8.30	CHA	AA(C*-C(N(CH3/CH3)))		CCL4
922M	B	8.00	CHA	AA(C*-C(N=C=O))		CDCL3
1950M	C	7.72	CHA	AA(C*-C(OH))		C3H6O
1952M	G	8.06	CHA	AA(C*-C(OH)-C(CH3))		CDCL3
1570M	F	8.33	CHA	AA(C*-C(O-CH2))		CDCL3
1569M	E	8.12	CHA	AA(C*-C(O-CH3))		CCL4
1241M	E	8.04	CHA	AA(C*-C(SH))		CDCL3
1310M	F	8.83	CHA	AA(C*-C(SO3-NA))		D2O
438M	D	7.99	CHA	AA(C*/CH-CH-C(I))		CDCL3
1569M	D	7.60	CHA	AA(C*/CH-CH-C(O-CH3))		CCL4
1952M	D	7.30	CHA	AA(C*/CH-C(CH3)-C(OH))		CDCL3
2340M	D	8.10	CHA	AA(C*/C(NH-C(=O)))		CDCL3
750M	B	7.72	CHA	ANAAN<CH-N-C*/CH-C*>		C3H6O
751M	B	7.47	CHA	ANAAN<C(CH3)-N-C*/CH-C*>		POLYSOL-D
750M	D	8.41	CHA	ANAAN<C*/CH-CH-N>		C3H6O
751M	D	8.13	CHA	ANAAN<C*/CH-C(CH3)-N>		POLYSOL-D
750M	E	9.19	CHA	ANAAN<N-C*-C*/CH-CH-C*>		C3H6O
749M	A	7.23	CHA	ANAA<CH-N-C</CH-C*-C*>		CDCL3
749M	F	8.55	CHA	ANAA<C*-C*/CH-CH-C>		CDCL3
746M	C	7.53	CHA	ANAA<C-C*-CH/C*-CH>		CCL4
749M	G	8.83	CHA	ANAA<N-C*/CH-CH-C*>		CDCL3
748M	E	9.18	CHA	ANAA<N-C*/C*>		CDCL3
718M	A	7.13	CHA	ANA<CH-N-C*/CH-C*>		CCL4
725M	A	7.22	CHA	ANA<CH-N-C*/CH-C*>		CCL4
723M	B	7.12	CHA	ANA<CH-N-C*/CH-C*>		CCL4
719M	B	7.05	CHA	ANA<C(CH3)-N-C*/CH-C*>		CCL4
1794M	I	7.50 APP.	CHA	ANA<C(CH(OH/R6R6N*BI))-C*/CH-N-C*>		POLYSOL-D
724M	A	7.29	CHA	ANA<C(CL)-N-C*/CH-C*>		CDCL3
764M	B	6.85	CHA	ANA<C(NH-NH2)-N-C*/CH-C*>		POLYSOL-D
1961M	A	6.57	CHA	ANA<C(OH)-N-C*/CH-C*>		DMSO
1963M	B	7.11	CHA	ANA<C(OH)-N-C*/C(CH3)-C*>		TFA
1174M	A	6.91	CHA	ANA<C(S-A)-N-C*/CH-C*>		CDCL3

BOOK NO.	ASSIGN-MENT	CHEM SHIFT - ppm -	PROTON GROUP	ENVIRONMENTAL GROUPS	S	SOLVENT
722M	D	7.82	CHA	ANA<C*/CH-CH-N>		CCL4
723M	D	7.84	CHA	ANA<C*/CH-CH-N>		CCL4
719M	D	7.82	CHA	ANA<C*/CH-C(CH3)-N>		CCL4
724M	C	7.95	CHA	ANA<C*/CH-C(CL)-N>		CDCL3
1961M	C	7.91	CHA	ANA<C*/CH-C(OH)-N>		DMSO
2183M	C	8.58	CHA	ANA<C*/C(C(=O)-H)-CH-N>		CDCL3
826M	B	8.46	CHA	ANA<C*/C(NH-NH2)-CH-N>	S	D20
723M	E	8.79	CHA	ANA<N-C*-C(CH3)/CH-CH-C*>		CCL4
725M	C	8.82	CHA	ANA<N-C*/CH-CH-C*>		CCL4
718M	C	8.84	CHA	ANA<N-C*/CH-CH-C*>		CCL4
722M	F	8.79	CHA	ANA<N-C*/CH-CH-C*>		CCL4
1794M	K	8.66	CHA	ANA<C*/CH-C(CH(OH/R6R6N*BI))-C*>		POLYSOL-D
2183M	D	9.31	CHA	ANA<N-C*/C(C(=O)-H)-CH-C*>		CDCL3
826M	C	8.95	CHA	ANA<N-C*/C(NH-NH2)-CH-C*>	S	D20
721M	B	7.15	CHA	ANA(CH-N-C*/CH-C*)		CDCL3
1962M	B	7.44	CHA	ANA(CH-N-C*/CH-C*)		CDCL3
720M	B	7.18	CHA	ANA(C(CH3)-C*/CH-N-C*)		CDCL3
721M	E	7.82	CHA	ANA(C*-CH-C(CH3)/CH-CH-N)		CDCL3
2868M	B	8.00	CHA	ANA(C*/CH-CH-N)		CDCL3
1962M	C	7.99	CHA	ANA(C*/CH-CH-N)		CDCL3
729M	A	7.35	CHA	ANA(C*/CH-N-C(CL))		CDCL3
1731M	E	8.03	CHA	ANA(C*/C(CH2-OH)-CH-N)		CDCL3
730M	B	7.11	CHA	ANA(C*/C(CH3)-N-C(CL))		CDCL3
727M	B	7.10	CHA	ANA(C*/C(NH2)-CH-N)		CDCL3
731M	D	9.02	CHA	ANA(N-CH-C(BR)/C*)		CDCL3
728M	B	8.43	CHA	ANA(N-CH-C*/CH-C*)		CCL4
731M	C	8.62	CHA	ANA(N-CH-C*/C(BR)-C*)		CDCL3
729M	D	8.16	CHA	ANA(N-C(CL)-C*/CH-C*)		CDCL3
1964M	E	7.93	CHA	ANA(N-C(OH)-C*/C(NO2)-C*)		DMSO
1962M	E	8.71	CHA	ANA(N-C*-C(OH)/CH-CH-C*)		CDCL3
2868M	C	8.62	CHA	ANA(N-C*-C(O-C(=O)-A)/CH-CH-C*)		CDCL3
721M	G	8.78	CHA	ANA(N-C*/CH-CH-C*)		CDCL3
720M	E	8.73	CHA	ANA(N-C*/CH-C(CH3)-C*)		CDCL3
1731M	F	8.75	CHA	ANA(N-C*/C(CH2-OH)-CH-C*)		CDCL3
727M	E	8.48	CHA	ANA(N-C*/C(NH2)-CH-C*)		CDCL3
1885M	F	7.17	CHA	ANC(C(CH2/CH3/CH3))/CH-C(OH))		CCL4
742M	C	9.55	CHA	ANNA(N-C(CL)-C*/N-C*)		TFA
734M	A	6.79	CHA	ANN<CH-N-C(NH2)/CH-N>		D20
1960M	A	6.40	CHA	ANN<CH-N-C(OH)/CH-N>		DMSO-D6
733M	A	7.52	CHA	ANN<C(CL)-N/C(CL)-N>		CDCL3
1582M	B	8.10	CHA	ANN<N-CH-C(O-CH3)/CH-N>		CDCL3
1732M	E	8.79	CHA	ANN<N-C(CH2.2-OH)-N/C(A)>		CDCL3
733M	B	8.89	CHA	ANN<N-C(CL)/N-C(CL)>		CDCL3
734M	B	8.39	CHA	ANN<N-C(NH2)-N>		D20
1960M	B	8.29	CHA	ANN<N-C(OH)-N>		DMSO-D6
1582M	C	8.21	CHA	ANN<N-C(O-CH3)/CH-N>		CDCL3
1582M	B	8.10	CHA	ANN<N/C(O-CH3)-N>		CDCL3
732M	B	7.62	CHA	ANN(C(A)-N/CH-N)		CDCL3
732M	D	8.70	CHA	ANN(N-CH-N/CH-C(A))		CDCL3
732M	E	9.28	CHA	ANN(N-C(A)/N)		CDCL3
1942M	B	8.52	CHA	AN<CH-CH-N>		POLYSOL-D
842M	C	8.72	CHA	AN<CH-CH-N(+)(CH3)>		POLYSOL-D
716M	B	7.77	CHA	AN<CH-C(AN<C-N>)-N>		CDCL3
703M	B	7.49 APP.	CHA	AN<CH-C(BR)-N>		CCL4
687M	G	7.45	CHA	AN<CH-C(CH2-CH2)-N>		CCL4
705M	E	7.35- 7.75	CHA	AN<CH-C(CH2-N)-N>		CDCL3
1728M	E	7.69	CHA	AN<CH-C(CH2-OH)-N>		CDCL3
712M	F	7.59	CHA	AN<CH-C(CH2-R6N)-N>		CDCL3
689M	F	7.47	CHA	AN<CH-C(CH(CH2.3/CH2.3))-N>		CCL4
702M	A	7.22	CHA	AN<CH-C(CL)-C(CL)/CH-N>		CDCL3
700M	C	7.68	CHA	AN<CH-C(CL)-N>		CCL4
694M	C	7.43	CHA	AN<CH-C(C(CH3/CH3/CH3))-N/CH-C(C(CH3/CH3/CH3))>		CCL4
2110M	C	7.81	CHA	AN<CH-C(C(=O)-CH3)-N>		CCL4
1334M	C	7.71	CHA	AN<CH-C(C(=S)-NH2)-N/CH-C(CH3)>		POLYSOL-D
699M	B	7.14	CHA	AN<CH-C(F)-N>		CCL4
708M	F	7.36	CHA	AN<CH-C(NH-CH2)-N>		CDCL3
2341M	C	7.70	CHA	AN<CH-C(NH-C(=O))-N>		CDCL3
1581M	F	7.58	CHA	AN<CH-C(O-CH2)-N>		CDCL3
882M	B	7.75	CHA	AN<CH-C(QN(QN(AN)))-N>		CDCL3
1942M	A	8.06	CHA	AN<CH-N>		POLYSOL-D
842M	B	8.26	CHA	AN<CH-N(+)(CH3)>		POLYSOL-D
844M	B	7.79 APP.	CHA	AN<CH-N(+)(CH3)/CH-C(NH2)>		D20
716M	A	7.25	CHA	AN<CH-N-C(AN<C-N>)>		CDCL3
697M	A	6.99	CHA	AN<CH-N-C(A)>		CDCL3
703M	A	7.20	CHA	AN<CH-N-C(BR)>		CCL4
687M	E	6.95	CHA	AN<CH-N-C(CH2-CH2)>		CCL4
705M	D	7.06	CHA	AN<CH-N-C(CH2-N)>		CDCL3
1728M	C	7.15	CHA	AN<CH-N-C(CH2-OH)>		CDCL3
712M	D	7.06	CHA	AN<CH-N-C(CH2-R6N)>		CDCL3
689M	E	6.97 APP.	CHA	AN<CH-N-C(CH(CH2.3/CH2.3))>		CCL4
700M	A	7.20	CHA	AN<CH-N-C(CL)>		CCL4

BOOK NO.	ASSIGN-MENT	CHEM SHIFT - ppm -	PROTON GROUP	ENVIRONMENTAL GROUPS	S	SOLVENT
2110M	B	7.39	CHA	AN<CH-N-C(C(=O)-CH3)>		CCL4
699M	A	6.89	CHA	AN<CH-N-C(F)>		CCL4
708M	E	6.45	CHA	AN<CH-N-C(NH-CH2)>		CDCL3
2341M	B	7.03	CHA	AN<CH-N-C(NH-C(=O))>		CDCL3
1581M	E	6.80	CHA	AN<CH-N-C(O-CH2)>		CDCL3
882M	A	7.31	CHA	AN<CH-N-C(QN(QN(AN)))>		CDCL3
713M	C	7.17	CHA	AN<CH-N/CH-C(CH2.2-AN)>		CDCL3
709M	C	6.91 APP.	CHA	AN<CH-N/CH-C(CH2-A)>		DMSO-D6
2346M	B	7.23	CHA	AN<CH-N/CH-C(C(=O)-NH)>		CDCL3
2409M	B	7.46	CHA	AN<CH-N/CH-C(C(=O)-NH)>		DMSO-D6
1002M	A	7.55	CHA	AN<CH-N/CH-C(C:N)>		CDCL3
1959M	A	7.23	CHA	AN<CH-N/CH-C(OH)>		DMSO-D6
716M	C	8.42	CHA	AN<C(AN<C-N>)-N>		CDCL3
703M	B	7.49 APP.	CHA	AN<C(BR)-N>		CCL4
821M	A	8.41	CHA	AN<C(BR)/CH-N>	S	D20
713M	D	7.43	CHA	AN<C(CH2.2-AN)-CH-N>		CDCL3
713M	B	7.06	CHA	AN<C(CH2.2-AN)/CH-N>		CDCL3
687M	F	7.02	CHA	AN<C(CH2-CH2)-N>		CCL4
685M	C	7.02	CHA	AN<C(CH2-CH3)/CH-N>		CCL4
705M	E	7.35- 7.75	CHA	AN<C(CH2-N)-N>		CDCL3
1728M	D	7.35	CHA	AN<C(CH2-OH)-N>		CDCL3
712M	E	7.40	CHA	AN<C(CH2-R6N)-N>		CDCL3
692M	B	7.17	CHA	AN<C(CH3)-CH-N/C(CH3)>		CCL4
695M	C	6.59	CHA	AN<C(CH3)-N-C(CH3)/C(CH3)>		CCL4
1334M	B	7.29	CHA	AN<C(CH3)-N-C(C(=S)-NH2)>		POLYSOL-D
689M	E	6.97 APP.	CHA	AN<C(CH(CH2.3/CH2.3))-N>		CCL4
686M	C	7.09	CHA	AN<C(CH(CH3/CH3))/CH-N>		CDCL3
707M	C	7.42	CHA	AN<C(CL)-CH-N/CH-C(NH2)>		DMSO-D6
702M	B	7.78	CHA	AN<C(CL)-C(CL)-N>		CDCL3
700M	B	7.29	CHA	AN<C(CL)-N>		CCL4
694M	B	7.04	CHA	AN<C(C(CH3/CH3/CH3))-N-C(C(CH3/CH3/CH3))>		CCL4
696M	C	6.90	CHA	AN<C(C(CH3/CH3/CH3))-N-C(C(CH3/CH3/CH3))/C(CH3)>		CDCL3
2112M	C	8.08	CHA	AN<C(C(=O)-A)-CH-N>		CDCL3
2110M	D	7.90	CHA	AN<C(C(=O)-CH3)-N>		CCL4
2409M	C	8.18	CHA	AN<C(C(=O)-NH)-CH-N>		DMSO-D6
2346M	E	8.09	CHA	AN<C(C(=O)-NH)-CH-N>		CDCL3
1334M	D	8.40	CHA	AN<C(C(=S)-NH2)-N-C(CH3)>		POLYSOL-D
1002M	B	8.11	CHA	AN<C(C:N)-CH-N>		CDCL3
699M	C	7.77	CHA	AN<C(F)-N>		CCL4
844M	B	7.79 APP.	CHA	AN<C(NH2)-CH-N(+)(CH3)>		D20
707M	B	6.58	CHA	AN<C(NH2)-N/CH-C(CL)>		DMSO-D6
709M	C	6.91 APP.	CHA	AN<C(NH-CH2)-CH-N>		DMSO-D6
708M	E	6.45	CHA	AN<C(NH-CH2)-N>		CDCL3
2341M	D	8.27 APP.	CHA	AN<C(NH-C(=O))-N>		CDCL3
710M	B	6.50	CHA	AN<C(N(CH3/CH3))/CH-N>		CDCL3
1959M	A	7.23	CHA	AN<C(OH)-CH-N>		DMSO-D6
1581M	E	6.80	CHA	AN<C(O-CH2)-N>		CDCL3
882M	C	8.13	CHA	AN<C(QN(QN(AN)))-N>		CDCL3
1172M	A	6.92	CHA	AN<C(S-A)/CH-N>		CDCL3
1942M	D	8.89	CHA	AN<N>		POLYSOL-D
842M	D	9.18	CHA	AN<N(+)(CH3)>		POLYSOL-D
844M	C	8.13 APP.	CHA	AN<N(+)(CH3)-CH-C(NH2)>		D20
844M	C	8.13 APP.	CHA	AN<N(+)(CH3)/C(NH2)>		D20
692M	C	8.12	CHA	AN<N-CH-C(CH3)/C(CH3)>		CCL4
2112M	D	8.78	CHA	AN<N-CH-C(C(=O)-A)>		CDCL3
2409M	D	8.70	CHA	AN<N-CH-C(C(=O)-NH)>		DMSO-D6
2346M	F	8.55	CHA	AN<N-CH-C(C(=O)-NH)>		CDCL3
1002M	C	8.89	CHA	AN<N-CH-C(C:N)>		CDCL3
709M	F	8.10	CHA	AN<N-CH-C(NH-CH2)>		DMSO-D6
1959M	B	8.09	CHA	AN<N-CH-C(OH)>		DMSO-D6
714M	C	8.59	CHA	AN<N-CH-C(Q2(AN<C-N>))>		CDCL3
716M	D	8.67	CHA	AN<N-C(AN<C-N>)>		CDCL3
697M	D	8.59	CHA	AN<N-C(A)>		CDCL3
703M	C	8.27	CHA	AN<N-C(BR)>		CCL4
687M	H	8.43	CHA	AN<N-C(CH2-CH2)>		CCL4
705M	F	8.52	CHA	AN<N-C(CH2-N)>		CDCL3
1728M	F	8.50	CHA	AN<N-C(CH2-OH)>		CDCL3
712M	G	8.52	CHA	AN<N-C(CH2-R6N)>		CDCL3
689M	G	8.49	CHA	AN<N-C(CH(CH2.3/CH2.3))>		CCL4
700M	D	8.37	CHA	AN<N-C(CL)>		CCL4
702M	C	8.30	CHA	AN<N-C(CL)-C(CL)>		CDCL3
2110M	E	8.71	CHA	AN<N-C(C(=O)-CH3)>		CCL4
699M	D	8.18	CHA	AN<N-C(F)>		CCL4
707M	D	7.94	CHA	AN<N-C(NH2)/C(CL)>		DMSO-D6
708M	G	8.07	CHA	AN<N-C(NH-CH2)>		CDCL3
2341M	D	8.27 APP.	CHA	AN<N-C(NH-C(=O))>		CDCL3
1581M	G	8.18	CHA	AN<N-C(O-CH3)>		CDCL3
882M	E	8.70	CHA	AN<N-C(QN(QN(AN)))>		CDCL3
714M	B	8.49	CHA	AN<N-C(Q2(AN<C-CH-N>))>		CDCL3
698M	B	8.63	CHA	AN<N/CH-C(A)>		CDCL3
821M	B	8.77	CHA	AN<N/CH-C(BR)>	S	D20

: REPRESENTS TRIPLE BOND, ¬ REPRESENTS AN ARROW AND < AND > REPRESENT BRACKETS.   PAGE   318

BOOK NO.	ASSIGN-MENT	CHEM SHIFT - ppm -	PROTON GROUP	ENVIRONMENTAL GROUPS	S	SOLVENT
685M	D	8.41	CHA	AN<N/CH-C(CH2-CH3)>		CCL4
686M	D	8.43	CHA	AN<N/CH-C(CH(CH3/CH3))>		CDCL3
710M	C	8.25	CHA	AN<N/CH-C(N(CH3/CH3))>		CDCL3
715M	B	8.52 APP.	CHA	AN<N/CH-C(Q2(AN))>		CDCL3
1172M	C	8.33	CHA	AN<N/CH-C(S-A)>		CDCL3
2112M	E	8.97	CHA	AN<N/C(C(=O)-A)>		CDCL3
2409M	E	9.04	CHA	AN<N/C(C(=O)-NH)>		DMSO-D6
2346M	G	8.92	CHA	AN<N/C(C(=O)-NH)>		CDCL3
1002M	D	8.93	CHA	AN<N/C(C:N)>		CDCL3
709M	E	7.79	CHA	AN<N/C(NH-CH2)>		DMSO-D6
1959M	C	8.21	CHA	AN<N/C(OH)>		DMSO-D6
714M	D	8.79	CHA	AN<N/C(Q2(AN<C-N>))>		CDCL3
1312M	I	8.38	CHA	AN(CH-CH-N(CH2-CH2))	S	CDCL3
847M	B	8.41	CHA	AN(CH-CH-N(>O))	S	D2O
845M	C	8.81	CHA	AN(CH-CH-N(+)(CH2-CH2))	S	D2O
843M	F	8.67	CHA	AN(CH-CH-N(+)(CH2-CH2))	S	DMSO-D6
681M	B	7.55	CHA	AN(CH-CH-N)		CCL4
2938M	E	7.61	CHA	AN(CH-C(CH2-C(=O)-O)-N)		CDCL3
682M	B	6.91 APP.	CHA	AN(CH-C(CH3)-N)		CCL4
2111M	D	7.69	CHA	AN(CH-C(C(=O)-CH3)-N/CH-C(CH3))		CDCL3
2408M	C	7.76	CHA	AN(CH-C(C(=O)-NH)-N)		CDCL3
706M	D	7.22	CHA	AN(CH-C(NH2)-N)		CDCL3
878M	D	7.71	CHA	AN(CH-C(QN(CH3/NH-A))-N)		DMSO-D6
1312M	H	7.99	CHA	AN(CH-N(CH2-CH2))	S	CDCL3
847M	A	8.10	CHA	AN(CH-N(>O))	S	D2O
845M	B	8.29	CHA	AN(CH-N(+)(CH2-CH2))	S	D2O
843M	E	8.19	CHA	AN(CH-N(+)(CH2-CH2))	S	DMSO-D6
681M	A	7.14	CHA	AN(CH-N)		CCL4
2938M	C	7.15	CHA	AN(CH-N-C(CH2-C(=O)-O))		CDCL3
682M	C	7.40	CHA	AN(CH-N-C(CH3))		CCL4
2408M	B	7.37	CHA	AN(CH-N-C(C(=O)-NH))		CDCL3
706M	C	6.48	CHA	AN(CH-N-C(NH2))		CDCL3
704M	A	7.10	CHA	AN(CH-N/CH-C(BR))		CCL4
683M	B	7.01	CHA	AN(CH-N/CH-C(CH3))		CCL4
683M	B	7.35	CHA	AN(CH-N/CH-C(CH3))		CCL4
701M	A	7.15	CHA	AN(CH-N/CH-C(CL))		CCL4
2606M	A	8.53	CHA	AN(CH-N/CH-C(C(=O)-OH))	S	D2O
2939M	E	7.38	CHA	AN(CH-N/CH-C(C(=O)-O-CH2))		CDCL3
711M	D	7.13	CHA	AN(CH-N/CH-C(R5N(CH-CH2/CH2)))		CCL4
717M	A	7.51	CHA	AN(C(AN(C-CH-CH-N))/CH-N)		CDCL3
704M	B	7.74	CHA	AN(C(BR)-CH-N)		CCL4
693M	D	7.31	CHA	AN(C(CH2.3-CH3)-CH-N/C(CH2.3-CH3))		CDCL3
688M	D	6.96	CHA	AN(C(CH2-CH2)/CH-N)		CCL4
2938M	D	7.29	CHA	AN(C(CH2-C(=O)-O)-N)		CDCL3
1729M	C	7.32	CHA	AN(C(CH2-OH)/CH-N)		CDCL3
690M	D	6.99	CHA	AN(C(CH3)-CH-C(CH3)/CH-N)		CDCL3
683M	C	7.01	CHA	AN(C(CH3)-CH-N)		CCL4
683M	C	7.35	CHA	AN(C(CH3)-CH-N)		CCL4
691M	D	7.28	CHA	AN(C(CH3)-CH-N/CH-C(CH3))		CDCL3
682M	B	6.91 APP.	CHA	AN(C(CH3)-N)		CCL4
2111M	C	7.30	CHA	AN(C(CH3)-N-C(C(=O)-CH3))		CDCL3
691M	C	6.95	CHA	AN(C(CH3)-N/CH-C(CH3))		CDCL3
684M	B	6.98	CHA	AN(C(CH3)/CH-N)		CCL4
701M	B	7.59	CHA	AN(C(CL)-CH-N)		CCL4
2111M	E	7.81	CHA	AN(C(C(=O)-CH3)-N-C(CH3))		CDCL3
2408M	D	8.15	CHA	AN(C(C(=O)-NH)-N)		CDCL3
895M	A	7.73	CHA	AN(C(C(=O)-NH)/CH-N)		DMSO
2606M	B	9.28 APP.	CHA	AN(C(C(=O)-OH)-CH-N)	S	D2O
2939M	F	8.29	CHA	AN(C(C(=O)-O-CH2)-CH-N)		CDCL3
706M	B	6.36	CHA	AN(C(NH2)-N)		CDCL3
878M	E	8.10	CHA	AN(C(QN(CH3/NH-A))-N)		DMSO-D6
711M	E	7.62	CHA	AN(C(R5N(CH-CH2/CH2))-CH-N)		CCL4
690M	C	6.97	CHA	AN(C/CH3)-N/C(CH3))		CDCL3
1312M	J	9.16	CHA	AN(N(CH2-CH2))	S	CDCL3
847M	C	8.68	CHA	AN(N(>O))	S	D2O
845M	D	9.01	CHA	AN(N(+)(CH2-CH2))	S	D2O
843M	G	9.18	CHA	AN(N(+)(CH2-CH2))	S	DMSO-D6
681M	C	8.51	CHA	AN(N)		CCL4
704M	C	8.48	CHA	AN(N-CH-C(BR))		CCL4
693M	E	8.30	CHA	AN(N-CH-C(CH2.3-CH3)/C(CH2.3-CH3))		CDCL3
683M	D	8.35	CHA	AN(N-CH-C(CH3))		CCL4
701M	C	8.41	CHA	AN(N-CH-C(CL))		CCL4
2606M	B	9.28 APP.	CHA	AN(N-CH-C(C(=O)-OH))	S	D2O
2939M	G	8.77	CHA	AN(N-CH-C(C(=O)-O-CH2))		CDCL3
711M	F	8.52	CHA	AN(N-CH-C(R5N(CH-CH2/CH2)))		CCL4
2938M	F	8.51	CHA	AN(N-C(CH2-C(=O)-O))		CDCL3
682M	D	8.37	CHA	AN(N-C(CH3))		CCL4
690M	E	8.35	CHA	AN(N-C(CH3)/CH-C(CH3))		CDCL3
691M	E	8.23	CHA	AN(N-C(CH3)/C(CH3))		CDCL3
2408M	E	8.53	CHA	AN(N-C(C(=O)-NH))		CDCL3
706M	E	7.93	CHA	AN(N-C(NH2))		CDCL3

BOOK NO.	ASSIGN-MENT	CHEM SHIFT - ppm -	PROTON GROUP	ENVIRONMENTAL GROUPS	S	SOLVENT
878M	F	8.51	CHA	AN(N-C(QN(CH3/NH-A)))		DMSO-D6
717M	B	8.71	CHA	AN(N/CH-C(AN(C-CH-CH-N)))		CDCL3
688M	E	8.36	CHA	AN(N/CH-C(CH2-CH2))		CCL4
1729M	D	8.41	CHA	AN(N/CH-C(CH2-OH))		CDCL3
684M	C	8.37	CHA	AN(N/CH-C(CH3))		CCL4
895M	B	8.76	CHA	AN(N/CH-C(C(=O)-NH))		DMSO
704M	D	8.66	CHA	AN(N/C(BR))		CCL4
683M	D	8.35	CHA	AN(N/C(CH3))		CCL4
701M	D	8.52	CHA	AN(N/C(CL))		CCL4
2606M	C	9.53	CHA	AN(N/C(C(=O)-OH))	S	D2O
2939M	H	9.24	CHA	AN(N/C(C(=O)-O-CH2))		CDCL3
711M	G	8.58	CHA	AN(N/C(R5N(CH-CH2/CH2)))		CCL4
2396M	C	7.81	CHA	ARSN(C*-C(=O)-N(CH2-A))		DMSO-D6
1727M	C	7.29 APP.	CHA	AR5A<CH-C*-CH(CH2-OH)/CH-CH-C*>		POLYSOL-D
2855M	D	7.64 APP.	CHA	AR5A<CH-C*-CH(C(=O)-O-CH3)/CH-CH-C*>		CDCL3
2136M	A	7.90	CHA	AR5A<CH-C*-C(=O)/CH-C*>		TFA
1727M	C	7.29 APP.	CHA	AR5A<CH-C*-C*/CH-CH-C*>		POLYSOL-D
2855M	C	7.32 APP.	CHA	AR5A<CH-C*-C*/CH-CH-C*>		CDCL3
2123M	A	7.01	CHA	AR5A<C(F)-CH-C*/CH-C*-C*>		CDCL3
1949M	B	6.82	CHA	AR5A<C(OH)-CH-C*/CH-C*-C*>		POLYSOL-D
1727M	D	7.69 APP.	CHA	AR5A<C*-CH(CH2-OH)-C*>		POLYSOL-D
2855M	C	7.32 APP.	CHA	AR5A<C*-CH(C(=O)-O-CH3)-C*>		CDCL3
2136M	C	8.32	CHA	AR5A<C*-C(=O)-C(=O)/CH-CH-C*>		TFA
2855M	D	7.64 APP.	CHA	AR5A<C*-C*>		CDCL3
1727M	D	7.69 APP.	CHA	AR5A<C*-C*>		POLYSOL-D
1949M	E	7.59	CHA	AR5A<C*-C*>		POLYSOL-D
1949M	D	7.56	CHA	AR5A<C*-C*/CH-C(OH)>		POLYSOL-D
2136M	B	8.10	CHA	AR5A<C*/CH-CH-C*>		TFA
612M	A	7.17	CHA	AR5NA<CH-C*-C*/CH-CH-C*>		C3H6O
2373M	B	7.15- 7.55	CHA	AR5NA<CH-C*-C*/CH-CH-C*>		CDCL3
612M	C	7.49	CHA	AR5NA<CH-C*-NH/CH-CH-C*>		C3H6O
2373M	B	7.15- 7.55	CHA	AR5NA<CH-C*-N(C(=O)-CH3)/CH-CH-C*>		CDCL3
745M	B	8.13	CHA	AR5NA<C*-C*>		CDCL3
2373M	C	7.83	CHA	AR5NA<C*-C*>		CDCL3
2373M	C	8.09	CHA	AR5NA<C*-C*>		CDCL3
612M	D	8.12	CHA	AR5NA<C*-C*>		C3H6O
612M	B	7.45 APP.	CHA	AR5NA<C*-NH-C*>		C3H6O
2373M	D	7.83	CHA	AR5NA<C*-N(C(=O)-CH3)-C*>		CDCL3
2373M	D	8.09	CHA	AR5NA<C*-N(C(=O)-CH3)-C*>		CDCL3
744M	D	8.04	CHA	AR5NA(C*-C*)		CDCL3
741M	A	7.44	CHA	AR5NNN<CH-C*-NH/CH-CH-C*>		CDCL3
741M	A	7.44	CHA	AR5NNN<CH-C*-N=/CH-CH-C*>		CDCL3
741M	B	8.01	CHA	AR5NNN<C*-NH-N=>		CDCL3
741M	B	8.01	CHA	AR5NNN<C*-N=N>		CDCL3
738M	B	7.66	CHA	AR5NN<CH-C*N=/CH-CH-C*>		DMSO-D6
738M	B	7.66	CHA	AR5NN<CH-C*-NH/CH-CH-C*>		DMSO-D6
739M	D	7.12	CHA	AR5NN<CH-C*-NH/CH-CH-C*>		POLYSOL-D
739M	D	7.12	CHA	AR5NN<CH-C*-N=/CH-CH-C*>		POLYSOL-D
738M	A	7.22	CHA	AR5NN<C*-NH-CH=>		DMSO-D6
739M	E	7.51	CHA	AR5NN<C*-NH-C(CH2.2-CH3)=>		POLYSOL-D
738M	A	7.22	CHA	AR5NN<C*-N=CH>		DMSO-D6
739M	E	7.51	CHA	AR5NN<C*-N=C(CH2.2-CH3)>		POLYSOL-D
1730M	B	7.19	CHA	AR5NN(CH-C*-NH/CH-CH-C*)		DMSO-D6
1730M	B	7.19	CHA	AR5NN(CH-C*-N=/CH-CH-C*)		DMSO-D6
740M	B	7.11	CHA	AR5NN(C(CH3)-CH-C*/CH-C*-NH)		CDCL3
740M	D	7.58	CHA	AR5NN(C*-NH-CH=/CH-C(CH3))		CDCL3
1730M	C	7.66	CHA	AR5NN(C*-NH-C(CH2-OH)=)		DMSO-D6
740M	C	7.49	CHA	AR5NN(C*-N=CH/C(CH3))		CDCL3
1730M	C	7.66	CHA	AR5NN(C*-N=C(CH2-OH))		DMSO-D6
1585M	D	7.20	CHA	AR5NO<C*-N=C(CH3)/C(CH3)-C(CH3)>		CDCL3
1585M	D	7.38	CHA	AR5NO<C*-N=C(CH3)/C(CH3)-C(CH3)>		CDCL3
1585M	C	7.20	CHA	AR5NO<C*-O-C(CH3)=/C(CH3)-C(CH3)>		CDCL3
1585M	C	7.38	CHA	AR5NO<C*-O-C(CH3)=/C(CH3)-C(CH3)>		CDCL3
2401M	A	8.07	CHA	AR5NR5N<C*-C(=O)-NH/C*-C(=O)-NH>		DMSO
611M	D	7.39	CHA	AR5NR6<C*-C*-CH2>		CDCL3
1177M	B	7.17	CHA	AR5NS<C(CL)-CH-C*/CH-C*-S>		CDCL3
1177M	D	7.86	CHA	AR5NS<C*-N=C(CH3)/C(CL)>		CDCL3
1177M	C	7.55	CHA	AR5NS<C*-S-C(CH3)=/CH-C(CL)>		CDCL3
1175M	B	7.08- 7.53	CHA	AR5NS(CH-C*-N=/CH-CH-C*)		CDCL3
1175M	B	7.08- 7.53	CHA	AR5NS(CH-C*-S/CH-CH-C*)		CDCL3
1176M	C	7.99 APP.	CHA	AR5NS(C*-N=C(A))		CDCL3
1175M	C	7.61- 8.04	CHA	AR5NS(C*-N=C(CH3))		CDCL3
1176M	B	7.67	CHA	AR5NS(C*-S-C(A)=)		CDCL3
1175M	C	7.61- 8.04	CHA	AR5NS(C*-S-C(CH3)=)		CDCL3
2395M	D	7.73	CHA	AR5N<CH-C*-C(=O)>		CDCL3
2402M	B	7.80 APP.	CHA	AR5N<CH-C*-C(=O)/CH-CH-C*>		DMSO
2391M	B	7.84	CHA	AR5N<CH-C*-C(=O)/CH-CH-C*>		TFA
2393M	B	7.84	CHA	AR5N<CH-C*-C(=O)/CH-CH-C*>		CDCL3
2397M	C	7.74	CHA	AR5N<CH-C*-C(=O)/CH-CH-C*>		CDCL3
2392M	C	7.76	CHA	AR5N<CH-C*-C(=O)/CH-CH-C*>		CDCL3
2398M	D	7.71	CHA	AR5N<CH-C*-C(=O)/CH-CH-C*>		CDCL3

REPRESENTS TRIPLE BOND, ¬ REPRESENTS AN ARROW AND < AND > REPRESENT BRACKETS.

BOOK NO.	ASSIGN-MENT	CHEM SHIFT - ppm -	PROTON GROUP	ENVIRONMENTAL GROUPS	S	SOLVENT
2381M	C	8.60	CHA	AR5N<C(NO2)-CH-C*/CH-C*-C(=O)>		POLYSOL-D
1020M	E	7.18	CHA	AR5N<C(S-C:N)-CH-C*/CH-C*-NH>		CDCL3
1020M	F	7.26	CHA	AR5N<C*-CH2-CH2/C(S-C:N)>		CDCL3
606M	D	7.42	CHA	AR5N<C*-CH=C(CH3)>		CDCL3
607M	E	7.59	CHA	AR5N<C*-C(CH3)=CH>		CDCL3
609M	D	7.41 APP.	CHA	AR5N<C*-C(CH3)=C(CH3)>		CDCL3
2381M	A	8.04	CHA	AR5N<C*-C(=O)-NH/CH-C(NO2)>		POLYSOL-D
2381M	B	8.49	CHA	AR5N<C*-C(=O)-NH/C(NO2)>		POLYSOL-D
2398M	E	7.83	CHA	AR5N<C*-C(=O)-N(A<C-CH-CH-C(O-CH3)>)>		CDCL3
2397M	D	7.91	CHA	AR5N<C*-C(=O)-N(A<C-C(CH3)>)>		CDCL3
2393M	C	7.99	CHA	AR5N<C*-C(=O)-N(CH2-BR)>		CDCL3
2392M	D	7.93	CHA	AR5N<C*-C(=O)-N(CH2-CH2)>		CDCL3
2391M	B	7.84	CHA	AR5N<C*-C(=O)-N(CH3)>		TFA
2402M	B	7.80 APP.	CHA	AR5N<C*-C(=O)-N(NH2)>		DMSO
2395M	E	7.82	CHA	AR5N<C*-C(=O)-N(Q3)>		CDCL3
1020M	D	6.50	CHA	AR5N<C*-NH-CH2/CH-C(S-C:N)>		DMSO
2380M	A	7.86	CHA	AR5N(CH-C*-C(=O)/CH-CH-C*)		CDCL3
2399M	C	7.70	CHA	AR5N(CH-C*-C(=O)/CH-CH-C*)		DMSO-D6
2396M	C	7.81	CHA	AR5N(CH-C*-C(=O)/CH-CH-C*)		CDCL3
2400M	D	7.50- 7.90	CHA	AR5N(CH-C*-C(=O)/CH-CH-C*)		CDCL3
2394M	E	7.82 APP.	CHA	AR5N(CH-C*-C(=O)/CH-CH-C*)		CCL4
605M	E	7.50	CHA	AR5N(C*)		DMSO
2380M	A	7.86	CHA	AR5N(C*-C(=O)-NH)		CDCL3
2399M	D	7.79	CHA	AR5N(C*-C(=O)-N(CH2-CH2))		CDCL3
2400M	D	7.50- 7.90	CHA	AR5N(C*-C(=O)-N(CH2-N))		CDCL3
2394M	E	7.82 APP.	CHA	AR5N(C*-C(=O)-N(HCH-R30))		POLYSOL-D
2608M	D	7.56	CHA	AR500<C(C(=O)-OH)-CH-C*/CH-C*-O>		POLYSOL-D
2608M	B	6.90	CHA	AR500<C*-O-CH2/CH-C(C(=O)-OH)>		POLYSOL-D
2608M	C	7.38	CHA	AR500<C*-O-CH2/C(O(=O)-OH)>		CDCL3
2186M	D	7.31	CHA	AR500(C(C(=O)-H)-CH-C*/CH-C*-O)		CDCL3
2186M	B	6.83	CHA	AR500(C*-O-CH2/CH-C(C(=O)-H))		CDCL3
2186M	C	7.24	CHA	AR500(C*-O-CH2/C(C(=O)-H))		DMSO-D6
2273M	A	8.61	CHA	AR50R50<C*-C(=O)-O/C*-C(=O)-O>		CCL4
1584M	B	7.00- 7.30	CHA	AR50<CH-C*-CH=/CH-CH-C*>		CCL4
1584M	C	7.30- 7.60	CHA	AR50<CH-C*-O/CH-CH-C*>		CDCL3
2956M	C	8.61	CHA	AR50<C(NO2)-CH-C*/CH-C*-CH2>		CDCL3
2956M	B	7.78	CHA	AR50<C*-CH2-O/CH-C(NO2)>		CCL4
1584M	C	7.30- 7.60	CHA	AR50<C*-CH=CH>		CDCL3
2956M	D	8.76	CHA	AR50<C*-C(=O)-O/C(NO2)>		CCL4
1584M	B	7.00- 7.30	CHA	AR50<C*-O-CH=>		CDCL3
2272M	A	7.72	CHA	AR50(C(F)-CH-C*/CH-C*C(=O))		CDCL3
2272M	B	7.79	CHA	AR50(C(F)/C*-C(=O)-O)		CDCL3
2272M	C	8.22	CHA	AR50(C*-C(=O)-O/CH-C(F))		DMSO
1180M	B	8.64	CHA	AR5SA<C-C(NO2)-CH-C*-S/CH-C*-C*>		DMSO
1180M	A	8.13	CHA	AR5SA<C-C*-C*/CH-C(NO2)-CH-C*-S>		DMSO
1180M	C	8.89	CHA	AR5SA<C-C*-S/C(NO2)-CH-CH-C*-C*>		DMSO
1179M	B	6.88	CHA	AR5SA<C(NH2)-CH-C*/CH-C*-C*)		DMSO
1278M	B	6.80	CHA	AR5SA<C(NH2)-CH-C*/CH-C*-SO2)		DMSO
1278M	C	7.19	CHA	AR5SA(C*-C*/C(NH2))		DMSO
1278M	D	7.62	CHA	AR5SA(C*-SO2-C*/CH-C(NH2))		CDCL3
195M	C	7.25 APP.	CHA	AR5<CH-C*-CH2/CH-CH-C*>		CCL4
2179M	D	7.52	CHA	AR5<C(C(=O)-H)-CH-C*/CH-C*-CH2>		CDCL3
195M	C	7.25 APP.	CHA	AR5<C*-CH2-CH2>		CCL4
2179M	C	7.20	CHA	AR5<C*-CH2-CH2/CH-C(C(=O)-H)>		CCL4
2179M	E	7.59	CHA	AR5<C*-CH2-CH2/C(C(=O)-H)>		CDCL3
863M	B	7.24 APP.	CHA	AR5(CH-C*-CH2/CH-CH-C*)		CDCL3
1948M	F	6.98	CHA	AR5(CH-C*-CH2/CH-C(OH)-C*)		DMSO
2150M	B	8.20	CHA	AR5(CH-C*-C(=O)/CH-CH-C*)		CDCL3
2108M	E	7.70	CHA	AR5(C(C(=O)-CH3)-CH-C*/CH-C*-CH2)		CDCL3
1948M	D	6.59	CHA	AR5(C(OH)-C*-CH2/CH-CH-C*)		CDCL3
1948M	E	6.75	CHA	AR5(C*-CH2-CH2/CH-CH-C(OH))		CDCL3
2108M	D	7.21	CHA	AR5(C*-CH2-CH2/CH-C(C(=O)-CH3))		CDCL3
2108M	F	7.76	CHA	AR5(C*-CH2-CH2/C(C(=O)-CH3))		CDCL3
863M	B	7.24 APP.	CHA	AR5(C*-CH2-C(=NOH))		DMSO
2150M	B	8.20	CHA	AR5(C*-C(=O)-C(OH/OH))		CDCL3
2128M	B	7.78	CHA	AR6A<CH-C*-C(VO)/CH-CH-C*>		CDCL3
2128M	D	8.30	CHA	AR6A<C*-C(=O)-C*>		CDCL3
2128M	C	8.00	CHA	AR6A<C*-C(=O)-C*/C(CH3)-C(CH3)>		CDCL3
211M	C	7.71	CHA	AR6A<C*-C*>		CDCL3
2127M	C	7.61	CHA	AR6A(CH-C*-C(=O)/CH-CH-C*)		CDCL3
2127M	B	7.21	CHA	AR6A(C(CH3)-C*-C*-C(=O)/CH-C(CH3)-C*)		CDCL3
2124M	C	8.38	CHA	AR6A(C*-C(=O)-C*)		CDCL3
2127M	D	8.03	CHA	AR6A(C*-C(=O)-C*)		DMSO-D6
1583M	B	6.35	CHA	AR6NSA<C(O-CH3)-CH-C*/CH-C*-NH>		DMSO-D6
1583M	C	6.39	CHA	AR6NSA<C*-S-C*/C(O-CH3)>		CDCL3
601M	F	6.57	CHA	AR6N<CH-C*-CH2/CH-CH-C*>		CDCL3
602M	G	6.54	CHA	AR6N<CH-C*-HCH/CH-CH-C*>		CDCL3
602M	H	6.75- 7.20	CHA	AR6N<CH-C*-NH/CH-CH-C*>		CDCL3
601M	H	6.92	CHA	AR6N<CH-C*-NH/CH-CH-C*>		CDCL3
601M	G	6.89	CHA	AR6N<C*-CH2-CH2>		CDCL3
602M	H	6.75- 7.20	CHA	AR6N<C*-HCH-HCH>		CDCL3

BOOK NO.	ASSIGN-MENT	CHEM SHIFT - ppm -	PROTON GROUP	ENVIRONMENTAL GROUPS	S	SOLVENT
601M	E	6.34	CHA	AR6N<C*-NH-CH2>		CDCL3
602M	F	6.39	CHA	AR6N<C*-NH-CH(CH3)>		CDCL3
1591M	A	6.79 APP.	CHA	AR600A<CH-C*-O/CH-CH-C*>		CDCL3
1591M	A	6.79 APP.	CHA	AR600A<C*-O-C*>		CDCL3
1590M	B	6.84	CHA	AR600<CH-C*-O/CH-CH-C*>		CDCL3
2109M	D	7.41 APP.	CHA	AR600<C(C(=O)-CH3)-CH-C*/CH-C*-O>		CDCL3
1590M	B	6.84	CHA	AR600<C*-O-CH2>		CDCL3
2109M	C	6.82	CHA	AR600<C*-O-CH2/CH-C(C(=O)-CH3)>		CDCL3
2109M	D	7.41 APP.	CHA	AR600<C*-O-CH2/C(C(=O)-CH3)>		CDCL3
1587M	C	7.61	CHA	AR60SA<CH-C*-O/CH-CH-C*>		TFA
1587M	B	7.40	CHA	AR60SA<CH-C*-SO2/CH-CH-C*>		TFA
1587M	A	7.32	CHA	AR60SA<C*-O-C*>		TFA
1587M	D	8.03	CHA	AR60SA<C*-SO2-C*>		TFA
2117M	E	7.28	CHA	AR60<C(CH3)-CH-C*/CH-C*-O>		CDCL3
2117M	F	7.69	CHA	AR60<C*-C(=O)-CH2/C(CH3)>		CDCL3
2117M	D	6.82	CHA	AR60<C*-O-CH2/CH-C(CH3)>		CDCL3
2118M	D	7.35	CHA	AR60(C(CL)-CH-C*/CH-C*-O)		CDCL3
2118M	E	7.74	CHA	AR60(C*-C(=O)-CH2/C(CL))		CDCL3
2118M	C	6.89	CHA	AR60(C*-O-CH2/CH-C(CL))		CDCL3
2121M	D	7.68 APP.	CHA	AR6<CH-C*-C(=O)/CH-CH-C*>		CDCL3
2115M	E	7.31	CHA	AR6<C(CH2-CH3)-CH-C*/CH-C*-CH2>		CDCL3
2116M	F	6.71	CHA	AR6<C(O-CH3)-CH-C*/CH-C*-CH2>		CDCL3
2115M	D	7.14	CHA	AR6<C*-CH2-CH2/CH-C(CH2-CH3)>		CDCL3
2116M	G	7.11	CHA	AR6<C*-CH2-CH2/CH-C(O-CH3)>		CDCL3
2116M	E	6.64	CHA	AR6<C*-CH2-C(=O)/C(O-CH3)>		CDCL3
2114M	E	7.89	CHA	AR6<C*-C(=O)-CH2>		CCL4
2115M	F	7.89	CHA	AR6<C*-C(=O)-CH2/C(CH2-CH3)>		CDCL3
2121M	E	7.96 APP.	CHA	AR6<C*-C(=O)-CH=>		CDCL3
2121M	E	7.96 APP.	CHA	AR6<C*-C(=O)-C(R6<CH-CH2/CH2>)=>		CDCL3
196M	C	7.02 APP.	CHA	AR6(CH-C*-CH2)		CDCL3
2120M	C	7.59- 7.87	CHA	AR6(CH-C*-C(=O)/CH-CH-C*)		CDCL3
196M	C	7.02 APP.	CHA	AR6(CH-CH2-CH2)		CDCL3
2120M	D	7.91- 8.20	CHA	AR6(C*-C(=O)-CH=)		CDCL3
2120M	D	7.91- 8.20	CHA	AR6(C*-C(=O)-C(C(CH3/CH3/CH3))=)		CDCL3
2125M	C	8.12	CHA	AR7A(C*-C(=O)-C*)		CCL4
736M	A	7.40- 7.90	CHA	A<CH-CH-C(ANNN<C-N-C(A)-N/N-C(A)>)>		TFA
381M	A	7.13 APP.	CHA	A<CH-CH-C(BR)>		CCL4
1819M	D	7.36	CHA	A<CH-CH-C(C(OH/C:C/CH3))>		CDCL3
1481M	D	6.90- 7.30	CHA	A<CH-CH-C(C(O/A/A))>		CDCL3
1486M	B	7.10- 7.40	CHA	A<CH-CH-C(C(O/O/A))>		CDCL3
2107M	A	7.32- 7.72	CHA	A<CH-CH-C(C(=O)-A)>		CDCL3
2221M	A	7.28- 7.90	CHA	A<CH-CH-C(C(=O)-BR)>		CCL4
2050M	E	7.20- 7.60	CHA	A<CH-CH-C(C(=O)-CH2.12)>		CDCL3
2051M	B	7.49 APP.	CHA	A<CH-CH-C(C(=O)-CH2)>		CDCL3
2052M	C	7.19- 7.69	CHA	A<CH-CH-C(C(=O)-CH2)>		CDCL3
2086M	C	7.25- 7.60	CHA	A<CH-CH-C(C(=O)-CH2)>		POLYSOL-D
2089M	C	7.30- 7.65	CHA	A<CH-CH-C(C(=O)-CH2)>		CDCL3
2047M	D	7.12- 7.55	CHA	A<CH-CH-C(C(=O)-CH2)>		CCL4
2090M	D	7.25- 7.55	CHA	A<CH-CH-C(C(=O)-CH)>		CDCL3
1865M	E	7.25- 7.68	CHA	A<CH-CH-C(C(=O)-CH)>		CDCL3
2220M	A	7.24- 7.78	CHA	A<CH-CH-C(C(=O)-CL)>		CCL4
2219M	A	7.25- 7.80	CHA	A<CH-CH-C(C(=O)-F)>		CCL4
2943M	C	7.45	CHA	A<CH-CH-C(C(=O)-O-A)>		CCL4
2863M	D	7.10- 7.60	CHA	A<CH-CH-C(C(=O)-O-CH2.2)>		CCL4
2865M	D	7.20- 7.60	CHA	A<CH-CH-C(C(=O)-O-CH2.2)>		CDCL3
2944M	B	7.41	CHA	A<CH-CH-C(C(=O)-O-CH2)>		CDCL3
2867M	C	7.13- 7.63	CHA	A<CH-CH-C(C(=O)-O-CH2)>		CCL4
2683M	A	7.52 APP.	CHA	A<CH-CH-C(C(=O)-O-NH4)>		D20
2995M	A	7.20- 7.80	CHA	A<CH-CH-C(C(=O)-O-O-C(=O))>		CDCL3
2095M	A	7.30- 7.70	CHA	A<CH-CH-C(C(=O)-Q2)>		POLYSOL-D
2083M	C	7.16- 7.60	CHA	A<CH-CH-C(C(=O)-R5)>		CCL4
2610M	B	7.22- 7.67	CHA	A<CH-CH-C(C(=O)-SH)>		CDCL3
1333M	A	7.10- 7.50	CHA	A<CH-CH-C(C(=S)-HNH)>		POLYSOL-D
2634M	B	6.60	CHA	A<CH-CH-C(NH-CH2)>		DMSO-D6
587M	G	6.64	CHA	A<CH-CH-C(NH-CH2)>		CDCL3
582M	D	6.57	CHA	A<CH-CH-C(NH-CH3)>		CCL4
2320M	B	6.90- 7.34	CHA	A<CH-CH-C(NH-C(=O))>		DMSO-D6
2317M	D	7.21	CHA	A<CH-CH-C(NH-C(=O)-CH)S		POLYSOL-D
760M	A	6.60	CHA	A<CH-CH-C(NH-NH)>		DMSO-D6
889M	B	6.75- 7.10	CHA	A<CH-CH-C(NH-QN)>		DMSO-D6
976M	C	6.71	CHA	A<CH-CH-C(N(CH2.2/CH2.2))>		DMSO-D6
656M	D	6.57	CHA	A<CH-CH-C(N(CH2/CH2))>		CCL4
653M	E	7.13	CHA	A<CH-CH-C(N(CH2/CH2))>		CDCL3
1706M	F	6.64	CHA	A<CH-CH-C(N(CH2/CH2))>		CDCL3
841M	C	7.40- 7.85	CHA	A<CH-CH-C(N(+)(CH2/CH2/CH2))>		CDCL3
1313M	B	7.20- 7.45	CHA	A<CH-CH-C(N(+)(CH3/CH3/CH3))>		POLYSOL-D
1490M	D	6.93 APP.	CHA	A<CH-CH-C(O-CH2.2)>		CDCL3
1492M	E	7.15	CHA	A<CH-CH-C(O-CH2.2)>		CCL4
1792M	F	6.83	CHA	A<CH-CH-C(O-CH2)>		CCL4
1488M	B	6.80	CHA	A<CH-CH-C(O-CH3)>		CCL4
2216M	D	6.93	CHA	A<CH-CH-C(O-CH)>		CCL4

BOOK NO.	ASSIGN-MENT	CHEM SHIFT - ppm -	PROTON GROUP	ENVIRONMENTAL GROUPS	S	SOLVENT
1659M	E	7.25- 7.62	CHA	A<CH-CH-C(P(=O/A/CH))>		POLYSOL-D
1366M	C	7.30- 7.60	CHA	A<CH-CH-C(QN(A<C-CH-CH-C(SO2-NH2)>))>		DMSO-D6
861M	A	7.46	CHA	A<CH-CH-C(QN(A/OH))>		CDCL3
866M	B	7.29	CHA	A<CH-CH-C(QN(CH3))>		CDCL3
859M	B	7.40 APP.	CHA	A<CH-CH-C(QN(CH3/OH))>		CCL4
1064M	B	7.20- 7.50	CHA	A<CH-CH-C(QN(NH-A))>		POLYSOL-D
879M	B	7.28 APP.	CHA	A<CH-CH-C(QN(QN/NH2))>		CDCL3
868M	B	7.35	CHA	A<CH-CH-C(QN)>		CDCL3
2858M	C	7.20- 7.60	CHA	A<CH-CH-C(Q1(C(=O)-CH2/C:N))>		CDCL3
2096M	C	7.30- 7.55	CHA	A<CH-CH-C(Q2(H/H/C(=O)-A))>		POLYSOL-D
674M	D	7.10- 7.35	CHA	A<CH-CH-C(R5NN<C=N/N(A)>)>		CDCL3
674M	C	6.80- 7.20	CHA	A<CH-CH-C(R5NN<N-C(A)=/CH2>)>		CDCL3
678M	B	7.00- 7.55	CHA	A<CH-CH-C(R5NN<N-N=/CH=>)>		CDCL3
641M	F	6.82	CHA	A<CH-CH-C(R6NN<N-CH(CH3)/CH2>)>		CDCL3
1157M	B	7.20- 7.48	CHA	A<CH-CH-C(R6SS(C=CH/S>)>		CDCL3
1594M	B	7.15- 7.45	CHA	A<CH-CH-C(SI(O/O/A))>		CDCL3
1270M	B	7.20- 7.65	CHA	A<CH-CH-C(SO2-A)>		CDCL3
1265M	C	7.50- 7.85	CHA	A<CH-CH-C(SO2-CH2)>		POLYSOL-D
1261M	E	7.20- 7.75	CHA	A<CH-CH-C(SO2-CH2)>		CDCL3
1361M	A	7.62 APP.	CHA	A<CH-CH-C(SO2-NH2)>		TFA
1371M	C	7.50- 7.80	CHA	A<CH-CH-C(SO2-NH)>		DMSO-D6
1313M	C	7.50- 7.70	CHA	A<CH-CH-C(SO3(-))>		POLYSOL-D
1300M	A	7.58	CHA	A<CH-CH-C(SO3-NA)>	S	D2O
736M	A	7.40- 7.90	CHA	A<CH-C(ANNN<C-N-C(A)-N/N-C(A)>)>		TFA
381M	A	7.13 APP.	CHA	A<CH-C(BR)>		CCL4
434M	A	6.90	CHA	A<CH-C(BR)-C(I)>		CCL4
1894M	B	6.74	CHA	A<CH-C(BR)-C(OH)>		CDCL3
1517M	C	6.71	CHA	A<CH-C(BR)-C(O-CH2)>		CCL4
397M	A	6.92	CHA	A<CH-C(BR)/CH-C(BR)>		CCL4
395M	B	7.10	CHA	A<CH-C(BR)/CH-C(CH2-BR)>		CDCL3
2068M	B	7.28	CHA	A<CH-C(BR)/CH-C(C(=O)-CH3)>		CCL4
2233M	A	7.39	CHA	A<CH-C(BR)/CH-C(C(=O)-CL)>		CCL4
993M	A	7.40	CHA	A<CH-C(BR)/CH-C(C:N)>		CDCL3
500M	E	6.64	CHA	A<CH-C(CH2-CH3)-C(NH2)/CH-C(CH3)>		CDCL3
929M	C	7.04	CHA	A<CH-C(CH2-CH3)-C(N=C=N)/CH-C(CH2-CH3)>		CDCL3
1504M	D	6.91	CHA	A<CH-C(CH2-NH2)-C(O-CH3)>		CDCL3
1918M	F	6.62	CHA	A<CH-C(CH2-Q3)-C(OH)/CH-C(CH3)>		CCL4
187M	C	7.00	CHA	A<CH-C(CH3)-C(CH3)/CH-C(CH3)>		CDCL3
595M	E	6.59	CHA	A<CH-C(CH3)-C(NH-CH2)>		CDCL3
501M	D	6.80	CHA	A<CH-C(CH(CH3/CH3))-C(NH2)/CH-C(CH(CH3/CH3))>		CDCL3
1018M	B	7.33 APP.	CHA	A<CH-C(CL)-C(CH2-S)/CH-C(CL)>		CDCL3
1922M	A	7.01	CHA	A<CH-C(CL)-C(OH)/CH-C(NO2)>		CDCL3
306M	A	7.22	CHA	A<CH-C(CL)/CH-C(CL)>		CCL4
2065M	B	7.15- 7.63	CHA	A<CH-C(CL)/CH-C(C(=O)-CH3)>		CCL4
2167M	A	7.60	CHA	A<CH-C(CL)/CH-C(C(=O)-H)>		CDCL3
2873M	B	7.30	CHA	A<CH-C(CL)/CH-C(C(=O)-O-CH3)>		CCL4
1057M	A	7.53	CHA	A<CH-C(CL)/CH-C(NO2)>		CDCL3
1882M	D	6.74	CHA	A<CH-C(C(CH3/CH3/CH3))-C(OH)>		CCL4
1819M	D	7.36	CHA	A<CH-C(C(OH/C:C/CH3))>		CDCL3
1481M	D	6.90- 7.30	CHA	A<CH-C(C(O/A/A))>		CDCL3
1486M	B	7.10- 7.40	CHA	A<CH-C(C(O/O/A))>		CDCL3
2107M	A	7.32- 7.72	CHA	A<CH-C(C(=O)-A)>		CDCL3
2221M	A	7.28- 7.90	CHA	A<CH-C(C(=O)-BR)>		CCL4
2050M	E	7.20- 7.60	CHA	A<CH-C(C(=O)-CH2.12)>		CDCL3
2051M	B	7.49 APP.	CHA	A<CH-C(C(=O)-CH2)>		CDCL3
2052M	C	7.19- 7.69	CHA	A<CH-C(C(=O)-CH2)>		CDCL3
2086M	C	7.25- 7.60	CHA	A<CH-C(C(=O)-CH2)>		POLYSOL-D
2089M	C	7.30- 7.65	CHA	A<CH-C(C(=O)-CH2)>		CDCL3
2047M	D	7.12- 7.55	CHA	A<CH-C(C(=O)-CH2)>		CCL4
2090M	D	7.25- 7.55	CHA	A<CH-C(C(=O)-CH)>		CDCL3
1865M	E	7.25- 7.68	CHA	A<CH-C(C(=O)-CH)>		CDCL3
2220M	A	7.24- 7.78	CHA	A<CH-C(C(=O)-CL)>		CCL4
2238M	C	7.10	CHA	A<CH-C(C(=O)-CL)-C(CH3)/CH-C(CH3)>		CCL4
2219M	A	7.25- 7.80	CHA	A<CH-C(C(=O)-F)>		CCL4
2165M.	B	7.37	CHA	A<CH-C(C(=O)-H)/CH-C(CH3)>		CCL4
2288M	A	7.35- 7.85	CHA	A<CH-C(C(=O)-NH2)>		TFA
2293M	A	6.96	CHA	A<CH-C(C(=O)-NH2)-C(OH)>		DMSO-D6
2575M	A	7.52	CHA	A<CH-C(C(=O)-OH)-C(I)>		C3D6O
2581M	A	7.75	CHA	A<CH-C(C(=O)-OH)-C(NO2)>		C3H6O
2587M	A	7.02	CHA	A<CH-C(C(=O)-OH)-C(OH)>		TFA
2585M	C	7.03	CHA	A<CH-C(C(=O)-OH)-C(O-CH2)>		CCL4
2678M	C	7.44	CHA	A<CH-C(C(=O)-ONA)-C(OH)>		D2O
2943M	C	7.45	CHA	A<CH-C(C(=O)-O-A)>		CCL4
2863M	D	7.10- 7.60	CHA	A<CH-C(C(=O)-O-CH2.2)>		CCL4
2865M	D	7.20- 7.60	CHA	A<CH-C(C(=O)-O-CH2.2)>		CDCL3
2897M	D	7.48	CHA	A<CH-C(C(=O)-O-CH2.4)-C(C(=O)-O-CH2.4)>		CCL4
2879M	E	6.51	CHA	A<CH-C(C(=O)-O-CH2.4)-C(NH2)>		DMSO-D6
2944M	B	7.41	CHA	A<CH-C(C(=O)-O-CH2)>		CDCL3
2867M	C	7.13- 7.63	CHA	A<CH-C(C(=O)-O-CH2)>		CCL4
2866M	D	7.30	CHA	A<CH-C(C(=O)-O-CH2)>		CCL4
2898M	D	7.41	CHA	A<CH-C(C(=O)-O-CH2)-C(C(=O)-O-CH2)>		CCL4

BOOK NO.	ASSIGN- MENT	CHEM SHIFT - ppm -	PROTON GROUP	ENVIRONMENTAL GROUPS	S	SOLVENT
2899M	E	7.48	CHA	A<CH-C(C(=0)-0-CH2)-C(C(=0)-0-CH2)>		CCL4
2877M	E	6.37- 6.71	CHA	A<CH-C(C(=0)-0-CH2)-C(NH2)>		CCL4
2890M	D	6.72	CHA	A<CH-C(C(=0)-0-CH2)-C(OH)>		CCL4
2902M	D	7.42	CHA	A<CH-C(C(=0)-0-CH2)/CH-C(C(=0)-0-CH2)>		CCL4
2903M	E	7.43	CHA	A<CH-C(C(=0)-0-CH2)/CH-C(C(=0)-0-CH2)>		CCL4
2904M	E	7.55	CHA	A<CH-C(C(=0)-0-CH2)/CH-C(C(=0)-0-CH2)>		CDCL3
2683M	A	7.52 APP.	CHA	A<CH-C(C(=0)-0-NH4)>		D20
2684M	A	6.97	CHA	A<CH-C(C(=0)-0-NH4)-C(OH)>		D20
2995M	A	7.20- 7.80	CHA	A<CH-C(C(=0)-0-0-C(=0))>		CDCL3
2878M	E	6.59	CHA	A<CH-C(C(=0)-0-R6)-C(NH2)>		CDCL3
2095M	A	7.30- 7.70	CHA	A<CH-C(C(=0)-02)>		POLYSOL-D
2083M	C	7.16- 7.60	CHA	A<CH-C(C(=0)-R5)>		CCL4
2610M	B	7.22- 7.67	CHA	A<CH-C(C(=0)-SH)>		CDCL3
1333M	A	7.10- 7.50	CHA	A<CH-C(C(=S)-HNH)>		POLYSOL-D
989M	B	7.87	CHA	A<CH-C(F)-C(C:N)/CH-C(F)>		DMSO-D6
1054M	B	7.66	CHA	A<CH-C(F)-C(NO2)>		CCL4
2871M	D	7.28	CHA	A<CH-C(F)/CH-C(C(=0)-0-CH2)>		CCL4
2326M	C	7.22	CHA	A<CH-C(F)/CH-C(NH-C(=0))>		CDCL3
434M	B	7.11	CHA	A<CH-C(I)-C(BR)>		CCL4
2575M	B	7.23	CHA	A<CH-C(I)-C(C(=0)-OH)>		C3D60
525M	B	6.47	CHA	A<CH-C(I)-C(NH2)>		CDCL3
431M	A	7.20	CHA	A<CH-C(I)/CH-C(CF3)>		CCL4
2069M	B	7.10	CHA	A<CH-C(I)/CH-C(C(=0)-0-CH3)>		CDCL3
2876M	B	7.00	CHA	A<CH-C(I)/CH-C(C(=0)-0-CH3)>		CDCL3
436M	A	6.79	CHA	A<CH-C(I)/CH-C(I)>		CDCL3
1897M	A	6.70- 7.00	CHA	A<CH-C(I)/CH-C(OH)>		POLYSOL-D
1520M	C	6.91	CHA	A<CH-C(I)/CH-C(0-CH3)>		CCL4
2879M	G	7.20	CHA	A<CH-C(NH2)-C(C(=0)-0-CH2.4)>		DMSO-D6
2877M	F	7.13	CHA	A<CH-C(NH2)-C(C(=0)-0-CH2)>		CCL4
2878M	F	7.20	CHA	A<CH-C(NH2)-C(C(=0)-0-R6)>		CDCL3
525M	D	7.12	CHA	A<CH-C(NH2)-C(I)>		CDCL3
1526M	B	7.00	CHA	A<CH-C(NH2)-C(0-CH3)>	S	POLYSOL-D
862M	D	7.11	CHA	A<CH-C(NH2)-C(QN(A/OH))>		POLYSOL-D
1236M	D	7.09	CHA	A<CH-C(NH2)-C(SH)>		CDCL3
1161M	D	6.99	CHA	A<CH-C(NH2)-C(S-CH3)>		CCL4
506M	E	7.20	CHA	A<CH-C(NH2)/CH-C(CF3)>		CDCL3
492M	G	7.05	CHA	A<CH-C(NH2)/CH-C(CH2-CH3)>		CDCL3
2880M	D	7.11	CHA	A<CH-C(NH2)/CH-C(C(=0)-0-CH3)>		CDCL3
2676M	B	7.27	CHA	A<CH-C(NH2)/CH-C(C(=0)-0-NA)>		D20
994M	C	7.19	CHA	A<CH-C(NH2)/CH-C(C:N)>		POLYSOL-D
1237M	E	6.97	CHA	A<CH-C(NH2)/CH-C(SH)>		CDCL3
2634M	D	7.11	CHA	A<CH-C(NH-CH2)>		DMSO-D6
587M	H	7.12	CHA	A<CH-C(NH-CH2)>		CDCL3
595M	F	6.90- 7.35	CHA	A<CH-C(NH-CH2)-C(CH3)>		CDCL3
1062M	C	6.53	CHA	A<CH-C(NH-CH2)-C(NO2)>		CCL4
582M	E	7.08	CHA	A<CH-C(NH-CH3)>		CCL4
590M	F	7.06	CHA	A<CH-C(NH-CH3)/CH-C(CH3)>		CDCL3
2320M	B	6.90- 7.34	CHA	A<CH-C(NH-C(=0))>		DMSO-D6
2333M	B	7.11	CHA	A<CH-C(NH-C(=0))-C(NO2)>		CDCL3
2317M	C	7.00	CHA	A<CH-C(NH-C(=0)-CH)>		POLYSOL-D
760M	C	7.07	CHA	A<CH-C(NH-NH)>		DMSO-D6
2581M	A	7.75	CHA	A<CH-C(NO2)-C(C(=0)-OH)>		C3H60
1054M	A	7.10- 7.50	CHA	A<CH-C(NO2)-C(F)>		CCL4
1062M	E	7.34	CHA	A<CH-C(NO2)-C(NH-CH2)>		CCL4
2333M	C	7.61	CHA	A<CH-C(NO2)-C(NH-C(=0))>		CDCL3
1066M	A	8.08	CHA	A<CH-C(NO2)-C(NO2)>		DMSO-D6
1903M	C	7.51	CHA	A<CH-C(NO2)-C(OH)>		CCL4
1534M	F	7.46	CHA	A<CH-C(NO2)-C(0-CH2)>		CCL4
1720M	C	7.48	CHA	A<CH-C(NO2)/CH-C(CH2-OH)>		CDCL3
2236M	A	7.85	CHA	A<CH-C(NO2)/CH-C(C(=0)-CL)>		CDCL3
2171M	A	7.85	CHA	A<CH-C(NO2)/CH-C(C(=0)-H)>		CDCL3
2885M	C	7.59	CHA	A<CH-C(NO2)/CH-C(C(=0)-0-CH2)>		CCL4
976M	E	7.19	CHA	A<CH-C(N(CH2.2/CH2.2))>		DMSO-D6
653M	E	7.13	CHA	A<CH-C(N(CH2/CH2))>		CDCL3
656M	F	7.07	CHA	A<CH-C(N(CH2/CH2))>		CCL4
1706M	H	7.18	CHA	A<CH-C(N(CH2/CH2))>		CDCL3
662M	E	6.91	CHA	A<CH-C(N(CH2/CH2))/CH-C(CH3)>		CCL4
1525M	F	6.98	CHA	A<CH-C(N(CH2/CH2))/CH-C(0-CH2)>		CCL4
841M	C	7.40- 7.85	CHA	A<CH-C(N(+)(CH2/CH2/CH2)>		CDCL3
1313M	B	7.20- 7.45	CHA	A<CH-C(N(+)(CH3/CH3/CH3))>		POLYSOL-D
897M	C	7.37	CHA	A<CH-C(N=N-A)/CH-C(CH3)>		CDCL3
1894M	D	7.07	CHA	A<CH-C(OH)-C(BR)>		CDCL3
1913M	F	6.94	CHA	A<CH-C(OH)-C(CH3)/CH-C(CH3)>		CDCL3
1882M	E	6.87	CHA	A<CH-C(OH)-C(C(CH3/CH3/CH3))>		CCL4
2293M	C	7.50	CHA	A<CH-C(OH)-C(C(=0)-NH2)>		DMSO-D6
2587M	C	7.59	CHA	A<CH-C(OH)-C(C(=0)-OH)>		TFA
2678M	B	7.00 APP.	CHA	A<CH-C(OH)-C(C(=0)-ONA)>		D20
2890M	F	7.32	CHA	A<CH-C(OH)-C(C(=0)-0-CH2)>		CCL4
2684M	C	7.46	CHA	A<CH-C(OH)-C(C(=0)-0-NH4)>		D20
1903M	A	6.90	CHA	A<CH-C(OH)-C(NO2)>		CCL4
1944M	B	7.23	CHA	A<CH-C(OH)-C(NO2)/CH-C(OH)>		POLYSOL-D

BOOK NO.	ASSIGN-MENT	CHEM SHIFT - ppm -	PROTON GROUP	ENVIRONMENTAL GROUPS	S	SOLVENT
1945M	A	6.47 APP.	CHA	A<CH-C(OH)-C(OH)/CH-C(OH)>		C3H6O
1880M	E	7.14	CHA	A<CH-C(OH)/CH-C(CH2-CH3)>		CDCL3
1911M	B	7.07	CHA	A<CH-C(OH)/CH-C(OH)>		C3H6O
1492M	E	7.15	CHA	A<CH-C(O-CH2.2)>		CCL4
1490M	E	7.22	CHA	A<CH-C(O-CH2.2)>		CDCL3
1502M	F	7.06	CHA	A<CH-C(O-CH2.4)/CH-C(CH3)>		CCL4
1792M	G	7.19	CHA	A<CH-C(O-CH2)>		CCL4
1517M	E	7.13	CHA	A<CH-C(O-CH2)-C(BR)>		CCL4
2585M	E	7.53	CHA	A<CH-C(O-CH2)-C(C(=O)-OH)>		CCL4
1534M	D	6.96	CHA	A<CH-C(O-CH2)-C(NO2)>		CCL4
1488M	C	7.19	CHA	A<CH-C(O-CH3)>		CCL4
1504M	F	7.23 APP.	CHA	A<CH-C(O-CH3)-C(CH2-NH2)>		CDCL3
1551M	F	7.07	CHA	A<CH-C(O-CH3)-C(CH3)/CH-C(CH3)>		CDCL3
1526M	D	7.39	CHA	A<CH-C(O-CH3)-C(NH2)>	S	POLYSOL-D
1545M	B	6.76	CHA	A<CH-C(O-CH3)-C(O-CH3)>		CCL4
1565M	C	7.00	CHA	A<CH-C(O-CH3)-C(O-CH3)/CH-C(O-CH3)>		CDCL3
1505M	F	7.21	CHA	A<CH-C(O-CH3)/CH-C(CH2-NH2)>		CDCL3
2216M	E	7.29	CHA	A<CH-C(O-CH)>		CCL4
1659M	E	7.25- 7.62	CHA	A<CH-C(P(=O/A/CH))>		POLYSOL-D
1366M	C	7.30- 7.60	CHA	A<CH-C(QN(A<C-CH-CH-C(SO2-NH2)>))>		DMSO-D6
861M	A	7.46	CHA	A<CH-C(QN(A/OH))>		CDCL3
862M	B	6.61	CHA	A<CH-C(QN(A/OH))-C(NH2)>		POLYSOL-D
866M	B	7.29	CHA	A<CH-C(QN(CH3))>		CDCL3
859M	B	7.40 APP.	CHA	A<CH-C(QN(CH3/OH))>		CCL4
1064M	B	7.20- 7.50	CHA	A<CH-C(QN(NH-A))>		POLYSOL-D
879M	B	7.28 APP.	CHA	A<CH-C(QN(QN/NH2))>		CDCL3
868M	B	7.35	CHA	A<CH-C(QN)>		CDCL3
2858M	C	7.20- 7.60	CHA	A<CH-C(Q1(C(=O)-O-CH2/C:N))>		CDCL3
2096M	C	7.30- 7.55	CHA	A<CH-C(Q2(H/H/C(=O)-A))>		POLYSOL-D
674M	D	7.10- 7.35	CHA	A<CH-C(R5NN<C=N/N(A)>)>		CDCL3
674M	C	6.80- 7.20	CHA	A<CH-C(R5NN<N-C(A)=/CH2>)>		CDCL3
678M	B	7.00- 7.55	CHA	A<CH-C(R5NN<N-N=/CH=>)>		CDCL3
641M	H	7.21	CHA	A<CH-C(R6NN<N-CH(CH3)/CH2>)>		CDCL3
1468M	E	7.12	CHA	A<CH-C(R6NO<N-CH2/CH2>)/CH-C(CH3)>		CDCL3
1157M	B	7.20- 7.48	CHA	A<CH-C(R6SS<C=CH/S>)>		CDCL3
1236M	C	6.64	CHA	A<CH-C(SH)-C(NH2)>		CDCL3
1594M	B	7.15- 7.45	CHA	A<CH-C(SI(O/O/A))>		CDCL3
1270M	B	7.20- 7.65	CHA	A<CH-C(SO2-A)>		CDCL3
1265M	C	7.50- 7.85	CHA	A<CH-C(SO2-CH2)>		POLYSOL-D
1261M	E	7.20- 7.75	CHA	A<CH-C(SO2-CH2)>		CDCL3
1361M	A	7.62 APP.	CHA	A<CH-C(SO2-NH2)>		TFA
1371M	C	7.50- 7.80	CHA	A<CH-C(SO2-NH)>		DMSO-D6
1313M	C	7.50- 7.70	CHA	A<CH-C(SO3(-))>		POLYSOL-D
1300M	A	7.58	CHA	A<CH-C(SO3-NA)>	S	D20
1161M	C	6.55 APP.	CHA	A<CH-C(S-CH3)-C(NH2)>		CCL4
2591M	A	7.59	CHA	A<CH-C(=O)-OH/CH-C(=O)-OH>		POLYSOL-D
1588M	B	6.78	CHA	A<CH-C*-O>		CCL4
982M	C	7.41	CHA	A<CNQ2(H/C:N/H)>		CCL4
736M	B	8.48	CHA	A<C(ANNN<C-N-C(A)-N/N-C(A)>)>		TFA
1732M	D	7.41 APP.	CHA	A<C(ANN<C-N-C(CH2.2-OH)/CH-N>)>		CDCL3
697M	C	7.93	CHA	A<C(AN<C-N>)>		CDCL3
996M	A	7.90	CHA	A<C(A<C-CH-CH-C(C:N)>)/CH-C(C:N)>		TFA
531M	C	7.24	CHA	A<C(A<C-CH-CH-C(NH2)>)/CH-C(NH2)>		DMSO-D6
1909M	B	7.43	CHA	A<C(A<C-CH-CH-C(OH)>)/CH-C(OH)>		DMSO-D6
1289M	B	7.39- 8.00	CHA	A<C(A<C-CH-CH-C(SO2-OH)>)>		DMSO
1934M	C	7.30 —	CHA	A<C(A<C-CH-CH-C(C(CH3/CH3/CH3))-C(OH)/CH-C(C(CH3/CH3/CH3))>-CH-C(C(CH3/CH3/CH3))/C(C(CH3/CH3/CH3))-C(OH)>		CDCL3
1930M	B	7.10- 7.70	CHA	A<C(A<C-CH-C-C(OH)>)>		POLYSOL-D
504M	C	7.43	CHA	A<C(A<C-C(NH2)>)>		DMSO-D6
1931M	C	7.30	CHA	A<C(A<C-C(OH)/CH-C(OH)>)>		CDCL3
1052M	B	7.79	CHA	A<C(A)-CH-C(NO2)>		CDCL3
186M	B	7.66	CHA	A<C(A)/CH-C(A)>		CDCL3
1053M	B	7.82	CHA	A<C(A)/CH-C(NO2)>		C3H6O
1289M	C	7.81 APP.	CHA	A<C(A)/CH-C(SO2-OH)>		DMSO
381M	B	7.41 APP.	CHA	A<C(BR)>		CCL4
397M	B	7.29	CHA	A<C(BR)-CH-C(BR)>		CCL4
523M	C	7.18	CHA	A<C(BR)-CH-C(BR)/CH-C(NH2)>		CDCL3
1921M	C	7.36	CHA	A<C(BR)-CH-C(BR)/CH-C(OH)>		CCL4
2068M	C	7.62	CHA	A<C(BR)-CH-C(C(=O)-CH3)>		CCL4
2233M	B	7.79	CHA	A<C(BR)-CH-C(C(=O)-CL)>		CCL4
375M	D	7.46	CHA	A<C(BR)-C(CH2-CH3)>		CCL4
434M	C	7.65	CHA	A<C(BR)-C(I)>		CCL4
434M	C	7.79	CHA	A<C(BR)-C(I)>		CCL4
524M	B	7.50	CHA	A<C(BR)-C(NH2)-C(BR)/C(BR)>		CDCL3
523M	D	7.51	CHA	A<C(BR)-C(NH2)/C(BR)>		CDCL3
1894M	E	7.43	CHA	A<C(BR)-C(OH)>		CDCL3
1921M	D	7.62	CHA	A<C(BR)-C(OH)/C(BR)>		CCL4
1517M	F	7.46	CHA	A<C(BR)-C(O-CH2)>		CCL4
398M	A	7.29	CHA	A<C(BR)/CH-C(BR)>		CDCL3
388M	B	7.60	CHA	A<C(BR)/CH-C(CF3)>		CCL4
2218M	E	7.33	CHA	A<C(BR)/CH-C(CH2-CH2)>		CDCL3

BOOK NO.	ASSIGN-MENT	CHEM SHIFT - ppm -	PROTON GROUP	ENVIRONMENTAL GROUPS	S	SOLVENT
394M	B	7.37	CHA	A<C(BR)/CH-C(CL)>		CCL4
2169M	A	7.68 APP.	CHA	A<C(BR)/CH-C(C(=O)-H)>		CDCL3
2574M	B	7.71	CHA	A<C(BR)/CH-C(C(=O)-OH)>		DMSO-D6
391M	B	7.40	CHA	A<C(BR)/CH-C(F)>		CCL4
435M	A	7.18	CHA	A<C(BR)/CH-C(I)>		CDCL3
2424M	B	7.37	CHA	A<C(BR)/CH-C(NH-C(=O))>		DMSO-D6
2331M	C	7.45	CHA	A<C(BR)/CH-C(NH-C(=O))>		DMSO-D6
2331M	C	7.61	CHA	A<C(BR)/CH-C(NH-C(=O))>		DMSO-D6
1542M	C	7.29	CHA	A<C(BR)/CH-C(O-A)>		CCL4
2388M	B	7.31	CHA	A<C(BR)/CH-C(R5N<N-C(=O)/C(=O)>)>		POLYSOL-D
1235M	C	7.30	CHA	A<C(BR)/CH-C(SH)>		CDCL3
1303M	A	7.68	CHA	A<C(BR)/CH-C(SO3-NA)>	S	D20
1160M	C	7.39	CHA	A<C(BR)/CH-C(S-CH3)>		CDCL3
397M	C	7.55	CHA	A<C(BR)/C(BR)>		CCL4
395M	E	7.47	CHA	A<C(BR)/C(CH2-BR)>		CDCL3
2068M	E	7.99	CHA	A<C(BR)/C(C(=O)-CH3)>		CCL4
2233M	D	8.19	CHA	A<C(BR)/C(C(=O)-CL)>		CCL4
395M	D	7.36	CHA	A<C(BR-CH-C(CH2-BR)>		CDCL3
431M	B	7.59	CHA	A<C(CF3)-CH-C(I)>		CCL4
506M	D	6.92	CHA	A<C(CF3)-CH-C(NH2)>		CDCL3
388M	A	7.49	CHA	A<C(CF3)/CH-C(BR)>		CCL4
300M	B	7.53	CHA	A<C(CF3)/CH-C(CL)>		CCL4
2226M	A	7.73	CHA	A<C(CF3)/CH-C(C(=O)-CL)>		CDCL3
229M	B	7.64	CHA	A<C(CF3)/CH-C(F)>		CCL4
507M	C	7.35	CHA	A<C(CF3)/CH-C(NH2)>		CDCL3
1272M	A	7.40- 8.35	CHA	A<C(CF3)/C(SO2-A)>		CDCL3
1928M	F	6.85	CHA	A<C(CH2.15-CH3)-C(OH)/CH-C(OH)>		POLYSOL-D
1503M	E	7.03	CHA	A<C(CH2.2-BR)/CH-C(O-CH3)>		CCL4
2212M	C	6.90- 7.40	CHA	A<C(CH2.2-C(=O)-CL)>		CCL4
1902M	E	7.03	CHA	A<C(CH2.2-C:N)/CH-C(OH)>		CDCL3
529M	D	6.98	CHA	A<C(CH2.2-NH2)/CH-C(NH2)>		CDCL3
2309M	E	7.21 APP.	CHA	A<C(CH2.2-NH)>		CDCL3
1718M	E	6.91	CHA	A<C(CH2.2-OH)/CH-C(NH2)>		POLYSOL-D
2836M	E	7.18 APP.	CHA	A<C(CH2.2-O-C(=O))>		CCL4
2385M	D	7.20 APP.	CHA	A<C(CH2.2-R5N)>		POLYSOL-D
2014M	C	7.22 APP.	CHA	A<C(CH2.2-R6N)>		CDCL3
2849M	E	7.11 APP.	CHA	A<C(CH2.3-C(=O)-O)>		CCL4
1884M	G	6.93	CHA	A<C(CH2.4-CH3)/CH-C(OH)>		CCL4
1933M	F	7.00	CHA	A<C(CH2-A)-C(OH)-C(C(CH3/CH3/CH3))/C(CH2-CH3)>		CDCL3
666M	D	7.01	CHA	A<C(CH2-A)/CH-C(N(CH3/CH3))>		CDCL3
918M	C	7.07	CHA	A<C(CH2-A)/CH-C(N=C=O)>		POLYSOL-D
1888M	C	7.00	CHA	A<C(CH2-A)/CH-C(OH)>		DMSO-D6
395M	C	7.22	CHA	A<C(CH2-BR)-CH-C(BR)>		CDCL3
373M	D	7.18	CHA	A<C(CH2-BR)/CH-C(CH3)>		CCL4
147M	C	7.14	CHA	A<C(CH2-CH2)>		CDCL3
2831M	C	7.16	CHA	A<C(CH2-CH2)>		CCL4
973M	C	7.16	CHA	A<C(CH2-CH2)>		CDCL3
1163M	C	7.17	CHA	A<C(CH2-CH2)>		CDCL3
2311M	C	7.22 APP.	CHA	A<C(CH2-CH2)>		CDCL3
137M	D	7.09	CHA	A<C(CH2-CH2)>		CCL4
143M	D	7.10	CHA	A<C(CH2-CH2)>		CCL4
141M	D	7.13	CHA	A<C(CH2-CH2)>		CCL4
482M	E	7.12	CHA	A<C(CH2-CH2)>		CCL4
2835M	E	7.19	CHA	A<C(CH2-CH2)>		CCL4
1927M	G	6.86	CHA	A<C(CH2-CH2)-C(OH)/CH-C(OH)>		CDCL3
2218M	D	6.98	CHA	A<C(CH2-CH2)/CH-C(BR)>		CDCL3
1501M	F	6.98	CHA	A<C(CH2-CH2)/CH-C(O-CH3)>		CCL4
190M	C	6.73	CHA	A<C(CH2-CH3)-CH-C(CH2-CH3)/C(CH2-CH3)>		CCL4
492M	F	6.55	CHA	A<C(CH2-CH3)-CH-C(NH2)>		CDCL3
503M	E	6.61	CHA	A<C(CH2-CH3)-C(NH2)-C(CH2-CH3)/C(CH3)>		CCL4
500M	F	6.90	CHA	A<C(CH2-CH3)-C(NH2)-C(CH3)>		CDCL3
929M	C	7.04	CHA	A<C(CH2-CH3)-C(N=C=N)-C(CH2-CH3)>		CDCL3
1050M	C	7.30	CHA	A<C(CH2-CH3)/CH-C(NO2)>		CCL4
1497M	E	7.03	CHA	A<C(CH2-CH3)/CH-C(O-CH3)>		CCL4
2544M	B	7.24 APP.	CHA	A<C(CH2-CH)>		CDCL3
2308M	C	7.27	CHA	A<C(CH2-CH)>		DMSO-D6
139M	D	6.98	CHA	A<C(CH2-CH)>		CDCL3
1791M	D	7.21 APP.	CHA	A<C(CH2-CH)>		CDCL3
804M	E	7.25	CHA	A<C(CH2-CH)>	S	CDCL3
311M	B	7.11	CHA	A<C(CH2-CL)-CH-C(CL)/CH-C(CL)>		CCL4
286M	D	7.20	CHA	A<C(CH2-CL)-C(CH3)/C(CH2-CL)-C(CH3)>		CDCL3
2312M	D	7.21	CHA	A<C(CH2-C(=O))>		CDCL3
2086M	B	7.21 APP.	CHA	A<C(CH2-C(=O)-A)/CH-C(CL)>		POLYSOL-D
2035M	D	7.15 APP.	CHA	A<C(CH2-C(=O)-CH)>		CCL4
2563M	E	7.19	CHA	A<C(CH2-C(=O)-OH)/CH-C(O-CH2)>		CDCL3
2673M	B	7.32	CHA	A<C(CH2-C(=O)-O)>	S	D20
2932M	D	7.20	CHA	A<C(CH2-C(=O)-O)>		CCL4
2848M	E	7.18 APP.	CHA	A<C(CH2-C(=O)-O)>		CCL4
2847M	E	7.21 APP.	CHA	A<C(CH2-C(=O)-O)>		CCL4
2933M	E	7.30	CHA	A<C(CH2-C(=O)-O)>		CDCL3
2561M	B	7.60	CHA	A<C(CH2-C(=O)-O)/CH-C(NO2)>		TFA

BOOK NO.	ASSIGN-MENT	CHEM SHIFT - ppm -	PROTON GROUP	ENVIRONMENTAL GROUPS	S	SOLVENT
1332M	B	7.05- 7.45	CHA	A<C(CH2-C(=S))>		POLYSOL-D
981M	B	7.24	CHA	A<C(CH2-C:N)/CH-C(CL)>		CCL4
425M	B	7.05- 7.45	CHA	A<C(CH2-I)>		CDCL3
782M	B	7.59	CHA	A<C(CH2-NH2)>	S	D2O
1505M	D	6.74 APP.	CHA	A<C(CH2-NH2)-CH-C(O-CH3)>		CDCL3
1504M	E	7.19	CHA	A<C(CH2-NH2)-C(n-CH3)>		CDCL3
486M	E	7.11 APP.	CHA	A<C(CH2-NH2)/CH-C(CH(CH3/CH3))>		CCL4
1505M	E	6.81	CHA	A<C(CH2-NH2)/C(n-CH3)>		CDCL3
805M	B	7.44	CHA	A<C(CH2-NH)>	S	TFA
581M	C	7.20	CHA	A<C(CH2-NH)>		CCL4
2432M	C	7.20 APP.	CHA	A<C(CH2-NH)>		POLYSOL-D
2346M	C	7.26	CHA	A<C(CH2-NH)>		CDCL3
580M	C	7.29 APP.	CHA	A<C(CH2-NH)>		D2O
709M	D	7.10- 7.50	CHA	A<C(CH2-NH)>		DMSO-D6
2422M	D	7.25 APP.	CHA	A<C(CH2-NH)>		POLYSOL-D
577M	E	7.18	CHA	A<C(CH2-NH)>		CCL4
579M	E	7.19	CHA	A<C(CH2-NH)>		CCL4
578M	F	7.19	CHA	A<C(CH2-NH)>		CCL4
596M	F	7.19 APP.	CHA	A<C(CH2-NH)>		CDCL3
595M	G	7.21 APP.	CHA	A<C(CH2-NH)>		POLYSOL-D
837M	C	7.40- 7.90	CHA	A<C(CH2-N(+))>		POLYSOL-D
838M	C	7.50 APP.	CHA	A<C(CH2-N(+))>		CDCL3
1005M	B	7.30	CHA	A<C(CH2-N)>		CCL4
644M	C	7.19	CHA	A<C(CH2-N)>		CDCL3
646M	D	7.10- 7.50	CHA	A<C(CH2-N)>		CDCL3
1704M	E	7.29 APP.	CHA	A<C(CH2-N)>		CDCL3
653M	F	7.22	CHA	A<C(CH2-N)>		CDCL3
1703M	F	7.30	CHA	A<C(CH2-N)>		CDCL3
937M	B	7.29 APP.	CHA	A<C(CH2-N=C=S)>		CCL4
1700M	C	7.19	CHA	A<C(CH2-OH)>		CDCL3
1720M	D	7.64	CHA	A<C(CH2-OH)-CH-C(NO2)>		DMSO-D6
1860M	C	7.27	CHA	A<C(CH2-OH)/CH-C(CH2-O')>		CCL4
1713M	D	7.01	CHA	A<C(CH2-OH)/CH-C(CH3)>		CCL4
1714M	E	7.07	CHA	A<C(CH2-OH)/CH-C(CH(CH3/CH3))>		C3H6O
1721M	B	7.62	CHA	A<C(CH2-OH)/CH-C(NO2)>		CCL4
1723M	E	7.10	CHA	A<C(CH2-OH)/CH-C(O-CH3)>		CDCL3
3000M	B	7.28	CHA	A<C(CH2-O)>		CDCL3
2844M	C	7.38 APP.	CHA	A<C(CH2-O-C(=O))>		CCL4
2845M	E	7.29	CHA	A<C(CH2-O-C(=O))>		CDCL3
2846M	E	7.31 APP.	CHA	A<C(CH2-O-C(=O))>		TFA
2633M	E	7.34	CHA	A<C(CH2-O-C(=O))>		CDCL3
2967M	B	7.60	CHA	A<C(CH2-O-C(=O))/CH-C(NO2)>		CCL4
2839M	E	7.20	CHA	A<C(CH2-O-C(=O))/CH-C(O-CH3)>		CCL4
154M	D	7.11	CHA	A<C(CH2-O2)>		CCL4
153M	E	7.14	CHA	A<C(CH2-O3)>		CCL4
1918M	G	6.80 APP.	CHA	A<C(CH2-O3)-C(OH)-C(CH3)>		CDCL3
144M	D	7.24	CHA	A<C(CH2-R3)>		CDCL3
2445M	D	7.30	CHA	A<C(CH2-R5NN)>		CDCL3
2015M	D	7.35 APP.	CHA	A<C(CH2-R6N)>		CCL4
1225M	C	7.14	CHA	A<C(CH2-SH)/CH-C(CL)>		POLYSOL-D
1267M	C	7.00- 7.30	CHA	A<C(CH2-SO2)>		POLYSOL-D
1279M	B	7.42 APP.	CHA	A<C(CH2-SO2-F)>		CS2
1191M	B	7.17	CHA	A<C(CH2-S)>		CDCL3
1017M	B	7.38	CHA	A<C(CH2-S)>		CCL4
1158M	C	7.20	CHA	A<C(CH2-S)>		POLYSOL-D
1162M	E	7.19 APP.	CHA	A<C(CH2-S)>		CDCL3
1068M	C	7.10	CHA	A<C(CH3)-CH-C(CH3)/CH-C(NO2)>		CDCL3
1552M	E	6.91 APP.	CHA	A<C(CH3)-CH-C(CH3)/CH-C(O-CH3)>		CCL4
189M	B	6.69	CHA	A<C(CH3)-CH-C(CH3)/C(CH3)>		CCL4
299M	B	6.87	CHA	A<C(CH3)-CH-C(CL)/CH-C(CH3)>		CCL4
2057M	C	7.07	CHA	A<C(CH3)-CH-C(C(=O)-CH3)/CH-C(CH3)>		CCL4
2165M	B	7.37	CHA	A<C(CH3)-CH-C(C(=O)-H)>		CCL4
430M	C	6.97 APP.	CHA	A<C(CH3)-CH-C(I)/CH-C(CH3)>		CCL4
497M	E	6.34	CHA	A<C(CH3)-CH-C(NH2)/CH-C(CH3)		CCL4
499M	D	6.29	CHA	A<C(CH3)-CH-C(NH2)/C(CH3)>		CDCL3
590M	E	6.50	CHA	A<C(CH3)-CH-C(NH-CH3)>		CDCL3
2339M	D	6.84	CHA	A<C(CH3)-CH-C(NH-C(=O))/CH-C(CH3)>		CDCL3
897M	B	7.28 APP.	CHA	A<C(CH3)-CH-C(N=N-A)>		POLYSOL-D
2596M	B	6.65	CHA	A<C(CH3)-CH-C(OH)/CH-C(C(=O)-OH)>		CDCL3
1926M	D	6.61	CHA	A<C(CH3)-CH-C(OH)/CH-C(OH)>		CCL4
1495M	D	7.00	CHA	A<C(CH3)-CH-C(O-CH3)>		CCL4
1284M	D	7.39	CHA	A<C(CH3)-CH-C(SO2-CL)/CH-C(CH3)>		DMSO-D6
1290M	B	7.40 APP.	CHA	A<C(CH3)-CH-C(SO2-OH)/CH-C(NH2)>		CCL4
204M	B	7.12	CHA	A<C(CH3)-CH-C*/CH-C*>		CDCL3
286M	C	6.98	CHA	A<C(CH3)-C(CH2-CL)/C(CH3)-C(CH2-CL)>		CDCL3
1932M	G	6.56	CHA	A<C(CH3)-C(CH2-O3)-C(OH)/C(CH3)>		CDCL3
187M	C	7.00	CHA	A<C(CH3)-C(CH3)>		CCL4
192M	B	6.69	CHA	A<C(CH3)-C(CH3)-C(CH3)/C(CH3)>		CDCL3
194M	B	6.81	CHA	A<C(CH3)-C(CH3)-C(CH3)/C(CH3)-C(CH3)>		CDCL3
2058M	D	6.90	CHA	A<C(CH3)-C(CH3)-C(C(=O)-CH3)/C(CH3)-C(CH3)>		CDCL3
2238M	D	7.28	CHA	A<C(CH3)-C(CH3)-C(C(=O)-CL)>		CCL4

BOOK NO.	ASSIGN-MENT	CHEM SHIFT - ppm -	PROTON GROUP	ENVIRONMENTAL GROUPS	S	SOLVENT
1913M	E	6.69	CHA	A<C(CH3)-C(CH3)-C(OH)>		CDCL3
1551M	D	6.68	CHA	A<C(CH3)-C(CH3)-C(O-CH3)>		CDCL3
2239M	B	7.13	CHA	A<C(CH3)-C(CH3)/CH-C(C(=O)-CL)>		CCL4
498M	E	6.93	CHA	A<C(CH3)-C(CH3)/CH-C(NH2)>		CDCL3
299M	C	7.02	CHA	A<C(CH3)-C(CL)/CH-C(CH3)>		CCL4
308M	B	7.04 APP.	CHA	A<C(CH3)-C(CL)/CH-C(CL)>		CCL4
304M	D	7.04	CHA	A<C(CH3)-C(CL)/CH-C(F)>		CCL4
2057M	C	7.07	CHA	A<C(CH3)-C(C(=O)-CH3)/CH-C(CH3)>		CCL4
430M	C	6.97 APP.	CHA	A<C(CH3)-C(I)/CH-C(CH3)>		CCL4
500M	F	6.90	CHA	A<C(CH3)-C(NH2)-C(CH2-CH3)>		CDCL3
502M	D	6.63	CHA	A<C(CH3)-C(NH2)-C(CH3)/C(CH3)>		CCL4
497M	F	6.76	CHA	A<C(CH3)-C(NH2)/CH-C(CH3)>		CCL4
536M	E	6.79	CHA	A<C(CH3)-C(NH2)/CH-C(NH2)>		CDCL3
2640M	E	6.77	CHA	A<C(CH3)-C(NH2)/C(CH3)-C(CH3)>		CCL4
595M	F	6.90- 7.35	CHA	A<C(CH3)-C(NH-CH2)>		CDCL3
2339M	E	7.01	CHA	A<C(CH3)-C(NH-C(=O))/CH-C(CH3)>		CDCL3
1070M	D	7.03	CHA	A<C(CH3)-C(NO2)/C(NH2)>		CDCL3
1068M	D	7.13	CHA	A<C(CH3)-C(NO2)/C(CH3)>		CDCL3
664M	G	6.99	CHA	A<C(CH3)-C(N(CH2/CH2))/CH-C(CH3)>		CCL4
1918M	G	6.80 APP.	CHA	A<C(CH3)-C(OH)-C(CH2-Q3)>		CCL4
1552M	E	6.91 APP.	CHA	A<C(CH3)-C(O-CH3)/C(CH3)>		CDCL3
1284M	C	7.29	CHA	A<C(CH3)-C(SO2-CL)/CH-C(CH3)>		CCL4
373M	C	6.99	CHA	A<C(CH3)/CH-C(CH2-BR)>		CCL4
1713M	D	7.01	CHA	A<C(CH3)/CH-C(CH2-OH)>		CCL4
182M	D	6.99	CHA	A<C(CH3)/CH-C(CH(CH3/CH3))>		CCL4
2060M	E	7.21	CHA	A<C(CH3)/CH-C(C(=O)-CH2.3)>		CDCL3
2223M	B	7.24	CHA	A<C(CH3)/CH-C(C(=O)-CL)>		CCL4
2567M	B	7.30	CHA	A<C(CH3)/CH-C(C(=O)-OH)>		TFA
490M	D	6.79	CHA	A<C(CH3)/CH-C(NH2)>		CCL4
596M	E	6.83	CHA	A<C(CH3)/CH-C(NH-CH2)>		CCL4
2423M	C	7.01	CHA	A<C(CH3)/CH-C(NH-C(=O))>		DMSO-D6
660M	D	6.89	CHA	A<C(CH3)/CH-C(N(CH3/CH3))>		CCL4
2362M	E	7.19	CHA	A<C(CH3)/CH-C(N(C(=O)-H/CH2))>		CDCL3
904M	C	7.10	CHA	A<C(CH3)/CH-C(N=N-NH)>		CDCL3
1878M	D	6.92	CHA	A<C(CH3)/CH-C(OH)>		CDCL3
2943M	B	7.07	CHA	A<C(CH3)/CH-C(O-C(=O)-A)>		CCL4
2933M	D	7.08	CHA	A<C(CH3)/CH-C(O-C(=O)-CH2)>		CDCL3
2925M	G	7.10	CHA	A<C(CH3)/CH-C(O-C(=O)-CH2)>		CCL4
2979M	D	7.14	CHA	A<C(CH3)/CH-C(O-C(=O)-NH2)>		DMSO-D6
2940M	B	7.05	CHA	A<C(CH3)/CH-C(O-C(=O)-O)>		CCL4
885M	D	6.88	CHA	A<C(CH3)/CH-C(QN(N(CH3/CH3)))>		CCL4
870M	B	7.08	CHA	A<C(CH3)/CH-C(QN(Q2))>		CDCL3
1821M	D	7.11	CHA	A<C(CH3)/CH-C(R6<C-(OH)-CH2/CH2>)>		CDCL3
184M	E	6.99	CHA	A<C(CH3)/CH-C(R6<C=CH/CH2>)>		CCL4
1264M	C	7.42	CHA	A<C(CH3)/CH-C(Sn2-CH2)>		POLYSOL-D
1267M	D	7.29	CHA	A<C(CH3)/CH-C(Sn2-CH2)>		POLYSOL-D
1709M	D	7.32	CHA	A<C(CH3)/CH-C(Sn2-CH2)>		CDCL3
1262M	F	7.34	CHA	A<C(CH3)/CH-C(Sn2-CH2)>		CDCL3
1283M	B	7.41	CHA	A<C(CH3)/CH-C(Sn2-CL)>		CDCL3
1708M	E	6.92	CHA	A<C(CH3)/CH-C(S-CH2.2)>		CCL4
1162M	C	7.01	CHA	A<C(CH3)/CH-C(S-CH2)>		POLYSOL-D
1196M	B	7.05	CHA	A<C(CH3)/CH-C(S-S)>		CDCL3
204M	C	7.35- 7.65	CHA	A<C(CH3)/C*>		CCL4
664M	E	6.71	CHA	A<C(CH3-CH-C(N(CH2/CH2))/CH-C(CH3)>		CCL4
667M	C	7.49	CHA	A<C(CH(A/A))/CH-C(N(CH3/CH3))>		TFA
1901M	E	7.00	CHA	A<C(CH(A/A))/CH-C(N(CH3/CH3))>		POLYSOL-D
1901M	E	7.00	CHA	A<C(CH(A/A))/CH-C(OH)>		POLYSOL-D
376M	B	7.15- 7.68	CHA	A<C(CH(BR/BR))>		CDCL3
479M	D	7.20 APP.	CHA	A<C(CH(CH2/CH3))>		CDCL3
501M	E	7.03	CHA	A<C(CH(CH3/CH3))-C(NH2)-C(CH(CH3/CH3))>		CDCL3
486M	E	7.11 APP.	CHA	A<C(CH(CH3/CH3))/CH-C(CH2-NH2)>		CCL4
1714M	E	7.07	CHA	A<C(CH(CH3/CH3))/CH-C(CH2-OH)>		CCL4
182M	D	6.99	CHA	A<C(CH(CH3/CH3))/CH-C(CH3)>		CCL4
493M	E	7.03	CHA	A<C(CH(CH3/CH3))/CH-C(NH2)>		CDCL3
592M	F	7.01	CHA	A<C(CH(CH3/CH3))/CH-C(NH-CH3)>		CDCL3
1881M	E	7.03	CHA	A<C(CH(CH3/CH3))/CH-C(OH)>		CDCL3
2213M	B	7.40	CHA	A<C(CH(CL/C(=O)))>		CCL4
631M	G	7.39	CHA	A<C(CH(C(=O)-O/CH2))>		D20
784M	D	7.51	CHA	A<C(CH(NH2/CH3))>		TFA
2310M	E	7.29	CHA	A<C(CH(NH/CH3))>	S	CDCL3
975M	C	7.20- 7.60	CHA	A<C(CH(N/C:N))>		CDCL3
1788M	E	7.18	CHA	A<C(CH(OH/CH2))>		CCL4
1791M	E	7.33 APP.	CHA	A<C(CH(OH/CH2))>		CDCL3
2850M	F	7.05- 7.45	CHA	A<C(CH(OH/CH2))>		CCL4
1480M	F	7.25	CHA	A<C(CH(O/CH2))>		CDCL3
1483M	E	7.16	CHA	A<C(CH(O/CH3))>		CCL4
1483M	E	7.21	CHA	A<C(CH(O/CH3))>		CCL4
1483M	F	7.21	CHA	A<C(CH(O/CH3))>		CCL4
2552M	C	7.15- 7.60	CHA	A<C(CH(O/C(=O)-OH))>		CDCL3
306M	A	7.22	CHA	A<C(CL)-CH-C(CL)>		CCL4
308M	B	7.04 APP.	CHA	A<C(CL)-CH-C(CL)/CH-C(CH3)>		CCL4

: REPRESENTS TRIPLE BOND, ¬ REPRESENTS AN ARROW AND < AND > REPRESENT BRACKETS.   PAGE   328

BOOK NO.	ASSIGN-MENT	CHEM SHIFT - ppm -	PROTON GROUP	ENVIRONMENTAL GROUPS	S	SOLVENT
2176M	A	7.31	CHA	A<C(CL)-CH-C(CL)/CH-C(C(=O)-H)>		CDCL3
516M	C	7.00	CHA	A<C(CL)-CH-C(CL)/CH-C(NH2)>		CDCL3
1919M	C	7.13	CHA	A<C(CL)-CH-C(CL)/CH-C(OH)>		CDCL3
314M	A	7.30	CHA	A<C(CL)-CH-C(CL)/C(CL)>		CDCL3
2065M	B	7.15- 7.63	CHA	A<C(CL)-CH-C(C(=O)-CH3)>		CCL4
2067M	B	7.32	CHA	A<C(CL)-CH-C(C(=O)-CH3)/CH-C(CL)>		CCL4
2079M	C	7.38	CHA	A<C(CL)-CH-C(C(=O)-CH3)/CH-C(OH)>		CDCL3
2167M	A	7.60	CHA	A<C(CL)-CH-C(C(=O)-H)>		CDCL3
2873M	C	7.46	CHA	A<C(CL)-CH-C(C(=O)-O-CH3)>		CCL4
757M	B	6.65	CHA	A<C(CL)-CH-C(NH-NH2)/CH-C(CL)>		CDCL3
1057M	B	7.67	CHA	A<C(CL)-CH-C(NO2)>		CDCL3
920M	A	7.09 APP.	CHA	A<C(CL)-CH-C(N=C=O)/CH-C(CL)>		CDCL3
1232M	B	6.99	CHA	A<C(CL)-CH-C(SH)/CH-C(CL)>		CCL4
1018M	B	7.33 APP.	CHA	A<C(CL)-C(CH2-S)-C(CL)>		CDCL3
299M	D	7.11	CHA	A<C(CL)-C(CH3)/C(CH3)>		CCL4
308M	C	7.30	CHA	A<C(CL)-C(CH3)/C(CL)>		CCL4
304M	C	6.99	CHA	A<C(CL)-C(CH3)/C(F)>		CCL4
311M	C	7.36	CHA	A<C(CL)-C(CL)/CH-C(CH2-CL)>		CCL4
2177M	A	7.58	CHA	A<C(CL)-C(CL)/CH-C(C(=O)-H)>		CDCL3
310M	C	7.32	CHA	A<C(CL)-C(CL)/CH-C(F)>		CCL4
1233M	C	7.24	CHA	A<C(CL)-C(CL)/CH-C(SH)>		CDCL3
1266M	C	7.70	CHA	A<C(CL)-C(CL)/CH-C(SO2-CH2)>		CDCL3
311M	D	7.39	CHA	A<C(CL)-C(CL)/C(CH2-CL)>		CCL4
315M	A	7.52	CHA	A<C(CL)-C(CL)/C(CL)-C(CL)>		CDCL3
2177M	B	7.68	CHA	A<C(CL)-C(CL)/C(C(=O)-H)>		CCL4
310M	B	7.15	CHA	A<C(CL)-C(CL)/C(F)>		CDCL3
1233M	D	7.29	CHA	A<C(CL)-C(CL)/C(SH)>		CCL4
1266M	E	8.10	CHA	A<C(CL)-C(CL)/C(SO2-CH2)>		CDCL3
2067M	B	7.32	CHA	A<C(CL)-C(C(=O)-CH3)/CH-C(CL)>		CCL4
2176M	B	7.40	CHA	A<C(CL)-C(C(=O)-H)/C(CL)>		CDCL3
517M	B	7.18	CHA	A<C(CL)-C(NH2)-C(CL)/C(CL)>		CDCL3
516M	D	7.22	CHA	A<C(CL)-C(NH2)/C(CL)>		CDCL3
796M	B	7.85	CHA	A<C(CL)-C(NH2)/C(NH2)>	S	D2O
757M	C	7.12 APP.	CHA	A<C(CL)-C(NH-NH2)/CH-C(CL)>		CDCL3
920M	B	7.26	CHA	A<C(CL)-C(N=C=O)/CH-C(CL)>		CDCL3
1943M	A	6.76	CHA	A<C(CL)-C(OH)-C(CL)/C(OH)>		POLYSOL-D
1922M	B	7.71	CHA	A<C(CL)-C(OH)-C(NO2)>		CDCL3
1919M	D	7.28	CHA	A<C(CL)-C(OH)/C(CL)>		CDCL3
1566M	B	7.29	CHA	A<C(CL)-C(O-CH3)-C(CL)/C(CL)>		CDCL3
296M	E	7.40	CHA	A<C(CL)-C(Q3)>		CCL4
1240M	D	7.11	CHA	A<C(CL)-C(SH)/CH-C(SH)>		CCL4
394M	A	7.13	CHA	A<C(CL)/CH-C(RR)>		CCL4
300M	A	7.42	CHA	A<C(CL)/CH-C(CF3)>		CCL4
2086M	B	7.21 APP.	CHA	A<C(CL)/CH-C(CH2-C(=O)-A)>		POLYSOL-D
981M	B	7.24	CHA	A<C(CL)/CH-C(CH2-C:N)>		CCL4
1225M	C	7.14	CHA	A<C(CL)/CH-C(CH2-SH)>		CCL4
2231M	A	7.46	CHA	A<C(CL)/CH-C(C(=O)-CL)>		CDCL3
2410M	C	7.30	CHA	A<C(CL)/CH-C(C(=O)-NH)>		CDCL3
2941M	B	7.35	CHA	A<C(CL)/CH-C(O-C(=O)-O)>		CDCL3
1707M	B	7.26	CHA	A<C(CL)/CH-C(QN(CH2.2-OH))>		CDCL3
1274M	A	7.42	CHA	A<C(CL)/CH-C(SO2-A)>		CDCL3
1263M	E	7.50	CHA	A<C(CL)/CH-C(SO2-CH2)>		CDCL3
1250M	D	7.53	CHA	A<C(CL)/CH-C(SO-CH2.2)>		CDCL3
1171M	A	7.28 APP.	CHA	A<C(CL)/CH-C(S-A)>		POLYSOL-D
1197M	A	7.20	CHA	A<C(CL)/CH-C(S-S)>		CDCL3
306M	B	7.39	CHA	A<C(CL)/C(CL)>		CCL4
2065M	D	7.82	CHA	A<C(CL)/C(C(=O)-CH3)		CCL4
2067M	C	7.49	CHA	A<C(CL)/C(C(=O)-CH3)-C(CL)>		CCL4
2079M	D	7.67	CHA	A<C(CL)/C(C(=O)-CH3)-C(OH)>		CDCL3
2167M	C	7.85	CHA	A<C(CL)/C(C(=O)-H)>		CDCL3
2873M	E	7.92	CHA	A<C(CL)/C(C(=O)-O-CH3)>		CCL4
2329M	C	7.70	CHA	A<C(CL)/C(NH-C(=O))>		CDCL3
757M	C	7.12 APP.	CHA	A<C(CL)/C(NH-NH2)-C(CL)>		CDCL3
1057M	C	8.10 APP.	CHA	A<C(CL)/C(NO2)>		CDCL3
920M	A	7.09 APP.	CHA	A<C(CL)/C(N=C=O)-C(CL)>		CDCL3
1580M	D	8.07	CHA	A<C(CL)/C(R5NO<C=N/O>)>		CCL4
1232M	C	7.20	CHA	A<C(Cl)-C(SH)/CH-C(CL)>		CCL4
1232M	D	7.28	CHA	A<C(Cl)/C(SH)-C(CL)>		POLYSOL-D
1908M	C	7.04	CHA	A<C(C(A/CH3/CH3))/CH-C(OH)>		CDCL3
1539M	G	7.13	CHA	A<C(C(A/CH3/CH3))/CH-C(O-CH2)>		CDCL3
977M	C	7.38 APP.	CHA	A<C(C(A/C:N/CH2))>		DMSO-D6
2543M	E	7.28 APP.	CHA	A<C(C(CH2/CH2.2/CH2.2))>		CCL4
1882M	F	7.19	CHA	A<C(C(CH3/CH3/CH3))-C(OH)>		CDCL3
2224M	B	7.52	CHA	A<C(C(CH3/CH3/CH3))/CH-C(C(=O)-CL)>		CCL4
2870M	D	7.36	CHA	A<C(C(CH3/CH3/CH3))/CH-C(C(=O)-O-CH2)>		DMSO-D6
2547M	A	6.90- 7.50	CHA	A<C(C(C(=O)-OH/A/A))>		CCL4
2852M	D	7.27	CHA	A<C(C(C(=O)-O/C(=O)-O/CH3))>		DMSO-D6
979M	C	7.49 APP.	CHA	A<C(C(C:N/CH2.2/CH2.2))>		CDCL3
925M	B	7.28 APP.	CHA	A<C(C(N=C=N/A/A))>		CDCL3
1822M	B	7.19	CHA	A<C(C(OH/A/A))>		CCL4
1820M	E	7.00- 7.40	CHA	A<C(C(OH/A/CH2.7))>		

: REPRESENTS TRIPLE BOND, ¬ REPRESENTS AN ARROW AND < AND > REPRESENT BRACKETS.

BOOK NO.	ASSIGN-MENT	CHEM SHIFT - ppm -	PROTON GROUP	ENVIRONMENTAL GROUPS	S	SOLVENT
2556M	B	7.23- 7.72	CHA	A<C(C(OH/C(=O)-OH/A))>		C3H6O
1819M	E	7.68	CHA	A<C(C(OH/C:C/CH3))>		CDCL3
1481M	C	7.12 APP.	CHA	A<C(C(O/A/A))>		CDCL3
1481M	E	7.43 APP.	CHA	A<C(C(O/A/A))>		CDCL3
1486M	C	7.49	CHA	A<C(C(O/O/A))>		CDCL3
1487M	B	7.20- 7.60	CHA	A<C(C(O/O/O))>		CCL4
2172M	A	8.09	CHA	A<C(C(=O))/CH-C(NO2)>		CDCL3
2112M	B	7.80	CHA	A<C(C(=O)-AN)>		CDCL3
2107M	B	7.88	CHA	A<C(C(=O)-A)>		CDCL3
2103M	D	7.30- 7.90	CHA	A<C(C(=O)-A)>		DMSO-D6
2107M	C	7.92	CHA	A<C(C(=O)-A)/CH-C(C(=O)-A))>		CDCL3
2221M	B	8.02	CHA	A<C(C(=O)-BR)>		CCL4
2050M	F	7.91	CHA	A<C(C(=O)-CH2.12)>		CDCL3
2070M	F	7.73	CHA	A<C(C(=O)-CH2.2)/CH-C(NH2)>		CDCL3
2077M	F	7.80	CHA	A<C(C(=O)-CH2.2)/CH-C(O-CH3)>		CCL4
2060M	F	7.83	CHA	A<C(C(=O)-CH2.3)/CH-C(CH3)>		CDCL3
2071M	F	7.75	CHA	A<C(C(=O)-CH2.3)/CH-C(NH2)>		CDCL3
2051M	C	7.90	CHA	A<C(C(=O)-CH2)>		CDCL3
2052M	D	7.88	CHA	A<C(C(=O)-CH2)>.		CDCL3
2086M	D	7.95	CHA	A<C(C(=O)-CH2)>		POLYSOL-D
2089M	D	7.98	CHA	A<C(C(=O)-CH2)>		CDCL3
2047M	E	7.87	CHA	A<C(C(=O)-CH2)>		CCL4
2068M	D	7.80	CHA	A<C(C(=O)-CH3)-CH-C(BR)>		CCL4
2069M	C	7.79	CHA	A<C(C(=O)-CH3)-CH-C(I)>		CDCL3
2055M	D	7.59	CHA	A<C(C(=O)-CH3)-C(CH3)>		CCL4
2078M	D	7.70	CHA	A<C(C(=O)-CH3)-C(CH3)/CH-C(OH)>		DMSO-D6
2057M	D	7.42	CHA	A<C(C(=O)-CH3)-C(CH3)/C(CH3)>		CCL4
2063M	C	7.86	CHA	A<C(C(=O)-CH3)-C(F)/CH-C(F)>		CCL4
2082M	B	8.05	CHA	A<C(C(=O)-CH3)/CH-C(C(=O)-CH3)>		CDCL3
2076M	E	7.91	CHA	A<C(C(=O)-CH3)/CH-C(O-CH2)>		CDCL3
2074M	C	7.81	CHA	A<C(C(=O)-CH3)/CH-C(S-CH3)>		POLYSOL-D
2087M	C	8.01	CHA	A<C(C(=O)-CH)>		CDCL3
2090M	E	8.03	CHA	A<C(C(=O)-CH)>		CDCL3
1865M	F	8.06	CHA	A<C(C(=O)-CH)>		CDCL3
2220M	B	8.04	CHA	A<C(C(=O)-CL)>		CCL4
2233M	C	8.03	CHA	A<C(C(=O)-CL)-CH-C(BR)>		CCL4
2239M	C	7.71 APP.	CHA	A<C(C(=O)-CL)-CH-C(CH3)/CH-C(CH3)>		CCL4
2065M	C	7.78	CHA	A<C(C(=O)-CL)-CH-C(CL)>		CCL4
2236M	B	8.49	CHA	A<C(C(=O)-CL)-CH-C(NO2)>		CDCL3
2236M	B	8.61	CHA	A<C(C(=O)-CL)-CH-C(NO2)>		CDCL3
2232M	B	8.00	CHA	A<C(C(=O)-CL)-C(BR)>		CCL4
2238M	E	7.84	CHA	A<C(C(=O)-CL)-C(CH3)-C(CH3)>		CCL4
2229M	B	8.01	CHA	A<C(C(=O)-CL)-C(CL)>		CCL4
2226M	B	8.20	CHA	A<C(C(=O)-CL)/CH-C(CF3)>		CDCL3
2223M	C	7.96	CHA	A<C(C(=O)-CL)/CH-C(CH3)>		CCL4
2231M	B	8.02	CHA	A<C(C(=O)-CL)/CH-C(CL)>		CDCL3
2224M	C	8.06	CHA	A<C(C(=O)-CL)/CH-C(C(CH3/CH3/CH3))>		CDCL3
2239M	C	7.71 APP.	CHA	A<C(C(=O)-CL)/C(CH3)-C(CH3)>		CCL4
2135M	C	7.94	CHA	A<C(C(=O)-C(=O))/CH-C(O-CH3)>		CDCL3
2219M	B	7.94	CHA	A<C(C(=O)-F)>		CCL4
2165M	C	7.60	CHA	A<C(C(=O)-H)-CH-C(CH3)>		CCL4
2167M	B	7.80	CHA	A<C(C(=O)-H)-CH-C(CL)>		CDCL3
2177M	C	7.89	CHA	A<C(C(=O)-H)-CH-C(CL)/CH-C(CL)>		CCL4
2171M	B	8.29	CHA	A<C(C(=O)-H)-CH-C(NO2)>		CDCL3
2171M	B	8.51	CHA	A<C(C(=O)-H)-CH-C(NO2)>		CDCL3
2168M	B	7.82	CHA	A<C(C(=O)-H)-C(BR)>		CCL4
2164M	C	7.72	CHA	A<C(C(=O)-H)-C(CH3)>		CCL4
2176M	C	7.80	CHA	A<C(C(=O)-H)-C(CL)/CH-C(CL)>		CDCL3
2169M	A	7.68 APP.	CHA	A<C(C(=O)-H)/CH-C(BR)>		CDCL3
2173M	E	7.69	CHA	A<C(C(=O)-H)/CH-C(O-CH2.2)>		CCL4
2175M	F	7.72	CHA	A<C(C(=O)-H)/CH-C(O-CH2)>		CCL4
2165M	C	7.60	CHA	A<C(C(=O)-H)/C(CH3)>		CCL4
2293M	D	8.02	CHA	A<C(C(=O)-NH2)-C(OH)>		DMSO-D6
2410M	D	7.69	CHA	A<C(C(=O)-NH)/CH-C(CL)>		CDCL3
2414M	B	7.00- 7.60	CHA	A<C(C(=O)-N)>		CDCL3
2370M	E	7.32 APP.	CHA	A<C(C(=O)-N)>		CDCL3
2591M	B	8.20	CHA	A<C(C(=O)-OH)-CH-C(C(=O)-OH)>		POLYSOL-D
2602M	A	8.80	CHA	A<C(C(=O)-OH)-CH-C(NO2)/C(C(=O)-OH)>		DMSO
2600M	B	7.52	CHA	A<C(C(=O)-OH)-CH-C(OH)/CH-C(OH)>		DMSO-D6
2598M	D	7.67	CHA	A<C(C(=O)-OH)-CH-C(O-CH3)/CH-C(OH)>		DMSO-D6
2601M	A	7.95	CHA	A<C(C(=O)-OH)-C(C(=O)-OH)/CH-C(NO2)>		D2O
2569M	B	8.02	CHA	A<C(C(=O)-OH)-C(F)>		POLYSOL-D
2575M	E	8.06	CHA	A<C(C(=O)-OH)-C(I)>		C3D6O
2581M	B	7.90	CHA	A<C(C(=O)-OH)-C(NO2)>		C3H6O
2587M	D	8.00	CHA	A<C(C(=O)-OH)-C(OH)>		TFA
2596M	D	7.72	CHA	A<C(C(=O)-OH)-C(OH)/CH-C(CH3)>		POLYSOL-D
2585M	F	8.08	CHA	A<C(C(=O)-OH)-C(O-CH2)>		CCL4
2574M	C	7.90	CHA	A<C(C(=O)-OH)/CH-C(BR)>		DMSO-D6
2567M	C	8.02	CHA	A<C(C(=O)-OH)/CH-C(CH3)>		TFA
2592M	A	8.11	CHA	A<C(C(=O)-OH)/CH-C(C(=O)-OH)>		DMSO-D6
2570M	B	8.11	CHA	A<C(C(=O)-OH)/CH-C(F)>		C3H6O

BOOK NO.	ASSIGN-MENT	CHEM SHIFT - ppm -	PROTON GROUP	ENVIRONMENTAL GROUPS	S	SOLVENT
2577M	B	7.90	CHA	A<C(C(=O)-OH)/CH-C(I)>		DMSO-D6
2578M	C	7.83	CHA	A<C(C(=O)-OH)/CH-C(NH2)>		C3H6O
2588M	B	8.11	CHA	A<C(C(=O)-OH)/CH-C(OH)>		C3H6O
2591M	D	11.70	CHA	A<C(C(=O)-OH)/C(C(=O)-OH)>		POLYSOL-D
2545M	C	7.23	CHA	A<C(C(=O)-OH/A/CH2.2)>		CDCL3
2678M	D	7.92	CHA	A<C(C(=O)-ONA)-C(OH)>		D2O
2677M	B	7.82	CHA	A<C(C(=O)-ONA)/CH-C(NH2)>		D2O
2943M	D	8.12	CHA	A<C(C(=O)-O-A)>		CCL4
2863M	E	8.01	CHA	A<C(C(=O)-O-CH2.2)>		CCL4
2865M	E	8.03	CHA	A<C(C(=O)-O-CH2.2)>		CDCL3
2897M	E	7.62	CHA	A<C(C(=O)-O-CH2.4)-C(C(=O)-O-CH2.4)>		CCL4
2879M	H	7.75	CHA	A<C(C(=O)-O-CH2.4)-C(NH2)>		DMSO-D6
2944M	C	8.04	CHA	A<C(C(=O)-O-CH2)>		CDCL3
2867M	D	8.00	CHA	A<C(C(=O)-O-CH2)>		CCL4
2902M	E	8.05 APP.	CHA	A<C(C(=O)-O-CH2)-CH-C(C(=O)-O-CH2)>		CCL4
2903M	F	8.12	CHA	A<C(C(=O)-O-CH2)-CH-C(C(=O)-O-CH2)>		CCL4
2904M	F	8.25	CHA	A<C(C(=O)-O-CH2)-CH-C(C(=O)-O-CH2)>		CDCL3
2871M	F	7.76	CHA	A<C(C(=O)-O-CH2)-CH-C(F)>		CCL4
2885M	D	10.00 APP.	CHA	A<C(C(=O)-O-CH2)-CH-C(NO2)>		CCL4
2898M	E	7.65	CHA	A<C(C(=O)-O-CH2)-C(C(=O)-O-CH2)>		CCL4
2899M	F	7.67	CHA	A<C(C(=O)-O-CH2)-C(C(=O)-O-CH2)>		CCL4
2877M	G	7.75	CHA	A<C(C(=O)-O-CH2)-C(NH2)>		CCL4
2890M	G	7.70	CHA	A<C(C(=O)-O-CH2)-C(OH)>		CCL4
2870M	E	7.88	CHA	A<C(C(=O)-O-CH2)/CH-C(C(CH3/CH3/CH3))>		CCL4
2907M	C	8.07	CHA	A<C(C(=O)-O-CH2)/CH-C(C(=O)-O-CH2)>		CDCL3
2908M	D	7.98	CHA	A<C(C(=O)-O-CH2)/CH-C(C(=O)-O-CH2)>		CCL4
2909M	E	8.11	CHA	A<C(C(=O)-O-CH2)/CH-C(C(=O)-O-CH2)>		CDCL3
2894M	E	7.80	CHA	A<C(C(=O)-O-CH2)/CH-C(OH)>		CCL4
2902M	F	8.53	CHA	A<C(C(=O)-O-CH2)/C(C(=O)-O-CH2)>		CCL4
2903M	G	8.56	CHA	A<C(C(=O)-O-CH2)/C(C(=O)-O-CH2)>		CCL4
2904M	G	8.78	CHA	A<C(C(=O)-O-CH2)/C(C(=O)-O-CH2)>		CDCL3
2866M	E	7.94	CHA	A<C(C(=O)-O-CH3)>		CCL4
2873M	D	7.89	CHA	A<C(C(=O)-O-CH3)-CH-C(CL)>		CCL4
2876M	D	7.94	CHA	A<C(C(=O)-O-CH3)-CH-C(I)>		CDCL3
2880M	F	7.36	CHA	A<C(C(=O)-O-CH3)-CH-C(NH2)>		CDCL3
2910M	C	7.05	CHA	A<C(C(=O)-O-CH3)-CH-C(NH2)/CH-C(C(=O)-O-CH3)>		POLYSOL-D
2905M	D	7.80	CHA	A<C(C(=O)-O-CH3)-CH-C(NH2)/C(C(=O)-O-CH3)>		POLYSOL-D
2920M	B	8.04	CHA	A<C(C(=O)-O-CH3)-C(C(=O)-O-CH3)/C(C(=O)-O-CH3)-C(C(=O)-O-CH3)>		CDCL3
2910M	E	7.77	CHA	A<C(C(=O)-O-CH3)-C(NH2)/CH-C(C(C=O)-O-CH3)>		POLYSOL-D
2882M	E	7.86	CHA	A<C(C(=O)-O-CH)/CH-C(NH2)>		CDCL3
2676M	D	7.45	CHA	A<C(C(=O)-O-NA)-CH-C(NH2)>		D2O
2679M	B	8.04	CHA	A<C(C(=O)-O-NA)/CH-C(OH)>		D2O
2683M	B	7.99	CHA	A<C(C(=O)-O-NH4)>		D2O
2684M	D	7.97	CHA	A<C(C(=O)-O-NH4)-C(OH)>		D2O
2995M	B	8.06	CHA	A<C(C(=O)-O-O-C(=O))>		CDCL3
2878M	G	7.89	CHA	A<C(C(=O)-O-R6)-C(NH2)>		CDCL3
2091M	D	8.01	CHA	A<C(C(=O)-Q2)>		CDCL3
2096M	E	8.11	CHA	A<C(C(=O)-Q2)/CH-C(O-CH3)>		POLYSOL-D
2083M	D	7.95	CHA	A<C(C(=O)-R5)>		CCL4
2369M	C	7.33	CHA	A<C(C(=O)-R6N)>		CCL4
2610M	C	7.90	CHA	A<C(C(=O)-SH)>		CDCL3
1333M	B	7.89	CHA	A<C(C(=S)-HNH)>		POLYSOL-D
1335M	B	7.70	CHA	A<C(C(=S)-NH)>		CDCL3
290M	B	7.88	CHA	A<C(C-CL3)/CH-C(F)>		CCL4
170M	A	7.10- 7.70	CHA	A<C(C:C)>		CDCL3
168M	D	7.05- 7.50	CHA	A<C(C:C)>		CCL4
1563M	E	7.20	CHA	A<C(C:N)-CH-C(O-CH3)/CH-C(O-CH3)>		CDCL3
987M	A	7.00- 7.90	CHA	A<C(C:N)-C(F)>		CDCL3
996M	A	7.90	CHA	A<C(C:N)/CH-C(A<C-CH-CH-C(C:N)>)>		TFA
995M	D	7.35	CHA	A<C(C:N)/CH-C(N(CH2/CH2))>		CDCL3
390M	A	6.97	CHA	A<C(F)-CH-C(BR)>		CCL4
304M	B	6.73	CHA	A<C(F)-CH-C(CL)/CH-C(CH3)>		CCL4
310M	A	6.91	CHA	A<C(F)-CH-C(CL)/CH-C(CL)>		CDCL3
2871M	C	7.13	CHA	A<C(F)-CH-C(C(=O)-O-CH2)>		CCL4
2063M	B	6.60- 7.10	CHA	A<C(F)-CH-C(F)/CH-C(C(=O)-CH3)>		CCL4
509M	C	6.97	CHA	A<C(F)-CH-C(NH2)>		CDCL3
2326M	D	7.52	CHA	A<C(F)-CH-C(NH-C(=O))>		CDCL3
2063M	B	6.60- 7.10	CHA	A<C(F)-C(C(=O)-CH3)/C(F)>		CCL4
2227M	A	7.17	CHA	A<C(F)-C(C(=O)-CL)>		CCL4
989M	A	7.31	CHA	A<C(F)-C(C:N)-C(F)>		DMSO-D6
1054M	A	7.10- 7.50	CHA	A<C(F)-C(NO2)>		CCL4
916M	A	6.75- 7.20	CHA	A<C(F)-C(N=C=O)>		CCL4
939M	A	6.85- 7.35	CHA	A<C(F)-C(N=C=S)>		CCL4
391M	A	6.90	CHA	A<C(F)/CH-C(BR)>		CCL4
229M	A	7.13	CHA	A<C(F)/CH-C(CF3)>		CCL4
2570M	A	7.27	CHA	A<C(F)/CH-C(C(=O)-OH)>		C3H6O
290M	A	7.05	CHA	A<C(F)/CH-C(C-CL3)>		CCL4
232M	A	6.95	CHA	A<C(F)/CH-C(F)>		CCL4
432M	A	6.78	CHA	A<C(F)/CH-C(I)>		CDCL3
510M	C	6.75	CHA	A<C(F)/CH-C(NH2)>		CCL4

BOOK NO.	ASSIGN-MENT	CHEM SHIFT - ppm -	PROTON GROUP	ENVIRONMENTAL GROUPS	S	SOLVENT
2327M	B	6.99	CHA	A<C(F)/CH-C(NH-C(=O))>		CDCL3
1891M	C	6.91	CHA	A<C(F)/CH-C(OH)>		CDCL3
1270M	A	7.12	CHA	A<C(F)/CH-C(SO2-A)>		CDCL3
2871M	E	7.63	CHA	A<C(F)/C(C(=O)-O-CH2)>		CCL4
2326M	C	7.22	CHA	A<C(F)/C(NH-C(=O))>		CDCL3
940M	A	6.75- 7.55	CHA	A<C(F)/C(N=C=S)>		CCL4
431M	C	7.90	CHA	A<C(I)-CH-C(CF3)>		CCL4
528M	D	7.12	CHA	A<C(I)-CH-C(CH3)/CH-C(NH2)>		POLYSOL-D
2069M	C	7.79	CHA	A<C(I)-CH-C(C(=O)-CH3)>		CDCL3
2876M	C	7.82	CHA	A<C(I)-CH-C(C(=O)-O-CH3)>		CDCL3
436M	B	7.60	CHA	A<C(I)-CH-C(I)>		CDCL3
1897M	B	7.12	CHA	A<C(I)-CH-C(OH)>		POLYSOL-D
1520M	D	7.19	CHA	A<C(I)-CH-C(O-CH3)>		CCL4
434M	D	7.65	CHA	A<C(I)-C(BR)>		CCL4
434M	D	7.79	CHA	A<C(I)-C(BR)>		CCL4
430M	D	7.55	CHA	A<C(I)-C(CH3)/C(CH3)>		CCL4
2575M	D	7.90	CHA	A<C(I)-C(C(=O)-OH)>		C3D6O
525M	E	7.63	CHA	A<C(I)-C(NH2)>		CDCL3
435M	B	7.50	CHA	A<C(I)/CH-C(BR)>		CDCL3
2577M	A	7.71	CHA	A<C(I)/CH-C(C(=O)-OH)>		DMSO-D6
432M	B	7.58	CHA	A<C(I)/CH-C(F)>		CDCL3
431M	D	7.97	CHA	A<C(I)/C(CF3)>		CCL4
528M	E	7.20	CHA	A<C(I)/C(CH3)-C(NH2)>		POLYSOL-D
2069M	D	8.17	CHA	A<C(I)/C(C(=O)-CH3)>		CDCL3
2876M	E	8.33	CHA	A<C(I)/C(C(=O)-O-CH3)>		CDCL3
436M	C	8.04	CHA	A<C(I)/C(I)>		CDCL3
1897M	C	7.28	CHA	A<C(I)/C(OH)>		POLYSOL-D
1520M	E	7.21	CHA	A<C(I)/C(O-CH3)>		CCL4
788M	A	7.51	CHA	A<C(NH2)>	S	TFA
787M	A	7.51	CHA	A<C(NH2)>	S	DMSO-D6
506M	B	6.75	CHA	A<C(NH2)-CH-C(CF3)>		CDCL3
492M	D	6.41	CHA	A<C(NH2)-CH-C(CH2-CH3)>		CDCL3
498M	C	6.49	CHA	A<C(NH2)-CH-C(CH3)/CH-C(CH3)>		CDCL3
1071M	D	6.50	CHA	A<C(NH2)-CH-C(CH3)/CH-C(NO2)>		POLYSOL-D
499M	C	6.09	CHA	A<C(NH2)-CH-C(C(CH3)>		CCL4
796M	A	7.59 APP.	CHA	A<C(NH2)-CH-C(CL)/CH-C(NH2)>	S	D2O
2103M	B	6.88	CHA	A<C(NH2)-CH-C(C(=O)-A)>		DMSO-D6
2880M	C	6.77	CHA	A<C(NH2)-CH-C(C(=O)-O-CH3)>		CDCL3
2905M	C	7.49	CHA	A<C(NH2)-CH-C(C(=O)-O-CH3)/C(C(=O)-O-CH3)>		POLYSOL-D
2676M	A	6.90	CHA	A<C(NH2)-CH-C(C(=O)-O-NA)>		D2O
536M	D	6.03	CHA	A<C(NH2)-CH-C(NH2)/CH-C(CH3)>		CDCL3
1070M	C	6.75	CHA	A<C(NH2)-CH-C(NO2)/CH-C(CH3)>		CDCL3
1237M	B	6.38	CHA	A<C(NH2)-CH-C(SH)>		CDCL3
523M	B	6.58	CHA	A<C(NH2)-C(BR)/CH-C(BR)>		CDCL3
538M	D	6.47	CHA	A<C(NH2)-C(CH2-CH3)/C(CH2-CH3)-C(NH2)>		CDCL3
528M	C	6.42	CHA	A<C(NH2)-C(CH3)/CH-C(I)>		POLYSOL-D
497M	D	6.25	CHA	A<C(NH2)-C(CH3)/C(CH3)>		CCL4
2640M	D	6.40	CHA	A<C(NH2)-C(CH3)/C(CH3)-C(CH3)>		CCL4
536M	C	5.97	CHA	A<C(NH2)-C(CH3)/C(NH2)>		CDCL3
494M	F	6.48	CHA	A<C(NH2)-C(CH(CH2/CH3))>		CCL4
516M	B	6.60	CHA	A<C(NH2)-C(CL)/CH-C(CL)>		CDCL3
796M	A	7.59 APP.	CHA	A<C(NH2)-C(CL)/CH-C(NH2)>	S	D2O
2595M	B	6.67	CHA	A<C(NH2)-C(C(=O)-OH)/CH-C(O-CH3)>		POLYSOL-D
2879M	F	6.76	CHA	A<C(NH2)-C(C(=O)-O-CH2.4)>		DMSO-D6
2877M	E	6.37- 6.71	CHA	A<C(NH2)-C(C(=O)-O-CH2)>		CCL4
2910M	D	7.43	CHA	A<C(NH2)-C(C(=O)-O-CH3)/C(C(=O)-O-CH3)>		POLYSOL-D
2878M	D	6.54	CHA	A<C(NH2)-C(C(=O)-O-R6)>		CDCL3
525M	C	6.71	CHA	A<C(NH2)-C(I)>		CDCL3
1562M	G	6.26	CHA	A<C(NH2)-C(O-CH2.3)/C(O-CH2.3)>		CDCL3
1526M	E	7.65	CHA	A<C(NH2)-C(O-CH3)>	S	POLYSOL-D
862M	C	6.79	CHA	A<C(NH2)-C(QN(A/OH))>		POLYSOL-D
1236M	B	6.59	CHA	A<C(NH2)-C(SH)>		CDCL3
1290M	B	7.40 APP.	CHA	A<C(NH2)-C(SO2-OH)/CH-C(CH3)>		DMSO-D6
1161M	C	6.55 APP.	CHA	A<C(NH2)-C(S-CH3)>		CCL4
531M	B	6.62	CHA	A<C(NH2)/CH-C(A<C-CH-CH-C(NH2)>)>		DMSO-D6
505M	B	6.73	CHA	A<C(NH2)/CH-C(A)>		C3H6O
507M	B	6.56	CHA	A<C(NH2)/CH-C(CF3)>		CDCL3
529M	C	6.61	CHA	A<C(NH2)/CH-C(CH2.2-NH2)>		CDCL3
1718M	D	6.53	CHA	A<C(NH2)/CH-C(CH2.2-OH)>		POLYSOL-D
490M	C	6.33	CHA	A<C(NH2)/CH-C(CH3)>		CCL4
493M	D	6.60	CHA	A<C(NH2)/CH-C(CH(CH3/CH3))>		CDCL3
2070M	E	6.58	CHA	A<C(NH2)/CH-C(C(=O)-CH2.2)>		CDCL3
2071M	E	6.59	CHA	A<C(NH2)/CH-C(C(=O)-CH2.3)>		CDCL3
2578M	B	6.76	CHA	A<C(NH2)/CH-C(C(=O)-OH)>		C3H6O
2677M	A	6.80	CHA	A<C(NH2)/CH-C(C(=O)-ONA)>		D2O
2882M	D	6.62	CHA	A<C(NH2)/CH-C(C(=O)-O-CH)>		CDCL3
510M	B	6.42	CHA	A<C(NH2)/CH-C(F)>		CCL4
535M	B	6.39	CHA	A<C(NH2)/CH-C(NH2)>		DMSO-D6
2688M	B	7.91	CHA	A<C(NH2)/CH-C(N(CH3/CH3))>		TFA
1238M	B	6.52	CHA	A<C(NH2)/CH-C(SH)>		CDCL3
1365M	B	6.64	CHA	A<C(NH2)/CH-C(SO2-NH2)>		DMSO-D6

BOOK NO.	ASSIGN- MENT	CHEM SHIFT - ppm -	PROTON GROUP	ENVIRONMENTAL GROUPS	S	SOLVENT
506M	C	6.81	CHA	A<C(NH2)/C(CF3)>		CDCL3
492M	E	6.49	CHA	A<C(NH2)/C(CH2-CH3)>		CDCL3
498M	D	6.53	CHA	A<C(NH2)/C(CH3)-C(CH3)>		CDCL3
1071M	C	6.43	CHA	A<C(NH2)/C(CH3)-C(NO2)S		POLYSOL-D
2880M	E	7.30	CHA	A<C(NH2)/C(C(=O)-O-CH3)>		CDCL3
2676M	C	7.39	CHA	A<C(NH2)/C(C(=O)-O-NA)>		D2O
1237M	C	6.45	CHA	A<C(NH2)/C(SH)>		CDCL3
480M	C	7.19	CHA	A<C(NH2/CH3/CH3)>		CCL4
2634M	B	6.60	CHA	A<C(NH-CH2)>		DMSO-D6
806M	C	7.55 APP.	CHA	A<C(NH-CH2)>	S	D2O
587M	F	6.50	CHA	A<C(NH-CH2)>		CDCL3
595M	D	6.52	CHA	A<C(NH-CH2)-C(CH3)>		CDCL3
1062M	D	6.75	CHA	A<C(NH-CH2)-C(NO2)>		CCL4
596M	D	6.32	CHA	A<C(NH-CH2)/CH-C(CH3)>		CCL4
582M	C	6.40	CHA	A<C(NH-CH3)>		CCL4
590M	D	6.39 APP.	CHA	A<C(NH-CH3)-CH-C(CH3)>		CDCL3
590M	D	6.39 APP.	CHA	A<C(NH-CH3)/CH3>		CDCL3
592M	E	6.47	CHA	A<C(NH-CH3)/CH-C(CH(CH3/CH3))>		CDCL3
1523M	D	6.45	CHA	A<C(NH-CH3)/CH-C(O-CH3)>		POLYSOL-D
598M	F	6.52	CHA	A<C(NH-CH)/CH-C(NH-CH)>		CDCL3
2320M	C	7.75	CHA	A<C(NH-C(=O))>		DMSO-D6
2326M	B	6.82	CHA	A<C(NH-C(=O))-CH-C(F)>		CDCL3
2339M	F	7.31	CHA	A<C(NH-C(=O))-C(CH3)/C(CH3)>		CDCL3
2328M	D	8.15	CHA	A<C(NH-C(=O))-C(CL)>		CDCL3
2333M	D	8.15	CHA	A<C(NH-C(=O))-C(NO2)>		CDCL3
2334M	C	7.68	CHA	A<C(NH-C(=O))-C(OH)>		DMSO-D6
2424M	B	7.37	CHA	A<C(NH-C(=O))/CH-C(BR)>		DMSO-D6
2331M	B	7.45	CHA	A<C(NH-C(=O))/CH-C(BR)>		DMSO-D6
2331M	B	7.61	CHA	A<C(NH-C(=O))/CH-C(BR)>		DMSO-D6
2423M	D	7.29	CHA	A<C(NH-C(=O))/CH-C(CH3)>		DMSO-D6
2327M	C	7.40	CHA	A<C(NH-C(=O))/CH-C(F)>		CDCL3
2211M	E	7.48	CHA	A<C(NH-C(=O))/CH-C(O-CH2)>		DMSO-D6
2337M	D	7.48	CHA	A<C(NH-C(=O))/CH-C(O-CH3)>		DMSO-D6
2336M	C	7.30	CHA	A<C(NH-C(=O)-CH3)/CH-C(OH)>		POLYSOL-D
2317M	E	7.60	CHA	A<C(NH-C(=O)-CH)>		POLYSOL-D
1351M	A	7.38	CHA	A<C(NH-C(=S))>		CDCL3
1348M	D	7.00- 7.70	CHA	A<C(NH-C(=S))>		CDCL3
588M	D	6.60- 7.40	CHA	A<C(NH-C)>		CDCL3
1527M	C	7.23	CHA	A<C(NH-NH2)-C(O-CH3)>	S	POLYSOL-D
760M	B	6.76	CHA	A<C(NH-NH)>		DMSO-D6
887M	A	6.90- 7.45	CHA	A<C(NH-QN)>		POLYSOL-D
889M	B	6.75- 7.10	CHA	A<C(NH-QN)>		DMSO-D6
1064M	A	7.19	CHA	A<C(NH-QN)/CH-C(NO2)>		POLYSOL-D
1063M	E	7.12	CHA	A<C(NH-QN)/CH-C(NO2)>		POLYSOL-D
1052M	C	8.08	CHA	A<C(NO2)-CH-C(A)>		CDCL3
1720M	E	8.05	CHA	A<C(NO2)-CH-C(CH2-OH)>		CDCL3
1057M	C	8.10 APP.	CHA	A<C(NO2)-CH-C(CL)>		CDCL3
2236M	C	8.49	CHA	A<C(NO2)-CH-C(C(=O)-CL)>		CDCL3
2236M	C	8.61	CHA	A<C(NO2)-CH-C(C(=O)-CL)>		CDCL3
2171M	C	8.29	CHA	A<C(NO2)-CH-C(C(=O)-H)>		CDCL3
2171M	C	8.51	CHA	A<C(NO2)-CH-C(C(=O)-H)>		CDCL3
2601M	B	8.46	CHA	A<C(NO2)-CH-C(C(=O)-OH)/CH-C(C(=O)-OH)>		D2O
2602M	A	8.80	CHA	A<C(NO2)-CH-C(C(=O)-OH)/C(C(=O)-OH)>		DMSO
2885M	D	10.00 APP.	CHA	A<C(NO2)-CH-C(C(=O)-O-CH2)>		CCL4
1557M	D	8.43	CHA	A<C(NO2)-CH-C(NO2)/CH-C(O-CH2)>		CDCL3
1555M	C	8.50	CHA	A<C(NO2)-CH-C(NO2)/CH-C(O-CH3)>		POLYSOL-D
1307M	B	8.57	CHA	A<C(NO2)-CH-C(NO2)/CH-C(SO3-NA)>		D2O
2911M	C	9.11 APP.	CHA	A<C(NO2)-CH-C(NO2)/C(C(=O)-O-CH2)>		CDCL3
2911M	C	9.11 APP.	CHA	A<C(NO2)-CH-C(NO2)/C(C(=O)-O-CH2)>		CDCL3
1076M	A	9.12	CHA	A<C(NO2)-CH-C(NO2)/C(NO2)>		DMSO-D6
1544M	C	7.90	CHA	A<C(NO2)-CH-C(O-A)>		CDCL3
1719M	D	8.05	CHA	A<C(NO2)-C(CH2-OH)>		CDCL3
1068M	E	7.84	CHA	A<C(NO2)-C(CH3)/CH-C(CH3)>		CDCL3
1071M	E	7.89	CHA	A<C(NO2)-C(CH3)/CH-C(NH2)>		POLYSOL-D
1070M	E	7.19	CHA	A<C(NO2)-C(CH3)/C(NH2)>		CDCL3
2072M	C	7.91	CHA	A<C(NO2)-C(C(=O)-CH3)>		CCL4
2235M	B	8.09	CHA	A<C(NO2)-C(C(=O)-CL)>		CCL4
2407M	C	8.02	CHA	A<C(NO2)-C(C(=O)-NH)>		DMSO-D6
2581M	B	7.90	CHA	A<C(NO2)-C(C(=O)-OH)>		C3H6O
1054M	C	8.03	CHA	A<C(NO2)-C(F)>		CCL4
1062M	G	8.06	CHA	A<C(NO2)-C(NH-CH2)>		CCL4
2333M	E	8.74	CHA	A<C(NO2)-C(NH-C(=O))>		CDCL3
1066M	B	8.26	CHA	A<C(NO2)-C(NO2)>		DMSO-D6
1903M	D	8.00	CHA	A<C(NO2)-C(OH)>		CCL4
1922M	C	8.05	CHA	A<C(NO2)-C(OH)-C(CL)>		CDCL3
1939M	B	9.13	CHA	A<C(NO2)-C(OH)-C(NO2)/C(NO2)>		C3D6O
1942M	C	8.54	CHA	A<C(NO2)-C(OH)-C(NO2)/C(NO2)>		POLYSOL-D
1543M	B	7.86	CHA	A<C(NO2)-C(O-A)>		CDCL3
1534M	G	7.70	CHA	A<C(NO2)-C(O-CH2)>		CCL4
1557M	E	8.69	CHA	A<C(NO2)-C(O-CH2)/C(NO2)>		CDCL3
1568M	B	8.93	CHA	A<C(NO2)-C(O-CH3)-C(NO2)/C(NO2)>		CDCL3

BOOK NO.	ASSIGN-MENT	CHEM SHIFT - ppm -	PROTON GROUP	ENVIRONMENTAL GROUPS	S	SOLVENT
1564M	E	7.98	CHA	A<C(NO2)-C(O-CH3)/CH-C(O-CH3)>		CDCL3
1555M	D	8.65	CHA	A<C(NO2)-C(O-CH3)/C(NO2)>		POLYSOL-D
1285M	B	8.29	CHA	A<C(NO2)-C(SO2-CL)>		CDCL3
1307M	C	8.62	CHA	A<C(NO2)-C(SO3-NA)/C(NO2)>		D20
1053M	C	8.26	CHA	A<C(NO2)/CH-C(A)>		C3H6O
1050M	D	8.03	CHA	A<C(NO2)/CH-C(CH2-CH3)>		CCL4
2561M	C	8.33	CHA	A<C(NO2)/CH-C(CH2-C(=0)-0)>		TFA
1721M	C	8.18	CHA	A<C(NO2)/CH-C(CH2-OH)>		C3H6O
2967M	C	8.27	CHA	A<C(NO2)/CH-C(CH2-O-C(=0))>		CDCL3
2172M	B	8.39	CHA	A<C(NO2)/CH-C(C(=0))>		CDCL3
1064M	E	8.10	CHA	A<C(NO2)/CH-C(NH-QN)>		POLYSOL-D
1063M	F	8.01	CHA	A<C(NO2)/CH-C(NH-QN)>		POLYSOL-D
1905M	B	8.15	CHA	A<C(NO2)/CH-C(OH)>		C3H6O
1532M	C	8.12	CHA	A<C(NO2)/CH-C(O-CH3)>		CCL4
2926M	C	8.29	CHA	A<C(NO2)/CH-C(O-C(=0)-CH3)>		CDCL3
2927M	C	8.28	CHA	A<C(NO2)/CH-C(O-C(=0)-C)>		CDCL3
1724M	E	8.07	CHA	A<C(NO2)/CH-C(Q2(CH2-OH))>		POLYSOL-D
2162M	D	8.23	CHA	A<C(NO2)/CH-C(Q2(H/C(=0)-H/H))>		DMSO-D6
1052M	D	8.30	CHA	A<C(NO2)/C(A)>		CDCL3
1720M	F	8.11	CHA	A<C(NO2)/C(CH2-OH)>		CDCL3
2236M	D	8.94	CHA	A<C(NO2)/C(C(=0)-CL)>		CDCL3
2171M	D	8.67	CHA	A<C(NO2)/C(C(=0)-H)>		CDCL3
2601M	C	8.52	CHA	A<C(NO2)/C(C(=0)-OH)-C(C(=0)-OH)>		D20
2885M	E	10.40	CHA	A<C(NO2)/C(C(=0)-O-CH2)>		CCL4
1544M	B	7.81	CHA	A<C(NO2)/C(O-A)>		CDCL3
2095M	D	8.52	CHA	A<C(NO2)/C(Q2(C(=0)-A))>		POLYSOL-D
976M	D	6.79	CHA	A<C(N(CH2.2/CH2.2))>		DMSO-D6
653M	D	6.69	CHA	A<C(N(CH2/CH2))>		CDCL3
656M	E	6.61	CHA	A<C(N(CH2/CH2))>		CCL4
1706M	G	6.72	CHA	A<C(N(CH2/CH2))>		CDCL3
664M	F	6.80	CHA	A<C(N(CH2/CH2))-C(CH3)/C(CH3)>		CCL4
995M	C	6.58	CHA	A<C(N(CH2/CH2))/CH-C(C:N)>		CDCL3
1024M	C	6.65	CHA	A<C(N(CH2/CH2))/CH-C(N=0)>		CDCL3
666M	C	6.62	CHA	A<C(N(CH3/CH3))/CH-C(CH2-A)>		CDCL3
660M	C	6.49	CHA	A<C(N(CH3/CH3))/CH-C(CH3)>		CCL4
1901M	C	6.63	CHA	A<C(N(CH3/CH3))/CH-C(CH(A/A))>		POLYSOL-D
667M	D	7.71	CHA	A<C(N(CH3/CH3))/CH-C(CH(A/A))>		TFA
2688M	B	7.91	CHA	A<C(N(CH3/CH3))/CH-C(NH2)>		TFA
1023M	B	6.60	CHA	A<C(N(CH3/CH3))/CH-C(N=0)>		CDCL3
2361M	C	7.00- 7.60	CHA	A<C(N(C(=0)-H/CH2))>		CDCL3
2362M	D	7.02	CHA	A<C(N(C(=0)-H/CH2))/CH-C(CH3)>		CDCL3
2427M	A	7.27 APP.	CHA	A<C(N(C(=0)-NH2/A))>		POLYSOL-D
2368M	B	7.33	CHA	A<C(N(C(=0)/A))>		CDCL3
2436M	C	7.25	CHA	A<C(N(C(=0)/A))>		CDCL3
2364M	D	7.50	CHA	A<C(N(C(=0)/CH2))>		CCL4
759M	B	6.70- 7.30	CHA	A<C(N(NH2/A))>		CDCL3
841M	D	8.11	CHA	A<C(N(+)(CH2/CH2/CH2))>		CDCL3
1313M	D	7.77	CHA	A<C(N(+)(CH3/CH3/CH3))>		POLYSOL-D
926M	A	6.80- 7.30	CHA	A<C(N=C=N)>		CDCL3
918M	B	6.98	CHA	A<C(N=C=O)/CH-C(CH2-A)>		POLYSOL-D
897M	D	7.52- 7.85	CHA	A<C(N=N-A)-CH-C(CH3)>		CDCL3
897M	D	7.52- 7.85	CHA	A<C(N=N-A)/C(CH3)>		CDCL3
904M	D	7.22	CHA	A<C(N=N-NH)/CH-C(CH3)>		CDCL3
1024M	D	7.79 APP.	CHA	A<C(N=0)/CH-C(N(CH2/CH2))>		CDCL3
1023M	C	7.70	CHA	A<C(N=0)/CH-C(N(CH3/CH3))>		CDCL3
2078M	C	6.70	CHA	A<C(OH)-CH-C(CH3)/CH-C(C(=0)-CH3)>		DMSO-D6
2080M	C	7.06	CHA	A<C(OH)-CH-C(C(=0)-CH3)/CH-C(OH)>		DMSO-D6
1897M	A	6.70- 7.00	CHA	A<C(OH)-CH-C(I)>		POLYSOL-D
1911M	A	6.49 APP.	CHA	A<C(OH)-CH-C(OH)>		C3H6O
1928M	D	6.29	CHA	A<C(OH)-CH-C(OH)/CH-C(CH2.15-CH3)>		POLYSOL-D
1927M	F	6.32	CHA	A<C(OH)-CH-C(OH)/CH-C(CH2-CH2)>		CDCL3
1947M	A	5.99	CHA	A<C(OH)-CH-C(OH)/C(OH)>		C3H6O
1894M	C	6.98	CHA	A<C(OH)-C(BR)>		CDCL3
1921M	B	6.91	CHA	A<C(OH)-C(BR)/CH-C(BR)>		CCL4
1928M	E	6.37	CHA	A<C(OH)-C(CH2.15-CH3)/C(OH)>		POLYSOL-D
1927M	E	6.28	CHA	A<C(OH)-C(CH2-CH2)/C(OH)>		CDCL3
1932M	F	6.43	CHA	A<C(OH)-C(CH2-Q3)/C(CH3)/C(CH3)>		CDCL3
1913M	D	6.58	CHA	A<C(OH)-C(CH3)-C(CH3)>		CDCL3
1923M	D	6.62	CHA	A<C(OH)-C(CH3)/CH-C(S-CH3)>		CDCL3
1919M	B	6.90	CHA	A<C(OH)-C(CL)/CH-C(CL)>		CDCL3
1882M	C	6.49	CHA	A<C(OH)-C(C(CH3/CH3/CH3))>		CCL4
2079M	B	6.89	CHA	A<C(OH)-C(C(=0)-CH3)/CH-C(CL)>		CDCL3
2080M	B	6.84	CHA	A<C(OH)-C(C(=0)-CH3)/CH-C(OH)>		DMSO-D6
2178M	B	6.79	CHA	A<C(OH)-C(C(=0)-H)/CH-C(O-CH3)>		CCL4
2293M	B	7.02	CHA	A<C(OH)-C(C(=0)-NH2)>		DMSO-D6
2587M	B	7.09	CHA	A<C(OH)-C(C(=0)-OH)>		TFA
2596M	C	6.71	CHA	A<C(OH)-C(C(=0)-OH)/C(CH3)>		POLYSOL-D
2678M	A	6.97 APP.	CHA	A<C(OH)-C(C(=0)-ONA)>		D20
2890M	E	6.85	CHA	A<C(OH)-C(C(=0)-O-CH2)>		CCL4
2684M	B	7.04	CHA	A<C(OH)-C(C(=0)-O-NH4)>		D20
1903M	B	7.09	CHA	A<C(OH)-C(NO2)>		CCL4

BOOK NO.	ASSIGN-MENT	CHEM SHIFT - ppm -	PROTON GROUP	ENVIRONMENTAL GROUPS	S	SOLVENT
1944M	A	6.54	CHA	A<C(OH)-C(NO2)-C(OH)>		POLYSOL-D
1945M	A	6.47 APP.	CHA	A<C(OH)-C(OH)-C(OH)>		C3H6O
2917M	D	7.20	CHA	A<C(OH)-C(OH)-C(OH)/C(C(=O)-O-CH2)>		C3D6O
2919M	E	7.01	CHA	A<C(OH)-C(OH)-C(OH)/C(C(=O)-O-CH2)>		C3D6O
2918M	E	7.23	CHA	A<C(OH)-C(OH)-C(OH)/C(C(=O)-O-CH2)>		C3D6O
2916M	B	7.12	CHA	A<C(OH)-C(OH)-C(OH)/C(C(=O)-O-CH3)>		POLYSOL-D
1926M	E	6.72	CHA	A<C(OH)-C(OH)/CH-C(CH3)>		CDCL3
2600M	A	6.99	CHA	A<C(OH)-C(OH)/CH-C(C(=O)-OH)>		DMSO-D6
1926M	C	6.55	CHA	A<C(OH)-C(OH)/C(CH3)>		CDCL3
2600M	C	7.61	CHA	A<C(OH)-C(OH)/C(C(=O)-OH)>		DMSO-D6
2598M	B	7.00	CHA	A<C(OH)-C(O-CH3)/CH-C(C(=O)-OH)>		DMSO-D6
1909M	A	6.88	CHA	A<C(OH)/CH-C(A<C-CH-CH-C(OH)>)>		DMSO-D6
1902M	D	6.77	CHA	A<C(OH)/CH-C(CH2.2-C:N)>		CDCL3
1884M	E	6.69	CHA	A<C(OH)/CH-C((CH2.4-CH3)>		CCL4
1888M	B	6.69	CHA	A<C(OH)/CH-C(CH2-A)>		DMSO-D6
1878M	C	6.69	CHA	A<C(OH)/CH-C(CH3)>		CDCL3
1901M	D	6.70	CHA	A<C(OH)/CH-C(CH(A/A))>		POLYSOL-D
1881M	D	6.78	CHA	A<C(OH)/CH-C(CH(CH3/CH3))>		CDCL3
1908M	B	6.70	CHA	A<C(OH)/CH-C(C(A/CH3/CH3))>		POLYSOL-D
2588M	A	7.07	CHA	A<C(OH)/CH-C(C(=O)-OH)>		C3H6O
2894M	D	6.84	CHA	A<C(OH)/CH-C(C(=O)-O-CH2)>		CCL4
2679M	A	7.06	CHA	A<C(OH)/CH-C(C(=O)-O-NA)>		D2O
1891M	B	6.79	CHA	A<C(OH)/CH-C(F)>		CDCL3
2336M	B	6.71	CHA	A<C(OH)/CH-C(NH-C(=O)-CH3)>		POLYSOL-D
1905M	A	7.06	CHA	A<C(OH)/CH-C(NO2)>		C3H6O
1887M	D	6.75	CHA	A<C(OH)/CH-C(R6<CH-CH2/CH2>)>		CDCL3
2078M	B	6.67	CHA	A<C(OH)/C(CH3)-C(C(=O)-CH3)>		DMSO-D6
2080M	D	7.24	CHA	A<C(OH)/C(C(=O)-CH3)-C(OH)>		DMSO-D6
1911M	A	6.49 APP.	CHA	A<C(OH)/C(OH)>		C3H6O
1548M	D	6.80- 7.40	CHA	A<C(O-A)>		CDCL3
1542M	A	6.75	CHA	A<C(O-A)/CH-C(BR)>		CCL4
1549M	B	6.90	CHA	A<C(O-A)/CH-C(O-CH3)>		POLYSOL-D
1548M	C	6.90	CHA	A<C(O-A)/CH-C(O-CH3)>		CDCL3
1492M	D	6.79 APP.	CHA	A<C(O-CH2.2)>		CCL4
1490M	D	6.93 APP.	CHA	A<C(O-CH2.2)>		CDCL3
2173M	D	6.89	CHA	A<C(O-CH2.2)/CH-C(C(=O)-H)>		CCL4
1562M	F	6.19	CHA	A<C(O-CH2.3)-CH-C(NH2)/CH-C(O-CH2.3)>		CDCL3
1562M	H	6.65	CHA	A<C(O-CH2.3)-C(NH2)/CH-C(O-CH2.3)>		CDCL3
2215M	B	6.70- 7.40	CHA	A<C(O-CH2)>		CCL4
2089M	B	6.80- 7.40	CHA	A<C(O-CH2)>		CDCL3
1792M	E	6.79	CHA	A<C(O-CH2)>		CCL4
1517M	D	6.76	CHA	A<C(O-CH2)-C(BR)>		CCL4
2585M	D	7.11	CHA	A<C(O-CH2)-C(C(=O)-OH)>		CCL4
1534M	E	7.03	CHA	A<C(O-CH2)-C(NO2)>		CCL4
1557M	C	7.25	CHA	A<C(O-CH2)-C(NO2)/CH-C(NO2)>		CDCL3
2563M	D	6.84	CHA	A<C(O-CH2)/CH-C(CH2-C(=O)-OH)>		CDCL3
1539M	F	6.81	CHA	A<C(O-CH2)/CH-C(C(A/CH3))>		CDCL3
2076M	D	6.91	CHA	A<C(O-CH2)/CH-C(C(=O)-CH3)>		CDCL3
2175M	E	6.92	CHA	A<C(O-CH2)/CH-C(C(=O)-H)>		CCL4
2211M	D	6.80	CHA	A<C(O-CH2)/CH-C(NH-C(=O))>		DMSO-D6
2565M	B	6.83	CHA	A<C(O-CH2)/CH-C(O-CH2)>		POLYSOL-D
1488M	B	6.80	CHA	A<C(O-CH3)>		CCL4
1505M	D	6.74 APP.	CHA	A<C(O-CH3)-CH-C(CH2-NH2)>		CDCL3
2178M	D	7.02	CHA	A<C(O-CH3)-CH-C(C(=O)-H)/CH-C(OH)>		CCL4
2595M	C	6.90	CHA	A<C(O-CH3)-CH-C(C(=O)-OH)/CH-C(NH2)>		POLYSOL-D
1520M	B	6.79	CHA	A<C(O-CH3)-CH-C(I)>		CCL4
1564M	C	6.49	CHA	A<C(O-CH3)-CH-C(O-CH3)/CH-C(NO2)>		CDCL3
1504M	C	6.84	CHA	A<C(O-CH3)-C(CH2-NH2)>		CDCL3
1551M	E	6.76	CHA	A<C(O-CH3)-C(CH3)>		CDCL3
1552M	D	6.69	CHA	A<C(O-CH3)-C(CH3)/CH-C(CH3)>		CDCL3
1526M	C	7.12	CHA	A<C(O-CH3)-C(NH2)>	S	POLYSOL-D
1555M	B	7.60	CHA	A<C(O-CH3)-C(NO2)/CH-C(NO2)>		POLYSOL-D
1564M	D	6.58	CHA	A<C(O-CH3)-C(NO2)/C(O-CH3)>		CDCL3
2915M	D	7.33	CHA	A<C(O-CH3)-C(OH)-C(O-CH3)/C(C(=O)-O-CH3)>		CDCL3
2598M	C	7.59	CHA	A<C(O-CH3)-C(OH)/C(C(=O)-OH)>		DMSO-D6
1545M	B	6.76	CHA	A<C(O-CH3)-C(O-CH3)>		CCL4
1565M	B	6.58	CHA	A<C(O-CH3)-C(O-CH3)-C(O-CH3)>		CDCL3
1563M	C	6.85	CHA	A<C(O-CH3)-C(O-CH3)/CH-C(C:N)>		CDCL3
1563M	D	7.02	CHA	A<C(O-CH3)-C(O-CH3)/C(C:N)>		CDCL3
1503M	D	6.71	CHA	A<C(O-CH3)/CH-C(CH2.2-BR)>		CCL4
1501M	E	6.71	CHA	A<C(O-CH3)/CH-C(CH2-CH2)>		CCL4
1497M	D	6.71	CHA	A<C(O-CH3)/CH-C(CH2-CH3)>		CCL4
1723M	D	6.73	CHA	A<C(O-CH3)/CH-C(CH2-OH)>		CCL4
2839M	D	6.75	CHA	A<C(O-CH3)/CH-C(CH2-O-C(=O))>		CCL4
2077M	E	6.81	CHA	A<C(O-CH3)/CH-C(C(=O)-CH2.2)>		CCL4
2135M	B	6.92	CHA	A<C(O-CH3)/CH-C(C(=O)-C(=O))>		CDCL3
2096M	B	7.03	CHA	A<C(O-CH3)/CH-C(C(=O)-Q2)>		POLYSOL-D
1523M	E	6.69	CHA	A<C(O-CH3)/CH-C(NH-CH3)>		POLYSOL-D
2337M	C	6.85	CHA	A<C(O-CH3)/CH-C(NH-C(=O))>		DMSO-D6
1532M	B	6.91	CHA	A<C(O-CH3)/CH-C(NO2)>		CCL4
1548M	B	6.80	CHA	A<C(O-CH3)/CH-C(O-A)>		CDCL3

BOOK NO.	ASSIGN-MENT	CHEM SHIFT - ppm -	PROTON GROUP	ENVIRONMENTAL GROUPS	S	SOLVENT
1549M	B	6.90	CHA	A<C(O-CH3)/CH-C(O-A)>>		POLYSOL-D
1528M	B	6.81	CHA	A<C(O-CH3)/CH-C(QN(A))>		CDCL3
2398M	B	6.97	CHA	A<C(O-CH3)/CH-C(R5NA<N-C(=O)/C(=O)>)>		CDCL3
1536M	C	6.81	CHA	A<C(O-CH3)/CH-C(SH)>		CDCL3
1538M	B	7.07	CHA	A<C(O-CH3)/CH-C(SO2-CL)>		CDCL3
2178M	C	6.91	CHA	A<C(O-CH3)/C(C(=O)-H)-C(OH)>		CCL4
2595M	D	7.29	CHA	A<C(O-CH3)/C(C(=O)-OH)-C(NH2)>		POLYSOL-D
2090M	C	6.70- 7.30	CHA	A<C(O-CH)>		CDCL3
2216M	C	6.82	CHA	A<C(O-CH)>		CCL4
2943M	B	7.07	CHA	A<C(O-C(=O)-A)/CH-C(CH3)>		CCL4
2923M	A	6.85- 7.50	CHA	A<C(O-C(=O)-CF3)>		CDCL3
2921M	C	6.90- 7.50	CHA	A<C(O-C(=O)-CH2)>		CCL4
2933M	C	6.90	CHA	A<C(O-C(=O)-CH2)/CH-C(CH3)>		CDCL3
2925M	F	6.88	CHA	A<C(O-C(=O)-CH2)/CH-C(CH3)>		CCL4
2929M	B	6.87	CHA	A<C(O-C(=O)-CH3)-CH-C(O-C(=O)-CH3)/C(O-C(=O)-CH3)>		CDCL3
2926M	B	7.32	CHA	A<C(O-C(=O)-CH3)/CH-C(NO2)>		CDCL3
2922M	B	6.90- 7.60	CHA	A<C(O-C(=O)-C)>		CDCL3
2927M	B	7.25	CHA	A<C(O-C(=O)-C)/CH-C(NO2)>		CDCL3
2979M	C	6.92	CHA	A<C(O-C(=O)-NH2)/CH-C(CH3)>		DMSO-D6
2991M	B	7.28	CHA	A<C(O-C(=O)-N)>		CDCL3
2940M	B	7.05	CHA	A<C(O-C(=O)-O)/CH-C(CH3)>		CCL4
2941M	A	7.19	CHA	A<C(O-C(=O)-O)/CH-C(CL)>		CDCL3
2859M	C	7.50- 8.10	CHA	A<C(P(=CH/A/A))>		TFA
1659M	F	7.89 APP.	CHA	A<C(P(=O/A/CH))>		POLYSOL-D
1528M	C	7.00- 7.40	CHA	A<C(QN(A<C-CH-CH-C(O-CH3)>))>		CDCL3
1366M	D	7.95	CHA	A<C(QN(A<C-CH-CH-C(SO2-NH2)>))>		DMSO-D6
871M	B	7.87	CHA	A<C(QN(A))>		CDCL3
872M	C	7.76	CHA	A<C(QN(A))/CH-C(CH3)>		CDCL3
1528M	D	7.73	CHA	A<C(QN(A))/CH-C(O-CH3)>		CDCL3
1366M	B	7.37	CHA	A<C(QN(A))/CH-C(SO2-NH2)>		DMSO-D6
861M	B	7.78	CHA	A<C(QN(A/OH))>		CDCL3
1707M	C	7.55	CHA	A<C(QN(CH2.2-OH))/CH-C(CL)>		CDCL3
866M	C	7.62	CHA	A<C(QN(CH3))>		CDCL3
859M	C	7.88	CHA	A<C(QN(CH3/OH))>		CCL4
887M	B	7.21 APP.	CHA	A<C(QN(NH-A))>		POLYSOL-D
1064M	C	7.69	CHA	A<C(QN(NH-A))>		POLYSOL-D
889M	D	7.91	CHA	A<C(QN(NH-A))>		DMSO-D6
885M	C	6.63	CHA	A<C(QN(N(CH3/CH3)))/CH-C(CH3)>		CCL4
879M	C	7.55 APP.	CHA	A<C(QN(QN/NH2))>		CDCL3
870M	B	7.08	CHA	A<C(QN(Q2))/CH-C(CH3)>		CDCL3
938M	A	7.20 APP.	CHA	A<C(QN(=S))>		CCL4
868M	C	7.67	CHA	A<C(QN)>		CDCL3
884M	B	6.70- 7.30	CHA	A<C(QN-N)>		CCL4
163M	B	7.08	CHA	A<C(Q1(A/A))>		CDCL3
163M	C	7.29	CHA	A<C(Q1(A/A))>		CDCL3
160M	E	6.90- 7.60	CHA	A<C(Q1(A/CH2.3-CH3))>		CCL4
161M	E	6.90- 7.50	CHA	A<C(Q1(A/CH2.6-CH3))>		CCL4
162M	E	7.00- 7.50	CHA	A<C(Q1(A/CH2.9-CH3))>		CDCL3
2042M	C	7.00- 7.50	CHA	A<C(Q1(A/C(=O)-CH3))>		CDCL3
164M	B	7.20	CHA	A<C(Q1(A/Q1))>		CDCL3
164M	B	7.38	CHA	A<C(Q1(A/Q1))>		CDCL3
164M	C	7.20	CHA	A<C(Q1(A/Q1))>		CDCL3
164M	C	7.38	CHA	A<C(Q1(A/Q1))>		CDCL3
1712M	E	7.18 APP.	CHA	A<C(Q1(CH3/CH2-OH/H))>		CDCL3
2856M	E	7.05- 7.55	CHA	A<C(Q1(CH3/C(=O)-O-CH2))>		CCL4
2858M	D	7.96	CHA	A<C(Q1(C(=O)-O-CH2/C:N))>		CDCL3
2161M	E	7.38	CHA	A<C(Q1(H/C(=O)-H/CH2-CH2))>		CCL4
1724M	D	7.49	CHA	A<C(Q2(CH2-OH))/CH-C(NO2)>		POLYSOL-D
157M	D	7.10- 7.52	CHA	A<C(Q2(CH3/H/H))>		CCL4
2842M	G	7.05- 7.45	CHA	A<C(Q2(H/CH2-O-C(=O)/H))>		CCL4
2843M	G	7.20 APP.	CHA	A<C(Q2(H/CH2-O-C(=O)/H))>		CCL4
1019M	D	7.25	CHA	A<C(Q2(H/CH2-S/H))>		CDCL3
2041M	E	7.20- 7.65	CHA	A<C(Q2(H/C(=O)-CH2.3/H))>		CDCL3
2162M	C	7.90	CHA	A<C(Q2(H/C(=O)-H/H))/CH-C(NO2)>		DMSO-D6
2269M	B	7.41	CHA	A<C(Q2(H/C(=O)-O-C(=O)/H))>		CDCL3
2857M	D	7.44	CHA	A<C(Q2(H/C(=O)-O-R6/H))>		CCL4
1360M	C	7.20- 7.70	CHA	A<C(Q2(H/SO2-NH2/H))>		POLYSOL-D
867M	C	7.05- 7.50	CHA	A<C(Q2(QN))>		CDCL3
158M	B	7.20	CHA	A<C(Q2)>		CDCL3
2398M	C	7.30	CHA	A<C(R5NA<N-C(=O)/C(=O)>)/CH-C(O-CH3)>		CDCL3
2441M	B	7.51	CHA	A<C(R5NA<N-C*/C(=O)>)>		DMSO-D6
2446M	B	7.33	CHA	A<C(R5NN<CH-NH/C(=O)>)>		DMSO-D6
2448M	D	7.31	CHA	A<C(R5NN<CH-NH/C(=O)>)>		CDCL3
2412M	F	7.40	CHA	A<C(R5NN<CH-NH/HCH>)>		DMSO-D6
674M	E	7.42	CHA	A<C(R5NN<C=N/N(A)>)>		CDCL3
674M	B	6.72	CHA	A<C(R5NN<N-C(A)=/CH2>)>		CDCL3
678M	C	7.50- 7.90	CHA	A<C(R5NN<N-N=/CH=>)>		CDCL3
1580M	C	7.95	CHA	A<C(R5NO<C=N/O>)-CH-C(CL)>		CDCL3
1151M	C	7.10- 7.65	CHA	A<C(R5NS<C=C(A)/N=>)>		CDCL3
1151M	C	7.29	CHA	A<C(R5NS<C=C(A)/N=>)>		CDCL3
1151M	B	7.10- 7.65	CHA	A<C(R5NS<C=C(A)/S>)>		CDCL3

BOOK NO.	ASSIGN-MENT	CHEM SHIFT - ppm -	PROTON GROUP	ENVIRONMENTAL GROUPS	S	SOLVENT
1151M	B	7.29	CHA	A<C(R5NS<C=C(A)/S)>		CDCL3
676M	C	7.05- 7.60	CHA	A<C(R5N<N-C(CH3)=/C(CH3)=>		CDCL3
2388M	C	7.64	CHA	A<C(R5N<N-C(=O)/C(=O)>)/CH-C(BR)>		POLYSOL-D
2951M	F	7.25 APP.	CHA	A<C(R5O<CH-HCH/HCH>)>		CDCL3
1157M	C	7.59	CHA	A<C(R5SS<C=CH/S>)>		CDCL3
2464M	C	7.39	CHA	A<C(R6NN<C(CH2-o3)-C(=O)/C(=O)>)>		DMSO-D6
641M	G	6.89	CHA	A<C(R6NN<N-CH(CH3)/CH2>)>		CDCL3
1887M	E	7.08	CHA	A<C(R6<CH-CH2/CH2>)/CH-C(OH)>		CDCL3
1775M	C	7.18 APP.	CHA	A<C(R6<CH-CH(OH)/CH2>)>		CCL4
1774M	E	7.20 APP.	CHA	A<C(R6<CH-CH(OH)/CH2>)>		CDCL3
1776M	F	6.90- 7.60	CHA	A<C(R6<C(A)-CH(OH)/CH2>)>		CDCL3
1821M	E	7.36	CHA	A<C(R6<C(OH)-CH2/CH2>)/CH-C(CH3)>		CDCL3
146M	D	7.00- 7.45	CHA	A<C(R6<C=CH/CH2>)>		CCL4
184M	F	7.16	CHA	A<C(R6<C=CH/CH2>)/CH-C(CH3)>		CCL4
2033M	B	7.47	CHA	A<C(R6<C=CH/C(=O)>)>		CDCL3
1233M	B	7.00	CHA	A<C(SH)-CH-C(CL)/CH-C(CL)>		CCL4
1237M	D	6.57	CHA	A<C(SH)-CH-C(NH2)>		CDCL3
1240M	C	6.87	CHA	A<C(SH)-CH-C(SH)/CH-C(CL)>		CCL4
1240M	E	7.17	CHA	A<C(SH)-C(CL)/C(SH)>		CCL4
1236M	E	7.32	CHA	A<C(SH)-C(NH2)		CDCL3
1235M	B	7.07	CHA	A<C(SH)/CH-C(BR)>		CDCL3
1238M	C	7.14	CHA	A<C(SH)/CH-C(NH2)>		CDCL3
1536M	D	7.30	CHA	A<C(SH)/CH-C(O-CH3)>		CDCL3
1090M	C	7.10- 7.60	CHA	A<C(SI(A/CH2.11/CH2.11))>		CCL4
1088M	C	7.28 APP.	CHA	A<C(SI(A/CH2/CH2))>		CDCL3
1594M	C	7.61	CHA	A<C(SI(O/O/A))>		CDCL3
1272M	B	7.40- 8.35	CHA	A<C(SO2-A)>		CDCL3
1270M	C	7.90 APP.	CHA	A<C(SO2-A)>		CDCL3
1270M	C	7.90 APP.	CHA	A<C(SO2-A)/CH-CH-C(F)>		CDCL3
1274M	B	7.82	CHA	A<C(SO2-A)/CH-C(CL)>		CDCL3
1265M	D	8.01	CHA	A<C(SO2-CH2)>		POLYSOL-D
1261M	F	7.89	CHA	A<C(SO2-CH2)>		CDCL3
1266M	D	7.88	CHA	A<C(SO2-CH2)-CH-C(CL)/CH-C(CL)>		CDCL3
1264M	D	7.81	CHA	A<C(SO2-CH2)/CH-C(CH3)>		POLYSOL-D
1267M	E	7.54	CHA	A<C(SO2-CH2)/CH-C(CH3)>		POLYSOL-D
1709M	E	7.79	CHA	A<C(SO2-CH2)/CH-C(CH3)>		CDCL3
1262M	G	7.78	CHA	A<C(SO2-CH2)/CH-C(CH3)>		CDCL3
1263M	F	7.81	CHA	A<C(SO2-CH2)/CH-C(CL)>		CDCL3
1284M	E	7.81	CHA	A<C(SO2-CL)-C(CH3)/C(CH3)>		CCL4
1283M	C	7.90	CHA	A<C(SO2-CL)/CH-C(CH3)>		CDCL3
1538M	C	7.98	CHA	A<C(SO2-CL)/CH-C(O-CH3)>		CDCL3
1361M	B	7.95 APP.	CHA	A<C(SO2-NH2)>		TFA
1362M	D	7.91	CHA	A<C(SO2-NH2)-C(CH3)>		DMSO-D6
1365M	D	7.50	CHA	A<C(SO2-NH2)/CH-C(NH2)>		DMSO-D6
1366M	E	7.97	CHA	A<C(SO2-NH2)/CH-C(QN(A))>		DMSO-D6
1371M	D	7.87	CHA	A<C(SO2-NH)>		DMSO-D6
1290M	C	7.77	CHA	A<C(SO2-OH)-C(NH2)/C(CH3)>		DMSO-D6
1289M	C	7.81 APP.	CHA	A<C(SO2-OH)/CH-C(A)>		DMSO
1376M	C	7.30- 8.00	CHA	A<C(SO2-R5NN)>		POLYSOL-D
1313M	E	8.01	CHA	A<C(SO3(-))>		POLYSOL-D
1320M	B	7.33 APP.	CHA	A<C(SO3-CH3)>		CDCL3
1300M	B	7.92	CHA	A<C(SO3-NA)>	S	D2O
1308M	A	8.45	CHA	A<C(SO3-NA)-CH-C(SO3-NA)/C(SO3-NA)>		D2O
1307M	A	8.29	CHA	A<C(SO3-NA)-C(NO2)/CH-C(NO2)>		D2O
1303M	B	7.79	CHA	A<C(SO3-NA)/CH-C(BR)>	S	D2O
1250M	E	7.60	CHA	A<C(SO-CH2.2)/CH-C(CL)>		CDCL3
1172M	B	7.20- 7.65	CHA	A<C(S-AN)>		CDCL3
1171M	A	7.28 APP.	CHA	A<C(S-A)/CH-C(CL)>		POLYSOL-D
1708M	F	7.14	CHA	A<C(S-CH2.2)/CH-C(CH3)>		CCL4
1162M	D	7.18	CHA	A<C(S-CH2)/CH-C(CH3)>		POLYSOL-D
1923M	E	7.03	CHA	A<C(S-CH3)-CH-C(CH3)/CH-C(OH)>		CDCL3
1161M	E	7.28	CHA	A<C(S-CH3)-C(NH2)>		CCL4
1160M	B	7.11	CHA	A<C(S-CH3)/CH-C(BR)>		CDCL3
2074M	B	7.24	CHA	A<C(S-CH3)/CH-C(=O)-CH3)>		POLYSOL-D
1923M	F	7.10	CHA	A<C(S-CH3)/C(CH3)-C(OH)>		CDCL3
1196M	C	7.34	CHA	A<C(S-S)/CH-C(CH3)>		CDCL3
1197M	B	7.38	CHA	A<C(S-S)/CH-C(CL)>		CCL4
204M	C	7.35- 7.65	CHA	A<C(C*-CH-C(CH3)/CH-C(CH3)>		CCL4
1588M	B	6.78	CHA	A<C(C*-O>		CCL4
291M	A	7.22 APP.	CHA	A<C-C(CL>		CCL4
288M	A	7.10- 7.85	CHA	A<C-C(CL/CL/A)>		CCL4
2288M	B	8.00	CHA	A<C-C(C(=O)-NH2)>		TFA
169M	A	7.10- 7.65	CHA	A<C-C(C:C-A)>		CCL4
2551M	C	7.38	CHA	A<C1(C(=O)-OH/CH2-CH3)>		CDCL3
732M	A	7.30- 7.55	CHA	A(CH-CH-C(ANN(C-N-CH-N)))		CDCL3
289M	A	7.34	CHA	A(CH-CH-C(CCL3))		CCL4
836M	C	7.30- 7.60	CHA	A(CH-CH-C(CH2-N(+)))	S	CDCL3
852M	A	7.28 APP.	CHA	A(CH-CH-C(CH=NOH))		CDCL3
2463M	A	7.46	CHA	A(CH-CH-C(CH=R6NN))		DMSO
2098M	A	7.47 APP.	CHA	A(CH-CH-C(C(=O)-A))		CDCL3
2099M	C	7.20- 7.50	CHA	A(CH-CH-C(C(=O)-A))		CCL4

: REPRESENTS TRIPLE BOND. - REPRESENTS AN ARROW AND < AND > REPRESENT BRACKETS.

BOOK NO.	ASSIGN-MENT	CHEM SHIFT - ppm -	PROTON GROUP	ENVIRONMENTAL GROUPS	S	SOLVENT
2054M	B	7.30- 7.70	CHA	A(CH-CH-C(C(=O)-CH2))		CDCL3
2840M	C	7.20- 7.70	CHA	A(CH-CH-C(C(=O)-CH2))		CDCL3
2085M	C	7.30- 7.60	CHA	A(CH-CH-C(C(=O)-CH2))		CDCL3
2046M	C	7.47 APP.	CHA	A(CH-CH-C(C(=O)-CH2))		CDCL3
2088M	D	7.30- 7.55	CHA	A(CH-CH-C(C(=O)-CH2))		CDCL3
2049M	E	7.15- 7.55	CHA	A(CH-CH-C(C(=O)-CH2))		CCL4
2045M	B	7.15- 7.50	CHA	A(CH-CH-C(C(=O)-CH3))		CCL4
2048M	C	7.33	CHA	A(CH-CH-C(C(=O)-CH))		CCL4
2134M	A	7.21- 7.65	CHA	A(CH-CH-C(C(=O)-C(=O)))		CCL4
2163M	A	7.20- 7.60	CHA	A(CH-CH-C(C(=O)-H))		CCL4
2411M	C	7.10- 7.50	CHA	A(CH-CH-C(C(=O)-NH))		CDCL3
2344M	C	7.30- 7.65	CHA	A(CH-CH-C(C(=O)-NH))		CDCL3
2851M	D	7.23- 7.58	CHA	A(CH-CH-C(C(=O)-NH))		CDCL3
2566M	A	7.52	CHA	A(CH-CH-C(C(=O)-OH))		CCL4
2864M	D	7.48	CHA	A(CH-CH-C(C(=O)-O-CH2))		CDCL3
2270M	A	7.57 APP.	CHA	A(CH-CH-C(C(=O)-O-C(=O)))		CDCL3
2675M	A	7.31- 7.64	CHA	A(CH-CH-C(C(=O)-O-NA))		D2O
2097M	A	7.52	CHA	A(CH-CH-C(C(=O)-Q2))		CDCL3
2084M	C	7.15- 7.60	CHA	A(CH-CH-C(C(=O)-R6))		CDCL3
426M	A	6.82- 7.45	CHA	A(CH-CH-C(I))		CCL4
487M	C	6.59 APP.	CHA	A(CH-CH-C(NH2))		CCL4
807M	A	6.88	CHA	A(CH-CH-C(NH-A))	S	DMSO
585M	F	6.61	CHA	A(CH-CH-C(NH-CH2.2))		CDCL3
594M	D	6.63	CHA	A(CH-CH-C(NH-CH2))		CDCL3
2318M	B	6.90- 7.50	CHA	A(CH-CH-C(NH-C(=O)))		DMSO-D6
2315M	C	6.90- 7.42	CHA	A(CH-CH-C(NH-C(=O)))		CDCL3
2435M	C	7.06	CHA	A(CH-CH-C(NH-C(=O)))		CDCL3
2316M	E	6.90- 7.70	CHA	A(CH-CH-C(NH-C(=O)))		CDCL3
2467M	A	6.82 APP.	CHA	A(CH-CH-C(NH-NH))		DMSO
878M	B	6.80	CHA	A(CH-CH-C(NH-QN))		DMSO-D6
586M	E	6.59	CHA	A(CH-CH-C(NH-R6))		CDCL3
655M	C	6.70	CHA	A(CH-CH-C(N(CH2.2/CH2.2)))		POLYSOL-D
2548M	B	6.45- 6.85	CHA	A(CH-CH-C(N(CH2/CH2)))		POLYSOL-D
654M	B	6.50- 6.80	CHA	A(CH-CH-C(N(CH2/CH2)))		CDCL3
649M	C	6.55 APP.	CHA	A(CH-CH-C(N(CH2/CH2)))		CCL4
652M	C	6.45- 6.75	CHA	A(CH-CH-C(N(CH2/CH3)))		CCL4
648M	B	6.42- 6.72	CHA	A(CH-CH-C(N(CH3/CH3)))		CCL4
896M	A	7.37	CHA	A(CH-CH-C(N=N))		CDCL3
1065M	A	7.40- 7.65	CHA	A(CH-CH-C(N=N-A))		CDCL3
1305M	A	7.50- 7.75	CHA	A(CH-CH-C(N=N-A))		DMSO
899M	C	7.15- 7.60	CHA	A(CH-CH-C(N=N-A))		CDCL3
900M	C	7.20- 7.60	CHA	A(CH-CH-C(N=N-A))		CDCL3
1491M	D	6.96	CHA	A(CH-CH-C(O-CH2.2))		CDCL3
2553M	B	6.92 APP.	CHA	A(CH-CH-C(O-CH2))		C3H6O
1710M	C	6.74	CHA	A(CH-CH-C(O-CH2))		CCL4
2554M	E	6.88 APP.	CHA	A(CH-CH-C(O-CH2))		CDCL3
2978M	A	6.82- 7.40	CHA	A(CH-CH-C(O-C(=O)-NH2))		DMSO
640M	D	7.05	CHA	A(CH-CH-C(R6NN(N/CH2-CH2-NH)))		CDCL3
1091M	C	7.09- 7.37	CHA	A(CH-CH-C(SI(A/A/CH2)))		CDCL3
1084M	B	7.15- 7.43	CHA	A(CH-CH-C(SI(A/H/H)))		CDCL3
1276M	A	7.39- 7.69	CHA	A(CH-CH-C(SO2-A))		CDCL3
1268M	C	7.30- 7.60	CHA	A(CH-CH-C(SO2-A))		CDCL3
1168M	A	7.29 APP.	CHA	A(CH-CH-C(S-C))		CDCL3
1194M	A	7.23	CHA	A(CH-CH-C(S-S))		CDCL3
732M	A	7.30- 7.55	CHA	A(CH-C(ANN(C-N-CH-N)))		CDCL3
176M	B	7.37	CHA	A(CH-C(A)-C(A))		CDCL3
396M	A	7.06	CHA	A(CH-C(BR)-C(BR))		CCL4
2572M	A	7.42 APP.	CHA	A(CH-C(BR)-C(C(=O)-OH))		DMSO
518M	B	6.54	CHA	A(CH-C(BR)-C(NH2))		CDCL3
1514M	B	6.80	CHA	A(CH-C(BR)-C(O-CH3))		CDCL3
393M	A	7.03	CHA	A(CH-C(BR)/CH-C(CL))		CCL4
2234M	A	7.38	CHA	A(CH-C(BR)/CH-C(C(=O)-BR))		CCL4
2573M	A	7.32	CHA	A(CH-C(BR)/CH-C(C(=O)-OH))		POLYSOL-D
519M	D	6.75- 7.06	CHA	A(CH-C(BR)/CH-C(NH2))		CDCL3
289M	A	7.34	CHA	A(CH-C(CCL3))		CCL4
836M	C	7.30- 7.60	CHA	A(CH-C(CH2-N(+)))	S	CDCL3
1722M	E	6.85	CHA	A(CH-C(CH2-OH)-C(O-CH3))		CDCL3
2593M	B	6.90- 7.35	CHA	A(CH-C(CH3)-C(C(=O)-OH)/CH-C(CH3))		CDCL3
427M	C	7.11 APP.	CHA	A(CH-C(CH3)-C(I))		CDCL3
589M	E	6.65	CHA	A(CH-C(CH3)-C(NH-CH3))		CDCL3
1372M	D	7.01 APP.	CHA	A(CH-C(CH3)-C(NH-SO2)/CH-C(CH3))		CDCL3
665M	C	6.91	CHA	A(CH-C(CH3)-C(N(CH3/CH3))/CH-C(CH3))		CDCL3
1916M	C	6.45- 6.95	CHA	A(CH-C(CH3)-C(OH)/CH-C(CH3))		CCL4
385M	D	7.08 APP.	CHA	A(CH-C(CH(CH3/CH3))-C(BR)/CH-C(CH3))		CDCL3
852M	A	7.28 APP.	CHA	A(CH-C(CH=NOH))		CDCL3
2463M	A	7.46	CHA	A(CH-C(CH=R6NN))		DMSO
309M	B	6.79- 7.28	CHA	A(CH-C(CL)-C(CH3)/CH-C(CL))		CCL4
305M	A	6.90- 7.55	CHA	A(CH-C(CL)-C(CL))		CCL4
312M	A	6.89- 7.46	CHA	A(CH-C(CL)-C(CL)/CH-C(CL))		CDCL3
433M	A	6.88	CHA	A(CH-C(CL)-C(I))		CCL4
1509M	B	6.85	CHA	A(CH-C(CL)-C(O-CH3))		CDCL3

BOOK NO.	ASSIGN-MENT	CHEM SHIFT - ppm -	PROTON GROUP	ENVIRONMENTAL GROUPS	S	SOLVENT
1553M	B	6.87	CHA	A(CH-C(CL)-C(O-CH3)/CH-C(CL))		CCL4
2230M	A	7.41	CHA	A(CH-C(CL)/CH-C(C(=O)-CL))		CCL4
898M	A	7.40 APP.	CHA	A(CH-C(CL)/CH-C(N=N-A))		CDCL3
1510M	C	7.11	CHA	A(CH-C(CL)/CH-C(O-CH3))		CCL4
2098M	A	7.47 APP.	CHA	A(CH-C(C(=O)-A))		CDCL3
2099M	C	7.20- 7.50	CHA	A(CH-C(C(=O)-A))		CCL4
2054M	B	7.30- 7.70	CHA	A(CH-C(C(=O)-CH2))		CDCL3
2840M	C	7.20- 7.70	CHA	A(CH-C(C(=O)-CH2))		CDCL3
2085M	C	7.30- 7.60	CHA	A(CH-C(C(=O)-CH2))		CDCL3
2046M	C	7.47 APP.	CHA	A(CH-C(C(=O)-CH2))		CDCL3
2088M	D	7.30- 7.55	CHA	A(CH-C(C(=O)-CH2))		CDCL3
2049M	E	7.15- 7.55	CHA	A(CH-C(C(=O)-CH2))		CCL4
2045M	B	7.15- 7.50	CHA	A(CH-C(C(=O)-CH3))		CCL4
2081M	B	7.57	CHA	A(CH-C(C(=O)-CH3/CH-C(C(=O)-CH3))		CDCL3
2048M	C	7.33	CHA	A(CH-C(C(=O)-CH))		CCL4
2237M	A	7.80	CHA	A(CH-C(C(=O)-CL)-C(C(=O)-CL))		CCL4
2134M	A	7.21- 7.65	CHA	A(CH-C(C(=O)-C(=O)))		CCL4
2163M	A	7.20- 7.60	CHA	A(CH-C(C(=O)-H))		CCL4
2289M	C	7.30	CHA	A(CH-C(C(=O)-NH2)/CH-C(CH3))		CDCL3
2411M	C	7.10- 7.50	CHA	A(CH-C(C(=O)-NH))		CDCL3
2344M	C	7.30- 7.65	CHA	A(CH-C(C(=O)-NH))		CDCL3
2851M	D	7.23- 7.58	CHA	A(CH-C(C(=O)-NH))		CDCL3
2370M	E	7.32 APP.	CHA	A(CH-C(C(=O)-N)>		CDCL3
2566M	A	7.52	CHA	A(CH-C(C(=O)-OH))		CCL4
2572M	A	7.42 APP.	CHA	A(CH-C(C(=O)-OH)-C(BR))		DMSO
2590M	A	7.51	CHA	A(CH-C(C(=O)-OH)-C(C(=O)-OH))		POLYSOL-D
2580M	A	7.74	CHA	A(CH-C(C(=O)-OH)/CH-C(C:N))		DMSO
2864M	D	7.48	CHA	A(CH-C(C(=O)-O-CH2))		CDCL3
2891M	F	7.42	CHA	A(CH-C(C(=O)-O-CH2)-C(OH))		CDCL3
2887M	B	6.75- 7.07	CHA	A(CH-C(C(=O)-O-CH3)-C(O-CH3))		CCL4
2901M	B	7.50	CHA	A(CH-C(C(=O)-O-CH3)/CH-C(C(=O)-O-CH3))		CDCL3
2889M	C	6.88	CHA	A(CH-C(C(=O)-O-CH)-C(OH))		CDCL3
2270M	A	7.57 APP.	CHA	A(CH-C(C(=O)-O-C(=O)))		CDCL3
2680M	A	7.61	CHA	A(CH-C(C(=O)-O-K)-C(C(=O)-O-K))		D2O
2675M	A	7.31- 7.64	CHA	A(CH-C(C(=O)-O-NA))		D2O
2097M	A	7.52	CHA	A(CH-C(C(=O)-Q2))		CDCL3
2084M	C	7.15- 7.60	CHA	A(CH-C(C(=O)-R6))		CDCL3
997M	A	8.00	CHA	A(CH-C(C:N)-C(C:N))		TFA
230M	A	6.90- 7.40	CHA	A(CH-C(F)-C(F))		CDCL3
231M	B	7.27	CHA	A(CH-C(F)/CH-C(F))		CDCL3
426M	A	6.82- 7.45	CHA	A(CH-C(I))		CCL4
427M	C	7.11 APP.	CHA	A(CH-C(I)-C(CH3))		CDCL3
433M	A	6.88	CHA	A(CH-C(I)-C(CL))		CCL4
1896M	B	6.59	CHA	A(CH-C(I)-C(OH))		CDCL3
1519M	B	6.65	CHA	A(CH-C(I)-C(O-CH3))		CDCL3
428M	B	6.90	CHA	A(CH-C(I)/CH-C(CH3))		CCL4
2576M	A	7.20	CHA	A(CH-C(I)/CH-C(C(=O)-OH))		POLYSOL-D
526M	C	6.79	CHA	A(CH-C(I)/CH-C(NH2))		CDCL3
1060M	A	7.50	CHA	A(CH-C(I)/CH-C(NO2))		DMSO
487M	D	6.99	CHA	A(CH-C(NH2))		CCL4
518M	D	7.03	CHA	A(CH-C(NH2)-C(BR))		CDCL3
495M	E	6.80	CHA	A(CH-C(NH2)-C(CH3)/CH-C(CH3))		CCL4
793M	A	7.66	CHA	A(CH-C(NH2)-C(NH2))	S	D2O
533M	B	6.67	CHA	A(CH-C(NH2)-C(NH2))		CDCL3
1198M	D	7.10	CHA	A(CH-C(NH2)-C(S-S))		CDCL3
489M	D	6.90	CHA	A(CH-C(NH2)/CH-C(CH3))		CCL4
534M	D	6.74	CHA	A(CH-C(NH2)/CH-C(NH2))		POLYSOL-D
1899M	D	6.78	CHA	A(CH-C(NH2)/CH-C(OH))		DMSO
1522M	E	6.98	CHA	A(CH-C(NH2)/CH-C(O-CH3))		CDCL3
807M	B	7.10- 7.40	CHA	A(CH-C(NH-A))	S	DMSO
585M	G	7.13	CHA	A(CH-C(NH-CH2.2))		CDCL3
594M	E	7.12	CHA	A(CH-C(NH-CH2))		CDCL3
589M	G	7.13	CHA	A(CH-C(NH-CH3)-C(CH3))		CDCL3
2318M	B	6.90- 7.50	CHA	A(CH-C(NH-C(=O)))		DMSO-D6
2315M	C	6.90- 7.42	CHA	A(CH-C(NH-C(=O)))		CDCL3
2435M	D	7.20- 7.50	CHA	A(CH-C(NH-C(=O)))		CDCL3
2316M	E	6.90- 7.70	CHA	A(CH-C(NH-C(=O)))		CDCL3
2322M	D	7.08	CHA	A(CH-C(NH-C(=O))/CH-C(CH3))		CDCL3
2335M	C	6.95- 7.20	CHA	A(CH-C(NH-C(=O))/CH-C(OH))		DMSO-D6
586M	F	7.12	CHA	A(CH-C(NH-R6))		CDCL3
2597M	A	7.00	CHA	A(CH-C(NO2)-C(OH)/CH-C(C(=O)-OH))		POLYSOL-D
1556M	B	7.31	CHA	A(CH-C(NO2)-C(O-CH3)/CH-C(NO2))		CDCL3
1047M	B	7.38	CHA	A(CH-C(NO2)/CH-C(CH3))		CCL4
2073M	B	7.67	CHA	A(CH-C(NO2)/CH-C(C(=O)-CH3))		CDCL3
1067M	A	7.89	CHA	A(CH-C(NO2)/CH-C(NO2))		CCL4
1531M	C	7.42	CHA	A(CH-C(NO2)/CH-C(O-CH3))		CDCL3
655M	D	7.19	CHA	A(CH-C(N(CH2.2/CH2.2)))		POLYSOL-D
654M	C	7.11	CHA	A(CH-C(N(CH2/CH2)))		CDCL3
2548M	C	7.14	CHA	A(CH-C(N(CH2/CH2)))		POLYSOL-D
649M	D	7.05 APP.	CHA	A(CH-C(N(CH2/CH2)))		CCL4
652M	D	7.03	CHA	A(CH-C(N(CH2/CH3)))		CCL4

BOOK NO.	ASSIGN-MENT	CHEM SHIFT - ppm -	PROTON GROUP	ENVIRONMENTAL GROUPS	S	SOLVENT
648M	C	7.10	CHA	A(CH-C(N(CH3/CH3)))		CCL4
659M	D	6.99	CHA	A(CH-C(N(CH3/CH3))/CH-C(CH3))		CCL4
896M	A	7.37	CHA	A(CH-C(N=N))		CDCL3
1065M	A	7.40- 7.65	CHA	A(CH-C(N=N-A))		CDCL3
1305M	A	7.50- 7.75	CHA	A(CH-C(N=N-A))		DMSO
899M	C	7.15- 7.60	CHA	A(CH-C(N=N-A))		CDCL3
900M	C	7.20- 7.60	CHA	A(CH-C(N=N-A))		CDCL3
2891M	C	6.85	CHA	A(CH-C(OH)-C(C(=O)-O-CH2))		CDCL3
2889M	E	7.42	CHA	A(CH-C(OH)-C(C(=O)-O-CH))		CDCL3
1896M	D	7.15	CHA	A(CH-C(OH)-C(I))		CDCL3
1910M	B	6.83	CHA	A(CH-C(OH)-C(OH))		POLYSOL-D
1877M	D	6.94	CHA	A(CH-C(OH)/CH-C(CH3))		CCL4
2892M	C	6.95- 7.48	CHA	A(CH-C(OH)/CH-C(C(=O)-O-CH3)		CDCL3
1491M	E	7.28	CHA	A(CH-C(O-CH2.2))		CDCL3
2553M	C	7.25	CHA	A(CH-C(O-CH2))		C3H6O
1710M	D	7.10	CHA	A(CH-C(O-CH2))		CCL4
2554M	F	7.22	CHA	A(CH-C(O-CH2))		CDCL3
1499M	F	7.00	CHA	A(CH-C(O-CH2)/CH-C(CH3))		CCL4
1514M	D	7.24	CHA	A(CH-C(O-CH3)-C(BR))		CDCL3
1722M	F	7.19	CHA	A(CH-C(O-CH3)-C(CH2-OH))		CDCL3
1509M	D	7.10- 7.50	CHA	A(CH-C(O-CH3)-C(CL))		CDCL3
2887M	C	7.37	CHA	A(CH-C(O-CH3)-C(C(=O)-O-CH3))		CCL4
1519M	D	7.20	CHA	A(CH-C(O-CH3)-C(I))		CDCL3
1529M	D	7.31	CHA	A(CH-C(O-CH3)-C(QN(OH)))		CDCL3
2583M	C	7.43	CHA	A(CH-C(O-CH3)/CH-C(C(=O)-OH))		DMSO-D6
1535M	D	7.10	CHA	A(CH-C(O-CH3)/CH-C(SH))		CDCL3
2978M	A	6.82- 7.40	CHA	A(CH-C(O-C(=O)-NH2))		DMSO
1529M	C	6.93	CHA	A(CH-C(QN(OH))-C(O-CH3))		CDCL3
640M	E	7.18	CHA	A(CH-C(R6NN(N/CH2-NH)))		CDCL3
1091M	C	7.09- 7.37	CHA	A(CH-C(SI(A/A/CH2)))		CDCL3
1084M	B	7.15- 7.43	CHA	A(CH-C(SI(A/H/H)))		CDCL3
1268M	C	7.30- 7.60	CHA	A(CH-C(SO2-A))		CDCL3
1276M	A	7.39- 7.69	CHA	A(CH-C(SO--A))		CDCL3
1168M	A	7.29 APP.	CHA	A(CH-C(S-C))		CDCL3
1194M	A	7.23	CHA	A(CH-C(S-S))		CDCL3
1198M	B	6.53	CHA	A(CH-C(S-S)-C(NH2))		CDCL3
200M	A	7.38	CHA	A(CH-C*/CH-CH-C*)		CCL4
860M	C	7.50	CHA	A(CQN(CH3/OH))/CH-C(CL))		CDCL3
732M	C	8.08 APP.	CHA	A(C(ANN(C-N-CH-N)))		CDCL3
762M	C	7.10- 7.68	CHA	A(C(A(C-CH-CH-C(N(N/CH3)))))		CDCL3
1508M	C	7.20- 7.70	CHA	A(C(A(C-CH-CH-C(O-CH3))))		CDCL3
532M	D	7.20	CHA	A(C(A(C-CH-C(CH3)-C(NH2)))-CH-C(CH3)/CH-C(NH2))		CDCL3
532M	E	7.23	CHA	A(C(A(C-CH-C(CH3)-C(NH2)))/C(CH3)-C(NH2))		CDCL3
176M	A	7.11	CHA	A(C(A(C-C(A))))		CDCL3
1889M	C	7.43	CHA	A(C(A)/CH-C(OH))		DMSO
1508M	D	7.49	CHA	A(C(A)/CH-C(O-CH3))		CDCL3
180M	B	7.78	CHA	A(C(A)/C(A))		CDCL3
393M	B	7.20 APP.	CHA	A(C(BR)-CH-C(CL))		CCL4
2234M	B	7.79	CHA	A(C(BR)-CH-C(C(=O)-BR))		CCL4
2573M	B	7.64	CHA	A(C(BR)-CH-C(C(=O)-OH))		POLYSOL-D
519M	D	6.75- 7.06	CHA	A(C(BR)-CH-C(NH2))		CDCL3
396M	B	7.49	CHA	A(C(BR)-C(BR))		CCL4
382M	C	7.46	CHA	A(C(BR)-C(CH3))		CCL4
386M	D	7.27	CHA	A(C(BR)-C(CH3)/C(CH3)-C(CH3))		CDCL3
385M	E	7.35	CHA	A(C(BR)-C(CH(CH3/CH3))/C(CH3))		CDCL3
522M	D	7.25	CHA	A(C(BR)-C(CL)/CH-C(NH2))		CDCL3
2291M	A	7.58 APP.	CHA	A(C(BR)-C(C(=O)-NH2))		TFA
2572M	B	7.69 APP.	CHA	A(C(BR)-C(C(=O)-OH))		DMSO
518M	E	7.34	CHA	A(C(BR)-C(NH2))		CDCL3
521M	E	7.19	CHA	A(C(BR)-C(NH2)/C(CH3))		CDCL3
1073M	A	8.09	CHA	A(C(BR)-C(NO2)/CH-C(NO2))		CDCL3
1937M	B	7.56	CHA	A(C(BR)-C(OH)-C(BR)/C(BR))		CCL4
1935M	C	7.29	CHA	A(C(BR)-C(OH)-C(BR)/C(C(A/CH3/CH3)))		CDCL3
1514M	E	7.49	CHA	A(C(BR)-C(O-CH3))		CDCL3
1567M	B	7.60	CHA	A(C(BR)-C(O-CH3)-C(BR)/C(BR))		CCL4
384M	C	7.30	CHA	A(C(BR)/CH-C(CH3))		CCL4
2102M	B	7.60	CHA	A(C(BR)/CH-C(C(=O)-A))		CDCL3
2406M	B	7.62	CHA	A(C(BR)/CH-C(C(=O)-NH))		DMSO
2875M	C	7.49	CHA	A(C(BR)/CH-C(C(=O)-O-CH2))		CCL4
520M	C	7.21	CHA	A(C(BR)/CH-C(NH2))		CDCL3
1378M	B	7.33	CHA	A(C(BR)/CH-C(NH-SO2))		POLYSOL-D
668M	C	7.25	CHA	A(C(BR)/CH-C(N(CH3/CH3)))		CDCL3
1895M	C	7.30	CHA	A(C(BR)/CH-C(OH))		CDCL3
1518M	D	7.31	CHA	A(C(BR)/CH-C(O-CH2))		CDCL3
1516M	C	7.29	CHA	A(C(BR)/CH-C(O-CH3))		CCL4
1275M	A	7.65	CHA	A(C(BR)/CH-C(SO2-A))		CDCL3
783M	C	7.81	CHA	A(C(BR)/C(CH2-NH2))	S	POLYSOL-D
393M	C	7.46	CHA	A(C(BR)/C(CL))		CCL4
2234M	D	8.07	CHA	A(C(BR)/C(C(=O)-BR))		CCL4
2573M	D	8.15	CHA	A(C(BR)/C(C(=O)-OH))		POLYSOL-D
519M	C	6.69	CHA	A(C(BR)/C(NH2))		CDCL3

BOOK NO.	ASSIGN-MENT	CHEM SHIFT - ppm -	PROTON GROUP	ENVIRONMENTAL GROUPS	S	SOLVENT
289M	B	7.83	CHA	A(C(CCL3))		CCL4
2243M	A	7.80	CHA	A(C(CE)-C(C(=O)-CE)/CH-C(NO2))		DMSO
185M	C	7.08	CHA	A(C(CH2.2-A)/CH-C(CH3))		CDCL3
135M	D	7.19 APP.	CHA	A(C(CH2.2-CH3))		CDCL3
2159M	C	7.20 APP.	CHA	A(C(CH2.2-C(=O)-H))		CDCL3
1485M	E	7.10 APP.	CHA	A(C(CH2.2-O))		CCL4
148M	B	7.07 APP.	CHA	A(C(CH2-A))		CCL4
1929M	E	7.19 APP.	CHA	A(C(CH2-A))		DMSO-D6
1929M	D	6.83	CHA	A(C(CH2-A)-C(OH)/CH-C(OH))		DMSO-D6
530M	D	6.81	CHA	A(C(CH2-A)/CH-C(NH2))		DMSO-D6
371M	B	7.22	CHA	A(C(CH2-RR))		CCL4
2862M	D	7.19	CHA	A(C(CH2-CH2)		CCL4
424M	C	6.90- 7.35	CHA	A(C(CH2-CH2))		CDCL3
2088M	C	7.20 APP.	CHA	A(C(CH2-CH2))		CDCL3
1218M	C	7.21	CHA	A(C(CH2-CH2))		CDCL3
2833M	D	7.11	CHA	A(C(CH2-CH2))		CCL4
477M	D	7.14	CHA	A(C(CH2-CH2))		CCL4
1484M	D	7.19	CHA	A(C(CH2-CH2))		CDCL3
1701M	D	7.19	CHA	A(C(CH2-CH2))		CDCL3
2036M	D	7.19 APP.	CHA	A(C(CH2-CH2))		CCL4
1702M	E	7.10	CHA	A(C(CH2-CH2))		CCL4
142M	E	7.15	CHA	A(C(CH2-CH2))		CDCL3
481M	E	7.20 APP.	CHA	A(C(CH2-CH2))		CDCL3
2891M	E	7.27	CHA	A(C(CH2-CH2))		CDCL3
2838M	F	7.16	CHA	A(C(CH2-CH2))		CCL4
155M	F	7.19	CHA	A(C(CH2-CH2))		CDCL3
2038M	D	6.75	CHA	A(C(CH2-CH2)/CH-C(OH))		CDCL3
134M	C	7.07	CHA	A(C(CH2-CH3))		CCL4
2059M	D	7.17	CHA	A(C(CH2-CH3)/CH-C(C(=O)-CH3))		CCL4
2324M	D	7.04	CHA	A(C(CH2-CH3)/CH-C(NH-C(=O)))		CDCL3
152M	C	7.18 APP.	CHA	A(C(CH2-CH))		CDCL3
978M	D	7.20	CHA	A(C(CH2-CH))		CDCL3
284M	B	7.28	CHA	A(C(CH2-CL))		CCL4
285M	D	7.18	CHA	A(C(CH2-CL)/CH-C(CH3))		CCL4
2085M	B	7.27	CHA	A(C(CH2-C(=O)))		CDCL3
2040M	B	7.00- 7.40	CHA	A(C(CH2-C(=O)-CH2))		CDCL3
2217M	B	7.18	CHA	A(C(CH2-C(=O)-CL)/CH-C(CL))		CDCL3
2405M	D	6.96	CHA	A(C(CH2-C(=O)-NH)/CH-C(NH2))		POLYSOL-D
2539M	B	7.27	CHA	A(C(CH2-C(=O)-OH))		CDCL3
2557M	C	7.12	CHA	A(C(CH2-C(=O)-O)/CH-C(CH3))		CDCL3
786M	C	7.31	CHA	A(C(CH2-C)/CH-C(CL))	S	D20
972M	B	7.27	CHA	A(C(CH2-C:N))		CCL4
221M	B	7.27	CHA	A(C(CH2-F))		CCL4
476M	C	7.29	CHA	A(C(CH2-NH2))		CDCL3
485M	D	7.04	CHA	A(C(CH2-NH2)/CH-C(CH3))		CCL4
2313M	E	7.25	CHA	A(C(CH2-NH))		CDCL3
1135M	E	7.28	CHA	A(C(CH2-NH))		CDCL3
594M	F	7.27	CHA	A(C(CH2-NH))		CDCL3
836M	C	7.69	CHA	A(C(CH2-N(+)))	S	CDCL3
839M	H	7.30- 7.80	CHA	A(C(CH2-N(+)))	S	CDCL3
2400M	C	6.90- 7.30	CHA	A(C(CH2-N))		CDCL3
654M	D	7.21 APP.	CHA	A(C(CH2-N))		CDCL3
652M	E	7.12	CHA	A(C(CH2-N))		CCL4
2853M	F	7.20	CHA	A(C(CH2-N))		CDCL3
1907M	D	7.31	CHA	A(C(CH2-OH)-C(OH))		DMSO-D6
1722M	G	7.24	CHA	A(C(CH2-OH)-C(O-CH3))		CDCL3
1716M	D	7.12	CHA	A(C(CH2-OH)/CH-C(F))		CDCL3
1482M	B	7.25	CHA	A(C(CH2-O))		CCL4
1479M	C	7.25 APP.	CHA	A(C(CH2-O))		CDCL3
1705M	E	7.33	CHA	A(C(CH2-O))		CDCL3
2913M	B	7.40	CHA	A(C(CH2-O-C(=O)))		CDCL3
2832M	C	7.20	CHA	A(C(CH2-O-C(=O)))		CCL4
2837M	D	7.20	CHA	A(C(CH2-O-C(=O)))		CCL4
1924M	F	6.53 APP.	CHA	A(C(CH2-O3)-CH-C(O-CH3)/CH-C(OH))		CCL4
2396M	B	7.29	CHA	A(C(CH2-R5NA))		DMSO-D6
2386M	C	7.29 APP.	CHA	A(C(CH2-R5N))		CDCL3
1224M	C	7.22	CHA	A(C(CH2-SH))		CCL4
1227M	D	7.03	CHA	A(C(CH2-SH)-C(CH2-SH)/C(CH3)-C(CH3))		CDCL3
1247M	B	7.29	CHA	A(C(CH2-S(=O)))		CDCL3
1173M	B	7.28	CHA	A(C(CH2-S))		CDCL3
133M	B	7.04	CHA	A(C(CH3))		CCL4
385M	D	7.08 APP.	CHA	A(C(CH3)-CH-C(BR)/CH-C(CH(CH3/CH3)))		CDCL3
521M	D	6.85	CHA	A(C(CH3)-CH-C(BR)/CH-C(NH2))		CDCL3
496M	E	6.66	CHA	A(C(CH3)-CH-C(CH3)/CH-C(NH2))		CCL4
2338M	D	6.84	CHA	A(C(CH3)-CH-C(CH3)/CH-C(NH-C(=O)))		CDCL3
1301M	C	7.00- 7.20	CHA	A(C(CH3)-CH-C(CH3)/CH-C(SO3NA))	S	D20
2240M	B	7.25	CHA	A(C(CH3)-CH-C(C(=O)-CL)/C(CH3))		CCL4
2289M	C	7.30	CHA	A(C(CH3)-CH-C(C(=O)-NH2))		CDCL3
428M	C	7.07	CHA	A(C(CH3)-CH-C(I))		CCL4
2322M	C	6.82	CHA	A(C(CH3)-CH-C(NH-C(=O)))		CDCL3
1047M	B	7.38	CHA	A(C(CH3)-CH-C(NO2))		CCL4

: REPRESENTS TRIPLE BOND, ¬ REPRESENTS AN ARROW AND < AND > REPRESENT BRACKETS.

BOOK NO.	ASSIGN-MENT	CHEM SHIFT - ppm -	PROTON GROUP	ENVIRONMENTAL GROUPS	S	SOLVENT
1917M	F	6.71	CHA	A(C(CH3)-CH-C(OH)/CH-C(CH(CH3/CH3)))		CDCL3
1915M	D	6.45	CHA	A(C(CH3)-CH-C(OH)/C(CH3))		CCL4
1499M	D	6.50	CHA	A(C(CH3)-CH-C(O-CH2))		CCL4
919M	B	6.74- 6.90	CHA	A(C(CH3)-CH-C(QN(=O))/CH-C(CH3))		CCL4
1239M	D	6.72	CHA	A(C(CH3)-CH-C(SH)/CH-C(SH))		CDCL3
387M	C	6.78	CHA	A(C(CH3)-C(BR)-C(CH3)/C(CH3))		CCL4
386M	C	6.98	CHA	A(C(CH3)-C(BR)/C(CH3)-C(CH3))		CDCL3
191M	C	6.72	CHA	A(C(CH3)-C(CH3)-C(CH3)/CH-C(CH3))		CCL4
495M	D	6.46	CHA	A(C(CH3)-C(CH3)-C(NH2))		CCL4
1914M	D	6.82	CHA	A(C(CH3)-C(CH3)/CH-C(OH))		CCL4
193M	B	6.87	CHA	A(C(CH3)-C(CH3)/C(CH3)-C(CH3))		CDCL3
823M	D	7.20	CHA	A(C(CH3)-C(CL)/CH-C(NH-NH2))	S	DMSO-D6
2593M	B	6.90- 7.35	CHA	A(C(CH3)-C(C(=O)-OH)-C(CH3))		CDCL3
427M	B	6.76	CHA	A(C(CH3)-C(I))		CDCL3
1291M	C	7.20	CHA	A(C(CH3)-C(NH2)/CH-C(SO3-H))		DMSO-D6
496M	F	6.72	CHA	A(C(CH3)-C(NH2)/C(CH3))		CCL4
589M	F	7.08	CHA	A(C(CH3)-C(NH-CH3))		CDCL3
2338M	E	6.90	CHA	A(C(CH3)-C(NH-C(=O))/C(CH3))		CDCL3
1372M	D	7.01 APP.	CHA	A(C(CH3)-C(NH-SO2)-C(CH3))		CDCL3
2241M	B	7.60	CHA	A(C(CH3)-C(NO2)/CH-C(C(=O)-CL))		CCL4
665M	C	6.91	CHA	A(C(CH3)-C(N(CH3/CH3))-C(CH3))		CDCL3
763M	D	6.79	CHA	A(C(CH3)-C(N(N/CH3))-C(CH3)/C(CH3))		CDCL3
921M	D	7.10	CHA	A(C(CH3)-C(N=C=O)/CH-C(N=C=O))		CCL4
1916M	C	6.45- 6.95	CHA	A(C(CH3)-C(OH)-C(CH3))		CCL4
919M	C	7.02	CHA	A(C(CH3)-C(QN(=O))/CH-C(CH3))		CCL4
1364M	C	7.04	CHA	A(C(CH3)-C(SO2-NH2)-C(CH3)/C(CH3))		TFA
1301M	C	7.00- 7.20	CHA	A(C(CH3)-C(SO3NA)/C(CH3))	S	D2O
384M	B	6.95	CHA	A(C(CH3)/CH-C(BR))		CCL4
185M	C	7.08	CHA	A(C(CH3)/CH-C(CH2.2-A))		CDCL3
285M	C	7.02	CHA	A(C(CH3)/CH-C(CH2-CL))		CCL4
2557M	C	7.12	CHA	A(C(CH3)/CH-C(CH2-C(=O)-O))		CDCL3
485M	D	7.04	CHA	A(C(CH3)/CH-C(CH2-NH2))		CCL4
181M	B	6.90	CHA	A(C(CH3)/CH-C(CH3))		CCL4
294M	B	6.98	CHA	A(C(CH3)/CH-C(CL))		CCL4
294M	B	7.12	CHA	A(C(CH3)/CH-C(CL))		CCL4
2101M	B	7.20	CHA	A(C(CH3)/CH-C(C(=O)-A))		CDCL3
2100M	B	7.22	CHA	A(C(CH3)/CH-C(C(=O)-A))		CDCL3
2062M	C	7.23	CHA	A(C(CH3)/CH-C(C(=O)-CH2))		CDCL3
2056M	C	7.09	CHA	A(C(CH3)/CH-C(C(=O)-CH3))		CCL4
2290M	B	7.43	CHA	A(C(CH3)/CH-C(C(=O)-NH2))		TFA
986M	B	7.23	CHA	A(C(CH3)/CH-C(C:N))		CCL4
226M	C	7.00	CHA	A(C(CH3)/CH-C(F))		CCL4
429M	B	6.89	CHA	A(C(CH3)/CH-C(I))		CDCL3
593M	F	6.96	CHA	A(C(CH3)/CH-C(NH-CH2))		CDCL3
591M	E	6.92	CHA	A(C(CH3)/CH-C(NH-CH3))		CDCL3
2345M	B	7.08	CHA	A(C(CH3)/CH-C(NH-C(=O)))		CDCL3
2323M	C	7.03	CHA	A(C(CH3)/CH-C(NH-C(=O)))		DMSO-D6
1368M	D	7.16 APP.	CHA	A(C(CH3)/CH-C(NH-SO2))		CDCL3
1048M	B	7.30	CHA	A(C(CH3)/CH-C(NO2))		CDCL3
663M	E	7.01	CHA	A(C(CH3)/CH-C(N(CH2/CH2)))		CDCL3
761M	D	7.05	CHA	A(C(CH3)/CH-C(N(N/CH3)))		CDCL3
1500M	E	6.95	CHA	A(C(CH3)/CH-C(O-CH2))		CCL4
1496M	D	7.09	CHA	A(C(CH3)/CH-C(O-CH3))		CDCL3
2924M	D	7.01	CHA	A(C(CH3)/CH-C(O-C(=O)-CH3))		CCL4
1099M	B	7.00- 7.40	CHA	A(C(CH3)/CH-C(P(A/A)))		CDCL3
881M	B	7.22	CHA	A(C(CH3)/CH-C(QN(QN)))		CDCL3
928M	B	7.06	CHA	A(C(CH3)/CH-C(QN(=N-A)))		CDCL3
2564M	C	7.21	CHA	A(C(CH3)/CH-C(Q?(H/C(=O)-OH/H)))		DMSO-D6
1230M	C	6.91	CHA	A(C(CH3)/CH-C(SH))		CDCL3
1269M	B	7.23	CHA	A(C(CH3)/CH-C(SO2-A))		CDCL3
1268M	B	7.26	CHA	A(C(CH3)/CH-C(SO2-A))		CDCL3
1363M	C	7.37	CHA	A(C(CH3)/CH-C(SO2-NH2))		TFA
1370M	C	7.15	CHA	A(C(CH3)/CH-C(SO2-NH))		CDCL3
1372M	E	7.19	CHA	A(C(CH3)/CH-C(SO2-NH))		CDCL3
1375M	C	7.34	CHA	A(C(CH3)/CH-C(SO2-N))		CDCL3
1369M	E	7.30	CHA	A(C(CH3)/CH-C(SO2-N))		CDCL3
1312M	F	7.12	CHA	A(C(CH3)/CH-C(SO3))	S	CDCL3
1302M	B	7.32	CHA	A(C(CH3)/CH-C(SO3-BA))	S	D2O
1322M	E	7.27	CHA	A(C(CH3)/CH-C(SO3-CH2))		CCL4
1321M	D	7.28	CHA	A(C(CH3)/CH-C(SO3-CH))		CCL4
1170M	B	7.07	CHA	A(C(CH3)/CH-C(S-A))		CDCL3
2037M	D	7.35 APP.	CHA	A(C(CH(BR/CH)))		CDCL3
378M	D	7.31	CHA	A(C(CH(BR/HCH)))		CDCL3
379M	C	7.19 APP.	CHA	A(C(CH(CH2/CH2)))		CCL4
138M	E	7.10	CHA	A(C(CH(CH2/CH3)))		CCL4
136M	C	7.09	CHA	A(C(CH(CH3/CH3)))		CCL4
1917M	G	7.07	CHA	A(C(CH(CH3/CH3))-C(OH)/CH-C(CH3))		CDCL3
152M	B	6.50- 7.30	CHA	A(C(CH(CH/CH2)))		CDCL3
2546M	B	7.32	CHA	A(C(CH(C(=O)-OH/A)))		CDCL3
2542M	C	7.26	CHA	A(C(CH(C(=O)-OH/CH2)))		DMSO
2541M	C	7.20 APP.	CHA	A(C(CH(C(=O)-OH/CH3)))		CCL4

BOOK NO.	ASSIGN-MENT	CHEM SHIFT - ppm -	PROTON GROUP	ENVIRONMENTAL GROUPS	S	SOLVENT
1790M	C	7.18	CHA	A(C(CH(OH/A)))		CCL4
1793M	E	7.50	CHA	A(C(CH(OH/CH3)-C(CL)/C(CL))		CCL4
2555M	B	7.15- 7.60	CHA	A(C(CH(OH/C(=O)-OH)))		DMSO
2834M	D	7.32	CHA	A(C(CH(O-C(=O)/CH3)))		CDCL3
852M	B	7.52	CHA	A(C(CH=NOH))		CDCL3
2463M	B	8.08	CHA	A(C(CH=R6NN))		DMSO
393M	B	7.20 APP.	CHA	A(C(CL)-CH-C(RR))		CCL4
515M	D	6.95 APP.	CHA	A(C(CL)-CH-C(CH3)/CH-C(NH2))		CCL4
1793M	D	7.15	CHA	A(C(CL)-CH-C(CH(OH/CH3)/CH-C(CL))		CCL4
313M	A	7.12	CHA	A(C(CL)-CH-C(CL)/CH-C(CL))		CCL4
1920M	B	6.71	CHA	A(C(CL)-CH-C(CL)/C(OH))		CDCL3
2230M	B	7.60	CHA	A(C(CL)-CH-C(C(=O)-CL))		CCL4
898M	A	7.40 APP.	CHA	A(C(CL)-CH-C(N=N-A))		CDCL3
1920M	C	6.92	CHA	A(C(CL)-CH-C(OH)/C(CL))		CDCL3
522M	C	6.69	CHA	A(C(CL)-C(BR)/C(NH2))		CDCL3
309M	B	6.79- 7.28	CHA	A(C(CL)-C(CH3)-C(CL))		CCL4
823M	C	7.14	CHA	A(C(CL)-C(CH3)/C(NH-NH2))		DMSO-D6
1793M	D	7.15	CHA	A(C(CL)-C(CH(OH/CH3)/CH-C(CL))	S	DMSO-D6
305M	A	6.90- 7.55	CHA	A(C(CL)-C(CL))		CCL4
312M	A	6.89- 7.46	CHA	A(C(CL)-C(CL)-C(CL))		CDCL3
313M	B	7.35	CHA	A(C(CL)-C(CL)/CH-C(CL))		CCL4
1069M	A	7.63	CHA	A(C(CL)-C(CL)/CH-C(NO2))		CCL4
313M	C	7.43	CHA	A(C(CL)-C(CL)/C(CL))		CCL4
1234M	C	7.39	CHA	A(C(CL)-C(CL)/C(CL)-C(SH))		CDCL3
1069M	C	8.30	CHA	A(C(CL)-C(CL)/C(NO2))		CCL4
1234M	B	7.35	CHA	A(C(CL)-C(CL)/C(SH)-C(CL))		CDCL3
301M	B	7.36	CHA	A(C(CL)-C(F))		CCL4
433M	B	7.38 APP.	CHA	A(C(CL)-C(I))		CCL4
758M	B	7.28	CHA	A(C(CL)-C(NH-NH2)-C(CL)/C(CL))		CDCL3
1509M	D	7.10- 7.50	CHA	A(C(CL)-C(O-CH3))		CDCL3
1553M	C	7.20	CHA	A(C(CL)-C(O-CH3)-C(CL))		CCL4
2217M	C	7.32	CHA	A(C(CL)/CH-C(CH2-C(=O)-CL))		CDCL3
786M	D	7.46	CHA	A(C(CL)/CH-C(CH2-C))	S	D20
294M	C	6.98	CHA	A(C(CL)/CH-C(CH3))		CCL4
294M	C	7.12	CHA	A(C(CL)/CH-C(CH3))		CCL4
307M	A	7.23	CHA	A(C(CL)/CH-C(CL))		CCL4
2066M	D	7.39	CHA	A(C(CL)/CH-C(C(=O)-CH2))		CDCL3
2571M	A	7.56	CHA	A(C(CL)/CH-C(C(=O)-OH))		DMSO
2874M.	B	7.38	CHA	A(C(CL)/CH-C(C(=O)-O-CH3))		CDCL3
991M	A	7.39	CHA	A(C(CL)/CH-C(C:N))		CDCL3
303M	B	7.19	CHA	A(C(CL)/CH-C(F))		CDCL3
514M	C	7.02	CHA	A(C(CL)/CH-C(NH2))		DMSO
2330M	B	7.32	CHA	A(C(CL)/CH-C(NH-C(=O)))		DMSO-D6
1058M	A	7.46	CHA	A(C(CL)/CH-C(NO2))		CDCL3
903M	A	7.39 APP.	CHA	A(C(CL)/CH-C(N(=N-A/=O)))		CDCL3
903M	A	7.39 APP.	CHA	A(C(CL)/CH-C(N=N(=O/A)))		CDCL3
1893M	C	7.10	CHA	A(C(CL)/CH-C(OH))		CDCL3
1513M	D	7.10	CHA	A(C(CL)/CH-C(O-CH2))		CCL4
1511M	C	7.18	CHA	A(C(CL)/CH-C(O-CH3))		CCL4
2562M	B	6.88	CHA	A(C(CL)/CH-C(O-C))		CDCL3
1100M	A	7.04- 7.50	CHA	A(C(CL)/CH-C(P(A/A)))		CDCL3
860M	B	7.29	CHA	A(C(CL)/CH-C(QN(CH3/OH)))		CDCL3
515M	D	6.95 APP.	CHA	A(C(CL)/C(CH3)-C(NH2))		CCL4
2230M	D	8.02	CHA	A(C(CL)/C(C(=O)-CL))		CCL4
898M	B	7.60- 7.90	CHA	A(C(CL)/C(N=N-A))		CDCL3
1273M	C	8.32	CHA	A(C(CL)/C(SO2-A)-C(CL))		CDCL3
2214M	A	7.10- 7.60	CHA	A(C(C(BR/C(=O)-RR/A)))		CDCL3
1886M	F	7.17	CHA	A(C(C(CH2/CH3/CH3))/CH-C(OH))		CDCL3
2325M	C	7.28	CHA	A(C(C(CH3/CH3/CH3))/CH-C(NH-C(=O)))		CDCL3
2325M	C	7.40	CHA	A(C(C(CH3/CH3/CH3))/CH-C(NH-C(=O)))		CDCL3
1883M	D	7.23	CHA	A(C(C(CH3/CH3/CH3))/CH-C(OH))		CDCL3
1231M	C	7.13	CHA	A(C(C(CH3/CH3/CH3))/CH-C(SH))		CCL4
2635M	A	7.50 APP.	CHA	A(C(C(NH2/C(=O)-OH/A)))		TFA
1817M	C	7.15- 7.60	CHA	A(C(C(OH/CH3/CH3)))		CDCL3
1226M	B	7.23 APP.	CHA	A(C(C(SH/A/A)))		CDCL3
2098M	B	7.44	CHA	A(C(C(=O)-A))		CDCL3
2099M	D	7.70	CHA	A(C(C(=O)-A))		CCL4
2102M	B	7.60	CHA	A(C(C(=O)-A)/CH-C(BR))		CDCL3
2101M	C	7.64	CHA	A(C(C(=O)-A)/CH-C(CH3))		CDCL3
2104M	D	7.75	CHA	A(C(C(=O)-A)/CH-C(N(CH2/CH2)))		CDCL3
2106M	B	8.11	CHA	A(C(C(=O)-A)/C(C(=O)-A))		POLYSOL-D
2234M	C	7.98	CHA	A(C(C(=O)-BR)-CH-C(BR))		CCL4
2054M	C	7.90	CHA	A(C(C(=O)-CH2))		CDCL3
2840M	D	7.89	CHA	A(C(C(=O)-CH2))		CDCL3
2046M	D	7.92 APP.	CHA	A(C(C(=O)-CH2))		CDCL3
2085M	D	7.98	CHA	A(C(C(=O)-CH2))		CDCL3
2088M	E	7.90	CHA	A(C(C(=O)-CH2))		CDCL3
2147M	F	7.82	CHA	A(C(C(=O)-CH2))		CDCL3
2049M	F	7.89	CHA	A(C(C(=O)-CH2))		CCL4
2062M	D	7.83	CHA	A(C(C(=O)-CH2)/CH-C(CH3))		CDCL3
2066M	E	7.89	CHA	A(C(C(=O)-CH2)/CH-C(CL))		CDCL3

BOOK NO.	ASSIGN-MENT	CHEM SHIFT - ppm -	PROTON GROUP	ENVIRONMENTAL GROUPS	S	SOLVENT
2045M	C	7.80	CHA	A(C(C(=O)-CH3))		CCL4
2081M	C	8.13	CHA	A(C(C(=O)-CH3)-CH-C(C(=O)-CH3))		CDCL3
2073M	C	8.28	CHA	A(C(C(=O)-CH3)-CH-C(NO2))		CDCL3
2059M	E	7.75	CHA	A(C(C(=O)-CH3)/CH-C(CH2-CH3))		CCL4
2056M	D	7.69	CHA	A(C(C(=O)-CH3)/CH-C(CH3))		CCL4
2075M	D	7.97	CHA	A(C(C(=O)-CH3)/CH-C(O-CH3))		CDCL3
2081M	D	8.49	CHA	A(C(C(=O)-CH3)/C(C(=O)-CH3))		CDCL3
2048M	D	7.85	CHA	A(C(C(=O)-CH))		CCL4
2240M	C	7.67	CHA	A(C(C(=O)-CL)-CH-C(CH3)/C(CH3))		CCL4
2230M	C	7.98	CHA	A(C(C(=O)-CL)-CH-C(CL))		CCL4
2228M	B	7.82	CHA	A(C(C(=O)-CL)-CH-C(F))		CCL4
2241M	C	8.18	CHA	A(C(C(=O)-CL)-CH-C(NO2)/CH-C(CH3))		CCL4
2222M	C	8.19	CHA	A(C(C(=O)-CL)-C(CH3))		CCL4
2237M	B	7.91	CHA	A(C(C(=O)-CL)-C(C(=O)-CL))		CCL4
2134M	B	7.67- 8.02	CHA	A(C(C(=O)-C(=O)))		CCL4
2163M	B	7.79	CHA	A(C(C(=O)-H))		CCL4
2166M	B	7.81 APP.	CHA	A(C(C(=O)-H)-C(CL))		CCL4
2170M	C	7.63	CHA	A(C(C(=O)-H)/CH-C(N(CH3/CH3)))		CDCL3
2174M	F	7.71	CHA	A(C(C(=O)-H)/CH-C(O-CH2))		CCL4
2289M	D	7.63	CHA	A(C(C(=O)-NH2)-CH-C(CH3))		CDCL3
2290M	C	7.92	CHA	A(C(C(=O)-NH2)/CH-C(CH3))		TFA
2292M	B	7.62	CHA	A(C(C(=O)-NH2)/CH-C(NO2))		DMSO
2289M	D	7.63	CHA	A(C(C(=O)-NH2)/C(CH3))		CDCL3
2342M	C	7.81	CHA	A(C(C(=O)-NH))		CDCL3
2343M	C	7.98	CHA	A(C(C(=O)-NH))		DMSO
2345M	D	7.76	CHA	A(C(C(=O)-NH))		CDCL3
2411M	D	7.82	CHA	A(C(C(=O)-NH))		CDCL3
2344M	D	7.89 APP.	CHA	A(C(C(=O)-NH))		CDCL3
2851M	E	7.80	CHA	A(C(C(=O)-NH))		CDCL3
2406M	C	7.88	CHA	A(C(C(=O)-NH)/CH-C(BR))		DMSO
2566M	B	8.14	CHA	A(C(C(=O)-OH))		CCL4
2573M	C	7.97	CHA	A(C(C(=O)-OH)-CH-C(BR))		POLYSOL-D
2591M	C	8.64	CHA	A(C(C(=O)-OH)-CH-C(C(=O)-OH)>		POLYSOL-D
2603M	A	8.72	CHA	A(C(C(=O)-OH)-CH-C(C(=O)-OH)/C(C(=O)-OH))		DMSO
2580M	C	8.18- 8.50	CHA	A(C(C(=O)-OH)-CH-C(C:N))		DMSO
2576M	C	8.00	CHA	A(C(C(=O)-OH)-CH-C(I))		POLYSOL-D
2583M	D	7.50- 7.80	CHA	A(C(C(=O)-OH)-CH-C(O-CH3))		DMSO-D6
2572M	B	7.69 APP.	CHA	A(C(C(=O)-OH)-C(BR))		DMSO
2590M	B	7.71	CHA	A(C(C(=O)-OH)-C(C(=O)-OH))		POLYSOL-D
2594M	A	8.09	CHA	A(C(C(=O)-OH)-C(NO2)/CH-C(NO2))		DMSO
2597M	B	8.09	CHA	A(C(C(=O)-OH)-C(OH)-C(NO2))		POLYSOL-D
2599M	C	7.71	CHA	A(C(C(=O)-OH)-C(OH)/CH-C(OH))		DMSO
2571M	B	8.00	CHA	A(C(C(=O)-OH)/CH-C(CL))		DMSO
2582M	A	8.21	CHA	A(C(C(=O)-OH)/CH-C(NO2))		DMSO-D6
2589M	B	8.09	CHA	A(C(C(=O)-OH)/CH-C(O-A))		DMSO
2586M	E	7.95	CHA	A(C(C(=O)-OH)/CH-C(O-CH2.2))		POLYSOL-D
2580M	C	8.18- 8.50	CHA	A(C(C(=O)-OH)/C(C:N))		DMSO
2868M	B	8.00	CHA	A(C(C(=O)-O-AAN))		CDCL3
2945M	B	8.01	CHA	A(C(C(=O)-O-A))		CDCL3
2942M	C	7.98	CHA	A(C(C(=O)-O-CH2))		CCL4
2864M	E	8.06	CHA	A(C(C(=O)-O-CH2))		CDCL3
2891M	G	7.80	CHA	A(C(C(=O)-O-CH2)-C(OH))		CDCL3
2875M	D	7.83	CHA	A(C(C(=O)-O-CH2)/CH-C(BR))		CCL4
2883M	D	8.32	CHA	A(C(C(=O)-O-CH2)/CH-C(NO))		CDCL3
2895M	F	7.90	CHA	A(C(C(=O)-O-CH2)/CH-C(OH))		CCL4
2884M	D	7.95	CHA	A(C(C(=O)-O-CH2)/CH-C(QN(=O)))		CDCL3
2901M	C	8.19	CHA	A(C(C(=O)-O-CH3)-CH-C(C(=O)-O-CH3))		CDCL3
2906M	B	8.98	CHA	A(C(C(=O)-O-CH3)-CH-C(NO2)/C(C(=O)-O-CH3))		CDCL3
2892M	D	7.62	CHA	A(C(C(=O)-O-CH3)-CH-C(OH))		CDCL3
2914M	C	6.95	CHA	A(C(C(=O)-O-CH3)-CH-C(OH)/C(OH))		DMSO-D6
2869M	D	7.90	CHA	A(C(C(=O)-O-CH3)-C(CH3))		CDCL3
2872M	C	7.73	CHA	A(C(C(=O)-O-CH3)-C(CL))		CCL4
2887M	D	7.69	CHA	A(C(C(=O)-O-CH3)-C(O-CH3))		CCL4
2874M	C	7.95	CHA	A(C(C(=O)-O-CH3)/CH-C(CL))		CDCL3
2881M	D	7.83	CHA	A(C(C(=O)-O-CH3)/CH-C(NH2))		CDCL3
2886M	B	8.26	CHA	A(C(C(=O)-O-CH3)/CH-C(NO2))		CDCL3
2888M	D	7.99	CHA	A(C(C(=O)-O-CH3)/CH-C(O-CH3))		CDCL3
2901M	D	8.63	CHA	A(C(C(=O)-O-CH3)/C(C(=O)-O-CH3))		CDCL3
2889M	F	7.84	CHA	A(C(C(=O)-O-CH)-C(OH)))		CDCL3
2893M	E	7.96	CHA	A(C(C(=O)-O-CH)/CH-C(OH))		CDCL3
2270M	B	8.11	CHA	A(C(C(=O)-O-C(=O)))		CDCL3
2680M	B	8.00	CHA	A(C(C(=O)-O-K)-C(C(=O)-O-K))		D2O
2675M	B	7.98	CHA	A(C(C(=O)-O-NA))		D2O
2147M	F	7.82	CHA	A(C(C(=O)-Q1))		CDCL3
2092M	B	8.00 APP.	CHA	A(C(C(=O)-Q2))		CDCL3
2097M	C	8.03	CHA	A(C(C(=O)-Q2))		CDCL3
2093M	C	7.98	CHA	A(C(C(=O)-Q2)/CH-C(CH3))		CDCL3
2084M	D	7.91	CHA	A(C(C(=O)-R6))		CDCL3
2971M	C	7.91	CHA	A(C(C(=O)-S))		CDCL3
167M	B	7.10- 7.50	CHA	A(C(C(C:C))		CDCL3
2044M	B	7.20- 7.70	CHA	A(C(C(C:C))		CDCL3

BOOK NO.	ASSIGN-MENT	CHEM SHIFT - ppm -	PROTON GROUP	ENVIRONMENTAL GROUPS	S	SOLVENT
2580M	B	8.10	CHA	A(C(C:N)-CH-C(C(=O)-OH))		DMSO
997M	A	8.00	CHA	A(C(C:N)-C(C:N))		TFA
986M	C	7.47	CHA	A(C(C:N)/CH-C(CH3))		CCL4
991M	B	7.57	CHA	A(C(C:N)/CH-C(CL))		CDCL3
988M	H	7.66	CHA	A(C(C:N)/CH-C(F))		CDCL3
231M	A	6.55- 7.10	CHA	A(C(F)-CH-C(F))		CDCL3
511M	D	6.69	CHA	A(C(F)-C(CH3)/CH-C(NH2))		CCL4
230M	A	6.90- 7.40	CHA	A(C(F)-C(F))		CDCL3
1072M	A	7.49	CHA	A(C(F)-C(NO2)/CH-C(NO2))		CDCL3
1716M	C	6.90	CHA	A(C(F)/CH-C(CH2-OH))		CDCL3
226M	B	6.81	CHA	A(C(F)/CH-C(CH3))		CCL4
303M	A	6.91	CHA	A(C(F)/CH-C(CL))		CDCL3
988M	A	7.17	CHA	A(C(F)/CH-C(C:N))		CDCL3
2327M	B	6.99	CHA	A(C(F)/CH-C(NH-C(=O)))		CDCL3
1055M	A	7.20	CHA	A(C(F)/CH-C(NO2))		CCL4
941M	A	6.90	CHA	A(C(F)/CH-C(N=C=S))		CCL4
1271M	A	7.18	CHA	A(C(F)/CH-C(SO2))		CDCL3
231M	A	6.55- 7.10	CHA	A(C(F)/C(F))		CDCL3
426M	B	7.65	CHA	A(C(I))		CCL4
428M	D	7.48	CHA	A(C(I)-CH-C(CH3))		CCL4
2576M	B	7.88	CHA	A(C(I)-CH-C(C(=O)-OH))		POLYSOL-D
526M	E	7.03	CHA	A(C(I)-CH-C(NH2))		CDCL3
1060M	B	8.21 APP.	CHA	A(C(I)-CH-C(NO2))		DMSO
433M	C	7.77 APP.	CHA	A(C(I)-C(CL))		CCL4
1896M	E	7.58	CHA	A(C(I)-C(OH))		CDCL3
1938M	B	8.02	CHA	A(C(I)-C(OH)-C(I)/C(I))		DMSO
1519M	E	7.71	CHA	A(C(I)-C(O-CH3))		CDCL3
429M	C	7.55	CHA	A(C(I)/CH-C(CH3))		CDCL3
437M	A	7.40	CHA	A(C(I)/CH-C(I))		CDCL3
527M	C	7.37	CHA	A(C(I)/CH-C(NH2))		CDCL3
1061M	A	8.01 APP.	CHA	A(C(I)/CH-C(NO2))		DMSO
1898M	C	7.48	CHA	A(C(I)/CH-C(OH))		CDCL3
1521M	C	7.53	CHA	A(C(I)/CH-C(O-CH3))		CDCL3
2389M	B	7.06	CHA	A(C(I)/CH-C(R5N(N-C(=O)/C(=O))))		TFA
1249M	B	7.36	CHA	A(C(I)/CH-C(SO-CH3))		CDCL3
428M	E	7.51	CHA	A(C(I)/C(CH3))		CCL4
2576M	D	8.35	CHA	A(C(I)/C(C(=O)-OH))		POLYSOL-D
526M	D	6.97	CHA	A(C(I)/C(NH2))		CDCL3
1060M	C	8.49	CHA	A(C(I)/C(NO2))		DMSO
1940M	A	7.49 APP.	CHA	A(C(NH2))		DMSO
487M	B	6.44	CHA	A(C(NH2))		CCL4
519M	B	6.41	CHA	A(C(NH2)-CH-C(BR))		CDCL3
511M	C	6.05- 6.37	CHA	A(C(NH2)-CH-C(CH3)/CH-C(F))		CCL4
537M	C	6.31	CHA	A(C(NH2)-CH-C(CH3)/C(CH3)-C(NH2))		CDCL3
522M	B	6.34	CHA	A(C(NH2)-CH-C(CL)/CH-C(BR))		CDCL3
526M	B	6.49	CHA	A(C(NH2)-CH-C(I))		CDCL3
534M	C	5.91	CHA	A(C(NH2)-CH-C(NH2))		POLYSOL-D
1899M	B	5.99 APP.	CHA	A(C(NH2)-CH-C(OH))		DMSO
1561M	E	6.18 APP.	CHA	A(C(NH2)-CH-C(O-CH2)/CH-C(O-CH2))		CDCL3
518M	C	6.60	CHA	A(C(NH2)-C(BR))		CDCL3
521M	C	6.55	CHA	A(C(NH2)-C(BR)/CH-C(CH3))		CDCL3
495M	D	6.46	CHA	A(C(NH2)-C(CH3)-C(CH3))		CCL4
532M	C	6.68	CHA	A(C(NH2)-C(CH3)/CH-C(A(C-CH-C(CH3)-C(NH2))))		CDCL3
496M	D	6.36	CHA	A(C(NH2)-C(CH3)/CH-C(CH3))		CCL4
515M	C	6.50	CHA	A(C(NH2)-C(CH3)/CH-C(CL))		CCL4
1291M	E	7.67	CHA	A(C(NH2)-C(CH3)/C(SO3-H))		DMSO-D6
793M	A	7.66	CHA	A(C(NH2)-C(NH2))	S	D20
533M	B	6.67	CHA	A(C(NH2)-C(NH2))		CDCL3
1198M	C	6.60	CHA	A(C(NH2)=C(S-S))		CDCL3
520M	B	6.57	CHA	A(C(NH2)/CH-C(BR))		CDCL3
530M	C	6.49	CHA	A(C(NH2)/CH-C(CH2-A))		DMSO-D6
2405M	C	6.51	CHA	A(C(NH2)/CH-C(CH2-C(=O)-NH))		POLYSOL-D
514M	B	6.60	CHA	A(C(NH2)/CH-C(CL))		DMSO
2881M	C	6.63	CHA	A(C(NH2)/CH-C(C(=O)-O-CH3))		CDCL3
527M	B	6.37	CHA	A(C(NH2)/CH-C(I))		CDCL3
795M.	A	7.78	CHA	A(C(NH2)/CH-C(NH2))	S	D20
670M	C	6.59	CHA	A(C(NH2)/CH-C(N(CH2/CH2)))		CDCL3
817M	D	7.40	CHA	A(C(NH2)/CH-C(N(CH2/CH2)))	S	D20
816M	B	7.65- 8.00	CHA	A(C(NH2)/CH-C(N(CH3/CH3)))	S	D20
669M	C	6.62 APP.	CHA	A(C(NH2)/CH-C(N(CH3/CH3)))		CDCL3
818M	C	7.79	CHA	A(C(NH2)/CH-C(N(CH3/CH3)))	S	D20
818M	C	7.99	CHA	A(C(NH2)/CH-C(N(CH3/CH3)))	S	D20
899M	B	6.60	CHA	A(C(NH2)/CH-C(N=N-A))		CDCL3
901M	C	6.70	CHA	A(C(NH2)/CH-C(N=N-A))		DMSO-D6
901M	C	6.76	CHA	A(C(NH2)/CH-C(N=N-A))		DMSO-D6
791M	C	7.44	CHA	A(C(NH2)/CH-C(O-CH3))	S	D20
1304M	A	6.79	CHA	A(C(NH2)/CH-C(SO3-NA))		D20
511M	C	6.05- 6.37	CHA	A(C(NH2)/C(CH3)-C(F))		CCL4
534M	B	5.84	CHA	A(C(NH2)/C(NH2))		POLYSOL-D
1899M	C	6.06	CHA	A(C(NH2)/C(OH))		DMSO
807M	B	7.10- 7.40	CHA	A(C(NH-A))	S	DMSO

BOOK NO.	ASSIGN-MENT	CHEM SHIFT - ppm -	PROTON GROUP	ENVIRONMENTAL GROUPS	S	SOLVENT
1306M	B	7.10- 7.65	CHA	A(C(NH-A))	S	DMSO
1306M	A	7.23	CHA	A(C(NH-A)-C(SO3NA)/CH-C(NO2))	S	DMSO
1022M	A	7.08	CHA	A(C(NH-A)/CH-C(N=O))		POLYSOL-D
585M	E	6.51	CHA	A(C(NH-CH2.2))		CDCL3
594M	C	6.58	CHA	A(C(NH-CH2))		CDCL3
593M	E	6.45	CHA	A(C(NH-CH2)/CH-C(CH3))		CDCL3
589M	D	6.60	CHA	A(C(NH-CH3)-C(CH3))		CDCL3
591M	D	6.40	CHA	A(C(NH-CH3)/CH-C(CH3))		CDCL3
2343M	B	7.81	CHA	A(C(NH-C(=0)))		DMSO
2467M	C	7.60	CHA	A(C(NH-C(=0)))		DMSO
2318M	C	7.61	CHA	A(C(NH-C(=0)))		DMSO-D6
2316M	D	7.09	CHA	A(C(NH-C(=0)))		CDCL3
2435M	D	7.20- 7.50	CHA	A(C(NH-C(=0)))		CDCL3
2315M	D	7.54	CHA	A(C(NH-C(=0)))		CDCL3
2322M	E	7.25	CHA	A(C(NH-C(=0))-CH-C(CH3))		CDCL3
2335M	C	6.95- 7.20	CHA	A(C(NH-C(=0))-CH-C(OH))		DMSO-D6
2338M	F	7.21	CHA	A(C(NH-C(=0))-C(CH3)/CH-C(CH3))		CDCL3
2324M	E	7.32	CHA	A(C(NH-C(=0))/CH-C(CH2-CH3))		CDCL3
2323M	D	7.45	CHA	A(C(NH-C(=0))/CH-C(CH3))		DMSO-D6
2330M	C	7.68	CHA	A(C(NH-C(=0))/CH-C(CL))		DMSO-D6
2325M	D	7.28	CHA	A(C(NH-C(=0))/CH-C(C(CH3/CH3/CH3)))		CDCL3
2325M	D	7.40	CHA	A(C(NH-C(=0))/CH-C(C(CH3/CH3/CH3)))		CDCL3
2327M	C	7.40	CHA	A(C(NH-C(=0))/CH-C(F))		CDCL3
2322M	F	7.29	CHA	A(C(NH-C(=0))/C(CH3))		CDCL3
2335M	D	7.30	CHA	A(C(NH-C(=0))/C(OH))		DMSO-D6
2332M	B	7.47	CHA	A(C(NH-C(=0)-CH3)/CH-C(QN(OH)))		POLYSOL-D
2425M	D	7.29	CHA	A(C(NH-C(=0)-NH2)/CH-C(O-CH3))		POLYSOL-D
2988M	C	6.80- 7.50	CHA	A(C(NH-C(=0)-0))		CDCL3
1340M	A	6.90- 7.60	CHA	A(C(NH-C(=S)))		DMSO
1350M	E	7.01- 7.59	CHA	A(C(NH-C(=S)))		CDCL3
823M	B	6.91	CHA	A(C(NH-NH2)-CH-C(CL)/CH-C(CH3))	S	DMSO-D6
824M	C	7.21	CHA	A(C(NH-NH2)/CH-C(O-CH3)))	S	D2O
2467M	A	6.82 APP.	CHA	A(C(NH-NH))		DMSO
1075M	C	7.94	CHA	A(C(NH-QN)-C(NO2)/CH-C(NO2))		CDCL3
586M	D	6.52	CHA	A(C(NH-R6))		CDCL3
1370M	B	7.12 APP.	CHA	A(C(NH-SO2))		CDCL3
1378M	A	7.09	CHA	A(C(NH-SO2)/CH-C(BR))		POLYSOL-D
1368M	D	7.16 APP.	CHA	A(C(NH-SO2)/CH-C(CH3))		CDCL3
1047M	C	7.94	CHA	A(C(NO2)-CH-C(CH3))		CCL4
1077M	C	7.88	CHA	A(C(NO2)-CH-C(CH3)/C(CH3)-C(NH2))		CDCL3
1069M	B	8.08	CHA	A(C(NO2)-CH-C(CL)/CH-C(CL))		CCL4
2243M	B	8.42	CHA	A(C(NO2)-CH-C(C(=0)-CE)/CH-C(CE))		DMSO
2073M	D	8.41	CHA	A(C(NO2)-CH-C(C(=0)-CH3))		CDCL3
2913M	C	9.13	CHA	A(C(NO2)-CH-C(C(=0)-0-CH2)/C(NO2))		CDCL3
2906M	B	8.98	CHA	A(C(NO2)-CH-C(C(=0)-0-CH3)/C(C(=0)-0-CH3))		CDCL3
2912M	C	9.19 APP.	CHA	A(C(NO2)-CH-C(C(=0)-0-R6)/C(NO2))		CDCL3
1060M	B	8.21 APP.	CHA	A(C(NO2)-CH-C(I))		DMSO
1067M	B	8.59	CHA	A(C(NO2)-CH-C(NO2))		CCL4
1073M	B	8.39	CHA	A(C(NO2)-CH-C(NO2)/CH-C(BR))		CDCL3
2594M	B	8.59	CHA	A(C(NO2)-CH-C(NO2)/CH-C(C(=0)-OH))		DMSO
1072M	B	8.60	CHA	A(C(NO2)-CH-C(NO2)/CH-C(F))		CDCL3
1075M	D	8.30	CHA	A(C(NO2)-CH-C(NO2)/CH-C(NH-QN)) ¬		CDCL3
2913M	C	9.13	CHA	A(C(NO2)-CH-C(NO2)/C(C(=0)-0-CH2))		CDCL3
2912M	C	9.19 APP.	CHA	A(C(NO2)-CH-C(NO2)/C(C(=0)-0-R6))		CDCL3
1531M	E	7.76	CHA	A(C(NO2)-CH-C(O-CH3))		CDCL3
1306M	C	8.08	CHA	A(C(NO2)-CH-C(SO3NA)/CH-C(NH-A))	S	DMSO
1073M	C	8.70	CHA	A(C(NO2)-C(BR)/C(NO2))		CDCL3
1049M	D	7.75	CHA	A(C(NO2)-C(CH2-CH3))		CCL4
2241M	D	8.49	CHA	A(C(NO2)-C(CH3)/C(C(=0)-CL))		CCL4
1056M	B	7.79	CHA	A(C(NO2)-C(CL))		CDCL3
2594M	C	8.70	CHA	A(C(NO2)-C(C(=0)-OH)/C(NO2))		DMSO
1072M	C	8.93	CHA	A(C(NO2)-C(F)/C(NO2))		CDCL3
1075M	E	9.11	CHA	A(C(NO2)-C(NH-QN)/C(NO2))		CDCL3
1074M	D	8.05	CHA	A(C(NO2)-C(NO2)/CH-C(N(CH3/CH3)))		DMSO-D6
1074M	C	7.11	CHA	A(C(NO2)-C(NO2)/C(N(CH3/CH3)))		DMSO-D6
2597M	B	8.09	CHA	A(C(NO2)-C(OH)-C(C(=0)-OH))		POLYSOL-D
1940M	C	8.66	CHA	A(C(NO2)-C(OH)-C(NO2)/C(NO2))		DMSO
1941M	C	8.69	CHA	A(C(NO2)-C(OH)-C(NO2)/C(NO2))		DMSO
1556M	C	8.00	CHA	A(C(NO2)-C(O-CH3)-C(NO2))		CDCL3
1048M	C	8.10	CHA	A(C(NO2)/CH-C(CH3))		CDCL3
1058M	B	8.09	CHA	A(C(NO2)/CH-C(CL))		CDCL3
2292M	C	7.78	CHA	A(C(NO2)/CH-C(C(=0)-NH2))		DMSO
2582M	B	8.30	CHA	A(C(NO2)/CH-C(C(=0)-OH))		DMSO-D6
2886M	B	8.26	CHA	A(C(NO2)/CH-C(C(=0)-0-CH3))		CDCL3
1055M	B	8.20	CHA	A(C(NO2)/CH-C(F))		CCL4
1061M	A	8.01 APP.	CHA	A(C(NO2)/CH-C(I))		DMSO
1065M	C	8.32	CHA	A(C(NO2)/CH-C(N≡N-A))		CDCL3
1533M	D	8.10	CHA	A(C(NO2)/CH-C(O-CH2))		CDCL3
2969M	B	8.12	CHA	A(C(NO2)/CH-C(O-C(=0)-CL))		DMSO-D6
1276M	D	8.30	CHA	A(C(NO2)/CH-C(SO2-A))		CDCL3
1047M	C	7.94	CHA	A(C(NO2)/C(CH3))		CCL4

BOOK NO.	ASSIGN-MENT	CHEM SHIFT - ppm -	PROTON GROUP	ENVIRONMENTAL GROUPS	S	SOLVENT
2073M	E	8.72	CHA	A(C(NO2)/C(C(=O)-CH3))		CDCL3
2243M	C	8.90	CHA	A(C(NO2)/C(C(=O)-CL)-C(CL))		DMSO
1067M	C	9.01	CHA	A(C(NO2)/C(NO2))		CCL4
1531M	D	7.69	CHA	A(C(NO2)/C(O-CH3))		CDCL3
1306M	D	8.51	CHA	A(C(NO2)/C(SO3NA)-C(NH-A))	S	DMSO
2883M	C	7.91	CHA	A(C(NO)/CH-C(C(=O)-O-CH2))		CDCL3
657M	A	6.80- 7.40	CHA	A(C(N(A/A)))		CDCL3
655M	B	6.63	CHA	A(C(N(CH2.2/CH2.2)))		POLYSOL-D
2548M	B	6.45- 6.85	CHA	A(C(N(CH2/CH2)))		POLYSOL-D
654M	B	6.50- 6.80	CHA	A(C(N(CH2/CH2)))		CDCL3
649M	C	6.55 APP.	CHA	A(C(N(CH2/CH2)))		CCL4
663M	D	6.59	CHA	A(C(N(CH2/CH2))/CH-C(CH3))		CDCL3
2104M	C	6.62	CHA	A(C(N(CH2/CH2))/CH-C(C(=O)-A))		CDCL3
670M	C	6.59	CHA	A(C(N(CH2/CH2))/CH-C(NH2))		CDCL3
817M	C	7.06	CHA	A(C(N(CH2/CH2))/CH-C(NH2))	S	D20
652M	C	6.45- 6.75	CHA	A(C(N(CH3/CH3)))		CCL4
648M	B	6.42- 6.72	CHA	A(C(N(CH3/CH3)))		CCL4
1074M	B	6.90	CHA	A(C(N(CH3/CH3))-CH-C(NO2)/CH-C(NO2))		DMSO-D6
668M	B	6.53	CHA	A(C(N(CH3/CH3))/CH-C(BR))		CDCL3
2170M	B	6.63	CHA	A(C(N(CH3/CH3))/CH-C(C(=O)-H))		CDCL3
816M	B	7.65- 8.00	CHA	A(C(N(CH3/CH3))/CH-C(NH2))	S	D20
818M	B	7.79	CHA	A(C(N(CH3/CH3))/CH-C(NH2))	S	D20
818M	B	7.99	CHA	A(C(N(CH3/CH3))/CH-C(NH2))	S	D20
669M	C	6.62 APP.	CHA	A(C(N(CH3/CH3))/CH-C(NH2))		CDCL3
819M	B	7.84	CHA	A(C(N(CH3/CH3))/CH-C(N(CH3/CH3)))	S	D20
900M	B	6.67	CHA	A(C(N(CH3/CH3))/CH-C(N=N-A))		CDCL3
901M	D	6.70	CHA	A(C(N(CH3/CH3))/CH-C(N=N-A))		DMSO-D6
901M	D	6.76	CHA	A(C(N(CH3/CH3))/CH-C(N=N-A))		DMSO-D6
2990M	F	6.90- 7.40	CHA	A(C(N(C(=O)-O/CH2)))		CCL4
2365M	E	7.07- 7.60	CHA	A(C(N(C(=O)/CH2))		CDCL3
1032M	A	7.01	CHA	A(C(N(N=O/A)))		CDCL3
1031M	B	7.20- 7.60	CHA	A(C(N(N=O/CH3)))		CDCL3
762M	B	6.90	CHA	A(C(N(N/CH3))/CH-C(A))		CDCL3
761M	C	6.72	CHA	A(C(N(N/CH3))/CH-C(CH3))		CDCL3
903M	C	8.18	CHA	A(C(N(=N-A/=O))/CH-C(CL))		CDCL3
902M	B	8.20 APP.	CHA	A(C(N(-O)=N))		CDCL3
921M	C	6.79	CHA	A(C(N=C=O)-CH-C(N=C=O)/CH-C(CH3))		CCL4
921M	B	6.71	CHA	A(C(N=C=O)-C(CH3)/C(N=C=O))		CCL4
941M	B	7.15	CHA	A(C(N=C=S)/CH-C(F))		CCL4
903M	B	8.09	CHA	A(C(N=N(=O/A))/CH-C(CL))		CDCL3
902M	B	8.20 APP.	CHA	A(C(N=N(-O)))		CDCL3
896M	B	7.88	CHA	A(C(N=N))		CDCL3
1065M	B	7.92 APP.	CHA	A(C(N=N-A))		CDCL3
899M	D	7.79 APP.	CHA	A(C(N=N-A))		CDCL3
900M	D	7.82	CHA	A(C(N=N-A))		CDCL3
898M	B	7.60- 7.90	CHA	A(C(N=N-A)-CH-C(CL))		CDCL3
899M	D	7.79 APP.	CHA	A(C(N=N-A)/CH-C(NH2))		CDCL3
901M	E	7.63	CHA	A(C(N=N-A)/CH-C(NH2))		DMSO-D6
901M	E	7.71	CHA	A(C(N=N-A)/CH-C(NH2))		DMSO-D6
1065M	B	7.92 APP.	CHA	A(C(N=N-A)/CH-C(NO2))		CDCL3
900M	D	7.82	CHA	A(C(N=N-A)/CH-C(N(CH3/CH3)))		CDCL3
901M	F	7.63	CHA	A(C(N=N-A)/CH-C(N(CH3/CH3)))		DMSO-D6
901M	F	7.71	CHA	A(C(N=N-A)/CH-C(N(CH3/CH3)))		DMSO-D6
1022M	C	7.77	CHA	A(C(N=O)/CH-C(NH-A))		POLYSOL-D
1914M	C	6.46 APP.	CHA	A(C(OH)-CH-C(CH3)/CH-C(CH3))		CCL4
1915M	C	6.33	CHA	A(C(OH)-CH-C(CH3)/C(CH3))		CCL4
2892M	C	6.95- 7.48	CHA	A(C(OH)-CH-C(C(=O)-O-CH3))		CDCL3
2914M	B	6.58	CHA	A(C(OH)-CH-C(C(=O)-O-CH3)/C(OH))		DMSO-D6
1899M	B	5.99 APP.	CHA	A(C(OH)-CH-C(NH2))		DMSO
2335M	B	6.55	CHA	A(C(OH)-CH-C(NH-C(=O)))		DMSO-D6
1904M	A	7.19	CHA	A(C(OH)-CH-C(NO2))		DMSO
1929M	B	6.21	CHA	A(C(OH)-CH-C(OH)/CH-C(CH2-A))		DMSO-D6
2599M	B	6.45	CHA	A(C(OH)-CH-C(OH)/CH-C(C(=O)-OH))		DMSO
1946M	A	6.49	CHA	A(C(OH)-CH-C(OH)/CH-C(OH))		D20
1929M	C	6.39	CHA	A(C(OH)-C(CH2-A)/C(OH))		DMSO-D6
1917M	E	6.53	CHA	A(C(OH)-C(CH(CH3/CH3))/C(CH3))		CDCL3
2599M	A	6.39	CHA	A(C(OH)-C(C(=O)-OH)/C(OH))		DMSO
2891M	D	6.95	CHA	A(C(OH)-C(C(=O)-O-CH2))		CDCL3
2889M	D	6.96	CHA	A(C(OH)-C(C(=O)-O-CH))		CDCL3
1896M	C	6.98	CHA	A(C(OH)-C(I))		CDCL3
1910M	A	6.69	CHA	A(C(OH)-C(OH))		POLYSOL-D
1946M	C	6.91	CHA	A(C(OH)-C(OH)/CH-C(OH))		D20
1946M	B	6.62	CHA	A(C(OH)-C(OH)/C(OH))		D20
1924M	G	6.71	CHA	A(C(OH)-C(O-CH3)/CH-C(CH2-Q3))		CCL4
1889M	A	6.87	CHA	A(C(OH)/CH-C(A))		DMSO
1895M	B	6.69	CHA	A(C(OH)/CH-C(BR))		CDCL3
2038M	E	6.99	CHA	A(C(OH)/CH-C(CH2-CH2))		CDCL3
1893M	B	6.71	CHA	A(C(OH)/CH-C(CL))		CDCL3
1886M	E	6.70	CHA	A(C(OH)/CH-C(C(CH2/CH3/CH3)))		CDCL3
1885M	E	6.74	CHA	A(C(OH)/CH-C(C(CH2/CH3/CH3)))		CCL4
1883M	C	6.75	CHA	A(C(OH)/CH-C(C(CH3/CH3/CH3)))		CDCL3

BOOK NO.	ASSIGN-MENT	CHEM SHIFT - ppm -	PROTON GROUP	ENVIRONMENTAL GROUPS	S	SOLVENT
2895M	D	6.87	CHA	A(C(OH)/CH-C(C(=O)-O-CH2))		CCL4
2893M	C	6.93	CHA	A(C(OH)/CH-C(C(=O)-O-CH))		CDCL3
1898M	B	6.59	CHA	A(C(OH)/CH-C(I))		CDCL3
1912M	A	6.79	CHA	A(C(OH)/CH-C(OH))		D2O
1914M	C	6.46 APP.	CHA	A(C(OH)/C(CH3)-C(CH3))		CCL4
2892M	D	7.62	CHA	A(C(OH)/C(C(=O)-O-CH3))		CDCL3
1818M	D	7.10- 7.60	CHA	A(C(OH/CH2/CH2))		CDCL3
2589M	A	7.20	CHA	A(C(O-A)OCH-C(C(=O)-OH))		DMSO
1550M	A	6.70 APP.	CHA	A(C(O-A)-CH-C(O-A))		CDCL3
1550M	A	6.70 APP.	CHA	A(C(O-A)/C(O-A))		CDCL3
1491M	C	6.88	CHA	A(C(O-CH2.2))		CDCL3
2586M	D	6.90	CHA	A(C(O-CH2.2)/CH-C(C(=O)-OH))		POLYSOL-D
1710M	B	6.71	CHA	A(C(O-CH2))		CCL4
2553M	B	6.92 APP.	CHA	A(C(O-CH2))		C3H6O
2554M	E	6.88 APP.	CHA	A(C(O-CH2))		CDCL3
1499M	D	6.50	CHA	A(C(O-CH2)-CH-C(CH3))		CCL4
1561M	F	6.70	CHA	A(C(O-CH2)-C(O-CH2)/CH-C(NH2))		CDCL3
1561M	E	6.18 APP.	CHA	A(C(O-CH2)-C(O-CH2)/C(NH2))		CDCL3
1518M	C	6.71	CHA	A(C(O-CH2)/CH-C(BR))		CDCL3
1500M	D	6.65	CHA	A(C(O-CH2)/CH-C(CH3))		CCL4
1513M	C	6.68	CHA	A(C(O-CH2)/CH-C(CL))		CCL4
2174M	E	6.92	CHA	A(C(O-CH2)/CH-C(C(=O)-H))		CCL4
1533M	C	6.91	CHA	A(C(O-CH2)/CH-C(NO2))		CDCL3
1499M	E	6.59	CHA	A(C(O-CH2)/C(CH3))		CCL4
1515M	B	6.77	CHA	A(C(O-CH3)-CH-C(BR))		CDCL3
2244M	B	6.61	CHA	A(C(O-CH3)-CH-C(C(=O)-CL)/C(O-CH3))		CCL4
2583M	B	7.20	CHA	A(C(O-CH3)-CH-C(C(=O)-OH))		DMSO-D6
1531M	B	7.21	CHA	A(C(O-CH3)-CH-C(NO2))		CDCL3
2244M	C	7.12	CHA	A(C(O-CH3)-CH-C(O-CH3)/C(C(=O)-CL))		CCL4
1507M	B	6.75	CHA	A(C(O-CH3)-C(A))		CCL4
1514M	C	6.88	CHA	A(C(O-CH3)-C(BR))		CDCL3
1722M	D	6.79	CHA	A(C(O-CH3)-C(CH2-OH))		CDCL3
1509M	C	6.91	CHA	A(C(O-CH3)-C(CL))		CDCL3
2887M	B	6.75- 7.07	CHA	A(C(O-CH3)-C(C(=O)-O-CH3))		CCL4
1519M	C	6.70	CHA	A(C(O-CH3)-C(I))		CDCL3
1924M	F	6.53 APP.	CHA	A(C(O-CH3)-C(OH)/C(CH2-Q3))		CCL4
1529M	B	6.87	CHA	A(C(O-CH3)-C(QN(OH)))		CDCL3
1508M	B	6.93	CHA	A(C(O-CH3)/CH-C(A))		CDCL3
1516M	B	6.69	CHA	A(C(O-CH3)/CH-C(BR))		CCL4
1496M	C	6.79	CHA	A(C(O-CH3)/CH-C(CH3))		CDCL3
1511M	B	6.72	CHA	A(C(O-CH3)/CH-C(CL))		CCL4
2075M	C	6.98	CHA	A(C(O-CH3)/CH-C(C(=O)-CH3))		CDCL3
2888M	C	6.88	CHA	A(C(O-CH3)/CH-C(C(=O)-O-CH3))		CDCL3
1521M	B	6.68	CHA	A(C(O-CH3)/CH-C(I))		CDCL3
791M	B	7.09	CHA	A(C(O-CH3)/CH-C(NH2))	S	D2O
2425M	C	6.77	CHA	A(C(O-CH3)/CH-C(NH-C(=O)-NH2))		POLYSOL-D
824M	B	7.08	CHA	A(C(O-CH3)/CH-C(NH-NH2))	S	D2O
1524M	C	6.79	CHA	A(C(O-CH3)/CH-C(N(CH3/CH3)))		CDCL3
1547M	B	6.79	CHA	A(C(O-CH3)/CH-C(O-CH3))		CDCL3
1506M	E	6.65	CHA	A(C(O-CH3)/CH-C(Q2(CH3)))		CCL4
1537M	B	6.91	CHA	A(C(O-CH3)/CH-C(SO2-A))		CDCL3
2583M	D	7.50- 7.80	CHA	A(C(O-CH3)/C(C(=O)-OH))		DMSO-D6
1493M	D	6.65- 7.40	CHA	A(C(O-CH))		CCL4
2924M	C	6.82	CHA	A(C(O-C(=O)-CH3)/CH-C(CH3))		CCL4
2969M	A	7.11	CHA	A(C(O-C(=O)-CL)/CH-C(NO2))		DMSO-D6
2978M	B	7.51	CHA	A(C(O-C(=O)-NH2))		DMSO
2562M	C	7.24	CHA	A(C(O-C)/CH-C(CL))		CDCL3
1608M	A	6.90- 7.50	CHA	A(C(O-P))		CDCL3
1099M	B	7.00- 7.40	CHA	A(C(P(A/A))/CH-C(CH3))		CDCL3
1100M	A	7.04- 7.50	CHA	A(C(P(A/A))/CH-C(CL))		CDCL3
1097M	C	7.10- 7.60	CHA	A(C(P(A/CH2)))		CDCL3
877M	D	7.94	CHA	A(C(QN(NH-A))-C(CL))		CDCL3
1529M	E	7.64	CHA	A(C(QN(OH))-C(O-CH3))		CDCL3
2332M	C	7.61	CHA	A(C(QN(OH))/CH-C(NH-C(=O)-CH3))		POLYSOL-D
881M	C	7.72	CHA	A(C(QN(QN))/CH-C(CH3))		CDCL3
928M	B	7.06	CHA	A(C(QN(=N-A))/CH-C(CH3))		CDCL3
919M	B	6.74- 6.90	CHA	A(C(QN(=O))-C(CH3)/C(CH3))		CCL4
2884M	C	7.06	CHA	A(C(QN(=O))/CH-C(C(=O)-O-CH2))		CDCL3
2160M	C	7.25- 7.65	CHA	A(C(Q1(C(=O)-H/CH3)))		CCL4
380M	C	7.19 APP.	CHA	A(C(Q2(BR)))		CCL4
2549M	D	7.30 APP.	CHA	A(C(Q2(CH2-C(=O)-OH)))		CDCL3
2841M	E	7.26	CHA	A(C(Q2(CH2-O-C(=O))))		CCL4
1506M	F	7.08	CHA	A(C(Q2(CH3))/CH-C(O-CH3))		CCL4
2201M	B	7.20- 7.60	CHA	A(C(Q2(C(=O)-OH)))		CDCL3
159M	B	7.15- 7.65	CHA	A(C(Q2(H/A/H)))		CDCL3
1711M	E	7.28	CHA	A(C(Q2(H/CH2-OH/H)))		CDCL3
2564M	D	7.59	CHA	A(C(Q2(H/C(=O)-OH/H))/CH-C(CH3))		DMSO-D6
2862M	E	7.31 APP.	CHA	A(C(Q2(H/C(=O)-O-CH2/H)))		CCL4
165M	A	7.10- 7.50	CHA	A(C(Q2/A))		CDCL3
1447M	D	7.21	CHA	A(C(R30))		CCL4
679M	B	7.42- 7.84	CHA	A(C(R5NNNN(C=N/N(CH3))))		CDCL3

BOOK NO.	ASSIGN-MENT	CHEM SHIFT - ppm -	PROTON GROUP	ENVIRONMENTAL GROUPS	S	SOLVENT
2447M	B	7.25- 7.60	CHA	A(C(R5NN(C(CH3)-NH/C(=0))))		DMSO-D6
1176M	C	7.99 APP.	CHA	A(C(R5NSA(C=N/S)))		CDCL3
2374M	D	6.90- 7.80	CHA	A(C(R5N(N-C(=0)/CH2)))		CDCL3
2389M	C	7.82	CHA	A(C(R5N(N-C(=0)/C(=0)))/CH-C(I))		TFA
640M	C	6.88	CHA	A(C(R6NN(N/CH2-CH2-NH)))		CDCL3
183M	C	7.11	CHA	A(C(R6)/CH-C(R6))		CDCL3
1239M	F	7.10	CHA	A(C(SH)-C(SH)/CH-C(CH3))		CDCL3
1239M	E	7.05	CHA	A(C(SH)-C(SH)/C(CH3))		CDCL3
1230M	D	7.09	CHA	A(C(SH)/CH-C(CH3))		CDCL3
1231M	C	7.13	CHA	A(C(SH)/CH-C(C(CH3/CH3/CH3)))		CCL4
1091M	D	7.48	CHA	A(C(SI(A/A/CH2)))		CDCL3
1084M	C	7.56	CHA	A(C(SI(A/H/H)))		CDCL3
1089M	B	7.20- 7.65	CHA	A(C(SI(CH3/CH3/CH3)))		CDCL3
1271M	B	7.95	CHA	A(C(SO2)/CH-C(F))		CDCL3
1276M	B	7.92	CHA	A(C(SO2-A))		CDCL3
1273M	B	7.94	CHA	A(C(SO2-A))		CDCL3
1268M	E	7.90	CHA	A(C(SO2-A))		CDCL3
1275M	B	7.82	CHA	A(C(SO2-A)/CH-C(BR))		CDCL3
1269M	C	7.80	CHA	A(C(SO2-A)/CH-C(CH3))		CDCL3
1268M	D	7.81	CHA	A(C(SO2-A)/CH-C(CH3))		CDCL3
1276M	C	8.08	CHA	A(C(SO2-A)/CH-C(NO2))		CDCL3
1537M	C	7.79	CHA	A(C(SO2-A)/CH-C(0-CH3))		CDCL3
1363M	D	7.84	CHA	A(C(SO2-NH2)/CH-C(CH3))		TFA
1370M	E	7.71	CHA	A(C(SO2-NH)/CH-C(CH3))		CDCL3
1372M	F	7.60	CHA	A(C(SO2-NH)/CH-C(CH3))		CDCL3
1375M	D	7.65	CHA	A(C(SO2-N)/CH-C(CH3))		CDCL3
1369M	F	7.69	CHA	A(C(SO2-N)/CH-C(CH3))		CDCL3
1301M	D	7.87	CHA	A(C(SO3NA)-C(CH3)/CH-C(CH3))	S	D20
1312M	G	7.75	CHA	A(C(SO3)/CH-C(CH3))	S	CDCL3
1302M	C	7.76	CHA	A(C(SO3-RA)/CH-C(CH3))	S	D20
1322M	F	7.71	CHA	A(C(SO3-CH2)/CH-C(CH3))		CCL4
1321M	E	7.70	CHA	A(C(SO3-CH)/CH-C(CH3))		CCL4
1291M	D	7.52	CHA	A(C(SO3-H)-CH-C(NH2)/CH-C(CH3))		DMSO-D6
1304M	B	7.62	CHA	A(C(SO3-NA)-CH-C(NH2))		D20
1249M	C	7.86	CHA	A(C(SO-CH3)/CH-C(I))		CDCL3
1170M	C	7.21	CHA	A(C(S-A)/CH-C(CH3))		CDCL3
1167M	B	7.05- 7.55	CHA	A(C(S-CH2))		CDCL3
1168M	B	7.65	CHA	A(C(S-C))		CDCL3
1192M	B	7.08- 7.55	CHA	A(C(S-S))		CCL4
1194M	B	7.48	CHA	A(C(S-S))		CDCL3
1198M	E	7.16	CHA	A(C(S-S)-C(NH2))		CDCL3
200M	B	7.68	CHA	A(C*)		CCL4
1046M	C	7.89	CHA	A(C-C(NO2)-C(CH3))		CCL4
427M	D	7.71	CHA	A(C-(I)-C(CH3))		CDCL3
746M	A	7.00- 7.80	CHA	UNSPECIFIED		CCL4
2228M	A	7.15- 7.70	CHA	UNSPECIFIED		CCL4
186M	A	7.30- 7.75	CHA	UNSPECIFIED		CDCL3
133M	B	7.04	CHA	UNSPECIFIED		CCL4
2093M	B	7.15- 7.75	CHA	UNSPECIFIED		CDCL3
216M	D	7.15- 7.80	CHA	UNSPECIFIED		CDCL3
2181M	B	9.96	CHR	AAAA(C*-C(C(=0)-H)/CH-C*)		CDCL3
2125M	A	6.85	CHR	AR7A(C*/CH-C*)		CCL4
1440M	E	2.70	CHR	R30<(CH2.5-CH3)/0-HCH>		CCL4
1441M	E	2.71	CHR	R30<(CH2.7-CH3)/0-HCH>		CCL4
1444M	D	3.40 APP.	CHR	R30<(CH2-BR)/0-HCH>		CCL4
1439M	E	2.69	CHR	R30<(CH2-CH3)/0-HCH>		CCL4
1540M	C	3.15	CHR	R30<(CH2-0)/0-HCH2>		CCL4
1445M	C	2.63	CHR	R30<(CH2-0)/0-HCH>		CCL4
1677M	C	3.27	CHR	R30<(HCH-OH)/0-HCH>		D20
1446M	C	3.30	CHR	R30<(Q3)/0-HCH>		CDCL3
1447M	C	3.69	CHR	R30((A)/0-HCH)		CCL4
1442M	E	2.74	CHR	R30((CH2-CH2)/0-HCH)		CCL4
1438M	D	2.80	CHR	R30((CH3)/0-HCH)		CCL4
1443M	C	3.17	CHR	R30((HCH-CL)-0-HCH)		CCL4
2394M	B	3.25	CHR	R30(HCH-R5NA)/0-CH2)		CDCL3
144M	B	0.98 APP.	CHR	R3<(CH2-A)/CH2-CH2>		CDCL3
41M	C	0.75 APP.	CHR	R3<(CH2-R3)/HCH-HCH>		CCL4
39M	C	0.90 APP.	CHR	R3<(CH3)/CH(CH3)-HCH>		CCL4
40M	B	0.33- 0.97	CHR	R3<(CH3)/C(CH3/CH3)-HCH>		CCL4
38M	B	0.31	CHR	R3<(CH(CH3/CH3))/HCH-HCH>		CCL4
1789M	B	0.98	CHR	R3<(CH(OH/A))/CH2-CH2>		CCL4
1761M	B	0.86	CHR	R3<(CH(OH/CH3))/CH2-CH2>		CDCL3
2786M	C	2.01	CHR	R3<(C(=0)-0-CH2)/CH(C(=0)-0-CH2)-CH2>		CCL4
1996M	B	2.00	CHR	R3((C(=0)-R3)-CH2/CH2)		CCL4
1454M	A	4.45- 5.00	CHR	R40((CL)/CH2-0/CH2)		CCL4
110M	E	5.17	CHR	R4R6BI(=C(CH3)-CH*/CH2-CH*)		CCL4
2513M	B	3.19	CHR	R4<(C(=0)-OH)/CH2-CH2/CH2>		CDCL3
772M	B	3.85	CHR	R4((NH2)/CH2-CH2/CH2)	S	D20
1763M	B	4.16	CHR	R4((OH)/CH2-CH2/CH2)		CCL4
1727M	A	3.60- 4.20	CHR	R5AA<(CH2-OH)/C*/C*>		POLYSOL-D
2855M	B	4.80	CHR	R5AA<(C(=0)-0-CH3)-C*/C*>		CDCL3

BOOK NO.	ASSIGN-MENT	CHEM SHIFT - ppm -	PROTON GROUP	ENVIRONMENTAL GROUPS	S	SOLVENT
199M	C	6.68	CHR	R5A(C*/=CH-CH2)		CCL4
199M	B	6.28	CHR	R5A(=CH-C*/CH2-C*)		CCL4
606M	B	6.18	CHR	R5NA<C*/=C(CH3)-NH>		CDCL3
607M	B	6.75	CHR	R5NA<N(H)-C*/=C(CH3)-C*>		CDCL3
608M	C	6.69	CHR	R5NA<=CH-C*/NH-C*>		CDCL3
608M	B	6.40	CHR	R5NA<=CH-NH/C*-C(CH3)>		CDCL3
605M	A	6.38	CHR	R5NA(C*/CH-NH)		CCL4
605M	B	6.76	CHR	R5NA(NH-C*/CH-C*)		CCL4
738M	C	8.30	CHR	R5NNA<NH-C*/=N-C*>		DMSO-D6
740M	E	8.12	CHR	R5NNA(=N-C*/NH-C*)		CDCL3
1156M	D	8.50	CHR	R5NNS<=N-N=/S-C(NH-CH2)=>		POLYSOL-D
2446M	A	5.14	CHR	R5NN<(A)/NH-C(=O)/C(=O)-NH>		DMSO-D6
2449M	C	4.93	CHR	R5NN<(A)/NH-C(=O)/C(=O)-N>		CDCL3
2448M	B	5.00	CHR	R5NN<(A)/NH-C(=O)/C(=O)-N(CH3)>		CDCL3
2412M	D	4.62	CHR	R5NN<(A)/NH-NH/HCH-C(=O)>		DMSO-D6
2451M	A	5.39	CHR	R5NN<(NH-C(=O)-NH2)/NH-C(=O)/C(=O)-NH>		DMSO-D6
678M	C	7.50- 7.90	CHR	R5NN<=CH-CH=/N(A)-N=>		CDCL3
678M	A	6.36	CHR	R5NN<=CH-N(A)/CH=N>		CDCL3
820M	C	7.58	CHR	R5NN(=C(CH2.2-NH2)-N=/NH-CH=)	S	D2O
820M	D	8.84	CHR	R5NN(=N-C(CH2.2-NH2)/NH-CH=)	S	D2O
1580M	B	7.39	CHR	R5NO<=C(A)-O/N=C(A<C-CH-C(CL)>)>		CDCL3
1579M	C	8.39	CHR	R5NO(=CH-C(CH3)=/O-N=)		CCL4
1579M	B	6.13	CHR	R5NO(=CH-O/C(CH3)=N)		CCL4
1148M	C	8.52	CHR	R5NS<S-N=/=CH-C(CH3)=>		CCL4
1150M	B	8.52	CHR	R5NS<S-N=/=C(A)-CH=>		CCL4
1150M	B	8.62	CHR	R5NS<S-N=/=C(A)-CH=>		CCL4
1149M	B	8.17	CHR	R5NS<=N=/=C(CH3)-CH=>		CCL4
1152M	A	7.27	CHR	R5NS<=CH-N=/S-C(BR)=>		CCL4
1152M	B	7.56	CHR	R5NS<=CH-S/N=C(BR)>		CCL4
1154M	C	5.97	CHR	R5NS<=C(CH3)-N=/S-C(NH2)=>	S	D2O
1148M	B	6.98	CHR	R5NS<=C-S/C(CH3)=N>		CCL4
1150M	C	8.52	CHR	R5NS<=N-S/C(A)=CH>		CCL4
1150M	C	8.62	CHR	R5NS<=N-S/C(A)=CH>		CCL4
1149M	B	8.17	CHR	R5NS<=N-S/C(CH3)=CH>		CCL4
1153M	A	6.48	CHR	R5NS(N=C(NH2)/=CH-S)		DMSO-D6
1153M	C	6.95	CHR	R5NS(S-C(NH2)=/=CH-N=)		DMSO-D6
2376M	C	2.60- 3.30	CHR	R5N<(CH3)/C(=O)-NH/HCH-C(=O)>		CDCL3
2636M	C	4.14	CHR	R5N<(C(=O)-OH)/NH-CH2/CH2-CH2>		D2O
677M	D	6.69	CHR	R5N<=CH-CH=/NH-C(CH2-N)=>		CDCL3
2182M	C	7.12	CHR	R5N<=CH-CH=/NH-C(C(=O)-H)=>		CDCL3
675M	C	6.57	CHR	R5N<=CH-N(CH3)-CH=>		CDCL3
2388M	A	7.07	CHR	R5N<=CH-C(=O)/C(=O)-N(A<C-CH-CH-C(BR)>)>		POLYSOL-D
2390M	A	7.15	CHR	R5N<=CH-C(=O)/C(=O)-N(A<C-CH-C(R5N<N-C(=O)/C(=O)>)>)>		DMSO-D6
2385M	C	6.78	CHR	R5N<=CH-C(=O)/C(=O)-N(CH2.2-A)>		POLYSOL-D
2384M	C	6.72	CHR	R5N<=CH-C(=O)/C(=O)-N(CH2-CH3)>		CDCL3
677M	C	6.09 APP.	CHR	R5N<=CH-NH/CH=C(CH2-N)>		CDCL3
2182M	A	6.29	CHR	R5N<=CH-NH/CH=C(C(=O)-H)>		CDCL3
675M	B	6.11	CHR	R5N<=CH-N(CH3)/CH=CH>		CDCL3
677M	C	6.09 APP.	CHR	R5N<=C(CH2-N)-NH/CH=CH>		CDCL3
676M	B	5.91	CHR	R5N<=C(CH3)-N(A)/CH=C(CH3)>		CDCL3
2182M	B	6.97	CHR	R5N<=C(C(=O)-H)-NH/CH=CH>		CDCL3
575M	B	6.41	CHR	R5N(NH-CH=/=CH-CH=)		CCL4
2637M	C	4.50- 4.90	CHR	R5N(OH/CH2-NH/CH2-CH(C(=O)-OH))		D2O
2637M	C	4.50- 4.90	CHR	R5N((C(=O)-OH)/NH-CH2/CH2-CH(OH))		D2O
2379M	A	6.79	CHR	R5N(=CH-C(=O)/C(=O)-NH)		POLYSOL-D
2389M	A	6.99	CHR	R5N(=CH-C(=O)/C(=O)-N(A(C-CH-CH-C(I))))		TFA
2387M	A	6.71	CHR	R5N(=CH-C(=O)/C(=O)-N(A(C-C(CL))))		CDCL3
2386M	B	6.63	CHR	R5N(=CH-C(=O)/C(=O)-N(CH2-A))		CDCL3
575M	A	6.07	CHR	R5N(=CH-NH/CH=CH)		CCL4
1584M	D	7.47	CHR	R5OA<=CH-C*/O-C*>		CCL4
1584M	A	6.59	CHR	R5OA<=CH-O/C*>		CCL4
1679M	E	3.60- 4.30	CHR	R5OO<(CH2-OH)/O-C(CH3/CH3)/CH2-O>		CCL4
1574M	D	7.15	CHR	R5O<O-C(CH3)=/=CH-CH=>		CCL4
2246M	C	7.82	CHR	R5O<O-C(C(=O)-CL)=/=CH-CH=>		CCL4
2133M	C	7.78	CHR	R5O<O-C(C(=O)-C(=O))/=CH-CH=>		CDCL3
2681M	C	7.64	CHR	R5O<O-C(C(=O)-O-K)=/=CH-CH>	S	D2O
2951M	C	3.69	CHR	R5O<(A)/HCH-O/HCH-C(=O)>		CDCL3
2947M	D	4.40 APP.	CHR	R5O<(CH2-CH2)/O-C(=O)/CH2-CH2>		CCL4
1457M	C	3.50- 4.08	CHR	R5O<(CH2-O)/O-CH2/CH2-CH2>		CCL4
2946M	B	1.68- 2.82	CHR	R5O<(CH3)/C(=O)-O/CH2-CH2>		CCL4
2256M	B	2.30- 3.55	CHR	R5O<(CH3)/C(=O)-O/CH2-C(=O)>		CDCL3
1456M	C	3.30- 4.00	CHR	R5O<(CH3)/O-CH2/CH2-CH2>		CCL4
2950M	C	3.71	CHR	R5O<(C(=O)-CH3)/C(=O)-O/HCH-CH2>		CCL4
2949M	D	4.22	CHR	R5O<(OH)/C(=O)-O/C(CH3/CH3)-CH2>		CDCL3
1866M	B	4.86- 5.16	CHR	R5O<(OH)/O-CH(CH2-OH)/CH(OH)-CH(OH)>		D2O
2935M	F	7.58	CHR	R5O<=CH-CH=/O-C(C(=O)-O-CH2.2)=>		CCL4
2936M	F	7.53	CHR	R5O<=CH-CH=/O-C(C(=O)-O-CH2.4)=>		CCL4
2141M	G	7.49	CHR	R5O<=CH-CH=/O-C(C(=O)-Q1)=>		CCL4
2605M	D	7.49	CHR	R5O<=CH-CH=/O-C(Q2(H/C(=O)-OH/H))=>		CDCL3
1578M	D	7.59	CHR	R5O<=CH-CH=/O-C(Q2(H/NO2/H))=>		CDCL3
2604M	B	7.60	CHR	R5O<=CH-C(C(=O)-OH)=/O-CH=>		POLYSOL-D

BOOK NO.	ASSIGN-MENT	CHEM SHIFT - ppm -	PROTON GROUP	ENVIRONMENTAL GROUPS	S	SOLVENT
1574M	C	6.13	CHR	R50<=CH-O/CH=C(CH3)>		CCL4
2246M	A	6.70	CHR	R50<=CH-O/CH=C(C(=O)-CL)>		CCL4
2133M	A	6.64	CHR	R50<=CH-O/CH=C(C(=O)-C(=O))>		CDCL3
2935M	D	6.47	CHR	R50<=CH-O/CH=C(C(=O)-O-CH2.2)>		CCL4
2936M	D	6.44	CHR	R50<=CH-O/CH=C(C(=O)-O-CH2.4)>		CCL4
2681M	A	6.59	CHR	R50<=CH-O/CH=C(C(=O)-K)>	S	D2O
2141M	E	6.46	CHR	R50<=CH-O/CH=C(C(=O)-Q1)>		CCL4
2091M	A	6.56	CHR	R50<=CH-O/CH=C(Q2(H/C(=O)-A/H))>		CDCL3
2605M	B	6.48	CHR	R50<=CH-O/CH=C(Q2(H/C(=O)-OH/H))>		CDCL3
1578M	A	6.58	CHR	R50<=CH-O/CH=C(Q2(H/NO2/H))>		CDCL3
2604M	A	6.83	CHR	R50<=CH-O/C(C(=O)-OH)=CH>		POLYSOL-D
2266M	A	7.21	CHR	R50<=C(BR)-C(=O)/C(=O)-O>		CDCL3
2954M	C	5.10	CHR	R50<=C(CH3)-O/CH2-C(=O)>		CCL4
1574M	B	5.83	CHR	R50<=C(CH3)-O/CH=CH>		CCL4
1575M	B	5.81	CHR	R50<=C(CH3)-O/CH=C(CH3)>		CDCL3
2246M	B	7.52	CHR	R50<=C(C(=O)-CL)-O/CH=CH>		CCL4
2133M	B	7.63	CHR	R50<=C(C(=O)-C(=O))-O/CH=CH>		CDCL3
2185M	A	7.62 APP.	CHR	R50<=C(C(=O)-H)-O/CH=C(NO2)>		CDCL3
2604M	C	8.20	CHR	R50<=C(C(=O)-OH)-CH=/O-CH=>		POLYSOL-D
2935M	E	7.11	CHR	R50<=C(C(=O)-O-CH2.2)-O/CH=CH>		CCL4
2936M	E	7.07	CHR	R50<=C(C(=O)-O-CH2.4)-O/CH=CH>		CCL4
2681M	B	7.05	CHR	R50<=C(C(=O)-O-K)-O/CH=CH>	S	D2O
2141M	F	7.06	CHR	R50<=C(C(=O)-Q1)-O/CH=CH>		CCL4
2185M	A	7.62 APP.	CHR	R50<=C(NO2)-O/CH=C(C(=O)-H)>		CDCL3
2091M	B	6.69	CHR	R50<=C(Q2(H/C(=O)-A/H))-O/CH=CH>		CDCL3
2605M	C	6.73	CHR	R50<=C(Q2(H/C(=O)-OH))-O/CH=CH>		CDCL3
1578M	B	6.92	CHR	R50<=C(Q2(H/NO2/H))-O/CH=CH>		CDCL3
2931M	D	7.30	CHR	R50(O-C(CH2-O-C(=O))/=CH-CH=)		CCL4
1576M	C	7.60	CHR	R50(O-C(C:N)/=/=CH)		CCL4
2948M	B	4.43 APP.	CHR	R50((BR)/C(=O)-O/CH2-CH2)		CCL4
1573M	B	7.37	CHR	R50(=CH-CH=/O-CH=)		CCL4
1733M	D	7.38	CHR	R50(=CH-CH=/O-C(CH2-OH)=)		CDCL3
1577M	E	7.30	CHR	R50(=CH-CH=/O-C(CH2-SH)=)		CDCL3
2023M	E	7.49 APP.	CHR	R50(=CH-CH=/O-C(CH(OH/C(=O)))=)		DMSO
2023M	F	7.89	CHR	R50(=CH-CH=/O-C(C(=O)-CH)=)		DMSO
2294M	D	7.82	CHR	R50(=CH-CH=/O-C(C(=O)-NH2))		DMSO
2934M	G	7.49	CHR	R50(=CH-CH=/O-C(Q2(H/C(=O)-O-CH2/H))=)		CDCL3
2263M	A	6.41	CHR	R50(=CH-C(=O)/C(=O)-O)		D2O
1573M	A	6.30	CHR	R50(=CH-O/CH=CH)		CCL4
1733M	C	6.29 APP.	CHR	R50(=CH-O/CH=C(CH2-OH))		CDCL3
2931M	C	6.29	CHR	R50(=CH-O/CH=C(CH2-O-C(=O)))		CCL4
1577M	D	6.25	CHR	R50(=CH-O/CH=C(CH2-SH))		CDCL3
2023M	C	6.40 APP.	CHR	R50(=CH-O/CH=C(CH(OH/C(=O))))		DMSO
2023M	D	6.64	CHR	R50(=CH-O/CH=C(C(=O)-CH))		DMSO
2294M	A	6.67	CHR	R50(=CH-O/CH=C(C(=O)-NH2))		DMSO
1576M	A	6.55	CHR	R50(=CH-O/CH=C(C:N))		CCL4
2934M	D	6.42	CHR	R50(=CH-O/CH=C(Q2(H/C(=O)-O-CH2/H)))		CDCL3
1733M	C	6.29 APP.	CHR	R50(=C(CH2-OH)-O/CH=CH)		CDCL3
2931M	C	6.29	CHR	R50(=C(CH2-O-C(=O))-O/CH=CH)		CCL4
1577M	C	6.14	CHR	R50(=C(CH2-SH)-O/CH=CH)		CDCL3
2023M	C	6.40 APP.	CHR	R50(=C(CH(OH)/C(=O)))-O/CH=CH)		DMSO
2023M	E	7.49 APP.	CHR	R50(=C(C(=O)-CH)-O/CH=CH)		DMSO
2294M	B	7.29	CHR	R50(=C(C(=O)-NH2)-O/CH=CH)		DMSO
2937M	C	7.32	CHR	R50(=C(C(=O)-O-CH2)-O/CH=C(NO2))		CDCL3
1576M	B	7.11	CHR	R50(=C(C:N)-O/CH=CH)		CCL4
2937M	C	7.32	CHR	R50(=C(NO2)-O/CH=C(C(=O)-O-CH2))		CDCL3
2934M	E	6.60	CHR	R50(=C(Q2(H/C(=O)-O-CH2/H))-O/CH=CH)		CDCL3
2264M	B	6.60	CHR	R50(O(CH3)-C(=O)/C(=O)-O)		CCL4
115M	D	5.41 APP.	CHR	R5R5BIR5<CH*/CH*(HCH)/=CH-CH*>		CCL4
115M	E	5.90 APP.	CHR	R5R5BIR5<CH*-CH*/=CH-CH2>		CCL4
115M	E	5.90 APP.	CHR	R5R5BIR5<=CH-CH*/CH2-CH*>		CCL4
1353M	D	4.05	CHR	R5R5BI<(NH-C(=S))/CH*(CH2/CH2)/CH2-CH*>		POLYSOL-D
1779M	D	4.00	CHR	R5R5BI<(OH)/C*((CH3)/C*/CH2)/CH2-CH*>		CDCL3
2824M	G	5.77- 6.22	CHR	R5R5BI<=CH-CH*/CH*(CH2/CH2)>		CCL4
2824M	G	5.77- 6.22	CHR	R5R5BI<=CH-CH*/CH*(CH(C(=O)-O-CH2)/CH2)>		CCL4
2537M	D	5.70- 6.40	CHR	R5R5BI(=CH-CH*/CH*(CH2/CH2))		CCL4
2537M	D	5.70- 6.40	CHR	R5R5BI(=CH-CH*/CH*(CH(C(=O)-OH)/CH2))		CCL4
1277M	B	7.16	CHR	R5SA(SO2-C*/=CH-C*)		CDCL3
1277M	A	6.62	CHR	R5SA(=CH-SO2/C*)		CDCL3
1260M	A	6.75	CHR	R5S<SO2-CH=/=C(CL)-C(CL)>		CDCL3
1141M	C	7.18	CHR	R5S<S-CH=/=CH-C(BR)=>		CDCL3
1146M	B	7.36	CHR	R5S<S-CH=/=CH-C(NO2)=>		CCL4
1146M	B	7.58	CHR	R5S<S-CH=/=CH-C(NO2)=>		CCL4
1141M	B	7.11	CHR	R5S<S-CH=/=C(BR)-CH=>		CDCL3
1146M	C	8.24	CHR	R5S<S-CH=/=C(NO2)-CH=>		CCL4
1140M	C	6.98	CHR	R5S<S-C(BR)=/=CH-CH=>		CCL4
1140M	C	7.12	CHR	R5S<S-C(BR)=/=CH-CH=>		CCL4
1145M	C	8.35	CHR	R5S<S-C(QN(OH))=/=CH-CH=>		TFA
1259M	D	3.80	CHR	R5S<(CH3)/SO2-CH2/CH2=C(CH3)>		CDCL3
1678M	F	7.00	CHR	R5S<=CH-CH=/S-C(CH2.2-OH)>		CCL4
2512M	C	7.13	CHR	R5S<=CH-CH=/S-C(CH2-C(=O)-OH)=>		CDCL3

BOOK NO.	ASSIGN-MENT	CHEM SHIFT - ppm -	PROTON GROUP	ENVIRONMENTAL GROUPS	S	SOLVENT
1143M	C	7.27	CHR	R5S<=CH-CH=/S-C(I)=>		CDCL3
1137M	C	7.05	CHR	R5S<=CH-C(CH3)=/S-CH=>		CCL4
1140M	A	6.79	CHR	R5S<=CH-S/CH=C(RR)>		CCL4
1678M	E	6.81	CHR	R5S<=CH-S/CH=C((CH2.2-OH)>		CCL4
2512M	B	6.89 APP.	CHR	R5S<=CH-S/CH=C((CH2-C(=O)-OH)>		CDCL3
1143M	A	6.72	CHR	R5S<=CH-S/CH=C(I)>		CDCL3
1145M	A	7.46	CHR	R5S<=CH-S/CH=C(QN(OH))>		TFA
1141M	A	6.91	CHR	R5S<=CH-S/C(BR)=CH>		CDCL3
1137M	B	6.77 APP.	CHR	R5S<=CH-S/C(CH3)=CH>		CCL4
1146M	A	7.36	CHR	R5S<=CH-S/C(NO2)=CH>		CCL4
1146M	A	7.58	CHR	R5S<=CH-S/C(NO2)=CH>		CCL4
1140M	B	6.98	CHR	R5S<=C(BR)-S/CH=CH>		CCL4
1140M	B	7.12	CHR	R5S<=C(BR)-S/CH=CH>		CCL4
1142M	A	6.71	CHR	R5S<=C(BR)-S/CH=C(BR)>		CCL4
1678M	D	6.71	CHR	R5S<=C(CH2.2-OH)-S/CH=CH>		CCL4
2512M	B	6.89 APP.	CHR	R5S<=C(CH2-C(=O)-OH)-S/CH=CH>		CDCL3
1259M	E	5.63	CHR	R5S<=C(CH3)-CH2/CH(CH3)-SO2>		CDCL3
1137M	B	6.77 APP.	CHR	R5S<=C(CH3)-CH=/S-CH=>		CCL4
1139M	A	6.64	CHR	R5S<=C(CL)-S/CH=C(CL)>		CCL4
1143M	B	7.19	CHR	R5S<=C(I)-S/CH=CH>		CDCL3
1145M	B	8.18	CHR	R5S<=C(QN(OH))-S/CH=CH>		TFA
2184M	B	6.87	CHR	R5S(C(CH3)-S/CH-C(C(=O)-H))		CDCL3
2184M	C	7.59	CHR	R5S(C(C(=O)-H)-S/CH-C(CH3))		CDCL3
1136M	B	7.10	CHR	R5S(S-CH=/=CH-CH=)		CCL4
1144M	B	7.60 APP.	CHR	R5S(S-C(C:N)=/=CH-CH=)		CCL4
1147M	C	7.09	CHR	R5S(=CH-CH=/S-C(CH2-R5S).=)		CDCL3
1136M	A	6.90	CHR	R5S(=CH-S/CH=CH)		CCL4
1147M	B	6.82 APP.	CHR	R5S(=CH-S/CH=C((CH2-R55))		CDCL3
1144M	A	7.10	CHR	R5S(=CH-S/CH=C(C:N))		CCL4
1147M	B	6.82 APP.	CHR	R5S(=C(CH2-R5S)-S/CH=CH)		CDCL3
1144M	B	7.60 APP.	CHR	R5S(=C(C:N)-S/CH=CH)		CCL4
363M	B	4.38	CHR	R5<(BR)/CH2-CH2/CH2-CH2>		CCL4
43M	C	1.81 APP.	CHR	R5<(CH3)/CH2-CH2/CH2-CH2>		CCL4
1765M	C	2.47 APP.	CHR	R5<(CH3)/CH(OH)-CH2/CH2-CH2>		CDCL3
266M	B	4.35	CHR	R5<(CL)/CH2-CH2>		CCL4
2083M	B	3.65	CHR	R5<(C(=O)-A)/CH2-CH2/CH2-CH2>		CCL4
2143M	D	3.35	CHR	R5<(C(=O)-CH3)-C/CH2-CH2>		CCL4
421M	C	4.32	CHR	R5<(I)/CH2-CH2/CH2-CH2>		CCL4
468M	C	3.31	CHR	R5<(NH2)/CH2-CH2/CH2-CH2>		CDCL3
1765M	D	3.71	CHR	R5<(OH)/CH(CH3)-CH2/CH2-CH2>		CDCL3
97M	C	5.66	CHR	R5<=CH-CH2/CH2-CH2>		CCL4
2024M	C	6.11	CHR	R5<=C(CL)-CH2/C(=O)-CH2>		CCL4
2204M	B	3.19	CHR	R5((C(=O)-CL)/CH2-CH2/CH2-CH2)		CCL4
1764M	C	4.21	CHR	R5((OH)/CH2-CH2/CH2-CH2)		CCL4
2121M	C	6.67	CHR	R6A<=C(R6<CH-CH2/CH2>)-C(=O)/C(=O)-C*>		CDCL3
197M	C	2.70	CHR	R6A((CH2-CH3)/C*/CH2-CH2)		CCL4
2120M	B	6.85	CHR	R6A(=C(C(CH3/CH3/CH3))-C(=O)/C(=O)-C*)		CDCL3
2372M	A	1.95	CHR	R6NA<CH2-N(C(=O)-CH3)/CH2-C*>		CDCL3
2372M	C	2.72	CHR	R6NA<C*/CH2-CH2>		CDCL3
2372M	D	3.79	CHR	R6NA<N(C(=O)-CH3)-C*/CH2-CH2>		CDCL3
602M	D	3.30	CHR	R6NA<(CH3)/NH-C*/HCH-HCH>		CDCL3
2453M	B	7.21	CHR	R6NN<NH-C(=O)/=C(CH3)-C(=O)>		DMSO-D6
567M	C	2.30- 3.10	CHR	R6NN<(CH3)/NH-CH2/CH2-NH>		CDCL3
2444M	B	4.03	CHR	R6NN<(CH3)/NH-C(=O)/C(=O)-NH>		POLYSOL-D
641M	E	3.67	CHR	R6NN<(CH3)/N(A)-CH2/CH2-NH>		CDCL3
2454M	B	6.02	CHR	R6NN<=C(CH3)-NH/C(=O)-NH>		TFA
2457M	A	7.88	CHR	R6NN<=C(I)-C(=O)/NH-C(=O)>		DMSO
2459M	D	2.33	CHR	R6NN((CH(CH2/CH3))/C(=O)-NH/C(=O)-NH)		DMSO-D6
2452M	D	7.29	CHR	R6NN(=CH-C(=O)/N(CH3)-C(=O))		CDCL3
2452M	C	5.71	CHR	R6NN(=CH-N(CH3)/C(=O)-N(CH3))		CDCL3
2456M	A	7.71	CHR	R6NN(=C(BR)-C(=O)/NH-C(=O))		DMSO
2458M	A	8.80	CHR	R6NN(=C(NO2)-C(=O)/NH-C(=O))		DMSO
1463M	C	3.30- 4.00	CHR	R6NO<(CH3)/O-CH(CH3)/CH2-NH>		CDCL3
563M	B	0.90- 1.80	CHR	R6N<(CH3)/CH2-HCH/CH2-HCH>		CCL4
814M	C	3.10- 3.95	CHR	R6N<(N(CH3/CH3)/CH2-CH2/CH2-CH2>	S	D20
673M	E	5.58	CHR	R6N<=CH-CH2/CH2-CH2>		CCL4
576M	E	5.76 APP.	CHR	R6N<=CH-CH2/CH2-CH2>		CDCL3
576M	E	5.76 APP.	CHR	R6N<=CH-CH2/CH2-NH>		CDCL3
673M	E	5.58	CHR	R6N<=CH-CH2/CH2-N(CH3)>		CCL4
562M	D	2.30- 3.20	CHR	R6N((CH3)/NH-CH2/CH2-CH2)		CCL4
564M	C	2.60	CHR	R6N((CH3)/N-CH(CH3)/CH2-CH2)		CCL4
2958M	B	6.50	CHR	R60A<=C(O-C(=O)-CH3)/C*/C(=O)-O>		CDCL3
2957M	B	7.88	CHR	R60A(C*/=C(CL)-C(=O))		CDCL3
1610M	E	6.40	CHR	R600R6BI<=CH-C*(CH3)/C*((CH(CH3/CH3))/O/CH2)>		CCL4
1610M	D	6.28	CHR	R600R6BI<=CH-C*(CH(CH3/CH3))/C*((CH3)/O/CH2)>		CCL4
1476M	D	4.29	CHR	R600R600SPI<(CH2-CH3)/O-HCH/O-CH2>		CCL4
1475M	D	4.58	CHR	R600R600SPI<(CH3)/O-HCH/O-CH2>		CDCL3
1472M	G	4.28	CHR	R600<(CH2.5-CH3)/O-HCH/O-HCH>		CCL4
2259M	B	2.04- 3.15	CHR	R60<(CH3)/CH2-C(=O)-O/CH2-C(=O)>		CDCL3
1867M	B	4.51	CHR	R60<(OH)/O-CH2/CH(OH)-CH(OH)>		D20
1868M	B	4.68	CHR	R60<(OH)/O-CH2/CH(OH)-CH(OH)>		D20

BOOK NO.	ASSIGN-MENT	CHEM SHIFT - ppm -	PROTON GROUP	ENVIRONMENTAL GROUPS	S	SOLVENT
1867M	C	5.24	CHR	R60<((OH)/O-CH2/CH(OH)-CH(OH)>		D20
1868M	C	5.28	CHR	R60<((OH)/O-CH(OH)-CH(OH)>		D20
1871M	B	4.60	CHR	R60<((OH)/O-CH(CH2-OH)/CH(OH)-CH(OH)>		D20
1871M	C	5.20	CHR	R60<((OH)/O-CH(CH2-OH)/CH(OH)-CH(OH)>		D20
1869M	C	4.81	CHR	R60<((OH)/O-CH(CH3)/CH(OH)-CH(OH)>		D20
1869M	D	5.10	CHR	R60<((OH)/O-CH(CH3)/CH(OH)-CH(OH)>		D20
1460M	D	4.56	CHR	R60<(O-CH2)/O-CH2/CH2-CH2>		CCL4
1874M	B	5.41	CHR	R60<(O-R50)/O-CH(CH2-OH)/CH(OH)-CH(OH)>		D20
756M	F	4.38	CHR	R60<=C(CH3)-O/C(CH3/CH3)-C(C(=O)-O-CH2)=>		CCL4
1872M	B	4.89	CHR	R60((OH)/O-CH(CH2-OH)/CH(OH)-CH(OH))		D20
1872M	C	5.19	CHR	R60((OH)/O-CH(CH2-OH)/CH(OH)-CH(OH))		D20
1461M	D	5.65	CHR	R60(=CH-CH2/CH2-O)		CCL4
1461M	D	5.80	CHR	R60(=CH-CH2/CH2-O)		CCL4
1461M	E	5.65	CHR	R60(=CH-CH2/CH2-O)		CCL4
1461M	E	5.80	CHR	R60(=CH-CH2/CH2-O)		CCL4
1692M	E	6.09	CHR	R60(=C(CH3)-CH2/O-C(CH2-OH/CH3))		CDCL3
1178M	B	7.89	CHR	R6R5NS<=CH-CH=/C*=N>		CDCL3
1178M	A	7.41	CHR	R6R5NS<=CH-CH*/CH=CH>		CDCL3
2268M	C	6.01 APP.	CHR	R6R50<=CH-CH2/CH2-CH*>		CDCL3
773M	D	3.60	CHR	R6R6BI((NH2)/CH*(CH2/CH2)/CH2-CH*)	S	D20
2129M	F	3.49	CHR	R6R6R6R5((OH)/CH2-C*=/CH2-CH2)		CDCL3
1780M	F	5.31	CHR	R6R6R6R5((OH)/CH2-C*/CH2-CH2)		CDCL3
2129M	F	3.49	CHR	R6R6R6R5(=C*-CH2/CH2-CH*)		CDCL3
2130M	G	5.70	CHR	R6R6R6R5(=C*-CH2/C(=O)-CH2)		CDCL3
269M	B	4.25- 4.75	CHR	R6R6R6TRI<(CL)/CH*(CH2/CH2)/CH*(CH2/CH2)>		CDCL3
1778M	B	3.48	CHR	R6R6<(OH)/CH2-CH*/CH2-CH2>		POLYSOL-D
1157M	A	6.53	CHR	R6SS<=C(A)-S/S-C(A)=>		CDCL3
1887M	B	2.47	CHR	R6<(A<C=CH-CH-C(OH)>)/CH2-CH2/CH2-CH2>		CDCL3
1774M	C	1.90- 2.70	CHR	R6<(A)/CH(OH)-HCH/CH2-CH2>		CCL4
2001M	C	2.22 APP.	CHR	R6<(CH3)/C(=O)-CH2/CH2-CH2>		CCL4
271M	A	4.10- 4.90	CHR	R6<(CL)/CH(CL)-CH(CL)/CH(CL)-CH(CL)>		POLYSOL-D
100M	C	1.00- 1.60	CHR	R6<(C(CH2/CH3/CH3))/CH2-CH=/CH2-CH2>		CCL4
2004M	B	1.20- 1.85	CHR	R6<(C(CH3/CH3/CH3))/HCH-CH2/HCH-CH2>		CDCL3
2205M	B	2.71	CHR	R6<(C(=O)-CL)/CH2-CH2/CH2-CH2>		CCL4
2515M	B	2.69	CHR	R6<(C(=O)-OH)/CH2-CH2/CH2-CH2>		TFA
2538M	B	3.09	CHR	R6<(C(=O)-OH)/CH(C(=O)-O)-CH2/CH2-CH=>		C3D60
2788M	C	2.70	CHR	R6<(C(=O)-O-CH2)/CH(C(=O)-O-CH2)-CH2/CH2-CH2>		CCL4
964M	B	2.64	CHR	R6<(C:N)/CH2-CH2/CH2-CH2>		CCL4
965M	B	2.71	CHR	R6<(C:N)/CH2-CH2/CH2-CH2>		CDCL3
422M	C	4.36	CHR	R6<(I)/CH2-CH2/CH2-CH2>		CDCL3
471M	D	2.20- 3.10	CHR	R6<(NH2)/CH2-CH2/CH2-CH2>		CCL4
470M	C	2.64	CHR	R6<(NH2)/CH2-CH2/C-CH2>		CCL4
570M	B	2.42 APP.	CHR	R6<(NH-CH2)/CH2-CH2/CH2-CH2>		POLYSOL-D
2421M	B	3.36	CHR	R6<(NH-C(=O)-NH2)/CH2-CH2/CH2-CH2>		POLYSOL-D
1377M	B	3.00	CHR	R6<(NH-SO2)/CH2-CH2/CH2-CH2>		CCL4
635M	C	2.39 APP.	CHR	R6<(N(CH2/CH2))/CH2-CH2/CH2-CH2>		CDCL3
1028M	B	3.75	CHR	R6<(N(NO/R6))/CH2-CH2/CH2-CH2>		CDCL3
1028M	B	4.83	CHR	R6<(N(NO/R6))/CH2-CH2/CH2-CH2>		CDCL3
1028M	C	3.75	CHR	R6<(N(NO/R6))/CH2-CH2/CH2-CH2>		CDCL3
1028M	C	4.83	CHR	R6<(N(NO/R6))/CH2-CH2/CH2-CH2>		CDCL3
1006M	B	3.60	CHR	R6<(N:C)/CH2-CH2/CH2-CH2>		CDCL3
1768M	D	3.51	CHR	R6<(OH)/CH2-CH2/CH2-CH2>		CDCL3
1769M	D	3.89	CHR	R6<(OH)/CH2-CH2/CH2-CH2>		CCL4
1775M	B	3.20- 4.00	CHR	R6<(OH)/CH(A)-CH2/CH2-CH2>		CDCL3
1774M	D	3.52	CHR	R6<(OH)/CH(A)-CH2/HCH-CH2>		CDCL3
1770M	D	3.19	CHR	R6<(OH)/CH(CH2-CH3)-CH2/CH2-CH2>		CDCL3
1770M	E	3.87	CHR	R6<(OH)/CH(CH2-CH3)-CH2/CH2-CH2>		CDCL3
1771M	C	3.04	CHR	R6<(OH)/CH(CH3)-CH2/CH2-CH2>		CDCL3
1767M	E	3.12	CHR	R6<(OH)/CH(CH3)-CH2/HCH-CH2>		CDCL3
1855M	C	3.75	CHR	R6<(OH)/CH(OH)-CH2/CH2-CH2>		CDCL3
1773M	B	3.43	CHR	R6<(OH)/CH(R6)-CH2/CH2-CH2>		CDCL3
1776M	E	4.55	CHR	R6<(OH)/C(A/A)-CH2/CH2-CH2>		CDCL3
2878M	B	4.99	CHR	R6<(O-C(=O)-A)/CH2-CH2/CH2-CH2>		CCL4
2714M	D	4.68	CHR	R6<(O-C(=O)-CH2)/CH2-CH2/CH2-CH2>		CCL4
2857M	B	4.87	CHR	R6<(O-C(=O)-Q2)/CH2-CH2/CH2-CH2>		CDCL3
883M	B	2.80 APP.	CHR	R6<(QN(N(CH3/CH3)))/CH2-CH2/CH2-CH2>		CDCL3
2121M	B	2.90	CHR	R6<(R6A<CH=CH/C(=O)>)/CH2-CH2/CH2-CH2>		CCL4
2158M	B	5.68	CHR	R6<=CH-CH2/CH2-CH2>		CCL4
99M	C	5.58	CHR	R6<=CH-CH2/CH2-CH2>		CCL4
101M	D	5.61	CHR	R6<=CH-CH2/CH2-CH2>		CCL4
100M	E	5.48	CHR	R6<=CH-CH2/CH2-CH2>		CCL4
100M	E	5.48	CHR	R6<=CH-CH2/CH2-CH(C(CH2/CH3/CH3))>		CCL4
2158M	B	5.68	CHR	R6<=CH-CH2/CH2-CH(C(=O)-H)>		C3D60
2538M	C	5.69	CHR	R6<=CH-CH2/CH2-CH(C(=O)-OH)>		CCL4
101M	D	5.61	CHR	R6<=CH-CH2/CH2-CH(Q3)>		CDCL3
113M	B	5.68	CHR	R6<=CH-CH2/CH2-CH=>		CDCL3
112M	B	5.83	CHR	R6<=CH-CH/CH=CH>		CCL4
2025M	B	5.88	CHR	R6<=CH-CH2/C(=O)-CH2>		CDCL3
112M	B	5.83	CHR	R6<=CH-CH=/CH2-CH2>		CCL4
2025M	C	6.91	CHR	R6<=CH-C(=O)/CH2-CH2>		CDCL3
2030M	C	6.78	CHR	R6<=CH-C(=O)/C(=O)-CH=>		CDCL3

BOOK NO.	ASSIGN-MENT	CHEM SHIFT - ppm -	PROTON GROUP	ENVIRONMENTAL GROUPS	S	SOLVENT
2030M	C	6.78	CHR	R6<=CH-C(=0)/C(=0)-C(CH3)=>		CDCL3
184M	D	5.98	CHR	R6<=C(A<C-CH-CH-C(CH3)>)-CH2/CH2-CH2>		CCL4
175M	D	5.49	CHR	R6<=C(A<C-C-C(CH3)>)-CH2/CH2-CH2>		CCL4
146M	C	6.01	CHR	R6<=C(A)-CH2/CH2-CH2>		CCL4
103M	D	5.23	CHR	R6<=C(CH2-CH3)-CH2/CH2-CH2>		CCL4
102M	C	5.30 APP.	CHR	R6<=C(CH3)-CH2/CH2-CH2>		CCL4
2027M	D	5.71	CHR	R6<=C(CH3)-CH2/C(=0)-CH2>		CCL4
2030M	B	6.63	CHR	R6<=C(CH3)-C(=0)/C(=0)-CH=>		CDCL3
2285M	D	5.66	CHR	R6<=C(CH(C(=0)/CH2))-CH2/CH2-CH2>		CDCL3
2026M	C	6.07	CHR	R6<=C(CL)-CH2/C(=0)-CH2>		CCL4
2029M	D	6.09	CHR	R6<=C(CL)-CH2/C(=0)-CH2>		CCL4
2022M	D	6.78	CHR	R6<=C(C(=0)-CH3)-CH2/CH2-CH2>		CCL4
1873M	B	4.60	CHR	R6(OH/O-CH/CH(OH))		D20
1873M	C	5.30	CHR	R6(OH/O-CH/CH(OH))		D20
183M	B	2.45	CHR	R6((A(C-CH-CH-C(R6)))/CH2-CH2/CH2-CH2)		CDCL3
145M	B	2.40 APP.	CHR	R6((A)/CH2-CH2/CH2-CH2)		CCL4
365M	B	4.13	CHR	R6((BR)/CH2-CH2/CH2-CH2)		CCL4
367M	B	4.32	CHR	R6((BR)/CH2-CH2/CH2-CH2)		CDCL3
366M	C	4.52	CHR	R6((BR)/CH2-CH(CH3)/CH2-CH2)		CCL4
2003M	B	1.18- 2.28	CHR	R6(CH3)/CH2-CH2/CH2-CH2)		CCL4
267M	B	3.95	CHR	R6((CL)/CH2-CH2/CH2-CH2)		CCL4
2084M	B	3.25	CHR	R6((C(=0)-A)/CH2-CH2/CH2-CH2)		CDCL3
970M	B	2.71 APP.	CHR	R6((C:N)/CH2-CH=/CH2-CH2)		CCL4
586M	B	3.21	CHR	R6((NH-A)/CH2-CH2/CH2-CH2)		CDCL3
1217M	C	2.29	CHR	R6((NH-CH2.2)/CH2-CH2/CH2-CH2)		CDCL3
559M	C	2.49	CHR	R6((NH-CH)/CH2-CH2/CH2-CH2)		CDCL3
1045M	B	4.29	CHR	R6((NO2)/CH2-CH2/CH2-CH2)		CCL4
924M	B	3.17	CHR	R6((N=C=N)/CH2-CH2/CH2-CH2)		CDCL3
1856M	B	3.30- 3.90	CHR	R6((OH)/CH2-CH2/CH2-CH2)		D20
1766M	B	3.49	CHR	R6((OH)/CH2-CH2/CH2-CH2)		CCL4
2912M	B	5.16	CHR	R6((O-C(=0)-A)/CH2-CH2/CH2-CH2)		CDCL3
2715M	D	4.70	CHR	R6((O-C(=0)-CH2)/CH2-CH2/CH2-CH2)		CCL4
2988M	B	4.79	CHR	R6((O-C(=0)-NH)/CH2-CH2/CH2-CH2)		CDCL3
970M	C	5.65	CHR	R6(=CH-CH2/CH2-CH2)		CCL4
970M	C	5.65	CHR	R6(=CH-CH2/CH2-CH(C:N))		CCL4
1808M	D	5.30	CHR	R6(=C(CH3)-CH2/CH2-CH(C(OH/CH3/CH3)))		CCL4
111M	E	5.39	CHR	R6(=C(CH3)-CH2/CH2-CH(Q2(CH3)))		CCL4
2031M	D	6.40	CHR	R6(=C(C(CH2/CH3))-C(=0)/C(=0)-CH=)		CDCL3
2210M	C	7.39	CHR	R6(=C(C(=0)-CL)-CH2/CH2-CH2)		CCL4
2535M	C	7.09 APP.	CHR	R6(=C(C(=0)-OH)-CH2/CH2-CH2)		CCL4
971M	C	6.58	CHR	R6(=C(C:N)-CH2/CH2-CH2)		CCL4
2144M	C	5.41	CHR	R6(=C(OH)-CH2/C(=0)-CH2)		CDCL3
105M	C	5.70 APP.	CHR	R6(=C(R6)-CH2/CH2-CH2)		CCL4
1772M	E	3.38	CHR	R6)(OH)/CH(CH(CH3/CH3))-CH2/CH2-CH(CH3))		CDCL3
472M	C	2.92	CHR	R7<(NH2)/CH2-CH2-CH2-CH2>		CDCL3
1777M	C	3.80	CHR	R7<(OH)/CH2-CH2/CH2-CH2>		CDCL3
1857M	B	3.77	CHR	R8<(OH)/CH2-CH2/CH2-CH2>		D20
2713M	C	4.83	CHR	R8<(O-C(=0)-CH3)/CH2-CH2/CH2-CH2>		CCL4
114M	B	5.48	CHR	R8<=CH-CH2/CH2-CH2>		CCL4
2536M	B	5.67 APP.	CHR	R8(=CH-CH2/CH2-CH2)		CDCL3
1873M	A	3.30- 4.30	CHR	UNSPECIFIED		D20
201M	B	3.03	CH2	AA<C-C*>/CH3		CCL4
1954M	B	3.37	CH2	AA<C-C*/C(OH)>/CH2-C:N		POLYSOL-D
998M	A	4.02	CH2	AA(C-CH-C*/CH-CH-C*)/C:N		POLYSOL-D
1725M	A	3.09	CH2	AA(C-C*/CH2-OH)		CCL4
1732M	A	3.22	CH2	ANN<C-N-CH-C(A)/N>/CH2-OH		CDCL3
685M	B	2.59	CH2	AN<C-CH-CH-N>/CH3		CCL4
713M	A	2.93	CH2	AN<C-CH-N>/CH2-AN		CDCL3
687M	D	2.73	CH2	AN<C-N>/CH2-CH2		CCL4
712M	C	3.62	CH2	AN<C-N>/R6N<N-CH2/CH2>		CDCL3
688M	C	2.57	CH2	AN(C-CH-CH-N)/CH2-CH2		CCL4
693M	C	2.60	CH2	AN(C-CH-N/CH-C(CH2.3-CH3))		CDCL3
845M	A	5.43	CH2	AN(N(+))/CH2-AN		D20
843M	D	4.71	CH2	AN(N(+))/CH2-CH2	S	DMSO-D6
1312M	E	4.61	CH2	AN(N)/CH2-CH2	S	CDCL3
173M	A	2.97	CH2	A<C-CH-CH-C(A)>/CH2-A	S	CDCL3
2218M	C	2.27	CH2	A<C-CH-CH-C(BR)>/CH2-CH2		CDCL3
2218M	C	2.57	CH2	A<C-CH-CH-C(BR)>/CH2-CH2		CDCL3
529M	A	2.61	CH2	A<C-CH-CH-C(NH2)>/CH2-NH2		CDCL3
1718M	A	2.63	CH2	A<C-CH-CH-C(NH2)>/CH2-OH		POLYSOL-D
1050M	B	2.74	CH2	A<C-CH-CH-C(NO2)>/CH3		CCL4
666M	B	3.78	CH2	A<C-CH-CH-C(N(CH3/CH3))>/A<C-CH-CH-C(N(CH3/CH3))>		CDCL3
918M	A	3.87	CH2	A<C-CH-CH-C(N=C=0)>/A<C-CH-CH-C(N=C=0)>		POLYSOL-D
1888M	A	3.70	CH2	A<C-CH-CH-C(OH)>/A<C-CH-CH-C(OH)>		DMSO-D6
1884M	D	2.48	CH2	A<C-CH-CH-C(OH)>/CH2.3-CH3		CCL4
1902M	B	2.75	CH2	A<C-CH-CH-C(OH)>/CH2-C:N		CDCL3
1503M	A	3.03	CH2	A<C-CH-CH-C(O-CH3)>/CH2-BR		CCL4
1501M	C	2.50	CH2	A<C-CH-CH-C(O-CH3)>/CH2-CH2		CCL4
1497M	B	2.53	CH2	A<C-CH-CH-C(O-CH3)>/CH3		CCL4
179M	B	2.58	CH2	A<C-CH-C(CH2-CH3)>/CH3		CCL4
190M	B	2.55	CH2	A<C-CH-C(CH2-CH3)/CH-C(CH2-CH3)>/CH3		CCL4

BOOK NO.	ASSIGN-MENT	CHEM SHIFT - ppm -	PROTON GROUP	ENVIRONMENTAL GROUPS	S	SOLVENT
178M	C	2.60	CH2	A<C-CH-C(CH3)>/CH3		CDCL3
1933M	C	2.57	CH2	A<C-CH-C(C(CH3/CH3/CH3))-C(OH)/CH-C(CH2-A)>		CDCL3
492M	B	2.52	CH2	A<C-CH-C(NH2)>/CH3		CDCL3
1880M	B	2.55	CH2	A<C-CH-C(OH)>/CH3		CDCL3
1560M	A	3.25	CH2	A<C-CH-C(O-CH3)-C(O-CH3)>/Q3		CCL4
375M	B	2.74	CH2	A<C-C(BR)>/CH3		CCL4
295M	B	2.73	CH2	A<C-C(CL)>/CH3		CCL4
2560M	C	2.87	CH2	A<C-C(NH2)>/CH2.2-C(=O)-OH	S	D20
538M	B	2.43	CH2	A<C-C(NH2)-C(CH2-CH3)-C(NH2)>/CH3		CDCL3
503M	C	2.40	CH2	A<C-C(NH2)-C(CH2-CH3)/CH-C(CH3)>/CH3		CCL4
500M	C	2.42	CH2	A<C-C(NH2)-C(CH3)>/CH3		CDCL3
929M	B	2.80	CH2	A<C-C(N=C=N)-C(CH2-CH3)>/CH3		CDCL3
1879M	B	2.57	CH2	A<C-C(OH)>/CH3		CCL4
1932M	B	3.36	CH2	A<C-C(OH)-CH-C(CH3)/C(CH3)>/Q3		CDCL3
1928M	C	2.50	CH2	A<C-C(OH)-CH-C(OH)>/CH2.14-CH3		POLYSOL-D
1927M	C	2.45	CH2	A<C-C(OH)-CH-C(OH)>/CH2-CH2		CDCL3
1933M	D	3.90	CH2	A<C-C(OH)-C(C(CH3/CH3/CH3))/CH-C(CH2-CH3)>/ A<C-C(OH)-C(C(CH3/CH3/CH3))/CH-C(CH2-CH3)>		CDCL3
185M	B	2.86	CH2	A(C-CH-CH-C(CH3))/CH2-A		CDCL3
786M	B	3.02	CH2	A(C-CH-CH-C(CL))/C(NH2/CH3/CH3)	S	D20
2059M	C	2.65	CH2	A(C-CH-CH-C(C(=O)-CH3))/CH3		CCL4
530M	A	3.57	CH2	A(C-CH-CH-C(NH2))/A(C-CH-CH-C(NH2))		DMSO-D6
2324M	C	2.56	CH2	A(C-CH-CH-C(NH-C(=O)))/CH3		CDCL3
2038M	A	2.11	CH2	A(C-CH-CH-C(OH))/CH2-C(=O)		CDCL3
1924M	A	3.21	CH2	A(C-CH-C(O-CH3)-C(OH))/Q3		CCL4
172M	C	2.59	CH2	A(C-C(A(C-CH-CH-C(CH3))))/CH3		CCL4
1227M	C	3.75	CH2	A(C-C(CH2-SH)-CH-C(CH3)/CH-C(CH3))/SH		CDCL3
491M	B	2.40	CH2	A(C-C(NH2))/CH3		CDCL3
1049M	B	2.88	CH2	A(C-C(NO2))/CH3		CCL4
1929M	A	3.80	CH2	A(C-C(OH)-CH-C(OH))/A		DMSO-D6
1936M	C	3.81	CH2	A(C-C(OH)-C(C(CH3/CH3/CH3))/CH-C(CH3))/A(C-C(OH)-C(CH2-A)/CH-C(CH3))		CDCL3
148M	A	3.82	CH2	A/A		CCL4
2544M	A	2.60- 3.30	CH2	A/CHNC(=O)-OH/CH2)/A		CDCL3
2849M	C	2.61	CH2	A/CH2.2-C(=O)-O		CCL4
149M	A	2.89	CH2	A/CH2-A		CDCL3
173M	A	2.97	CH2	A/CH2-A		CDCL3
785M	C	2.83	CH2	A/CH2-CH	S	TFA
1702M	B	2.62	CH2	A/CH2-CH2		CCL4
147M	B	2.70	CH2	A/CH2-CH2		CDCL3
143M	C	2.57	CH2	A/CH2-CH2		CCL4
141M	C	2.58	CH2	A/CH2-CH2		CCL4
137M	C	2.58	CH2	A/CH2-CH2		CCL4
481M	C	2.64	CH2	A/CH2-CH2		CDCL3
1164M	C	2.69	CH2	A/CH2-CH2		CCL4
1164M	C	2.80	CH2	A/CH2-CH2		CCL4
142M	D	2.59	CH2	A/CH2-CH2		CDCL3
482M	D	2.60	CH2	A/CH2-CH2		CCL4
135M	C	2.58	CH2	A/CH2-CH3		CDCL3
2088M	A	3.08	CH2	A/CH2-C(=O)		CDCL3
2088M	A	3.20	CH2	A/CH2-C(=O)		CDCL3
2036M	C	2.81	CH2	A/CH2-C(=O)		CCL4
2212M	A	2.89	CH2	A/CH2-C(=O)-CL		CCL4
2159M	B	2.89	CH2	A/CH2-C(=O)-H		CDCL3
2540M	B	2.93	CH2	A/CH2-C(=O)-OH		CDCL3
973M	B	2.73	CH2	A/CH2-C:N		CDCL3
424M	A	3.08	CH2	A/CH2-I		CDCL3
2311M	A	2.83	CH2	A/CH2-NH		CDCL3
2986M	B	2.73	CH2	A/CH2-NH		CCL4
2309M	B	2.79	CH2	A/CH2-NH		CDCL3
2986M	B	3.32	CH2	A/CH2-NH		CCL4
477M	B	2.68 APP.	CH2	A/CH2-NH2		CCL4
1484M	A	2.73	CH2	A/CH2-O		CDCL3
1485M	B	2.71	CH2	A/CH2-O		CCL4
1701M	B	2.77	CH2	A/CH2-OH		CDCL3
2860M	A	2.79	CH2	A/CH2-O-C(=O)		CCL4
2831M	A	2.90	CH2	A/CH2-O-C(=O)		CCL4
2862M	A	2.94	CH2	A/CH2-O-C(=O)		CCL4
2866M	A	2.96	CH2	A/CH2-O-C(=O)		CCL4
2891M	A	3.07	CH2	A/CH2-O-C(=O)		CDCL3
2835M	C	2.88	CH2	A/CH2-O-C(=O)		CCL4
2836M	C	2.89	CH2	A/CH2-O-C(=O)		CCL4
2838M	D	2.85	CH2	A/CH2-O-C(=O)		CCL4
155M	B	2.67	CH2	A/CH2-Q3		CDCL3
2385M	A	2.87	CH2	A/CH2-R5N		POLYSOL-D
2014M	A	2.43	CH2	A/CH2-R6N		CDCL3
1163M	A	2.90	CH2	A/CH2-S		CDCL3
134M	B	2.53	CH2	A/CH3		CCL4
151M	A	3.35	CH2	A/CH(A/A)		CDCL3
152M	A	2.50- 3.30	CH2	A/CH(A/CH)		CDCL3
139M	C	2.39	CH2	A/CH(CH3/CH3)		CDCL3

BOOK NO.	ASSIGN-MENT	CHEM SHIFT - ppm -	PROTON GROUP	ENVIRONMENTAL GROUPS	S	SOLVENT
2308M	A	2.82	CH2	A/CH(NH/CH2)		DMSO-D6
804M	D	3.51	CH2	A/CH(NH/CH3)	S	CDCL3
2146M	D	3.43	CH2	A/C(=0)-CH2		CCL4
2539M	A	3.61	CH2	A/C(=0)-OH		CDCL3
2146M	D	3.43	CH2	A/C(=0)-Q1		CCL4
972M	A	3.62	CH2	A/C:N		CCL4
2146M	E	3.60	CH2	A/Q1(OH/C(=0)-CH3)		CCL4
154M	B	3.27	CH2	A/Q2(CH3)		CCL4
144M	C	2.53	CH2	A/R3		CDCL3
2462M	A	3.30	CH2	A/R6NN(C(CH2-A)-C(=0)/C(=0))		DMSO-D6
371M	A	4.34	CH2	BR/A		CCL4
373M	B	4.32	CH2	BR/A<C-CH-CH-C(CH3)>		CCL4
395M	A	4.33	CH2	BR/A<C-CH-C(BR)>		CDCL3
372M	B	4.39	CH2	BR/A(C-C(CH3))		CCL4
346M	A	4.94	CH2	BR/BR		CCL4
339M	D	3.35	CH2	BR/CH2.14-CH3		CCL4
340M	D	3.41	CH2	BR/CH2.15-CH3		CDCL3
1640M	B	3.51	CH2	BR/CH2.2-OH		CDCL3
364M	B	3.30	CH2	BR/CH2.2-R6		CCL4
2197M	C	3.40	CH2	BR/CH2.4-C(=0)-CL		CCL4
1503M	B	3.41	CH2	BR/CH2-A		CCL4
348M	A	3.68	CH2	BR/CH2-BR		CDCL3
379M	B	2.75- 3.40	CH2	BR/CH2-CH		CCL4
328M	C	3.33	CH2	BR/CH2-CH		CCL4
358M	C	3.52	CH2	BR/CH2-CH		CCL4
360M	B	3.38	CH2	BR/CH2-CH2		CCL4
359M	B	3.41	CH2	BR/CH2-CH2		CCL4
354M	B	3.51	CH2	BR/CH2-CH2		CCL4
362M	C	3.37	CH2	BR/CH2-CH2		CCL4
957M	C	3.40	CH2	BR/CH2-CH2		CCL4
338M	D	3.31	CH2	BR/CH2-CH2		CCL4
335M	D	3.32	CH2	BR/CH2-CH2		CCL4
326M	D	3.33	CH2	BR/CH2-CH2		CCL4
332M	D	3.33	CH2	BR/CH2-CH2		CCL4
336M	D	3.34	CH2	BR/CH2-CH2		CCL4
337M	D	3.34	CH2	BR/CH2-CH2		CCL4
333M	D	3.35	CH2	BR/CH2-CH2		CCL4
330M	D	3.38	CH2	BR/CH2-CH2		CCL4
322M	D	3.39	CH2	BR/CH2-CH2		CCL4
341M	D	3.39	CH2	BR/CH2-CH2		CDCL3
320M	C	3.36	CH2	BR/CH2-CH3		CCL4
343M	A	3.56	CH2	BR/CH2-CL		CCL4
2196M	A	3.51 APP.	CH2	BR/CH2-C(=0)		CCL4
956M	B	3.53	CH2	BR/CH2-C:N		CCL4
1491M	A	3.52	CH2	BR/CH2-0		CDCL3
1639M	A	3.45	CH2	BR/CH2-OH		CCL4
1296M	B	3.66	CH2	BR/CH2-SO3	S	D20
319M	B	3.34	CH2	BR/CH3		CCL4
351M	A	4.09	CH2	BR/CH(BR/BR)		CCL4
355M	A	3.82	CH2	BR/CH(BR/CH2)		CCL4
344M	C	3.55	CH2	BR/CH(CH2/CH3)		CDCL3
324M	C	3.24	CH2	BR/CH(CH3/CH3)		CCL4
1751M	B	3.59	CH2	BR/CH(OH/CH2)		CDCL3
1426M	B	3.28	CH2	BR/CH(0/0)		CCL4
349M	A	4.02	CH2	BR/C(BR/F2)		CCL4
1841M	A	3.56	CH2	BR/C(CH2/CH2/CH2)		POLYSOL-D
329M	B	3.15	CH2	BR/C(CH3/CH3/CH3)		CCL4
350M	A	4.40	CH2	BR/C(CL/CL/CL)		CCL4
2053M	A	4.43	CH2	BR/C(=0)-A		CDCL3
2062M	B	4.39	CH2	BR/C(=0)-A		CDCL3
2844M	A	3.83	CH2	BR/C(=0)-CH2		CDCL3
2485M	A	3.92	CH2	BR/C(=0)-OH		CDCL3
2728M	A	3.77	CH2	BR/C(=0)-0-CH3		CCL4
369M	A	3.99	CH2	BR/Q2(CH2-BR)		CDCL3
368M	A	3.88	CH2	BR/Q3		CCL4
1444M	C	3.22	CH2	BR/R30<CH-0/HCH>		CCL4
2393M	A	5.54	CH2	BR/R5NA<N-C(=0)/C(=0)>		CDCL3
2354M	C	1.58	CH2	CH2.N/CH3		CDCL3
693M	B	1.10- 1.90	CH2	CH2.2-AN/CH3		CDCL3
1884M	B	1.10- 1.50	CH2	CH2.2-A/CH2-CH3		CCL4
689M	B	0.95- 1.50	CH2	CH2.2-CH/CH3		CCL4
2732M	C	1.10- 1.70	CH2	CH2.2-CH/CH3		CDCL3
2060M	B	1.00- 2.05	CH2	CH2.2-C(=0)-A/CH3		CDCL3
2071M	B	1.10- 2.00	CH2	CH2.2-C(=0)-A/CH3		CDCL3
1969M	B	1.35 APP.	CH2	CH2.2-C(=0)-CH3/CH3		CCL4
2252M	B	1.10- 1.55	CH2	CH2.2-C(=0)-0/CH2-CH3		CDCL3
2041M	B	1.00- 2.00	CH2	CH2.2-C(=0)-Q2/CH3		CDCL3
407M	B	1.40 APP.	CH2	CH2.2-I/CH3		CCL4
779M	A	1.50 APP.	CH2	CH2.2-NH2/CH2.3-NH2	S	D20
768M	B	1.10- 2.20	CH2	CH2.2-NH2/CH3	S	CDCL3
1215M	B	1.10- 1.80	CH2	CH2.2-NH/CH3		CDCL3

BOOK NO.	ASSIGN-MENT	CHEM SHIFT - ppm -	PROTON GROUP	ENVIRONMENTAL GROUPS	S	SOLVENT
799M	B	1.00- 2.00	CH2	CH2.2-NH/CH3	S	D2O
828M	B	1.10- 2.00	CH2	CH2.2-N(+)/CH3		CDCL3
931M	B	1.20- 2.10	CH2	CH2.2-N=C=S/CH3		CCL4
1652M	B	1.10- 1.80	CH2	CH2.2-N/CH3		CDCL3
1653M	B	1.10- 1.60	CH2	CH2.2-N/CH3		CDCL3
2351M	C	1.10- 1.90	CH2	CH2.2-N/CH3		CDCL3
2765M	B	1.00- 2.00	CH2	CH2.2-O-C(=O)-O/CH3		CDCL3
2743M	B	1.00- 1.85	CH2	CH2.2-O-C(=O)/CH3		CCL4
2896M	B	1.10- 2.00	CH2	CH2.2-O-C(=O)/CH3		CDCL3
2847M	B	1.10- 1.90	CH2	CH2.2-O-C(=O)/CH3		CCL4
2766M	B	1.10- 2.05	CH2	CH2.2-O-C(=O)/CH3		CDCL3
2775M	B	1.10- 1.80	CH2	CH2.2-O-C(=O)/CH3		CCL4
1082M	B	1.10- 1.60	CH2	CH2.2-O-NO2/CH2-CH3		CDCL3
1327M	B	1.00- 1.60	CH2	CH2.2-O-SO3-NA/CH2-CH3		D2O
1599M	B	1.00- 1.70	CH2	CH2.2-O/CH3		CCL4
1965M	B	1.10- 2.00	CH2	CH2.2-O/CH3		CDCL3
1413M	B	1.10- 1.70	CH2	CH2.2-O/CH3		CCL4
1380M	B	1.10- 1.75	CH2	CH2.2-O/CH3		CDCL3
1562M	B	1.15- 2.08	CH2	CH2.2-O/CH3		CDCL3
1382M	C	1.20- 1.80	CH2	CH2.2-O/CH3		CCL4
160M	B	1.10- 1.80	CH2	CH2.2-Q1/CH3		CCL4
2433M	B	1.10- 1.65	CH2	CH2.2-R5NN/CH3		CDCL3
1254M	B	1.15- 2.15	CH2	CH2.2-SO2/CH3		CCL4
1281M	B	1.50	CH2	CH2.2-SO2/CH3		CDCL3
1315M	B	1.10- 2.10	CH2	CH2.2-SO3/CH3		CCL4
1187M	B	1.10- 1.60	CH2	CH2.2-S/CH2-CH3		CCL4
1884M	B	1.10- 1.50	CH2	CH2.3-A/CH3		CCL4
2252M	B	1.10- 1.55	CH2	CH2.3-C(=O)-O/CH3		CDCL3
1082M	B	1.10- 1.60	CH2	CH2.3-O-NO2/CH3		CDCL3
1327M	B	1.00- 1.60	CH2	CH2.3-O-SO3-NA/CH3		D2O
1187M	B	1.10- 1.60	CH2	CH2.3-S/CH3		CCL4
553M	C	1.27	CH2	CH2.8		CCL4
687M	C	1.72 APP.	CH2	CH2-AN/CH2-CH2		CDCL3
1312M	C	1.82	CH2	CH2-AN/CH2-CH2	S	DMSO-D6
843M	C	1.98	CH2	CH2-AN/CH2-CH2	S	CDCL3
693M	B	1.10- 1.90	CH2	CH2-AN/CH2-CH3		CCL4
1884M	C	1.52	CH2	CH2-A/CH2.2-CH3		CCL4
482M	B	1.49 APP.	CH2	CH2-A/CH2-CH2		CDCL3
142M	C	1.59	CH2	CH2-A/CH2-CH2		CCL4
137M	B	1.10- 1.80	CH2	CH2-A/CH2-CH3		CCL4
1501M	B	1.10- 1.92	CH2	CH2-A/CH3		CDCL3
135M	B	1.63	CH2	CH2-A/CH3		CCL4
339M	C	1.86	CH2	CH2-BR/CH2.13-CH3		CDCL3
340M	C	1.88	CH2	CH2-BR/CH2.14-CH3		CCL4
354M	A	2.36	CH2	CH2-BR/CH2-BR		CCL4
359M	A	2.04	CH2	CH2-BR/CH2-CH2		CCL4
362M	B	1.89 APP.	CH2	CH2-BR/CH2-CH2		CDCL3
341M	C	1.80	CH2	CH2-BR/CH2-CH2		CCL4
338M	C	1.84	CH2	CH2-BR/CH2-CH2		CCL4
326M	C	1.85	CH2	CH2-BR/CH2-CH2		CCL4
332M	C	1.85	CH2	CH2-BR/CH2-CH2		CCL4
335M	C	1.86	CH2	CH2-BR/CH2-CH2		CCL4
333M	C	1.87	CH2	CH2-BR/CH2-CH2		CCL4
336M	C	1.87	CH2	CH2-BR/CH2-CH2		CCL4
337M	C	1.87	CH2	CH2-BR/CH2-CH2		CCL4
330M	C	1.88	CH2	CH2-BR/CH2-CH2		CCL4
322M	C	1.82	CH2	CH2-BR/CH2-CH3		CCL4
1640M	A	2.10	CH2	CH2-BR/CH2-OH		CDCL3
320M	B	1.89	CH2	CH2-BR/CH3		CCL4
331M	C	1.60 APP.	CH2	CH2-CH		CCL4
2501M	A	1.35	CH2	CH2-CH2/CH2-CH2		DMSO-D6
1127M	A	1.42	CH2	CH2-CH2/CH2-CH2		CCL4
420M	A	1.50	CH2	CH2-CH2/CH2-CH2		CCL4
362M	A	1.52 APP.	CH2	CH2-CH2/CH2-CH2		CCL4
963M	A	1.69	CH2	CH2-CH2/CH2-CH2		CDCL3
2174M	B	1.10- 1.60	CH2	CH2-CH2/CH2-CH3		CCL4
326M	B	1.16- 1.70	CH2	CH2-CH2/CH2-CH3		CCL4
2M	B	1.25	CH2	CH2-CH2/CH2-CH3		CCL4
2721M	B	1.35 APP.	CH2	CH2-CH2/CH2-CH3		CDCL3
687M	B	1.37 APP.	CH2	CH2-CH2/CH2-CH3		CCL4
240M	B	1.18- 2.01	CH2	CH2-CH2/CH2/CH3		CCL4
1668M	B	0.65- 1.90	CH2	CH2-CH2/CH3		CDCL3
2066M	B	1.00- 2.00	CH2	CH2-CH2/CH3		CDCL3
1675M	B	1.06- 1.78	CH2	CH2-CH2/CH3		CCL4
1322M	B	1.08- 2.70	CH2	CH2-CH2/CH3		D2O
2297M	B	1.10- 1.70	CH2	CH2-CH2/CH3		CCL4
236M	B	1.10- 2.00	CH2	CH2-CH2/CH3		CCL4
137M	B	1.10- 1.80	CH2	CH2-CH2/CH3		CCL4
651M	B	1.10- 1.85	CH2	CH2-CH2/CH3		CDCL3
1978M	B	1.10- 1.90	CH2	CH2-CH2/CH3		CCL4
1614M	B	1.10- 1.70	CH2	CH2-CH2/CH3		CCL4

BOOK NO.	ASSIGN-MENT	CHEM SHIFT - ppm -	PROTON GROUP	ENVIRONMENTAL GROUPS	S	SOLVENT
2174M	B	1.10- 1.60	CH2	CH2-CH2/CH3		CCL4
1414M	B	1.10- 1.72	CH2	CH2-CH2/CH3		CCL4
1404M	B	1.10- 1.80	CH2	CH2-CH2/CH3		CCL4
1384M	B	1.10- 1.70	CH2	CH2-CH2/CH3		CCL4
2429M	B	1.10- 1.70	CH2	CH2-CH2/CH3		CDCL3
2250M	B	1.11- 1.97	CH2	CH2-CH2/CH3		CDCL3
1245M	B	1.11- 2.08	CH2	CH2-CH2/CH3		CDCL3
2982M	B	1.12- 1.64	CH2	CH2-CH2/CH3		CCL4
2792M	B	1.14- 1.95	CH2	CH2-CH2/CH3		CCL4
326M	B	1.16- 1.70	CH2	CH2-CH2/CH3		CCL4
1009M	B	1.16- 2.13	CH2	CH2-CH2/CH3		CCL4
441M	B	1.17- 1.57	CH2	CH2-CH2/CH3		CDCL3
544M	B	1.17- 1.63	CH2	CH2-CH2/CH3		D20
2917M	B	1.17- 1.89	CH2	CH2-CH2/CH3		C3D60
240M	B	1.18- 2.01	CH2	CH2-CH2/CH3		CCL4
118M	B	1.18- 1.65	CH2	CH2-CH2/CH3		CCL4
2908M	B	1.18- 1.93	CH2	CH2-CH2/CH3		CCL4
2959M	B	1.19- 2.05	CH2	CH2-CH2/CH3		CCL4
1534M	B	1.19- 2.08	CH2	CH2-CH2/CH3		CCL4
2902M	B	1.20- 2.08	CH2	CH2-CH2/CH3		CCL4
1183M	B	1.20- 2.14	CH2	CH2-CH2/CH3		CDCL3
1417M	B	1.20- 1.70	CH2	CH2-CH2/CH3		CCL4
70M	B	1.20- 1.60	CH2	CH2-CH2/CH3		CCL4
2M	B	1.25	CH2	CH2-CH2/CH3		CCL4
1M	B	1.25 APP.	CH2	CH2-CH2/CH3		CCL4
1104M	B	1.26	CH2	CH2-CH2/CH3		CDCL3
1103M	B	1.27	CH2	CH2-CH2/CH3		CDCL3
120M	B	1.30	CH2	CH2-CH2/CH3		CCL4
617M	B	1.30	CH2	CH2-CH2/CH3		CCL4
688M	B	1.33 APP.	CH2	CH2-CH2/CH3		CCL4
57M	B	1.35	CH2	CH2-CH2/CH3		CCL4
2721M	B	1.35 APP.	CH2	CH2-CH2/CH3		CDCL3
687M	B	1.37 APP.	CH2	CH2-CH2/CH3		CCL4
334M	B	1.38	CH2	CH2-CH2/CH3		CDCL3
2366M	B	1.38	CH2	CH2-CH2/CH3		CCL4
2438M	B	1.39	CH2	CH2-CH2/CH3		CCL4
2161M	B	1.40	CH2	CH2-CH2/CH3		CCL4
2349M	B	1.41	CH2	CH2-CH2/CH3		CCL4
579M	B	1.41 APP.	CH2	CH2-CH2/CH3		CCL4
322M	B	1.43 APP.	CH2	CH2-CH2/CH3		CCL4
2717M	B	1.45	CH2	CH2-CH2/CH3		CCL4
1110M	B	1.47	CH2	CH2-CH2/CH3		CCL4
1421M	B	1.48	CH2	CH2-CH2/CH3		CCL4
2767M	B	1.50	CH2	CH2-CH2/CH3		CCL4
800M	B	1.53	CH2	CH2-CH2/CH3		D20
946M	B	1.59	CH2	CH2-CH2/CH3		CCL4
946M	B	1.59	CH2	CH2-CH2/CH3		CCL4
2894M	B	1.60	CH2	CH2-CH2/CH3		CCL4
2890M	B	1.62 APP.	CH2	CH2-CH2/CH3		CCL4
832M	B	1.19- 2.10	CH2	CH2-CH2/CH3	S	CDCL3
2990M	C	1.10- 1.70	CH2	CH2-CH2/CH3		CCL4
71M	C	1.10- 1.70	CH2	CH2-CH2/CH3		CCL4
2984M	C	1.20- 1.75	CH2	CH2-CH2/CH3		CCL4
2702M	C	1.26- 1.84	CH2	CH2-CH2/CH3		CCL4
1424M	C	1.30- 1.69	CH2	CH2-CH2/CH3		CCL4
2998M	C	1.30- 1.91	CH2	CH2-CH2/CH3		CCL4
1755M	C	1.38 APP.	CH2	CH2-CH2/CH3		CCL4
2701M	C	1.54 APP.	CH2	CH2-CH2/CH3		CCL4
1244M	C	1.63 APP.	CH2	CH2-CH2/CH3		CCL4
547M	D	1.17- 1.65	CH2	CH2-CH2/CH3		CDCL3
1M	B	1.25 APP.	CH2	CH2-CH3/CH2-CH3		CCL4
689M	B	0.95- 1.50	CH2	CH2-CH/CH2-CH3		CCL4
2732M	C	1.10- 1.70	CH2	CH2-CH/CH2-CH3		CDCL3
327M	B	1.10- 2.10	CH2	CH2-CH/CH3		CCL4
2191M	B	1.10- 2.10	CH2	CH2-CH/CH3		CCL4
1784M	B	1.10- 1.65	CH2	CH2-CH/CH3		CDCL3
1659M	B	1.10- 2.00	CH2	CH2-CH/CH3		POLYSOL-D
2479M	B	1.10- 2.00	CH2	CH2-CH/CH3		CCL4
2618M	B	1.16- 2.10	CH2	CH2-CH/CH3		D20
1740M	B	1.20- 1.70	CH2	CH2-CH/CH3		CDCL3
2486M	B	1.49	CH2	CH2-CH/CH3		CDCL3
2522M	C	1.10- 1.70	CH2	CH2-CH/CH3		CCL4
2745M	C	1.30- 2.10	CH2	CH2-CH/CH3		CDCL3
1744M	C	1.37 APP.	CH2	CH2-CH/CH3		CCL4
235M	B	1.77	CH2	CH2-CL/CH2		CCL4
247M	C	1.74	CH2	CH2-CL/CH2.13-CL		CCL4
1502M	A	1.89	CH2	CH2-CL/CH2.2-0		CCL4
263M	A	1.92	CH2	CH2-CL/CH2-CH2		CCL4
248M	C	1.70 APP.	CH2	CH2-CL/CH2-CH2		CCL4
244M	C	1.74	CH2	CH2-CL/CH2-CH2		CCL4
243M	C	1.76	CH2	CH2-CL/CH2-CH2		CCL4

: REPRESENTS TRIPLE BOND, ¬ REPRESENTS AN ARROW AND < AND > REPRESENT BRACKETS.   PAGE   358

BOOK NO.	ASSIGN-MENT	CHEM SHIFT - ppm -	PROTON GROUP	ENVIRONMENTAL GROUPS	S	SOLVENT
240M	C	1.77	CH2	CH2-CL/CH2-CH2		CCL4
245M	C	1.77	CH2	CH2-CL/CH2-CH2		CCL4
236M	B	1.10- 2.00	CH2	CH2-CL/CH2-CH3		CCL4
2195M	A	2.14	CH2	CH2-CL/CH2-C(=0)		CCL4
955M	A	2.09	CH2	CH2-CL/CH2-C:N		CCL4
1637M	A	1.97	CH2	CH2-CL/CH2-OH		CCL4
2050M	C	1.72	CH2	CH2-C(=0)-A/CH2.10-CH3		CDCL3
2060M	B	1.00- 2.05	CH2	CH2-C(=0)-A/CH2-CH3		CDCL3
2071M	B	1.10- 2.00	CH2	CH2-C(=0)-A/CH2-CH3		CDCL3
2077M	B	1.72	CH2	CH2-C(=0)-A/CH3		CCL4
2070M	B	1.72	CH2	CH2-C(=0)-A/CH3		CDCL3
1984M	C	1.56	CH2	CH2-C(=0)-CH2.2/CH2.6-CH3		CCL4
1981M	C	1.54	CH2	CH2-C(=0)-CH2.5/CH3		CCL4
1984M	C	1.56	CH2	CH2-C(=0)-CH2.8/CH3		CCL4
1970M	C	1.59	CH2	CH2-C(=0)-CH2/CH3		CDCL3
1969M	C	1.51 APP.	CH2	CH2-C(=0)-CH3/CH2-CH3		CCL4
2194M	C	1.72	CH2	CH2-C(=0)-CL/CH2.14-CH3		CCL4
2202M	B	1.71	CH2	CH2-C(=0)-CL/CH2.6-C(=0)-CL		CCL4
2188M	B	1.75	CH2	CH2-C(=0)-CL/CH3		CDCL3
2151M	B	1.61	CH2	CH2-C(=0)-H/CH3		CCL4
2404M	A	1.61	CH2	CH2-C(=0)-NH/CH2.2-C(=0)-NH		D20
2352M	B	1.59	CH2	CH2-C(=0)-N/CH3		D20
2353M	B	1.63	CH2	CH2-C(=0)-N/CH3		D20
2482M	C	1.70	CH2	CH2-C(=0)-OH/CH2.12-CH3		CDCL3
2503M	B	1.58	CH2	CH2-C(=0)-OH/CH2.12-C(=0)-OH		POLYSOL-D
2749M	C	1.63	CH2	CH2-C(=0)-OH/CH2.6-C(=0)-0		CDCL3
2560M	A	2.00	CH2	CH2-C(=0)-OH/CH2-A	S	D20
2689M	A	1.60	CH2	CH2-C(=0)-OH/CH2-CH2		D20
2554M	B	1.70 APP.	CH2	CH2-C(=0)-OH/CH2-CH2		CDCL3
2579M	C	1.60	CH2	CH2-C(=0)-OH/CH2-CH2		CDCL3
2761M	C	1.61	CH2	CH2-C(=0)-0/CH2.14-CH3		CDCL3
2252M	C	1.63	CH2	CH2-C(=0)-0/CH2.2-CH3		CDCL3
2254M	C	1.63	CH2	CH2-C(=0)-0/CH2.3-CH3		CCL4
2749M	C	1.63	CH2	CH2-C(=0)-0/CH2.6-C(=0)-OH		CDCL3
2849M	A	1.90	CH2	CH2-C(=0)-0/CH2-A		CCL4
2499M	A	1.52	CH2	CH2-C(=0)-0/CH2-CH2		DMSO-D6
2781M	B	1.55 APP.	CH2	CH2-C(=0)-0/CH2-CH2		CCL4
2785M	B	1.59	CH2	CH2-C(=0)-0/CH2-CH2		CDCL3
2777M	B	1.61	CH2	CH2-C(=0)-0/CH2-CH2		CCL4
2779M	B	1.61	CH2	CH2-C(=0)-0/CH2-CH2		CCL4
2501M	B	1.62	CH2	CH2-C(=0)-0/CH2-CH2		DMSO-D6
2760M	C	1.59	CH2	CH2-C(=0)-0/CH2-CH2		CCL4
2480M	C	1.60	CH2	CH2-C(=0)-0/CH2-CH2		CCL4
2704M	C	1.61	CH2	CH2-C(=0)-0/CH2-CH2		CCL4
2780M	C	1.62	CH2	CH2-C(=0)-0/CH2-CH2		CDCL3
2758M	C	1.62	CH2	CH2-C(=0)-0/CH2-CH2		CDCL3
2925M	C	1.70	CH2	CH2-C(=0)-0/CH2-CH2		CCL4
2712M	C	1.71 APP.	CH2	CH2-C(=0)-0/CH2-CH2		CDCL3
2250M	B	1.11- 1.97	CH2	CH2-C(=0)-0/CH2-CH3		CDCL3
2701M	C	1.54 APP.	CH2	CH2-C(=0)-0/CH2-CH3		CCL4
2498M	A	1.80	CH2	CH2-C(=0)-0/CH2-C(=0)-0		DMSO-D6
2778M	B	1.50- 2.10	CH2	CH2-C(=0)-0/CH2-C(=0)-0		CCL4
2775M	C	1.85	CH2	CH2-C(=0)-0/CH2-C(=0)-0		CCL4
2778M	C	2.29	CH2	CH2-C(=0)-0/CH2-C(=0)-0		CCL4
2842M	B	1.67	CH2	CH2-C(=0)-0/CH3		CCL4
2249M	B	1.69	GROUP	CH2-C(=0)-0/CH3		CCL4
2700M	C	1.70	CH2	CH2-C(=0)-0/CH3		CCL4
2490M	B	2.74 APP.	CH2	CH2-C(=0)-0/SH		CDCL3
2041M	B	1.00- 2.00	CH2	CH2-C(=0)-Q2/CH2-CH3		CDCL3
1989M	C	1.54	CH2	CH2-C(=0)/CH2.9-CH3		CDCL3
2218M	A	1.87	CH2	CH2-C(=0)/CH2-A		CDCL3
2199M	A	1.77	CH2	CH2-C(=0)/CH2-CH2		CCL4
2206M	B	1.78	CH2	CH2-C(=0)/CH2-CH2		CDCL3
2279M	C	1.60	CH2	CH2-C(=0)/CH2-CH2		CDCL3
2278M	C	1.60 APP.	CH2	CH2-C(=0)/CH2-CH2		CDCL3
2298M	C	1.62 APP.	CH2	CH2-C(=0)/CH2-CH2		CCL4
2049M	C	1.69	CH2	CH2-C(=0)/CH2-CH2		CDCL3
2193M	C	1.70	CH2	CH2-C(=0)/CH2-CH2		CCL4
2192M	C	1.72	CH2	CH2-C(=0)/CH2-CH2		TFA
892M	C	1.76	CH2	CH2-C(=0)/CH2-CH2		CCL4
2153M	C	2.35	CH2	CH2-C(=0)/CH2-CH2		CDCL3
2066M	B	1.00- 2.00	CH2	CH2-C(=0)/CH2-CH3		CDCL3
1978M	B	1.10- 1.90	CH2	CH2-C(=0)/CH2-CH3		CDCL3
2302M	D	1.92- 2.61	CH2	CH2-C(=0)/CH2-C(=0)		CCL4
1972M	B	1.58	CH2	CH2-C(=0)/CH3		DMSO-D6
2413M	B	1.58	CH2	CH2-C(=0)/CH3		CDCL3
2316M	B	1.64	CH2	CH2-C(=0)/CH3		CCL4
2047M	B	1.72	CH2	CH2-C(=0)/CH3		CCL4
118M	B	1.18- 1.65	CH2	CH2-C:CH/CH2-CH3		CCL4
117M	B	1.55	CH2	CH2-C:CH/CH3		CDCL3
963M	A	1.69	CH2	CH2-C:N/CH2-CH2		CDCL3

BOOK NO.	ASSIGN-MENT	CHEM SHIFT - ppm -	PROTON GROUP	ENVIRONMENTAL GROUPS	S	SOLVENT
953M	C	1.55	CH2	CH2-C:N/CH2-CH2		CDCL3
946M	B	1.59	CH2	CH2-C:N/CH2-CH3		CCL4
946M	B	1.59	CH2	CH2-C:N/CH2-CH3		CCL4
944M	B	1.67	CH2	CH2-C:N/CH3		CCL4
131M	B	1.52	CH2	CH2-C:/CH2.2-C:		CCL4
123M	A	1.68	CH2	CH2-C:/CH2-CH2		CDCL3
1787M	C	1.10- 1.90	CH2	CH2-C:/CH3		CCL4
130M	B	1.36	CH2	CH2-C:/CH(CH3/CH3)		CCL4
2545M	A	0.70- 1.40	CH2	CH2-C/CH3		CDCL3
2543M	B	1.20- 1.40	CH2	CH2-C/CH3		DMSO-D6
1624M	C	1.00- 1.40	CH2	CH2-C/CH3		CDCL3
21M	C	1.03- 1.45	CH2	CH2-C/CH3		CDCL3
2190M	C	1.10- 2.00	CH2	CH2-C/CH3		CCL4
219M	C	1.86	CH2	CH2-F/CH2.3-CH3		CCL4
220M	C	1.88	CH2	CH2-F/CH2-CH2		CCL4
414M	C	1.82	CH2	CH2-I/CH2.13-CH3		CCL4
413M	C	1.83	CH2	CH2-I/CH2.9-CH3		CCL4
418M	A	1.94	CH2	CH2-I/CH2-CH2		CCL4
420M	B	1.88	CH2	CH2-I/CH2-CH2		CCL4
412M	C	1.81	CH2	CH2-I/CH2-CH2		CCL4
411M	C	1.82	CH2	CH2-I/CH2-CH2		CCL4
407M	C	1.80 APP.	CH2	CH2-I/CH2-CH3		CCL4
417M	A	2.29	CH2	CH2-I/CH2-I		CCL4
405M	B	1.85	CH2	CH2-I/CH3		CCL4
439M	B	1.48	CH2	CH2-NH2		CCL4
779M	B	1.70	CH2	CH2-NH2/CH2.4-NH2	S	D20
481M	B	1.80	CH2	CH2-NH2/CH2-A		CDCL3
2644M	A	1.42- 2.28	CH2	CH2-NH2/CH2-CH	S	D20
461M	A	1.47	CH2	CH2-NH2/CH2-CH2		D20
777M	A	1.78	CH2	CH2-NH2/CH2-CH2	S	D20
482M	B	1.49 APP.	CH2	CH2-NH2/CH2-CH2		CCL4
2623M	B	1.64	CH2	CH2-NH2/CH2-CH2		D20
770M	C	1.70	CH2	CH2-NH2/CH2-CH2	S	D20
441M	B	1.17- 1.57	CH2	CH2-NH2/CH2-CH3		CDCL3
768M	B	1.10- 2.20	CH2	CH2-NH2/CH2-CH3	S	CDCL3
458M	A	1.55	CH2	CH2-NH2/CH2-NH2		D20
1656M	A	1.91	CH2	CH2-NH2/CH2-OH	S	D20
1466M	B	1.54	CH2	CH2-NH2/CH2-R6N0		CCL4
1121M	A	1.72	CH2	CH2-NH2/CH2-S		D20
439M	B	1.48	CH2	CH2-NH2/CH3		CCL4
767M	B	1.64	CH2	CH2-NH2/CH3	S	DMSO-D6
2629M	A	1.62	CH2	CH2-NH/CH2-CH		D20
1215M	B	1.10- 1.80	CH2	CH2-NH/CH2-CH3		CDCL3
2429M	B	1.10- 1.70	CH2	CH2-NH/CH2-CH3		CDCL3
2297M	B	1.10- 1.70	CH2	CH2-NH/CH2-CH3		D20
2982M	B	1.12- 1.64	CH2	CH2-NH/CH2-CH3		CCL4
544M	B	1.17- 1.63	CH2	CH2-NH/CH2-CH3		D20
579M	B	1.41 APP.	CH2	CH2-NH/CH2-CH3		CCL4
800M	B	1.53	CH2	CH2-NH/CH2-CH3		D20
799M	B	1.00- 2.00	CH2	CH2-NH/CH2-CH3	S	D20
547M	D	1.17- 1.65	CH2	CH2-NH/CH2-CH3		CDCL3
464M	A	1.58	CH2	CH2-NH/CH2-NH2		D20
466M	B	1.63	CH2	CH2-NH/CH2-NH2		CDCL3
542M	B	1.49	CH2	CH2-NH/CH3		CDCL3
584M	B	1.54	CH2	CH2-NH/CH3		CCL4
2981M	C	1.45	CH2	CH2-NH/CH3		CCL4
578M	C	1.47	CH2	CH2-NH/CH3		CCL4
2299M	C	1.51	CH2	CH2-NH/CH3		CDCL3
549M	B	1.07- 1.81	CH2	CH2-NH/CH(CH3/CH3)		CCL4
585M	B	1.20- 2.10	CH2	CH2-NH/CH(CH3/CH3)		CDCL3
1041M	B	2.00	CH2	CH2-NO2/CH3		CCL4
831M	C	1.81	CH2	CH2-N(+)/CH2-CH2	S	CDCL3
839M	C	1.83	CH2	CH2-N(+)/CH2-CH2	S	CDCL3
828M	B	1.10- 2.00	CH2	CH2-N(+)/CH2-CH3		CDCL3
832M	B	1.19- 2.10	CH2	CH2-N(+)/CH2-CH3	S	CDCL3
908M	B	1.61	CH2	CH2-N=C=0/CH3		CDCL3
933M	C	1.74	CH2	CH2-N=C=S/CH2-CH2		CCL4
931M	B	1.20- 2.10	CH2	CH2-N=C=S/CH2-CH3		CCL4
810M	C	1.84	CH2	CH2-N/CH2.5-CH3		CDCL3
626M	C	1.10- 1.70	CH2	CH2-N/CH2-CH		CDCL3
1652M	B	1.10- 1.80	CH2	CH2-N/CH2-CH3		CDCL3
651M	B	1.10- 1.85	CH2	CH2-N/CH2-CH3		CCL4
1653M	B	1.10- 1.60	CH2	CH2-N/CH2-CH3		CDCL3
617M	B	1.30	CH2	CH2-N/CH2-CH3		CCL4
2438M	B	1.39	CH2	CH2-N/CH2-CH3		CCL4
2349M	B	1.41	CH2	CH2-N/CH2-CH3		CCL4
2990M	C	1.10- 1.70	CH2	CH2-N/CH2-CH3		CCL4
2351M	C	1.10- 1.90	CH2	CH2-N/CH2-CH3		CDCL3
2984M	C	1.20- 1.75	CH2	CH2-N/CH2-CH3		CCL4
1755M	C	1.38 APP.	CH2	CH2-N/CH2-CH3		CCL4
958M	B	1.69	CH2	CH2-N/CH2-C:N		CCL4

BOOK NO.	ASSIGN-MENT	CHEM SHIFT - ppm -	PROTON GROUP	ENVIRONMENTAL GROUPS	S	SOLVENT
634M	A	1.67	CH2	CH2-N/CH2-N		CDCL3
627M	A	1.60	CH2	CH2-N/CH2-NH2		CDCL3
1649M	A	1.60	CH2	CH2-N/CH2-OH		CCL4
1369M	A	1.81	CH2	CH2-N/CH2-OH		CDCL3
1653M	C	1.69	CH2	CH2-N/CH2-OH		CDCL3
615M	B	1.11- 1.75	CH2	CH2-N/CH3		CCL4
2365M	B	1.56	CH2	CH2-N/CH3		CDCL3
650M	B	1.58	CH2	CH2-N/CH3		CCL4
1027M	C	1.00- 2.05	CH2	CH2-N/CH3		CCL4
1702M	A	1.82	CH2	CH2-OH/CH2-A		CCL4
1849M	A	1.10- 2.00	CH2	CH2-OH/CH2-CH		POLYSOL-D
1614M	B	1.10- 1.70	CH2	CH2-OH/CH2-CH3		CCL4
1643M	A	1.68	CH2	CH2-OH/CH2-NH2		D20
1824M	A	1.78	CH2	CH2-OH/CH2-OH		D20
1613M	B	1.49	CH2	CH2-OH/CH3		CCL4
1038M	C	1.74	CH2	CH2-ONO/CH2-CH2		CCL4
2765M	B	1.00- 2.00	CH2	CH2-0-C(=0)-0/CH2-CH3		CDCL3
2961M	C	1.71 APP.	CH2	CH2-0-C(=0)/CH2-CH2		CCL4
2721M	C	1.75	CH2	CH2-0-C(=0)/CH2-CH2		CDCL3
2939M	C	1.79	CH2	CH2-0-C(=0)/CH2-CH2		CDCL3
2909M	C	1.80	CH2	CH2-0-C(=0)/CH2-CH2		CDCL3
2708M	D	1.67	CH2	CH2-0-C(=0)/CH2-CH2		CCL4
2743M	B	1.00- 1.85	CH2	CH2-0-C(=0)/CH2-CH3		CCL4
2766M	B	1.10- 2.05	CH2	CH2-0-C(=0)/CH2-CH3		CDCL3
2775M	B	1.10- 1.80	CH2	CH2-0-C(=0)/CH2-CH3		CCL4
2896M	B	1.10- 2.00	CH2	CH2-0-C(=0)/CH2-CH3		CDCL3
2847M	B	1.10- 1.90	CH2	CH2-0-C(=0)/CH2-CH3		CCL4
2792M	B	1.14- 1.95	CH2	CH2-0-C(=0)/CH2-CH3		CCL4
2917M	B	1.17- 1.89	CH2	CH2-0-C(=0)/CH2-CH3		C3D6O
2908M	B	1.18- 1.93	CH2	CH2-0-C(=0)/CH2-CH3		CCL4
2959M	B	1.19- 2.05	CH2	CH2-0-C(=0)/CH2-CH3		CCL4
2902M	B	1.20- 2.08	CH2	CH2-0-C(=0)/CH2-CH3		CCL4
2767M	B	1.50	CH2	CH2-0-C(=0)/CH2-CH3		CCL4
2894M	B	1.60	CH2	CH2-0-C(=0)/CH2-CH3		CCL4
2890M	B	1.62 APP.	CH2	CH2-0-C(=0)/CH2-CH3		CCL4
2702M	C	1.26- 1.84	CH2	CH2-0-C(=0)/CH2-CH3		CCL4
2798M	A	1.74	CH2	CH2-0-C(=0)/CH2-Q3		CCL4
2987M	B	1.68	CH2	CH2-0-C(=0)/CH3		CDCL3
2935M	B	1.72	CH2	CH2-0-C(=0)/CH3		CCL4
2863M	B	1.73	CH2	CH2-0-C(=0)/CH3		CCL4
2900M	B	1.80	CH2	CH2-0-C(=0)/CH3		CDCL3
1082M	C	1.74	CH2	CH2-0-NO2/CH2.2-CH3		CDCL3
1080M	B	1.75	CH2	CH2-0-NO2/CH3		CCL4
1033M	B	1.72	CH2	CH2-0-N=0/CH3		CCL4
1327M	C	1.69	CH2	CH2-0-S03-NA/CH2.2-CH3		D20
1502M	A	1.89	CH2	CH2-0/CH2.2-CL		CCL4
2998M	C	1.30- 1.91	CH2	CH2-0/CH2CH3		CCL4
2554M	B	1.70 APP.	CH2	CH2-0/CH2-CH2		CDCL3
1581M	C	1.80	CH2	CH2-0/CH2-CH2		CDCL3
2174M	C	1.80	CH2	CH2-0/CH2-CH2		CCL4
1668M	B	0.65- 1.90	CH2	CH2-0/CH2-CH3		CCL4
1599M	B	1.00- 1.70	CH2	CH2-0/CH2-CH3		CCL4
1675M	B	1.06- 1.78	CH2	CH2-0/CH2-CH3		CDCL3
1965M	B	1.10- 2.00	CH2	CH2-0/CH2-CH3		CDCL3
1414M	B	1.10- 1.72	CH2	CH2-0/CH2-CH3		CCL4
1413M	B	1.10- 1.70	CH2	CH2-0/CH2-CH3		CCL4
1404M	B	1.10- 1.80	CH2	CH2-0/CH2-CH3		CCL4
1384M	B	1.10- 1.70	CH2	CH2-0/CH2-CH3		CCL4
1380M	B	1.10- 1.75	CH2	CH2-0/CH2-CH3		CDCL3
1562M	B	1.15- 2.08	CH2	CH2-0/CH2-CH3		CDCL3
1534M	B	1.19- 2.08	CH2	CH2-0/CH2-CH3		CCL4
1417M	B	1.20- 1.70	CH2	CH2-0/CH2-CH3		CCL4
2717M	B	1.45	CH2	CH2-0/CH2-CH3		CCL4
1421M	B	1.48	CH2	CH2-0/CH2-CH3		CCL4
1382M	C	1.20- 1.80	CH2	CH2-0/CH2-CH3		CCL4
1424M	C	1.30- 1.69	CH2	CH2-0/CH2-CH3		CCL4
1667M	B	1.59	CH2	CH2-0/CH3		CDCL3
1381M	B	1.60	CH2	CH2-0/CH3		CDCL3
2999M	B	1.70	CH2	CH2-0/CH3		CDCL3
1490M	B	1.71	CH2	CH2-0/CH3		CDCL3
2586M	B	1.71	CH2	CH2-0/CH3		POLYSOL-D
1329M	B	1.75	CH2	CH2-0/CH3		CCL4
2173M	B	1.76	CH2	CH2-0/CH3		CCL4
1394M	C	1.50	CH2	CH2-0/CH3		CCL4
1097M	A	1.70	CH2	CH2-P/CH2-P		CDCL3
874M	B	1.51	CH2	CH2-QN/CH3		CCL4
854M	B	1.56	CH2	CH2-QN/CH3		CDCL3
1063M	B	1.59	CH2	CH2-QN/CH3		POLYSOL-D
160M	B	1.10- 1.80	CH2	CH2-Q1/CH2-CH3		CCL4
2161M	B	1.40	CH2	CH2-Q1/CH2-CH3		CCL4
93M	B	1.29	CH2	CH2-Q1/CH3		CCL4

BOOK NO.	ASSIGN-MENT	CHEM SHIFT - ppm -	PROTON GROUP	ENVIRONMENTAL GROUPS	S	SOLVENT
92M	B	1.33	CH2	CH2-Q1/CH3		CCL4
2523M	C	1.50	CH2	CH2-Q1/CH3		CCL4
2157M	C	1.58	CH2	CH2-Q1/CH3		CCL4
70M	B	1.20- 1.60	CH2	CH2-Q2/CH2-CH3		CCL4
71M	C	1.10- 1.70	CH2	CH2-Q2/CH2-CH3		CCL4
2800M	B	1.41	CH2	CH2-Q2/CH3		CCL4
2521M	B	1.41	CH2	CH2-Q2/CH3		CCL4
2799M	B	1.50	CH2	CH2-Q2/CH3		CCL4
2156M	B	1.54	CH2	CH2-Q2/CH3		CDCL3
2520M	B	1.54	CH2	CH2-Q2/CH3		CCL4
82M	C	1.31	CH2	CH2-Q2/CH3		CCL4
57M	B	1.35	CH2	CH2-Q3/CH2-CH3		CCL4
2399M	A	1.10- 2.00	CH2	CH2-R5NA/CH2-CH2		CDCL3
739M	B	1.90	CH2	CH2-R5NNA/CH3		POLYSOL-D
2433M	B	1.10- 1.65	CH2	CH2-R5NN/CH2-CH3		CCL4
1211M	C	1.60	CH2	CH2-SH/CH2.6-CH3		CDCL3
1220M	B	1.69	CH2	CH2-SH/CH2-CH2		CCL4
1201M	C	1.67	CH2	CH2-SH/CH3		CDCL3
1254M	B	1.15- 2.15	CH2	CH2-SO2/CH2-CH3		CDCL3
1281M	C	2.01	CH2	CH2-SO2/CH2-CH3		CCL4
1253M	B	1.81	CH2	CH2-SO2/CH3		CCL4
1280M	B	2.09	CH2	CH2-SO2/CH3		CCL4
1295M	C	1.71	CH2	CH2-SO3-NA/CH2.4-CH3		D2O
1322M	B	1.08- 2.70	CH2	CH2-SO3/CH2-CH3		CCL4
1315M	B	1.10- 2.10	CH2	CH2-SO3/CH2-CH3		CDCL3
1244M	C	1.63 APP.	CH2	CH2-SO/CH2-CH3		CCL4
1248M	B	1.66	CH2	CH2-SO/CH3		CCL4
1245M	B	1.11- 2.08	CH2	CH2-S(=O)/CH2-CH3		CDCL3
1187M	C	1.68 APP.	CH2	CH2-S/CH2.2-CH3		CCL4
1189M	C	1.68	CH2	CH2-S/CH2.9-CH3		CDCL3
1012M	C	1.81	CH2	CH2-S/CH2.9-CH3		CCL4
1164M	A	1.92	CH2	CH2-S/CH2-A		CCL4
1127M	A	1.42	CH2	CH2-S/CH2-CH2		CCL4
1016M	A	2.01	CH2	CH2-S/CH2-CH2		CDCL3
1125M	B	1.69	CH2	CH2-S/CH2-CH2		CDCL3
1011M	C	1.82	CH2	CH2-S/CH2-CH2		CCL4
1010M	C	1.83	CH2	CH2-S/CH2-CH2		CCL4
1009M	B	1.16- 2.13	CH2	CH2-S/CH2-CH3		CCL4
1183M	B	1.20- 2.14	CH2	CH2-S/CH2-CH3		CDCL3
1110M	B	1.47	CH2	CH2-S/CH2-CH3		CCL4
1109M	B	1.59	CH2	CH2-S/CH3		CCL4
1124M	B	1.60	CH2	CH2-S/CH3		CCL4
1112M	B	1.20- 2.00	CH2	CH2-S/CH(CH3/CH3)		CDCL3
23M	C	1.20	CH2	CH3/C(CH3/CH3/CH2)		CDCL3
689M	C	1.68 APP.	CH2	CH(AN/CH2.3)/CH2.2-CH3		CCL4
494M	C	1.53	CH2	CH(A/CH3)/CH3		CCL4
138M	C	1.59 APP.	CH2	CH(A/CH3)/CH3		CCL4
978M	A	3.25	CH2	CH(A/CH)/A		CDCL3
331M	D	1.80 APP.	CH2	CH(BR/CH2.2)/CH3		CCL4
331M	D	1.80 APP.	CH2	CH(BR/CH2)/CH2-CH3		CCL4
358M	B	2.28	CH2	CH(BR/CH3)/CH2-BR		CCL4
361M	B	1.98	CH2	CH(BR/CH3)/CH2-CH		CDCL3
334M	D	1.81 APP.	CH2	CH(BR/CH3)/CH2-CH2		CCL4
327M	B	1.10- 2.10	CH2	CH(BR/CH3)/CH2-CH3		CCL4
323M	C	1.82	CH2	CH(BR/CH3)/CH3		CDCL3
2487M	C	2.01	CH2	CH(BR/C(=O)-OH)/CH2-CH2		CCL4
2486M	C	2.06	CH2	CH(BR/C(=O)-OH)/CH2-CH3		CDCL3
2732M	D	2.04	CH2	CH(BR/C(=O)-O)/CH2.2-CH3		CDCL3
2733M	D	1.93	CH2	CH(BR/C(=O)-O)/CH2.6-CH3		CCL4
357M	B	1.40- 2.50	CH2	CH(BR/HCH)/CH3		CDCL3
379M	A	2.11	CH2	CH(CH2/A)/CH2-BR		CCL4
2695M	B	1.10- 1.70	CH2	CH(CH2/CH2)/CH3		CCL4
2691M	B	1.10- 1.80	CH2	CH(CH2/CH2)/CH3		CDCL3
1622M	B	1.30	CH2	CH(CH2/CH2)/CH3		CDCL3
1601M	B	1.34	CH2	CH(CH2/CH2)/CH3		CCL4
1832M	B	1.53	CH2	CH(CH2/CH3)/CH2-OH		CDCL3
20M	B	1.00- 1.50	CH2	CH(CH2/CH3)/CH3		CCL4
58M	C	1.00- 1.80	CH2	CH(CH2/CH3)/CH3		CCL4
445M	C	1.09- 1.68	CH2	CH(CH2/CH3)/CH3		CDCL3
31M	B	1.08- 1.83	CH2	CH(CH3/CH3)/CH2-CH		CCL4
328M	B	1.76	CH2	CH(CH3/CH3)/CH2-CH2		CCL4
410M	B	1.73 APP.	CH2	CH(CH3/CH3)/CH2-I		CCL4
619M	B	1.10- 1.88	CH2	CH(CH3/CH3)/CH2-N		CDCL3
446M	B	1.32	CH2	CH(CH3/CH3)/CH2-NH2		CDCL3
1037M	B	1.00- 2.20	CH2	CH(CH3/CH3)/CH2-NO2		CDCL3
1385M	B	1.20- 2.00	CH2	CH(CH3/CH3)/CH2-O		CCL4
1618M	B	1.10- 1.90	CH2	CH(CH3/CH3)/CH2-OH		CCL4
2747M	B	1.25- 1.95	CH2	CH(CH3/CH3)/CH2-O-C(=O)		CCL4
856M	B	1.44	CH2	CH(CH3/CH3)/CH2-QN		CDCL3
1188M	B	1.30- 2.05	CH2	CH(CH3/CH3)/CH2-S		CCL4
1205M	C	1.78- 1.92	CH2	CH(CH3/CH3)/CH2-SH		CCL4

BOOK NO.	ASSIGN-MENT	CHEM SHIFT - ppm -	PROTON GROUP	ENVIRONMENTAL GROUPS	S	SOLVENT
17M	C	0.90- 1.60	CH2	CH(CH3/CH3)/CH3		CCL4
22M	B	1.09	CH2	CH(CH3/CH3)/CH(CH3/CH3)		CCL4
262M	B	1.88	CH2	CH(CL/CH2)/CH3		CCL4
237M	C	1.72	CH2	CH(CL/CH3)/CH3		CCL4
2484M	B	2.04	CH2	CH(CL/C(=0)-OH)/CH3		CDCL3
2137M	C	1.85	CH2	CH(C(=0)-CH3/C(=0)-CH3)/CH3		CDCL3
2191M	B	1.10- 2.10	CH2	CH(C(=0)-CL/CH2.2)/CH2-CH3		CCL4
2542M	A	1.79	CH2	CH(C(=0)-OH/A)/CH2-CH		DMSO
2479M	B	1.10- 2.20	CH2	CH(C(=0)-OH/CH2)/CH2-CH3		CCL4
2796M	A	1.96	CH2	CH(C(=0)-O-CH3/C(=0)-O-CH3)/CH2-CH		CDCL3
2651M	B	1.00- 1.75	CH2	CH(C(=0)-O/CH2.3)/CH3		POLYSOL-D
2757M	B	1.10- 1.91	CH2	CH(C(=0)-O/CH2)/CH3		CDCL3
2253M	B	1.60	CH2	CH(C(=0)-O/CH2)/CH3		CCL4
2477M	C	1.16- 1.90	CH2	CH(C(=0)-O/CH2)/CH3		CCL4
2475M	C	1.56 APP.	CH2	CH(C(=0)-O/CH3)/CH3		CDCL3
1865M	B	2.60	CH2	CH(C(=0)-O/C(=0))/CH(C(=0)-O/C(=0))		CDCL3
2745M	C	1.30- 2.10	CH2	CH(C(=0)-O/C(=0)-CH3)/CH2-CH3		CDCL3
2744M	C	1.82	CH2	CH(C(=0)-O/C(=0)-CH3)/CH3		CCL4
2770M	D	1.77	CH2	CH(C(=0)-O/C(=0)-O)/CH2-CH2		CCL4
25M	B	1.10- 1.90	CH2	CH(C/CH3)/CH3		CCL4
1617M	C	1.05- 1.81	CH2	CH(HCH/CH3)/CH3		CCL4
408M	B	1.75	CH2	CH(I/CH3)/CH3		CDCL3
626M	C	1.10- 1.70	CH2	CH(NH2/CH3)/CH2.2-N		CDCL3
785M	B	2.19	CH2	CH(NH2/CH3)/CH2-A	S	TFA
443M	D	1.31	CH2	CH(NH2/CH3)/CH3		CDCL3
450M	C	1.20	CH2	CH(NH2/CH3)/CH(CH3/CH3)		CCL4
2644M	A	1.42- 2.28	CH2	CH(NH2/C(=0)-OH)/CH2-CH2	S	D2O
2632M	A	2.20	CH2	CH(NH2/C(=0)-OH)/CH2-C(=0)		D2O
2643M	A	2.30	CH2	CH(NH2/C(=0)-OH)/CH2-NH2	S	D2O
2629M	A	1.62	CH2	CH(NH2/C(=0)-O)/CH2-CH2		D2O
2615M	B	1.88	CH2	CH(NH2/C(=0)-O)/CH3		D2O
2618M	B	1.16- 2.10	CH2	CH(NH2/C(=0)-O/CH2-CH3		D2O
1644M	B	1.36 APP.	CH2	CH(NH/HCH)/CH3		CDCL3
2633M	A	2.49	CH2	CH(NH3(+)/C(=0)-OH)/CH2-C(=0)-O		TFA
545M	C	1.00- 1.70	CH2	CH(NH/CH3)/CH3		CCL4
598M	C	1.10- 1.80	CH2	CH(NH/CH3)/CH3		CDCL3
2627M	A	1.94 APP.	CH2	CH(NH/C(=0)-OH)/CH2-S		POLYSOL-D
2621M	B	1.59 APP.	CH2	CH(NH/C(=0)-OH)/CH(CH3/CH3)		POLYSOL-D
1791M	B	2.97	CH2	CH(OH/A)/A		CDCL3
1788M	B	1.57	CH2	CH(OH/A)/CH3		CCL4
1740M	B	1.20- 1.70	CH2	CH(OH/CH2.2)/CH2-CH3		CDCL3
1849M	A	1.10- 2.00	CH2	CH(OH/CH2.3)/CH2.2-OH		POLYSOL-D
1784M	B	1.10- 1.65	CH2	CH(OH/CH2)/CH2-CH3		CDCL3
1829M	B	1.10- 1.80	CH2	CH(OH/CH2)/CH3		CDCL3
1737M	B	1.39	CH2	CH(OH/CH2)/CH3		CCL4
1787M	C	1.10- 1.90	CH2	CH(OH/CH2)/CH3		CCL4
1748M	C	1.25	CH2	CH(OH/CH3)/CH2-CH2		CCL4
1736M	C	1.38	CH2	CH(OH/CH3)/CH3		CCL4
1830M	B	1.49	CH2	CH(OH/CH3)/CH(OH/CH3)		CCL4
2741M	C	1.49 APP.	CH2	CH(OH/C(=0)-O)/CH(CH3/CH3)		CCL4
1744M	C	1.37 APP.	CH2	CH(OH/C)/CH2-CH3		CCL4
1659M	B	1.10- 2.00	CH2	CH(OH/P=)/CH2-CH3		POLYSOL-D
2698M	D	1.55	CH2	CH(O-C(=0)/CH3)/CH3		CDCL3
1034M	C	1.73	CH2	CH(O-N=0/CH3)/CH3		CCL4
1480M	B	1.97	CH2	CH(O/A)/CH2-C:N		CDCL3
1429M	A	1.80	CH2	CH(O/O)/CH(O/O)		CCL4
2021M	B	1.50	CH2	CH(Q2/CH2)/CH3		CCL4
2522M	C	1.10- 1.70	CH2	CH(Q2/CH3)/CH2-CH3		CCL4
56M	B	1.10- 2.10	CH2	CH(Q3/CH2)/CH3		CDCL3
55M	C	1.31	CH2	CH(Q3/CH3)/CH3		CCL4
1203M	D	1.50	CH2	CH(SH/CH3)/CH3		CCL4
1184M	C	1.60	CH2	CH(S/CH3)/CH3		CCL4
277M	B	4.20	CH2	CL(Q2(H/H/CL)		CDCL3
284M	A	4.48	CH2	CL/A		CCL4
316M	A	4.83	CH2	CL/AA<C-C*>		CCL4
311M	A	4.42	CH2	CL/A<C-CH-C(CL)-C(CL)>		CCL4
286M	B	4.50	CH2	CL/A<C-C(CH3)-CH-C(CH3)/CH-C(CH2-CL)>		CDCL3
1181M	A	4.60	CH2	CL/A<C-C(CL)>		CCL4
285M	B	4.40	CH2	CL/A(C-CH-CH-C(CH3))		CCL4
247M	D	3.48	CH2	CL/CH2.1J-CH3		CCL4
1502M	C	3.52	CH2	CL/CH2.3-O		CCL4
343M	B	3.70	CH2	CL/CH2-BR		CCL4
264M	B	3.51	CH2	CL/CH2-CH2		CCL4
263M	B	3.52	CH2	CL/CH2-CH2		CCL4
242M	C	3.44	CH2	CL/CH2-CH2		CCL4
246M	C	3.46	CH2	CL/CH2-CH2		CCL4
236M	C	3.49	CH2	CL/CH2-CH2		CCL4
2195M	C	3.55	CH2	CL/CH2-CH2		CCL4
955M	C	3.60	CH2	CL/CH2-CH2		CCL4
1637M	C	3.72	CH2	CL/CH2-CH2		CCL4
240M	D	3.40	CH2	CL/CH2-CH2		CCL4

: REPRESENTS TRIPLE BOND, ¬ REPRESENTS AN ARROW AND < AND > REPRESENT BRACKETS.   PAGE 363

BOOK NO.	ASSIGN-MENT	CHEM SHIFT - ppm -	PROTON GROUP	ENVIRONMENTAL GROUPS	S	SOLVENT
243M	D	3.43	CH2	CL/CH2-CH2		CCL4
244M	D	3.44	CH2	CL/CH2-CH2		CCL4
245M	D	3.46	CH2	CL/CH2-CH2		CCL4
248M	D	3.46	CH2	CL/CH2-CH2		CCL4
2727M	D	3.51	CH2	CL/CH2-CH2		CCL4
235M	C	3.45	CH2	CL/CH2-CH3		CCL4
252M	A	3.67	CH2	CL/CH2-CL		CCL4
2313M	B	3.68	CH2	CL/CH2-C(=0)		CDCL3
2052M	B	3.87	CH2	CL/CH2-C(=0)		CDCL3
2724M	C	3.71	CH2	CL/CH2-C(=0)-0		CCL4
2725M	C	3.73	CH2	CL/CH2-C(=0)-0		CCL4
954M	B	3.70	CH2	CL/CH2-C:N		CCL4
655M	A	3.61 APP.	CH2	CL/CH2-N		POLYSOL-D
811M	C	3.91	CH2	CL/CH2-N	S	D20
812M	D	3.99	CH2	CL/CH2-N	S	D20
1607M	A	3.67	CH2	CL/CH2-0		CDCL3
2996M	A	3.71	CH2	CL/CH2-0		CCL4
1330M	A	3.80	CH2	CL/CH2-0		CDCL3
1411M	B	3.79	CH2	CL/CH2-0		CCL4
1636M	B	3.63	CH2	CL/CH2-OH		CDCL3
1636M	B	3.79	CH2	CL/CH2-OH		CDCL3
2962M	A	3.72	CH2	CL/CH2-0-C(=0)		CDCL3
2392M	A	3.80	CH2	CL/CH2-R5NA		CDCL3
2392M	A	4.06	CH2	CL/CH2-R5NA		CDCL3
815M	D	3.98	CH2	CL/CH2-R6N	S	D20
1282M	A	4.01	CH2	CL/CH2-S02		CCL4
355M	B	3.96	CH2	CL/CH(BR/CH2)		CCL4
344M	C	3.55	CH2	CL/CH(CH2/CH3)		CDCL3
238M	C	3.32	CH2	CL/CH(CH3/CH3)		CCL4
259M	A	3.88	CH2	CL/CH(CL/CH2)		CCL4
262M	C	3.31- 4.16	CH2	CL/CH(CL/CH2)		CCL4
257M	B	3.28- 3.78	CH2	CL/CH(CL/CH3)		CCL4
254M	A	3.97	CH2	CL/CH(CL/CL)		CDCL3
1840M	A	3.66 APP.	CH2	CL/CH(OH/CH2)		D20
1750M	A	3.69	CH2	CL/CH(OH/CH2)		CDCL3
249M	A	5.28	CH2	CL/CL		CCL4
2655M	B	3.93	CH2	CL/C(CL/C(=0)-0/CH3)	S	D20
2051M	A	4.66	CH2	CL/C(=0)-A		CDCL3
2318M	A	4.27	CH2	CL/C(=0)-NH		DMSO-D6
2281M	A	4.18	CH2	CL/C(=0)-NH2		D20
2483M	A	4.05	CH2	CL/C(=0)-OH		CCL4
2804M	A	4.03	CH2	CL/C(=0)-0-CH2		CCL4
283M	B	4.06	CH2	CL/C:CH		CCL4
1399M	A	5.51	CH2	CL/0-CH2		CDCL3
278M	B	4.12	CH2	CL/Q1(CL/CH3)		CCL4
1786M	B	4.13	CH2	CL/Q1(CL/H/OH)		CCL4
1786M	C	4.34	CH2	CL/Q1(CL/OH/H)		CCL4
276M	A	4.05	CH2	CL/Q2(CH2-CL)		CCL4
274M	D	4.07	CH2	CL/Q2(CH2-C)		CDCL3
277M	A	4.03	CH2	CL/Q2(H/CL/H)		CDCL3
277M	A	4.20	CH2	CL/Q2(H/CL/H)		CDCL3
277M	B	4.03	CH2	CL/Q2(H/H/CL)		CDCL3
272M	A	3.99	CH2	CL/Q3		CCL4
1604M	B	2.75	CH2	CL/SI(0/CH3/CH3)		CDCL3
1120M	A	4.83	CH2	CL/S-CH2		CDCL3
1013M	A	4.92	CH2	CL/S-C:N		CCL4
977M	B	2.41	CH2	C(A/A/C:N)/CH3		CDCL3
2543M	C	1.89	CH2	C(A/CH2/CH2)/CH2-CH3		DMSO-D6
1885M	C	1.60	CH2	C(A/CH3/CH3)/CH3		CCL4
1886M	C	1.70	CH2	C(A/CH3/CH3)/C(CH3/CH3/CH3)		CDCL3
979M	A	2.34 APP.	CH2	C(A/C:N/CH2.2)/CH2-C:N		DMSO-D6
1835M	B	1.29	CH2	C(CH2/CH2/CH2)/CH3		CDCL3
1624M	C	1.00- 1.40	CH2	C(CH2/CH3/CH3)/CH2-CH3		CDCL3
274M	B	1.28	CH2	C(CH2/CH3/CH3)/C(CH3/CH3/CH3)		CDCL3
21M	C	1.03- 1.45	CH2	C(CH3/CH3/CH3)/CH2-CH3		CDCL3
27M	C	1.12	CH2	C(CH3/CH3/CH3)/CH(CH3/CH3)		CCL4
265M	B	2.28	CH2	C(CH3/CH3/CH3)/CH(CL/CL)		CCL4
26M	C	1.00- 1.82	CH2	C(CH/CH3/CH3)/CH3		CCL4
241M	C	1.73	CH2	C(CL/CH3/CH3)/CH3		CCL4
2190M	C	1.10- 2.00	CH2	C(C(=0)-CL/CH3/CH3)/CH2-CH3		CCL4
2545M	B	2.31	CH2	C(C(=0)-OH/A/A)/CH2-CH3		CDCL3
2771M	B	1.85	CH2	C(C(=0)-0/C(=0)-0/CH2)/CH3		CCL4
1645M	B	1.56	CH2	C(NH2/CH3/CH3)/CH2-OH		CDCL3
447M	D	1.35	CH2	C(NH2/CH3/CH3)/CH3		CDCL3
2419M	C	1.61	CH2	C(NH/CH3/CH3)/CH3		DMSO-D6
2302M	C	1.70	CH2	C(NH/CH3/CH3)/CH3		CDCL3
2305M	C	1.82	CH2	C(NH/CH3/CH3)/C(CH3/CH3/CH3)		CDCL3
1820M	D	2.15	CH2	C(OH/A/A)/CH2.6-CH3		CCL4
1818M	C	1.82	CH2	C(OH/A/CH2)/CH3		CDCL3
1837M	C	1.48	CH2	C(OH/CH2/CH3)/C(CH3/CH3/CH3)		CDCL3
1796M	C	1.46	CH2	C(OH/CH3/CH3)/CH3		CCL4

BOOK NO.	ASSIGN-MENT	CHEM SHIFT - ppm -	PROTON GROUP	ENVIRONMENTAL GROUPS	S	SOLVENT
1803M	C	1.49	CH2	C(OH/CH/CH2)/CH3		CCL4
1814M	C	1.61	CH2	C(OH/C:C/CH3)/CH3		CCL4
1815M	C	1.58	CH2	C(OH/C:C/CH3)/CH(CH3/CH3)		CDCL3
100M	B	1.26	CH2	C(R6/CH3/CH3)/CH3		CCL4
2031M	C	1.77	CH2	C(R6/CH3/CH3)/CH3		CDCL3
1223M	B	1.20- 1.60	CH2	C(SH/CH2.3/CH3)/CH3		CDCL3
2085M	A	4.21	CH2	C(=O)-A/A		TFA
2086M	A	4.27	CH2	C(=O)-A/A<C-CH-CH-C(CL)>		POLYSOL-D
2050M	D	2.93	CH2	C(=O)-A/CH2.11-CH3		CDCL3
2071M	C	2.82	CH2	C(=O)-A/CH2.2-CH3		CDCL3
2060M	D	2.90	CH2	C(=O)-A/CH2.2-CH3		CDCL3
2088M	B	3.08	CH2	C(=O)-A/CH2-A		CDCL3
2088M	B	3.20	CH2	C(=O)-A/CH2-A		CDCL3
2066M	C	2.90	CH2	C(=O)-A/CH2-CH2		CDCL3
2049M	D	2.86	CH2	C(=O)-A/CH2-CH2		CCL4
2077M	C	2.79	CH2	C(=O)-A/CH2-CH3		CCL4
2070M	C	2.81	CH2	C(=O)-A/CH2-CH3		CDCL3
2047M	C	2.82	CH2	C(=O)-A/CH2-CH3		CCL4
2052M	A	3.39	CH2	C(=O)-A/CH2-CL		CDCL3
2046M	B	2.94	CH2	C(=O)-A/CH3		CDCL3
2147M	C	4.03	CH2	C(=O)-A/C(=O)-CH3		CDCL3
2148M	B	4.36	CH2	C(=O)-A/C(=O)-Q1		POLYSOL-D
2054M	A	4.14	CH2	C(=O)-A/C:N		CDCL3
2148M	A	4.20	CH2	C(=O)-A/Q1(OH/C(=O)-A)		POLYSOL-D
1981M	D	2.30 APP.	CH2	C(=O)-CH2.2/CH2.4-CH3		CCL4
1984M	D	2.30	CH2	C(=O)-CH2.2/CH2.7-CH3		CCL4
1970M	D	2.29	CH2	C(=O)-CH2.2/CH3		CDCL3
2139M	E	3.41	CH2	C(=O)-CH2.2/C(=O)-CH2.2		CCL4
1975M	E	2.43	CH2	C(=O)-CH2.4/CH3		CDCL3
1981M	D	2.30 APP.	CH2	C(=O)-CH2.5/CH2-CH3		CCL4
1984M	D	2.30	CH2	C(=O)-CH2.8/CH2-CH3		CCL4
1988M	D	2.34 APP.	CH2	C(=O)-CH2.9/CH3		CCL4
2040M	A	3.67	CH2	C(=O)-CH2/A		CDCL3
2034M	C	3.53	CH2	C(=O)-CH2/A		CCL4
1975M	D	2.38	CH2	C(=O)-CH2/CH2.3-CH3		CDCL3
1988M	D	2.34 APP.	CH2	C(=O)-CH2/CH2.8-CH3		CCL4
1985M	C	2.31	CH2	C(=O)-CH2/CH2-CH2		CCL4
1983M	C	2.31	CH2	C(=O)-CH2/CH2-CH2		CCL4
1987M	C	2.39	CH2	C(=O)-CH2/CH2-CH2		CDCL3
1978M	C	2.40	CH2	C(=O)-CH2/CH2-CH2		CDCL3
1986M	C	2.40	CH2	C(=O)-CH2/CH2-CH2		CDCL3
2495M	C	2.40 APP.	CH2	C(=O)-CH2/CH2-CH2		CDCL3
1980M	D	2.34	CH2	C(=O)-CH2/CH2-CH2		CCL4
2139M	C	2.21	CH2	C(=O)-CH2/CH2-CH3		CCL4
1972M	C	2.31	CH2	C(=O)-CH2/CH2-CH3		CCL4
1970M	E	2.37	CH2	C(=O)-CH2/CH2-CH3		CDCL3
2495M	D	2.67	CH2	C(=O)-CH2/CH2-C(=O)		CDCL3
2034M	B	2.34	CH2	C(=O)-CH2/CH3		CCL4
2138M	C	2.26	CH2	C(=O)-CH2/CH3		CCL4
1980M	E	2.36	CH2	C(=O)-CH2/CH3		CCL4
1979M	B	1.96- 2.34	CH2	C(=O)-CH2/CH(CH3/CH3)		CCL4
2138M	E	3.47	CH2	C(=O)-CH2/C(=O)-CH2		CCL4
2146M	C	3.32	CH2	C(=O)-CH2/C(=O)-CH3		CCL4
2039M	B	3.48	CH2	C(=O)-CH3/AR500(C-CH-C*-O/CH-CH-C*)		CCL4
1989M	E	2.43	CH2	C(=O)-CH3/CH2.10		CDCL3
1969M	E	2.37	CH2	C(=O)-CH3/CH2.2-CH3		CCL4
2748M	B	2.33	CH2	C(=O)-CH3/CH2.4-C(=O)-CL		CDCL3
2038M	A	2.11	CH2	C(=O)-CH3/CH2-A		CDCL3
2036M	B	2.64	CH2	C(=O)-CH3/CH2-A		CCL4
1976M	D	2.34	CH2	C(=O)-CH3/CH2-CH2		CCL4
1974M	D	2.36	CH2	C(=O)-CH3/CH2-CH2		CCL4
1995M	B	2.60	CH2	C(=O)-CH3/CH2-C(=O)		CCL4
2746M	B	2.50	CH2	C(=O)-CH3/CH2-C(=O)-O		CCL4
2494M	B	2.59 APP.	CH2	C(=O)-CH3/CH2-C(=O)-O		CDCL3
2747M	D	2.45	CH2	C(=O)-CH3/CH2-C(=O)-O		CCL4
2019M	B	2.40 APP.	CH2	C(=O)-CH3/CH2-Q3		CCL4
1968M	C	2.40	CH2	C(=O)-CH3/CH3		CCL4
1971M	C	1.90- 2.37	CH2	C(=O)-CH3/CH(CH3/CH3)		CCL4
1973M	C	2.28	CH2	C(=O)-CH3/C(CH3/CH3/CH3)		CCL4
1997M	C	2.38 APP.	CH2	C(=O)-CH3/R5		CCL4
2035M	A	3.61	CH2	C(=O)-CH/A		CCL4
1982M	D	2.35	CH2	C(=O)-CH/CH2.4-CH3		CCL4
2217M	A	4.10	CH2	C(=O)-CL/A(C-CH-CH-C(CL))		CDCL3
2194M	D	2.85	CH2	C(=O)-CL/CH2.15-CH3		CCL4
2197M	B	2.92	CH2	C(=O)-CL/CH2.4-BR		CCL4
2748M	C	2.94	CH2	C(=O)-CL/CH2.4-C(=O)-O		CDCL3
2202M	C	2.88	CH2	C(=O)-CL/CH2.7-C(=O)-CL		CCL4
2212M	B	3.02	CH2	C(=O)-CL/CH2-A		CCL4
2196M	A	3.51 APP.	CH2	C(=O)-CL/CH2-BR		CCL4
2218M	B	2.27	CH2	C(=O)-CL/CH2-CH2		CDCL3
2218M	B	2.57	CH2	C(=O)-CL/CH2-CH2		CDCL3

BOOK NO.	ASSIGN-MENT	CHEM SHIFT - ppm -	PROTON GROUP	ENVIRONMENTAL GROUPS	S	SOLVENT
2200M	B	2.89	CH2	C(=O)-CL/CH2-CH2		CCL4
2199M	B	2.94	CH2	C(=O)-CL/CH2-CH2		CDCL3
2195M	B	3.09	CH2	C(=O)-CL/CH2-CH2		CCL4
2193M	D	2.86	CH2	C(=O)-CL/CH2-CH2		CDCL3
2192M	D	2.87	CH2	C(=O)-CL/CH2-CH2		CCL4
2206M	D	2.92	CH2	C(=O)-CL/CH2-CH2		CCL4
2188M	C	2.88	CH2	C(=O)-CL/CH2-CH3		CDCL3
2198M	A	3.28	CH2	C(=O)-CL/CH2-C(=O)-CL		CDCL3
2203M	B	2.88	CH2	C(=O)-CL/CH2-R5		CCL4
2187M	B	2.93	CH2	C(=O)-CL/CH3		CDCL3
2189M	B	2.79	CH2	C(=O)-CL/C(CH3/CH3/CH3)		CCL4
2131M	C	2.71	CH2	C(=O)-C(=O)/CH3		CCL4
2277M	C	1.85- 2.25	CH2	C(=O)-HNH/CH2-CH2		DMSO-D6
2159M	A	2.69	CH2	C(=O)-H/CH2-A		CDCL3
2154M	C	2.34	CH2	C(=O)-H/CH2-CH2		CDCL3
2153M	D	4.78	CH2	C(=O)-H/CH2-CH2		CCL4
2151M	C	2.36	CH2	C(=O)-H/CH2-CH3		CCL4
2287M	A	4.19	CH2	C(=O)-NH2/AA<C-C*>		TFA
2280M	C	2.63	CH2	C(=O)-NH2/CH2.11-CH3		TFA
2632M	B	2.47	CH2	C(=O)-NH2/CH2-CH		D20
2278M	D	2.21	CH2	C(=O)-NH2/CH2-CH2		CDCL3
2279M	D	2.21	CH2	C(=O)-NH2/CH2-CH2		CDCL3
2276M	B	2.23	CH2	C(=O)-NH2/CH3		CDCL3
2405M	A	3.28	CH2	C(=O)-NH-NH2/A(C-CH-CH-C(NH2))		POLYSOL-D
2314M	A	3.55	CH2	C(=O)-NH/A		CDCL3
2312M	B	3.48	CH2	C(=O)-NH/A		CDCL3
2404M	B	2.28	CH2	C(=O)-NH/CH2.3-C(=O)-NH		D20
891M	C	2.20	CH2	C(=O)-NH/CH2-CH2		CDCL3
2302M	D	1.92- 2.61	CH2	C(=O)-NH/CH2-CH2		CDCL3
2298M	D	2.20	CH2	C(=O)-NH/CH2-CH2		CDCL3
2299M	D	2.21	CH2	C(=O)-NH/CH2-CH2		CDCL3
892M	D	2.51	CH2	C(=O)-NH/CH2-CH2		TFA
2413M	C	2.11	CH2	C(=O)-NH/CH2-CH3		DMSO-D6
2316M	C	2.29	CH2	C(=O)-NH/CH2-CH3		CDCL3
2313M	A	2.56	CH2	C(=O)-NH/CH2-CL		CDCL3
2296M	B	2.24	CH2	C(=O)-NH/CH3		CDCL3
2315M	B	2.35	CH2	C(=O)-NH/CH3		CDCL3
2319M	C	3.56	CH2	C(=O)-NH/C(=O)-CH3		DMSO-D6
2320M	A	3.51	CH2	C(=O)-NH/C(=O)-NH		DMSO-D6
2354M	D	2.29	CH2	C(=O)-N/CH2.7-CH3		CDCL3
2355M	C	2.20	CH2	C(=O)-N/CH2-CH2		CCL4
2356M	D	2.19	CH2	C(=O)-N/CH2-CH2		CCL4
2353M	C	2.38	CH2	C(=O)-N/CH2-CH3		D20
2352M	C	2.41	CH2	C(=O)-N/CH2-CH3		D20
2350M	C	2.41	CH2	C(=O)-N/CH3		D20
2351M	D	2.31	CH2	C(=O)-N/CH3		CDCL3
2358M	F	3.51	CH2	C(=O)-N/C(=O)-CH3		CDCL3
2561M	A	3.96	CH2	C(=O)-OH/A<C-CH-CH-C(NO2)>		TFA
2563M	B	3.59	CH2	C(=O)-OH/A<C-CH-CH-C(O-CH2)>		CDCL3
2558M	A	3.69	CH2	C(=O)-OH/A<C-C(F)>		CDCL3
2557M	B	3.57	CH2	C(=O)-OH/A(C-CH-CH-C(CH3))		CDCL3
2559M	A	3.58	CH2	C(=O)-OH/A(C-CH-C(F))		CDCL3
2503M	C	2.27	CH2	C(=O)-OH/CH2.13		POLYSOL-D
2482M	D	2.37	CH2	C(=O)-OH/CH2.13-CH3		CDCL3
2560M	B	2.55	CH2	C(=O)-OH/CH2.2-A	S	D20
2749M	D	2.32 APP.	CH2	C(=O)-OH/CH2.7-C(=O)-O		CDCL3
2540M	A	2.67	CH2	C(=O)-OH/CH2-A		CDCL3
2622M	B	2.15	CH2	C(=O)-OH/CH2-CH2		D20
2499M	B	2.21	CH2	C(=O)-OH/CH2-CH2		DMSO-D6
2502M	B	2.22	CH2	C(=O)-OH/CH2-CH2		DMSO-D6
2498M	B	2.26	CH2	C(=O)-OH/CH2-CH2		DMSO-D6
2689M	B	2.27	CH2	C(=O)-OH/CH2-CH2		D20
2623M	C	2.14	CH2	C(=O)-OH/CH2-CH2		D20
2501M	C	2.20	CH2	C(=O)-OH/CH2-CH2		DMSO-D6
2554M	C	2.31	CH2	C(=O)-OH/CH2-CH2		CDCL3
2495M	C	2.40 APP.	CH2	C(=O)-OH/CH2-CH2		CDCL3
2528M	D	2.30	CH2	C(=O)-OH/CH2-CH2		CCL4
2579M	D	2.32	CH2	C(=O)-OH/CH2-CH2		CDCL3
2480M	D	2.33	CH2	C(=O)-OH/CH2-CH2		CCL4
2529M	D	2.34	CH2	C(=O)-OH/CH2-CH2		CDCL3
2494M	C	2.70	CH2	C(=O)-OH/CH2-C(=O)		CDCL3
2497M	A	2.43	CH2	C(=O)-OH/CH2-C(=O)-O		DMSO-D6
2617M	A	2.53	CH2	C(=O)-OH/CH2-NH2		D20
2527M	D	2.33	CH2	C(=O)-OH/CH2-Q2		CCL4
2525M	D	2.37 APP.	CH2	C(=O)-OH/CH2-Q2		CCL4
2526M	D	2.37 APP.	CH2	C(=O)-OH/CH2-Q2		CCL4
2518M	A	2.20- 2.70	CH2	C(=O)-OH/CH2-Q3		CDCL3
2490M	B	2.74 APP.	CH2	C(=O)-OH/CH2-SH		CCL4
2473M	B	2.37	CH2	C(=O)-OH/CH3		CDCL3
2510M	A	2.78	CH2	C(=O)-OH/CH(C(=O)-O/CH2)		D20
2507M	A	2.91	CH2	C(=O)-OH/CH(OH/C(=O)-OH)		D20

BOOK NO.	ASSIGN-MENT	CHEM SHIFT - ppm -	PROTON GROUP	ENVIRONMENTAL GROUPS	S	SOLVENT
2543M	D	2.99	CH2	C(=O)-OH/C(A/CH2/CH2.2)		DMSO-D6
2500M	B	2.31	CH2	C(=O)-OH/C(CH2/CH3/CH3)		POLYSOL-D
2496M	A	3.37	CH2	C(=O)-OH/C(=O)-OH		POLYSOL-D
2549M	A	3.25	CH2	C(=O)-OH/Q2(A)		CDCL3
2521M	D	3.03	CH2	C(=O)-OH/Q2(CH2-CH2)		CCL4
2516M	A	3.12	CH2	C(=O)-OH/Q3		CDCL3
2607M	A	3.64	CH2	C(=O)-OH/R5NA<C-C*/=CH>		DMSO
2512M	A	3.79	CH2	C(=O)-OH/R5S<C=CH/S>		CDCL3
2674M	A	4.25	CH2	C(=O)-ONA/AA<C-C*>		D2O
2932M	B	3.63	CH2	C(=O)-O-A/A	S	D2O
2933M	B	3.79	CH2	C(=O)-O-A/A		CCL4
2925M	E	2.45	CH2	C(=O)-O-A/CH2-CH2		CDCL3
2921M	B	2.47	CH2	C(=O)-O-A/CH3		CCL4
2649M	B	2.30	CH2	C(=O)-O-CD/CH3		CCL4
2783M	C	2.28	CH2	C(=O)-O-CH2.11/CH2.7-C(=O)-O		D2O
2711M	C	2.28	CH2	C(=O)-O-CH2.11/CH2.9-CH3		CDCL3
2709M	D	2.20	CH2	C(=O)-O-CH2.2/CH2.4-CH3		CDCL3
2747M	E	2.62	CH2	C(=O)-O-CH2.2/CH2-C(=O)-CH3		CCL4
2847M	C	3.51	CH2	C(=O)-O-CH2.3/A		CCL4
2775M	D	2.29	CH2	C(=O)-O-CH2.3/CH2.2-C(=O)-O		CCL4
2819M	D	2.29	CH2	C(=O)-O-CH2.3/CH2.6-Q2		CCL4
2743M	E	3.30	CH2	C(=O)-O-CH2.3/C(=O)-CH3		CDCL3
2705M	C	2.22	CH2	C(=O)-O-CH2.4		CCL4
2848M	C	3.48	CH2	C(=O)-O-CH2.7/A		CCL4
2860M	B	3.44	CH2	C(=O)-O-CH2/A		CCL4
2854M	C	3.50	CH2	C(=O)-O-CH2/A<C-C(CH3)>		CCL4
2801M	C	2.24	CH2	C(=O)-O-CH2/CH2.6-CH3		CCL4
2782M	C	2.29	CH2	C(=O)-O-CH2/CH2.7-C(=O)-O		CCL4
2749M	D	2.32 APP.	CH2	C(=O)-O-CH2/CH2.7-C(=O)-OH		CDCL3
2763M	C	2.30	CH2	C(=O)-O-CH2/CH2.9-CH3		CDCL3
2633M	B	2.89	CH2	C(=O)-O-CH2/CH2-CH		CDCL3
2777M	C	2.27	CH2	C(=O)-O-CH2/CH2-CH2		TFA
2784M	C	2.27	CH2	C(=O)-O-CH2/CH2-CH2		CCL4
2719M	C	2.33	CH2	C(=O)-O-CH2/CH2-CH2		CCL4
2759M	C	2.35 APP.	CH2	C(=O)-O-CH2/CH2-CH2		CDCL3
2818M	D	1.73- 2.30	CH2	C(=O)-O-CH2/CH2-CH2		CDCL3
2817M	D	1.96	CH2	C(=O)-O-CH2/CH2-CH2		CCL4
2823M	D	2.28	CH2	C(=O)-O-CH2/CH2-CH2		CCL4
2780M	D	2.29	CH2	C(=O)-O-CH2/CH2-CH2		CCL4
2701M	D	2.30	CH2	C(=O)-O-CH2/CH2-CH2		CDCL3
2758M	D	2.36	CH2	C(=O)-O-CH2/CH2-CH2		CCL4
2842M	C	2.24	CH2	C(=O)-O-CH2/CH2-CH3		CDCL3
2724M	B	2.71	CH2	C(=O)-O-CH2/CH2-CL		CCL4
2806M	A	2.60	CH2	C(=O)-O-CH2/CH2-C(=O)-O		CCL4
2774M	C	2.51	CH2	C(=O)-O-CH2/CH2-C(=O)-O		CCL4
2853M	B	2.38	CH2	C(=O)-O-CH2/CH2-N		CDCL3
2835M	B	2.22	CH2	C(=O)-O-CH2/CH3		CCL4
2753M	B	2.37	CH2	C(=O)-O-CH2/CH3		CDCL3
2730M	C	2.82 APP.	CH2	C(=O)-O-CH2/CH(BR/CH3)		CCL4
2837M	B	2.10	CH2	C(=O)-O-CH2/CH(CH3/CH3)		CCL4
2838M	B	2.08	CH2	C(=O)-O-CH2/CH(CH3/CH3)		CCL4
2843M	C	2.12 APP.	CH2	C(=O)-O-CH2/CH(CH3/CH3)		CCL4
2706M	C	2.18	CH2	C(=O)-O-CH2/CH(CH3/CH3)		CDCL3
2850M	B	2.59	CH2	C(=O)-O-CH2/CH(OH/A)		CCL4
2762M	D	3.18	CH2	C(=O)-O-CH2/C(O-C(=O)-O/C(=O)-O/CH2)		CCL4
2767M	C	3.22	CH2	C(=O)-O-CH2/C(=O)-O-CH2		CCL4
2938M	B	3.84	CH2	C(=O)-O-CH3/AN(C-N)		CDCL3
2849M	B	2.21	CH2	C(=O)-O-CH3/CH2.2-A		CCL4
2707M	C	2.21	CH2	C(=O)-O-CH3/CH2-CH2		CCL4
2781M	C	2.23	CH2	C(=O)-O-CH3/CH2-CH2		CCL4
2710M	C	2.23	CH2	C(=O)-O-CH3/CH2-CH2		CCL4
2779M	C	2.28	CH2	C(=O)-O-CH3/CH2-CH2		CDCL3
2785M	C	2.30	CH2	C(=O)-O-CH3/CH2-CH2		CCL4
2704M	D	2.25	CH2	C(=O)-O-CH3/CH2-CH2		CDCL3
2712M	D	2.30	CH2	C(=O)-O-CH3/CH2-CH2		CCL4
2746M	C	2.66	CH2	C(=O)-O-CH3/CH2-C(=O)		CCL4
2737M	A	2.62	CH2	C(=O)-O-CH3/CH2-C:N		CDCL3
2793M	A	2.43	CH2	C(=O)-O-CH3/CH2-N		CDCL3
2738M	B	2.40- 3.00	CH2	C(=O)-O-CH3/CH2-SH		CCL4
2699M	C	2.12	CH2	C(=O)-O-CH3/CH(CH3/CH3)		CCL4
2791M	A	2.49	CH2	C(=O)-O-CH3/CH(OH/CH2)		CDCL3
2790M	A	2.84	CH2	C(=O)-O-CH3/CH(OH/C(=O)-O)		CCL4
2776M	B	2.35	CH2	C(=O)-O-CH3/C(CH2/CH3/CH3)		CDCL3
2742M	B	3.37	CH2	C(=O)-O-CH3/C(=O)-CH3		CDCL3
2761M	D	2.30	CH2	C(=O)-O-CH/CH2.15-CH3		CCL4
2727M	C	2.23	CH2	C(=O)-O-CH/CH2-CH2		CCL4
2823M	D	2.28	CH2	C(=O)-O-CH/CH2-CH2		CCL4
2760M	D	2.29	CH2	C(=O)-O-CH/CH2-CH2		CCL4
2700M	D	2.18	CH2	C(=O)-O-CH/CH2-CH3		CCL4
2725M	B	2.70	CH2	C(=O)-O-CH/CH2-CL		CCL4
2773M	B	2.49	CH2	C(=O)-O-CH/CH2-C(=O)-O		CCL4

BOOK NO.	ASSIGN-MENT	CHEM SHIFT - ppm -	PROTON GROUP	ENVIRONMENTAL GROUPS	S	SOLVENT
2698M	E	2.30	CH2	C(=0)-0-CH/CH3		CDCL3
2252M	D	2.37	CH2	C(=0)-0-C(=0)-CH2.4/CH2.3-CH3		CDCL3
2254M	D	2.40	CH2	C(=0)-0-C(=0)-CH2.5/CH2.4-CH3		CCL4
2250M	C	2.48	CH2	C(=0)-0-C(=0)/CH2-CH2		CDCL3
2249M	C	2.40	CH2	C(=0)-0-C(=0)/CH2-CH3		CCL4
2248M	B	2.43	CH2	C(=0)-0-C(=0)/CH3		CCL4
2768M	B	3.06	CH2	C(=0)-0-C/C(=0)-0-C		CCL4
2761M	D	2.30	CH2	C(=0)-0-HCH/CH2.15-CH3		CDCL3
2760M	D	2.29	CH2	C(=0)-0-HCH/CH2-CH2		CCL4
2670M	B	2.09	CH2	C(=0)-0-K/CH2-CH2	S	D20
2673M	A	3.55	CH2	C(=0)-0-NA/A	S	D20
2664M	A	2.38	CH2	C(=0)-0-NA/CH2-C(=0)-0		D20
2660M	A	2.41	CH2	C(=0)-0-NA/CH2-OH		D20
2663M	A	3.11	CH2	C(=0)-0-NA/C(=0)-0-NA	S	D20
2682M	A	2.50	CH2	C(=0)-0-NH4/CH2-C(=0)-0	S	D20
2652M	C	2.13	CH2	C(=0)-0-NO/CH2CH2		CCL4
2802M	C	2.38	CH2	C(=0)-0-Q3/CH2-CH2		CDCL3
2797M	B	2.36	CH2	C(=0)-0-Q3/CH3		CCL4
2714M	C	2.20	CH2	C(=0)-0-R6/CH2-CH3		CCL4
2715M	C	2.09 APP.	CH2	C(=0)-0-R6/CH(CH3/CH3)		CCL4
2769M	C	3.34	CH2	C(=0)-0/CH2.11/C(=0)-0-CH2.11		CDCL3
2139M	C	2.21	CH2	C(=0)-Q1/CH2-CH3		CCL4
2138M	C	2.26	CH2	C(=0)-Q1/CH3		CCL4
2041M	C	2.61	CH2	C(=0)-Q2/CH2.2-CH3		CDCL3
2141M	C	3.86	CH2	C(=0)-R50/C(=0)-CH3		CCL4
1332M	A	3.92	CH2	C(=S)-NH2/A		POLYSOL-D
122M	D	2.11	CH2	C:CH/CH2.14-CH3		CCL4
121M	D	2.15	CH2	C:CH/CH2.7-CH3		CCL4
124M	C	2.20	CH2	C:CH/CH2-CH2		CDCL3
123M	C	2.22	CH2	C:CH/CH2-CH2		CDCL3
119M	D	2.09 APP.	CH2	C:CH/CH2-CH2		CCL4
120M	D	2.10	CH2	C:CH/CH2-CH2		CCL4
118M	D	2.11	CH2	C:CH/CH2-CH2		CCL4
117M	D	2.12	CH2	C:CH/CH2-CH3		CCL4
1695M	B	2.38	CH2	C:CH/CH2-OH		CCL4
127M	D	2.10	CH2	C:C-CH2.2/CH2.3-CH3		CCL4
127M	D	2.10	CH2	C:C-CH2.4/CH2-CH3		CCL4
1250M	B	2.55	CH2	C:C-CH3/CH2-SO		CDCL3
129M	C	2.09	CH2	C:C/CH2.3-CH3		CCL4
1698M	C	2.15	CH2	C:C/CH2.3-CH3		CCL4
131M	C	2.11 APP.	CH2	C:C/CH2.3-C:		CCL4
1699M	C	2.12	CH2	C:C/CH2.4-CH3		CCL4
1697M	C	2.20	CH2	C:C/CH2.4-CH3		CCL4
168M	C	2.37	CH2	C:C/CH2.5-CH3		CCL4
128M	D	2.10 APP.	CH2	C:C/CH2.5-CH3		CCL4
130M	D	2.10	CH2	C:C/CH2-CH		CCL4
1787M	D	1.90- 2.40	CH2	C:C/CH2-CH3		CCL4
1699M	D	2.32	CH2	C:C/CH2-OH		CCL4
1698M	D	2.38	CH2	C:C/CH2-OH		CCL4
1696M	B	2.23	CH2	C:C/CH3		CCL4
131M	C	2.11 APP.	CH2	C:C/CH3		CCL4
128M	D	2.10 APP.	CH2	C:C/CH3		CCL4
1787M	D	1.90- 2.40	CH2	C:C/CH(OH/CH2)		CCL4
981M	A	3.62	CH2	C:N/A<C-CH-CH-C(CL)>		CCL4
980M	A	3.62	CH2	C:N/A<C-C(F)>		CCL4
958M	C	2.30	CH2	C:N/CH2.2-N		CCL4
950M	C	2.29	CH2	C:N/CH2.4-CH3		CCL4
951M	C	2.31	CH2	C:N/CH2.5-CH3		CCL4
952M	C	2.29	CH2	C:N/CH2.7-CH3		CCL4
973M	A	2.36	CH2	C:N/CH2-A		CDCL3
1902M	A	2.50	CH2	C:N/CH2-A		CDCL3
1954M	A	2.64	CH2	C:N/CH2-AA		POLYSOL-D
956M	A	2.97	CH2	C:N/CH2-BR		CCL4
979M	B	2.49 APP.	CH2	C:N/CH2-C		DMSO-D6
1480M	C	2.39 APP.	CH2	C:N/CH2-CH		CDCL3
957M	B	2.33	CH2	C:N/CH2-CH2		CCL4
963M	B	2.40	CH2	C:N/CH2-CH2		CDCL3
955M	B	2.51	CH2	C:N/CH2-CH2		CCL4
946M	C	2.30	CH2	C:N/CH2-CH2		CCL4
946M	C	2.30	CH2	C:N/CH2-CH2		CCL4
949M	C	2.33	CH2	C:N/CH2-CH2		CDCL3
953M	D	2.31	CH2	C:N/CH2-CH2		CDCL3
959M	D	2.48	CH2	C:N/CH2-CH2		CCL4
959M	D	2.48	CH2	C:N/CH2-CH2		CCL4
944M	C	2.27	CH2	C:N/CH2-CH3		CCL4
954M	A	2.80	CH2	C:N/CH2-CL		CCL4
2737M	A	2.62	CH2	C:N/CH2-C(=0)-0		CCL4
962M	A	2.78	CH2	C:N/CH2-C:N		CDCL3
976M	A	2.69	CH2	C:N/CH2-N		DMSO-D6
2613M	A	3.01	CH2	C:N/CH2-NH		D20
960M	B	2.55	CH2	C:N/CH2-NH		CDCL3

BOOK NO.	ASSIGN-MENT	CHEM SHIFT - ppm -	PROTON GROUP	ENVIRONMENTAL GROUPS	S	SOLVENT
1400M	B	2.56	CH2	C:N/CH2-O		CDCL3
1658M	A	2.61	CH2	C:N/CH2-OH		CDCL3
1122M	A	2.75	CH2	C:N/CH2-S		CDCL3
1122M	A	2.88	CH2	C:N/CH2-S		CDCL3
1297M	A	2.96 APP.	CH2	C:N/CH2-SO3		D20
947M	C	2.21	CH2	C:N/CH(CH3/CH3)		CCL4
974M	B	2.48	CH2	C:N/C(A/CH3/CH3)		CCL4
961M	A	4.21	CH2	C:N/C:N		DMSO-D6
221M	A	5.24	CH2	F/A		CCL4
219M	D	4.35	CH2	F/CH2.4-CH3		CCL4
220M	D	4.31	CH2	F/CH2-CH2		CCL4
1990M	A	5.11	CH2	F/C(=O)-CH2		CDCL3
2653M	A	4.73	CH2	F/C(=O)-O-NA		D20
425M	A	4.38	CH2	I/A		CDCL3
413M	D	3.14	CH2	I/CH2.10-CH3		CCL4
414M	D	3.14	CH2	I/CH2.14-CH3		CCL4
407M	D	3.19	CH2	I/CH2.2-CH3		CCL4
419M	B	3.20	CH2	I/CH2.4-I		CDCL3
424M	B	3.19	CH2	I/CH2-A		CDCL3
410M	C	3.17	CH2	I/CH2-CH		CCL4
418M	B	3.17	CH2	I/CH2-CH2		CCL4
417M	B	3.29	CH2	I/CH2-CH2		CCL4
420M	C	3.20	CH2	I/CH2-CH2		CCL4
412M	D	3.12	CH2	I/CH2-CH2		CCL4
411M	D	3.14	CH2	I/CH2-CH2		CCL4
405M	C	3.15	CH2	I/CH2-CH3		CCL4
416M	A	3.70	CH2	I/CH2-I		CDCL3
404M	B	3.13	CH2	I/CH3		CCL4
409M	C	3.10	CH2	I/CH(CH3/CH3)		CCL4
2488M	A	3.71	CH2	I/C(=O)-OH		CDCL3
2734M	B	3.69	CH2	I/C(=O)-O-CH2		CCL4
2656M	A	3.63	CH2	I/C(=O)-O-NA	S	D20
415M	A	3.88	CH2	I/I		CCL4
423M	A	3.80	CH2	I/Q3		CCL4
782M	A	4.27	CH2	NH2/A	S	D20
476M	B	3.85	CH2	NH2/A		CDCL3
486M	D	3.71	CH2	NH2/A<C-CH-CH-C(CH(CH3/CH3))>		CCL4
484M	C	3.80	CH2	NH2/A<C-CH-C(CH3)>		CDCL3
1505M	C	3.79	CH2	NH2/A<C-CH-C(O-CH3)>		CDCL3
483M	C	3.79	CH2	NH2/A<C-C(CH3)>		CDCL3
1504M	B	3.88 APP.	CH2	NH2/A<C-C(O-CH3)>		CCL4
485M	C	3.72	CH2	NH2/A(C-CH-CH-C(CH3))		POLYSOL-D
783M	A	4.06	CH2	NH2/A(C-CH-C(BR))	S	D20
771M	A	3.89	CH2	NH2/CF3	S	D20
2686M	D	2.79	CH2	NH2/CH2.10-CH3		CDCL3
462M	C	2.68	CH2	NH2/CH2.11-NH2		CDCL3
768M	C	3.09	CH2	NH2/CH2.2-CH3	S	CDCL3
1656M	B	3.17	CH2	NH2/CH2.2-OH	S	D20
1121M	D	2.68	CH2	NH2/CH2.2-S		D20
1597M	D	2.68	CH2	NH2/CH2.2-SI		CDCL3
779M	C	3.05	CH2	NH2/CH2.5-NH2	S	D20
2685M	D	2.80	CH2	NH2/CH2.8-CH3		CDCL3
529M	B	2.86	CH2	NH2/CH2-A		CDCL3
477M	C	2.82 APP.	CH2	NH2/CH2-A		CCL4
2643M	B	3.31	CH2	NH2/CH2-CH	S	D20
446M	E	2.71	CH2	NH2/CH2-CH		CDCL3
461M	B	2.60	CH2	NH2/CH2-CH2		D20
458M	B	2.62	CH2	NH2/CH2-CH2		D20
1643M	B	2.70	CH2	NH2/CH2-CH2		D20
2628M	B	2.90	CH2	NH2/CH2-CH2		D20
778M	B	3.00- 3.70	CH2	NH2/CH2-CH2	S	TFA
777M	B	3.07	CH2	NH2/CH2-CH2	S	D20
2644M	B	3.10	CH2	NH2/CH2-CH2	S	D20
482M	C	2.54	CH2	NH2/CH2-CH2		CCL4
466M	C	2.70	CH2	NH2/CH2-CH2		CDCL3
2622M	C	2.98	CH2	NH2/CH2-CH2		D20
627M	D	2.40	CH2	NH2/CH2-CH2		CDCL3
464M	D	2.61	CH2	NH2/CH2-CH2		D20
441M	D	2.61	CH2	NH2/CH2-CH2		CDCL3
439M	D	2.65	CH2	NH2/CH2-CH2		CCL4
444M	D	2.69	CH2	NH2/CH2-CH2		CDCL3
1466M	D	2.70	CH2	NH2/CH2-CH2		CCL4
481M	D	2.70	CH2	NH2/CH2-CH2		CDCL3
451M	D	2.70	CH2	NH2/CH2-CH2		CDCL3
2623M	D	2.98	CH2	NH2/CH2-CH2		D20
770M	D	3.03	CH2	NH2/CH2-CH2	S	D20
465M	E	2.68	CH2	NH2/CH2-CH2		CCL4
767M	C	2.75	CH2	NH2/CH2-CH3	S	DMSO-D6
439M	D	2.65	CH2	NH2/CH2-CH3		CCL4
2617M	B	3.18	CH2	NH2/CH2-C(=O)-O		D20
580M	A	2.60 APP.	CH2	NH2/CH2-NH		D20

BOOK NO.	ASSIGN- MENT	CHEM SHIFT - ppm -	PROTON GROUP	ENVIRONMENTAL GROUPS	S	SOLVENT
463M	C	2.65 APP.	CH2	NH2/CH2-NH		D2O
775M	A	3.40	CH2	NH2/CH2-NH2		D2O
2690M	A	3.41	CH2	NH2/CH2-NH2		D2O
776M	A	3.42	CH2	NH2/CH2-NH2	S	D2O
457M	B	2.60	CH2	NH2/CH2-NH2		CCL4
1672M	B	2.83	CH2	NH2/CH2-O		CDCL3
1642M	A	2.73	CH2	NH2/CH2-OH		CDCL3
1655M	A	3.18	CH2	NH2/CH2-OH	S	D2O
820M	B	3.49	CH2	NH2/CH2-R5NN	S	D2O
780M	B	3.07	CH2	NH2/CH2-S		D2O
780M	B	3.39	CH2	NH2/CH2-S		D2O
766M	B	3.08	CH2	NH2/CH3	S	D2O
479M	C	2.71 APP.	CH2	NH2/CH(A/CH3)		CDCL3
454M	C	2.61	CH2	NH2/CH(CH2/CH2)		CDCL3
445M	E	2.57	CH2	NH2/CH(CH2/CH3)		CDCL3
442M	D	2.49	CH2	NH2/CH(CH3/CH3)		CDCL3
459M	C	2.20- 2.65	CH2	NH2/CH(NH2/CH3)		CDCL3
625M	C	2.29- 2.95	CH2	NH2/CH(N/CH3)		D2O
1844M	A	2.63	CH2	NH2/CH(OH/CH2)		D2O
1427M	B	2.69	CH2	NH2/CH(O/O)		CCL4
1428M	B	2.76	CH2	NH2/CH(O/O)		CDCL3
460M	C	2.40	CH2	NH2/C(NH2/CH3/CH3)		CCL4
2638M	A	3.84	CH2	NH2/C(=O)-NH		D2O
2638M	A	3.90	CH2	NH2/C(=O)-NH		D2O
2641M	A	3.98	CH2	NH2/C(=O)-NH		D2O
2646M	A	3.92	CH2	NH2/C(=O)-NH	S	D2O
2611M	A	3.58	CH2	NH2/C(=O)-OH		D2O
475M	C	3.12	CH2	NH2/Q2(CH3/H/H)		CCL4
781M	A	3.60	CH2	NH2/Q3	S	POLYSOL-D
474M	B	3.30	CH2	NH2/Q3		CDCL3
469M	.C	2.52	CH2	NH2/R6		CDCL3
473M	E	2.31	CH2	NH2/R6R6TRI<C*(CH2/CH2/CH2)>		CDCL3
600M	B	3.20	CH2	NH-AA/CH3		CCL4
709M	A	4.29	CH2	NH-AN/A		DMSO-D6
708M	C	3.36	CH2	NH-AN/CH2-N		CDCL3
594M	B	4.22	CH2	NH-A/A		CDCL3
596M	C	4.07	CH2	NH-A/A		CCL4
595M	C	6.18	CH2	NH-A/A		CDCL3
585M	C	3.04	CH2	NH-A/CH2-CH		CDCL3
584M	C	2.97	CH2	NH-A/CH2-CH3		CCL4
583M	C	3.03	CH2	NH-A/CH3		CCL4
1062M	B	3.30	CH2	NH-A/CH3		CCL4
806M	B	3.51	CH2	NH-A/CH3	S	D2O
593M	C	3.01	CH2	NH-A/CH3		CDCL3
2634M	A	3.81	CH2	NH-A/C(=O)-OH		DMSO-D6
587M	B	3.60	CH2	NH-A/Q3		CDCL3
1966M	E	5.01	CH2	NH-A/R5NN<N-C(=O)/C(=O)>		CDCL3
554M	D	2.59	CH2	NH-CH2.12/CH2.11-CH3		CDCL3
580M	B	3.64	CH2	NH-CH2.2/A		D2O
542M	C	2.58	CH2	NH-CH2.2/CH2-CH3		CDCL3
555M	C	2.65	CH2	NH-CH2.2/CH3		CDCL3
548M	C	2.60	CH2	NH-CH2.4/CH2.3-CH3		CDCL3
805M	A	4.37	CH2	NH-CH2/A	S	TFA
581M	B	3.70	CH2	NH-CH2/A		CCL4
579M	D	3.69	CH2	NH-CH2/A		CCL4
577M	D	3.70	CH2	NH-CH2/A		CCL4
578M	E	3.68	CH2	NH-CH2/A		CCL4
549M	D	2.52	CH2	NH-CH2/CH2-CH		CCL4
1757M	D	3.06	CH2	NH-CH2/CH2-CH		CDCL3
579M	C	2.57	CH2	NH-CH2/CH2-CH2		CCL4
466M	C	2.70	CH2	NH-CH2/CH2-CH2		CDCL3
800M	C	3.03	CH2	NH-CH2/CH2-CH2		D2O
551M	D	2.40	CH2	NH-CH2/CH2-CH2		CDCL3
550M	D	2.40	CH2	NH-CH2/CH2-CH2		CDCL3
553M	D	2.51	CH2	NH-CH2/CH2-CH2		CCL4
544M	D	2.52	CH2	NH-CH2/CH2-CH2		D2O
1757M	D	3.06	CH2	NH-CH2/CH2-CH2		CDCL3
578M	D	2.53	CH2	NH-CH2/CH2-CH3		CCL4
2613M	B	3.43	CH2	NH-CH2/CH2-C:N		D2O
960M	C	2.96	CH2	NH-CH2/CH2-C:N		CDCL3
1843M	A	2.72	CH2	NH-CH2/CH2-NH		D2O
555M	D	2.72	CH2	NH-CH2/CH2-NH		CDCL3
580M	A	2.60 APP.	CH2	NH-CH2/CH2-NH2		D2O
463M	C	2.65 APP.	CH2	NH-CH2/CH2-NH2		D2O
1843M	A	2.72	CH2	NH-CH2/CH2-OH		D2O
1842M	A	2.74	CH2	NH-CH2/CH2-OH		D2O
463M	B	2.60	CH2	NH-CH2/CH3		D2O
797M	B	3.03	CH2	NH-CH2/CH3	S	CDCL3
574M	C	2.56	CH2	NH-CH2/CH3		CCL4
577M	C	2.60	CH2	NH-CH2/CH3		CCL4
546M	D	2.31	CH2	NH-CH2/CH(CH3/CH3)		CCL4

BOOK NO.	ASSIGN-MENT	CHEM SHIFT - ppm -	PROTON GROUP	ENVIRONMENTAL GROUPS	S	SOLVENT
2613M	C	3.68	CH2	NH-CH2/C(=O)-OH		D2O
2789M	C	3.38	CH2	NH-CH2/C(=O)-O-CH2		CCL4
573M	D	3.19	CH2	NH-CH2/Q1(CH3/CH3)		CDCL3
574M	D	3.12	CH2	NH-CH2/Q2(CH2-NH)		CCL4
572M	C	3.13	CH2	NH-CH2/Q2(CH3)		CDCL3
571M	B	3.22	CH2	NH-CH2/Q3		CDCL3
464M	C	2.53	CH2	NH-CH3/CH2-CH2		D2O
552M	E	2.54	CH2	NH-CH3/CH2-CH2		CDCL3
1288M	B	3.14- 3.58	CH2	NH-CH3/CH2-SO3H		D2O
2612M	B	3.62	CH2	NH-CH3/C(=O)-OH		D2O
556M	B	2.62	CH2	NH-CH/CH2-NH		D2O
557M	E	2.70	CH2	NH-CH/CH2-NH		CDCL3
1647M	B	2.66	CH2	NH-CH/CH2-OH		CCL4
2309M	C	3.48	CH2	NH-C(=O)-CH3/CH2-A		CDCL3
2301M	B	3.24	CH2	NH-C(=O)-CH3/CH2-NH		POLYSOL-D
2639M	B	3.81	CH2	NH-C(=O)-CH/C(=O)-OH		D2O
2422M	A	4.25	CH2	NH-C(=O)-NH2/A		POLYSOL-D
2418M	C	2.91	CH2	NH-C(=O)-NH2/CH(CH3/CH3)		POLYSOL-D
2432M	A	4.28	CH2	NH-C(=O)-NH/A		POLYSOL-D
2982M	C	3.09	CH2	NH-C(=O)-O/CH2-CH2		CCL4
2981M	D	3.08	CH2	NH-C(=O)-O/CH2-CH3		CCL4
2983M	C	4.51	CH2	NH-C(=O)-O/NH-C(=O)-O		CDCL3
2346M	A	4.54	CH2	NH-C(=O)/A		CDCL3
2314M	B	4.32	CH2	NH-C(=O)/A		CDCL3
2313M	C	4.34	CH2	NH-C(=O)/A		CDCL3
2311M	B	3.52	CH2	NH-C(=O)/CH2-A		CDCL3
2986M	C	2.73	CH2	NH-C(=O)/CH2-A		CCL4
2986M	C	3.32	CH2	NH-C(=O)/CH2-A		CCL4
2429M	C	3.15	CH2	NH-C(=O)/CH2-CH2		CDCL3
2297M	D	3.19	CH2	NH-C(=O)/CH2-CH2		D2O
2299M	E	3.20	CH2	NH-C(=O)/CH2-CH3		CDCL3
2420M	A	3.04	CH2	NH-C(=O)/CH2-NH		DMSO-D6
2295M	B	3.29	CH2	NH-C(=O)/CH3		D2O
2428M	B	3.50	CH2	NH-C(=O)/CH3		CDCL3
2638M	B	3.84	CH2	NH-C(=O)/C(=O)-OH		D2O
2638M	B	3.90	CH2	NH-C(=O)/C(=O)-OH		D2O
2646M	B	4.10	CH2	NH-C(=O)/C(=O)-OH	S	D2O
2751M	B	3.79	CH2	NH-C(=O)/C(=O)-O-CH2		DMSO-D6
2851M	B	4.20	CH2	NH-C(=O)/C(=O)-O-CH3		CDCL3
2300M	A	5.01	CH2	NH-C(=O)/NH-C(=O)		TFA
2430M	A	4.51	CH2	NH-C(=O)/OH		DMSO-D6
2306M	A	3.91	CH2	NH-C(=O)/Q3		CDCL3
1347M	C	3.39	CH2	NH-C(=S)/CH2.8-CH3		POLYSOL-D
1339M	B	3.28	CH2	NH-C(=S)/CH3		DMSO-D6
1344M	B	3.51	CH2	NH-C(=S)/CH3		CCL4
1348M	B	3.66	CH2	NH-C(=S)/CH3		CDCL3
1346M	C	3.30	CH2	NH-C(=S)/CH(CH3/CH3)		CDCL3
1350M	A	4.22	CH2	NH-C(=S)/Q3		CDCL3
547M	E	2.56	CH2	NH-C/CH2-CH2		CDCL3
1654M	A	2.93	CH2	NH-NH2/CH2-OH		D2O
2629M	B	3.22	CH2	NH-QNH(NH2)/CH2-CH2		D2O
1156M	B	3.39	CH2	NH-R5NNS/CH3		POLYSOL-D
1135M	C	4.45	CH2	NH-R5NS/A		CDCL3
1217M	D	2.50- 3.10	CH2	NH-R6/CH2-SH		CDCL3
570M	C	3.20	CH2	NH-R6/Q3		CCL4
799M	C	3.07	CH2	NH/CH2.2-CH3	S	D2O
1037M	C	4.70	CH2	NO2/CH2-CH		CDCL3
1041M	C	4.31	CH2	NO2/CH2-CH3		CCL4
1040M	B	4.40	CH2	NO2/CH3		CDCL3
672M	B	3.12	CH2	N(AA/CH2)/CH3		CCL4
737M	D	3.43	CH2	N(ANNN/CH2)/CH(CH2/CH2)		CCL4
655M	A	3.61 APP.	CH2	N(A/CH2.2)/CH2-CL		POLYSOL-D
976M	B	3.69	CH2	N(A/CH2.2)/CH2-C:N		DMSO-D6
654M	A	4.59	CH2	N(A/CH2)/A		CDCL3
653M	C	4.48	CH2	N(A/CH2)/A		CDCL3
651M	C	3.22	CH2	N(A/CH2)/CH2-CH2		CCL4
650M	C	3.17	CH2	N(A/CH2)/CH2-CH3		CCL4
1706M	D	3.30	CH2	N(A/CH2)/CH2-OH		CDCL3
670M	B	3.17	CH2	N(A/CH2)/CH3		CDCL3
649M	B	3.27	CH2	N(A/CH2)/CH3		CCL4
995M	B	3.36	CH2	N(A/CH2)/CH3		CDCL3
2104M	B	3.38	CH2	N(A/CH2)/CH3		CDCL3
653M	B	3.43	CH2	N(A/CH2)/CH3		CDCL3
1024M	B	3.48	CH2	N(A/CH2)/CH3		CDCL3
817M	B	3.63	CH2	N(A/CH2)/CH3	S	D2O
661M	C	2.98	CH2	N(A/CH2)/CH3		CDCL3
661M	C	2.98	CH2	N(A/CH2)/CH3		CDCL3
662M	C	3.22	CH2	N(A/CH2)/CH3		CCL4
663M	C	3.23	CH2	N(A/CH2)/CH3		CDCL3
1525M	C	3.29	CH2	N(A/CH2)/CH3		CCL4
1706M	C	3.30	CH2	N(A/CH2)/CH3		CDCL3

BOOK NO.	ASSIGN-MENT	CHEM SHIFT - ppm -	PROTON GROUP	ENVIRONMENTAL GROUPS	S	SOLVENT
664M	D	2.93	CH2	N(A/CH2)/CH3		CCL4
2548M	A	4.08	CH2	N(A/CH2)/C(=O)-OH		POLYSOL-D
656M	A	3.85	CH2	N(A/CH2)/Q3		CCL4
652M	B	4.41	CH2	N(A/CH3)/A		CCL4
2366M	D	3.65	CH2	N(A/C(=O))/CH2-CH2		CCL4
621M	C	2.38	CH2	N(CH2.11/CH2.11)/CH2.10-CH3		CDCL3
2793M	B	2.79	CH2	N(CH2.2/CH2.2)/CH2-C(=O)-O		CDCL3
1652M	C	2.48	CH2	N(CH2.2/CH2.3)/CH2.2-CH3		CDCL3
812M	B	3.32	CH2	N(CH2.2/CH3)/CH3	S	D2O
1653M	D	2.42	CH2	N(CH2.3/CH2.3)/CH2.2-CH3		CDCL3
1653M	E	2.63	CH2	N(CH2.3/CH2.3)/CH2.2-OH		CDCL3
1652M	D	2.57	CH2	N(CH2.3/CH2.3)/CH2-OH		CDCL3
626M	E	2.50 APP.	CH2	N(CH2.3/CH2)/CH3		CDCL3
618M	C	2.40	CH2	N(CH2.4/CH2.4)/CH2.3-CH3		CCL4
620M	C	2.29	CH2	N(CH2.7/CH2.7)/CH2.6-CH3		CCL4
810M	D	3.01	CH2	N(CH2.7/CH2.7)/CH2.6-CH3		CDCL3
623M	D	2.31	CH2	N(CH2.7/CH3)/CH2.6-CH3		CDCL3
1704M	D	3.61	CH2	N(CH2/CH2.2)/A		CDCL3
2668M	B	3.90	CH2	N(CH2/CH2.2)/C(=O)-O-K		D2O
647M	A	3.51	CH2	N(CH2/CH2)/A		CCL4
2400M	A	4.02	CH2	N(CH2/CH2)/A		CDCL3
645M	C	3.56	CH2	N(CH2/CH2)/A		CDCL3
646M	C	3.56	CH2	N(CH2/CH2)/A		CDCL3
2853M	D	3.56	CH2	N(CH2/CH2)/A		CDCL3
705M	C	3.75	CH2	N(CH2/CH2)/AN<C-N>		CDCL3
619M	C	2.38 APP.	CH2	N(CH2/CH2)/CH2-CH		CDCL3
465M	C	1.61	CH2	N(CH2/CH2)/CH2-CH2		CCL4
617M	C	2.30	CH2	N(CH2/CH2)/CH2-CH2		CCL4
959M	C	2.38	CH2	N(CH2/CH2)/CH2-CH2		CCL4
959M	C	2.38	CH2	N(CH2/CH2)/CH2-CH2		CCL4
465M	D	2.10- 2.55	CH2	N(CH2/CH2)/CH2-CH2		CCL4
615M	C	2.31	CH2	N(CH2/CH2)/CH2-CH3		CCL4
812M	C	3.57	CH2	N(CH2/CH2)/CH2-CL	S	D2O
2853M	C	2.73	CH2	N(CH2/CH2)/CH2-C(=O)-O		CDCL3
1854M	A	2.62 APP.	CH2	N(CH2/CH2)/CH2-N		CDCL3
2668M	A	3.64	CH2	N(CH2/CH2)/CH2-N		D2O
1854M	A	2.62 APP.	CH2	N(CH2/CH2)/CH2-OH		CDCL3
1850M	A	2.70	CH2	N(CH2/CH2)/CH2-OH		D2O
1852M	A	3.50	CH2	N(CH2/CH2)/CH2-OH	S	D2O
1650M	B	2.50	CH2	N(CH2/CH2)/CH2-OH		CCL4
1704M	B	2.63	CH2	N(CH2/CH2)/CH2-OH		CDCL3
614M	B	2.42	CH2	N(CH2/CH2)/CH3		CCL4
646M	B	2.49	CH2	N(CH2/CH2)/CH3		CDCL3
645M	B	2.52	CH2	N(CH2/CH2)/CH3		CDCL3
705M	B	2.59	CH2	N(CH2/CH2)/CH3		CDCL3
2657M	B	2.69	CH2	N(CH2/CH2)/CH3		D2O
809M	B	3.21	CH2	N(CH2/CH2)/CH3	S	CDCL3
1650M	C	2.52	CH2	N(CH2/CH2)/CH3		CCL4
631M	E	3.17	CH2	N(CH2/CH2)/CH3		D2O
1851M	B	2.48	CH2	N(CH2/CH2)/CH(OH/CH3)		CDCL3
631M	D	2.98	CH2	N(CH2/CH2)/C(CH2/CH3/CH3)		D2O
2794M	B	3.67	CH2	N(CH2/CH2)/C(=O)-O-CH2		CDCL3
2666M	A	3.09	CH2	N(CH2/CH2)/C(=O)-O-NA		D2O
2665M	A	3.74	CH2	N(CH2/CH2)/C(=O)-O-NA		D2O
2657M	C	3.19	CH2	N(CH2/CH2)/C(=O)-O-NA		D2O
2400M	B	4.92	CH2	N(CH2/CH2)/R5NA(N-C(=O)/C(=O))		CDCL3
1703M	D	3.55	CH2	N(CH2/CH3)/A		CDCL3
627M	E	2.71	CH2	N(CH2/CH3)/CH2-CH2		CDCL3
633M	C	2.35 APP.	CH2	N(CH2/CH3)/CH2-N		CCL4
1703M	B	2.59	CH2	N(CH2/CH3)/CH2-OH		CDCL3
633M	C	2.35 APP.	CH2	N(CH2/CH3)/CH3		CCL4
1430M	B	2.52	CH2	N(CH2/CH3)/CH(O/O)		CCL4
1431M	C	2.64	CH2	N(CH2/CH3)/CH(O/O)		CDCL3
1755M	F	2.42 APP.	CH2	N(CH2/HCH)/CH2-CH2		CCL4
635M	D	2.48	CH2	N(CH2/R6)/CH3		CCL4
644M	B	3.33	CH2	N(CH3/CH3)/A		CCL4
624M	C	2.21 APP.	CH2	N(CH3/CH3)/CH2.20-CH3		CDCL3
622M	D	2.23	CH2	N(CH3/CH3)/CH2.8-CH3		CDCL3
634M	C	2.29 APP.	CH2	N(CH3/CH3)/CH2-CH2		CDCL3
1649M	C	2.41	CH2	N(CH3/CH3)/CH2-CH2		CCL4
811M	B	3.56	CH2	N(CH3/CH3)/CH2-CL	S	D2O
708M	B	2.51	CH2	N(CH3/CH3)/CH2-NH		CDCL3
2865M	B	2.70	CH2	N(CH3/CH3)/CH2-O-C(=O)		CDCL3
613M	C	2.33	CH2	N(CH3/CH3)/CH3		CDCL3
1754M	B	2.17	CH2	N(CH3/CH3)/CH(OH/CH3)		CDCL3
2642M	B	3.98	CH2	N(CH3/CH3)/C(=O)-OH	S	D2O
630M	B	2.72	CH2	N(CH3/CH3)/N(CH3/CH3)		CDCL3
642M	B	2.93	CH2	N(CH3/CH3)/Q3		CDCL3
610M	B	3.52	CH2	N(CH3/CH3)/R5NA(C=CH/C*)		DMSO-D6
677M	B	3.43	CH2	N(CH3/CH3)/R5N<C=CH/NH>		CDCL3
1406M	B	2.51	CH2	N(CH3/CH3/CH2-O		CCL4

BOOK NO.	ASSIGN-MENT	CHEM SHIFT - ppm -	PROTON GROUP	ENVIRONMENTAL GROUPS	S	SOLVENT
958M	D	2.58	CH2	N(CH/CH)/CH2.2-C:N		CCL4
616M	B	2.48	CH2	N(CH/CH)/CH3		CCL4
2370M	C	3.28	CH2	N(C(=O)-A/CH2)/CH3		CDCL3
2370M	D	3.49	CH2	N(C(=O)-A/CH2)/CH3		CDCL3
2353M	D	3.36	CH2	N(C(=O)-CH2.2/CH2)/CH3		D20
2353M	E	3.41	CH2	N(C(=O)-CH2.2/CH2)/CH3		D20
2354M	E	3.17	CH2	N(C(=O)-CH2.8/CH2.2)/CH2-CH3		CDCL3
2354M	F	3.21	CH2	N(C(=O)-CH2.8/CH2.2)/CH2-CH3		CDCL3
2350M	D	3.36	CH2	N(C(=O)-CH2-CH2)/CH3		D20
2351M	E	3.29	CH2	N(C(=O)-CH2/CH2.3)/CH2.2-CH3		CDCL3
2358M	E	3.10- 3.60	CH2	N(C(=O)-CH2/CH2>		CDCL3
2350M	E	3.40	CH2	N(C(=O)-CH2/CH2)/CH3		D20
2361M	B	3.81	CH2	N(C(=O)-H/A)/CH3		CDCL3
2362M	C	3.80	CH2	N(C(=O)-H/A)/CH3		CDCL3
2347M	C	3.31	CH2	N(C(=O)-H/CH2)/CH3		CDCL3
2347M	D	3.37	CH2	N(C(=O)-H/CH2)/CH3		CDCL3
2990M	D	3.61	CH2	N(C(=O)-O/A)/CH2-CH2		CCL4
2984M	D	3.19	CH2	N(C(=O)-O/CH2)/CH2-CH2		CCL4
2358M	E	3.10- 3.60	CH2	N(C(=O)-O1/CH2>		CDCL3
2365M	D	3.69	CH2	N(C(=O)/A)/CH2-CH3		CDCL3
2364M	C	3.69	CH2	N(C(=O)/A)/CH3		CCL4
2438M	C	3.02	CH2	N(C(=O)/CH2)/CH2-CH2		CCL4
2349M	D	3.22	CH2	N(C(=O)/CH2)/CH2-CH2		CCL4
2356M	E	3.27	CH2	N(C(=O)/CH2)/CH3		CCL4
1356M	B	3.52	CH2	N(C(=S)/CH2)/CH3		CDCL3
1005M	A	4.06	CH2	N(C:N/CH2)/A		CDCL3
827M	B	3.24	CH2	N(&)(CH2/CH2/CH2)/CH3	S	D20
1078M	C	3.58	CH2	N(NO2/CH2)/CH(CH3/CH3)		CDCL3
1026M	C	3.60	CH2	N(NO/CH2)/CH3		CDCL3
1026M	D	4.12	CH2	N(NO/CH2)/CH3		CDCL3
1027M	D	3.48	CH2	N(N=O/CH2.2)/CH2-CH3		CCL4
1027M	E	4.06	CH2	N(N=O/CH2.2)/CH2-CH3		CCL4
2998M	D	2.91	CH2	N(P/CH2)/CH3		CCL4
2998M	D	3.10	CH2	N(P/CH2)/CH3		CCL4
2998M	E	2.91	CH2	N(P/CH2)/CH3		CCL4
2998M	E	3.10	CH2	N(P/CH2)/CH3		CCL4
1369M	C	3.24	CH2	N(SO2/CH2)/CH2-OH		CDCL3
827M	B	3.24	CH2	N(T)(CH2/CH2/CH2)/CH3	S	D20
841M	B	4.14	CH2	N(+)(A/CH2/CH2)/CH3		CDCL3
828M	C	3.20	CH2	N(+)(CH2.3/CH2.3/CH2.3)/CH2.2-CH3		CDCL3
832M	C	3.42 APP.	CH2	N(+)(CH2/CH2/CH2)/CH2-CH2	S	CDCL3
834M	B	3.40	CH2	N(+)(CH2/CH2/CH2)/CH3		POLYSOL-D
834M	D	4.39	CH2	N(+)(CH2/CH2/CH2)/C:CH		POLYSOL-D
839M	G	4.99	CH2	N(+)(CH2/CH3/CH3)/A	S	CDCL3
839M	F	3.50 APP.	CH2	N(+)(CH2/CH3/CH3)/CH2-CH2	S	CDCL3
838M	B	4.48	CH2	N(+)(CH3/CH3/CH3)/A		POLYSOL-D
837M	B	4.93	CH2	N(+)(CH3/CH3/CH3)/A		POLYSOL-D
836M	B	5.06	CH2	N(+)(CH3/CH3/CH3)/A	S	CDCL3
829M	D	3.52	CH2	N(+)(CH3/CH3/CH3)/CH2.10-CH3	S	CDCL3
830M	D	3.67	CH2	N(+)(CH3/CH3/CH3)/CH2.10-CH3	S	CDCL3
833M	D	3.58	CH2	N(+)(CH3/CH3/CH3)/CH2.16-CH3	S	CDCL3
831M	E	3.69	CH2	N(+)(CH3/CH3/CH3)/CH2-CH2	S	CDCL3
1657M	B	3.56	CH2	N(+)(CH3/CH3/CH3)/CH2-OH	S	CDCL3
1004M	A	3.60	CH2	N-C:N/Q3		CCL4
910M	C	3.29	CH2	N=C=O/CH2.10-CH3		CCL4
909M	C	3.24	CH2	N=C=O/CH2.4-CH3		CDCL3
908M	C	3.29	CH2	N=C=O/CH2-CH3		CDCL3
937M	A	4.59	CH2	N=C=S/A		CDCL3
934M	C	3.51	CH2	N=C=S/CH2.16-CH3		CDCL3
931M	C	3.55	CH2	N=C=S/CH2.2-CH3		CCL4
933M	D	3.51	CH2	N=C=S/CH2-CH2		CCL4
936M	A	4.15	CH2	N=C=S/Q3		CCL4
2662M	A	3.74	CH2	OH(CH(OH/CH)	S	D20
1700M	B	4.41	CH2	OH/A		CCL4
1731M	A	4.80	CH2	OH/ANA(C-CH-N-C*/CH-C*)		CDCL3
1728M	A	4.78	CH2	OH/AN<C-N>		CDCL3
1729M	A	4.71	CH2	OH/AN(C-CH-CH-N)		CDCL3
1734M	B	4.43	CH2	OH/AR500<C-CH-C*-O/CH-CH-C*>		CDCL3
1860M	A	4.51	CH2	OH/A<C-CH-CH-C(CH2-OH)>		DMSO-D6
1713M	C	4.37	CH2	OH/A<C-CH-CH-C(CH3)>		CCL4
1714M	D	4.35	CH2	OH/A<C-CH-CH-C(CH(CH3/CH3))>		CCL4
1721M	A	4.79	CH2	OH/A<C-CH-CH-C(NO2)>		C3H60
1723M	C	4.40	CH2	OH/A<C-CH-CH-C(O-CH3)>		CCL4
1720M	B	4.78	CH2	OH/A<C-CH-C(NO2)>		CDCL3
1717M	B	4.65	CH2	OH/A<C-C(CL)>		CDCL3
1719M	B	4.99	CH2	OH/A<C-C(NO2)>		CDCL3
1716M	A	4.40	CH2	OH/A(C-CH-CH-C(F))		CDCL3
1715M	A	4.46	CH2	OH/A(C-C(F))		CCL4
1907M	A	4.55	CH2	OH/A(C-C(OH))		DMSO-D6
1722M	C	4.60	CH2	OH/A(C-C(O-CH3))		CDCL3
1827M	B	3.40	CH2	OH/CH2.15-OH		DMSO-D6

BOOK NO.	ASSIGN-MENT	CHEM SHIFT - ppm -	PROTON GROUP	ENVIRONMENTAL GROUPS	S	SOLVENT
1635M	D	3.48	CH2	OH/CH2.22-CH3		POLYSOL-D
1640M	C	3.72	CH2	OH/CH2.2-BR		CDCL3
1849M	B	3.56	CH2	OH/CH2.2-CH		POLYSOL-D
1621M	C	3.50	CH2	OH/CH2.2-CH		CCL4
1653M	F	3.78	CH2	OH/CH2.2-N		CDCL3
1656M	C	3.73	CH2	OH/CH2.2-NH2	S	D20
1625M	D	3.60	CH2	OH/CH2.3-CH		CDCL3
1718M	B	3.64	CH2	OH/CH2-A		POLYSOL-D
1701M	C	3.71	CH2	OH/CH2-A		CDCL3
1725M	C	3.69	CH2	OH/CH2-AA		CCL4
1732M	C	4.11	CH2	OH/CH2-ANN		CDCL3
1639M	B	3.85	CH2	OH/CH2-BR		CCL4
1645M	D	3.81	CH2	OH/CH2-C		CDCL3
1618M	C	3.52	CH2	OH/CH2-CH		CCL4
1620M	D	3.56	CH2	OH/CH2-CH		CCL4
1629M	D	3.65	CH2	OH/CH2-CH		CDCL3
1832M	D	3.65	CH2	OH/CH2-CH		CDCL3
1826M	B	3.56	CH2	OH/CH2-CH2		CDCL3
1825M	B	3.60	CH2	OH/CH2-CH2		D20
1637M	B	3.62	CH2	OH/CH2-CH2		CCL4
1824M	B	3.65	CH2	OH/CH2-CH2		D20
1626M	C	3.49	CH2	OH/CH2-CH2		CCL4
1616M	C	3.50	CH2	OH/CH2-CH2		CCL4
1619M	C	3.50	CH2	OH/CH2-CH2		CCL4
1630M	C	3.50	CH2	OH/CH2-CH2		CCL4
1702M	C	3.51	CH2	OH/CH2-CH2		CCL4
1614M	C	3.52	CH2	OH/CH2-CH2		CCL4
1643M	C	3.63	CH2	OH/CH2-CH2		D20
1623M	D	3.50	CH2	OH/CH2-CH2		CCL4
1631M	D	3.51	CH2	OH/CH2-CH2		CCL4
1628M	D	3.55	CH2	OH/CH2-CH2		CCL4
1649M	D	3.59	CH2	OH/CH2-CH2		CCL4
1633M	D	3.59	CH2	OH/CH2-CH2		CDCL3
1632M	D	3.61	CH2	OH/CH2-CH2		CDCL3
1634M	D	3.62	CH2	OH/CH2-CH2		CDCL3
1689M	E	3.49	CH2	OH/CH2-CH2		CCL4
1613M	C	3.50	CH2	OH/CH2-CH3		CCL4
1636M	A	3.63	CH2	OH/CH2-CL		CDCL3
1636M	A	3.79	CH2	OH/CH2-CL		CDCL3
2660M	B	3.79	CH2	OH/CH2-C(=O)-O		D20
1699M	F	3.60	CH2	OH/CH2-C:		CCL4
1698M	F	3.60	CH2	OH/CH2-C:		CCL4
1695M	C	3.67	CH2	OH/CH2-C:CH		CCL4
1658M	C	3.85	CH2	OH/CH2-C:N		CDCL3
1854M	B	3.63	CH2	OH/CH2-N		CDCL3
1850M	B	3.64	CH2	OH/CH2-N		D20
1852M	B	3.97	CH2	OH/CH2-N	S	D20
1704M	C	3.54	CH2	OH/CH2-N		CDCL3
1650M	D	3.45	CH2	OH/CH2-N		CCL4
1652M	E	3.54	CH2	OH/CH2-N		CDCL3
1703M	E	3.61	CH2	OH/CH2-N		CDCL3
1706M	E	3.62	CH2	OH/CH2-N		CDCL3
1646M	B	3.60	CH2	OH/CH2-NH		CDCL3
1843M	B	3.69	CH2	OH/CH2-NH		D20
1842M	B	3.69	CH2	OH/CH2-NH		D20
1654M	B	3.74	CH2	OH/CH2-NH		D20
1647M	E	3.58	CH2	OH/CH2-NH		CCL4
1655M	B	3.85	CH2	OH/CH2-NH2	S	D20
1642M	C	3.54	CH2	OH/CH2-NH2		CDCL3
1657M	C	4.05	CH2	OH/CH2-N(+)	S	CDCL3
1847M	A	3.55	CH2	OH/CH2-O		CCL4
1845M	A	3.65	CH2	OH/CH2-O		CDCL3
1726M	B	3.98	CH2	OH/CH2-O		CDCL3
1665M	C	3.51	CH2	OH/CH2-O		CDCL3
1705M	C	3.60	CH2	OH/CH2-O		CCL4
1705M	C	3.70	CH2	OH/CH2-O		CCL4
1665M	C	3.71	CH2	OH/CH2-O		CDCL3
1672M	D	3.40- 3.80	CH2	OH/CH2-O		CDCL3
1823M	A	3.68	CH2	OH/CH2-OH		D20
1688M	B	1.80- 2.45	CH2	OH/CH2-Q2		CCL4
1687M	C	3.65	CH2	OH/CH2-Q3		CDCL3
1664M	C	4.70	CH2	OH/CH2-R5NN		TFA
1678M	B	3.67	CH2	OH/CH2-R5S		CCL4
1682M	C	3.56	CH2	OH/CH2-R6		CCL4
2465M	A	3.60	CH2	OH/CH2-R6N3		DMSO-D6
1708M	D	3.57	CH2	OH/CH2-S		CCL4
2972M	D	3.72	CH2	OH/CH2-S		CCL4
1660M	F	3.71	CH2	OH/CH2-S		CDCL3
1661M	B	3.69	CH2	OH/CH2-SH		D20
1663M	B	3.93	CH2	OH/CH2-SO3-K		D20
1612M	B	3.58	CH2	OH/CH3		CCL4

BOOK NO.	ASSIGN-MENT	CHEM SHIFT - ppm -	PROTON GROUP	ENVIRONMENTAL GROUPS	S	SOLVENT
1622M	D	3.54	CH2	OH/CH(CH2/CH2)		CDCL3
1627M	E	3.43	CH2	OH/CH(CH2/CH2)		CCL4
1615M	C	3.27	CH2	OH/CH(CH3/CH3)		CCL4
1638M	A	3.97	CH2	OH/CH(CL/CL)		CCL4
1994M	E	3.71	CH2	OH/CH(C(=0)-CH3/CH3)		CDCL3
2641M	B	3.99	CH2	OH/CH(NH/C(=0)-OH)		D20
1651M	C	3.60	CH2	OH/CH(N/CH3)		CCL4
1840M	A	3.66 APP.	CH2	OH/CH(OH/CH2)		D20
1844M	B	3.30- 3.90	CH2	OH/CH(OH/CH2)		D20
2718M	B	3.50- 4.00	CH2	OH/CH(OH/CH2)		CDCL3
1848M	B	3.62	CH2	OH/CH(OH/CH2)		D20
1829M	C	3.10- 3.80	CH2	OH/CH(OH/CH2)		CDCL3
2719M	E	3.69	CH2	OH/CH(OH/CH2)		CDCL3
1863M	A	3.59- 3.81	CH2	OH/CH(OH/CH)		CDCL3
1861M	A	3.74 APP.	CH2	OH/CH(OH/CH)		D20
2661M	A	3.75 APP.	CH2	OH/CH(OH/CH)	S	D20
1662M	F	3.77	CH2	OH/CH(SH/CH2)		CDCL3
1641M	B	4.28	CH2	OH/C(BR/BR/BR)		CDCL3
1853M	A	3.62	CH2	OH/C(CH2/CH2/CH2)		D20
1841M	B	3.68	CH2	OH/C(CH2/CH2/CH2)		POLYSOL-D
1835M	C	3.50	CH2	OH/C(CH2/CH2/CH2)		CDCL3
1839M	D	3.47	CH2	OH/C(CH2/CH2/CH2)		C3D60
1624M	E	3.27	CH2	OH/C(CH2/CH3/CH3)		CDCL3
1837M	F	3.93	CH2	OH/C(OH/CH2/CH3)		CDCL3
2492M	A	4.29	CH2	OH/C(=0)-OH		D20
1696M	D	4.17	CH2	OH/C:C		CCL4
1697M	E	4.19	CH2	OH/C:C		CCL4
1693M	C	4.23	CH2	OH/C:CH		CDCL3
1694M	C	4.11	CH2	OH/C:C-CH3		CCL4
1690M	F	4.02	CH2	OH/Q1(CH2.3-CH/CH3)		CCL4
1712M	C	4.09	CH2	OH/Q1(H/A/CH3)		CDCL3
1724M	A	4.29	CH2	OH/Q2(A<C-CH-CH-C(NO2)>)		POLYSOL-D
1686M	B	3.92	CH2	OH/Q2(CH3)		CCL4
1711M	B	4.22	CH2	OH/Q2(H/A/H)		CDCL3
1685M	A	4.05	CH2	OH/Q3		CCL4
1858M	A	4.29	CH2	OH/Q3-CH2		D20
1727M	A	3.60- 4.20	CH2	OH/R5AA<CH-C*/C*>		POLYSOL-D
1730M	A	4.95	CH2	OH/R5NNA(C=N/NH)		DMSO-D6
1679M	D	3.53	CH2	OH/R500<CH-0/CH2>		CCL4
1733M	B	4.50	CH2	OH/R50(C=CH/0)		CDCL3
1683M	D	3.37	CH2	OH/R6N(CH-CH2/CH2)		CDCL3
1692M	D	3.49 APP.	CH2	OH/R60(C(CH3)-0/CH2)		CDCL3
1684M	D	3.07	CH2	OH/R6R6R6TRI<C*(CH2/CH2/CH2)>		POLYSOL-D
1680M	B	3.32	CH2	OH/R6<CH-CH2/CH2>		CCL4
1681M	C	3.32	CH2	OH/R6<CH-CH2/CH2>		CCL4
1709M	C	4.61	CH2	OH/S02-A		CDCL3
1038M	D	4.62	CH2	ONO/CH2-CH2		CCL4
1572M	A	5.10	CH2	O-AA/A		CDCL3
1726M	C	4.09	CH2	O-AA/CH2-OH		CDCL3
1570M	B	3.95	CH2	O-AA/CH3		CDCL3
1571M	B	4.11	CH2	O-AA/CH3		CDCL3
1581M	D	4.30	CH2	O-AN/CH2-CH2		CDCL3
1562M	D	3.82	CH2	O-A/CH2.2-CH3		CDCL3
1562M	E	3.89	CH2	O-A/CH2.2-CH3		CDCL3
1502M	D	3.88	CH2	O-A/CH2.3-CL		CCL4
1491M	B	4.19	CH2	O-A/CH2-BR		CDCL3
1534M	C	4.06	CH2	O-A/CH2-CH2		CCL4
2554M	D	3.92	CH2	O-A/CH2-CH2		CDCL3
2174M	D	3.99	CH2	O-A/CH2-CH2		CCL4
1490M	C	3.85	CH2	O-A/CH2-CH3		CDCL3
2586M	C	3.91	CH2	O-A/CH2-CH3		POLYSOL-D
2173M	C	3.93	CH2	O-A/CH2-CH3		CCL4
1492M	C	4.00	CH2	O-A/CH2-0		CCL4
1513M	B	3.90	CH2	O-A/CH3		CCL4
1518M	B	3.90	CH2	O-A/CH3		CDCL3
1489M	B	3.91	CH2	O-A/CH3		CCL4
1517M	B	3.99	CH2	O-A/CH3		CCL4
1512M	B	4.02	CH2	O-A/CH3		CCL4
1533M	B	4.11	CH2	O-A/CH3		CDCL3
2585M	B	4.28	CH2	O-A/CH3		CCL4
1557M	B	4.37	CH2	O-A/CH3		CDCL3
1499M	C	3.81	CH2	O-A/CH3		CCL4
1522M	C	3.82	CH2	O-A/CH3		CDCL3
2211M	C	3.91	CH2	O-A/CH3		DMSO-D6
1500M	C	3.91	CH2	O-A/CH3		CCL4
1498M	C	3.92	CH2	O-A/CH3		CCL4
2563M	C	4.02	CH2	O-A/CH3		CDCL3
2076M	C	4.09	CH2	O-A/CH3		CDCL3
1525M	D	3.94	CH2	O-A/CH3		CCL4
1561M	D	3.97	CH2	O-A/CH3		CDCL3
1792M	C	3.72	CH2	O-A/CH(OH/CH3)		CCL4

BOOK NO.	ASSIGN-MENT	CHEM SHIFT - ppm -	PROTON GROUP	ENVIRONMENTAL GROUPS	S	SOLVENT
2089M	A	5.21	CH2	O-A/C(=O)-A		CDCL3
2215M	A	4.80	CH2	O-A/C(=O)-CL		CCL4
2565M	A	4.52	CH2	O-A/C(=O)-OH		POLYSOL-D
2553M	A	4.67	CH2	O-A/C(=O)-OH		C3H6O
2175M	A	4.57	CH2	O-A/Q3		CCL4
1539M	B	4.48	CH2	O-A/Q3		CDCL3
1540M	D	3.95	CH2	O-A/R30<CH-O/CH2>		CCL4
1393M	B	4.05	CH2	O-CF2/CH3		CCL4
1390M	E	3.46	CH2	O-CH2.17/CH3		CDCL3
1413M	C	3.39	CH2	O-CH2.2/CH2.2-CH3		CCL4
1385M	C	3.32	CH2	O-CH2.2/CH2-CH		CCL4
1381M	C	3.37	CH2	O-CH2.2/CH2-CH3		CDCL3
1667M	C	3.43	CH2	O-CH2.2/CH2-CH3		CDCL3
1672M	C	3.52	CH2	O-CH2.2/CH2-NH2		CDCL3
1674M	D	3.56	CH2	O-CH2.2/CH2-O		CCL4
1674M	C	3.50	CH2	O-CH2.2/CH2-OH		CCL4
1672M	D	3.40- 3.80	CH2	O-CH2.2/CH2-OH		CDCL3
1412M	B	3.42	CH2	O-CH2.2/CH3		CCL4
1674M	C	3.50	CH2	O-CH2.2/CH3		CCL4
1691M	B	3.97	CH2	O-CH2.2/Q3		CCL4
1413M	D	3.48	CH2	O-CH2.3/CH2-O		CCL4
1382M	E	3.39	CH2	O-CH2.3/CH3		CCL4
1389M	C	3.60	CH2	O-CH2.9/CH2.8-CH3		CCL4
1482M	A	4.47	CH2	O-CH2/A		CCL4
1705M	D	4.54	CH2	O-CH2/A		CCL4
1390M	D	3.40	CH2	O-CH2/CH2.16-CH3		CDCL3
1382M	D	3.35	CH2	O-CH2/CH2.2-CH3		CCL4
1384M	C	3.29	CH2	O-CH2/CH2-CH2		CCL4
1386M	C	3.29	CH2	O-CH2/CH2-CH2		CCL4
1388M	C	3.31	CH2	O-CH2/CH2-CH2		CCL4
1392M	C	3.38	CH2	O-CH2/CH2-CH2		CDCL3
1391M	C	3.40	CH2	O-CH2/CH2-CH2		CDCL3
1417M	C	3.40	CH2	O-CH2/CH2-CH2		CCL4
1421M	C	3.41	CH2	O-CH2/CH2-CH2		CCL4
2784M	D	3.29- 3.68	CH2	O-CH2/CH2-CH2		CCL4
2717M	D	3.38	CH2	O-CH2/CH2-CH2		CCL4
1675M	D	3.44	CH2	O-CH2/CH2-CH2		CDCL3
1411M	A	3.59	CH2	O-CH2/CH2-CL		CCL4
1418M	A	3.79 APP.	CH2	O-CH2/CH2-O		CDCL3
1419M	B	3.46 APP.	CH2	O-CH2/CH2-O		CCL4
1420M	B	3.48 APP.	CH2	O-CH2/CH2-O		CCL4
1415M	B	3.49	CH2	O-CH2/CH2-O		CCL4
1847M	B	3.60	CH2	O-CH2/CH2-O		CCL4
2756M	B	3.64	CH2	O-CH2/CH2-O		CDCL3
1412M	C	3.47	CH2	O-CH2/CH2-O		CCL4
1419M	C	3.50	CH2	O-CH2/CH2-O		CCL4
1420M	C	3.52	CH2	O-CH2/CH2-O		CCL4
1416M	C	3.63 APP.	CH2	O-CH2/CH2-O		CDCL3
1417M	D	3.50	CH2	O-CH2/CH2-O		CCL4
1421M	D	3.55 APP.	CH2	O-CH2/CH2-O		CCL4
1674M	D	3.56	CH2	O-CH2/CH2-O		CCL4
2757M	D	3.66	CH2	O-CH2/CH2-O		CDCL3
2717M	E	3.50	CH2	O-CH2/CH2-O		CCL4
1845M	A	3.65	CH2	O-CH2/CH2-OH		CDCL3
1705M	B	3.60	CH2	O-CH2/CH2-OH		CCL4
1847M	B	3.60	CH2	O-CH2/CH2-OH		CCL4
1705M	B	3.70	CH2	O-CH2/CH2-OH		CCL4
2867M	A	3.79	CH2	O-CH2/CH2-O-C(=O)		CCL4
2756M	C	3.68	CH2	O-CH2/CH2-O-C(=O)		CDCL3
2784M	D	3.29- 3.68	CH2	O-CH2/CH2-O-C(=O)		CCL4
2757M	E	3.70	CH2	O-CH2/CH2-O-C(=O)		CDCL3
2717M	F	3.58	CH2	O-CH2/CH2-O-C(=O)		CCL4
1402M	C	3.55	CH2	O-CH2/CH2-SH		CCL4
1401M	E	3.59	CH2	O-CH2/CH2-SH		CDCL3
1410M	B	3.15	CH2	O-CH2/CH3		CDCL3
1379M	B	3.38	CH2	O-CH2/CH3		CCL4
1403M	B	3.49	CH2	O-CH2/CH3		CDCL3
1416M	B	3.50 APP.	CH2	O-CH2/CH3		CDCL3
1401M	D	3.52	CH2	O-CH2/CH3		CDCL3
1383M	E	3.38	CH2	O-CH2/CH3		CCL4
1387M	D	3.19	CH2	O-CH2/CH(CH2/CH2)		CCL4
1383M	D	3.09	CH2	O-CH2/CH(CH3/CH3)		CCL4
1676M	B	4.23	CH2	O-CH2/C:C		CDCL3
1410M	C	4.55	CH2	O-CH2/O-CH2		CDCL3
1411M	C	4.70	CH2	O-CH2/O-CH2		CCL4
1407M	A	3.90	CH2	O-CH2/Q3		CCL4
1403M	C	3.97	CH2	O-CH2/Q3		CDCL3
1479M	B	4.35	CH2	O-CH3/A		CDCL3
1380M	D	3.37	CH2	O-CH3/CH2.2-CH3		CDCL3
1484M	C	3.53	CH2	O-CH3/CH2-A		CDCL3
1419M	B	3.46 APP.	CH2	O-CH3/CH2-O		CCL4

BOOK NO.	ASSIGN-MENT	CHEM SHIFT - ppm -	PROTON GROUP	ENVIRONMENTAL GROUPS	S	SOLVENT
1420M	B	3.48 APP.	CH2	O-CH3/CH2-O		CCL4
1415M	B	3.49	CH2	O-CH3/CH2-O		CCL4
1492M	B	3.59	CH2	O-CH3/CH2-O		CCL4
1665M	D	3.51	CH2	O-CH3/CH2-OH		CDCL3
1665M	D	3.71	CH2	O-CH3/CH2-OH		CDCL3
2491M	B	4.10	CH2	O-CH3/C(EO)-OH		D2O
2284M	B	3.89	CH2	O-CH3/C(=O)-NH2		CDCL3
2739M	C	3.90	CH2	O-CH3/C(=O)-O-CH3		CCL4
1409M	B	4.40	CH2	O-CH3/O-CH3		CCL4
1457M	B	3.31	CH2	O-CH3/R50<CH-O/CH2>		CCL4
1485M	C	3.49 APP.	CH2	O-CH/CH2-A		CCL4
1400M	C	3.63	CH2	O-CH/CH2-C		CDCL3
1424M	D	3.40	CH2	O-CH/CH2-CH2		CCL4
1394M	D	3.31	CH2	O-CH/CH2-CH3		CCL4
1436M	B	3.52	CH2	O-CH/CH3		CCL4
1493M	B	3.68	CH2	O-CH/CH3		CCL4
1428M	C	3.20- 3.90	CH2	O-CH/CH3		CDCL3
1426M	C	3.58 APP.	CH2	O-CH/CH3		CCL4
1480M	D	3.31	CH2	O-CH/CH3		CDCL3
1431M	D	3.32- 3.90	CH2	O-CH/CH3		CDCL3
1445M	E	3.15- 3.90	CH2	O-CH/R30<CH-O/HCH>		CCL4
2913M	A	5.44	CH2	O-C(=O)-A		CDCL3
2939M	D	4.35	CH2	O-C(=O)-AN/CH2-CH2		CDCL3
2942M	A	5.21	CH2	O-C(=O)-A/A		CCL4
2896M	C	4.37	CH2	O-C(=O)-A/CH2.2-CH3		CDCL3
2897M	C	4.21	CH2	O-C(=O)-A/CH2.3-CH3		CCL4
2879M	C	4.21	CH2	O-C(=O)-A/CH2.3-CH3		DMSO-D6
2866M	B	4.41	CH2	O-C(=O)-A/CH2-A		CCL4
2891M	B	4.53	CH2	O-C(=O)-A/CH2-A		CDCL3
2919M	C	4.14	CH2	O-C(=O)-A/CH2-CH2		C3D6O
2877M	C	4.21	CH2	O-C(=O)-A/CH2-CH2		CCL4
2917M	C	4.25	CH2	O-C(=O)-A/CH2-CH2		C3D6O
2894M	C	4.27	CH2	O-C(=O)-A/CH2-CH2		CCL4
2908M	C	4.28	CH2	O-C(=O)-A/CH2-CH2		CCL4
2890M	C	4.29	CH2	O-C(=O)-A/CH2-CH2		CCL4
2902M	C	4.30	CH2	O-C(=O)-A/CH2-CH2		CCL4
2895M	C	4.30	CH2	O-C(=O)-A/CH2-CH2		CCL4
2909M	D	4.35	CH2	O-C(=O)-A/CH2-CH2		CDCL3
2863M	C	4.22	CH2	O-C(=O)-A/CH2-CH3		CCL4
2900M	C	4.30	CH2	O-C(=O)-A/CH2-CH3		CDCL3
2865M	C	4.41	CH2	O-C(=O)-A/CH2-N		CDCL3
2867M	B	4.41	CH2	O-C(=O)-A/CH2-O		CCL4
2944M	A	4.63	CH2	O-C(=O)-A/CH2-O-C(=O)		CDCL3
2871M	B	4.31	CH2	O-C(=O)-A/CH3		CCL4
2875M	B	4.31	CH2	O-C(=O)-A/CH3		CCL4
2884M	B	4.34	CH2	O-C(=O)-A/CH3		CDCL3
2907M	B	4.39	CH2	O-C(=O)-A/CH3		CDCL3
2885M	B	4.40	CH2	O-C(=O)-A/CH3		CCL4
2883M	B	4.45	CH2	O-C(=O)-A/CH3		CDCL3
2911M	B	4.51	CH2	O-C(=O)-A/CH3		CDCL3
2870M	C	4.29	CH2	O-C(=O)-A/CH3		CCL4
2898M	C	4.19	CH2	O-C(=O)-A/CH(CH2/CH2)		CCL4
2903M	D	4.22	CH2	O-C(=O)-A/CH(CH2/CH2)		CCL4
2918M	C	4.04	CH2	O-C(=O)-A/CH(CH3/CH3)		C3D6O
2864M	C	4.10	CH2	O-C(=O)-A/CH(CH3/CH3)		CDCL3
2899M	A	4.72	CH2	O-C(=O)-A/Q3		CCL4
2904M	A	4.88	CH2	O-C(=O)-A/Q3		CDCL3
2721M	D	4.32	CH2	O-C(=O)-CF3/CH2-CH2		CDCL3
2711M	D	4.05	CH2	O-C(=O)-CH2.10/CH2.10-CH3		CDCL3
2763M	D	4.10	CH2	O-C(=O)-CH2.10/C(CH2/CH2/CH2)		CDCL3
2633M	D	5.22	CH2	O-C(=O)-CH2.2/A		TFA
2747M	F	4.03	CH2	O-C(=O)-CH2.2/CH2-CH		CCL4
2842M	D	4.66	CH2	O-C(=O)-CH2.2/Q2(H/A/H)		CCL4
2806M	B	4.53	CH2	O-C(=O)-CH2.2/Q3		CCL4
2775M	E	4.00	CH2	O-C(=O)-CH2.3/CH2.2-CH3		CCL4
2705M	D	4.01	CH2	O-C(=O)-CH2.3/CH2.3-CH3		CCL4
2778M	D	3.80	CH2	O-C(=O)-CH2.3/CH(CH3/CH3)		CCL4
2709M	E	4.03	CH2	O-C(=O)-CH2.5/CH2-CH		CCL4
2819M	E	4.06	CH2	O-C(=O)-CH2.7/CH2.2-CH3		CDCL3
2801M	D	4.48	CH2	O-C(=O)-CH2.7/Q3		CCL4
2783M	D	4.05	CH2	O-C(=O)-CH2.8/CH2.10-CH3		CDCL3
2749M	E	4.13	CH2	O-C(=O)-CH2.8/CH3		CDCL3
2782M	D	4.02	CH2	O-C(=O)-CH2.8/CH(CH2/CH2.3)		CDCL3
2844M	B	5.20	CH2	O-C(=O)-CH2/A		CDCL3
2837M	C	4.99	CH2	O-C(=O)-CH2/A		CCL4
2769M	D	4.13	CH2	O-C(=O)-CH2/CH2.10-CH3		CDCL3
2847M	D	4.03	CH2	O-C(=O)-CH2/CH2.2-CH3		CCL4
2743M	F	4.07	CH2	O-C(=O)-CH2/CH2.2-CH3		CCL4
2848M	D	3.99	CH2	O-C(=O)-CH2/CH2.6-CH3		CCL4
2860M	C	4.18	CH2	O-C(=O)-CH2/CH2-A		CCL4
2835M	D	4.22	CH2	O-C(=O)-CH2/CH2-A		CCL4

BOOK NO.	ASSIGN-MENT	CHEM SHIFT - ppm -	PROTON GROUP	ENVIRONMENTAL GROUPS	S	SOLVENT
2838M	E	4.20	CH2	O-C(=0)-CH2/CH2-A		CCL4
2774M	D	4.01	CH2	O-C(=0)-CH2/CH2-CH2		CCL4
2706M	D	4.07	CH2	O-C(=0)-CH2/CH2-CH2		CDCL3
2767M	D	4.10	CH2	O-C(=0)-CH2/CH2-CH2		CCL4
2784M	E	4.11	CH2	O-C(=0)-CH2/CH2-O		CCL4
2753M	C	4.30	CH2	O-C(=0)-CH2/CH2-O-C(=0)		CDCL3
2750M	B	4.19	CH2	O-C(=0)-CH2/CH3	S	D20
2751M	C	4.11	CH2	O-C(=0)-CH2/CH3		DMSO-D6
2734M	C	4.14	CH2	O-C(=0)-CH2/CH3		CCL4
2794M	C	4.19	CH2	O-C(=0)-CH2/CH3		CDCL3
2850M	D	4.06.	CH2	O-C(=0)-CH2/CH3		CCL4
2777M	D	4.06	CH2	O-C(=0)-CH2/CH3		CCL4
2854M	D	4.08	CH2	O-C(=0)-CH2/CH3		CCL4
2789M	D	4.13	CH2	O-C(=0)-CH2/CH3		CCL4
2730M	D	4.13	CH2	O-C(=0)-CH2/CH3		CCL4
2724M	D	4.14	CH2	O-C(=0)-CH2/CH3		CCL4
2818M	E	4.04	CH2	O-C(=0)-CH2/CH3		CCL4
2853M	E	4.05	CH2	O-C(=0)-CH2/CH3		CDCL3
2780M	E	4.11	CH2	O-C(=0)-CH2/CH3		CDCL3
2701M	E	4.19	CH2	O-C(=0)-CH2/CH3		CCL4
2817M	F	4.06	CH2	O-C(=0)-CH2/CH3		CCL4
2762M	E	3.98 APP.	CH2	O-C(=0)-CH2/CH(CH2.3/CH2)		CCL4
2759M	D	4.13 APP.	CH2	O-C(=0)-CH2/CH(OH/CH2)		CDCL3
2758M	F	4.19	CH2	O-C(=0)-CH2/CH(OH/CH2)		CDCL3
2719M	G	4.13	CH2	O-C(=0)-CH2/CH(OH/CH2)		CDCL3
2823M	E	3.87- 4.42	CH2	O-C(=0)-CH2/CH(O-C(=0)/CH2)		CCL4
2843M	D	4.62	CH2	O-C(=0)-CH2/Q2(H/A/H)		CCL4
2804M	B	4.62	CH2	O-C(=0)-CH2/Q3		CCL4
2832M	B	4.99	CH2	O-C(=0)-CH3/A		CCL4
2839M	C	4.91	CH2	O-C(=0)-CH3/A<C-CH-CH-C(O-CH3)>		CCL4
2755M	C	4.02	CH2	O-C(=0)-CH3/CH2-CH2		CCL4
2697M	D	3.98	CH2	O-C(=0)-CH3/CH2-CH2		CCL4
2798M	D	4.00	CH2	O-C(=0)-CH3/CH2-CH2		CCL4
2756M	D	4.21	CH2	O-C(=0)-CH3/CH2-O		CDCL3
2717M	G	4.12	CH2	O-C(=0)-CH3/CH2-O		CCL4
2752M	B	4.19	CH2	O-C(=0)-CH3/CH2-O-C(=0)		CCL4
2696M	D	3.90	CH2	O-C(=0)-CH3/CH(CH2/CH2)		CCL4
2695M	D	3.92	CH2	O-C(=0)-CH3/CH(CH2/CH2)		CCL4
2718M	C	4.10	CH2	O-C(=0)-CH3/CH(OH/CH2>		CDCL3
2840M	B	5.30	CH2	O-C(=0)-CH3/C(=0)-A		CDCL3
2716M	B	4.69	CH2	O-C(=0)-CH3/C:N		CDCL3
2841M	B	4.61	CH2	O-C(=0)-CH3/Q2(A)		CCL4
2800M	E	4.41	CH2	O-C(=0)-CH3/Q2(H/CH2.2-CH3/H)		CCL4
2931M	B	4.94	CH2	O-C(=0)-CH3/R50(C-O/=CH)		CCL4
2836M	D	4.21	CH2	O-C(=0)-CH/CH2-A		CCL4
2792M	D	4.22	CH2	O-C(=0)-CH/CH2-CH2		CCL4
2702M	E	4.00	CH2	O-C(=0)-CH/CH2-CH2		CCL4
2708M	F	4.11	CH2	O-C(=0)-CH/CH2-CH2		CCL4
2757M	F	4.25	CH2	O-C(=0)-CH/CH2-O		CDCL3
2795M	C	4.20	CH2	O-C(=0)-CH/CH3		CDCL3
2720M	C	4.20	CH2	O-C(=0)-CH/CH3		CCL4
1865M	C	4.21	CH2	O-C(=0)-CH/CH3		CDCL3
2736M	D	4.30	CH2	O-C(=0)-CH/CH3	S	D20
2770M	F	4.13	CH2	O-C(=0)-CH/CH3		CCL4
2744M	F	4.14	CH2	O-C(=0)-CH/CH3		CCL4
2733M	F	4.19	CH2	O-C(=0)-CH/CH3		CCL4
2745M	F	4.20	CH2	O-C(=0)-CH/CH3		CDCL3
2731M	F	4.22	CH2	O-C(=0)-CH/CH3		CDCL3
2732M	F	4.22	CH2	O-C(=0)-CH/CH3		CDCL3
2741M	G	4.20	CH2	O-C(=0)-CH/CH3		CCL4
2967M	A	5.41	CH2	O-C(=0)-CL/A<C-CH-CH-C(NO2)>		CDCL3
2959M	C	4.31	CH2	O-C(=0)-CL/CH2-CH2		CCL4
2961M	D	4.26	CH2	O-C(=0)-CL/CH2-CH2		CCL4
2966M	D	4.27	CH2	O-C(=0)-CL/CH2-CH2		CCL4
2962M	B	4.54	CH2	O-C(=0)-CL/CH2-CL		CDCL3
2960M	C	4.20	CH2	O-C(=0)-CL/CH(CH2/CH2)		CCL4
2964M	B	4.11	CH2	O-C(=0)-CL/C(CH2/CH3/CH3)		CCL4
2963M	A	4.87	CH2	O-C(=0)-CL/C-CL3		CCL4
2965M	A	4.78	CH2	O-C(=0)-CL/Q3(H/H/H)		CCL4
2766M	C	4.27	CH2	O-C(=0)-C(=0)-O/CH2.2-CH3		CDCL3
2805M	A	4.71	CH2	O-C(=0)-C(=0)-O/Q3		CCL4
2772M	B	4.34	CH2	O-C(=0)-C/CH3		CCL4
2723M	B	4.41	CH2	O-C(=0)-C/CH3		CDCL3
2703M	C	4.07	CH2	O-C(=0)-C/CH3		CCL4
2852M	C	4.16	CH2	O-C(=0)-C/CH3		CCL4
2729M	C	4.21	CH2	O-C(=0)-C/CH3		CDCL3
2831M	B	4.30	CH2	O-C(=0)-H/CH2-A		CCL4
2692M	C	4.10	CH2	O-C(=0)-H/CH2-CH2		CCL4
2693M	C	4.10	CH2	O-C(=0)-H/CH2-CH2		CCL4
2691M	C	4.10	CH2	O-C(=0)-H/CH(CH2/CH2)		CDCL3
2976M	C	4.04	CH2	O-C(=0)-NH2/CH2-CH2		CDCL3

BOOK NO.	ASSIGN-MENT	CHEM SHIFT - ppm -	PROTON GROUP	ENVIRONMENTAL GROUPS	S	SOLVENT
2977M	A	4.48	CH2	O-C(=O)-NH2/Q3		CCL4
2987M	C	4.10	CH2	O-C(=O)-NH/CH2-CH3		CDCL3
2983M	B	4.14	CH2	O-C(=O)-NH/CH3		CDCL3
2980M	C	4.11	CH2	O-C(=O)-NH/CH3·		CDCL3
2986M	D	4.00	CH2	O-C(=O)-NH/CH3		CCL4
2981M	E	4.03	CH2	O-C(=O)-NH/CH3		CCL4
2990M	E	4.03	CH2	O-C(=O)-N/CH3		CCL4
2984M	E	4.07	CH2	O-C(=O)-N/CH3		CCL4
2765M	C	4.11	CH2	O-C(=O)-O-CH2.3/CH2.2-CH3		CDCL3
2830M	B	4.30	CH2	O-C(=O)-Q		CDCL3
2743M	F	4.07	CH2	O-C(=O)-Q1/CH2.2-CH3		CCL4
2858M	B	4.34	CH2	O-C(=O)-Q1/CH3		CDCL3
2856M	C	4.11	CH2	O-C(=O)-Q1/CH3		CCL4
2861M	A	5.17	CH2	O-C(=O)-Q2/A		CCL4
2846M	B	5.17	CH2	O-C(=O)-Q2/A		CDCL3
2862M	B	4.32	CH2	O-C(=O)-Q2/CH2-A		CCL4
2827M	C	4.17	CH2	O-C(=O)-Q2/CH2-CH2		CCL4
2813M	D	4.10	CH2	O-C(=O)-Q2/CH2-CH2		CCL4
2934M	B	4.21	CH2	O-C(=O)-Q2/CH3		CDCL3
2820M	B	4.29	CH2	O-C(=O)-Q2/CH3		CCL4
2814M	C	4.11	CH2	O-C(=O)-Q2/CH3		CCL4
2810M	C	4.15	CH2	O-C(=O)-Q2/CH3		CCL4
2812M	D	3.89	CH2	O-C(=O)-Q2/CH(CH3/CH3)		CCL4
2829M	A	4.58	CH2	O-C(=O)-Q2/Q3		CCL4
2845M	A	5.11	CH2	O-C(=O)-Q3/A		CCL4
2809M	C	4.10	CH2	O-C(=O)-Q3/CH2-CH2		CCL4
2808M	C	4.03	CH2	O-C(=O)-Q3/CH(CH2/CH2)		CCL4
2807M	C	3.89	CH2	O-C(=O)-Q3/CH(CH3/CH3)		CCL4
2786M	D	4.08	CH2	O-C(=O)-R3/CH3		CCL4
2936M	C	4.22	CH2	O-C(=O)-R50/CH2.3-CH3		CCL4
2935M	C	4.20	CH2	O-C(=O)-R50/CH2-CH3		CCL4
2937M	B	4.44	CH2	O-C(=O)-R50/CH3		CDCL3
2824M	E	4.01	CH2	O-C(=O)-R5R5BI/CH3		CCL4
2824M	E	4.09	CH2	O-C(=O)-R5R5BI/CH3		CCL4
2824M	F	4.01	CH2	O-C(=O)-R5R5BI/CH3		CCL4
2824M	F	4.09	CH2	O-C(=O)-R5R5BI/CH3		CDCL3
2985M	C	4.14	CH2	O-C(=O)-R6NN/CH3		CCL4
756M	E	4.13	CH2	O-C(=O)-R60/CH3		CCL4
2788M	D	3.94	CH2	O-C(=O)-R6/CH(CH2.3/CH2)		CCL4
2972M	E	4.27	CH2	O-C(=O)-S/CH3		CCL4
1481M	B	3.12	CH2	O-C/CH3		CDCL3
1397M	C	3.32	CH2	O-C/CH3		CCL4
1434M	B	3.89	CH2	O-C/Q3		CCL4
1082M	D	4.47	CH2	O-NO2/CH2.3-CH3		CDCL3
1080M	C	4.40	CH2	O-NO2/CH2-CH3		CCL4
1033M	C	4.61	CH2	O-N=O/CH2-CH3		CCL4
1035M	C	4.45	CH2	O-N=O/CH(CH3/CH3)		CCL4
3000M	A	4.98	CH2	O-P=/A		CDCL3
1965M	C	4.03	CH2	O-P=/CH2.2-CH3		CDCL3
2997M	B	4.06	CH2	O-P=/CH3		CCL4
2998M	F	3.86	CH2	O-P/CH2-CH2		CCL4
2999M	C	3.99	CH2	O-P/CH2-CH3		CDCL3
1607M	B	4.10	CH2	O-P/CH2-CL		CDCL3
2996M	B	4.20 APP.	CH2	O-P/CH2-CL		CCL4
1606M	C	3.62	CH2	O-P/CH(CH2/CH2)		CCL4
1408M	C	3.71	CH2	O-Q2/CH3		CCL4
1404M	C	3.60	CH2	O-Q3/CH2-CH2		CCL4
1406M	C	3.70	CH2	O-Q3/CH2-N		CCL4
1418M	A	3.79 APP.	CH2	O-Q3/CH2-O		CDCL3
1405M	C	3.38	CH2	O-Q3/CH(CH3/CH3)		CCL4
1599M	C	3.71	CH2	O-SI/CH2.2-CH3		CCL4
1600M	C	3.67	CH2	O-SI/CH2-CH2		CCL4
1593M	C	3.59	CH2	O-SI/CH3		CDCL3
1595M	C	3.81	CH2	O-SI/CH3		CCL4
1596M	D	3.76	CH2	O-SI/CH3		CCL4
1601M	C	3.66	CH2	O-SI/CH(CH2/CH2)		CCL4
1602M	C	3.67	CH2	O-SI/CH(CH2/CH2)		CCL4
1329M	C	4.15	CH2	O-SO2-O/CH2-CH3		D20
1326M	B	4.12	CH2	O-SO3-K/CH3		POLYSOL-D
1328M	C	3.82	CH2	O-SO3-NA/CH2.12-CH3		D20
1327M	D	4.06	CH2	O-SO3-NA/CH2.3-CH3		CDCL3
1330M	B	4.52	CH2	O-SO3/CH2-CL		CCL4
1325M	C	3.94	CH2	O-S(=O)-O/CH2-CH2		CDCL3
1597M	E	3.80	CH2	O/SI/CH3		CDCL3
1097M	B	2.21	CH2	P(A/A)/CH2-CH2		CDCL3
1096M	B	1.99	CH2	P(A/A)/CH3		CDCL3
1104M	D	1.58 APP.	CH2	P(=O/CH3/CH3)/CH2-CH2		CDCL3
1103M	D	1.60 APP.	CH2	P(=O/CH3/CH3)/CH2-CH2		CDCL3
1101M	B	2.52	CH2	P(+)(CH2/CH2/CH2)/CH3	S	CDCL3
868M	A	3.96	CH2	QN(A)/CH2-QN		POLYSOL-D
1063M	D	2.27	CH2	QN(CH3/NH-A)/CH2-CH3		POLYSOL-D

BOOK NO.	ASSIGN- MENT	CHEM SHIFT - ppm -	PROTON GROUP	ENVIRONMENTAL GROUPS	S	SOLVENT
2470M	D	2.20	CH2	QN(CH3/NH-C(=O))/CH2-CH2		CDCL3
857M	D	2.21	CH2	QN(CH3/OH)/CH2-CH2		CDCL3
856M	D	2.28 APP.	CH2	QN(CH3/OH)/CH2-CH2		CDCL3
854M	D	2.25	CH2	QN(CH3/OH)/CH2-CH3		CDCL3
853M	C	2.22	CH2	QN(CH3/OH)/CH3		CDCL3
853M	D	2.40	CH2	QN(CH3/OH)/CH3		CDCL3
855M	C	1.98- 2.40	CH2	QN(CH3/OH)/CH(CH3/CH3)		CDCL3
849M	C	2.00- 2.60	CH2	QN(H/OH)/CH2.4-CH3		CDCL3
874M	C	2.12	CH2	QN(NH-A)/CH2-CH3		CCL4
1358M	C	2.30	CH2	QN(NH-C(=S))/CH2-CH2		CDCL3
867M	A	3.80	CH2	QN(Q2(A))/CH2-QN		CDCL3
160M	C	2.09	CH2	Q1(A/A)/CH2.2-CH3		CCL4
161M	C	2.08	CH2	Q1(A/A)/CH2.5-CH3		CCL4
162M	C	2.10	CH2	Q1(A/A)/CH2.8-CH3		CDCL3
2551M	B	2.58	CH2	Q1(A/C(=O)-OH)/CH3		CDCL3
1690M	D	1.96	CH2	Q1(CH3/CH2-OH)/CH2.2-CH		CCL4
94M	D	1.26- 2.08	CH2	Q1(CH3/CH3)/CH(CH3/CH3)		CCL4
92M	E	1.97	CH2	Q1(CH3/H/CH3)/CH2-CH3		CCL4
2157M	D	2.32	CH2	Q1(C(=O)-H/CH2-CH3)/CH2-CH3		CCL4
2161M	C	2.48	CH2	Q1(C(=O)-H/H/A)/CH2-CH2		CCL4
2523M	D	2.27	CH2	Q1(C(=O)-OH/CH2-CH2)/CH3		CCL4
2523M	D	2.27	CH2	Q1(C(=O)-OH/CH2-CH3)/CH2-CH3		CCL4
93M	E	1.95	CH2	Q1(H/CH3/CH3)/CH2-CH3		CCL4
2139M	D	2.40	CH2	Q1(OH/C(=O)-CH2.2)/CH2-CH3		CCL4
2138M	D	2.47	CH2	Q1(OH/C(=O)-CH2)/CH3		CCL4
85M	C	1.95	CH2	Q2(CH2)/CH2-CH2		CCL4
86M	C	1.96	CH2	Q2(CH2-CH2)/CH2-CH2		CDCL3
2818M	D	1.73- 2.30	CH2	Q2(CH2-CH2)/CH2-CH2		CCL4
71M	D	1.80- 2.25	CH2	Q2(CH2-CH3/CH2)/CH2-CH2		CCL4
274M	C	2.05	CH2	Q2(CH2-CL)/C(CH2/CH3/CH3)		CDCL3
2521M	C	2.02	CH2	Q2(CH2-C(=O)-OH)/CH2-CH3		CCL4
2257M	C	1.99	CH2	Q2(CH2-R50)/CH2.7-CH3		CDCL3
83M	D	1.95 APP.	CH2	Q2(CH3)/CH2-CH2		CCL4
72M	D	1.99	CH2	Q2(CH3)/CH2-CH2		CCL4
70M	D	2.00	CH2	Q2(CH3)/CH2-CH2		CCL4
75M	C	1.98	CH2	Q2(CH3)/CH3		CCL4
88M	C	1.80- 2.40	CH2	Q2(CH3)/CH(Q3/CH3)		CCL4
69M	C	2.01	CH2	Q2(CH3/H/H)/CH3		CCL4
2524M	C	2.20	CH2	Q2(C(=O)-OH)/CH2-CH2		CCL4
1257M	B	3.86	CH2	Q2(H/A/H)/SO2-CH3		CDCL3
2525M	C	1.99	CH2	Q2(H/CH2.2-C(=O)-OH/H)/CH2.3-CH3		CCL4
2526M	C	2.00	CH2	Q2(H/CH2.2-C(=O)-OH/H)/CH2.4-CH3		CCL4
2527M	C	1.97	CH2	Q2(H/CH2.2-C(=O)-OH/H)/CH2.6-CH3		CCL4
2525M	D	2.37 APP.	CH2	Q2(H/CH2.4-CH3/H)/CH2-C(=O)-OH		CCL4
2526M	D	2.37 APP.	CH2	Q2(H/CH2.5-CH3/H)/CH2-C(=O)-OH		CCL4
2819M	C	1.95 APP.	CH2	Q2(H/CH2.7-CH3/H)/CH2.6-C(=O)-O		CDCL3
2527M	D	2.33	CH2	Q2(H/CH2.7-CH3/H)/CH2-C(=O)-OH		CCL4
2819M	C	1.95 APP.	CH2	Q2(H/CH2.7-C(=O)-O/H)/CH2.7-CH3		CDCL3
84M	C	1.97 APP.	CH2	Q2(H/CH2-CH2/H)/CH2-CH2		CCL4
2529M	C	1.98	CH2	Q2(H/CH2-CH2/H)/CH2-CH2		CDCL3
84M	C	1.97 APP.	CH2	Q2(H/CH2-CH2/H)/CH2-CH3		CCL4
79M	B	1.70- 2.24	CH2	Q2(H/CH2-CH3/H)/CH3		CCL4
2800M	D	2.01 APP.	CH2	Q2(H/CH2-O-C(=O)/H)/CH2-CH3		CCL4
82M	D	1.96	CH2	Q2(H/C(CH3/CH3/CH3)/H)/CH2-CH3		CCL4
2156M	C	2.33	CH2	Q2(H/C(=O)-H/H)/CH2-CH3		CDCL3
2520M	C	2.21	CH2	Q2(H/C(=O)-OH/H)/CH2-CH3		CCL4
2815M	C	2.16	CH2	Q2(H/C(=O)-O-CH3/H)/CH2.5-CH3		CCL4
2799M	C	2.16	CH2	Q2(H/C(=O)-O-CH3/H)/CH2-CH3		CCL4
2966M	C	1.97	CH2	Q2(H/H/CH2-CH2)/CH2-CH2		CCL4
1689M	C	1.97	CH2	Q2(H/H/CH2-CH2)/CH2-CH2		CCL4
2528M	C	2.00	CH2	Q2(H/H/CH2-CH2)/CH2-CH2		CCL4
2823M	C	2.01 APP.	CH2	Q2(H/H/CH2-CH2)/CH2-CH2		CCL4
2817M	E	2.20	CH2	Q2(H/H/CH2-CH2)/CH2-CH2		CCL4
1688M	A	0.95	CH2	Q2(H/H/CH2-CH2)/CH3		CCL4
78M	B	2.03	CH2	Q2(H/H/CH2-CH3)		CDCL3
1688M	C	3.52	CH2	Q2(H/H/CH2-CH3)/CH2-OH		CCL4
2816M	D	2.71	CH2	Q2(H/H/CH2-Q2)/Q2(H/H/CH2-CH3)		CCL4
2670M	B	2.09	CH2	Q3(H/H/H)/CH2-CH2	S	D2O
60M	C	1.78- 2.47	CH2	Q3(H/H/H)/CH2-CH2		CCL4
65M	C	2.00	CH2	Q3(H/H/H)/CH2-CH2		CCL4
57M	C	2.04	CH2	Q3(H/H/H)/CH2-CH2		CCL4
2798M	C	2.06	CH2	Q3(H/H/H)/CH2-CH2		CCL4
2019M	B	2.40 APP.	CH2	Q3(H/H/H)/CH2-C(=O)		CCL4
66M	A	2.11	CH2	Q3(H/H/H)/CH2-Q3		CCL4
153M	A	3.33	CH2	Q3/A		CCL4
1918M	B	3.26	CH2	Q3/A<C-C(OH)-C(CH3)>		CCL4
155M	A	2.39	CH2	Q3/CH2-A		CDCL3
63M	C	2.00	CH2	Q3/CH2-CH2		CCL4
59M	C	2.03	CH2	Q3/CH2-CH2		CCL4
62M	C	2.04	CH2	Q3/CH2-CH2		CCL4
61M	C	2.05	CH2	Q3/CH2-CH2		CCL4

BOOK NO.	ASSIGN-MENT	CHEM SHIFT - ppm -	PROTON GROUP	ENVIRONMENTAL GROUPS	S	SOLVENT
64M	C	2.08	CH2	Q3/CH2-CH2		CCL4
2206M	C	2.10	CH2	Q3/CH2-CH2		CCL4
2518M	A	2.20- 2.70	CH2	Q3/CH2-C(=O)-OH		CDCL3
1687M	A	2.37	CH2	Q3/CH2-OH		CDCL3
58M	D	1.98	CH2	Q3/CH(CH2/CH3)		CCL4
1784M	C	2.21	CH2	Q3/CH(OH/CH2.2)		CDCL3
1785M	A	2.30	CH2	Q3/CH(OH/Q3)		CDCL3
67M	B	1.90- 2.50	CH2	Q3/CH(Q3/CH3)		CCL4
968M	A	3.10	CH2	Q3/C:N		CCL4
2464M	A	3.09	CH2	Q3/R6NN<C(A)-C(=O)/C(=O)>		DMSO-D6
2461M	A	2.60	CH2	Q3/R6NN<C(CH2-Q3)-C(=O)/C(=O)>		DMSO-D6
2137M	E	2.29	CH2	Q(C(=O)-CH3/OH/CH3)/CH3		CDCL3
1439M	B	1.50	CH2	R30<CH-O/HCH>/CH3		CCL4
41M	D	1.19	CH2	R3<CH-CH2/CH2>/R3<CH-CH2/CH2>		CCL4
109M	D	4.57 APP.	CH2	R4R6BI(=C-CH*/CH2)		CDCL3
744M	B	4.10	CH2	R5NAA(N-C*/C*)		CDCL3
2392M	B	3.80	CH2	R5NA<N-C(=O)/C(=O)>/CH2-CL		CDCL3
2392M	B	4.06	CH2	R5NA<N-C(=O)/C(=O)>/CH2-CL		DMSO-D6
2396M	A	4.78	CH2	R5NA(N-C(=O)/C(=O))/A		CDCL3
2399M	B	3.69	CH2	R5NA(N-C(=O)/C(=O))/CH2-CH2		POLYSOL-D
739M	C	2.90	CH2	R5NNA<C=N/NH>/CH2-CH3		TFA
1155M	B	2.99	CH2	R5NNS<C=N/S>/CH3		CCL4
2433M	C	3.10	CH2	R5NN<N-C(=O)/CH2>/CH2.2-CH3		POLYSOL-D
2434M	B	3.77	CH2	R5NN<N-C(=O)/CH2>/Q3		CDCL3
2445M	B	4.64	CH2	R5NN<N-C(=O)/C(=O)>/A		CDCL3
2449M	B	3.47	CH2	R5NN<N-C(=O)/C(=O)>/CH3		TFA
1664M	A	3.94	CH2	R5NN<N-C(=S)/CH2>/CH2-OH	S	D20
820M	A	3.32	CH2	R5NN(C=CH/N)/CH2-NH2		CDCL3
1756M	C	1.90- 2.90	CH2	R5N<N-CH2/CH2>/CH(OH/CH3)		CDCL3
2382M	D	3.49	CH2	R5N<N-C(=O)/C(=O)>/CH2.3-CH3		POLYSOL-D
2385M	B	3.69	CH2	R5N<N-C(=O)/C(=O)>/CH2-A		CDCL3
2384M	B	3.55	CH2	R5N<N-C(=O)/C(=O)>/CH3		CDCL3
2386M	A	4.63	CH2	R5N(N-C(=O)/C(=O))/A		CCL4
1459M	C	1.55	CH2	R500<C(CH3)/O/O>/CH3		CCL4
1678M	A	2.91	CH2	R5S<C=CH/S>/CH2-OH		CDCL3
1147M	A	4.28	CH2	R5S(C=CH/S)/R5S(=CH/S)		CDCL3
2466M	B	4.02	CH2	R6NNN(N-C(=O)/C(=O))/CH3		TFA
2460M	B	2.22	CH2	R6NN<C(CH2-CH3)-C(=O)/C(=O)>/CH3		CDCL3
1465M	B	3.00	CH2	R6NO<N-CH2/CH2>/Q3		CDCL3
1473M	A	2.00- 2.70	CH2	R6NO<N-CH2/CH2>/R600<CH-O/CH2>		CCL4
1466M	C	2.35	CH2	R6NO(N-CH2/CH2)/CH2-CH2		CCL4
1464M	B	2.34 APP.	CH2	R6NO(N-CH2/CH2)/CH3		DMSO-D6
2465M	B	3.83	CH2	R6N3<N-C(=O)/C(=O)-N>/CH2-OH		CDCL3
2015M	C	3.60	CH2	R6N<N-CH2/CH2>/A	S	D20
815M	C	3.53	CH2	R6N(N-CH2/CH2)/CH2-CL		CCL4
638M	C	2.71	CH2	R6N(N-CH2/CH2)/R6N(N-CH2/CH2)		CCL4
1476M	B	1.55	CH2	R600R600SPI<CH-O/O>/CH3		CCL4
107M	C	4.51	CH2	R6<=C-CH(CH3)/CH(CH3)>		CCL4
47M	B	0.90- 1.90	CH2	R6/CH3		CCL4
1224M	B	3.64	CH2	SH/A		CCL4
1225M	B	3.57	CH2	SH/A<C-CH-CH-C(CL)>		CCL4
1206M	D	2.49	CH2	SH/CH2.4-CH3		CDCL3
1204M	D	2.47	CH2	SH/CH2.5		CDCL3
1211M	D	2.53	CH2	SH/CH2.7-CH3		CCL4
1205M	D	2.49	CH2	SH/CH2-CH		CCL4
1222M	C	2.49	CH2	SH/CH2-CH2		CCL4
1221M	C	2.50	CH2	SH/CH2-CH2		CCL4
1220M	C	2.51 APP.	CH2	SH/CH2-CH2		CCL4
1213M	D	2.45	CH2	SH/CH2-CH2		CCL4
1209M	D	2.49	CH2	SH/CH2-CH2		CDCL3
1208M	D	2.53	CH2	SH/CH2-CH2		CDCL3
1212M	D	2.55	CH2	SH/CH2-CH2		CDCL3
1201M	D	2.52	CH2	SH/CH2-CH3		CDCL3
2738M	B	2.40- 3.00	CH2	SH/CH2-C(=O)-O		CDCL3
1217M	D	2.50- 3.10	CH2	SH/CH2-NH		CCL4
1402M	B	2.70	CH2	SH/CH2-O		CDCL3
1401M	C	2.69	CH2	SH/CH2-O		D20
1661M	A	2.68	CH2	SH/CH2-OH		CCL4
1200M	C	2.52	CH2	SH/CH3		CCL4
1207M	E	2.49	CH2	SH/CH(CH2/CH2)		D20
2624M	A	3.10	CH2	SH/CH(NH2/C(=O)-OH)		D20
2645M	A	3.21	CH2	SH/CH(NH2/C(=O)-OH)	S	CDCL3
1662M	C	2.83	CH2	SH/CH(SH/CH2)		CDCL3
1219M	D	2.71	CH2	SH/CH(SH/CH3)		D20
2658M	A	3.51	CH2	SH/C(=O)-O-NA	S	CDCL3
1577M	B	3.70	CH2	SH/R50(C=CH/O)		CDCL3
1083M	A	0.90 APP.	CH2	SIH3/CH2.4-CH3		CDCL3
1091M	B	1.22	CH2	SI(A/A/A)/CH3		CDCL3
1088M	A	2.59	CH2	SI(A/A/CH2)/A		CCL4
1085M	A	0.59	CH2	SI(CH2/CH2/CH2)/A		CL2C=CCL2
1087M	B	1.52	CH2	SI(CH2/CH3/CH3)/Q3(H/H/H)		

BOOK NO.	ASSIGN-MENT	CHEM SHIFT - ppm -	PROTON GROUP	ENVIRONMENTAL GROUPS	S	SOLVENT
1086M	B	1.56	CH2	SI(CH3/CH3/CH3)/Q3		CCL4
1597M	A	0.64	CH2	SI(0/0/0)/CH2.2-NH2		CDCL3
1596M	A	0.53	CH2	SI(0/0/0)/CH3		CCL4
1267M	B	4.44	CH2	SO2-A/A		POLYSOL-D
1266M	B	4.06	CH2	SO2-A/C:CH		CDCL3
1265M	B	4.35	CH2	SO2-A/C:CH		POLYSOL-D
1261M	A	3.80	CH2	SO2-A/Q3		CDCL3
1263M	A	3.81	CH2	SO2-A/Q3		CDCL3
1262M	B	3.81	CH2	SO2-A/Q3		CDCL3
1264M	B	4.88	CH2	SO2-A/SO2-A		POLYSOL-D
1254M	C	2.95	CH2	SO2-CH2.3/CH2.2-CH3		CDCL3
1255M	C	2.84	CH2	SO2-CH2/CH2-CH2		CCL4
1253M	C	2.91	CH2	SO2-CH2/CH2-CH3		CCL4
1281M	D	3.69	CH2	SO2-CL/CH2.2-CH3		CCL4
1280M	C	3.68	CH2	SO2-CL/CH2-CH3		CCL4
1282M	A	4.01	CH2	SO2-CL/CH2-CL		CCL4
1279M	A	5.07	CH2	SO2-F/A		POLYSOL-D
1368M	C	3.10	CH2	SO2-NH/CH3		CDCL3
1256M	B	2.97	CH2	SO2-Q3/CH3		CCL4
1288M	B	3.14- 3.58	CH2	SO3H/CH2-NH		D2O
1322M	D	3.94	CH2	SO3-A/CH2-CH2		CCL4
1324M	B	4.04	CH2	SO3-CH2/CH3		CCL4
1315M	D	4.23	CH2	SO3-CH3/CH2.2-CH3		CDCL3
1317M	D	4.20	CH2	SO3-CH3/CH2-CH2		CDCL3
1316M	B	3.09	CH2	SO3-CH3/CH3		CCL4
1287M	B	3.26	CH2	SO3-H/CH3		CDCL3
1663M	A	3.12	CH2	SO3-K/CH2-OH		D2O
1294M	C	2.89	CH2	SO3-NA/CH2.3-CH3		D2O
1295M	D	2.81	CH2	SO3-NA/CH2.5-CH3		D2O
1296M	A	3.41	CH2	SO3-NA/CH2-BR	S	D2O
1297M	B	3.15 APP.	CH2	SO3-NA/CH2-C:N		D2O
1298M	A	3.27	CH2	SO3-NA/CH2-SO3-NA		D2O
1299M	A	3.68	CH2	SO3-NA/Q3		D2O
1248M	C	2.67	CH2	SO-A/CH2-CH3		CCL4
1250M	C	2.94	CH2	SO-A/CH2-C:C		CDCL3
1244M	D	2.56 APP.	CH2	SO-CH2/CH2-CH2		CCL4
1244M	D	2.56 APP.	CH2	SO-CH2/CH3		CCL4
1247M	A	3.85	CH2	S(=O)-CH2/A		CDCL3
1245M	C	2.68	CH2	S(=O)-CH2/CH2-CH2		CDCL3
1246M	B	1.82- 2.80	CH2	S(=O)-CH2/CH(CH3/CH3)		CCL4
1173M	A	4.18	CH2	S-AA/A		CDCL3
1165M	A	4.07	CH2	S-A/A		POLYSOL-D
1162M	B	4.05	CH2	S-A/A		POLYSOL-D
1163M	B	3.07	CH2	S-A/CH2-A		CDCL3
1164M	B	2.69	CH2	S-A/CH2-CH2		CCL4
1164M	B	2.80	CH2	S-A/CH2-CH2		CCL4
1708M	B	2.89	CH2	S-A/CH2-OH		CCL4
1167M	B	4.25	CH2	S-A/S-A		CDCL3
1660M	E	2.71	CH2	S-CH2.11/CH2-OH		CDCL3
1117M	E	2.43	CH2	S-CH2.11/CH3		CCL4
1119M	E	2.54	CH2	S-CH2.17/CH3		CDCL3
1660M	D	2.52	CH2	S-CH2.2/CH2.10-CH3		CDCL3
1109M	C	2.44	CH2	S-CH2.2/CH2-CH3		CCL4
1122M	B	2.75	CH2	S-CH2.2/CH2-C:N		CDCL3
1122M	B	2.88	CH2	S-CH2.2/CH2-C:N		CDCL3
1123M	B	2.56	CH2	S-CH2.2/CH3		CCL4
1114M	C	2.43	CH2	S-CH2.5/CH2.4-CH3		CCL4
1115M	C	2.45	CH2	S-CH2.6/CH2.5-CH3		CCL4
1191M	A	3.46	CH2	S-CH2/A		CS2
1159M	C	3.62	CH2	S-CH2/A		CCL4
1117M	D	2.41	CH2	S-CH2/CH2.10-CH3		CCL4
1119M	D	2.49	CH2	S-CH2/CH2.16-CH3		CDCL3
1112M	C	2.53	CH2	S-CH2/CH2-CH		CDCL3
1118M	C	2.41	CH2	S-CH2/CH2-CH2		CCL4
1110M	C	2.42	CH2	S-CH2/CH2-CH2		CCL4
1126M	C	2.43	CH2	S-CH2/CH2-CH2		CCL4
1125M	C	2.52	CH2	S-CH2/CH2-CH2		CDCL3
1126M	C	2.43	CH2	S-CH2/CH2-CH3		CCL4
1124M	C	2.49	CH2	S-CH2/CH2-CH3		CCL4
1123M	C	2.71	CH2	S-CH2/CH2-S		CCL4
1124M	D	2.61	CH2	S-CH2/CH2-S		CCL4
1159M	B	2.32	CH2	S-CH2/CH3		CCL4
1108M	B	2.47	CH2	S-CH2/CH3		CCL4
1113M	D	2.37	CH2	S-CH2/CH(CH2/CH2)		CCL4
1111M	C	2.32	CH2	S-CH2/CH(CH3/CH3)		CCL4
1158M	B	3.58	CH2	S-CH3/A		CCL4
1116M	D	2.41	CH2	S-CH3/CH2.10-CH3		CCL4
1121M	C	2.57	CH2	S-CH3/CH2.2-NH2		D2O
2627M	C	2.54	CH2	S-CH3/CH2-CH		POLYSOL-D
1127M	C	2.42	CH2	S-CH3/CH2-CH2		CCL4
1107M	C	2.43	CH2	S-CH3/CH3		CCL4

BOOK NO.	ASSIGN-MENT	CHEM SHIFT - ppm -	PROTON GROUP	ENVIRONMENTAL GROUPS	S	SOLVENT
1128M	B	2.69	CH2	S-CH/CH3		CCL4
2970M	C	2.83	CH2	S-C(=O)-CH3/CH3		CCL4
2972M	B	2.98	CH2	S-C(=O)-O/CH2-OH		CCL4
2971M	A	4.25	CH2	S-C(=O)/A		CDCL3
1017M	A	4.15	CH2	S-C:N/A		CDCL3
1018M	A	4.51	CH2	S-C:N/A<C-C(CL)/C(CL)>		CDCL3
1012M	D	2.94	CH2	S-C:N/CH2.10-CH3		CCL4
1016M	B	3.01	CH2	S-C:N/CH2-CH2		CDCL3
1009M	C	2.97	CH2	S-C:N/CH2-CH2		CCL4
1011M	D	2.93	CH2	S-C:N/CH2-CH2		CCL4
1010M	D	2.93	CH2	S-C:N/CH2-CH2		CCL4
1015M	A	3.38	CH2	S-C:N/CH2-S		POLYSOL-D
1008M	B	3.00	CH2	S-C:N/CH3		CDCL3
1019M	A	3.58	CH2	S-C:N/Q2(H/A/H)		CDCL3
1014M	A	4.40	CH2	S-C:N/S-C:N		CDCL3
1189M	D	2.70	CH2	S-S/CH2.10-CH3		CDCL3
1187M	D	2.64	CH2	S-S/CH2.3-CH3		CCL4
1188M	C	2.69	CH2	S-S/CH2-CH		CCL4
1183M	C	2.96	CH2	S-S/CH2-CH2		CDCL3
780M	A	3.07	CH2	S-S/CH2-NH2		D20
780M	A	3.39	CH2	S-S/CH2-NH2		D20
1193M	B	2.66	CH2	S-S/CH3		CCL4
1185M	C	2.55	CH2	S-S/CH(CH3/CH3)		CCL4
1190M	A	3.29	CH2	S-S/Q3		CCL4
2976M	B	1.28 APP.	CH2.X	CH2.10		CDCL3
2503M	A	1.29	CH2.X	CH2.10		POLYSOL-D
462M	A	1.30 APP.	CH2.X	CH2.10		CDCL3
1116M	B	1.10- 1.80	CH2.X	CH2.10		CCL4
2769M	B	1.10- 1.90	CH2.X	CH2.10		CDCL3
2895M	B	1.26	CH2.X	CH2.10		CCL4
8M	B	1.27	CH2.X	CH2.10		CCL4
2697M	B	1.28	CH2.X	CH2.10		CCL4
2919M	B	1.29	CH2.X	CH2.10		C3D60
2050M	B	1.29 APP.	CH2.X	CH2.10		CDCL3
621M	B	1.29 APP.	CH2.X	CH2.10		CDCL3
1212M	B	1.30	CH2.X	CH2.10		CDCL3
2809M	B	1.30	CH2.X	CH2.10		CCL4
63M	B	1.30 APP.	CH2.X	CH2.10		CCL4
830M	B	1.10- 2.20	CH2.X	CH2.10	S	CDCL3
829M	B	1.10- 2.10	CH2.X	CH2.10	S	CDCL3
1090M	B	0.90- 1.60	CH2.X	CH2.11		CCL4
2280M	B	1.10- 2.10	CH2.X	CH2.11		TFA
910M	B	1.10- 1.90	CH2.X	CH2.11		CCL4
9M	B	1.26	CH2.X	CH2.11		CCL4
1118M	B	1.28	CH2.X	CH2.11		CCL4
337M	B	1.29 APP.	CH2.X	CH2.11		CCL4
953M	B	1.10- 1.50	CH2.X	CH2.12		CDCL3
10M	B	1.25	CH2.X	CH2.12		CCL4
338M	B	1.25 APP.	CH2.X	CH2.12		CCL4
1757M	B	1.26 APP.	CH2.X	CH2.12		CDCL3
64M	B	1.27 APP.	CH2.X	CH2.12		CCL4
1632M	B	1.28	CH2.X	CH2.12		CDCL3
2758M	B	1.29	CH2.X	CH2.12		CDCL3
246M	B	1.29 APP.	CH2.X	CH2.12		CCL4
1804M	C	1.10- 1.60	CH2.X	CH2.12		CDCL3
1104M	B	1.26	CH2.X	CH2.13		CDCL3
11M	B	1.26	CH2.X	CH2.13		CCL4
247M	B	1.28 APP.	CH2.X	CH2.13		CCL4
414M	B	1.29 APP.	CH2.X	CH2.13		CCL4
339M	B	1.29 APP.	CH2.X	CH2.13		CCL4
1581M	B	1.30	CH2.X	CH2.13		CDCL3
843M	B	1.28	CH2.X	CH2.13	S	DMSO-D6
839M	B	1.29 APP.	CH2.X	CH2.13	S	CDCL3
831M	B	1.29 APP.	CH2.X	CH2.13	S	CDCL3
122M	B	1.10- 1.70	CH2.X	CH2.14		CCL4
892M	B	1.10- 1.60	CH2.X	CH2.14		TFA
2710M	B	1.27	CH2.X	CH2.14		CCL4
65M	B	1.28	CH2.X	CH2.14		CCL4
2761M	B	1.28 APP.	CH2.X	CH2.14		CDCL3
2194M	B	1.28 APP.	CH2.X	CH2.14		CCL4
1391M	B	1.29	CH2.X	CH2.14		CDCL3
340M	B	1.29 APP.	CH2.X	CH2.14		CDCL3
1213M	C	1.29	CH2.X	CH2.14		CCL4
2759M	B	1.26	CH2.X	CH2.15		CDCL3
2719M	B	1.26	CH2.X	CH2.15		CDCL3
248M	B	1.28	CH2.X	CH2.15		CCL4
2802M	B	1.29	CH2.X	CH2.15		CDCL3
934M	B	1.10- 1.90	CH2.X	CH2.16		CDCL3
552M	B	1.23 APP.	CH2.X	CH2.16		CDCL3
1633M	B	1.25 APP.	CH2.X	CH2.16		CDCL3
1392M	B	1.27	CH2.X	CH2.16		CDCL3

BOOK NO.	ASSIGN-MENT	CHEM SHIFT - ppm -	PROTON GROUP	ENVIRONMENTAL GROUPS	S	SOLVENT
12M	B	1.28	CH2.X	CH2.16		CDCL3
341M	B	1.29 APP.	CH2.X	CH2.16		CDCL3
833M	B	1.10- 2.10	CH2.X	CH2.16	S	CDCL3
1390M	C	1.25 APP.	CH2.X	CH2.16		CDCL3
1119M	C	1.27 APP.	CH2.X	CH2.16		CDCL3
13M	B	1.25	CH2.X	CH2.18		CDCL3
1634M	B	1.26	CH2.X	CH2.18		CDCL3
2712M	B	1.27	CH2.X	CH2.19		CDCL3
688M	B	1.33 APP.	CH2.X	CH2.2		CCL4
624M	B	1.26 APP.	CH2.X	CH2.20		CDCL3
14M	B	1.29	CH2.X	CH2.20		CDCL3
15M	B	1.24	CH2.X	CH2.21		CCL4
2628M	A	1.11- 2.00	CH2.X	CH2.3		D20
419M	A	1.20- 2.20	CH2.X	CH2.3		CDCL3
2200M	A	1.20- 2.05	CH2.X	CH2.3		CCL4
2197M	A	1.20- 2.20	CH2.X	CH2.3		CCL4
2755M	A	1.20- 1.90	CH2.X	CH2.3		CCL4
360M	A	1.32- 2.20	CH2.X	CH2.3		CCL4
264M	A	1.35- 2.12	CH2.X	CH2.3		CCL4
1825M	A	1.49 APP.	CH2.X	CH2.3		D20
124M	A	1.52 APP.	CH2.X	CH2.3		CDCL3
778M	A	1.30- 2.30	CH2.X	CH2.3	S	TFA
2525M	B	1.00- 1.70	CH2.X	CH2.3		CCL4
548M	B	1.00- 1.90	CH2.X	CH2.3		CDCL3
2277M	B	1.00- 1.80	CH2.X	CH2.3		DMSO-D6
2049M	B	1.00- 1.60	CH2.X	CH2.3		CCL4
83M	B	1.05- 1.50	CH2.X	CH2.3		CCL4
2470M	B	1.06- 1.68	CH2.X	CH2.3		CDCL3
141M	B	1.08- 1.91	CH2.X	CH2.3		CCL4
444M	B	1.09- 1.66	CH2.X	CH2.3		CDCL3
1616M	B	1.09- 1.80	CH2.X	CH2.3		CCL4
2487M	B	1.10- 1.75	CH2.X	CH2.3		CCL4
2382M	B	1.10- 1.90	CH2.X	CH2.3		CDCL3
618M	B	1.10- 1.80	CH2.X	CH2.3		CCL4
411M	B	1.10- 1.65	CH2.X	CH2.3		CCL4
142M	B	1.10- 1.50	CH2.X	CH2.3		CDCL3
129M	B	1.10- 1.80	CH2.X	CH2.3		CCL4
330M	B	1.10- 1.80	CH2.X	CH2.3		CCL4
2254M	B	1.10- 1.60	CH2.X	CH2.3		CCL4
1698M	B	1.10- 1.85	CH2.X	CH2.3		CCL4
1983M	B	1.10- 1.80	CH2.X	CH2.3		CCL4
59M	B	1.10- 1.70	CH2.X	CH2.3		CCL4
933M	B	1.10- 1.60	CH2.X	CH2.3		CCL4
2897M	B	1.10- 2.00	CH2.X	CH2.3		CCL4
2757M	B	1.10- 1.91	CH2.X	CH2.3		CDCL3
1255M	B	1.12- 2.15	CH2.X	CH2.3		CCL4
1325M	B	1.15- 2.00	CH2.X	CH2.3		CCL4
891M	B	1.15- 1.94	CH2.X	CH2.3		CDCL3
72M	B	1.31 APP.	CH2.X	CH2.3		CCL4
2153M	B	1.34	CH2.X	CH2.3		CCL4
1600M	B	1.38	CH2.X	CH2.3		CCL4
1783M	B	1.38 APP.	CH2.X	CH2.3		CCL4
2780M	B	1.38 APP.	CH2.X	CH2.3		CDCL3
2774M	B	1.44	CH2.X	CH2.3		CCL4
949M	B	1.49	CH2.X	CH2.3		CDCL3
2727M	B	1.65 APP.	CH2.X	CH2.3		CCL4
2770M	C	0.65- 1.55	CH2.X	CH2.3		CCL4
2477M	C	1.16- 1.90	CH2.X	CH2.3		CCL4
1738M	C	1.18- 1.71	CH2.X	CH2.3		CCL4
1826M	A	1.10- 1.80	CH2.X	CH2.4		CDCL3
2623M	A	1.10- 1.60	CH2.X	CH2.4		D20
2622M	A	1.10- 1.90	CH2.X	CH2.4		D20
957M	A	1.20- 2.10	CH2.X	CH2.4		CCL4
2781M	A	1.32 APP.	CH2.X	CH2.4		CCL4
2202M	A	1.37	CH2.X	CH2.4		CCL4
332M	B	1.08- 1.60	CH2.X	CH2.4		CCL4
2481M	B	1.10- 2.00	CH2.X	CH2.4		CCL4
2526M	B	1.10- 1.65	CH2.X	CH2.4		CCL4
849M	B	1.10- 1.80	CH2.X	CH2.4		CDCL3
857M	B	1.10- 1.70	CH2.X	CH2.4		CDCL3
550M	B	1.10- 1.80	CH2.X	CH2.4		CDCL3
1114M	B	1.10- 1.90	CH2.X	CH2.4		CCL4
1699M	B	1.10- 1.80	CH2.X	CH2.4		CCL4
1697M	B	1.10- 1.80	CH2.X	CH2.4		CCL4
1386M	B	1.10- 1.70	CH2.X	CH2.4		CCL4
1987M	B	1.10- 1.80	CH2.X	CH2.4		CDCL3
950M	B	1.10- 2.00	CH2.X	CH2.4		CCL4
2749M	B	1.10- 1.55	CH2.X	CH2.4		CDCL3
2827M	B	1.10- 1.99	CH2.X	CH2.4		CCL4
2760M	B	1.10- 1.45	CH2.X	CH2.4		CCL4
2877M	B	1.11- 1.96	CH2.X	CH2.4		CCL4

BOOK NO.	ASSIGN-MENT	CHEM SHIFT - ppm -	PROTON GROUP	ENVIRONMENTAL GROUPS	S	SOLVENT
1974M	B	1.12- 1.72	CH2.X	CH2.4		CCL4
1927M	B	1.29 APP.	CH2.X	CH2.4		CDCL3
334M	B	1.30	CH2.X	CH2.4		CCL4
85M	B	1.30	CH2.X	CH2.4		CCL4
44M	B	1.30	CH2.X	CH2.4		CCL4
2279M	B	1.31 APP.	CH2.X	CH2.4		CDCL3
60M	B	1.32 APP.	CH2.X	CH2.4		CCL4
2704M	B	1.33	CH2.X	CH2.4		CCL4
1358M	B	1.34	CH2.X	CH2.4		CDCL3
1619M	B	1.35 APP.	CH2.X	CH2.4		CCL4
2925M	B	1.36	CH2.X	CH2.4		CCL4
1206M	C	1.10- 2.00	CH2.X	CH2.4		CCL4
1739M	C	1.30 APP.	CH2.X	CH2.4		CCL4
2206M	A	1.39	CH2.X	CH2.5		CCL4
2822M	B	1.06- 1.78	CH2.X	CH2.5		CCL4
242M	B	1.06- 2.03	CH2.X	CH2.5		CCL4
2692M	B	1.08- 1.91	CH2.X	CH2.5		CCL4
219M	B	1.10- 1.65	CH2.X	CH2.5		CCL4
333M	B	1.10- 1.60	CH2.X	CH2.5		CCL4
1115M	B	1.10- 1.90	CH2.X	CH2.5		CCL4
951M	B	1.10- 1.90	CH2.X	CH2.5		CCL4
1038M	B	1.10- 1.60	CH2.X	CH2.5		CCL4
2816M	B	1.10- 1.80	CH2.X	CH2.5		CCL4
810M	B	1.10- 1.60	CH2.X	CH2.5		CDCL3
551M	B	1.10- 1.80	CH2.X	CH2.5		CDCL3
168M	B	1.10- 2.00	CH2.X	CH2.5		CCL4
3M	B	1.29	CH2.X	CH2.5		CCL4
1208M	B	1.29	CH2.X	CH2.5		CDCL3
120M	B	1.30	CH2.X	CH2.5		CCL4
2005M	B	1.30	CH2.X	CH2.5		CDCL3
2524M	B	1.31	CH2.X	CH2.5		CCL4
119M	B	1.32	CH2.X	CH2.5		CCL4
2532M	B	1.32	CH2.X	CH2.5		CCL4
1010M	B	1.33	CH2.X	CH2.5		CCL4
2909M	B	1.35	CH2.X	CH2.5		CDCL3
1623M	B	1.39 APP.	CH2.X	CH2.5		CCL4
770M	B	1.34	CH2.X	CH2.5	S	D20
128M	C	1.10- 1.75	CH2.X	CH2.5		CCL4
1980M	C	1.28	CH2.X	CH2.5		CCL4
1742M	C	1.31	CH2.X	CH2.5		CCL4
451M	C	1.35	CH2.X	CH2.5		CDCL3
2708M	C	1.39	CH2.X	CH2.5		CCL4
2502M	A	1.02- 1.88	CH2.X	CH2.6		DMSO-D6
2785M	A	1.28 APP.	CH2.X	CH2.6		CDCL3
2554M	A	1.31 APP.	CH2.X	CH2.6		CDCL3
2670M	A	1.31	CH2.X	CH2.6	S	D20
2527M	B	1.10- 1.65	CH2.X	CH2.6		CCL4
2939M	B	1.10- 1.60	CH2.X	CH2.6		CDCL3
620M	B	1.10- 1.70	CH2.X	CH2.6		CCL4
623M	B	1.10- 1.80	CH2.X	CH2.6		CDCL3
412M	B	1.10- 1.60	CH2.X	CH2.6		CCL4
2192M	B	1.10- 1.60	CH2.X	CH2.6		CCL4
1221M	B	1.10- 1.91	CH2.X	CH2.6		CCL4
1211M	B	1.10- 1.50	CH2.X	CH2.6		CDCL3
4M	B	1.28	CH2.X	CH2.6		CCL4
143M	B	1.28	CH2.X	CH2.6		CCL4
1689M	B	1.29	CH2.X	CH2.6		CCL4
1626M	B	1.29 APP.	CH2.X	CH2.6		CCL4
61M	B	1.30	CH2.X	CH2.6		CCL4
2966M	B	1.30	CH2.X	CH2.6		CCL4
2693M	B	1.31	CH2.X	CH2.6		CCL4
1388M	B	1.31	CH2.X	CH2.6		CCL4
1209M	C	1.15- 1.85	CH2.X	CH2.6		CCL4
952M	B	1.00- 1.90	CH2.X	CH2.7		CCL4
220M	B	1.10- 1.60	CH2.X	CH2.7		CCL4
2707M	B	1.10- 1.90	CH2.X	CH2.7		CCL4
121M	B	1.10- 1.85	CH2.X	CH2.7		CCL4
1222M	B	1.21- 1.98	CH2.X	CH2.7		CCL4
5M	B	1.28	CH2.X	CH2.7		CDCL3
243M	B	1.30	CH2.X	CH2.7		CCL4
1011M	B	1.30	CH2.X	CH2.7		CCL4
2257M	B	1.30	CH2.X	CH2.7		CDCL3
2154M	B	1.30	CH2.X	CH2.7		CDCL3
1628M	B	1.30	CH2.X	CH2.7		CCL4
2354M	B	1.30 APP.	CH2.X	CH2.7		CDCL3
1216M	B	1.10- 1.90	CH2.X	CH2.8		CDCL3
1347M	B	1.10- 1.80	CH2.X	CH2.8		POLYSOL-D
1389M	B	1.10- 1.70	CH2.X	CH2.8		CCL4
244M	B	1.28	CH2.X	CH2.8		CCL4
62M	B	1.28	CH2.X	CH2.8		CCL4
6M	B	1.28	CH2.X	CH2.8		CCL4

BOOK NO.	ASSIGN-MENT	CHEM SHIFT - ppm -	PROTON GROUP	ENVIRONMENTAL GROUPS	S	SOLVENT
1317M	B	1.28 APP.	CH2.X	CH2.8		CDCL3
2480M	B	1.29	CH2.X	CH2.8		CCL4
2298M	B	1.29	CH2.X	CH2.8		CDCL3
335M	B	1.29 APP.	CH2.X	CH2.8		CCL4
622M	B	1.29 APP.	CH2.X	CH2.8		CDCL3
2813M	B	1.30	CH2.X	CH2.8		CCL4
2193M	B	1.30	CH2.X	CH2.8		CDCL3
1630M	B	1.30	CH2.X	CH2.8		CCL4
2763M	B	1.10- 1.90	CH2.X	CH2.9		CDCL3
2299M	B	1.10- 1.50	CH2.X	CH2.9		CDCL3
1442M	B	1.18- 1.55	CH2.X	CH2.9		CCL4
7M	B	1.25	CH2.X	CH2.9		CCL4
1103M	B	1.27	CH2.X	CH2.9		CDCL3
2961M	B	1.28	CH2.X	CH2.9		CCL4
2355M	B	1.28	CH2.X	CH2.9		CCL4
336M	B	1.29	CH2.X	CH2.9		CCL4
2652M	B	1.29	CH2.X	CH2.9		D20
1189M	B	1.29 APP.	CH2.X	CH2.9		CDCL3
1989M	B	1.29 APP.	CH2.X	CH2.9		CDCL3
1012M	B	1.29 APP.	CH2.X	CH2.9		CCL4
1631M	B	1.30	CH2.X	CH2.9		CCL4
245M	B	1.30 APP.	CH2.X	CH2.9		CCL4
1312M	B	1.21 APP.	CH2.X	CH2.9	S	CDCL3
1748M	C	1.25	CH2.X	CH2.9		CCL4
2356M	C	1.29	CH2.X	CH2.9		CCL4
2579M	B	1.29	CH2.X	CH2-8		CDCL3
86M	B	1.27	CH2.X	UNSPECIFIED		CDCL3
2686M	B	1.10- 1.80	CH2.10	CH2-NH2/CH3		CDCL3
1670M	B	1.10- 1.85	CH2.10	CH2-0/CH3		CDCL3
1660M	B	1.10- 2.00	CH2.10	CH2-S/CH3		CDCL3
1117M	C	1.10- 1.80	CH2.10	CH2-S/CH3		CCL4
554M	B	1.10- 1.80	CH2.11	CH2-NH/CH3		CDCL3
2482M	B	1.27 APP.	CH2.12	CH2-CH2-C(=0)-OH/CH3		CDCL3
1328M	B	1.10- 1.90	CH2.12	CH2-0-S03-NA/CH3		POLYSOL-D
1928M	B	1.10- 1.80	CH2.14	CH2-A/CH3		POLYSOL-D
1827M	A	1.31 APP.	CH2.14	CH2-OH/CH2-OH		DMSO-D6
1635M	B	1.29 APP.	CH2.22	CH2-OH/CH3		POLYSOL-D
1975M	C	1.00- 1.90	CH2.3	CH2-C(=0)-CH2/CH3		CDCL3
2748M	A	1.10- 2.10	CH2.3	CH2-C(=0)-CL/CH2-C(=0)-0		CDCL3
2879M	B	1.10- 2.00	CH2.3	CH2-0-C(=0)/CH3		DMSO-D6
2936M	B	1.10- 2.00	CH2.3	CH2-0-C(=0)/CH3		CCL4
1294M	B	1.10- 2.10	CH2.3	CH2-S03-NA/CH3		D20
2651M	B	1.00- 1.75	CH2.3	CH(C(=0)-0/CH2)/CH3		POLYSOL-D
1798M	C	1.37 APP.	CH2.3	C(OH/CH3/CH3)/CH3		CCL4
1223M	E	1.57	CH2.3	C(SH/CH2/CH3)/C(SH/CH3/CH3)		CDCL3
1095M	B	1.00- 1.90	CH2.3	P(CH2.3/CH2.3)/CH3		CDCL3
16M	B	1.29	CH2.34	CH3/CH3		POLYSOL-D
1295M	B	1.10- 1.60	CH2.4	CH2.2-S03-NA/CH3		D20
1981M	B	1.00- 1.50	CH2.4	CH2-C(=0)-CH2.2/CH3		CCL4
1982M	C	1.00- 1.90	CH2.4	CH2-C(=0)-CH/CH3		CCL4
2709M	C	1.10- 2.00	CH2.4	CH2-C(=0)-0/CH3		CCL4
909M	B	1.10- 1.90	CH2.4	CH2-N=C=0/CH3		CDCL3
1669M	B	1.00- 1.80	CH2.4	CH2-0/CH3		CCL4
1083M	B	1.00- 1.70	CH2.4	CH2-SIH3/CH3		CDCL3
161M	B	1.00- 1.70	CH2.5	CH2-Q1/CH3		CCL4
2815M	B	1.10- 1.75	CH2.5	CH2-Q2/CH3		CCL4
1204M	B	1.10- 1.90	CH2.5	CH2-SA/CH3		CDCL3
1800M	C	1.10- 1.60	CH2.5	C(OH/CH3/CH3)/CH3		CDCL3
1440M	B	1.10- 1.80	CH2.5	R30<CH-0/HCH>/CH3		CCL4
1472M	D	1.10- 1.70	CH2.5	R600<CH-0/0>/CH3		CCL4
1984M	B	1.10- 1.50	CH2.6	CH2.2-C(=0)-CH2.2/CH3		CCL4
2733M	C	1.30 APP.	CH2.6	CH2-CH/CH3		CCL4
2801M	B	1.10- 1.90	CH2.6	CH2-C(=0)-0/CH3		CCL4
1820M	B	1.00- 1.60	CH2.6	CH2-C/CH3		CCL4
2848M	B	1.10- 1.90	CH2.6	CH2-0-C(=0)/CH3		CCL4
1441M	B	1.10- 1.60	CH2.7	R30<CH-0/HCH>/CH3		CCL4
1988M	C	1.10- 1.90	CH2.8	CH2-C(=0)-CH2/CH3		CCL4
2685M	B	1.27 APP.	CH2.8	CH2-NH2/CH3		CDCL3
162M	B	1.10- 1.70	CH2.8	CH2-Q1/CH3		CDCL3
413M	B	1.28 APP.	CH2.9	CH2.2-I/CH3		CCL4
208M	A	3.76	CH2R	AR5A(C*/C*)		CDCL3
565M	B	1.39 APP.	CH2R	R13N<CH2-CH2/CH2-CH2>		CDCL3
565M	B	1.39 APP.	CH2R	R13N<CH2-NH/CH2-CH2>		CDCL3
565M	C	2.64	CH2R	R13N<NH-CH2/CH2-CH2>		CDCL3
2010M	A	1.29	CH2R	R13(CH2-CH2/CH2-CH2)		CCL4
2010M	B	1.40- 1.95	CH2R	R13(CH2-C(=0)/CH2-CH2)		CCL4
2010M	C	2.36	CH2R	R13(C(=0)-CH2/CH2-CH2)		CCL4
2953M	B	2.31	CH2R	R150<C(=0)-0/CH2-CH2>		CDCL3
2953M	C	4.11	CH2R	R150<0-C(=0)/CH2-CH2>		CDCL3
2011M	B	1.64	CH2R	R15<CH2-C(=0)/CH2-CH2>		CDCL3
2011M	C	2.43	CH2R	R15<C(=0)-CH2/CH2-CH2>		CDCL3

BOOK NO.	ASSIGN-MENT	CHEM SHIFT - ppm -	PROTON GROUP	ENVIRONMENTAL GROUPS	S	SOLVENT
1540M	B	2.65	CH2R	R30<O-CH(CH2-O)>		CCL4
2394M	A	2.58- 2.95	CH2R	R30(O-CH(HCH-R5NA))		CDCL3
144M	A	0.08- 0.74	CH2R	R3<CH(CH2-A)-CH2>		CDCL3
1789M	A	0.09- 0.64	CH2R	R3<CH(CH(OH/A))-CH2>		CCL4
1761M	A	0.10- 0.80	CH2R	R3<CH(CH(OH/CH3))-CH2>		CDCL3
2786M	B	1.31	CH2R	R3<CH(C(=O)-O-CH2)-CH(C(=O)-O-CH2)>		CCL4
1996M	A	0.60- 1.10	CH2R	R3(CH(C(=O)-R3)-CH2)		CCL4
1454M	A	4.45- 5.00	CH2R	R40(O-CH2/CH(CL))		CDCL3
1129M	A	3.00	CH2R	R4S<CH2-S/CH2>		CDCL3
1129M	B	3.23	CH2R	R4S<S-CH2/CH2>		CDCL3
2513M	A	1.60- 2.70	CH2R	R4<CH2-CH(C(=O)-OH)/CH2>		CDCL3
2513M	A	1.60- 2.70	CH2R	R4<CH(C(=O)-OH)-CH2/CH2>		CDCL3
772M	A	1.50- 2.60	CH2R	R4(CH2-CH(NH2)/CH2)	S	D20
1763M	A	1.10- 2.50	CH2R	R4(CH2-CH(OH)/CH2)		CCL4
772M	A	1.50- 2.60	CH2R	R4(CH(NH2)-CH2/CH2)	S	D20
1763M	A	1.10- 2.50	CH2R	R4(CH(OH)-CH2/CH2)		CCL4
209M	B	3.82	CH2R	R5AA<C*-CH-C(CH3)/C*>		CDCL3
1949M	A	3.78	CH2R	R5AA<C*/C*>		POLYSOL-D
2180M	A	3.72	CH2R	R5AA(C*-CH-C(C(=O)-H)/C*)		CDCL3
207M	A	3.30	CH2R	R5AA(C*/CH2-C*)		CDCL3
198M	B	2.50- 3.00	CH2R	R5AR6(C*/CH2-CH*)		CCL4
195M	A	2.02	CH2R	R5A<CH2-C*/CH2-C*>		CDCL3
2179M	A	2.12	CH2R	R5A<CH2-C*/CH2-C*>		CCL4
2149M	A	3.63	CH2R	R5A<C(=O)-C*/C(=O)-C*>		TFA
195M	B	2.90	CH2R	R5A<C*/CH2-CH2>		CDCL3
2179M	B	2.91	CH2R	R5A<C*/CH2-CH2>		CCL4
1948M	A	1.92	CH2R	R5A(CH2-C*/CH2-C*)		CDCL3
2108M	A	2.03	CH2R	R5A(CH2-C*/CH2-C*)		CDCL3
1948M	B	2.78 APP.	CH2R	R5A(C*-C(OH)/CH2-CH2)		CDCL3
1948M	B	2.78 APP.	CH2R	R5A(C*/CH2-CH2)		CDCL3
2108M	C	2.89	CH2R	R5A(C*/CH2-CH2)		CDCL3
199M	A	3.12	CH2R	R5A(C*/CH=CH)		CCL4
863M	A	3.83 APP.	CH2R	R5A(C*/C(=NOH)-CH2)		CDCL3
1020M	A	2.99	CH2R	R5NA<C*/CH2-NH>		CDCL3
1020M	B	3.56	CH2R	R5NA<NH-C*/CH2-C*>		CDCL3
2431M	A	3.50	CH2R	R5NN<NH-C(=O)/CH2-NH>		CCL4
2433M	D	3.38	CH2R	R5NN<NH-C(=O)/CH2-N(CH2,3-CH3)>		POLYSOL-D
2434M	A	3.39	CH2R	R5NN<NH-C(=O)/CH2-N(CH2-Q3)>		TFA
2443M	A	4.29	CH2R	R5NN<NH-C(=O)/C(=O)-NH>		TFA
1664M	B	4.11 APP.	CH2R	R5NN<NH-C(=S)/CH2-N(CH2-CH2)>		CDCL3
674M	A	4.00	CH2R	R5NN<N(A)-C(A)=/CH2-N=>		CCL4
2433M	D	3.38	CH2R	R5NN<N(CH2,3-CH3)-C(=O)/CH2-NH>		TFA
1664M	B	4.11 APP.	CH2R	R5NN<N(CH2-CH2)-C(=S)/CH2-NH>		POLYSOL-D
2434M	A	3.39	CH2R	R5NN<N(CH2-Q3)-C(=O)/CH2-NH>		POLYSOL-D
1376M	A	3.27	CH2R	R5NN<N(SO2-A)-CH2/CH2-N(SO2-A)>		POLYSOL-D
1376M	B	4.56	CH2R	R5NN<N(SO2-A)-CH2/N(SO2-A)-CH2>		CDCL3
674M	A	4.00	CH2R	R5NN<N=C(A)/CH2-N(A)>		CDCL3
2450M	A	4.22	CH2R	R5NN(N(A)-C(=O)/C(=O)-N(A))		CDCL3
2992M	A	3.62	CH2R	R5NO<NH-C(=O)/CH2-O>		CDCL3
2994M	A	3.90	CH2R	R5NO<N(A)-C(=O)/CH2-O>		CDCL3
2992M	B	4.48	CH2R	R5NO<O-C(=O)/CH2-NH>		CDCL3
2994M	B	4.36	CH2R	R5NO<O-C(=O)/CH2-N(A)>		CCL4
1134M	B	3.27	CH2R	R5NS<N=C(CH3)/CH2-S>		CCL4
1134M	C	4.11	CH2R	R5NS<S-C(CH3)=/CH2-N=>		CDCL3
1135M	B	4.00	CH2R	R5NS(N=C(NH-CH2)/CH2-S)		CDCL3
1135M	A	3.29	CH2R	R5NS(S-C(NH-CH2)=/CH2-N=)		CDCL3
712M	A	1.10- 1.80	CH2R	R5N<CH2-CH2/CH2-CH2>		C6H6
560M	A	1.45	CH2R	R5N<CH2-NH/CH2-CH2>		D20
2636M	A	1.74- 2.60	CH2R	R5N<CH2-NH/CH2-CH(C(=O)-OH)>		CDCL3
712M	A	1.10- 1.80	CH2R	R5N<CH2-N(CH2-AN)/CH2-CH2>		CDCL3
1756M	B	1.76	CH2R	R5N<CH2-N(CH2-CH)/CH2-CH2>		CDCL3
636M	A	1.78	CH2R	R5N<CH2-N(CH3)/CH2-CH2>		D20
1029M	A	2.08	CH2R	R5N<CH2-N(NO)/CH2-CH2>		D20
2636M	A	1.74- 2.60	CH2R	R5N<CH(C(=O)-OH)-NH/CH2-CH2>		D20
2375M	A	2.79	CH2R	R5N<C(=O)-NH/CH2-C(=O)>		CDCL3
2382M	C	2.70	CH2R	R5N<C(=O)-N(CH2,4-CH3)/CH2-C(=O)>		C6H6
560M	C	2.69	CH2R	R5N<NH-CH2/CH2-CH2>		D20
2636M	B	3.39	CH2R	R5N<NH-CH(C(=O)-OH)/CH2-CH2>		CDCL3
712M	B	2.43	CH2R	R5N<N(CH2-AN)-CH2/CH2-CH2>		CDCL3
1756M	C	1.90- 2.90	CH2R	R5N<N(CH2-CH)-CH2/CH2-CH2>		CDCL3
636M	C	2.48	CH2R	R5N<N(CH3)-CH2/CH2-CH2>		D20
1029M	B	3.52	CH2R	R5N<N(NO)-CH2/CH2-CH2>		D20
1029M	C	4.21	CH2R	R5N<N(NO)-CH2/CH2-CH2>		CDCL3
2374M	A	2.10	CH2R	R5N(CH2-N(A)/CH2-C(=O))		D20
2637M	A	2.00- 2.80	CH2R	R5N(CH(OH)-CH2/CH(C(=O)-OH)-NH)		CDCL3
2374M	B	2.55	CH2R	R5N(C(=O)-N(A)/CH2-CH2)		D20
2637M	B	3.54 APP.	CH2R	R5N(NH-CH(C(=O)-OH)/CH(OH)-CH2)		CDCL3
2374M	C	3.78	CH2R	R5N(N(A)-C(=O)/CH2-CH2)		CCL4
711M	C	3.12	CH2R	R5N(N(CH3)-CH2/CH(AN(C-CH-N))-CH2)		CDCL3
2955M	A	3.59	CH2R	R5OA<C*/C(=O)-O>		CDCL3
2956M	A	5.48	CH2R	R5OA<O-C(=O)/C*>		CDCL3

BOOK NO.	ASSIGN-MENT	CHEM SHIFT - ppm -	PROTON GROUP	ENVIRONMENTAL GROUPS	S	SOLVENT
1588M	A	5.89	CH2R	R500A<0-C*/0-C*>		CCL4
2608M	A	6.08	CH2R	R500A<0-C*/0-C*>		POLYSOL-D
1734M	C	5.85	CH2R	R500A<0-C*/0-C*>		CDCL3
2186M	A	6.01	CH2R	R500A(0-C*/0-C*)		CDCL3
2039M	C	5.85	CH2R	R500A(0-C*/0-C*)		CCL4
1458M	A	3.79	CH2R	R500<0-CH2/CH2-0>		CCL4
1458M	B	4.80	CH2R	R500<0-CH2/0-CH2>		CCL4
1679M	E	3.60- 4.30	CH2R	R500<0-C(CH3/CH3)/CH(CH2-OH)-0>		CCL4
1459M	D	3.82	CH2R	R500<0-C/CH2-0>		CCL4
1318M	A	2.61	CH2R	R50S<CH2-0/CH2-S02>		CDCL3
1318M	C	4.50	CH2R	R50S<0-S02/CH2-CH2>		CDCL3
1318M	B	3.23	CH2R	R50S<S02-0/CH2-CH2>		CDCL3
1457M	A	1.60- 2.12	CH2R	R50<CH2-0/CH2-CH(CH2-0)>		CCL4
1460M	B	1.70- 2.40	CH2R	R50<CH2-0/CH2-CH(CH2-0)>		CCL4
1456M	B	1.20- 2.20	CH2R	R50<CH2-0/CH2-CH(CH3)>		CCL4
1457M	A	1.60- 2.12	CH2R	R50<CH(CH2-0)-0/CH2-CH2>		CCL4
1460M	B	1.70- 2.40	CH2R	R50<CH(CH2-0)-0/CH2-CH2>		CCL4
2946M	B	1.68- 2.82	CH2R	R50<CH(CH3)-C(=0)/CH2-0>		CCL4
1456M	B	1.20- 2.20	CH2R	R50<CH(CH3)-0/CH2-CH2>		CCL4
2947M	C	2.07- 2.66	CH2R	R50<C(=0)-0/CH2-CH(CH2-CH2)>		CCL4
2255M	A	3.00	CH2R	R50<C(=0)-0/CH2-C(=0)>		CDCL3
2256M	B	2.30- 3.55	CH2R	R50<C(=0)-0/CH(CH3)-C(=0)>		CDCL3
2954M	B	3.08	CH2R	R50<C(=0)-0/CH=C(CH3)>		CCL4
2258M	A	3.62	CH2R	R50<C(=0)-0/C(=HCH)-C(=0)>		CDCL3
1457M	C	3.50- 4.08	CH2R	R50<0-CH(CH2-0)/CH2-CH2>		CCL4
1456M	C	3.30- 4.00	CH2R	R50<0-CH(CH3)/CH2-CH2>		CCL4
2946M	C	4.02- 4.42	CH2R	R50<0-C(=0)/CH2-CH(CH3)>		CCL4
2949M	C	3.97	CH2R	R50<0-C(=0)/C(CH3/CH3)-CH(OH)>		CDCL3
2950M	D	4.29	CH2R	R50<0-C(=0)/HCH-CH(C(=0)-CH3)>		CCL4
1455M	A	1.81	CH2R	R50(CH2-0/CH2-CH2)		CDCL3
2948M	A	2.20- 3.27	CH2R	R50(CH(BR)-C(=0)/CH2-0)		CCL4
1455M	B	3.71	CH2R	R50(0-CH2/CH2-CH2)		CDCL3
2948M	B	4.43 APP.	CH2R	R50(0-C(=0)/CH2-CH(BR))		CCL4
2824M	C	1.40- 2.30	CH2R	R5R5BI<CH*(CH=/CH2)/CH(C(=0)-0-CH2)-CH*>		CCL4
2824M	C	1.40- 2.30	CH2R	R5R5BI<CH*(CH=/CH2)/CH*(CH=/CH(C(=0)-0-CH2))>		CCL4
2132M	C	1.40- 2.40	CH2R	R5R5BI<CH*(C(=0)/C(CH3/CH3)/CH2-C*(CH3)>		POLYSOL-D
2008M	D	1.40- 2.30	CH2R	R5R5BI<C(=0)-C*(CH3)/CH*(C(=0)/C)>		CDCL3
2132M	C	1.40- 2.40	CH2R	R5R5BI<C*(CH3)-C(=0)/C(CH3/CH3)/CH2-CH*>		POLYSOL-D
2008M	D	1.40- 2.30	CH2R	R5R5BI<C*((CH3)/C(=0)/C)/C(=0)-CH*>		CDCL3
2537M	B	1.50-22.40	CH2R	R5R5BI(CH(C(=0)-OH)-CH*/CH*(CH=/CH2))		CCL4
2537M	A	1.10- 1.60	CH2R	R5R5BI(CH*(CH(C(=0)-OH)/CH=)		CCL4
108M	A	0.82	CH2R	R5R5BI(CH*(Q2/CH2))		CDCL3
2262M	D	1.80- 2.60	CH2R	R5R60BI<CH*(C/C(=0))/CH2-C*(CH3)>		CDCL3
2262M	D	1.80- 2.60	CH2R	R5R60BI<C*(C(=0)/C/CH3)/CH2-CH*>		CDCL3
2129M	D	2.00- 2.50	CH2R	R5R6R6R6(C(=0)-C*(CH3)/CH2-CH*)		CDCL3
1130M	A	1.90	CH2R	R5S<CH2-S/CH2-CH2>		CCL4
1259M	C	3.64	CH2R	R5S<S02-CH(CH3)/C(CH3)=CH>		CDCL3
1130M	B	2.77	CH2R	R5S<S-CH2/CH2-CH2>		CCL4
42M	A	1.50	CH2R	R5<CH2-CH2/CH2-CH2>		CCL4
363M	A	1.40- 2.32	CH2R	R5<CH2-CH(BR)/CH2-CH2>		CCL4
43M	B	1.60 APP.	CH2R	R5<CH2-CH(CH3)/CH2-CH2>		CCL4
266M	A	1.38- 2.30	CH2R	R5<CH2-CH(CL)/CH2-CH2>		CCL4
2083M	A	1.38- 2.15	CH2R	R5<CH2-CH(C(=0)-A)/CH2-CH2>		CCL4
421M	A	1.78	CH2R	R5<CH2-CH(I)/CH2-CH2>		CCL4
468M	A	1.00- 2.10	CH2R	R5<CH2-CH(NH2)/CH2-CH2>		CDCL3
97M	A	1.85	CH2R	R5<CH2-CH=/CH2-CH=>		CCL4
98M	B	1.48- 1.97	CH2R	R5<CH2-C(CH3)=/CH2-C(CH3)>		CCL4
1999M	A	2.02 APP.	CH2R	R5<CH2-C(=0)/CH2-CH2>		CCL4
363M	A	1.40- 2.32	CH2R	R5<CH(BR)-CH2/CH2-CH2>		CCL4
43M	B	1.60 APP.	CH2R	R5<CH(CH3)-CH2/CH2-CH2>		CCL4
266M	A	1.38- 2.30	CH2R	R5<CH(CL)-CH2/CH2-CH2>		CCL4
2083M	A	1.38- 2.15	CH2R	R5<CH(C(=0)-A)-CH2/CH2-CH2>		CCL4
421M	B	2.03	CH2R	R5<CH(I)-CH2/CH2-CH2>		CCL4
468M	A	1.00- 2.10	CH2R	R5<CH(NH2)-CH2/CH2-CH2>		CDCL3
97M	B	2.29	CH2R	R5<CH=CH/CH2-CH2>		CCL4
98M	C	2.22	CH2R	R5<C(CH3)=C(CH3)/CH2-CH2>		CCL4
2024M	B	2.85	CH2R	R5<C(CL)=CH/CH2-C(=0)>		CCL4
1999M	A	2.02 APP.	CH2R	R5<C(=0)-CH2/CH2-CH2>		CCL4
2024M	A	2.49	CH2R	R5<C(=0)-CH=/CH2-C(CL)=>		CCL4
2204M	A	1.40- 2.25	CH2R	R5(CH2-CH(C(=0)-CL)/CH2-CH2)		CCL4
1764M	A	1.61 APP.	CH2R	R5(CH2-CH(OH)/CH2-CH2)		CCL4
2204M	A	1.40- 2.25	CH2R	R5(CH(C(=0)-CL)-CH2/CH2-CH2)		CCL4
1764M	A	1.61 APP.	CH2R	R5(CH(OH)-CH2/CH2-CH2)		CCL4
211M	A	2.86	CH2R	R6AA<C*/CH2-C*>		CDCL3
2124M	A	4.31	CH2R	R6AA(C*/C*)		CDCL3
198M	B	2.50- 3.00	CH2R	R6AR5(C*/CH2-CH2)		CCL4
2114M	A	2.07	CH2R	R6A<CH2-C*/CH2-C(=0)>		CCL4
2115M	B	2.10	CH2R	R6A<CH2-C*/CH2-C(=0)>		CDCL3
2116M	A	2.49	CH2R	R6A<C(=0)-CH2/CH2-C*>		CDCL3
2114M	B	2.52	CH2R	R6A<C(=0)-C*/CH2-CH2>		CCL4
2114M	C	2.90	CH2R	R6A<C*/CH2-CH2>		CCL4

BOOK NO.	ASSIGN-MENT	CHEM SHIFT - ppm -	PROTON GROUP	ENVIRONMENTAL GROUPS	S	SOLVENT
2116M	B	2.97	CH2R	R6A<C*/CH2-C(=O)>		CDCL3
2116M	C	3.51	CH2R	R6A<C*/C(=O)-CH2>		CDCL3
196M	A	1.79	CH2R	R6A(CH2-C*/CH2-CH2)		CDCL3
196M	B	2.75	CH2R	R6A(C*/CH2-CH2)		CDCL3
197M	C	2.70	CH2R	R6A(C*/CH2-CH2)		CCL4
601M	A	1.83	CH2R	R6NA<CH2-NH/CH2-C*>		CDCL3
2371M	A	1.92	CH2R	R6NA<CH2-N(C(=O)-H)/CH2-C*>		CDCL3
601M	B	2.69	CH2R	R6NA<C*/CH2-CH2>		CDCL3
2371M	B	2.81	CH2R	R6NA<C*/CH2-CH2>		CDCL3
601M	C	3.14	CH2R	R6NA<NH-C*/CH2-CH2>		CDCL3
2371M	C	3.80	CH2R	R6NA<N(C(=O)-H)-C*/CH2-CH2>		CDCL3
603M	B	2.61	CH2R	R6NA(C*/CH2-NH)		CCL4
603M	C	2.91	CH2R	R6NA(NH-CH2/CH2-C*)		CCL4
603M	D	3.80	CH2R	R6NA(NH-CH2/C*)		CCL4
801M	A	1.49- 2.18	CH2R	R6NH<CH2-CH2/CH2-CH2>	S	CDCL3
801M	A	1.49- 2.18	CH2R	R6NH<CH2-NH/CH2-CH2>	S	CDCL3
801M	B	3.20	CH2R	R6NH<NH-CH2/CH2-CH2>	S	CDCL3
2993M	B	5.11	CH2R	R6NN<N(C(=O)-O-CH3)-CH2/N(C(=O)-O-CH3)-CH2>		CDCL3
566M	B	2.83	CH2R	R6NN<NH-CH2/CH2-NH>		CDCL3
641M	D	3.01 APP.	CH2R	R6NN<NH-CH2/CH2-N(A)>		CDCL3
641M	C	2.60- 3.26	CH2R	R6NN<NH-CH2/CH(CH3)-N(A)>		CDCL3
567M	C	2.30- 3.10	CH2R	R6NN<NH-CH(CH3)/CH(CH3)-NH>		CDCL3
2442M	B	3.19	CH2R	R6NN<NH-C(=O)/C(CH3/CH3)-CH2>		TFA
641M	D	3.01 APP.	CH2R	R6NN<N(A)-CH(CH3)/CH2-NH>		CDCL3
639M	B	2.42	CH2R	R6NN<N(CH3)-CH2/CH2-N(CH(A/A))>		CDCL3
755M	B	2.20- 3.30	CH2R	R6NN<N(CH3)-CH2/CH2-N(NH2)>		CDCL3
639M	B	2.42	CH2R	R6NN<N(CH(A/A))-CH2/CH2-N(CH3)>		CDCL3
2985M	B	3.44	CH2R	R6NN<N(C(=O)-O-CH2)-CH2/CH2-N(C(=O)-O-CH2)>		CDCL3
755M	B	2.20- 3.00	CH2R	R6NN<N(NH2)-CH2/CH2-N(CH3)>		CDCL3
1079M	A	4.10	CH2R	R6NN<N(NO2)-CH2/CH2-N(NO2)>		DMSO-D6
1374M	B	3.31	CH2R	R6NN<N(SO2-N)-CH2/CH2-N(SO2-N)>		CDCL3
802M	A	3.14	CH2R	R6NN(NH-CH2/CH2-NH)	S	D20
803M	A	3.25	CH2R	R6NN(NH-CH2/CH2-NH)	S	D20
2689M	C	3.30	CH2R	R6NN(NH-CH2/CH2-NH)		D20
640M	B	3.08	CH2R	R6NN(NH/CH2-N)		CDCL3
640M	B	3.08	CH2R	R6NN(N(A)/CH2-NH)		CDCL3
1463M	B	2.20- 3.20	CH2R	R6NO<NH-CH2/CH(CH3)-O>		CDCL3
1468M	B	3.05	CH2R	R6NO<N(A<C-CH-C(CH3)>)-CH2/CH2-O>		CDCL3
1465M	A	2.45	CH2R	R6NO<N(CH2-Q3)-CH2/CH2-O>		CDCL3
1473M	A	2.00- 2.70	CH2R	R6NO<N(CH2-R600)-CH2/CH2-O>		CDCL3
1467M	B	2.61	CH2R	R6NO<N(C(C:N/CH3/CH3))-CH2/CH2-O>		CDCL3
2360M	B	3.45	CH2R	R6NO<N(C(=O)-CH3)-CH2/CH2-O>		CCL4
2360M	B	3.53	CH2R	R6NO<N(C(=O)-CH3)-CH2/CH2-O>		CCL4
1468M	C	3.79	CH2R	R6NO<O-CH2/CH2-N(A<C-CH-C(CH3)>)>		CDCL3
1465M	C	3.70	CH2R	R6NO<O-CH2/CH2-N(CH2-Q3)>		CDCL3
1467M	C	3.70	CH2R	R6NO<O-CH2/CH2-N(C(C:N/CH3/CH3))>		CDCL3
2360M	C	3.45	CH2R	R6NO<O-CH2/CH2-N(C(=O)-CH3)>		CCL4
2360M	C	3.53	CH2R	R6NO<O-CH2/CH2-N(C(=O)-CH3)>		CCL4
1462M	B	2.72	CH2R	R6NO(NH-CH2/CH2-O)		CCL4
1469M	B	3.98	CH2R	R6NO(NH-CH2/CH2-O)	S	D20
1464M	B	2.34 APP.	CH2R	R6NO(N(CH2-CH3)-CH2/CH2-O)		CCL4
1466M	C	2.35	CH2R	R6NO(N-CH2/CH2-O)		CCL4
1469M	A	3.33	CH2R	R6NO(O-CH2/CH2-NH)	S	D20
1462M	C	3.52	CH2R	R6NO(O-CH2/CH2-NH)		CCL4
1464M	C	3.57	CH2R	R6NO(O-CH2/CH2-N(CH2-CH3))		CCL4
1466M	E	3.58	CH2R	R6NO(O-CH2/CH2-N)		CCL4
2378M	B	2.50	CH2R	R6NR6SPI<C*(CH2/CH2)-CH2/C(=O)-NH>		CDCL3
569M	D	2.40- 3.27	CH2R	R6NR6(NH-CH*/CH2-CH2)		CDCL3
637M	A	1.42 APP.	CH2R	R6N<CH2-CH2/CH2-CH2>		CCL4
886M	A	1.54	CH2R	R6N<CH2-CH2/CH2-CH2>		CCL4
2439M	A	1.60 APP.	CH2R	R6N<CH2-CH2/CH2-CH2>		CDCL3
2369M	A	1.62	CH2R	R6N<CH2-CH2/CH2-CH2>		CCL4
1355M	A	1.63	CH2R	R6N<CH2-CH2/CH2-CH2>		CDCL3
2303M	A	1.77	CH2R	R6N<CH2-C(=O)/CH2-CH2>		CCL4
2377M	A	2.12	CH2R	R6N<CH2-C(=O)/CH2-C(=O)>		TFA
2303M	B	2.20	CH2R	R6N<CH2-NH/CH2-CH2>		CCL4
637M	A	1.42 APP.	CH2R	R6N<CH2-N(CH3)/CH2-CH2>		CCL4
2369M	A	1.62	CH2R	R6N<CH2-N(C(=O)-A)/CH2-CH2>		CCL4
2439M	A	1.60 APP.	CH2R	R6N<CH2-N(C(=O)-R6N)/CH2-CH2>		CDCL3
886M	A	1.54	CH2R	R6N<CH2-N(QN(A))/CH2-CH2>		CCL4
1355M	A	1.63	CH2R	R6N<CH2-N/CH2-CH2>		CDCL3
563M	B	0.90- 1.80	CH2R	R6N<CH(CH3)-CH2/HCH-NH>		CCL4
814M	A	1.60- 2.70	CH2R	R6N<CH(N(CH3/CH3))-CH2/CH2-NH>	S	D20
576M	B	2.08 APP.	CH2R	R6N<CH=CH/CH2-NH>		CDCL3
673M	A	2.14 APP.	CH2R	R6N<CH=CH/CH2-N(CH3)>		CCL4
576M	D	3.30	CH2R	R6N<CH=CH/NH-CH2>		CDCL3
2015M	A	2.41	CH2R	R6N<C(=O)-CH2/CH2-N(CH2-A)>		CDCL3
2013M	B	2.80	CH2R	R6N<C(=O)-CH2/C(CH3/CH3)-NH>	S	CDCL3
2303M	B	2.20	CH2R	R6N<C(=O)-NH/CH2-CH2>		CCL4
2377M	B	2.79	CH2R	R6N<C(=O)-NH/CH2-CH2>		TFA
814M	C	3.10- 3.95	CH2R	R6N<NH-CH2/CH2-CH(N(CH3/CH3))>	S	D20

BOOK NO.	ASSIGN-MENT	CHEM SHIFT - ppm -	PROTON GROUP	ENVIRONMENTAL GROUPS	S	SOLVENT
576M	C	2.97	CH2R	R6N<NH-CH2/CH2-CH=>		CDCL3
2303M	C	3.23	CH2R	R6N<NH-C(=O)/CH2-CH2>		CCL4
2015M	B	2.71	CH2R	R6N<N(CH2-A)-CH2/CH2-C(=O)>		CDCL3
637M	C	2.23 APP.	CH2R	R6N<N(CH3)-CH2/CH2-CH2>		CCL4
673M	C	2.37 APP.	CH2R	R6N<N(CH3)-CH2/CH2-CH=>		CCL4
673M	D	2.79	CH2R	R6N<N(CH3)-CH2/CH=CH>		CCL4
2369M	B	3.47	CH2R	R6N<N(C(=O)-A)-CH2/CH2-CH2>		CCL4
2439M	B	3.19	CH2R	R6N<N(C(=O)-R6N)-CH2/CH2-CH2>		CDCL3
1355M	C	3.73	CH2R	R6N<N(C(=S)-NH)-CH2/CH2-CH2>		CDCL3
886M	B	3.31	CH2R	R6N<N(QN(A))-CH2/CH2-CH2>		CCL4
638M	A	1.20- 1.80	CH2R	R6N(CH2-CH2/CH2-CH2)		CCL4
1030M	A	1.30- 2.00	CH2R	R6N(CH2-CH2/CH2-CH2)		CDCL3
815M	A	1.30- 2.20	CH2R	R6N(CH2-CH2/CH2-CH2)	S	D20
564M	B	0.71- 1.89	CH2R	R6N(CH2-CH(CH3)/CH2-CH2)		CCL4
564M	B	0.71- 1.89	CH2R	R6N(CH2-CH(CH3)/CH2-CH(CH3))		CCL4
815M	A	1.30- 2.20	CH2R	R6N(CH2-N(CH2-CH2)/CH2-CH2)	S	D20
638M	A	1.20- 1.80	CH2R	R6N(CH2-N(CH2-R6N)/CH2-CH2)		CCL4
1030M	A	1.30- 2.20	CH2R	R6N(CH2-N(=O)/CH2-CH2)		CDCL3
561M	B	2.80	CH2R	R6N(NH-CH2/CH2-CH2)		CDCL3
1683M	C	2.80- 3.30	CH2R	R6N(NH-CH2/CH2-CH2)		CDCL3
1683M	B	2.10- 2.70	CH2R	R6N(NH-CH2/CH(CH2-OH)-CH2)		CDCL3
562M	D	2.30- 3.20	CH2R	R6N(NH-CH(CH3)/CH2-CH2)		CCL4
815M	B	2.70- 3.80	CH2R	R6N(N(CH2-CH2)-CH2/CH2-CH2)	S	D20
638M	B	2.39 APP.	CH2R	R6N(N(CH2-R6N)-CH2/CH2-CH2)		CCL4
1030M	B	3.78	CH2R	R6N(N(N=O)-CH2/CH2-CH2)		CDCL3
1030M	C	4.19	CH2R	R6N(N(N=O)-CH2/CH2-CH2)		CDCL3
2117M	B	2.75	CH2R	R60A<C(=O)-C*/CH2-O>		CDCL3
1589M	A	2.69	CH2R	R60A<C*/CH2-O>		CCL4
1589M	B	3.79	CH2R	R60A<O-CH2/CH2-C*>		CCL4
1589M	C	4.60	CH2R	R60A<O-CH2/C*>		CCL4
2117M	C	4.48	CH2R	R60A<O-C*/CH2-C(=O)>		CDCL3
2118M	A	2.77	CH2R	R60A(C(=O)-C*/CH2-O)		CDCL3
2118M	B	4.53	CH2R	R60A(O-C*/CH2-C(=O))		CDCL3
1590M	A	4.23	CH2R	R600A<O-C*/CH2-O>		CDCL3
2109M	B	4.27	CH2R	R600A<O-C*/CH2-O>		CDCL3
1477M	A	5.12	CH2R	R6000<O-CH2/O-CH2>		DMSO-D6
1476M	C	3.09- 3.82	CH2R	R600R600SPI<C*(HCH/CH2)-HCH/O-CH(CH2-CH3)>		CCL4
1474M	A	3.76	CH2R	R600R600SPI<O-CH2/C*(CH2/CH2-CH2)		CDCL3
1474M	B	4.80	CH2R	R600R600SPI<O-CH2/O-CH2>		CDCL3
1475M	B	3.19- 3.69	CH2R	R600R600SPI<O-CH(CH3)/C*(HCH/CH2)-HCH>		CDCL3
1471M	A	3.63	CH2R	R600<O-CH2/CH2-O>		CCL4
1319M	A	1.60- 2.50	CH2R	R60S<CH2-O/CH2-CH2>		CDCL3
1319M	A	1.60- 2.50	CH2R	R60S<CH2-SO2/CH2-CH2>		CDCL3
1470M	B	3.81	CH2R	R60S<O-CH2/CH2-S>		CCL4
1319M	C	4.55	CH2R	R60S<O-SO2/CH2-CH2>		CDCL3
1319M	B	3.17	CH2R	R60S<SO2-O/CH2-CH2>		CDCL3
1470M	A	2.55	CH2R	R60S<S-CH2/CH2-O>		CCL4
2259M	B	2.04- 3.15	CH2R	R60<C(=O)-O-C(=O)/CH(CH3)-CH2>		CDCL3
2952M	B	2.59	CH2R	R60<C(=O)-O/CH2-CH2>		CCL4
1867M	B	4.51	CH2R	R60<O-CH(OH)/CH(OH)-CH(OH)>		D20
2952M	C	4.20	CH2R	R60<O-C(=O)/CH2-CH2>		CCL4
1461M	A	2.08	CH2R	R60(CH=CH/CH2-O)		CCL4
1692M	C	1.00- 1.90	CH2R	R60(C(CH2-OH/CH3)-O/CH2-C(CH3)=)		CDCL3
1692M	C	1.00- 1.90	CH2R	R60(C(CH3)=CH/CH2-C(CH2-OH/CH3))		CDCL3
2260M	B	1.92	CH2R	R60(C(CH3/CH3)-C(=O)/CH2-C(=O))		CDCL3
2260M	C	2.42	CH2R	R60(C(=O)-O/CH2-C(CH3/CH3))		CDCL3
1461M	B	3.69	CH2R	R60(O-CH2/CH2-CH=)		CCL4
1461M	C	4.01	CH2R	R60(O-CH2/CH=CH)		CCL4
1448M	A	0.91- 1.60	CH2R	R6R30BI<CH2-CH*/CH2-CH2>		CCL4
1448M	B	1.82 APP.	CH2R	R6R30BI<CH*-O/CH2-CH2>		CCL4
611M	A	1.83	CH2R	R6R5NA<CH2-C*=/CH2-CH2>		CDCL3
611M	B	2.60	CH2R	R6R5NA<C*-C*/CH2-CH2>		CDCL3
611M	B	2.60	CH2R	R6R5NA<C*-NH/CH2-CH2>		CDCL3
2267M	A	1.82	CH2R	R6R50<CH2-C*=/CH2-CH2>		CDCL3
2268M	A	2.00- 2.90	CH2R	R6R50<CH*-C(=O)/CH=CH>		CDCL3
2267M	B	2.45	CH2R	R6R50<C*-C(=O)/CH2-CH2>		CDCL3
2261M	A	1.20- 2.30	CH2R	R6R50(CH2-CH*/CH2-CH2)		CDCL3
2261M	A	1.20- 2.30	CH2R	R6R50(CH*-C(=O)/CH2-CH2)		CDCL3
911M	A	1.90	CH2R	R6R6I<C*(N=C=O/CH2)/CH2-C*(N=C(O)>		CDCL3
2129M	D	2.00- 2.50	CH2R	R6R6R6R5(CH*-CH*/CH=C*)		CDCL3
2130M	F	2.10- 2.55	CH2R	R6R6R6R5(C(=O)-CH=/CH2-C*(CH3))		CDCL3
1684M	A	1.51 APP.	CH2R	R6R6R6TRI<CH*(CH2/CH2)/CH*(CH2/CH2)>		POLYSOL-D
935M	A	1.69	CH2R	R6R6R6TRI<CH*(CH2/CH2)/CH*(CH2/CH2)>		CDCL3
268M	A	1.71	CH2R	R6R6R6TRI<CH*(CH2/CH2)/CH*(CH2/CH2)>		CDCL3
473M	B	1.48	CH2R	R6R6R6TRI<CH*(CH2/CH2)/CH*(CH2/CH2)>		CDCL3
473M	C	1.71	CH2R	R6R6R6TRI<C*(CH2-NH2)-CH2/CH*(CH2/CH2)>		CDCL3
935M	B	2.02	CH2R	R6R6R6TRI<C*(QN(=S)/CH2/CH2)/CH*(CH2/CH2)>		CDCL3
1684M	B	1.72 APP.	CH2R	R6R6R6TRI<C*((CH2-OH)/CH2/CH2)/CH*(CH2/CH2)>		POLYSOL-D
268M	B	2.16 APP.	CH2R	R6R6R6TRI<C*((CL)/CH2/CH2)/CH*(CH2/CH2)>		CDCL3
2359M	A	1.72	CH2R	R6R6R6TRI(CH*(CH2/CH2)/CH*(CH2/CH2))		CDCL3
835M	A	1.69	CH2R	R6R6R6TRI(CH*(CH2/CH2)/CH*(CH2/CH2))	S	D20

BOOK NO.	ASSIGN-MENT	CHEM SHIFT - ppm -	PROTON GROUP	ENVIRONMENTAL GROUPS	S	SOLVENT
813M	A	1.70	CH2R	R6R6R6TRI(CH*(CH2/CH2)/CH*(CH2/CH2))	S	D20
2359M	B	2.02	CH2R	R6R6R6TRI(C*(C(=0)-N/CH2/CH2)/CH*(CH2/CH2))		CDCL3
813M	B	1.94	CH2R	R6R6R6TRI(C*(N(CH3/CH3)/CH2/CH2)/CH*(CH2/CH2))	S	D20
835M	B	2.07	CH2R	R6R6R6TRI(C*(N(+)(CH3/CH3/CH3))-CH2/CH*(CH2/CH2))	S	D20
835M	B	2.07	CH2R	R6R6R6TRI(C*(N(+)(CH3/CH3/CH3)/CH2/CH2)/CH*(CH2/CH2))	S	D20
813M	B	1.94	CH2R	R6R6R6TRI(G*(N(CH3/CH3))-CH2/CH*(CH2/CH2))	S	D20
1132M	A	2.02	CH2R	R6SS<CH2-S/CH2-S>		POLYSOL-D
1132M	B	2.83	CH2R	R6SS<S-CH2/CH2-CH2>		POLYSOL-D
1132M	C	3.80	CH2R	R6SS<CH2-S/S-CH2>		POLYSOL-D
1133M	A	2.85	CH2R	R6SS(S-CH2/CH2-S)		CCL4
1131M	A	1.30- 2.10	CH2R	R6S<CH2-CH2/CH2-CH2>		CCL4
1131M	A	1.30- 2.10	CH2R	R6S<CH2-S/CH2-CH2>		CCL4
1131M	B	2.58	CH2R	R6S<S-CH2/CH2-CH2>		CCL4
2016M	A	2.67	CH2R	R6S(C(=0)-CH2/CH2-S)		CDCL3
2016M	B	2.98	CH2R	R6S(S-CH2/CH2-C(=0))		CDCL3
422M	A	1.00- 2.00	CH2R	R6<CH2-CH2/CH2-CH2>		CDCL3
45M	A	1.42	CH2R	R6<CH2-CH2/CH2-CH2>		CCL4
422M	A	1.00- 2.00	CH2R	R6<CH2-CH(I)/CH2-CH2>		CDCL3
1855M	A	1.00- 2.09	CH2R	R6<CH2-CH(OH)/CH2-CH2>		CDCL3
1776M	A	1.10- 1.80	CH2R	R6<CH2-CH(OH)/CH2-CH2>		CDCL3
146M	A	1.30- 2.00	CH2R	R6<CH2-CH=/CH2-CH2>		CCL4
184M	A	1.30- 2.00	CH2R	R6<CH2-CH=/CH2-CH2>		CCL4
2022M	A	1.60	CH2R	R6<CH2-CH=/CH2-CH2>		CCL4
99M	A	1.62 APP.	CH2R	R6<CH2-CH=/CH2-CH2>		CCL4
175M	A	1.69 APP.	CH2R	R6<CH2-CH=/CH2-CH2>		CCL4
103M	B	1.57	CH2R	R6<CH2-CH=/CH2-CH2>		CCL4
184M	A	1.30- 2.00	CH2R	R6<CH2-C(A<C-CH-CH-C(CH3)>)=/CH2-CH2>		CCL4
175M	A	1.69 APP.	CH2R	R6<CH2-C(A<C-C(CH3)>)=/CH2-CH2>		CCL4
146M	A	1.30- 2.00	CH2R	R6<CH2-C(A)=/CH2-CH2>		CCL4
1776M	A	1.10- 1.80	CH2R	R6<CH2-C(A/A)/CH2-CH2>		CDCL3
103M	B	1.57	CH2R	R6<CH2-C(CH2-CH3)=/CH2-CH2>		CCL4
2022M	A	1.60	CH2R	R6<CH2-C(C(=0)-CH3)=/CH2-CH2>		CCL4
104M	A	1.40- 1.69	CH2R	R6<CH2-C(=0)=/CH2-CH2>		CCL4
2026M	A	1.70- 2.50	CH2R	R6<CH2-C(=0)/CH2-C(CL)=>		CCL4
2028M	B	2.01 APP.	CH2R	R6<CH2-C(=0)/CH2-C(CL)=>		CCL4
100M	C	1.00- 1.60	CH2R	R6<CH(C(CH2/CH3/CH3))-CH2/CH2-CH=>		CCL4
100M	D	1.90 APP.	CH2R	R6<CH(C(CH2/CH3/CH3))-CH2/CH=CH>		CCL4
2515M	A	1.30- 2.30	CH2R	R6<CH(C(=0)-OH)-CH2/CH2-CH(C(=0)-OH)>		TFA
2538M	A	2.51 APP.	CH2R	R6<CH(C(=0)-OH)-CH(C(=0)-OH)/CH2-CH>		C3D60
965M	A	1.40- 2.35	CH2R	R6<CH(C:N)-CH2/CH2-CH(C:N)>		CDCL3
422M	B	2.08 APP.	CH2R	R6<CH(I)-CH2/CH2-CH2>		CDCL3
1855M	A	1.00- 2.09	CH2R	R6<CH(OH)-CH(OH)/CH2-CH2>		CDCL3
1776M	D	2.37 APP.	CH2R	R6<CH(OH)-C(A/A)/CH2-CH2>		CDCL3
99M	B	1.97	CH2R	R6<CH=CH/CH2-CH2>		CCL4
100M	D	1.90 APP.	CH2R	R6<CH=CH/CH2-CH2-CH(C(CH2/CH3/CH3))>		CCL4
112M	A	2.14	CH2R	R6<CH=CH/CH2-CH=>		CDCL3
113M	A	2.65	CH2R	R6<CH=CH/CH=CH>		CDCL3
184M	B	2.00- 2.50	CH2R	R6<CH=C(A<C-CH-CH-C(CH3)>)/CH2-CH2>		CCL4
175M	B	2.15 APP.	CH2R	R6<CH=C(A<C-C(CH3)>)/CH2-CH2>		CCL4
146M	B	2.00- 2.50	CH2R	R6<CH=C(A)/CH2-CH2>		CCL4
102M	B	1.88	CH2R	R6<CH=C(CH3)/CH2-CH2>		CCL4
2022M	C	2.19	CH2R	R6<CH=C(C(=0)-CH3)/CH2-CH2>		CCL4
184M	B	2.00- 2.50	CH2R	R6<C(A<C-CH-CH-C(CH3)>)=CH/CH2-CH2>		CCL4
175M	B	2.15 APP.	CH2R	R6<C(A<C-C(CH3)>)=CH/CH2-CH2>		CCL4
146M	B	2.00- 2.50	CH2R	R6<C(A)=CH/CH2-CH2>		CCL4
1776M	C	1.90 APP.	CH2R	R6<C(A/A)-CH(OH)/CH2-CH2>		CDCL3
102M	B	1.88	CH2R	R6<C(CH3)=CH/CH2-CH2>		CCL4
104M	C	1.84	CH2R	R6<C(CH3)=C(CH3)/CH2-CH2>		CCL4
2026M	B	2.70	CH2R	R6<C(CL)=CH/CH2-CH2>		CCL4
2029M	C	2.49	CH2R	R6<C(CL)=CH/C(CH3/CH3)-CH2>		CCL4
2028M	D	2.71	CH2R	R6<C(CL)=C(CH3)/CH2-CH2>		CCL4
2022M	C	2.19	CH2R	R6<C(C(=0)-CH3)=CH/CH2-CH2>		CCL4
2004M	C	1.85- 2.60	CH2R	R6<C(=0)-CH2/HCH-CH(C(CH3/CH3/CH3))>		CDCL3
2001M	C	2.22 APP.	CH2R	R6<C(=0)-CH(CH3)/CH2-CH2>		CCL4
2026M	A	1.70- 2.50	CH2R	R6<C(=0)-CH/CH2-CH2>		CCL4
2029M	B	2.13	CH2R	R6<C(=0)-CH=/C(CH3/CH3)-CH2>		CCL4
2028M	C	2.32	CH2R	R6<C(=0)-C(CH3)=CH/CH2-CH2>		CCL4
2411M	A	1.60 APP.	CH2R	R6(CH2-CH2/CH2-CH2)		CDCL3
2000M	A	1.79	CH2R	R6(CH2-CH2/CH2-CH2)		CCL4
105M	A	1.00- 1.90	CH2R	R6(CH2-CH=/CH2-CH2)		CCL4
2535M	A	1.40- 1.90	CH2R	R6(CH2-CH=/CH2-CH2)		CCL4
971M	A	1.68 APP.	CH2R	R6(CH2-CH=/CH2-CH2)		CCL4
2210M	A	1.69 APP.	CH2R	R6(CH2-CH=/CH2-CH2)		CCL4
2210M	A	1.69 APP.	CH2R	R6(CH2-C(C(=0)-CL)/CH2-CH2)		CCL4
2535M	A	1.40- 1.90	CH2R	R6(CH2-C(C(=0)-OH)=/CH2-CH2)		CCL4
971M	A	1.68 APP.	CH2R	R6(CH2-C(C:N)=/CH2-CH2)		CCL4
105M	A	1.00- 1.90	CH2R	R6(CH2-C(R6)=/CH2-CH2)		CCL4
2411M	A	1.60 APP.	CH2R	R6(CH2-C(=N-NH)/CH2-CH2)		CDCL3
865M	A	1.87 APP.	CH2R	R6(CH2-C(=N-OH)/CH2-CH2)		CDCL3
2000M	A	1.79	CH2R	R6(CH2-C(=0)/CH2-CH2)		CCL4
2145M	A	1.98	CH2R	R6(CH2-C(=0)/CH2-C(OH)=)		CCL4

: REPRESENTS TRIPLE BOND, ¬ REPRESENTS AN ARROW AND < AND > REPRESENT BRACKETS.

BOOK NO.	ASSIGN-MENT	CHEM SHIFT - ppm -	PROTON GROUP	ENVIRONMENTAL GROUPS	S	SOLVENT
367M	A	1.10- 2.60	CH2R	R6(CH(BR)-CH2/CH2-CH(BR))		CDCL3
2003M	B	1.18- 2.28	CH2R	R6(CH(CH3)-CH2/CH2-C(=0))		CCL4
1856M	A	1.00- 2.20	CH2R	R6(CH(OH)-CH2/CH2-CH(OH))		D20
2210M	B	2.32 APP.	CH2R	R6(CH=C(C(=0)-CL)/CH2-CH2)		CCL4
971M	B	2.22 APP.	CH2R	R6(CH=C(C:N)/CH2-CH2)		CCL4
105M	B	1.90- 2.50	CH2R	R6(CH=C(R6)/CH2-CH2)		CCL4
2535M	B	2.00- 2.50	CH2R	R6(C(C(=0)-OH)=CH/CH2-CH2)		CCL4
971M	B	2.22 APP.	CH2R	R6(C(C:N)=CH/CH2-CH2)		CCL4
2144M	B	2.02	CH2R	R6(C(OH)=CH/C(CH3/CH3)-CH2)		CDCL3
2145M	D	2.39	CH2R	R6(C(OH)=C(C(=0)-CH3)/CH2-CH2)		CCL4
2145M	D	2.61	CH2R	R6(C(OH)=C(C(=0)-CH3)/CH2-CH2)		CCL4
105M	B	1.90- 2.50	CH2R	R6(C(R6)=CH/CH2-CH2)		CCL4
2411M	B	2.38 APP.	CH2R	R6(C(=N-NH)-CH2/CH2-CH2)		CDCL3
865M	B	2.89 APP.	CH2R	R6(C(=N-OH)-C(=N-OH)/CH2-CH2)		CDCL3
2000M	B	2.25	CH2R	R6(C(=0)-CH2/CH2-CH2)		CCL4
2003M	C	2.21 APP.	CH2R	R6(C(=0)-CH2/CH2-CH(CH3))		CCL4
2144M	B	2.02	CH2R	R6(C(=0)-CH=/C(CH3/CH3)-CH2)		CDCL3
2210M	B	2.32 APP.	CH2R	R6(C(=0)-CL)=CH/CH2-CH2)		CCL4
2145M	B	2.39	CH2R	R6(C(=0)-C(C(=0)-CH3)=/CH2-CH2)		CCL4
2145M	B	2.61	CH2R	R6(C(=0)-C(C(=0)-CH3)/CH2-CH2)		CCL4
2383M	C	2.70	CH2R	R7N(C(=0)-N(C(=0)-CH3)/CH2-CH2)		CDCL3
2383M	D	3.91	CH2R	R7N(N(C(=0)-CH3)-C(=0)/CH2-CH2)		CDCL3
1478M	A	1.65	CH2R	R700<CH2-0/CH2-CH2>		CCL4
1478M	B	3.67	CH2R	R700<0-CH2/CH2-CH2>		CCL4
1478M	C	4.62	CH2R	R700<0-CH2/0-CH2>		CCL4
1450M	A	0.70- 1.70	CH2R	R7R30<CH2-CH2/CH2-CH2>		CCL4
1450M	A	0.70- 1.70	CH2R	R7R30<CH2-CH*/CH2-CH2>		CCL4
1450M	B	1.93 APP.	CH2R	R7R30<CH*-0/CH2-CH2>		CCL4
50M	A	1.53	CH2R	R7<CH2-CH2/CH2-CH2>		CDCL3
2009M	A	1.71 APP.	CH2R	R7<CH2-CH2/CH2-CH2>		CDCL3
2009M	A	1.71 APP.	CH2R	R7<CH2-C(=0)/CH2-CH2>		CDCL3
2009M	B	2.49	CH2R	R7<C(=0)-CH2/CH2-CH2>		CDCL3
1452M	A	1.45- 2.02	CH2R	R8R30R30(CH*-0/CH2-CH*)		CCL4
1857M	A	1.00- 2.20	CH2R	R8<CH2-CH(OH)/CH2-CH(OH)>		D20
1857M	A	1.00- 2.20	CH2R	R8<CH(OH)-CH2/CH2-CH2>		D20
114M	A	2.33	CH2R	R8<CH=CH/CH2-CH=>		CCL4
51M	A	1.52	CH2R	R8(CH2-CH2/CH2-CH2)		CCL4
106M	A	1.52	CH2R	R8(CH=CH/CH2-CH2)		CCL4
106M	B	2.12	CH2R	R8(CH=CH-CH2/CH2.5)		CCL4
858M	B	2.10- 2.65	CH2R	R8(C(=NOH)-CH2/CH2-CH2)		CDCL3
133M	A	2.29	CH3	A		CCL4
215M	A	2.44	CH3	AAA<C-CH-C*/CH-CH-C*>		CDCL3
216M	B	2.29	CH3	AAA<C-C*-CH/CH-CH-CH-C*-C*>		CDCL3
722M	A	2.40	CH3	AAN<C-CH-C*-N/CH-CH-C*>		CCL4
723M	A	2.80	CH3	AAN<C-C*-N>		CCL4
721M	A	2.36	CH3	AAN(C-CH-C*/CH-CH-C*)		CDCL3
204M	A	2.42	CH3	AA<C-CH-C*>		CCL4
202M	A	2.49	CH3	AA<C-CH-C*/CH-CH-C*>		CDCL3
205M	B	2.40	CH3	AA<C-CH-C*/CH-CH-C*>		CDCL3
203M	A	2.31	CH3	AA<C-C(CH3)-CH-C*/CH-C*>		CDCL3
205M	A	2.31	CH3	AA<C-C(CH3)-CH-C*/CH-C*>		CDCL3
2119M	A	2.15	CH3	AA<C-C(=0)-C*/CH-C(=0)-C*>		CDCL3
1952M	A	2.21	CH3	AA(C-C(OH)-C*/CH-CH-C*)		CDCL3
751M	A	2.89	CH3	ANAAN<C-N-C*-C*/CH-CH-C*>		POLYSOL-D
1963M	A	2.80	CH3	ANA<C-C*/CH-C(OH)-N>		TFA
719M	A	2.64	CH3	ANA<C-N-C*/CH-CH-C*>		CCL4
720M	A	2.67	CH3	ANA(C-C*/CH-CH-N)		CDCL3
730M	A	2.50	CH3	ANA(C-N-C(CL)-C*/CH-C*)		CDCL3
735M	A	2.43	CH3	ANN(C-N-C(CH3)-C(CH3)-N)		CDCL3
695M	A	2.18	CH3	AN<C-CH-C(CH3)-N/CH-C(CH3)>		CCL4
696M	B	2.31	CH3	AN<C-CH-C((C(CH3/CH3/CH3))-N/CH-C(C(CH3/CH3/CH3))>		CDCL3
692M	A	2.24	CH3	AN<C-CH-N/CH-C(CH3)>		CCL4
695M	B	2.37	CH3	AN<C-N-C(CH3)/CH-C(CH3)>		CCL4
1334M	A	2.53	CH3	AN<C-N-C(C(=S)-NH2)>		POLYSOL-D
842M	A	4.54	CH3	AN<N(+)>		POLYSOL-D
844M	A	4.34	CH3	AN<N(+)-CH-C(NH2)>		D20
684M	A	2.29	CH3	AN(C-CH-CH-N)		CCL4
690M	A	2.29	CH3	AN(C-CH-C(CH3)-N)		CDCL3
683M	A	2.27	CH3	AN(C-CH-N)		CCL4
691M	A	2.20	CH3	AN(C-CH-N-C(CH3))		CDCL3
682M	A	2.47	CH3	AN(C-N)		CCL4
691M	B	2.46	CH3	AN(C-N-CH-C(CH3))		CDCL3
2111M	A	2.60	CH3	AN(C-N-C(C(=0)-CH3))		CDCL3
690M	B	2.50	CH3	AN(C-N/CH-C(CH3))		CDCL3
209M	A	2.41	CH3	AR5A<C-CH-C*/CH-CH-C*>		CDCL3
740M	A	2.47	CH3	AR5NN(C-CH-C*-N=/CH-CH-C*)		CDCL3
1585M	A	2.32	CH3	AR5N0<C-C(CH3)-CH-C*/CH-C*-N=>		CDCL3
1585M	A	2.32	CH3	AR5N0<C-C(CH3)-CH-C*/CH-C*-0>		CDCL3
608M	A	2.48	CH3	AR5N<C-C*-CH=CH>		CDCL3
2271M	A	2.63	CH3	AR50<C-CH-C*-C(=0)/CH-CH-C*>		CDCL3
2126M	A	2.45	CH3	AR6A<C-CH-C*-C(=0)/CH-CH-C*>		CCL4

BOOK NO.	ASSIGN-MENT	CHEM SHIFT - ppm -	PROTON GROUP	ENVIRONMENTAL GROUPS	S	SOLVENT
2128M	A	2.38	CH3	AR6A<C-C(CH3)-CH-C*/CH-C*-C(=O)>		CDCL3
2127M	A	2.66	CH3	AR6A(C-C*-C(=O)-C*/CH-CH-C(CH3))		CDCL3
2117M	A	2.30	CH3	AR6O<C-CH-C*-C(=O)/CH-CH-C*>		CDCL3
187M	A	2.19	CH3	A<C(CH3)/C(CH3)>		CDCL3
373M	A	2.29	CH3	A<C-CH-CH-C(CH2-BR)>		CCL4
1713M	A	2.28	CH3	A<C-CH-CH-C(CH2-OH)>		CCL4
182M	B	2.28	CH3	A<C-CH-CH-C(CH(CH3/CH3))>		CCL4
2060M	C	2.40	CH3	A<C-CH-CH-C(C(=O)-CH2.3)>		CDCL3
2223M	A	2.44	CH3	A<C-CH-CH-C(C(=O)-CL)>		CCL4
2567M	A	2.47	CH3	A<C-CH-CH-C(C(=O)-OH)		TFA
490M	A	2.18	CH3	A<C-CH-CH-C(NH2)>		CCL4
596M	A	2.14	CH3	A<C-CH-CH-C(NH-CH2)>		CCL4
2423M	A	2.21	CH3	A<C-CH-CH-C(NH-C(=O))>		DMSO-D6
660M	A	2.19	CH3	A<C-CH-CH-C(N(CH3/CH3))>		CCL4
2362M	B	2.36	CH3	A<C-CH-CH-C(N(C(=O)-H/CH2))>		CDCL3
904M	A	2.30	CH3	A<C-CH-CH-C(N=N-NH)>		CDCL3
1878M	A	2.20	CH3	A<C-CH-CH-C(OH)>		CDCL3
2943M	A	2.34	CH3	A<C-CH-CH-C(O-C(=O)-A)>		CCL4
2933M	A	2.29	CH3	A<C-CH-CH-C(O-C(=O)-CH2)>		CDCL3
2925M	D	2.32	CH3	A<C-CH-CH-C(O-C(=O)-CH2)>		CCL4
2979M	A	2.27	CH3	A<C-CH-CH-C(O-C(=O)-NH2)>		DMSO-D6
2940M	A	2.31	CH3	A<C-CH-CH-C(O-C(=O)-O)>		CCL4
872M	A	2.35	CH3	A<C-CH-CH-C(QN(A))>		CDCL3
885M	A	2.24	CH3	A<C-CH-CH-C(QN(N(CH3/CH3))>		CCL4
870M	A	2.30	CH3	A<C-CH-CH-C(QN(O2))>		CDCL3
1821M	B	2.34	CH3	A<C-CH-CH-C(R6<C(OH)-CH2/CH2>)>		CDCL3
184M	C	2.30	CH3	A<C-CH-CH-C(R6<C=CH/CH2>)>		CCL4
1267M	A	2.39	CH3	A<C-CH-CH-C(SO2-CH2)>		POLYSOL-D
1262M	A	2.40	CH3	A<C-CH-CH-C(SO2-CH2)>		CDCL3
1709M	A	2.42	CH3	A<C-CH-CH-C(SO2-CH2)>		CDCL3
1264M	A	2.44	CH3	A<C-CH-CH-C(SO2-CH2)>		POLYSOL-D
1283M	A	2.49	CH3	A<C-CH-CH-C(SO2-CL)>		CDCL3
1708M	A	2.22	CH3	A<C-CH-CH-C(S-CH2.2)>		CCL4
1162M	A	2.21	CH3	A<C-CH-CH-C(S-CH2)>		POLYSOL-D
1196M	A	2.30	CH3	A<C-CH-CH-C(S-S)>		CDCL3
178M	B	2.31	CH3	A<C-CH-C(CH2-CH3)>		CDCL3
503M	B	2.18	CH3	A<C-CH-C(CH2-CH3)-C(NH2)/CH-C(CH2-CH3)>		CCL4
484M	B	2.33	CH3	A<C-CH-C(CH2-NH2)>		CDCL3
2061M	B	2.13	CH3	A<C-CH-C(CH3)-C(C(=O)-C)>		CCL4
502M	B	2.16	CH3	A<C-CH-C(CH3)-C(NH2)/CH-C(CH3)>		CCL4
1966M	C	2.21	CH3	A<C-CH-C(CH3)-C(NH-CH2)>		CDCL3
1068M	A	2.40	CH3	A<C-CH-C(CH3)-C(NO2)>		CDCL3
1552M	A	2.19	CH3	A<C-CH-C(CH3)-C(O-CH3)>		CDCL3
189M	A	2.23	CH3	A<C-CH-C(CH3)/CH-C(CH3)>		CCL4
377M	A	2.29	CH3	A<C-CH-C(CH(BR/BR))>		CCL4
293M	A	2.30	CH3	A<C-CH-C(CL)>		CCL4
299M	A	2.31	CH3	A<C-CH-C(CL)-C(CH3)>		CCL4
2057M	A	2.33	CH3	A<C-CH-C(C(=O)-CH3)-C(CH3)>		CCL4
2165M	A	2.42	CH3	A<C-CH-C(C(=O)-H)>		CCL4
430M	A	2.18	CH3	A<C-CH-C(I)-C(CH3)>	S	POLYSOL-D
790M	A	2.29	CH3	A<C-CH-C(NH2)>		CCL4
497M	B	2.17	CH3	A<C-CH-C(NH2)-C(CH3)>		CCL4
792M	B	2.43	CH3	A<C-CH-C(NH2)-C(CH3)>	S	D20
499M	A	2.15	CH3	A<C-CH-C(NH2)/CH-C(CH3)>		CCL4
590M	A	2.24	CH3	A<C-CH-C(NH-CH3)>		CDCL3
2339M	A	2.07	CH3	A<C-CH-C(NH-C(=O))-C(CH3)>		CDCL3
1355M	B	2.32	CH3	A<C-CH-C(NH-C(=S))>		CCL4
662M	B	2.23	CH3	A<C-CH-C(N(CH2/CH2))>		CCL4
664M	C	2.28	CH3	A<C-CH-C(N(CH2/CH2))-C(CH3)>		CDCL3
897M	A	2.40	CH3	A<C-CH-C(N=N-A)>		CDCL3
1932M	A	2.22	CH3	A<C-CH-C(OH)-C(CH2-Q3)/CH-C(CH3)>		POLYSOL-D
2596M	A	2.31	CH3	A<C-CH-C(OH)-C(C(=O)-OH)>		CDCL3
1926M	A	2.17	CH3	A<C-CH-C(OH)-C(OH)>		CCL4
1502M	B	2.31	CH3	A<C-CH-C(O-CH2.4)>		CCL4
1540M	A	2.31	CH3	A<C-CH-C(O-CH2)>		CCL4
1495M	A	2.28	CH3	A<C-CH-C(O-CH3)>		CCL4
2932M	A	2.21	CH3	A<C-CH-C(O-C(=O)-CH2)>		CDCL3
1106M	A	2.35	CH3	A<C-CH-C(P(=O/A/A))>		CDCL3
1468M	A	2.30	CH3	A<C-CH-C(R6NO<N-CH2/CH2>)>		CDCL3
1229M	A	2.30	CH3	A<C-CH-C(SH)>		CCL4
1284M	A	2.41	CH3	A<C-CH-C(SO2-CL)-C(CH3)>		CCL4
1290M	A	2.39	CH3	A<C-CH-C(SO2-OH)-C(NH2)>		DMSO-D6
286M	A	2.34	CH3	A<C-C(CH2-CL)-CH-C(CH2-CL)/CH-C(CH3)>		CDCL3
2854M	B	2.30	CH3	A<C-C(CH2-C(=O)-O)>		CCL4
483M	B	2.30	CH3	A<C-C(CH2-NH2)>		CDCL3
1932M	A	2.22	CH3	A<C-C(CH2-Q3)-C(OH)/CH-C(CH3)>		CDCL3
2640M	A	2.09	CH3	A<C-C(CH3)-CH-C(CH3)/CH-C(NH2)>		CCL4
2239M	A	2.31 APP.	CH3	A<C-C(CH3)-CH-C(C(=O)-CL)>		CCL4
498M	A	2.19	CH3	A<C-C(CH3)-CH-C(NH2)>		CDCL3
2640M	B	2.15	CH3	A<C-C(CH3)-CH-C(NH2)/CH-C(CH3)>		CCL4
187M	B	2.29	CH3	A<C-C(CH3)-C(CH3)>		CDCL3

BOOK NO.	ASSIGN-MENT	CHEM SHIFT - ppm -	PROTON GROUP	ENVIRONMENTAL GROUPS	S	SOLVENT
2058M	A	2.08	CH3	A<C-C(CH3)-C(C(=O)-CH3)-C(CH3)/CH-C(CH3)>		CDCL3
2238M	A	2.33	CH3	A<C-C(CH3)-C(C(=O)-CL)>		CCL4
1913M	B	2.24	CH3	A<C-C(CH3)-C(OH)>		CDCL3
1551M	B	2.27	CH3	A<C-C(CH3)-C(O-CH3)>		CDCL3
2239M	A	2.31 APP.	CH3	A<C-C(CH3)/CH-C(C(=O)-CL)>		CCL4
498M	A	2.19	CH3	A<C-C(CH3)/CH-C(NH2)>		CDCL3
299M	A	2.31	CH3	A<C-C(CL)-CH-C(CH3)>		CCL4
308M	A	2.34	CH3	A<C-C(CL)-CH-C(CL)>		CCL4
304M	A	2.29	CH3	A<C-C(CL)-CH-C(F)>		CCL4
2055M	A	2.49	CH3	A<C-C(C(=O)-CH3)>		CCL4
2057M	B	2.44 APP.	CH3	A<C-C(C(=O)-CH3)-CH-C(CH3)>		CCL4
2058M	B	2.19	CH3	A<C-C(C(=O)-CH3)-CH-C(CH3)-C(CH3)/C(CH3)>		CDCL3
2078M	A	2.48	CH3	A<C-C(C(=O)-CH3)/CH-C(OH)>		DMSO-D6
2238M	B	2.39	CH3	A<C-C(C(=O)-CL)/C(CH3)>		CCL4
2061M	C	2.30	CH3	A<C-C(C(=O)-C)/CH-C(CH3)>		CCL4
2164M	A	2.65	CH3	A<C-C(C(=O)-H)>		CCL4
430M	B	2.30	CH3	A<C-C(I)-CH-C(CH3)>		CCL4
497M	A	2.00	CH3	A<C-C(NH2)-CH-C(CH3)>		CCL4
792M	A	2.32	CH3	A<C-C(NH2)-CH-C(CH3)>	S	D2O
2640M	B	2.15	CH3	A<C-C(NH2)-CH-C(CH3)/CH-C(CH3)>		CCL4
536M	A	2.03	CH3	A<C-C(NH2)-CH-C(NH2)>		CDCL3
500M	B	2.08	CH3	A<C-C(NH2)-C(CH2-CH3)>		CDCL3
502M	A	2.07	CH3	A<C-C(NH2)-C(CH3)-CH-C(CH3)>		CCL4
528M	A	2.04	CH3	A<C-C(NH2)/CH-C(I)>		POLYSOL-D
595M	A	2.00	CH3	A<C-C(NH-CH2)>		CDCL3
1966M	B	2.12	CH3	A<C-C(NH-CH2)/CH-C(CH3)>		CDCL3
2339M	B	2.13	CH3	A<C-C(NH-C(=O))-CH-C(CH3)>		CDCL3
2339M	B	2.26	CH3	A<C-C(NH-C(=O))-CH-C(CH3)>		CDCL3
2974M	A	2.15	CH3	A<C-C(NH-C(=O))/CH-C(BR)>		CDCL3
1341M	A	2.24	CH3	A<C-C(NH-C(=S))>		DMSO-D6
1371M	A	2.11	CH3	A<C-C(NH-SO2)>		DMSO-D6
1070M	A	2.41	CH3	A<C-C(NO2)-CH-C(NH2)>		CDCL3
1068M	B	2.58	CH3	A<C-C(NO2)/CH-C(CH3)>		CDCL3
1071M	A	2.51	CH3	A<C-C(NO2)/CH-C(NH2)S		POLYSOL-D
664M	B	2.22	CH3	A<C-C(N(CH2/CH2)-CH-C(CH3)>		CCL4
658M	A	2.28	CH3	A<C-C(N(CH3/CH3))>		CCL4
927M	A	2.34	CH3	A<C-C(N=C=N)>		CCL4
1876M	A	2.17	CH3	A<C-C(OH)>		CCL4
1918M	A	2.12	CH3	A<C-C(OH)-C(CH2-Q3)>		CCL4
1925M	A	2.21	CH3	A<C-C(OH)-C(OH)>		CDCL3
1923M	A	2.20	CH3	A<C-C(OH)/CH-C(S-CH3)>		CDCL3
1913M	A	2.14	CH3	A<C-C(OH)/C(CH3)>		CDCL3
1498M	B	2.18	CH3	A<C-C(O-CH2)>		CCL4
1552M	B	2.24	CH3	A<C-C(O-CH3)/CH-C(CH3)>		CDCL3
1558M	A	2.18	CH3	A<C-C(O-CH3)/CH-C(O-CH3)>		CCL4
1551M	A	2.13	CH3	A<C-C(O-CH3)/C(CH3)>		CDCL3
1105M	A	2.52	CH3	A<C-C(P(=O/A/A))>		CDCL3
2397M	A	2.21	CH3	A<C-C(R5NA<N-C(=O)/C(=O)>)>		CDCL3
175M	C	2.24	CH3	A<C-C(R6<C=CH/CH2>)>		CCL4
1228M	A	2.32	CH3	A<C-C(SH)>		CDCL3
1284M	B	2.70	CH3	A<C-C(SO2-CL)-CH-C(CH3)>		CCL4
1362M	A	2.65	CH3	A<C-C(SO2-NH2)>		DMSO-D6
1195M	A	2.24	CH3	A<C-C(S-S)>		CDCL3
387M	B	2.32	CH3	A(C(BR)-C(CH3)/CH-C(CH3))		CCL4
172M	B	2.38	CH3	A(C-CH-CH-C(A(C-C(CH2-CH3))))		CCL4
384M	A	2.25	CH3	A(C-CH-CH-C(BR))		CCL4
185M	A	2.30	CH3	A(C-CH-CH-C(CH2.2-A))		CDCL3
285M	A	2.28	CH3	A(C-CH-CH-C(CH2-CL))		CCL4
2557M	A	2.31	CH3	A(C-CH-CH-C(CH2-C(=O)-O))		CDCL3
485M	B	2.30	CH3	A(C-CH-CH-C(CH2-NH2))		CCL4
181M	A	2.27	CH3	A(C-CH-CH-C(CH3))		CCL4
294M	A	2.29	CH3	A(C-CH-CH-C(CL))		CCL4
2101M	A	2.36	CH3	A(C-CH-CH-C(C(=O)-A))		CDCL3
2105M	A	2.38	CH3	A(C-CH-CH-C(C(=O)-A))		CDCL3
2100M	A	2.39	CH3	A(C-CH-CH-C(C(=O)-A))		CDCL3
2062M	A	2.39	CH3	A(C-CH-CH-C(C(=O)-CH2))		CDCL3
2056M	A	2.32	CH3	A(C-CH-CH-C(C(=O)-CH3))		CCL4
2093M	A	2.36	CH3	A(C-CH-CH-C(C(=O)-Q2))		CDCL3
986M	A	2.41	CH3	A(C-CH-CH-C(C:N))		CCL4
226M	A	2.23	CH3	A(C-CH-CH-C(F))		CCL4
429M	A	2.26	CH3	A(C-CH-CH-C(I))		CDCL3
593M	B	2.20	CH3	A(C-CH-CH-C(NH-CH2))		CDCL3
591M	A	2.21	CH3	A(C-CH-CH-C(NH-CH2))		CDCL3
2345M	A	2.30	CH3	A(C-CH-CH-C(NH-C(=O)))		CDCL3
2323M	B	2.22	CH3	A(C-CH-CH-C(NH-C(=O)))		DMSO-D6
1368M	B	2.30	CH3	A(C-CH-CH-C(NH-SO2))		CDCL3
1048M	A	2.45	CH3	A(C-CH-CH-C(NO2))		CDCL3
663M	B	2.21	CH3	A(C-CH-CH-C(N(CH2/CH2)))		CDCL3
761M	A	2.25	CH3	A(C-CH-CH-C(N(N/CH3)))		CDCL3
1500M	B	2.26	CH3	A(C-CH-CH-C(O-CH2))		CCL4
2924M	B	2.28	CH3	A(C-CH-CH-C(O-C(=O)-CH3))		CCL4

: REPRESENTS TRIPLE BOND. ¬ REPRESENTS AN ARROW AND < AND > REPRESENT BRACKETS.   PAGE 394

BOOK NO.	ASSIGN-MENT	CHEM SHIFT - ppm -	PROTON GROUP	ENVIRONMENTAL GROUPS	S	SOLVENT
1099M	A	2.21	CH3	A(C-CH-CH-C(P(A/A)))		CDCL3
881M	A	2.38	CH3	A(C-CH-CH-C(QN(QN)))		CDCL3
928M	A	2.30	CH3	A(C-CH-CH-C(QN(=N-A)))		CDCL3
2564M	A	2.33	CH3	A(C-CH-CH-C(Q2(H/C(=O)-OH/H)))		DMSO-D6
1230M	A	2.20	CH3	A(C-CH-CH-C(SH))		CDCL3
1268M	A	2.30	CH3	A(C-CH-CH-C(SO2-A))		CDCL3
1269M	A	2.31	CH3	A(C-CH-CH-C(SO2-A))		CDCL3
1363M	A	2.46	CH3	A(C-CH-CH-C(SO2-NH2))		TFA
1370M	A	2.29	CH3	A(C-CH-CH-C(SO2-NH))		CDCL3
1372M	B	2.38	CH3	A(C-CH-CH-C(SO2-NH))		CDCL3
1375M	A	2.43	CH3	A(C-CH-CH-C(SO2-N))		CDCL3
1369M	B	2.40	CH3	A(C-CH-CH-C(SO2-N))		CDCL3
1312M	D	2.31	CH3	A(C-CH-CH-C(SO3))	S	CDCL3
1302M	A	2.37	CH3	A(C-CH-CH-C(SO3-BA))	S	D20
1322M	C	2.42	CH3	A(C-CH-CH-C(SO3-CH2))		CCL4
1321M	B	2.40	CH3	A(C-CH-CH-C(SO3-CH))		CCL4
1170M	A	2.30	CH3	A(C-CH-CH-C(S-A))		CDCL3
2290M	A	2.49	CH3	A(C-CH-CH-(C(=O)-NH2))		TFA
383M	A	2.30	CH3	A(C-CH-C(BR))		CCL4
385M	B	2.26	CH3	A(C-CH-C(BR)-C(CH(CH3/CH3)))		CDCL3
521M	A	2.17	CH3	A(C-CH-C(BR)-C(NH2))		CDCL3
1936M	B	2.21	CH3	A(C-CH-C(CH2-A)-C(OH)/CH-C(CH2-A))		CDCL3
177M	A	2.28	CH3	A(C-CH-C(CH3))		CCL4
387M	A	2.21	CH3	A(C-CH-C(CH3)-C(BR)/CH-C(CH3))		CCL4
496M	B	2.16	CH3	A(C-CH-C(CH3)-C(NH2))		CCL4
2338M	A	1.99	CH3	A(C-CH-C(CH3)-C(NH-C(=O)))		CDCL3
763M	A	2.21	CH3	A(C-CH-C(CH3)-C(N(N/CH3))/CH-C(CH3))		CDCL3
1364M	A	2.31	CH3	A(C-CH-C(CH3)-C(SO2-NH2)/CH-C(CH3))		TFA
1301M	A	2.24	CH3	A(C-CH-C(CH3)-C(SO3NA))	S	D20
1936M	B	2.21	CH3	A(C-CH-C(C(CH3/CH3/CH3))-C(OH)/CH-C(CH2-A))		CDCL3
2240M	A	2.35	CH3	A(C-CH-C(C(=O)-CL)/CH-C(CH3))		CCL4
2289M	A	2.34	CH3	A(C-CH-C(C(=O)-NH2))		CDCL3
985M	A	2.39	CH3	A(C-CH-C(C:N))		CCL4
225M	A	0.32	CH3	A(C-CH-C(F))		CCL4
428M	A	2.24	CH3	A(C-CH-C(I))		CCL4
489M	A	2.20	CH3	A(C-CH-C(NH2))		CCL4
2322M	B	2.20	CH3	A(C-CH-C(NH-C(=O)))		CDCL3
1047M	A	2.45	CH3	A(C-CH-C(NO2))		CCL4
659M	A	2.25	CH3	A(C-CH-C(N(CH3/CH3)))		CCL4
1877M	A	2.18	CH3	A(C-CH-C(OH))		CCL4
1917M	B	2.21	CH3	A(C-CH-C(OH)-C(CH(CH3/CH3)))		CDCL3
1915M	A	2.18	CH3	A(C-CH-C(OH)/CH-C(CH3))		CCL4
1499M	B	2.24	CH3	A(C-CH-C(O-CH2))		CCL4
919M	A	2.29	CH3	A(C-CH-C(QN(=O))-C(CH3))		CCL4
1239M	A	2.17	CH3	A(C-CH-C(SH)-C(SH))		CDCL3
382M	A	2.36	CH3	A(C-C(BR))		CCL4
386M	B	2.31	CH3	A(C-C(BR)-CH-C(CH3)/CH-C(CH3))		CDCL3
372M	A	2.36	CH3	A(C-C(CH2-BR))		CCL4
174M	A	2.20	CH3	A(C-C(CH3))		CCL4
386M	A	2.16	CH3	A(C-C(CH3)-CH-C(BR)/CH-C(CH3))		CDCL3
1227M	B	2.19	CH3	A(C-C(CH3)-CH-C(CH2-SH)/CH-C(CH2-SH))		CDCL3
386M	A	2.16	CH3	A(C-C(CH3)-CH-C(CH3)/CH-C(BR))		CDCL3
193M	A	2.17	CH3	A(C-C(CH3)-CH-C(CH3)/CH-C(CH3))		CDCL3
1914M	A	2.12	CH3	A(C-C(CH3)-CH-C(OH))		CCL4
191M	B	2.19	CH3	A(C-C(CH3)-C(CH3)-C(CH3))		CCL4
191M	A	2.13	CH3	A(C-C(CH3)-C(CH3)/C(CH3))		CCL4
495M	B	2.00	CH3	A(C-C(CH3)-C(NH2))		CCL4
495M	B	2.21	CH3	A(C-C(CH3)-C(NH2))		CCL4
1914M	A	2.12	CH3	A(C-C(CH3)/CH-C(OH))		CCL4
292M	A	2.37	CH3	A(C-C(CL))		CDCL3
823M	A	2.25	CH3	A(C-C(CL)-CH-C(NH-NH2))	S	DMSO-D6
309M	A	2.41	CH3	A(C-C(CL)/C(CL))		CCL4
2099M	A	2.29	CH3	A(C-C(C(=O)-A))		CCL4
2222M	A	2.51	CH3	A(C-C(C(=O)-CL))		CCL4
2593M	A	2.41	CH3	A(C-C(C(=O)-OH)-C(CH3))		CDCL3
2869M	A	2.59	CH3	A(C-C(C(=O)-O-CH3))		CDCL3
984M	A	2.51	CH3	A(C-C(C:N))		CCL4
224M	A	2.22	CH3	A(C-C(F))		CCL4
511M	A	2.11	CH3	A(C-C(F)/CH-C(NH2))		CCL4
427M	A	2.36	CH3	A(C-C(I))		CDCL3
1077M	A	2.21	CH3	A(C-C(NHI)-C(CH3)/CH-C(NO2))		CDCL3
488M	A	2.04	CH3	A(C-C(NH2))		CCL4
789M	A	2.49	CH3	A(C-C(NH2))	S	D20
1291M	A	2.30	CH3	A(C-C(NH2)-CH-C(SO3-H))		DMSO-D6
537M	A	2.10	CH3	A(C-C(NH2)-C(CH3)/CH-C(NH2))		CDCL3
532M	A	2.19	CH3	A(C-C(NH2)/CH-C(A(C-CH-C(CH3)-C(NH2))))		CDCL3
496M	A	2.02	CH3	A(C-C(NH2)/CH-C(CH3))		CCL4
515M	A	2.08	CH3	A(C-C(NH2)/CH-C(CL))		CCL4
495M	A	2.00	CH3	A(C-C(NH2)/C(CH3))		CCL4
495M	A	2.21	CH3	A(C-C(NH2)/C(CH3))		CCL4
589M	A	2.10	CH3	A(C-C(NH-CH3))		CDCL3

BOOK NO.	ASSIGN-MENT	CHEM SHIFT - ppm -	PROTON GROUP	ENVIRONMENTAL GROUPS	S	SOLVENT
2344M	A	2.31	CH3	A(C-C(NH-C(=O)))		CDCL3
2321M	B	2.05	CH3	A(C-C(NH-C(=O)))		CDCL3
2321M	B	2.15	CH3	A(C-C(NH-C(=O)))		CDCL3
2338M	C	2.09	CH3	A(C-C(NH-C(=O))/CH-C(CH3))		CDCL3
2338M	C	2.22	CH3	A(C-C(NH-C(=O))/CH-C(CH3))		CDCL3
1372M	A	2.02	CH3	A(C-C(NH-S02)-C(CH3))		CDCL3
1046M	A	2.57	CH3	A(C-C(NO2))		CCL4
2241M	A	2.70	CH3	A(C-C(NO2)-CH-C(C(=O)-CL))		CCL4
661M	B	2.29	CH3	A(C-C(N(CH2/CH2)))		CDCL3
661M	B	2.29	CH3	A(C-C(N(CH2/CH2)))		CDCL3
665M	A	2.26	CH3	A(C-C(N(CH3/CH3))-C(CH3))		CDCL3
763M	B	2.30	CH3	A(C-C(N(N/CH3))-C(CH3)/CH-C(CH3))		CDCL3
913M	A	2.29	CH3	A(C-C(N=C=O))		CCL4
921M	A	2.29	CH3	A(C-C(N=C=O)-CH-C(N=C=O))		CCL4
1916M	A	2.18	CH3	A(C-C(OH)-C(CH3))		CCL4
1494M	A	2.18	CH3	A(C-C(O-CH3))		CCL4
1098M	A	2.39	CH3	A(C-C(P(A/A)))		CDCL3
919M	A	2.29	CH3	A(C-C(QN(=O))-CH-C(CH3))		CCL4
1364M	B	2.64	CH3	A(C-C(S02-NH2)-C(CH3)/CH-C(CH3))		TFA
1301M	B	2.65	CH3	A(C-C(S03NA)/CH-C(CH3))	S	D20
1496M	A	2.28	CH3	A(C/CH-CH-C(O-CH3))		CDCL3
2151M	A	0.95	CH3	CHI.2-C(=O)-H		CCL4
1630M	A	0.90	CH3	CH2.CH2		CCL4
2254M	A	0.90	CH3	CH2.S-C(=O)-O		CCL4
629M	A	0.90	CH3	CH2.10-CH		CDCL3
2711M	A	0.90	CH3	CH2.10-CH3		CDCL3
2763M	A	0.89	CH3	CH2.10-C(=O)-O		CDCL3
1989M	A	0.89	CH3	CH2.11-C(=O)		CDCL3
413M	A	0.89	CH3	CH2.11-I		CCL4
621M	A	0.90	CH3	CH2.11-N		CDCL3
2686M	A	0.90	CH3	CH2.11-NH2		CDCL3
829M	A	0.89	CH3	CH2.11-N(+)	S	CDCL3
830M	A	0.89	CH3	CH2.11-N(+)	S	CDCL3
910M	A	0.90	CH3	CH2.11-N=C=O		CCL4
1670M	A	0.88	CH3	CH2.11-O		CDCL3
2783M	A	0.89	CH3	CH2.11-O-C(=O)		CDCL3
2769M	A	0.89	CH3	CH2.11-O-C(=O)		CDCL3
2711M	A	0.90	CH3	CH2.11-O-C(=O)		CDCL3
1189M	A	0.89	CH3	CH2.11-S		CDCL3
1660M	A	0.89	CH3	CH2.11-S		CDCL3
1012M	A	0.90	CH3	CH2.11-S		CCL4
1116M	A	0.90	CH3	CH2.11-S		CCL4
1117M	A	0.90	CH3	CH2.11-S		CCL4
1090M	A	0.89	CH3	CH2.11-SI		CCL4
2050M	A	0.89	CH3	CH2.12-C(=O)-A		CDCL3
2280M	A	0.92	CH3	CH2.12-C(=O)-NH2		TFA
554M	A	0.88	CH3	CH2.12-NH		CDCL3
1328M	A	0.89	CH3	CH2.13-O-S03-NA		POLYSOL-D
2482M	A	0.90	CH3	CH2.14-C(=O)-OH		CDCL3
1928M	A	0.89	CH3	CH2.15-A		POLYSOL-D
339M	A	0.89	CH3	CH2.15-BR		CCL4
247M	A	0.89	CH3	CH2.15-CL		CCL4
122M	A	0.90	CH3	CH2.15-C:		CCL4
414M	A	0.89	CH3	CH2.15-I		CCL4
340M	A	0.90	CH3	CH2.16-BR		CDCL3
2194M	A	0.90	CH3	CH2.16-C(=O)-CL		CCL4
833M	A	0.89	CH3	CH2.17-N(+)	S	CDCL3
934M	A	0.90	CH3	CH2.17-N=		CDCL3
1390M	A	0.89	CH3	CH2.17-O		CDCL3
1119M	A	0.88	CH3	CH2.17-S		CDCL3
624M	A	0.89	CH3	CH2.21-N		CDCL3
1635M	A	0.89	CH3	CH2.23-OH		POLYSOL-D
135M	A	0.93	CH3	CH2.2-A		CDCL3
2545M	A	0.70- 1.40	CH3	CH2.2-C		CDCL3
2543M	A	0.87	CH3	CH2.2-C		DMSO-D6
1797M	A	0.94	CH3	CH2.2-C		CCL4
2190M	A	0.95	CH3	CH2.2-C		CCL4
21M	B	0.90	CH3	CH2.2-C		CDCL3
1659M	A	0.87	CH3	CH2.2-CH		POLYSOL-D
1740M	A	0.93	CH3	CH2.2-CH		CDCL3
2522M	A	0.93	CH3	CH2.2-CH		CCL4
331M	A	0.94	CH3	CH2.2-CH		CCL4
327M	A	0.95	CH3	CH2.2-CH		CCL4
1836M	A	0.95	CH3	CH2.2-CH		CDCL3
1784M	A	0.95	CH3	CH2.2-CH		CDCL3
2745M	A	0.95	CH3	CH2.2-CH		CDCL3
2191M	A	0.95	CH3	CH2.2-CH		CCL4
2486M	A	0.98	CH3	CH2.2-CH		CDCL3
2070M	A	0.98	CH3	CH2.2-C(=O)-A		CDCL3
2077M	A	0.98	CH3	CH2.2-C(=O)-A		CCL4
1970M	A	0.92	CH3	CH2.2-C(=O)-CH2		CDCL3

BOOK NO.	ASSIGN-MENT	CHEM SHIFT - ppm -	PROTON GROUP	ENVIRONMENTAL GROUPS	S	SOLVENT
1981M	A	0.93 APP.	CH3	CH2.2-C(=O)-CH2.5		CCL4
1984M	A	0.91	CH3	CH2.2-C(=O)-CH2.8		CCL4
2188M	A	0.99	CH3	CH2.2-C(=O)-CL		CDCL3
2353M	A	0.85- 1.35	CH3	CH2.2-C(=O)-N		D2O
2352M	A	0.96	CH3	CH2.2-C(=O)-N		D2O
2842M	A	0.95	CH3	CH2.2-C(=O)-O		CCL4
2700M	A	0.95	CH3	CH2.2-C(=O)-O		CCL4
1787M	A	0.95	CH3	CH2.2-C:		CCL4
127M	B	0.98	CH3	CH2.2-C:C		CCL4
1027M	A	0.88	CH3	CH2.2-N		CCL4
2354M	A	0.89 APP.	CH3	CH2.2-N		CDCL3
1027M	B	0.97	CH3	CH2.2-N		CCL4
542M	A	0.90 APP.	CH3	CH2.2-NH		CDCL3
1490M	A	0.90	CH3	CH2.2-O		CDCL3
1394M	A	0.91	CH3	CH2.2-O		CCL4
1667M	A	0.93	CH3	CH2.2-O		CDCL3
1381M	A	0.93	CH3	CH2.2-O		CDCL3
2586M	A	1.02	CH3	CH2.2-O		POLYSOL-D
2173M	A	1.04	CH3	CH2.2-O		CCL4
2987M	A	0.94	CH3	CH2.2-O-C(=O)		CDCL3
2863M	A	1.00	CH3	CH2.2-O-C(=O)		CCL4
2935M	A	1.01	CH3	CH2.2-O-C(=O)		CCL4
1033M	A	0.97	CH3	CH2.2-O-N=O		CCL4
1063M	A	0.95	CH3	CH2.2-QN		POLYSOL-D
2800M	A	0.91	CH3	CH2.2-Q2		CCL4
2799M	A	0.94	CH3	CH2.2-Q2		CCL4
2520M	A	0.98	CH3	CH2.2-Q2		CCL4
2156M	A	0.98	CH3	CH2.2-Q2		CDCL3
739M	A	1.00	CH3	CH2.2-R5NNA		POLYSOL-D
1109M	A	0.98	CH3	CH2.2-S		CCL4
1201M	A	0.99	CH3	CH2.2-SH		CDCL3
1280M	A	1.17	CH3	CH2.2-SO2		CCL4
16M	A	0.89	CH3	CH2.34-CH3		POLYSOL-D
693M	A	0.93	CH3	CH2.3-AN		CDCL3
452M	A	0.91	CH3	CH2.3-C		CDCL3
1798M	A	0.92	CH3	CH2.3-C		CCL4
456M	A	0.93	CH3	CH2.3-C		CDCL3
689M	A	0.88	CH3	CH2.3-CH		CCL4
1749M	A	0.88 APP.	CH3	CH2.3-CH		CCL4
2651M	A	0.89	CH3	CH2.3-CH		POLYSOL-D
2650M	A	0.89 APP.	CH3	CH2.3-CH		D2O
2782M	A	0.90	CH3	CH2.3-CH		CDCL3
2732M	A	0.92	CH3	CH2.3-CH		CDCL3
455M	A	0.92	CH3	CH2.3-CH		CDCL3
2762M	A	0.93 APP.	CH3	CH2.3-CH		CCL4
2788M	A	0.94	CH3	CH2.3-CH		CCL4
29M	B	0.90	CH3	CH2.3-CH		CDCL3
2071M	A	0.93	CH3	CH2.3-C(=O)-A		CDCL3
2060M	A	0.96	CH3	CH2.3-C(=O)-A		CDCL3
1969M	A	0.91	CH3	CH2.3-C(=O)-CH3		CCL4
2705M	A	0.92	CH3	CH2.3-C(=O)-O		CCL4
2041M	A	0.92	CH3	CH2.3-C(=O)-Q2		CDCL3
407M	A	0.99	CH3	CH2.3-I		CCL4
1652M	A	0.91	CH3	CH2.3-N		CDCL3
1653M	A	0.92	CH3	CH2.3-N		CDCL3
2351M	A	0.95	CH3	CH2.3-N		CDCL3
1215M	A	0.93	CH3	CH2.3-NH		CDCL3
799M	A	0.93	CH3	CH2.3-NH	S	D2O
768M	A	0.98	CH3	CH2.3-NH2	S	CDCL3
828M	A	1.00	CH3	CH2.3-N(+)		CDCL3
931M	A	0.99	CH3	CH2.3-N=C=S		CCL4
1380M	A	0.91	CH3	CH2.3-O		CDCL3
1413M	A	0.91	CH3	CH2.3-O		CCL4
1382M	A	0.93	CH3	CH2.3-O		CCL4
1599M	A	0.94	CH3	CH2.3-O		CCL4
1562M	A	0.95	CH3	CH2.3-O		CDCL3
1965M	A	0.95	CH3	CH2.3-O		CDCL3
2819M	A	0.90	CH3	CH2.3-O-C(=O)		CDCL3
2847M	A	0.91	CH3	CH2.3-O-C(=O)		CCL4
2775M	A	0.95	CH3	CH2.3-O-C(=O)		CCL4
2743M	A	0.95	CH3	CH2.3-O-C(=O)		CCL4
2896M	A	0.95	CH3	CH2.3-O-C(=O)		CDCL3
2766M	A	0.96	CH3	CH2.3-O-C(=O)		CDCL3
2765M	A	0.93	CH3	CH2.3-O-C(=O)-O		CDCL3
1095M	A	0.94	CH3	CH2.3-P		CCL4
160M	A	0.88	CH3	CH2.3-Q1		CCL4
2433M	A	0.95	CH3	CH2.3-R5NN		CCL4
1254M	A	0.97	CH3	CH2.3-SO2		CDCL3
1281M	A	1.02	CH3	CH2.3-SO2		CCL4
1315M	A	0.97	CH3	CH2.3-SO3		CDCL3
1884M	A	0.89	CH3	CH2.4-A		CCL4

BOOK NO.	ASSIGN-MENT	CHEM SHIFT - ppm -	PROTON GROUP	ENVIRONMENTAL GROUPS	S	SOLVENT
2481M	A	0.90	CH3	CH2.4-CH		CCL4
1975M	A	0.92	CH3	CH2.4-C(=O)-CH2		CDCL3
2252M	A	0.91	CH3	CH2.4-C(=O)-O		CDCL3
129M	A	0.91	CH3	CH2.4-C:		CCL4
1698M	A	0.92	CH3	CH2.4-C:		CCL4
127M	A	0.91	CH3	CH2.4-C:C		CCL4
618M	A	0.90	CH3	CH2.4-N		CCL4
548M	A	0.90	CH3	CH2.4-NH		CDCL3
2879M	A	0.90	CH3	CH2.4-O-C(=O)		DMSO-D6
2705M	A	0.92	CH3	CH2.4-O-C(=O)		CCL4
2897M	A	0.92	CH3	CH2.4-O-C(=O)		CCL4
2936M	A	0.93	CH3	CH2.4-O-C(=O)		CCL4
1082M	A	0.95	CH3	CH2.4-O-NO2		CDCL3
1327M	A	0.92	CH3	CH2.4-O-SO3-NA		D2O
2525M	A	1.90	CH3	CH2.4-Q2		CCL4
2382M	A	0.90	CH3	CH2.4-R5N		CDCL3
1187M	A	0.95	CH3	CH2.4-S		CCL4
1294M	A	0.91	CH3	CH2.4-SO3-NA		D2O
1204M	A	0.88	CH3	CH2.5		CDCL3
219M	A	0.92	CH3	CH2.5		CCL4
1800M	A	0.90	CH3	CH2.5-C		CDCL3
1210M	A	0.90	CH3	CH2.5-CH		CDCL3
1982M	A	0.90	CH3	CH2.5-C(=O)-CH		CCL4
1981M	A	0.93 APP.	CH3	CH2.5-C(=O)-CH2.2		CCL4
2709M	A	0.90	CH3	CH2.5-C(=O)-O		CCL4
1699M	A	0.90	CH3	CH2.5-C:		CCL4
1697M	A	0.92	CH3	CH2.5-C:		CCL4
950M	A	0.92	CH3	CH2.5-C:N		CCL4
909M	A	0.90	CH3	CH2.5-N=C=O		CDCL3
1669M	A	0.92	CH3	CH2.5-O		CCL4
849M	A	0.89	CH3	CH2.5-QN		CDCL3
2526M	A	0.90	CH3	CH2.5-Q2		CCL4
1440M	A	0.91	CH3	CH2.5-R30		CCL4
2005M	A	0.99 APP.	CH3	CH2.5-R6		CDCL3
1472M	B	0.90	CH3	CH2.5-R600		CCL4
1114M	A	0.91	CH3	CH2.5-S		CCL4
1206M	A	0.90	CH3	CH2.5-SH		CCL4
1083M	A	0.90 APP.	CH3	CH2.5-SIH3		CDCL3
168M	A	0.90	CH3	CH2.6-C:		CCL4
128M	A	0.91	CH3	CH2.6-C:		CCL4
951M	A	0.90	CH3	CH2.6-C:N		CCL4
161M	A	0.89	CH3	CH2.6-Q1		CCL4
2815M	A	0.89	CH3	CH2.6-Q2		CCL4
1115M	A	0.90	CH3	CH2.6-S		CCL4
1295M	A	0.89	CH3	CH2.6-SO3-NA		D2O
1820M	A	0.88	CH3	CH2.7-C		CCL4
2733M	A	0.90	CH3	CH2.7-CH		CCL4
2801M	A	0.90	CH3	CH2.7-C(=O)-O		CCL4
810M	A	0.89	CH3	CH2.7-N		CDCL3
623M	A	0.90	CH3	CH2.7-N		CDCL3
620M	A	0.90	CH3	CH2.7-N		CCL4
2848M	A	0.89	CH3	CH2.7-O-C(=O)		CCL4
2527M	A	0.89	CH3	CH2.7-Q2		CCL4
2819M	A	0.90	CH3	CH2.7-Q2		CDCL3
1441M	A	0.90	CH3	CH2.7-R30		CCL4
121M	A	0.90	CH3	CH2.8-C:		CCL4
952M	A	0.90	CH3	CH2.8-C:N		CCL4
2257M	A	0.89	CH3	CH2.8-Q2		CDCL3
1211M	A	0.90	CH3	CH2.8-SH		CDCL3
1988M	A	0.90	CH3	CH2.9-C(=O)-CH2		CCL4
622M	A	0.89	CH3	CH2.9-N		CDCL3
1216M	A	0.89	CH3	CH2.9-NH		CDCL3
1347M	A	0.89	CH3	CH2.9-NH		POLYSOL-D
2685M	A	0.90	CH3	CH2.9-NH2		CDCL3
1389M	A	0.89	CH3	CH2.9-O		CCL4
162M	A	0.89	CH3	CH2.9-Q1		CDCL3
103M	A	0.96	CH3	CH2-A		CCL4
172M	A	1.09	CH3	CH2-A		CCL4
1880M	A	1.16	CH3	CH2-A		CDCL3
1879M	A	1.17	CH3	CH2-A		CCL4
2324M	A	1.18	CH3	CH2-A		CDCL3
491M	A	1.18	CH3	CH2-A		CDCL3
500M	A	1.19	CH3	CH2-A		CDCL3
134M	A	1.19	CH3	CH2-A		CCL4
179M	A	1.20	CH3	CH2-A		CCL4
1497M	A	1.20	CH3	CH2-A		CCL4
178M	A	1.21	CH3	CH2-A		CDCL3
1933M	A	1.21	CH3	CH2-A		CDCL3
295M	A	1.22	CH3	CH2-A		CCL4
375M	A	1.22	CH3	CH2-A		CCL4
2059M	A	1.22	CH3	CH2-A		CCL4

BOOK NO.	ASSIGN-MENT	CHEM SHIFT - ppm -	PROTON GROUP	ENVIRONMENTAL GROUPS	S	SOLVENT
190M	A	1.23	CH3	CH2-A		CCL4
929M	A	1.26	CH3	CH2-A		CDCL3
1049M	A	1.26	CH3	CH2-A		CCL4
1050M	A	1.27	CH3	CH2-A		CCL4
503M	A	1.19	CH3	CH2-A		CCL4
538M	A	1.20	CH3	CH2-A		CDCL3
492M	A	1.21	CH3	CH2-A		CDCL3
201M	A	1.37	CH3	CH2-AA		CCL4
685M	A	1.21	CH3	CH2-AN		CCL4
2115M	A	1.22	CH3	CH2-AR6		CDCL3
319M	A	1.66	CH3	CH2-BR		CCL4
1885M	A	0.68	CH3	CH2-C		CCL4
2031M	A	0.71	CH3	CH2-C		CDCL3
1818M	A	0.77	CH3	CH2-C		CDCL3
2771M	A	0.80	CH3	CH2-C		CCL4
2419M	A	0.81	CH3	CH2-C		DMSO-D6
2302M	A	0.83	CH3	CH2-C		CDCL3
1835M	A	0.83	CH3	CH2-C		CDCL3
1839M	A	0.83	CH3	CH2-C		C3D6O
447M	A	0.89	CH3	CH2-C		CDCL3
1803M	A	0.89	CH3	CH2-C		CCL4
1802M	A	0.89 APP.	CH3	CH2-C		CCL4
1801M	A	0.90	CH3	CH2-C		CCL4
1796M	A	0.90	CH3	CH2-C		CCL4
1223M	A	0.98	CH3	CH2-C		CDCL3
241M	A	1.01	CH3	CH2-C		CCL4
100M	A	0.79	CH3	CH2-C		CCL4
26M	A	0.79 APP.	CH3	CH2-C		CCL4
1814M	A	1.01	CH3	CH2-C		CCL4
977M	A	1.07	CH3	CH2-C		CDCL3
20M	A	0.62- 1.00	CH3	CH2-CH		CCL4
138M	A	0.80	CH3	CH2-CH		CCL4
1788M	A	0.81	CH3	CH2-CH		CCL4
17M	A	0.86	CH3	CH2-CH		CCL4
56M	A	0.86	CH3	CH2-CH		CDCL3
1620M	A	0.87	CH3	CH2-CH		CCL4
55M	A	0.88	CH3	CH2-CH		CCL4
494M	A	0.88	CH3	CH2-CH		CCL4
2285M	A	0.88	CH3	CH2-CH		CDCL3
1622M	A	0.88	CH3	CH2-CH		CDCL3
1749M	A	0.88 APP.	CH3	CH2-CH		CCL4
1746M	A	0.88 APP.	CH3	CH2-CH		CCL4
2021M	A	0.89	CH3	CH2-CH		CCL4
2650M	A	0.89 APP.	CH3	CH2-CH		D20
454M	A	0.90	CH3	CH2-CH		CDCL3
2696M	A	0.90	CH3	CH2-CH		CCL4
2695M	A	0.90	CH3	CH2-CH		CCL4
2698M	A	0.90	CH3	CH2-CH		CDCL3
2691M	A	0.90	CH3	CH2-CH		CDCL3
1736M	A	0.90	CH3	CH2-CH		CCL4
1737M	A	0.90	CH3	CH2-CH		CCL4
1743M	A	0.90	CH3	CH2-CH		CCL4
1627M	A	0.90	CH3	CH2-CH		CCL4
545M	A	0.90	CH3	CH2-CH		CCL4
737M	A	0.90	CH3	CH2-CH		CCL4
2782M	A	0.90	CH3	CH2-CH		CDCL3
1745M	A	0.91	CH3	CH2-CH		CDCL3
2137M	A	0.91	CH3	CH2-CH		CDCL3
443M	A	0.92	CH3	CH2-CH		CDCL3
598M	A	0.92	CH3	CH2-CH		CDCL3
1601M	A	0.92	CH3	CH2-CH		CCL4
1606M	A	0.92	CH3	CH2-CH		CCL4
1602M	A	0.92 APP.	CH3	CH2-CH		CCL4
2475M	A	0.93	CH3	CH2-CH		CDCL3
2960M	A	0.93	CH3	CH2-CH		CCL4
2744M	A	0.93	CH3	CH2-CH		CCL4
2788M	A	0.94	CH3	CH2-CH		CCL4
1644M	A	0.95	CH3	CH2-CH		CDCL3
1836M	A	0.95	CH3	CH2-CH		CDCL3
2808M	A	0.95 APP.	CH3	CH2-CH		CCL4
1034M	A	0.96	CH3	CH2-CH		CCL4
2253M	A	0.97	CH3	CH2-CH		CCL4
1829M	A	0.97	CH3	CH2-CH		CDCL3
1203M	A	0.98	CH3	CH2-CH		CCL4
408M	A	0.99	CH3	CH2-CH		CDCL3
2615M	A	0.99	CH3	CH2-CH		D20
1184M	A	0.99	CH3	CH2-CH		CCL4
323M	A	1.00	CH3	CH2-CH		CDCL3
237M	A	1.01	CH3	CH2-CH		CCL4
262M	A	1.05	CH3	CH2-CH		CCL4
357M	A	1.08	CH3	CH2-CH		CDCL3

BOOK NO.	ASSIGN-MENT	CHEM SHIFT - ppm -	PROTON GROUP	ENVIRONMENTAL GROUPS	S	SOLVENT
2484M	A	1.08	CH3	CH2-CH		CDCL3
1113M	B	0.90	CH3	CH2-CH		CCL4
1387M	B	0.90	CH3	CH2-CH		CCL4
24M	B	0.91	CH3	CH2-CH		CCL4
1747M	B	0.91	CH3	CH2-CH		CCL4
58M	B	0.92	CH3	CH2-CH		CCL4
1617M	B	0.92	CH3	CH2-CH		CCL4
445M	B	0.94	CH3	CH2-CH		CDCL3
1745M	B	0.94	CH3	CH2-CH		CDCL3
1743M	B	0.94	CH3	CH2-CH		CCL4
2477M	B	0.97	CH3	CH2-CH		CCL4
1787M	B	0.98	CH3	CH2-CH		CCL4
2478M	B	0.99	CH3	CH2-CH		CCL4
2903M	B	1.00	CH3	CH2-CH		CCL4
331M	B	1.07	CH3	CH2-CH		CCL4
1207M	C	0.99	CH3	CH2-CH		CCL4
1927M	A	0.84	CH3	CH2-CH2		CDCL3
2277M	A	0.85	CH3	CH2-CH2		DMSO-D6
1747M	A	0.85	CH3	CH2-CH2		CCL4
1744M	A	0.85	CH3	CH2-CH2		CCL4
2652M	A	0.86	CH3	CH2-CH2		D2O
552M	A	0.86	CH3	CH2-CH2		CDCL3
13M	A	0.87	CH3	CH2-CH2		CDCL3
449M	A	0.87	CH3	CH2-CH2		CDCL3
1113M	A	0.87	CH3	CH2-CH2		CCL4
86M	A	0.88	CH3	CH2-CH2		CDCL3
5M	A	0.88	CH3	CH2-CH2		CDCL3
143M	A	0.88	CH3	CH2-CH2		CCL4
60M	A	0.88	CH3	CH2-CH2		CCL4
11M	A	0.88	CH3	CH2-CH2		CCL4
62M	A	0.88	CH3	CH2-CH2		CCL4
120M	A	0.88	CH3	CH2-CH2		CCL4
64M	A	0.88	CH3	CH2-CH2		CCL4
7M	A	0.88	CH3	CH2-CH2		CCL4
15M	A	0.88	CH3	CH2-CH2		CCL4
467M	A	0.88	CH3	CH2-CH2		CCL4
412M	A	0.88	CH3	CH2-CH2		CCL4
244M	A	0.88	CH3	CH2-CH2		CCL4
2355M	A	0.88	CH3	CH2-CH2		CCL4
2470M	A	0.88	CH3	CH2-CH2		CDCL3
2579M	A	0.88	CH3	CH2-CH2		CDCL3
2712M	A	0.88	CH3	CH2-CH2		CDCL3
1626M	A	0.88	CH3	CH2-CH2		CCL4
1632M	A	0.88	CH3	CH2-CH2		CDCL3
1633M	A	0.88	CH3	CH2-CH2		CDCL3
2M	A	0.89	CH3	CH2-CH2		CCL4
8M	A	0.89	CH3	CH2-CH2		CCL4
83M	A	0.89	CH3	CH2-CH2		CCL4
9M	A	0.89	CH3	CH2-CH2		CCL4
119M	A	0.89	CH3	CH2-CH2		CCL4
57M	A	0.89	CH3	CH2-CH2		CCL4
1M	A	0.89	CH3	CH2-CH2		CCL4
92M	A	0.89	CH3	CH2-CH2		CCL4
10M	A	0.89	CH3	CH2-CH2		CCL4
14M	A	0.89	CH3	CH2-CH2		CDCL3
341M	A	0.89	CH3	CH2-CH2		CDCL3
338M	A	0.89	CH3	CH2-CH2		CCL4
2356M	A	0.89	CH3	CH2-CH2		CCL4
2278M	A	0.89	CH3	CH2-CH2		CDCL3
2495M	A	0.89	CH3	CH2-CH2		CDCL3
2528M	A	0.89	CH3	CH2-CH2		CCL4
2459M	A	0.89	CH3	CH2-CH2		DMSO-D6
2365M	A	0.89	CH3	CH2-CH2		CDCL3
2480M	A	0.89	CH3	CH2-CH2		CCL4
2366M	A	0.89	CH3	CH2-CH2		CCL4
2524M	A	0.89	CH3	CH2-CH2		CCL4
2710M	A	0.89	CH3	CH2-CH2		CCL4
2719M	A	0.89	CH3	CH2-CH2		CDCL3
2697M	A	0.89	CH3	CH2-CH2		CCL4
1118M	A	0.89	CH3	CH2-CH2		CCL4
1213M	A	0.89	CH3	CH2-CH2		CCL4
1689M	A	0.88	CH3	CH2-CH2		CCL4
1980M	A	0.88	CH3	CH2-CH2		CCL4
2976M	A	0.88	CH3	CH2-CH2		CDCL3
1322M	A	0.88	CH3	CH2-CH2		CCL4
1387M	A	0.88	CH3	CH2-CH2		CCL4
615M	A	0.88	CH3	CH2-CH2		CCL4
688M	A	0.88	CH3	CH2-CH2		CCL4
2817M	A	0.88	CH3	CH2-CH2		CCL4
2818M	A	0.88	CH3	CH2-CH2		CCL4
1746M	A	0.88 APP.	CH3	CH2-CH2		CCL4

BOOK NO.	ASSIGN-MENT	CHEM SHIFT - ppm -	PROTON GROUP	ENVIRONMENTAL GROUPS	S	SOLVENT
1623M	A	0.89	CH3	CH2-CH2		CCL4
1628M	A	0.89	CH3	CH2-CH2		CCL4
1634M	A	0.89	CH3	CH2-CH2		CDCL3
1739M	A	0.89	CH3	CH2-CH2		CCL4
1748M	A	0.89	CH3	CH2-CH2		CCL4
2049M	A	0.89	CH3	CH2-CH2		CCL4
1987M	A	0.89	CH3	CH2-CH2		CDCL3
2193M	A	0.89	CH3	CH2-CH2		CDCL3
2919M	A	0.89	CH3	CH2-CH2		C3D60
2990M	A	0.89	CH3	CH2-CH2		CCL4
2939M	A	0.89	CH3	CH2-CH2		CDCL3
2966M	A	0.89	CH3	CH2-CH2		CCL4
2961M	A	0.89	CH3	CH2-CH2		CCL4
2895M	A	0.89	CH3	CH2-CH2		CCL4
1392M	A	0.89	CH3	CH2-CH2		CDCL3
579M	A	0.89	CH3	CH2-CH2		CCL4
1757M	A	0.89	CH3	CH2-CH2		CDCL3
2822M	A	0.89	CH3	CH2-CH2		CCL4
2802M	A	0.89	CH3	CH2-CH2		CDCL3
2758M	A	0.89	CH3	CH2-CH2		CDCL3
2759M	A	0.89	CH3	CH2-CH2		CDCL3
953M	A	0.89	CH3	CH2-CH2		CDCL3
1011M	A	0.89	CH3	CH2-CH2		CCL4
1104M	A	0.89	CH3	CH2-CH2		CDCL3
1103M	A	0.89	CH3	CH2-CH2		CDCL3
1010M	A	0.90	CH3	CH2-CH2		CCL4
933M	A	0.90	CH3	CH2-CH2		CCL4
1675M	A	0.90	CH3	CH2-CH2		CDCL3
1619M	A	0.90	CH3	CH2-CH2		CCL4
1742M	A	0.90	CH3	CH2-CH2		CCL4
1631M	A	0.90	CH3	CH2-CH2		CCL4
1972M	A	0.90	CH3	CH2-CH2		CCL4
1985M	A	0.90	CH3	CH2-CH2		CCL4
1986M	A	0.90	CH3	CH2-CH2		CDCL3
2153M	A	0.90	CH3	CH2-CH2		CCL4
2925M	A	0.90	CH3	CH2-CH2		CCL4
2909M	A	0.90	CH3	CH2-CH2		CDCL3
578M	A	0.90	CH3	CH2-CH2		CCL4
550M	A	0.90	CH3	CH2-CH2		CDCL3
551M	A	0.90	CH3	CH2-CH2		CDCL3
650M	A	0.90	CH3	CH2-CH2		CCL4
617M	A	0.90	CH3	CH2-CH2		CCL4
857M	A	0.90	CH3	CH2-CH2		CDCL3
737M	A	0.90	CH3	CH2-CH2		CCL4
1581M	A	0.90	CH3	CH2-CH2		CDCL3
1501M	A	0.90	CH3	CH2-CH2		CCL4
1600M	A	0.90	CH3	CH2-CH2		CCL4
1804M	A	0.90	CH3	CH2-CH2		CDCL3
1783M	A	0.90	CH3	CH2-CH2		CCL4
2813M	A	0.90	CH3	CH2-CH2		CCL4
2823M	A	0.90	CH3	CH2-CH2		CCL4
2809M	A	0.90	CH3	CH2-CH2		CCL4
2760M	A	0.90	CH3	CH2-CH2		CCL4
2770M	A	0.90	CH3	CH2-CH2		CCL4
82M	A	0.90	CH3	CH2-CH2		CCL4
4M	A	0.90	CH3	CH2-CH2		CCL4
93M	A	0.90	CH3	CH2-CH2		CCL4
59M	A	0.90	CH3	CH2-CH2		CCL4
63M	A	0.90	CH3	CH2-CH2		CDCL3
12M	A	0.90	CH3	CH2-CH2		CCL4
65M	A	0.90	CH3	CH2-CH2		CCL4
6M	A	0.90	CH3	CH2-CH2		CDCL3
142M	A	0.90	CH3	CH2-CH2		CCL4
141M	A	0.90	CH3	CH2-CH2		CCL4
44M	A	0.90	CH3	CH2-CH2		CCL4
465M	A	0.90	CH3	CH2-CH2		CDCL3
444M	A	0.90	CH3	CH2-CH2		CDCL3
454M	A	0.90	CH3	CH2-CH2		CDCL3
451M	A	0.90	CH3	CH2-CH2		CCL4
411M	A	0.90	CH3	CH2-CH2		CCL4
332M	A	0.90	CH3	CH2-CH2		CCL4
243M	A	0.90	CH3	CH2-CH2		CCL4
248M	A	0.90	CH3	CH2-CH2		CCL4
242M	A	0.90	CH3	CH2-CH2		CCL4
220M	A	0.90	CH3	CH2-CH2		CCL4
336M	A	0.90	CH3	CH2-CH2		CCL4
334M	A	0.90	CH3	CH2-CH2		CCL4
335M	A	0.90	CH3	CH2-CH2		CCL4
2297M	A	0.90	CH3	CH2-CH2		D20
2298M	A	0.90	CH3	CH2-CH2		CDCL3
2279M	A	0.90	CH3	CH2-CH2		CDCL3

BOOK NO.	ASSIGN-MENT	CHEM SHIFT - ppm -	PROTON GROUP	ENVIRONMENTAL GROUPS	S	SOLVENT
2413M	A	0.90	CH3	CH2-CH2		DMSO-D6
2529M	A	0.90	CH3	CH2-CH2		CDCL3
2487M	A	0.90	CH3	CH2-CH2		CCL4
2521M	A	0.90	CH3	CH2-CH2		CCL4
2532M	A	0.90	CH3	CH2-CH2		CCL4
2721M	A	0.90	CH3	CH2-CH2		CDCL3
2693M	A	0.90	CH3	CH2-CH2		CCL4
2707M	A	0.90	CH3	CH2-CH2		CCL4
2696M	A	0.90	CH3	CH2-CH2		CCL4
2692M	A	0.90	CH3	CH2-CH2		CCL4
1208M	A	0.90	CH3	CH2-CH2		CDCL3
1212M	A	0.90	CH3	CH2-CH2		CDCL3
1209M	A	0.90	CH3	CH2-CH2		CCL4
2981M	A	0.90	CH3	CH2-CH2		CCL4
2299M	A	0.90 APP.	CH3	CH2-CH2		CDCL3
72M	A	0.91	CH3	CH2-CH2		CCL4
891M	A	0.91	CH3	CH2-CH2		CDCL3
892M	A	0.91	CH3	CH2-CH2		TFA
1110M	A	0.91	CH3	CH2-CH2		CCL4
1038M	A	0.91	CH3	CH2-CH2		CCL4
1614M	A	0.91	CH3	CH2-CH2		CCL4
1616M	A	0.91	CH3	CH2-CH2		CCL4
1738M	A	0.91	CH3	CH2-CH2		CCL4
1978M	A	0.91	CH3	CH2-CH2		CDCL3
1974M	A	0.91	CH3	CH2-CH2		CCL4
1983M	A	0.91	CH3	CH2-CH2		CCL4
2192M	A	0.91	CH3	CH2-CH2		CCL4
2154M	A	0.91	CH3	CH2-CH2		CDCL3
2898M	A	0.91	CH3	CH2-CH2		CCL4
2877M	A	0.91	CH3	CH2-CH2		CCL4
2903M	A	0.91	CH3	CH2-CH2		CCL4
687M	A	0.91	CH3	CH2-CH2		CCL4
800M	A	0.91	CH3	CH2-CH2		D20
854M	A	0.91	CH3	CH2-CH2		CDCL3
2757M	A	0.91	CH3	CH2-CH2		CDCL3
85M	A	0.91	CH3	CH2-CH2		CCL4
61M	A	0.91	CH3	CH2-CH2		CCL4
441M	A	0.91	CH3	CH2-CH2		CDCL3
1317M	A	0.89	CH3	CH2-CH2		CDCL3
1384M	A	0.90	CH3	CH2-CH2		CCL4
1386M	A	0.90	CH3	CH2-CH2		CCL4
1391M	A	0.90	CH3	CH2-CH2		CDCL3
1358M	A	0.90	CH3	CH2-CH2		CDCL3
1417M	A	0.91	CH3	CH2-CH2		CCL4
1388M	A	0.91	CH3	CH2-CH2		CCL4
1404M	A	0.91	CH3	CH2-CH2		CCL4
439M	A	0.91	CH3	CH2-CH2		CCL4
439M	A	0.91	CH3	CH2-CH2		CCL4
337M	A	0.91	CH3	CH2-CH2		CCL4
245M	A	0.91	CH3	CH2-CH2		CCL4
333M	A	0.91	CH3	CH2-CH2		CCL4
246M	A	0.91	CH3	CH2-CH2		CCL4
2479M	A	0.91	CH3	CH2-CH2		CCL4
84M	A	0.91 APP.	CH3	CH2-CH2		CCL4
1325M	A	0.92	CH3	CH2-CH2		CCL4
1421M	A	0.92	CH3	CH2-CH2		CCL4
137M	A	0.92	CH3	CH2-CH2		CCL4
70M	A	0.92	CH3	CH2-CH2		CCL4
71M	A	0.92	CH3	CH2-CH2		CCL4
959M	A	0.92	CH3	CH2-CH2		CCL4
959M	A	0.92	CH3	CH2-CH2		CCL4
2161M	A	0.92	CH3	CH2-CH2		CCL4
2947M	A	0.92	CH3	CH2-CH2		CCL4
2984M	A	0.92	CH3	CH2-CH2		CCL4
584M	A	0.92	CH3	CH2-CH2		CCL4
1606M	A	0.92	CH3	CH2-CH2		CCL4
544M	A	0.92	CH3	CH2-CH2		D20
326M	A	0.92	CH3	CH2-CH2		CCL4
2316M	A	0.92	CH3	CH2-CH2		CDCL3
2477M	A	0.92	CH3	CH2-CH2		CCL4
2704M	A	0.92	CH3	CH2-CH2		CCL4
2717M	A	0.92	CH3	CH2-CH2		CCL4
2827M	A	0.92	CH3	CH2-CH2		CCL4
1602M	A	0.92 APP.	CH3	CH2-CH2		CCL4
1442M	A	0.93	CH3	CH2-CH2		CCL4
118M	A	0.93	CH3	CH2-CH2		CCL4
240M	A	0.93	CH3	CH2-CH2		CCL4
330M	A	0.93	CH3	CH2-CH2		CCL4
2714M	A	0.93	CH3	CH2-CH2		CCL4
949M	A	0.93	CH3	CH2-CH2		CDCL3
2174M	A	0.93	CH3	CH2-CH2		CCL4

BOOK NO.	ASSIGN-MENT	CHEM SHIFT - ppm -	PROTON GROUP	ENVIRONMENTAL GROUPS	S	SOLVENT
1755M	A	0.93	CH3	CH2-CH2		CCL4
1668M	A	0.93	CH3	CH2-CH2		CCL4
2960M	A	0.93	CH3	CH2-CH2		CCL4
2774M	A	0.93	CH3	CH2-CH2		CCL4
2706M	A	0.93 APP.	CH3	CH2-CH2		CDCL3
1613M	A	0.94	CH3	CH2-CH2		CCL4
2438M	A	0.94	CH3	CH2-CH2		CCL4
2708M	A	0.94	CH3	CH2-CH2		CCL4
2066M	A	0.94	CH3	CH2-CH2		CDCL3
2982M	A	0.94	CH3	CH2-CH2		CCL4
2784M	A	0.94	CH3	CH2-CH2		CCL4
1424M	A	0.95	CH3	CH2-CH2		CCL4
1414M	A	0.95	CH3	CH2-CH2		CCL4
2767M	A	0.95	CH3	CH2-CH2		CCL4
236M	A	0.95	CH3	CH2-CH2		CCL4
2250M	A	0.95	CH3	CH2-CH2		CDCL3
2618M	A	0.95	CH3	CH2-CH2		D2O
2047M	A	0.95	CH3	CH2-CH2		CCL4
2998M	A	0.95	CH3	CH2-CH2		CCL4
651M	A	0.95	CH3	CH2-CH2		CCL4
2808M	A	0.95 APP.	CH3	CH2-CH2		CCL4
2429M	A	0.96	CH3	CH2-CH2		CDCL3
2523M	A	0.96	CH3	CH2-CH2		CCL4
1245M	A	0.96	CH3	CH2-CH2		CDCL3
1126M	A	0.96	CH3	CH2-CH2		CCL4
2917M	A	0.96	CH3	CH2-CH2		C3D6O
874M	A	0.96	CH3	CH2-CH2		CCL4
1534M	A	0.96	CH3	CH2-CH2		CCL4
946M	A	0.97	CH3	CH2-CH2		CCL4
2894M	A	0.97	CH3	CH2-CH2		CCL4
2349M	A	0.97	CH3	CH2-CH2		CCL4
946M	A	0.97	CH3	CH2-CH2		CCL4
2701M	A	0.98	CH3	CH2-CH2		CCL4
1255M	A	0.98	CH3	CH2-CH2		CCL4
908M	A	0.98	CH3	CH2-CH2		CDCL3
2157M	A	0.98	CH3	CH2-CH2		CCL4
2890M	A	0.98	CH3	CH2-CH2		CCL4
3M	A	0.99	CH3	CH2-CH2		CCL4
2792M	A	0.99	CH3	CH2-CH2		CCL4
1183M	A	0.99	CH3	CH2-CH2		CDCL3
1124M	A	0.99	CH3	CH2-CH2		CCL4
1244M	A	0.99	CH3	CH2-CH2		CCL4
1009M	A	0.99	CH3	CH2-CH2		CCL4
2999M	A	0.99	CH3	CH2-CH2		CDCL3
557M	A	0.99	CH3	CH2-CH2		CDCL3
322M	A	0.99	CH3	CH2-CH2		CCL4
1329M	A	1.00	CH3	CH2-CH2		CCL4
2902M	A	1.00	CH3	CH2-CH2		CCL4
2908M	A	1.00	CH3	CH2-CH2		CCL4
405M	A	1.00	CH3	CH2-CH2		CCL4
117M	A	1.01	CH3	CH2-CH2		CCL4
2249M	A	1.01	CH3	CH2-CH2		CCL4
1041M	A	1.01	CH3	CH2-CH2		CCL4
1080M	A	1.01	CH3	CH2-CH2		CCL4
2900M	A	1.01	CH3	CH2-CH2		CDCL3
2959M	A	1.01	CH3	CH2-CH2		CCL4
1248M	A	1.02	CH3	CH2-CH2		CCL4
320M	A	1.02	CH3	CH2-CH2		CCL4
235M	A	1.05	CH3	CH2-CH2		CCL4
944M	A	1.07	CH3	CH2-CH2		CCL4
2702M	A	1.09	CH3	CH2-CH2		CCL4
1253M	A	1.09	CH3	CH2-CH2		CCL4
843M	A	0.88	CH3	CH2-CH2	S	DMSO-D6
1312M	A	0.89	CH3	CH2-CH2	S	CDCL3
770M	A	0.89	CH3	CH2-CH2	S	D2O
831M	A	0.90	CH3	CH2-CH2	S	CDCL3
839M	A	0.90	CH3	CH2-CH2	S	CDCL3
767M	A	0.90	CH3	CH2-CH2	S	DMSO-D6
832M	A	1.01	CH3	CH2-CH2	S	CDCL3
1624M	B	0.89	CH3	CH2-CH2		CDCL3
35M	B	0.89	CH3	CH2-CH2		CDCL3
19M	B	0.89	CH3	CH2-CH2		CCL4
553M	B	0.89	CH3	CH2-CH2		CCL4
32M	B	0.91	CH3	CH2-CH2		CCL4
34M	B	0.91	CH3	CH2-CH2		CCL4
1207M	B	0.92	CH3	CH2-CH2		CCL4
1839M	B	0.93	CH3	CH2-CH2		C3D6O
547M	B	0.93	CH3	CH2-CH2		CDCL3
23M	A	0.82	CH3	CH2-C(CH3/CH3)		CDCL3
2034M	A	0.93	CH3	CH2-C(=O)		CCL4
1968M	A	0.99	CH3	CH2-C(=O)		CCL4

BOOK NO.	ASSIGN-MENT	CHEM SHIFT - ppm -	PROTON GROUP	ENVIRONMENTAL GROUPS	S	SOLVENT
2131M	A	1.03	CH3	CH2-C(=0)		CCL4
2276M	A	1.12	CH3	CH2-C(=0)		CDCL3
2046M	A	1.18	CH3	CH2-C(=0)		CDCL3
2315M	A	1.19	CH3	CH2-C(=0)		CDCL3
1980M	B	1.00	CH3	CH2-C(=0)		CCL4
2138M	B	1.11	CH3	CH2-C(=0)-CH2		CCL4
1970M	B	1.03	CH3	CH2-C(=0)-CH2.2		CDCL3
1975M	B	1.07	CH3	CH2-C(=0)-CH2.4		CDCL3
1988M	B	1.01	CH3	CH2-C(=0)-CH2.9		CCL4
2187M	A	1.22	CH3	CH2-C(=0)-CL		CDCL3
2351M	B	1.16	CH3	CH2-C(=0)-N		CDCL3
2350M	B	1.21	CH3	CH2-C(=0)-N		D20
2296M	A	1.17	CH3	CH2-C(=0)-NH		CDCL3
2761M	A	0.89	CH3	CH2-C(=0)-0		CDCL3
2835M	A	1.09	CH3	CH2-C(=0)-0		CCL4
2649M	A	1.09	CH3	CH2-C(=0)-0		D20
2473M	A	1.14	CH3	CH2-C(=0)-0		CDCL3
2753M	A	1.15	CH3	CH2-C(=0)-0		CDCL3
2797M	A	1.16	CH3	CH2-C(=0)-0		CCL4
2248M	A	1.17	CH3	CH2-C(=0)-0		CCL4
2921M	A	1.20	CH3	CH2-C(=0)-0		CCL4
2698M	B	1.16	CH3	CH2-C(=0)-0		CDCL3
2138M	B	1.11	CH3	CH2-C(=0)-Q1		CCL4
131M	A	1.11	CH3	CH2-C:		CCL4
1696M	A	1.15	CH3	CH2-C:		CCL4
128M	B	1.11	CH3	CH2-C:		CCL4
404M	A	1.84	CH3	CH2-I		CCL4
2353M	A	0.85- 1.35	CH3	CH2-N		D20
1651M	A	0.88- 1.28	CH3	CH2-N		CCL4
664M	A	0.95	CH3	CH2-N		CCL4
616M	A	0.97	CH3	CH2-N		CCL4
661M	A	0.97	CH3	CH2-N		CDCL3
661M	A	0.97	CH3	CH2-N		CDCL3
632M	A	0.97	CH3	CH2-N		CCL4
614M	A	0.98	CH3	CH2-N		CCL4
672M	A	0.99	CH3	CH2-N		CCL4
633M	A	1.00	CH3	CH2-N		CCL4
635M	A	1.00	CH3	CH2-N		CCL4
626M	A	1.00	CH3	CH2-N		CDCL3
1650M	A	1.00	CH3	CH2-N		CCL4
646M	A	1.02	CH3	CH2-N		CDCL3
645M	A	1.02	CH3	CH2-N		CDCL3
2657M	A	1.06	CH3	CH2-N		D20
662M	A	1.07	CH3	CH2-N		CCL4
705M	A	1.07	CH3	CH2-N		CDCL3
670M	A	1.08	CH3	CH2-N		CDCL3
663M	A	1.08	CH3	CH2-N		CDCL3
2364M	A	1.08	CH3	CH2-N		CCL4
613M	A	1.09	CH3	CH2-N		CDCL3
1706M	A	1.09	CH3	CH2-N		CDCL3
2370M	A	1.09	CH3	CH2-N		CDCL3
649M	A	1.10	CH3	CH2-N		CCL4
2350M	A	1.11	CH3	CH2-N		D20
2361M	A	1.11	CH3	CH2-N		CDCL3
1026M	A	1.11	CH3	CH2-N		CDCL3
2358M	A	1.12	CH3	CH2-N		CDCL3
2347M	A	1.12	CH3	CH2-N		CDCL3
1525M	A	1.13	CH3	CH2-N		CCL4
2362M	A	1.14	CH3	CH2-N		CDCL3
653M	A	1.17	CH3	CH2-N		CDCL3
2104M	A	1.17	CH3	CH2-N		CDCL3
1356M	A	1.20	CH3	CH2-N		CDCL3
1024M	A	1.23	CH3	CH2-N		CDCL3
995M	A	1.28	CH3	CH2-N		CDCL3
834M	A	1.30	CH3	CH2-N		POLYSOL-D
817M	A	1.14	CH3	CH2-N	S	D20
812M	A	1.38	CH3	CH2-N	S	D20
809M	A	1.45	CH3	CH2-N	S	CDCL3
629M	B	1.00	CH3	CH2-N		CDCL3
2998M	B	1.06	CH3	CH2-N		CCL4
2356M	B	1.11	CH3	CH2-N		CCL4
2358M	B	1.19 APP.	CH3	CH2-N		CDCL3
2347M	B	1.20	CH3	CH2-N		CDCL3
2370M	B	1.20	CH3	CH2-N		CDCL3
1026M	B	1.41	CH3	CH2-N		CDCL3
631M	C	1.29	CH3	CH2-N		D20
1339M	A	1.04	CH3	CH2-NH		DMSO-D6
463M	A	1.07	CH3	CH2-NH		D20
593M	A	1.10	CH3	CH2-NH		CDCL3
555M	A	1.11	CH3	CH2-NH		CDCL3
583M	A	1.12	CH3	CH2-NH		CCL4

BOOK NO.	ASSIGN-MENT	CHEM SHIFT - ppm -	PROTON GROUP	ENVIRONMENTAL GROUPS	S	SOLVENT
2295M	A	1.15	CH3	CH2-NH		D2O
1348M	A	1.19	CH3	CH2-NH		CDCL3
1344M	A	1.22	CH3	CH2-NH		CCL4
2428M	A	1.22	CH3	CH2-NH		CDCL3
1156M	A	1.25	CH3	CH2-NH		POLYSOL-D
600M	A	1.32	CH3	CH2-NH		CCL4
1062M	A	1.38	CH3	CH2-NH		CCL4
806M	A	1.39	CH3	CH2-NH	S	D2O
797M	A	1.45	CH3	CH2-NH	S	CDCL3
574M	B	1.04	CH3	CH2-NH		CCL4
577M	B	1.07	CH3	CH2-NH		CCL4
766M	A	1.30	CH3	CH2-NH2	S	D2O
1040M	A	1.55	CH3	CH2-NO2		CDCL3
827M	A	1.26	CH3	CH2-N(&)	S	D2O
827M	A	1.26	CH3	CH2-N(T)	S	D2O
841M	A	1.30	CH3	CH2-N(+)		CDCL3
1397M	A	1.11	CH3	CH2-O		CCL4
1379M	A	1.13	CH3	CH2-O		CCL4
1480M	A	1.13	CH3	CH2-O		CDCL3
1410M	A	1.16	CH3	CH2-O		CDCL3
1481M	A	1.16	CH3	CH2-O		CDCL3
1412M	A	1.17	CH3	CH2-O		CCL4
1666M	A	1.18	CH3	CH2-O		CCL4
1436M	A	1.19	CH3	CH2-O		CCL4
1426M	A	1.19	CH3	CH2-O		CCL4
1493M	A	1.19	CH3	CH2-O		CCL4
1674M	A	1.20	CH3	CH2-O		CCL4
1431M	A	1.20	CH3	CH2-O		CDCL3
1416M	A	1.20	CH3	CH2-O		CDCL3
1401M	A	1.20	CH3	CH2-O		CDCL3
1403M	A	1.20	CH3	CH2-O		CDCL3
1408M	A	1.23	CH3	CH2-O		CCL4
1428M	A	1.23	CH3	CH2-O		CDCL3
1522M	A	1.29	CH3	CH2-O		CDCL3
2211M	A	1.30	CH3	CH2-O		DMSO-D6
1499M	A	1.30	CH3	CH2-O		CCL4
1561M	A	1.31	CH3	CH2-O		CDCL3
2997M	A	1.33	CH3	CH2-O		CCL4
1489M	A	1.34	CH3	CH2-O		CCL4
1513M	A	1.35	CH3	CH2-O		CCL4
1518M	A	1.35	CH3	CH2-O		CDCL3
1393M	A	1.35	CH3	CH2-O		CCL4
1498M	A	1.36	CH3	CH2-O		CCL4
1500M	A	1.36	CH3	CH2-O		CCL4
1570M	A	1.37	CH3	CH2-O		CDCL3
1517M	A	1.40	CH3	CH2-O		CCL4
2563M	A	1.40	CH3	CH2-O		CDCL3
2076M	A	1.42	CH3	CH2-O		CDCL3
1533M	A	1.42	CH3	CH2-O		CDCL3
1512M	A	1.42	CH3	CH2-O		CCL4
1571M	A	1.45	CH3	CH2-O		CDCL3
2585M	A	1.49	CH3	CH2-O		CCL4
1557M	A	1.54	CH3	CH2-O		CDCL3
1593M	B	1.13	CH3	CH2-O		CCL4
1383M	B	1.15	CH3	CH2-O		CCL4
1382M	B	1.16	CH3	CH2-O		CCL4
1390M	B	1.19	CH3	CH2-O		CDCL3
1595M	B	1.22	CH3	CH2-O		CDCL3
1597M	B	1.22	CH3	CH2-O		CDCL3
1561M	B	1.36	CH3	CH2-O		CDCL3
1525M	B	1.38	CH3	CH2-O		CCL4
1596M	C	1.19	CH3	CH2-O		CCL4
1612M	A	1.17	CH3	CH2-OH		CCL4
2986M	A	1.15	CH3	CH2-O-C(=O)		CCL4
2850M	A	1.19	CH3	CH2-O-C(=O)		CCL4
2751M	A	1.20	CH3	CH2-O-C(=O)		DMSO-D6
2853M	A	1.20	CH3	CH2-O-C(=O)		CDCL3
2824M	A	1.20	CH3	CH2-O-C(=O)		CCL4
1865M	A	1.20	CH3	CH2-O-C(=O)		CDCL3
2854M	A	1.21	CH3	CH2-O-C(=O)		CCL4
2852M	A	1.21	CH3	CH2-O-C(=O)		CCL4
2786M	A	1.22	CH3	CH2-O-C(=O)		CCL4
2777M	A	1.23	CH3	CH2-O-C(=O)		CCL4
2856M	A	1.23	CH3	CH2-O-C(=O)		CCL4
2983M	A	1.23	CH3	CH2-O-C(=O)		CDCL3
2780M	A	1.24	CH3	CH2-O-C(=O)		CDCL3
2824M	A	1.24	CH3	CH2-O-C(=O)		CCL4
2814M	A	1.24	CH3	CH2-O-C(=O)		CCL4
2724M	A	1.25	CH3	CH2-O-C(=O)		CCL4
2749M	A	1.27	CH3	CH2-O-C(=O)		CDCL3
2795M	A	1.27	CH3	CH2-O-C(=O)		CDCL3

BOOK NO.	ASSIGN-MENT	CHEM SHIFT - ppm -	PROTON GROUP	ENVIRONMENTAL GROUPS	S	SOLVENT
2810M	A	1.29	CH3	CH2-O-C(=O)		CCL4
2789M	A	1.29	CH3	CH2-O-C(=O)		CCL4
2794M	A	1.29	CH3	CH2-O-C(=O)		CDCL3
2734M	A	1.29	CH3	CH2-O-C(=O)		CCL4
2730M	A	1.29	CH3	CH2-O-C(=O)		CCL4
2830M	A	1.30	CH3	CH2-O-C(=O)		CDCL3
2720M	A	1.30	CH3	CH2-O-C(=O)		CCL4
2729M	A	1.31	CH3	CH2-O-C(=O)		CDCL3
2820M	A	1.33	CH3	CH2-O-C(=O)		CCL4
2858M	A	1.36	CH3	CH2-O-C(=O)		CDCL3
2772M	A	1.37	CH3	CH2-O-C(=O)		CCL4
2871M	A	1.39	CH3	CH2-O-C(=O)		CCL4
2723M	A	1.41	CH3	CH2-O-C(=O)		CDCL3
2750M	A	1.26	CH3	CH2-O-C(=O)	S	D2O
2736M	A	1.30	CH3	CH2-O-C(=O)	S	D2O
2980M	A	1.24	CH3	CH2-O-C(=O)		CDCL3
2985M	A	1.26	CH3	CH2-O-C(=O)		CDCL3
2934M	A	1.29	CH3	CH2-O-C(=O)		CDCL3
2972M	A	1.31	CH3	CH2-O-C(=O)		CCL4
2875M	A	1.34	CH3	CH2-O-C(=O)		CCL4
2884M	A	1.38	CH3	CH2-O-C(=O)		CDCL3
2907M	A	1.40	CH3	CH2-O-C(=O)		CDCL3
2937M	A	1.40	CH3	CH2-O-C(=O)		CDCL3
2885M	A	1.42	CH3	CH2-O-C(=O)		CCL4
2883M	A	1.45	CH3	CH2-O-C(=O)		CDCL3
2911M	A	1.49	CH3	CH2-O-C(=O)		CDCL3
2990M	B	1.11	CH3	CH2-O-C(=O)		CCL4
2981M	B	1.20	CH3	CH2-O-C(=O)		CCL4
2824M	B	1.20	CH3	CH2-O-C(=O)		CCL4
2984M	B	1.21	CH3	CH2-O-C(=O)		CCL4
2818M	B	1.21	CH3	CH2-O-C(=O)		CCL4
2817M	B	1.22	CH3	CH2-O-C(=O)		CCL4
2703M	B	1.23	CH3	CH2-O-C(=O)		CCL4
2824M	B	1.24	CH3	CH2-O-C(=O)		CCL4
2770M	B	1.25	CH3	CH2-O-C(=O)		CCL4
2701M	B	1.29	CH3	CH2-O-C(=O)		CCL4
2733M	B	1.29	CH3	CH2-O-C(=O)		CCL4
2744M	B	1.29	CH3	CH2-O-C(=O)		CCL4
2745M	B	1.29	CH3	CH2-O-C(=O)		CDCL3
2741M	B	1.30	CH3	CH2-O-C(=O)		CCL4
2732M	B	1.30	CH3	CH2-O-C(=O)		CDCL3
756M	B	1.30	CH3	CH2-O-C(=O)		CCL4
2870M	B	1.37	CH3	CH2-O-C(=O)		CCL4
2731M	C	1.30	CH3	CH2-O-C(=O)		CDCL3
1326M	A	1.31	CH3	CH2-O-SO3-K		D2O
1096M	A	1.05	CH3	CH2-P		CDCL3
1101M	A	1.33	CH3	CH2-P(+)	S	CDCL3
2137M	B	1.03	CH3	CH2-Q		CDCL3
853M	A	1.09	CH3	CH2-QN		CDCL3
2138M	A	1.00	CH3	CH2-Q1		CCL4
2551M	A	1.20	CH3	CH2-Q1		CDCL3
2157M	B	1.01	CH3	CH2-Q1		CCL4
2523M	B	1.03	CH3	CH2-Q1		CCL4
2816M	A	0.90	CH3	CH2-Q2		CCL4
79M	A	0.92	CH3	CH2-Q2		CCL4
78M	A	0.95	CH3	CH2-Q2		CDCL3
75M	A	0.95	CH3	CH2-Q2		CCL4
69M	A	1.00	CH3	CH2-Q2		CCL4
71M	B	1.01	CH3	CH2-Q2		CCL4
1688M	B	1.80- 2.45	CH3	CH2-Q2		CCL4
1439M	A	0.98	CH3	CH2-R30		CCL4
2384M	A	1.18	CH3	CH2-R5N		CDCL3
744M	A	1.21	CH3	CH2-R5NAA		CDCL3
2449M	A	1.12	CH3	CH2-R5NN		CDCL3
1155M	A	1.44	CH3	CH2-R5NNS		TFA
1459M	A	0.88	CH3	CH2-R500		CCL4
47M	A	0.87	CH3	CH2-R6		CCL4
1810M	A	0.89	CH3	CH2-R6		C3F60
1770M	A	1.00 APP.	CH3	CH2-R6		CDCL3
197M	A	0.95	CH3	CH2-R6A		CCL4
2460M	A	1.01	CH3	CH2-R6NN		TFA
2466M	A	1.29	CH3	CH2-R6NNN		CDCL3
1464M	A	1.02	CH3	CH2-R6NO		CCL4
1476M	A	0.90	CH3	CH2-R600R600SPI		CCL4
1159M	A	1.19	CH3	CH2-S		CCL4
1108M	A	1.23	CH3	CH2-S		CCL4
1107M,	A	1.23	CH3	CH2-S		CCL4
2970M	A	1.23	CH3	CH2-S		CCL4
1125M	A	1.25	CH3	CH2-S		CDCL3
1193M	A	1.25	CH3	CH2-S		CCL4
1123M	A	1.28	CH3	CH2-S		CCL4

BOOK NO.	ASSIGN-MENT	CHEM SHIFT - ppm -	PROTON GROUP	ENVIRONMENTAL GROUPS	S	SOLVENT
1128M	A	1.29	CH3	CH2-S		CCL4
1008M	A	1.51	CH3	CH2-S		CDCL3
1117M	B	1.21	CH3	CH2-S		CCL4
1119M	B	1.24	CH3	CH2-S		CDCL3
1200M	B	1.31	CH3	CH2-SH		CCL4
1091M	A	1.10	CH3	CH2-SI		CDCL3
1085M	B	0.91	CH3	CH2-SI		CCL4
1596M	B	0.98	CH3	CH2-SI		CCL4
1244M	B	1.28	CH3	CH2-SO		CCL4
1256M	A	1.26	CH3	CH2-SO2		CCL4
1368M	A	1.33	CH3	CH2-SO2		CDCL3
1324M	A	1.34	CH3	CH2-SO3		CCL4
1316M	A	1.39	CH3	CH2-SO3		CCL4
1287M	A	1.45	CH3	CH2-SO3-H		CDCL3
686M	A	1.21	CH3	CH(AN/CH3)		CDCL3
138M	B	1.20	CH3	CH(A/CH2)		CCL4
494M	B	1.20	CH3	CH(A/CH2)		CCL4
479M	B	1.21	CH3	CH(A/CH2)		CDCL3
1881M	A	1.20	CH3	CH(A/CH3)		CDCL3
1714M	A	1.21	CH3	CH(A/CH3)		CCL4
486M	A	1.21	CH3	CH(A/CH3)		CCL4
182M	A	1.21	CH3	CH(A/CH3)		CCL4
385M	A	1.21	CH3	CH(A/CH3)		CDCL3
1917M	A	1.22	CH3	CH(A/CH3)		CDCL3
592M	A	1.22	CH3	CH(A/CH3)		CDCL3
136M	A	1.22	CH3	CH(A/CH3)		CCL4
493M	A	1.22	CH3	CH(A/CH3)		CDCL3
501M	A	1.25	CH3	CH(A/CH3)		CDCL3
353M	A	1.84	CH3	CH(BR)-HCH		CCL4
327M	C	1.71	CH3	CH(BR/CH2.2)		CCL4
361M	A	1.76	CH3	CH(BR/CH2)		CDCL3
358M	A	1.78	CH3	CH(BR/CH2)		CCL4
323M	B	1.70	CH3	CH(BR/CH2)		CDCL3
2730M	B	1.76	CH3	CH(BR/CH2)		CCL4
334M	C	1.69	CH3	CH(BR/CH2)		CCL4
321M	A	1.70	CH3	CH(BR/CH3)		CCL4
1992M	A	1.71	CH3	CH(BR/C(=0))		CCL4
1620M	B	0.95	CH3	CH(CH2.2/CH2)		CCL4
453M	A	0.89	CH3	CH(CH2.2/CH3)		CDCL3
1385M	A	0.90	CH3	CH(CH2.2/CH3)		CCL4
130M	A	0.90	CH3	CH(CH2.2/CH3)		CCL4
585M	A	0.91	CH3	CH(CH2.2/CH3)		CDCL3
2747M	A	0.93	CH3	CH(CH2.2/CH3)		CCL4
1188M	A	0.95	CH3	CH(CH2.2/CH3)		CCL4
1037M	A	0.97	CH3	CH(CH2.2/CH3)		CDCL3
1801M	B	0.93	CH3	CH(CH2.2/CH3)		CCL4
2709M	B	0.96	CH3	CH(CH2.2/CH3)		CCL4
29M	A	0.88	CH3	CH(CH2.3/CH3)		CDCL3
1690M	A	0.89 APP.	CH3	CH(CH2.3/CH3)		CCL4
1621M	A	0.91	CH3	CH(CH2.3/CH3/CH3)		CCL4
1625M	A	0.90	CH3	CH(CH2.4/CH3)		CDCL3
20M	A	0.62- 1.00	CH3	CH(CH2/CH2)		CCL4
35M	A	0.84	CH3	CH(CH2/CH2)		CDCL3
37M	A	0.86	CH3	CH(CH2/CH2)		CCL4
1629M	A	0.89	CH3	CH(CH2/CH2)		CDCL3
58M	A	0.89	CH3	CH(CH2/CH2)		CCL4
1832M	A	0.92	CH3	CH(CH2/CH2)		CDCL3
445M	A	0.92	CH3	CH(CH2/CH2)		CDCL3
893M	A	0.93	CH3	CH(CH2/CH2)		CDCL3
344M	A	1.17	CH3	CH(CH2/CH2)		CDCL3
19M	A	0.85	CH3	CH(CH2/CH3)		CCL4
37M	A	0.86	CH3	CH(CH2/CH3)		CCL4
22M	A	0.86	CH3	CH(CH2/CH3)		CCL4
1799M	A	0.88	CH3	CH(CH2/CH3)		CCL4
31M	A	0.88	CH3	CH(CH2/CH3)		CCL4
1615M	A	0.89	CH3	CH(CH2/CH3)		CCL4
619M	A	0.89	CH3	CH(CH2/CH3)		CDCL3
1383M	A	0.89	CH3	CH(CH2/CH3)		CCL4
48M	A	0.89	CH3	CH(CH2/CH3)		CCL4
34M	A	0.89	CH3	CH(CH2/CH3)		CCL4
32M	A	0.89	CH3	CH(CH2/CH3)		CCL4
1979M	A	0.90	CH3	CH(CH2/CH3)		CCL4
1976M	A	0.90	CH3	CH(CH2/CH3)		CCL4
139M	A	0.90	CH3	CH(CH2/CH3)		CDCL3
94M	A	0.90	CH3	CH(CH2/CH3)		CCL4
2837M	A	0.90	CH3	CH(CH2/CH3)		CCL4
2838M	A	0.90	CH3	CH(CH2/CH3)		CCL4
549M	A	0.90	CH3	CH(CH2/CH3)		CCL4
442M	A	0.90	CH3	CH(CH2/CH3)		CDCL3
2418M	A	0.90	CH3	CH(CH2/CH3)		POLYSOL-D
2621M	A	0.91	CH3	CH(CH2/CH3)		POLYSOL-D

BOOK NO.	ASSIGN-MENT	CHEM SHIFT - ppm -	PROTON GROUP	ENVIRONMENTAL GROUPS	S	SOLVENT
1971M	A	0.91	CH3	CH(CH2/CH3)		CCL4
856M	A	0.91	CH3	CH(CH2/CH3)		CDCL3
1618M	A	0.91	CH3	CH(CH2/CH3)		CCL4
446M	A	0.91	CH3	CH(CH2/CH3)		CDCL3
450M	A	0.91	CH3	CH(CH2/CH3)		CCL4
1112M	A	0.92	CH3	CH(CH2/CH3)		CDCL3
855M	A	0.92	CH3	CH(CH2/CH3)		CDCL3
2478M	A	0.92	CH3	CH(CH2/CH3)		CCL4
2140M	A	0.92 APP.	CH3	CH(CH2/CH3)		CCL4
2706M	A	0.93 APP.	CH3	CH(CH2/CH3)		CDCL3
328M	A	0.94	CH3	CH(CH2/CH3)		CCL4
2741M	A	0.94	CH3	CH(CH2/CH3)		CCL4
2715M	A	0.95	CH3	CH(CH2/CH3)		CCL4
1346M	A	0.95	CH3	CH(CH2/CH3)		CDCL3
2699M	A	0.96	CH3	CH(CH2/CH3)		CCL4
2778M	A	0.96	CH3	CH(CH2/CH3)		CCL4
2807M	A	0.96	CH3	CH(CH2/CH3)		CCL4
410M	A	0.96	CH3	CH(CH2/CH3)		CCL4
2843M	A	0.97	CH3	CH(CH2/CH3)		CCL4
1078M	A	0.98	CH3	CH(CH2/CH3)		CDCL3
1035M	A	0.98	CH3	CH(CH2/CH3)		CCL4
2812M	A	0.98	CH3	CH(CH2/CH3)		CCL4
1111M	A	0.99	CH3	CH(CH2/CH3)		CCL4
2864M	A	1.00	CH3	CH(CH2/CH3)		CDCL3
2918M	A	1.00	CH3	CH(CH2/CH3)		C3D6O
1815M	A	1.01	CH3	CH(CH2/CH3)		CDCL3
409M	A	1.01	CH3	CH(CH2/CH3)		CCL4
1205M	A	0.91	CH3	CH(CH2/CH3)		CCL4
1185M	A	1.01	CH3	CH(CH2/CH3)		CCL4
238M	A	1.03	CH3	CH(CH2/CH3)		CCL4
1246M	A	1.08	CH3	CH(CH2/CH3)		CCL4
324M	A	1.08	CH3	CH(CH2/CH3)		CCL4
947M	A	1.08	CH3	CH(CH2/CH3)		CCL4
17M	B	0.87	CH3	CH(CH2/CH3)		CCL4
1780M	B	0.88	CH3	CH(CH2/CH3)		CDCL3
546M	B	0.88	CH3	CH(CH2/CH3)		CCL4
2130M	B	0.89	CH3	CH(CH2/CH3)		CDCL3
1802M	B	0.90	CH3	CH(CH2/CH3)		CCL4
1627M	B	0.91	CH3	CH(CH2/CH3)		CCL4
27M	B	0.92	CH3	CH(CH2/CH3)		CCL4
1405M	A	0.97	CH3	CH(CH2/CH3)		CCL4
28M	A	0.58- 1.07	CH3	CH(CH/CH3)		CCL4
24M	A	0.86	CH3	CH(CH/CH3)		CCL4
18M	A	0.88	CH3	CH(CH/CH3)		CCL4
2620M	A	0.92	CH3	CH(CH/CH3)		DMSO-D6
1741M	A	0.92	CH3	CH(CH/CH3)		CDCL3
2619M	A	0.99	CH3	CH(CH/CH3)		D2O
2731M	A	1.02	CH3	CH(CH/CH3)		CDCL3
2619M	B	1.05	CH3	CH(CH/CH3)		D2O
2731M	B	1.11	CH3	CH(CH/CH3)		CDCL3
28M	A	0.58- 1.07	CH3	CH(CH/CH)		CCL4
257M	A	1.60	CH3	CH(CL/CH2)		CCL4
237M	B	1.49	CH3	CH(CL/CH2)		CCL4
251M	A	2.07	CH3	CH(CL/CL)		CCL4
1991M	A	1.57	CH3	CH(CL/C(=0)-CH3)		CCL4
260M	A	1.88	CH3	CH(CL/C)		CCL4
1044M	A	2.02	CH3	CH(CL/NO2)		CCL4
1982M	B	1.05	CH3	CH(C(=0)-CH2.5/CH3)		CCL4
2035M	A	1.01	CH3	CH(C(=0)-CH2/CH3)		CCL4
1994M	A	1.12	CH3	CH(C(=0)-CH3/CH2)		CDCL3
1977M	A	1.00	CH3	CH(C(=0)-C/CH3)		CCL4
2317M	A	1.12	CH3	CH(C(=0)-NH/CH3)		POLYSOL-D
2541M	A	1.47	CH3	CH(C(=0)-OH/A)		CCL4
2475M	B	1.17	CH3	CH(C(=0)-0/CH2)		CDCL3
2836M	A	1.12	CH3	CH(C(=0)-0/CH3)		CCL4
2474M	A	1.20	CH3	CH(C(=0)-0/CH3)		CCL4
2702M	B	1.13	CH3	CH(C(=0)-0/CH3)		CCL4
2708M	B	1.20	CH3	CH(C(=0)-0/CH3)		CCL4
2152M	A	1.12	CH3	CH(C(=0)/CH3)		CCL4
2048M	A	1.18	CH3	CH(C(=0)/CH3)		CCL4
945M	A	1.30	CH3	CH(C:N/CH3)		CCL4
26M	B	0.82	CH3	CH(C/CH3)		CCL4
2720M	B	1.50	CH3	CH(F/C(=0)-0)		CCL4
1617M	A	0.90	CH3	CH(HCH/CH2)		CCL4
408M	C	1.90	CH3	CH(I/CH2)		CDCL3
406M	A	1.91	CH3	CH(I/CH3)		CCL4
478M	A	1.29	CH3	CH(NH2/A)		CCL4
784M	A	1.87	CH3	CH(NH2/A)	S	TFA
453M	B	1.06	CH3	CH(NH2/CH2.2)		CDCL3
626M	B	1.05	CH3	CH(NH2/CH2.3)		CDCL3
459M	A	1.07	CH3	CH(NH2/CH2)		CDCL3

BOOK NO.	ASSIGN-MENT	CHEM SHIFT - ppm -	PROTON GROUP	ENVIRONMENTAL GROUPS	S	SOLVENT
785M	A	1.52	CH3	CH(NH2/CH2)	S	TFA
449M	B	1.05	CH3	CH(NH2/CH2)		CDCL3
443M	B	1.05	CH3	CH(NH2/CH2)		CDCL3
450M	B	1.08	CH3	CH(NH2/CH2)		CCL4
440M	A	1.01	CH3	CH(NH2/CH3)		D20
1753M	A	0.93- 1.25	CH3	CH(NH2/CH)		CDCL3
2639M	A	1.56	CH3	CH(NH2/C(=O)-NH)		D20
2614M	A	1.48	CH3	CH(NH2/C(=O)-O)		D20
2735M	A	0.57	CH3	CH(NH2/C(=O)-O)	S	D20
2736M	B	1.60	CH3	CH(NH2/C(=O)-O)	S	D20
448M	B	0.96	CH3	CH(NH2/C)		CCL4
2307M	A	1.36	CH3	CH(NH/A)		CCL4
2310M	A	1.45	CH3	CH(NH/A)		CDCL3
804M	A	1.38	CH3	CH(NH/CH2)	S	CDCL3
545M	B	1.00 APP.	CH3	CH(NH/CH2)		CCL4
557M	B	1.03	CH3	CH(NH/CH2)		CDCL3
598M	B	1.12	CH3	CH(NH/CH2)		CDCL3
559M	A	1.01	CH3	CH(NH/CH3)		CDCL3
556M	A	1.03	CH3	CH(NH/CH3)		D20
1647M	A	1.08	CH3	CH(NH/CH3)		CCL4
2417M	A	1.09	CH3	CH(NH/CH3)		POLYSOL-D
1349M	A	1.18	CH3	CH(NH/CH3)		POLYSOL-D
1345M	A	1.24	CH3	CH(NH/CH3)		CDCL3
798M	A	1.33	CH3	CH(NH/CH3)	S	D20
543M	B	1.00	CH3	CH(NH/CH3)		CCL4
1042M	A	1.57	CH3	CH(NO2/CH3)		CDCL3
923M	A	1.22	CH3	CH(N=C=/CH3)		CDCL3
1651M	A	0.88- 1.28	CH3	CH(N/CH2)		CCL4
625M	A	1.00	CH3	CH(N/CH2)		D20
616M	A	0.97	CH3	CH(N/CH3)		CCL4
958M	A	1.00	CH3	CH(N/CH3)		CCL4
2348M	A	1.29	CH3	CH(N/CH3)		CCL4
1648M	A	1.00	CH3	CH(N/HCH)		D20
1833M	A	1.15	CH3	CH(OH)-HCH		CCL4
1793M	A	1.41	CH3	CH(OH/A)		CCL4
1760M	A	1.09	CH3	CH(OH/CH2)		CCL4
1851M	A	1.10	CH3	CH(OH/CH2)		CDCL3
1754M	A	1.11	CH3	CH(OH/CH2)		CDCL3
1756M	A	1.13	CH3	CH(OH/CH2)		CDCL3
1830M	A	1.19	CH3	CH(OH/CH2)		CCL4
1792M	A	1.21	CH3	CH(OH/CH2)		CCL4
1738M	B	0.98	CH3	CH(OH/CH2)		CCL4
1748M	B	1.10	CH3	CH(OH/CH2)		CCL4
1736M	B	1.11	CH3	CH(OH/CH2)		CCL4
1739M	B	1.11	CH3	CH(OH/CH2)		CCL4
1742M	B	1.12	CH3	CH(OH/CH2)		CCL4
1746M	B	1.12 APP.	CH3	CH(OH/CH2)		CCL4
1757M	B	1.26 APP.	CH3	CH(OH/CH2)		CDCL3
1735M	A	1.29	CH3	CH(OH/CH3)		CCL4
1753M	A	0.93- 1.25	CH3	CH(OH/CH)		CDCL3
2626M	A	1.29	CH3	CH(OH/CH)		D20
2357M	A	1.22	CH3	CH(OH/C(=O))		CCL4
2283M	A	1.38	CH3	CH(OH/C(=O))		D20
2493M	A	1.43	CH3	CH(OH/C(=O)-OH)		D20
2659M	A	1.30	CH3	CH(OH/C(=O)-O)		CCL4
2740M	A	1.36	CH3	CH(OH/C(=O)-O)		CDCL3
1758M	A	1.59	CH3	CH(OH/C:N)		CDCL3
1759M	A	1.03	CH3	CH(OH/HCH)		CCL4
1831M	A	1.12	CH3	CH(OH/HCH)		CDCL3
1828M	A	1.13	CH3	CH(OH/HCH)		CCL4
1755M	B	1.02	CH3	CH(OH/HCH)		CCL4
1782M	A	1.20	CH3	CH(OH/Q2)		CDCL3
1761M	C	1.29	CH3	CH(OH/R3)		CCL4
1762M	A	1.07	CH3	CH(OH/R6)		CDCL3
1432M	A	1.37	CH3	CH(O-CH/O-CH)		CDCL3
2834M	A	1.52	CH3	CH(O-C(=O)/A)		CDCL3
2698M	C	1.21	CH3	CH(O-C(=O)/CH2)		CCL4
2727M	A	1.21	CH3	CH(O-C(=O)/CH3)		CDCL3
2973M	A	1.22	CH3	CH(O-C(=O)/CH3)		CCL4
2773M	A	1.22	CH3	CH(O-C(=O)/CH3)		CCL4
2725M	A	1.25	CH3	CH(O-C(=O)/CH3)		CCL4
2811M	A	1.27	CH3	CH(O-C(=O)/CH3)		CCL4
2828M	A	1.27	CH3	CH(O-C(=O)/CH3)		CCL4
2826M	A	1.29	CH3	CH(O-C(=O)/CH3)		CDCL3
2882M	A	1.32	CH3	CH(O-C(=O)/CH3)		CDCL3
2893M	A	1.36	CH3	CH(O-C(=O)/CH3)		CDCL3
2889M	A	1.39	CH3	CH(O-C(=O)/CH3)		CCL4
2700M	B	1.22	CH3	CH(O-C(=O)/CH3)		CCL4
2754M	A	1.25	CH3	CH(O-C(=O)/HCH)		CCL4
1081M	A	1.37	CH3	CH(O-NO2/CH3)		CCL4
1034M	B	1.39	CH3	CH(O-N=O/CH2)		CCL4

BOOK NO.	ASSIGN-MENT	CHEM SHIFT - ppm -	PROTON GROUP	ENVIRONMENTAL GROUPS	S	SOLVENT
1483M	A	1.34	CH3	CH(O/A)		CCL4
1483M	A	1.36	CH3	CH(O/A)		CCL4
1483M	B	1.34	CH3	CH(O/A)		CCL4
1483M	B	1.36	CH3	CH(O/A)		CCL4
1760M	A	1.09	CH3	CH(O/CH2)		CCL4
1398M	A	1.04	CH3	CH(O/CH3)		CCL4
1395M	A	1.05	CH3	CH(O/CH3)		CCL4
1445M	A	1.12	CH3	CH(O/CH3)		CCL4
1400M	A	1.18	CH3	CH(O/CH3)		CDCL3
1394M	B	1.12	CH3	CH(O/CH3)		CCL4
2090M	A	1.64	CH3	CH(O/C(=O)-A)		CDCL3
2216M	A	1.71	CH3	CH(O/C(=O)-CL)		CCL4
1485M	A	1.19	CH3	CH(O/O)		CCL4
1422M	A	1.20	CH3	CH(O/O)		CCL4
1423M	B	1.21	CH3	CH(O/O)		CCL4
1424M	B	1.22	CH3	CH(O/O)		CCL4
848M	A	1.08	CH3	CH(QN/CH3)		CCL4
2469M	A	1.09	CH3	CH(QN/CH3)		CDCL3
848M	B	1.10	CH3	CH(QN/CH3)		CCL4
2522M	B	1.08	CH3	CH(Q2/CH2.2)		CCL4
80M	A	0.95	CH3	CH(Q2/CH3)		CCL4
77M	A	0.96	CH3	CH(Q2/CH3)		CCL4
76M	A	0.97	CH3	CH(Q2/CH3)		CCL4
81M	A	0.98	CH3	CH(Q2/CH3)		CCL4
89M	A	1.10	CH3	CH(Q2/Q3)		CCL4
88M	A	0.97	CH3	CH(Q3/CH2)		CCL4
67M	A	1.00	CH3	CH(Q3/CH2)		CCL4
55M	B	0.97	CH3	CH(Q3/CH2)		CCL4
38M	C	0.90 APP.	CH3	CH(R3/CH3)		CCL4
2130M	C	0.91	CH3	CH(R5R6R6R6/CH2)		CDCL3
1780M	C	0.91	CH3	CH(R5R6R6R6/CH2)		CDCL3
2459M	B	1.00	CH3	CH(R6NN/CH2)		DMSO-D6
1610M	A	0.96	CH3	CH(R600R6BI/CH3)		CCL4
1772M	B	0.91	CH3	CH(R6/CH3)		CDCL3
1210M	B	1.30	CH3	CH(SH/CH2.5)		CDCL3
1219M	A	1.41	CH3	CH(SH/CH2)		CDCL3
1203M	C	1.30	CH3	CH(SH/CH2)		CCL4
1202M	A	1.31	CH3	CH(SH/CH3)		CCL4
2489M	A	1.52	CH3	CH(SH/C(=O)-OH)		CCL4
1321M	A	1.23	CH3	CH(SO3/CH3)		CCL4
1184M	B	1.28	CH3	CH(S/CH2)		CCL4
216M	A	1.22	CH3	CH/CH3/AAA		CDCL3
2803M	A	4.11	CH3	CL/C(=O)-O-Q3		CDCL3
696M	A	1.32	CH3	C(AN/CH3/CH3)		CDCL3
694M	A	1.36	CH3	C(AN/CH3/CH3)		CCL4
1908M	A	1.57	CH3	C(A/A/CH3)		POLYSOL-D
1935M	A	1.60	CH3	C(A/A/CH3)		CDCL3
1539M	A	1.63	CH3	C(A/A/CH3)		CDCL3
974M	A	1.47	CH3	C(A/CH2/CH3)		CCL4
1885M	B	1.23	CH3	C(A/CH2/CH3)		CCL4
1886M	B	1.32	CH3	C(A/CH2/CH3)		CDCL3
1231M	A	1.28	CH3	C(A/CH3/CH3)		CCL4
1883M	A	1.28	CH3	C(A/CH3/CH3)		CDCL3
2325M	A	1.29	CH3	C(A/CH3/CH3)		CDCL3
140M	A	1.32	CH3	C(A/CH3/CH3)		CCL4
2870M	A	1.34	CH3	C(A/CH3/CH3)		CCL4
1936M	A	1.38	CH3	C(A/CH3/CH3)		CDCL3
2224M	A	1.39	CH3	C(A/CH3/CH3)		CDCL3
1882M	A	1.40	CH3	C(A/CH3/CH3)		CCL4
1934M	A	1.48	CH3	C(A/CH3/CH3)		CDCL3
1933M	B	1.40	CH3	C(A/CH3/CH3)		CDCL3
325M	A	1.77	CH3	C(BR/CH3/CH3)		CCL4
2729M	B	1.94	CH3	C(BR/C(=O)-O/CH3)		CDCL3
21M	A	0.89	CH3	C(CH2.2/CH3/CH3)		CDCL3
2776M	A	1.07	CH3	C(CH2-C(=O)-O/CH2-C(=O)-O/CH3		CCL4
1624M	A	0.85	CH3	C(CH2/CH2/CH3)		CDCL3
274M	A	1.00	CH3	C(CH2/CH2/CH3)		CDCL3
631M	A	1.08	CH3	C(CH2/CH2/CH3)		D20
2500M	A	1.10	CH3	C(CH2/CH2/CH3)		POLYSOL-D
631M	B	1.12	CH3	C(CH2/CH2/CH3)		D20
2305M	A	1.00	CH3	C(CH2/CH3-CH3)		CDCL3
1886M	A	0.73	CH3	C(CH2/CH3/CH3)		CDCL3
1629M	A	0.89	CH3	C(CH2/CH3/CH3)		CDCL3
27M	A	0.90	CH3	C(CH2/CH3/CH3)		CCL4
274M	A	1.00	CH3	C(CH2/CH3/CH3)		CDCL3
329M	A	1.02	CH3	C(CH2/CH3/CH3)		CCL4
1973M	A	1.02	CH3	C(CH2/CH3/CH3)		CCL4
1837M	A	1.02	CH3	C(CH2/CH3/CH3)		CDCL3
265M	A	1.07	CH3	C(CH2/CH3/CH3)		CCL4
2964M	A	1.08	CH3	C(CH2/CH3/CH3)		CCL4
2189M	A	1.10	CH3	C(CH2/CH3/CH3)		CCL4

BOOK NO.	ASSIGN-MENT	CHEM SHIFT - ppm -	PROTON GROUP	ENVIRONMENTAL GROUPS	S	SOLVENT
23M	B	0.84	CH3	C(CH3/CH2/CH2)		CDCL3
26M	A	0.79 APP.	CH3	C(CH/CH2/CH3)		CCL4
1744M	A	0.85	CH3	C(CH/CH3/CH3)		CCL4
448M	A	0.85	CH3	C(CH/CH3/CH3)		CCL4
1838M	A	1.02	CH3	C(CH/CH3/CH3)		CDCL3
241M	B	1.51	CH3	C(CL/CH2/CH3)		CCL4
239M	A	1.61	CH3	C(CL/CH3/CH3)		CCL4
258M	A	2.20	CH3	C(CL/CL/CH3)		CCL4
2655M	A	1.75	CH3	C(CL/C(=O)-O/CH2)	S	D2O
2061M	A	1.21	CH3	C(C(=O)-A/CH3/CH3)		CCL4
1977M	B	1.11	CH3	C(C(=O)-CH/CH3/CH3)		CCL4
2190M	B	1.29	CH3	C(C(=O)-CL/CH2.2/CH3)		CCL4
2476M	A	1.21	CH3	C(C(=O)-OH/CH3/CH3)		CDCL3
2922M	A	1.34	CH3	C(C(=O)-O-A/CH3/CH3)		CDCL3
2703M	A	1.17	CH3	C(C(=O)-O/CH3/CH3)		CCL4
2251M	A	1.25	CH3	C(C(=O)-O/CH3/CH3)		CCL4
2927M	A	1.38	CH3	C(C(=O)-O/CH3/CH3)		CDCL3
2852M	B	1.77	CH3	C(C(=O)-O/C(=O)-O/A)		CCL4
126M	A	1.18	CH3	C(C:C/CH3/CH3)		CCL4
948M	A	1.39	CH3	C(C:N/CH3/CH3)		CCL4
116M	A	1.21	CH3	C(C:/CH3/CH3)		CCL4
480M	A	2.19	CH3	C(NH2/A/CH3)		CCL4
452M	B	1.11	CH3	C(NH2/CH2.3/CH3)		CDCL3
460M	A	1.00	CH3	C(NH2/CH2/CH3)		CCL4
1645M	A	1.22	CH3	C(NH2/CH2/CH3)		CDCL3
786M	A	1.40	CH3	C(NH2/CH2/CH3)	S	D2O
447M	B	1.10	CH3	C(NH2/CH2/CH3)		CDCL3
769M	A	1.30	CH3	C(NH2/CH3/CH3)		CDCL3
2625M	A	1.46	CH3	C(NH2/C(=O)-OH/HCH)		D2O
2616M	A	1.50	CH3	C(NH2/C(=O)-O/CH3)		D2O
2419M	B	1.17	CH3	C(NH/CH2/CH3)		DMSO-D6
2302M	B	1.29	CH3	C(NH/CH2/CH3)		CDCL3
2305M	B	1.47	CH3	C(NH/CH2/CH3)		CDCL3
2304M	A	1.40	CH3	C(NH/CH3/CH3)		CDCL3
547M	C	1.00	CH3	C(NH/CH3/CH3)		CDCL3
588M	A	1.61	CH3	C(NH/C:CH/CH3)		CDCL3
1043M	A	1.61	CH3	C(NO2/CH3/CH3)		CCL4
925M	A	0.98	CH3	C(N=C=N/CH3/CH3)		CDCL3
1021M	A	1.21	CH3	C(N=O/CH3/CH3)		CDCL3
1817M	A	1.51	CH3	C(OH/A/CH3)		CDCL3
1819M	A	1.75	CH3	C(OH/A/C:C)		CDCL3
1805M	A	1.77	CH3	C(OH/CBR3/CH3)		CDCL3
1801M	C	1.12	CH3	C(OH/CH2.2/CH2)		CCL4
1797M	B	1.18	CH3	C(OH/CH2.2/CH3)		CCL4
1798M	B	1.17	CH3	C(OH/CH2.3/CH3)		CCL4
1800M	B	1.21	CH3	C(OH/CH2.5/CH3)		CDCL3
1837M	B	1.27	CH3	C(OH/CH2/CH2)		CDCL3
1802M	C	1.10	CH3	C(OH/CH2/CH2)		CCL4
1799M	B	1.12	CH3	C(OH/CH2/CH3)		CCL4
1796M	B	1.15	CH3	C(OH/CH2/CH3)		CCL4
1795M	A	1.20	CH3	C(OH/CH3/CH3)		CCL4
1838M	B	1.30	CH3	C(OH/CH/CH3)		CDCL3
1993M	A	1.37	CH3	C(OH/C(=O)/CH3)		CDCL3
1813M	A	1.53	CH3	C(OH/C:CH/CH3)		CDCL3
1814M	B	1.41	CH3	C(OH/C:C/CH2)		CCL4
1815M	B	1.49	CH3	C(OH/C:C/CH2)		CDCL3
1806M	A	1.61	CH3	C(OH/C:N/CH3)		CDCL3
1859M	A	1.39	CH3	C(OH/C:/CH3)		DMSO-D6
1834M	A	1.26	CH3	C(OH/C/CH3)		CDCL3
1831M	B	1.18	CH3	C(OH/HCH/CH3)		CCL4
1831M	C	1.23	CH3	C(OH/HCH/CH3)		CCL4
1812M	A	1.23	CH3	C(OH/Q3/CH3)		CCL4
1808M	A	1.12	CH3	C(OH/R6/CH3)		CCL4
1807M	A	1.54	CH3	C(OH/SO3-NA/CH3)		D2O
1398M	B	1.12	CH3	C(O-CH/CH3/CH3)		CCL4
2768M	A	1.44	CH3	C(O-C(=O)/CH3/CH3)		CCL4
2975M	A	1.45	CH3	C(O-C(=O)/CH3/CH3)		CDCL3
1036M	A	1.57	CH3	C(O-NO/CH3/CH3)		CDCL3
1396M	A	1.12	CH3	C(O/CH3/CH3)		CCL4
1609M	A	1.19	CH3	C(O/CH3/CH3)		CCL4
1592M	A	1.33	CH3	C(O/CH3/CH3)		CDCL3
1397M	B	1.13	CH3	C(O/CH3/CH3)		CCL4
2562M	A	1.59	CH3	C(O/C(=O)-OH/CH3)		CDCL3
1759M	B	1.18	CH3	C(O/HCH/CH3)		CCL4
1759M	C	1.21	CH3	C(O/HCH/CH3)		CCL4
1433M	A	1.23	CH3	C(O/OCH3)		CCL4
1434M	A	1.32	CH3	C(O/O/CH3)		CCL4
1437M	A	1.31	CH3	C(O/O/O)		CCL4
91M	A	1.09	CH3	C(Q1/CH3/CH3)		CCL4
82M	B	1.00	CH3	C(Q2/CH3/CH3)		CCL4
54M	A	1.00	CH3	C(Q3/CH3/CH3)		CCL4

: REPRESENTS TRIPLE BOND, ¬ REPRESENTS AN ARROW AND < AND > REPRESENT BRACKETS.   PAGE 411

BOOK NO.	ASSIGN-MENT	CHEM SHIFT - ppm -	PROTON GROUP	ENVIRONMENTAL GROUPS	S	SOLVENT
2120M	A	1.39	CH3	C(R6A/CH3/CH3)		CDCL3
1467M	A	1.47	CH3	C(R6N0/C:N/CH3)		CDCL3
100M	A	0.79	CH3	C(R6/CH2/CH3)		CCL4
2031M	B	1.21	CH3	C(R6/CH2/CH3)		CDCL3
2004M	A	0.95	CH3	C(R6/CH3/CH3)		CDCL3
1223M	C	1.31	CH3	C(SH/CH2.3/CH2)		CDCL3
1223M	D	1.40	CH3	C(SH/CH2.3/CH3)		CDCL3
1186M	A	1.30	CH3	C(S/CH3/CH3)		CCL4
2045M	A	2.43	CH3	C(=O)-A		CCL4
2072M	A	2.46	CH3	C(=O)-A		CCL4
2078M	A	2.48	CH3	C(=O)-A		DMSO-D6
2068M	A	2.50	CH3	C(=O)-A		CCL4
2069M	A	2.50	CH3	C(=O)-A		CDCL3
2065M	A	2.50	CH3	C(=O)-A		CCL4
2074M	A	2.52	CH3	C(=O)-A		POLYSOL-D
2063M	A	2.53	CH3	C(=O)-A		CCL4
2064M	A	2.55	CH3	C(=O)-A		CCL4
2075M	A	2.56	CH3	C(=O)-A		CDCL3
2080M	A	2.59	CH3	C(=O)-A		DMSO-D6
2067M	A	2.59	CH3	C(=O)-A		CCL4
2079M	A	2.62	CH3	C(=O)-A		CDCL3
2082M	A	2.63	CH3	C(=O)-A		CDCL3
2081M	A	2.64	CH3	C(=O)-A		CDCL3
2073M	A	2.68	CH3	C(=O)-A		CDCL3
2056M	B	2.42	CH3	C(=O)-A		CCL4
2059M	B	2.42	CH3	C(=O)-A		CCL4
2057M	B	2.44 APP.	CH3	C(=O)-A		CCL4
2055M	B	2.49	CH3	C(=O)-A		CCL4
2076M	B	2.51	CH3	C(=O)-A		CDCL3
2058M	C	2.40	CH3	C(=O)-A		CDCL3
2113M	A	2.60	CH3	C(=O)-AA		CCL4
2110M	A	2.62	CH3	C(=O)-AN		CCL4
2111M	B	2.69	CH3	C(=O)-AN		CDCL3
2108M	B	2.48	CH3	C(=O)-AR5		CDCL3
2109M	A	2.49	CH3	C(=O)-AR600		CDCL3
1993M	B	2.23	CH3	C(=O)-C		CDCL3
2037M	A	2.42	CH3	C(=O)-CH		CDCL3
1994M	B	2.21	CH3	C(=O)-CH		CCL4
1991M	B	2.29	CH3	C(=O)-CH		CCL4
1992M	B	2.31	CH3	C(=O)-CH		CCL4
2744M	D	2.12	CH3	C(=O)-CH		CCL4
2745M	D	2.21	CH3	C(=O)-CH		CDCL3
2036M	A	2.00	CH3	C(=O)-CH2		CCL4
2039M	A	2.09	CH3	C(=O)-CH2		CCL4
2019M	A	2.09	CH3	C(=O)-CH2		CCL4
2746M	A	2.11	CH3	C(=O)-CH2		CCL4
1995M	A	2.12	CH3	C(=O)-CH2		CCL4
2494M	A	2.17	CH3	C(=O)-CH2		CDCL3
2742M	A	2.19	CH3	C(=O)-CH2		CDCL3
1971M	B	2.01	CH3	C(=O)-CH2		CCL4
1997M	B	2.05	CH3	C(=O)-CH2		CCL4
1968M	B	2.05	CH3	C(=O)-CH2		CCL4
1973M	B	2.06	CH3	C(=O)-CH2		CCL4
2141M	B	2.20	CH3	C(=O)-CH2		CCL4
2319M	B	2.21	CH3	C(=O)-CH2		DMSO-D6
2147M	B	2.24	CH3	C(=O)-CH2		CDCL3
1974M	C	2.06	CH3	C(=O)-CH2		CCL4
1976M	C	2.06	CH3	C(=O)-CH2		CCL4
2038M	C	2.77	CH3	C(=O)-CH2		CDCL3
2743M	D	2.19	CH3	C(=O)-CH2		CCL4
2358M	D	2.26	CH3	C(=O)-CH2		CDCL3
1989M	D	2.13	CH3	C(=O)-CH2.11		CDCL3
2747M	C	2.10	CH3	C(=O)-CH2.2		CCL4
1969M	D	2.07	CH3	C(=O)-CH2.3		CCL4
1967M	A	2.11	CH3	C(=O)-CH3		CDCL3
2131M	B	2.26	CH3	C(=O)-C(=O)		CCL4
2044M	A	2.40	CH3	C(=O)-C:		CDCL3
2363M	A	1.86	CH3	C(=O)-N		CDCL3
2368M	A	2.06	CH3	C(=O)-N		CDCL3
2364M	B	1.72	CH3	C(=O)-N		CCL4
2348M	B	1.97	CH3	C(=O)-N		CCL4
2366M	C	1.72	CH3	C(=O)-N		CCL4
2365M	C	1.82	CH3	C(=O)-N		CDCL3
2349M	C	1.98	CH3	C(=O)-N		CCL4
2301M	A	1.90	CH3	C(=O)-NH		POLYSOL-D
2309M	A	1.90	CH3	C(=O)-NH		CDCL3
2403M	A	1.93	CH3	C(=O)-NH		CDCL3
2337M	A	2.02	CH3	C(=O)-NH		DMSO-D6
2336M	A	2.03	CH3	C(=O)-NH		POLYSOL-D
2323M	A	2.05	CH3	C(=O)-NH		DMSO-D6
2321M	A	2.05	CH3	C(=O)-NH		CDCL3

BOOK NO.	ASSIGN-MENT	CHEM SHIFT - ppm -	PROTON GROUP	ENVIRONMENTAL GROUPS	S	SOLVENT
2322M	A	2.06	CH3	C(=0)-NH		CDCL3
2335M	A	2.09	CH3	C(=0)-NH		DMSO-D6
2331M	A	2.10	CH3	C(=0)-NH		DMSO-D6
2330M	A	2.10	CH3	C(=0)-NH		DMSO-D6
2327M	A	2.11	CH3	C(=0)-NH		CDCL3
2334M	A	2.11	CH3	C(=0)-NH		DMSO-D6
2332M	A	2.11	CH3	C(=0)-NH		CDCL3
2327M	A	2.11	CH3	C(=0)-NH		CDCL3
2340M	A	2.11	CH3	C(=0)-NH		CDCL3
2321M	A	2.15	CH3	C(=0)-NH		CDCL3
2329M	A	2.16	CH3	C(=0)-NH		CDCL3
2328M	A	2.17	CH3	C(=0)-NH		CDCL3
2326M	A	2.17	CH3	C(=0)-NH		CDCL3
2341M	A	2.20	CH3	C(=0)-NH		CDCL3
2333M	A	2.27	CH3	C(=0)-NH		CDCL3
273M	A	2.28	CH3	C(=0)-NH		DMSO-D6
2310M	B	1.90	CH3	C(=0)-NH		CDCL3
2620M	B	1.92	CH3	C(=0)-NH		DMSO-D6
2211M	B	2.02	CH3	C(=0)-NH		DMSO-D6
2324M	B	2.07	CH3	C(=0)-NH		CDCL3
2627M	B	2.08	CH3	C(=0)-NH		POLYSOL-D
2338M	B	2.09	CH3	C(=0)-NH		CDCL3
2325M	B	2.10	CH3	C(=0)-NH		CDCL3
2974M	B	2.21	CH3	C(=0)-NH		CDCL3
2338M	B	2.22	CH3	C(=0)-NH		CDCL3
2621M	C	1.91	CH3	C(=0)-NH		POLYSOL-D
2297M	C	1.99	CH3	C(=0)-NH		D2O
2339M	C	2.13	CH3	C(=0)-NH		CDCL3
2339M	C	2.26	CH3	C(=0)-NH		CDCL3
2275M	A	1.98	CH3	C(=0)-NH2		D2O
2472M	A	2.06	CH3	C(=0)-OH		CCL4
2687M	A	1.99	CH3	C(=0)-OH	S	D2O
2685M	C	1.90	CH3	C(=0)-OH		CDCL3
2686M	C	1.91	CH3	C(=0)-OH		CDCL3
2924M	A	2.12	CH3	C(=0)-O-A		CCL4
2928M	A	2.18	CH3	C(=0)-O-A		CCL4
2929M	A	2.22	CH3	C(=0)-O-A		CDCL3
2926M	A	2.35	CH3	C(=0)-O-A		CDCL3
2930M	A	2.19	CH3	C(=0)-O-AA		CDCL3
2762M	C	1.99	CH3	C(=0)-O-C		CCL4
2834M	B	2.03	CH3	C(=0)-O-CH		CDCL3
2754M	B	2.07 APP.	CH3	C(=0)-O-CH		CCL4
2822M	C	1.95	CH3	C(=0)-O-CH		CCL4
2833M	A	1.90	CH3	C(=0)-O-CH2		CCL4
2839M	A	1.93	CH3	C(=0)-O-CH2		CCL4
2832M	A	1.96	CH3	C(=0)-O-CH2		CCL4
2841M	A	1.99	CH3	C(=0)-O-CH2		CCL4
2931M	A	2.00	CH3	C(=0)-O-CH2		CCL4
2756M	A	2.08	CH3	C(=0)-O-CH2		CDCL3
2718M	A	2.11	CH3	C(=0)-O-CH2		CDCL3
2840M	A	2.13	CH3	C(=0)-O-CH2		CDCL3
2716M	A	2.14	CH3	C(=0)-O-CH2		CDCL3
2798M	B	1.96	CH3	C(=0)-O-CH2		CCL4
2755M	B	1.97	CH3	C(=0)-O-CH2		CCL4
2696M	C	1.94	CH3	C(=0)-O-CH2		CCL4
2697M	C	1.95	CH3	C(=0)-O-CH2		CCL4
2695M	C	1.96	CH3	C(=0)-O-CH2		CCL4
2800M	C	1.97	CH3	C(=0)-O-CH2		CCL4
2717M	C	1.98	CH3	C(=0)-O-CH2		CCL4
2752M	A	2.01	CH3	C(=0)-O-CH2.2		CCL4
2694M	A	2.00	CH3	C(=0)-O-CH3		CCL4
2247M	A	2.20	CH3	C(=0)-O-C(=0)		CCL4
2754M	B	2.07 APP.	CH3	C(=0)-O-HCH		CCL4
2958M	A	2.43	CH3	C(=0)-O-R60A		CDCL3
2713M	B	1.95	CH3	C(=0)-O-R8		CCL4
2146M	A	1.88	CH3	C(=0)-Q1		CCL4
2042M	A	1.89	CH3	C(=0)-Q1		CDCL3
2319M	A	1.93	CH3	C(=0)-Q1		DMSO-D6
2020M	B	2.15 APP.	CH3	C(=0)-Q1		CDCL3
2821M	A	2.37	CH3	C(=0)-Q2		CDCL3
2018M	B	2.12	CH3	C(=0)-Q2		CCL4
2021M	D	2.14	CH3	C(=0)-Q2		CCL4
2017M	A	2.20	CH3	C(=0)-Q3		CCL4
2143M	B	2.21	CH3	C(=0)-R5		CCL4
2373M	A	2.70	CH3	C(=0)-R5NAA		CDCL3
2950M	B	2.39	CH3	C(=0)-R50		CCL4
1998M	B	2.11 APP.	CH3	C(=0)-R5R5BI		CDCL3
2022M	B	2.15	CH3	C(=0)-R6		CCL4
2145M	C	2.51	CH3	C(=0)-R6		CCL4
2372M	B	2.21	CH3	C(=0)-R6NA		CDCL3
2360M	A	1.98	CH3	C(=0)-R6NO		CCL4

BOOK NO.	ASSIGN-MENT	CHEM SHIFT - ppm -	PROTON GROUP	ENVIRONMENTAL GROUPS	S	SOLVENT
2383M	B	2.49	CH3	C(=O)-R7N		CDCL3
2970M	B	2.28	CH3	C(=O)-S		CCL4
2609M	A	2.37	CH3	C(=O)-5H		CCL4
2143M	A	1.94	CH3	C(=R5/OH)		CCL4
1337M	A	2.62	CH3	C(=S)-N		CDCL3
1331M	A	2.40	CH3	C(=S)-NH2		DMSO-D6
1331M	A	2.40	CH3	C(=S)-NH2		DMSO-D6
1021M	B	1.58	CH3	C(+)(N/CH3/CH3)		CDCL3
253M	A	2.70	CH3	C-CL3		CCL4
2796M	C	3.75	CH3	C-C(=O)-CH		CDCL3
1694M	A	1.83	CH3	C:C		CCL4
167M	A	1.99	CH3	C:C		CDCL3
126M	B	1.71	CH3	C:C-C		CCL4
1250M	A	1.75	CH3	C:C-CH2.2		CDCL3
125M	A	1.70	CH3	C:C-CH3		CCL4
943M	A	1.94	CH3	C:N		CCL4
2286M	A	0.83	CH3	HCH-CH		CCL4
1423M	A	1.14	CH3	HCH-O		CCL4
1425M	A	1.16	CH3	HCH-O		CCL4
403M	A	2.20	CH3	I		CDCL3
765M	A	2.62	CH3	NH2	S	D2O
1523M	A	2.63	CH3	NH-A		POLYSOL-D
582M	A	2.67	CH3	NH-A		CCL4
591M	B	2.62	CH3	NH-A		CDCL3
590M	B	2.69	CH3	NH-A		CDCL3
592M	B	2.70	CH3	NH-A		CDCL3
589M	B	2.85	CH3	NH-A		CDCL3
599M	A	2.79	CH3	NH-AA		CDCL3
804M	B	2.78	CH3	NH-CH	S	CDCL3
2612M	A	2.77	CH3	NH-CH2		D2O
1288M	A	2.79	CH3	NH-CH2		D2O
464M	B	2.29	CH3	NH-CH2		D2O
544M	C	2.32	CH3	NH-CH2		D2O
552M	D	2.40	CH3	NH-CH2		CDCL3
2312M	A	2.66	CH3	NH-C(=O)		CDCL3
2436M	A	2.78	CH3	NH-C(=O)		CDCL3
2342M	A	2.97	CH3	NH-C(=O)		CDCL3
2298M	E	2.80	CH3	NH-C(=O)		CDCL3
2296M	C	2.80	CH3	NH-C(=O)-CH2		CDCL3
2416M	A	2.70	CH3	NH-C(=O)-NH2		D2O
2980M	B	2.78	CH3	NH-C(=O)-O		CDCL3
1338M	A	2.80	CH3	NH-C(=S)		DMSO-D6
774M	A	2.81	CH3	NH-NH	S	D2O
753M	A	2.61	CH3	NH-NH2		CCL4
822M	A	2.91	CH3	NH-NH2	S	D2O
904M	B	3.21	CH3	NH-N=N-A		CDCL3
558M	B	2.39	CH3	NH-R6		CDCL3
1039M	A	4.22	CH3	NO2		CCL4
671M	A	2.81	CH3	N(AA/CH3)		CCL4
710M	A	2.97	CH3	N(AN/CH3)		CDCL3
652M	A	2.90	CH3	N(A/CH2)		CCL4
669M	A	2.80	CH3	N(A/CH3)		CDCL3
1900M	A	2.81	CH3	N(A/CH3)		CDCL3
666M	A	2.85	CH3	N(A/CH3)		CDCL3
648M	A	2.85	CH3	N(A/CH3)		CCL4
1524M	A	2.85	CH3	N(A/CH3)		CDCL3
668M	A	2.86	CH3	N(A/CH3)		CDCL3
1901M	A	2.89	CH3	N(A/CH3)		POLYSOL-D
900M	A	2.98	CH3	N(A/CH3)		CDCL3
901M	A	2.98	CH3	N(A/CH3)		DMSO-D6
2170M	A	3.01	CH3	N(A/CH3)		CDCL3
1074M	A	3.11	CH3	N(A/CH3)		DMSO-D6
1023M	A	3.11	CH3	N(A/CH3)		CDCL3
667M	A	3.52	CH3	N(A/CH3)		TFA
2688M	A	3.52	CH3	N(A/CH3)		TFA
819M	A	3.36	CH3	N(A/CH3)	S	D2O
816M	A	3.43	CH3	N(A/CH3)	S	D2O
818M	A	3.44	CH3	N(A/CH3)	S	D2O
658M	B	2.62	CH3	N(A/CH3)		CCL4
660M	B	2.79	CH3	N(A/CH3)		CCL4
665M	B	2.79	CH3	N(A/CH3)		CDCL3
659M	B	2.79	CH3	N(A/CH3)		CCL4
624M	C	2.21 APP.	CH3	N(CH2.21/CH3)		CDCL3
1406M	A	2.21	CH3	N(CH2.2/CH3)		CCL4
2865M	A	2.31	CH3	N(CH2.2/CH3)		CDCL3
623M	C	2.21	CH3	N(CH2.7/CH2.7)		CDCL3
622M	C	2.21	CH3	N(CH2.9-CH3/CH3)		CDCL3
1703M	A	2.22	CH3	N(CH2/CH2)		CDCL3
1430M	A	2.34	CH3	N(CH2/CH2)		CCL4
627M	B	1.69	CH3	N(CH2/CH2)		CDCL3
633M	B	2.12	CH3	N(CH2/CH2)		CCL4

: REPRESENTS TRIPLE BOND, ¬ REPRESENTS AN ARROW AND < AND > REPRESENT BRACKETS.   PAGE 414

BOOK NO.	ASSIGN-MENT	CHEM SHIFT - ppm -	PROTON GROUP	ENVIRONMENTAL GROUPS	S	SOLVENT
1431M	B	2.40	CH3	N(CH2/CH2)		CDCL3
610M	A	2.14	CH3	N(CH2/CH3)		DMSO-D6
644M	A	2.14	CH3	N(CH2/CH3)		CCL4
628M	A	2.19	CH3	N(CH2/CH3)		D2O
642M	A	2.21	CH3	N(CH2/CH3)		CDCL3
630M	A	2.22	CH3	N(CH2/CH3)		CDCL3
677M	A	2.22	CH3	N(CH2/CH3)		CDCL3
708M	A	2.24	CH3	N(CH2/CH3)		CDCL3
811M	A	2.92	CH3	N(CH2/CH3)	S	D2O
2642M	A	2.97	CH3	N(CH2/CH3)	S	D2O
632M	B	2.12	CH3	N(CH2/CH3)		CDCL3
634M	B	2.20	CH3	N(CH2/CH3)		CCL4
1649M	B	2.20	CH3	N(CH2/CH3)		CDCL3
613M	B	2.27	CH3	N(CH2/CH3)		CCL4
1754M	C	2.29	CH3	N(CH2/CH3)		CDCL3
808M	A	2.94	CH3	N(CH3/CH3)	S	D2O
975M	A	2.33	CH3	N(CH/CH3)		CDCL3
625M	B	2.19	CH3	N(CH/CH3)		D2O
1648M	B	2.20	CH3	N(CH/CH3)		D2O
2352M	D	2.94	CH3	N(C(=O)-CH2.2/CH3)		D2O
2352M	E	3.11	CH3	N(C(=O)-CH2.2/CH3)		D2O
2440M	A	3.16	CH3	N(C(=O)-N/A)		CDCL3
2991M	A	3.06	CH3	N(C(=O)-O/CH3)		CDCL3
2363M	B	3.23	CH3	N(C(=O)/A)		CDCL3
2437M	A	2.75	CH3	N(C(=O)/CH3)		1.25
2426M	A	2.91	CH3	N(C(=O)/CH3)		CDCL3
2435M	A	2.97	CH3	N(C(=O)/CH3)		CDCL3
2357M	B	2.99	CH3	N(C(=O)/CH3)		CCL4
2359M	C	3.04	CH3	N(C(=O)/CH3)		CDCL3
2355M	D	2.91 APP.	CH3	N(C(=O)/CH3)		CCL4
1336M	A	3.27	CH3	N(C(=S)-H/CH3)		CDCL3
1336M	B	3.30	CH3	N(C(=S)-H/CH3)		CDCL3
1354M	A	3.29	CH3	N(C(=S)/CH3)		POLYSOL-D
1337M	B	3.31	CH3	N(C(=S)/CH3)		CDCL3
1337M	C	3.48	CH3	N(C(=S)/CH3)		CDCL3
1003M	A	2.88	CH3	N(C:N/CH3)		CCL4
840M	A	3.69	CH3	N(&)(A/CH3/CH3)	S	D2O
754M	A	2.35	CH3	N(NH2/CH3)		CCL4
2410M	A	2.66	CH3	N(NH/CH3)		CDCL3
1353M	C	2.51	CH3	N(NH/CH3)		POLYSOL-D
1025M	A	2.95	CH3	N(NO/CH3)		CCL4
1025M	B	3.71	CH3	N(NO/CH3)		CCL4
1031M	A	3.39	CH3	N(N=O/A)		CDCL3
906M	A	3.23	CH3	N(N=/CH3)		CCL4
762M	A	3.02	CH3	N(N/A)		CDCL3
761M	B	2.89	CH3	N(N/A)		CDCL3
763M	C	2.89	CH3	N(N/A)		CDCL3
2414M	A	3.14	CH3	N(N/C(=O)-A)		CDCL3
884M	A	2.90	CH3	N(QN/CH3)		CCL4
883M	B	2.80 APP.	CH3	N(QN/CH3)		CDCL3
885M	B	2.87	CH3	N(QN/CH3)		CCL4
643M	B	2.39	CH3	N(Q1/CH3)		CDCL3
814M	B	2.97	CH3	N(R6N/CH3)	S	D2O
813M	D	2.78	CH3	N(R6R6R6TRI/CH3)	S	D2O
1374M	A	2.83	CH3	N(SO2/CH3)		CDCL3
1375M	B	2.69	CH3	N(SO2/CH3)		CDCL3
1373M	B	2.85	CH3	N(SO2/CH3)	S	CDCL3
1313M	A	3.70	CH3	N(+)(A/CH3/CH3)		POLYSOL-D
829M	C	3.41	CH3	N(+)(CH2.11/CH3/CH3)	S	CDCL3
830M	C	3.48	CH3	N(+)(CH2.11/CH3/CH3)	S	CDCL3
833M	C	3.50	CH3	N(+)(CH2.17/CH3/CH3)	S	CDCL3
839M	E	3.29	CH3	N(+)(CH2/CH2/CH3)	S	CDCL3
838M	A	3.10	CH3	N(+)(CH2/CH3/CH3)		POLYSOL-D
1657M	A	3.23	CH3	N(+)(CH2/CH3/CH3)	S	CDCL3
836M	A	3.40	CH3	N(+)(CH2/CH3/CH3)	S	CDCL3
831M	D	3.49	CH3	N(+)(CH2/CH3/CH3)	S	CDCL3
835M	D	2.99	CH3	N(+)(R6R6R6TRI/CH3/CH3)	S	D2O
837M	A	3.30	CH3	N(+)(CH2/CH3/CH3)		POLYSOL-D
907M	A	3.01	CH3	N=C=O		CDCL3
930M	A	3.30	CH3	N=C=S		CDCL3
1611M	A	3.34	CH3	OH		CCL4
1546M	A	3.29	CH3	O-A		CCL4
1507M	A	3.53	CH3	O-A		CCL4
1528M	A	3.65	CH3	O-A		CDCL3
1510M	A	3.68	CH3	O-A		CCL4
1515M	A	3.69	CH3	O-A		CDCL3
1488M	A	3.70	CH3	O-A		CCL4
1511M	A	3.70	CH3	O-A		CCL4
1520M	A	3.70	CH3	O-A		CCL4
2595M	A	3.70	CH3	O-A		POLYSOL-D
2178M	A	3.70	CH3	O-A		CCL4

BOOK NO.	ASSIGN-MENT	CHEM SHIFT - ppm -	PROTON GROUP	ENVIRONMENTAL GROUPS	S	SOLVENT
1547M	A	3.71	CH3	O-A		CDCL3
1516M	A	3.71	CH3	O-A		CCL4
1519M	A	3.71	CH3	O-A		CDCL3
1548M	A	3.71	CH3	O-A		CDCL3
2425M	A	3.71	CH3	O-A		POLYSOL-D
1545M	A	3.72	CH3	O-A		CCL4
1554M	A	3.72	CH3	O-A		CDCL3
1521M	A	3.74	CH3	O-A		CDCL3
1549M	A	3.75	CH3	O-A		POLYSOL-D
1508M	A	3.76	CH3	O-A		CDCL3
1906M	A	3.78	CH3	O-A		CDCL3
1537M	A	3.79	CH3	O-A		CDCL3
2244M	A	3.80	CH3	O-A		CCL4
2398M	A	3.80	CH3	O-A		CDCL3
2887M	A	3.80	CH3	O-A		CCL4
1567M	A	3.81	CH3	O-A		CCL4
1529M	A	3.82	CH3	O-A		CDCL3
2584M	A	3.82	CH3	O-A		DMSO-D6
1563M	A	3.83	CH3	O-A		CDCL3
2135M	A	3.83	CH3	O-A		CDCL3
1553M	A	3.84	CH3	O-A		CCL4
1514M	A	3.84	CH3	O-A		CDCL3
2583M	A	3.85	CH3	O-A		DMSO-D6
1565M	A	3.86	CH3	O-A		CDCL3
1531M	A	3.86	CH3	O-A		CDCL3
1509M	A	3.87	CH3	O-A		CDCL3
1566M	A	3.88	CH3	O-A		CDCL3
1564M	A	3.89	CH3	O-A		CDCL3
1532M	A	3.89	CH3	O-A		CCL4
1530M	A	3.89	CH3	O-A		CCL4
2096M	A	3.89	CH3	O-A		POLYSOL-D
1538M	A	3.92	CH3	O-A		CDCL3
2598M	A	3.92	CH3	O-A		DMSO-D6
1556M	A	4.04	CH3	O-A		CDCL3
1555M	A	4.19	CH3	O-A		POLYSOL-D
1568M	A	4.19	CH3	O-A		CDCL3
1527M	A	3.84	CH3	O-A	S	POLYSOL-D
791M	A	3.84	CH3	O-A	S	D20
824M	A	3.85	CH3	O-A	S	D20
1526M	A	3.97	CH3	O-A	S	POLYSOL-D
1506M	B	3.61	CH3	O-A		CCL4
1523M	B	3.61	CH3	O-A		POLYSOL-D
1558M	B	3.62	CH3	O-A		CCL4
1495M	B	3.68	CH3	O-A		CCL4
2839M	B	3.68	CH3	O-A		CCL4
1722M	B	3.69	CH3	O-A		CDCL3
1723M	B	3.69	CH3	O-A		CCL4
2337M	B	3.70	CH3	O-A		DMSO-D6
1924M	B	3.70	CH3	O-A		CCL4
1560M	B	3.71	CH3	O-A		CCL4
1535M	B	3.71	CH3	O-A		CDCL3
1494M	B	3.73	CH3	O-A		CCL4
1505M	B	3.74	CH3	O-A		CDCL3
1524M	B	3.75	CH3	O-A		CDCL3
1536M	B	3.76	CH3	O-A		CDCL3
1496M	B	3.77	CH3	O-A		CDCL3
2888M	B	3.82	CH3	O-A		CDCL3
1559M	B	3.84	CH3	O-A		CDCL3
1563M	B	3.87	CH3	O-A		CDCL3
2888M	B	3.87	CH3	O-A		CDCL3
2075M	B	3.88	CH3	O-A		CDCL3
1504M	B	3.88 APP.	CH3	O-A		CDCL3
1564M	B	3.92	CH3	O-A		CDCL3
2915M	B	3.92	CH3	O-A		CDCL3
1497M	C	3.69	CH3	O-A		CCL4
1558M	C	3.69	CH3	O-A		CCL4
1503M	C	3.71	CH3	O-A		CCL4
1551M	C	3.79	CH3	O-A		CDCL3
1552M	C	3.79	CH3	O-A		CDCL3
1559M	C	3.87	CH3	O-A		CDCL3
1501M	D	3.64	CH3	O-A		CCL4
2077M	D	3.80	CH3	O-A		CCL4
1569M	A	3.72	CH3	O-AA		CCL4
1794M	C	3.90	CH3	O-AAN		POLYSOL-D
1582M	A	3.97	CH3	O-ANN		CDCL3
2116M	D	3.78	CH3	O-AR6		CDCL3
1583M	A	3.70	CH3	O-AR6NSA		DMSO-D6
1487M	A	3.09	CH3	O-C		CCL4
1486M	A	3.11	CH3	O-C		CDCL3
1433M	B	3.10	CH3	O-C		CCL4
1396M	B	3.11	CH3	O-C		CCL4

BOOK NO.	ASSIGN-MENT	CHEM SHIFT - ppm -	PROTON GROUP	ENVIRONMENTAL GROUPS	S	SOLVENT
1437M	B	3.19	CH3	O-C		CCL4
1759M	E	3.18	CH3	O-C		CCL4
1435M	A	3.22	CH3	O-CH		CCL4
2552M	A	3.32	CH3	O-CH		CDCL3
1422M	B	3.21	CH3	O-CH		CCL4
1429M	B	3.23	CH3	O-CH		CCL4
1427M	C	3.30	CH3	O-CH		CCL4
1430M	C	3.30	CH3	O-CH		CCL4
1409M	A	3.23	CH3	O-CH2		CCL4
1419M	A	3.29	CH3	O-CH2		CCL4
1479M	A	3.29	CH3	O-CH2		CDCL3
1420M	A	3.30	CH3	O-CH2		CCL4
1415M	A	3.31	CH3	O-CH2		CCL4
2739M	A	3.38	CH3	O-CH2		CCL4
2491M	A	3.40	CH3	O-CH2		D2O
2284M	A	3.43	CH3	O-CH2		CDCL3
1484M	B	3.26	CH3	O-CH2		CDCL3
1760M	B	3.30	CH3	O-CH2		CCL4
1457M	B	3.31	CH3	O-CH2		CCL4
1665M	B	3.38	CH3	O-CH2		CDCL3
1673M	B	3.40	CH3	O-CH2		CDCL3
1492M	A	3.30	CH3	O-CH2.2		CCL4
1380M	C	3.30	CH3	O-CH2.3		CDCL3
2880M	A	3.80	CH3	O-C(=O)-A		CDCL3
2887M	A	3.80	CH3	O-C(=O)-A		CCL4
2916M	A	3.80	CH3	O-C(=O)-A		POLYSOL-D
2881M	A	3.82	CH3	O-C(=O)-A		CDCL3
2888M	A	3.82	CH3	O-C(=O)-A		CDCL3
2910M	A	3.84	CH3	O-C(=O)-A		POLYSOL-D
2872M	A	3.85	CH3	O-C(=O)-A		CCL4
2914M	A	3.86	CH3	O-C(=O)-A		DMSO-D6
2888M	A	3.87	CH3	O-C(=O)-A		CDCL3
2873M	A	3.88	CH3	O-C(=O)-A		CCL4
2915M	A	3.89	CH3	O-C(=O)-A		CDCL3
2905M	A	3.89	CH3	O-C(=O)-A		POLYSOL-D
2874M	A	3.89	CH3	O-C(=O)-A		CDCL3
2876M	A	3.89	CH3	O-C(=O)-A		CDCL3
2892M	A	3.91	CH3	O-C(=O)-A		CDCL3
2901M	A	3.94	CH3	O-C(=O)-A		CDCL3
2920M	A	3.96	CH3	O-C(=O)-A		CDCL3
2886M	A	3.97	CH3	O-C(=O)-A		CDCL3
2906M	A	4.02	CH3	O-C(=O)-A		CDCL3
2869M	B	3.81	CH3	O-C(=O)-A		CDCL3
2771M	C	3.67	CH3	O-C(=O)-C		CCL4
2726M	B	3.85	CH3	O-C(=O)-CH		CCL4
2735M	B	3.84	CH3	O-C(=O)-CH	S	D2O
2740M	C	3.74	CH3	O-C(=O)-CH		CCL4
2790M	C	3.79	CH3	O-C(=O)-CH		CDCL3
2938M	A	3.67	CH3	O-C(=O)-CH2		CDCL3
2851M	A	3.73	CH3	O-C(=O)-CH2		CDCL3
2728M	A	3.77	CH3	O-C(=O)-CH2		CCL4
2739M	B	3.69	CH3	O-C(=O)-CH2		CCL4
2790M	B	3.71	CH3	O-C(=O)-CH2		CDCL3
2776M	C	3.59	CH3	O-C(=O)-CH2		CCL4
2742M	C	3.67	CH3	O-C(=O)-CH2		CDCL3
2791M	C	3.69	CH3	O-C(=O)-CH2		CCL4
2707M	D	3.59	CH3	O-C(=O)-CH2		CCL4
2781M	D	3.60	CH3	O-C(=O)-CH2		CCL4
2746M	D	3.61	CH3	O-C(=O)-CH2		CCL4
2710M	D	3.61	CH3	O-C(=O)-CH2		CCL4
2779M	D	3.61	CH3	O-C(=O)-CH2		CCL4
2699M	D	3.61	CH3	O-C(=O)-CH2		CCL4
2785M	D	3.65	CH3	O-C(=O)-CH2		CDCL3
2822M	E	3.60	CH3	O-C(=O)-CH2		CCL4
2704M	E	3.61	CH3	O-C(=O)-CH2		CCL4
2712M	E	3.63	CH3	O-C(=O)-CH2		CDCL3
2737M	B	3.72	CH3	O-C(=O)-CH2.2		CCL4
2793M	C	3.64	CH3	O-C(=O)-CH2.2		CDCL3
2738M	C	3.71	CH3	O-C(=O)-CH2.2		CDCL3
2849M	D	3.60	CH3	O-C(=O)-CH2.3		CCL4
2748M	D	3.67	CH3	O-C(=O)-CH2.5		CDCL3
2816M	E	3.59	CH3	O-C(=O)-CH2.7-Q2		CCL4
2694M	B	3.65	CH3	O-C(=O)-CH3		CCL4
2859M	A	3.77	CH3	O-C(=O)-CH=		TFA
2722M	A	4.00	CH3	O-C(=O)-C-CL3		CCL4
2982M	D	3.60	CH3	O-C(=O)-NH		CCL4
2825M	A	3.80	CH3	O-C(=O)-Q2		CDCL3
2821M	B	3.82	CH3	O-C(=O)-Q2		CDCL3
2799M	D	3.62	CH3	O-C(=O)-Q2		CCL4
2815M	D	3.63	CH3	O-C(=O)-Q2		CCL4
2855M	A	3.65	CH3	O-C(=O)-R5AA		CDCL3

BOOK NO.	ASSIGN-MENT	CHEM SHIFT - ppm -	PROTON GROUP	ENVIRONMENTAL GROUPS	S	SOLVENT
2787M	B	3.60	CH3	O-C(=O)-R6		CCL4
2787M	C	3.63	CH3	O-C(=O)-R6		CCL4
2993M	A	3.77	CH3	O-C(=O)-R6NNN		CDCL3
846M	A	3.89	CH3	O-NH2	S	D2O
1598M	A	3.60	CH3	O-SI		CDCL3
1594M	A	3.61	CH3	O-SI		CDCL3
1314M	A	3.80	CH3	O-SO3-K		D2O
1323M	A	3.59	CH3	O-S(=O/O)		CCL4
1104M	C	1.41	CH3	P(=O/CH2/CH3)		CDCL3
1103M	C	1.44	CH3	P(=O/CH2/CH3)		CDCL3
1102M	A	3.27	CH3	P(+)(A/A/A)	S	CDCL3
878M	A	2.39	CH3	QN(AN(C-N)/NH-A)		DMSO-D6
866M	A	3.41	CH3	QN(A)		CDCL3
860M	A	2.25	CH3	QN(A/OH)		CDCL3
859M	A	2.48	CH3	QN(A/OH)		CCL4
1063M	C	1.95 APP.	CH3	QN(CH2.2-CH3/NH-A)		POLYSOL-D
2470M	C	1.82	CH3	QN(CH2-CH2/NH-C(=O))		CDCL3
857M	C	1.88	CH3	QN(CH2-CH2/OH)		CDCL3
854M	C	1.88	CH3	QN(CH2-CH2/OH)		CDCL3
856M	C	1.90	CH3	QN(CH2-CH2/OH)		CDCL3
853M	B	1.89	CH3	QN(CH2-CH3/OH)		CDCL3
855M	B	1.89	CH3	QN(CH2-CH/OH)		CDCL3
932M	A	1.45	CH3	QN(CH3/CH3/=C=S)		CCL4
1075M	A	2.09	CH3	QN(CH3/NH-A)		CDCL3
1075M	A	2.18	CH3	QN(CH3/NH-A)		CDCL3
1075M	B	2.09	CH3	QN(CH3/NH-A)		CDCL3
1075M	B	2.18	CH3	QN(CH3/NH-A)		CDCL3
2469M	B	1.81	CH3	QN(CH(CH3/CH3)/NH-C(=O))		CDCL3
888M	A	1.90	CH3	QN(NH-A/A)		CDCL3
864M	A	2.01	CH3	QN(QN(OH/CH3)/OH)		POLYSOL-D
2856M	B	2.51	CH3	Q1(A/C(=O)-O-CH2)		CCL4
1712M	A	1.81	CH3	Q1(A/H/CH2-OH)		CDCL3
1690M	C	1.67 APP.	CH3	Q1(CH2.3-CH/CH2-OH)		CCL4
92M	D	1.59	CH3	Q1(CH2-CH2/CH3/H)		CCL4
893M	B	1.59	CH3	Q1(CH3/CH2-CH2)		CDCL3
893M	B	1.68	CH3	Q1(CH3/CH2-CH2)		CDCL3
893M	C	1.59	CH3	Q1(CH3/CH2-CH2)		CDCL3
893M	C	1.68	CH3	Q1(CH3/CH2-CH2)		CDCL3
93M	C	1.60	CH3	Q1(CH3/CH2-CH2/H)		CCL4
93M	C	1.69	CH3	Q1(CH3/CH2-CH2/H)		CCL4
94M	B	1.60	CH3	Q1(CH3/CH2-CH)		CCL4
94M	B	1.70	CH3	Q1(CH3/CH2-CH)		CCL4
94M	C	1.60	CH3	Q1(CH3/CH2-CH)		CCL4
94M	C	1.70	CH3	Q1(CH3/CH2-CH)		CCL4
573M	B	1.68	CH3	Q1(CH3/CH2-NH)		CDCL3
573M	C	1.72	CH3	Q1(CH3/CH2-NH)		CDCL3
90M	A	1.48	CH3	Q1(CH3/CH3)		CCL4
90M	B	1.58 APP.	CH3	Q1(CH3/CH3)		CCL4
2020M	A	1.90	CH3	Q1(CH3/C(=O)-CH3)		CDCL3
2020M	B	2.15 APP.	CH3	Q1(CH3/C(=O)-CH3)		CDCL3
91M	B	1.65- 1.71	CH3	Q1(CH3/C)		CCL4
91M	C	1.71- 1.65	CH3	Q1(CH3/C)		CCL4
93M	D	1.60	CH3	Q1(CH3/H/CH2-CH2)		CCL4
93M	D	1.69	CH3	Q1(CH3/H/CH2-CH2)		CCL4
2519M	A	1.95	CH3	Q1(CH3/H/C(=O)-OH)		CCL4
2519M	B	2.19	CH3	Q1(CH3/H/C(=O)-OH)		CCL4
643M	A	1.65	CH3	Q1(CH3/N)		CDCL3
278M	A	2.19	CH3	Q1(CL/CH2-CL)		CCL4
280M	A	1.73	CH3	Q1(CL/CL)		CDCL3
2160M	A	1.99	CH3	Q1(C(=O)-H/A)		CCL4
2534M	A	2.41	CH3	Q1(C(=O)-OH/H/C(=O)-OH)		TFA
92M	C	1.55	CH3	Q1(H/CH3/CH2-CH2)		CCL4
2147M	A	2.13	CH3	Q1(OH/C(=O)-A)		CDCL3
2146M	B	1.98	CH3	Q1(OH/C(=O)-CH2)		CCL4
2358M	C	1.92	CH3	Q1(OH/C(=O)-N)		CDCL3
2743M	C	1.90	CH3	Q1(OH/C(=O)-O-CH2.3)		CCL4
2141M	A	2.08	CH3	Q1(OH/C(=O)-R50)		CCL4
95M	A	1.71	CH3	Q1(Q1/CH3)		CCL4
95M	B	1.78	CH3	Q1(Q1/CH3)		CCL4
1506M	A	1.78	CH3	Q2(A(C-CH-CH-C(n-CH3))/CH3		CCL4
157M	A	2.10	CH3	Q2(A/H/H)		CCL4
154M	A	1.68	CH3	Q2(CH2-A)		CCL4
83M	C	1.57	CH3	Q2(CH2-CH2)		CCL4
70M	C	1.70	CH3	Q2(CH2-CH2)		CCL4
72M	C	1.70	CH3	Q2(CH2-CH2)		CCL4
75M	B	1.60	CH3	Q2(CH2-CH3)		CCL4
69M	B	1.69	CH3	Q2(CH2-CH3/H/H)		CCL4
88M	B	1.63	CH3	Q2(CH2-CH)		CCL4
475M	B	1.73	CH3	Q2(CH2-NH2/H/H)		CCL4
572M	B	1.78	CH3	Q2(CH2-NH)		CDCL3
1686M	A	1.69	CH3	Q2(CH2-OH)		CCL4

: REPRESENTS TRIPLE BOND, ⌐ REPRESENTS AN ARROW AND < AND > REPRESENT BRACKETS.   PAGE 418

BOOK NO.	ASSIGN-MENT	CHEM SHIFT - ppm -	PROTON GROUP	ENVIRONMENTAL GROUPS	S	SOLVENT
68M	A	1.72	CH3	Q2(CH3/H/H)		CDCL3
76M	B	1.59	CH3	Q2(CH(CH3/CH3))		CCL4
1782M	B	1.70	CH3	Q2(CH(OH/CH3)/H/H)		CCL4
2810M	B	1.91	CH3	Q2(C(=O)-O-CH2/H/H)		CCL4
2813M	C	1.92	CH3	Q2(C(=O)-O-CH2/H/H)		CCL4
2812M	C	1.92	CH3	Q2(C(=O)-O-CH2/H/H)		CCL4
2811M	B	1.90	CH3	Q2(C(=O)-O-CH/H/H)		CCL4
967M	A	1.98	CH3	Q2(C:N/H/H)		CCL4
1559M	A	1.86	CH3	Q2(H/A<C-CH-C(O-CH3)-C(O-CH3)>/H)		CDCL3
77M	B	1.62	CH3	Q2(H/CH(CH3/CH3)/H)		CCL4
2018M	A	1.89	CH3	Q2(H/C(=O)-CH3/H)		CCL4
2814M	B	1.89	CH3	Q2(H/C(=O)-O-CH2/H)		CCL4
2517M	A	1.89	CH3	Q2(H/C(=O)-O/H)		CDCL3
1408M	B	1.53	CH3	Q2(H/H/O-CH2)		CCL4
2671M	A	1.82	CH3	Q2(H/H/Q2)		D20
894M	A	1.81	CH3	Q2(H/Q2/H)		POLYSOL-D
87M	A	1.73	CH3	Q2(Q2(CH3))		CCL4
74M	A	1.87	CH3	Q2(Q2(CH3/H/H)/H/H)		CCL4
2208M	A	1.92	CH3	Q2(Q2(C(=O)-CL))		CCL4
2530M	A	1.89	CH3	Q2(Q2-C(=O)-OH)		CDCL3
73M	A	1.82	CH3	Q2(Q3/H/H)		CCL4
111M	A	1.63	CH3	Q2(R6(CH-CH2/CH2))		CCL4
1408M	B	1.53	CH3	Q3(H/O-CH2/H)		CCL4
96M	A	1.62	CH3	Q(CH3/CH3/CH3)		CDCL3
1449M	A	0.97	CH3	R3OR6R4BI<C*(O/CH*)>		CCL4
1438M	A	1.24	CH3	R3O(CH-O/HCH)		CCL4
39M	D	1.15	CH3	R3<CH-CH(CH3)/HCH>		CCL4
40M	C	1.14	CH3	R3<CH-C(CH3/CH3)/HCH>		CCL4
40M	C	1.14	CH3	R3<C(CH3)-CH(CH3)/HCH>		CCL4
1449M	B	1.30	CH3	R4R6IR3O<C(CH3)-CH*/CH*>		CCL4
109M	A	0.72	CH3	R4R6BI(C(CH3)-CH*/CH*)		CCL4
110M	A	0.84	CH3	R4R6BI(C(CH3)-CH*/CH*)		CCL4
109M	B	1.25	CH3	R4R6BI(C(CH3)-CH*/CH*)		CCL4
110M	B	1.27	CH3	R4R6BI(C(CH3)-CH*/CH*)		CCL4
110M	C	1.65	CH3	R4R6BI(C=CH/CH*)		CCL4
2142M	A	1.32	CH3	R4<C(CH3)-C(=O)/C(=O)>		CDCL3
606M	A	2.30	CH3	R5NA<C-NH/=CH>		CDCL3
607M	A	2.29	CH3	R5NA<C=CH/C*>		CDCL3
609M	A	2.21	CH3	R5NA<C=C(CH3)/C*>		CDCL3
609M	B	2.23	CH3	R5NA<C=C(CH3)/NH>		CDCL3
2391M	A	3.23	CH3	R5NA<N-C(=O)/C(=O)>		TFA
679M	A	4.16	CH3	R5NNNN(N-N=/C(A)=)		CDCL3
1966M	A	1.30	CH3	R5NN<C(CH3)-NH/C(=O)>		CDCL3
2445M	A	1.38	CH3	R5NN<C(CH3)-NH/C(=O)>		CDCL3
2448M	A	3.00	CH3	R5NN<N-C(=O)/C(=O)>		CDCL3
2447M	A	1.68	CH3	R5NN(C(A)-NH/C(=O))		DMSO-D6
1585M	B	2.56	CH3	R5NOA<C=N/O>		CDCL3
1579M	A	2.27	CH3	R5NO(C=N/CH=)		CCL4
1177M	A	2.71	CH3	R5NSA<C=N/S>		CDCL3
1175M	A	2.77	CH3	R5NSA(C=N/S)		CDCL3
1149M	A	2.32	CH3	R5NS<C=CH/CH=>		CCL4
1154M	A	2.15	CH3	R5NS<C=CH/N=>	S	D20
1148M	A	2.50	CH3	R5NS<C=N/CH=>		CCL4
1134M	A	2.12	CH3	R5NS<C=N/S>		CCL4
1151M	A	2.70	CH3	R5NS<C=N/S>		CDCL3
2376M	A	1.31	CH3	R5N<CH-C(=O)/HCH>		CDCL3
676M	A	2.02	CH3	R5N<C=CH/N(A)>		CDCL3
636M	B	2.34	CH3	R5N<N-CH2/CH2>		CDCL3
675M	A	3.62	CH3	R5N<N-CH=/CH=>		CDCL3
711M	B	2.15	CH3	R5N(N-CH2/CH2)		CCL4
1459M	B	1.20	CH3	R500<C(CH2-CH3)-O/O>		CCL4
1679M	A	1.31	CH3	R500<C(CH3)-O/O>		CCL4
1679M	B	1.37	CH3	R500<C(CH3)-O/O>		CCL4
2946M	A	1.21	CH3	R50<CH-C(=O)/CH2>		CCL4
2256M	A	1.41	CH3	R50<CH-C(=O)/CH2>		CDCL3
1456M	A	1.13	CH3	R50<CH-O/CH2>		CCL4
2949M	A	1.02	CH3	R50<C(CH3)-CH(OH)/CH2>		CDCL3
2949M	A	1.18	CH3	R50<C(CH3)-CH(OH)/CH2>		CDCL3
2949M	B	1.02	CH3	R50<C(CH3)-CH(OH)/CH2>		CDCL3
2949M	B	1.18	CH3	R50<C(CH3)-CH(OH)/CH2>		CDCL3
2954M	A	1.99	CH3	R50<C-O/=CH>		CCL4
1574M	A	2.22	CH3	R50<C-O/=CH>		CCL4
1575M	A	2.23	CH3	R50<C=CH/O>		CDCL3
2264M	A	2.19	CH3	R50(C=CH/C(=O))		CCL4
2265M	A	2.09	CH3	R50(C=C(CH3)/C(=O))		CDCL3
1779M	A	0.89	CH3	R5R5BI<C(CH3)-C*(CH3)/CH*>		CDCL3
2132M	A	0.91	CH3	R5R5BI<C(CH3)-C*(CH3)/CH*>		POLYSOL-D
2008M	A	0.93	CH3	R5R5BI<C(CH3)-C*(CH3)/CH*>		CDCL3
2008M	B	1.05	CH3	R5R5BI<C(CH3)-C*(CH3)/CH*>		CDCL3
2132M	B	1.09	CH3	R5R5BI<C(CH3)-C*(CH3)/CH*>		POLYSOL-D
2007M	A	0.89	CH3	R5R5BI<C(CH3)-C*(HCH-SO3-NA)/CH*>		D20

BOOK NO.	ASSIGN-MENT	CHEM SHIFT - ppm -	PROTON GROUP	ENVIRONMENTAL GROUPS	S	SOLVENT
2007M	B	1.10	CH3	R5R5BI<C(CH3)-C*(HCH-S03-NA)/CH*>		D20
2132M	B	1.09	CH3	R5R5BI<C*(C(CH3/CH3))-C(=0)/CH2>		POLYSOL-D
1779M	A	0.89	CH3	R5R5BI<C*-C(CH3/CH3)/CH(OH)/CH2>		CDCL3
2008M	C	1.11	CH3	R5R5BI<C*-C(=0)/C(CH3/CH3)/CH2>		CDCL3
2006M	A	1.01	CH3	R5R5BI(C(CH3)-CH*/C(=0)-C*(CH3))		CCL4
2207M	A	0.83	CH3	R5R5BI(C(CH3)-C*(HCH-S03H)/CH*)		D20
2207M	B	1.03	CH3	R5R5BI(C(CH3)-C*(HCH-S03H)/CH*)		D20
2006M	B	1.09	CH3	R5R5BI(C*(C(=0)/CH2/CH2))		CCL4
2262M	A	1.01	CH3	R5R60RI<C(CH3)-C*(CH3)/CH*>		CDCL3
2262M	B	1.10	CH3	R5R60RI<C(CH3)-C*(CH3)/CH*>		CDCL3
2262M	C	1.26	CH3	R5R60RI<C*-C(=0)/C(CH3/CH3)/CH2>		CDCL3
2130M	A	0.72	CH3	R5R6R6R6(C*-CH(CH/CH2)/CH2)		CDCL3
1780M	A	0.80	CH3	R5R6R6R6(C*-CH*(CH(CH2/CH3)))		CDCL3
2129M	A	0.90	CH3	R5R6R6R6(C*-C(=0)/CH2)		CDCL3
1259M	A	1.39	CH3	R5S<CH-S02/CH=>		CDCL3
1259M	B	1.88	CH3	R5S<C=CH/CH2>		CDCL3
1137M	A	2.22	CH3	R5S<C=CH/CH=>		CCL4
2184M	A	2.54	CH3	R5S(C-S/CH-CH)		CDCL3
43M	A	0.97	CH3	R5<CH-CH2/CH2>		CCL4
1765M	A	0.96	CH3	R5<CH-CH(OH)/CH2>		CDCL3
98M	A	1.57	CH3	R5<C=C(CH3)/CH2>		CCL4
602M	A	1.16	CH3	R6NA<CH-NH/HCH>		CDCL3
567M	A	1.13	CH3	R6NN<CH-NH/CH2>		CDCL3
2444M	A	1.31	CH3	R6NN<CH-NH/C(=0)>		POLYSOL-D
641M	A	1.01	CH3	R6NN<CH-N(A)/CH2>		CDCL3
2442M	A	1.13	CH3	R6NN<C(CH3)-CH2/CH2>		TFA
2454M	A	2.39	CH3	R6NN<C-NH/=CH>		TFA
2455M	B	2.38	CH3	R6NN<C-NH/=C(CH3)>		TFA
2453M	A	1.75	CH3	R6NN<C=CH/C(=0)>		DMSO-D6
2455M	A	2.05	CH3	R6NN<C=C(CH3)/C(=0)>		TFA
639M	A	2.26	CH3	R6NN<N-CH2/CH2>		CDCL3
755M	A	2.29	CH3	R6NN<N-CH2/CH2>		CDCL3
568M	A	0.99	CH3	R6NN(CH-NH/HCH)		CDCL3
2452M	B	3.41	CH3	R6NN(N-C(=0)/CH=)		CDCL3
2452M	A	3.30	CH3	R6NN(N-C(=0)/C(=0))		CDCL3
1463M	A	1.05- 1.30	CH3	R6N0<CH-0/CH2>		CDCL3
563M	A	0.91	CH3	R6N<CH-CH2/CH2>		CCL4
2013M	A	1.74	CH3	R6N<C(CH3)-NH/CH2>	S	CDCL3
637M	B	2.10	CH3	R6N<N-CH2/CH2>		CCL4
673M	B	2.21	CH3	R6N<N-CH2/CH2>		CCL4
562M	A	1.00	CH3	R6N(CH-NH/CH2)		CCL4
564M	A	1.00	CH3	R6N(CH-N/CH2)		CCL4
1610M	B	1.29	CH3	R600R6BI<C*-0/CH=/CH2>		CCL4
1475M	A	1.30	CH3	R600R600SPI<CH-0/0>		CDCL3
1472M	A	0.70	CH3	R600<C(CH3)-HCH/HCH>		CCL4
1472M	C	1.17	CH3	R600<C(CH3)-HCH/HCH>		CCL4
2259M	A	1.12	CH3	R60<CH-CH2/CH2>		CDCL3
1869M	A	1.27	CH3	R60<CH-0/CH(OH)>		D20
756M	A	1.20	CH3	R60<C(CH3)-C(C(=0)-0-CH2)=/CH=>		CCL4
756M	C	1.75	CH3	R60<C-0/=CH>		CCL4
756M	D	2.00	CH3	R60<C-0/=C(C(=0)-0-CH2)>		CCL4
1692M	A	1.16	CH3	R60(C(CH2-OH)-0/CH2-CH2)		CDCL3
2260M	A	1.21	CH3	R60(C(CH3)-C(=0)/CH2)		CDCL3
1692M	B	1.56	CH3	R60(C=CH/CH2)		CDCL3
2129M	B	1.05	CH3	R6R6R6R5(C*-CH*/CH2)		CDCL3
1780M	D	0.80- 2.40	CH3	R6R6R6R5(C*-CH*/CH2)		CDCL3
2130M	D	1.20	CH3	R6R6R6R5(C*-CH*/CH2)		CDCL3
1771M	A	0.70- 1.15	CH3	R6<CH-CH2/CH2>		CDCL3
1768M	A	0.89	CH3	R6<CH-CH2/CH2>		CDCL3
1681M	A	0.92	CH3	R6<CH-CH2/CH2>		CCL4
471M	A	0.92 APP.	CH3	R6<CH-CH2/CH2>		CDCL3
1769M	A	0.93	CH3	R6<CH-CH2/CH2>		CDCL3
2027M	A	1.07	CH3	R6<CH-CH2/CH2>		CCL4
1771M	A	0.70- 1.15	CH3	R6<CH-CH(OH)/CH2>		CDCL3
1767M	A	1.03	CH3	R6<CH-CH(OH)/CH2>		CDCL3
107M	A	1.03	CH3	R6<CH-C(=CH2)/CH2>		CCL4
2001M	A	0.94	CH3	R6<CH-C(=0)/CH2>		CCL4
2029M	A	1.11	CH3	R6<C(CH3)-CH2/CH2>		CCL4
1809M	A	1.21	CH3	R6<C(OH)-CH2/CH2>		CDCL3
2027M	B	1.97	CH3	R6<C=CH/CH2>		CCL4
2030M	A	2.08	CH3	R6<C=CH/C(=0)>		CDCL3
104M	B	1.56	CH3	R6<C=C(CH3)/CH2>		CCL4
2032M	A	2.01	CH3	R6<C=C(CH3)/C(=0)>		CDCL3
2028M	A	1.85	CH3	R6<C=C(CL)/C(=0)>		CCL4
1772M	A	0.80	CH3	R6(CH-CH2/CH2)		CDCL3
46M	A	0.90	CH3	R6(CH-CH2/CH2)		CCL4
366M	A	0.91	CH3	R6(CH-CH2/CH2)		CCL4
2005M	A	0.99 APP.	CH3	R6(CH-CH2/CH2)		CDCL3
2002M	A	1.02	CH3	R6(CH-CH2/CH2)		CCL4
2003M	A	1.02	CH3	R6(CH-CH2/CH2)		CCL4
2144M	A	1.09	CH3	R6(C(CH3)-CH2/CH2)		CDCL3

BOOK NO.	ASSIGN-MENT	CHEM SHIFT - ppm -	PROTON GROUP	ENVIRONMENTAL GROUPS	S	SOLVENT
111M	B	1.71	CH3	R6(C=CH/CH2)		CCL4
1808M	C	1.61	CH3	R6(C=CH/CH2)		CCL4
1811M	A	1.16	CH3	R7<C(OH)-CH2/CH2>		CCL4
1605M	A	0.08	CH3	R8OOOOSISISISI<SI(CH3)-O/O>		CCL4
1199M	B	2.07	CH3	SH		CDCL3
1089M	A	0.29	CH3	SI(A/CH3/CH3)		CDCL3
1087M	A	0.01	CH3	SI(CH2/CH2/CH3)		CL2C=CCL2
1086M	A	0.03	CH3	SI(CH2/CH3/CH3)		CCL4
1092M	A	1.17	CH3	SI(CL/CL/CL)		CCL4
1092M	A	1.17	CH3	SI(CL/CL/CL)		CCL4
1093M	A	0.04	CH3	SI(NH/CH3/CH3)		CCL4
1604M	A	0.23	CH3	SI(O/CH2/CH3)		CDCL3
1603M	A	0.04	CH3	SI(O/CH3/CH3)		CCL4
1593M	A	0.08	CH3	SI(O/CH3/CH3)		CCL4
1595M	A	0.13	CH3	SI(O/O/O)		CDCL3
1094M	A	0.04	CH3	SI(SI/CH3/CH3)		CCL4
1257M	A	2.87	CH3	SO2-CH2		CDCL3
1252M	A	3.11	CH3	SO2-CH3		D2O
1373M	A	2.78	CH3	SO2-N	S	CDCL3
1359M	A	3.03	CH3	SO2-NH2		POLYSOL-D
1320M	A	3.07	CH3	SO3-A		CDCL3
1317M	C	2.97	CH3	SO3-CH2		CDCL3
1316M	C	3.85	CH3	SO3-CH2		CCL4
1315M	C	3.00	CH3	SO3-CH2.3		CDCL3
1249M	A	2.70	CH3	SO-A		CDCL3
1243M	A	2.52	CH3	S(=O)-CH3		CCL4
1161M	A	2.29	CH3	S-A		CCL4
1160M	A	2.45	CH3	S-A		CDCL3
2074M	A	2.52	CH3	S-A		POLYSOL-D
1923M	B	2.38	CH3	S-A		CDCL3
1158M	A	1.90	CH3	S-CH2		CCL4
1127M	B	2.00	CH3	S-CH2		CCL4
1107M	B	2.04	CH3	S-CH2		CCL4
1116M	C	2.01	CH3	S-CH2.11		CCL4
2627M	A	1.94 APP.	CH3	S-CH2.2		POLYSOL-D
1121M	B	2.10	CH3	S-CH2.3		D2O
1007M	A	2.61	CH3	S-C:N		CCL4
1192M	A	2.36	CH3	S-S		CCL4
2278M	B	1.31	CH3.X	CH2.3		CDCL3
1449M	D	2.89	CH*	R30R6R4BI<O-C*(CH3)/CH2-CH*>		CCL4
1448M	C	2.94	CH*	R6R30BI<O-CH*/CH2-CH2>		CCL4
935M	B	2.02	CH*	R6R6R6TRI<CH2-C*(QN(=S))/CH2-CH*/CH2-CH*>		CDCL3
1453M	D	4.01	CH*R	R30R5A<O-CH*/C*>		CCL4
1453M	C	3.87	CH*R	R30R5A<O-CH*/HCH-C*>		CCL4
1452M	B	2.84 APP.	CH*R	R30R8R30(O-CH*/CH2-CH2)		CCL4
1353M	B	2.31 APP.	CH*R	R5R5BI<CH2-CH*/CH2-CH(NH-C(=S))/CH2-CH2>		POLYSOL-D
1353M	B	2.31 APP.	CH*R	R5R5BI<CH(NH-C(=S))-CH2/CH2-CH*/CH2-CH2>		POLYSOL-D
2008M	E	2.61	CH*R	R5R5BI<C(=O)-CH2/C(CH3/CH3)-C*/CH2-C(=O)>		CDCL3
2132M	D	2.60	CH*R	R5R5BI<C(=O)-C(=O)/C(CH3/CH3)-C*(CH3)/CH2-CH2>		POLYSOL-D
2262M	E	2.84	CH*R	R5R50BI<C(=O)-O/C(CH3/CH3)-C*/CH2-CH2>		CDCL3
569M	C	2.09	CH*R	R6NR6(CH2-CH2/CH2-CH2)		CDCL3
569M	D	2.40- 3.27	CH*R	R6NR6(NH-CH2/CH2-CH2)		CDCL3
2268M	B	3.48 APP.	CH*R	R6R50<C(=O)-O/CH2-CH=>		CDCL3
2261M	B	3.22	CH*R	R6R50(C(=O)-O/CH2-CH2)		CDCL3
773M	B	2.29	CH*R	R6R6BI(CH2-CH*/CH2-CH(NH2)/CH2-CH2)	S	D2O
773M	C	2.56	CH*R	R6R6BI(CH(NH2)-CH2/CH2-CH*/CH2-CH2)	S	D2O
473M	D	1.97	CH*R	R6R6R6TRI<CH2-C*(CH2-NH2)/CH2-CH*/CH2-CH*>		CDCL3
1684M	C	1.93	CH*R	R6R6R6TRI<CH2-C*(CH2-OH)/CH2-CH*/CH2-CH*>		POLYSOL-D
268M	B	2.16 APP.	CH*R	R6R6R6TRI<CH2-C*(CL)/CH2-CH*/CH2-CH*>		CDCL3
2012M	B	2.54	CH*R	R6R6R6TRI<C(=O)-CH*/CH2-CH*/CH2-CH*>		CDCL3
2359M	B	2.02	CH*R	R6R6R6TRI(CH2-C*(C(=O)-N)/CH2-CH*/CH2-CH*)		CDCL3
813M	C	2.22	CH*R	R6R6R6TRI(CH2-C*(N(CH3/CH3))/CH2-CH*/CH2-CH*)	S	D2O
835M	C	2.29	CH*R	R6R6R6TRI(CH2-C*(N(+)(CH3/CH3/CH3))/CH2-CH*/CH2-CH*)	S	D2O
1450M	C	2.91	CH*R	R7R30<O-CH*/CH2-CH2>		CCL4
1451M	B	2.78 APP.	CH*R	R8R30<O-CH*/CH2-CH2>		CDCL3
2859M	B	4.53	CH=	=P(A/A/A)/C(=O)-O-CH3		TFA
834M	C	3.88	CH:	:C-CH2		POLYSOL-D
588M	B	2.33	CH:	:C-C(NH/CH3/CH3)		CDCL3
1935M	B	5.81	DH	A(C-C(BR)-CH=C(C(A/CH3/CH3))/C(BR))		CDCL3
769M	B	3.79	H	BH2		CDCL3
790M	C	10.31	H	CL	S	POLYSOL-D
781M	D	6.00	H	CL	S	POLYSOL-D
768M	D	8.07	H	CL	S	CDCL3
783M	D	8.29	H	CL	S	POLYSOL-D
810M	E	11.51	H	CL		CDCL3
785M	E	5.40- 7.00	H	CL	S	TFA
1526M	F	9.80	H	CL	S	POLYSOL-D
2169M	B	9.97	H	C(=O)-A		CDCL3
2163M	C	9.94	H	C(=O)-A		CCL4
2172M	C	10.18	H	C(=O)-A		CDCL3
2168M	C	10.30	H	C(=O)-A		CCL4

BOOK NO.	ASSIGN-MENT	CHEM SHIFT - ppm -	PROTON GROUP	ENVIRONMENTAL GROUPS	S	SOLVENT
2166M	C	10.48	H	C(=O)-A		CCL4
2170M	D	9.66	H	C(=O)-A		CDCL3
2165M	D	9.91	H	C(=O)-A		CCL4
2177M	D	9.95	H	C(=O)-A		CCL4
2167M	D	10.00	H	C(=O)-A		CDCL3
2164M	D	10.22	H	C(=O)-A		CCL4
2176M	D	10.35	H	C(=O)-A		CDCL3
2171M	E	10.19	H	C(=O)-A		CDCL3
2173M	F	9.78	H	C(=O)-A		CCL4
2178M	F	10.50	H	C(=O)-A		CCL4
2174M	G	9.80	H	C(=O)-A		CCL4
2175M	G	9.82	H	C(=O)-A		CCL4
2181M	C	10.39	H	C(=O)-AAAA		CDCL3
2183M	E	10.23	H	C(=O)-ANA		CDCL3
2179M	F	9.82	H	C(=O)-AR5		CCL4
2180M	D	9.93	H	C(=O)-AR5A		CDCL3
2186M	E	9.72	H	C(=O)-AR500		CDCL3
2152M	C	9.58	H	C(=O)-CH		CCL4
2154M	D	9.73	H	C(=O)-CH2		CDCL3
2153M	E	9.72	H	C(=O)-CH2		CCL4
2151M	D	9.68	H	C(=O)-CH2.2		CCL4
2159M	D	9.71	H	C(=O)-CH2.2		CDCL3
2361M	D	8.30	H	C(=O)-N		CDCL3
2347M	E	8.08	H	C(=O)-N		CDCL3
2362M	F	8.27	H	C(=O)-N		CDCL3
2295M	C	8.02	H	C(=O)-NH		D20
2300M	C	8.38	H	C(=O)-NH		TFA
2308M	E	7.95	H	C(=O)-NH		DMSO-D6
2471M	A	8.22	H	C(=O)-OH		D20
2647M	A	8.48	H	C(=O)-O-CA		D20
2831M	D	7.90	H	C(=O)-O-CH2	S	D20
2692M	D	7.91	H	C(=O)-O-CH2		CCL4
2693M	D	7.96	H	C(=O)-O-CH2		CCL4
2691M	D	8.07	H	C(=O)-O-CH2		CDCL3
2648M	A	8.46	H	C(=O)-O-LI		D20
2160M	D	9.57	H	C(=O)-Q1		CCL4
2157M	F	9.33	H	C(=O)-Q1		CCL4
2161M	F	9.47	H	C(=O)-Q1		CCL4
2162M	E	9.76	H	C(=O)-Q2		DMSO-D6
2156M	F	9.53	H	C(=O)-Q2		CDCL3
2182M	D	9.48	H	C(=O)-R5N		CDCL3
2185M	B	9.87	H	C(=O)-R50		CDCL3
2155M	B	9.66	H	C(=O)-R6		CDCL3
2158M	C	9.64	H	C(=O)-R6		CCL4
2371M	E	8.81	H	C(=O)-R6NA		CDCL3
1336M	C	9.19	H	C(=S)-N		CDCL3
839M	D	3.05	H	OH		CDCL3
829M	E	3.57	H	OH	S	CDCL3
1965M	D	5.99 APP.	H	P(=O/O/O)	S	CDCL3
848M	E	6.44	H	QN(OH/CH)		CDCL3
848M	F	7.23	H	QN(OH/CH)		CCL4
1083M	C	3.52	H	SIH2-CH2.5		CCL4
1084M	A	4.92	H	SI(A/A/H)		CDCL3
1291M	B	7.15 APP.	H	S03-A		CDCL3
1287M	C	10.70	H	S03-CH2		DMSO-D6
378M	A	3.89 APP.	HCH	BR/CH(BR/A)		CDCL3
378M	B	4.09 APP.	HCH	BR/CH(BR/A)		CDCL3
357M	C	3.60	HCH	BR/CH(BR/CH2)		CDCL3
357M	D	3.81	HCH	BR/CH(BR/CH2)		CDCL3
353M	B	3.48	HCH	BR/CH(BR/CH3)		CCL4
353M	B	3.80	HCH	BR/CH(BR/CH3)		CCL4
353M	C	3.48	HCH	BR/CH(BR/CH3)		CCL4
353M	C	3.80	HCH	BR/CH(BR/CH3)		CCL4
356M	A	3.80	HCH	BR/CH(BR/HCH)		CCL4
356M	A	3.90	HCH	BR/CH(BR/HCH)		CCL4
356M	B	3.80	HCH	BR/CH(BR/HCH)		CCL4
356M	B	3.90	HCH	BR/CH(BR/HCH)		CCL4
2286M	B	1.75 APP.	HCH	CH(C(=O)/A)/CH3		CCL4
2286M	B	2.07 APP.	HCH	CH(C(=O)/A)/CH3		CCL4
2286M	C	1.75 APP.	HCH	CH(C(=O)/A)/CH3		CCL4
2286M	C	2.07 APP.	HCH	CH(C(=O)/A)/CH3		CCL4
1833M	B	1.48	HCH	CH(OH/CH3)/HCH-CH		CCL4
1833M	B	1.55	HCH	CH(OH/CH3)/HCH-CH		CCL4
1833M	C	1.48	HCH	CH(OH/CH3)/HCH-CH		CCL4
1833M	C	1.55	HCH	CH(OH/CH3)/HCH-CH		CCL4
2726M	A	3.50- 4.15	HCH	CL/CH(CL/C(=O)-O)		CCL4
275M	A	3.61	HCH	CL/CH(CL/Q3)		CCL4
275M	A	3.78	HCH	CL/CH(CL/Q3)		CCL4
275M	B	3.61	HCH	CL/CH(CL/Q3)		CCL4
275M	B	3.78	HCH	CL/CH(CL/Q3)		CCL4
1214M	C	3.71	HCH	CL/CH(SH/HCH)		CCL4

BOOK NO.	ASSIGN-MENT	CHEM SHIFT - ppm -	PROTON GROUP	ENVIRONMENTAL GROUPS	S	SOLVENT
1214M	D	3.92	HCH	CL/CH(SH/HCH)		CCL4
1443M	D	3.48	HCH	CL/R30		CCL4
1443M	D	3.56	HCH	CL/R30		CCL4
1443M	E	3.48	HCH	CL/R30		CCL4
1443M	E	3.56	HCH	CL/R30		CCL4
1831M	D	1.41	HCH	C(OH/CH3/CH3)/CH(OH/CH3)		CCL4
1831M	E	1.55	HCH	C(OH/CH3/CH3)/CH(OH/CH3)		CCL4
1759M	D	1.39- 2.11	HCH	C(O/CH3/CH3)/CH(OH/CH3)		CCL4
2631M	A	2.83	HCH	C(=O)-NH2/CH(NH2/C(=O)-OH)		D2O
2631M	B	2.97	HCH	C(=O)-NH2/CH(NH2/C(=O)-OH)		D2O
2630M	A	2.84 APP.	HCH	C(=O)-NH2/CH(NH2/C(=O)-OH)>		D2O
2630M	B	2.95 APP.	HCH	C(=O)-NH2/CH(NH2/C(=O)-OH)>		D2O
2505M	A	2.83	HCH	C(=O)-OH/CH(CL/HCH)		D2O
2505M	B	3.08	HCH	C(=O)-OH/CH(CL/HCH)		D2O
2511M	A	2.90	HCH	C(=O)-OH/C(OH/C(=O)-O/HCH)		D2O
2511M	B	3.08	HCH	C(=O)-OH/C(OH/C(=O)-O/HCH)		D2O
2667M	A	2.44	HCH	C(=O)-O-K/C(OH/C(=O)-O-K/HCH)	S	D2O
2667M	A	2.70	HCH	C(=O)-O-K/C(OH/C(=O)-O-K/HCH)	S	D2O
2667M	B	2.44	HCH	C(=O)-O-K/C(OH/C(=O)-O-K/HCH)	S	D2O
2667M	B	2.70	HCH	C(=O)-O-K/C(OH/C(=O)-O-K/HCH)	S	D2O
1752M	A	2.50	HCH	NH2/CH(OH/HCH)		D2O
1752M	B	2.62	HCH	NH2/CH(OH/HCH)		D2O
1755M	D	2.18	HCH	N(CH2/CH2)/CH(OH/CH3)		CCL4
1755M	E	2.28	HCH	N(CH2/CH2)/CH(OH/CH3)		CCL4
1617M	D	3.40	HCH	OH/CH(CH2/CH3)		CCL4
1617M	D	3.52	HCH	OH/CH(CH2/CH3)		CCL4
1617M	E	3.40	HCH	OH/CH(CH2/CH3)		CCL4
1617M	E	3.52	HCH	OH/CH(CH2/CH3)		CCL4
1644M	E	3.28	HCH	OH/CH(NH2/CH2)		CDCL3
1644M	F	3.62	HCH	OH/CH(NH2/CH)		CDCL3
1648M	D	3.46	HCH	OH/CH(N/CH3)		D2O
1648M	E	3.62	HCH	OH/CH(N/CH3)		D2O
1828M	B	3.37	HCH	OH/CH(OH/CH3)		CDCL3
1828M	C	3.50	HCH	OH/CH(OH/CH3)		CDCL3
2625M	B	3.63	HCH	OH/C(NH2/C(=O)-OH/CH3)		D2O
2625M	C	3.91	HCH	OH/C(NH2/C(=O)-OH/CH3)		D2O
1677M	D	3.49	HCH	OH/R30<CH-O/HCH>		D2O
1677M	E	3.92	HCH	OH/R30<CH-O/HCH>		D2O
1425M	B	3.42	HCH	O-CH/CH3		CCL4
1423M	C	3.36	HCH	O-CH/CH3		CCL4
1425M	C	3.50	HCH	O-CH/CH3		CCL4
1423M	D	3.52	HCH	O-CH/CH3		CCL4
2761M	E	4.15	HCH	O-C(=O)-CH2.16/CH(O-C(=O)/HCH)		CDCL3
2761M	F	4.29	HCH	O-C(=O)-CH2.16/CH(O-C(=O)/HCH)		CDCL3
2760M	E	4.10	HCH	O-C(=O)-CH2/CH(O-C(=O)/HCH)		CCL4
2760M	F	4.23	HCH	O-C(=O)-CH2/CH(O-C(=O)/HCH)		CCL4
2754M	C	4.00	HCH	O-C(=O)-CH3/CH(O-C(=O)/CH3)		CCL4
2754M	D	4.13	HCH	O-C(=O)-CH3/CH(O-C(=O)/CH3)		CCL4
2394M	C	3.81	HCH	R5NA(N-C(=O)/C(=O))/R30(CH-O/CH2)		CDCL3
2394M	D	3.94	HCH	R5NA(N-C(=O)/C(=O))/R30(CH-O/CH2)		CDCL3
115M	A	1.27	HCH	R5R5BIR5<CH*(CH*/CH=)/CH*(CH*/CH)>		CCL4
115M	A	1.50	HCH	R5R5BIR5<CH*(CH*/CH=)/CH*(CH*/CH)>		CCL4
115M	B	1.27	HCH	R5R5BIR5<CH*(CH*/CH=)/CH*(CH*/CH)>		CCL4
115M	B	1.50	HCH	R5R5BIR5<CH*(CH*/CH=)/CH*(CH*/CH)>		CCL4
2207M	D	2.81	HCH	SO3H/R5R5BI(C*(C(=O)/C/CH2))		D2O
2207M	E	3.27	HCH	SO3H/R5R5BI(C*(C(=O)/C/CH2))		D2O
2007M	D	2.80	HCH	SO3-NA/R5R5BI<C*-C(=O)/C(CH3/CH3)/CH2>		D2O
2007M	E	3.27	HCH	SO3-NA/R5R5BI<C*-C(=O)/C(CH3/CH3)/CH2>		D2O
2258M	B	5.94	HCH	=R50<C-C(=O)/CH2-C(=O)>		CDCL3
2258M	B	6.53	HCH	=R50<C-C(=O)/CH2-C(=O)>		CDCL3
2258M	C	5.94	HCH	=R50<C-C(=O)/CH2-C(=O)>		CDCL3
2258M	C	6.53	HCH	=R50<C-C(=O)/CH2-C(=O)>		CDCL3
1440M	C	2.29	HCHR	R30<O-CH(CH2.5-CH3)>		CCL4
1440M	D	2.56	HCHR	R30<O-CH(CH2.5-CH3)>		CCL4
1441M	C	2.29	HCHR	R30<O-CH(CH2.7-CH3)>		CCL4
1441M	D	2.54	HCHR	R30<O-CH(CH2.7-CH3)>		CCL4
1444M	A	2.58	HCHR	R30<O-CH(CH2-BR)>		CCL4
1444M	B	2.84	HCHR	R30<O-CH(CH2-BR)>		CCL4
1439M	C	2.31	HCHR	R30<O-CH(CH2-CH3)>		CCL4
1439M	D	2.55	HCHR	R30<O-CH(CH2-CH3)>		CCL4
1445M	B	2.46	HCHR	R30<O-CH(CH2-O)>		CCL4
1445M	D	2.98	HCHR	R30<O-CH(CH2-O)>		CCL4
1677M	A	2.79	HCHR	R30<O-CH(HCH-OH)>		D2O
1677M	B	2.91	HCHR	R30<O-CH(HCH-OH)>		D2O
1446M	A	2.60	HCHR	R30<O-CH(Q3)>		CDCL3
1446M	B	2.90	HCHR	R30<O-CH(Q3)>		CDCL3
1447M	B	2.96	HCHR	R30(O-CH(A))		CCL4
1442M	C	2.28	HCHR	R30(O-CH(CH2-CH2))		CCL4
1442M	D	2.56	HCHR	R30(O-CH(CH2-CH2))		CCL4
1443M	A	2.58	HCHR	R30(O-CH(HCH-CL))		CCL4
1443M	A	2.79	HCHR	R30(O-CH(HCH-CL))		CCL4

BOOK NO.	ASSIGN-MENT	CHEM SHIFT - ppm -	PROTON GROUP	ENVIRONMENTAL GROUPS	S	SOLVENT
1443M	B	2.58	HCHR	R30(O-CH(HCH-CL))		CCL4
1443M	B	2.79	HCHR	R30(O-CH(HCH-CL))		CCL4
1447M	A	2.61	HCHR	R30(O-CH(A))		CCL4
1438M	B	2.23	HCHR	R30(O-CH(CH3))		CCL4
1438M	C	2.59	HCHR	R30(O-CH(CH3))		CCL4
41M	A	0.03	HCHR	R3<CH(CH2-R3)-HCH>		CCL4
41M	B	0.41	HCHR	R3<CH(CH2-R3)-HCH>		CCL4
39M	A	0.11	HCHR	R3<CH(CH3)-CH(CH3)>		CCL4
39M	B	0.75	HCHR	R3<CH(CH3)-CH(CH3)>		CCL4
38M	A	0.02	HCHR	R3<CH(CH(CH3/CH3))-HCH>		CCL4
38M	B	0.31	HCHR	R3<CH(CH(CH3/CH3))-HCH>		CCL4
40M	A	0.05	HCHR	R3<C(CH3/CH3)-CH(CH3)>		CCL4
40M	B	0.33- 0.97	HCHR	R3<C(CH3/CH3)-CH(CH3)>		CCL4
2412M	A	2.39	HCHR	R5NN<C(=O)-NH/CH(A)-NH>		DMSO-D6
2412M	A	2.79	HCHR	R5NN<C(=O)-NH/CH(A)-NH>		DMSO-D6
2412M	B	2.39	HCHR	R5NN<C(=O)-NH/CH(A)-NH>		DMSO-D6
2412M	B	2.79	HCHR	R5NN<C(=O)-NH/CH(A)-NH>		DMSO-D6
2376M	B	2.38	HCHR	R5N<C(=O)-NH/CH(CH3)-C(=O)>		CDCL3
2376M	C	2.60- 3.30	HCHR	R5N<C(=O)-NH/CH(CH3)-C(=O)>		CDCL3
2950M	A	1.92- 3.02	HCHR	R50<CH(C(=O)-CH3)-C(=O)/CH2-O>		CCL4
2951M	A	2.58	HCHR	R50<C(=O)-O/CH(A)-HCH>		CDCL3
2951M	A	2.80	HCHR	R50<C(=O)-O/CH(A)-HCH>		CDCL3
2951M	B	2.58	HCHR	R50<C(=O)-O/CH(A)-HCH>		CDCL3
2951M	B	2.80	HCHR	R50<C(=O)-O/CH(A)-HCH>		CDCL3
2951M	D	4.16	HCHR	R50<O-C(=O)/CH(A)-HCH>		CDCL3
2951M	D	4.58	HCHR	R50<O-C(=O)/CH(A)-HCH>		CDCL3
2951M	E	4.16	HCHR	R50<O-C(=O)/CH(A)-HCH>		CDCL3
2951M	E	4.58	HCHR	R50<O-C(=O)/CH(A)-HCH>		CDCL3
1453M	A	2.71	HCHR	R5R30A<C*/CH*(O/CH*)>		CCL4
1453M	B	3.09	HCHR	R5R30A<C*/CH*(O/CH*)>		CCL4
602M	B	1.20- 2.15	HCHR	R6NA<CH(CH3)-NH/HCH-C*>		CDCL3
602M	C	2.40- 2.90	HCHR	R6NA<C*/HCH-CH(CH3)>		CDCL3
568M	C	2.08- 3.09	HCHR	R6NN(NH-HCH/CH(CH3)-NH)		CDCL3
563M	D	2.49	HCHR	R6N<NH-HCH/CH2-CH(CH3)>		CCL4
563M	E	2.96	HCHR	R6N<NH-HCH/CH2-CH(CH3)>		CCL4
1476M	C	3.09- 3.82	HCHR	R600R600SPI<C*(HCH/CH2)-CH2/O-CH(CH2-CH3)>		CCL4
1476M	E	4.55	HCHR	R600R600SPI<C*(HCH/CH2)-CH2/O-CH(CH2-CH3)>		CCL4
1475M	B	3.19- 3.69	HCHR	R600R600SPI<O-CH(CH3)/C*(HCH/CH2)-CH2>		CDCL3
1475M	C	4.52	HCHR	R600R600SPI<O-CH(CH3)/C*(HCH/CH2)-CH2>		CDCL3
1472M	E	3.28	HCHR	R600<O-CH(CH2.5-CH3)/C(CH3/CH3)>		CCL4
1472M	F	3.51	HCHR	R600<O-CH(CH2.5-CH3)/C(CH3/CH3)>		CCL4
1781M	B	2.63 APP.	HCHR	R6S(S-HCH/CH2-CH2)		CDCL3
1781M	B	2.63 APP.	HCHR	R6S(S-HCH/CH(OH)-CH2)		CDCL3
2004M	B	1.20- 1.85	HCHR	R6<CH(C(CH3/CH3/CH3))-HCH/CH2-C(=O)>		CDCL3
2004M	C	1.85- 2.60	HCHR	R6<CH(C(CH3/CH3/CH3))-HCH/CH2-C(=O)>		CDCL3
1774M	C	1.90- 2.70	HCHR	R6<CH(OH)-CH(A)/CH2-CH2>		CDCL3
1767M	C	1.86	HCHR	R6<CH(OH)-CH(CH3)/CH2-CH2>		CDCL3
2286M	E	5.86	HNH	C(=O)-CH		CCL4
2286M	E	6.45	HNH	C(=O)-CH		CCL4
2286M	F	5.86	HNH	C(=O)-CH		CCL4
2286M	F	6.45	HNH	C(=O)-CH		CCL4
2277M	D	6.65 APP.	HNH	C(=O)-CH2		DMSO-D6
2277M	E	7.15 APP.	HNH	C(=O)-CH2		DMSO-D6
1333M	C	9.32	HNH	C(=S)-A		POLYSOL-D
1333M	D	9.65	HNH	C(=S)-A		POLYSOL-D
600M	C	3.95	NH	AA<C-C*>/CH2-CH3		CCL4
599M	B	4.03	NH	AA(C-C*)		CDCL3
604M	A	5.61	NH	AA/A		CCL4
709M	B	6.23	NH	AN<C-CH-N>/CH2-A		DMSO-D6
708M	D	3.69	NH	AN<C-N>/CH2-CH2		CDCL3
596M	B	3.48	NH	A<C-CH-CH-C(CH3)>/CH2-A		CCL4
592M	D	3.36	NH	A<C-CH-CH-C(CH(CH3/CH3))>/CH3		CDCL3
598M	D	2.63	NH	A<C-CH-CH-C(NH-CH)>/CH(CH2/CH3)>		CDCL3
1523M	C	4.47	NH	A<C-CH-CH-C(O-CH3)>/CH3		POLYSOL-D
590M	C	3.39	NH	A<C-CH-C(CH3)>/CH3		CDCL3
595M	B	3.62	NH	A<C-C(CH3)>/CH2-A		CDCL3
1966M	F	6.65	NH	A<C-C(CH3)-CH-C(CH3)>/CH2-R5NN		CDCL3
1062M	F	7.84	NH	A<C-C(NO2)>/CH2-CH3		CCL4
593M	D	3.20	NH	A(C-CH-CH-C(CH3))/CH2-CH3		CDCL3
591M	C	3.29	NH	A(C-CH-CH-C(CH3))/CH3		CDCL3
589M	C	3.39	NH	A(C-C(CH3))/CH3		CDCL3
1306M	E	9.24	NH	A(C-C(SO3NA)-CH-C(NO2))/A	S	DMSO
597M	A	5.42	NH	A/A		CDCL3
807M	C	10.26	NH	A/A	S	DMSO
585M	D	3.35	NH	A/CH2.2-CH		CDCL3
594M	A	3.78	NH	A/CH2-A		CDCL3
584M	D	3.31	NH	A/CH2-CH2		CCL4
583M	C	3.23	NH	A/CH2-CH3		CCL4
2634M	C	6.81 APP.	NH	A/CH2-C(=O)-O		DMSO-D6
587M	A	3.59	NH	A/CH2-Q3		CDCL3
582M	B	3.34	NH	A/CH3		CCL4

BOOK NO.	ASSIGN-MENT	CHEM SHIFT - ppm -	PROTON GROUP	ENVIRONMENTAL GROUPS	S	SOLVENT
588M	C	3.41	NH	A/C(C:CH/CH3/CH3)		CDCL3
586M	C	3.38	NH	A/R6		CDCL3
554M	C	1.59	NH	CH2.12-CH3/CH2.12-CH3		CDCL3
555M	B	1.23	NH	CH2.2-NH/CH2-CH3		CDCL3
1215M	C	1.61	NH	CH2.2-SH/CH2.3-CH3		CDCL3
1216M	C	1.42	NH	CH2.2-SH/CH2.9-CH3		CDCL3
548M	B	1.00- 1.90	NH	CH2.4-CH3/CH2.4-CH3		CDCL3
581M	A	1.32	NH	CH2-A/CH2-A		CCL4
805M	C	7.60 APP.	NH	CH2-A/CH2-A	S	TFA
578M	B	1.00	NH	CH2-A/CH2-CH2		CCL4
577M	A	0.91	NH	CH2-A/CH2-CH3		CCL4
553M	A	0.66	NH	CH2-CH2/CH2-CH2		CCL4
466M	A	1.18	NH	CH2-CH2/CH2-CH2		CDCL3
1218M	A	1.58	NH	CH2-CH2/CH2-CH2		CDCL3
960M	A	1.80	NH	CH2-CH2/CH2-CH2		CDCL3
551M	C	1.59	NH	CH2-CH2/CH2-CH2		CDCL3
549M	C	1.68	NH	CH2-CH2/CH2-CH2		CCL4
550M	C	1.79	NH	CH2-CH2/CH2-CH2		CDCL3
552M	C	1.49	NH	CH2-CH2/CH3		CDCL3
797M	C	9.35	NH	CH2-CH3/CH2-CH3	S	CDCL3
546M	A	0.79	NH	CH2-CH/CH2-CH		CCL4
2789M	B	2.07	NH	CH2-C(=O)-O/CH2-C(=O)-O		CCL4
573M	A	1.34	NH	CH2-Q1/CH2-Q1		CDCL3
574M	A	0.86	NH	CH2-Q2/CH2-CH3		CCL4
572M	A	1.39	NH	CH2-Q2/CH2-Q2		CDCL3
571M	A	1.56	NH	CH2-Q3		CDCL3
557M	D	2.58	NH	CH(CH2/CH3)/CH2-CH2		CDCL3
804M	F	9.21	NH	CH(CH2/CH3)/CH3	S	CDCL3
1647M	D	3.19	NH	CH(CH3/CH3)/CH2.2-OH		CCL4
543M	A	0.67	NH	CH(CH3/CH3)/CH(CH3/CH3)		CCL4
547M	A	0.74	NH	C(CH3/CH3/CH3)/CH2-CH2		CDCL3
2346M	D	7.29	NH	C(=O)-AN/CH2-A		CDCL3
2343M	D	10.21	NH	C(=O)-A/A		DMSO
2345M	E	8.04	NH	C(=O)-A/A(C-CH-CH-C(CH3))		CDCL3
2344M	D	7.89 APP.	NH	C(=O)-A/A(C-C(CH3))		CDCL3
2851M	C	7.06	NH	C(=O)-A/CH2-C(=O)-O		CDCL3
2311M	D	7.40	NH	C(=O)-CF3/CH2-CH2		CDCL3
2320M	D	9.93	NH	C(=O)-CH2/A		DMSO-D6
2318M	D	10.27	NH	C(=O)-CH2/A		DMSO-D6
2315M	E	8.38	NH	C(=O)-CH2/A		CDCL3
2316M	F	8.45	NH	C(=O)-CH2/A		CDCL3
2319M	F	10.05	NH	C(=O)-CH2/A		DMSO-D6
2314M	C	5.95	NH	C(=O)-CH2/CH2-A		CDCL3
2313M	D	6.96 APP.	NH	C(=O)-CH2/CH2-A		CDCL3
2299M	F	6.80	NH	C(=O)-CH2/CH2-CH2		CDCL3
2312M	C	6.62	NH	C(=O)-CH2/CH3		CDCL3
2296M	D	6.76	NH	C(=O)-CH2/CH3		CDCL3
2298M	F	6.23	NH	C(=O)-CH2/CH3		CDCL3
2302M	E	5.64	NH	C(=O)-CH2/C(CH2/CH3/CH3)		CDCL3
2340M	E	8.24	NH	C(=O)-CH3/AA(C-CH-C*)		CDCL3
2341M	E	9.94	NH	C(=O)-CH3/AN<C-N>		CDCL3
2331M	D	10.04	NH	C(=O)-CH3/A<C-CH-CH-C(BR)>		DMSO-D6
2327M	D	7.45 APP.	NH	C(=O)-CH3/A<C-CH-CH-C(F)>		CDCL3
2336M	E	9.21	NH	C(=O)-CH3/A<C-CH-CH-C(OH)>		POLYSOL-D
2211M	F	9.71	NH	C(=O)-CH3/A<C-CH-CH-C(O-CH2)>		DMSO-D6
2337M	E	9.71	NH	C(=O)-CH3/A<C-CH-CH-C(O-CH3)>		DMSO-D6
2329M	D	8.74	NH	C(=O)-CH3/A<C-CH-C(CL)>		CDCL3
2326M	E	8.50	NH	C(=O)-CH3/A<C-CH-C(F)>		CDCL3
2339M	G	7.62	NH	C(=O)-CH3/A<C-C(CH3)/CH-C(CH3)>		CDCL3
2328M	C	7.83	NH	C(=O)-CH3/A<C-C(CL)>		CDCL3
2333M	F	10.27	NH	C(=O)-CH3/A<C-C(NO2)>		CDCL3
2334M	E	9.37	NH	C(=O)-CH3/A<C-C(OH)>		DMSO-D6
2334M	E	9.75	NH	C(=O)-CH3/A<C-C(OH)>		DMSO-D6
2323M	E	9.74	NH	C(=O)-CH3/A(C-CH-CH-C(CH3))		DMSO-D6
2330M	D	10.03	NH	C(=O)-CH3/A(C-CH-CH-C(CL))		DMSO-D6
2325M	E	7.80	NH	C(=O)-CH3/A(C-CH-CH-C(C(CH3/CH3/CH3)))		CDCL3
2327M	D	7.45 APP.	NH	C(=O)-CH3/A(C-CH-CH-C(F))		CDCL3
2322M	G	8.72	NH	C(=O)-CH3/A(C-CH-C(CH3))		CDCL3
2335M	E	9.43	NH	C(=O)-CH3/A(C-CH-C(OH))		DMSO-D6
2321M	D	7.43	NH	C(=O)-CH3/A(C-C(CH3))		CDCL3
2338M	G	7.96	NH	C(=O)-CH3/A(C-C(CH3)-CH-C(CH3))		CDCL3
2309M	D	6.58	NH	C(=O)-CH3/CH2.2-A		CDCL3
2301M	C	7.36	NH	C(=O)-CH3/CH2.2-NH		POLYSOL-D
2310M	D	6.68	NH	C(=O)-CH3/CH(A/CH3)		CDCL3
2627M	E	8.06	NH	C(=O)-CH3/CH(C(=O)-OH/CH2.2)		POLYSOL-D
2621M	E	7.91	NH	C(=O)-CH3/CH(C(=O)-OH/CH2)		POLYSOL-D
2620M	E	7.93	NH	C(=O)-CH3/CH(C(=O)-O/CH)		DMSO-D6
2317M	F	9.58	NH	C(=O)-CH/A		POLYSOL-D
2300M	B	8.10	NH	C(=O)-H/CH2-NH		TFA
2307M	D	7.65	NH	C(=O)-H/CH(A/CH3)		CCL4
2308M	D	6.70- 7.80	NH	C(=O)-H/CH(CH2/CH2)		DMSO-D6

BOOK NO.	ASSIGN- MENT	CHEM SHIFT - ppm -	PROTON GROUP	ENVIRONMENTAL GROUPS	S	SOLVENT
2424M	C	8.62	NH	C(=0)-NH2/A<C-CH-CH-C(BR)>		DMSO-D6
2423M	E	8.39	NH	C(=0)-NH2/A<C-CH-C(CH3)>		DMSO-D6
2425M	E	8.19	NH	C(=0)-NH2/A(C-CH-CH-C(O-CH3))		POLYSOL-D
2422M	C	6.35	NH	C(=0)-NH2/CH2-A		POLYSOL-D
2418M	E	6.00	NH	C(=0)-NH2/CH2-CH		POLYSOL-D
2420M	C	6.01	NH	C(=0)-NH2/CH2-CH2		DMSO-D6
2751M	E	6.29	NH	C(=0)-NH2/CH2-C(=0)-0		DMSO-D6
2417M	D	5.74	NH	C(=0)-NH2/CH(CH3/CH3)		POLYSOL-D
2419M	E	5.63	NH	C(=0)-NH2/C(CH2/CH3/CH3)		DMSO-D6
2451M	B	5.70 APP.	NH	C(=0)-NH2/R5NN<CH-NH/C(=0)>		DMSO-D6
2421M	D	5.92	NH	C(=0)-NH2/R6		POLYSOL-D
2467M	F	8.67	NH	C(=0)-NH/A		DMSO
2432M	B	6.16	NH	C(=0)-NH/CH2-A		POLYSOL-D
2429M	D	5.71	NH	C(=0)-NH/CH2-CH2		CDCL3
2428M	C	6.53	NH	C(=0)-NH/CH2-CH3		CDCL3
2430M	C	6.71	NH	C(=0)-NH/CH2-0H		DMSO-D6
2435M	B	6.47	NH	C(=0)-N/A		CDCL3
2436M	B	4.48	NH	C(=0)-N/CH3		CDCL3
2986M	E	5.00 APP.	NH	C(=0)-0-CH2/CH2-CH2		CCL4
2981M	F	5.25	NH	C(=0)-0-CH2/CH2-CH2		CCL4
2983M	D	6.42	NH	C(=0)-0-CH2/CH2-NH		CDCL3
2980M	D	5.09	NH	C(=0)-0-CH2/CH3		CDCL3
2982M	E	5.30	NH	C(=0)-0-CH3/CH2-CH2		CCL4
894M	F	8.24	NH	C(=0)-Q2/OH		POLYSOL-D
2306M	G	7.29	NH	C(=0)-Q3/CH2-Q3		CDCL3
2305M	E	5.81	NH	C(=0)-Q3/C(CH2/CH3/CH3)		CDCL3
2304M	C	6.03	NH	C(=0)-Q3/C(CH3/CH3/CH3)		CDCL3
1335M	C	9.22	NH	C(=S)-A/A		CDCL3
1340M	C	9.66	NH	C(=S)-NH2/A		DMSO
1342M	D	9.61	NH	C(=S)-NH2/AA<C-C*>		POLYSOL-D
1341M	D	8.96	NH	C(=S)-NH2/A<C-C(CH3)>		DMSO-D6
1339M	D	7.50	NH	C(=S)-NH2/CH2-CH3		DMSO-D6
1338M	B	5.00- 8.00	NH	C(=S)-NH2/CH3		DMSO-D6
1349M	D	9.13	NH	C(=S)-NH/A		POLYSOL-D
1348M	E	8.62	NH	C(=S)-NH/A		CDCL3
1350M	F	8.49	NH	C(=S)-NH/A		CDCL3
1352M	B	9.60	NH	C(=S)-NH/A(C-C(CL))		DMSO
1347M	D	7.10	NH	C(=S)-NH/CH2.9-CH3		POLYSOL-D
1346M	D	6.50	NH	C(=S)-NH/CH2-CH		CDCL3
1348M	C	6.19	NH	C(=S)-NH/CH2-CH3		CDCL3
1344M	C	6.67	NH	C(=S)-NH/CH2-CH3		CCL4
1350M	D	6.20 APP.	NH	C(=S)-NH/CH2-Q3		CDCL3
1345M	C	6.10	NH	C(=S)-NH/CH(CH3/CH3)		CDCL3
1353M	E	7.19	NH	C(=S)-NH/R5R5BI<CH-CH*/CH2>		POLYSOL-D
1354M	C	8.78	NH	C(=S)-N/A<C-C(CL)>		POLYSOL-D
1351M	B	7.97 APP.	NH	C=S-NH/A		CDCL3
764M	A	4.87	NH	NH2/ANA<C-N-C*/CH-CH-C*>		POLYSOL-D
757M	A	3.87 APP.	NH	NH2/A<C-C(CL)/CH-C(CL)>		CDCL3
823M	E	7.50- 9.50	NH	NH2/A(C-CH-C(CL)-C(CH3))	S	DMSO-D6
758M	A	4.18 APP.	NH	NH2/A(C-C(CL)-CH-C(CL)/C(CL))		CDCL3
753M	B	3.36	NH	NH2/CH3		CCL4
2406M	A	4.52	NH	NH2/C(=0)-A		DMSO
2407M	A	4.55 APP.	NH	NH2/C(=0)-A		DMSO-D6
2408M	A	4.60 APP.	NH	NH2/C(=0)-AN		CDCL3
2405M	E	8.38	NH	NH2/C(=0)-CH2		POLYSOL-D
2403M	B	5.02	NH	NH2/C(=0)-CH3		CDCL3
2468M	B	5.90	NH	NH2/C(=0)-N		CDCL3
760M	D	7.49	NH	NH-A/A		DMSO-D6
2467M	E	8.18	NH	NH-A/C(=0)-NH		DMSO
2467M	D	7.69	NH	NH-C(=0)/A		DMSO
2413M	D	9.60	NH	NH-C(=0)/C(=0)-CH2		DMSO-D6
2410M	B	6.50- 8.50	NH	N(CH3/CH3)/C(=0)-A		CDCL3
1353M	F	8.31	NH	N(CH3/CH3)/C(=S)-NH		POLYSOL-D
904M	E	8.01	NH	N=N-A/CH3		CDCL3
2411M	E	9.55	NH	N=R6/C(=0)-A		CDCL3
891M	D	8.60	NH	OH/C(=0)-CH2		CDCL3
893M	F	8.69	NH	OH/C(=0)-CH2		CDCL3
878M	G	9.43	NH	QN(AN(C-N)/CH3)/A		DMSO-D6
877M	B	7.59	NH	QN(A(C-C(CL)))/A		CDCL3
889M	A	5.71	NH	QN(A)/A		DMSO-D6
876M	C	9.16	NH	QN(A)/A		C3H60
887M	D	8.30- 9.30	NH	QN(A)/A		POLYSOL-D
1064M	F	11.14	NH	QN(A)/A<C-CH-CH-C(NO2)>		POLYSOL-D
1063M	G	9.52	NH	QN(CH2.2-CH3/CH3)/A<C-CH-CH-C(NO2)>		POLYSOL-D
1358M	E	10.10	NH	QN(CH2-CH2)/C(=S)-NH		CDCL3
2470M	F	8.76	NH	QN(CH2-CH2/CH3)/C(=0)-NH2		CDCL3
888M	B	6.21	NH	QN(CH3/A)/A		CDCL3
1075M	F	11.00	NH	QN(CH3/CH3)/A(C-C(NO2-CH-C(NO2))		CDCL3
2469M	E	8.58	NH	QN(CH(CH3/CH3)/CH3)/C(=0)-NH2		CDCL3
890M	A	5.89	NH	QN(NH-A/A)/A		CDCL3
875M	C	8.04	NH	QN(Q2(A))/A		DMSO

: REPRESENTS TRIPLE BOND, ¬ REPRESENTS AN ARROW AND < AND > REPRESENT BRACKETS.   PAGE   426

BOOK NO.	ASSIGN-MENT	CHEM SHIFT - ppm -	PROTON GROUP	ENVIRONMENTAL GROUPS	S	SOLVENT
2319M	F	10.05	NH	O1(OH)-C(=O)/A		DMSO-D6
1156M	C	7.69	NH	R5NNS<C=N/S>/CH2-CH3		POLYSOL-D
1664M	A	3.94	NH	R5NN<C(=S)-N(CH2-CH2)/CH2-CH2>		TFA
1135M	D	4.62	NH	R5NS(C=N/S)/CH2-A		CDCL3
2182M	E	11.20 APP.	NH	R5N<=C(C(=O)-H-CH/CH=CH>		CDCL3
801M	C	8.15	NH	R6NH<CH2-CH2/CH2-CH2>	S	CDCL3
2455M	C	10.10	NH	R6NN<C(=O)-NH/C(CH3)=(CH3)>		TFA
2455M	C	10.10	NH	R6NN<C(=O)-NH/C(=O)-C(CH3)=>		TFA
1217M	B	1.83	NH	R6/CH2.2-SH		CDCL3
1370M	D	7.65	NH	SO2-A/A		CDCL3
1371M	E	9.36	NH	SO2-A/A<C-C(CH3)>		DMSO-D6
1372M	C	6.56	NH	SO2-A/A(C-CH-CH-C(CH3))		CDCL3
1368M	E	7.36	NH	SO2-CH2/A(C-CH-CH-C(CH3))		CDCL3
1378M	C	10.11	NH	SO2-NH/A(C-CH-CH-C(BR))		POLYSOL-D
1377M	C	6.28	NH	SO2-NH/R6		POLYSOL-D
565M	A	0.95	NHR	R13N<CH2-CH2/CH2-CH2>		CDCL3
2401M	B	11.42	NHR	R5NAR5N<C(=O)-C*/C(=O)-C*>		DMSO
611M	D	7.39	NHR	R5NAR6<C*-CH2/C*>		CDCL3
2381M	D	11.33	NHR	R5NA<C(=O)-C*/C(=O)-C*>		POLYSOL-D
1020M	C	4.18	NHR	R5NA<C*/CH2-CH2>		CDCL3
608M	E	7.19 APP.	NHR	R5NA<C*/CH=CH>		CDCL3
607M	D	7.49	NHR	R5NA<C*/CH=C>		CDCL3
606M	E	7.56	NHR	R5NA<C*/C(CH3)=CH>		CDCL3
609M	D	7.41 APP.	NHR	R5NA<C*/C(CH3)=C(CH3)>		CDCL3
2441M	C	11.10	NHR	R5NA<C*/C(=O)-N(A)>		DMSO-D6
2380M	B	11.29	NHR	R5NA(C(=O)-C*/C(=O)-C*)		DMSO
605M	D	7.04 APP.	NHR	R5NA<C*/CH-CH)		CCL4
610M	D	10.83	NHR	R5NA(C*/CH=C(CH2-N)-C*)		DMSO-D6
1357M	D	12.62	NHR	R5NNAA(C*/C(=S)-NH)		DMSO-D6
739M	F	11.58	NHR	R5NNA<C*/C(CH2.2-CH3)=N>		POLYSOL-D
740M	F	12.49	NHR	R5NNA(C*/CH=N)		CDCL3
1730M	D	8.70	NHR	R5NNA(C*/C(CH2-OH)=N)		DMSO-D6
741M	C	14.49	NHR	R5NNNA<N=N-C*/C*>		CDCL3
2431M	B	5.30	NHR	R5NN<C(=O)-NH/CH2-CH2>		CDCL3
2446M	C	8.34	NHR	R5NN<C(=O)-NH/CH(A)-C(=O)>		DMSO-D6
2451M	C	6.94	NHR	R5NN<C(=O)-NH/CH(NH-C(=O)-NH2)-C(=O)>		DMSO-D6
2446M	D	10.74	NHR	R5NN<C(=O)-NH/C(=O)-CH(A)>		DMSO-D6
2451M	D	7.92	NHR	R5NN<C(=O)-NH/CH(NH-C(=O)-NH2)>		DMSO-D6
2433M	E	6.69	NHR	R5NN<C(=O)-N(CH2.3-CH3)/CH2-CH2>		CCL4
2445M	C	7.13	NHR	R5NN<C(=O)-N(CH2-A)/C(CH3/CH3)-C(=O)>		CDCL3
1966M	D	4.60	NHR	R5NN<C(=O)-N(CH2-NH)/C(CH3/CH3)-C(=O)>		CDCL3
2434M	E	6.42	NHR	R5NN<C(=O)-N(CH2-Q3)/CH2-CH2>		POLYSOL-D
2448M	C	6.61	NHR	R5NN<C(=O)-N(CH3)/CH(A)-C(=O)>		CDCL3
2412M	E	5.58	NHR	R5NN<NH-CH(A)/C(=O)-HCH>		DMSO-D6
2412M	C	3.48	NHR	R5NN<NH-C(=O)/CH(A)-HCH>		DMSO-D6
2447M	C	8.52	NHR	R5NN(C(=O)-NH/C(A/CH3)-C(=O))		DMSO-D6
2992M	C	6.42	NHR	R5NO<C(=O)-O/CH2-CH2>		CDCL3
560M	B	2.39	NHR	R5N<CH2-CH2/CH2-CH2>		C6H6
2376M	D	9.51	NHR	R5N<C(=O)-CH(CH3)/C(=O)-HCH		CDCL3
575M	C	7.48	NHR	R5N(CH=CH/CH=CH)		CCL4
2379M	B	10.60	NHR	R5N(C(=O)-CH=/C(=O)-CH=)		POLYSOL-D
601M	D	3.62	NHR	R6NA<C*/CH2/CH2>		CDCL3
602M	E	3.48	NHR	R6NA<C*/CH-(CH3)-HCH>		CDCL3
603M	A	2.08	NHR	R6NA(CH2-C*/CH2-CH2)		CCL4
752M	A	6.49	NHR	R6NNNAA(N=N/C*)		DMSO
566M	A	2.03	NHR	R6NN<CH2-CH2/CH2-CH2>		CDCL3
641M	B	1.90	NHR	R6NN<CH2-CH(CH3)/CH2-CH2>		CDCL3
567M	B	1.49	NHR	R6NN<CH(CH3)-CH2/CH2-CH(CH3)>		CDCL3
2457M	B	9.10	NHR	R6NN<C(=O)-C(I)=/C(=O)-NH>		DMSO
2444M	C	7.44	NHR	R6NN<C(=O)-NH/CH(CH3)-C(=O)>		POLYSOL-D
2457M	B	9.10	NHR	R6NN<C(=O)-NH/CH=C(I)>		DMSO
2454M	C	10.19	NHR	R6NN<C(=O)-NH/C(CH3)=CH>		TFA
2444M	D	9.52	NHR	R6NN<C(=O)-NH/C(=O)-CH(CH3)>		POLYSOL-D
2454M	D	10.19	NHR	R6NN<C(=O)-NH/C(=O)-CH=>		TFA
2464M	D	11.64	NHR	R6NN<C(=O)-NH/C(=O)-C(A/CH2-Q3)>		DMSO-D6
2461M	C	11.38	NHR	R6NN<C(=O)-NH/C(=O)-C(CH2-Q3/CH2-Q3)>		DMSO-D6
640M	A	1.78	NHR	R6NN(CH2-CH2-N)		CDCL3
568M	B	1.43	NHR	R6NN(CH(CH3)-HCH/HCH-CH(CH3))		CDCL3
2456M	B	10.65	NHR	R6NN(C(=O)-C(BR)=/C(=O)-NH)		DMSO
2458M	B	11.69	NHR	R6NN(C(=O)-NH/CH=C(NO2))		DMSO
2458M	B	11.69	NHR	R6NN(C(=O)-NH/C(=O)-C(NO2)=)		DMSO
1462M	A	1.78	NHR	R6NO(CH2-CH2/CH2-CH2)		CCL4
2378M	C	8.42	NHR	R6NR6SPI<C(=O)-CH2/C(=O)-CH2>		CDCL3
569M	B	1.34	NHR	R6NR6(CH*-CH2/CH2-CH2)		CDCL3
1182M	B	8.61	NHR	R6NSAA<C*/C*>		DMSO-D6
1583M	E	8.34	NHR	R6NSAA<C*/C*>		DMSO-D6
576M	A	1.94	NHR	R6N<CH2-CH=/CH2-CH2>		CDCL3
2013M	C	7.90-11.20	NHR	R6N<C(CH3/CH3)-CH2/C(CH3/CH3)-CH2>	S	CDCL3
2303M	D	8.09	NHR	R6N<C(=O)-CH2/CH2-CH2>		CCL4
563M	C	1.55	NHR	R6N<HCH-CH2/HCH-CH2>		CCL4
562M	C	2.31	NHR	R6N(CH(CH3)-CH2/CH2-CH2)		CCL4

BOOK NO.	ASSIGN-MENT	CHEM SHIFT - ppm -	PROTON GROUP	ENVIRONMENTAL GROUPS	S	SOLVENT
487M	A	3.32	NH2	A		CCL4
1940M	B	7.91	NH2	A		DMSO
787M	B	9.78	NH2	A	S	DMSO-D6
541M	A	5.76	NH2	AAA<C-C*/CH-C*>		DMSO
540M	A	4.42	NH2	AA<C-CH-C*/CH-CH-C*>		POLYSOL-D
1953M	A	4.71	NH2	AA<C-CH-C*/CH-CH-C*>		DMSO-D6
1293M	G	9.53	NH2	AA<C-C(SO2-OH)-C*/CH-CH-C*>		DMSO-D6
539M	A	3.81	NH2	AA(C-C*)		CDCL3
727M	A	3.99	NH2	ANA(C-CH-N-C*/CH-C*)		CDCL3
707M	A	6.11	NH2	AN-C-N-CH-C(CL)>		DMSO-D6
706M	A	5.10	NH2	AN(C-N)		CDCL3
1278M	A	6.29	NH2	AR5SA(C-CH-C*-C*/CH-CH-C*)		DMSO
1179M	A	5.47	NH2	AR5SA(C-CH-C*-S/CH-CH-C*)		DMSO
531M	A	4.41	NH2	A<C-CH-CH-C(A<C-CH-CH-C(NH2)>)>		DMSO-D6
505M	A	3.93	NH2	A<C-CH-CH-C(A)>		C3H6O
507M	A	3.77	NH2	A<C-CH-CH-C(CF3)>		CDCL3
1718M	C	4.05	NH2	A<C-CH-CH-C(CH2.2-OH)>		POLYSOL-D
490M	B	3.25	NH2	A<C-CH-CH-C(CH3)>		CCL4
493M	C	3.43	NH2	A<C-CH-CH-C(CH(CH3/CH3))>		CDCL3
2070M	D	4.30	NH2	A<C-CH-CH-C(C(=O)-CH2.2)>		CDCL3
2071M	D	4.38	NH2	A<C-CH-CH-C(C(=O)-CH2.3)>		CDCL3
2578M	A	6.55	NH2	A<C-CH-CH-C(C(=O)-OH)>		C3H6O
2882M	B	4.22	NH2	A<C-CH-CH-C(C(=O)-O-CH)>		CDCL3
510M	A	3.33	NH2	A<C-CH-CH-C(F)>		CCL4
535M	A	4.00	NH2	A<C-CH-CH-C(NH2)>		DMSO-D6
1238M	A	3.52	NH2	A<C-CH-CH-C(SH)>		CDCL3
1365M	A	5.69	NH2	A<C-CH-CH-C(SO2-NH2)>		DMSO-D6
506M	A	3.70	NH2	A<C-CH-C(CF3)>		CDCL3
492M	C	3.47	NH2	A<C-CH-C(CH2-CH3)>		CDCL3
790M	C	10.31	NH2	A<C-CH-C(CH3)>	S	POLYSOL-D
498M	B	3.43	NH2	A<C-CH-C(CH3)-C(CH3)>		CDCL3
1071M	B	6.12	NH2	A<C-CH-C(CH3)-C(NO2)>		POLYSOL-D
499M	B	3.29	NH2	A<C-CH-C(CH3)/CH-C(CH3)>		CCL4
2103M	A	5.39	NH2	A<C-CH-C(C(=O)-A)>		DMSO-D6
2880M	B	3.88	NH2	A<C-CH-C(C(=O)-O-CH3)>		CDCL3
2905M	B	5.23	NH2	A<C-CH-C(C(=O)-O-CH3)/CH-C(C(=O)-O-CH3)>		POLYSOL-D
994M	A	5.29	NH2	A<C-CH-C(C:N)>		POLYSOL-D
509M	A	3.60	NH2	A<C-CH-C(F)>		CDCL3
536M	B	3.39	NH2	A<C-CH-C(NH2)-C(CH3)>		CDCL3
1070M	B	3.80	NH2	A<C-CH-C(NO2)-C(CH3)>		CDCL3
1237M	A	3.50	NH2	A<C-CH-C(SH)>		CDCL3
504M	A	4.58	NH2	A<C-C(A)>		DMSO-D6
523M	A	3.99	NH2	A<C-C(BR)-CH-C(BR)>		CDCL3
524M	A	4.59	NH2	A<C-C(BR)-CH-C(BR)/C(BR)>		CDCL3
503M	D	3.21	NH2	A<C-C(CH2-CH3)-CH-C(CH3)/C(CH2-CH3)>		CCL4
538M	C	3.23	NH2	A<C-C(CH2-CH3)-CH-C(NH2)/CH-C(CH2-CH3)>		CDCL3
500M	D	3.38	NH2	A<C-C(CH2-CH3)/C(CH3)>		CDCL3
2640M	C	3.27	NH2	A<C-C(CH3)-CH-C(CH3)/CH-C(CH3)>		CCL4
502M	C	3.19	NH2	A<C-C(CH3)-CH-C(CH3)/C(CH3)>		CCL4
528M	B	4.56	NH2	A<C-C(CH3)-CH-C(I)>		POLYSOL-D
497M	C	3.21	NH2	A<C-C(CH3)/CH-C(CH3)>		CCL4
536M	B	3.39	NH2	A<C-C(CH3)/CH-C(NH2)>		CDCL3
494M	E	3.34	NH2	A<C-C(CH(CH2/CH3))>		CCL4
501M	C	3.58	NH2	A<C-C(CH(CH3/CH3))/C(CH(CH3/CH3))>		CDCL3
516M	A	3.99	NH2	A<C-C(CL)-CH-C(CL)>		CDCL3
517M	A	4.39	NH2	A<C-C(CL)-CH-C(CL)/C(CL)>		CDCL3
2595M	E	7.87	NH2	A<C-C(C(=O)-OH)-CH-C(O-CH3)>		POLYSOL-D
2879M	D	6.32	NH2	A<C-C(C(=O)-O-CH2.4)>		DMSO-D6
2877M	D	5.73	NH2	A<C-C(C(=O)-O-CH2)>		CCL4
2910M	B	6.11	NH2	A<C-C(C(=O)-O-CH3)/CH-C(C(=O)-O-CH3)>		POLYSOL-D
2878M	C	5.71	NH2	A<C-C(C(=O)-O-R6)>		CDCL3
508M	A	3.50	NH2	A<C-C(F)>		CCL4
525M	A	4.02	NH2	A<C-C(I)>		CDCL3
1562M	C	3.72	NH2	A<C-C(O-CH2.3)/CH-C(O-CH2.3)>		CDCL3
1526M	F	9.80	NH2	A<C-C(O-CH3)>	S	POLYSOL-D
862M	A	4.62	NH2	A<C-C(QN(A/OH))>		POLYSOL-D
1236M	A	3.68	NH2	A<C-C(SH)>		CDCL3
1290M	D	9.20 APP.	NH2	A<C-C(SO2-OH)-CH-C(CH3)>		DMSO-D6
1161M	B	4.11	NH2	A<C-C(S-CH3)>		CCL4
520M	A	3.53	NH2	A(C-CH-CH-C(BR))		CDCL3
530M	B	4.63	NH2	A(C-CH-CH-C(CH2-A))		DMSO-D6
2405M	B	4.05	NH2	A(C-CH-CH-C(CH2-C(=O)-NH))		POLYSOL-D
514M	A	5.03	NH2	A(C-CH-CH-C(CL))		DMSO
2881M	B	4.03	NH2	A(C-CH-CH-C(C(=O)-O-CH3))		CDCL3
527M	A	3.59	NH2	A(C-CH-CH-C(I))		CDCL3
669M	B	3.29	NH2	A(C-CH-CH-C(N(CH3/CH3)))		CDCL3
899M	A	3.84	NH2	A(C-CH-CH-C(N=N-A))		CDCL3
901M	B	5.70	NH2	A(C-CH-CH-C(N=N-A))		DMSO-D6
519M	A	3.58	NH2	A(C-CH-C(BR))		CDCL3
489M	B	3.32	NH2	A(C-CH-C(CH3))		CCL4
511M	B	3.32	NH2	A(C-CH-C(CH3)-C(F))		CCL4

BOOK NO.	ASSIGN-MENT	CHEM SHIFT - ppm -	PROTON GROUP	ENVIRONMENTAL GROUPS	S	SOLVENT
537M	B	3.17	NH2	A(C-CH-C(CH3)-C(NH2)/CH-C(CH3))		CDCL3
513M	A	3.58	NH2	A(C-CH-C(CL))		CDCL3
522M	A	3.65	NH2	A(C-CH-C(CL)-C(BR))		CDCL3
526M	A	3.54	NH2	A(C-CH-C(I))		CDCL3
534M	A	4.08	NH2	A(C-CH-C(NH2))		POLYSOL-D
1899M	A	4.71	NH2	A(C-CH-C(OH))		DMSO
1522M	B	3.62	NH2	A(C-CH-C(O-CH2))		CDCL3
1561M	C	3.43	NH2	A(C-CH-C(O-CH2)-C(O-CH2))		CDCL3
518M	A	3.95	NH2	A(C-C(BR))		CDCL3
521M	B	3.82	NH2	A(C-C(BR)-CH-C(CH3))		CDCL3
491M	C	3.30	NH2	A(C-C(CH2-CH3))		CDCL3
488M	B	3.23	NH2	A(C-C(CH3))		CCL4
532M	B	3.45	NH2	A(C-C(CH3)-CH-C(A(C-CH-C(CH3)-C(NH2))))		CDCL3
496M	C	3.16	NH2	A(C-C(CH3)-CH-C(CH3))		CCL4
515M	B	3.49	NH2	A(C-C(CH3)-CH-C(CL))		CCL4
537M	B	3.17	NH2	A(C-C(CH3)-CH-C(NH2)/C(CH3))		CDCL3
1077M	B	4.30	NH2	A(C-C(CH3)-CH-C(NO2)/C(CH3))		CDCL3
495M	C	3.35	NH2	A(C-C(CH3)-C(CH3))		CCL4
1291M	B	7.15 APP.	NH2	A(C-C(CH3)/CH-C(SO3-H))		DMSO-D6
512M	A	3.81	NH2	A(C-C(CL))		CCL4
1941M	B	7.90	NH2	A(C-C(CL))		DMSO
533M	A	3.28	NH2	A(C-C(NH2))		CDCL3
1554M	B	3.78	NH2	A(C-C(O-CH3)-CH-C(CL))		CDCL3
1198M	A	4.24	NH2	A(C-C(S-S))		CDCL3
462M	B	1.59	NH2	CH2.11-NH2		CDCL3
2686M	E	7.98	NH2	CH2.11-CH3		CDCL3
1672M	A	2.63	NH2	CH2.2-O		CDCL3
768M	D	8.07	NH2	CH2.3-CH3	S	CDCL3
2685M	E	8.14	NH2	CH2.9-CH3		CDCL3
485M	A	1.18	NH2	CH2-A		CCL4
483M	A	1.31	NH2	CH2-A		CDCL3
1505M	A	1.50	NH2	CH2-A		CDCL3
476M	A	1.52	NH2	CH2-A		CDCL3
1504M	A	1.72	NH2	CH2-A		CDCL3
484M	A	1.80	NH2	CH2-A		CDCL3
486M	B	1.51	NH2	CH2-A		CCL4
783M	D	8.29	NH2	CH2-A	S	POLYSOL-D
460M	B	1.14	NH2	CH2-C		CCL4
479M	A	0.99	NH2	CH2-CH		CDCL3
1428M	A	1.23	NH2	CH2-CH		CDCL3
1427M	A	1.69	NH2	CH2-CH		CCL4
459M	B	1.20	NH2	CH2-CH		CDCL3
442M	C	1.82	NH2	CH2-CH		CDCL3
445M	D	1.21	NH2	CH2-CH		CDCL3
477M	A	0.93 APP.	NH2	CH2-CH2		CCL4
482M	A	0.99	NH2	CH2-CH2		CCL4
481M	A	1.01	NH2	CH2-CH2		CDCL3
466M	A	1.18	NH2	CH2-CH2		CDCL3
457M	A	1.19	NH2	CH2-CH2		CCL4
1466M	A	1.25 APP.	NH2	CH2-CH2		CCL4
451M	B	1.20	NH2	CH2-CH2		CDCL3
1642M	B	2.82	NH2	CH2-CH2		CDCL3
446M	C	1.49	NH2	CH2-CH2		CDCL3
444M	C	1.51	NH2	CH2-CH2		CDCL3
441M	C	1.60	NH2	CH2-CH2		CDCL3
439M	C	1.80- 2.40	NH2	CH2-CH2		CCL4
439M	C	1.80- 2.40	NH2	CH2-CH2		CCL4
627M	C	2.20	NH2	CH2-CH2		CDCL3
778M	C	6.95 APP.	NH2	CH2-CH2	S	TFA
465M	D	2.10- 2.55	NH2	CH2-CH2		CCL4
767M	D	8.32	NH2	CH2-CH2	S	DMSO-D6
475M	A	1.10	NH2	CH2-O2		CCL4
474M	A	1.21	NH2	CH2-O3		CDCL3
781M	D	6.00	NH2	CH2-O3	S	POLYSOL-D
469M	B	1.49	NH2	CH2-R6		CDCL3
473M	A	1.21	NH2	CH2-R6R6R6TRI		CDCL3
478M	B	1.47	NH2	CH(A/CH3)		CCL4
784M	C	7.18 APP.	NH2	CH(A/CH3)	S	TFA
455M	B	1.29	NH2	CH(CH2.3/CH2.3)		CDCL3
626M	D	1.39 APP.	NH2	CH(CH2.3/CH3)		CDCL3
459M	B	1.20	NH2	CH(CH2/CH3)		CDCL3
443M	C	1.17	NH2	CH(CH2/CH3)		CDCL3
449M	D	3.20	NH2	CH(CH2/CH3)		CDCL3
450M	E	2.19 APP.	NH2	CH(CH2/CH3)		CCL4
785M	E	5.40- 7.00	NH2	CH(CH2/CH3)	S	TFA
1753M	B	2.22	NH2	CH(CH/CH3)		CDCL3
448M	C	1.37	NH2	CH(C/CH3)		CCL4
1644M	D	3.02	NH2	CH(HCH/CH2)		CDCL3
480M	B	3.35	NH2	C(A/CH3/CH3)		CCL4
1645M	C	2.71	NH2	C(CH2.2/CH3/CH3)		CDCL3
456M	B	1.19	NH2	C(CH2.3/CH2.3/CH2.3)		CDCL3

BOOK NO.	ASSIGN-MENT	CHEM SHIFT - ppm -	PROTON GROUP	ENVIRONMENTAL GROUPS	S	SOLVENT
460M	B	1.14	NH2	C(CH2/CH3/CH3)		CCL4
447M	C	1.22	NH2	C(CH2/CH3/CH3)		CDCL3
769M	B	3.79	NH2	C(CH3/CH3/CH3)		CDCL3
2635M	B	8.17	NH2	C(C(=0)-OH/A/A)		TFA
2292M	A	7.20	NH2	C(=0)-A		DMSO
2289M	B	6.50 APP.	NH2	C(=0)-A		CDCL3
2290M	D	11.70 APP.	NH2	C(=0)-A		TFA
2293M	E	8.20 APP.	NH2	C(=0)-A		DMSO-D6
2282M	B	7.35 APP.	NH2	C(=0)-CH		C3H60
2285M	E	6.20 APP.	NH2	C(=0)-CH		CDCL3
2276M	C	6.00- 7.50	NH2	C(=0)-CH2		CDCL3
2284M	C	6.62 APP.	NH2	C(=0)-CH2		CDCL3
2279M	E	6.11	NH2	C(=0)-CH2		CDCL3
2278M	E	6.25	NH2	C(=0)-CH2		CDCL3
2426M	B	4.38	NH2	C(=0)-N		CDCL3
2424M	A	5.88	NH2	C(=0)-NH		DMSO-D6
2422M	B	5.29	NH2	C(=0)-NH		POLYSOL-D
2420M	B	5.48	NH2	C(=0)-NH		DMSO-D6
2425M	B	5.53	NH2	C(=0)-NH		POLYSOL-D
2451M	B	5.70 APP.	NH2	C(=0)-NH		DMSO-D6
2423M	B	5.79	NH2	C(=0)-NH		DMSO-D6
2417M	C	5.21 APP.	NH2	C(=0)-NH		POLYSOL-D
2421M	C	5.39	NH2	C(=0)-NH		POLYSOL-D
1339M	C	6.93	NH2	C(=0)-NH		DMSO-D6
2419M	D	5.21	NH2	C(=0)-NH		DMSO-D6
2418M	D	5.22	NH2	C(=0)-NH		POLYSOL-D
2751M	D	5.61	NH2	C(=0)-NH		DMSO-D6
2469M	D	5.89	NH2	C(=0)-NH		CDCL3
2470M	E	5.92	NH2	C(=0)-NH		CDCL3
2415M	A	6.79	NH2	C(=0)-NH2		POLYSOL-D
2979M	B	6.80	NH2	C(=0)-0-A		DMSO-D6
2978M	C	8.64	NH2	C(=0)-0-A		DMSO
2975M	R	4.88	NH2	C(=0)-0-C		CDCL3
2973M	C	4.97	NH2	C(=0)-0-CH		CDCL3
2976M	D	4.92	NH2	C(=0)-0-CH2		CDCL3
2977M	D	5.71 APP.	NH2	C(=0)-0-CH2		CCL4
2294M	C	7.72	NH2	C(=0)-R50		DMSO
1334M	E	9.79 APP.	NH2	C(=S)-AN		POLYSOL-D
1332M	C	8.45 APP.	NH2	C(=S)-CH2		POLYSOL-D
1331M	B	9.20	NH2	C(=S)-CH3		DMSO-D6
1331M	B	9.20	NH2	C(=S)-CH3		DMSO-D6
1342M	A	7.00	NH2	C(=S)-NH		POLYSOL-D
1338M	B	5.00- 8.00	NH2	C(=S)-NH		DMSO-D6
1341M	B	6.88	NH2	C(=S)-NH		DMSO-D6
1340M	B	7.38	NH2	C(=S)-NH		DMSO
757M	A	3.87 APP.	NH2	NH-A		CDCL3
758M	A	4.18 APP.	NH2	NH-A		CDCL3
823M	E	7.50- 9.50	NH2	NH-A	S	DMSO-D6
764M	A	4.87	NH2	NH-ANA		POLYSOL-D
753M	B	3.36	NH2	NH-CH3		CCL4
2468M	A	3.50	NH2	NH-C(=0)		CDCL3
2409M	A	4.51	NH2	NH-C(=0)		DMSO-D6
2406M	A	4.52	NH2	NH-C(=0)		DMSO
2408M	A	4.60 APP.	NH2	NH-C(=0)		CDCL3
2403M	B	5.02	NH2	NH-C(=0)		CDCL3
2407M	A	4.55 APP.	NH2	NH-C(=0)-A		DMSO-D6
2405M	B	4.05	NH2	NH-C(=0)-CH2		POLYSOL-D
759M	A	3.97	NH2	N(A/A)		CDCL3
754M	B	3.00	NH2	N(CH3/CH3)		CCL4
873M	A	5.37	NH2	QN(AA<C-C*>)		POLYSOL-D
879M	A	5.35	NH2	QN(QN/A)		CDCL3
969M	A	7.57	NH2	Q1(C:N/C:N)		DMSO-D6
2402M	A	4.93	NH2	R5NA<N-C(=0)/C(=0)>		DMSO
1155M	C	7.00- 9.00	NH2	R5NNS<C=N/S>		TFA
1154M	B	5.87	NH2	R5NS<C=N/S>	S	D20
1153M	B	6.87	NH2	R5NS(C=N/S)		DMSO-D6
468M	B	1.47	NH2	R5<CH-CH2/CH2>		CDCL3
755M	C	3.21	NH2	R6NN<N-CH2/CH2)		CDCL3
471M	B	1.31	NH2	R6<CH-CH2/CH2>		CDCL3
470M	B	1.51	NH2	R6<CH-CH2/CH2>		CCL4
472M	A	1.36	NH2	R7<CH-CH2/CH2>		CDCL3
1366M	A	7.11	NH2	S02-A		DMSO-D6
1363M	B	4.05 APP.	NH2	S02-A		TFA
1362M	B	7.21	NH2	S02-A		DMSO-D6
1365M	C	6.89	NH2	S02-A		DMSO-D6
1367M	A	7.11	NH2	S02-AA		POLYSOL-D
1359M	B	6.38	NH2	S02-CH3		POLYSOL-D
1360M	A	6.50 APP.	NH2	S02-Q2		POLYSOL-D
273M	B	8.22	NH2	S02-R5NNS		DMSO-D6
2633M	F	7.70	NH3(+)	CH(C(=0)-OH/CH2.2)		TFA
1875M	A	6.11	OH	A		CDCL3

BOOK NO.	ASSIGN-MENT	CHEM SHIFT - ppm -	PROTON GROUP	ENVIRONMENTAL GROUPS	S	SOLVENT
1962M	D	8.61	OH	AAN(C-C*-N)		CDCL3
1951M	B	8.35	OH	AA<C-CH-C*/CH-CH-C*>		C3H6O
1958M	D	8.32	OH	AA<C-CH-C*/CH-CH-C*>		C3D6O
1956M	E	8.48	OH	AA<C-CH-C*/CH-C(OH)-C*>		C3H6O
1954M	H	8.99 APP.	OH	AA<C-C(CH2.2-C:N)-C*/CH-CH-C*>		POLYSOL-D
1953M	A	4.71	OH	AA<C-C*>		DMSO-D6
1957M	D	9.58	OH	AA<C-C*>		DMSO-D6
1956M	F	8.98	OH	AA<C-C*/CH-C(OH)>		C3H6O
1950M	E	8.92	OH	AA(C-C*)		C3H6O
1952M	B	5.20	OH	AA(C-C*/C(CH3))		CDCL3
1961M	D	11.78	OH	ANA<C-N-C*/CH-CH-C*>		DMSO
1960M	C	10.30	OH	ANN<C-N/N>		DMSO-D6
1959M	D	9.93	OH	AN<C-CH-N>		DMSO-D6
1949M	F	8.99	OH	AR5A<C-CH-C*-CH2/CH-CH-C*>		POLYSOL-D
1948M	C	6.15	OH	AR5(C-C*-CH2-CH2)		CDCL3
1909M	C	9.20	OH	A<C-CH-CH-C(A<C-CH-CH-C(OH)>)>		DMSO-D6
1902M	C	6.34	OH	A<C-CH-CH-C(CH2.2-C:N)>		CDCL3
1884M	F	6.79	OH	A<C-CH-CH-C(CH2.4-CH3)>		CCL4
1888M	D	8.97	OH	A<C-CH-CH-C(CH2-A)>		DMSO-D6
1878M	B	6.45	OH	A<C-CH-CH-C(CH3)>		CDCL3
1881M	C	6.39	OH	A<C-CH-CH-C(CH(CH3/CH3))>		CDCL3
1908M	D	7.60	OH	A<C-CH-CH-C(C(A/CH3/CH3))>		POLYSOL-D
2588M	C	9.76	OH	A<C-CH-CH-C(C(=O)-OH)>		C3H6O
2894M	F	8.00	OH	A<C-CH-CH-C(C(=O)-O-CH2)>		CCL4
1891M	A	6.53	OH	A<C-CH-CH-C(F)>		CDCL3
2336M	D	8.76	OH	A<C-CH-CH-C(NH-C(=O)-CH3)>		POLYSOL-D
1905M	C	9.32	OH	A<C-CH-CH-C(NO2)>		C3H6O
1887M	C	4.95	OH	A<C-CH-CH-C(R6<CH-CH2/CH2>)>		CDCL3
1931M	A	5.28	OH	A<C-CH-C(A)-C(OH)>		CDCL3
1880M	C	6.09	OH	A<C-CH-C(CH2-CH3)>		CDCL3
2078M	E	8.20-10.20	OH	A<C-CH-C(CH3)-C(C(=O)-CH3)>		DMSO-D6
1943M	B	8.95	OH	A<C-CH-C(CL)-C(OH)/CH-C(CL)>		POLYSOL-D
2080M	E	9.14	OH	A<C-CH-C(C(=O)-CH3)-C(OH)>		DMSO-D6
1897M	D	9.24	OH	A<C-CH-C(I)>		POLYSOL-D
1911M	C	8.16	OH	A<C-CH-C(OH)>		C3H6O
1928M	G	7.70	OH	A<C-CH-C(OH)-C(CH2.15-CH3)>		POLYSOL-D
1927M	D	5.85	OH	A<C-CH-C(OH)-C(CH2-CH2)>		CDCL3
1947M	B	6.01	OH	A<C-CH-C(OH)/CH-C(OH)>		C3H6O
1931M	A	5.28	OH	A<C-C(A)-CH-C(OH)>		CDCL3
1894M	A	5.08	OH	A<C-C(BR)>		CDCL3
1921M	A	5.41	OH	A<C-C(BR)-CH-C(BR)>		CCL4
1928M	G	7.70	OH	A<C-C(CH2.15-CH3)/CH-C(OH)>		POLYSOL-D
1927M	D	5.85	OH	A<C-C(CH2-CH2)/CH-C(OH)>		CDCL3
1879M	C	5.52	OH	A<C-C(CH2-CH3)>		CCL4
1932M	C	4.91 APP.	OH	A<C-C(CH2-Q3)-C(CH3)/CH-C(CH3)>		CDCL3
1918M	C	4.79	OH	A<C-C(CH2-Q3)/C(CH3)>		CCL4
1876M	B	5.18	OH	A<C-C(CH3)>		CCL4
1923M	C	5.31	OH	A<C-C(CH3)-CH-C(S-CH3)>		CDCL3
1913M	C	4.84	OH	A<C-C(CH3)-C(CH3)>		CDCL3
1892M	A	5.37	OH	A<C-C(CL)>		CDCL3
1919M	A	5.68	OH	A<C-C(CL)-CH-C(CL)>		CDCL3
1943M	C	9.37	OH	A<C-C(CL)-CH-C(OH)/C(CL)>		POLYSOL-D
1922M	D	10.97	OH	A<C-C(CL)/C(NO2)>		CDCL3
1882M	B	4.48	OH	A<C-C(C(CH3/CH3/CH3))>		CCL4
1933M	E	5.71 APP.	OH	A<C-C(C(CH3/CH3/CH3))-CH-C(CH2-CH3)/C(CH2-A)>		CDCL3
1934M	B	5.13	OH	A<C-C(C(CH3/CH3/CH3))/CH-C(A<C-CH-C(C(CH3/CH3/CH3))-C(OH)/CH-C(C(CH3/CH3/CH3))>/C(C(CH3/CH3/CH3))>		CDCL3
2079M	E	12.02	OH	A<C-C(C(=O)-CH3)-CH-C(CL)>		CDCL3
2080M	F	11.40	OH	A<C-C(C(=O)-CH3)-CH-C(CL)>		DMSO-D6
2178M	E	9.70	OH	A<C-C(C(=O)-H)-CH-C(O-CH3)>		CCL4
2293M	F	13.10	OH	A<C-C(C(=O)-NH2)>		DMSO-D6
2596M	E	10.90	OH	A<C-C(C(=O)-OH)/CH-C(CH3)>		POLYSOL-D
1890M	A	5.32	OH	A<C-C(F)>		CCL4
2334M	D	9.37	OH	A<C-C(NH-C(=O))>		DMSO-D6
2334M	D	9.75	OH	A<C-C(NH-C(=O))>		DMSO-D6
1903M	E	10.46	OH	A<C-C(NO2)>		CCL4
1939M	A	6.73	OH	A<C-C(NO2)-CH-C(NO2)/C(NO2)>		C3D6O
1944M	C	10.35	OH	A<C-C(NO2)-C(OH)>		POLYSOL-D
1930M	C	8.86	OH	A<C-C(OH)-CH-C(A)>		POLYSOL-D
1926M	B	5.87	OH	A<C-C(OH)-CH-C(CH3)>		CDCL3
2919M	D	6.47	OH	A<C-C(OH)-CH-C(C(=O)-O-CH2)/C(OH)>		C3D6O
2918M	D	6.60 APP.	OH	A<C-C(OH)-CH-C(C(=O)-O-CH2)/C(OH)>		C3D6O
2917M	E	7.72	OH	A<C-C(OH)-CH-C(C(=O)-O-CH2)/C(OH)>		C3D6O
2916M	C	8.19	OH	A<C-C(OH)-CH-C(C(=O)-O-CH3)/C(OH)>		POLYSOL-D
1925M	B	5.78	OH	A<C-C(OH)-C(CH3)>		CDCL3
1945M	B	7.54	OH	A<C-C(OH)-C(OH)>		C3H6O
2919M	D	6.47	OH	A<C-C(OH)-C(OH)/CH-C(C(=O)-O-CH2)>		C3D6O
2918M	D	6.60 APP.	OH	A<C-C(OH)-C(OH)/CH-C(C(=O)-O-CH2)>		C3D6O
2917M	E	7.72	OH	A<C-C(OH)-C(OH)/CH-C(C(=O)-O-CH2)>		C3D6O
2916M	C	8.19	OH	A<C-C(OH)-C(OH)/CH-C(C(=O)-O-CH3)>		POLYSOL-D
1930M	C	8.86	OH	A<C-C(OH)/CH-C(A)>		POLYSOL-D

BOOK NO.	ASSIGN-MENT	CHEM SHIFT - ppm -	PROTON GROUP	ENVIRONMENTAL GROUPS	S	SOLVENT
1926M	B	5.87	OH	A<C-C(OH)/CH-C(CH3)>		CDCL3
1925M	B	5.78	OH	A<C-C(OH)/C(CH3)>		CDCL3
1945M	B	7.54	OH	A<C-C(OH)/C(OH)>		C3H60
2598M	E	10.63	OH	A<C-C(O-CH3)-CH-C(C(=O)-OH)>		DMSO-D6
2915M	C	5.92	OH	A<C-C(O-CH3)-CH-C(C(=O)-O-CH3)/C(O-CH3)>		CDCL3
1889M	D	9.49	OH	A(C-CH-CH-C(A))		DMSO
1895M	A	5.20	OH	A(C-CH-CH-C(BR))		CDCL3
2038M	B	2.71	OH	A(C-CH-CH-C(CH2-CH2))		CDCL3
1893M	A	6.33	OH	A(C-CH-CH-C(CL))		CDCL3
1886M	D	4.67	OH	A(C-CH-CH-C(C(CH2/CH3/CH3)))		CDCL3
1885M	D	5.46	OH	A(C-CH-CH-C(C(CH2/CH3/CH3)))		CCL4
1883M	B	4.91	OH	A(C-CH-CH-C(C(CH3/CH3/CH3)))		CDCL3
2895M	E	7.70	OH	A(C-CH-CH-C(C(=O)-O-CH2))		CCL4
2893M	D	7.31	OH	A(C-CH-CH-C(C(=O)-O-CH))		CDCL3
1898M	A	5.41	OH	A(C-CH-CH-C(I))		CDCL3
1914M	B	5.40	OH	A(C-CH-C(CH3)-C(CH3))		CCL4
1915M	B	5.73	OH	A(C-CH-C(CH3)/CH-C(CH3))		CCL4
1920M	A	5.28	OH	A(C-CH-C(CL)/CH-C(CL))		CDCL3
2892M	B	6.72 APP.	OH	A(C-CH-C(C(=O)-O-CH3))		CDCL3
2914M	D	9.59	OH	A(C-CH-C(C(=O)-O-CH3)/CH-C(OH))		DMSO-D6
1899M	E	8.78	OH	A(C-CH-C(NH2))		DMSO
1904M	E	10.31	OH	A(C-CH-C(NO2))		DMSO
1929M	F	9.08	OH	A(C-CH-C(OH)-C(CH2-A))		DMSO-D6
1937M	A	5.71	OH	A(C-C(BR)-CH-C(BR)/C(BR))		CCL4
1936M	D	6.44	OH	A(C-C(CH2-A)-CH-C(CH3)/C(CH2-A))		CDCL3
1929M	F	9.08	OH	A(C-C(CH2-A)/CH-C(OH))		DMSO-D6
1907M	E	9.22	OH	A(C-C(CH2-OH))		DMSO-D6
1916M	B	4.39	OH	A(C-C(CH3)/C(CH3))		CCL4
1917M	D	4.77	OH	A(C-C(CH(CH3/CH3))/CH-C(CH3))		CDCL3
1936M	D	6.44	OH	A(C-C(C(CH3/CH3/CH3))-CH-C(CH3)/C(CH2-A))		CDCL3
2105M	G	12.00	OH	A(C-C(C(=O)-A))		CDCL3
2891M	H	10.72	OH	A(C-C(C(=O)-O-CH2))		CDCL3
2889M	G	10.92	OH	A(C-C(C(=O)-O-CH))		CDCL3
1896M	A	5.55	OH	A(C-C(I))		CDCL3
1938M	A	7.80 APP.	OH	A(C-C(I)-CH-C(I)/C(I))		DMSO
1941M	B	7.90	OH	A(C-C(NO2)-CH-C(NO2)/C(NO2))		DMSO
1940M	B	7.91	OH	A(C-C(NO2)-CH-C(NO2)/C(NO2))		DMSO
2597M	C	12.49	OH	A(C-C(NO2)/C(C(=O)-OH))		POLYSOL-D
1910M	C	7.51	OH	A(C-C(OH))		POLYSOL-D
1924M	D	5.40	OH	A(C-C(O-CH3)-CH-C(CH2-Q3))		CCL4
1827M	C	3.92	OH	CH2.16-OH		DMSO-D6
1635M	C	2.71	OH	CH2.23-CH3		POLYSOL-D
1718M	C	4.05	OH	CH2.2-A		POLYSOL-D
1725M	B	3.41	OH	CH2.2-AA		CCL4
1732M	B	3.96	OH	CH2.2-ANN		CDCL3
1645M	C	2.71	OH	CH2.2-C		CDCL3
1620M	E	3.79	OH	CH2.2-CH		CCL4
1699M	E	3.30 APP.	OH	CH2.2-C:		CCL4
1698M	E	3.31	OH	CH2.2-C:		CCL4
1704M	A	2.31	OH	CH2.2-N		CDCL3
1652M	F	3.64	OH	CH2.2-N		CDCL3
1647M	D	3.19	OH	CH2.2-NH		CCL4
1672M	A	2.63	OH	CH2.2-O		CDCL3
1674M	B	3.12	OH	CH2.2-O		CCL4
1670M	C	2.10	OH	CH2.2-O		CDCL3
1669M	C	2.75	OH	CH2.2-O		CCL4
1678M	C	3.78	OH	CH2.2-R5S		CCL4
1682M	B	3.49	OH	CH2.2-R6		CCL4
1660M	C	2.07	OH	CH2.2-S		CDCL3
1708M	C	3.28	OH	CH2.2-S		CCL4
1640M	D	4.21	OH	CH2.3-BR		CDCL3
1849M	C	4.53	OH	CH2.3-CH		POLYSOL-D
1621M	D	4.13	OH	CH2.3-CH		CCL4
1653M	G	5.19	OH	CH2.3-N		CDCL3
1625M	C	2.85	OH	CH2.4-CH		CDCL3
1723M	A	3.09	OH	CH2-A		CCL4
1700M	A	3.10	OH	CH2-A		CCL4
1722M	A	3.11	OH	CH2-A		CDCL3
1719M	A	3.12	OH	CH2-A		CDCL3
1717M	A	3.30	OH	CH2-A		CDCL3
1720M	A	4.20	OH	CH2-A		CDCL3
1713M	B	2.94	OH	CH2-A		CCL4
1715M	B	4.51	OH	CH2-A		CCL4
1907M	B	4.69	OH	CH2-A		DMSO-D6
1716M	B	4.88	OH	CH2-A		CDCL3
1860M	B	5.10	OH	CH2-A		DMSO-D6
1714M	C	4.05	OH	CH2-A		CCL4
1728M	B	5.02	OH	CH2-AN		CDCL3
1729M	B	6.27	OH	CH2-AN		CDCL3
1731M	B	5.49	OH	CH2-ANA		CDCL3
1734M	A	2.83	OH	CH2-AR500		CDCL3

BOOK NO.	ASSIGN-MENT	CHEM SHIFT - ppm -	PROTON GROUP	ENVIRONMENTAL GROUPS	S	SOLVENT
1641M	A	3.28	OH	CH2-C		CDCL3
1693M	B	4.01	OH	CH2-C		CDCL3
1841M	C	3.93	OH	CH2-C		POLYSOL-D
1624M	D	2.59	OH	CH2-C		CDCL3
1835M	D	4.09	OH	CH2-C		CDCL3
1837M	E	2.60	OH	CH2-C		CDCL3
1839M	E	3.71	OH	CH2-C		C3D6O
1638M	B	4.19	OH	CH2-CH		CCL4
1622M	C	1.56	OH	CH2-CH		CDCL3
1627M	D	1.97	OH	CH2-CH		CCL4
2719M	D	2.38 APP.	OH	CH2-CH		CDCL3
1994M	D	3.11	OH	CH2-CH		CDCL3
1615M	D	3.98	OH	CH2-CH		CCL4
1829M	D	4.30	OH	CH2-CH		CDCL3
2718M	D	4.30	OH	CH2-CH		CDCL3
1662M	E	3.33	OH	CH2-CH		CDCL3
1701M	A	2.44	OH	CH2-CH2		CDCL3
1665M	A	2.49	OH	CH2-CH2		CDCL3
1726M	A	2.49	OH	CH2-CH2		CDCL3
1705M	A	2.59	OH	CH2-CH2		CCL4
1673M	A	3.27	OH	CH2-CH2		CDCL3
1846M	A	3.48	OH	CH2-CH2		CDCL3
1687M	B	2.57	OH	CH2-CH2		CDCL3
1642M	B	2.82	OH	CH2-CH2		CDCL3
1706M	B	2.91	OH	CH2-CH2		CDCL3
1658M	B	3.42	OH	CH2-CH2		CDCL3
1845M	B	4.22	OH	CH2-CH2		CDCL3
1634M	C	1.62	OH	CH2-CH2		CDCL3
1632M	C	1.64	OH	CH2-CH2		CDCL3
1629M	C	1.74	OH	CH2-CH2		CDCL3
1633M	C	2.05	OH	CH2-CH2		CDCL3
1628M	C	2.33	OH	CH2-CH2		CCL4
1703M	C	2.89	OH	CH2-CH2		CDCL3
1675M	C	3.07	OH	CH2-CH2		CDCL3
1631M	C	3.24	OH	CH2-CH2		CCL4
1668M	C	3.25	OH	CH2-CH2		CCL4
1623M	C	3.40	OH	CH2-CH2		CCL4
1832M	C	3.47	OH	CH2-CH2		CDCL3
1630M	C	3.50	OH	CH2-CH2		CCL4
2972M	C	3.61	OH	CH2-CH2		CCL4
1695M	C	3.67	OH	CH2-CH2		CCL4
1639M	C	4.29	OH	CH2-CH2		CCL4
1636M	C	4.50	OH	CH2-CH2		CDCL3
1826M	C	4.52	OH	CH2-CH2		CDCL3
2465M	C	4.54	OH	CH2-CH2		DMSO-D6
1854M	C	4.61	OH	CH2-CH2		CDCL3
1689M	D	2.87	OH	CH2-CH2		CCL4
1702M	D	3.63 APP.	OH	CH2-CH2		CCL4
1619M	D	3.67	OH	CH2-CH2		CCL4
1613M	D	3.71	OH	CH2-CH2		CCL4
1626M	D	3.90	OH	CH2-CH2		CCL4
1614M	D	4.11	OH	CH2-CH2		CCL4
1618M	D	4.11	OH	CH2-CH2		CCL4
1688M	D	4.21	OH	CH2-CH2		CCL4
1616M	D	4.41	OH	CH2-CH2		CCL4
1657M	D	4.61	OH	CH2-CH2	S	CDCL3
1650M	E	3.52	OH	CH2-CH2		CCL4
1649M	E	3.74	OH	CH2-CH2		CCL4
1612M	C	4.40	OH	CH2-CH3		CCL4
1696M	C	4.01	OH	CH2-C:		CCL4
1697M	D	3.61 APP.	OH	CH2-C:		CCL4
2430M	B	5.27	OH	CH2-NH		DMSO-D6
1712M	B	3.38	OH	CH2-Q1		CDCL3
1690M	E	2.30	OH	CH2-Q1		CCL4
1711M	A	2.33	OH	CH2-Q2		CDCL3
1724M	B	4.42	OH	CH2-Q2		POLYSOL-D
1686M	C	4.11	OH	CH2-Q2		CCL4
1685M	B	4.60	OH	CH2-Q3		CCL4
1727M	B	4.93	OH	CH2-R5AA		POLYSOL-D
1730M	D	8.70	OH	CH2-R5NNA		DMSO-D6
1733M	A	3.32	OH	CH2-R5O		CDCL3
1679M	C	3.46	OH	CH2-R5OO		CCL4
1680M	C	3.48	OH	CH2-R6		CCL4
1681M	D	4.05	OH	CH2-R6		CCL4
1692M	D	3.49 APP.	OH	CH2-R6O		CDCL3
1684M	E	3.49	OH	CH2-R6R6R6TRI		POLYSOL-D
1709M	B	4.45	OH	CH2-SO2		CDCL3
1611M	B	4.11	OH	CH3		CCL4
1794M	F	5.20- 5.60	OH	CH(ANA/R6R6N*RI)		POLYSOL-D
1790M	A	2.28	OH	CH(A/A)		CCL4
1791M	A	2.10	OH	CH(A/CH2)		CDCL3

: REPRESENTS TRIPLE BOND, ¬ REPRESENTS AN ARROW AND < AND > REPRESENT BRACKETS.

BOOK NO.	ASSIGN-MENT	CHEM SHIFT - ppm -	PROTON GROUP	ENVIRONMENTAL GROUPS	S	SOLVENT
1788M	C	2.67	OH	CH(A/CH2)		CCL4
2850M	C	3.50	OH	CH(A/CH2)		CCL4
1793M	B	2.82	OH	CH(A/CH3)		CCL4
1789M	C	3.22	OH	CH(A/R3)		CCL4
1749M	C	2.02	OH	CH(CH2.2/CH2.2)		CCL4
1740M	C	2.18	OH	CH(CH2.2/CH2.2)		CDCL3
1849M	C	4.53	OH	CH(CH2.3/CH2.3)		POLYSOL-D
1784M	D	2.43	OH	CH(CH2/CH2.2)		CDCL3
1751M	A	3.27	OH	CH(CH2/CH2)		CDCL3
2791M	B	2.90	OH	CH(CH2/CH2)		CCL4
2759M	C	2.35 APP.	OH	CH(CH2/CH2)		CDCL3
1737M	C	3.30	OH	CH(CH2/CH2)		CCL4
1750M	C	3.40- 4.40	OH	CH(CH2/CH2)		CDCL3
2719M	D	2.38 APP.	OH	CH(CH2/CH2)		CDCL3
1745M	D	2.71	OH	CH(CH2/CH2)		CDCL3
1747M	D	2.97	OH	CH(CH2/CH2)		CCL4
1829M	D	4.30	OH	CH(CH2/CH2)		CDCL3
2718M	D	4.30	OH	CH(CH2/CH2)		CDCL3
2758M	E	2.50 APP.	OH	CH(CH2/CH2)		CDCL3
1787M	E	2.86	OH	CH(CH2/CH2)		CCL4
2532M	F	7.17	OH	CH(CH2/CH2)		CCL4
1792M	B	3.41	OH	CH(CH2/CH3)		CCL4
1748M	D	1.67	OH	CH(CH2/CH3)		CCL4
1746M	D	2.42	OH	CH(CH2/CH3)		CCL4
1738M	D	2.81	OH	CH(CH2/CH3)		CCL4
1742M	D	3.11	OH	CH(CH2/CH3)		CCL4
1754M	D	3.19	OH	CH(CH2/CH3)		CDCL3
1739M	D	3.39	OH	CH(CH2/CH3)		CCL4
1756M	D	3.40	OH	CH(CH2/CH3)		CDCL3
1830M	D	4.51- 4.88	OH	CH(CH2/CH3)		CCL4
1851M	D	4.70	OH	CH(CH2/CH3)		CDCL3
1736M	E	3.99	OH	CH(CH2/CH3)		CCL4
1735M	B	2.90	OH	CH(CH3/CH3)		CCL4
1743M	D	2.05	OH	CH(CH/CH2)		CCL4
1753M	B	2.22	OH	CH(CH/CH3)		CDCL3
1741M	B	1.64	OH	CH(CH/CH)		CDCL3
2555M	C	7.72 APP.	OH	CH(C(=O)-OH/A)		DMSO
2741M	E	2.72	OH	CH(C(=O)-O/CH2)		CCL4
2790M	E	5.19	OH	CH(C(=O)-O/CH2)		CDCL3
2740M	B	3.24	OH	CH(C(=O)-O/CH3)		CCL4
2792M	C	3.70	OH	CH(C(=O)-O/CH)		CCL4
2357M	C	3.83	OH	CH(C(=O)/CH3)		CCL4
2023M	A	5.31	OH	CH(C(=O)/R50)		DMSO
1758M	B	4.05	OH	CH(C:N/CH3)		CDCL3
1744M	B	1.32	OH	CH(C/CH2)		CCL4
1838M	D	2.58	OH	CH(C/C)		CDCL3
1833M	E	4.28	OH	CH(HCH/CH3)		CCL4
1828M	E	4.38	OH	CH(HCH/CH3)		CDCL3
1759M	F	3.40	OH	CH(HCH/CH3)		CCL4
1755M	G	3.20	OH	CH(HCH/CH3)		CCL4
1831M	H	4.87	OH	CH(HCH/CH3)		CCL4
1659M	D	5.52	OH	CH(P=/CH2.2)		POLYSOL-D
1782M	C	3.09	OH	CH(Q2/CH3)		CCL4
1785M	B	3.15	OH	CH(Q3/CH2)		CDCL3
1783M	C	2.78	OH	CH(Q3/CH2)		CCL4
1761M	D	2.77	OH	CH(R3/CH3)		CDCL3
1762M	C	3.05	OH	CH(R6/CH3)		CCL4
1822M	A	2.70 APP.	OH	C(A/A/A)		CDCL3
1820M	C	1.87	OH	C(A/A/CH2.7)		CCL4
1818M	B	1.79	OH	C(A/CH2/CH2)		CDCL3
1817M	B	2.34	OH	C(A/CH3/CH3)		CDCL3
1819M	C	2.72	OH	C(A/C:C/CH3)		CDCL3
1805M	B	2.62	OH	C(CBR3/CH3/CH3)		CDCL3
1801M	E	2.00	OH	C(CH2.2/CH2/CH3)		CCL4
1798M	D	1.78	OH	C(CH2.3/CH3/CH3)		CCL4
1800M	D	1.89	OH	C(CH2.5/CH3/CH3)		CDCL3
1804M	B	1.16	OH	C(CH2/CH2/CH2)		CDCL3
1837M	D	2.15	OH	C(CH2/CH2/CH3)		CDCL3
1802M	E	2.19	OH	C(CH2/CH2/CH3)		CCL4
1796M	D	2.89	OH	C(CH2/CH3/CH3)		CCL4
1795M	B	2.40	OH	C(CH3/C(3/CH3)		CCL4
1838M	C	2.29	OH	C(CH/CH3/CH3)		CDCL3
2556M	A	6.27	OH	C(C(=O)-OH/A/A)		C3H6O
1993M	C	3.30	OH	C(C(=O)/CH3/CH3)		CDCL3
1813M	B	2.30	OH	C(C:CH/CH3/CH3)		CDCL3
1815M	D	1.93	OH	C(C:C/CH2/CH3)		CDCL3
1814M	E	2.70	OH	C(C:C/CH2/CH3)		CCL4
1806M	B	3.49	OH	C(C:N/CH3/CH3)		CDCL3
1859M	B	5.47	OH	C(C:/CH3/CH3)		DMSO-D6
1834M	B	2.10	OH	C(C/CH3/CH3)		CDCL3
1831M	G	4.72	OH	C(HCH/CH3/CH3)		CCL4

BOOK NO.	ASSIGN-MENT	CHEM SHIFT - ppm -	PROTON GROUP	ENVIRONMENTAL GROUPS	S	SOLVENT
2575M	A	6.41	OH	C(=O)-A		C3D60
2578M	A	6.55	OH	C(=O)-A		C3H60
2574M	A	7.28 APP.	OH	C(=O)-A		DMSO-D6
2592M	B	9.41	OH	C(=O)-A		DMSO-D6
2603M	B	11.53	OH	C(=O)-A		DMSO
2602M	B	12.01	OH	C(=O)-A		DMSO
2568M	B	12.70	OH	C(=O)-A		POLYSOL-D
2571M	C	8.27	OH	C(=O)-A		DMSO
2572M	C	9.11	OH	C(=O)-A		DMSO
2570M	C	9.72	OH	C(=O)-A		C3H60
2588M	C	9.76	OH	C(=O)-A		C3H60
2581M	C	10.67	OH	C(=O)-A		C3H60
2593M	C	11.40	OH	C(=O)-A		CDCL3
2590M	C	11.90	OH	C(=O)-A		POLYSOL-D
2589M	C	12.02	OH	C(=O)-A		DMSO
2597M	C	12.49	OH	C(=O)-A		POLYSOL-D
2569M	C	12.57	OH	C(=O)-A		POLYSOL-D
2566M	C	12.82	OH	C(=O)-A		CCL4
2594M	D	9.61	OH	C(=O)-A		DMSO
2580M	D	10.32	OH	C(=O)-A		DMSO
2595M	E	7.87	OH	C(=O)-A		POLYSOL-D
2598M	E	10.63	OH	C(=O)-A		DMSO-D6
2596M	E	10.90	OH	C(=O)-A		POLYSOL-D
2573M	E	11.21	OH	C(=O)-A		POLYSOL-D
2576M	E	11.86	OH	C(=O)-A		POLYSOL-D
2896M	E	12.48	OH	C(=O)-A		CDCL3
2583M	E	12.80	OH	C(=O)-A⁺		DMSO-D6
2586M	F	10.95	OH	C(=O)-A		POLYSOL-D
2585M	G	10.59	OH	C(=O)-A		CCL4
2608M	E	10.80	OH	C(=O)-AR500		POLYSOL-D
2556M	A	6.27	OH	C(=O)-C		C3H60
2476M	B	12.01	OH	C(=O)-C		CDCL3
2562M	D	9.48	OH	C(=O)-C		CDCL3
2545M	D	10.48	OH	C(=O)-C		CDCL3
2504M	A	12.53	OH	C(=O)-CF2		POLYSOL-D
1155M	C	7.00- 9.00	OH	C(=O)-CF3		TFA
2555M	C	7.72 APP.	OH	C(=O)-CH		DMSO
2544M	C	10.58	OH	C(=O)-CH		CDCL3
2546M	C	10.60	OH	C(=O)-CH		CDCL3
2489M	D	11.09	OH	C(=O)-CH		CCL4
2481M	D	11.50	OH	C(=O)-CH		CCL4
2541M	D	11.50	OH	C(=O)-CH		CCL4
2484M	D	11.57	OH	C(=O)-CH		CDCL3
2552M	D	11.58	OH	C(=O)-CH		CDCL3
2479M	D	12.23	OH	C(=O)-CH		CCL4
2475M	E	10.60	OH	C(=O)-CH		CDCL3
2486M	E	11.78	OH	C(=O)-CH		CDCL3
2478M	E	12.01	OH	C(=O)-CH		CCL4
2477M	E	12.09	OH	C(=O)-CH		CCL4
2487M	E	12.13	OH	C(=O)-CH		CCL4
2621M	F	11.01	OH	C(=O)-CH		POLYSOL-D
2627M	F	11.80	OH	C(=O)-CH		POLYSOL-D
2620M	F	11.85	OH	C(=O)-CH		DMSO-D6
2485M	B	10.59	OH	C(=O)-CH2		CDCL3
2488M	B	10.80	OH	C(=O)-CH2		CDCL3
2483M	B	11.22	OH	C(=O)-CH2		CCL4
2496M	B	11.50	OH	C(=O)-CH2		POLYSOL-D
2497M	B	11.80	OH	C(=O)-CH2		DMSO-D6
2634M	C	6.81 APP.	OH	C(=O)-CH2		DMSO-D6
2500M	C	9.74	OH	C(=O)-CH2		POLYSOL-D
2473M	C	10.49	OH	C(=O)-CH2		CDCL3
2607M	C	10.66	OH	C(=O)-CH2		DMSO
2539M	C	10.88	OH	C(=O)-CH2		CDCL3
2558M	C	11.00	OH	C(=O)-CH2		CDCL3
2502M	C	11.05	OH	C(=O)-CH2		DMSO-D6
2499M	C	11.32	OH	C(=O)-CH2		DMSO-D6
2490M	C	11.50	OH	C(=O)-CH2		CCL4
2498M	C	11.74	OH	C(=O)-CH2		DMSO-D6
2565M	C	11.79	OH	C(=O)-CH2		POLYSOL-D
2559M	C	11.89	OH	C(=O)-CH2		CDCL3
2553M	D	8.78	OH	C(=O)-CH2		C3H60
2557M	D	9.07	OH	C(=O)-CH2		CDCL3
2494M	D	9.33	OH	C(=O)-CH2		CDCL3
2540M	D	10.92	OH	C(=O)-CH2		CDCL3
2512M	D	11.49	OH	C(=O)-CH2		CDCL3
2501M	D	11.67	OH	C(=O)-CH2		DMSO-D6
2548M	D	11.68	OH	C(=O)-CH2		POLYSOL-D
2495M	E	10.03	OH	C(=O)-CH2		CDCL3
2516M	E	10.08	OH	C(=O)-CH2		CDCL3
2518M	E	10.81	OH	C(=O)-CH2		CDCL3
2579M	E	10.88	OH	C(=O)-CH2		CDCL3

BOOK NO.	ASSIGN-MENT	CHEM SHIFT - ppm -	PROTON GROUP	ENVIRONMENTAL GROUPS	S	SOLVENT
2480M	E	10.96	OH	C(=0)-CH2		CCL4
2549M	E	11.28	OH	C(=0)-CH2		CDCL3
2532M	F	7.17	OH	C(=0)-CH2		CCL4
2543M	F	10.59	OH	C(=0)-CH2		DMSO-D6
2563M	F	10.70	OH	C(=0)-CH2		CDCL3
2528M	F	11.86	OH	C(=0)-CH2		CCL4
2554M	G	10.68	OH	C(=0)-CH2		CDCL3
2503M	D	8.97	OH	C(=0)-CH2.14		POLYSOL-D
2482M	E	7.90- 8.90	OH	C(=0)-CH2.14-CH3		CDCL3
2526M	F	11.73	OH	C(=0)-CH2.2		CCL4
2525M	F	11.80	OH	C(=0)-CH2.2		CCL4
2527M	F	11.91	OH	C(=0)-CH2.2		CCL4
2749M	F	11.60	OH	C(=0)-CH2.8		CDCL3
2472M	B	11.90	OH	C(=0)-CH3		CCL4
2686M	E	7.98	OH	C(=0)-CH3		CDCL3
2685M	E	8.14	OH	C(=0)-CH3	·	CDCL3
2650M	C	2.07	OH	C(=0)-0-NA/CH2.3-CH3/CH2-CH3		D20
2519M	D	12.22	OH	C(=0)-Q1		CCL4
2551M	E	11.76	OH	C(=0)-Q1		CDCL3
2523M	F	12.34	OH	C(=0)-Q1		CCL4
2531M	C	12.27	OH	C(=0)-Q2		POLYSOL-D
2517M	D	11.79	OH	C(=0)-Q2		CDCL3
2550M	D	11.90	OH	C(=0)-Q2		CDCL3
2530M	E	10.04	OH	C(=0)-Q2		CDCL3
2605M	F	10.32	OH	C(=0)-Q2		CDCL3
2520M	F	11.91	OH	C(=0)-Q2		CCL4
2524M	F	12.35	OH	C(=0)-Q2		CCL4
2522M	G	12.15	OH	C(=0)-Q2		CCL4
2533M	B	12.28	OH	C(=0)-Q2(H/C(=0)-0H/H)		DMSO-D6
2513M	C	11.99	OH	C(=0)-R4		CDCL3
2604M	D	9.19	OH	C(=0)-R50		POLYSOL-D
2537M	E	11.70	OH	C(=0)-R5R5BI		CCL4
2514M	B	12.00	OH	C(=0)-R6		CCL4
2538M	D	9.17	OH	C(=0)-R6		C3D60
2535M	D	12.42	OH	C(=0)-R6		CCL4
2536M	C	11.72	OH	C(=0)-R8		CDCL3
2143M	E	13.27	OH	C(=R5/CH3)		CCL4
1644M	D	3.02	OH	HCH-CH		CDCL3
1828M	E	4.38	OH	HCH-CH		CDCL3
1617M	F	3.90	OH	HCH-CH		CCL4
891M	D	8.60	OH	NH-C(=0)		CDCL3
894M	F	8.24	OH	NH-C(=0)-Q2		POLYSOL-D
852M	D	9.91	OH	N=CH		CDCL3
2997M	C	11.06	OH	P(=0/0/0)		CCL4
2332M	E	9.50	OH	QN(A(C-CH-CH-C(NH-C(=0)-CH3)))		POLYSOL-D
1529M	G	9.34	OH	QN(A(C-C(0-CH3)ĵ))		CDCL3
860M	D	9.33	OH	QN(A/CH3)		CDCL3
849M	F	9.80	OH	QN(CH2.5-CH3)		CDCL3
854M	E	9.08	OH	QN(CH2-CH2/CH3)		CDCL3
857M	E	9.39	OH	QN(CH2-CH2/CH3)		CDCL3
856M	E	9.83	OH	QN(CH2-CH2/CH3)		CDCL3
853M	E	9.55	OH	QN(CH2-CH3/CH3)		CDCL3
855M	D	9.08	OH	QN(CH2-CH/CH3)		CDCL3
853M	E	9.55	OH	QN(CH3/CH2-CH3)		CDCL3
848M	G	8.45	OH	QN(H/CH)		CCL4
864M	B	10.48	OH	QN(QN(0H/CH3)/CH3)		POLYSOL-D
2139M	G	15.24	OH	Q1(CH2.2-CH3/C(=0)-CH2.2)		CCL4
2138M	G	15.16	OH	Q1(CH2-CH3/C(=0)-CH2)		CCL4
2146M	H	15.02	OH	Q1(CH3/C(=0)-CH2)		CCL4
2743M	H	11.93	OH	Q1(CH3/C(=0)-0-CH2.3)		CCL4
2141M	H	15.03	OH	Q1(CH3/C(=0)-R50)		CCL4
1786M	A	4.02	OH	Q1(H/CH2-CL/CL)		CCL4
1786M	A	4.02	OH	Q1(H/CL/CH2-CL)		CCL4
2137M	G	16.60	OH	Q(CH3/C(=0)-CH3/CH2-CH3)		CDCL3
1763M	C	5.48	OH	R4(CH-CH2/CH2)		CCL4
2150M	A	7.72	OH	R5A(C(0H)-C(=0)/C(=0))		DMSO
2949M	E	4.43	OH	R50<CH-C(=0)/C(CH3/CH3)>		CDCL3
1779M	C	1.53	OH	R5R5BI<CH-C*(CH3)/CH2>		CDCL3
2143M	E	13.27	OH	R5<C=C(C(=0)-CH3)/CH2>		CCL4
1764M	B	3.58	OH	R5(CH-CH2/CH2)		CCL4
2129M	E	2.92	OH	R6R6R6R5(CH-CH2/CH2)		CDCL3
1778M	C	3.81	OH	R6R6<CH-CH2/CH2>		POLYSOL-D
1768M	C	2.60	OH	R6<CH-CH2/CH2>		CDCL3
1769M	C	2.86	OH	R6<CH-CH2/CH2>		CDCL3
1774M	B	1.89	OH	R6<CH-CH(A)/HCH>		CDCL3
1770M	C	2.39	OH	R6<CH-CH(CH2-CH3)/CH2>		CDCL3
1771M	D	3.11	OH	R6<CH-CH(CH3)/CH2>		CDCL3
1771M	E	3.75	OH	R6<CH-CH(CH3)/CH2>		CDCL3
1767M	D	2.54	OH	R6<CH-CH(CH3)/HCH>		CDCL3
1855M	B	3.20	OH	R6<CH-CH(0H)/CH2>		CDCL3
1773M	C	4.12	OH	R6<CH-CH(R6)/CH2>		CDCL3

BOOK NO.	ASSIGN- MENT	CHEM SHIFT - ppm -	PROTON GROUP	ENVIRONMENTAL GROUPS	S	SOLVENT
1776M	B	1.49	OH	R6<CH-C(A/A)/CH2>		CDCL3
1821M	C	2.36	OH	R6<C(A<C-CH-CH-C(CH3)>)-CH2/CH2>		CDCL3
1809M	B	1.33	OH	R6<C(OH)-CH2/CH2>		CDCL3
1766M	C	4.20	OH	R6(CH-CH2/CH2)		CCL4
1772M	D	2.23	OH	P6(CH-CH(CH(CH3/CH3))/CH2)		CDCL3
1810M	B	1.10 APP.	OH	R6(C(CH2-CH3)-CH2/CH2-CH2)		C3F60
1816M	C	3.08	OH	R6(C(C:CH)-CH2/CH2)		CDCL3
2144M	D	10.00	OH	R6(C=CH/CH2)		CDCL3
1777M	B	2.69	OH	R7<CH-CH2/CH2>		CDCL3
1289M	A	6.83	OH	SO2-A		DMSO
1290M	D	9.20 APP.	OH	SO2-A		DMSO-D6
1293M	G	9.53	OH	SO2-AA		DMSO-D6
873M	D	8.14	QN	AA<C-C#>/NH2		POLYSOL-D
882M	D	8.67	QN	AN<C-N>/QN(AN<C-N>)		CDCL3
872M	D	8.39	QN	A<C-CH-CH-C(CH3)>/A		CDCL3
1707M	D	8.12	QN	A<C-CH-CH-C(CL)>/CH2.2-OH		CDCL3
1528M	E	8.23	QN	A<C-CH-CH-C(O-CH3)>/A		CDCL3
881M	D	8.62	QN	A(C-CH-CH-C(CH3)/QN(A))		CDCL3
2332M	D	8.04	QN	A(C-CH-CH-C(NH-C(=O)-CH3))/OH		POLYSOL-D
877M	C	7.90	QN	A(C-C(CL))/NH-A		CDCL3
1529M	F	8.49	QN	A(C-C(OH))/OH		CDCL3
871M	C	8.40	QN	A/A		CDCL3
1366M	F	8.59	QN	A/A<C-CH-CH-C(SO2-NH2)>		DMSO-D6
868M	D	8.28	QN	A/CH2-CH2		CDCL3
866M	D	8.11	QN	A/CH3		CDCL3
876M	B	7.73	QN	A/NH-A		C3H60
1064M	D	8.06	QN	A/NH-A		POLYSOL-D
849M	D	6.71	QN	CH2.5-CH3/OH		CDCL3
849M	E	6.44	QN	CH2.5-CH3/OH		CDCL3
1358M	D	7.42	QN	CH2-CH2/NH-C(=S)		CDCL3
887M	C	8.11	QN	NH-A/A		POLYSOL-D
884M	C	7.35	QN	N(CH3/CH3)/A		CCL4
885M	E	7.29	QN	N(CH3/CH3)/A<C-CH-CH-C(CH3)>		CCL4
883M	C	7.30	QN	N(CH3/CH3)/R6<CH-CH2/CH2>		CDCL3
850M	A	7.82	QN	QN(OH)/OH		DMSO
869M	B	8.15	QN	Q2(A)/A		CDCL3
870M	D	8.14	QN	Q2(A)/A<C-CH-CH-C(CH3)>		CDCL3
867M	D	7.95	QN	Q2(A)/CH2.2-QN		CDCL3
875M	B	7.80	QN	Q2(A)/NH-A		DMSO
880M	A	7.11	QN	Q2(A)/QN(Q2)		CDCL3
1145M	D	8.55	QN	R5S<C-S/=CH>/OH		TFA
886M	D	7.28	QN	R6N<N-CH2/CH2>/A		CCL4
889M	A	5.71	QNH	NH-A/A		DMSO-D6
163M	A	6.99	Q1	A/A/A		CDCL3
2161M	D	7.10	Q1	A/C(=O)-H/CH2-CH2		CCL4
2160M	B	7.19	Q1	A/C(=O)-H/CH3		CCL4
2551M	D	7.80	Q1	A/C(=O)-OH/CH2-CH3		CDCL3
2858M	E	8.20	Q1	A/C(=O)-O-CH2/C:N		CDCL3
160M	D	5.99	Q1	CH2.3-CH3/A/A		CCL4
161M	D	5.98	Q1	CH2.6-CH3/A/A		CCL4
162M	D	6.07	Q1	CH2.9-CH3/A/A		CDCL3
2523M	E	6.88	Q1	CH2-CH2/CH2-CH3/C(=O)-OH		CCL4
893M	E	5.05	Q1	CH2-CH2/CH3/CH3		CDCL3
93M	F	5.09	Q1	CH2-CH2/CH3/CH3		CCL4
2157M	E	6.37	Q1	CH2-CH2/C(=O)-H/CH2-CH3		CCL4
94M	E	5.10	Q1	CH2-CH/CH3/CH3		CCL4
278M	C	5.71	Q1	CH2-CL/CL/CH3		CCL4
573M	E	5.26	Q1	CH2-NH/CH3/CH3		CDCL3
1690M	G	5.35	Q1	CH2-OH/CH2.3-CH/CH3		CCL4
1712M	D	6.46	Q1	CH2-OH/CH3/A		CDCL3
92M	F	5.16	Q1	CH3/CH2-CH2/CH3		CCL4
90M	C	5.12	Q1	CH3/CH3/CH3		CCL4
280M	B	5.86	Q1	CH3/CL/CL		CDCL3
282M	A	6.49	Q1	CL/CL/CL		CCL4
91M	D	5.11	Q1	C(CH3/CH3)/CH3/CH3		CCL4
2148M	C	6.28	Q1	C(=O)-A/OH/CH2-C(=O)-A		POLYSOL-D
2147M	D	6.12	Q1	C(=O)-A/OH/CH3		CDCL3
2139M	F	5.39	Q1	C(=O)-CH2.2/OH/CH2.2-CH3		CCL4
2148M	D	6.51	Q1	C(=O)-CH2/OH/A		POLYSOL-D
2138M	F	5.42	Q1	C(=O)-CH2/OH/CH2-CH3		CCL4
2146M	F	5.29	Q1	C(=O)-CH2/OH/CH3		CCL4
2042M	B	6.54	Q1	C(=O)-CH3/A/A		CDCL3
2020M	C	6.10	Q1	C(=O)-CH3/CH3/CH3		CDCL3
2146M	F	5.29	Q1	C(=O)-CH3/OH/CH2-A		CCL4
2319M	D	5.21	Q1	C(=O)-CH3/OH/NH-A		DMSO-D6
2358M	G	5.10	Q1	C(=O)-N/OH/CH3		CDCL3
2519M	C	5.69	Q1	C(=O)-OH/CH3/CH3		CCL4
2534M	B	7.04	Q1	C(=O)-OH/CH3/C(=O)-OH		TFA
2743M	G	4.88	Q1	C(=O)-O-CH2.3/OH/CH3		CCL4
2856M	D	6.03	Q1	C(=O)-O-CH2/A/CH3		CCL4
2141M	D	6.00	Q1	C(=O)-R50/OH/CH3		CCL4

BOOK NO.	ASSIGN-MENT	CHEM SHIFT - ppm -	PROTON GROUP	ENVIRONMENTAL GROUPS	S	SOLVENT
969M	B	7.63	Q1	NH2/C:N/C:N		DMSO-D6
643M	C	5.31	Q1	N(CH3/CH3)/CH3/CH3		CDCL3
1786M	E	6.45	Q1	OH/CH2-CL/CL		CCL4
1786M	D	6.23	Q1	OH/CL/CH2-CL		CCL4
164M	A	6.80	Q1	Q1(A/A)/A/A		CDCL3
95M	C	5.89	Q1	Q1(CH3/CH3)/CH3/CH3		CCL4
1166M	A	6.83	Q1	S-A/A/A		CDCL3
1724M	C	6.61 APP.	Q2	A<C-CH-CH-C(NO2)>/CH2-OH		POLYSOL-D
2162M	B	7.79	Q2	A<C-CH-CH-C(NO2)>/H/C(=O)-H		DMSO-D6
1559M	E	6.39	Q2	A<C-CH-C(O-CH3)-C(O-CH3)>/H/CH3		CDCL3
2564M	E	7.61	Q2	A(C-CH-CH-C(CH3))/H/C(=O)-OH		DMSO-D6
1506M	D	6.21	Q2	A(C-CH-CH-C(O-CH3))/CH3		CCL4
158M	A	6.58	Q2	A/A/H		CDCL3
380M	B	7.02	Q2	A/BR		CCL4
2549M	C	6.53	Q2	A/CH2-C(=O)-OH		CDCL3
2841M	D	6.62	Q2	A/CH2-O-C(=O)		CCL4
2201M	C	7.80	Q2	A/C(=O)-OH		CDCL3
159M	A	7.08	Q2	A/H/A		CDCL3
1711M	D	6.57	Q2	A/H/CH2-OH		CDCL3
2843M	F	6.55	Q2	A/H/CH2-O-C(=O)		CCL4
2842M	F	6.61	Q2	A/H/CH2-O-C(=O)		CCL4
1019M	C	6.59	Q2	A/H/CH2-S		CDCL3
1257M	D	6.72	Q2	A/H/CH2-SO2		CDCL3
2041M	F	7.51	Q2	A/H/C(=O)-CH2.3		CDCL3
2550M	C	7.73	Q2	A/H/C(=O)-OH		CDCL3
2861M	D	7.63	Q2	A/H/C(=O)-O-CH2		CCL4
2862M	F	7.57	Q2	A/H/C(=O)-O-CH2		CCL4
2269M	C	7.80	Q2	A/H/C(=O)-O-C(=O)		CDCL3
2857M	E	7.67	Q2	A/H/C(=O)-O-R6		CCL4
2043M	C	7.72	Q2	A/H/C(=O)-Q2		CDCL3
982M	B	7.36	Q2	A/H/C:N		CCL4
1360M	B	7.10	Q2	A/H/SO2-NH2		POLYSOL-D
1258M	B	7.40 APP.	Q2	A/H/SO2-Q2		CDCL3
867M	B	6.81 APP.	Q2	A/QN(CH2.2-QN)		CDCL3
880M	A	7.11	Q2	A/QN(QN)		CDCL3
380M	A	6.61	Q2	BR/A		CCL4
370M	A	6.64	Q2	BR/BR/H		CCL4
370M	B	7.04	Q2	BR/H/BR		CCL4
2800M	F	5.61 APP.	Q2	CH2.2-CH3/H/CH2-O-C(=O)		CCL4
2156M	E	6.87	Q2	CH2.2-CH3/H/C(=O)-H		CDCL3
2520M	E	7.03	Q2	CH2.2-CH3/H/C(=O)-OH		CCL4
2799M	F	6.83	Q2	CH2.2-CH3/H/C(=O)-O-CH3		CCL4
2525M	E	5.48	Q2	CH2.2-C(=O)-OH/H/CH2.4-CH3		CCL4
2526M	E	5.47	Q2	CH2.2-C(=O)-OH/H/CH2.5-CH3		CCL4
2527M	E	5.43	Q2	CH2.2-C(=O)-OH/H/CH2.7-CH3		CCL4
2525M	E	5.48	Q2	CH2.4-CH3/H/CH2.2-C(=O)-OH		CCL4
2526M	E	5.47	Q2	CH2.5-CH3/H/CH2.2-C(=O)-OH		CCL4
2815M	F	6.84	Q2	CH2.6-CH3/H/C(=O)-O-CH3		CCL4
2527M	E	5.43	Q2	CH2.7-CH3/H/CH2.2-C(=O)-OH		CCL4
2819M	F	5.38	Q2	CH2.7-CH3/H/CH2.7-C(=O)-O		CDCL3
2819M	F	5.38	Q2	CH2.7-C(=O)-O/H/CH2.7-CH3		CDCL3
2257M	E	5.41 APP.	Q2	CH2.8-CH3/CH2-R50		CDCL3
154M	C	5.47 APP.	Q2	CH2-A/CH3		CCL4
369M	B	6.01	Q2	CH2-BR/CH2-BR		CDCL3
86M	D	5.33	Q2	CH2-CH2/CH2-CH2		CDCL3
85M	D	5.34	Q2	CH2-CH2/CH2-CH2		CCL4
2818M	F	5.30	Q2	CH2-CH2/CH2-CH2		CCL4
2528M	E	5.28	Q2	CH2-CH2/CH2-CH2/H		CCL4
2966M	E	5.30	Q2	CH2-CH2/CH2-CH2/H		CCL4
2823M	F	5.00- 5.60	Q2	CH2-CH2/CH2-CH2/H		CCL4
1689M	F	5.25	Q2	CH2-CH2/CH2-CH2/H		CCL4
2817M	G	5.28	Q2	CH2-CH2/CH2-CH2/H		CCL4
1688M	E	5.05- 5.70	Q2	CH2-CH2/CH2-CH3/H		CCL4
2532M	E	5.40	Q2	CH2-CH2/CH2-CH/H		CCL4
2521M	E	5.54 APP.	Q2	CH2-CH2/CH2-C(=O)-OH		CCL4
83M	E	1.95 APP.	Q2	CH2-CH2/CH3		CCL4
70M	E	4.61	Q2	CH2-CH2/CH3		CCL4
72M	E	4.62	Q2	CH2-CH2/CH3		CCL4
2524M	E	7.04	Q2	CH2-CH2/C(=O)-OH		CCL4
84M	D	5.32 APP.	Q2	CH2-CH2/H/CH2-CH2		CCL4
2529M	E	5.39	Q2	CH2-CH2/H/CH2-CH2		CDCL3
82M	E	5.24	Q2	CH2-CH2/H/C(CH3/CH3/CH3)		CCL4
71M	E	4.66	Q2	CH2-CH3/CH2-CH2		CCL4
1688M	E	5.05- 5.70	Q2	CH2-CH3/CH2-CH2/H		CCL4
78M	C	5.30	Q2	CH2-CH3/CH2-CH3/H		CDCL3
75M	D	5.34 APP.	Q2	CH2-CH3/CH3		CCL4
79M	C	5.37	Q2	CH2-CH3/H/CH2-CH3		CCL4
2822M	G	5.35 APP.	Q2	CH2-CH/CH2-CH2		CCL4
2532M	E	5.40	Q2	CH2-CH/CH2-CH2/H		CCL4
88M	F	5.35 APP.	Q2	CH2-CH/CH3		CCL4
274M	E	5.30- 6.15	Q2	CH2-CL/CH2-C		CDCL3

BOOK NO.	ASSIGN-MENT	CHEM SHIFT - ppm -	PROTON GROUP	ENVIRONMENTAL GROUPS	S	SOLVENT
276M	B	5.93	Q2	CH2-CL/CH2-CL		CCL4
2549M	B	6.14	Q2	CH2-C(=O)-OH/A		CDCL3
2521M	E	11.47	Q2	CH2-C(=O)-OH/CH2-CH2		CCL4
274M	E	5.30- 6.15	Q2	CH2-C/CH2-CL		CDCL3
574M	E	5.55	Q2	CH2-NH/CH2-NH		CCL4
572M	D	4.87	Q2	CH2-NH/CH3		CDCL3
1724M	C	6.61 APP.	Q2	CH2-OH/A<C-CH-CH=C(NO2)>		POLYSOL-D
1686M	D	5.57 APP.	Q2	CH2-OH/CH3		CCL4
1711M	C	6.31	Q2	CH2-OH/H/A		CDCL3
2841M	C	6.16	Q2	CH2-O-C(=O)/A		CCL4
2843M	E	6.18	Q2	CH2-O-C(=O)/H/A		CCL4
2842M	E	6.19	Q2	CH2-O-C(=O)/H/A		CCL4
2800M	F	5.61 APP.	Q2	CH2-O-C(=O)/H/CH2.2-CH3		CCL4
2257M	E	5.41 APP.	Q2	CH2-R50/CH2.8-CH3		CDCL3
1257M	C	6.27	Q2	CH2-SO2/H/A		CDCL3
1019M	B	6.10 APP.	Q2	CH2-S/H/A		CDCL3
1506M	C	5.91	Q2	CH3/A(C-CH-CH=C(O-CH3))		CCL4
154M	C	5.47 APP.	Q2	CH3/CH2-A		CCL4
88M	F	5.35 APP.	Q2	CH3/CH2-CH		CCL4
83M	E	1.95 APP.	Q2	CH3/CH2-CH2		CCL4
75M	D	5.34 APP.	Q2	CH3/CH2-CH3		CCL4
475M	D	4.70	Q2	CH3/CH2-NH2/H		CCL4
1686M	D	5.57 APP.	Q2	CH3/CH2-OH		CCL4
76M	D	4.90- 5.41	Q2	CH3/CH(CH3/CH3)		CCL4
1559M	D	5.91	Q2	CH3/H/A<C-CH=C(O-CH3)-C(O-CH3)>		CDCL3
77M	D	5.31	Q2	CH3/H/CH(CH3/CH3)		CCL4
2018M	D	6.70	Q2	CH3/H/C(=O)-CH3		CCL4
2517M	C	7.04	Q2	CH3/H/C(=O)-OH		CDCL3
2814M	E	6.90	Q2	CH3/H/C(=O)-O-CH2		CCL4
1408M	E	4.68	Q2	CH3/H/O-CH2		CCL4
894M	C	6.06 APP.	Q2	CH3/H/Q2(H/C(=O)-NH/H)		POLYSOL-D
1408M	D	4.27	Q2	CH3/O-CH2/H		CCL4
87M	B	5.20- 5.80	Q2	CH3/Q2(CH3)		CCL4
2530M	D	7.30	Q2	CH3/Q2(C(=O)-OH		CDCL3
2671M	C	6.01- 6.53	Q2	CH3/Q2(C(=O)-OK)		D2O
2522M	F	6.93	Q2	CH(CH2.2/CH3)/H/C(=O)-OH		CCL4
2021M	F	6.47	Q2	CH(CH2/CH2)/H/C(=O)-CH3		CCL4
76M	D	4.90- 5.41	Q2	CH(CH3/CH3)/CH3		CCL4
80M	C	5.00	Q2	CH(CH3/CH3)/CH(CH3/CH3)/H		CCL4
77M	D	5.31	Q2	CH(CH3/CH3)/H/CH3		CCL4
81M	C	5.27	Q2	CH(CH3/CH3)/H/CH(CH3/CH3)		CCL4
279M	A	5.50	Q2	CL/CL		CCL4
2531M	B	6.84	Q2	CL/C(=O)-OH/H		POLYSOL-D
281M	A	6.36	Q2	CL/H/CL		CCL4
82M	F	5.40	Q2	C(CH3/CH3/CH3)/H/CH2-CH2		CCL4
2097M	B	7.95	Q2	C(=O)-A/H/C(=O)-A		CDCL3
2041M	D	6.68	Q2	C(=O)-CH2.3/H/A		CDCL3
2018M	C	6.00	Q2	C(=O)-CH3/H/CH3		CCL4
2021M	E	5.92	Q2	C(=O)-CH3/H/CH(CH2/CH2)		CCL4
2821M	D	7.03	Q2	C(=O)-CH3/H/C(=O)-O-CH3		CDCL3
2209M	A	7.08	Q2	C(=O)-CL/H/C(=O)-CL		CCL4
2162M	A	6.91	Q2	C(=O)-H/H/A<C-CH-CH=C(NO2)>		DMSO-D6
2156M	D	6.13	Q2	C(=O)-H/H/CH2.2-CH3		CDCL3
894M	B	5.91	Q2	C(=O)-NH/H/Q2(H/CH3/H)		POLYSOL-D
2201M	A	6.41	Q2	C(=O)-OH/A		CDCL3
2524M	D	5.76	Q2	C(=O)-OH/CH2-CH2		CCL4
2531M	A	6.27	Q2	C(=O)-OH/CL/H		POLYSOL-D
2550M	A	6.41	Q2	C(=O)-OH/H/A		CDCL3
2564M	B	6.49	Q2	C(=O)-OH/H/A(C-CH-CH=C(CH3))		DMSO-D6
2520M	D	5.77	Q2	C(=O)-OH/H/CH2.2-CH3		CCL4
2517M	B	5.82	Q2	C(=O)-OH/H/CH3		CDCL3
2522M	E	5.71	Q2	C(=O)-OH/H/CH(CH2.2/CH3)		CCL4
2533M	A	6.66	Q2	C(=O)-OH/H/C(=O)-OH		DMSO-D6
2605M	A	6.28	Q2	C(=O)-OH/H/R50<C=CH/O>		CDCL3
2530M	B	5.73	Q2	C(=O)-OH/Q2(CH3)		CDCL3
2530M	C	6.01- 6.51	Q2	C(=O)-OH/Q2(CH3)		CDCL3
2671M	B	5.83	Q2	C(=O)-OK/Q2(CH3)		D2O
2672M	A	6.10	Q2	C(=O)-ONA/C(=O)-ONA/H		D2O
2829M	E	6.15	Q2	C(=O)-O-CH2/C(=O)-O-CH2		CCL4
2861M	B	6.38	Q2	C(=O)-O-CH2/H/A		CCL4
2862M	C	6.30	Q2	C(=O)-O-CH2/H/A		CCL4
2814M	D	5.79	Q2	C(=O)-O-CH2/H/CH3		CCL4
2827M	D	6.79	Q2	C(=O)-O-CH2/H/C(=O)-O-CH2		CCL4
2846M	A	1.94	Q2	C(=O)-O-CH2/H/H		CDCL3
2934M	C	6.28	Q2	C(=O)-O-CH2/H/R50(C=OH/O)		CDCL3
2799M	E	5.71	Q2	C(=O)-O-CH3/H/CH2.2-CH3		CCL4
2815M	E	5.71	Q2	C(=O)-O-CH3/H/CH2.6-CH3		CCL4
2821M	C	6.59	Q2	C(=O)-O-CH3/H/C(=O)-CH3		CDCL3
2825M	B	6.86	Q2	C(=O)-O-CH3/H/C(=O)-O-CH3		CDCL3
2828M	C	6.09	Q2	C(=O)-O-CH/C(=O)-O-CH/H		CCL4
2826M	C	6.71	Q2	C(=O)-O-CH/H/C(=O)-O-CH		CCL4

BOOK NO.	ASSIGN-MENT	CHEM SHIFT - ppm -	PROTON GROUP	ENVIRONMENTAL GROUPS	S	SOLVENT
2828M	D	6.73	Q2	C(=O)-O-CH/H/C(=O)-O-CH		CCL4
2269M	A	6.49	Q2	C(=O)-O-C(=O)/H/A		CDCL3
2857M	C	6.40	Q2	C(=O)-O-R6/H/A		CCL4
2043M	A	7.05	Q2	C(=O)-Q2/H/A		CDCL3
982M	A	5.84	Q2	C:N/H/A		CCL4
157M	B	5.01	Q2	H/A/CH3		CCL4
69M	D	4.62	Q2	H/CH2-CH3/CH3		CCL4
157M	C	5.31	Q2	H/CH3/A		CCL4
69M	D	4.62	Q2	H/CH3/CH2-CH2		CCL4
475M	E	4.80	Q2	H/CH3/CH2-NH2		CCL4
1782M	F	4.70	Q2	H/CH3/CH(OH/CH3)		CCL4
1782M	F	4.89	Q2	H/CH3/CH(OH/CH3)		CCL4
2811M	E	5.99	Q2	H/CH3/C(=O)-O-CH		CCL4
2846M	D	6.12	Q2	H/CH3/C(=O)-O-CH2		CDCL3
2810M	E	6.06	Q2	H/CH3/C(=O)-O-CH2		CCL4
2812M	F	6.04	Q2	H/CH3/C(=O)-O-CH2		CCL4
967M	B	5.79 APP.	Q2	H/CH3/C:N		CCL4
2813M	F	6.02	Q2	H/CH3/O-C(=O)-CH2		CCL4
74M	B	4.90	Q2	H/CH3/Q2(CH3/H/H)		CCL4
73M	B	4.93	Q2	H/CH3/Q3		CCL4
1782M	E	4.70	Q2	H/CH(OH/CH3)/CH3		CCL4
1782M	E	4.89	Q2	H/CH(OH/CH3)/CH3		CCL4
2820M	D	6.51	Q2	H/CL/C(=O)-O-CH2		CCL4
2846M	C	5.52	Q2	H/C(=O)-O-CH2-CH3		CDCL3
2810M	D	5.49	Q2	H/C(=O)-O-CH2/CH3		CCL4
2812M	E	5.47	Q2	H/C(=O)-O-CH2/CH3		CCL4
2820M	C	5.99	Q2	H/C(=O)-O-CH2/CL		CCL4
2811M	D	5.43	Q2	H/C(=O)-O-CH/CH3		CCL4
967M	B	5.79 APP.	Q2	H/C:N/CH3		CCL4
2813M	E	5.39	Q2	H/O-C(=O)-CH2/CH3		CCL4
74M	C	5.00	Q2	H/Q2(CH3/H/H)/CH3		CCL4
73M	B	4.93	Q2	H/Q3/CH3		CCL4
1578M	E	7.78	Q2	NO2/H/R50<C=CH/O>		CDCL3
1408M	F	5.82	Q2	O-CH2/CH3/H		CCL4
1408M	G	6.12	Q2	O-CH2/H/CH3		CCL4
867M	B	6.81 APP.	Q2	QN(CH2.2-QN)/A		CDCL3
851M	A	7.04	Q2	QN(OH)/A		DMSO
880M	C	8.41	Q2	QN(QN)/A		CDCL3
87M	C	5.93	Q2	Q2(CH3)/CH3		CCL4
2208M	C	7.38	Q2	Q2(CH3)/C(=O)-Cl		CCL4
2671M	D	7.00	Q2	Q2(CH3)/C(=O)-OK)		D2O
2530M	C	6.01- 6.51	Q2	Q2(C(=O)-OH)/CH3		CDCL3
2671M	C	6.01- 6.53	Q2	Q2(C(=O)-OK)/CH3		D2O
68M	B	4.61	Q2	Q2(H/CH3/CH3)		CDCL3
894M	E	7.11	Q2	Q2(H/CH3/H)/H/C(=O)-NH		POLYSOL-D
894M	D	6.26	Q2	Q2(H/C(=O)-NH/H)/H/CH3		POLYSOL-D
2605M	E	7.51	Q2	R50<C=CH/O>/H/C(=O)-OH		CDCL3
1578M	C	7.48	Q2	R50<C=CH/O>/H/NO2		CDCL3
2934M	F	7.41	Q2	R50(C=CH/O)/H/C(=O)-O-CH2		CDCL3
111M	D	4.69	Q2	R6(CH-CH2/CH2)/CH3		CCL4
106M	C	5.54	Q2	R8(CH2-CH2/CH2-CH2/H)		CCL4
1360M	D	7.41	Q2	SO2-NH2/H/A		POLYSOL-D
1258M	A	6.82	Q2	SO2-Q2/H/A		CDCL3
296M	C	7.08	Q3	A<C-C(CL)>/H/H		CCL4
156M	C	6.59	Q3	A/H/H		CCL4
1924M	C	4.98	Q3	CH2-A		CCL4
1560M	C	5.02 APP.	Q3	CH2-A		CCL4
1918M	D	5.02 APP.	Q3	CH2-A		CCL4
1560M	D	5.87	Q3	CH2-A		CCL4
1924M	E	5.80	Q3	CH2-A		CCL4
1918M	E	5.84	Q3	CH2-A		CCL4
153M	D	5.85 APP.	Q3	CH2-A/H/H		CCL4
1932M	E	5.86	Q3	CH2-A/H/H		CDCL3
368M	D	5.91	Q3	CH2-RR/H/H		CCL4
67M	C	4.75- 5.20	Q3	CH2-CH		CCL4
1785M	D	4.85- 5.38	Q3	CH2-CH		CDCL3
67M	D	5.45- 6.15	Q3	CH2-CH		CCL4
58M	E	4.91 APP.	Q3	CH2-CH		CCL4
1785M	E	5.78 APP.	Q3	CH2-CH		CDCL3
1784M	F	5.06 APP.	Q3	CH2-CH		CDCL3
58M	F	5.72	Q3	CH2-CH		CCL4
1784M	G	5.82	Q3	CH2-CH		CDCL3
62M	D	4.77- 6.06	Q3	CH2-CH2		CCL4
66M	D	5.70	Q3	CH2-CH2/H/H		CCL4
2518M	D	5.80	Q3	CH2-CH2/H/H		CDCL3
2019M	E	5.75	Q3	CH2-CH2/H/H		CCL4
155M	E	5.81	Q3	CH2-CH2/H/H		CDCL3
2670M	E	5.78	Q3	CH2-CH2/H/H	S	D2O
59M	F	5.66 APP.	Q3	CH2-CH2/H/H		CCL4
64M	F	5.66 APP.	Q3	CH2-CH2/H/H		CCL4
65M	F	5.66 APP.	Q3	CH2-CH2/H/H		CCL4

: REPRESENTS TRIPLE BOND, ¬ REPRESENTS AN ARROW AND < AND > REPRESENT BRACKETS.   PAGE   440

BOOK NO.	ASSIGN-MENT	CHEM SHIFT - ppm -	PROTON GROUP	ENVIRONMENTAL GROUPS	S	SOLVENT
57M	F	5.67 APP.	Q3	CH2-CH2/H/H		CCL4
60M	F	5.68 APP.	Q3	CH2-CH2/H/H		CCL4
63M	F	5.70	Q3	CH2-CH2/H/H		CCL4
61M	F	5.72	Q3	CH2-CH2/H/H		CCL4
1687M	F	5.80	Q3	CH2-CH2/H/H		CDCL3
2798M	G	5.67	Q3	CH2-CH2/H/H		CCL4
2206M	G	5.84	Q3	CH2-CH2/H/H		CCL4
272M	D	5.90 APP.	Q3	CH2-CL/H/H		CCL4
2516M	D	5.87	Q3	CH2-C(=O)-OH/H/H		CDCL3
968M	C	5.77	Q3	CH2-C:N/H/H		CCL4
423M	D	5.98	Q3	CH2-I/H/H		CCL4
656M	B	5.10 APP.	Q3	CH2-N		CCL4
656M	C	5.77	Q3	CH2-N		CCL4
1350M	B	5.10	Q3	CH2-NH		CDCL3
1350M	C	5.52- 6.20	Q3	CH2-NH		CDCL3
474M	E	6.00	Q3	CH2-NH2/H/H		CDCL3
781M	E	8.56	Q3	CH2-NH2/H/H	S	POLYSOL-D
587M	E	5.80	Q3	CH2-NH/H/H		CDCL3
571M	E	5.83	Q3	CH2-NH/H/H		CDCL3
2306M	E	5.88	Q3	CH2-NH/H/H		CDCL3
570M	F	5.75 APP.	Q3	CH2-NH/H/H		CCL4
936M	D	5.80 APP.	Q3	CH2-N=/H/H		CCL4
1004M	D	5.80 APP.	Q3	CH2-N/H/H		CCL4
642M	E	5.82	Q3	CH2-N/H/H		CDCL3
1685M	E	5.88	Q3	CH2-OH/H/H		CCL4
2829M	D	5.80	Q3	CH2-O-C(=O)/H/H		CCL4
2965M	D	5.90	Q3	CH2-O-C(=O)/H/H		CCL4
2899M	D	5.90	Q3	CH2-O-C(=O)/H/H		CCL4
2805M	D	5.92	Q3	CH2-O-C(=O)/H/H		CCL4
2904M	D	6.01	Q3	CH2-O-C(=O)/H/H		CDCL3
2977M	E	5.79	Q3	CH2-O-C(=O)/H/H		CCL4
2806M	E	5.87	Q3	CH2-O-C(=O)/H/H		CCL4
2804M	E	5.89	Q3	CH2-O-C(=O)/H/H		CCL4
2801M	G	5.82	Q3	CH2-O-C(=O)/H/H		CCL4
1691M	C	5.10	Q3	CH2-O/H/H		CCL4
1407M	D	5.82	Q3	CH2-O/H/H		CCL4
2175M	D	5.94	Q3	CH2-O/H/H		CCL4
1434M	E	5.80	Q3	CH2-O/H/H		CCL4
1539M	E	6.06	Q3	CH2-O/H/H		CDCL3
1403M	F	5.94	Q3	CH2-O/H/H		CDCL3
2434M	C	5.19	Q3	CH2-R5NN		POLYSOL-D
2434M	C	5.75	Q3	CH2-R5NN		POLYSOL-D
2461M	B	4.89- 5.91	Q3	CH2-R6NN		DMSO-D6
2464M	B	4.96- 6.13	Q3	CH2-R6NN		DMSO-D6
1465M	F	5.86	Q3	CH2-R6NO/H/H		CDCL3
1086M	C	4.86 APP.	Q3	CH2-SI		CCL4
1086M	D	5.83	Q3	CH2-SI		CCL4
1087M	D	5.69 APP.	Q3	CH2-SI/H/H		CL2C=CCL2
1263M	D	5.76	Q3	CH2-SO2/H/H		CDCL3
1261M	D	5.77	Q3	CH2-SO2/H/H		CDCL3
1262M	E	5.79	Q3	CH2-SO2/H/H		CDCL3
1299M	B	5.34 APP.	Q3	CH2-SO3-NA		D2O
1299M	C	6.00	Q3	CH2-SO3-NA		D2O
1190M	D	5.72	Q3	CH2-S/H/H		CCL4
56M	E	5.60	Q3	CH(CH2/CH2)/H/H		CDCL3
67M	C	4.75- 5.20	Q3	CH(CH2/CH3)		CCL4
67M	D	5.45- 6.15	Q3	CH(CH2/CH3)		CCL4
88M	G	5.63 APP.	Q3	CH(CH2/CH3)/H/H		CCL4
55M	G	5.70	Q3	CH(CH2/CH3)/H/H		CCL4
275M	F	5.95 APP.	Q3	CH(CL/HCH)/H/H		CCL4
1785M	D	4.85- 5.38	Q3	CH(OH/CH2)		CDCL3
1785M	E	5.78 APP.	Q3	CH(OH/CH2)		CDCL3
1783M	G	5.78 APP.	Q3	CH(OH/CH2)/H/H		CCL4
1425M	E	5.00- 5.50	Q3	CH(O/O)		CCL4
1425M	F	5.67	Q3	CH(O/O)		CCL4
89M	C	5.02 APP.	Q3	CH(Q2/CH3)		CCL4
54M	D	5.80	Q3	C(CH3/CH3/CH3)/H/H		CCL4
1812M	E	5.92	Q3	C(OH/CH3/CH3)/H/H		CCL4
2017M	B	5.82 APP.	Q3	C(=O)-CH3/H/H		CCL4
2304M	B	5.40- 6.50	Q3	C(=O)-NH		CDCL3
2305M	F	6.09 APP.	Q3	C(=O)-NH/H/H		CDCL3
2305M	F	6.19 APP.	Q3	C(=O)-NH/H/H		CDCL3
2306M	F	6.29 APP.	Q3	C(=O)-NH/H/H		CDCL3
2845M	C	6.19 APP.	Q3	C(=O)-O-CH2/H/H		CCL4
2808M	E	6.03 APP.	Q3	C(=O)-O-CH2/H/H		CCL4
2807M	E	6.09 APP.	Q3	C(=O)-O-CH2/H/H		CCL4
2809M	E	6.18	Q3	C(=O)-O-CH2/H/H		CCL4
966M	A	5.40- 6.10	Q3	C:N/H/H		CCL4
296M	A	5.29	Q3	H/A<C-C(CL)>/H		CCL4
156M	A	5.11	Q3	H/A/H		CCL4
153M	C	5.02	Q3	H/CH2-A/H		CCL4

BOOK NO.	ASSIGN-MENT	CHEM SHIFT - ppm -	PROTON GROUP	ENVIRONMENTAL GROUPS	S	SOLVENT
1932M	D	5.00	Q3	H/CH2-A/H		CDCL3
368M	B	5.09	Q3	H/CH2-BR/H		CCL4
66M	B	4.91	Q3	H/CH2-CH2/H		CCL4
2518M	B	5.02	Q3	H/CH2-CH2/H		CDCL3
2019M	C	4.91	Q3	H/CH2-CH2/H		CCL4
155M	C	4.97	Q3	H/CH2-CH2/H		CDCL3
2670M	C	4.91	Q3	H/CH2-CH2/H	S	D20
57M	D	4.86	Q3	H/CH2-CH2/H		CCL4
64M	D	4.86	Q3	H/CH2-CH2/H		CCL4
59M	D	4.87	Q3	H/CH2-CH2/H		CCL4
60M	D	4.87	Q3	H/CH2-CH2/H		CCL4
63M	D	4.88	Q3	H/CH2-CH2/H		CCL4
65M	D	4.88	Q3	H/CH2-CH2/H		CCL4
61M	D	4.89	Q3	H/CH2-CH2/H		CCL4
1687M	D	5.10	Q3	H/CH2-CH2/H		CDCL3
2798M	E	4.95	Q3	H/CH2-CH2/H		CCL4
2206M	E	5.01	Q3	H/CH2-CH2/H		CCL4
272M	B	5.15	Q3	H/CH2-CL/H		CCL4
2516M	C	5.18	Q3	H/CH2-C(=O)-OH/H		CDCL3
968M	B	5.10- 5.65	Q3	H/CH2-C:N/H		CCL4
423M	B	4.91	Q3	H/CH2-I/H		CCL4
781M	B	5.32	Q3	H/CH2-NH2/H	S	POLYSOL-D
474M	C	5.08	Q3	H/CH2-NH2/H		CDCL3
2306M	B	5.11	Q3	H/CH2-NH/H		CDCL3
571M	C	5.03	Q3	H/CH2-NH/H		CDCL3
587M	C	5.08	Q3	H/CH2-NH/H		CDCL3
570M	D	5.00 APP.	Q3	H/CH2-NH/H		CCL4
936M	B	5.27	Q3	H/CH2-N=/H		CCL4
1004M	B	5.25	Q3	H/CH2-N/H		CCL4
642M	C	5.11	Q3	H/CH2-N/H		CDCL3
1685M	C	5.07	Q3	H/CH2-OH/H		CCL4
2977M	B	5.14	Q3	H/CH2-O-C(=O)/H		CCL4
2829M	B	5.15	Q3	H/CH2-O-C(=O)/H		CCL4
2899M	B	5.21	Q3	H/CH2-O-C(=O)/H		CCL4
2805M	B	5.22	Q3	H/CH2-O-C(=O)/H		CCL4
2904M	B	5.31	Q3	H/CH2-O-C(=O)/H		CDCL3
2965M	B	5.39	Q3	H/CH2-O-C(=O)/H		CCL4
2806M	C	5.17	Q3	H/CH2-O-C(=O)/H		CCL4
2804M	C	5.21	Q3	H/CH2-O-C(=O)/H		CCL4
2801M	E	5.13	Q3	H/CH2-O-C(=O)/H		CCL4
1407M	B	5.11	Q3	H/CH2-O/H		CCL4
2175M	B	5.28	Q3	H/CH2-O/H		CCL4
1434M	C	5.01	Q3	H/CH2-O/H		CCL4
1539M	C	5.22	Q3	H/CH2-O/H		CDCL3
1403M	D	5.16	Q3	H/CH2-O/H		CDCL3
1691M	D	5.16	Q3	H/CH2-O/H		CCL4
1465M	D	5.15	Q3	H/CH2-R6NO/H		CDCL3
1087M	C	4.79 APP.	Q3	H/CH2-SI/H		CL2C=CCL2
1263M	C	5.29	Q3	H/CH2-SO2/H		CDCL3
1261M	C	5.30	Q3	H/CH2-SO2/H		CDCL3
1262M	D	5.29	Q3	H/CH2-SO2/H		CDCL3
1190M	B	5.05	Q3	H/CH2-S/H		CCL4
56M	D	4.99	Q3	H/CH(CH2/CH2)/H		CDCL3
88M	D	4.83	Q3	H/CH(CH2/CH3)/H		CCL4
55M	E	4.88	Q3	H/CH(CH2/CH3)/H		CCL4
275M	D	5.46 APP.	Q3	H/CH(CL/HCH)/H		CCL4
1783M	E	4.93	Q3	H/CH(OH/CH2)/H		CCL4
54M	C	4.82	Q3	H/C(CH3/CH3/CH3)/H		CCL4
1812M	C	4.88	Q3	H/C(OH/CH3/CH3)/H		CCL4
2017M	C	6.18 APP.	Q3	H/C(=O)-CH3		CCL4
2017M	D	6.28 APP.	Q3	H/C(=O)-CH3		CCL4
2305M	D	5.51	Q3	H/C(=O)-NH/H		CDCL3
2306M	D	5.61 APP.	Q3	H/C(=O)-NH/H		CDCL3
2845M	B	5.72	Q3	H/C(=O)-O-CH2/H		CCL4
2809M	D	5.71	Q3	H/C(=O)-O-CH2/H		CCL4
2808M	D	5.73	Q3	H/C(=O)-O-CH2/H		CCL4
2807M	F	6.34	Q3	H/C(=O)-O-CH2/H		CCL4
966M	A	5.40- 6.10	Q3	H/C:N/H		CCL4
1812M	D	5.11	Q3	H/H C(OH/CH3/CH3)		CCL4
2305M	G	6.19 APP.	Q3	H/HC(=O)-NH		CDCL3
156M	B	5.59	Q3	H/H/A		CCL4
296M	B	5.60	Q3	H/H/A<C-C(CL)>		CCL4
153M	B	4.99	Q3	H/H/CH2-A		CCL4
1932M	C	4.91 APP.	Q3	H/H/CH2-A		CDCL3
368M	C	5.26	Q3	H/H/CH2-BR		CCL4
66M	C	4.96	Q3	H/H/CH2-CH2		CCL4
2518M	C	5.08	Q3	H/H/CH2-CH2		CDCL3
2019M	D	4.97	Q3	H/H/CH2-CH2		CCL4
155M	D	5.01	Q3	H/H/CH2-CH2		CDCL3
2670M	D	4.97	Q3	H/H/CH2-CH2	S	D20
65M	E	4.90	Q3	H/H/CH2-CH2		CCL4

BOOK NO.	ASSIGN-MENT	CHEM SHIFT - ppm -	PROTON GROUP	ENVIRONMENTAL GROUPS	S	SOLVENT
57M	E	4.90	Q3	H/H/CH2-CH2		CCL4
64M	E	4.90	Q3	H/H/CH2-CH2		CCL4
59M	E	4.91	Q3	H/H/CH2-CH2		CCL4
60M	E	4.91	Q3	H/H/CH2-CH2		CCL4
63M	E	4.92	Q3	H/H/CH2-CH2		CCL4
61M	E	4.94	Q3	H/H/CH2-CH2		CCL4
1687M	E	5.14	Q3	H/H/CH2-CH2		CDCL3
2798M	F	5.00	Q3	H/H/CH2-CH2		CCL4
2206M	F	5.07	Q3	H/H/CH2-CH2		CCL4
272M	C	5.29	Q3	H/H/CH2-CL		CCL4
2516M	B	5.12	Q3	H/H/CH2-C(=O)-OH		CDCL3
968M	B	5.10- 5.65	Q3	H/H/CH2-C:N		CCL4
423M	C	5.16	Q3	H/H/CH2-I		CCL4
1004M	C	5.33	Q3	H/H/CH2-N		CCL4
642M	D	5.16	Q3	H/H/CH2-N		CDCL3
2306M	C	5.18	Q3	H/H/CH2-NH		CDCL3
571M	D	5.11	Q3	H/H/CH2-NH		CDCL3
587M	D	5.13	Q3	H/H/CH2-NH		CDCL3
570M	E	5.05 APP.	Q3	H/H/CH2-NH		CCL4
781M	C	5.50	Q3	H/H/CH2-NH2	S	POLYSOL-D
474M	D	5.12	Q3	H/H/CH2-NH2		CDCL3
936M	C	5.35	Q3	H/H/CH2-N=		CCL4
1407M	C	5.19	Q3	H/H/CH2-O		CCL4
2175M	C	5.35	Q3	H/H/CH2-O		CCL4
1434M	D	5.16	Q3	H/H/CH2-O		CCL4
1539M	D	5.35	Q3	H/H/CH2-O		CDCL3
1403M	E	5.21	Q3	H/H/CH2-O		CDCL3
1691M	E	5.81	Q3	H/H/CH2-O		CCL4
1685M	D	5.21	Q3	H/H/CH2-OH		CCL4
2977M	C	5.21	Q3	H/H/CH2-O-C(=O)		CCL4
2829M	C	5.23	Q3	H/H/CH2-O-C(=O)		CCL4
2899M	C	5.31	Q3	H/H/CH2-O-C(=O)		CCL4
2805M	C	5.33	Q3	H/H/CH2-O-C(=O)		CCL4
2965M	C	5.42	Q3	H/H/CH2-O-C(=O)		CCL4
2904M	C	5.42	Q3	H/H/CH2-O-C(=O)		CDCL3
2806M	D	5.23	Q3	H/H/CH2-O-C(=O)		CCL4
2804M	D	5.30	Q3	H/H/CH2-O-C(=O)		CCL4
2801M	F	5.20	Q3	H/H/CH2-O-C(=O)		CCL4
1465M	E	5.19	Q3	H/H/CH2-R6NO		CDCL3
1190M	C	5.11	Q3	H/H/CH2-S		CCL4
1087M	C	4.79 APP.	Q3	H/H/CH2-SI		CL2C=CCL2
1261M	B	5.11	Q3	H/H/CH2-SO2		CDCL3
1263M	B	5.11	Q3	H/H/CH2-SO2		CDCL3
1262M	C	5.12	Q3	H/H/CH2-SO2		CDCL3
56M	C	4.90	Q3	H/H/CH(CH2/CH2)		CDCL3
88M	E	4.95	Q3	H/H/CH(CH2/CH3)		CCL4
55M	F	4.91	Q3	H/H/CH(CH2/CH3)		CCL4
275M	E	5.58 APP.	Q3	H/H/CH(CL/HCH)		CCL4
1783M	F	5.15	Q3	H/H/CH(OH/CH2)		CCL4
54M	B	4.78	Q3	H/H/C(CH3/CH3/CH3)		CCL4
2306M	F	6.29 APP.	Q3	H/H/C(=O)-NH		CDCL3
2305M	G	6.09 APP.	Q3	H/H/C(=O)-NH		CDCL3
2807M	D	5.72	Q3	H/H/C(=O)-O-CH2		CCL4
2845M	D	6.39	Q3	H/H/C(=O)-O-CH2		CCL4
2808M	F	6.37	Q3	H/H/C(=O)-O-CH2		CCL4
2809M	F	6.39	Q3	H/H/C(=O)-O-CH2		CCL4
966M	B	6.22	Q3	H/H/C:N		CCL4
1418M	C	4.16	Q3	H/H/O-CH2		CDCL3
1404M	E	4.01	Q3	H/H/O-CH2		CCL4
1405M	E	4.03	Q3	H/H/O-CH2		CCL4
1414M	E	4.09	Q3	H/H/O-CH2		CCL4
1406M	E	4.08	Q3	H/H/O-CH2.2		CCL4
2803M	C	4.94	Q3	H/H/O-C(=O)-CH2		CDCL3
2797M	D	4.77	Q3	H/H/O-C(=O)-CH2		CCL4
2802M	E	4.82	Q3	H/H/O-C(=O)-CH2		CDCL3
73M	D	5.10	Q3	H/H/O2		CCL4
2395M	B	6.02	Q3	H/H/R5NA<N-C(=O)/C(=O)>		CDCL3
1794M	E	4.91	Q3	H/H/R6R6N*BI<CH-CH*/CH2>		POLYSOL-D
101M	C	4.98	Q3	H/H/R6<CH-CH2/CH2>		CCL4
1406M	D	3.89	Q3	H/O-CH2.2/H		CCL4
1418M	B	4.00	Q3	H/O-CH2/H		CDCL3
1404M	D	3.84	Q3	H/O-CH2/H		CCL4
1405M	D	3.86	Q3	H/O-CH2/H		CCL4
1414M	D	3.91	Q3	H/O-CH2/H		CCL4
2803M	B	4.66	Q3	H/O-C(=O)-CH2/H		CDCL3
2797M	C	4.47	Q3	H/O-C(=O)-CH2/H		CCL4
2802M	D	4.51	Q3	H/O-C(=O)-CH2/H		CDCL3
73M	C	5.02	Q3	H/O2/H		CCL4
2395M	A	5.01	Q3	H/R5NA<N-C(=O)/C(=O)>/H		CDCL3
1794M	D	4.89	Q3	H/R6R6N*BI<CH-CH*/CH2>/H		POLYSOL-D
101M	B	4.90	Q3	H/R6<CH-CH2/CH2>/H		CCL4

BOOK NO.	ASSIGN- MENT	CHEM SHIFT - ppm -	PROTON GROUP	ENVIRONMENTAL GROUPS	S	SOLVENT
1406M	F	6.35	Q3	O-CH2.2/H/H		CCL4
1418M	D	6.48	Q3	O-CH2/H/H		CDCL3
1404M	F	6.32	Q3	O-CH2/H/H		CCL4
1405M	F	6.37	Q3	O-CH2/H/H		CCL4
1414M	F	6.38	Q3	O-CH2/H/H		CCL4
2803M	D	7.21	Q3	O-C(=O)-CH2/H/H		CDCL3
2797M	E	7.24	Q3	O-C(=O)-CH2/H/H		CCL4
2802M	F	7.23	Q3	O-C(=O)-CH2/H/H		CDCL3
2996M	C	5.65- 6.88	Q3	P(=O/O/O)		CCL4
89M	C	5.02 APP.	Q3	Q2(CH(Q3/CH3))		CCL4
73M	E	6.34 APP.	Q3	Q2/H/H		CCL4
1446M	D	5.10- 5.70	Q3	R30<CH-O/HCH>		CDCL3
2395M	C	6.83	Q3	R5NA<N-C(=O)/C(=O)>/H/H		CDCL3
1794M	G	5.80	Q3	R6R6N*BI<CH-CH*/CH2>/H/H		POLYSOL-D
101M	E	5.88	Q3	R6<CH-CH2/CH2>/H/H		CCL4
1242M	A	3.45	SH	AA(C-CH-C*/CH-CH-C*)		CDCL3
1241M	A	3.35	SH	AA(C-C*)		CDCL3
1235M	A	3.42	SH	A<C-CH-CH-C(BR)>		CDCL3
1238M	A	3.52	SH	A<C-CH-CH-C(NH2)>		CDCL3
1536M	A	3.37	SH	A<C-CH-CH-C(O-CH3)>		CDCL3
1229M	B	3.39	SH	A<C-CH-C(CH3)>		CDCL3
1233M	A	3.38	SH	A<C-CH-C(CL)-C(CL)>		CCL4
1237M	A	3.50	SH	A<C-CH-C(NH2)>		CDCL3
1240M	A	3.31	SH	A<C-CH-C(SH)-C(CL)>		CCL4
1240M	A	3.79	SH	A<C-CH-C(SH)-C(CL)>		CCL4
1228M	B	3.26	SH	A<C-C(CH3)>		CDCL3
1232M	A	3.84	SH	A<C-C(CL)/CH-C(CL)>		CCL4
1240M	B	3.31	SH	A<C-C(CL)/CH-C(SH)>		CCL4
1240M	B	3.79	SH	A<C-C(CL)/CH-C(SH)>		CCL4
1236M	A	3.68	SH	A<C-C(NH2)>		CDCL3
1230M	B	3.30	SH	A(C-CH-CH-C(CH3))		CDCL3
1231M	B	3.16	SH	A(C-CH-CH-C(C(CH3/CH3/CH3)))		CCL4
1535M	A	3.43	SH	A(C-CH-C(O-CH3))		CDCL3
1234M	A	3.85	SH	A(C-C(CL)-CH-C(CL)/CH-C(CL))		CDCL3
1239M	B	3.52	SH	A(C-C(SH)-CH-C(CH3))		CDCL3
1239M	C	3.69	SH	A(C-C(SH)-CH-C(CH3))		CDCL3
1201M	B	1.31	SH	CH2.2-CH3		CDCL3
2738M	A	1.68	SH	CH2.2-C(=O)-O		CDCL3
1217M	B	1.83	SH	CH2.2-NH		CDCL3
1215M	C	1.61	SH	CH2.2-NH		CDCL3
1206M	B	1.19	SH	CH2.5-CH3		CCL4
1204M	C	1.41	SH	CH2.6-CH3		CDCL3
1211M	B	1.10- 1.50	SH	CH2.8-CH3		CDCL3
1224M	A	1.50	SH	CH2-A		CCL4
1225M	A	1.58	SH	CH2-A		CCL4
1227M	A	1.81	SH	CH2-A		CDCL3
1207M	A	0.89	SH	CH2-CH		CCL4
1662M	A	1.79	SH	CH2-CH		CDCL3
1219M	B	1.68	SH	CH2-CH		CDCL3
1222M	A	1.16	SH	CH2-CH2		CCL4
1221M	A	1.18	SH	CH2-CH2		CCL4
1220M	A	1.18	SH	CH2-CH2		CCL4
1218M	A	1.58	SH	CH2-CH2		CDCL3
2490M	A	1.58	SH	CH2-CH2		CCL4
1402M	A	1.60	SH	CH2-CH2		CCL4
1205M	B	1.11	SH	CH2-CH2		CCL4
1209M	B	1.11	SH	CH2-CH2		CCL4
1213M	B	1.20	SH	CH2-CH2		CCL4
1401M	B	1.60	SH	CH2-CH2		CDCL3
1212M	C	1.46	SH	CH2-CH2		CDCL3
1208M	C	2.09	SH	CH2-CH2		CDCL3
1200M	A	1.17	SH	CH2-CH3		CCL4
1577M	A	1.90	SH	CH2-R50		CDCL3
1199M	A	1.24	SH	CH3		CDCL3
1662M	B	1.85	SH	CH(CH2/CH2)		CDCL3
1203M	B	1.24	SH	CH(CH2/CH3)		CCL4
1219M	C	1.86	SH	CH(CH2/CH3)		CDCL3
1202M	B	1.40	SH	CH(CH3/CH3)		CCL4
2489M	B	2.22	SH	CH(C(=O)-OH/CH3)		CCL4
1214M	A	2.12	SH	CH(HCH/HCH)		CCL4
1226M	A	3.05	SH	C(A/A/A)		CDCL3
1223M	F	1.70	SH	C(CH2.3/CH2/CH3)		CDCL3
1223M	F	1.70	SH	C(CH2.3/CH3/CH3)		CDCL3
2610M	A	5.35	SH	C(=O)-A		CDCL3
2609M	B	4.83	SH	C(=O)-CH3		CCL4
1877M	B	6.51	OH	A(C-CH-C(CH3))		CCL4
1683M	E	3.67	OH	CH2-R6N		CDCL3
1812M	B	2.14	OH	C(Q3/CH3/CH3)		CCL4
2201M	D	11.21	OH	C(=O)-Q2		CDCL3
893M	F	8.69	OH	NH-C(=O)		CDCL3
1483M	F	7.16		A<C(CH(O/CH3))>		CCL4

BOOK NO.	ASSIGN-MENT	CHEM SHIFT - ppm -	PROTON GROUP	ENVIRONMENTAL GROUPS	S	SOLVENT
679M	B	7.42- 7.84		UN		CDCL3
1468M	D	6.50- 6.85		UNSEPCIFIED		CDCL3
1348M	D	7.00- 7.70		UNSEPCIFIED		CDCL3
2834M	D	7.32		UNSPECIED		CDCL3
364M	A	0.50- 2.15		UNSPECIFIED		CCL4
2421M	A	0.70- 2.10		UNSPECIFIED		POLYSOL-D
586M	A	0.70- 2.20		UNSPECIFIED		CDCL3
49M	A	0.71- 2.00		UNSPECIFIED		CCL4
1217M	A	0.80- 2.10		UNSPECIFIED		CDCL3
469M	A	0.80- 2.00		UNSPECIFIED		CDCL3
470M	A	0.80- 2.02		UNSPECIFIED		CCL4
569M	A	0.80- 1.90		UNSPECIFIED		CDCL3
52M	A	0.80- 1.90		UNSPECIFIED		CCL4
145M	A	0.80- 2.10		UNSPECIFIED		CCL4
198M	A	0.80- 2.60		UNSPECIFIED		CCL4
33M	A	0.81 APP.		UNSPECIFIED		CCL4
883M	A	0.82- 1.98		UNSPECIFIED		CDCL3
558M	A	0.82- 2.07		UNSPECIFIED		CDCL3
2121M	A	0.83- 2.17		UNSPECIFIED		CDCL3
2203M	A	0.85- 2.11		UNSPECIFIED		CCL4
25M	A	0.88 APP.		UNSPECIFIED		CCL4
30M	A	0.89 APP.		UNSPECIFIED		CCL4
924M	A	0.89- 2.13		UNSPECIFIED		CDCL3
36M	A	0.90 APP.		UNSPECIFIED		CCL4
2155M	A	0.90- 2.60		UNSPECIFIED		CDCL3
1997M	A	0.90- 2.60		UNSPECIFIED		CCL4
570M	A	0.90- 2.20		UNSPECIFIED		CCL4
270M	A	0.90- 2.50		UNSPECIFIED		CCL4
183M	A	0.90- 2.10		UNSPECIFIED		CDCL3
2878M	A	0.90- 2.20		UNSPECIFIED		CDCL3
1006M	A	0.90- 2.27		UNSPECIFIED		CDCL3
1887M	A	0.91- 2.18		UNSPECIFIED		CDCL3
1028M	A	0.91- 2.20		UNSPECIFIED		CDCL3
53M	A	0.93- 2.17		UNSPECIFIED		CDCL3
2139M	A	0.95		UNSPECIFIED		CCL4
101M	A	0.98- 2.51		UNSPECIFIED		CDCL3
2536M	A	1.00- 2.80		UNSPECIFIED		CCL4
2205M	A	1.00- 2.45		UNSPECIFIED		CDCL3
1816M	A	1.00- 2.20		UNSPECIFIED		CDCL3
2084M	A	1.00- 2.20		UNSPECIFIED		CDCL3
1998M	A	1.00- 2.00		UNSPECIFIED		CDCL3
2988M	A	1.00- 2.20		UNSPECIFIED		CCL4
1045M	A	1.00- 2.50		UNSPECIFIED		CCL4
2857M	A	1.08- 2.18		UNSPECIFIED		CCL4
2514M	A	1.10- 2.60		UNSPECIFIED		CCL4
2787M	A	1.10- 2.80		UNSPECIFIED		CCL4
365M	A	1.10- 2.40		UNSPECIFIED		CCL4
964M	A	1.10- 2.10		UNSPECIFIED		CDCL3
2953M	A	1.20- 2.00		UNSPECIFIED		CDCL3
2912M	A	1.20- 2.30		UNSPECIFIED		CDCL3
858M	A	1.20- 2.10		UNSPECIFIED		CCL4
2713M	A	1.30- 2.05		UNSPECIFIED		CDCL3
1821M	A	1.30- 2.10		UNSPECIFIED		CDCL3
269M	A	1.30- 2.50		UNSPECIFIED		CDCL3
2011M	A	1.33 APP.		UNSPECIFIED		CCL4
2779M	A	1.40 APP.		UNSPECIFIED		CCL4
2158M	A	1.40- 2.72		UNSPECIFIED		CCL4
2952M	A	1.40- 2.00		UNSPECIFIED		CDCL3
2378M	A	1.51 APP.		UNSPECIFIED		CDCL3
561M	A	1.53 APP.		UNSPECIFIED		CCL4
102M	A	1.60 APP.		UNSPECIFIED		CDCL3
147M	A	1.60- 2.33		UNSPECIFIED		CCL4
267M	A	1.65 APP.		UNSPECIFIED		CCL4
2025M	A	1.72- 2.58		UNSPECIFIED		CDCL3
2383M	A	1.77		UNSPECIFIED		CDCL3
2764M	A	2.00- 2.20		UNSPECIFIED		CCL4
192M	A	2.01- 2.28		UNSPECIFIED		CDCL3
2012M	A	2.04		UNSPECIFIED		CCL4
970M	A	2.10 APP.		UNSPECIFIED		CCL4
188M	A	2.19 APP.		UNSPECIFIED		CDCL3
194M	A	2.22		UNSPECIFIED		CDCL3
1646M	A	2.50- 2.90		UNSPECIFIED		D20
1871M	A	3.00- 4.10		UNSPECIFIED		D20
1868M	A	3.16- 4.19		UNSPECIFIED		D20
1872M	A	3.20- 4.00		UNSPECIFIED		D20
1867M	A	3.30- 4.20		UNSPECIFIED		D20
1874M	A	3.35- 4.33		UNSPECIFIED		D20
1862M	A	3.40- 3.80		UNSPECIFIED		D20
1864M	A	3.49- 4.05		UNSPECIFIED		D20
2669M	A	5.50- 6.30		UNSPECIFIED		CDCL3
905M	A	6.50- 8.05		UNSPECIFIED		CDCL3

BOOK NO.	ASSIGN-MENT	CHEM SHIFT - ppm -	PROTON GROUP	ENVIRONMENTAL GROUPS	S	SOLVENT
876M	A	6.50- 7.70		UNSPECIFIED		C3H6O
875M	A	6.54- 7.66		UNSPECIFIED		DMSO
1182M	A	6.55- 7.20		UNSPECIFIED		DMSO-D6
917M	A	6.60- 7.42		UNSPECIFIED		CDCL3
234M	A	6.60- 7.80		UNSPECIFIED		CDCL3
1138M	A	6.62- 7.01		UNSPECIFIED		CDCL3
877M	A	6.64- 7.39		UNSPECIFIED		CDCL3
302M	A	6.67- 7.40		UNSPECIFIED		CCL4
389M	A	6.70- 7.60		UNSPECIFIED		CCL4
223M	A	6.71- 7.43		UNSPECIFIED		CCL4
1541M	A	6.78- 7.40		UNSPECIFIED		CDCL3
392M	A	6.78- 7.60		UNSPECIFIED		CCL4
1543M	A	6.80- 7.60		UNSPECIFIED		CDCL3
227M	A	6.80- 7.70		UNSPECIFIED		CCL4
301M	A	6.80- 7.25		UNSPECIFIED		CCL4
233M	A	6.80- 7.81		UNSPECIFIED		CDCL3
210M	A	6.80- 7.80		UNSPECIFIED		CDCL3
2923M	A	6.85- 7.50		UNSPECIFIED		CDCL3
297M	A	6.85- 7.55		UNSPECIFIED		CCL4
228M	A	6.90- 7.65		UNSPECIFIED		CDCL3
1544M	A	6.90- 7.65		UNSPECIFIED		CDCL3
1608M	A	6.90- 7.50		UNSPECIFIED		CDCL3
2343M	A	6.90- 7.70		UNSPECIFIED		DMSO
2569M	A	6.90- 7.82		UNSPECIFIED		POLYSOL-D
2547M	A	6.90- 7.50		UNSPECIFIED		DMSO-D6
887M	A	6.90- 7.45		UNSPECIFIED		POLYSOL-D
1586M	A	6.92		UNSPECIFIED		CDCL3
922M	A	7.00- 7.90		UNSPECIFIED		CDCL3
869M	A	7.00- 7.60		UNSPECIFIED		CDCL3
180M	A	7.00- 7.70		UNSPECIFIED		CDCL3
1176M	A	7.01- 7.55		UNSPECIFIED		CDCL3
2441M	A	7.02 APP.		UNSPECIFIED		DMSO-D6
2868M	A	7.02- 7.54		UNSPECIFIED		CDCL3
2122M	A	7.05- 7.70		UNSPECIFIED		CCL4
2945M	A	7.08- 7.63		UNSPECIFIED		CDCL3
745M	A	7.10- 7.70		UNSPECIFIED		CDCL3
902M	A	7.10- 7.59		UNSPECIFIED		CDCL3
914M	A	7.10- 7.80		UNSPECIFIED		CDCL3
2214M	A	7.10- 7.60		UNSPECIFIED		CDCL3
165M	A	7.10- 7.50		UNSPECIFIED		CDCL3
170M	A	7.10- 7.70		UNSPECIFIED		CCL4
1150M	A	7.10- 7.64		UNSPECIFIED		CDCL3
399M	A	7.11- 7.63		UNSPECIFIED		CDCL3
171M	A	7.12- 7.63		UNSPECIFIED		CDCL3
912M	A	7.13		UNSPECIFIED		CDCL3
298M	A	7.15- 7.60		UNSPECIFIED		CDCL3
915M	A	7.15- 7.55		UNSPECIFIED		CDCL3
2957M	A	7.15- 7.70		UNSPECIFIED		CDCL3
212M	A	7.15- 7.90		UNSPECIFIED		CDCL3
1169M	A	7.18		UNSPECIFIED		CCL4
1056M	A	7.19- 7.59		UNSPECIFIED		CDCL3
938M	A	7.20 APP.		UNSPECIFIED		CCL4
1580M	A	7.20- 7.80		UNSPECIFIED		CDCL3
1052M	A	7.20- 7.65		UNSPECIFIED		CDCL3
942M	A	7.21 APP.		UNSPECIFIED		CCL4
2367M	A	7.22		UNSPECIFIED		CCL4
2968M	A	7.23 APP.		UNSPECIFIED		CCL4
401M	A	7.23- 7.80		UNSPECIFIED		CCL4
1059M	A	7.23- 7.95		UNSPECIFIED		CDCL3
2427M	A	7.27 APP.		UNSPECIFIED		POLYSOL-D
990M	A	7.29- 7.85		UNSPECIFIED		CDCL3
222M	A	7.30- 7.70		UNSPECIFIED		CCL4
731M	A	7.30- 7.85		UNSPECIFIED		CDCL3
2568M	A	7.30- 8.00		UNSPECIFIED		POLYSOL-D
1053M	A	7.32- 7.89		UNSPECIFIED		C3H6O
992M	A	7.33- 7.90		UNSPECIFIED		7.90
871M	A	7.34		UNSPECIFIED		CDCL3
1000M	A	7.36- 7.97		UNSPECIFIED		CDCL3
2635M	A	7.50 APP.		UNSPECIFIED		TFA
983M	A	7.50 APP.		UNSPECIFIED		CCL4
1001M	A	7.50- 8.00		UNSPECIFIED		CDCL3
2291M	A	7.58 APP.		UNSPECIFIED		TFA
214M	A	7.60		UNSPECIFIED		CCL4
742M	A	7.70- 8.30		UNSPECIFIED		TFA
1051M	A	7.75		UNSPECIFIED		CDCL3
743M	A	8.60- 9.12		UNSPECIFIED		DMSO-D6
773M	A	0.80- 2.20		UNSPECIFIED		D20
825M	A	7.15- 7.60		UNSPECIFIED	S	DMSO-D6
48M	B	0.70- 2.00		UNSPECIFIED	S	CCL4
107M	B	0.80- 2.30		UNSPECIFIED		CCL4
559M	B	0.80- 2.10		UNSPECIFIED		CDCL3

BOOK NO.	ASSIGN-MENT	CHEM SHIFT - ppm -	PROTON GROUP	ENVIRONMENTAL GROUPS	S	SOLVENT
47M	B	0.90- 1.90		UNSPECIFIED		CCL4
1629M	B	0.95- 1.70		UNSPECIFIED		CDCL3
46M	B	1.00- 1.80		UNSPECIFIED		CCL4
30M	B	1.00- 1.60		UNSPECIFIED		CCL4
1621M	B	1.00- 1.90		UNSPECIFIED		CCL4
2762M	B	1.00- 1.75		UNSPECIFIED		CCL4
2650M	B	1.00- 1.75		UNSPECIFIED		D2O
472M	B	1.00- 2.20		UNSPECIFIED		CDCL3
711M	A	1.46- 2.55		UNSPECIFIED		CCL4
657M	A	6.80- 7.40		UNSPECIFIED		CDCL3
714M	A	6.90- 7.90		UNSPECIFIED		CDCL3
715M	A	6.90- 7.70		UNSPECIFIED		CDCL3
728M	A	7.18- 7.89		UNSPECIFIED		CCL4
680M	A	7.19- 7.69		UNSPECIFIED		CDCL3
726M	A	7.20- 7.80		UNSPECIFIED		CDCL3
698M	A	7.32- 7.73		UNSPECIFIED		CDCL3
635M	B	1.00- 2.00		UNSPECIFIED		CCL4
562M	B	1.00- 1.90		UNSPECIFIED		CCL4
465M	B	1.06- 1.50		UNSPECIFIED		CCL4
366M	B	1.09- 2.44		UNSPECIFIED		CCL4
84M	B	1.10- 1.70		UNSPECIFIED		CDCL3
1625M	B	1.10- 1.80		UNSPECIFIED		CCL4
1602M	B	1.10- 1.60		UNSPECIFIED		CCL4
2715M	B	1.10- 2.50		UNSPECIFIED		CDCL3
2706M	B	1.10- 1.90		UNSPECIFIED		CCL4
2696M	B	1.10- 1.60		UNSPECIFIED		CCL4
2705M	B	1.10- 1.90		UNSPECIFIED		CDCL3
2783M	B	1.10- 1.90		UNSPECIFIED		CCL4
2788M	B	1.10- 2.30		UNSPECIFIED		CDCL3
2782M	B	1.10- 2.00		UNSPECIFIED		CDCL3
2711M	B	1.10- 2.00		UNSPECIFIED		CDCL3
2495M	B	1.10- 2.00		UNSPECIFIED		CCL4
2808M	B	1.10- 1.87		UNSPECIFIED		CDCL3
2819M	B	1.10- 1.80		UNSPECIFIED		CCL4
2898M	B	1.10- 1.90		UNSPECIFIED		CCL4
959M	B	1.12- 2.08		UNSPECIFIED		CCL4
959M	B	1.12- 2.08		UNSPECIFIED		CCL4
2947M	B	1.14- 2.07		UNSPECIFIED		CCL4
2714M	B	1.14- 2.00		UNSPECIFIED		CCL4
2784M	B	1.15- 1.91		UNSPECIFIED		CCL4
33M	B	1.20 APP.		UNSPECIFIED		CCL4
1126M	B	1.21- 1.91		UNSPECIFIED		CCL4
37M	B	1.22 APP.		UNSPECIFIED		CCL4
467M	B	1.27 APP.		UNSPECIFIED		CDCL3
454M	B	1.29		UNSPECIFIED		CCL4
36M	B	1.29 APP.		UNSPECIFIED		CCL4
2528M	B	1.30		UNSPECIFIED		CCL4
2823M	B	1.30 APP.		UNSPECIFIED		CCL4
1606M	B	1.32		UNSPECIFIED		CDCL3
2529M	B	1.32		UNSPECIFIED		CCL4
2960M	B	1.32 APP.		UNSPECIFIED	S	D2O
826M	A	7.50- 8.15		UNSPECIFIED	S	DMSO-D6
787M	A	7.51		UNSPECIFIED	S	TFA
788M	A	7.51		UNSPECIFIED	S	D2O
794M	A	7.67 APP.		UNSPECIFIED		CCL4
737M	B	1.27 APP.		UNSPECIFIED		CCL4
197M	B	1.40- 2.10		UNSPECIFIED		CCL4
1651M	B	2.12- 2.89		UNSPECIFIED		D2O
628M	B	2.30- 2.81		UNSPECIFIED		CDCL3
2764M	B	4.10- 4.40		UNSPECIFIED		CCL4
1546M	B	5.90- 7.40		UNSPECIFIED		CDCL3
509M	B	6.15- 6.60		UNSPECIFIED		CCL4
508M	B	6.29- 7.10		UNSPECIFIED		CCL4
512M	B	6.40- 7.30		UNSPECIFIED		CCL4
225M	B	6.50- 7.40		UNSPECIFIED		CDCL3
152M	B	6.50- 7.30		UNSPECIFIED		CCL4
1510M	B	6.55- 6.95		UNSPECIFIED		DMSO-D6
504M	B	6.58- 7.20		UNSPECIFIED		CCL4
604M	B	6.60- 7.55		UNSPECIFIED		DMSO-D6
2334M	B	6.60- 7.08		UNSPECIFIED		CCL4
177M	B	6.62- 7.08		UNSPECIFIED		CDCL3
1098M	B	6.64- 7.30		UNSPECIFIED		CCL4
224M	B	6.65- 7.27		UNSPECIFIED		CDCL3
1088M	B	6.66- 7.09		UNSPECIFIED		CDCL3
597M	B	6.68- 7.38		UNSPECIFIED		CDCL3
2440M	B	6.68- 7.18		UNSPECIFIED		CDCL3
759M	B	6.70- 7.30		UNSPECIFIED		CCL4
884M	B	6.70- 7.30		UNSPECIFIED		CDCL3
2559M	B	6.70- 7.50		UNSPECIFIED		POLYSOL-D
994M	B	6.70- 7.05		UNSPECIFIED		CDCL3
2989M	B	6.75- 7.50		UNSPECIFIED		CDCL3

BOOK NO.	ASSIGN-MENT	CHEM SHIFT - ppm -	PROTON GROUP	ENVIRONMENTAL GROUPS	S	SOLVENT
2328M	B	6.78- 7.40		UNSPECIFIED		CDCL3
188M	B	6.79 APP.		UNSPECIFIED		CCL4
980M	B	6.79- 7.52		UNSPECIFIED		CCL4
890M	B	6.80- 7.40		UNSPECIFIED		CDCL3
671M	B	6.80- 8.30		UNSPECIFIED		CCL4
2928M	B	6.80- 7.43		UNSPECIFIED		CCL4
1542M	B	6.80- 7.30		UNSPECIFIED		CCL4
2342M	B	6.80- 7.70		UNSPECIFIED		CDCL3
2558M	B	6.81- 7.45		UNSPECIFIED		CDCL3
2607M	B	6.82- 7.70		UNSPECIFIED		DMSO
1530M	B	6.83- 7.85		UNSPECIFIED		CCL4
872M	B	6.85- 7.55		UNSPECIFIED		CDCL3
2955M	B	6.85- 7.46		UNSPECIFIED		CDCL3
1105M	B	6.87- 7.62		UNSPECIFIED		CDCL3
906M	B	6.88- 7.50		UNSPECIFIED		CCL4
913M	B	6.90- 7.20		UNSPECIFIED		CCL4
1550M	B	6.90- 7.40		UNSPECIFIED		CDCL3
174M	B	6.95		UNSPECIFIED		CCL4
383M	B	6.95- 7.30		UNSPECIFIED		CCL4
2462M	B	6.95- 7.40		UNSPECIFIED		DMSO-D6
752M	B	6.98- 7.37		UNSPECIFIED		DMSO
140M	B	7.00- 7.35		UNSPECIFIED		CCL4
2971M	B	7.00- 7.50		UNSPECIFIED		CDCL3
2344M	B	7.00- 7.50		UNSPECIFIED		CDCL3
2414M	B	7.00- 7.60		UNSPECIFIED		CDCL3
2329M	B	7.00- 7.50		UNSPECIFIED		CDCL3
2467M	B	7.00- 7.45		UNSPECIFIED		DMSO
2942M	B	7.01- 7.49		UNSPECIFIED		CCL4
984M	B	7.02- 7.66		UNSPECIFIED		CCL4
374M	B	7.02- 7.51		UNSPECIFIED		CDCL3
425M	B	7.05- 7.45		UNSPECIFIED		CDCL3
2450M	B	7.05- 7.65		UNSPECIFIED		CDCL3
927M	B	7.07		UNSPECIFIED		CCL4
293M	B	7.07 APP.		UNSPECIFIED		CCL4
148M	B	7.07 APP.		UNSPECIFIED		CCL4
163M	B	7.08		UNSPECIFIED		CDCL3
2872M	B	7.08- 7.50		UNSPECIFIED		CCL4
390M	B	7.09- 7.43		UNSPECIFIED		CCL4
382M	B	7.10		UNSPECIFIED		CCL4
1022M	B	7.10- 7.50		UNSPECIFIED		POLYSOL-D
1151M	B	7.10- 7.65		UNSPECIFIED		CDCL3
873M	B	7.10- 7.55		UNSPECIFIED		POLYSOL-D
697M	B	7.10- 7.65		UNSPECIFIED		CDCL3
167M	B	7.10- 7.50		UNSPECIFIED		CDCL3
211M	B	7.10- 7.50		UNSPECIFIED		CDCL3
173M	B	7.10- 7.70		UNSPECIFIED		CDCL3
2397M	B	7.10- 7.40		UNSPECIFIED		CDCL3
202M	B	7.12- 7.91		UNSPECIFIED		CDCL3
1572M	B	7.14- 7.53		UNSPECIFIED		CDCL3
150M	B	7.15 APP.		UNSPECIFIED		CDCL3
1032M	B	7.15- 7.58		UNSPECIFIED		CDCL3
376M	B	7.15- 7.68		UNSPECIFIED		CDCL3
159M	B	7.15- 7.65		UNSPECIFIED		CDCL3
2555M	B	7.15- 7.60		UNSPECIFIED		DMSO
2387M	B	7.16- 7.60		UNSPECIFIED		CDCL3
2550M	B	7.17- 7.69		UNSPECIFIED		CDCL3
1292M	A	7.20- 8.30		UNSPECIFIED		TFA
1273M	A	7.25- 7.70		UNSPECIFIED		CDCL3
1286M	A	7.30- 7.80		UNSPECIFIED		POLYSOL-D
1251M	A	7.30- 7.80		UNSPECIFIED		CDCL3
1285M	A	7.70- 8.05		UNSPECIFIED		CDCL3
1218M	B	2.40- 3.16		UNSPECIFIED		CDCL3
1195M	B	7.02 APP.		UNSPECIFIED		POLYSOL-D
1332M	B	7.05- 7.45		UNSPECIFIED		CDCL3
1167M	B	7.05- 7.55		UNSPECIFIED		CCL4
1181M	B	7.06- 7.51		UNSPECIFIED		CCL4
1192M	B	7.08- 7.55		UNSPECIFIED		CDCL3
1166M	B	7.10- 7.55		UNSPECIFIED		CDCL3
1174M	B	7.10- 7.80		UNSPECIFIED		CS2
1191M	B	7.17		UNSPECIFIED		CDCL3
292M	B	7.18		UNSPECIFIED		CCL4
316M	B	7.18- 8.12		UNSPECIFIED		CCL4
317M	B	7.18- 7.77		UNSPECIFIED		CDCL3
149M	B	7.19		UNSPECIFIED		CDCL3
164M	B	7.20		UNSPECIFIED		POLYSOL-D
1165M	B	7.20 APP.		UNSPECIFIED		CDCL3
1172M	B	7.20- 7.65		UNSPECIFIED		CDCL3
1031M	B	7.20- 7.60		UNSPECIFIED		CDCL3
1089M	B	7.20- 7.65		UNSPECIFIED		CDCL3
438M	B	7.20- 7.60		UNSPECIFIED		CCL4
371M	B	7.22		UNSPECIFIED		

BOOK NO.	ASSIGN-MENT	CHEM SHIFT - ppm -	PROTON GROUP	ENVIRONMENTAL GROUPS	S	SOLVENT
851M	B	7.22- 7.82		UNSPECIFIED		DMSO
1226M	B	7.23 APP.		UNSPECIFIED		CDCL3
2556M	B	7.23- 7.72		UNSPECIFIED		C3H6O
2544M	B	7.24 APP.		UNSPECIFIED		CDCL3
1106M	B	7.25- 7.75		UNSPECIFIED		CDCL3
880M	B	7.25- 7.70		UNSPECIFIED		CDCL3
718M	B	7.25- 8.30		UNSPECIFIED		CCL4
2390M	B	7.25- 7.70		UNSPECIFIED		DMSO-D6
2447M	B	7.25- 7.60		UNSPECIFIED		DMSO-D6
972M	B	7.27		UNSPECIFIED		CCL4
647M	B	7.27		UNSPECIFIED		CCL4
221M	B	7.27		UNSPECIFIED		CCL4
2539M	B	7.27		UNSPECIFIED		CDCL3
1173M	B	7.28		UNSPECIFIED		CDCL3
284M	B	7.28		UNSPECIFIED		CCL4
2991M	B	7.28		UNSPECIFIED		CDCL3
3000M	B	7.28		UNSPECIFIED		CDCL3
925M	B	7.28 APP.		UNSPECIFIED		CDCL3
1377M	A	0.70- 2.20		UNSPECIFIED		POLYSOL-D
1353M	A	0.80- 2.10		UNSPECIFIED		POLYSOL-D
1451M	A	0.80- 2.30		UNSPECIFIED		CDCL3
1460M	A	1.17- 1.70		UNSPECIFIED		CCL4
1340M	A	6.90- 7.60		UNSPECIFIED		DMSO
1352M	A	6.90- 7.80		UNSPECIFIED		DMSO
1335M	A	7.10- 7.70		UNSPECIFIED		CDCL3
1343M	A	7.10- 7.60		UNSPECIFIED		DMSO
1351M	A	7.38		UNSPECIFIED		CDCL3
1473M	B	3.30- 4.00		UNSPECIFIED		CDCL3
1354M	B	7.00- 7.60		UNSPECIFIED		POLYSOL-D
1370M	B	7.12 APP.		UNSPECIFIED		CDCL3
1371M	B	7.19 APP.		UNSPECIFIED		DMSO-D6
1487M	B	7.20- 7.60		UNSPECIFIED		CCL4
1342M	B	7.20- 7.65		UNSPECIFIED		POLYSOL-D
1482M	B	7.25		UNSPECIFIED		CCL4
1247M	B	7.29		UNSPECIFIED		CDCL3
1151M	B	7.29		UNSPECIFIED		CDCL3
2396M	B	7.29		UNSPECIFIED		DMSO-D6
937M	B	7.29 APP.		UNSPECIFIED		CDCL3
1005M	B	7.30		UNSPECIFIED		CDCL3
749M	B	7.30- 7.80		UNSPECIFIED		CDCL3
2546M	B	7.32		UNSPECIFIED		CDCL3
2368M	B	7.33		UNSPECIFIED		CDCL3
2446M	B	7.33		UNSPECIFIED		DMSO-D6
1320M	B	7.33 APP.		UNSPECIFIED		CDCL3
1046M	B	7.33 APP.		UNSPECIFIED		CCL4
985M	B	7.37		UNSPECIFIED		CCL4
287M	B	7.37 APP.		UNSPECIFIED		CCL4
1017M	B	7.38		UNSPECIFIED		CDCL3
164M	B	7.38		UNSPECIFIED		CDCL3
1289M	B	7.39- 8.00		UNSPECIFIED		DMSO
2913M	B	7.40		UNSPECIFIED		CDCL3
999M	B	7.40- 8.08		UNSPECIFIED		CDCL3
724M	B	7.40- 7.82		UNSPECIFIED		CDCL3
729M	B	7.40- 7.65		UNSPECIFIED		CDCL3
2407M	B	7.40- 7.90		UNSPECIFIED		DMSO-D6
1279M	B	7.42 APP.		UNSPECIFIED		POLYSOL-D
993M	B	7.50- 7.95		UNSPECIFIED		CDCL3
725M	B	7.50- 8.05		UNSPECIFIED		CCL4
2441M	B	7.51		UNSPECIFIED		DMSO-D6
1305M	B	7.80- 8.07		UNSPECIFIED		DMSO
2662M	B	3.60- 4.10		UNSPECIFIED	S	D2O
2661M	B	3.70- 4.20		UNSPECIFIED	S	D2O
1527M	B	6.65- 7.05		UNSPECIFIED	S	POLYSOL-D
790M	B	7.05- 7.40		UNSPECIFIED	S	POLYSOL-D
1306M	B	7.10- 7.65		UNSPECIFIED	S	DMSO
783M	B	7.20- 7.75		UNSPECIFIED	S	POLYSOL-D
2673M	B	7.32		UNSPECIFIED	S	D2O
789M	B	7.38		UNSPECIFIED	S	D2O
805M	B	7.44		UNSPECIFIED	S	TFA
840M	B	7.55- 8.00		UNSPECIFIED	S	D2O
782M	B	7.59		UNSPECIFIED	S	D2O
2674M	B	7.60- 8.50		UNSPECIFIED	S	D2O
1102M	B	7.62- 8.08		UNSPECIFIED	S	CDCL3
1309M	B	7.89 APP.		UNSPECIFIED	S	DMSO-D6
471M	C	0.80- 2.20		UNSPECIFIED		CDCL3
1210M	C	1.00- 2.00		UNSPECIFIED		CDCL3
24M	C	1.00- 2.00		UNSPECIFIED		CCL4
29M	C	1.00- 1.80		UNSPECIFIED		CDCL3
1620M	C	1.00- 1.90		UNSPECIFIED		CCL4
455M	C	1.00- 1.60		UNSPECIFIED		CDCL3
453M	C	1.00- 1.90		UNSPECIFIED		CDCL3

BOOK NO.	ASSIGN-MENT	CHEM SHIFT - ppm -	PROTON GROUP	ENVIRONMENTAL GROUPS	S	SOLVENT
1627M	C	1.04- 1.83		UNSPECIFIED		CCL4
19M	C	1.05- 1.90		UNSPECIFIED		CCL4
1387M	C	1.09- 1.62		UNSPECIFIED		CCL4
629M	C	1.10- 1.90		UNSPECIFIED		CDCL3
127M	C	1.10- 1.80		UNSPECIFIED		CCL4
2459M	C	1.10- 1.80		UNSPECIFIED		DMSO-D6
2478M	C	1.10- 2.00		UNSPECIFIED		CCL4
2903M	C	1.17- 1.99		UNSPECIFIED		CCL4
449M	C	1.25		UNSPECIFIED		CDCL3
35M	C	1.25 APP.		UNSPECIFIED		CDCL3
32M	C	1.26		UNSPECIFIED		CCL4
2818M	C	1.28 APP.		UNSPECIFIED		CCL4
2817M	C	1.29		UNSPECIFIED		CCL4
34M	C	1.29 APP.		UNSPECIFIED		CCL4
452M	C	1.29 APP.		UNSPECIFIED		CDCL3
456M	C	1.30 APP.		UNSPECIFIED		CDCL3
1610M	C	1.30- 2.15		UNSPECIFIED		CCL4
557M	C	1.31		UNSPECIFIED		CDCL3
1113M	C	1.31 APP.		UNSPECIFIED		CCL4
109M	C	1.31- 2.60		UNSPECIFIED		CCL4
44M	C	1.40- 2.00		UNSPECIFIED		CCL4
1597M	C	1.40- 1.90		UNSPECIFIED		CDCL3
115M	C	1.50- 3.40		UNSPECIFIED		CCL4
1680M	A	0.25- 2.82		UNSPECIFIED		CCL4
1682M	A	0.50- 2.00		UNSPECIFIED		CCL4
1773M	A	0.50- 2.20		UNSPECIFIED		CDCL3
1778M	A	0.70- 2.10		UNSPECIFIED		POLYSOL-D
1775M	A	0.80- 2.90		UNSPECIFIED		CCL4
1766M	A	0.83- 2.43		UNSPECIFIED		CCL4
1683M	A	0.85- 2.00		UNSPECIFIED		CDCL3
1774M	A	0.90- 2.20		UNSPECIFIED		CDCL3
1794M	A	1.00- 2.00		UNSPECIFIED		POLYSOL-D
1781M	A	1.00- 2.60		UNSPECIFIED		CDCL3
1777M	A	1.20- 2.30		UNSPECIFIED		CDCL3
1691M	A	3.30- 3.75		UNSPECIFIED		CCL4
1707M	A	3.40- 4.00		UNSPECIFIED		CDCL3
1676M	A	3.40- 4.10		UNSPECIFIED		CDCL3
1671M	A	3.50- 3.90		UNSPECIFIED		CDCL3
1710M	A	3.50- 4.00		UNSPECIFIED		CCL4
1771M	B	0.50- 2.10		UNSPECIFIED		CDCL3
1770M	B	0.70- 2.10		UNSPECIFIED		CDCL3
1681M	B	0.70- 2.00		UNSPECIFIED		CCL4
1767M	B	0.70- 1.80		UNSPECIFIED		CDCL3
1803M	B	0.80- 1.50		UNSPECIFIED		CCL4
1779M	B	1.00- 2.60		UNSPECIFIED		CDCL3
1690M	B	1.00- 1.60		UNSPECIFIED		CCL4
1768M	B	1.00- 2.20		UNSPECIFIED		CDCL3
1765M	B	1.10- 2.20		UNSPECIFIED		CDCL3
1769M	B	1.10- 2.00		UNSPECIFIED		CDCL3
1749M	B	1.10- 1.70		UNSPECIFIED		CCL4
1808M	B	1.24- 2.29		UNSPECIFIED		CCL4
1811M	B	1.54		UNSPECIFIED		CCL4
1762M	B	1.76		UNSPECIFIED		CCL4
1794M	B	2.00- 3.70		UNSPECIFIED		POLYSOL-D
1666M	B	3.51 APP.		UNSPECIFIED		CCL4
1743M	C	1.00- 1.70		UNSPECIFIED		CCL4
1772M	C	1.08- 2.48		UNSPECIFIED		CDCL3
1745M	C	1.10- 1.80		UNSPECIFIED		CDCL3
1797M	C	1.20- 1.60		UNSPECIFIED		CCL4
1747M	C	1.25		UNSPECIFIED		CCL4
1746M	C	1.25 APP.		UNSPECIFIED		CCL4
1799M	C	1.29		UNSPECIFIED		CCL4
1810M	C	1.34		UNSPECIFIED		C3F60
1809M	C	1.51 APP.		UNSPECIFIED		CDCL3
1449M	C	1.51- 2.11		UNSPECIFIED		CCL4
111M	C	1.60- 2.40		UNSPECIFIED		CCL4
1870M	A	3.50- 4.20		UNSPECIFIED		D20
1866M	A	3.50- 4.30		UNSPECIFIED		D20
1930M	A	6.97		UNSPECIFIED		POLYSOL-D
1951M	A	7.01- 7.86		UNSPECIFIED		C3H60
1941M	A	7.43 APP.		UNSPECIFIED		DMSO
1940M	A	7.49 APP.		UNSPECIFIED		DMSO
1836M	B	1.00- 1.80		UNSPECIFIED		CDCL3
1869M	B	3.20- 4.10		UNSPECIFIED		D20
1846M	B	3.67		UNSPECIFIED		CDCL3
1931M	B	6.40- 6.85		UNSPECIFIED		CDCL3
1890M	B	6.50- 7.20		UNSPECIFIED		CCL4
1892M	B	6.60- 7.38		UNSPECIFIED		CDCL3
1875M	B	6.65- 7.32		UNSPECIFIED		CDCL3
1961M	B	7.03- 7.81		UNSPECIFIED		DMSO
1930M	B	7.10- 7.70		UNSPECIFIED		POLYSOL-D

BOOK NO.	ASSIGN-MENT	CHEM SHIFT - ppm -	PROTON GROUP	ENVIRONMENTAL GROUPS	S	SOLVENT
1889M	B	7.13- 7.70		UNSPECIFIED		DMSO
1822M	B	7.19		UNSPECIFIED		CDCL3
1950M	B	7.22- 7.60		UNSPECIFIED		C3H6O
1955M	B	7.39- 7.65		UNSPECIFIED		CDCL3
1839M	C	1.00- 1.60		UNSPECIFIED		C3D6O
2532M	C	1.79- 2.47		UNSPECIFIED		CCL4
2816M	C	1.80- 2.40		UNSPECIFIED		CCL4
103M	C	1.89		UNSPECIFIED		CCL4
1757M	C	1.91		UNSPECIFIED		CDCL3
467M	C	2.32- 2.88		UNSPECIFIED		CCL4
632M	C	2.40 APP.		UNSPECIFIED		CCL4
2537M	C	2.75- 3.30		UNSPECIFIED		CCL4
1760M	C	2.81- 4.09		UNSPECIFIED		CCL4
1460M	C	3.15- 4.10		UNSPECIFIED		CCL4
1414M	C	3.30- 3.80		UNSPECIFIED		CDCL3
1836M	C	3.40- 4.20		UNSPECIFIED		CDCL3
1781M	C	3.50- 4.05		UNSPECIFIED		CDCL3
1673M	C	3.63		UNSPECIFIED		CDCL3
2764M	C	4.75- 5.80		UNSPECIFIED		CDCL3
277M	C	5.80- 6.50		UNSPECIFIED.		CCL4
1256M	C	6.00- 7.00		UNSPECIFIED		CCL4
489M	C	6.15- 6.55		UNSPECIFIED		CCL4
488M	C	6.30- 7.10		UNSPECIFIED		CCL4
1877M	C	6.36- 6.70		UNSPECIFIED		CCL4
659M	C	6.41 APP.		UNSPECIFIED		CCL4
1876M	C	6.45- 7.12		UNSPECIFIED		CCL4
1494M	C	6.50- 7.20		UNSPECIFIED		CDCL3
1535M	C	6.55- 6.95		UNSPECIFIED		CDCL3
2033M	A	6.84		UNSPECIFIED		CDCL3
1962M	A	7.04- 7.41		UNSPECIFIED		CDCL3
2112M	A	7.18- 7.69		UNSPECIFIED		CDCL3
2094M	A	7.20- 8.00		UNSPECIFIED		POLYSOL-D
2092M	A	7.22- 7.80		UNSPECIFIED		CDCL3
2106M	A	7.25- 8.08		UNSPECIFIED		CCL4
2102M	A	7.30- 7.80		UNSPECIFIED		CCL4
2001M	B	1.00- 2.10		UNSPECIFIED		CCL4
1976M	B	1.02- 1.90		UNSPECIFIED		CCL4
2002M	B	1.10- 2.40		UNSPECIFIED		CDCL3
1985M	B	1.10- 1.85		UNSPECIFIED		CDCL3
1986M	B	1.10- 1.90		UNSPECIFIED		CDCL3
2014M	B	2.79 APP.		UNSPECIFIED		CDCL3
2089M	B	6.80- 7.40		UNSPECIFIED		CDCL3
2040M	B	7.00- 7.40		UNSPECIFIED		CCL4
2043M	B	7.14- 7.80		UNSPECIFIED		CCL4
2064M	B	7.15- 7.60		UNSPECIFIED		CDCL3
2099M	B	7.19 APP.		UNSPECIFIED		CDCL3
2044M	B	7.20- 7.70		UNSPECIFIED		CCL4
2087M	B	7.20- 7.70		UNSPECIFIED		CCL4
2072M	B	7.25- 7.80		UNSPECIFIED		CDCL3
2113M	B	7.30- 8.09		UNSPECIFIED		CDCL3
2033M	B	7.47		UNSPECIFIED		POLYSOL-D
2124M	B	7.53		UNSPECIFIED		CDCL3
2095M	B	7.79 APP.		UNSPECIFIED		CCL4
2005M	C	1.10- 2.60		UNSPECIFIED		D2O
2006M	C	1.20- 2.20		UNSPECIFIED		CCL4
2007M	C	1.30- 2.70		UNSPECIFIED		CDCL3
2027M	C	1.70- 2.60		UNSPECIFIED		CDCL3
1998M	C	2.00- 3.10		UNSPECIFIED		CCL4
2115M	C	2.40- 3.10		UNSPECIFIED		CCL4
886M	C	6.58- 7.25		UNSPECIFIED		CDCL3
1495M	C	6.60		UNSPECIFIED		CCL4
1554M	C	6.60		UNSPECIFIED		CCL4
1489M	C	6.60- 7.30		UNSPECIFIED		CCL4
198M	C	6.60- 7.10		UNSPECIFIED		CCL4
2932M	C	6.60- 7.38		UNSPECIFIED		CCL4
1512M	C	6.60- 7.35		UNSPECIFIED		DMSO-D6
1715M	C	6.65- 7.45		UNSPECIFIED		CDCL3
1907M	C	6.65- 7.20		UNSPECIFIED		CDCL3
1925M	C	6.68		UNSPECIFIED		DMSO-D6
2090M	C	6.70- 7.30		UNSPECIFIED		CCL4
2103M	C	6.70- 7.30		UNSPECIFIED		CCL4
2168M	A	7.20- 7.70		UNSPECIFIED		CCL4
2245M	A	7.20- 7.80		UNSPECIFIED		CCL4
2229M	A	7.21- 7.58		UNSPECIFIED		CCL4
2232M	A	7.23- 7.83		UNSPECIFIED		CCL4
2166M	A	7.40 APP.		UNSPECIFIED		CDCL3
2183M	A	7.40- 8.10		UNSPECIFIED		CDCL3
2181M	A	7.48- 8.07		UNSPECIFIED		CCL4
2225M	A	7.59- 8.12		UNSPECIFIED		CCL4
2235M	A	7.70- 7.99		UNSPECIFIED		CDCL3
2242M	A	8.15- 8.45		UNSPECIFIED		

BOOK NO.	ASSIGN- MENT	CHEM SHIFT - ppm -	PROTON GROUP	ENVIRONMENTAL GROUPS	S	SOLVENT
2140M	B	1.10- 2.10		UNSPECIFIED		CCL4
2285M	B	1.17- 2.30		UNSPECIFIED		CDCL3
2139M	B	1.62 APP.		UNSPECIFIED		CCL4
2208M	B	5.70- 6.70		UNSPECIFIED		CCL4
2215M	B	6.70- 7.40		UNSPECIFIED		CCL4
2222M	B	7.10- 7.65		UNSPECIFIED		CCL4
2123M	B	7.10- 7.65		UNSPECIFIED		CDCL3
2180M	B	7.19- 7.51		UNSPECIFIED		CDCL3
2201M	B	7.20- 7.60		UNSPECIFIED		CDCL3
2287M	B	7.20- 7.65		UNSPECIFIED		TFA
2126M	B	7.29- 8.38		UNSPECIFIED		CCL4
2227M	B	7.30- 8.30		UNSPECIFIED		CCL4
2164M	B	7.31		UNSPECIFIED		CCL4
2125M	B	7.40		UNSPECIFIED		CCL4
2213M	B	7.40		UNSPECIFIED		CCL4
2269M	B	7.41		UNSPECIFIED		CDCL3
2271M	B	7.65- 8.10		UNSPECIFIED		CDCL3
2149M	B	8.07 APP.		UNSPECIFIED		TFA
2129M	C	1.10- 2.10		UNSPECIFIED		CDCL3
2207M	C	1.20- 2.65		UNSPECIFIED		CDCL3
2143M	C	1.65- 2.70		UNSPECIFIED		CCL4
2140M	C	2.16 APP.		UNSPECIFIED		CCL4
658M	C	6.70- 7.18		UNSPECIFIED		CCL4
610M	C	6.76- 7.71		UNSPECIFIED		DMSO-D6
375M	C	6.79- 7.23		UNSPECIFIED		CCL4
1349M	C	6.80- 7.55		UNSPECIFIED		POLYSOL-D
888M	C	6.80- 7.50		UNSPECIFIED		CDCL3
151M	C	6.80- 7.30		UNSPECIFIED		CDCL3
377M	C	6.80- 7.35		UNSPECIFIED		CCL4
2988M	C	6.80- 7.50		UNSPECIFIED		CDCL3
1229M	C	6.81- 7.33		UNSPECIFIED		CDCL3
2212M	C	6.90- 7.40		UNSPECIFIED		CCL4
1507M	C	6.90- 7.55		UNSPECIFIED		CCL4
609M	C	6.90- 7.25		UNSPECIFIED		CDCL3
424M	C	6.90- 7.35		UNSPECIFIED		CDCL3
2994M	C	6.90- 7.60		UNSPECIFIED		CDCL3
2921M	C	6.90- 7.50		UNSPECIFIED		CCL4
1515M	C	6.90- 7.20		UNSPECIFIED		CDCL3
2400M	C	6.90- 7.30		UNSPECIFIED		CDCL3
209M	C	6.91- 7.98		UNSPECIFIED		CDCL3
179M	C	6.92 APP.		UNSPECIFIED		CCL4
1228M	C	6.92- 7.40		UNSPECIFIED		CDCL3
672M	C	6.93- 8.42		UNSPECIFIED		CCL4
2055M	C	6.95- 7.45		UNSPECIFIED		CCL4
1949M	C	6.95- 7.50		UNSPECIFIED		POLYSOL-D
870M	C	6.95- 7.56		UNSPECIFIED		CDCL3
1096M	C	6.99- 7.44		UNSPECIFIED		CDCL3
1569M	C	6.99- 7.50		UNSPECIFIED		CCL4
2042M	C	7.00- 7.50		UNSPECIFIED		CDCL3
1571M	C	7.00- 7.90		UNSPECIFIED		CDCL3
1267M	C	7.00- 7.30		UNSPECIFIED		POLYSOL-D
744M	C	7.00- 7.60		UNSPECIFIED		CDCL3
764M	C	7.00- 7.85		UNSPECIFIED		POLYSOL-D
539M	C	7.00- 7.85		UNSPECIFIED		CDCL3
2869M	C	7.00- 7.40		UNSPECIFIED		CDCL3
1528M	C	7.00- 7.40		UNSPECIFIED		CDCL3
2361M	C	7.00- 7.60		UNSPECIFIED		CDCL3
2974M	C	7.01- 7.72		UNSPECIFIED		CDCL3
1717M	C	7.02- 7.51		UNSPECIFIED		CDCL3
605M	C	7.03 APP.		UNSPECIFIED		CCL4
606M	C	7.04		UNSPECIFIED		CDCL3
978M	C	7.05		UNSPECIFIED		CDCL3
867M	C	7.05- 7.50		UNSPECIFIED		CDCL3
676M	C	7.05- 7.60		UNSPECIFIED		CDCL3
505M	C	7.05- 7.62		UNSPECIFIED		C3H6O
878M	C	7.06- 7.46		UNSPECIFIED		DMSO-D6
134M	C	7.07		UNSPECIFIED		CCL4
2363M	C	7.07- 7.59		UNSPECIFIED		CDCL3
2321M	C	7.08		UNSPECIFIED		CDCL3
1956M	C	7.08- 7.85		UNSPECIFIED		C3H6O
611M	C	7.09		UNSPECIFIED		CDCL3
136M	C	7.09		UNSPECIFIED		CCL4
145M	C	7.09		UNSPECIFIED		CCL4
372M	C	7.10 APP.		UNSPECIFIED		CCL4
1193M	C	7.10- 7.50		UNSPECIFIED		CCL4
1179M	C	7.10- 7.53		UNSPECIFIED		DMSO
1090M	C	7.10- 7.60		UNSPECIFIED		CCL4
1097M	C	7.10- 7.60		UNSPECIFIED		CDCL3
1151M	C	7.10- 7.65		UNSPECIFIED		CCL4
1049M	C	7.10- 7.60		UNSPECIFIED		DMSO-D6
889M	C	7.10- 7.50		UNSPECIFIED		

BOOK NO.	ASSIGN-MENT	CHEM SHIFT - ppm -	PROTON GROUP	ENVIRONMENTAL GROUPS	S	SOLVENT
762M	C	7.10- 7.68		UNSPECIFIED		CDCL3
541M	C	7.10- 7.80		UNSPECIFIED		DMSO
201M	C	7.10- 7.55		UNSPECIFIED		CCL4
1481M	C	7.12 APP.		UNSPECIFIED		CDCL3
1173M	C	7.12- 7.58		UNSPECIFIED		CDCL3
147M	C	7.14		UNSPECIFIED		CDCL3
2866M	C	7.15		UNSPECIFIED		CCL4
295M	C	7.15 APP.		UNSPECIFIED		CCL4
1817M	C	7.15- 7.60		UNSPECIFIED		CDCL3
1242M	C	7.15- 7.75		UNSPECIFIED		CDCL3
2552M	C	7.15- 7.60		UNSPECIFIED		CDCL3
2466M	C	7.15- 7.60		UNSPECIFIED		CDCL3
2468M	C	7.15- 7.40		UNSPECIFIED		CDCL3
973M	C	7.16		UNSPECIFIED		CDCL3
2831M	C	7.16		UNSPECIFIED		CCL4
1163M	C	7.17		UNSPECIFIED		CDCL3
607M	C	7.17		UNSPECIFIED		CDCL3
1790M	C	7.18		UNSPECIFIED		CCL4
1775M	C	7.18 APP.		UNSPECIFIED		CCL4
152M	C	7.18 APP.		UNSPECIFIED		CDCL3
2307M	C	7.19		UNSPECIFIED		CCL4
1700M	C	7.19		UNSPECIFIED		CCL4
644M	C	7.19		UNSPECIFIED		CCL4
1341M	C	7.19 APP.		UNSPECIFIED		DMSO-D6
379M	C	7.19 APP.		UNSPECIFIED		CCL4
380M	C	7.19 APP.		UNSPECIFIED		CCL4
1241M	C	7.19- 7.50		UNSPECIFIED		CDCL3
1158M	C	7.20		UNSPECIFIED		CCL4
581M	C	7.20		UNSPECIFIED		CCL4
164M	C	7.20		UNSPECIFIED		CDCL3
2832M	C	7.20		UNSPECIFIED		CCL4
2159M	C	7.20 APP.		UNSPECIFIED		CDCL3
2088M	C	7.20 APP.		UNSPECIFIED		CDCL3
2541M	C	7.20 APP.		UNSPECIFIED		CCL4
2432M	C	7.20 APP.		UNSPECIFIED		POLYSOL-D
2091M	C	7.20- 7.80		UNSPECIFIED		CDCL3
1508M	C	7.20- 7.70		UNSPECIFIED		CDCL3
1360M	C	7.20- 7.70		UNSPECIFIED		POLYSOL-D
975M	C	7.20- 7.60		UNSPECIFIED		CDCL3
723M	C	7.20- 7.60		UNSPECIFIED		CCL4
730M	C	7.20- 7.50		UNSPECIFIED		CDCL3
1218M	C	7.21		UNSPECIFIED		CDCL3
1224M	C	7.22		UNSPECIFIED		CCL4
974M	C	7.22		UNSPECIFIED		CCL4
2540M	C	7.22		UNSPECIFIED		CDCL3
2311M	C	7.22 APP.		UNSPECIFIED		CDCL3
2014M	C	7.22 APP.		UNSPECIFIED		CDCL3
1731M	C	7.22- 7.80		UNSPECIFIED		CDCL3
727M	C	7.22- 7.65		UNSPECIFIED		CDCL3
2958M	C	7.22- 7.79		UNSPECIFIED		CDCL3
2545M	C	7.23		UNSPECIFIED		CDCL3
2436M	C	7.25		UNSPECIFIED		CDCL3
1479M	C	7.25 APP.		UNSPECIFIED		CDCL3
2160M	C	7.25- 7.65		UNSPECIFIED		CCL4
1719M	C	7.25- 7.90		UNSPECIFIED		CDCL3
1362M	C	7.25- 7.50		UNSPECIFIED		DMSO-D6
1277M	C	7.25- 7.77		UNSPECIFIED		CDCL3
2346M	C	7.26		UNSPECIFIED		CDCL3
2542M	C	7.26		UNSPECIFIED		DMSO
719M	C	7.26- 7.70		UNSPECIFIED		CCL4
2308M	C	7.27		UNSPECIFIED		DMSO-D6
1088M	C	7.28 APP.		UNSPECIFIED		CDCL3
2345M	C	7.28- 7.59		UNSPECIFIED		CDCL3
1151M	C	7.29		UNSPECIFIED		CDCL3
476M	C	7.29		UNSPECIFIED		CDCL3
163M	C	7.29		UNSPECIFIED		CDCL3
2386M	C	7.29 APP.		UNSPECIFIED		CDCL3
580M	C	7.29 APP.		UNSPECIFIED		D20
2930M	C	7.29- 7.90		UNSPECIFIED		CDCL3
1931M	C	7.30		UNSPECIFIED		CDCL3
2989M	C	7.30 APP.		UNSPECIFIED		CDCL3
1376M	C	7.30- 8.00		UNSPECIFIED		POLYSOL-D
2861M	C	7.31		UNSPECIFIED		CCL4
2100M	C	7.32- 7.84		UNSPECIFIED		CDCL3
2369M	C	7.33		UNSPECIFIED		CCL4
164M	C	7.38		UNSPECIFIED		CDCL3
2551M	C	7.38		UNSPECIFIED		CDCL3
977M	C	7.38 APP.		UNSPECIFIED		CDCL3
2844M	C	7.38 APP.		UNSPECIFIED		CDCL3
2464M	C	7.39		UNSPECIFIED		DMSO-D6
1963M	C	7.40- 7.90		UNSPECIFIED		TFA

BOOK NO.	ASSIGN-MENT	CHEM SHIFT - ppm -	PROTON GROUP	ENVIRONMENTAL GROUPS	S	SOLVENT
982M	C	7.41		UNSPECIFIED		CCL4
504M	C	7.43		UNSPECIFIED		DMSO-D6
215M	C	7.46- 7.87		UNSPECIFIED		CDCL3
979M	C	7.49 APP.		UNSPECIFIED		DMSO-D6
838M	C	7.50 APP.		UNSPECIFIED		POLYSOL-D
2859M	C	7.50- 8.10		UNSPECIFIED		TFA
2180M	C	7.53- 7.91		UNSPECIFIED		CDCL3
873M	C	7.55- 8.00		UNSPECIFIED		POLYSOL-D
720M	C	7.58 APP.		UNSPECIFIED		CDCL3
1258M	C	7.60		UNSPECIFIED		CDCL3
2340M	C	7.61 APP.		UNSPECIFIED		CDCL3
1342M	C	7.65- 8.20		UNSPECIFIED		POLYSOL-D
998M	C	7.70- 8.00		UNSPECIFIED		POLYSOL-D
1572M	C	7.71		UNSPECIFIED		CDCL3
2287M	C	7.80 APP.		UNSPECIFIED		TFA
2095M	C	8.00- 8.30		UNSPECIFIED		POLYSOL-D
792M	C	7.00- 7.50		UNSPECIFIED	S	D20
806M	C	7.55 APP.		UNSPECIFIED	S	D20
1801M	D	1.10- 1.70		UNSPECIFIED		CCL4
893M	D	1.11- 2.33		UNSPECIFIED		CDCL3
1802M	D	1.13- 1.78		UNSPECIFIED		CCL4
1207M	D	1.32		UNSPECIFIED		CCL4
110M	D	1.80- 2.60		UNSPECIFIED		CCL4
2822M	D	1.95- 2.42		UNSPECIFIED		CCL4
2137M	D	2.20 APP.		UNSPECIFIED		CDCL3
2257M	D	2.27- 3.40		UNSPECIFIED		CDCL3
1216M	D	2.40- 3.10		UNSPECIFIED		CDCL3
1215M	D	2.40- 3.00		UNSPECIFIED		CDCL3
629M	D	2.50 APP.		UNSPECIFIED		CDCL3
2824M	D	2.69- 3.28		UNSPECIFIED		CCL4
1669M	D	3.20- 3.80		UNSPECIFIED		CCL4
1668M	D	3.30- 3.74		UNSPECIFIED		CCL4
1670M	D	3.30- 3.80		UNSPECIFIED		CDCL3
1667M	D	3.30- 3.85		UNSPECIFIED		CDCL3
1369M	D	3.30- 4.20		UNSPECIFIED		CDCL3
89M	D	5.30- 6.60		UNSPECIFIED		CCL4
1522M	D	6.20 APP.		UNSPECIFIED		CDCL3
874M	D	6.26- 7.40		UNSPECIFIED		CCL4
651M	D	6.30- 7.25		UNSPECIFIED		CCL4
491M	D	6.30- 7.10		UNSPECIFIED		CDCL3
583M	D	6.32- 7.23		UNSPECIFIED		CCL4
662M	D	6.35 APP.		UNSPECIFIED		CCL4
650M	D	6.36- 7.20		UNSPECIFIED		CCL4
2039M	D	6.45- 6.76		UNSPECIFIED		CCL4
1879M	D	6.50- 7.20		UNSPECIFIED		CCL4
1498M	D	6.52- 7.18		UNSPECIFIED		CCL4
1880M	D	6.56- 6.90		UNSPECIFIED		CDCL3
1558M	D	6.59 APP.		UNSPECIFIED		CCL4
1583M	D	6.60- 7.15		UNSPECIFIED		DMSO-D6
1589M	D	6.60- 7.15		UNSPECIFIED		CCL4
588M	D	6.60- 7.40		UNSPECIFIED		CDCL3
2987M	D	6.60- 7.50		UNSPECIFIED		CDCL3
1493M	D	6.65- 7.40		UNSPECIFIED		CCL4
1355M	D	6.70- 7.40		UNSPECIFIED		CDCL3
1734M	D	6.71 APP.		UNSPECIFIED		CDCL3
1548M	D	6.80- 7.40		UNSPECIFIED		CDCL3
608M	D	6.80- 7.20		UNSPECIFIED		CDCL3
661M	D	6.80- 7.30		UNSPECIFIED		CDCL3
661M	D	6.80- 7.30		UNSPECIFIED		CDCL3
178M	D	6.87- 7.39		UNSPECIFIED		CDCL3
2374M	D	6.90- 7.80		UNSPECIFIED		CDCL3
199M	D	6.90- 7.40		UNSPECIFIED		CCL4
2061M	D	6.91 APP.		UNSPECIFIED		CCL4
139M	D	6.98		UNSPECIFIED		CDCL3
197M	D	6.99		UNSPECIFIED		CCL4
1163M	D	6.99- 7.51		UNSPECIFIED		CDCL3
2114M	D	7.00- 7.50		UNSPECIFIED		CCL4
1725M	D	7.00- 8.00		UNSPECIFIED		CCL4
156M	D	7.00- 7.40		UNSPECIFIED		CCL4
296M	D	7.00- 7.30		UNSPECIFIED		CCL4
146M	D	7.00- 7.45		UNSPECIFIED		CCL4
639M	D	7.03- 7.53		UNSPECIFIED		CDCL3
483M	D	7.03- 7.32		UNSPECIFIED		CDCL3
1726M	D	7.04- 7.60		UNSPECIFIED		CDCL3
168M	D	7.05- 7.50		UNSPECIFIED		CCL4
172M	D	7.08- 7.28		UNSPECIFIED		CCL4
137M	D	7.09		UNSPECIFIED		CCL4
143M	D	7.10		UNSPECIFIED		CCL4
1818M	D	7.10- 7.60		UNSPECIFIED		CDCL3
1570M	D	7.10- 7.55		UNSPECIFIED		CDCL3
646M	D	7.10- 7.50		UNSPECIFIED		CDCL3

BOOK NO.	ASSIGN-MENT	CHEM SHIFT - ppm -	PROTON GROUP	ENVIRONMENTAL GROUPS	S	SOLVENT
709M	D	7.10- 7.50		UNSPECIFIED		DMSO-D6
599M	D	7.10- 7.85		UNSPECIFIED		CDCL3
157M	D	7.10- 7.52		UNSPECIFIED		CCL4
154M	D	7.11		UNSPECIFIED		CCL4
2833M	D	7.11		UNSPECIFIED		CCL4
1164M	D	7.12		UNSPECIFIED		CCL4
484M	D	7.12		UNSPECIFIED		CDCL3
141M	D	7.13		UNSPECIFIED		CCL4
477M	D	7.14		UNSPECIFIED		CCL4
2860M	D	7.15		UNSPECIFIED		CCL4
2035M	D	7.15 APP.		UNSPECIFIED		CCL4
2034M	D	7.17		UNSPECIFIED		CCL4
2371M	D	7.18		UNSPECIFIED		CDCL3
1701M	D	7.19		UNSPECIFIED		CDCL3
1484M	D	7.19		UNSPECIFIED		CDCL3
2862M	D	7.19		UNSPECIFID		CCL4
2036M	D	7.19 APP.		UNSPECIFIED		CCL4
135M	D	7.19 APP.		UNSPECIFIED		CDCL3
978M	D	7.20		UNSPECIFIFD		CDCL3
2932M	D	7.20		UNSPECIFIED		CCL4
2837M	D	7.20		UNSPECIFIED		CCL4
2385M	D	7.20 APP.		UNSPECIFIED		POLYSOL-D
479M	D	7.20 APP.		UNSPECIFIED		CDCL3
2312M	D	7.21		UNSPECIFIED		CDCL3
1447M	D	7.21		UNSPFCIFIED		CCL4
1159M	D	7.21		UNSPECIFIED		CCL4
478M	D	7.21		UNSPECIFIED		CCL4
1791M	D	7.21 APP.		UNSPFCIFIED		CDCL3
2314M	D	7.21 APP.		UNSPECIFIED		CDCL3
654M	D	7.21 APP.		UNSPECIFIED		CDCL3
1019M	D	7.25		UNSPECIFIED		CDCL3
2422M	D	7.25 APP.		UNSPECIFIED		POLYSOL-D
2852M	D	7.27		UNSPECIFIED		CCL4
645M	D	7.30		UNSPECIFIED		CDCL3
2445M	D	7.30		UNSPECIFIFD		CDCL3
2549M	D	7.30 APP.		UNSPECIFIED		CDCL3
2103M	D	7.30- 7.90		UNSPECIFIED		DMSO-D6
1248M	D	7.30- 7.70		UNSPECIFIED		CCL4
2896M	D	7.30- 8.05		UNSPECIFIED		CDCL3
378M	D	7.31		UNSPECIFIED		CDCL3
2448M	D	7.31		UNSPECIFIED		CDCL3
2449M	D	7.33		UNSPECIFIED		CDCL3
2015M	D	7.35 APP.		UNSPECIFIED		CDCL3
2037M	D	7.35 APP.		UNSPECIFIED		CDCL3
205M	D	7.38 APP.		UNSPECIFIED		CDCL3
1732M	D	7.41 APP.		UNSPECIFIED		CDCL3
2857M	D	7.44		UNSPECIFIED		CCL4
2364M	D	7.50		UNSPECIFIED		CCL4
1173M	D	7.60- 7.85		UNSPECIFIED		CDCL3
1179M	D	7.61- 8.16		UNSPECIFIED		DMSO
2096M	D	7.77 APP.		UNSPECIFIED		POLYSOL-D
2600M	D	9.27 APP.		UNSPECIFIED		DMSO-D6
2599M	D	10.20		UNSPECIFIED		DMSO
2560M	D	7.10- 7.60		UNSPECIFIED	S	D2O
1527M	D	7.40		UNSPECIFIED	S	POLYSOL-D
784M	D	7.51		UNSPECIFIED	S	TFA
825M	D	9.63		UNSPECIFIED	S	DMSO-D6
2130M	E	0.80- 2.10		UNSPECIFIED		CDCL3
1780M	E	3.49		UNSPECIFIED		CDCL3
1675M	E	3.60 APP.		UNSPECIFIED		CDCL3
1525M	E	6.00- 6.30		UNSPECIFIED		CCL4
584M	E	6.32- 7.25		UNSPECIFIED		CCL4
1502M	E	6.40- 6.80		UNSPECIFIED		CCL4
1540M	E	6.45- 7.25		UNSPECIFIED		CCL4
1560M	E	6.60		UNSPECIFIED		CCL4
603M	E	6.70- 7.20		UNSPECIFIED		CCL4
1453M	E	6.85- 7.50		UNSPECIFIED		CCL4
2319M	E	6.90- 7.75		UNSPECIFIED		DMSO-D6
160M	E	6.90- 7.60		UNSPECIFIED		CCL4
161M	E	6.90- 7.50		UNSPECIFIED		CCL4
1936M	E	6.92		UNSPECIFIED		CDCL3
1820M	E	7.00- 7.40		UNSPECIFIED		CCL4
600M	E	7.00- 7.50		UNSPECIFIED		CCL4
162M	E	7.00- 7.50		UNSPECIFIED		CDCL3
175M	E	7.01 APP.		UNSPECIFIED		CCL4
1350M	E	7.01- 7.59		UNSPECIFIED		CDCL3
2856M	E	7.05- 7.55		UNSPECIFIED		CCL4
2372M	E	7.06- 7.40		UNSPECIFIFD		CDCL3
2365M	E	7.07- 7.60		UNSPECIFIED		CDCL3
2854M	E	7.08		UNSPECIFIED		CCL4
1702M	E	7.10		UNSPECIFIED		CCL4

BOOK NO.	ASSIGN-MENT	CHEM SHIFT - ppm -	PROTON GROUP	ENVIRONMENTAL GROUPS	S	SOLVENT
138M	E	7.10		UNSPECIFIED		CCL4
1485M	E	7.10 APP.		UNSPECIFIED		CCL4
862M	E	7.10- 7.60		UNSPECIFIED		POLYSOL-D
2849M	E	7.11 APP.		UNSPECIFIED		CCL4
652M	E	7.12		UNSPECIFIED		CCL4
482M	E	7.12		UNSPECIFIED		CCL4
153M	E	7.14		UNSPECIFIED		CCL4
142M	E	7.15		UNSPECIFIED		CDCL3
1483M	E	7.16		UNSPECIFIED		CCL4
1788M	E	7.18		UNSPECIFIED		CCL4
577M	E	7.18		UNSPECIFIED		CCL4
1712M	E	7.18 APP.		UNSPECIFIED		CDCL3
2836M	E	7.18 APP.		UNSPECIFIED		CCL4
2848M	E	7.18 APP.		UNSPECIFIED		CCL4
579M	E	7.19		UNSPECIFIED		CCL4
2835M	E	7.19		UNSPECIFIED		CCL4
1929M	E	7.19 APP.		UNSPECIFIED		DMSO-D6
1162M	E	7.19 APP.		UNSPECIFIED		POLYSOL-D
1774M	E	7.20 APP.		UNSPECIFIED		CDCL3
481M	E	7.20 APP.		UNSPECIFIED		CDCL3
2148M	E	7.20- 7.65		UNSPECIFIED		POLYSOL-D
2041M	E	7.20- 7.65		UNSPECIFIED		CDCL3
1483M	E	7.21		UNSPECIFIED		CCL4
2847M	E	7.21 APP.		UNSPECIFIED		CCL4
2309M	E	7.21 APP.		UNSPECIFIED		CDCL3
2313M	E	7.25		UNSPECIFIED		CDCL3
2841M	E	7.26		UNSPECIFIED		CCL4
2891M	E	7.27		UNSPECIFIED		CDCL3
1789M	E	7.27		UNSPECIFIED		CCL4
1135M	E	7.28		UNSPECIFIED		CDCL3
1711M	E	7.28		UNSPECIFIED		CDCL3
2543M	E	7.28 APP.		UNSPECIFIED		DMSO-D6
2310M	E	7.29		UNSPECIFIED		CDCL3
2845M	E	7.29		UNSPECIFIED		CCL4
1704M	E	7.29 APP.		UNSPECIFIED		CDCL3
2933M	E	7.30		UNSPECIFIED		CDCL3
2846M	E	7.31 APP.		UNSPECIFIED		CDCL3
2862M	E	7.31 APP.		UNSPECIFIED		CCL4
1705M	E	7.33		UNSPECIFIED		CCL4
1791M	E	7.33 APP.		UNSPECIFIED		CDCL3
2633M	E	7.34		UNSPECIFIED		TFA
1257M	E	7.36 APP.		UNSPECIFIED		CDCL3
1278M	E	7.50- 8.05		UNSPECIFIED		DMSO
1726M	E	7.70 APP.		UNSPECIFIED		CDCL3
713M	E	8.49 APP.		UNSPECIFIED		CDCL3
804M	E	7.25		UNSPECIFIED	S	CDCL3
631M	F	4.04 APP.		UNSPECIFIED		D20
2816M	F	5.29 APP.		UNSPECIFIED		CCL4
1559M	F	6.85 APP.		UNSPECIFIED		CDCL3
2990M	F	6.90- 7.40		UNSPECIFIED		CCL4
1776M	F	6.90- 7.60		UNSPECIFIED		CDCL3
2850M	F	7.05- 7.45		UNSPECIFIED		CCL4
2986M	F	7.13		UNSPECIFIED		CCL4
1483M	F	7.16		UNSPECIFIED		CCL4
2838M	F	7.16		UNSPECIFIED		CCL4
578M	F	7.19		UNSPECIFIED		CCL4
155M	F	7.19		UNSPECIFIED		CDCL3
596M	F	7.19 APP.		UNSPECIFIED		CCL4
2853M	F	7.20		UNSPECIFIED		CDCL3
1483M	F	7.21		UNSPECIFIED		CCL4
653M	F	7.22		UNSPECIFIED		CDCL3
1480M	F	7.25		UNSPECIFIED		CDCL3
2951M	F	7.25 APP.		UNSPECIFIED		CDCL3
594M	F	7.27		UNSPECIFIED		CDCL3
1703M	F	7.30		UNSPECIFIED		CDCL3
2412M	F	7.40		UNSPECIFIED		DMSO-D6
2148M	F	7.70- 8.15		UNSPECIFIED		POLYSOL-D
785M	F	7.31		UNSPECIFIED	S	TFA
494M	G	6.60- 7.11		UNSPECIFIED		CCL4
1966M	G	6.88		UNSPECIFIED		CDCL3
2842M	G	7.05- 7.45		UNSPECIFIED		CCL4
2146M	G	7.12 APP.		UNSPECIFIED		CCL4
2843M	G	7.20 APP.		UNSPECIFIED		CCL4
595M	G	7.21 APP.		UNSPECIFIED		CDCL3
2286M	G	7.22		UNSPECIFIED		CCL4
631M	G	7.39		UNSPECIFIED		D20
839M	H	7.30- 7.80		UNSPECIFIED	S	CDCL3